GUIDE AGREEMENT

I _____ on this _____ day in _____ acknowledge and agree to take responsibility for my future and will commit the time, energy and resources necessary to find a college or university that will fit my academic, athletic, financial and geographic needs.

I understand that the task involved will enable me to obtain a college education and pursue my athletic endeavors.

The Official Guides To College Athletic Scholarship Programs
1845 Summit Ave ~ Suite 402~ Plano, Texas 75074 Toll Free: 1-800-862-3092
Telephone: 972-509-5707 Fax: 972-516-1754 Email: sports@thesportsource.com

THE OFFICIAL ATHLETIC COLLEGE SCHOLARSHIP GUIDES

Yes! I am interested in receiving the current edition of:

TITLES	PRICE	# OF BOOKS
The Official Athletic College Guide: SOCCER	$34.95 x	_____
The Official Athletic College Guide: BASEBALL	$34.95 x	_____
The Official Athletic College Kit: SOFTBALL	$34.95 x	_____
The Official Athletic College Guide: VOLLEYBALL	$34.95 x	_____
Freshman College Kit: Includes Workbook and 1 Match-Fit online access code.	$23.95 +$7 S&H x	_____
Sophomore College Kit: Includes Workbook and three Match-Fit online access codes.	$42.95 +$7 S&H x	_____
Junior College Kit: Includes College Guide, Workbook and 4 Match-Fit online access codes.	$64.85 +$9 S&H x	_____
Senior College Kit: Includes College Guide, Workbook and 2 Match-Fit online access codes.	$55.85 +$9 S&H x	_____

PAYMENT: ☐ CHECK ☐ MONEY ORDER ☐ VISA ☐ MASTERCARD ☐ AMEX

Card#:_____ Exp. Date:_____

Name on card: _____

Signature: _____

(product): _____ x (price):$_____ =$_____

TAX (8.25% Texas residence only) =$_____

Shipping & handling ($7.00 per guide) =$_____

Total amount being billed =$_____

☐ Please include information regarding "Plan for Success" College Seminars

Ship to:

Name:_____

Address: _____

City: _____ State: _____

Zip:_____

Phone: _____

E-mail: _____

Fax your order to:
972-516-1754

Toll Free: 1-800-862-3092
(972)509-5707
1845 Summit Ave~Suite
402~Plano,Texas 75074

web-site:
http://www.thesportsource.com
E-mail:
sports@thesportsource.com

MATCH FIT ™

ONLINE COLLEGE IDENTIFICATION SERVICE

Jump-start your own college search with MATCHFIT™ our new online college identification service offered exclusively at **www.thesportsource.com**. Confidentially enter personal biographical data including your G.P.A., class rank, and standardized test scores, along with information specific to the type of college or university you would like to attend. Your information is matched against our extensive database to identify ten (10) college programs which match your selection criteria. Then make changes to your data and re-run the search two (2) additional times.

The net effect is three (3) sets of ten (10) colleges and universities which are compatible with your requirements for a college athletic program. Any duplications further validate that particular program as one you will want to pursue. You may select any college or university and download information specific to that program directly to your PC. This includes both a general academic profile, and a detailed athletic profile with the coach's name, mailing address, office number, fax, e-mail address, and the college web address. MATCHFIT™ is available for $34.95 and can be ordered at **www.thesportsource.com** with a MasterCard, VISA, American Express, by E-check,or order by phone.

"PLAN FOR SUCCESS" COLLEGE SEMINARS

"PLAN FOR SUCCESS" - COLLEGE SEMINARS ™ are conducted throughout the U.S. for teams, clubs, schools, and sports organizations. Our network of presenters include college coaches and experts within the field of collegiate athletics who will discuss in detail:

* *THE SPORT SOURCE*™ "Action Plan for Success"
* What college coaches look for in a player
* NCAA / NAIA recruiting rules
* Evaluating colleges and athletic programs
* Writing resumes and cover letters
* Conducting campus visits
* Opportunities for obtaining a college athletic scholarship

"PLAN FOR SUCCESS" - COLLEGE SEMINARS™ pricing varies by group size. For more information call:

1-800-862-3092

website:http://www.thesportsource.com

THE SPORT SOURCE, INC. is pleased to present the *Official Athletic College Guide: Volleyball.* With over eleven years of assisting high school athletes in their pursuit of playing at the collegiate level, we continue to explore ways to improve our College Guides. They are the definitive guides to sports Colleges and sports Scholarships for Soccer, Baseball, Volleyball and Softball, functioning as both a reference handbook and self-promotional tool. Our commitment to providing the most current and comprehensive information available to our readers remains a priority!

The Official Athletic College Guides were created, in part, to allow college coaches an effective medium for disseminating information about their programs to high school athletes, their parents, youth and high school coaches, and guidance counselors. The information provided is systematically organized and packaged in the College Guides to provide concise, accurate, and timely data for the prospective student-athlete and his/her family. If fully utilized, it will assist your son or daughter in making the best choice to meet specific academic interests while continuing his/her athletic career. In addition, this publication will supplement the numerous other handbooks that offer more complete information regarding academics, on-campus facilities, and student lifestyles - publications that are available directly from the various colleges and universities.

The original premise for the College Guide was to provide a comprehensive reference tool to college and university academic and athletic programs. The idea was to provide individual profiles for each institution's academic and athletic environment. It became a starting point from which student-athletes could begin to gauge the academic and athletic environment of colleges and universities of their interest. In effect, the College Guide became a barometer of various collegiate "climates." To this end, we consider our publications to be a tremendous success! We continue to get feedback from student-athletes currently enrolled in various colleges and universities who used the College Guide to assist them in choosing their particular school.

All of our publications have been well received by college coaches, parents and student athletes that have gone through the process of college selection. For the prospective student-athlete, one of the keys to communicating effectively with a college coach and university admissions counselor is to be able to converse intelligently about their athletic and academic programs. Accordingly, we have been advised that prospective players who have used our publications are submitting resumes and cover letters that are professional and comprehensive. Also, these players are better informed about a prospective college or university and its academic and athletic program.

The Official Athletic College Guide: WORKBOOK is another tool to use for your college research. The workbook can help you identify and select schools that meet a student's athletic and academic program needs. We believe this workbook is the perfect companion to our sport-specific guides to colleges and universities offering athletic/academic scholarships. The data compiled in this book was gathered through phone inquiries and detailed questionnaires mailed to college and university coaches throughout the United States.

As we continue to grow and expand, a few things have been learned about selecting the appropriate college. We have found that the college selection process for the student athlete becomes a two-fold issue. First, it is sometimes difficult to evaluate one's own ability as a player. All prospective student-athletes know where they would like to play, but the question becomes can they honestly be successful in that situation? Second, it becomes difficult to determine a university that will meet the specific academic needs of the individual student. Remember: When you participate in athletics at the collegiate level, you are a student-athlete. This means that you are a student--first, and an athlete-- second. This is the cornerstone of intercollegiate athletics. Therefore, there needs to be an interactive way that will allow the prospective student-athlete to find the right balance of both academics and athletics. This is why we have created this workbook. This workbook will allow student-athletes to assess not only a university's academic strengths, but also where they fit in to this competitive athletic and scholastic environment. This is a detailed and complete "Action - Plan for Success" that has been proven to work time and time again.

THE SPORT SOURCE, INC., publisher of the *Official Athletic College Guides*, is pleased to announce the addition of an exciting new service to assist student athletes in identifying prospective college and university programs. As an industry leader in providing informational assistance to high school athletes, **THE SPORT SOURCE, INC.** is aggressively expanding its "Plan For Success" college seminar programs and offering its new **MATCHFIT**TM online college identification service. For more information regarding **MATCHFIT**TM or college seminars in your area, please contact The Sport Source Seminar Division Toll Free at (800) 862-3092 or visit our website at http://www.thesportsource.com.

THE PUBLISHER

As founder of **THE SPORT SOURCE, INC.**, Charlie Kadupski continues to annually compile, edit, and publish the _Official Athletic College Guides: SOCCER, BASEBALL, VOLLEYBALL and SOFTBALL._ Mr. Kadupski is a former collegiate soccer player having also played professionally with the San Jose Earthquakes, Houston Hurricanes, and Ft. Lauderdale Strikers of the North American Soccer League (NASL), the Los Angeles Lazers of the Major Indoor Soccer League (MISL), and the Dallas Americans of the American Soccer League (ASL). While at Hartwick College, he was an All-American selection in 1977 - the same year his college men's team won the NCAA Division I National Championship.

Charlie currently holds a USSF "A" License and serves on the United States Soccer Federation (USSF) National Coaching Staff and Editorial Board. He is also the full-time Coaching Director for the Storm Soccer Club in Plano, Texas.

ACKNOWLEDGMENTS

The Sport Source™ would like to recognize Coach Jack Cohen for his valuable assistance and input in this publication. Jack has devoted his his teaching and coaching the Volleyball. Coach Cohen has been coaching volleyball at all levels in Canada for over 20 years. Jack currently is the Head Coach for the Senior Girls Volleyball team at J.G. Diefenbaker High School in Calagary Alberta, Canada.

Recognition: **THE SPORT SOURCE**™ would like to thank all of the organizations who are committed to education and youth in sports.

Special acknowledgment for their help each year with the production of the **Official Athletic College Guides and WORKBOOKS.**

Editor in Chief - Charlie Kadupski
Corporate Editor - Cathie Pyle
Contributing Editor-at-Large - Micheal Jago -_Goal Magazine International_

THE SPORT SOURCE ®

1845 Summit Avenue, Ste. 402
Plano, TX 75074
Telephone: 972-509-5707 Fax: 972-516-1754
Email: sports@thesportsource.com
Web Address: www.thesportsource.com

THE SPORT SOURCE GROUP	RESEARCH DEPARTMENT	NATIONAL DIVISION
Chairman, CEO - Charlie Kadupski	**Production -** Shauna Green	**National Seminar Director -** Chad Blake
Strategic Relations - Jeff Solem	**Production -** Robyn Martin	ccb@thesportsource.com
Corporate Liaison - William Gazonas		
Controller - Frank Pyle	**PRODUCTION**	**REGIONAL REPRESENTATIVES**
Special Initiatives - Jim Randolph		
	Creative Director - Tal Hollingsworth	**Southeastern -** John Webb
SPORTS INFORMATION DIVISION	**Associate Production Director -** Dave Barrett	jw@thesportsource.com
	Technical Supervisor - Rod Emerson	**South-** Jeff Solem
	Printing - Brenda Cockrell	js@thesportsource.om
Director - Dave Barrett	_Dallas Offset Inc._	**East Coast -** Bill Gazonas
dlb@thesportsource.com		sports@thesportsource.com
Assistant Director - Tara Hewko	**COMMUNICATIONS**	
tdh@thesportsource.com		**Special Representative-High School**
	Consumer Marketing/New Media	George Phillips - Staff Services
	Lisa Lavelle	gp@thesportsource.com
	ldl@thesportsource.com	

INTRODUCTION

Selecting the best college or university to meet your needs may seem like an enormous and intimidating task. The prospect of choosing one school over another may produce intense feelings of anxiety, panic, and even fear of making the wrong decision. But fear and panic are products of the unknown. There is no reason for this process to be overwhelming. By being organized and diligent, and surrounding yourself with the right resources and materials, you will be able to make an informed decision - a decision that you can truly feel good about!

Most people travel from the known to the unknown. The known is that you are a junior or senior in high school with a certain GPA and test scores. The unknown is, "Where am I going to college?" The task is not impossible. You will simply need to identify a school that offers the academic programs that best suit your needs, and a volleyball program that is compatible with your athletic ability. You may have as many as 20 schools on your initial list, but only target those schools where the minimum test scores and required GPA fit your own.

Use the College Guide extensively, but don't make it your only resource. Consult other reference materials. Ask questions of your parents, guidance counselors, coaches and other administrators at the colleges that interest you. Gather your information carefully; then examine your options. With regard to your own athletic and academic career, this may be the single biggest decision you will make to this point in your life. While it requires careful consideration, the process itself should never be a stumbling block, but rather a fun and exciting time to share with your parents in planning for your future. It does require a focused and concerted effort, however, a lack of follow-through may create roadblocks, forcing you to make unnecessary compromises in the type of school or sports program you may be seeking.

The process of identifying your interests and selecting the appropriate colleges should begin early. Your freshman year in high school is not too soon to begin the process. Those especially talented players will have less to worry about - the college coaches will be pursuing them. However, it is the greater majority of student-athletes who need to be prepared. As a prospective college player, it is critical that you do your research, and are identified by college coaches as early as possible. Your high school varsity volleyball program and summer leagues are the best vehicles for college coaches to spot you as a prospective recruit. "All-Star," and college showcase events are also effective activities for personal recognition and identification by college coaches. Those student-athletes who make a conscious effort to evaluate college programs, and narrow those choices as they progress through their high school career will have identified two to three solid choices by December of their senior year.

Most college coaches begin to identify student-athletes as high school juniors - your year to shine as both a player and a student. But even if you have delayed the process of selecting a college until your senior year, all hope is not lost. High school coaches who are well-connected will be able to pinpoint tournaments or showcase events where college coaches will be present. You must take the initiative to contact the coach at the school or schools that interest you by sending them your resume. Preface it with a personalized cover letter and be sure to mention your game schedule and the dates of any showcase events where you might be playing. In this situation, time is very critical - you will need to be seen quickly by college coaches in order for them to fairly evaluate your abilities before they make commitments to other players. (This topic is discussed further in the section titled The Student Athlete's Role in Choosing a College.)

Throughout the evaluation process, be advised that college coaches are selling their programs. They are going to tell you all the best things about their school and their team. Remember also, that college coaches are not just promoting their program to you, but to 25 or more other players as well. It is important to make sure the information you hear is accurate. If you do your homework, you won't overestimate your ability, or underestimate the competition for the position you wish to play. There may also be weaknesses and shortcomings in the program that you will be forced to identify on your own. If you make a mistake in your quest to join a high-profile program, you may end up riding the bench for four years or transferring to another school. This is the reason it is so very important to take an analytical approach to this process. Do your homework and be sure to do a thorough job.

As previously mentioned, one of the most critical steps in the recruitment process is your direct correspondence with the college coach. Because there are often coaching changes, it is highly recommended that you contact the college athletic department to verify the current coach and the correct spelling of the name before mailing any correspondence. Compose your resume and address a personalized cover letter directly to the volleyball coach. Be sure to include specific information about the program - information contained in the academic and athletic profiles listed in the ***Official Athletic College Guide: Volleyball***.

****

The first step in the identification and evaluation process is to thoroughly explore this guide. It contains much of the information you will need to make an informed decision. Choosing the best avenue to continue your education and athletic development is not as hard as it really seems. We hope the ***Official Athletic College Guide: Volleyball*** will assist you in making the right choice. We believe there is a program to fit everyone's needs. With proper research, you will find the program that is right for you.

Much success to you in the classroom and on the field of play!

Editor's Note: The following sections, **"THE COLLEGE IDENTIFICATION AND SELECTION PROCESS"** and **"THE STUDENT ATH-LETE'S ROLE IN CHOOSING A COLLEGE"**, both have one goal; to prepare you, the prospective student athlete, for college athletics. Although similar in many ways, these methods have various distinctions that make them unique. They are all positive techniques. You are encouraged to examine them all and choose one or more methods that you feel will work for you.

OFFICIAL ATHLETIC COLLEGE GUIDE: VOLLEYBALL

Table of Content

SELECTING A COLLEGE

YOUR FIRST CONSIDERATION MUST BE ACADEMIC

FIELDS OF STUDY

- Identify your general and specific interest
- Do you prefer a research institute or one committed to undergraduate studies?
- Do you prefer innovative programs or traditional, structured programs

COLLEGE SIZE

- Do you want a broad range of activities?(i.e., larger schools offer more)
- Do you require a broad range of courses or special ized training?
- Are graduate students acceptable as instructors in lower level course?
- Do you prefer a big name program?

LOCATION

- Would you like to be close to home?
- Do you prefer a rural or urban campus?
- Do you prefer a specific climate?
- Do you wish to play in a particular conference?

COLLEGE ENVIRONMENT

- Do you prefer a particular religious affiliation?
- Conservative or liberal environment?
- Coed or single-sex institution?
- Private or State University?
- Are sororities and fraternities important?

Identify up to 10 colleges that meet your individual needs

NOW CONSIDER THE VOLLEYBALL PROGRAM

IDENTIFY YOUR SKILLS

- What are your strengths? (Do you have speed,quickness, strength, etc.)
- Is your style compatible with the program your interested in?
- What is your potential to contribute to the program and when?

IDENTIFY POTENTIAL COLLEGES

- Can you be competitive at the college's level of play?
- Competitiveness of schedule?
- Chance of making the team?
- Potential playing time in first year?
- Competence and personality of coach?

Identify 7-10 schools that meet your academic and athletic requirements

CONTACT SCHOOLS

COVER LETTER
Handwritten or typed
RESUME
Neatly typed and concise

CAMPUS VISIT:
Be prepared
Dress appropriately
Ask the right questions

KNOW THE RECRUITING RULES!

This chapter provides hints on how to make the selection process more manageable. There are many possible options, but if you are methodical, organized, and willing to spend the necessary time reviewing the available data, you will soon find that only a handful of schools offer exactly what you want. Your first task is to determine the type of college you wish to attend. If you follow the guidelines outlined in this chapter, you should be able to eliminate a great number of choices. In many cases, this process will allow you to better define your own wants, needs, and goals.

COLLEGE ACADEMIC LIFE

As a volleyball player with proven skills, you are probably more interested in quality volleyball programs than any other aspect of university life. Indeed, that is one of the main themes of the College Guide. **Nevertheless, your chances of making a career out of your volleyball playing abilities are limited.** Even those who eventually find a place on a professional roster often find their careers can be very short-lived. The average professional volleyball player retires in their late twenties and must rely on alternative skills to earn a living. This might seem a bleak picture to someone whose life revolves around the volleyball court, but it is realistic. Put simply: professional volleyball players are few; professional careers are many.

With this in mind, your search for the right university should revolve around **education first, and volleyball second.** While your volleyball skills will deteriorate with age, an education and the degree that seals it can open the door to new opportunities continuously.

Perhaps the most important aspect of university selection is flexibility. If you are reasonably sure you know what you want to study (engineering, for example), thoroughly research those institutions that offer the best programs. Compile a list of colleges maintaining quality engineering departments and compare their strong and weak points. Remember, however, that most students change majors at least once; some change many times before finding the right field. So be mindful not to lock yourself into a system that inhibits your ability to change and grow.

There are many different types of programs. Some, for example, stress traditional curriculum, basing studies on a liberal arts foundation. Others are better equipped to train students in particular trades, offering courses of study as diverse as finance and horticulture. To decide which is right for you, ask yourself a series of questions:

What are your main interests? In systematic fashion, list those subjects that interest you most. If you have many varied interests, look for schools with a comprehensive selection of programs. This will allow you to change majors freely without having to transfer to different colleges or universities.

Do you have one specific interest or skill? If so, look for schools specializing in that area, but keep in mind that if you do change majors you might be forced to transfer.

Do you prefer a faculty that is dedicated to teaching undergraduate courses? Institutions with large graduate populations are sometimes more committed to research than to teaching. Professors at those institutions generally have less time to spend on undergraduate activities outside the classroom. On the other hand, the ideas they do bring to the classroom represent current research.

THE COLLEGE IDENTIFICATION AND SELECTION PROCESS

Do you prefer more innovative programs? These programs offer unique opportunities such as overseas studies, cooperative work/study programs, and individually created majors stressing independent study.

Do you prefer a more structured traditional program? These programs are generally built around certain university core requirements which must be satisfied before a student embarks on a single major.

UNIVERSITY SIZE

You can eliminate many colleges and universities by determining the environment in which you feel most comfortable. In other words, do you prosper in larger classes or in a smaller, more personal atmosphere? To pick a school based primarily on its size, you will undoubtedly have to make some trade-offs. Large institutions generally have large classes. This often means that instruction is less personal and interaction among students and professors is limited. On the other hand, larger institutions usually offer more extracurricular activities and broader educational possibilities. Conversely, at small universities, classes tend to be smaller allowing students to more readily exchange ideas with professors and other students during class discussions. There are potential draw-backs though. Because the enrollment is small, the student population may be less diverse than at a larger college or university. Additionally, small schools do not have the resources necessary to offer a wide array of career options; therefore, the curriculum is usually more focused. If you do not know what you want to study, a small school might not be right for you. Ask yourself the following questions when determining the university size most appropriate for you:

What kind of environment exists at your high school? Are you more comfortable in large or small classes? Do you want to expe-rience a different kind of environment or do you prefer to stick to what you already know?

Do you want to meet and interact with many of your classmates personally? This is more likely at a small school.

Is a wide range of activities outside the classroom important? If you answer yes, then a larger university may better suit your needs.

Would you like an academic program which offers specialized training in many fields, or one that focuses on a limited curriculum? Large universities obviously offer a wider range of courses. That, however, does not automatically ensure a better institution. Small universities can sometimes compensate for the lack of fields with more one-on-one instruction and better access to resources.

Are you concerned with the expertise of the faculty? Though the size of an institution does not determine faculty qualifications, there are some things you should research and consider. For example, at large universities, graduate students sometimes teach lower level courses. Though generally well-qualified, they do not have the experience or knowledge most professors possess.

Do you want to play volleyball at a big-name university? Or, would you do better to target a smaller school where your chances to play might be better?

THE COLLEGE IDENTIFICATION AND SELECTION PROCESS

UNIVERSITY LOCATION

Another way to narrow your prospective list of schools is to determine geographically where you may want to spend the next four years. Some questions you should try to answer include:

Do you want to stay close to home or do you want the challenge of living far from your family in a distant environment?

Would you rather experience a rural or an urban campus? If you grew up in a small town, it may be beneficial for you to experi-ence life in a big city for several years. On the contrary, if you are from a large city, can you see yourself adapting to a rural envi-ronment?

Do you prefer a particular climate? If you dislike cold weather, you might eliminate universities in the North and Northeast. On the other hand, you might want to consider those areas if you also enjoy winter recreational sports.

As a volleyball player, do you prefer the competition a particular conference offers? Do the West Coast universities play a style more compatible with your skills? East Coast? North?

UNIVERSITY ENVIRONMENT

Each university or college offers a unique environment. Though hard to grasp from brochures and handbooks, each institution has distinct social, religious, and political attitudes. In order to better assess the information provided in printed materials, be sure to ask specific questions when speaking with college representatives.

Do you want to attend an institution with a particular religious affiliation?

Are you more comfortable in a conservative or liberal environment? You can gather insights about predominant political trends by reading campus newspapers, talking to university representatives, finding documentation written by faculty members, and asking questions of students when making campus visits.

Do you want to attend a university that considers fraternities and sororities important aspects of social life? Many volleyball players consider their team an adequate substitute for organized social activities. Others might want a social life apart from their volleyball team.

Do you prefer a coed or single sex institution?

Would you like to attend a private school or a public institution? Though private schools are generally more expensive, cost alone should not deter you from pursuing the university of your choice. Financial aid is available for many qualified applicants.

COLLEGE VOLLEYBALL

If you have followed the guidelines presented , you can now compile a preliminary list of schools based on academic, philosophical, social, and other prerequisites. Now you can start looking at college volleyball programs.

Does the school have special academic counseling for athletes? This is very important because academic counselors who deal specifically with athletes can give you a slight edge. He or she can help you select the right courses and the best professors to allow you the flexibility you will need for training, games, and travel. Along the same lines, does the college have tutors available to athletes? If tutors are available, ask if they are free, or if you are required to pay for their services. Depending on your financial situation, it may make a difference, particularly if you are a marginal student. Also, are there required study sessions for athletes? These study sessions can be helpful in making sure you are devoting enough time to your studies. Many freshmen simply do not know how to budget their time.

How many players from the program have graduated and earned degrees in the last five years? This may give you an indication of the amount of emphasis a school puts on academics. Check to see what percentage of athletes graduate, and then weigh that against the percentage who graduate from the entire student body. Keep in mind that not all schools are alike, so strict comparisons of these numbers may sometimes be misleading.

What is the total number of players on athletic scholarship? Consider what effect this will have on your chances for a scholarship and on your playing time. There are other important questions to ask with regard to scholarships. What will the complete financial aid package include? Depending on how much need-based aid for which you will qualify, you may find a variety of sources comprising your total financial aid package. Grants-in-aid, loans, work study and other aid programs can be combined with scholarship money to meet your needs. You will need to know how to renew the scholarship each year there is no such thing as a four-year scholarship. It must be renewed every year. If you hear something about the renewal process you don't understand, ask for an explanation. You won't want to deal with surprises later on. Finally, you should determine what happens if you get injured and can't play for all, or part of a season.

How many games does a team play each year? You have to balance your desire to play as much volleyball as possible with the realization that you can't get in over your head academically. Is there a fall season? A fall season is a good way to get into shape and make a determination about how much playing time you might see during your sophomore year.

How successful has the school's program been in recent years? Obviously, everybody wants to play for a winner. But the more successful a program is, the stronger the competition will be for playing time. The school's conference and playoff record can give yet another indication of its success. Is there a current upswing that indicates the program has turned the corner, or a down trend, indicating a turn for the worse.

Are you being recruited for a specific position? If so, find out who is ahead of you at that position. This can help determine your chances for playing time. If there are two sophomores ahead of you, there's a better chance of you being in the middle of the bench than in the middle of the line-up. Or, you may be asked to switch positions. Ask yourself honestly if you'll be happy moving to another position.

What kind of athletic facilities does the school have? Sure you're going to be a student, but you're also going to be an athlete. It's best to find out where you will be playing and training. Poor facilities may contribute to injuries, stifle development, or adversely affect your mental approach to the game. On the other hand, don't let a shiny new stadium color your judgment if you are not comfortable with the coaching staff.

Find out also if they have indoor training facilities. Does the program have a weight room and strength coach? Your physical development will play a major role in your success as a college player, and proper training facilities and professional coaching can help elevate your game to the next level. Find out what kind of in-season and off-season conditioning program you can expect.

Does the school offer a junior varsity volleyball program? If so, how many players are on the junior varsity and varsity teams? If a junior varsity program is offered, find out if it is used as a feeder for the varsity, and if there is any movement to and from each program.

Who comprises the coaching staff? It is important to know who you will be "working for" during your college career. Find out if one specific coach will be working with players at your position, or if it will be the head coach.

Now that you have identified some of the things you want out of a volleyball program, look at the list of schools you have already compiled for academic and other considerations. Try to find those schools among the university profiles listed in this guide. Are their volleyball programs also compatible? If so, these are the schools you definitely want to pursue. If not, you might have to make some trade-offs. For example, can you adapt to a new position if a particular coach says you may have to switch?

If you are flexible, you can expand the list of schools that interest you. Remember, there are many quality schools with good volleyball programs. Everyone should be able to find a number of match-ups that qualify for their final list.

At this point, attempt to identify up to ten colleges or universities that really interest you. Focus on these schools. The section on Admissions and Paying For College describe how to prepare information that will assist you with college admission requirements. Economic factors generally prohibit visiting all the campuses. Nevertheless, if you can afford the cost, visit as many schools and talk to as many coaches as you can. The section on The Importance of Campus Visits explains what the coach may be looking for, and how you can prepare yourself for this important meeting.

SUMMARY

It is important to remember that your final selection of a college or university should be based primarily on your educational needs. _The Official Athletic College Guide: Volleyball_ does not describe individual academic programs in detail. For academic and other information, you should consult other handbooks devoted to that purpose by looking at individual college brochures, and consulting with parents, guidance counselors, current and former players, and college officials. Compile your list of schools from those resources. The volleyball profiles in the College Guide should assist you in reducing the number of universities on your list to a more manageable size. Together with the school's complete academic profile you will be able to determine the right college to meet both your academic and athletic needs.

THE STUDENT ATHLETES ROLE IN CHOOSING A COLLEGE

The diversity and abundance of opportunities for young men and women to participate in a college volleyball program is overwhelming when considering the full range of classifications from NCAA Division I, II, III, NAIA, and NJCAA. To date there are 1200+ colleges and universities that sponsor Women's Volleyball programs. There are 80+ colleges and universities that sponsor universities that sponsor Men's Volleyball Programs.

Each of these schools is unique in three key areas: academic programs, social and environmental factors, and athletic standards. The obvious result of any comprehensive search is that a positive match for the prepared and well-informed student-athlete does certainly exist.

The recommended process involves a focused effort in three areas. These are simply referred to as **THE THREE P's**.

I) BE PROACTIVE: Take a proactive approach to gathering information beginning the sophomore year. This should involve a system for prioritizing choices and a continuous evaluation of personal athletic and academic goals.

II) BE PERSISTENT: Once prioritized, be persistent in communicating your goals and personal interests to the program(s) of choice.

III) BE PREPARED: Prepare both athletically and academically to meet necessary eligibility and admission requirements.

THE WELL-INFORMED STUDENT ATHLETE

What are the variables to consider in selecting a college? The most frequent questions and discussion topics encountered may be generally categorized as academic, social, and athletic related. Essentially, the student-athlete should be attempting to set a variety of immediate and long-term goals for their own personal growth in each of these key areas. Matching a college opportunity to these goals is a vital step in achieving them.

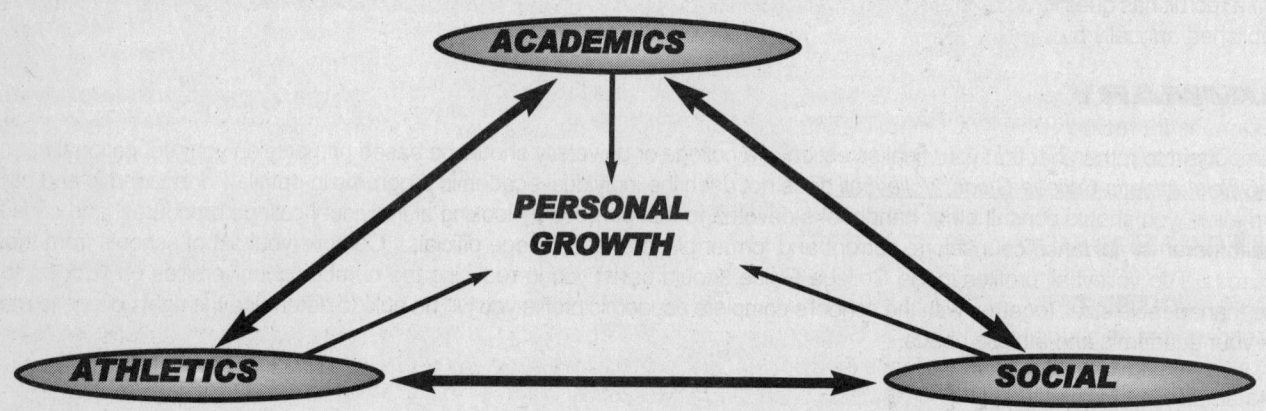

ESSENTIAL QUESTIONS TO CONSIDER

ACADEMICALLY...Will I have the desire, support, and ability to succeed here?

SOCIALLY...Will I be comfortable with my surroundings and able to grow as a person?

ATHLETICALLY...Will I contribute and become a better player?

THE STUDENT ATHLETE'S ROLE IN CHOOSING A COLLEGE

ACADEMIC ELIGIBILITY & ADMISSION REQUIREMENTS

Each Division (I, II, III) of the NCAA has some variability in eligibility requirements. The NAIA and NJCAA are significantly different from the NCAA. As well, the admissions requirements for various colleges and universities may be unique and vary greatly from one to another. However, it is possible to generally view the following items as essential elements for admission criteria to most colleges.

KNOW THE RECRUITING RULES

A recruit should know a few basic NCAA rules:

A college coach may not have off-campus contact with a recruit until July 1st after his junior year in high school.

A recruit may not practice with an NCAA Division I college team on a campus visit.

A player may not accept payments for playing for any club team.

A recruit should not accept any financial rewards for attending an institution outside the formal scholarship opportunities.

Recruitment must be by members of the institution's academic and athletic staff only.

Rules for NAIA and junior college associations are different. Therefore, the recruit should always seek advice directly from the association's governing body if something seems too good to be legal. Also, NCAA Division III rules vary from NCAA rules at other levels. If a recruit has questions, he/she should obtain a current copy of the NCAA Guide for the College-Bound Student-Athlete which is published annually by the NCAA.

Choosing a college or university is a big decision and should not be taken lightly. As a student-athlete you need to enhance your opportunities for recruitment by helping in the process. The more knowledgeable and organized you are, the better your chances will be. Obviously, this process doesn't take the place of pure athletic ability and hard work, but if you have the talent and dedication to play at the collegiate level you need to freely communicate this to the coaches.

ADMISSION STEPS

STANDARDIZED TEST RESULTS: (SAT or ACT) These standardized tests represent common admission criteria. It is recommended, that as a student-athlete, you take the preliminary (PSAT or PACT) exam as a junior for two very important reasons. One, students have a tendency to improve their scores by repeated attempts at the exam, and secondly, the exam is a prerequisite to an official campus visit to NCAA Division I and Division II schools.

PHOTOCOPIES OF UNOFFICIAL HIGH SCHOOL TRANSCRIPTS: Once you have established an open dialogue with a coaching staff, you should provide a copy of your academic history. Many athletic departments have access to qualified people who will analyze these transcripts and assess the probability of admission to the school well in advance of the official notification.

COLLEGE ELIGIBILITY REQUIREMENTS FOR THE STUDENT-ATHLETE

THE ADMISSIONS APPLICATION: This step must be completed during the first few months of the senior year. College coaches are not the admissions officials - the final decision for admission lies with a college official outside of the athletic department. In this regard, the volleyball coaching staff is typically delighted when notified that a student-athlete has been responsible for completing the admission process on his own.

Be aware that in some cases an application may be "coded" by the athletic department in order to speed the process, or in some special cases to aid in the admission process. This is a specific question that should be asked of the coaching staff prior to making application.

ATHLETIC ELIGIBILITY REQUIREMENTS

This section is categorized separately because it is, in fact, a separate issue. While the athlete may be "admitted" to a college, this does not guarantee athletic eligibility - more rules to play by!

The NCAA has established a National Clearinghouse from which all decisions regarding an athlete's initial eligibility at an in-situation will be determined. If the athlete is not registered and certified through the Clearinghouse he or she will not be able to participate in Division I or Division II Volleyball.

The key steps:

The key steps:

Freshman through Senior Year: Academic Requirements

1) Earn a minimum GPA of 2.5 on a 4.0 scale

2) Credit in at least 13 core academic courses, including:
> 4 years of English (3 years for Division II)
> 2 years of Math
> 2 years of Social Science
> 2 years of Science (minimum 1 lab science)
> 1 year additional English, Math, Science
> 2 years additional any of above or foreign language

3) NCAA - Division I & II: Earn a summary score of at least 68 on the ACT or a combined score of 820 on the SAT. (Note: these scores may be higher based upon a sliding scale relative to the student's cumulative GPA.)

GPA	SAT	ACT SUM
2.5	820	68
2.0	1010	86

NCAA - Division III: Based on eligibility requirements set by the member institution and the college's participating athletic conference.

COLLEGE ELIGIBILITY REQUIREMENTS FOR THE STUDENT-ATHLETE

NAIA: Qualification criteria is based on any 2 of the 3 requirements outlined below.
> 1. A minimum GPA of 2.0 on a 4.0 scale
> 2. A combined score for the SAT of 860 or ACT of 18
> 3. Rank in the top 50% of high school graduating class

Junior Year: Registration with Clearinghouse

Immediately after the completion of the second semester the student-athlete should register with the Clearinghouse. This is accomplished by requesting a Clearinghouse "Student Release Form" from the high school counselor's office. The student should provide two copies of the form to the high school counselor for processing.

Senior Year: Verification of Standardized Test Scores

Verify that the standardized test scores and official transcripts have been sent to the Clearinghouse.

Finally, there are other valuable reference materials to aid in the student-athlete's pursuit of college playing opportunities. These publications will provide additional specific information:

NCAA RULES
NCAA Guide For The College-Bound Student-Athlete

National Collegiate Athletic Association
700 W. Washington Ave.
P.O. Box 6222
Indianapolis, Indiana 46206-6222
Phone: 317/917-6222   Fax: 317/917-6888
Website http://www.ncaa.org

NAIA RULES
NAIA Guide For The College-Bound Student

NAIA Headquarters
6120 South Yale, Suite 1450
Tulsa, OK 74136
Phone (918) 494-8828
Website http://www.naia.org

NCAA CLEARINGHOUSE
NCAA Clearinghouse
2255 North Dubuque Rd.
P.O. Box 4044
Iowa City, IA 52243-4404
Phone (319) 337-1492

ACADEMIC RATINGS OF COLLEGES
Gourman Report, Dr. Jack Gourman

Editor's Note: Please be aware that NCAA and NAIA rules and regulations regarding recruitment of high school athletes are under constant review. Annually request the current edition of the NCAA Guide for the College-Bound Student-Athlete and NAIA Guide For The College-Bound Student, but don't assume that you have definitive information - when in doubt, contact the NCAA or NAIA directly for clarification of any rules regarding recruiting practices.

COLLEGE EVALUATION TABLE

SELECTION FACTORS	1	2	3	4	5
SCHOOL NAMES					
ACADEMICS					
Academic Focus - Degree of Difficulty					
Academic Offering in Selected Major					
Size - Total Enrollment					
Athlete Tutoring					
Student-Athlete Support Service					
Quarter / Semester System					
Admissions - GPA Requirement					
Admissions - SAT/ACT Standard					
Coaches Academic "Perspective"					
Requirements for Selected Major					
Tuition (In-State)					
Tuition (Non-resident)					
ATHLETIC PROGRAM					
NCAA / NAIA Affiliation (i.e. Div I, II, III)					
Immediate Contribution / Playing Time					
Player Turnover (Number of Juniors/Seniors)					
Distribution of Scholarship Monies					
Coaching Staff Qualification					
Total Staff & Time Commitment					
Competitive Schedule					
Athletic Department Commitment					
Facilities					
Training Schedule (Traditional Season)					
Training Schedule (Fall / Non-Traditional season)					
Coaches Interest in Me?					
Team Atmosphere (Players Perspective)					
Travel Requirements					
Coach's Contacts to Higher Levels (All Star Teams)					
SOCIAL / ENVIRONMENT					
Metropolitan / City / Suburban / Rural					
Ethnic Diversity					
Cultural Environment					
Coed					
Fraternity / Sorority System					
Distance from Immediate Family					
Recreational Activities Available					
Campus Atmosphere					
Climate					
Team Social Atmosphere					
Employment Opportunities					
Totals (based on 1 to 5 - 5 being best) **Highest Total - Best Fit**					

COMMUNICATING WITH COLLEGE COACHES

NARROWING YOUR FOCUS

Student athletes should contact a number of colleges. There are many factors to be considered when choosing colleges: **location, size, public or private, academic difficulty, courses of study, cost, availability of academic and/or athletic scholarships, and opportunities for need based financial aid.** Added to these are factors regarding the Volleyball program: level of play, competitive-ness of the schedule, chance of making the team, and the competence and personality of the coach.

Once you have determined what your personal needs will be, some additional research is required. Obtain other college reference guides from a bookstore or a local library to assist you in your evaluation. Realistically, student-athletes should not expect to find a college that is tailor-made for them, but rather ones that provide a reasonable fit.

STEP I: WRITTEN COMMUNICATION

Having identified 7 - 10 schools of interest, entering your junior year of high school you should begin contacting the coaches for each program. Initially, this should be written communication that supplies the coaching staff with important information regarding you as a student-athlete.

CONTACTING THE VOLLEYBALL COACH

Take the time to prepare your resume and write a letter to each college coach. A personal cover letter is more effective than a generic version for all coaches. The cover letter should explain your expectations in terms of education, the Volleyball program, financial need, and scholarship requirements. Be sure to request literature about the college, and specifically, the Volleyball program. The cover letter should also be typed (although more recently, college coaches have given special consideration to neat handwritten letters) and, of course, have correct spelling and proper grammar.

Remember that the resume should be one typed page that presents only pertinent information. Coaches would rather read concise information about a player than page after page of trivia. If a player has a videotape it may be listed on the Resume, but should be sent only at the request of the coach. The resume should be sent to all the selected colleges and contain the following sections:

- ◎ A personal section with name, address, phone number, date of birth, height, weight, social security number, and high school graduation year.

- ◎ An academic section with high school name, address and phone number; grade point average and/or class rank and standardized test information (SAT, PSAT, ACT scores).

- ◎ An athletic section with a list of all Volleyball teams on which the student athlete currently plays (high school, club, league, etc.), positions played, coaches names and team records. List any Volleyball honors that have been received. This section should include any other sports that the athlete plays and any honors in those sports. Volleyball camps recently attended are also helpful.

- ◎ A reference section with the names of 3 or 4 people who can accurately gauge the player's character and ability. In other words, those who are knowledgeable of the game and the player as a person. References' addresses and phone numbers are necessary.

STEP II: TELEPHONE CONTACT

The single key variable that separates a single student-athlete from all of the other solicitation letters received by a college coach is regular follow-up. Be sure to call once or twice each month after sending your resume and cover letter. The majority of letters received by college coaches are form letters mailed to numerous programs with the hope that some interest will be generated. **A specific letter followed by a telephone call indicates a sincere interest in a given program.**

The athlete should have a specific purpose in calling; most often it is to update the coaching staff on key games, tournaments, or other opportunities to see you compete. It is also an effective way to directly express interest in the program and to ask questions regarding information not readily available from published sources such as college brochures or the College Guide. Most coaches will be happy to answer questions that aid in the decision process, but may be less enthusiastic regarding information that is readily available from other sources, i.e. school size, degree programs, and athletic conference. Remember - Direct conversation allows the coach and athlete to assess personalities and interest levels.

The well-prepared student-athlete will have assembled this information prior to the telephone call. NCAA rules permit high school athletes to call the coach without restrictions. However, be aware that a college coach may not call the student including returning messages until after July 1st following the completion of your junior year in high school.

SAMPLE RESUME

Your Name
Your Address
City, State ZIP
Home Phone
E-mail

Date of Birth: March 9, 1984
SSN: 446-29-1999
Height: 6' 1"
Weight: 145 lbs.

ACADEMICS

High School:

W.T. White High School
1244 Forest Ln.
Dallas, TX 57228
(214) 385-5660

Graduation Date:

Class of 2000

GPA/Class Rank:

3.28 GPA (4.0)
Top 25% in class
Honors program - Math

SAT/ACT Scores:

610 Math, 560 Verbal: 1170 - SAT Total
11 Math, 12 Verbal: 23 - ACT Total

ATHLETICS

High School Volleyball:

W.T. White Longhorns
Varsity team, 1999-2001
All-District Honorable Mention - Sophomore
All-District - Junior

Volleyball Club:

Dallas Mustangs
Coach: Jim Turner / Bill Thacker
3-Time Regional All-Star

REFERENCES

Coaches:

Kevin McGhee
Head coach, W.T. White High School
12345 Inwood Rd.
Dallas, TX 75228
(214) 827-9951

Judy Suarez
Former Coach, Mustangs
(214) 696-9642

Personal:

Heron Hieronymus
Counselor
W.T. White High School
(214)385-5660

SAMPLE COVER LETTER

YOUR NAME
Address
City, State Zip
Home Telephone
E-mail Address

Date

Coach's Name
Men's/Women's Volleyball Coach
Name of College
Address
City, State, Zip

Dear (Coach's Name):

Based on my research in preparation for choosing a college, (name of college) has both an excellent reputation, and the types of academic and athletic programs I hope to pursue after graduation from high school.

The enclosed resume details my academic standing and Volleyball experience. I am currently a junior, with a GPA of ___ on a 4.0 scale, and taking college preparatory classes with an emphasis on (list core courses). The strength and variety of courses offered at (name of college) provide several degree plans of interest to me, although I have not yet decided on a specific major area of study.

More specifically, your Volleyball program is of primary interest to me. I believe my skills and abilities would fit well into your program, and enable me to contribute to the success of the (team name) while continuing to develop my Volleyball talents under your style of play.

I would like to pursue all available means for financial aid, and I believe my academic standing should qualify me for scholarship assistance.

Thank you for any consideration you can give me as a future (team name). Please send me information on your program, and any suggestions you may have on how best to prepare for attendance at (name of school) in the fall of (your graduation year).

Sincerely,

(Your Name)

Editor's Note: The sample cover letter is for illustration purposes only. Please be original and write your own letter. College coaches tell us they have seen this one a few times and are likely to file it in the trash!

CONDUCTING CAMPUS VISITS

To get the best feel for a college, it is best to plan a minimum of two visits to the campus - an initial visit and a second or "paid" visit. If this were to occur, you should plan an initial visit sometime in your junior year. The second visit would then occur during your senior year. Sometimes, because of distance or a late start in the college search process, this is not possible and the visits will have to be combined.

The initial visit is a way for you to get acquainted with the college and for the coaches and players to get acquainted with you - their recruit. Many athletes schedule a number of college visits on the same trip, as each visit will take only a short time. The initial visit should include a tour of the campus, an admissions interview (if available) and a talk with the volleyball coach or a representative of the volleyball program. As a student-athlete, you will need to call ahead and arrange interview times with the admissions department and the volleyball coach.

Come prepared for both of these interviews, and be appropriately dressed since first impressions can mean a great deal. You should also have a list of specific questions to be asked of coaches, players, and college administrators. Coaches and admissions personnel are looking for individuals who have some substance. You should ask pertinent questions that fill in the gaps of your knowledge about the college and its volleyball program.

Sample questions to ask the Volleyball coach:

*What is the status of the returning team, including eligibility of players at the same position as the recruit?
*What are your chances of making the team and/or significant playing time as a freshman, sophomore, etc.?
*What is the availability and chances for a scholarship?
*What is the general practice schedule?
*How much time does Volleyball require?
*Does Volleyball interfere with a player's ability to complete academic work?
*How does the red-shirt program work?
*What are the coaches' goals for the team in the next four years?
*What equipment is provided for each player?

Many admissions department personnel will ask difficult questions that will require you to give thoughtful, unprepared responses. Think through your answers and give serious intuitive answers. Most of these questions will be about personal experiences so no preparation is required. It is helpful, however, to gain experience in an interview situation, be completely up-front with the coach and ask questions that will help you to better understand the level of commitment required for participation in the volleyball program.

Most coaches will not bring up the subject of volleyball scholarships unless asked, so find out what is available and what your own chances might be. As a recruit, be persistent but tactful in seeking answers to all your questions. The coach will want to get a feel for your personality - the type of player and competitor you are and may ask for your own assessment of personal strengths and weaknesses. The coach may also want to know where his program stands on the your list of colleges and universities, and information regarding other schools of interest. Be sure to answer these questions thoroughly and honestly.

The second visit, which can be a paid visit, should occur after you have narrowed your choices to a smaller number of schools. Paid visits can only be made after a student has started their senior year. Each student is allowed five paid visits by NCAA rules to different NCAA schools and only one paid visit per school. A visit would be considered "paid" if the volleyball program provides anything free for the recruit (i.e., meals, lodging, etc.) The college may pay for transportation to and from the school and any expenses incurred during normal living arrangements as long as these expenses are not excessive. Paid visits can last up to 48 hours.

On the second visit the recruit will probably be staying with a varsity volleyball team member. If this occurs, you are encouraged to go to class with the player to experience the full flavor of campus life, and get questions answered from a player's perspective. Be aware, however, that the coach will be observing you, so please act responsibly. At NCAA institutions, a recruit may not practice with the team while on a paid visit.

Editor's Note: If the two visits have to be combined, be ready to evaluate the college on a one-shot basis. Do as much as possible in this visit. Remember, you will spend almost four years of your life at your chosen college. An insightful visit limits the chances of making a mistake.

THE WORLD WIDE WEB AND YOUR COLLEGE SEARCH

ADVANTAGES OF THE INTERNET

With the low cost of computers and ease of Internet access almost anyone can now get "online", whether it be from your high school, home, public library, or the workplace. What previously was a medium for use only by computer enthusiasts has now become a medium for the masses. A simple message can easily be viewed by millions of people - almost instantly. That's a "reach" more powerful than any television network or metro newspaper could ever have dreamed about even 5 years ago. And that message could be your message!

This rapidly-evolving medium continues to open the door of opportunity to both student-athletes and college coaches alike. Taking a proactive approach to the recruiting process in today's marketplace means using all the tools current technology has to offer. Your ability to promote yourself to college coaches should not be limited to a well-written resume and personal cover letter. E-mail and personal Web sites have become an effective and viable means of communicating with busy college coaches caught balancing games and training sessions, a hectic travel and recruiting schedule, and their personal life. With a laptop computer and Internet access a coach can literally take his office with him. The net effect has been to stretch recruiting budgets and provide alternate means of locating and tracking potential recruits. A quick e-mail to or from a college coach shows genuine interest and opens the door for future direct contact either by telephone or in person.

Through extensive recruiting budgets, and both academic and athletic scholarships, colleges commit significant funds annually to the students and athletes they attract. To minimize these costs and to attract both the top students and top athletes, colleges and sports information directors have jumped into the Internet with both feet, making available vast resources. Realistically, they have only just begun to really explore the capacity of the Internet to help people learn and communicate about their programs. This new wealth of information has allowed student-athletes to explore how they match up with other scholarship candidates, and where playing opportunities may exist.

WHY YOU SHOULD HAVE YOUR OWN WEB SITE

As a result of recent technology developments, you can easily become part of this online community, have your own Web site, and explore the benefits of the Internet during the recruiting process. Your personal Web site will allow you to promote your abilities directly to coaches and college selection committees. Maintaining your site will provide a "fresh look" with new information and your accomplishments, including game highlights, honors, and personal stats. And you can manage this site on your own without depending on third party assistance - i.e. recruiting services or a Webmaster. You control the information being published and the timely release of updated information. Remember, the recruiting process represents a narrow window from your sophomore through senior year in high school. If playing college athletics remains your primary goal, you will want to create a chronological overview of your athletic career to assist college coaches in evaluating your abilities as both a player and student-athlete.

Your Web site can also be a powerful networking tool. Learn to use it effectively to interact with other people in your respective sport, such as your prep or club coach, and to assist you in creating your own online community. Having your information readily available will help others in promoting your abilities directly to various contacts at the collegiate level. To maximize your site's effectiveness, be sure to promote it through your personal e-mail account. (There are various providers who offer free e-mail accounts.) By building a private directory of your contacts, you can provide quick and effective notification of updates to your site.

Also encourage your team to build and maintain its own Web site. Information about the other players including the competitiveness and overall success of your team will all contribute to a college coach's evaluation of you as a player, and whether you are the "right fit" for his / her athletic program.

TIPS FOR DEVELOPING YOUR WEB SITE

Just like any good advertisement, your site must effectively convey your message to your target audience - in this case college coaches. Make it concise, well organized, and informative. Use your creativity to effectively communicate your message, and try to minimize the entertainment value associated with all the "gimmicky" shooting stars, fireballs, flashing signs, and scrolling message screens in more commercial sites.

THE WORLD WIDE WEB AND
YOUR COLLEGE SEARCH

Treat your Web site as print medium. Lay it out like a news magazine and use color highlights, font styles, photographs, and subtle graphics to dress your page and not to dominate it. The college coaches will appreciate being able to quickly get the information they need, and are more likely to thoroughly read the material you present, if they are not being bombarded by technical enhancements.

WHAT SHOULD APPEAR ON YOUR WEB SITE

When building your site, it is of primary importance for you to provide as much information about yourself both as an athlete and student without jeopardizing your own right to privacy. Remember, anyone with a computer and Internet access will be able to log-on and visit your Web site. Although you will want to include a resume of your accomplishments, do not include your home address, telephone number, and social security number, which should not be a part of your biographical information on the Internet.

If you want to include a contact number, use your e-mail address or a third party telephone number such as a parent's work number or (with permission) that of your coach. While your most important personal contact will be directly with the college coach, if interested he / she will likely ask permission from your parents' before speaking with you, or leave a telephone number where you can call back. College coaches are recruiting you - not your parents, so be sure you take the time to speak with them personally and return their calls. As a quick overview your Web site should include the following:

Your name, city of residence, e-mail address, third party contact number, high school and its address, graduation year, GPA, class rank, standardized test scores, a listing of your extra-curricular activities, religious preference (if pertinent to your college search), accomplishments - both academically and athletically, other sports you participate in, current coaches -high school and club teams, win-loss records on those teams, current game schedule, any tournaments or showcase events you know you will be participating in, and personal references (again with permission only).

A current photograph - in your uniform works fine as long as your face is plainly visible!

Team photograph and action shot of yourself

In addition to the above, take time to describe some of your personal goals both on and off the field of play; possible degree plans; what you are looking for in a college environment - urban v. rural, larger v. smaller enrollment, on-campus v. off-campus housing, geographic location, climate, social aspects-fraternities/sororities, religious affiliation, etc.; and athletically - under what coaching style you best excel; your style of play; level of competition - NCAA Division I, II, III, NAIA, NCCAA, or NJCAA; and basically, anything a college coach and admissions department can use to evaluate you as a potential student-athlete for their college or university.

WHEN TO LAUNCH AND UPDATE YOUR WEB SITE

Your Web site is a personal snap shot of you as a student and potential college athlete. Much of the information you publish on your site will remain static (unchanged), however, any pertinent information including changes in your e-mail address and contact numbers, updated grades, standardized test scores, class rank, team and personal accomplishments, certain photographs, etc. should be updated. This information should be reviewed at least semi-annually beginning your sophomore year, and as available beginning your junior year in high school.

THE WORLD WIDE WEB AND YOUR COLLEGE SEARCH

PROMOTING YOURSELF AND YOUR WEB SITE

Identify the colleges you wish to target using one of the various student-athlete college handbooks currently available, or by directly visiting college Web sites on the Internet. Develop a Name & Address Book of college coaches capturing college Web sites and coaches e-mail addresses within the directory of your e-mail service. Prepare a more extensive resume with your home address, telephone numbers, birth date, and your Social Security Number along with a personal cover letter to be sent both e-mail and hard copy directly to college coaches beginning your sophomore year in high school. Be sure to include your Web address and do encourage the coaches to visit it periodically for updates. You will want to follow-up the initial distribution of resumes and cover letters with a personal phone call directly to the coach 7-10 days after it is sent. Remember, due to NCAA restrictions, college coaches may talk to you if they receive your call, but will not be able to return your telephone calls until after July 1st going into your senior year in high school.

Do not overlook the importance of hyper links to other Web sites. You will want to initiate link requests to your team or club for permission to link to their Web site. College coaches who are attracted to a particular team or club because of their reputation for competitiveness, or developing college level players in the past, may just "stumble" on your site. You will not want to miss-out on the opportunity to be "front and center" with your Web site if you fit their criteria as a player.

SUMMARY

From your Web site, coaches can view your player statistics, accomplishments, etc. and extend their recruiting efforts beyond the limits of their budgets. So what does this mean to you as a student-athlete? With only limited resources invested, you can systematically identify college programs, evaluate scholarship opportunities, review college admission requirements, view the campuses and athletic facilities, and create a personal profile to share with coaches both in the U.S. and around the world - all without ever leaving your desktop computer!

Editor's Note: These are merely guidelines and suggestions for using the Internet and building your own Web site. It is strongly recommended that any decision to build and maintain your own personal site be something that you discuss with your parents, coaches, and academic advisers. As well, you will need to refer to current collegiate recruiting guidelines with regard to use of the Internet and as outlined in the NCAA Guide For The College-Bound Student-Athlete - for more information call 913.339.1906, or visit their Web site at www.ncaa.org. Also, please refer to the NAIA Guide For the College-Bound Student - for more information call 918.494.8828, or visit their Web site at www.naia.org.

COLLEGE PLANNING CHECKLIST

Jul Aug Sep — FRESHMEN YEAR

ACTIVITY	Date Planned	Date Scheduled	Date Completed	NOTES
Participate in High School Orientation				
Student meeting with counselor				
Set Academic Plan for Freshman Year				
Evaluate your Time Management Skills				
Explore possible Community Service Opportunities				
Do your homework				

Oct Nov Dec — FRESHMEN YEAR

ACTIVITY	Date Planned	Date Scheduled	Date Completed	NOTES
Parent/Student meeting with counselor				
Use MatchFit to begin to assess your academic and athletic needs				
Write a letter to a college coach				
Write a description of your "ideal" College Program				
Student Meeting with coaches to evaluate athletic development				
Participate with a Community Service Organization				
Don't forget to study				

Jan Feb Mar — FRESHMEN YEAR

ACTIVITY	Date Planned	Date Scheduled	Date Completed	NOTES
Start a college file				
Research possible camps to attend				
Review progress with parents				
Identify the NCAA "Core Courses"				
Set Individual athletic goals for the summer				
Perform on the court				

Apr May Jun — FRESHMEN YEAR

ACTIVITY	Date Planned	Date Scheduled	Date Completed	NOTES
Student meeting with counselor to review goals-progress-interest				
Review progress with parents				
Set academic plan for next year				
Pick college campus to visit				
Attend a college camp				
Finish the school year strong				

COLLEGE PLANNING CHECKLIST

Jul Aug Sep

ACTIVITY	Date Planned	Date Scheduled	Date Completed	NOTES
Student meeting with counselor				
Set academic plan for Junior year				
Check with counselor for PSAT & PACT registration deadline				
Purchase *Official Athletic College Guide*				
Obtain current *Guide for the College Bound Student Athlete* from NCAA				
Complete a practice admission application				
Set-up files - begin to assemble college information				
Do your homework				

Oct Nov Dec

ACTIVITY	Date Planned	Date Scheduled	Date Completed	NOTES
Parent/Student meeting with counselor				
Verify PSAT & PACT test dates				
Use academic & CPN to write for admis-sions information for several schools				
Review progress with parents				
Attend College Night at high school - gather college information brochures				
Begin to identify 7-10 college programs				
Student meeting with coaches to evaluate athletic development				
Don't forget to study				

Jan Feb Mar

ACTIVITY	Date Planned	Date Scheduled	Date Completed	NOTES
Review material in college file				
Continue requesting information				
Review progress with parents				
Become familiar with financial aid publications from counselor				
Begin to identify 7-10 college programs				
Perform on the field				

Apr May Jun

ACTIVITY	Date Planned	Date Scheduled	Date Completed	NOTES
Parent/Student meeting with counselor to review goals-progress-interest				
Review progress with parents				
Begin a College Contact List				
Review academic progress				
Plan next year's academic program				
Begin investigating sources for financial aid				
Continue to update list of potential colleges				
Do your homework				

COLLEGE PLANNING CHECKLIST

JUNIOR YEAR

Jul Aug Sep

ACTIVITY	Date Planned	Date Scheduled	Date Completed	NOTES
Student meeting with counselor				
Review academic plan for Junior year				
Check with counselor for Oct. & Nov. SAT & ACT registration deadlines				
Purchase **MATCHFIT** *Online Identification Service*				
Develop more selective college contact list-begin writing to college coaches				
Review Achievement Test results				
Purchase updated edition of the *Official Athletic College Guide*				
Relay event schedule to college coaches				

Oct Nov Dec

ACTIVITY	Date Planned	Date Scheduled	Date Completed	NOTES
Review potential college list				
Verify & schedule SAT & ACT test dates				
Explore opportunities for college / high school joint enrollment credit				
Achievement Test given in Nov. nationally				
Verify December SAT registration deadline with counselor				
Visit College Nights / College Fairs				
Complete at least (2) two admission applications for practice only				
Get Letters of Recommendation/References				

Jan Feb Mar

ACTIVITY	Date Planned	Date Scheduled	Date Completed	NOTES
Organize your personal portfolio				
Visit local colleges of different types & sizes				
Review Achievement Test results				
Check with counselor for re-test schedule pending on first testing results				
Develop your preferred college list				
Arrange for spring/summer visits & interviews at colleges from preferred college list				
Research internet for financial aid information				
Perform in the classroom and on the field				

Apr May Jun

ACTIVITY	Date Planned	Date Scheduled	Date Completed	NOTES
Parent/Student meeting with counselor to review goals-progress-interest				
Take SAT and ACT				
Develop academic plan for senior year				
Achievement Test given in May				
Explore possibility of enrolling in AP courses during senior year for college credit				
Review admission applications questions & concerns with counselors				
Register with NCAA National Clearinghouse				

COLLEGE PLANNING CHECKLIST

Jul Aug Sep

ACTIVITY	Date Planned	Date Scheduled	Date Completed	NOTES
Finalize application essay topics				
Relay fall schedule to college coaches				
College coaches coaches can make contact & receive calls after Junior year after July 1				
Purchase *Official Athletic College Guide*				
Obtain current *Guide for the College Bound Student Athlete* from NCAA				
Parent/student meeting with counselor				
Verify SAT/ ACT retake schedule and registration dates				
Arrange for college visits & interviews				

Oct Nov Dec

ACTIVITY	Date Planned	Date Scheduled	Date Completed	NOTES
Update student-athlete portfolio				
Request referrals from teachers/coaches				
Review application essays with teachers-parents for suggestions & proofing				
Get tax records to prepare financial aid forms				
If applying for early admissions, complete and send applications				
Obtain all financial aid forms(national & from schools)				
Narrow list to (5) five schools for possible admissions application				
Apply to at (3) three schools				
Inform counselor of applications sent				
National Letter of Intent Signing in November				
Achievement Test in November nationally				

Jan Feb Mar

ACTIVITY	Date Planned	Date Scheduled	Date Completed	NOTES
File financial Aid Forms ASAP after Jan. 1				
Final visits to schools where applied				
Make sure all applications have been sent				
Parent / student meeting with counselor to verify all transcript verification is complete				
Re-submit any necessary information				
Re-take SAT & ACT if necessary				
Decision Time - "Good Luck"				
National Letter of Intent Signing Day in Feb				

Apr May Jun

ACTIVITY	Date Planned	Date Scheduled	Date Completed	NOTES
Review acceptances and offers-choose college you wish to attend				
AP Examination given in May				
If put on waiting lists, contact college admissions officers & guidance counselor				
Submit necessary deposits to college chosen				
Notify college you have chosen to attend				
Notify colleges applied not attending				
Notify counselor of final choice and have final grades, proof of graduation,etc. sent				

COLLEGE ADMISSIONS

APPLYING TO SELECTIVE COLLEGES:
The Admissions Committee

What makes applying to selective colleges and universities more of a challenge is that they are in fact selective; that is to say, they have many applicants to choose from and have therefore established selection criteria to determine worthy candidates. Students are not chosen solely on the basis of academic credentials, but also based on what the college is looking for in terms of filling academic and athletic programs. As a volleyball player, you will not be evaluated like other candidates; your ability, as well as the needs of the team will be taken into careful consideration. Although the coach will have input, he will not have the authority to make the final decision regarding your admission request.

The matching approach to college admissions requires two basic steps: getting a realistic view of what is available, and an accurate assessment of your abilities. The number of selective colleges is small and can be defined easily by looking at any of the readily available guidebooks. Although definitions of "selective" may vary, most knowledgeable sources would say there are perhaps two hundred such institutions in the country. Of these, not all schools offer volleyball programs, compete in NCAA Division I, offer scholarships or have strong winning traditions. The point is that by evaluating academic admission requirements and strength of the volleyball program, you can separate institutions into categories and place them in a simple matrix or grid. (See page 23.) The programs more suitable to your abilities will appear with the higher accumulated values.

You can, and should, undertake a similar exercise for yourself looking at your academic achievements and standardized test scores, and rank them along with your volleyball abilities. As an example, assign values for your SAT scores with a ranking from a high of 1600 = 10, to 1000 = 4 or a top 20% class ranking being worth an 8. Create similar values for playing on district or state level teams, all league and MVP honors, invitational opportunities, and so on through your senior year. You can then roughly determine where you stand. Keep in mind that there are relatively few institutions or individuals that score high in all areas. Just as it is very difficult to find institutions that have high academic standards and offer competitive volleyball with a strong winning tradition, it is very difficult to find "blue chip" athletes that are similarly "blue chip" scholars. In fact, college administrators concede that there are only a limited number of gifted volleyball players with superb academic credentials to fill the needs of their institutions. The resulting compromise is to balance academic standards with athletic abilities in order to find qualified student-athletes to fill college rosters. If your volleyball abilities are stronger than your academics, try to match-up with those schools that are stronger in volleyball than academics, and vice versa.

Once you have identified compatible colleges and universities, you can begin to eliminate schools from this list based on standard evaluation criteria - academic programs offered, distance from home, cost, and so on. This will further narrow your choices and give you an idea of where you might want to make initial contacts. Of course, while you are looking at colleges, coaches may be contacting you, which may continue to expand the number of colleges on your list.

Further elimination will occur by looking at particulars of your given situation - how much a college may want you to enroll, and whether your academic credentials deviate too far from their norm. In other words, are you as qualified as other applicants? If not, how far might an admissions committee be willing to compromise to get a talented volleyball athlete?

COLLEGE ADMISSIONS

First, try to gauge your value to the volleyball program. Keep in mind that not all institutions apply the same admission standards to their athletes as other students. Look at your position - what is the depth of the team at that position, and graduation year of the starters? Is their skill level far greater than yours? In short, do they need help, and do they need it right away? If the answer is clearly yes, an admissions committee may be likely to compromise on the academic side. However, there is a limit to how far they will go, even for a marquee player!

This "flexibility" can only be estimated, and the only truly reliable way to know is to ask the players. The coach should be willing to give you their phone numbers. If you have any questions, do not hesitate to contact them about their background and their experience academically on campus. Of course, be sure to ask how many hours they commit to their studies, so that you can fairly assess both their ability and willingness to work. If your credentials are well below key players, your chances are not good; if they are the same as average players, they are good; and if they are better than average players, your chances are excellent.

This should give you a pretty clear picture of your chances. Thus allowing you to direct your inquiries accordingly. Your chances for success will increase when your academic credentials are similiar to current players, and your volleyball ability is within two years of making a contribution at your position. Be wary of long shots because they are just that and rarely pan out. Be aware, also, that any time you show a college both athletic and academic promise, you not only assure your chances of admission, but greatly increase your chances for a merit scholarship.

PRESENTING YOURSELF:
The Application and Interview

How can you improve your chances at any selective institution? Present yourself well. It will not always be the difference, but it does make a difference and you want as much on your side as possible. You have only one, two, and possibly three bona fide opportunities to do this. The first, and most important, is the application itself; the second is a campus interview or visit that you initiate; the third is the campus visit that may be initiated by the athletic department, and for some selective schools, the fourth may be an interview with a review board. For all of these the basics are the same: you want to create the most positive impression that you can without giving up spontaneity or sincerity. Fake it and you will be found out - guaranteed!

The application should be organized, neat, complete, and returned early. The appearance cannot be over-emphasized. Admissions officers and committees will form an impression of you based on the application. Never send in anything that is not first rate. Make sure that all words are correctly spelled and use proper grammar. Be sure to type it, and think of it as a professional resume.

The same rules apply for personal meetings or interviews. Dress appropriately, neatly, and with good taste. Also, make sure that you are properly groomed. Being over-dressed is always better than being under-dressed, and take into account the appropriate style of clothes for the season and region of the country you will be visiting. Make your appointment well in advance and be on time. Better yet, be slightly early. If you are unavoidably detained, call and let the person know you will be late. A good rule of thumb is to prepare yourself as though your interview is with a potential employer. Do your homework on the school you are visiting and master the basic information to minimize dialogue about programs the institution does not have.

COLLEGE ADMISSIONS

Different individuals and institutions will conduct interviews in different ways, however, most selective institutions are interested in some very basic things: What interests you? How do you invest your time? With what results? What have you gained from this? Have you pursued any outside interests in depth, and have you been recognized by others for this effort? Can you ask intelligent questions? Can you respond intelligently to intuitive questions? The outcome will be to discern excellence, dedication, motivation and enthusiasm. Or to put it another way, they are designed to find out if you are as good in the classroom as you are on the field!

Above all, spend some time collecting your thoughts before the interview. Why are you interested in this particular college or university? What is important for your own personal growth? If you need to, write down your questions. Try to word them in a way that will reveal useful information. For example, ask how many of the classes during your freshman year will have less than 25 students. Ask whether specific classes are taught by tenured senior faculty. Ask how many volleyball players graduated in the top third of their class and what the grade point average is for the volleyball team. Be as particular and specific as possible. The more thorough you are, the more likely it is that you will be remembered in a positive way. And of course, keep in mind that although the interview will rarely get you crossed off the list; if done well, it will most certainly put you at or near the top.

IMPORTANT DIFFERENCES AMONG SELECTIVE INSTITUTIONS: The Six Categories

It is worthwhile to identify the various types of colleges and universities, and to learn more about their admissions criteria. **The six types of institutions are private colleges and universities (including the Ivy League), and state or public universities, the U.S. Service Academies, state and private military academies, and junior colleges.** While there are clearly differences among the various members within each group, understanding the common characteristics is beneficial to understanding the admissions process. As a group, the private selective colleges including the Ivy League have the most freedom in pursuing any type of mission that they choose, and almost total freedom in choosing whatever students they wish to admit to achieve that mission. This freedom is occasionally curbed by athletic league affiliations, but more generally is curbed by faculty review of the admissions activities, usually by setting higher academic standards as a part of the admission policy. Although it is extremely rare for faculty to be involved in selecting candidates, it does happen in some instances, and you need to be aware of this in researching schools.

Faculty members generally put more weight on academic indicators and objective test scores than admissions officers. Most admissions officers are very reluctant to admit athletes who are significantly less qualified academically than other candidates because of the negative opinion that will be formed. Be sure as well that your references include high school faculty can vouch for your character, integrity, and academic accomplishments.

The Ivy League is an association of private colleges comprising a specific athletic conference; it is the only athletic association founded on the premise that athletes should not be given scholarships. While this may be important if you are looking for an athletic scholarship, it has even more important ramifications for admissions. As an athletic conference, each member institution is required to report the academic qualifications of recruited athletes to other member institutions such that all athletes are within certain guidelines for the general population of admitted and enrolled students.

COLLEGE ADMISSIONS

Of all selective institutions, *state* and *public colleges* and **universities** will typically have lower academic admission standards for residents of their state; however, they often have higher standards for those out-of-state applicants. Applying to a selective university in your state always makes good sense. Applying to a public college or university out-of-state should be carefully evaluated since private selectives may be more generous in terms of admissions standards and financial aid. One way to gauge this is to look at the geographic composition of the members of the volleyball team. If a large number of the players come from out-of-state you know that the admission committee has sufficient leeway to give you reasonable consideration; if the converse is true you may want to place your bets elsewhere. Remember, too, that the number of public selective institutions is rather small. This is due to the fact that, by their public nature, tuition and admission requirements must be affordable for residents, yet still attractive to qualified out-of-state applicants. For this reason, your residence may be as much a factor in determining your chance for admission as your credentials. View this, of course, in light of the geographic composition of the athletic teams as indicated above.

The U.S. Service Academies differ from the other groups in several important respects, not the least of which is the fact that they are free to those student athlete's who gain appointment. While the Ivy League offers no merit scholarships, although they are very generous with those demonstrating need, the service academies offer all appointees a merit scholarship. Of course, the hitch is that applicants must be sure they want the discipline and lifestyle that these institutions offer, and also willing to accept military service requirements after graduation. The other salient difference is that although these institutions are selective, they conduct their admissions business very differently from all the rest. Essentially, almost everyone who is admitted attends. As a result, the number of students admitted is very small compared to other institutions where (as a general rule) fewer than half of the admitted students will choose to enroll. Since the general admission procedures are readily available, there is no need to cover them here. Be sure, however, that you understand the singular nature of these institutions, the unique environment and curriculum, and the difficulty of transferring to another college or university later if you find it's not for you.

State and Private Military Academies have the same characteristics as other state and private colleges and universities for admissions and available financial aid, but offer similar discipline and lifestyle as the U.S. Service Academies without the mandatory military service requirements after graduation.

JUNIOR COLLEGES

There are many paths to following your pursuit of higher education. A junior college is often a viable alternative to beginning a college education at a four-year school. A student-athlete may make a more comfortable transition to campus life in a smaller, friendlier and more familiar setting. The junior college also offers an Associate Degree for those who are seeking to gain employment after only two years of study.

Most junior colleges build a solid academic foundation for students who wish to move on to a four-year degree program and for those who have not fully applied themselves in previous settings. They allow students to acclimate themselves more slowly to the rigors of college life relieving some of the academic pressure by adding a personal touch that may not be found at larger universities. This does not mean, however, that they are less demanding than four-year institutions.

COLLEGE ADMISSIONS

Junior colleges almost always offer a smaller student-instructor ratio than that of a larger state school. And, because building the "academic foundation" is paramount, the junior college normally excels in support services. Resource rooms, tutoring, labs, mentoring programs, and academic counseling are staples of a junior college education.

When selecting a college, money may be a primary concern. Attending a nearby community college while living at home for the first year or two can significantly cut the cost of a four-year degree. The junior college offers a very affordable tuition that allows students and their parents some breathing room in the first two years. Moving away from home to attend a junior college offer the advantage of lower tuition, however housing, food and miscellaneous living expenses may match the costs for room and board while attending an in-state university.

Many junior college programs are serious about athletics, recognizing that they are valuable in the overall education of an individual. It is also widely recognized that through athletics an individual can increase his or her market value as a prospective student-athlete to a four-year school.

Junior college athletics are geared towards the continuation of skill development for an individual in a particular sport. Some athletes do not reach their full potential in high school. As in the academic areas, the junior college athletic program is also geared to improving the student's physical abilities. NJCAA intercollegiate athletic competition is very keen, with the various conference, district, regional and national play-offs and tournaments providing a great proving ground and barometer for student-athletes who want to pursue their sport at the NCAA Division I, II, and III levels, or in the NAIA.

Many student-athletes fall through the cracks of the recruiting process, while others are simply unable to make a decision about their future in education and athletics. For some, the financial situation is appealing; for others, the need to develop academically is a priority. These are all reasons that may best describe the cross section of student-athletes found in many junior colleges. Junior college affords them the opportunity to play volleyball at the collegiate level. For the most part, these student-athletes continue their education and playing careers at four-year schools. Many are recruited from the junior college setting, and many receive scholarships. These are success stories that cannot be ignored or discounted.

SUMMARY

Evaluate yourself and selective institutions on two dimensions - athletic and academic, then match them as closely as possible. Apply early and try your best to leave a good first impression both on the application and during interviews or visits. Understand the differences that exist in the general grouping of selective institutions. Use this information to your advantage as you attempt to choose the best match possible.

Above all, do not get caught up thinking this is a "life or death" decision, or that, only one college could possibly be the "right" one for you. The fact is, if a college can provide the educational opportunities you want for your future and offer you an opportunity to play volleyball, it is really hard to see how you can lose!

PAYING FOR COLLEGE

GORDON PECK
FORMER ASSOCIATE DEAN OF ADMISSIONS AND FINANCIAL AID
DAVIDSON COLLEGE

As you begin the important process of selecting a college, you and your parents will probably be influenced by the stated cost of each institution. Please do not be! At least, not at first.

Too many students rule out a college that may be well suited to meet their needs because of that college's apparent high price. They assume that a student must be from a low-income family in order to qualify for financial aid. They are unaware of student employment opportunities, creative payment plans, and low interest loans. Some have not turned over enough stones in search of competitive scholarships and restricted grants. Others are simply bewildered by the perceived complexities of the financial aid application process.

In the pages that follow, we will attempt to dispel these misconceptions and to provide you with the information you need to plan the financing of the most important investment you may make in your lifetime: your college education. We will focus on three general areas of assistance:

> **Need-Based Financial Aid**
> **Non Need-Based Aid Including Merit Scholarships**
> **Family Financial Planning**

Need-based aid will receive the most attention because, as the foundation of most college financial aid programs, it provides the largest dollar volume of assistance. Before we guide you through the analysis, it is important that you accurately interpret the college price tag.

COLLEGE COSTS

No matter where you enroll, your expenses will include direct educational costs and living expenses. Financial aid assistance is generally determined by your school year budget using five categories:

> **Tuition And Fees**
> **Room And Board**
> **Books And Supplies**
> **Personal Expenses (Clothing, Laundry, Medical, etc.)**
> **Transportation**

Typically the first category represents fixed costs payable directly to the college.

Room and board will be set by the college in the case of resident (on campus) students, but expenses may vary greatly for students living off campus.

Books, supplies, and personal expenses will vary with the student's academic program and personal spending habits.

Transportation costs for resident students are generally estimated on the basis of two round-trips home during the academic year while commuting students must estimate gasoline, parking and other related costs.

PAYING FOR COLLEGE

To be certain that you are comparing oranges with oranges when determining estimated college costs, we suggest that you use a chart similar to X1(below) to record actual and estimated costs in each category for each college you are considering. Be sure you are comparing costs for the same academic year. College A may be publishing 1998-99 costs while College B may be listing 1999-2000 costs.

X1 - ESTIMATING COLLEGE COSTS

Items of Expense	College A	College B	College C	College D
Tuition	_____	_____	_____	_____
Fees	_____	_____	_____	_____
Books/supplies	_____	_____	_____	_____
Room	_____	_____	_____	_____
Board	_____	_____	_____	_____
Personal expenses	_____	_____	_____	_____
Transportation	_____	_____	_____	_____
Other	_____	_____	_____	_____
TOTAL	_____	_____	_____	_____

Most colleges will provide estimates of costs in each category based on annual student surveys. Insist that the colleges you are considering provide these figures in updated form.

YOUR FAMILY CONTRIBUTION

Now that you have determined the estimated annual costs of your top choice of colleges, let us take a close look at how colleges determine your family's contribution toward college costs. Remember: do not rule out any college until you have analyzed all the possible means of reducing the real costs.

All colleges and government agencies expect you to pay something toward college expenses according to your family's financial strength. Most college financial aid offices will determine your family's ability to pay based on a standard financial aid "need analysis" system called Congressional Methodology. The analysis will examine your parents' income and assets as well as your own savings and summer earnings

You may assume that families with higher incomes will be expected to contribute more to college expenses, but the methodology also considers family assets (home equity, investments, savings) and family expenses. A family with six dependents and unusual medical expenses will be expected to contribute less than a family of three even though their annual income is similar.

In addition to the parent's contribution, you, the student, will be expected to contribute at least $700 towards your annual educational costs. The actual amount will depend on your earnings for the previous year and the savings you have been able to accumulate.

PAYING FOR COLLEGE

To the extent that each family's situation is unique, financial aid officers invite you to provide documentation which may substantiate unusual expenses or circumstances which cannot be adequately demonstrated on the FAF. Usually, high consumer debt may not be a legitimate basis for adjusting the results of the standard formula, but many other uncontrollable drains on income may be worth sharing with each aid office.

Table X2 provides an approximation of what many college, state, and private student aid programs will expect parents to pay at various income levels.

TABLE X2				ESTIMATED PARENTS CONTRIBUTION											
This chart of typical expected family contributions derives from Financial Aid Form (FAF)															
Net assets $20000				$4000				$6000				$8000			
Family Size: 3	4	5	6	3	4	5	6	3	4	5	6	3	4	5	6
INCOME Before Taxes															
$8,000	0	0	0	0	0	0	0	0	0	0	0	314	0	0	0
12000	0	0	0	0	0	0	0	417	0	0	0	999	493	0	0
16000	266	0	0	562	72	0	0	1090	600	139	0	1618	1128	1284	130
20000	916	398	0	0	1176	687	228	0	1706	1215	756	236	2316	1750	916	784
24000	1567	1049	563	13	1804	1302	843	323	2430	1848	1371	851	3183	2481	1927	1379
28000	2296	1700	1214	663	2544	1947	1458	937	3317	2585	2025	1456	4265	3376	2686	2034
32000	3216	2471	1888	1314	3451	2709	2124	1552	4451	3517	2801	2133	5579	4533	3643	2813
36000	4388	3420	2688	2001	4636	3674	2935	2231	5764	4718	3800	2947	6892	5846	4866	3814
40000	5546	4616	3711	2824	5784	4864	3958	3061	6922	5992	5051	3972	8050	7120	6179	5068
44000	6621	5691	4276	3852	6869	5939	5076	4091	7997	7067	6204	5208	9125	8195	7332	6336
48000	7834	6895	6031	5035	8072	7143	6278	5283	9200	8271	7407	6411	10328	9399	8535	7539
52000	9027	8098	7234	6238	9276	8346	7482	6487	10404	9474	8610	7615	11532	10602	9738	8743
56000	1018	930111	8437	7442	10428	9549	8685	7690	11556	10677	9813	8818	12684	11805	10941	9946
60000	11252	0384	9583	8645	11500	10633	9831	8893	12620	11761	10959	10021	13756	12889	12087	11149

Figures on the chart are based on the following assumptions:
One Child In College
Only One Parent Working
No Unusual Financial Circumstances

Your actual circumstances could lead to an increase or decrease. Please use these figures as a general guide only.

Add a minimum student contribution of $700-$1000 to the parent contribution you derived from the table and you will have a rough estimate of the total family contribution you may be expected to pay at each of the colleges where you are accepted. Remember that the parents' contribution, as derived through the need analysis system, is a measure of the family's capacity to pay over time; it is not an amount that is expected to come solely from current income. While a few families may be able to provide the entire parent contribution from current income, most families use some combination of savings and borrowing to satisfy their share of the annual college costs. Supplemental loan programs, financing, and other options will be discussed later.

PAYING FOR COLLEGE

COLLEGE COST-FAMILY CONTRIBUTION = FINANCIAL AID ELIGIBILITY

Once your estimated family contribution has been determined, it should be subtracted from the total costs of the various colleges you are considering (remember, we are talking about need-base aid; "merit" aid is another matter). Because the majority of colleges will base their analysis on the same methodology, the expected family contribution will be about the same at each college.

Knowing the total college costs at the schools you are considering (Table X1) and knowing your estimated parents' contribution (Table X2), you are now able to begin the comparison of net costs of the colleges you are considering. For purposes of illustration, let us say that your family of six is supported on an income of $52,000 and that net assets are valued at $40,000. Using Table X2, you estimate that your parents' contribution would be $6,187. You then subtract that $6,187 and $1,000 (student contribution), a total family contribution of $7,187 from the total costs at colleges A, B, C and D as follows:

	COLLEGE A	COLLEGE B	COLLEGE C	COLLEGE D
Total Costs	$ 8,000	$12,000	$16,000	$20,000
Family Contribution	7,487	7,487	7,487	7,487
Aid Eligibility	513	4,513	8,513	12,813

As the various college financial aid offices use the standardized need analysis formula, family's annual contribution to your college costs should remain constant while your "need" or financial aid eligibility will vary with college costs. College D at $20,000 will be no less affordable than College A at $8,000 for the family used in this illustration. Knowing that the family contribution will be the same at Colleges A, B, C and D, this family can concentrate on important non-financial considerations in choosing the most appropriate college.

PACKAGING

After your financial aid eligibility is determined, the next task for the financial aid office is to determine which financial aid resources should be combined to form your financial aid "package". Packages may contain grants, scholarships, student loans, and campus employment. Sources of these may include federal and state funds, independent agencies, and college itself. Not all colleges are able to offer you a package that meets all of your financial need, and among those schools that do meet 100% of financial need, aid packages may vary greatly. To illustrate, look at three possible packages that might be offered to meet the $12,813 need of a student attending College D in the previous illustration.

	SHORTFALL PACKAGE	HIGH SELF-HELP	LOW SELF-HELP
Loan	$2,500	$3,000	$2,000
Job	1,500	1,500	800
State Grant	1,000	1,000	1,000
College Grant	1,000	7,313	9,013
Total	$6,000	$12,813	$12,813

PAYING FOR COLLEGE

The **"shortfall package"** provides $6,000 of financial aid but that amount falls $6,813 short of the calculated need. Most colleges will not offer you a package that falls so far short of your need unless your application materials arrive late or the institution simply has inadequate funds to provide full need for all its students. The "high self-help" package starts with a combination of loan and job (self-help) which totals $4,500 or 35% of the package. The "low self-help" package includes a total of $2,800 in self-help or 22% of the package, a more favorable package because the student's repayment and employment responsibilities are reduced. Both of these $12,813 packages meet 100% of the student's calculated need while holding the family contribution at $7,187.

You will be informed about your calculated need and the resulting financial aid package by way of an "award letter." Each college where you have been accepted for admission, applied for aid, and provided on-time financial aid application forms, will send you an "award letter" informing you of the amount and type of aid you will receive. This letter should reach you well before the deadline date for making your admissions deposit so that you will have time to compare packages and ask questions about your package.

NON-NEED BASED ASSISTANCE

In spite of our encouragement and your family's best efforts, the need analysis system may determine that you are not eligible for need-based financial aid, or perhaps your parents feel they cannot come up with all of the family contribution calculated by your top choice colleges. What then? There may still be hope in the form of grants-in-aid, merit scholarships, payment plans, alternative loan programs, and other creative financing options.

Grants and merit scholarships--As discussed earlier, many need-based financial aid packages will include grants or scholarships. Many colleges also offer gift aid (grants and scholarships) without regard to financial need to recognize outstanding accomplishments and potential in academics, performing arts, athletics, and other special talents. These special awards may be offered to no more than ten percent of the students at a particular college and may range in value from a hundred dollars to full cost.

Competition for these college-sponsored scholarships is keen and frequently requires a separate application. You should ask each college you are considering about the requirements and procedures that apply to merit scholarships at that institution. You should explore the possibility of scholarships and grants from private organizations. Your parents' employers, professional organizations, service organizations, churches, local PTA groups, veterans' organizations, charitable societies, and many other groups frequently provide aid for college-bound students. Begin your search for these private scholarships in your school's guidance library. Also check with the public library for such guides as "The College Blue Book: Scholarships, Fellowships, Grants and Loans or Financial Aid for Higher Education," Oreon Keesler, Editor.

Again, you might turn to individual college financial aid offices about outside sources of scholarships that have been used by their students in the past.

Alternative loan program--The loans referred to in our earlier discussion of packaging are subsidized student loans, available only to students who demonstrate need. These need-based loans are provided through the Perkins or Stafford loan programs, and they are generally included within a student's need-based package.

PAYING FOR COLLEGE

In this section, we want to make you aware of educational loan options available to parents and students who may not qualify for need- based aid or who may need assistance meeting the family contribution expected by the financial aid office.

At the federal level, Congress has authorized two programs: Parent Loans for Undergraduate Students (PLUS) and Supplemental Loans for Students (SLS). PLUS loans are available for parents of dependent students, and SLS loans are for independent students. Unlike the Perkins and Stafford loan programs, there is no in-school interest subsidy and very limited opportunity to postpone payments until after college. However, the programs offer interest rates and repayment advantages over most consumer loans.

Several alternative loan programs have been developed in the private sector over the past few years. Some are supported by nonprofit organizations such as The Education Resources Institute (TERI) in Boston, and Concern: Loans for Education in Washington, D.C. These loans offer high annual limits (as much as $25,000 annually) to credit-worthy families, plus options for postponing principal repayment while the student remains in school. Banks and other for-profit organizations also sponsor loan programs. Some of these arrangements establish a line of credit which families may draw against as needed for educational costs. Other loan plans may be tied to tuition payment plans.

Tuition payment plans--Some colleges, plus a number of private financial institutions provide payment plans which allow families to spread the cost of attending college over the entire school year. Such plans provide a budget-wise option to the traditional lump sum payment at the beginning of each semester. Generally, the only charge for such programs is an application fee, unless the program is combined with an educational loan. Organizations such as Academic Management Services of Pawtucket, RI and the Knight Tuition Payment Plan of Boston work closely with several colleges in arranging individual payment plans for families.

Other options--A number of other creative options are being developed to help families better plan and manage the costs of higher education. Federal agencies, state governments, colleges, financial institutions, and various consortia are involved in the creation of savings plans, prepayment plans, tuition guarantee plans, and other alternatives too numerous to mention here. Our advice is to gather all the facts you can through your guidance office from publications such as "The College Cost Book" published by The College Board and Peterson's, "The College Money Handbook," and especially from the financial aid offices at the colleges you are considering.

SCHEDULE FOR FINANCIAL AID APPLICANTS

Junior Year

As you investigate colleges, check each college's literature for financial aid application requirements, deadlines, and any special programs for which you may be eligible. When planning your college visits, try to set an appointment to see a financial aid officer. Be prepared with specific questions about application requirements, competitive scholarship programs, packaging policies, alternative loan programs, and other questions important to your family.

Senior Year

September - get a copy of "Meeting College Costs," a publication of the College Scholarship Service, available in most guidance offices. Use the charts in this handy guide to estimate your family contribution and financial needs.

PAYING FOR COLLEGE

December - get the FAF (Financial Aid Form), the SAAC (Student Aid Application for California) or the FFS (Family Financial Statement) from the guidance office. The form may not be submitted before January 1, but you should familiarize yourself with requested information and begin to gather the financial records you will need to complete the form.

January / February - complete and submit the FAF (or SAAC or FFS). Make a copy for your records before sending them. Complete other financial aid application materials and send them to the colleges to which you are applying. Make one last check for forms you may also need to submit to be considered for private scholarship programs or other outside aid. If you anticipate that you may not be eligible or receive enough need-based aid, you should complete your investigation of alternative loan programs and other sources of non-need based aid. Be sure to include college financial aid officers as you seek advice on these matters.

April/May - carefully compare the bottom line costs to your family from each of the colleges offering you financial aid. As you inform your first choice of colleges of your decision to attend, respond also to school's offer of financial aid. Be sure to let the other colleges know of your decision to attend the first choice college.

May/June - by now your family should have submitted copies of its federal tax returns, promissory notes for student loans and other required documents to the appropriate financial aid office. If suggested by your college, the Stafford loan application should be submitted at that time.

WHOM CAN I TRUST

While your high school coach and the college athletic recruiter may be very helpful and eager to assist you in the college search, it is important that you and your family maintain direct contact with the college financial aid offices. Do not send your financial aid application materials through the coach and do not rely on his or her interpretation of your eligibility for financial aid. Too many lost documents, missed deadlines, and misinterpreted financial aid packages have been attributed to well-meaning but unnecessary intercession by athletic recruiters.

While some high school officers may not have as much time or good information as you would like, they are still the best place to start when seeking financial aid advice. At a minimum, they can put valuable material into your hands and guide you to other people who can help. Financial aid officers at the college you are considering are probably in the best position to analyze your circumstances and lead you to the best sources of need-based and non need-based financial assistance.

Editors note:Some of the publications referred to earlier can provide you with excellent guidance as you contemplate the serious matter of financing your education. We especially recommend:**The College Cost Book, 13th Edition, New York: College Entrance Examination Board**

PAYING FOR COLLEGE

FOREIGN STUDENTS

THE SPORT SOURCE, INC. has learned through its first ten years of publications that many student-athletes outside of the U.S. are using this College Guide. Because of this, we continue to include a brief outline of the steps necessary for international students to apply to schools in the U.S.

As an international applicant it is important to begin the process as early as possible. You should apply no later than 6 months prior to the semester in which you wish to begin your studies. You will need the extra time to obtain your official school records, arrange for the required examinations, forward bank verification of your financial resources, for your application to be reviewed, and to obtain your visa.

It is important to note that many U.S. colleges and universities require international students applying for undergraduate studies (bachelor's degree) to pay all expenses themselves. Many universities do not give scholarships or financial aid to international students seeking undergraduate studies.

REQUIREMENTS

International students usually are required to be proficient in the English language, and good students in their own countries before they will be considered for admission into a college in the U.S. Students usually should have 12 years of study in their own country, beginning at age six. The last four or five years should include the study of English, history, mathematics and science. Although each university may be different, this is a basic overview of what many universities require for application from international students:

An Application Form: Answer every question. Your principal or headmaster may also be asked to answer questions on the form. There may or may not be an application fee.

Financial Certification: The student or his/her parents must often submit proof that the family or sponsor can pay for the schooling. This amount can range anywhere from $14,000-$20,000 per year, including tuition, room, food, books, and other miscellaneous expenses. The university needs an official statement from a bank, employer, sponsor, or other official affidavit of support.

School Records: These are transcripts or certificates of satisfactory study. Records should include an English translation of the subjects the student has studied and grades the student has made in each subject. It is very important to explain the grading system of each school attended.

Test of English as a Foreign Language (TOEFL): This is usually required for all international students except those whose native language is English. Information about this test can be found at U.S. Embassies, Consulates, offices of the United States Information Services, or at schools in your home country.

Aptitude Tests (SAT/ACT): These tests, such as the Scholastic Aptitude Test (SAT) or American College Testing's (ACT) Assessment Program which measure verbal and mathematical ability are required for both international students and American students.

PAYING FOR COLLEGE

VISA

After you have been admitted and have submitted the financial certification information with bank statements, the university will send you a visa qualifying document. In most cases, you will be sent an I-20 Form which is used to get an F-I student visa. To get the visa, you will need to go to your nearest American Embassy or Consulate and show the following three items:

> **Your Passport**
> **Your I-20**
> **Your Current Financial Certification**

Because you may be asked to prove your financial resources, you should retain certified copies of the original financial information that you are sending to U. S. colleges when applying.

If you already are in the United States, you will not need to get a new visa; you will receive a transfer, which will extend your time to the dates of the appropriate academic program. An I-20 will be sent for you to do your transfer.

PAYING FOR COLLEGE

IF YOU HAVE MORE TIME

If college is still several years away for you, your family has the advantage of planning and saving for your college education. Remember, colleges will consider the student and their family as the first and primary source of funds for education, and the bulk of financial aid awards will continue to be given on the basis of financial need. Therefore, it behooves you to do all you can in advance to painlessly provide the calculated family contribution when the time comes.

Educational financial planning can be complicated, but it is not as cumbersome as paying for college when there has been no planning at all. Start your savings plans knowing that college choices will be more numerous for those who have planned.

Government Organizations and web sites that may be helpful in the search for financial aid:

1. **Federal Student Aid Information Center**
   PO Box 84, Washington DC 20044, (800) 433-3234, 8 am- 8 pm EST,
   Funding Your Education (free publication) www.ed.gov/prog_info/SFA/FYE
   The Student Guide (free publication) www.ed.gov/prog_info/SFA/StudentGuide

2. **U.S. Department of Education, Office of Student Financial Assistance**
   400 Maryland Avenue, Washington, DC 20202, (800) USA-LEARN
   www.ed.gov/finaid.html

Helpful Publications:

1. **Best Buys in College Education by Lucia Solorzano**
   Barron's Educational Series, Inc., 250 Wireless Blvd., Hauppauge, NY 11788,
   (800) 645-3476, www.barronseduc.com

2. **Financial Aids for Higher Education by Judy K. Santamaria & Oreon Keeslar**
   McGraw-Hill Higher Education, P.O. Box 182605, Columbus, OH 43218,
   (800) 262-4729, www.mhhe.com

3. **College Money Handbook 2001**
   Peterson's Guides, 2200 Lenox Drive, Lawrenceville, NJ 08648,
   (800) 338-3282 ext. 5333, www.petersons.com

4. **Winning Money for College**
   Peterson's Guides, 2200 Lenox Drive, Lawrenceville, NJ 08648,
   (800) 338-3282 ext. 5333, www.petersons.com

5. **The Scholarship Book 2001: The Complete Guide to Private-Sector Scholarships, Fellowships, Grants, and Loans for the Undergraduate**
   Prentice Hall Press, P.O. Box 11075, Des Moines, IA 50336,
   (800) 947-7700, www.phdirect.com

MATCHING YOUR SKILLS TO THE PROGRAM
THAT FITS YOUR NEEDS

matchfit

 ## ONLINE COLLEGE IDENTIFICATION SERVICE

Jump-start your own college search with **MATCHFIT**™ our new online college identification service offered exclusively at **www.thesportsource.com**. Confidentially enter personal biographical data including your G.P.A., class rank, and standardized test scores, along with information specific to the type of college or university you would like to attend. Your information is matched against our extensive database to identify ten (10) college programs which match your selection criteria. Then make changes to your data and re-run the search two (2) additional times.

The net effect is three (3) sets of ten (10) colleges and universities which are compatible with your requirements for a college athletic program. Any duplications further validate that particular program as one you will want to pursue. You may select any college or university and download information specific to that program directly to your PC. This includes both a general academic profile, and a detailed athletic profile with the coach's name, mailing address, office number, fax, e-mail address, and the college web address. **MATCHFIT**™ is available **www.thesportsource.com**

AN ORGANIZED APPROACH TO "THE COLLEGE CHOICE"

The following pages represent a checklist for the prospective college athlete. Along with your parents, use these guidelines in assembling your college selection criteria beginning with your sophomore year. By using these guidelines as a planning tool you will have a road map that will keep you pointed in the right direction throughout the selection process.

A simple but complete analysis is critical to filtering the information that the student-athlete will discover as you begin to look at each program. The diagrams that follows is intended to help rank each variable that may be valuable in the decision-making process. As you begin to gather information from a variety of sources you should assign a ranking - numerical value for that specific variable. Quantitatively, begin to rank your top six colleges (1 - 5) according to personal criteria with the top choice being a "5."

evaluation

evaluating the college & volleyball program

academic /athletic college profiles

ALABAMA

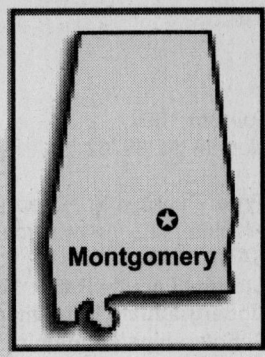

Montgomery

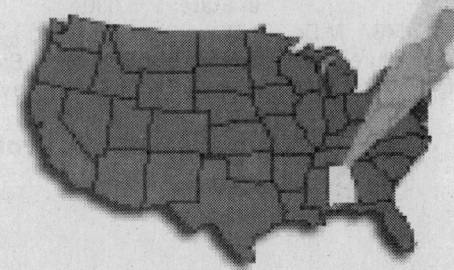

SCHOOL	CITY	AFFILIATION	PAGE
Alabama A&M University	Normal	NCAA II	41
Alabama State University	Montgomery	NCAA I	41
Auburn University	Auburn	NCAA I	42
Bevill State Community College	Fayette	NJCAA II	42
Birmingham Southern College	Birmingham	NAIA	43
Faulkner University	Montgomery	NCAA II	44
Huntingdon College	Montgomery	NAIA	44
Jacksonville State University	Jacksonville	NCAA I	45
Judson College	Marion	NCCAA	45
Miles College	Birmingham	NCAA II	46
Samford University	Birmingham	NCAA I	46
Stillman College	Tuscaloosa	NCAA III	47
Talladega College	Talledaga	NAIA	47
Troy State University	Troy	NCAA I	48
Tuskegee University	Tuskegee	NCAA II	49
University of Alabama-Tuscaloosa	Tuscaloosa	NCAA I	49
University of Alabama-Birmingham	Birmingham	NCAA I	
University of Alabama-Huntsville	Huntsville	NCAA II	50
University of Montevallo	Montevallo	NCAA II	50
University of North Alabama	Florence	NCAA II	51
University of South Alabama	Mobile	NCAA I	52
University of West Alabama	Livingston	NCAA II	52
			53

Alabama A&M University
Academic Profile

P.O Box 1597
Normal, AL 35762

Phone: (256) 851-5000

Type: Public, 4 Yr., Coed
Website: http://www.aamu.edu
SAT/ACT/GPA: 700/17
Student/Faculty Ratio: 17:1
Undergraduate Enrollment: 4,000
Scholarships/Academic:
Expenses By: Year
Degrees Conferred: AA, AS, BA, MS, MBA, M.Ed., PHD

Founded: 1875
Religion: Non-Affiliated
Housing: No
Male/Female: 48:52
Graduate Enrollment: 1,300
Athletic: Yes　　**Financial Aid:** Yes
In State: $ 5,000　　**Out of State:** $ 6,700

Programs of Study: Accounting, Agriculture, Animal Science, Art Education, Biology, Business Administration, Chemistry, Computer Science, English, History, Marketing, Physical Education, Political Science, PreVeterinary, Psychology,Telecommunications, Zoology

Women's Athletic Profile

P.O. Box 1597
Normal, AL 35762
Coach: Betty Austin
Email:

NCAA I
Lady Bulldogs, Maroon, White
Phone: (256) 858-4267
Fax: (256) 851-5369

Estimated # of Women's Volleyball Scholarships: N/A
Conference: Southern Intercollegiate Conference
Freshman Receiving Financial Aid/Academic:
Roster In State: 5
Sophomores on Team:
Most Recent Record: 15-8-0
Camp of Clinic Dates: July 2001
Positions Needed: MB, RS

Athletic: 4
Out of State: 6　　**Out of Country:** 1
Seniors on Team: 1　　**Graduation %:** 100

Schedule: U.S Naval Academy, University of Maine, Eastern Illinois, Seattle Pacific, Western Washington, Alaska Anchorage, Northwest Nazarene, Western Oregon, Central Washington, Cal State Stanislaus
Style of Play: Aggressive ball control very up tempo, but calculated.

Alabama State University
Academic Profile

915 S Jackson St.

Montgomery, AL 36101

Phone: (334) 229-4291

Type: Public, 4 Yr., Coed
Website: http://www.alasu.edu
SAT/ACT/GPA: 700/17
Student/Faculty Ratio: 17:1
Undergraduate Enrollment: 4,500
Scholarships/Academic: Yes
Expenses By: Year
Degrees Conferred: AA, AS, BA, BS, MA

Founded: 1874
Religion: Non-Affiliated
Housing: No
Male/Female: 1:14
Graduate Enrollment: 400
Athletic: Yes　　**Financial Aid:** Yes
In State: $ 3,500　　**Out of State:** $ 5,000

Programs of Study: Accounting, Banking/Finance, Biological Science, Business Administration, Computer Science, Criminal Justice, Education, Engineering, English, Fine Arts, History, Journalism, Marketing, Math, Music, Physics, Political Science, Psychology, Social Science, Visual/Performing Arts

Women's Athletic Profile

915 S. Jackson Street
Montgomery, AL 36101-0271
Coach: Sonia Price
Email: sports@hornet.alasu.edu

NCAA I
Lady Hornet, Black, Old Gold
Phone: (334) 229-7618
Fax: (334) 229-4992

Estimated # of Women's Volleyball Scholarships: N/A
Conference: Southwestern Athletic Conference

Auburn University
Academic Profile

P.O. Box 351
Auburn, AL 36831-0351

Phone: 334-844-4080

Type: Public, 4 Yr., Liberal Arts, Coed
Website: http://www.auburn.edu
SAT/ACT/GPA: 1100/24/3.2
Student/Faculty Ratio: 30:1
Undergraduate Enrollment: 22,000
Scholarships/Academic: Yes   **Athletic:** Yes
Expenses By: Year   **In State:** $ 7,935
Specializes In: Veterinary Medicine, Business, Education, Arts & Science
Degrees Conferred: BS, BA, MA, MS
Programs of Study: 150 areas of baccalaureate study including Agriculture, Agronomy, Animal Production, Entomology, Horticulture, Architecture, Business, Marketing, Management, Engineering, Accounting

Founded: 1856
Religion: Non-Affiliated
Housing: No
Male/Female: 55:45
Graduate Enrollment: N/A
Financial Aid: No
Out of State: $ 13,600

Women's Athletic Profile

P.O. Box 351
Auburn, AL 36831
Coach: Kris Grunwald
Email: grunwkr@mail.auburn.ca

NCAA I
Lady Tigers, Navy, Orange
Phone: (334) 844-9794
Fax: (334) 844-4255

Estimated # of Women's Volleyball Scholarships: 2/12
Conference: Southeastern Conference
Program Profile: Our season goes from August 11 through November 25 and possibly into December for NCAA Tournament. We play in a student activities center that holds 2,000. Our program has 12 full scholarships and is in its 10th year.
History: The program is going to its 11th season, it began in 1988. It has been in the top two of SEC for the past four years. We were Co-Champions of the SEC West in 1997.
Achievements: Co-Champions of the SEC West in 1997.
Coaching: Kris Grunwald, Head Coach, is in his first year with the program.. He played at George Mason and was named All-American. Jenn McCall, Assistant Coach, played at Florida State. Jane Belanger Thomas, Assistant Coach, played at Kentucky and was named All-American.
Freshman Receiving Financial Aid/Academic: **Athletic:** 3
Roster In State: 3   **Out of State:** 9   **Out of Country:** 0
Sophomores on Team: 4   **Seniors on Team:** 3   **Graduation %:** Unknown
Most Recent Record: 22-9-0   **Fall Games:** 31   **Spring Games:** 0
Camp of Clinic Dates: July 16-19; July 30-August 2
Schedule: Florida, Georgia, Arkansas, Kansas, Florida State, Louisiana State

Bevill State Community College
Academic Profile

2631 Temple Avenue N
Fayette, AL 35555

Phone: (205) 932-3221

Type: Public, 2 Yr., Jr. College, Coed
Website: http://www.bevillst.cc.al.us
SAT/ACT/GPA: High School Diploma
Student/Faculty Ratio: 30:1
Undergraduate Enrollment: 1,100
Scholarships/Academic: Yes   **Athletic:** Yes
Expenses By: Year   **In State:** $ 2,500-appr.
Degrees Conferred: AA, AS, AAS, Certificates
Programs of Study: Most students enter into a university parallel program of their choice.

Founded: 1969
Religion: Non-Affiliated
Housing: Yes
Male/Female: 40:60
Graduate Enrollment: N/A
Financial Aid: Yes
Out of State: $ 2,500-appr.

Women's Athletic Profile

2631 Temple Avenue North
Fayette, AL 35555
Coach: Sandra Holliman
Email:

NCAA I
Lady Bears, Royal Blue, Green
Phone: (205) 932-3221
Fax: (205) 932-3271

Estimated # of Women's Volleyball Scholarships: 14

Conference: Alabama Junior Community College Conference

Program Profile: The program is designed as a stepping stone for advancement into a 4-year school and volleyball programs. We travel to 2 out-of-state tournaments per year for exposure and national competition. Our gymnasium has 750 people.

History: Our program began in 1990. We won 3 consecutive AJCCC Titles in 1990, 1991 and 1992. We also made a trip to the NJCAA Tournament in 1990. We have finished in the top half of the Conference every year. Melanie Davis was head coach from 1990-1992. Her overall record was 92-19. Pam Howell was head coach from 1993 to 1994. Her overall record was 24-38.

Achievements: Melanie Davis-3 AJCCC Titles, 3 AJCCC Coach of the Year Awards; One Honorable Mention All-American in 1992; 12 All-Region Selections; 10 Players signed with 4-yr programs in the last 3 years; Team GPA in 1996 of 3.31 (11th in a national publication by AVCA)

Coaching: Sandra Holliman has been Head Coach from 1995 to the present. She helped lead Mantec CC to 3rd place at the NJCAF National Tournament in 1988.

Freshman Receiving Financial Aid/Academic: **Athletic:** 4

Roster In State: 14	**Out of State:** 0	**Out of Country:** 0
Sophomores on Team: 0	**Seniors on Team:** 9	**Graduation %:** 85
Most Recent Record: 22-22-0	**Fall Games:** 45	**Spring Games:** 4

Camp of Clinic Dates: July 19-22, 1999

Positions Needed: Setter, (3) Middle Hitters, (3) Outsides/Right Side Hitters, Defense Specialist

Schedule: NW-Shoals CC, Wallace St.Hanceville CC, Florida CC-Jacksonville, Tyler, TX CC, Opponents at FCC Jacksonville Tournament, Opponents at NW-Schools CC

Style of Play: Our program is based on sound fundamentals.

Birmingham Southern College
Academic Profile

Box 549035
Birmingham, AL 35254

Phone: (205) 226-4944

Type: Private, 4 Yr., Liberal Arts, Coed   **Founded:** 1856

Website: http://www.bsc.edu   **Religion:** Methodist

SAT/ACT/GPA: 26   **Housing:** Yes

Student/Faculty Ratio: 13:1   **Male/Female:** 46:54

Undergraduate Enrollment: 1,150   **Graduate Enrollment:** 350

Scholarships/Academic: Yes   **Athletic:** Yes   **Financial Aid:** Yes

Expenses By: Year   **In State:** $ 20,886   **Out of State:** $ 20,886

Specializes In: PreMed, PreLaw

Degrees Conferred: BA, BS, BF, BM, M.Ed.

Programs of Study: Accounting, Biology, Business, Chemistry, Computer, Economics, Education, English, Fine Arts, Graphic Design, Health, History, Information Science, International Marketing, Math, Music, Philosophy, Political, Psychology, Social Science, Visual and Performing Arts

Women's Athletic Profile

900 Arkadelphia Rd. Box 549041
Birmingham, AL 35254
Coach: Cecilla Patterson West
Email: cpatters@bsc.edu

NCAA I
Lady Panthers, Black, Gold
Phone: (205) 226-4944
Fax: (205) 226-3059

Estimated # of Women's Volleyball Scholarships: 7

Conference: Tran South Athletic Conference

Program Profile: We play matches in the new Striplin Physical Fitness and Recreation Center. It is a 8.4 million dollar facility. The team competes in the fall term.

History: We just finished the first year of the program with an overall record of 6-28. We had a record at Tran South Conference of 2-10.

Achievements: 1997 NAIA Southeast Region Coach of the Year

Coaching: Cecilla Patterson West, Head Coach, compiled a record of 44-31 in two years at another school.

Freshman Receiving Financial Aid/Academic: **Athletic:** 4

Roster In State: 6	**Out of State:** 5	**Out of Country:** 1
Sophomores on Team: 2	**Seniors on Team:** 2	**Graduation %:** 100
Most Recent Record: 7-21-0	**Fall Games:** 30	**Spring Games:** 0

Camp of Clinic Dates: June 10-12, 1999; July 26 - August 3, 1999

Positions Needed: Setter, Middle Hitter

Schedule: Union University, Lee University, Lipscomb University, Huntington College, LaGrange

Faulkner University
Academic Profile

5345 Atlanta Hwy.

Montgomery, AL 36109

Phone: 334-386-7240

Type: Private, 4 Yr., Liberal Arts, Coed
Website: http://www.faulkner.edu
SAT/ACT/GPA: 860/18
Student/Faculty Ratio: 18:1
Undergraduate Enrollment: 750
Scholarships/Academic: Yes
Expenses By: Year
Degrees Conferred: BA, BS

Athletic: Yes
In State: $ 10,400

Founded: 1942
Religion: Church of Christ
Housing: No
Male/Female: Not Available
Graduate Enrollment: N/A
Financial Aid: Yes
Out of State: $ 10,400

Programs of Study: Biology, Business Administration, Education, English, General Studies, Liberal Arts, Optometry, PreLaw, Religion, Sports Management

Women's Athletic Profile

5345 Atlanta Hwy.
Montgomery, AL 36109
Coach: Rayla Black
Email:

NCAA I
Lady Eagles, Blue, Grey, White
Phone: (800) 879-9816
Fax: (334) 260-6268

Estimated # of Women's Volleyball Scholarships: N/A
Conference: GLIAC
Program Profile: We play at Davis Gymnasium. In just two seasons, the Faulkner Lady Eagles took strides seldom seen on the NAIA level. Winners of just six matches a year ago, the Lady Eagles won 23 matches in 1998. They finished second in the always-tough Georgia-Alabama-Carolina Conference.
History: We are in our second season of intercollegiate competition.
Achievements: 1998 American Volleyball Coaches Association National Academic Award.
Coaching: Terina Odom - Head Coach. She was named the Georgia-Alabama-Carolina Conference Volleyball Coach of the Year. She is starting her second year here. The team won 23 matches this year, earning them second place in the conference. She is a 1994 Faulkner graduate.
Freshman Receiving Financial Aid/Academic: N/A
Roster In State: 9
Sophomores on Team: 4
Most Recent Record: 23-0-0

Athletic: N/A
Out of State: 2
Seniors on Team: 2

Out of Country: 0
Graduation %: Unknown

Schedule: Pensacola Christian, Belhaven, Huntingdon, Judson, West Georgia, Valdosta State, LaGrande, Williams Baptist, Flagler, Webber

Huntingdon College
Academic Profile

1500 East Fairview Avenue
Montgomery, AL 36106

Phone: 334-833-4497

Type: Private, 4 Yr., Liberal Arts, Coed
Website: http://www.huntingdon.edu
SAT/ACT/GPA: 920 combined/490 verbal/202.5
Student/Faculty Ratio: 9:1
Undergraduate Enrollment: 750
Scholarships/Academic: Yes
Expenses By: Year
Specializes In: Premed, Prelaw programs
Degrees Conferred: BS

Athletic: No
In State: $ 17,450

Founded: 1854
Religion: Methodist
Housing: Yes
Male/Female: 1:2
Graduate Enrollment: N/A
Financial Aid: Yes
Out of State: $ 17,450

Programs of Study: Accounting, American Studies, Art, Biology, Business Administration, Chemistry, Computer Information Systems, Computer Science, Dance, Drama, Education, European Studies, Health Science, International Studies, Kinesiology, Mathematics, Music, Musical Theatre, Philosophy, Physical Education, Political Science, Psychology, Public Administration, Public Affairs, Public Policy, Religion, Social Science

Women's Athletic Profile

1500 El Fairview Avenue
Montgomery, AL 36106
Coach: Yvette Williamson
Email: ywilliamson@huntington.edu

NCAA I
Lady Hawks, Maroon, White
Phone: (334) 833-4411
Fax: (334) 833-4486

Did Not Return Profile

Jacksonville State University
Academic Profile

700 Pelham Rd. N
Jacksonville, AL 36265

Phone: (256) 782-5268

Type: Public, 4 Yr., Coed
Website: http://www.jsu.edu
SAT/ACT/GPA: 900/19/2.5
Student/Faculty Ratio: 22:1
Undergraduate Enrollment: 6,477
Scholarships/Academic: Yes   **Athletic:** Yes
Expenses By: Year   **In State:** $ 5,720
Specializes In: Education, Nursing, Criminal Justice
Degrees Conferred: BA, BS, BFA, BMU, MA, MS

Founded: 1883
Religion: Non-Affiliated
Housing: Yes
Male/Female: 44:56
Graduate Enrollment: 1,142
Financial Aid: Yes
Out of State: $ 7,960

Programs of Study: Art, Biology, Business, Chemistry, Communications, Computer Science, Drama, English, Exercise Science, Family & Consumer Science, Foreign Languages, General Studies, Geography, History, Mathematics, Music, Physics, Political Science, PreProfessional Programs, Psychology, Recreation Administration, Social Work, Sociology, Technology

Women's Athletic Profile

700 Pelham Road N
Jacksonville, AL 32656-1602
Coach: Jose Rivera
Email: jrivera@jsucc.jsu.edu

NCAA I
Lady Gamecocks, Red, White
Phone: (256) 782-5521
Fax: (256) 782-5666

Estimated # of Women's Volleyball Scholarships: 12
Conference: Trans America Athletic Conference
Program Profile: We play at Pete Mathews Coliseum, a multi-purpose facility with a seating capacity of 5,500. Opened in 1974, renovated in 1987. Plays tough and competitive while competing in the TAAC.
History: Our program began in 1978 and has an overall record of 477-309.
Achievements: We were 1995 & 1998 TAAC Tournament Participant.
Coaching: Jose Rivera is our Head Coach. He compiled a record 39-19 in 1997. He led team to 1998 TAAC Tournament. Angel Mauterer is our Assistant Coach.
Freshman Receiving Financial Aid/Academic: **Athletic:** 3
Roster In State: 4   **Out of State:** 6   **Out of Country:** 0
Sophomores on Team: 0   **Seniors on Team:** 4   **Graduation %:** N/A
Most Recent Record: 14-16-0
Positions Needed: Setter, Middle Blocker, Outside Hitter
Schedule: Syracuse, Kansas Street, Weber State, New Mexico State, Alabama, Auburn
Style of Play: We play fast and aggressive style.

Judson College
Academic Profile

P.O. Box 120
Marion, AL 36756

Phone: (800) 447-9472

Type: Private, 4 Yr., Liberal Arts
Website: http://www.home.judson.edu
SAT/ACT/GPA: 870/18/2.0
Student/Faculty Ratio: 12:1
Undergraduate Enrollment: 375
Scholarships/Academic: Yes   **Athletic:** Yes

Founded: 1838
Religion: Southern Baptist
Housing: Yes
Male/Female: 100%-F
Graduate Enrollment: N/A
Financial Aid: Yes

Expenses By: Year   **In State:** $ 12,420   **Out of State:** $ 12,42

Degrees Conferred: BA, BS

Programs of Study: Art, Biology, Business Administration and Management of Information Systems, Chemistry, Criminal Justice, Education, K-12, Environmental Science, Fashion Merchandising, Fitness Management, History, Human Performance, Mathematics, Modern Foreign Languages, Music, Psychology, Religious Studies, Preprofessional Programs: PreDentistry, PreEngineering, PreLaw, PreMedical Technology, PreNursing, PrePharmacy, PrePhysical Therapy, PreSeminary, PreVeterinary Medicine

Women's Athletic Profile

Bibb Street
Marion, AL 36756
Coach: Jeff Edwards
Email:

NCAA I
Lady Eagles, Red, Black, White
Phone: (334) 683-5159
Fax:

Did Not Return Profile

Miles College
Academic Profile

P. O. Box 3800
Birmingham, AL 35208

Phone: 205-929-1000

Type: Private, 4 Yr., Coed
Website: http://www.miles.edu
SAT/ACT/GPA: Open
Student/Faculty Ratio: 22:1
Undergraduate Enrollment: 1,442
Scholarships/Academic: Yes   **Athletic:** Yes
Expenses By: Year   **In State:** $ 7,570
Degrees Conferred: AA, AB, BS

Founded: 1905
Religion: None-affiliated
Housing: No
Male/Female: 48:82
Graduate Enrollment: N/A
Financial Aid: Yes
Out of State: $ 7,570

Programs of Study: Accounting, Biology, Biology Education, Business Administration, Business Management, Chemistry, Communications, Elementary Education, English, Environmental Science, Language Arts Education, Mathematics, Mathematics Education, Music, Natural Science, Political Science, PreDentistry, PreEngineering, PreVeterinary Medicine, Social Science, Social Work

Women's Athletic Profile

5500 Myron Massey Boulevard
Birmingham, AL 35208
Coach:
Email:

NCAA I
Golden Bears, Purple, Gold
Phone: (205) 929-1000
Fax:

Did Not Return Profile

Samford University
Academic Profile

800 Lakeshore Drive
Birmingham, AL 35229

Phone: 205-726-2901

Type: Private, 4 Yr., Liberal Arts, Coed
Website: http://www.samford.edu
SAT/ACT/GPA: 1000/24
Student/Faculty Ratio: 14:1
Undergraduate Enrollment: 3,200
Scholarships/Academic: Yes   **Athletic:** Yes
Expenses By: Year   **In State:** $ 12,500
Degrees Conferred: BA, BGS, BM, BS, BSEd, BSN, MBA, Mmus

Founded: 1841
Religion: Southern Baptist
Housing: No
Male/Female: 38:62
Graduate Enrollment: 1,350
Financial Aid: Yes
Out of State: $ 12,500

Programs of Study: Accounting, Athletic Training, Art, Biology, Church Recreation, Computer Science, Dramatic Arts, Early Childhood Education, Engineering, Physics, Environmental Science, Fashion Merchandising, International Relations, Management, Languages, Journalism, Professional Programs, Speech, Theatre, Voice

Women's Athletic Profile

800 Lakeshore Drive
Birmingham, AL 35229
Coach: Vicki Nichols
Email: maashcra@samford.edu

NCAA I
Lady Bulldogs, Crimson, Blue
Phone: (205) 870-2969
Fax: (205) 870-2132

Estimated # of Women's Volleyball Scholarships: N/A
Conference: Trans America Athletic Conference
Program Profile: Lady Bulldogs play in Seibert Hall with capacity of 4,000.
History: Volleyball began in 1986 and since 1988 have a record of 158-240.
Schedule: Mississippi State, Central Florida, Alabama, Troy State.

Stillman College
Academic Profile

3600 Stillman Boulevard
Tuscaloosa, AL 35403

Phone: 205-366-8816

Type: Private, 4 Yr., Liberal Arts, Coed
Website: http://www.stillman.edu
SAT/ACT/GPA: Open/2.0
Student/Faculty Ratio: 13:1
Undergraduate Enrollment: 1,017
Scholarships/Academic: Yes   **Athletic:** No
Expenses By: Year   **In State:** $ 9,492
Degrees Conferred: BA, BS

Founded: 1876
Religion: Presbyterian
Housing: Yes
Male/Female: 1:12
Graduate Enrollment: N/A
Financial Aid: Yes
Out of State: $ 9,492

Programs of Study: Biology, Business Administration, Chemistry, Communications, Computer Science, Education, English, History, Interdisciplinary Studies, International Studies, Management, Mathematics, Music, Philosophy, Physical Education, Physics, Religion, Sociology

Women's Athletic Profile

3600 Stilmann Blvd.
Tuscaloosa, AL 35403
Coach: Jake Irby, III
Email:

NCAA I
Lady Tigers, Old Gold, Blue
Phone: (205) 349-4240
Fax: (205) 366-8996

Estimated # of Women's Volleyball Scholarships: N/A
Conference: None
Program Profile: We have a moderate program and play about 25 games a season. We win about 45% of our games. We play in the basketball gym which has about 1,000 seats.
History: Dr. Betty Smith started the program in 1972. The program stopped in 1981 and started again in 1984.
Coaching: Jake Irby, III, Head Coach, has been here from 1984 to the present.
Freshman Receiving Financial Aid/Academic: **Athletic:** 0
Roster In State: 8   **Out of State:** 3   **Out of Country:** 1
Sophomores on Team: 2   **Seniors on Team:** 1   **Graduation %:** 65
Most Recent Record: 8-11-0   **Fall Games:** 19   **Spring Games:** 0
Positions Needed: Setters, Middle Blockers, Outside Hitters
Schedule: Mississippi, Miles
Style of Play: We use the 5-1 offense and sometimes the 4-2 offense. We try to use quick hitting short sets. We use a lot of singles blocking because we are short in height.

Talladega College
Academic Profile

627 West Battle Street
Talladega, AL 35160

Phone: 256-761-6219

Type: Private, 4 Yr., Liberal Arts, Coed
Website: http://www.talladega.edu
SAT/ACT/GPA: Open
Student/Faculty Ratio: 13:1

Founded: 1867
Religion: Non-Affiliated
Housing: Yes
Male/Female: 43:57

Undergraduate Enrollment: 647

Scholarships/Academic: Yes   **Athletic:** Yes

Expenses By: Year   **In State:** $ 9,048

Graduate Enrollment: N/A

Financial Aid: Yes

Out of State: $ 9,048

Degrees Conferred: BA

Programs of Study: Biology, Business Administration, Chemistry, Computer Science, Education, English, Journalism, Management, Mathematics, Music, Physics, Social Science

Women's Athletic Profile

627 W. Battle Street
Talledaga, AL 35160
Coach: Natasha McCrary
Email:

NCAA I
Tornadoes, Crimson, Blue
Phone: (800) 633-2440
Fax: (265) 761-6460

Estimated # of Women's Volleyball Scholarships: Yes
Conference: Independent
Freshman Receiving Financial Aid/Academic: N/A   **Athletic:** N/A

Roster In State: 6   **Out of State:** 6   **Out of Country:** 0

Sophomores on Team: 2   **Seniors on Team:** 2   **Graduation %:** Unknown

Most Recent Record: 3-9-0   **Fall Games:** 12   **Spring Games:** 0

Positions Needed: Middle Blocker, Middle Hitter
Schedule: Clark-Atlanta, Morris Brown, Miles, Lane, Judson, Belhaven
Style of Play: Defense but still timid.

Troy State University
Academic Profile

100 S. George Wallace Drive
Troy, AL 36082

Phone: (334) 670-3926

Type: Public, 4 Yr., Coed
Website: http://www.troyst.edu
SAT/ACT/GPA: 870+/18+/2.0
Student/Faculty Ratio: 21:1
Undergraduate Enrollment: 5,500
Scholarships/Academic: Yes   **Athletic:** Yes
Expenses By: Year   **In State:** $ 7,500

Founded: 1887
Religion: Non-Affiliated
Housing: Yes
Male/Female: 52:48
Graduate Enrollment: 1,500
Financial Aid: Yes
Out of State: $ 10,400

Degrees Conferred: Bachelors, Masters, Specialist
Programs of Study: Accounting, Art, Athletic Training, Biology, Chemistry, Computer Information Science, Criminal Justice, Economics, Education (Elementary & Secondary), English, Environmental Science, Finance, History, Journalism (Broadcast & Print), Management, Marketing, Nursing, Physical Science, Psychology, Rehabilitation, Social Science, Sociology, Sports Medicine, Sport & Fitness Management, Special Education, Social Work, Social Science, Sociology, Sport and Fitness Management, Studio Art

Women's Athletic Profile

University Avenue & Geo. Wallace
Troy, AL 36082
Coach: Ginger Lowe
Email: glowe@trojan.troyst.edu

NCAA I
Trojans, Cardinal, Silver, Black
Phone: (334) 670-3926
Fax: (334) 670-3876

Estimated # of Women's Volleyball Scholarships: 12
Conference: Trans America Athletic Conference
Program Profile: We play at Trojan Arena which seats 4,000. Our season goes from August to November.
History: We have one of the top programs in the area. We are traditionally in the conference.
Achievements: Vickie Paciski led the nation in digs per game in 1997; 20 All-Academic players in the last 3 seasons; many All-Conference Players; various conference winners in different conferences.
Coaching: Ginger Lowe, Head Coach, has coached here from 1978-1988 and from 1996 to the present. She is Troy State's winningest coach with 268 career wins. She has 720 winning seasons. She produced 19 All-Americans. In the past 3 seasons, she has placed 20 girls in Academic All-Conference. Pam Summer is Assistant Coach.
Freshman Receiving Financial Aid/Academic: **Athletic:** 3

Roster In State: 0   **Out of State:** 14   **Out of Country:** 0

Sophomores on Team: 5   **Seniors on Team:** 1   **Graduation %:** Unknown

Most Recent Record: 15-18-0　　　　　　**Fall Games:** 33　　　　　　**Spring Games:** 9
Camp of Clinic Dates: July 26-29
Schedule: Southern Mississippi, Arkansas State, Georgia State, Florida Atlantic University, Central Florida, Western Kentucky, Austin-Peay, University of New Orleans
Style of Play: Tough serving; scrappy defense; traditionally, a well passing team.

Tuskegee University
Academic Profile

321 Chappie James Center
Tuskegee, AL 36088

Phone: (800) 622-6531

Type: Private, 4 Yr., Coed
Website: http://www.tusk.edu
SAT/ACT/GPA: 800/18/2.50
Student/Faculty Ratio: 13:1
Undergraduate Enrollment: 2,932
Scholarships/Academic: Yes　　　　**Athletic:** Yes
Expenses By: Year　　　　**In State:** $ 15,098

Founded: 1881
Religion: Non-Affiliated
Housing: Yes
Male/Female: 40:60
Graduate Enrollment: 148
Financial Aid: Yes
Out of State: $ 15,098

Degrees Conferred: BA, BS, B Arch, DVM,MS, M Ed, Ph D
Programs of Study: Accounting, Agriculture, Animal Science, Banking, Business Administration, Chemistry, Construction Engineering, Economics, (Early Childhood, Elementary, General Science, Mathematics, Physical) Education , (Aerospace, Architectural, Chemical, Electrical, Mechanical) Engineering, English, Finance, History, Horticulture, Hospitality Management, Language Arts, Marketing, Mathematics, Medical Technology, Nursing, Occupational Therapy, Political Science, Plant and Soil Sciences, Psychology, Social Science, Social Work, Sociology, Veterinary Science.

Women's Athletic Profile

James Center Room 321
Tuskegee, AL 36088
Coach: Terence Polmer
Email:

NCAA I
Lady Tigerettes, Crimson, Gold
Phone: (334) 727-8680
Fax: (334) 724-4233

Did Not Return Profile

University of Alabama
Academic Profile

P.O Box 870393
Tuscaloosa, AL 35487

Phone: 800-933-2262

Type: Public, 4 Yr., Liberal Arts, Engineering, Coed
Website: http://www.ua.edu
SAT/ACT/GPA: 1010/20
Student/Faculty Ratio: 20:1
Undergraduate Enrollment: 15,000
Scholarships/Academic: Yes　　　　**Athletic:** Yes
Expenses By: Year　　　　**In State:** $ 7,420

Founded: 1831
Religion: Non-Affiliated
Housing: Yes
Male/Female: 1:1
Graduate Enrollment: 4,000
Financial Aid: Yes
Out of State: $ 11,300

Degrees Conferred: BA, BS, BM, MS, MBA, MD
Programs of Study: Accounting, Advertising, Athletic Training, Banking/Finance, Communications, Communication Disorders, Computer Science, Education, Engineering, English, Fashion Design, Foreign Languages, Journalism, Management, Marine Science, Marketing, Math, Medical

Women's Athletic Profile

Box 870323
Tuscaloosa, AL 35487
Coach: Judy Green
Email:

NCAA I
Crimson Tide, Crimson, White
Phone: (205) 348-3829
Fax: (205) 345-2196

Estimated # of Women's Volleyball Scholarships: N/A
Conference: Southeastern Conference

University of Alabama - Birmingham
Academic Profile

617 S. 13th St., Bartow Arena
Birmingham, AL 35294

Phone: (205) 934-8066

Type: Public, 4 Yr., Coed
Website: http://www.uab.edu
SAT/ACT/GPA: 950/20/2.0
Student/Faculty Ratio: 17:1
Undergraduate Enrollment: 11,000
Scholarships/Academic: Yes
Expenses By: Year

Athletic: Yes
In State: $ 6,750

Founded: 1969
Religion: Non-Affiliated
Housing: Yes
Male/Female: 45:55
Graduate Enrollment: 6,000
Financial Aid: Yes
Out of State: $ 9.750

Specializes In: Business, Education, Engineering, Medicine, Research and Technology
Degrees Conferred: BA, BS, BFA, MA, MS, MBA, MEd, Ph D, Ed D, DDS, MD
Programs of Study: Over 70 degree programs available: Business, Education, Engineering, Health Sciences, Life Sciences, Social Science, Etc.

Women's Athletic Profile

1530 Third Ave. South
Birmingham, AL 35294-1160
Coach: Melinda Claiborne
Email: melindac@uab.edu

NCAA I
Lady Blazers, Green, Gold
Phone: (205) 975-8010
Fax: (205) 934-7505

Estimated # of Women's Volleyball Scholarships: 12
Conference: Conference USA
Program Profile: UAB Volleyball competes at Bartow Arena, an on-campus facility. The volleyball season typically runs from September until November. UAB volleyball competes on a wood floor at Bartow Arena that has a maximum capacity of 8,500.
History: The program started in 1978 and was an original member of the Sun belt Conference and Great Midwest Conference. We won 3 straight conference championships in the early 1990's (1989-1990, 1990-1991, 1991-1992) as a part of the Sun Belt and Great Midwest Conferences.
Achievements: UAB volleyball has won three Conference Championships, The Great Midwest in 1991-92 and the Sun Belt in 1990. The Blazers have had 20 All-Conference performers, four All-Freshman performers, two Academic All-Americans, Four Academic All-District performers, three conference Player of the year and three AVCA All-South Region.
Coaching: Melinda Claiborne (Head Coach), Tonya Larson (Assistant Coach).

Roster In State: 3
Seniors on Team: 2
Most Recent Record: 5-17-0

Out of State: 7
Graduation %: 95

Out of Country: 2

Camp of Clinic Dates: July 15-22 (various camps)
Positions Needed: Setter, middle blockers, outside hitters
Schedule: Georgia, Houston, South Florida, Cincinnati, Mississippi State
Style of Play: Our team is disciplined and plays with a very dynamic style, utilizing quickness, agility and athleticism.

University of Alabama - Huntsville
Academic Profile

205 Spragins Hall
Huntsville, AL 35899

Phone: (256) 824-6144

Type: Public, 4 Yr., Liberal Arts, Engineering, Coed
Website: http://www.uah.edu
SAT/ACT/GPA: 840172.5
Student/Faculty Ratio: 20:1
Undergraduate Enrollment: 2,953
Scholarships/Academic: Yes
Expenses By: Year

Athletic: Yes
In State: $ 8,941

Founded: 1969
Religion: Non-Affiliated
Housing: Yes
Male/Female: 48:53
Graduate Enrollment: 1,500
Financial Aid: Yes
Out of State: $ 11,817

Specializes In: Engineering, Business, Sciences
Degrees Conferred: BS, BA, MA, MS, Ph.D.
Programs of Study: Engineering: Electrical, Mechanical, Optical, Computer, Environmental, Civil, Aerospace; Business: Marketing, MIS, Accounting, Administration, Management, Finance; Nursing; Liberal Arts: Art, Communications, Education, English, Spanish, German, French, History, Music, Political Science, Philosophy, Psychology, Sociology; Sciences: Biology, Chemistry, Computer

Science, Mathematics, Physics, Optical Science

Women's Athletic Profile

205 Spragins Hall
Huntsville, AL 35899
Coach: Laura Taube
Email: taubel@email.uah.edu

NCAA I
Lady Chargers, Blue, White
Phone: (256) 824-2203
Fax: (256) 824-7306

Estimated # of Women's Volleyball Scholarships: 3.5
Conference: Gulf South Conference
Program Profile: Enrollment is approximately 8000. Nice playing facility with wood floor, weight room, pool, and locker rooms. Winning tradition in our program 2 NCAA Tournament Appearances.
History: Volleyball at UAH has come along way since its rocky beginning. The program began in1986. Throughout its history the UAH volleyball program won over 60% of its games. That percentage has improved to over 71% during the last 10 seasons. Overall record under 4 coaches 320-195-2.
Achievements: Laura Taube- Overall record in seven years 210-72. Coach of the Year in GSC in 1995 and 1999.
Coaching: Head Coach Laura Taube. Assistant Coach Holly Richards.
Freshman Receiving Financial Aid/Academic: | | **Athletic:** 5
Roster In State: 5 | **Out of State:** 6 | **Out of Country:** 0
Most Recent Record: 22-19
Camp of Clinic Dates: June 25-30
Positions Needed: Outside Hitter
Schedule: Tampa, South Dakota, North Alabama, Central Missouri State, Missouri Western, North Florida
Style of Play: Fast paced offense, we run slides. One's in the middle and low outside sets. We are a good defensive team.

University of Montevallo
Academic Profile

Station 6600
Montevallo, AL 35115

Phone: 205-665-6030

Type: Public, 4 Yr., Liberal Arts, Coed
Website: http://www.montevallo.edu
SAT/ACT/GPA: 850/18
Student/Faculty Ratio: 18:1
Undergraduate Enrollment: 3,000
Scholarships/Academic: Yes | **Athletic:** Yes
Expenses By: Year | **In State:** $ 4,980
Specializes In: Education
Degrees Conferred: BA, BS, MEd

Founded: 1896
Religion: Non-Affiliated
Housing: Yes
Male/Female: 1:2
Graduate Enrollment: 500
Financial Aid: Yes
Out of State: $ 7,480

Programs of Study: Accounting, Banking & Finance, Broadcasting, Chemistry, Communications, Education, English, Fine Arts, French, Government, Health Science, History, Management, Marketing, Mathematics, Medical Technology, Music, Optometry, Photography, Political Science, PreDentistry, PreMed, PreLaw, Public Health, Social Science, Psychology, Spanish, Speech Pathology, Visual and Performing Arts

Women's Athletic Profile

Station 6600
Montevallo, AL 35115-6001
Coach: C.J Sherman
Email: shermanm@montevallo.edu

NCAA I
Lady Falcons, Purple, Gold
Phone: (205) 665-6598
Fax: (205) 665-6587

Estimated # of Women's Volleyball Scholarships: .75
Conference: Gulf South Conference
Program Profile: NCAA II South Central Region ranking #5, NCAA South Central Region Volleyball Championships, 30-9 record overall. Myrick Hall has a wood floor and seating for 2,000, season begins Aug 25.
History: Started as intercollegiate program in 1972. Attended 14 consecutive NAIA National Tournament between 1982 and 1995, moved from NAIA to NCAA in 1995.
Achievements: 18 Athletic and Academic NAIA All-Americans.
Freshman Receiving Financial Aid/Academic: | | **Athletic:** 4
Roster In State: 4 | **Out of State:** 8 | **Out of Country:** 2

Most Recent Record: 30-9
Camp of Clinic Dates: June 4-7, July 9-13 2001
Positions Needed: Middle, Setter, DS
Schedule: Colorado Christian, Univ. of North Alabama, Truman State, Valdosta State
Style of Play: Fun, disciplined basic skill volleyball. We are good athletes and we pride ourselves on our ball control.

University of North Alabama
Academic Profile

UNA Box 5121
Florence, AL 35632-0001

Phone: (256) 765-4221

Type: Public, 4 Yr., Coed
Website: http://www.unanov.edu
SAT/ACT/GPA: 830 or higher18/2.0
Student/Faculty Ratio: 22:1
Undergraduate Enrollment: 5,000
Scholarships/Academic: Yes   **Athletic:** Yes
Expenses By: Year   **In State:** $ 6,608

Founded: 1830
Religion: Non-Affiliated
Housing: Yes
Male/Female: 42:58
Graduate Enrollment: 500
Financial Aid: Yes
Out of State: $ 8,744

Specializes In: Business, Education, Nursing
Degrees Conferred: BA, BS, BFA, BAM, BGS, BM, BMMEd, BSEd., BSM, BSN, MA, MBA
Programs of Study: Art, Accounting, Banking/Finance, Biology, Broadcasting, Business, Chemistry, Communications, Criminal Justice, Economics, Education, English, Fine Arts, French, General Studies, Geography, German, Health and Physical Education, History, Home Economics, Information Science, Journalism, Management, Marketing, Mathematics, Physical Sciences, Psychology

Women's Athletic Profile

UNA Box 5121
Florence, AL 35632
Coach: Matt Peck
Email: mpeck@unanov.una.edu

NCAA I
Lady Lions, Purple, Gold
Phone: (205) 765-4397
Fax: (205) 765-4685

Estimated # of Women's Volleyball Scholarships: 8
Conference: Gulf South Conference
Program Profile: Maximally founded high profile NCAA II since 1996. Arena seats 3,850 air conditioned, wood floor, six courts in facility
History: Began 1969. Overall Record since 1974 605-350. 69-1 in South Central Region since 1996. Highest national finish 5th (1998) 1st NCAA school in Alabama to participate in NCSS volleyball postseason in all divisions I,II,III.
Achievements: AVCA South Central Region Coach of the Year (1998), conference Coach of the Year (1987,1996,1997,1998) 3 GSC titles won 46 matches in a row. One 1st team All-American, 3 2nd team All-Americans
Coaching: Matt Peck, 1984 Wayne St. University 16th season as Head Coach, career overall record of 373-170. Record at UNA of 142-35, 5 NCAA tournament appearances. Sweet 16 twice, elite eight once, AVCA top 10 finish.
Freshman Receiving Financial Aid/Academic: **Athletic:** 4
Roster In State: 3   **Out of State:** 11   **Out of Country:** 2
Sophomores on Team: 2   **Seniors on Team:** 2   **Graduation %:** 90
Most Recent Record: 38-5   **Fall Games:** 43   **Spring Games:** 10
Camp of Clinic Dates: indiv. July 18-21, Setters July 23-24, team July 25-31
Positions Needed: Swing hitter, Opposite
Schedule: Tampa, Barry, Central Missouri, Rockhurst, Minnesota State
Style of Play: Swing offense with outside hitters and opposite hitting from inside/out. Very fast tempo, utilizing primarily play sets for all attackers. Opposite hits first and second tempo sets exclusively.

University of South Alabama
Academic Profile

307 University Blvd.
Mobile, AL 36688

Phone: 334-460-6141

Type: Public, 4 Yr., Liberal Arts, Coed
Website: http://www.usouthal.edu
SAT/ACT/GPA: 820/19
Student/Faculty Ratio: 14:1
Undergraduate Enrollment: 9,500

Founded: 1963
Religion: Non-Affiliated
Housing: Yes
Male/Female: 43:57
Graduate Enrollment: 3,000

Scholarships/Academic: Yes   **Athletic:** Yes   **Financial Aid:** Yes
Expenses By: Year   **In State:** $ 7,000   **Out of State:** $ 8,900
Degrees Conferred: Bachelors to Ph.D.
Programs of Study: College of Arts and Sciences, College of Business and Management Studies, College of Education, College of Engineering, School of Continuing Education and Special Programs, College of Allied Health Professions, College of Medicine, College of Nursing, School of Computer and Information Sciences

Women's Athletic Profile

1107 HPELS Bldg.   NCAA I
Mobile, AL 36688   Lady Jaguars, Red, White, Blue
Coach: Ginger Mayson   **Phone:** (334) 460-7124
Email: gmayson@usamail.usouthal.edu   **Fax:** (334) 460-7297

Estimated # of Women's Volleyball Scholarships: N/A
Conference: Sun Belt West Conference
Program Profile: The Jaguars train, practice and play all at a central location on campus. The program is based in the physical education building. Players work out in a two-year old training room in the Mitchell center, a $30 million basketball arena. Games are played in Jaguar gymnasium, inside the P.E. building. The capacity is 500.
History: The Jaguars fielded their first program in 1974 and have had a team every year since. The school has the longest running relationship with the Sun Belt Conference. The team's best season was under current head coach Ginger Mayson in 1982 when she led USA to a 42-13 record.
Achievements: The school has had two Sun Belt Coach of the Year honors, six players named to the First Team All Sun Belt and five named to the Sun Belt Conference All-Tournament Team.
Roster In State: 6   **Out of State:** 2   **Out of Country:** 1
Seniors on Team: 4
Most Recent Record: 8-21
Camp of Clinic Dates: July 24-26, 2000
Positions Needed: OH, S
Schedule: Arkansas State, Arkansas Little Rock, Denver, Auburn, Alabama, Southern Mississippi
Style of Play: South Alabama will play physical this year because of the team's height and size. The Jaguars have the size in the front court to stay on the attack.

University of West Alabama
Academic Profile

Station 5   **Phone:** 205-652-3578
Livingston, AL 35470

Type: Public, 4 Yr., Coed   **Founded:** 1835
Website: http://www.westal.edu   **Religion:** Non-Affiliated
SAT/ACT/GPA: 18   **Housing:** Yes
Student/Faculty Ratio: 18:1   **Male/Female:** 1:1.3
Undergraduate Enrollment: 2,153   **Graduate Enrollment:** N/A
Scholarships/Academic: Yes   **Athletic:** Yes   **Financial Aid:** Yes
Expenses By: Year   **In State:** $ 5,826   **Out of State:** $ 8,106
Specializes In: Business, Liberal Arts, Education
Degrees Conferred: AS, BA, BS, BMEd, BT, MA, M.Ed.
Programs of Study: College of Business, Division of Technology, College of Education, College of Natural Science, Division of Nursing, College of Liberal Arts, PreProfessional Programs, Allied Health Programs

Women's Athletic Profile

Station 5   NCAA I
Livingston, AL 35470   Lady Tigers, Red, White
Coach: Shawna Laurendine   **Phone:** (205) 652-3784
Email: **Fax:** (205) 652-3600

Estimated # of Women's Volleyball Scholarships: Yes
Conference: Gulf South Conference
Program Profile: We are a member of the Gulf South Conference which has 16 members. Our home volleyball games are played at Pruitt Hall which has 1,500 seats.

History: The volleyball program began in 1982.

Achievements: In 1977, we got the most wins: 32. We had 17 consecutive match wins, most of them in the Gulf South Conference.

Coaching: Shawna Lauerdine, Head Coach, finished her 3rd season with an overall record of 63-59. She is a graduate of the University of Montreal.

Freshman Receiving Financial Aid/Academic: | **Athletic:** 3

Roster In State: 9 | **Out of State:** 1 | **Out of Country:** 0

Sophomores on Team: 0 | **Seniors on Team:** 2 | **Graduation %:** Unknown

Most Recent Record: 12-26-0 | **Fall Games:** 38 | **Spring Games:** 0

Positions Needed: Setter, Middle Hitter, Outside Hitter

Schedule: University of North Alabama, University of Alabama-Huntsville, Valdosta, Montevallo

Style of Play: Defense, defense, defense. Try to keep our game quick. Very scrappy. Able to pick up any ball anywhere.

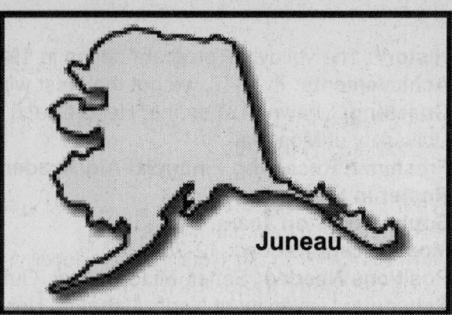

Juneau

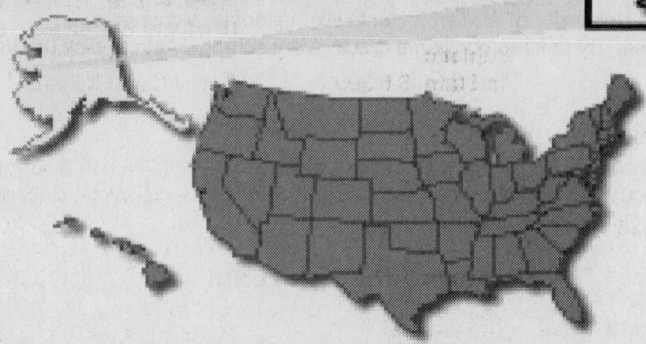

SCHOOL	CITY	AFFILIATION	PAGE
University of Alaska - Anchorage	Anchorage	NCAA I	56
University of Alaska - Fairbanks	Fairbanks	NCAA I	56

University of Alaska - Anchorage
Academic Profile

3211 Providence Dr.
Anchorage, AK 99508

Phone: 907-786-1480

Type: Public, 4 Yr., Coed
Website: http://www.alaska.net/~apu
SAT/ACT/GPA: Either Required for Placement
Student/Faculty Ratio: 15:1
Undergraduate Enrollment: 14,300
Scholarships/Academic:
Expenses By: Year
Specializes In: Engineering

Athletic:
In State: $ 6,300

Founded: 1954
Religion: Non-Affiliated
Housing: No
Male/Female: 1:1.41
Graduate Enrollment: 520
Financial Aid: Yes
Out of State: $ 8,600

Degrees Conferred: AA, AS, BA, BS, BBA, BEd, BFA, BMus, BSW, MA, MS
Programs of Study: Accounting, Anthropology, Art, Biology, Chemistry, Civil Engineering, Health Science, History, Music, Mathematics, Communications, Psychology, Political Science, Secondary Education, Social Work, Sociology, Nursing Science, Theatre, Economics, Education, Natural Science, Physical Education

Women's Athletic Profile

3211 Providence
Anchorage, AK 99508
Coach: Kim Lauwers
Email: ankal@uaa.alaska.edu

NCAA I
Lady Seawolves, Green, Gold
Phone: (970) 786-1226
Fax: (907) 786-4565

Estimated # of Women's Volleyball Scholarships: N/A
Conference: Pacific West Conference
Program Profile: UAA plays in the 1500 seat UAA Sports Center on campus. The Seawolves have a regular playing season from late August through early November. UAA Played eight teams that were ranked in the Top 25 last season. UAA annually ranks in the top 10 in NCAA D. II in attendance.
History: Program began in 1980. Coach Kim Lauwers is the fourth head coach in UAA history.
Coaching: Head Coach Kim Lauwers 3 season record of 44-47. Assistant Coach Nicky Rose and Julie Weber.
Roster In State: 9   **Out of State:** 5   **Out of Country:** 0
Seniors on Team: 3
Most Recent Record: 14-18
Positions Needed: OH, MB

University of Alaska - Fairbanks
Academic Profile

Box 757480
Fairbanks, AK 99775-7480

Phone: 800-478-1823

Type: Public, 4 Yr., Liberal Arts, Coed
Website: http://www.uaf.alaska.edu
SAT/ACT/GPA: 900
Student/Faculty Ratio: 7:1
Undergraduate Enrollment: 7,000
Scholarships/Academic:
Expenses By: Year

Athletic: Yes
In State: $ 4,500

Founded: 1917
Religion: Non-Affiliated
Housing: No
Male/Female: Not N/A
Graduate Enrollment: 700
Financial Aid: Yes
Out of State: $ 7,000

Specializes In: Engineering, Wildlife Management
Degrees Conferred: AA, AS, BA, BS, BBA, BEd, BFA, BTech, MA, MS, Ph.D.
Programs of Study: Accounting, Art, Anthropology, Applied Physics, Business Administration, Chemistry, Computer Science, General Science, English, Music, Natural Science, Geography, Art, Biological Science, Journalism, Geology, Psychology, Political Science, Justice, Journalism, Physical Education, Speech Communications, Mathematics, Northern Studies

Women's Athletic Profile

P.O. Box 757440
Fairbanks, AK 99775
Coach: Phil Shoemaker
Email: phil.shoemaker@uaf.edu

NCAA I
Lady Nanooks, Blue, Gold
Phone: (907) 474-6809
Fax: (907) 474-5162

Estimated # of Women's Volleyball Scholarships: 3
Conference: Great Northwest
Program Profile: The Nanooks home is the Patty Center and it has a seating capacity of 2, 000. It's a modern facility which is located on UAF campus with maple wood courts, swimming pool, and weight training facilities.
History: UAF has sponsored volleyball as a varsity sport since 1979. A much stronger commitment to the team has been made since 1991 and results have become more impressive including a 15-8 mark in 2000.
Achievements: 2000 was Coach Shoemaker's first year at UAF, but his past records include 243 Division I wins as Head Coach at Wichita State and 75 as Assistant coach at Missouri. 1991 Conference Coach of the Year.
Coaching: Phil Shoemaker is the Head Coach. Kevin Raap is the Assistant Coach.

ARIZONA

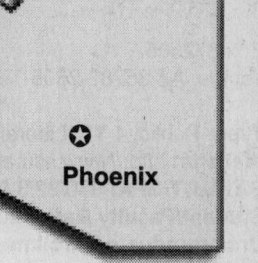

Phoenix

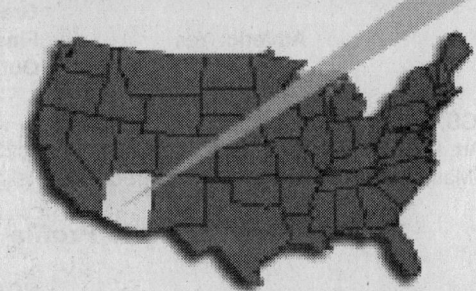

SCHOOL	CITY	AFFILIATION	PAGE
Arizona State University	Tempe	NCAA I	59
Grand Canyon University	Phoenix	NCAA II	59
Northern Arizona University	Flagstaff	NCAA I	60
Phoenix College	Phoenix	NJCAA	61
Southwestern College	Phoenix	NCCAA	61
University of Arizona	Tucson	NCAA I	62
Yavapai College	Prescott	NJCAA	63

Arizona State University
Academic Profile

Box 872505
Tempe, AZ 85287-2505

Phone: 480-965-7788

Type: Public, 4 Yr., Liberal Arts, Engineering, Coed
Website: http://www.asu.edu
SAT/ACT/GPA: 930/22/3.0
Student/Faculty Ratio: 20:1
Undergraduate Enrollment: 43,732
Scholarships/Academic: Yes   **Athletic:** Yes
Expenses By: Year   **In State:** $ 11,000
Specializes In: Business, Education, Nurses
Degrees Conferred: BS, BS, BM, BGS, BSN, MA, MBA, MEd
Programs of Study: Anthropology, Art, Broadcasting, Chemistry, Education, Music, Science, History, Geology, Economics, English, Geography, Humanities, Journalism, Math, Music, Philosophy, Political Science, Religious, Sociology

Founded: 1885
Religion: Non-Affiliated
Housing: Yes
Male/Female: 38:62
Graduate Enrollment: 100
Financial Aid: Yes
Out of State: $ 17,000

Women's Athletic Profile

ICA Building, 5th Street
Tempe, AZ 85287-2505
Coach: Patti Snyder-Park
Email: pspvball@asu.edu

NCAA I
Lady Sun Devils, Maroon, Gold
Phone: (602) 965-2035
Fax: (602) 965-7398

Estimated # of Women's Volleyball Scholarships: 3
Conference: Pacific 10 Conference
Program Profile: All matches in Wells Fargo Arena, capacity 13,000. Sport Court Playing surface, brand new multipurpose practice facility for 2002 season
History: Program began 1973, Intermountain Conf. 1973-78, Western Collegiate Athletic Assoc. 1979-84, Pacific 10 conf. 1985-present, history great players.
Achievements: 1997 All-PAC 10 All-Academic Team; 1997 All-PAC 10 Freshman, Sweet 16 appearances in 1994-95, Snyder-Park Pac-10 Coach of the Year in 1990-92.
Coaching: Patti Snyder-Park started her 10th season as Head Coach. She has guided the Lady Sun Devils to post-season competition in five of the last seasons here. Mindy Rich started her second season as Associate Head Coach. She graduated Summa Cum Laude from Arizona State in 1994. She was GTE Academic All-American twice in her volleyball career. Scott Swanson is Assistant Coach. He has been here three years. He was 1995 Cactus Region Male Coach of the Year.
Freshman Receiving Financial Aid/Academic: **Athletic:** 4
Roster In State: 10   **Out of State:** 2   **Out of Country:** 0
Seniors on Team: 3   **Graduation %:** 100
Most Recent Record: 14-13-0
Camp of Clinic Dates: July 17-21 (individual camps), 24-28 (team camp)2001
Positions Needed: outside hitter, middle blocker, opposite
Schedule: Stanford, UCLA, USC, Arizona, Oregon State.
Style of Play: Ball control, defensive-oriented, emphasis on all-around skill and hustle.

Grand Canyon University
Academic Profile

3300 W Camelback Road
Phoenix, AZ 85287

Phone: 602-589-2885

Type: Private, 4 Yr., Liberal Arts, Coed
Website: http://www.grand-canyon.edu
SAT/ACT/GPA: 1050/22/3.0
Student/Faculty Ratio: 17:1
Undergraduate Enrollment: 1,594
Scholarships/Academic: Yes   **Athletic:** Yes
Expenses By: Year   **In State:** $ 13,406
Specializes In: Nursing, Education, Science
Degrees Conferred: BA, BS, BM, BGS, BSN, MA, MBA, MEd
Programs of Study: Accounting, Banking/Finance, Biology, Business, Chemistry, Communications, Criminal Justice, Economics, Education, English, Graphic Design, History, International Business, Management, Marketing, Mathematics, Music, Nursing, Religion, Speech, Science, Visual and Performing Arts

Founded: 1949
Religion: Southern Baptist
Housing: Yes
Male/Female: 1:2
Graduate Enrollment: 862
Financial Aid: Yes
Out of State: $ 13,406

Women's Athletic Profile

3300 W. Camelback
Phoenix, AZ 85017
Coach: Kris Naber
Email: vball@grand-canyon.edu

NCAA I
Lady Antelopes, Purple, White
Phone: (602) 589-2791
Fax: (602) 589-2529

Estimated # of Women's Volleyball Scholarships: 6.5
Conference: California College Athletic Assocation.
Program Profile: Playing season is from Aug-Nov. We play on a wooden surface with a seating capacity of 2,000
Achievements: Amber Letarte Canyons All-Time leader in kills and digs.
Coaching: Kris Naber Head Coach. Overall record of 100-58 She was named the first volleyball All-American for the Asics Tiger Teams. Assistant Coach Kathy Nevill returned to the program for which she played from 1990-93.
Freshman Receiving Financial Aid/Academic: **Athletic:** 2
Roster In State: 7   **Out of State:** 4   **Out of Country:** 0
Seniors on Team: 5   **Graduation %:** 93
Most Recent Record: 19-12
Camp of Clinic Dates: 6/18-22, 6/25-29
Positions Needed: MH, DS, Setter
Schedule: CS Bakersfield, CS Los Angeles, Northwood, SW State, Seattle Pacific
Style of Play: Quick, aggressive defense and fast offense.

Northern Arizona University
Academic Profile

P.O. Box 15400
Flagstaff, AZ 86011

Phone: 520-523-6792

Type: Public, 4 Yr., Coed
Website: http://www.nau.edu
SAT/ACT/GPA: 1040222.5
Student/Faculty Ratio: 22:1
Undergraduate Enrollment: 13,905
Scholarships/Academic: Yes
Expenses By: Semester
Specializes In: Education, Engineering, Forestry, Hotel Management
Degrees Conferred: Bachelors, Masters, Doctorates

Founded: 1899
Religion: Non-Affiliated
Housing: Yes
Male/Female: 44:56
Graduate Enrollment: 6,059
Athletic: Yes   **Financial Aid:** Yes
In State: $3,474   **Out of State:** $ 5,554

Programs of Study: College of Arts & Sciences, College of Business Administration, School of Communications, College of Ecosystem Science and Management, College of Engineering and Technology, Center for Excellence in Education, College of Professions, School of Hotel and Restaurant Management, Museum Faculty of Fine Art, School of Performing Arts, College of Social and Behavioral Sciences, Interdisciplinary Studies.

Women's Athletic Profile

Box 15400
Flagstaff, AZ 86011
Coach: Kelley Silva
Email: kelley.sliva@nau.edu

NCAA I
Lady Lumberjacks, Blue, Gold
Phone: (520) 523-5649
Fax: (520) 523-6035

Estimated # of Women's Volleyball Scholarships: N/A
Conference: Big Sky Conference
Program Profile: The NAU program just finished its 27th season of intercollegiate varsity play. It is housed in the Rolle Activity Center, a multipurpose facility with a hardwood floor and bleachers and VIP tables to hold 1, 066 spectators on match nights. The NCAA I season runs from preseason camp in August through the national tournament in December. The Lumberjack have played in Rolle Activity Center since 1989.
History: Varsity program began in 1974, joined the Mountain West/Big Sky Conference in 1987. 20-win seasons 1983 and 1991, NIVC tournament berth in 1991, NCAA tournament berth in 1999, Big Sky Tournament Champion in 1999. Is currently on a record streak of four straight winning seasons, with an average of 18 wins per season.
Achievements: Kelley Silva, 1999 Big Sky Conference Coach of the Year, NAU won the 1999 Big Sky Tournament title and is a 2000 regular season co-champion. Program has produced two regular season league MVPs, and I tournament MVP. Program also has produced 3 All-Region Picks.
Coaching: Head Coach Kelley Sliva just finished her 8th season at NAU, is the winningest coach in program history (127 wins) and is

second in win percentage. Prior to NAU, had a successful tenure as an assistant at USC and Texas-Arlington. Assistant Robin Davis just finished his second season with the program after 10 years at Biola, where he was the programs winningest coach and produced 15 NAIA All-Americans and 6 20 win seasons.

Freshman Receiving Financial Aid/Academic: **Athletic:** 2

Roster In State: 3   **Out of State:** 9   **Out of Country:** 0

Sophomores on Team: 0   **Seniors on Team:** 0   **Graduation %:** 100

Most Recent Record: 18-7-0

Positions Needed: Middle Blocker

Schedule: Fresno State, Florida State, Oregon State, Arizona State, Pepperdine, Sacramento State

Style of Play: NAU plays an aggressive offensive style (5-1) with a complex system, athletes are as talented as any in the conference and plays with maximum effort, taking pride in defense. Is very good in transition and is one of the best side-out teams around, giving its offense plenty of opportunities to score.

Phoenix College
Academic Profile

1202 W Thomas Road   **Phone:** (602) 285-7137
Phoenix, AZ 85013-4234

Type: Public, 2 Yr., Coed   **Founded:** 1920
Website: http://pc.maricopa.edu   **Religion:** Non-Affiliated
SAT/ACT/GPA: Recommend   **Housing:** No
Student/Faculty Ratio: 18/1   **Male/Female:** 1:1
Undergraduate Enrollment: 12,000   **Graduate Enrollment:** N/A
Scholarships/Academic: Yes   **Athletic:** Yes   **Financial Aid:** Yes
Expenses By: Semester   **In State:** $600   **Out of State:** $3,500
Specializes In: General Studies
Degrees Conferred: AA, AGS, AAS

Programs of Study: Certificates in EMT, Fire Sciences, Nursing, Dental Hygiene, Phlebotomy, Computers, Culinary Arts as well as two-year degrees in all listed. Above is only a sampling.

Women's Athletic Profile

1202 W. Thomas Rd.   **NCAA I**
Phoenix, AZ 85013   Lady Bears, Blue, Gold
Coach: Patrick Mooney   **Phone:** (602) 285-7137
Email: mooney@pc.maricopa.edu   **Fax:** (602) 285-7333

Estimated # of Women's Volleyball Scholarships: 12
Conference: Arizona Community Colleges Athletic Conference
Program Profile: The playing season is from August 25th through November 25th. We play approximately 60 matches. Games are played in the Cave (Phoenix College North Gym). We are a 2 year school that has 100% of graduating sophomores that obtain 4 year scholarships.
History: The Phoenix college program has and is undergoing a rebirth into making it a respectable program. The best year of our program was in 1994 when the record was 19-11. The last 3 years, all eligible sophomores have been placed at a 4 year school.
Achievements: 3 Academic All-Americans; 3 Scholar Athletes of the Year Award.
Coaching: Patrick Mooney is entering his 4th year as Head Coach. His overall record is 41-86.

Freshman Receiving Financial Aid/Academic: **Athletic:** 100%

Roster In State: 15   **Out of State:** 0   **Out of Country:** 0

Sophomores on Team: 0   **Seniors on Team:** 6   **Graduation %:** 100

Most Recent Record: 15-25-0   **Fall Games:** 55   **Spring Games:** 2

Positions Needed: 6

Schedule: College of Southern Idaho, Ricks College, Utah Valley State, Glendale, Scottsdale, Salt Lake

Style of Play: We like to run a quick offense while relying on defense and ball control for success. Technique/fundamentals and footwork are a large part of our practices. Our athletes learn a hardworking, aggressive style of practice and play.

Southwestern College
Academic Profile

2625 E. Cactus Road   **Phone:** 800-247-2697 x 100
Phoenix, AZ 85032

Type: Private, 4 yr.,   **Founded:** 1960

Website: www.southwesterncollege.edu
SAT/ACT/GPA: Required
Student/Faculty Ratio: 9:1
Undergraduate Enrollment: 258
Scholarships/Academic: Yes
Expenses By: Year
Degrees Conferred: Bachelors & Associates
Programs of Study: Contact school for more information.

Athletic: No
In State: $ 12,980

Religion: Baptist
Housing: Yes
Male/Female: 53:47
Graduate Enrollment: N/A
Financial Aid: Yes
Out of State: $ 12,980

Women's Athletic Profile

2625 E Cactus Road
Phoenix, AZ 85032
Coach: Deborah Robbins
Email: swc@southwesterncollege.edu

NCAA I
Lady Eagles, Blue, White
Phone: 602-992-6101
Fax: 602-404-2159

Estimated # of Women's Volleyball Scholarships: Non-Scholarship
Conference: Independent
Program Profile: Southwestern College is an NCCAA II school. We are a Bible college, accredited by the Commission of Institutions of Higher Education of the North Central Association of Colleges amd Schools, and by the Accrediting Association of Bible Colleges. We have a beautiful modern gymnasium, that will seat 750-1,000 when permanent seating is put in. We have a maple wood floor.
`**Achievements:** We placed 2nd in last seasons NCCAA West Regional Tournament. 2000 Coach of the Year.
Coaching: Deborah Robbins is our Head Coach.
Freshman Receiving Financial Aid/Academic:
Roster In State: 8
Sophomores on Team:
Most Recent Record: 8-18-0
Camp of Clinic Dates: Not Available
Positions Needed: All
Schedule: Life Bible College, California Institute of Technology, Chandler-Gilbert CC, Yavapai, San Jose Christian, Eastern Arizona
Style of Play: We play a 5-1 offense and occassionally a 6-2. We have a strong emphasis on defense and basic skills and techniques.

Out of State: 5
Seniors on Team: 0

Athletic: 0
Out of Country: 0
Graduation %: N/A

University of Arizona
Academic Profile

McKale Center, Rm. 311
Tucson, AZ 85721

Phone: 520-621-3237

Type: Public, 4 Yr., Coed
Website: http//www.arizona.edu
SAT/ACT/GPA: 23
Student/Faculty Ratio: 19:1
Undergraduate Enrollment: 35,306
Scholarships/Academic: Yes
Expenses By: Year
Degrees Conferred: BA, BS, BFA, BM, MA, MBA, MFA, JD
Programs of Study: Accounting, Anthropology, Banking/Finance, Communications, Computer Engineering, Education, Horticulture, Languages, Journalism, Medical, PreProfessional Programs, Religion, Social Science, Speech

Athletic: Yes
In State: $ 3,000

Founded: 1885
Religion: Non-Affiliated
Housing: No
Male/Female: 49:1
Graduate Enrollment: N/A
Financial Aid: Yes
Out of State: $ 8,600

Women's Athletic Profile

211 McKale Center
Tucson, AZ 85721-0096
Coach: David Rubio
Email: cmj@u.arizona.edu

NCAA I
Lady Wildcats, Cardinal, Navy
Phone: (520) 621-2856
Fax: (520) 626-7018

Estimated # of Women's Volleyball Scholarships: 4
Conference: Pacific 10 Conference
Program Profile: Top 5 program in 2000. Team trains and plays in state of the art Mckale Center, which seats 14, 489 fans. The fall season starts in late Aug-early Sept, concluding with the NCAA Finals in Mid Dec. New academic services and athletic training and weight facility to open 2001.

History: Program began 1966, joined Pac-10 in 1986. Made NCAA Tournament 7 of 9 years under David Rubio. Won Pac-10 Championship in 2000, only 1 of 3 teams ever to do so.
Achievements: David Rubio: AVCA West Region Coach of the Year (93), Co-PAC-10 Coach of the Year (00), PAC-10 Champions (00) 1st Team All-American Dana Burkholder (00), 5 All-Americans, and 2 Olympians.
Coaching: David Rubio Head Coach. Charita Johnson and AJ Malis are the Assistant Coaches.
Freshman Receiving Financial Aid/Academic: **Athletic:** 4
Roster In State: 5   **Out of State:** 11   **Out of Country:** 0
Seniors on Team: 3
Most Recent Record: 28-5
Camp of Clinic Dates: Call Volleyball office
Positions Needed: OH, MB
Schedule: Florida, UCLA, USC, Stanford, Utah, Louisville, Arizona State
Style of Play: Highest level of play that emphasizes attacking and blocking.

Yavapai College
Academic Profile

1100 East Sheldon Street
Prescott, AZ 86301

Phone: (520) 776-2242

Type: Public, 2 Yr., Coed   **Founded:** 1969
Website: http://www.yavapai.cc.az.us   **Religion:** Non-Affiliated
SAT/ACT/GPA: Open   **Housing:** Yes
Student/Faculty Ratio: 19:1   **Male/Female:** 3:5
Undergraduate Enrollment: 3,800   **Graduate Enrollment:** N/A
Scholarships/Academic: Yes   **Athletic:** Yes   **Financial Aid:** Yes
Expenses By: Sem   **In State:** $2,750   **Out of State:** $3,000
Degrees Conferred: AA, AAS
Programs of Study: 67 programs from A (Accounting) to Z (Zoology) with credits transferring to four-year institutions.

Women's Athletic Profile

1100 E. Sheldon St.
Prescott, AZ 86301
Coach: Dalton Overstreet
Email: Dalton_Overstreet@yapavai.cc.az.us

NCAA I
Lady Roughriders, Green, Gold
Phone: (520) 776-2235
Fax: (520) 776-2243

Estimated # of Women's Volleyball Scholarships: 9
Conference: Arizona C. C. Athletic
Program Profile: We have excellent facilities. We play from August 1st through the middle of November. Our gym has a capacity of 1,000.
History: We began in 1969. In six seasons, we have won three Conference Championships and have been Regional Runner-Up twice.
Achievements: Conference Coach of the Year 4 times; 3 Titles; 4 All-Americans and 4 Academic All-Americans.
Coaching: Dalton Overstreet became Head Coach in 1993. Fay Matsumoto is Assistant Coach.
Freshman Receiving Financial Aid/Academic: **Athletic:** 7
Roster In State: 13   **Out of State:** 0   **Out of Country:** 0
Sophomores on Team: 0   **Seniors on Team:** 5   **Graduation %:** 33-80
Most Recent Record: 22-29-0   **Fall Games:** 54   **Spring Games:** 4
Positions Needed: 2 Middle Hitters , 1 Setter, 3 Outside Hitters
Schedule: College of South Idaho, Miami Dade, Utah Valley, Ricks, Jefferson, Barton County, Gendale-Arizona
Style of Play: We play with aggressive defense and multiple attack patterns.

ARKANSAS

Little Rock

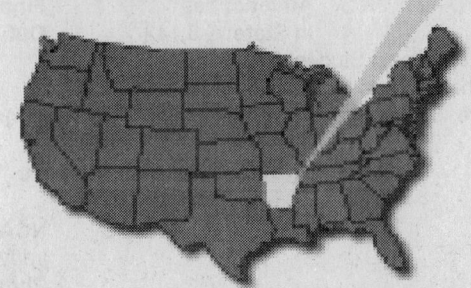

Arkansas State University
Academic Profile

PO Box 1630
State University, AR 72467

Phone: (870) 972-3876

Type: Public, 4 Yr., Liberal Arts, Coed
Website: http://www.astate.edu
SAT/ACT/GPA: 19/2.5
Student/Faculty Ratio: 1:25
Undergraduate Enrollment: 7,500
Scholarships/Academic: Yes   **Athletic:** Yes
Expenses By: Year   **In State:** $ 3,142
Specializes In: Radio/TV, Nursing, International Student Program
Degrees Conferred: Associates, Bachelors (Arts & Sciences), Masters, Doctoral
Programs of Study: 99 undergraduate, 30 masters, 3 doctoral; contact admission for more information.

Founded: 1906
Religion: Non-Affiliated
Housing: Yes
Male/Female: 46:54
Graduate Enrollment: 2,500
Financial Aid: Yes
Out of State: $ 4,595

Women's Athletic Profile

P.O. Box 1630
State University, AR 72467-1000
Coach: Craig Cummings
Email: ccummings@mohawk.astate.edu

NCAA I
Lady Indians, Scarlet, Black
Phone: (870) 972-3876
Fax: (870) 972-3367

Estimated # of Women's Volleyball Scholarships: 5
Conference: Sun Belt Conference
Program Profile: We are a Division I NCAA volleyball program. We compete in the Sun Belt Conference. Our facility is Convocation Center which has 8,000 seats.
History: Our program began in 1975. We have a program record of 737-268-5 (0.703).
Achievements: Sun Belt Conference Champions in 1991, 1992, 1993, 1994, 1995, 1996 and 1998; 17 All-Conference Performers; 4 Conference Players of the Year.
Coaching: Craig Cummings started as Head Coach in 1996. His overall record in 10 seasons 177-149 (.543). His best active record in the Sun Belt Conference of 27-5 (0.844). He was Conference Coach of the Year in 1996 and 1998.
Roster In State: 2   **Out of State:** 9   **Out of Country:** 0
Sophomores on Team: 1   **Seniors on Team:** 4   **Graduation %:** 100
Most Recent Record: 28-7-0   **Fall Games:** 30   **Spring Games:** 8
Camp of Clinic Dates: Individual Camp: July 14-16; Team Camp: July 29-31
Positions Needed: Outside Hitter, Middle Hitter
Schedule: Missouri, Texas Tech, Mississippi, New Mexico State

Arkansas Technical University
Academic Profile

Tucker Coliseum, ATU
Russellville, AR 72801-2222

Phone: 501-968-0343

Type: Public, 4 Yr., Coed
Website: http://www.atu.edu
SAT/ACT/GPA: 800/17
Student/Faculty Ratio: 18:1
Undergraduate Enrollment: 4,166
Scholarships/Academic: Yes   **Athletic:** Yes
Expenses By: Year   **In State:** $ 1,902
Degrees Conferred: AA, AS, BA, BS, BFA, M
Programs of Study: Accounting, Agriculture, Art, Biological Science, Business, Chemistry, Computer, Creative Writing, Economics, Engineering, Geology, Health, Journalism, Medical, Music, Natural Science, Parks/Recreation, Physical Science, Psychology

Founded: 1909
Religion: Non-Affiliated
Housing: Yes
Male/Female: 41:59
Graduate Enrollment: 190
Financial Aid: Yes
Out of State: $ 2,732

Women's Athletic Profile

Hwy. 7
Russellville, AR 72801-2222
Coach: Tracy McWilliams
Email: tracy.mcwilliams@mail.atu.edu

NCAA I
Lady Golden Suns, Green, Gold
Phone: (501) 964-0513
Fax: (501) 964-0829

Estimated # of Women's Volleyball Scholarships: N/A
Conference: Gulf South Conference

Harding University
Academic Profile

PO Box 12281
Searcy, AR 72149

Phone: 501-279-4761

Type: Private, 4 Yr., Coed
Website: http://www.harding.edu
SAT/ACT/GPA: 1000/24
Student/Faculty Ratio: 18/1
Undergraduate Enrollment: 4500
Scholarships/Academic: Yes
Expenses By: Year
Specializes In: Liberal Arts
Degrees Conferred: AA, BA, BS, BFA, M

Athletic: Yes
In State: $11,000

Founded: 1924
Religion: Church of Christ
Housing: Yes
Male/Female: 51/49
Graduate Enrollment: 200
Financial Aid: Yes
Out of State: $11,000

Programs of Study: Advertising, Art, Biblical, Biology, Business, Chemistry, Dietetics, Economics, Fashion, Finance, Journalism, PreProfessional Programs, Religious, Science, Speech, Special Education

Women's Athletic Profile

Box 12281
Searcy, AR 72149-0001
Coach: Keith Giboney
Email: kgiboney@harding.edu

NCAA I
Lady Bisons, Black, Gold
Phone: (501) 279-4176
Fax: (501) 279-4138

Estimated # of Women's Volleyball Scholarships: 7.5
Conference: Gulf-South
Program Profile: Facility- Rhodes Fieldhouse, Seating of 3,000
History: Began in 1983.
Achievements: 3 Years in a row of post season play
Freshman Receiving Financial Aid/Academic:
Roster In State: 1
Sophomores on Team: 2
Most Recent Record: 21-16-0

Athletic: 5
Out of State: 11
Seniors on Team: 5

Out of Country: 0
Graduation %: 90

Schedule: North Alabama, Arkansas Tech, Univ of Montevollo
Style of Play: Strong defense, highly motivated, academic players. Stresses in discipline, high moral character and strong achievement in all endeavors. Awesome team Chemistry.

Henderson State University
Academic Profile

Box 7891, HSU
Arkadelphia, AR 71999

Phone: 800-228-7333

Type: Public, 4 Yr., Coed
Website: http://www.hsu.edu
SAT/ACT/GPA: 500/21
Student/Faculty Ratio: 19/1
Undergraduate Enrollment: 3,252
Scholarships/Academic: Yes
Expenses By: Year
Degrees Conferred: AA, BA, BFA, BS, BM, BME

Athletic: Yes
In State: $ 1,860

Founded: 1890
Religion: Non-Affiliated
Housing: Yes
Male/Female: 45:55
Graduate Enrollment: 290
Financial Aid: Yes
Out of State: $ 2,270

Programs of Study: Accounting, Biological Science, Business, Chemistry, Communications, English, Pharmacy, Physics, Political, PreProfessional Programs, Recreation, Social Science, Speech Pathology

Women's Athletic Profile

Box 7630
Arkadelphia, AR 71999-0001
Coach: Rhonda Thigpen
Email: thigpen@oaks.hsu.edu

NCAA I
Lady Reddies, Red, Grey
Phone: (870) 230-5194
Fax: (870) 230-5408

Estimated # of Women's Volleyball Scholarships: 4
Conference: Gulf South Conference
Program Profile: The program has been in 2 final four in the NAIA in the early 1990's before making the change to NCAA. Since

then been conference division champs and runner-up. We play on a wood floor and have 2 courts.

Achievements: Coach of the Year 3 times, 2 Conference titles, 5 Division titles, 3 All-Americans, 3 NCAA All-Region Players.

Coaching: Rhonda Thigpen Head Coach

Freshman Receiving Financial Aid/Academic: **Athletic:** 1

Roster In State: 1   **Out of State:** 9   **Out of Country:** 1

Seniors on Team: 2

Most Recent Record: 21-13

Camp of Clinic Dates: June

Positions Needed: Setter, OH, MB

Schedule: Univ. of North Alabama, Truman State, Univ. of Alabama Huntsville, Missouri Western

Style of Play: Fast tempo, very aggressive, hard working and a family like environment.

Hendrix College
Academic Profile

1600 Washington Avenue
Conway, AR 72032

Phone: 800-277-9017

Type: Private, 4 Yr., Liberal Arts, Coed
Website: http://www.hendrix.edu
SAT/ACT/GPA: Open
Student/Faculty Ratio: 13:1
Undergraduate Enrollment: 1,047
Scholarships/Academic: Yes
Expenses By: Year
Specializes In: Liberal Arts
Degrees Conferred: BA, Masters in Accounting

Founded: 1876
Religion: United Methodist
Housing: Yes
Male/Female: 45:55
Graduate Enrollment: 11
Athletic: No   **Financial Aid:** Yes
In State: $ 17,680   **Out of State:** $ 17,680

Programs of Study: Art, Biology, Chemistry, Computer Science, Business, Economics, Elementary Education, English, French, German, History, Interdisciplinary Studies, International Relations & Global Studies, Mathematics, Music, Philosophy, Philosophy & Religion, Physical Education, Physics, Politics, Psychology, Religion, Sociology, Spanish, Theater Arts, PreProfessional Programs: PreDentistry, PreEngineering, PreLaw, PreMedicine, PreMinistry, PrePharmacy, PrePhysical Therapy, PreVeterinary, PreSocial Work. Teacher Certification.

Women's Athletic Profile

1600 Washington Avenue
Conway, AR 72032
Coach: Beverly Robison
Email: robison@mercury.hendrix.edu

NCAA I
Warriors/Black, Orange
Phone: (501) 450-3899
Fax: (501) 450-3805

Estimated # of Women's Volleyball Scholarships: 0

Conference: Southern California Athletic Conference

Program Profile: Program is in it's 24th year, play 22 date (approx.30 matches), play in the fall. Games are held in the Mabee Center

History: 24th year for program. Finished 8th in 1999 in SCAC

Achievements: Coach =2nd year at Hendrix

Coaching: Head Coach-Beverly Robison-2nd year team had best SCAC Finish with history of program in 1999. Karl Talcott-Assistant-1st year-was head coach at Cardinal Stritch College 93-97

Roster In State: 6   **Out of State:** 6   **Out of Country:**

Sophomores on Team: **Seniors on Team:** 1   **Graduation %:** 100

Most Recent Record: 13-14-0

Positions Needed: All

Schedule: Trinity University, DePauw, Austin College, Southwestern, Millsaps

Style of Play: Will play to strength of personnel

John Brown University
Academic Profile

2000 West University
Siloam Springs, AR 72761

Phone: 877-528-4636

Type: Private, 4 Yr., Liberal Arts, Coed
Website: http://www.jbu.edu

Founded: 1919
Religion: Non-Affiliated

SAT/ACT/GPA: 900/40
Student/Faculty Ratio: 18:1
Undergraduate Enrollment: 1,200
Scholarships/Academic: Yes
Expenses By: Year
Degrees Conferred: BA, BS, BSE, BMus, AA, AS

Athletic: Yes
In State: $ 13,510

Housing: Yes
Male/Female: 45:55
Graduate Enrollment: N/A
Financial Aid: Yes
Out of State: $ 13,510

Programs of Study: Accounting, Art, Biochemistry, Biology, Business Administration, Chemistry, Church Ministry, Construction Management, Elementary Education, Engineering, English, Environmental Science, History, Journalism, Mathematics, Medical Technology, Music, Physical Education, PreLaw, PreMed, Psychology, Sports Medicine

Women's Athletic Profile

2000 W. University Street
Siloam Springs, AR 72761
Coach: Robyn Gordon
Email: rgordan@jbu.edu

NCAA I
Golden Eagles, Royal, Gold
Phone: (501) 524-7301
Fax: (501) 524-7412

Estimated # of Women's Volleyball Scholarships: 5.4
Conference: Sooner Athletic Conference
Program Profile: Fall season, Murray Sells Gymnasium and has a wooden floor.
History: Began in 1976
Achievements: 2000 Conference title, 1999 sub regional champions, 1999 region runner up.
Coaching: Robyn Gordan 11th season. 188-172 through 10 seasons, second in region 5 in 1999 (28-13).
Freshman Receiving Financial Aid/Academic: **Athletic:** 4
Roster In State: 1   **Out of State:** 11   **Out of Country:**
Sophomores on Team: **Seniors on Team:** 3   **Graduation %:** 90
Most Recent Record: 29-11
Camp of Clinic Dates: Summer 2001 team camp
Positions Needed: Outside and Middle hitter, Right side player.
Schedule: Lubbock Christian, Palm Beach Atlantic, Master's College, Houston Baptist.
Style of Play: Quick offense and solid rotational defense, aggressive serving and a solid serve reception.

Lyon College
Academic Profile

P.O Box 2317
Batesville, AR 75203-2317

Phone: 800-423-2542

Type: Private, 4 Yr., Liberal Arts, Coed
Website: http://www.lyon.edu
SAT/ACT/GPA: 20
Student/Faculty Ratio: 12:1
Undergraduate Enrollment: 500
Scholarships/Academic: Yes
Expenses By: Year
Specializes In: Sciences, Business, Education
Degrees Conferred: BA, BS

Athletic: Yes
In State: $ 15,325

Founded: 1872
Religion: Presbyterian
Housing: Yes
Male/Female: 1:2
Graduate Enrollment: N/A
Financial Aid: Yes
Out of State: $ 15,325

Programs of Study: Accounting, Art, Biology, Chemistry, Economics, Elementary Education, English, History, Psychology, Journalism, Management, Mathematics, Music, Politics, Religion & Philosophy, Secondary Education, Spanish, Theatre

Women's Athletic Profile

Highland Avenue
Batesville, AR 72501
Coach: Laura Kozella
Email: lkozella@lyon.edu

NCAA I
Lady Pipers, Red, White
Phone: (870) 698-4223
Fax: (870) 793-1763

Did Not Return Profile

Ouachita Baptist University
Academic Profile

410 Ouachita St.
Arkadelphia, AR 71998-0001

Phone: 800-342-5628

Type: Private, 4 Yr., Coed
Website: Not Available
SAT/ACT/GPA: 950/23
Student/Faculty Ratio: 11:1
Undergraduate Enrollment: 1,604
Scholarships/Academic: Yes
Expenses By: Year
Degrees Conferred: BA, BS, BME, BM, M

Athletic: Yes
In State: $ 10,620

Founded: 1886
Religion: Non-Affiliated
Housing: Yes
Male/Female: 48:52
Graduate Enrollment: N/A
Financial Aid: Yes
Out of State: $ 10,620

Programs of Study: Accounting, Art, Biology, Business, Chemistry, Communications, Computer, Dietetics, Economics, Education, English, Languages, Health, History, Math, Medical, PreProfessional Programs, Speech

Women's Athletic Profile

410 Quachita Street
Arkadelphia, AR 71998
Coach: Bill Sutton
Email: suttonb@alpha.obu.edu

NCAA I
Lady Tigers, Purple, Gold
Phone: (870) 245-5104
Fax: (870) 245-5598

Estimated # of Women's Volleyball Scholarships: 8
Conference: Gulf South
Program Profile: Our facility has a new sport court. We play a fall season and a spring season.
History: 30 years of Ouachita Volleyball
Achievements: 2000 Gulf South Freshman of the Year, 3 players on All-Conference team, 5 players All-Academic.
Coaching: Biss Sutton Head Coach and Graduate Assistant Danny Precott
Freshman Receiving Financial Aid/Academic:
Roster In State: 1
Seniors on Team: 4
Most Recent Record: 23-8
Camp of Clinic Dates: July 2001
Positions Needed: Setter, OH

Out of State: 11
Graduation %: 85

Athletic: 3
Out of Country: 3

Schedule: Univ. North Alabama, Arkansas Tech, Harding, Rockhurst, East Texas Baptist, Dallas Baptist, Henderson State, Central Arkansas
Style of Play: Fast pace, quick set offense.

Southern Arkansas University
Academic Profile

100 East University
Magnolia, AR 71753-5000

Phone: (870) 235-4000

Type: Public, 4 Yr., Coed
Website: http://www.saumag.edu
SAT/ACT/GPA: 16
Student/Faculty Ratio: 20:1
Undergraduate Enrollment: 2,785
Scholarships/Academic: Yes
Expenses By:
Degrees Conferred: AA, AS, BA, BS, BME, BSE, MED

Athletic: Yes
In State: $3,092

Founded: 1906
Religion: Non-Affiliated
Housing: Yes
Male/Female: 41/59
Graduate Enrollment: 252
Financial Aid: Yes
Out of State: $ 3,716

Programs of Study: School of Business Administration, School of Liberal Arts and Performing Arts, General Studies, School of Science and Technology, School of Education, Master of Education

Women's Athletic Profile

100 E. University, Box 9213
Magnolia, AR 71753-5000
Coach: Allison Kelley
Email: amkeeley@saumag.edu

NCAA I
Lady Riderettes, Blue, Gold
Phone: (870) 235-4128
Fax: (870) 235-4988

Estimated # of Women's Volleyball Scholarships: 8
Conference: Gulf South West Conference
Program Profile: The SAU Riderettes have access to two gym facilities and the athletic weight room. Both gyms have wood floors

and the competition gym seats 1,500 fans. The program seeks to play the highest competition available and to compete at the NCAA regional and national levels.

History: SAU has had a volleyball program since 1977. Under Coach Ginger Hurst the team had 10 winning seasons, multiple conference titles, and All-Conference and All-Regional players. In 1995, the program became Division II under the leadership of Michelle Shoppach and continued it's winning ways with 6 winning seasons and a conference championship.

Coaching: Allison Kelley is in her third season at Southern Arkansas. She previously coached at Chaffey Community College in California and was the club director and under 18's coach for Gene's team.

Freshman Receiving Financial Aid/Academic:

Athletic: 2

Roster In State: 0   **Out of State:** 17   **Out of Country:** 0

Seniors on Team: 2   **Graduation %:** 85

Most Recent Record: 10-18-0

Positions Needed: Setter, middle blockers, defensive specialist

Schedule: Arkansas Tech, Henderson State, Harding, Christian Brothers, Ouachita Baptist, Emporia State, Truman State, North Alabama, Northwest Missouri, Central Missouri.

Style of Play: Offense is tailored to personnel, aggressive, perimeter defense.

University of Arkansas - Fayetteville
Academic Profile

131 Barnhill Arena
Fayetteville, AR 72701

Phone: (501) 575-2348

Type: Public, 4 Yr., Coed
Website: http://www.uark.edu
SAT/ACT/GPA: 23/3.0
Student/Faculty Ratio: 15:1
Undergraduate Enrollment: 14,161
Scholarships/Academic: Yes
Expenses By: Year

Founded: 1871
Religion: Non-Affiliated
Housing: Yes
Male/Female: 52:48
Graduate Enrollment: 2,600

Athletic: Yes   **Financial Aid:** Yes
In State: $ 7,722   **Out of State:** $ 12,706

Degrees Conferred: BS,BA,BFA,BM,BSBA, BSIM,BSPA, BSE, A-Architect, BSHES, BID

Programs of Study: Colleges - many programs of study within each Agricultural, Food & Life Sciences, Architecture, College of Arts & Sciences, Business, Education & Health Professions, Engineering, Law

Women's Athletic Profile

131 Barnhill Arena
Fayetteville, AR 72701
Coach: Chris Poole
Email: cpoole@comp.uark.edu

NCAA I
Razorbacks, Cardinal, White
Phone: (501) 575-3814
Fax: (501) 575-7501

Estimated # of Women's Volleyball Scholarships: 0

Conference: Southeastern Conference

Program Profile: We are a top 15 program funded at the highest level. We play in the Barnhill Arena which has 9,000 seats. It is a volleyball-only arena. It also houses an academic center, a training room and a locker room.

History: Our program began in 1994. We were the West Division SEC Champions for 5 consecutive years. We had NCAA appearances in 1996,1997 and 1998. We were SEC Tournament Champions in 1997. We were in the NCAA Sweet 16 in 1998. We were ranked in the Top 25 all of 1997 and 1998. We went up as high as #13 when 1998 ended.

Achievements: Chris Poole-1994 SEC Coach of the Year; 1997 District 4 Coach of the Year; 2 All-Americans, 2 Gatorade Players of the Year; 3 High School All-Americans

Coaching: Chris Poole, Head Coach, has a record here of 129-55. At Arkansas, he had a 397-120 overall record. He got seven Division I Coach of the Year Honors. He has 11 Conference Titles and 10 post-season appearances. Beth Nuneviller and Holly Graham are Assistant Coaches. Beth Nuneviller was Coach of the Year and an MVP American at Arkansas State in 1988.

Freshman Receiving Financial Aid/Academic:

Athletic: 12

Roster In State: 0   **Out of State:** 11   **Out of Country:** 2

Sophomores on Team: 0   **Seniors on Team:** 2   **Graduation %:** 100

Most Recent Record: 29-6-0   **Fall Games:** 35   **Spring Games:** 4

Camp of Clinic Dates: July 18-30

Positions Needed: Outside, Middle

Schedule: Pepperdine, Florida, Oral Roberts, Michigan ,Clemson, Georgia, Tennessee, Kentucky

Style of Play: Very tall/athletic power team. Average height of 1999 team is 6'1 (including DS's) We have been one of the top teams in the nation the past two years in blocks per game, hitting efficiency and kills per game. Highly motivated players.

University of Arkansas - Little Rock
Academic Profile

2801 S. University
Little Rock, AR 72204

Phone: 501-569-3127

Type: Public, 4 Yr., Coed
Website: http://www.ualr.edu
SAT/ACT/GPA: 870/21/2.00
Student/Faculty Ratio: 16:1
Undergraduate Enrollment: 9,500
Scholarships/Academic: Yes   **Athletic:** Yes
Expenses By: Year   **In State:** $ 8,000

Founded: 1927
Religion: Non-Affiliated
Housing: Yes
Male/Female: 46:54
Graduate Enrollment: 2,500
Financial Aid: Yes
Out of State: $ 12,000

Specializes In: Business, Engineering, PreMed, PreLaw, Information Tech
Programs of Study: Accounting, Advertising, Art, Biology, Business, Chemistry, Communicative Disorders, Computer, Construction, Criminal, Economics, Engineering, Finance, Geology, Health, Journalism, Science, Technology

Women's Athletic Profile

2801 S. University
Little Rock, AR 72204-1099
Coach: Van Compton
Email: vxcompton@ualr.edu

NCAA I
Lady Trojans, Maroon, Silver
Phone: (501) 569-3371
Fax: (501) 569-3030

Estimated # of Women's Volleyball Scholarships: 9
Conference: Sun Belt Conference
Program Profile: Our gym is called Trojan Fieldhouse with a seating capacity of 1,000. Our playing season is August through December.
History: Our first year was in 1988 with an overall all-time record of 134-102 (.568). Our last post-season opponent was Wisconsin with a result of 3-0 in 1998.
Achievements: Coach of the Year in 1993, Conference Tournament Title in 1995, 1997 & 1998; Conference Co-Champions in 1997, Academic All-American in 1997.
Coaching: Van Compton, Head Coach, started with the program in 1988. He has an overall record of 178-127. Danijela Tomic is our Assistant Coach, played in 1995 & 1996 for WALR. She was a student assistant coach for two years. Became an assistant coach in 1999. She was named All-Conference and All-Conference tournament.

Roster In State: 1   **Out of State:** 5   **Out of Country:** 5
Seniors on Team: 3   **Graduation %:** 85-90
Most Recent Record: 20-9-0   **Fall Games:** 30   **Spring Games:** 0
Positions Needed: Setter, Middle, Outside
Style of Play: Fast, aggressive offense and serving.

University of Arkansas - Pine Bluff
Academic Profile

North University Drive
Pine Bluff, AR 71601

Phone: 800-264-6585

Type: 4 Yr., Coed
Website: http://www.uapb.edu
SAT/ACT/GPA: Open
Student/Faculty Ratio:
Undergraduate Enrollment: N/A
Scholarships/Academic: **Athletic:**
Expenses By: Year   **In State:**
Degrees Conferred:

Founded:
Religion: Non-Affiliated
Housing: No
Male/Female:
Graduate Enrollment: N/A
Financial Aid:
Out of State:

Programs of Study: Contact school for programs of study.

Women's Athletic Profile

N. University Drive
Pine Bluff, AR 71611
Coach: Betty Hayes
Email:

NCAA I
Lady Lionettes, Black, Gold
Phone: (870) 543-8695
Fax: (501) 543-8114

Estimated # of Women's Volleyball Scholarships: N/A
Conference: Southwestern Athletic Conference
Program Profile: Kenneth Johnson HPER Complex was built in 1980, a multi-facilities with three volleyball court, indoor track, racquetball, dance and swimming. Arena has a seating capacity of 4,500, while stadium has a seating capacity of 8,000. Our playing season is in the Fall that starts September-November.
History: Our women's volleyball program began in the Fall of 1997. Entering one at the Southwestern Athletic Conference.
Coaching: Betty Hayes, Head Coach, a 1980 graduate of University of Arkansas-Pine Bluff. She has a three-year overall record: 1997-1998 was 5-24, 1998-1999 was 10-23 and SWAC Conference Tournament in 1998-1999 that placed her team into 7th.

Roster In State: 7	**Out of State:** 7	**Out of Country:** 0
Sophomores on Team: 3	**Seniors on Team:** 1	**Graduation %:**
Most Recent Record: 10-23-0	**Fall Games:** 42	**Spring Games:** 0

Positions Needed: Defensive specialist
Schedule: Southern University, Grambling State University, Prairie View, Alcorn State, Alabama A&M, Alabama State
Style of Play: New group and new mix of players. In 1998, our skill level varied from position to position. We hope to execute more challenging offensive-defensive plays and be more competitive. Second year team with a lot of growing to do.

University of Central Arkansas
Academic Profile

UCA Box 5004
Conway, AR 72035

Phone: (501) 450-3258

Type: Public, 4 Yr., Coed
Website: http://www.uca.edu
SAT/ACT/GPA: 890/17/3.0
Student/Faculty Ratio: 19:1
Undergraduate Enrollment: 9,000
Scholarships/Academic: Yes   **Athletic:** Yes
Expenses By: Year   **In State:** $ 6,638

Founded: 1907
Religion: Non-Affiliated
Housing: Yes
Male/Female: 2.3:1
Graduate Enrollment: 1,000
Financial Aid: Yes
Out of State: $ 7,136

Specializes In: Liberal Arts, Physical Therapy, Teacher Education
Degrees Conferred: AA, AS. AAS, BA, BBA, BS, BSE, MA, MS, MSE, MSN, MM, Ph.D. (Physical Therapy)
Programs of Study: Athletic Training, Business, Communications, Education, Kinesiology (Physical Education), Liberal Arts, Music, Nursing, Occupational Therapy, Physical Therapy, Science, Speech(Language) Pathology

Women's Athletic Profile

201 Donaghey & Bruce St.
Conway, AR 72035-5003
Coach: Mary Ann Schlientz
Email: maryanns@maul.uca.edu

NCAA I
Lady Bears, Purple, Grey
Phone: (501) 450-3154
Fax: (501) 450-3151

Estimated # of Women's Volleyball Scholarships: 8
Conference: Gulf South Conference
Program Profile: Traditionally, we are a competitive program within the conference. We had 4 appearances at the conference tournament in the last 5 years of membership in GSC. We compete in the Farris Center, with a seating capacity of 5,000.

Roster In State: 6	**Out of State:** 6	**Out of Country:** 0
Most Recent Record: 19-20-0	**Fall Games:** 39	**Spring Games:** 4

Positions Needed: Setter, Outside Hitter, Middle Blocker

Williams Baptist College
Academic Profile

60 West Fulbright Avenue
Walnut Ridge, AR 72476

Phone: 870-886-6741

Type: Private, 4 Yr., Coed
Website: http://www.wb2.wbcoll.edu
SAT/ACT/GPA: Open
Student/Faculty Ratio: 10:1
Undergraduate Enrollment: N/A
Scholarships/Academic: Yes   **Athletic:** Yes
Expenses By: Year   **In State:** $ 4,800

Founded: 1941
Religion: Non-Affiliated
Housing: No
Male/Female: 43:57
Graduate Enrollment: N/A
Financial Aid: Yes
Out of State: $ 4,800

Programs of Study: Art, Bible Studies, Business and Management, Education, English, History, Music, Physical Education, Psychology, Theological Studies

Women's Athletic Profile

60 W. Fulbright Avenue
Walnut Ridge, AR 72476
Coach: Judy Johnson
Email: jjohnson@wbcoll.edu

NCAA I
Lady Eagles, Blue, White
Phone: (870) 886-6741
Fax: (870) 886-9924

Did Not Return Profile

CALIFORNIA

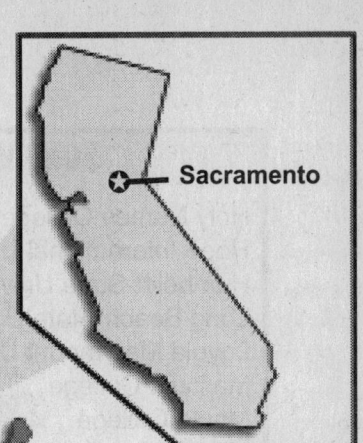

Sacramento

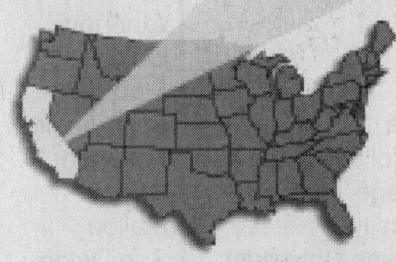

SCHOOL	CITY	AFFILIATION	PAGE
Azusa Pacific University	Azusa	NAIA	76
Bethany College	Scotts Valley	NAIA	76
Biola University	La Mirada	NAIA	77
California Baptist College	Riverside	NAIA	77
California Institute of Technology	Pasadena	NCAA III	78
California Lutheran University	Thousand Oaks	NCAA III	78
California Maritime Academy	Vallejo	NAIA	79
Cal State Polytechnic U - SLO	San Luis Obispo	NCAA I	79
Cal State Polytechnic U-Pomona	Pomona	NCAA II	80
Cal State University - Bakersfield	Bakersfield	NCAA II	81
Cal State University - Chico	Chico	NCAA II	81
Cal State University - D.H.	Carson	NCAA II	82
Cal State University - Fresno	Fresno	NCAA I	82
Cal State University - Fullerton	Fullerton	NCAA I	82
Cal State University - Hayward	Hayward	NCAA III	83
Cal State University - Los Angeles	Los Angeles	NCAA II	83
Cal State University - Monterey Bay	Seaside	NAIA	84
Cal State University - Northridge	Northridge	NCAA I	84
Cal State University - Sacramento	Sacramento	NCAA I	86
Cal State University - San Bern.	San Bernardino	NCAA II	86
Cal State University - Stanislaus	Turlock	NCAA II	87
Chapman University	Orange	NCAA III	88
Christian Heritage College	El Cajon	NCCAA I/NAIA	88
Claremont-Mudd-Scripps Colleges	Claremont	NCAA III	89
College of Notre Dame	Belmont	NCAA II	89
Concordia University	Irvine	NAIA	90
Dominican College	San Rafael	NAIA	91
Fresno Pacific University	Fresno	NAIA	91

SCHOOL	CITY	AFFILIATION	PAGE
Holy Names College	Oakland	NAIA	92
Hope International University	Fullerton	NAIA	92
Humboldt State University	Arcata	NCAA II	93
Long Beach State University	Long Beach	NCAA I	94
Loyola Marymount University	Los Angeles	NCAA I	95
Master's College	Santa Clarita	NAIA I	96
Menlo College	Atherton	NCAA III/NAIA	96
Mills College	Oakland	NCAA III	97
Moorpark College	Moorpark	NJCAA	97
Occidental College	Los Angeles	NCAA III	98
Pacific Christian College	Fullerton	NCCAA/NAIA	99
Pacific Union College	Angwin		99
Pepperdine University	Malibu	NCAA I	100
Point Loma Nazarene University	San Diego	NAIA	100
Pomona-Pitzer Colleges	Claremont	NCAA III	101
Saint Mary's College - California	Moraga	NCAA I	102
San Diego State University	San Diego	NCAA I	102
San Francisco State University	San Francisco	NCAA II	103
San Jose State University	San Jose	NCAA I	104
Santa Clara University	Santa Clara	NCAA I	104
Simpson College	Redding	NCCAA/NAIA	105
Solano Community College	Suisun City	CCCAA	106
Sonoma State University	Rohnert Park	NCAA II	106
Stanford University	Stanford	NCAA I	107
University of Cal - Berkeley	Berkeley	NCAA I	108
University of Cal - Davis	Davis	NCAA II	108
University of Cal - Irvine	Irvine	NCAA I	109
University of Cal - Los Angeles	Los Angeles	NCAA I	109
University of Cal - Riverside	Riverside	NCAA II	110
University of Cal - San Diego	La Jolla	NCAA III	111
University of Cal - Santa Barbara	Santa Barbara	NCAA I	112
University of Cal - Santa Cruz	Santa Cruz	NCAA III	113
University of LaVerne	La Verne	NCAA III	114
University of Redlands	Redlands	NCAA III	115
University of San Diego	San Diego	NCAA I	115
University of San Francisco	San Francisco	NCAA I	116
University of Southern California	Los Angeles	NCAA I	116
University of the Pacific	Stockton	NCAA I	117
Vanguard University	Costa Mesa	NAIA	118
Westmont College	Santa Barbara	NAIA	118
Whittier College	Whittier	NCAA III	119

Azusa Pacific University
Academic Profile

901E Acosta Avenue
Azusa, CA 91702

Phone: (626) 815-6000 ext.3269

Type: Private, 4 Yr., Liberal Arts, Coed
Website: http://www.apu.edu
SAT/ACT/GPA: 920/18/2.5
Student/Faculty Ratio: 15:1
Undergraduate Enrollment: 2,500
Scholarships/Academic: Yes   **Athletic:** Yes
Expenses By: Year   **In State:** $ 18,000

Founded: 1899
Religion: Evangelical
Housing: Yes
Male/Female: 1:3
Graduate Enrollment: 2,400
Financial Aid: Yes
Out of State: $ 18,000

Degrees Conferred: 40+ undergraduate:18 Masters Degree; 3 Doctorates; CA Teaching Credentials
Programs of Study: Accounting, Applied Health, Art, Athletic Training, Biblical Studies, Biochemistry, Biology, Business Administration, Chemistry, Christian Ministries, Communications, Computer Science, English, Global Studies, History, International Business, Life Science, Liberal Studies, Mathematics, Marketing, Music, Nursing, Philosophy, Physical Education, Physics, Political Science, PreDentistry, PreEngineering, PreLaw, PreM.Ed., PreVeterinary, Psychology, Social Science, Social Work, Sociology, Spanish, Theology

Women's Athletic Profile

901 E. Alosta
Azusa, CA 91702
Coach: Gerry Gregory
Email: ggregory@apu.edu

NCAA I
Lady Cougars, Orange, Black
Phone: (626) 815-6000x5184
Fax: (626) 815-5084

Estimated # of Women's Volleyball Scholarships: 2
Conference: Golden State Athletic Conference
Program Profile: Moving into the new on-campus, 3700-seat Fleix event center at the beginning of the 2001 season, houses 4 courts and 4 teams rooms, will be an ideal setting for any tournament including the NAIAs.
History: Won the 1980 NAIA National Championship (the NAIAs first-ever women's sports), returned to the NAIA Championship tournament in 1991, and again in 1994. Won the 1979 AIAW Division III national championship and was runner-up in 1980
Roster In State: 12   **Out of State:** 1   **Out of Country:**
Sophomores on Team: **Seniors on Team:** 1   **Graduation %:** 80
Most Recent Record: 15-13
Schedule: Fresno Pacific, Point Loma Nazarene, Biola

Bethany College
Academic Profile

800 Bethany Drive
Scotts Valley, CA 95066

Phone: 831-438-3800

Type: Private, 4 Yr., Coed
Website: http://www.bethany.edu
SAT/ACT/GPA: Open
Student/Faculty Ratio: 25:1
Undergraduate Enrollment: 617
Scholarships/Academic: Yes   **Athletic:** Yes
Expenses By: Year   **In State:** $ 13,155

Founded: 1919
Religion: Assemblies of God
Housing: Yes
Male/Female: 45:55
Graduate Enrollment: N/A
Financial Aid: Yes
Out of State: $ 13,155

Degrees Conferred: AA, AS, BA, BS
Programs of Study: Biblical Languages, Biblical Studies, Business Administration, Commerce, Management, Drug and Alcohol/Substance Abuse Counseling, Early Childhood Education, Education, Elementary Education, English, International Studies, Liberal Arts, General Studies, International Studies, Music, Music Education, Psychology, Sacred Music, Social Science, Theatre Arts/Drama, Theology

Women's Athletic Profile

800 Bethany Drive
Scotts Valley, CA 95066
Coach: Butch Mandon
Email:

NCAA I
Lady Bruins, Blue, White
Phone: (831) 438-3800
Fax:

Did Not Return Profile

Biola University
Academic Profile

13800 Biola Avenue
La Mirada, CA 90639

Phone: 800-652-4652

Type: Private, 4 Yr., Liberal Arts, Coed
Website: http://www.biola.edu
SAT/ACT/GPA: Open
Student/Faculty Ratio: 18:1
Undergraduate Enrollment: 2,200
Scholarships/Academic: Yes   **Athletic:** Yes
Expenses By: Year   **In State:** $ 22,924
Specializes In: Liberal Arts

Founded: 1908
Religion: Non-Denominational
Housing: Yes
Male/Female: 40:60
Graduate Enrollment: 1,100
Financial Aid: Yes
Out of State: $ 22,924

Degrees Conferred: BA, BS, Masters, Ph.D.
Programs of Study: Art, Biochemistry, Biological Science, Accounting, Computer Information Systems, Economics, Business Administration, Philosophy, Management, Marketing, Nursing, History, Humanities, Education, Sociology, Computer Science, Communications, Psychology

Women's Athletic Profile

13800 Biola Avenue
La Mirada, CA 90639
Coach: Ryan McGuyre
Email: ryan.mcguyre@bubbs.biola.edu

NCAA I
Lady Eagles, Red, White
Phone: (562)944-0351
Fax: (562) 903-4890

Estimated # of Women's Volleyball Scholarships: N/A
Conference: GSAC

California Baptist College
Academic Profile

8432 Magnolia Avenue
Riverside, CA 92504

Phone: 877-228-8866

Type: Private, 4 Yr., Liberal Arts, Coed
Website: http://www.calbaptist.edu
SAT/ACT/GPA: 870/20/2.3
Student/Faculty Ratio: 14:1
Undergraduate Enrollment: 850
Scholarships/Academic: Yes   **Athletic:** Yes
Expenses By: Year   **In State:** $ 15,000
Specializes In: Education, Liberal Studies, Physical Education

Founded: 1950
Religion: Southern Baptist
Housing: Yes
Male/Female: 50:50
Graduate Enrollment: 45
Financial Aid: Yes
Out of State: $ 15,000

Degrees Conferred: BA, BS, MS, BM
Programs of Study: Biology, Communications, Art, Business, Physical Education, Education, Liberal Arts, Religion, PreMed, PreNursing, PreDentistry, English, History, Psychology, Sociology

Women's Athletic Profile

8432 Magnolia Avenue
Riverside, CA 92504
Coach: Wayne White
Email:

NCAA I
Lady Lancers, White, Blue
Phone: (909) 343-4596
Fax: (909) 689-4754

Estimated # of Women's Volleyball Scholarships: N/A
Conference: Golden State
Program Profile: Playing season is in the fall, home gym is the Van Dyne Gym (on campus). Capacity 1,100. Very competitive conference (GSAC) four teams ranked in the top 25 annually, last years NAIA runner-up came from the GSAC, playing surface is hardwood.
History: Began in 1975, advanced to the NAIA championships on six different occasions. Finished 5th in the nation in 1989, was the 1992 NAIA runner-up, also advanced to the 1999 NAIA Quarterfinals was an NAIA women's volleyball power in the late 80s and early 90s and now again in the late 90s and into 2000.
Achievements: Former head coach, Mike Neece, was named 1999 GSAC Coach of the Year, Yue-Ming Li was named 1999 GSAC

Player of the Year and 1999 All-American she was a member of the 1988 and 1992 Chinese Olympic Teams.

Coaching: Head coach Wayne White is in his first year as the women's head coach. He guided the men's team to a 1999 NAIA/SSI National Championship in the first year of the program. He played at UCLA in the early 80s with Karch Kirlay before transferring to Long Beach State. He is assisted by wife Becky, who was a four-time All-American at Biola University in the early 80s.

Freshman Receiving Financial Aid/Academic: **Athletic:** 2

Roster In State: 9   **Out of State:** 3   **Out of Country:** 1

Seniors on Team: 3

Most Recent Record: 5-6

Schedule: Fresno Pacific, Westmont, CS San Bernardino, UC San Diego, CS Los Angeles, Point Loma, Azusa Pacific.

Style of Play: Very aggressive offensively, defensively find your spots and stay there and dig.

California Institute of Technology
Academic Profile

1201 East California Boulevard   **Phone:** 800-568-8324
Pasadena, CA 91125

Type: Private, 4 Yr., Engineering, Coed   **Founded:** 1891
Website: http://www.caltech.edu   **Religion:** Non-Affiliated
SAT/ACT/GPA: Top 1%   **Housing:** Yes
Student/Faculty Ratio: 10:1   **Male/Female:** 3:1
Undergraduate Enrollment: 800   **Graduate Enrollment:** 1,000
Scholarships/Academic: Yes   **Athletic:** No   **Financial Aid:** Yes
Expenses By: Year   **In State:** $ 25,000   **Out of State:** $ 25,000
Specializes In: Engineering, Science, Mathematics
Degrees Conferred: BA, BS, MS, Ph.D.
Programs of Study: Aeronautical Engineering, Astronomy, Biology, Chemical Engineering, Chemistry, Civil Engineering, Economics, Electrical Engineering, Engineering, Geochemistry, Geology, Geophysics, History, Literature, Mathematics, Mechanical Engineering, Physics, Planetary Science, Political Science, Seismology, Social Science, Space Science

Women's Athletic Profile

1201 E. California Boulevard   **NCAA I**
Pasadena, CA 91125   Beavers, Orange, White, Navy
Coach: Brent Reger   **Phone:** (626) 395-3262
Email: breger@caltech.edu   **Fax:** (626) 584-0589

Estimated # of Women's Volleyball Scholarships: 0
Conference: SCIAC
Program Profile: 3 month season in 500 seat capacity gym. Academics is the main focus point of this University.
History: 1979 women's volleyball began, that's when women were able to attend this University.
Roster In State: 3   **Out of State:** 6   **Out of Country:** 4
Seniors on Team: 2   **Graduation %:** 100
Most Recent Record: 5-15-0
Positions Needed: All
Schedule: La Verne, Cal Lutherian, Whittier, Pamona pitzer
Style of Play: Aggressive but inexperienced.

California Lutheran University
Academic Profile

60 W Olsen Road   **Phone:** (877) 256-3678
Thousands Oaks, CA 91360

Type: Private, 4 Yr., Liberal Arts, Coed   **Founded:** 1959
Website: http://www.callutheran.edu   **Religion:** Lutheran
SAT/ACT/GPA: 1000/21/2.75   **Housing:** Yes
Student/Faculty Ratio: 15:1   **Male/Female:** 45:55
Undergraduate Enrollment: 1,600   **Graduate Enrollment:** 900
Scholarships/Academic: Yes   **Athletic:** No   **Financial Aid:** Yes
Expenses By: Year   **In State:** $ 16,020   **Out of State:** $ 16,020
Specializes In: Biology, Business, Criminal Justice, Education, Psychology
Degrees Conferred: BA, BS, MA, MS
Programs of Study: Master of Business Education, Master of Public Administration, Master of Education, Master in Clinical Psychology, Master in Arts Education, Master of Science in Counseling and Guidance, Master of Special Education, Master in Marital

and Family Therapy

Women's Athletic Profile

60 W. Olsen Rd.
Thousand Oaks, CA 91360
Coach: James Park
Email:

NCAA I
Lady Regals, Purple, Gold
Phone: (805) 493-3832
Fax: (805) 493-3860

Estimated # of Women's Volleyball Scholarships: N/A
Conference: Southern California Intercollegiate Athletic Conference

California Maritime Academy
Academic Profile

200 Maritime Dr.
Vallejo, CA 94590

Phone: 707-654-1330

Type: Public, 4 Yr., Engineering, Coed
Website: http://www.csum.edu
SAT/ACT/GPA: Open/2.0 Min.
Student/Faculty Ratio: 15:1
Undergraduate Enrollment: 1,160
Scholarships/Academic: Yes   **Athletic:** Yes
Expenses By: Year   **In State:** $ 11,000
Specializes In: Engineering, Business
Degrees Conferred: BA, BS

Founded: 1929
Religion: Non-affiliated
Housing: Yes
Male/Female: 9:1
Graduate Enrollment: N/A
Financial Aid: Yes
Out of State: $ 11,000

Programs of Study: Business Administration, Engineering, Facilities Engineering, Marine Engineering, Marine Transportation, Maritime Transportation, Mechanical Engineering

Women's Athletic Profile

200 Maritime Drive
Vallejo, CA 94590
Coach: Jerry Carter
Email:

NCAA I
Sea Hags, Silver, Red, Black
Phone: (707) 654-1050
Fax: (707) 654-1051

Estimated # of Women's Volleyball Scholarships: 4
Conference: California Pacific Conference
Program Profile: Our program is trying to grow. We are just now beginning to recruit.
Roster In State: 8   **Out of State:** 1   **Out of Country:** 0
Graduation %: 100
Most Recent Record: 3-19-0   **Fall Games:** 22   **Spring Games:** 0
Positions Needed: 6
Schedule: Notre Dame, Holy Names, Simpson, Dominican, Pacific Union College

California State Polytechnic University - San Louis Obispo
Academic Profile

One Grand Avenue
San Luis Obispo, CA 93405-2002

Phone: 805-756-2311

Type: Public, 4 Yr., Liberal Arts, Coed
Website: http://www.calpoly.edu.
SAT/ACT/GPA: 1000
Student/Faculty Ratio: 19:1
Undergraduate Enrollment: 15,540
Scholarships/Academic: Yes   **Athletic:** Yes
Expenses By: Year   **In State:** $ 7,542
Specializes In: Agriculture, Architecture Business
Degrees Conferred: BA, BS, BLA, BAR, MA, MS, MBA, MCRP

Founded: 1901
Religion: Non-Affiliated
Housing: Yes
Male/Female: 58:42
Graduate Enrollment: 1,200
Financial Aid: Yes
Out of State:

Programs of Study: College of Agriculture (Business, Engineering, Systems Management, Science, Animal Science, Crop Science, Dairy/Food/Fruit Science, Forestry and Natural Resources, Nutritional, Horticulture, Plant Protection, Recreation, Soil Science),

College of Architecture and Environmental Design (Engineering, Architecture, City and Regional Planning, Construction, Landscape), College of Business (Business Administration, Economics, Industrial Technology), College of Engineering (Aeronautical, Civil, Computer, Computer Science, Electrical, Engineering Science, Environmental, Industrial, Manufacturing, Materials, Mechanical), College of Liberal Arts (Applied Art and Design, English, Graphic Communication, History, Human Development, Journalism, Liberal Studies, Music, Philosophy, Political, Psychology, Social Science, Speech), College of Science and Mathematics (Biochemistry, Biological Sciences, Chemistry, Ecology and Systematic Biology, Math, Microbiology, Physical Education, Physical Science, Physics, Statistics)

Women's Athletic Profile

1 Grand Avenue
San Luis Obispo, CA 93407
Coach: Steve Schlick
Email:

NCAA I
Lady Broncos, Green, Gold
Phone: (909) 869-2822
Fax: (909) 869-2814

Estimated # of Women's Volleyball Scholarships: N/A
Conference: Big West Conference
History: Our team has been a strong team in the competitive NCAA Division II.
Camp of Clinic Dates: General Skills: July 26-30

California State Polytechnic University - Pomona
Academic Profile

3801 W. Temple Avenue
Pomona, CA 91768

Phone: (909) 869-2810

Type: Public, 4 Yr., Coed
Website: http://www.csupomona.edu
SAT/ACT/GPA: 820/68 sum/2.0
Student/Faculty Ratio: 18/1
Undergraduate Enrollment: 18,100
Scholarships/Academic: Yes   **Athletic:** Yes
Expenses By: Year   **In State:** $9,000

Founded: 1938
Religion: Non-Affiliated
Housing: Yes
Male/Female: 55:45
Graduate Enrollment: 2,000
Financial Aid: Yes
Out of State: $14,000

Specializes In: Engineering, Agriculture, Hotel/Restaurant Mgmt, Business
Degrees Conferred: BA, BS, BArch, MA, MS, MBA
Programs of Study: Accounting, Aerospace Engineering, Agricultural Biology, Agricultural Business Management, Apparel Merchandising, Architecture, Chemistry, Behavioral Science, Construction Engineering, Computer Engineering, Industrial Engineering, Horticulture, Marketing Management, Physics, Political Science, Sociology, Soil Science, Zoology

Women's Athletic Profile

3801 W. Temple Avenue
Pomona, CA 91768
Coach: Rosie Wegrich
Email: rwegrich@csupomona.edu

NCAA I
Lady Broncos, Green, Gold
Phone: (909) 869-2822
Fax: (909) 768-2814

Estimated # of Women's Volleyball Scholarships: 5-6
Conference: California Collegiate Athletic Association
Program Profile: We are a Division II, Collegiate Athletic Association member which is arguably one of the best NCAA D.II conferences in the nation. CPP is a competitive program regionally and nationally athletically and academically. CPP plays its home matches in 500 seat Darlene May Gym, named after the legendary Women's Basketball coach guided the Broncos to three national titles. The playing season is fall and off-season competition occurs in the spring.
History: We started in 1979.
Achievements: CPP has 12 national postseason appearances, 2 CCAA titles, 10 All-America Awards, 5 Academic All-America Awards and numerous All-CCAA honorees.
Coaching: Rosie Wegrich, Head Coach, came to Pomona after spending the majority of her career at the University of Arizona plus a pair of seasons at the University of Minnesota. She was named the Northwest Regional Coach of the Year by the American Volleyball Coaches Association. Assitant Coach, Vinh Nguyen.
Freshman Receiving Financial Aid/Academic: **Athletic:** 2-3
Roster In State: 10   **Out of State:** 1   **Out of Country:** 0
Sophomores on Team: 0   **Seniors on Team:** 2   **Graduation %:** 95-98
Camp of Clinic Dates: July

Positions Needed: Setter, Outside Hitter
Schedule: Cal State- Bakersfield, University of California- Riverside, California University- Davis, Cal State- Los Angeles, Cal State- San Bernardino
Style of Play: Swing offense, OH pass middle of court, and approach parallel to the net. Middles hit back row attack, and 1st or 2nd tempo transitional attack. Setter's are trained to be deceptive, hit 2nd ball contact, jump set as often as possible.

California State University - Bakersfield
Academic Profile

9001 Stockdale Hwy.
Bakersfield, CA 93311-1099

Phone: (661) 664-2188

Type: Public, 4 Yr., Liberal Arts, Coed
Website: http://www.csubak.edu
SAT/ACT/GPA: Sliding Scale
Student/Faculty Ratio: 17:1
Undergraduate Enrollment: 4,900
Scholarships/Academic: Yes
Expenses By: Year
Specializes In: Education, Business
Degrees Conferred: BA, BS, MA, MS, MBA

Founded: 1970
Religion: Non-Affiliated
Housing: Yes
Male/Female: 35:65
Graduate Enrollment: 1,000
Athletic: Yes **Financial Aid:** Yes
In State: $ 6,800 **Out of State:** $ 13,800

Programs of Study: Accounting, Agriculture, Anthropology, Banking & Finance, Biochemistry, Biology, Business Administration, Chemistry, Clinical Science, Communications, Computer Science, Criminal Justice, Economics, Education, English, Environmental Science, Fine Arts, Geology, History, Information Science, Land Resource Management, Management, Marketing, Math, Medical Technology, Nursing, Petroleum Engineering, Philosophy, Physics, Political Science, PreProfessional, Public Health, Religion, Social Science, Spanish

Women's Athletic Profile

9001 Stockdale Hwy.
Bakersfield, CA 93311-1099
Coach: John Price
Email: jprice@csubak.edu

NCAA I
Lady Roadrunners, Blue, Gold
Phone: (805) 664-2269
Fax: (805) 664-2376

Estimated # of Women's Volleyball Scholarships: N/A
Conference: California Collegiate Athletic Association

California State University - Chico
Academic Profile

First & Normal
Chico, CA 95929

Phone: (530) 898-6470

Type: Public, 4 Yr., Liberal Arts, Engineering, Coed
Website: http://www.csuchio.edu
SAT/ACT/GPA: TBA
Student/Faculty Ratio: 18:1
Undergraduate Enrollment: 13,600
Scholarships/Academic: Yes
Expenses By: Year
Specializes In: Business, Education, Communications, Engineering
Degrees Conferred: BS, MA

Founded: 1887
Religion: Non-Affiliated
Housing: Yes
Male/Female: 49:51
Graduate Enrollment: 1,200
Athletic: Yes **Financial Aid:** Yes
In State: $ 5,250 **Out of State:** $ 7,030

Programs of Study: Business, Education, Communication, Science, PreMed, Engineering, Art, Language, History, Accounting, Anthropology, Botany, Liberal Arts

Women's Athletic Profile

First & Orange
Chico, CA 95929-0300
Coach: Zach Shaver
Email: volleyballoffice@csuchico.edu

NCAA I
Lady Wildcats, Cardinal, White
Phone: (530) 898-6180
Fax: (530) 898-4699

Did Not Return Profile

California State University - Dominguez Hills
Academic Profile

1000 E Victoria Avenue
Carson, CA 90747

Phone: 310-243-3600

Type: Public, 4 Yr., Liberal Arts, Coed
Website: http://www.csudh.edu
SAT/ACT/GPA: 1200
Student/Faculty Ratio: 30:1
Undergraduate Enrollment: 11,000
Scholarships/Academic: Yes   **Athletic:** Yes
Expenses By: Year   **In State:** $ 1,900
Degrees Conferred: BS, MA

Founded: 1960
Religion: Non-Affiliated
Housing: Yes
Male/Female: 1:2
Graduate Enrollment: 1,500
Financial Aid: Yes
Out of State: $ Varies

Programs of Study: Anthropology, Biology, Business Administration, Chemistry, Clinical Science, Communication, Computer Science, Economics, English, Fine Arts, French, Geology, Health Science, History, Human Services, Mathematics, Nursing, Physical Education, Physics, Political Science, Psychology

Women's Athletic Profile

1000 E. Victoria Street
Carson, CA 90747
Coach: Henry Chen
Email: hchen@csudh.edu

NCAA I
Lady Toros, Cardinal, Gold
Phone: (310) 243-2222
Fax: (310) 217-6975

Estimated # of Women's Volleyball Scholarships: N/A
Conference: California Collegiate Athletic Association

California State University - Fresno
Academic Profile

1620 E Bulldog Lane
Fresno, CA 93740-7400

Phone: (559) 278-8302

Type: Public, 4 Yr., Coed
Website: http://www.csufresno.edu
SAT/ACT/GPA: 900/3.0
Student/Faculty Ratio: 14:1
Undergraduate Enrollment: 17,400
Scholarships/Academic: Yes   **Athletic:** Yes
Expenses By: Year   **In State:** $ 3,700
Specializes In: Business, Agriculture

Founded: 1911
Religion: Non-Affiliated
Housing: Yes
Male/Female: 2:3
Graduate Enrollment: 3,345
Financial Aid: Yes
Out of State: $ 7,387

Degrees Conferred: BS, BA, 56 undergraduate programs, 41 graduate programs
Programs of Study: Architecture, PreMed, PreDental, Aerospace, Agricultural Business, Animal Science, Anthropology, Business, Kinesiology, Biology, Chemistry, Chicago Studies, Communications, Computer Science, Criminology, Dance, Ecology, Education, Engineering, Enology, Linguistics, Marine Science, Music, Philosophy, Physical Therapy, Sociology, Spanish, Speech Comm.

Women's Athletic Profile

5305 N. Campus
Fresno, CA 93749-0048
Coach: Lindy Vivas
Email:

NCAA I
Lady Bulldogs, Cardinal, Blue
Phone: (209) 278-2837
Fax: (209) 278-6611

Estimated # of Women's Volleyball Scholarships: N/A
Conference: Western Athletic Conference

California State University - Fullerton
Academic Profile

P.O. Box 6810
Fullerton, CA 92834

Phone: (714) 278-3495

Type: Public, 4 Yr., Coed
Website: http://www.fullerton.edu
SAT/ACT/GPA: Sliding Scale
Student/Faculty Ratio: 19:1
Undergraduate Enrollment: 24,175
Scholarships/Academic: Yes
Expenses By: Year
Specializes In: Athletic Training, Communications, Business
Degrees Conferred: BA, BS, BFA, BM, MA, MS, MFA
Programs of Study: Seven Schools - Arts, Business Education/Economics, Communications, Engineering/Computer Sciences, Human Development/ Community Services, Humanities/Social Sciences, Natural Sciences and Mathematics

Founded: 1957
Religion: Non-Affiliated
Housing: Yes
Male/Female: 42:58
Graduate Enrollment: 4,000
Financial Aid: Yes
Athletic: Yes
In State: $ 8,331
Out of State: $ 12,729

Women's Athletic Profile

P.O. Box 6810
Fullerton, CA 92834-000
Coach: Mary Ellen Murchison
Email: mmurchinson@fullerton.edu

NCAA I
Titans, Blue, Orange, White
Phone: (714) 278-3052
Fax: (714)278-5396

California State University - Hayward
Academic Profile

25800 Carlos Bee Blvd.
Hayward, CA 94542

Phone: (510) 885-4805

Type: Public, 4 Yr., Liberal Arts, Coed
Website: http://www.csuhayward.edu
SAT/ACT/GPA: 1300/30/2.0
Student/Faculty Ratio: 25:1
Undergraduate Enrollment: 10,000
Scholarships/Academic: Yes
Expenses By: Year
Specializes In: Liberal Arts, Business, Kinesiology, Physical Therapy
Degrees Conferred: BA, BS, MA, MS, MBA
Programs of Study: Biology, Business, Chemistry, Communications, Computer, Criminal, Dramatic Art, Ecology, Economics, English, Environmental, Ethnic, Management, Math, Nursing, Philosophy, Physical, Recreation, Statistics, Taxation

Founded: 1957
Religion: Non-Affiliated
Housing: Yes
Male/Female: 40:60
Graduate Enrollment: 2,000
Financial Aid: Yes
Athletic: No
In State: $ 5,500
Out of State: $ 8,750

Women's Athletic Profile

25800 Carlos Bee Boulevard
Hayward, CA 94542
Coach: Jim Spagle
Email: jspagle@csuhayward.edu

NCAA I
Pioneers, Red, Black, White
Phone: (510) 885-4805
Fax: (510) 885-2282

Estimated # of Women's Volleyball Scholarships: 0
Conference: Independent
Program Profile: We play at a 5,500 seat gymnasium, that includes a training room, a team room and a weight room.
History: We ranked 12th in the nation in 1998.
Coaching: Jim Spagle, Head Coach, compiled a record of 20-13 in 1996. In 1997, the team's record was 24-9 and in 1998 and he had compiled a record of 31-7. California State Hayward had never had a winning record prior to his arrival in 1996. Meg Kilday and Detlev Rothe are assistant coaches.
Roster In State: 14
Sophomores on Team: 0
Most Recent Record: 31-7-0
Out of State: 0
Seniors on Team: 4
Fall Games: 38
Out of Country: 0
Graduation %: 86
Spring Games: 2-4
Schedule: University of California-San Diego, California Lutheran, Willamette University, George Fox, Puget Sound, Linfield
Style of Play: We are aggressive, fast paced and fun.

California State University - Los Angeles
Academic Profile

5151 State University Drive
Los Angeles, CA 90032-8240

Phone: (323)343-3080

Type: Public, 4 Yr., Yes Yes Coed
Website: http://www.calstatela.edu
SAT/ACT/GPA: Varies 2.0
Student/Faculty Ratio:
Undergraduate Enrollment: 13,732
Scholarships/Academic: Yes   **Athletic:** Yes
Expenses By: Year   **In State:**
Specializes In: Engineering, dance, elementary and secondary education
Degrees Conferred: BS, BA, MS, MA, Ph.D.
Programs of Study: 50 Academic departments and divisions. Liberal Arts, Physical Sciences, Social Sciences, Business, Education, Physical Education

Founded: 1947
Religion: Non-Affiliated
Housing: Yes
Male/Female: 39/61
Graduate Enrollment: 5,797
Financial Aid: Yes
Out of State:

Women's Athletic Profile

5151 State University Drive
Los Angeles, CA 90032-8240
Coach: Bill Lawler
Email: blawler@calstatela.edu

NCAA I
Golden Eagles, Black, Gold
Phone: (213) 343-3087
Fax: (213) 343-6535

Estimated # of Women's Volleyball Scholarships: N/A
Conference: CCAA
Program Profile: Fall playing season-play in 5,000 seat gym one of the top Div.II programs. Consistently in top 20 during the 1990's, ranked 5th in NCAA as of Oct 17, 2000
History: Hold the NCAA team record for most kills in 5-game match (114), 6 NCAA tournament appearances from 1992-1999, 4th place in NCAA tournament in 1992.
Achievements: Won CCAA title in 1999, 1999 West Region Freshman of the Year and numerous All-Americans
Coaching: Head Coach played Volleyball at San Diego State. Asst. Coach is a former Player of the Year Mid-America Conference.
Roster In State: 13   **Out of State:** 1   **Out of Country:** 0
Seniors on Team: 3
Most Recent Record: 26-4
Positions Needed: ALL
Schedule: Cal State Bakersfield, North Dakota State, UC San Diego

California State University - Monterey Bay
Academic Profile

100 Campus Center, Building 21
Seaside, CA 93955

Phone: 831-582-3518

Type: 4 Yr.,
Website: http://www.monterey.edu
SAT/ACT/GPA: Open
Student/Faculty Ratio:
Undergraduate Enrollment: N/A
Scholarships/Academic: **Athletic:**
Expenses By: **In State:**
Degrees Conferred:
Programs of Study: Contact school for programs of study.

Founded:
Religion: Non-Affiliated
Housing: No
Male/Female:
Graduate Enrollment: N/A
Financial Aid:
Out of State:

Women's Athletic Profile

100 Campus Center
Seaside, CA 93955
Coach: Sean Madden
Email: sean_madden@monterey.edu

NCAA I
Lady Otters, Green, Gold, Teal
Phone: (831) 582-3309
Fax: (831) 582-4023

Estimated # of Women's Volleyball Scholarships: N/A
Conference: California Pacific Conference

California State University - Northridge
Academic Profile

18111 Nordhoff

Phone: (818) 677-4512

Northridge, CA 91330-8276
Type: Public, 4 Yr., Liberal Arts, Engineering, Coed
Website: http://www.csub.edu
SAT/ACT/GPA: Combination of GPA and SAT scores2.00 to 3.00
Student/Faculty Ratio: 21:1
Undergraduate Enrollment: 22,189
Scholarships/Academic: Yes   **Athletic:** Yes
Expenses By: Year   **In State:** $ 8,530
Specializes In: Substantial programs in technological and professional fields
Degrees Conferred: BA, BS, BM, MA, MS, MBA
Programs of Study: Accounting, Anthropology, Astrophysics, Banking/Finance, Biochemistry, Biology, Broadcasting, Business, Chemistry, Computer, Criminology, Dietetics, Earth Science, Economics, Engineering, Mathematics, Music, Nursing, Physics, Radio and Television, Religion, Seismology, Etc.

Founded: 1958
Religion: Non-Affiliated
Housing: Yes
Male/Female: 40:60
Graduate Enrollment: 5,464
Financial Aid: Yes
Out of State: $ 14,265

Men's Athletic Profile

1811 Nordhoff Street
Northridge, CA 91330
Coach: Jeff Cambell
Email: jeff.campbell@csun.edu

NCAA I
Matadors/Red, White, Black
Phone: (818) 677-4512
Fax: (818) 677-2661

Estimated # of Men's Volleyball Scholarships: N/A
Conference: Mountain Pacific Sports Federation
Program Profile: We play in the best league in the nation against the top teams in the nation. We play in the Maradome which seats 1,600.
History: Our program began in 1977. We were National Championship runner-up in 1993. We got our highest NCAA ranking as 3rd in 1991. We made league playoffs seven years straight. (1990-1996).
Achievements: Coach of the Year in 1993; 17 All-Americans; 1 Bronze medal Olympian; MPSF Tournament Champions in 1993.
Coaching: Jeff Campbell served as Assistant Coach for 7 years and Jeff started as Head Coach in 1997. Jeff was an All-American in 1988.
Roster In State: 10   **Out of State:** 3   **Out of Country:** 2
Sophomores on Team: 2   **Seniors on Team:** 2   **Graduation %:** 80%
Most Recent Record: 10-14   **Fall Games:** 0   **Spring Games:** 25
Camp or Clinic Dates: July 26-30
Positions Needed: Outside Hitter, Opposite, Middle Blocker, Setter
Schedule: Brigham Young, UCLA, Pepperdine, Long Beach State, Hawaii, Stanford

Women's Athletic Profile

18111 Nordhof Street
Northridge, CA 91330
Coach: Lian Kang Lu
Email: lkl32338@csun.edu

NCAA I
Matadors, Red, White, Black
Phone: (818) 677-3221
Fax: (818) 677-2661

Estimated # of Women's Volleyball Scholarships: N/A
Conference: Big West
Program Profile: Playing season begins in middle of August, and runs through November. We have 2 gyms, a practice gym with 3 courts with wood floors, a game gym with wood floors. Our Spring season starts in February and runs through May concentrates on strength training.
History: The volleyball program began in 1975. It started to compete in Division I in 1990 and competed as an independent for 5 years before joining the Big Sky Conference. Competed in Big Sky for 5 years from 1996-2000.
Achievements: 1994 NIVC National Champions, 1996 Big Sky Conference Champions and Coach of the Year, 1999 Big Sky Championship Runner-up, 1999 NCAA Statistical Dig Champion, 2000 NCAA Statistical Dig Champion.
Coaching: Lian Lu has coached 7 season at Northridge. He has been an instructor and guest lecturer in over 100 clinics and camps in over 30 countries. Renowned international coaches instructor in Federation of International Volleyball. Assistant Coach at UCSB for 10 years before Northridge.
Freshman Receiving Financial Aid/Academic: **Athletic:** 6
Roster In State: 7   **Out of State:** 2   **Out of Country:** 2
Seniors on Team: 1   **Graduation %:** 100
Most Recent Record: 16-10
Camp of Clinic Dates: Nike camp July 12-15

Positions Needed: MB, OH
Schedule: University of Santa Barbara, University of Pacific, Long Beach State, Utah State, Cal Poly San Luis Obispo, University of Oregon, Eastern Washington.
Style of Play: Defensive and strong serving.

California State University - Sacramento
Academic Profile

6000 J Street
Sacramento, CA 95819-6099

Phone: (916) 278-6427

Type: Public, 4 Yr., Liberal Arts, Coed
Website: http://www.csus.edu
SAT/ACT/GPA: Sliding Scale/2.5
Student/Faculty Ratio:
Undergraduate Enrollment: 22,000
Scholarships/Academic: Yes   **Athletic:** Yes
Expenses By: Year   **In State:** $ 7,500
Specializes In: Many fields of study
Degrees Conferred: BA, BS, MBA, MS

Founded: 1947
Religion: Non-Affiliated
Housing: Yes
Male/Female:
Graduate Enrollment: N/A
Financial Aid: Yes
Out of State: $ 7,500

Programs of Study: Accounting, Anthropology, Art, Biochemistry, Biology, Business, Chemistry, Communication, Computer Science, Criminal Justice, Education, Finance, Engineering, Geography, Journalism, Nursing, Physics, Political Science, PreLaw, Philosophy, Microbiology, Public Administration

Women's Athletic Profile

6000 J. Street
Sacramento, CA 95819
Coach: Debby Colberg
Email: dcolberg@saclinc.scus.edu

NCAA I
Lady Hornets, Green, Gold
Phone: (916) 278-6427
Fax: (916) 278-5429

Estimated # of Women's Volleyball Scholarships: 12
Conference: Big Sky Conference
Program Profile: We have a top 35 Division I program. We complete on campus at a 1200 seat gymnasium, renovated in 1999.
History: Our program began in 1966. We have competed in Division I since 1991. We have been a member of the Big Sky Conference since 1996.
Achievements: 1997 and 1998 Big Sky Champions; Jill Haas-2nd Team All-American
Coaching: Debby Colberg has been Head Coach since 1996. Her overall record is 607-206. Liz Gilbert became Assistant Coach in 1999. Weidi Zhang has been Assistant Coach since 1986.
Freshman Receiving Financial Aid/Academic: **Athletic:** 4
Roster In State: 9   **Out of State:** 4   **Out of Country:** 1
Sophomores on Team: 3   **Seniors on Team:** 2   **Graduation %:** 76
Most Recent Record: 25-8-0   **Fall Games:**   **Spring Games:** 3
Camp of Clinic Dates: August 2-6; August 9-13
Positions Needed: Outside Hitters
Schedule: UOP, Arizona, Washington, Fresno State, San Diego, Eastern Washington
Style of Play: Good ball control team with strong passing and defensive skills.

California State University - San Bernardino
Academic Profile

5500 University Parkway
San Bernardino, CA 92407

Phone: 909-880-5200

Type: Public, 4 Yr., Coed
Website: http://www.csusb.edu
SAT/ACT/GPA: 820+ varies w/GPA
Student/Faculty Ratio: 18:1
Undergraduate Enrollment: 10,000
Scholarships/Academic: Yes   **Athletic:** Yes
Expenses By: Year   **In State:** $ 7,943
Specializes In: Education, Physical Education, Kinesiology, Business
Degrees Conferred: Bachelors, Master's

Founded: 1965
Religion: Non-Affiliated
Housing: Yes
Male/Female: 40:60
Graduate Enrollment: 3,059
Financial Aid: Yes
Out of State: $ 13,847

Programs of Study: Accounting, Afro-American Studies, American Studies, Anthropology, Art, Biochemistry, Biological Science, Business Administration, Chemistry, Child Psychology, Communications, Computer Science, Creative Writing, Criminal Justice, Dietetics, Economics, English, Environmental Studies, Finance, French, Geography, Geology, Graphic Art, Health Services Administration, Health Education, Health Science, History, Humanities, Human Development, Human Services, Information Science, Interdisciplinary Studies, Liberal Arts, Management, Management Information Systems, Marketing, Mathematics, Music, Natural Science, Nursing, Nutrition, Philosophy, Physical Education, Physics, Political Science, Psychology, Public Administration, Social Science, Spanish, Theatre, Vocational Education

Women's Athletic Profile

5500 University Parkway
San Bernardino, CA 92407-2397
Coach: Kim Cherniss
Email: kcyotevb@csusb.edu
Estimated # of Women's Volleyball Scholarships: 4
Conference: CCAA

NCAA I
Lady Coyotes, Blue, Black
Phone: (909) 880-5050
Fax: (909) 880-7605

Program Profile: CSUSB women's volleyball competes in the prestigious CCAA. This is the best volleyball in NCAA Division II. The team plays in fabulous coussoulis arena, a spectacular 5000 seat arena.
History: We just completed our 10th year of NCAA II volleyball. The program has been in existence for 18 years the first 8 as an NCAA III school. The program just concluded it's 4th consecutive 20 win season.
Achievements: Kim Cherniss 1997 CCAA Coach of the Year, 3 All-American Selections, 7 All-Region Selection.
Coaching: Head Coach Kim Cherniss

Freshman Receiving Financial Aid/Academic:		**Athletic:** 6
Roster In State: 14	**Out of State:** 0	**Out of Country:** 0
Seniors on Team: 2	**Graduation %:** 100	

Most Recent Record: 26-8
Camp of Clinic Dates: August 1-4
Positions Needed: 1 OH, 1 MB
Schedule: Cal State Los Angeles, Cal State Bakersfield, Augustana College, West Texas A & M, UC San Diego
Style of Play: Dynamic offense paired with outstanding team defense and ball control.

California State University - Stanislaus
Academic Profile

801 West Monte Vista Avenue
Turlock, CA 95382-0299

Phone: 209-667-3151

Type: Public, 4 Yr., Liberal Arts, Coed
Website: http://www.lead.csustan.edu
SAT/ACT/GPA: 820
Student/Faculty Ratio: 18:1
Undergraduate Enrollment: 4,500
Scholarships/Academic: Yes
Expenses By: Year
Degrees Conferred: BA, BS, MA, MS, MBA

Athletic: No
In State: $ 7,000

Founded: 1961
Religion: Non-Affiliated
Housing: No
Male/Female: 40:60
Graduate Enrollment: 1,500
Financial Aid: Yes
Out of State: $ 14,000

Programs of Study: Accounting, Anthropology, Applied Mathematics, Art, Bilingual Education, Biology, Botany, Business, Chemistry, Communications, Computer Information Systems, Entomology, Criminal Justice, Environmental Studies, History, International Studies, Journalism, Liberal Arts, Physics, PreLaw, PreMed, PreVet, Spanish, Statistics, Theatre, Urban Studies

Women's Athletic Profile

801 W. Monte Vista
Turlock, CA 95382-0299
Coach: Cindy Nikkel
Email: cnikkel@stan.csustan.edu

NCAA I
Lady Warriors, Red, Gold
Phone: (209) 667-3803
Fax: (209) 667-3084

Estimated # of Women's Volleyball Scholarships: N/A
Conference: California Collegiate Athletic Association (CCAA)
Program Profile: This is the third year for Cindy Nikkel as head coach. We run the program with high expectations for our student-athletes. This year we are currently 10-9 and looking at our second round of CCAA play with enthusiasm. We practice and play in Warrior Arena (Capacity 2500) and we are able to run camps and clinics with 6 to 7 courts. Our fall season runs from August through November. The Spring is February through April.
History: The program went from Div.III (where they saw regional and final round play) with no scholarships, to Div II (no scholarship for 6 years and poor results), to moving to the most winning conference in the nation and some scholarships. The team placed 11th

the first year in 1998. The second year the team finished ahead of all Northern CA schools and upset two regionally ranked Southern CA schools (Cal Poly Pomona and Cal State San Bernardino).

Achievements: The 1999 team held a 3.1 GPA. Cindy Nikkel has coached high school for 10 years (selected as coach of the year 5 times, won 5 league titles, 6 section championships and brought the team to 2nd in State in 1992 and 1996).

Freshman Receiving Financial Aid/Academic: **Athletic:** 3

Roster In State: 11   **Out of State:** 1   **Out of Country:** 0

Sophomores on Team: **Seniors on Team:** 3   **Graduation %:** 100

Most Recent Record: 10-9

Camp of Clinic Dates: 3rd and 4th week of July

Positions Needed: MB, OH, S

Schedule: Cal State LA, UC San Diego, Cal State San Bernardino, Cal State Bakersfield, Cal Poly Pomona, Grand Canyon, UC Davis.

Style of Play: We like to run a quick tempo offense with front and back slides. We run shoots in the middle and out to our left fronts. We are focusing on more ball control and running a new defense.

Chapman University
Academic Profile

1 University Drive
Orange, CA 92866

Phone: (714) 997-6815

Type: Private, 4 Yr., Liberal Arts, Coed   **Founded:** 1861

Website: http://www.chapman.edu   **Religion:** Disciples of Christ

SAT/ACT/GPA: 960/19/2.5   **Housing:** Yes

Student/Faculty Ratio: 15:1   **Male/Female:** N/A

Undergraduate Enrollment: 2,800   **Graduate Enrollment:** 1,200

Scholarships/Academic: Yes   **Athletic:** No   **Financial Aid:** Yes

Expenses By: Year   **In State:** $27,500   **Out of State:** $27,500

Specializes In: Business, Economics

Degrees Conferred: BA, BS, BFA, BM, MA, MS, MBA, MFA

Programs of Study: Accounting, American Studies, Art, Biology, Business and Economics, Communication, Criminal Justice, Education, Kinesiology, Languages, Liberal Studies, Music, Movement and Exercise Sciences, Nutrition, Philosophy, Psychology, Religion, Social Science, Sociology, Theatre & Dance

Women's Athletic Profile

333 N. Glassell
Orange, CA 92866
Coach: Mary Cahill
Email:

NCAA I
Lady Panthers, Cardinal, Grey
Phone: (714) 997-6691
Fax: (714) 532-6010

Estimated # of Women's Volleyball Scholarships: N/A

Conference: Independent

Program Profile: Our volleyball team is very competitive with other California Division III teams. We have qualified for Regional 3 of the past 5 years. Being an independent university, our playing schedule is mixed with Division III, II and NAIA matches. We play one tournament out of state.

Achievements: 1985 Second Team Academic All-American.

Coaching: Mary Cahill, Head Coach, is in her 10th year here. Her career record is 151-120. She graduated from Chapman in 1986. John Cahill is Assistant Coach. He graduated from Fullerton in 1996.

Roster In State: 10   **Out of State:** 2   **Out of Country:** 0

Sophomores on Team: 4   **Seniors on Team:** 4   **Graduation %:** 90

Most Recent Record: 13-13-0   **Fall Games:** 24   **Spring Games:** 0

Positions Needed: Middle, Outside Swing Hitters

Schedule: University of California-San Diego, California Lutheran, Wittenberg-Ohio

Style of Play: 5-1 offense, ball control and strong defensively.

Christian Heritage College
Academic Profile

2100 Greenfield Drive
El Cajon, CA 92019

Phone: 619-588-7747

Type: Private, 4 Yr., Liberal Arts, Coed   **Founded:** 1970

Website: http://www.christianHeritage.edu   **Religion:** Baptist

SAT/ACT/GPA: 900/20/2.5
Student/Faculty Ratio: 15:1
Undergraduate Enrollment: 630
Scholarships/Academic: Yes **Athletic:** Yes
Expenses By: Year **In State:** $ 15,200
Specializes In: Biblical Studies, Counseling, Teaching Education

Housing: Yes
Male/Female: 45:55
Graduate Enrollment: N/A
Financial Aid: Yes
Out of State: $ 15,200

Programs of Study: Biblical Studies, Business, Clinical Psychology, Communications, Computer Information Systems, Economics, Education, Elementary Education, English, History, International Business, Management, Mathematics, Ministries, Music, Pastoral Studies, Physical Education, Psychology, Secondary Education, Social Science, Theology, Voice, Women's Studies

Women's Athletic Profile

2100 Greenfield Drive
El Cajon, CA 92019
Coach: Carrie Wright
Email:

NCAA I
Lady Hawks, Royal Blue, Gold
Phone: (619) 441-2200x1731
Fax: (619) 590-1734

Did Not Return Profile

Claremont - Mudd - Scripps College
Academic Profile

500 E. 9th Street
Claremont, CA 91711

Phone: (909) 607-3565

Type: Private, 4 Yr., Liberal Arts, Engineering, Coed
Website: http://www.mckenna.edu - www.scrippscol.edu
SAT/ACT/GPA: 1300/4.0
Student/Faculty Ratio: 20:1
Undergraduate Enrollment: 900
Scholarships/Academic: Yes **Athletic:** No
Expenses By: Year **In State:** $ 28,000
Specializes In: Business, Engineering, History, Mathematics, Sciences
Degrees Conferred: BA, BS

Founded: 1946
Religion: Non-Affiliated
Housing: Yes
Male/Female: 60:40
Graduate Enrollment: N/A
Financial Aid: Yes
Out of State: $ 28,000

Programs of Study: Business, Economics, English, Letters/Literature, Mathematics, Multi/Interdisciplinary Studies, Psychology, Sciences, Social Sciences

Women's Athletic Profile

500 E. 9th Street
Claremont, CA 91711
Coach: Penny Graves
Email: pgraves@benson.mckenna.edu

NCAA I
Athena's, Cardinal, Gold
Phone: (909) 607-3565
Fax: (909) 621-8848

Estimated # of Women's Volleyball Scholarships: N/A
Conference: Southern California Intercollegiate Athletic Conference
Program Profile: We are a Competitive Division III program, We have great facilities and we play from September through November.
Achievements: Back to back Conference Champions; NCAA Regional playoffs in 1997.
Coaching: Penny Graves, Head Coach, started with the program in 1996.
Roster In State: 6 **Out of State:** 6 **Out of Country:** 0
Sophomores on Team: 0 **Seniors on Team:** 2 **Graduation %:** 100
Most Recent Record: 12-11-0 **Fall Games:** 23 **Spring Games:** 0
Positions Needed: Setter, Middle Hitter
Schedule: University of California at San Diego, California Lutheran, La Verne, Concordia, Colorado College, Chapman
Style of Play: Quick and tough on defense.

College of Notre Dame
Academic Profile

1500 Ralston Avenue
Belmont, CA 94002-1997

Phone: (650) 508-3590

Type: Private, 4 Yr., Liberal Arts, Coed

Founded: 1851

Website: http://www.cnd.edu
SAT/ACT/GPA: 790+/2.0
Student/Faculty Ratio: 14:1
Undergraduate Enrollment: 990
Scholarships/Academic: Yes   **Athletic:** Yes
Expenses By: Year   **In State:** $ 23,076
Degrees Conferred: BA, BS, BFA, MA, MS, MBA, MFA, M.Ed.

Religion: Roman Catholic
Housing: Yes
Male/Female: 30:70
Graduate Enrollment: 772
Financial Aid: Yes
Out of State: $ 23,076

Programs of Study: Art, Biochemistry, Biology, Business Management, Communication, Computer Science, Economics, Education, Elementary Education, English, Environmental Studies, Finance, French, Graphic Art, History, Humanities, Human Services, Interior Design, International Business, Latin American Studies, Liberal Arts, Marketing, Music, Philosophy, Physical Science, PreDentistry, PreLaw, PreMed, Psychology, Religion, Secondary Education, Social Science, Sociology, Theatre, Voice

Women's Athletic Profile

1500 Ralston Avenue
Belmont, CA 94002
Coach: Tonia Moe
Email: admission@cnd.edu

NCAA I
Argonauts, Gold, White, Blue
Phone: (650) 508-3590
Fax: (650) 508-3691

Estimated # of Women's Volleyball Scholarships: 4
Conference: California Pacific Conference
Program Profile: The team plays at Walter Gleason Center which has 900 seats. Our playing season goes from September through November.
Achievements: Conference Coach of the Year in 1998; Conference Champions in 1998.
Coaching: Tonia Moe, Head Coach, is entering her tenth year with the program. She was a former coach in high school. She was named North Peninsula League Coach of the Year in 1983. She was inducted into the Sports Hall of Fame (Pacific) in 1991. She was named California Pacific Coach of the Year in 1998. Jared Sellers is Assistant Coach. Doreen Letti, Assistant Coach, was North Peninsula League Player of the Year in 1983.

Roster In State: 3   **Out of State:** 4   **Out of Country:** 1
Sophomores on Team: 1   **Seniors on Team:** 1   **Graduation %:** 100
Most Recent Record: 23-11-0   **Fall Games:** 34   **Spring Games:** 0
Positions Needed: Setter, Outside Hitter, DS
Style of Play: We are a defense oriented team and a Conference leader in digs and service aces. Offensive standout-2 time Olympian and 1998 Conference Player of the Year. Ranked #1 nationally in kills percentages.

Concordia University - Irvine

Academic Profile

1530 Concordia West
Irvine, CA 92612-3299

Phone: (949)854-8002

Type: Private, 4 Yr., Liberal Arts, Coed
Website: http://www.cui.edu
SAT/ACT/GPA: 86018/2.5
Student/Faculty Ratio: 20/1
Undergraduate Enrollment: 950
Scholarships/Academic: Yes   **Athletic:** Yes
Expenses By: Year   **In State:** $21,000
Specializes In: Education and Business
Degrees Conferred: BA, Masters

Founded: 1972
Religion: Lutheran
Housing: Yes
Male/Female: 40/60
Graduate Enrollment: 250
Financial Aid: Yes
Out of State: $21,000

Programs of Study: Art, Behavioral Science, Biology, Business Administration, Communications, Elementary Education, English, History, Mathematics, Music, Liberal Studies, PreLaw, Humanities, Religion, Psychology, Sports Management

Women's Athletic Profile

1530 Concordia West
Irvine, CA 92612-3299
Coach: Jody Wise
Email: jody.wise@cui.edu

NCAA I
Lady Eagles, Green, Gold
Phone: (949) 854-8002
Fax: (949) 854-6771

Estimated # of Women's Volleyball Scholarships: 2
Conference: Golden State Athletic Conference

Program Profile: Our program has 26 Fall matches and 4 Spring dates. There are 13-15 members in our team. Playing season begins August 15, while national games begin December 2-5. We have a 2,500-seat arena.

History: The program began in 1981 and has had only four head coaches. We have been to play-offs 2 of the last 4 seasons. Our 1998 season was the second best in history. Last 3 years have been the most successful in schools history. Program is growing.

Achievements: 3 Academic All-Americans last year, 1 All-American, Head coach has 627 collegiate wins

Coaching: Jody Wise, Head Coach, compiled a record of 591-465 in college. She has been coaching from 1978 to the present. She started coaching at Concordia University three years ago. Sherry Ringer is Assistant Coach.

Freshman Receiving Financial Aid/Academic: **Athletic:** 3

Roster In State: 10   **Out of State:** 2   **Out of Country:** 0

Sophomores on Team: 0   **Seniors on Team:** 3   **Graduation %:** 99

Most Recent Record: 17-13-0

Positions Needed: Right side, Def.spec.

Schedule: Fresno Pacific, Biola University, Azusa Pacific, Pt. Loma Nazarene, Lewis & Clark-Idaho

Dominican College
Academic Profile

50 Acacia Ave.   **Phone:** 888-323-6763
San Rafael, CA 94901-8008

Type: Private, 4 Yr., Liberal Arts, Coed   **Founded:** 1890
Website: http://www.dominican.edu   **Religion:** Catholic
SAT/ACT/GPA: 810+   **Housing:** No
Student/Faculty Ratio: 6:1   **Male/Female:** 23:77
Undergraduate Enrollment: 515   **Graduate Enrollment:** 284
Scholarships/Academic: Yes   **Athletic:** Yes   **Financial Aid:** Yes
Expenses By: Year   **In State:** $ 18,996   **Out of State:** $ 18,996
Degrees Conferred: BA, BS, BFA, MA, MS, MBA
Programs of Study: Contact school for programs of study.

Women's Athletic Profile

50 Acacia Avenue   **NCAA I**
San Rafael, CA 94901   Penguins, Black, Gold, White
Coach: Susan Huffman   **Phone:** (415) 257-1306
Email: shuffman@dominican.edu   **Fax:** (415) 485-9746

Estimated # of Women's Volleyball Scholarships: N/A
Conference: California Pacific Conference

Fresno Pacific University
Academic Profile

1717 S. Chestnut Avenue   **Phone:** 559-453-2039
Fresno, CA 93702

Type: Private, 4 Yr., Liberal Arts, Coed   **Founded:** 1944
Website: http://www.fresno.edu   **Religion:** Mennonite Brethren
SAT/ACT/GPA: 900/3.1   **Housing:** Yes
Student/Faculty Ratio: 14:1   **Male/Female:** 40:60
Undergraduate Enrollment: 800   **Graduate Enrollment:** 690
Scholarships/Academic: Yes   **Athletic:** Yes   **Financial Aid:** Yes
Expenses By: Year   **In State:** $ 14,665   **Out of State:** $ 14,665
Degrees Conferred: AA, BA, MA
Programs of Study: Accounting, Business & Management, Education, Communications, Computer Sciences, Mathematics, Social Sciences

Women's Athletic Profile

1717 S. Chestnut Avenue   **NCAA I**
Fresno, CA 93702   Sunbirds, Blue, White, Orange
Coach: Dennis Janzen   **Phone:** (209) 453-2074

Email: djanzen@fresno.edu
Estimated # of Women's Volleyball Scholarships: N/A
Conference: Golden Athletic Conference

Fax: (209) 453-2005

Holy Names College
Academic Profile

3500 Mountain Blvd.
Oakland, CA 94619

Phone: 800-430-1321

Type: Private, 4 YR Liberal Arts, Coed
Website: Liberal Arts & Sciences
SAT/ACT/GPA: 850-1060/3.37
Student/Faculty Ratio: 12:1
Undergraduate Enrollment: 600
Scholarships/Academic: yes   **Athletic:** yes
Expenses By: Year   **In State:** $21,348
Specializes In: Liberal Arts and Sciences
Degrees Conferred: BA, BM, BS, BSN, MA, MBA, M Ed, MM, MSN
Programs of Study: Applied Computing & Communication, Biological Science, Business Management & Communication, English, History, Liberal Studies (Teacher K-6), Music, PreLaw, Psychology, Religion/Philosophy, Sociology, Spanish

Founded: 1868
Religion: Catholic
Housing: Yes
Male/Female: 1:3
Graduate Enrollment: 324
Financial Aid: yes
Out of State: $21,348

Women's Athletic Profile

5305 N. Campus Drive
Fresno, CA 93740-8020
Coach: Lindy Vivas
Email:

NCAA I
Bulldogs, Red & Blue
Phone: 559-278-2837
Fax: 559-278-6583

Estimated # of Women's Volleyball Scholarships: 12
Conference: Western Athletic
Program Profile: Presently play in "North Gym" (1551 Capacity) will move into a new arena "The Savemart Center", (16, 000 Capacity) in fall 2002. Ranked among nation's top 30 in attendance twice in last five years, regional ranked program, 3 NCAA Appearances, 3 NIVC Appearances, 1984 quarter finalist (top 5 in nation), 2 All-Americans, 2 US National Players.
History: Began in 1965, 5 postseason showings, 6 20 win seasons in the last 10 years, averages 19 wins a season.
Achievements: 2 time WAC Coach of the Year, 1 NCAA Coach of the Year.
Freshman Receiving Financial Aid/Academic: N/A   **Athletic:** N/A
Roster In State: 13   **Out of State:** 3   **Out of Country:** 1
Seniors on Team: 3   **Graduation %:** 100
Most Recent Record: 13-17-0
Camp of Clinic Dates: TBA
Positions Needed: All
Style of Play: 100% work ethic, flexible but demands commitment, tough love, teaching & showing, show improvement, learn & study the game and opponents.

Hope International U (Pacific Christian C)
Academic Profile

2500 E. Nutwood Ave.
Fullerton, CA 92831

Phone: (714) 879-3901

Type: Private, 4 Yr., Coed
Website: http://www.hiu.edu
SAT/ACT/GPA: 890/18/2.00
Student/Faculty Ratio: 1:18
Undergraduate Enrollment: 598
Scholarships/Academic: Yes   **Athletic:** Yes
Expenses By: Year   **In State:** $ 14,965
Specializes In: Christian Service
Degrees Conferred: AA, BA, BS, MA, MBA, MSM
Programs of Study: Biblical Studies, Biological Science, Business Administration, Church Ministry, Children's Ministry, Communications, Disability Ministry, Education, Health Science, Linguistics, Ministry of Older Adults, Mathematics, Music, Political Science, Social Science, Sports Ministry, Theatre Arts, Women's Ministry, Youth Ministry

Founded: 1928
Religion: Independent Christian
Housing: Yes
Male/Female: 5:6
Graduate Enrollment: 178
Financial Aid: Yes
Out of State: $ 14,965

Men's Athletic Profile

2500 E. Nutwood Ave.
Fullerton, CA 92831
Coach: TBA
Email: mklunder@aol.com

NCAA I
Royals/Royal/Grey
Phone: 714-879-3901
Fax: 714-879-1041

Estimated # of Men's Volleyball Scholarships: Yes
Conference: None
Program Profile: We are a small, supportive school. We have a growing program as NAIA adds men's volleyball. We will have a new facility in 2001.
History: We began in 1980. We have competed in several local organizations. We have been varsity for each year. NAIA is planning to add men's volleball, so the sport at this level is just beginning to take off.
Freshman Receiving Financial Aid/Academic: 3   **Athletic:** 3
Sophomores on Team: **Seniors on Team:** 3   **Graduation %:** 80%
Most Recent Record: 8-17   **Fall Games:** 0   **Spring Games:** 28
Positions Needed: Middle Blocker, Outside Hitter
Schedule: California Baptist University, University of California-Santa Cruz, Simpson College

Women's Athletic Profile

2500 Nutwood Ave.
Fullerton, CA 92831
Coach: Mike Klunder
Email: mklunder@aol.com

NCAA I
Lady Royals, Royal/Grey
Phone: (714) 879-3901
Fax: (714) 879-1041

Estimated # of Women's Volleyball Scholarships: 4
Conference: GSAC
Program Profile: We run a small, supportive school. We will have new facilities by the year 2001. We are in a tough Conference.
History: We began in 1960. We competed in the NCAA for many years. We joined the NAIA in 1996. We joined the GSAC in 1998.
Coaching: Mike Klunder, Head Coach, has been coaching the men's team for three years. (1996-1999). He has coached the women's team for one year. (1998)
Freshman Receiving Financial Aid/Academic: **Athletic:** 4
Roster In State: 8   **Out of State:** 4   **Out of Country:** 0
Sophomores on Team: 0   **Seniors on Team:** 4   **Graduation %:** 90
Most Recent Record: 7-21-0   **Fall Games:** 33   **Spring Games:** 2
Positions Needed: 6 - Middle Blockers & Setters
Schedule: Fresno Pacific University, Biola University, Cal State San Bernardino, Christian Heritage College, Westmont College, Point Loma Nazarene University
Style of Play: Very dedicated athletes, both to each other and to the game.

Humboldt State University
Academic Profile

1 Harpst Street
Arcata, CA 95521-4757

Phone: (707) 826-5941

Type: Public, 4 Yr., Liberal Arts, Engineering, Coed
Website: http://www.humboldt.edu
SAT/ACT/GPA: 1000/3.0
Student/Faculty Ratio: 18:1
Undergraduate Enrollment: 6,535
Scholarships/Academic: Yes   **Athletic:** Yes
Expenses By: Year   **In State:** $ 8,500

Founded: 1913
Religion: Non-Affiliated
Housing: Yes
Male/Female: 50:50
Graduate Enrollment: 940
Financial Aid: Yes
Out of State: $ 13,500

Specializes In: Biology, Forestry, Marine Biology, Natural Science
Degrees Conferred: BA, BS, MA, MS, MBA, MFA
Programs of Study: Business, Computer Science, Education, Environmental Engineering, Forestry, Kinesiology, Marine Biology, Natural Resources, Range Management, Psychology, Wildlife, plus a broad range of Liberal Arts programs.

Women's Athletic Profile

1 Harpst Street
Arcata, CA 95521
Coach: Tina Raddish
Email: tmr1@axe.humboldt.edu

NCAA I
Lady Lumberjacks, Green, Gold
Phone: (707) 826-5974
Fax: (707) 826-5446

Estimated # of Women's Volleyball Scholarships: 1.5
Conference: Pacific West
Program Profile: Normally a successful program, the team saw a down year in 2000 due to major injuries, key players lost to graduation and overall youth… finished 2-23 in 2000. It was the first time since 1994 that the team had less than 10 wins. HSU was 31-7 in 1990 and 21-10 in 1991. Home court is HSU East Gym with a capacity 1400.
History: Program began competing at the intercollegiate level in 1973 when HSU joined the Northern California Intercollegiate Athletic Conference todate. The program has an overall record of 311-328 with six consecutive 10 plus win season prior to 2000. Winningest season was in 1990 when the Jacks went 31-7 and 11-3 in Conference.
Achievements: 2 Conference Players of the Year 1994, 1995.
Coaching: Head Coach Tina Raddish has a 91-104 overall record in seven years. Turned the program from a 5-23 team in 1993 to a 18-9 record in 1995. Raddish has had four winning seasons and six seasons with 10 wins or more.
Freshman Receiving Financial Aid/Academic: | | **Athletic:** 1
Roster In State: 10 | **Out of State:** 3 | **Out of Country:** 0
Seniors on Team: 3 | **Graduation %:** 90 |
Most Recent Record: 2-23-0
Camp of Clinic Dates: July 15-19, July 22-26, July 27-28
Positions Needed: Middle Hitters, OH, Setter
Schedule: Seattle Pacific, Western Washington, Central Washington, UC Davis
Style of Play: Strong serving and defensive team. Offensively working on new style of play.

Long Beach State University
Academic Profile

4901 E. Carson St.
Long Beach, CA 90808

Phone:

Type: Public, 4 Yr., Liberal Arts, Coed
Website: http://www.lbcc.cc.ca.us
SAT/ACT/GPA: Open
Student/Faculty Ratio:
Undergraduate Enrollment: 30,000
Scholarships/Academic: Yes
Expenses By: Year
Degrees Conferred: Bachelors, Masters

Founded: 1949
Religion: Non-Affiliated
Housing: Yes
Male/Female:
Graduate Enrollment: N/A

Athletic: Yes | **Financial Aid:** Yes
In State: $ 8,000 | **Out of State:** $ 10,000

Programs of Study: Accounting, Advertising, Architectural, Art, Automotive, Aviation, Biology, Clothing/Textiles, Fashion Design/Technology, Flight Training, General Engineering, Horticulture, Insurance, Interior, Photography, Retail, Theatre, Travel/Tourism, Welding

Men's Athletic Profile

1250 Bellflower Blvd.
Long Beach, CA 90840-0118
Coach: Ray Ratelle
Email:

NCAA I
49ers/Black, Gold
Phone: (562) 985-5064
Fax: (562) 985-8197

Estimated # of Men's Volleyball Scholarships: N/A
Conference: Mountain Pacific Sports Federation

Women's Athletic Profile

1250 Bellflower Boulevard
Long Beach, CA 90840-0118
Coach: Brian Gimmillaro
Email:

NCAA I
Lady 49ers, Black, Gold
Phone: (562) 985-8366
Fax: (562) 985-1911

Estimated # of Women's Volleyball Scholarships: 12

Conference: Big West Conference

Program Profile: We have a top program. Our VB team is the main sport on campus, we have produced 6 Players of the Year, we are consider to be one of the best women's programs in College. We play in the Pyramid which seats 5,000 with wood floor.

History: Program began in 1964. 5 National Championship in NCAA and in AIAW, 7 Final Four Appearances, 6 of the last 12 National Players of the Year, 25 Trips to the National Tournament, 7 Big West Conference Titles, Only undefeated team in D. I history in 1998 36-0

Achievements: 6 National AVCA Players of the Year, 22 AVCA All-Americans, 9 Big West Conference Players of the Year, 3 indoor Olympians and 1 outdoor.

Coaching: Head Coach Gimmillaro VB Magazine U.S Olympic Committee National Coach of the Year, AVCA Coach of the Year in 1998, 1990 Asics Tiger National Coach of the Year. Have an overall record of 425-97. Assistant Coaches Debbie Green-Vargas Coached 6 All-American setters at LBSU in 13 yrs. U.S Olympic team in 1980-84. Joy Mckenzie All-American Setter from LBSU

Freshman Receiving Financial Aid/Academic:		**Athletic:** 2
Roster In State: 6	**Out of State:** 8	**Out of Country:** 0

Seniors on Team: 2

Most Recent Record: 31-4-0

Camp of Clinic Dates: 1st week in Aug.

Positions Needed: OH, MB

Schedule: Stanford, Penn State, Nebraska, BYU, UOP, UCSB

Style of Play: Fast offense, aggressive, defense is an important part of our style.

Loyola Marymount University
Academic Profile

7900 Loyola Boulevard
Los Angeles, CA 90045-8235

Phone: (310) 338-2700

Type: Private, 4 Yr., Coed
Website: http://www.lmu.edu
SAT/ACT/GPA: 1000/3.0
Student/Faculty Ratio: 22:1
Undergraduate Enrollment: 3,968
Scholarships/Academic: Yes   **Athletic:** Yes
Expenses By: Year   **In State:** $ 26,751
Specializes In: Liberal Arts

Founded: 1911
Religion: Jesuit
Housing: Yes
Male/Female: 1:4
Graduate Enrollment: 1,155
Financial Aid: Yes
Out of State: $ 26,751

Degrees Conferred: BA, BS, BBA, BSA, BSE, MA, MS, MBA, M.Ed., JD

Programs of Study: Accounting, Biochemistry, Biology, Business Administration, Civil Engineering, Communications, Dramatic Arts, Economics, Electrical Engineering, English, French, History, Humanities, Mathematics, Mechanical Engineering, Music, Philosophy, Physics, Political Science, Psychology, Religion, Social Science

Men's Athletic Profile

7900 Loyola Blvd.
Los Angeles, CA 90045-8235
Coach: Rick McLaughlin
Email: whusak.lmumail.lmu.edu

NCAA I
Lions/Navy, White
Phone: (310) 338-2935
Fax: (310) 338-2703

Estimated # of Men's Volleyball Scholarships: N/A

Conference: Mountain Pacific Sports Federation

Women's Athletic Profile

7900 Loyola Blvd.
Los Angeles, CA 90045-8235
Coach: Steve Stratos
Email: sstratos@lmumail.lmu.edu

NCAA I
Lady Lions, Crimson, Navy Blue
Phone: (310) 338-2700
Fax: (310) 338-5915

Estimated # of Women's Volleyball Scholarships: 12

Conference: West Coast Conference

Program Profile: We play at Gersten Pavillion Arena which, has a capacity of 4,156. The facility includes a volleyball weight room, a training room and locker rooms.

History: Our first season of NCAA Division Competition was in 1982. Our first season of competition as a West Coast Conference member was in 1985.

Achievements: 5 WCC Championships; 36 All-WCC Athletes; I AVICA All-American; 5 WCC Players of the Year; 4 WCC Coach of the Year; 5 Volleyball Magazine All-Americans; 1 WCC Scholar-Athlete of the Year; 2 GTE Academic All-Americans

Coaching: Steve Stratos has been Head Coach from 1990 to the present. His overall record is 192-81. His WCC record is 90-27. His teams have won 3 WCC Championships and participated in 4 NCAA post-season appearances. Larry Smoot and Heather Collins are Assistant Coaches.

Roster In State: 7	**Out of State:** 5	**Out of Country:** 1
Seniors on Team: 2	**Graduation %:** 100	
Most Recent Record: 20-11-0	**Fall Games:** 30	**Spring Games:** 0

Schedule: Brigham Young, UC-Santa Barbara, San Diego, Hawaii, Colorado State, Texas Tech, Ohio State, Pepperdine

Style of Play: We play a 5-1 offense, utilize varied attack options (including back row) and practice intense defense.

Master's College
Academic Profile

21726 Placerita Canyon
Santa Clarita, CA 91321

Phone: 800-568-6248

Type: Private, 4 Yr., Liberal Arts, Coed
Website: http://www.masters.edu
SAT/ACT/GPA: 1000/20/2.5
Student/Faculty Ratio: 17:1
Undergraduate Enrollment: 900
Scholarships/Academic: Yes   **Athletic:** Yes
Expenses By: Year   **In State:** $ 9,000

Founded: 1927
Religion: Christian
Housing: Yes
Male/Female: 47:53
Graduate Enrollment: 280
Financial Aid: Yes
Out of State: $ 9,000

Specializes In: Christian, Liberal Arts, Education

Degrees Conferred: BA, BS, MD in Biblical Counseling, Theology, Divinity

Programs of Study: Biblical Studies, Biological Science, Business Administration, Communications, English, History, Home Economics, Liberal Studies, Mathematics, Music, Natural Science, Physical Education, Political Studies

Women's Athletic Profile

21726 Placerita Canyon Rd.
Santa Clarita, CA 91321-1200
Coach: Karen Peterson
Email: kpete@masters.edu

NCAA I
Lady Mustangs, Blue, Gold
Phone: (661) 259-3540
Fax: (661) 254-6129

Estimated # of Women's Volleyball Scholarships: Yes

Conference: Independent

Program Profile: We play our matches on campus in Bross Gymnasium during the months of September, October and November. Our gymnasium has seats for approximately 800-1,000 people.

History: Our program has been here from 1975 to the present. We are members of the Far West Region. We were nationally ranked in 1998.

Achievements: Coach Karen Peterson received Coach of the Year in 1995 and 1997; one All-American, two Academic All-Americans; Her teams have earned the Team All-Academic Award twice and are on their way to a third time.

Coaching: Karen Peterson, Head Coach, started here in 1997. Her overall record is 33-33. She was Coach of the Year in 1995 and 1997. She has a Cap Level II Rating.

Freshman Receiving Financial Aid/Academic: N/A		**Athletic:** 1
Roster In State: 8	**Out of State:** 4	**Out of Country:** 0
Sophomores on Team: 5	**Seniors on Team:** 1	**Graduation %:** 100
Most Recent Record: 18-15-0	**Fall Games:** 33	**Spring Games:** 4-8
Positions Needed: 4		

Style of Play: 5-1 possibly a 6-2 offense. Aggressive style but emphasis on high percentage offense.

Menlo College
Academic Profile

1000 El Camino Real
Atherton, CA 94027

Phone: 800-556-3656

Type: Private, 4 Yr., Liberal Arts, Coed
Website: http://www.menlo.edu
SAT/ACT/GPA: 850/18/2.5

Founded: 1927
Religion: Non-Affiliated
Housing: Yes

Student/Faculty Ratio: 15:1
Undergraduate Enrollment: 466
Scholarships/Academic: Yes　　　　**Athletic:** No
Expenses By: Year　　　　**In State:** $ 25,510
Specializes In: Management, Mass Communications
Degrees Conferred: BM, BMC, Liberal Arts
Programs of Study: Business Management, International Business, Environmental Resources Management, Management Information Systems, Media Studies, Media Management, Electronic Communications, Psychology, Humanities, International Policy and Planning or Environmental Policy and Planning

Male/Female: 55:45
Graduate Enrollment: N/A
Financial Aid: Yes
Out of State: $ 25,510

Women's Athletic Profile

1000 El Camino Real
Atherton, CA 94027
Coach: Antonio Veloso
Email:

NCAA I
Lady Oaks, Navy Blue, White
Phone: (650) 688-3777
Fax: (650) 688-3769

Did Not Return Profile

Mills College
Academic Profile

5000 MacArthur Blvd.
Oakland, CA 94613

Phone: 800-876-4557

Type: Private, 4 Yr., Women Only
Website: http://www.mills.edu
SAT/ACT/GPA: 940+
Student/Faculty Ratio: 11:1
Undergraduate Enrollment: 850
Scholarships/Academic: Yes　　　　**Athletic:** No
Expenses By: Year　　　　**In State:** $ 22,030
Degrees Conferred: BA, MA, MFA
Programs of Study: American Studies, Anthropology, Art, Art History, Biochemistry, Biology, Education, Elementary Education, English, Environmental Science

Founded: 1852
Religion: Non-Affiliated
Housing: No
Male/Female: Female
Graduate Enrollment: 300
Financial Aid: Yes
Out of State: $ 22,030

Women's Athletic Profile

5000 MacArthur Boulevard
Oakland, CA 94613
Coach: Marla Mundis
Email:

NCAA I
Cyclones, Navy, Gold, White
Phone: (510) 430-3283
Fax: (510) 430-2276

Estimated # of Women's Volleyball Scholarships: N/A
Conference: Cal Pac
Program Profile: We are dual members of NCAA and NAIA. With a 22 match schedule typically we have a standard hard wood floor, with one or two courts set-up.
History: Began in 1980.
Achievements: Conference Champions 1985, 1986.
Coaching: Head Coach Marla Mundis is an alumni of Mills. She played four years at Mills and has been the assistant coach at Mills for five years.
Roster In State: 9　　　　**Out of State:** 3　　　　**Out of Country:** 0
Most Recent Record: 3-18
Positions Needed: MH,OH,DS, Setter
Schedule: College of Notre Dame, Pacific Union, Holy Names
Style of Play: Mills is a hustling team with multiple offensive and defensive approches.

Moorpark College
Academic Profile

7075 Campus Rd.
Moorpark, CA 93015

Phone: (805) 378-1400

Type: Public, 2 Yr., Jr. College, Coed
Website: http://www.vcccd.cc.ca.us

Founded: 1967
Religion: Non-Affiliated

SAT/ACT/GPA: Open
Student/Faculty Ratio: 26:1
Undergraduate Enrollment: 13,000
Scholarships/Academic: No
Expenses By: Year

Athletic: No
In State: $ Varies

Housing: No
Male/Female: 40:60
Graduate Enrollment: N/A
Financial Aid: Yes
Out of State: $ Varies

Programs of Study: Accounting, Animal Science, Anthropology, Art/Fine Arts, Behavioral Science, Biology, Biological Science, Broadcasting, Business Administration, Commerce, Management, Business Machine Technology, Chemistry, Commercial Art, Computer Information System, Computer Science, Corrections, Criminal Justice, Data Processing, Early Childhood Education, Engineering Technology, Fashion Design, and Technology, Film Studies, Geology, Graphic Design, Journalism, Law Enforcement, Marketing, Retailing, Law Enforcement, Optical Technology, Wildlife Management

Women's Athletic Profile

7075 Campus Rd.
Moorpark, CA 93015
Coach: Steve Burkart
Email:

NCAA I
Raiders, Blue, Black, White
Phone: (805) 378-1400 x1711
Fax: (805) 378-1539

Estimated # of Women's Volleyball Scholarships: N/A
Conference: Western State Conference
Program Profile: We have a fall season. We travel throughout California. We play quality volleyball.
History: We ranked in the Top 15 in the state of California for the last 5 years.
Achievements: 2 WSC Coach of the Year; Over 10 Division I, II Players after completions.
Coaching: Steve Burkhart, Head Coach, has been coaching for 20 years. He was Illinois Coach of the Year. Kevin Judd is Assistant Coach.
Freshman Receiving Financial Aid/Academic: N/A   **Athletic:** N/A
Roster In State: 13   **Out of State:** 1   **Out of Country:** 0
Sophomores on Team: 8   **Seniors on Team:** 6   **Graduation %:** 90
Most Recent Record: 13-7-0   **Fall Games:** 24   **Spring Games:** 0
Schedule: Cuesta, Santa Barbara, Golden West, Ventura
Style of Play: Aggressive, quality, quick tempo.

Occidental College
Academic Profile

1600 Campus Road
Los Angeles, CA 90041

Phone: 800-825-5262

Type: Private, 4 Yr., Liberal Arts, Coed
Website: http://www.oxy.edu
SAT/ACT/GPA: 1000
Student/Faculty Ratio: 12:1
Undergraduate Enrollment: 1,585
Scholarships/Academic: Yes
Expenses By: Year

Athletic: No
In State: $ 25,356

Founded: 1887
Religion: Non-Affiliated
Housing: No
Male/Female: 55%:45%
Graduate Enrollment: 50
Financial Aid: Yes
Out of State: $ 25,356

Degrees Conferred: BA, Graduate program: MA
Programs of Study: Anthropology, Art, Biology, Chemistry, Economics, Education, Engineering, Geology, History, International, Languages, Mathematics, Physical Fitness/Movement, Physics, Political, Religion, Seismology

Women's Athletic Profile

1600 Campus Rd
Los Angeles, CA 90041
Coach: Jenna Panatier
Email: panatier@oxy.edu

NCAA I
Lady Tigers, Orange, Black
Phone: (323) 259-2702
Fax: (323) 341-4993

Estimated # of Women's Volleyball Scholarships: N/A
Conference: Southern California Intercollegiate Athletic Conference
Achievements: 9 Conference Titles, 3 All-Americans.
Seniors on Team: 1   **Graduation %:** 100
Most Recent Record: 16-9-0
Positions Needed: Outside, Middle
Schedule: Univ. of La Verne, Cal Lutheran, Linfield, CS-Hayward

Pacific Christian C(Hope International U)
Academic Profile

2500 N. Nutwood Avenue
Fullerton, Ca 92361

Phone: 800-762-1294

Type: 4 Yr., Coed
Website: http://www.hiv.edu
SAT/ACT/GPA: Open
Student/Faculty Ratio: 16:1
Undergraduate Enrollment: 841
Scholarships/Academic:
Expenses By: Year
Degrees Conferred: Associates

Founded: 1928
Religion: Non-Affiliated
Housing: Yes
Male/Female: Not Available
Graduate Enrollment: N/A
Financial Aid:

Athletic:
In State: $ 8,950+

Out of State: $ 8,950+

Programs of Study: Biblical Studies, Business Administration, Commerce, Management, Child Psychology, Child Development, Early Childhood Education, Elementary Education, English, Health Science, Liberal Arts, General Studies, Ministries, Music, Music Education, Pastoral Studies, Psychology, Religious Education, Religious Studies, Secondary Education, Social Science, Social Work, Sport Medicine

Women's Athletic Profile

2500 E. Nutwood Avenue
Fullerton, CA 92631
Coach: Mike Klunder
Email: mklunder@aol.com

NCAA I
Lady Royals, Blue, Silver, White
Phone: 714-879-3901
Fax: (714) 879-1041

Did Not Return Profile

Pacific Union College
Academic Profile

One Angwin Ave.
Angwin, CA 94508

Phone: 800-862-7080

Type: Coed
Website: http://www.puc.edu
SAT/ACT/GPA: Open
Student/Faculty Ratio: 13:1
Undergraduate Enrollment: 1,544
Scholarships/Academic:
Expenses By: Year
Degrees Conferred: Bachelors, Masters

Founded: 1882
Religion: Non-Affiliated
Housing: No
Male/Female: Not Available
Graduate Enrollment: N/A
Financial Aid:

Athletic:
In State: $ Varies

Out of State: $ Varies

Programs of Study: Accounting, Advertising, Applied Mathematics, Art/Fine Arts, Art History, Astrophysics, Behavioral Science, Biblical Studies, Biochemistry, Business Administration, Commerce, Management, Business Education, Chemistry, Communications, Computer Information Systems, Industrial Arts, Data Processing, Electrical and Electronics, Management Information System, Religious Study, Music Education, Nursing, Physical Education, Public Relations, Recreation and Leisure

Women's Athletic Profile

100 Howell Mt.
Angwin, CA 94508
Coach: Bob Paulson
Email: bpaulson@puc.edu

NCAA I
Pioneers, green and yellow
Phone: (707) 965-6348
Fax: (707) 965-6780

Estimated # of Women's Volleyball Scholarships: 0
Conference: Cal Pac
Program Profile: Pacific Union College plays as both a club and varsity team. We participate in the Northern Cal. Club league and the California Pacific Athletic Conference.
Coaching: Five years at Pacific Union College
Freshman Receiving Financial Aid/Academic:
Roster In State: 10
Graduation %: 100
Most Recent Record: 25-4

Out of State: 2

Fall Games: 0

Athletic: 0
Out of Country: 0

Spring Games: 29

Positions Needed: Outside Middle, Offside, and a Middle. We will also be looking for a setter for the 2000/2001season
Schedule: UC Davis, St. Mary's College, Air force Academy, Sac State, Oregon State, Chico State
Style of Play: Fundamental

Pepperdine University
Academic Profile

24255 Pacific Coast Hwy.
Malibu, CA 90263

Phone: (310) 456-4322

Type: Private, 4 Yr., Liberal Arts, Coed
Website: http://www.pepperdine.edu
SAT/ACT/GPA: 1100
Student/Faculty Ratio: 13:1
Undergraduate Enrollment: 2,900
Scholarships/Academic: Yes
Expenses By: Year

Athletic: Yes
In State: $32,000

Founded: 1937
Religion: Church of Christ
Housing: Yes
Male/Female: 42/58
Graduate Enrollment: 5,100
Financial Aid: Yes
Out of State: $32,000

Specializes In: Liberal Arts, Business, Professional Programs, Communications
Degrees Conferred: BA, BS, MBA, MA, JD, MS, Mdiv
Programs of Study: Business, Communication, Sports Medicine There are 36 total.

Men's Athletic Profile

24255 Pacific Coast Hwy.
Malibu, CA 90263
Coach: Marv Dunphy
Email: jgwatson@pepperdine.edu

NCAA I
Waves/Blue, Orange
Phone: (310) 456-4517
Fax: (310) 456-4322

Estimated # of Men's Volleyball Scholarships: N/A
Conference: Mountain Pacific Sports Federation

Women's Athletic Profile

24255 Pacific Coast Hwy.
Malibu, CA 90263
Coach: Nina Matthies
Email:

NCAA I
Lady Waves, Blue, Orange
Phone: (310) 456-4150
Fax: (310) 456-4322

Estimated # of Women's Volleyball Scholarships: N/A
Conference: West Coast Conference
Program Profile: We are a Top 20 ranked NCAA Division I program. Out team plays a highly competitive schedule. All home matches are played at the Firestone Field house which seats 3,104. Our season goes from August to December.
History: Our program began in 1975. We are a member of the West Coast Conference. Our team consistently ranked in the National Top 20 and advanced to the NCAA Championships.
Achievements: Program advanced to the "Sweet 16" at the 1998 NCAA Championships.
Coaching: Nina Mathies, Head Coach, is recognized as one of the world's top beach volleyball players. Her overall record is 285-211 in 16 seasons at Pepperdine. She is a former collegiate player and captain at UCLA, She began her coaching career in 1977, serving as an assistant coach for six seasons to Andy Banachowski at UCLA. John Wallace, Assistant Coach, was a former standout setter at the University of California-Santa Barbara. He is beginning his seventh season.
Freshman Receiving Financial Aid/Academic:

Athletic: 6

Roster In State: 10
Sophomores on Team: 2
Most Recent Record: 19-11-0

Out of State: 2
Seniors on Team: 3
Fall Games: 30

Out of Country: 0
Graduation %: 100
Spring Games: 4

Positions Needed: Middle Blocker
Schedule: University of California-Santa Barbara, University of California-Los Angeles, California State University-Long Beach, University of California-San Diego, Loyola Marymount
Style of Play: Pepperdine teams rely heavily on the overall athleticism and team speed along with a strong hitting attack.

Point Loma Nazarene College
Academic Profile

3900 Lomaland Drive
San Diego, CA 92106

Phone: (619) 849-2200

Type: Private, 4 Yr., Liberal Arts, Coed

Founded: 1902

Website: http://www.ptloma.edu
SAT/ACT/GPA: Open
Student/Faculty Ratio: 18:1
Undergraduate Enrollment: 2,000
Scholarships/Academic: Yes   **Athletic:** Yes
Expenses By: Year   **In State:** $ 17,000
Specializes In: Liberal Arts
Degrees Conferred: BA, BSN, MA, MED, EDS
Programs of Study: Business and Management, Health Science, Home Economics, Letters/Literature, Multi/Interdisciplinary Studies, Social Science, Visual and Performing Arts

Religion: Nazarene
Housing: Yes
Male/Female: 1:2
Graduate Enrollment: 400
Financial Aid: Yes
Out of State: $ 17,000

Women's Athletic Profile

3900 Lomaland Rd.
San Diego, CA 92106
Coach: Barbara Wnek
Email: wnek.pe@oa.ptloma.edu

NCAA I
Lady Crusaders, Green, Gold
Phone: (619) 849-2589
Fax: (619) 849-2553

Did Not Return Profile

Pomona - Pitzer Colleges
Academic Profile

220 E 6th Street
Claremont, CA 91711

Phone: (909) 621-8427

Type: Private, 4 Yr., Liberal Arts, Coed
Website: http://www.pomona.edu
SAT/ACT/GPA: Varies/3.0+
Student/Faculty Ratio: 10:1
Undergraduate Enrollment: 1,400
Scholarships/Academic: No   **Athletic:** No
Expenses By: Year   **In State:** $ 27,200
Specializes In: Liberal Arts Colleges
Degrees Conferred: BA, BS

Founded: 1887
Religion: Non-Affiliated
Housing: Yes
Male/Female: 1:1
Graduate Enrollment: N/A
Financial Aid: Yes
Out of State: $ 27,200

Programs of Study: American Studies, Anthropology, Art, Asian Languages, Astronomy, Biology, Black Studies, Chemistry, Chicano Studies, Computer Science, Economics, Education, English, Geology, German and Russian, History, International Relations, Latin American Studies, Linguistics, Mathematics, Media Studies, Music, Neuroscience, Philosophy, Politics, Physical Education, Physics, Public Policy Analysis, Religious Studies, Romance Languages, Science, Technology and Society, Sociology, Theatre and Dance , Women's Studies

Women's Athletic Profile

Rains Center, 220 E. 6th St.
Claremont, CA 91711
Coach: Pam Havlick
Email: phavlick@pomona.edu

NCAA I
Sagehens, Navy, White, Orange
Phone: (909) 621-8427
Fax: (909) 621-8863

Estimated # of Women's Volleyball Scholarships: 0
Conference: Southern California Intercollegiate Athletic Conference
Program Profile: We recruit highly academic student athletes. Our facility is Voelkel Gymnasium, which has 2,000 seats. Our season starts on September 7th and ends November 4th.
History: We began in 1976. We were invited to the NCAA tournaments 5 times.
Achievements: 1984 Western Region AVCA Coach of the Year; 2 SCIAC Conference titles; 2 1st team All-Americans; 1 2nd Team All-American
Coaching: Pam Havlick, Head Coach, was in the Final Four at Pepperdine University. She was an IVA player and a senior All-American and the Player of the Year in college.
Freshman Receiving Financial Aid/Academic:
Roster In State: 4   **Out of State:** 7   **Athletic:** 0
Sophomores on Team: 0   **Seniors on Team:** 5   **Out of Country:** 0
Most Recent Record: 17-8-0   **Graduation %:** 100
Positions Needed: 2 Middle Blockers, 1 Setter, 2 Outside Hitters

Schedule: Cal Lutheran, Nebraska Wesleyan, Elmhurst College, LaVerne, Chapman

Saint Mary's College
Academic Profile

1928 Saint Mary's Rd
Moraga, CA 94575

Phone: (925) 631-4444

Type: Private, 4 Yr., Liberal Arts, Coed
Website: http://www.stmarys-ca.edu
SAT/ACT/GPA: 1000/3.0
Student/Faculty Ratio: 20:1
Undergraduate Enrollment: 2,100
Scholarships/Academic: Yes
Expenses By: Year
Specializes In: Liberal Arts

Athletic: Yes
In State: $ 24,695

Founded: 1863
Religion: Catholic (Christian Brothers)
Housing: Yes
Male/Female: 45:56
Graduate Enrollment: 2,000
Financial Aid: Yes
Out of State: $ 24,695

Degrees Conferred: BA, BS, Nursing, MA, MS, MBA, M.Ed.
Programs of Study: Anthropology, Art, Biology, Business, Classical Languages, Chemistry, Communications, Economics, Engineering, Government, History, Mathematics, Nursing, Philosophy, Psychology, Sociology

Women's Athletic Profile

1928 St. Mary's Rd.
Moraga, CA 94575
Coach: Ron Twomey
Email: rtwomey@St.mary-ca.edu

NCAA I
Lady Gaels, Red, Blue
Phone: (925) 631-4444
Fax: (925) 376-0829

Estimated # of Women's Volleyball Scholarships: 11
Conference: West Coast Conference
Program Profile: We play against top Division I teams in the pre-season and in our Conference. Our athletic facilities have a total of 5 courts and we play in the McKeon Pavilion which has 4,000 seats.
History: Our program started in 1978 as an NAIA school and we won the National Championship in 1985. The program joined NCAA Division I and the West Coast Conference in 1987.
Achievements: Ron Twomey was named Big East Conference Co-Coach of the Year in 1995.
Coaching: Ron Twomey, Head Coach, started in 1996 with an overall record of 25-59. Jody Paperno is Assistant Coach. She is in her third year here. She played at the University of North Dakota.
Freshman Receiving Financial Aid/Academic:

Athletic: 3
Roster In State: 10
Sophomores on Team: 6
Most Recent Record: 9-19-0
Camp of Clinic Dates: July 4-8
Positions Needed: Middle Blocker, Setter

Out of State: 2
Seniors on Team: 3
Fall Games: 28

Out of Country: 1
Graduation %: 100
Spring Games: 0

Schedule: University of Pacific, University of Washington, Fresno State, Pepperdine, Loyola Marymount, University of San Diego
Style of Play: We are defensive oriented and have a quick offense.

San Diego State University
Academic Profile

5500 Campanile Drive
San Diego, CA 92182-4328

Phone: (619) 594-5200

Type: Public, 4 Yr., Coed
Website: http://www.sdsu.edu
SAT/ACT/GPA: 1058/22/3.48
Student/Faculty Ratio: 19:1
Undergraduate Enrollment: 25,800
Scholarships/Academic: Yes
Expenses By: Year
Specializes In: Business, Engineering, Education

Athletic: Yes
In State: $ 8,542

Founded: 1897
Religion: Non-Affiliated
Housing: Yes
Male/Female: 49:51
Graduate Enrollment: 3,200
Financial Aid: Yes
Out of State: $ 14,446

Degrees Conferred: BA, BS, MA, MS, MBA, MFA, Ph.D.
Programs of Study: Business Management, Computer Sciences, Education, Engineering, Exercise and Nutritional Sciences, Mathematics, Physical Therapy, Psychology, Telecommunications

Men's Athletic Profile

5500 Campanile Drive
San Diego, CA 92115
Coach: Jack Henn
Email: henn@mail.sdsu.edu

NCAA I
Aztecs/Scarlet, Black
Phone: (619) 594-4444
Fax: (619) 582-6541

Estimated # of Men's Volleyball Scholarships: 3
Conference: Mountain Pacific Sports Federation
Program Profile: We are a Charter member of MPSF. We were formerly WIVA-CIVA and So.Cal.I.V.A. The team plays at Peterson Gym with a seating capacity of 3,500. The season starts in January and goes through May.
History: The program began in 1961.
Achievements: NCAA Champions, USVBA Collegiate Champions; 5 Conference Titles; 5 Olympians, and 12 AVP pros.
Coaching: Jack Henn, Head Coach, was named All-American, Collegiate MVP and an Olympian. Tim Klauda, Assistant Coach, was named Coach of the Year and Section Champion Team.
Freshman Receiving Financial Aid/Academic: 0   **Athletic:** 2
Sophomores on Team: 6   **Seniors on Team:** 2   **Graduation %:** 92.7%
Most Recent Record: 9-14-0   **Fall Games:** 0   **Spring Games:** 25
Camp or Clinic Dates: August 1-5
Positions Needed: 4
Schedule: University of California-Los Angeles, Stanford, University of Southern California, Long Beach State, Brigham Young University, Hawaii

Women's Athletic Profile

5500 Campanile Drive
San Diego, CA 92182
Coach: Mark Warner
Email: warner@mail.sdsu

NCAA I
Lady Aztecs, Scarlet, Black
Phone: (619) 594-5064
Fax: (619) 582-6541

Estimated # of Women's Volleyball Scholarships: 2
Conference: Mountain West Athletic Conference
Program Profile: We play in Peterson Gym which has 3,668 seats. Occasionally, we play at Cox Arena which has 12,414 seats .
History: Our program started in 1976. In 22 years, we have produced 20 winning seasons (10 straight). We had 12 NCAA Tournament Appearances and 14 All-Americans. We were 3rd in the NCAA'S in 1981 and 1982 and made the Final Four both years. We were in NCAA "Sweet 16" in 1995.
Achievements: Mark Warner was WAL Coach of the Year in 1995; 1995 WAC Champions; 1979,1981,1982 WCAA Champions.
Coaching: Mark Warner has been Head Coach since 1995. As a player, he won the 1968 Collegiate National Championship at SDSU. He is a 12 time USVBA All-American. He was 1993 MVP of the USVBA National Championships.
Freshman Receiving Financial Aid/Academic: **Athletic:** 2
Roster In State: 17   **Out of State:** 2   **Out of Country:** 0
Sophomores on Team: 0   **Seniors on Team:** 2   **Graduation %:** Unknown
Camp of Clinic Dates: August 1-5
Positions Needed: Already signed; 1 Middle Blocker and 1 Outside Hitter
Schedule: Long Beach State, Nebraska, Arizona, BYU, USD, Loyola Marymount
Style of Play: Aggressive, fast offense; very physical and play hard.

San Francisco State University
Academic Profile

1600 Halloway Ave.
San Francisco, CA 94132

Phone: (415) 338-1100

Type: Public, 4 Yr., Coed
Website: http://www.sfsu.edu
SAT/ACT/GPA: 820/26+/2.0
Student/Faculty Ratio: 18:1
Undergraduate Enrollment: 19,000
Scholarships/Academic: Yes   **Athletic:** Yes
Expenses By: Year   **In State:** $ 8,500
Specializes In: Business, Psychology, Sciences
Degrees Conferred: BA, BS, MA, MS, MBA

Founded: 1899
Religion: Non-Affiliated
Housing: Yes
Male/Female: 45:65
Graduate Enrollment: 6,000
Financial Aid: Yes
Out of State: $ 14,500

Programs of Study: Accounting, American Studies, Anthropology, Art, Astronomy, Biology, Broadcasting, Chemistry, Cinema, Communications, Computer Information Systems, Computer Science, Creative Writing, Dance, Ecology, Economics, Education, Engineering, Gerontology, Journalism, Management, Marketing, Mathematics, Music, Nursing, Philosophy, Political Science, Psychology, Social Science, Sociology, Physics

Women's Athletic Profile

1600 Holloway Avenue
San Francisco, CA 94132
Coach: Kathy Argo
Email: kargo@sfsu.edu

NCAA I
Lady Gators, Purple, Gold
Phone: (415) 338-2707
Fax: (415) 338-1967

Did Not Return Profile

San Jose State University
Academic Profile

One Washington Square
San Jose, CA 95192-0062

Phone: (408) 924-1291

Type: Public, 4 Yr., Liberal Arts, Engineering, Coed
Website: http://www.spartnas.sjsu.edu
SAT/ACT/GPA: 820/2.0
Student/Faculty Ratio: 30:1
Undergraduate Enrollment: 19,000
Scholarships/Academic: Yes
Expenses By: Year

Athletic: Yes
In State: $ 15,000

Founded: 1865
Religion: Non-Affiliated
Housing: Yes
Male/Female: 53:47
Graduate Enrollment: 8,000
Financial Aid: Yes
Out of State: $ 21,000

Specializes In: Business, Education, Communications, Engineering
Degrees Conferred: BA, BS, BFA, MA, MS, MBA, MFA
Programs of Study: Top 10 majors - Computer Science, Art & Design, Accounting, Management, Electrical Engineering, Management Information Systems, Computer Engineering, Psychology, Criminal Justice, Administration, Biology, Child Development

Women's Athletic Profile

One Washington Square
San Jose, CA 95192-0062
Coach: Craig Choate
Email: gmano@email.sjsu.edu

NCAA I
Lady Spartans, Gold, Blue
Phone: (408) 924-1444
Fax: (408) 924-1291

Estimated # of Women's Volleyball Scholarships: 12
Conference: Western Athletic Conference
Program Profile: Hawaii, Washington State, Santa Clara, University of San Diego, California, Northwestern
History: The team went 21-12 last year. We were semifinalists of the WAC Tournament and made it to the NCAA Tournament. We play in the SJSU Event Center which has 5,000 seats.
Coaching: Craig Choate is starting his 6th season as Head Coach. His overall record is 101-88. He was head coach at New Mexico State for three seasons.
Freshman Receiving Financial Aid/Academic:
Roster In State: 8
Sophomores on Team: 0
Most Recent Record: 21-12-0
Camp of Clinic Dates: July 16-18

Out of State: 4
Seniors on Team: 3
Fall Games: 30

Athletic: 2
Out of Country: 0
Graduation %: Unknown
Spring Games: 10

Positions Needed: Setter, Outside Hitter, Right Side Hitter
Schedule: Hawaii, Washington State, Santa Clara, University of San Diego, California, North Western

Santa Clara University
Academic Profile

500 El Camino
Santa Clara, CA 95053

Phone: (707) 864-7000

Type: Private, 4 Yr., Liberal Arts, Engineering, Coed
Website: http://www.SantaClaraBroncos.com
SAT/ACT/GPA: 1210/3.5

Founded: 1851
Religion: Catholic-Jesuit
Housing: Yes

Student/Faculty Ratio: 13:1
Undergraduate Enrollment: 4,200
Scholarships/Academic: Yes
Expenses By: Year
Specializes In: Liberal Arts, Business, Law
Degrees Conferred: BA, BS, MA, MS, MBA, Ph.D., JD
Programs of Study: Business and Management, Communications, Engineering, International, Letters/Literature, Multi/Interdisciplinary, PreProfessional Programs, Psychology, Social Sciences

Athletic: Yes
In State: $ 25,713

Male/Female: 50:50
Graduate Enrollment: 4,000
Financial Aid: Yes
Out of State: $ 25,713

Women's Athletic Profile

500 El Camino Real - Leavey Activities Ctr.
Santa Clara, CA 95053
Coach: Annie Feller
Email: afeller@scu.edu

NCAA I
Lady Broncos, Burgundy, White
Phone: (408) 554-6981
Fax: (408) 554-6969

Estimated # of Women's Volleyball Scholarships: N/A
Conference: West Coast Conference
Program Profile: We are a fully funded Division I program that competes in the fall in the WCC. Toso Pavillion is our home arena with a seating capacity of 5,000. It is ideal for women's volleyball.
History: In 1997 season, the Broncos had a 19-9 record, which marked the most victories by a Santa Clara team since 1993 and the fifth-highest victory total in school history. For the first time ever, the Broncos finished in single digits in the loss column. Santa Clara netted its sixth upper division West Coast Conference finish in seven years, as the Broncos placed fourth in the WCC with a 8-6 record.
Achievements: 7 1st team All-WCC players in 1997; 6 2nd team All-WCC players in 1997; 10 Honorable Mention is Sarah Noriega was named Player of the Year; Sue Synder was named Coach of the Year; Cathy Cook was named Freshman of the Year.
Coaching: Annie Feller, Head Coach, former Broncos' assistant for three seasons, took over the program duties for the 1993 seasons when Laurie Corbelli resigned her position. She came to Santa Clara after serving as an assistant coach on Dave Shojji's staff at the University of Hawaii. She is a former All-American and received a Broderick Award nominee in 1986. She was named Female Athlete of the Year in 1985 and 1986. Dave Hollaway, Assistant Coach, enters his second season after heading up the very successful girls program at Dana Hills High School in Southern California. He served as an assistant coach at Golden West College for two seasons. Dustin Moore, Assistant Coach, enters his second season as a volunteer coach. He has spent eight years as a coach on the high school, club and collegiate level. He served as the head coach at Menlo College.

Roster In State: 13
Graduation %: 100
Most Recent Record: 20-9-0
Camp of Clinic Dates: August 2-5
Schedule: Stanford, UCP, Texas A & M, Florida State, Arizona, Pepperdine
Style of Play: Big at the net with an outstanding ball control team.

Out of State: 2

Fall Games: 29

Out of Country: 1

Spring Games: 0

Simpson College - California
Academic Profile

2211 College View Dr.
Redding, CA 96003

Phone: (530) 224-5600

Type: Private, 4 Yr., Coed
Website: http://www.simpsonca.edu
SAT/ACT/GPA: Required/2.0
Student/Faculty Ratio: 17:1
Undergraduate Enrollment: 1,169
Scholarships/Academic: Yes
Expenses By: Year
Specializes In: Christian Ministry, Professional Studies
Degrees Conferred: Bachelors, Masters
Programs of Study: Accounting, Biblical Studies, Business Administration, Commerce, Management, Communications, Education, Elementary Education, English, History, Human Resources, Liberal Arts, General Studies, Mathematics, Ministries, Music, Music Education, Pastoral Studies, Psychology, Religious Studies, Sacred Music, Secondary Education, Social Science

Athletic: No
In State: $ 8,040

Founded: 1921
Religion: Christian & Missionary Alliance
Housing: Yes
Male/Female: 40:60
Graduate Enrollment: N/A
Financial Aid: Yes
Out of State: $8,010

Women's Athletic Profile

2211 College View Drive
Redding, CA 96003
Coach: TBA
Email:

NCAA I
Vanguards, Red, White, Black
Phone: (530) 224-5600
Fax: (530) 224-2053

Did Not Return Profile

Solano Community College
Academic Profile

4000 Suisun Valley Rd.
Suisun City, CA 94585

Phone: (707) 864-7000

Type: Public, 2 Yr., Jr. College, Coed
Website: http://www.solano.cc.ca.us
SAT/ACT/GPA: High School Diploma
Student/Faculty Ratio: 30:1
Undergraduate Enrollment: 10,000
Scholarships/Academic: Yes
Expenses By: Year
Specializes In: Transfer courses to UC and CSU Systems
Degrees Conferred: Associates

Athletic: No
In State: $ 1,385

Founded: 1947
Religion: Non-Affiliated
Housing: No
Male/Female: Not Available
Graduate Enrollment: N/A
Financial Aid: Yes
Out of State: $ 2,210

Programs of Study: Accounting, African Studies, Aircraft and Missile Maintenance, Art/Fine Arts, Automotive Technology, Aviation Technology, Biology, Biotechnology, Black American Studies, Business Administration, Business Machines Technology, Chemistry, Commerce, Commercial Art, Computer Programming, Cosmetology, Criminal Justice, Drafting and Design, Early Childhood Education, Education, Electrical and Electronic Technology, English, Ethnic Studies, Fashion Merchandising, Finance/Banking Fire Science, French, German, History, Home Economics, Journalism, Legal Specialist, Management, Mathematics, Medical Office Specialist, Nursing, Physical Education, Physics, Political Science, Psychology, Public Administration, Science, Social Science, Spanish, Sports Medicine, Telecommunications, Theatre Arts, Transcriptionist, Welding Technology

Women's Athletic Profile

4000 Suisn Valley Road
Suisun City, CA 94484
Coach: Jason Zocteman
Email: jzoetema@solano.cc.ca.us

NCAA I
Lady Falcons, Royal, White
Phone: (707) 864-7000
Fax: (707) 864-7156

Estimated # of Women's Volleyball Scholarships: 0
Conference: Bay Valley Conference
Program Profile: We play at a 3 court gymnasium with one of the highest ceilings in the league. The season starts in August and runs through December.
History: Our program rejuvenated in 1998.
Achievements: (1) All-Conference Selection and (1) Honorable Mention in 1998
Coaching: Jason Zocteman became Head Coach in 1998. The assistant coach will be announced.
Freshman Receiving Financial Aid/Academic:
Roster In State: 12
Sophomores on Team: 0
Most Recent Record: 4-12-0
Camp of Clinic Dates: August 9,10,11
Positions Needed: Setters, Middle Hitters

Out of State: 0
Seniors on Team: 2
Fall Games: 24

Athletic: 0
Out of Country: 0
Graduation %: 90
Spring Games: 0

Schedule: Santa Rosa Junior College, American River Junior Colette, Napa Valley College, Butte College
Style of Play: Nothing hits the floor at Solano! Aggressive play is encouraged, teamwork is a must.

Sonoma State University
Academic Profile

1801 E. Cotati Avenue
Rohnert Park, CA 94928
Type: Public, 4 Yr., Coed
Website: http://www.sonoma.edu
SAT/ACT/GPA: 820/18
Student/Faculty Ratio: 20:1
Undergraduate Enrollment: 7,000

Phone: 707-664-2778

Founded: 1960
Religion: Non-Affiliated
Housing: Yes
Male/Female: 40:60
Graduate Enrollment: 1,000

Scholarships/Academic: Yes   **Athletic:** Yes   **Financial Aid:** No
Expenses By: Year   **In State:** $ 8,500   **Out of State:** $ 14,900
Degrees Conferred: BA, BS, MA, MS
Programs of Study: Accounting, Anthropology, Art, Banking/Finance, Biology, Botany, Cell Biology, Chemistry, Communications, Computer Science, Criminal Justice, Dance, Dramatic Arts, Economics, English, Geography, Geology, German, History, Marine Biology, Marketing, Math, Microbiology, Music, Nursing, Philosophy, Physics, Political Science, Psychology, Social Science

Women's Athletic Profile

1801 E. Cotati Avenue
Rohnert Park, CA 94928-3609
Coach: Jon Stevenson
Email: jon.stevenson@sonoma.edu

NCAA I
Lady Cossacks, Blue, White
Phone: (707) 664-2656
Fax: (707) 664-4101

Did Not Return Profile

Stanford University
Academic Profile

Arrillaga Sports Center
Stanford, CA 94305-6150

Phone: (650) 725-0736

Type: Private, 4 Yr., Liberal Arts, Coed
Website: http://www.gostanford.com
SAT/ACT/GPA: 1300+
Student/Faculty Ratio: 10:1
Undergraduate Enrollment: 6,500
Scholarships/Academic: Yes
Expenses By: Year

Founded: 1891
Religion: Non-Affiliated
Housing: Yes
Male/Female: 55:45
Graduate Enrollment: 6,500
Athletic: Yes   **Financial Aid:** Yes
In State: $ 31,599   **Out of State:** $ 31,599
Degrees Conferred: BA, BS, MA, MS, MBA, MFA, MEd, Ph.D., EdD
Programs of Study: African - American Studies, Anthropology, Art, Asian Languages, Biological Sciences, Chemistry, Classics, Communication, Comparative Literature, Computer Science, Drama, Earth Science, East Asian Studies, Economics, Engineering, English, Feminist Studies, French, German Studies, History, Human Biology, International Relations, Italian, Latin American Studies, Linguistics, Math, Music, Philosophy, Physics, Political Science, Psychology, Public Policy, Religion, Sociology, Spanish, Portuguese

Men's Athletic Profile

Department of Athletics
Stanford, CA 94305
Coach: Ruben Nieves
Email:

NCAA I
Cardinal/Cardinal, White
Phone: (650) 725-0763
Fax: (650) 725-8642

Estimated # of Men's Volleyball Scholarships: N/A
Conference: Pacific 10 Conference

Women's Athletic Profile

Arrillaga Sports Center
Stanford, CA 94305-6150
Coach: Don Shaw
Email:

NCAA I
Lady Cardinals, Cardinal, White
Phone: (650) 723-0561
Fax: (650) 725-9515

Estimated # of Women's Volleyball Scholarships: 12
Conference: Pacific 10 Conference
Program Profile: We provide a top academic atmosphere. We play our matches in Maples Pavilion which has a capacity of 7,500.
History: Our program went varsity in 1976. We have gone to 11 Final Fours in the last 17 years. We were National Champions in 1992, 1994,1996 and 1997.
Achievements: Pac 10 Titles: 1987,1991,1994,1995, 1996, 1997 and 1998; Second place on other years; 16 All-Americans; Kim Oden-Player of the Decades for the 1980's; 4 National Player of the Year.
Coaching: Don Shaw has been Head Coach here for 14 years and has an overall record of 409-67. Denise Corlett has been Associate Head Coach here for 10 years. Josh Cohen in his first year here as Assistant Coach.

Freshman Receiving Financial Aid/Academic: | | **Athletic:** 3
Roster In State: 10 | **Out of State:** 4 | **Out of Country:** 1
Sophomores on Team: 0 | **Seniors on Team:** 1 | **Graduation %:** 99
Most Recent Record: 27-4-0 | **Fall Games:** 27 | **Spring Games:** 4
Camp of Clinic Dates: Coach Clinic: 9-11-99
Schedule: Brigham Young University, University of Texas, University of Pennsylvania, University of Hawaii, University of California-LA, University of Arizona
Style of Play: Aggressive and fundamentally sound; more of a blocking team; win with block and defense.

University of California - Berkeley
Academic Profile

2223 Fulton St.
Berkeley, CA 94720

Phone: (510) 643-8100

Type: Public, 4 Yr., Coed
Website: http://www.berkeley.edu
SAT/ACT/GPA: 600-710/3.89
Student/Faculty Ratio: 17:1
Undergraduate Enrollment: 14,578
Scholarships/Academic: Yes
Expenses By: Year

Founded: 1869
Religion: Non-Affiliated
Housing: Yes
Male/Female: 1:1
Graduate Enrollment: 24,172

Athletic: Yes
In State: $ 14,598

Financial Aid: Yes
Out of State: $ 24,172

Degrees Conferred: BA, BS, MA, MS, MBA, Ph.D., EdD, OD, JD
Programs of Study: Anthropology, Art, Architecture, Astronomy, BioEngineering, Biology, Business Administration, Chemistry, Communications, Computer Science, Earth Science, Economics, Engineering, Geology, Sociology, Political Science, Psychology, Physics

Women's Athletic Profile

210 Memorial Stadium
Berkeley, CA 94720
Coach: Rich Feller
Email: calyball@uclink4.berkelay.edu

NCAA I
Lady Golden Bears, Blue, Gold
Phone: (510) 643-0978
Fax: (510) 643-5344

Estimated # of Women's Volleyball Scholarships: N/A
Conference: Pacific 10 Conference
Program Profile: Games are played in Haas Pavilion which seats 12,172.
Freshman Receiving Financial Aid/Academic: N/A | **Athletic:** N/A
Roster In State: 15 | **Out of State:** 3 | **Out of Country:** 0
Seniors on Team: 6

University of California - Davis
Academic Profile

One Shields Avenue
Davis, CA 95616

Phone: (530) 752-2971

Type: Public, 4 Yr., Coed
Website: http://www.ucdavis.edu
SAT/ACT/GPA: 1000/3.4
Student/Faculty Ratio: 18:1
Undergraduate Enrollment: 19,500
Scholarships/Academic: Yes
Expenses By: Year

Founded: 1906
Religion: Non-Affiliated
Housing: Yes
Male/Female: 48:52
Graduate Enrollment: 4,600

Athletic: Yes
In State: $ 10,988

Financial Aid: Yes
Out of State: $ 20,372

Specializes In: PreMed, PreVet, Hard Sciences, Social Sciences
Degrees Conferred: All
Programs of Study: More than 100 undergraduate majors available.

Women's Athletic Profile

Athletic Department
Davis, CA 95616
Coach: Stephaine Hawbecker
Email: shawbecker@ucdavis.edu

NCAA I
Lady Aggies, Yale blue, Gold
Phone: (530) 752-0644
Fax: (530) 752-2676

Did Not Return Profile

University of California - Irvine
Academic Profile

204 Administration Bldg.
Irvine, CA 92697-1075

Phone: (949) 824-6703

Type: Public, 4 Yr., Coed
Website: http://www.uci.edu
SAT/ACT/GPA: 1200/3.0
Student/Faculty Ratio: 19:1
Undergraduate Enrollment: 17,395
Scholarships/Academic: Yes   **Athletic:** Yes
Expenses By: Year   **In State:** $ 10,109.50
Degrees Conferred: BA, BS, BFA, MA, MS, MBA, Ph.D., MD

Founded: 1965
Religion: Non-Affiliated
Housing: Yes
Male/Female: 1:1
Graduate Enrollment: 2,373
Financial Aid: Yes
Out of State: $ 19,093.50

Programs of Study: Anthropology, Biological Sciences, Chemistry, Computer Science, Dance, Drama, Economics, Engineering, Fine Arts, Geography, Humanities, Mathematics, Music, Philosophy, Physical Science, Political Sciences, Psychology, Social Ecology, Social Sciences, Sociology

Men's Athletic Profile

West Peltason & California
Irvine, CA 92697-4125
Coach: Charlie Brande
Email: dgguerre@uci.edu
Estimated # of Men's Volleyball Scholarships: N/A
Conference: Big West Conference

NCAA I
Anteaters/Blue, Gold
Phone: (949) 824-6682
Fax: (949) 824-8492

Women's Athletic Profile

Crawford Hall
Irvine, CA 92697-4125
Coach: Merja Connolly-Freund
Email: Mcconnol@uci.edu

NCAA I
Lady Anteaters, Blue, Gold
Phone: (949) 824-3447
Fax: (949) 824-8492

Estimated # of Women's Volleyball Scholarships: 12
Conference: Big West Conference
Program Profile: Volleyball only facility-Crawford hall seats 2,000. Fully funded program competes in one of the nation's top conferences-the Big West Conference.
History: We are entering 14 years in the Big West Conference. UC-Irvine is one of the up and coming programs in the conference. Finishing in 8th place in 1998-UC-Irvine is aiming to go to the NCAA Tournament by finishing within the top 4.
Achievements: Larissa Carter - Junior was named All-Big West Selection-second team and All-Freshman team in 1997. Michelle Wong was All-Freshman team selection last season. Cavie Janisch-Sophomore was WPVA.
Coaching: Merja Connolly-Freundl is entering her fourth season as a Head Coach, was a UCLA All-American and national team member. Professional player in Italy and in the MVL (major league Volleyball-Minnesota Monarchs). Doug Tuttle and Travis Tudrie are the Assistant Coaches.

Freshman Receiving Financial Aid/Academic: **Athletic:** 3
Roster In State: 11   **Out of State:** 2   **Out of Country:** 0
Sophomores on Team: 2   **Seniors on Team:** 1   **Graduation %:** 100
Most Recent Record: 9-21-0   **Fall Games:** 28   **Spring Games:** 4
Camp of Clinic Dates: 1st week in August 2000
Schedule: Long Beach State, UCSB, University of Pacific, NAU, CPSLO, University of Nevada-Reno
Style of Play: Ball control and defense are our key focus. Fast offense - middle transition first. Hard work and attitude are stressed.

University of California - Los Angeles
Academic Profile

P.O. Box 24044
Los Angeles, CA 90024-0044

Phone: 310-825-3101

Type: Public, 4 Yr., Coed
Website: http://www.ucla.edu
SAT/ACT/GPA: 1000/21/3.0
Student/Faculty Ratio: 10:1
Undergraduate Enrollment: 23,000

Founded: 1919
Religion: Non-Affiliated
Housing: Yes
Male/Female: 1:1
Graduate Enrollment: 11,000

Scholarships/Academic: Yes   **Athletic:** Yes   **Financial Aid:** Yes

Expenses By: Year   **In State:** $ 12,000   **Out of State:** $ 21,000

Specializes In: Medical School, Business, Communications

Degrees Conferred: BA, BS, MA, MS, MBA

Programs of Study: Anthropology, Art, AstroPhysics, Biology, Classics, Computer, Cybernetics, Earth Science, English, Languages, Geology, GeoPhysics, History, International, Meteorology, Nursing, Religion, Seismology

Men's Athletic Profile

325 Westwood Plaza

Los Angeles, CA 90095-1405

Coach: Al Scates

Email:

NCAA I

Bruins/Blue, Gold

Phone: (310) 825-8699

Fax: (310) 206-7047

Estimated # of Men's Volleyball Scholarships: N/A

Conference: Mountain Pacific Sports Federation

Women's Athletic Profile

P.O. Box 24044

Los Angeles, CA 90095

Coach: Andy Banachowski

Email: wv@athletics.ucla.edu

NCAA I

Lady Bruins, Blue, Gold

Phone: (310) 206-6190

Fax: (310) 206-4269

Estimated # of Women's Volleyball Scholarships: 12

Conference: PAC-10 Conference

History: We have won 6 of the last National Championships.

Achievements: All-time win leader; 1998 Coach of the Year.

Coaching: Andy Banachowski, Head Coach, is an all-time winnings coach. Kim Jagd and Burt Fuller are Assistant Coaches.

Freshman Receiving Financial Aid/Academic: **Athletic:** 4

Roster In State: 13   **Out of State:** 5   **Out of Country:** 0

Sophomores on Team: 6   **Seniors on Team:** 2   **Graduation %:** Unknown

Most Recent Record: 15-11-0   **Fall Games:** 26   **Spring Games:** 5

Camp of Clinic Dates: Summer

Positions Needed: Setter, Hitter

Schedule: Top National schedule

Style of Play: We play fast rated, motivational caliber volleyball. We want to play and recruit to the best of our ability.

University of California - Riverside
Academic Profile

900 University Avenue

Riverside, CA 92521

Phone: (909) 787-5432

Type: Public, 4 Yr., Liberal Arts, Coed   **Founded:** 1954

Website: http://www.ucr.edu   **Religion:** Non-Affiliated

SAT/ACT/GPA: 3.4   **Housing:** Yes

Student/Faculty Ratio: 15:1   **Male/Female:** 45:54

Undergraduate Enrollment: 10,120   **Graduate Enrollment:**

Scholarships/Academic: Yes   **Athletic:** Yes   **Financial Aid:** Yes

Expenses By: Year   **In State:** $ 12,028   **Out of State:** $ 22,272

Specializes In: Biological Science, Liberal Arts, Entomology, Business

Degrees Conferred: BA, BS, MA, MS, MBA

Programs of Study: Anthropology, BioChemistry, Biology, Botany, Business, Comparative Literature, Classical Studies, Creative Writing, Engineering, Entomology, Geography, Geology, Languages, Law, Linguistic, Management, Music, Philosophy, Religion, Seismology, Soil Science, Sociology, Statistics, Theatre, Women's Studies

Women's Athletic Profile

900 University Avenue

Riverside, CA 92571

Coach: Sue Gozansky

Email: gozansky@math.ucr.edu

NCAA I

Lady Highlanders, Blue, Gold

Phone: (909) 787-5432

Fax: (909) 787-3569

Estimated # of Women's Volleyball Scholarships: 7
Conference: California Collegiate Athletic Association
Program Profile: Our Student Recreation Center has 3,000 seats. We participate in a 12 team conference and do a double round robin.
History: We have 3 National Championships. We received an NCAA record for consecutive appearances at the regional championships.
Achievements: 10 All-Americans; 2 National Players of the Year; 5 time Coach of the Year CCAA; 1 National Coach of the Year; 5 Professional players Europe and USA League.
Coaching: Sue Gozanzky has been Head Coach from 1970 to the present. Monica Trainer has been Assistant Coach from 1985 to the present.
Freshman Receiving Financial Aid/Academic: **Athletic:** 10
Roster In State: 12   **Out of State:** 0   **Out of Country:** 0
Sophomores on Team: 0   **Seniors on Team:** 4   **Graduation %:** 90
Most Recent Record: 24-9-0
Camp of Clinic Dates: August 16-21
Positions Needed: Middle Hitter, Outside Hitter
Schedule: Bakersfield, Irvine, California State University-Los Angeles, Brigham Young University, Hawaii Pacific
Style of Play: Quick tempo, scrambling defense, creative.

University of California - San Diego
Academic Profile

9500 Gillman Dr.
La Jolla, CA 92093

Phone: 619-534-4831

Type: Public, 4 Yr., Liberal Arts, Coed
Website: http://www.ucsd.edu
SAT/ACT/GPA: Required
Student/Faculty Ratio: 22:1
Undergraduate Enrollment: 13,500
Scholarships/Academic: Yes   **Athletic:** No
Expenses By: Year   **In State:** $ 1,629

Founded: 1959
Religion: Non-Affiliated
Housing: Yes
Male/Female: 51:49
Graduate Enrollment: 3,500
Financial Aid: Yes
Out of State: $ 4,426

Degrees Conferred: BA, BS,MA,MS, MFA, MD
Programs of Study: Anthropology, Art, Biochemistry, Biology, BioPhysics, Communications, Computer Science, Dramatic Arts, Earth Science, Ecology, Engineering, English, Foreign Languages, Linguistics, Mathematics, Microbiology, Molecular Biology, Music, Philosophy, Physics, Physiology, Political Science, Psychology, Quantitative Methods, Religion, Social Science, Visual Performing Arts

Men's Athletic Profile

9500 Gilman Drive
La Jolla, CA 92093
Coach: Jon Stevenson
Email:

NCAA III
Tritons/Blue, Gold
Phone: (619) 534-4211
Fax: (619) 534-8172

Estimated # of Men's Volleyball Scholarships: N/A
Conference: Independent

Women's Athletic Profile

0531, 9500 Gillman Drive
La Jolla, CA 92093
Coach: Duncan McFarland
Email: dncfarland@ucsd.edu

NCAA I
Lady Tritons, Blue, Gold
Phone: (619) 534-8443
Fax: (619) 534-8172

Did Not Return Profile

University of California - Santa Barbara
Academic Profile

University of California-Santa Barbara
Santa Barbara, CA 93106

Phone: (805) 893-2200

Type: Public, 4 Yr., Engineering, Coed
Website: http://www.gogauchos.ucsb.edu
SAT/ACT/GPA: 1200/20/3.7
Student/Faculty Ratio: 20:1
Undergraduate Enrollment: 17,059
Scholarships/Academic: Yes   **Athletic:** Yes
Expenses By: Year   **In State:** $ 13,700

Founded: 1909
Religion: Non-Affiliated
Housing: Yes
Male/Female: 47:53
Graduate Enrollment: 2,304
Financial Aid: Yes
Out of State: $ 23,274

Specializes In: Engineering & Sciences, English & Languages, Drama, Music
Degrees Conferred: BA, BS, BFA, MA, MS, MFA, Ph.D.
Programs of Study: Anthropology, Art, Art History, BioChemistry, Biology, Chemistry, Composition, Computer Science, Criminal Justice, Dance, Dramatic Art, Ecology & Evolution, Engineering, Economics, Film, Film Studies, French, Geography, History, Literature, Mathematics, Music, Physics Philosophy, Physics, Pharmacology, Physiology, Political Science, Psychology, Religion

Men's Athletic Profile

Dept. Athletics
Santa Barbara, CA 93106
Coach: Ken Preston
Email: media.relations@athletics.ucsb.edu

NCAA I
Gauchos/Blue, Gold
Phone: (805) 893-3291
Fax: (805) 893-7738

Estimated # of Men's Volleyball Scholarships: 4.5
Conference: Mountain Pacific Sports Federation
Program Profile: Our Events Center seats 6,000. Pre-Season is from October to November. Our playing season is from January through the NCAA Championships in May.
History: Our program began in the 1960's. We got second place in four different NCAA Championships.
Achievements: All-Americans : Eric Fonoimoana, Todd Rogers, Donny Harris, Robert Treachy
Coaching: Ken Preston has been Head Coach from 1979 to the present. He had an overall record of 382-235. Jon Roberts started here in 1995. Lee Nelson started here in 1998.
Freshman Receiving Financial Aid/Academic: **Athletic:** 2
Roster In State: 22   **Out of State:** 1   **Out of Country:** 2
Sophomores on Team: 4   **Seniors on Team:** 1   **Graduation %:** 94%
Most Recent Record: 10-13-0   **Fall Games:** 4   **Spring Games:** 26
Camp or Clinic Dates: Boy's Camp: July 12-16; Co-ed: July 24-28
Positions Needed: Middle Blockers
Schedule: University of California-Los Angeles, Stanford, Hawaii, Pepperdine, Long Beach State, University of Southern California

Women's Athletic Profile

Dept. of Athletics
Santa Barbara, CA 93106
Coach: Kathy Gregory
Email:

NCAA I
Lady Gauchos, Blue, Gold
Phone: (805) 893-3291
Fax: (805) 893-7738

Estimated # of Women's Volleyball Scholarships: 12
Conference: Big West Conference
Program Profile: We are a perennial top 10 program playing in the Big West Conference. We participated in every NCAA Tournament and finished in the top 8 in 1997. We received 3rd ranking in the nation in 1998. Our home matches are in the Thunder dome, a 6,000 seat arena.. We are 18 time NCAA qualifiers and one of 4 schools to compete in all 18. We play from August 12 to December 20.
History: The program has been in existence for 24 years, all of which Kathy Gregory has been Head Coach. We have participated in all NCAA Championships. We compete in the Big West Conference. We have more National Championships than any other team.
Achievements: 1998 Ranked #3 in the Nation Sweet Sixteen; 1 All-American, 1997 Ranked #4 in the Nation Elite Eight; 2 All-Americans; 1993 NCAA Coach of the Year.
Coaching: Kathy Gregory, Head Coach, started coaching the program in 1974. She compiled a record of 599-262. She has a 700% winning percentage. She was named Women's Beach Player of the Year in 1976, 1977, 1978, 1981 & 1982. She was named to the Volleyball Hall of Fame.
Freshman Receiving Financial Aid/Academic: **Athletic:** 5
Roster In State: 10   **Out of State:** 2   **Out of Country:** 0
Sophomores on Team: 0   **Seniors on Team:** 4   **Graduation %:** 90
Most Recent Record: 28-6-0   **Fall Games:** 34   **Spring Games:** 0
Camp of Clinic Dates: July 21-24, 1999
Positions Needed: Middle, Outside Hitter
Schedule: University of Pacific, Long Beach State, University of Florida, Pepperdine, Florida State, Oral Roberts
Style of Play: Ball control and defense. Aggressive physical, dynamic, excellent work ethic, relentless pursuit, fast and fun.

University of California - Santa Cruz
Academic Profile

1056 High Street
Santa Cruz, CA 95064

Phone: (831) 459-2531

Type: Public, 4 Yr., Liberal Arts, Engineering, Coed
Website: http://www.ucsc.edu
SAT/ACT/GPA: 1000/3.4
Student/Faculty Ratio: 13:1
Undergraduate Enrollment: 10,000
Scholarships/Academic: Yes
Expenses By: Year
Specializes In: Natural Sciences, Engineering
Degrees Conferred: BA, BS, Masters, Doctoral
Programs of Study: Over 150 programs of study.

Athletic: No
In State: $ 14,598

Founded: 1965
Religion: Non-Affiliated
Housing: Yes
Male/Female: 40:60
Graduate Enrollment: 1,000
Financial Aid: Yes
Out of State: $ 25,110

Men's Athletic Profile

1156 High Street
Santa Cruz, CA 95064
Coach: Ralph Smith
Email:

NCAA III
Banana Slug/Navy Blue, Gold
Phone: (408) 459-2531
Fax: (408) 459-4070

Estimated # of Men's Volleyball Scholarships: 0
Conference: Independent
Program Profile: We primarily play Division I Schools. We play in the Slug Dome, also known as the West Field House, which seats 300 people.
History: We have a fairly young program which has only existed since 1980. Last year, the Slugs were ranked 10th in the Division III. Two years ago, the Slugs had their best ranking of 5th in the Nation.
Coaching: Ralph Smith is entering his second year as Head Coach of the Slugs. He is a former National player. He was an All-American on the Long Beach State team. Jay Hosack is assistant coach.
Freshman Receiving Financial Aid/Academic:

Athletic:

Roster In State: 8
Sophomores on Team: 2

Out of State: 4
Seniors on Team: 3

Out of Country: 1
Graduation %: 100%

Schedule: Brigham Young University, University of California-LA, University of Southern California, Cal Tech, Pepperdine, Ohio State University

Women's Athletic Profile

East Field House
Santa Cruz, CA 95064
Coach: Cindy Mori
Email:

NCAA I
Lady Banana Slugs, Blue, Gold
Phone: (831) 459-2531
Fax: (831) 459-4070

Estimated # of Women's Volleyball Scholarships: 0
Conference: Independent
Program Profile: We are consistently one of the top teams in the West Region. The Slugs play in a loud gym, known as the West Field House which seats about 300.
Achievements: Cindy Mori was All-PAC Conference Setter for the University of Arizona Wildcats.
Coaching: Cindy Mori has been head coach here for 15 years. She played volleyball at the University of Arizona where she was named Most Valuable Player in 1979.
Freshman Receiving Financial Aid/Academic:

Athletic: Yes

Roster In State: 13
Sophomores on Team: 6
Most Recent Record: 10-16-0

Out of State: 0
Seniors on Team: 1
Fall Games: 26

Out of Country: 0
Graduation %: 100
Spring Games: 0

Camp of Clinic Dates: General Skills: July 12-16; General Skills: July 19-23; General Skills/High School: July 26-30
Positions Needed: All
Schedule: University of California-San Diego, Willamette University, Linfield College, George Fox College, California State University-Hayward, College of Notre Dame
Style of Play: Aggressive and defensive.

University of La Verne
Academic Profile

1950 Third Street
La Verne, CA 91750

Phone: 800-876-4858

Type: Private, 4 Yr., Liberal Arts, Coed
Website: http://www.uv.edu
SAT/ACT/GPA: Open
Student/Faculty Ratio: 15:1
Undergraduate Enrollment: 1,100
Scholarships/Academic: Yes   **Athletic:** No
Expenses By: Year   **In State:** $ 18,100
Specializes In: Business, Teacher
Degrees Conferred: BA, BS, MA, MS, MBA, EdD, JD

Founded: 1891
Religion: Non-Affiliated
Housing: Yes
Male/Female: 3:1
Graduate Enrollment: 3,000
Financial Aid: Yes
Out of State: $ 18,100

Programs of Study: Arts and Sciences, Athletic, Business Management, Communications, Computer, Economics, Engineering, Law, Physical, PreProfessional, Social Sciences, Teacher Preparation, Visual and Performing Arts

Men's Athletic Profile

1950 3rd Street
La Verne, CA 91750
Coach: Jack Coberly
Email:

NCAA III
Leopards/Dark Green, Orange
Phone: (909) 593-3511
Fax: (909) 392-2760

Estimated # of Men's Volleyball Scholarships: N/A
Conference: Southern California Intercollegiate Athletic Conference

Women's Athletic Profile

1950 Third Street
La Verne, CA 91750
Coach: Don Flora
Email: florad@ulv.edu

NCAA I
Lady Leopards, Green, Orange
Phone: (909) 593-3511
Fax: (909) 392-2760

Estimated # of Women's Volleyball Scholarships: 0
Conference: SCIAC
Program Profile: We play a traditional season. We have a new wood court and a 500 seat gym. We have a long tradition of winning conference championships and getting national ranking.
History: Our program started in the 1960's. In 1981, we were NAIA National Champions. In 1982, we were NCAA III National Champions. Since 1980, we have won 13 Conference Championships and have been to the National playoffs for 15 years.
Achievements: 13 Conference Championships; 16 All-Americans; Jimmy Paschal was Coach of the Year in 1982 and Regional Coach of the Year in 1989.
Coaching: Don Flora became head coach in 1998 and was assistant coach from 1993 to 1997. His overall record here is 12-13. Randi Winn has been Assistant Coach since 1998.
Freshman Receiving Financial Aid/Academic: **Athletic:** 0
Roster In State: 12   **Out of State:** 0   **Out of Country:** 0
Sophomores on Team: 2   **Seniors on Team:** 2   **Graduation %:** 90
Most Recent Record: 12-13-0   **Fall Games:** 25   **Spring Games:** 0
Camp of Clinic Dates: First three weeks in August
Positions Needed: Setters, Middles, OPP
Schedule: University of California-San Diego, Cal Lutheran, Wisconsin Stout, Illinois Benedictine, Azusa Pacific, Wisconsin Stevens Point
Style of Play: We play a fast tempo, intense, competitive style. We stress strong ball control and aggressive blocking tactics.

University of Redlands
Academic Profile

1200 E Colton Avenue
Redlands, CA 92373

Phone: (909) 793-2121

Type: Private, 4 Yr., Liberal Arts, Coed
Website: http://www.redlands.edu
SAT/ACT/GPA: 1100/19/3.2
Student/Faculty Ratio: 13:1

Founded: 1909
Religion: Non-Affiliated
Housing: Yes
Male/Female: 56:44

Undergraduate Enrollment: 1,560

Graduate Enrollment: 500

Scholarships/Academic: Yes   **Athletic:** No   **Financial Aid:** Yes

Expenses By: Year   **In State:** $ 27,000   **Out of State:** $ 27,000

Specializes In: Liberal Arts

Degrees Conferred: BS, BA

Programs of Study: Accounting, Art, History/Studio Art, Asian Studies, Biology, Business Administration, Chemistry, Communicative Disorders, Computer Science, Creative Writing, Economics, English Literature, Environmental Studies, French, German, Government, History, International Relations, Latin American Studies, Math, Music, Philosophy, Physics, PreLaw, PreMed, Psychology, Race and Ethnic Studies, Religion, Sociology, Anthropology, Spanish, Theatre, Women's Studies, Interdisciplinary Minor

Women's Athletic Profile

P.O. Box 3080, 1200 E. Colton Avenue

Redlands, CA 92373

Coach: Paul Gianni

Email: gianni@jasper.uor.edu

NCAA I

Lady Bulldogs, Maroon, Grey

Phone: (909) 793-2121

Fax: (909) 335-4088

Estimated # of Women's Volleyball Scholarships: N/A

Conference: Southern California Intercollegiate Athletic Conference

University of San Diego
Academic Profile

5998 Alcala Park

San Diego, CA 92111

Type: Private, 4 Yr., Coed

Website: http://www.acusd.edu

SAT/ACT/GPA: 1150/3.7

Student/Faculty Ratio: 15:1

Undergraduate Enrollment: 4,000

Scholarships/Academic: No   **Athletic:** No

Expenses By: Year   **In State:** $ 26,205

Phone: (619) 260-2306

Founded: 1949

Religion: Roman Catholic

Housing: Yes

Male/Female: 45:55

Graduate Enrollment: 2,500

Financial Aid: Yes

Out of State: $ 26,205

Degrees Conferred: BA, BS, MA, MS, MFA, MEd, EdD, JD

Programs of Study: Accounting, Art, Biology, Business Administration, Chemistry, Communications, Computer Science, Diversified Liberal Arts, Broadcasting, Chemical Engineering, Economics, Electrical Engineering, English, Exercise & Sports Science, Geology, Health Education, Hispanic/Latin Studies, History, Humanities, Journalism, Mathematics, Music, Nursing, Ocean Studies, Pharmacy, Political Science, Psychology, Religious Studies, Sociology, Zoology

Women's Athletic Profile

5998 Alcala Park

San Diego, CA 92110-2492

Coach: Jennifer Torns

Email: mturley@acusd.edu

NCAA I

Lady Toreros, Blue, White

Phone: (619) 260-5909

Fax: (619) 260-2990

Estimated # of Women's Volleyball Scholarships: 12

Conference: West Coast Conference

Program Profile: We play at Jenny Craig Pavilion which opened in October of 2000 and seats 5,100.

History: The program began 1975.

Achievements: 3 Coach of the Year honors-Sue Snyder; 2 West Coast Conference Championships; 5 trips to the NCAA.

Coaching: Jennifer Torns, Head Coach, began coaching at USD in 1990. She produced six All-West region players. She has an average of 21 wins per season. She was WCC Coach of the Year and serves on the AVCA Ranking committee and the NCAA All-Region Selection Committee. She captured the first WCC Championship in the program's history.

Roster In State: 12   **Out of State:** 11   **Out of Country:** 0

Seniors on Team: 1   **Graduation %:** 100

Positions Needed: Outside hitter

Schedule: Arizona, Maryland, Georgetown, Loyola Marymount, Pepperdine, Santa Clara

University of San Francisco
Academic Profile

2130 Fulton St. Ignatian Hts

San Francisco, CA 94117-1080

Phone: (415) 422-6563

Type: Private, 4 Yr., Liberal Arts,Coed
Website: http://www.usfca.edu
SAT/ACT/GPA: Yes
Student/Faculty Ratio: 18-25:1
Undergraduate Enrollment: 5,000
Scholarships/Academic: Yes   **Athletic:** Yes
Expenses By: Year   **In State:** $ 26,348
Founded: 1855
Religion: Catholic (Jesuit)
Housing: Yes
Male/Female: 40:60
Graduate Enrollment: 2,000
Financial Aid: Yes
Out of State: $ 26,348
Specializes In: Business, International Business, Broadcasting, Nursing, Biology
Degrees Conferred: BS, MS, Ph.D.
Programs of Study: Biology, Business, Chemistry, Communications, Computer Economics, Environmental Science, English, History, Law , (MBA), Nursing, PrePhysical Therapy, Psychology, Sports Science, Exercise Sports Science, Communications

Women's Athletic Profile

2130 Fulton Street
San Francisco, CA 94117
Coach: David Noble
Email: nobled@usfca.edu

NCAA I
Lady Dons, Green, Gold
Phone: (415) 422-2908
Fax: (415) 422-2510

Estimated # of Women's Volleyball Scholarships: N/A
Conference: West Coast Conference
Achievements: USJO Outstanding Coach Award
Coaching: David Noble has been Head Coach for two years. He is building the program. He led the NIKE team to the Gold Medal at the USAV Olympics in 1995.
Freshman Receiving Financial Aid/Academic: N/A   **Athletic:** N/A
Camp of Clinic Dates: General Skills: July 8-11; High Potential: July 15-18

University of Southern California
Academic Profile

1026 W 34th Street
Los Angeles, CA 90059-2511

Phone: 213-740-1111

Type: Private, 4 Yr., Coed
Website: http://www.usctrojans.com
SAT/ACT/GPA: Open
Undergraduate Enrollment: 14,470
Scholarships/Academic: Yes   **Athletic:** Yes
Expenses By: Year   **In State:** $ 30,126
Founded: 1880
Religion: Non-Affiliated
Housing: No
Graduate Enrollment: N/A
Financial Aid: Yes
Out of State:
Degrees Conferred:
Programs of Study: 197 Undergraduate Majors: 31 Graduate and Professional Programs, 110 Areas of Study including Business and Management, Communications, Engineering, Social Science, Visual and Performing Arts

Men's Athletic Profile

103 Heritage Hall
Los Angeles, CA 90089-0012
Coach: Pat Powers
Email:

NCAA I
Trojans/Cardinal, Gold
Phone: (213) 740-6829
Fax: (213) 740-1306

Estimated # of Men's Volleyball Scholarships: N/A
Conference: Mountain Pacific Sports Federation

Women's Athletic Profile

Heritage Hall
Los Angeles, CA 90089-0012
Coach: Jerritt Elliott
Email: Llove@almaak.usc.edu

NCAA I
Lady Trojans, Cardinal Gold
Phone: (213) 740-6560
Fax: (213) 740-1306

Estimated # of Women's Volleyball Scholarships: 4
Conference: Pacific 10 Conference

Program Profile: We are one of the premier volleyball programs in the country with 4 National Titles. We compete in the Pacific 10 Conference.

Achievements: We have 22 Olympians, 10 Freshman of the Year, 39 All-Americans, 5 Academic All-Americans, 53 All-Conference and 1 Valedictorian players.

Coaching: Jerritt Elliott, Interim Head Coach. Erikka Gorranson and Paula Weihoffe are the Assistant Coaches.

Freshman Receiving Financial Aid/Academic: **Athletic:** 3

Roster In State: 11

raduation %: 100

Most Recent Record: 24-6-0

Positions Needed: Middle Blocker, Outside Hitters

Schedule: Stanford, UCLA, LB State, Arizona, Hawaii, Arizona State

Style of Play: We have tremendous ball control, which will allow us to run a highly excellent offense.

University of the Pacific
Academic Profile

3601 Pacific Avenue   **Phone:** (209) 926-2497
Stockton, CA 95211

Type: Private, 4 Yr., Liberal Arts, Coed   **Founded:** 1851
Website: http://www.pacifictigers.com   **Religion:** Non-Affiliated
SAT/ACT/GPA: No minimum   **Housing:** Yes
Student/Faculty Ratio: 13:6   **Male/Female:** 43:57
Undergraduate Enrollment: 2,805   **Graduate Enrollment:** 562
Scholarships/Academic: Yes   **Athletic:** Yes   **Financial Aid:** Yes
Expenses By: Year   **In State:** $ 25,485   **Out of State:** $ 25,485
Specializes In: Art & Sciences, Business, Education, Engineering, Nursing
Degrees Conferred: BA, BS, BFA, MA, MS, Ph.D., PharmD
Programs of Study: Accounting, Advertising, Athletic Training, Behavioral, Biology, Broadcasting, Business, Computer, Criminal, Engineering, Environmental Sciences, Finance, Geology, Linguistics, Ministries, Natural Science, Pharmacy, Spanish

Men's Athletic Profile

3601 Pacific Avenue   **NCAA I**
Stockton, CA 95211   Tigers/Orange, Black
Coach: Joe Wortmann   **Phone:** (209) 946-2724
Email: **Fax:** (209) 946-2731

Estimated # of Men's Volleyball Scholarships: N/A
Conference: Mountain Pacific Sports Federation

Women's Athletic Profile

3601 Pacific Avenue   **NCAA I**
Stockton, CA 95211   Tigers, Orange, Black
Coach: John Dunning   **Phone:** (209) 946-2479
Email: uopathl@inreach.com   **Fax:** (209) 946-2757
Estimated # of Women's Volleyball Scholarships: Yes
Conference: Big West Conference

Program Profile: We are a nationally recognized program. We have a Fall competitive season. We have first-class facilities that include the Alex G. Spanos Center (6,150 seats), an athletic performance center, an athletic training center and a student-athlete resource center.

History: The Pacific women's volleyball program began in 1975. Over the past, 24 years, Pacific has been in NCAA Championships (18 total), 16 NCAA Regional and 6 NCAA Final Fours. We have posted 20 or more wins in each of the last 21 seasons.

Achievements: Pacific boasts two former Olympians; 4 U.S. National members; 40 All-American selections; 3 National Coach of the Year awards; 16 Academic All-American ; 90 All-Conference picks.

Coaching: John Dunning, Head Coach, started here in 1985. His overall record is 377-95. He was 1985 National Coach of the Year. Associate Coach Jayne Gibson-McHugh started here in 1989. She was a 1988 Olympian. Assistant Coach Mas Shibata began coaching here in 1990.

Freshman Receiving Financial Aid/Academic: **Athletic:** 3

Roster In State: 11	**Out of State:** 4	**Out of Country:** 1
Sophomores on Team: 2	**Seniors on Team:** 2	**Graduation %:** 99
Most Recent Record: 26-6-0	**Fall Games:** 32	**Spring Games:** varies

Camp of Clinic Dates: Setter Camps: July 15-18, July 20-23; Advance All-Skills: July 9-13;Excell All-Skills:July25-28
Positions Needed: None
Schedule: Long Beach State, Nebraska, Penn State, Florida, Louisville, University of California- Santa Barbara, Stanford

Vanguard University of Southern California
Academic Profile

55 Fair Drive
Costa Mesa, CA 92626

Phone: (714) 556-3610

Type: Private, 4 Yr., Liberal Arts, Coed
Website: http://www.vanguard.edu
SAT/ACT/GPA: 740+/18+/2.8
Student/Faculty Ratio: 16:1
Undergraduate Enrollment: 1,181
Scholarships/Academic: Yes   **Athletic:** Yes
Expenses By: Year   **In State:** $ 14,500
Specializes In: Liberal Arts
Degrees Conferred: BA, MA, MS, MTS

Founded: 1920
Religion: Assembly of God
Housing: Yes
Male/Female: 2:3
Graduate Enrollment: 134
Financial Aid: Yes
Out of State: $ 14,500

Programs of Study: Accounting, Biology, Anthropology, Broadcasting, Chemistry, Communications, Education, English, Finance, Humanities, Journalism, Management, Marketing, Mathematics, Physical Education, PreLaw, PreMed, Social Science, Sociology

Women's Athletic Profile

55 Fair Drive
Costa Mesa, CA 92626
Coach: Carin Avery
Email:

NCAA I
Lady Vanguards, Blue, Gold
Phone: (714) 556-3610
Fax: (714) 668-6144

Did Not Return Profile

Westmont College
Academic Profile

955 La Paz Road
Santa Barbara, CA 93108

Phone: (805) 565-6221

Type: Private, 4 Yr., Liberal Arts, Coed
Website: http://www.westmont.edu
SAT/ACT/GPA: 1200/3.0
Student/Faculty Ratio: 15:1
Undergraduate Enrollment: Yes
Scholarships/Academic: Yes   **Athletic:** Yes
Expenses By: Year   **In State:** $ 25,000
Specializes In: Liberal Arts
Degrees Conferred: BS, BA

Founded: 1937
Religion: Non-Denominational
Housing: Yes
Male/Female: 40:60
Graduate Enrollment: N/A
Financial Aid: Yes
Out of State: $ 25,000

Programs of Study: Art, Biology, Business, Chemistry, Communications, Computer Science, Economics, Education, Engineering, English, French, History, Kinesiology, Mathematics, Music, Natural Sciences, Philosophy, Physics, Political Science, Psychology, Religious Studies, Social Science, Sociology, Spanish, Theatre Arts

Women's Athletic Profile

955 La Paz Rd.
Santa Barbara, CA 93108
Coach: Jim Smoot
Email:

NCAA I
Lady Warriors, Maroon, White
Phone: (805) 565-7303
Fax: (805) 565-6220

Did Not Return Profile

Whittier College
Academic Profile

13406 E. Philadelphia

Phone: 562-907-4238

Whittier, CA 90608

Type: Private, 4 Yr., Liberal Arts, Coed
Website: http://www.whittier.edu
SAT/ACT/GPA: 1100/21/3.0
Student/Faculty Ratio: 13:1
Undergraduate Enrollment: 1,300
Scholarships/Academic: Yes
Expenses By: Year
Specializes In: Liberal Arts
Degrees Conferred: BA, BS, MA, MS, JD

Athletic: No
In State: $ 26,096

Founded: 1887
Religion: Non-Affiliated
Housing: Yes
Male/Female: 50:50
Graduate Enrollment: 100
Financial Aid: Yes
Out of State:

Programs of Study: Anthropology, Art, Athletic Training, Biochemistry, Biology, Business & Management, Chemistry, Economics, Education, English, Fine Arts, French, Geology, History, International Studies, Liberal Arts, Literature, Mathematics, Modern Languages, Music, Philosophy, Physical Education, Physical Science, Physics, Political Science, PreDentistry, PreLaw, PreMed, PreVet, Psychology, Religion, Social Science, Spanish, Speech Pathology, Theatre

Women's Athletic Profile

13406 E. Philadelphia
Whittier, CA 90608
Coach: Kristi Vandenberg
Email: kvandenberg@whittier.edu

NCAA I
Lady Poets, Purple, Gold
Phone: (562) 907-4976
Fax: (562) 945-8024

Estimated # of Women's Volleyball Scholarships: N/A
Conference: Southern California Intercollegiate Athletic Conference

COLORADO

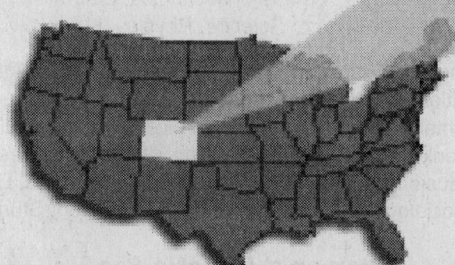

Denver

SCHOOL	CITY	AFFILIATION	PAGE
Adams State College	Alamosa	NCAA II	121
Colorado Christian University	Lakewood	NCAA II	121
Colorado College	Colorado Springs	NCAA III	122
Colorado School of Mines	Golden	NCAA II	123
Colorado State University	Fort Collins	NCAA I	123
Fort Lewis College	Durango	NCAA II	124
Mesa State college	Grand Junction	NCAA II	124
Metropolitan State College	Denver	NCAA II	125
Northeastern Junior College	Sterling	NJCAA	126
Regis University	Denver	NCAA II	126
United States Air Force Academy	Colorado Springs	NCAA I	127
University of Colorado	Boulder	NCAA I	128
Univ of Colorado-CO Springs	Colorado Springs	NCAA II	128
University of Denver	Denver	NCAA I	129
University of Northern Colorado	Greeley	NCAA II	130
University of Southern Colorado	Pueblo	NCAA II	130
Western State College	Gunnison	NCAA II	131

Adams State College
Academic Profile

208 Edgemont
Alamosa, CO 81102

Phone: 719-587-7712

Type: Public, 4 Yr., Liberal Arts, Coed
Website: http://www.adams.edu
SAT/ACT/GPA: Not required/21.4/3.21
Student/Faculty Ratio: 20/1
Undergraduate Enrollment: 2500
Scholarships/Academic: Yes   **Athletic:** Yes
Expenses By: Year   **In State:** $8006
Specializes In: Education
Degrees Conferred: BA, BS, MA, M.Ed.

Founded: 1921
Religion: Non-Affiliated
Housing: Yes
Male/Female: 1/2
Graduate Enrollment: 300
Financial Aid: Yes
Out of State: $12,402

Programs of Study: Accounting, Advertising, Art Education, Art/Fine Arts, Art History, Athletic Training, Biology, Biological Science, Botany, Plant Science, Business Administration, Commerce, Management, Business Education, Chemistry, Communications, Computer Science, Criminal Justice, PreDental, Earth Science, Economics, Education, Elementary Education, PreEngineering, English, Environmental Science, Finance/Banking, Geology, Liberal Arts, General Studies, History, International Business, Journalism, Mathematics, Medical Technology, Music, Music Education, Painting, Drawing, Physical Education, Physical Fitness, Physics, Political Science, Psychology, Science Education, Sociology, Spanish, Secondary Education, Studio Art, Theatre Art/Drama

Women's Athletic Profile

Stadium Drive
Alamosa, CO 81102
Coach: Penny Groves
Email:

NCAA I
Lady Grizzles, Green, White
Phone: (719) 587-7842
Fax: (719) 587-7276

Estimated # of Women's Volleyball Scholarships: 4
Conference: Rocky Mountain Athletic Conference
Program Profile: Competitive Division II program. Very nice stadium and field house for tournament and camps. Play both fall and spring seasons.
Achievements: New Coach
Coaching: P. Groves 1st year 10th over all college 115-124.
Chris Rodgers 2nd year At Adams
Joann Branno 1st year at Adams
Freshman Receiving Financial Aid/Academic: **Athletic:** 2
Roster In State: 9   **Out of State:** 5   **Out of Country:**
Seniors on Team: 1   **Graduation %:** 95
Most Recent Record: 8-18   **Fall Games:** 26   **Spring Games:** 4 Dates
Camp of Clinic Dates: July
Positions Needed: Setter
Style of Play: New Coach-will have to see the personality of this team.

Colorado Christian University
Academic Profile

180 S Garrison St.
Lakewood, CO 80226

Phone: 800-443-2484

Type: Private, 4 Yr., Liberal Arts, Coed
Website: http://www.ccu.edu
SAT/ACT/GPA: NCAA Requirements
Student/Faculty Ratio: 16:1
Undergraduate Enrollment: 850
Scholarships/Academic: Yes   **Athletic:** Yes
Expenses By: Year   **In State:** $ 15,680
Degrees Conferred: BA, BS

Founded: 1914
Religion: Non-denominational
Housing: Yes
Male/Female: 48:52
Graduate Enrollment: 2000
Financial Aid: Yes
Out of State: $ 15,680

Programs of Study: Accounting, American Studies, Art, Biblical Studies, Biology, Broadcasting, Business Administration, Christian Leadership, Communication, Computer Applications, Computer Information Systems, Computer Information Systems Management, English, ESOL, Family Studies, Health and Physical Education, History-Political Science, Latin American Studies, Liberal Arts, Management of Human Resources, Mathematics, Middle East Studies, Missions, Music, Organizational Management, Professional Counseling Certificate, Psychology, Russian Studies, Science, Youth Ministries

Women's Athletic Profile

180 S. Garrison
Lakewood, CO 80226
Coach: Dave Foster
Email:

NCAA I
Cougars, Blue, White, Gold
Phone: (303) 238-5388x221
Fax: (303) 234-1217

Estimated # of Women's Volleyball Scholarships: Open
Conference: Rocky Mountain Athletic Conference
Program Profile: We are a "Christ-centered" program with a strong push for education. We receive the largest crowds out of any CCU sport. Training is year round, with an emphasis on strength and conditioning.
History: Volleyball began in 1990. Since that time CCU volleyball has established itself as a powerhouse in NCAA volleyball. We have been national ranked for the past 7 years and continue to make post-season play.
Achievements: 3 All-Region, 5 All-Conference, 1998 Co-Champions for RMAC Title Top 25 in the Nation, Continue to make post-Season play.
Coaching: Ed Garrett-Coaching for the past 12 years, 1994-97-Assistant with USA Men's Olympic team, 1996 Manager of USA Beach Teams in Atlanta, ASICS Clinician, coaching philosophy-"Christ, education, volleyball-in that order".
Freshman Receiving Financial Aid/Academic: | | **Athletic:** 4
Roster In State: 5 | **Out of State:** 5 | **Out of Country:**
Seniors on Team: 2 | **Graduation %:** 95
Most Recent Record: 12-2
Camp of Clinic Dates: Call for information
Positions Needed: Open
Schedule: Regis University, Nebraska Kearny, West Texas A&M, Florida Southern, Abilene Christian University of North Colorado, Metro State, Western State, University of Southern Colorado
Style of Play: We are a family before we are a team. We practice hard and we play even harder!

Colorado College
Academic Profile

14 E Cache La Poudre
Colorado Springs, CO 80903

Phone: (719) 389-6000

Type: Private, 4 Yr., Liberal Arts, Coed
Website: http://www.cc.colorado.edu
SAT/ACT/GPA: 1200-1350/25-30
Student/Faculty Ratio: 11:1
Undergraduate Enrollment: 1,900
Scholarships/Academic: Yes
Expenses By: Year
Specializes In: Sciences, Education
Degrees Conferred: BA, MAT
Programs of Study: Liberal Arts and Sciences

Founded: 1874
Religion: Non-Affiliated
Housing: Yes
Male/Female: 42:58
Graduate Enrollment: N/A
Athletic: Yes | **Financial Aid:** Yes
In State: $ 27,390 | **Out of State:** $ 27,390

Women's Athletic Profile

14 E. Cache La Poudre
Colorado Springs, CO 80903
Coach: Rick Swan
Email: rswan@cc.colorado.edu

NCAA I
Lady Tigers, Black, Gold
Phone: (719) 389-6485
Fax: (719) 389-6256

Estimated # of Women's Volleyball Scholarships: N/A
Conference: Independent
History: Our program began in 1979 and had 11 post-season appearances.
Achievements: We have had 8 All-Americans.
Coaching: Rick Swan is our Head Coach. He compiled a record of 15-11 in 1998. Karen Warnock is our Assistant Coach.
Freshman Receiving Financial Aid/Academic: | | **Athletic:** 0
Roster In State: 7 | **Out of State:** 8 | **Out of Country:** 0
Sophomores on Team: 3 | **Seniors on Team:** 4 | **Graduation %:** 95
Most Recent Record: 15-11-0 | **Fall Games:** 26 | **Spring Games:** 10
Positions Needed: Setter, Outside Hitter
Schedule: Wartburg, George Fox, Linfield, Willamette, Eastern Community State University, Pomona Pitzer
Style of Play: Quick offense, scrappy defense and great ball control.

Colorado School of Mines
Academic Profile

1500 Illinois Street
Golden, CO 80401

Phone: 303-273-3220

Type: Public, 4 Yr., Engineering, Coed
Website: http://www.gn.mines.colorado.edu
SAT/ACT/GPA: 1100/3.3
Student/Faculty Ratio: 25:1
Undergraduate Enrollment: 2,200
Scholarships/Academic: Yes   **Athletic:** Yes
Expenses By: Year   **In State:** $ 10,000
Specializes In: Engineering, Math, Science, Computers
Degrees Conferred: BS, MS, MEng, Ph.D.
Programs of Study: Engineering (Chemical, Geological, Geophysical, Metallurgical/Materials, Mining, Petroleum), Chemistry, Economics, Mathematics, Physics

Founded: 1870
Religion: Non-Affiliated
Housing: Yes
Male/Female: 70:30
Graduate Enrollment: 800
Financial Aid: Yes
Out of State: $ 20,000

Women's Athletic Profile

1500 Illinois Street
Golden, CO 80401
Coach: Michelle Harris
Email: mharris@mines.edu

NCAA I
Lady Orediggers, Silver, Blue
Phone: (303) 273-337
Fax: (303) 273-3362

Did Not Return Profile

Colorado State University
Academic Profile

Department of Athletics
Fort Collins, CO 80523

Phone: (970) 491-0214

Type: Public, 4 Yr., Coed
Website: http://www.colostate.edu
SAT/ACT/GPA: All areas are evaluated for admissions
Student/Faculty Ratio: 22:1
Undergraduate Enrollment: 22,000
Scholarships/Academic: Yes   **Athletic:** Yes
Expenses By: Year   **In State:** $ 9,199
Specializes In: Agricultural
Degrees Conferred: BA, BS, BFA, BMus, MA, MS, MBA, MFA, M.Ed., Ph.D.
Programs of Study: Accounting, Actuarial Science, Agricultural Business, Agricultural Economics, Agricultural Education, Agricultural Engineering, Agricultural Science, Agronomy, Soil and Crop Sciences, American Studies, Animal Science, Anthropology, Applied Mathematics, Art Education, Ceramic Art, Biology, Biological Science, Art History, Family Studies, Civil Engineering, Computer Information Systems, Computer Science, Construction Technology, Economics, Electrical Engineering, Creative Writing, Physics, Entomology, Farm and Ranch Management, Human Development, Humanities, Journalism, Fish and Game Management, Home Economics, Philosophy, MicroBiology, Natural Resources, Occupational Therapy, Photography, Food Science, Political Science, Real Estate, Textile Arts, Social Work, Social Science, Veterinary Medicine, Water Resources

Founded: 1862
Religion: Non-Affiliated
Housing: Yes
Male/Female: 50:50
Graduate Enrollment: 3,630
Financial Aid: Yes
Out of State: $ 16,892

Women's Athletic Profile

203 McGraw Athletic Center
Fort Collins, CO 80523-0100
Coach: Tom Hilbert
Email: ramvball@lamar.colostate.edu

NCAA I
Rams, Green, Gold
Phone: (970) 491-6582
Fax: (970) 491-7725

Estimated # of Women's Volleyball Scholarships: 4
Conference: Mountian West
Program Profile: CSU Volleyball has made 6 consecutive trips to the NCAA Championships with two straight years in the sweet sixteen. CSU has been nationally ranked each of those years (highest ranking 3rd). We play in Moby Arena and average over 2000 fans per match (8th national in attendance).
History: Program started in 1977. Program has been nationally ranked and in the NCAA tourney 12 times since 1983. CSU has strong history as one of the nations best programs.

Achievements: CSU Volleyball has had 6 All-Americans since 1985 and one Olympian. We have won our conference title 5 times 84, 85, 98, 00. We have won our conference tournament once in 99. Tom Hilbert has been named conference Coach of the Year 3 times.

Coaching: Tom Hilbert has been coaching at CSU since 1997. Priorto that he spent 8 years at the University of Idaho and 5 years as an Assistant at Oklahoma. Karrie Larsen was a member of the US womens national team in 1997-98. Spent one year at Clemson before joining Tom Hilberts Staff. Andy Klussman was a two time national champion at UCLA then a member of the AVP and Bud Light four man tour for eight years. He joined the CSU staff in 2000.

Freshman Receiving Financial Aid/Academic: **Athletic:** 3

Roster In State: 4   **Out of State:** 6   **Out of Country:** 2

Seniors on Team: 3   **Graduation %:** 95

Most Recent Record: 32-5

Camp of Clinic Dates: July 8-11, July 27-30

Positions Needed: 2 MB, OH

Schedule: BYU, Utah, Arkansas, San Diego, Georgia Tech

Style of Play: Intense and Fast.

Fort Lewis College
Academic Profile

1000 Rim Drive   **Phone:** (970) 247-7571
Durango, CO 81301

Type: Public, 4 Yr., Liberal Arts, Coed   **Founded:** 1892

Website: http://www.fortlewis.edu   **Religion:** Non-Affiliated

SAT/ACT/GPA: Sliding Scale   **Housing:** Yes

Student/Faculty Ratio: 23:1   **Male/Female:** 51:49

Undergraduate Enrollment: 4,314   **Graduate Enrollment:** N/A

Scholarships/Academic: Yes   **Athletic:** Yes   **Financial Aid:** Yes

Expenses By: Year   **In State:** $ 5,322   **Out of State:** $ 11,744

Specializes In: Business School

Degrees Conferred: BA, BS

Programs of Study: Agriculture, Anthropology, Art, Biology, Chemistry, Communications, Community Services, Computer Science Information Systems, Engineering, English, Forestry, French, General Sciences, Geography, Geology, German, Health, History, Humanities, International Studies, Japanese, Latin, Mathematics & Statistics, Music, Philosophy, Exercise Science, Physics, Physical Science, Political Science, Sociology, Southwest Studies, Spanish, Theatre, Women's Studies, Writing, Accounting, Agricultural Business, Business Administration, Economics, Engineering Management,Operation Management, Tourism & Resort Management, Teacher Education, Psychology

Women's Athletic Profile

1000 Rim Drive   **NCAA I**
Durango, CO 81301   Lady Skyhawks, Navy, Gold

Coach: Pam Adams   **Phone:** (970) 247-7516

Email: adams_p@fortlewis.edu   **Fax:** (970) 247-7655

Did Not Return Profile

Mesa State College
Academic Profile

1175 Texas Avenue   **Phone:** 800-982-6372
Grand Junction, CO 81501

Type: Public, 4 Yr., Liberal Arts, Coed   **Founded:** 1925

Website: http://www.mesastate.edu   **Religion:** Non-Affiliated

SAT/ACT/GPA: 880/19/2.5   **Housing:** Yes

Student/Faculty Ratio: 28:1   **Male/Female:** 47:53

Undergraduate Enrollment: 4,500   **Graduate Enrollment:** 50

Scholarships/Academic: Yes   **Athletic:** Yes   **Financial Aid:** Yes

Expenses By: Year   **In State:** $ 8,240   **Out of State:** $ 12,120

Specializes In: Liberal Arts

Degrees Conferred: Cert, AS, BA, BS, MBA

Programs of Study: Accounting, Biological Science, Business, Communications, Computer, Criminal, Dramatic Arts, Economics, English, Fine Arts, Geology, History, Human Services, Management, Marketing, Parks/Recreation, Physics, Science, Social Science

Women's Athletic Profile

1175 Texas Avenue
Grand Junction, CO 81501
Coach: Rusty Crick
Email: crick@wpogate.mesastate.edu

NCAA I
Mavericks, Cardinal, Gold
Phone: (970) 248-1020
Fax: (970) 248-1980

Estimated # of Women's Volleyball Scholarships: 6
Conference: Rocky Mountain Athletic Conference
Program Profile: We have a strong, contending program with excellent support. Our team plays at a 2,500 seat arena.
History: The program started in 1972 and has had only two coaches. Karen Perrin was coach from 1972 to 1980. Rusty Crick has been our coach from 1981 to the present.
Achievements: Won five times Coach of the Year honors; 9 Conference Titles, 6 All-American players.
Coaching: Rusty Crick, Head Coach, has coached here from 1981 to the present. His overall record is 470-203. Jamie Cup is Assistant Coach.
Freshman Receiving Financial Aid/Academic: N/A   **Athletic:** 3

Roster In State: 8	**Out of State:** 4	**Out of Country:** 0
Sophomores on Team: 3	**Seniors on Team:** 1	**Graduation %:** 95
Most Recent Record: 15-12-0	**Fall Games:** 27	**Spring Games:** 12

Camp of Clinic Dates: Throughout summer
Positions Needed: Setter, Middle, Outside, Right side
Schedule: Regis, Metro, Kearney, Colorado Christian University, Davis, Tampa
Style of Play: Quick, update, swing offense.

Metropolitan State College - Denver
Academic Profile

P.O Box 173362
Denver, CO 80217-3362

Phone: 303-556-3058

Type: Public, 4 Yr., Coed
Website: http://www.mscd.edu
SAT/ACT/GPA: 820/18/2.5
Student/Faculty Ratio: 22:1
Undergraduate Enrollment: 17,500
Scholarships/Academic: Yes   **Athletic:** Yes
Expenses By: Year   **In State:** $ 7,250
Degrees Conferred: BA, BS, BFA

Founded: 1963
Religion: Non-Affiliated
Housing: No
Male/Female: 1:1
Graduate Enrollment: N/A
Financial Aid: Yes
Out of State: $ 12,450

Programs of Study: Accounting, Anthropology, Art, Behavioral Science, Biology, Chemistry, Computer Information System, Computer Science, Criminalistics, Economics, English, Geography, Geology, Journalism, Land Use, Management, Marketing, Music, Philosophy, Physics, Political Science, Psychology, Public Administration, Social Work, Sociology, Spanish, Speech Communications, Theoretical Physics

Women's Athletic Profile

Campus Box 9
Denver, CO 80217
Coach: Jonelle Duvall
Email:

NCAA I
Roadrunners, Navy, Red
Phone: (303) 556-3832
Fax: (303) 556-2720

Estimated # of Women's Volleyball Scholarships: 8
Conference: Rocky Mountain Athletic Conference
Program Profile: We play at Aurora Events Center with a seating capacity of 2,100.
History: Our program began in 1974.
Achievements: Seven NCAA Regional Appearances, 10 All-Americans, RMAC Title in 1999, 2 CAC Champs in 1992 & 1993.
Coaching: Jonelle Duvall, Head Coach, is entering first year with the program. He was named Big East Player of the Year and All-American. Todd Raasc is our Assistant Coach, entering first year with the program. Frederick Wagner, is entering first year.
Freshman Receiving Financial Aid/Academic: N/A   **Athletic:** 4

Roster In State: 7	**Out of State:** 3	**Out of Country:** 3
Sophomores on Team: 3	**Seniors on Team:** 2	**Graduation %:** N/A

Most Recent Record: 26-11-0
Camp of Clinic Dates: TBA
Positions Needed: Middle Blocker
Schedule: Regis, Nebraska-Kearney, Colorado Christian, West Texas A&M, Minnesota-Duluth, Barry

Northeastern Junior College
Academic Profile

100 College Dr.
Sterling, CO 80751

Phone: 970-521-7000

Type: 2 Yr.,
Website: nejc.cc.co.us
SAT/ACT/GPA: Open
Student/Faculty Ratio: 43:1
Undergraduate Enrollment: 3,408
Scholarships/Academic:
Expenses By:
Degrees Conferred:
Programs of Study: Contact school for programs of study.

Founded: 1941
Religion: Non-Affiliated
Housing: No
Male/Female: Not Available
Graduate Enrollment: N/A
Athletic: **Financial Aid:**
In State: **Out of State:**

Women's Athletic Profile

10 College Drive
Sterling, CO 80751
Coach: Marci Henry
Email: Marci.henry@njc.ccoes.ed

NCAA I
Plainswomen, Black and Gold
Phone: (970) 521-6617
Fax: (970)522-4945

Estimated # of Women's Volleyball Scholarships: 14
Conference: Region IX South Sub.Region
Program Profile: Quick offense lifting swing. 1998 7.5 million facility with courts and wood suspension floor. 40-50 matches per year. 3000 seating with over half stadium theater seating
History: A national appearances with 4th ,6th,7th and 8th place finishes. Program began in 1974. Coached by Sheila Worley until 1987. She was selected to NJCAA Volleyball Hall of Fame in 1999. Then by Sue Pollaut 1988-1998, 1999 Present coach Marci Henry
Achievements: Marci Henry 1999 South Region Coach of the Year. South Sub. Region title 1999. Several All Tournament and All regional Players. Also several Academic All Americans.
Coaching: Marci Henry 10yrs experience, 2nd at NSE. Rob Haley 3rd season NJC, Tanya Baird 1st season, experience playing for 4th UNC Bears. DII
Freshman Receiving Financial Aid/Academic: N/A   **Athletic:** 11
Roster In State: 12   **Out of State:** 2   **Out of Country:**
Seniors on Team: 3   **Graduation %:** 100
Most Recent Record: 10-2
Positions Needed: Middle hitter, outside hitter and setter
Schedule: Western NE, Eastern WY, Seward County, Sheridan College, Caspa College, Central CC Platter,NE
Style of Play: Fast , Utilizing our quickness and seen swing offense.

Regis University
Academic Profile

3333 Regis Blvd.
Denver, CO 80221

Phone: 303-458-4900

Type: Private, 4 Yr., Liberal Arts, Coed
Website: http://www.regis.edu
SAT/ACT/GPA: 1100/20/3.0
Student/Faculty Ratio: 15:1
Undergraduate Enrollment: 1,200
Scholarships/Academic: Yes   **Athletic:** Yes
Expenses By: Year   **In State:** $ 22,800
Specializes In: Liberal Arts, Business, Preprofessional (Sciences)
Degrees Conferred: BA, BS, MBA, Nursing, Physical Therapy, MSL, MACL, MIS
Programs of Study: Business and Management, Communications, Life Sciences, Religion, Mathematics, Philosophy, Social Sciences, Theology

Founded: 1877
Religion: Roman Catholic-Jesuit
Housing: Yes
Male/Female: 45:55
Graduate Enrollment: 7,000
Financial Aid: Yes
Out of State: $ 22,800

Women's Athletic Profile

333 Regis Blvd., A-12
Denver, CO 80221
Coach: Frank Lavrisha
Email: flavrisha@regis.edu

NCAA I
Lady Rangers, Navy Blue, Gold
Phone: (800) 388-2366
Fax: (303) 964-5534

Estimated # of Women's Volleyball Scholarships: 1.5
Conference: Rocky Mountain Athletic Conference
Program Profile: Our facilities include: a field house with 2,400-seats, a volleyball locker-room with wood lockers, an athletic weight room, an up-to-date training room, a full-time trainer and a volleyball media guide.
History: Our initial year was 1977. We had 13 post-season appearances and a 14-13 playoffs record. Our overall record is 340-136. Our conference record is 164-25.
Achievements: Won 9 Conference Championships; 6 time Conference Coach of the Year; 39 All-Conference players; 26 All-Region players; 13 All-Americans; 6 Academic All-American; AVCA team Academic Award three times.
Coaching: Frank Lavrisha, Head Coach, has coached the team from 1986 to the present. He has a record of 340-136. He was named Coach of the Year in 1988 and Olympic Festival Coach of the Year in 1989 & 1991 (Gold Medal). He got USA "B" Team Coach in 1994 (Japan & China). Frank Gray is assistant coach.

Freshman Receiving Financial Aid/Academic:		**Athletic:** 1
Roster In State: 7	**Out of State:** 8	**Out of Country:** 0
Sophomores on Team: 7	**Seniors on Team:** 4	**Graduation %:** 100
Most Recent Record: 31-4-0	**Fall Games:** 35	**Spring Games:** 4

Camp of Clinic Dates: Camp - June 7-11; July 11-15; 19-21; 22-24; June 12, July 10, July 17
Positions Needed: Setter
Schedule: Brigham Young University-Hawaii, Northern Michigan, Central Missouri State, Augustana, Barry, Metro State, Barry
Style of Play: Competitive, consistent, intense and enjoying the experience! We want to take great swings at the ball and go after it on defense.

United States Air Force Academy
Academic Profile

2169 Field House Drive
Colorado Springs, CO 80840-9500

Phone: (719) 333-2897

Type: Public, 4 Yr., Engineering, Coed
Website: http://www.airforcesports.com
SAT/ACT/GPA: 1140/25/3.0
Student/Faculty Ratio: 15:1
Undergraduate Enrollment: 4,000
Scholarships/Academic: Yes
Expenses By: Year
Specializes In: Sciences
Degrees Conferred: BS
Programs of Study: Has 27 academic majors, mostly Sciences, Languages (Foreign) and Political Science.

Founded: 1954
Religion: Non-Affiliated
Housing: Yes
Male/Female: 85:15
Graduate Enrollment: N/A

	Athletic: Yes	**Financial Aid:** Yes
	In State: $ 100% free	**Out of State:** $ 100% free

Women's Athletic Profile

2169 Field House Drive, Suite 212
Colorado Springs, CO 80840-9500
Coach: Penny-Lucas White
Email: julatonvd.ah@usafa.af.mil

NCAA I
Falcons, Blue, Silver
Phone: (719) 333-2897
Fax: (719) 333-2599

Estimated # of Women's Volleyball Scholarships: Yes
Conference: Mountain West
Program Profile: We have spectacular facilities and our school sits on over 18,000 acres. We have a beautiful new sport court solely for volleyball.
History: We are starting our 4th season as Division I program. This coming year will be our first as members of the Mountain West Conference after leaving WAC.
Achievements: WAC Player of the Week
Coaching: Penny Lucas-White, Head Coach, was a National Team Member and an MVP of the NVL in 1997. She played professionally in Europe for several years. Verna Julaton and Paul Larger are assistant coaches.

Freshman Receiving Financial Aid/Academic:		**Athletic:** All
Roster In State: 3	**Out of State:** 14	**Out of Country:** 0
Sophomores on Team: 0	**Seniors on Team:** 1	**Graduation %:** 100
Most Recent Record: 10-21-0	**Fall Games:** 27	**Spring Games:** 4 tournaments

Camp of Clinic Dates: June 14-18, June 21-25, June 28-July 2
Positions Needed: Middle Hitter, Outside Right, Setter
Schedule: Colorado State University, Brigham Young University, University of Nevada-Las Vegas, University of Utah, University of Wyoming, San Diego State University
Style of Play: Intense defense & quick transitions/offense to offset diminutive player size!

University of Colorado - Boulder
Academic Profile

Campus Box 372
Boulder, CO 80309-0372

Phone: (303) 492-6141

Type: Public, 4 Yr., Coed
Website: http://www.buffaloes.colorado.edu
SAT/ACT/GPA: 1080-1250/23-27/3.2-3.7
Student/Faculty Ratio: 14:1
Undergraduate Enrollment: 20,595
Scholarships/Academic: Yes
Expenses By: Year
Specializes In: Many

Founded: 1876
Religion: Non-Affiliated
Housing: Yes
Male/Female: 53:47
Graduate Enrollment: 4,530

Athletic: Yes
In State: $ 8,621

Financial Aid: Yes
Out of State: $ 21,103

Degrees Conferred: BA, BS, BFA, MA, MS, MBA, MFA, Ph.D., EdD, PharmD
Programs of Study: All: Business, Communications, Environmental Design, Engineering, Journalism, Liberal Arts

Women's Athletic Profile

Campus Box 369
Boulder, CO 80309
Coach: Pii Aiu
Email: cuvb@moonshine.colorado.edu

NCAA I
Lady Buffaloes, Gold, Black
Phone: (303) 492-6141
Fax: (303) 492-5363

Estimated # of Women's Volleyball Scholarships: 12
Conference: Big 12 Conference
Program Profile: We have two gyms: Carlson is our practice gym and Coors Event Center is our game gym. Dal Ward Center includes: administration, academics, a training table, a weight room and a training room. We play a Fall season.
History: We began in 1986 and went to the NCAA Tournaments nine times. We have won two Conference Championships.
Achievements: 2 All-Americans, Big 12 1997 Coach of the Year; 2 Conference Titles.
Coaching: Pii Aiu has been Head Coach from 1997 to the present. He was Assistant Coach from 1989 to 1996. He was Coach of the Year in 1997. Carrie Appleman and Robyn Read are assistant coaches.
Freshman Receiving Financial Aid/Academic:

Roster In State: 0	**Out of State:** 10	**Athletic:** 2
Sophomores on Team: 3	**Seniors on Team:** 4	**Out of Country:** 2
Most Recent Record: 22-8-0	**Fall Games:** 30	**Graduation %:** 100
		Spring Games: 4

Camp of Clinic Dates: July 11-18
Positions Needed: Outside Hitter, Right side Setter, Middle Blocker
Schedule: Nebraska, Texas, Long Beach, Washington State, California-Berkeley, Hawaii

University of Colorado - Colorado Springs
Academic Profile

1420 Austin Bluffs Pkwy.
Colorado Springs, CO 80933-7150

Phone: (719) 262-3679

Type: Public, 4 Yr., Coed
Website: http://www.uccs.edu
SAT/ACT/GPA: 850/18/3.4
Student/Faculty Ratio: 17:1
Undergraduate Enrollment: 6,000
Scholarships/Academic: Yes
Expenses By: Year

Founded: 1965
Religion: Non-Affiliated
Housing: Yes
Male/Female: 2:3
Graduate Enrollment: 1,000

Athletic: Yes
In State: $ 7,800

Financial Aid: Yes
Out of State: $ 14,600

Degrees Conferred: BA, BS, MA, MS, MBA, MPA, MEngineering, MBasic Science, BSN, MSN
Programs of Study: College of Business, College of Engineering and Applied Sciences, School of Education, College of Letters Arts and Sciences, Graduate School of Public Affairs

Women's Athletic Profile

1420 Austin Bluffs Parkway
Colorado Springs, CO 80933
Coach: Sharon Garus
Email: sgarus@mail.uccs.edu

NCAA I
Mountain Lions, Black, Gold
Phone: (719) 262-3679
Fax: (719) 262-3029

Estimated # of Women's Volleyball Scholarships: 3
Conference: Rocky Mountain Athletic Conference
Program Profile: We have a new program. Our facilities are small with a seating capacity of only 500. We are in a tough conference with two tournaments.
History: Our overall records were: 1993:19-15, 1994:13-24, 1995: 6-26, 1996:3-30, 1997:7-18, 1998:4-26.
Coaching: Sharon Garus, Head Coach, is in his first year here. She moved to Colorado from California.
Freshman Receiving Financial Aid/Academic: **Athletic:** 5

Roster In State: 12	**Out of State:** 3	**Out of Country:** 0
Sophomores on Team: 2	**Seniors on Team:** 2	**Graduation %:** 85
Most Recent Record: 4-26-0	**Fall Games:** 30	**Spring Games:** 4 Tournaments

Camp of Clinic Dates: July 26-30
Positions Needed: Outside Hitter, Middle Blocker, Setter, OP
Schedule: Regis University, Metro State College, Colorado Christian, Nebraska-Kearney, Mesa State, Fort Hayes State
Style of Play: Ball control and smart play.

University of Denver
Academic Profile

2250 E. Jewell Avenue   **Phone:** (303) 871-3944
Denver, CO 80208

Type: Private, 4 Yr., Coed	**Founded:** 1864
Website: http://www.du.edu	**Religion:** Non-Affiliated
SAT/ACT/GPA: 610 U & M /273.4	**Housing:** Yes
Student/Faculty Ratio: 13:1	**Male/Female:** 48:52
Undergraduate Enrollment: 3,000	**Graduate Enrollment:** 3,175

Scholarships/Academic: Yes   **Athletic:** Yes   **Financial Aid:** Yes
Expenses By: Year   **In State:** $ 25,000   **Out of State:** $ 25,000
Specializes In: Business, Hotel & Restaurant Management, Science
Degrees Conferred: BA, BFA, BM, BSBA, MA, MBA, MFA, MS, MIM, MRCM, MSLA, MT, Ph.D.,
Programs of Study: Art, Art History, Education, English, Finance, Finance-Marketing, Finance-Real Estate, General Business, Hotel/Restaurant & Tourism Management, Languages & Literature, History, Law, Management, Management Information Systems, Marketing, Music, Philosophy, Real Estate & Construction Management, Religious Studies, Statistics & Operations Research, Theatre, Pre-law, Pre-M.Ed.

Women's Athletic Profile

2201 E. Asbury Avenue   **NCAA I**
Denver, CO 80208   Lady Pioneers, Crimson, Gold
Coach: Beth Kuwata   **Phone:** (303) 871-3944
Email: bkuwata@du.edu   **Fax:** (303) 871-3759

Estimated # of Women's Volleyball Scholarships: 4
Conference: Sun Belt Conference
Program Profile: We are an up and coming Division I program. Our first year in Division I was in 1998. Daniel L. Ritchie Center for Sports and Wellness was built March of 1999. It is a 400,000 square foot building. It includes Hamilton Gymnasium that has 2,800 seats. The Hagness Arena has 7,200 seats. We have an Olympic size pool called Ed Ponar Natatorium which has 300 seats.
History: Our program began in 1983. It has been a Division II program until 1998, playing in the Continental Divide Conference, the Colorado Athletic Conference and the Rocky Mountain Conference.
Achievements: 1994 Western Athletic Conference Co-Coach of the Year; NCAA Tournament Appearance in 1995.
Coaching: Beth Kuwata, Head Coach, started in 1996. Her records were: 11-24 in 1996, 21-11 in 1997 and 8-17 in 1998. Her 1994 record in Wyoming was 17-13. Jill Thomason and Amy Kleyweg are Assistant Coaches.
Freshman Receiving Financial Aid/Academic: **Athletic:** 3

Roster In State: 8	**Out of State:** 6	**Out of Country:** 0
Sophomores on Team: 1	**Seniors on Team:** 2	**Graduation %:** 100
Most Recent Record: 8-17-0	**Fall Games:** 28	**Spring Games:** 0

Camp of Clinic Dates: June 14 - 18, 1999; July 19-23
Positions Needed: (2) Middle Hitters, Setter, Outside Hitter
Schedule: Colorado, California - Berkeley, University of California-Los Angeles, Wyoming, Arkansas-Little Rock, Arkansas State, Minnesota, Colorado, Colorado State, Arkansas-Little Rock, Arkansas State
Style of Play: Medium tempo, balanced offensive attack, perimeter read offense.

University of Northern Colorado
Academic Profile

501 20th Street, Athletic Dept.
Greeley, CO 80639
Type: Public, 4 Yr., Liberal Arts, Coed
Website: http://www.uncBears.edu
SAT/ACT/GPA: 1000/21/2.8
Student/Faculty Ratio: 30:1
Undergraduate Enrollment: 10,000
Scholarships/Academic: Yes
Expenses By: Year
Specializes In: Business, Education, Nursing
Degrees Conferred: MA, MS, Ph.D., EdD, BA, BS, MM, MME

Phone: (970) 351-1719

Founded: 1889
Religion: Non-Affiliated
Housing: Yes
Male/Female: 50:50
Graduate Enrollment: 1,500
Financial Aid: Yes

Athletic: Yes
In State: $ 7,649

Out of State: $ 14,679

Programs of Study: Biology, Business, Communication Disorders, Dietetics, Earth Science, Economics, English, Geography, Gerontology, Health, History, Human Rehabilitation, Services, Interdisciplinary, Journalism, PreProfessional Programs, Psychology, Recreation, Visual Arts

Women's Athletic Profile

501 20th Street Athletic Department
Greeley, CO 80639
Coach: Linda Delk
Email: ldelk@athletics.unc.edu

NCAA I
Lady Bears, Blue, Gold
Phone: (970) 351-1719
Fax: (970) 351-2018

Estimated # of Women's Volleyball Scholarships: 3
Conference: North Central Collegiate Athletic Conference
Program Profile: Butler-Hancock Hall is a 4,500-seat athletic arena, capable of holding 7 full courts. Our home court record is 211-45 (82%). We have a home winning streak of 33 straight matches from 9/28/85 to 11/8/87. We have the highest match attendance of 1,368. We have been Regional NCAA Volleyball Host for 3 years.
History: We began in the 1970's as a Division I school. Coach Delk took the helm in 1976. Her overall record is 633-260 (70%). We have had 14 National Tournament Appearances since 1979. We are 3rd in the nation in career victories in Division II.
Achievements: 10 Conference Titles; 14 National Tournament Appearances; 2 pro players; 10 Coach of the Year Awards either Regional or in the Conference. 21 All-Americans; 5 Academic All-American; Team GPA 3.21.
Coaching: Linda Delk, Head Coach, started in 1976 with a record of 633-260. She has had 18 straight winning seasons. She is a former member of NCAA National Volleyball Committee. She is a graduate of Ohio State University. Cathy Brelt is Assistant Coach.
Freshman Receiving Financial Aid/Academic:
Roster In State: 9
Sophomores on Team: 3
Most Recent Record: 19-13-0
Out of State: 5
Seniors on Team: 1
Fall Games: 32
Athletic: 6
Out of Country: 0
Graduation %: 98
Spring Games: 15
Camp of Clinic Dates: 6-7/9 Camp, 7/19-7/22 Camp; 7/10Setter; 7/16 Blocker; 7/17 Defense; 7/18 Hitter Clinics
Positions Needed: Outside Hitter, Middle Hitter, Setter
Schedule: North Dakota State, Augustana College, Metro State, Regis University, Colorado Christian, Southern Colorado
Style of Play: Quick play set offense; swing hitter system; great mobility; strong block and defense.

University of Southern Colorado
Academic Profile

2200 N. Bonforte Blvd.
Pueblo, CO 81001-4901

Phone: 719-549-2461

Type: Public, 4 Yr., Coed
Website: http://www.uscolo.edu
SAT/ACT/GPA: 820/17
Student/Faculty Ratio: 17:1
Undergraduate Enrollment: 3,940
Scholarships/Academic: Yes
Expenses By: Year
Degrees Conferred: BA, BS, MS, MBA

Founded: 1969
Religion: Non-Affiliated
Housing: Yes
Male/Female: 46:54
Graduate Enrollment: 130
Financial Aid: Yes

Athletic: Yes
In State: $ 6,880

Out of State: $ 7,880

Programs of Study: Accounting, Art, Automotive Parts and Service Management, Biology, Business, Chemistry, Civil Engineering Technology, Computer Information Systems, Electrical Engineering, Electronic Engineering Technology, Computer Engineering, Elementary and Secondary Certification, English, Exercise Science, Athletic Training, Health Promotions, Foreign Languages, History, Industrial Engineering, Mass Communications, Mathematics, Mechanical Engineering, Music, Nursing, Political Science, PreProfessional Programs, Psychology, Recreation, Social Science, Sociology, Speech Communications

Women's Athletic Profile

2200 N. Bonforte Blvd.
Pueblo, CO 81001
Coach: Tom Shoji
Email: shoji@uscolo.edu

NCAA I
Thundervolves, Red, Blue White
Phone: (719) 549-2794
Fax: (719) 549-2750

Estimated # of Women's Volleyball Scholarships: 3
Conference: Rocky Mountain Athletic Conference
Program Profile: Has qualified for NCAA II Tournament 2 out of the last 3 years. Games played in Massani Arena (5,500). The season runs from the last weekend in August to the second weekend in Nov.
History: Started in 1978. All Time record is 296-397.
Achievements: 1 All-American
Tom Shoji 1996 Region Coach of the Year
Coaching: Tom Shoji, 1994, 293-209
Freshman Receiving Financial Aid/Academic: **Athletic:** 4
Roster In State: 10   **Out of State:** 4   **Out of Country:**
Sophomores on Team: 3   **Seniors on Team:** 3   **Graduation %:** 90
Most Recent Record: 11-18
Positions Needed: MH
Schedule: Northern Michigan, Augustana, Reges, Metro State, Texas Women's, Colorado Christian
Style of Play: Quick Tempo

Western State College
Academic Profile

Paul Wright Gym-Athletics
Gunnison, CO 81231

Phone: (970) 943-2079

Type: Public, 4 Yr., Liberal Arts, Coed
Website: http://www.western.edu
SAT/ACT/GPA: 950 combined/202.5
Student/Faculty Ratio: 20:1
Undergraduate Enrollment: 2.400
Scholarships/Academic: Yes   **Athletic:** Yes
Expenses By: Year   **In State:** $ 7,563
Programs of Study: Contact school for programs of study.

Founded: 1901
Religion: Non-Affiliated
Housing: Yes
Male/Female: 60:40
Graduate Enrollment: N/A
Financial Aid: Yes
Out of State: $ 12,943

Women's Athletic Profile

1 College Heights
Gunnison, CO 81231
Coach: Darin Weber
Email: dweber@western.edu
Estimated # of Women's Volleyball Scholarships: 2.3
Conference: Rocky Mountain Athletic Conference
Program Profile: We play at Paul Wright Gym, which has a seating capacity of 1,800.
History: Our program started in 1972.
Coaching: Darin Weber, Head Coach, was Assistant Coach in 1994. He was interim coach in 1995, and became Head Coach in 1996.

NCAA I
Lady Mountaineers, Crimson
Phone: (970) 943-2079
Fax: (970) 943-2754

Roster In State: 4   **Out of State:** 10   **Out of Country:** 1
Sophomores on Team: 0   **Seniors on Team:** 1   **Graduation %:** Unknown
Most Recent Record: 4-13-0
Positions Needed: Right side hitter
Schedule: Regis, Metro, Colorado Christian, Cameron University, Mesa State, University of Southern Colorado
Style of Play: Power volleyball.

CONNECTICUT

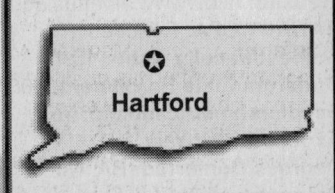

Hartford

SCHOOL	CITY	AFFILIATION	PAGE
Albertus Magnus College	New Haven	NCAA III	133
Central Connecticut State Univ.	New Britain	NCAA I	133
Connecticut College	New London	NCAA III	134
Eastern Connecticut State Univ.	Willimantic	NCAA III	134
Fairfield University	Fairfield	NCAA I	135
Quinnipiac College	Hamden	NCAA I	136
Sacred Heart University	New Haven	NCAA II	136
Southern Connecticut State Univ.	New Haven	NCAA II	137
Teikyo Post University	Waterbury	NCAA II/NAIA	137
Trinity College	Hartford	NCAA III	138
US Coast Guard Academy	New London	NCAA III	138
University of Bridgeport	Bridgeport	NCAA II	139
University of Connecticut	Storrs	NCAA I	139
University of Hartford	West Hartford	NCAA I	140
University of New Haven	West Haven	NCAA II	140
Wesleyan University	Middletown	NCAA III	141
Western Connecticut State Univ.	Danbury	NCAA III	141
Yale University	New Haven	NCAA I	142

Albertus Magnus College
Academic Profile

700 Prospect St.
New Haven, CT 06511

Phone: 203-773-8501

Type: Private, 4 Yr., Liberal Arts, Coed
Website: http://www.albertus.edu
SAT/ACT/GPA: Required
Student/Faculty Ratio: 15:1
Undergraduate Enrollment: 400+
Scholarships/Academic: Yes   **Athletic:** No
Expenses By: Year   **In State:** $ 20,000
Degrees Conferred: BA, MA

Founded: 1925
Religion: Catholic
Housing: Yes
Male/Female: 3:1
Graduate Enrollment: 100+
Financial Aid: Yes
Out of State: $ 20,000

Programs of Study: Accounting, Biology, Business and Management, Communications, Economics, Management/Administration, English, Finance, Fine Arts, Mathematics, History, Human Services, Philosophy, Political Science, PreLaw, PreMed, Psychology, Religion, Sociology

Women's Athletic Profile

700 Prospect Street
New Haven, CT 06511
Coach: Mark Giordano
Email: mgiord3583@aol.com

NCAA I
Lady Falcons, Blue, White
Phone: (203) 773-8596
Fax: (203) 776-7533

Estimated # of Women's Volleyball Scholarships: N/A
Conference: The Great Northeast Athletic Conference
Program Profile: This year, we won our first game and added four more victories during this season.
History: We are improving. This year we won five games and proved that our volleyball program is on the rise.
Coaching: Heather Beler, Head Coach, started in 1998. Joe Defrancesco and Nicole Klarides-Ditria are trainers.
Roster In State: 7   **Out of State:** 1   **Out of Country:** 0
Sophomores on Team: 3   **Seniors on Team:** 2   **Graduation %:** 100
Schedule: Becker, Bridgeport, Emerson, Southern Connecticut, Daniel Webster, Suffolk, Sacred Heart, Teikyo Post, Emmanuel

Central Connecticut State University
Academic Profile

1615 Stanley Street
New Britain, CT 06050

Phone: 860-832-2285

Type: Public, 4 Yr., Liberal Arts, Coed
Website: http://www.ccsu.ctsateu.edu
SAT/ACT/GPA: 930 combined SAT
Student/Faculty Ratio: 17:1
Undergraduate Enrollment: 9,551
Scholarships/Academic: Yes   **Athletic:** Yes
Expenses By: Year   **In State:** $ 4,457
Specializes In: Education

Founded: 1849
Religion: Non-Affiliated
Housing: Yes
Male/Female: 45:55
Graduate Enrollment: 2,495
Financial Aid: Yes
Out of State: $ 7,196

Degrees Conferred: BS, BA, MA, MB, MS-Industrial Technical Management, Sixth Year Certificate
Programs of Study: Accounting, American Studies, Actuarial Science, Anthropology, Archaeology, Astronomy, Art, Biology, Computer Science, Business, Chemistry, Communication, Engineering, Math, General Studies

Women's Athletic Profile

1615 Stanley St.
New Britain, CT 06050-4010
Coach: Leo Uzcategui
Email: uzcateguil@ccsu.edu

NCAA I
Lady Blue Devils, Blue, White
Phone: (860) 832-3268
Fax: (860) 832-3754

Estimated # of Women's Volleyball Scholarships: N/A
Conference: Mid-Continent Conference
History: Our program became Division I in 1986. We joined the East Coast Conference in 1990. In 1994 we joined the Mid-Continent Conference.

Achievements: In 1991, we ranked 11th nationally; In 1993 ,we ranked 7th nationally; Melissa Phelps 1993 All-ECC First Team; 3 players named to 1993 All-ECC Second Team; Christine Dadducci 1993 ECC All-Tournament Team; 4 times Mid-Conference Player of the Week; 3 players named 1995 All-Mid-Continent Conference First Team.

Coaching: Leo Uzcategui became Head Coach four seasons ago. In 1993, he guided the Florida Atlantic University volleyball team to its first Division I competition and its first year as a member of the Trans-America Athletic Conference. Nancy Ringrose started as our Assistant Coach in 1996. She is a CCSU graduate.

Roster In State: 1   **Out of State:** 9   **Out of Country:** 0
Sophomores on Team: 2   **Seniors on Team:** 2   **Graduation %:** Unknown
Style of Play: Team chemistry; team members respect and understand each other.

Connecticut College
Academic Profile

270 Mohegan Ave.
New London, CT 06320

Phone: (860) 439-2507

Type: Private, 4 Yr., Liberal Arts, Coed
Website: http://www.camel.conncoll.edu
SAT/ACT/GPA: Not required
Student/Faculty Ratio: 11:1
Undergraduate Enrollment: 1,700
Scholarships/Academic: No   **Athletic:** No
Expenses By: Year   **In State:** $ 28,475
Specializes In: Liberal Arts
Degrees Conferred: BA, MA

Founded: 1911
Religion: Non-Affiliated
Housing: Yes
Male/Female: 45:55
Graduate Enrollment: 100
Financial Aid: Yes
Out of State: $ 28,475

Programs of Study: Anthropology, Art, Art History, Asian Studies, Biochemistry, Biology, Botany, Chemistry, Chinese, Classics, Dance, Economics, European Studies, French, German, Hispanic Studies, History, Human Ecology, Interdisciplinary Studies, International Studies, Italian, Japanese, Marine Biology, Mathematics, Medieval Studies, Music, Philosophy, Physics, Political Science, Psychology, Religion, Russian, Sociology, Theatre, Urban Studies, Zoology

Women's Athletic Profile

270 Mohegan Avenue
New London, CT 06320
Coach: Melody Davidson
Email:

NCAA I
Lady Camels, Blue, White
Phone: (860) 439-2550
Fax: (860) 439-2516

Estimated # of Women's Volleyball Scholarships: N/A
Conference: NESCAC
Program Profile: Charles B. Luce Field House was upgraded in 1992 and contains 2 wood floor basketball/volleyball courts. Our main field house consists of 22,000 square feet playing surface. There are 3 multi-purpose courts for badminton, basketball, tennis and volleyball.
History: Our program started in 1972. We made ECAC Appearances in 1993 and 1994. We made 3 NIAC Appearances in 1981, 1982, and 1983. We were Connecticut State Champions in 1978.
Achievements: Won 30 matches in a row
Coaching: Melody Davidson, Head Coach, started coaching in 1998 with a record of 4-23. Stanton Ching, Assistant Coach, started in 1991.

Roster In State: 1   **Out of State:** 12   **Out of Country:** 0
Sophomores on Team: 5   **Seniors on Team:** 5   **Graduation %:** 100
Most Recent Record: 4-23-0   **Fall Games:** 27   **Spring Games:** 0
Positions Needed: Setter, Outside Hitter
Schedule: Wesleyan, Trinity, Colby, Bowdoin, Amherst, Coast Guard
Style of Play: Aggressive, strong serving and tough defense.

Eastern Connecticut State University
Academic Profile

83 Windham St.
Willimantic, CT 06226-2295

Phone: 877-353-3278

Type: Public, 4 Yr., Liberal Arts, Coed
Website: http://www.ecsu.ctstateu.edu
SAT/ACT/GPA: 900/2.5
Student/Faculty Ratio: 17:1

Founded: 1889
Religion: Non-Affiliated
Housing: Yes
Male/Female: 43:57

Undergraduate Enrollment: 4,335
Scholarships/Academic: Yes
Expenses By: Year
Specializes In: Education
Degrees Conferred: AS, BA, BS, BGS, MS

Athletic: No
In State: $ 10,000

Graduate Enrollment: 297
Financial Aid: Yes
Out of State: $ 15,000

Programs of Study: Accounting, Art, Biology, Business, Communications, Computer, Earth Science, Economics, Education, English, Environmental, History, Finance, Management, Microbiology, Sociology, Social Work

Women's Athletic Profile

Windham Street
Willimantic, CT 06226
Coach: Thomas York
Email: yorkt@ecsu.ctstateu.edu

NCAA I
Lady Warriors, Royal, White
Phone: (860) 456-5182
Fax: (860) 465-4695

Estimated # of Women's Volleyball Scholarships: N/A
Conference: Little East Conference
Program Profile: We are one of the Top Ten teams in New England. We have excellent facilities and a 40 matches season.
History: We began in 1975. Our program has a 23 year history. We have won 640 games and lost 307 games (67.6). We have had 13 NCAA appearances. We played in 23 post-season tournaments. The program is considered the winningest program in New England.
Achievements: The program produced 2 All-Americans; 20 All-Region; 27 All-New England; 1 Coach of the Year in East Region.
Coaching: Thomas York, Head Coach, has been with the program from 1997 to the present. He has compiled an overall record of 58-20. Floretta Crabtree, Assistant Coach, has a career coaching record of 616-295 overall (1975 to 1996).

Roster In State: 5
Sophomores on Team: 2
Most Recent Record: 34-8-0

Out of State: 8
Seniors on Team: 4
Fall Games: 42

Out of Country: 0
Graduation %: Unknown
Spring Games: 0

Positions Needed: 2 Middle Hitters, 2 Outside Hitters
Schedule: Springfield College, Wheaton College, MIT, Wellesley College, Amherst College, Williams College
Style of Play: Fast multiple offense and defense.

Fairfield University
Academic Profile

1073 North Benson Road
Fairfield, CT 06430-5195

Phone: (201) 254-4000

Type: Private, 4 Yr., Liberal Arts, Coed
Website: http://www.fairfield.edu
SAT/ACT/GPA: 1100-1250/23-28/3.0
Student/Faculty Ratio: 13:1
Undergraduate Enrollment: 3,100
Scholarships/Academic: Yes
Expenses By: Year
Degrees Conferred: BA, BS

Athletic: Yes
In State: $ 27,815

Founded: 1942
Religion: Jesuit
Housing: Yes
Male/Female: 46:54
Graduate Enrollment: 900
Financial Aid: Yes
Out of State: $ 27,815

Programs of Study: Accounting, American Studies, Biology, Business, Chemistry, Communications, Computer Information Systems, Computer Science, Economics, Engineering, English, Family Health, Finance, History, Human Resources Management, International Business, International Taxation, International Studies, Management, Marketing, Mathematics, Mental Health, Modern Languages and Literature, Neuroscience, Philosophy, Physics Politics, Psychology, Religious Studies, Sociology and Anthropology, Visual and Performing Arts

Women's Athletic Profile

N. Benson Road
Fairfield, CT 06430-5195
Coach: Todd Kress
Email:

NCAA I
Lady Stags, Red, White
Phone: (203) 254-4000x2362
Fax: (203) 254-4270

Estimated # of Women's Volleyball Scholarships: N/A
Conference: Metro Atlantic Athletic Conference
Program Profile: Our program has jumped from a bottom half program to "top 30" nationally in the past three years. We play in Alumni Hall with a capacity of 2,700. We practice in the University's new Athletic Center.

History: The first year of the program was 1985. We have compiled an 82-23 record the past 3 seasons, including back to back MAAC Championships and NCAA Tournament Appearances.

Achievements: MAAC Coach of the Year in 1996, 1997 & 1998; Regular Season title in 1996, 1997, & 1998; Conference Champions in 1997 & 1998.

Coaching: Todd Kress, Head Coach, joined the program in 1995 with an overall record of 94-42. He was named MAAC Coach of the Year in 1996, 1997 & 1998. John Spinney is Assistant Coach.

Freshman Receiving Financial Aid/Academic: **Athletic:** 3

Roster In State: 0   **Out of State:** 11   **Out of Country:** 1

Graduation %: 100

Most Recent Record: 35-1-0   **Fall Games:** 36   **Spring Games:** 2

Camp of Clinic Dates: July 5 - 9

Positions Needed: Middle Block, Setter (top priority)

Schedule: Oregon State, Notre Dame, Connecticut, Air Force, Ohio State, Illinois

Style of Play: We are very aggressive and intense. Our motto is to get the most of every minute of practice and competition.

Quinnipiac College
Academic Profile

275 Mount Carmel Avenue
Hamden, CT 06518

Phone: (800) 462-1944

Type: Private, 4 Yr., Liberal Arts, Coed
Website: http://www.quinnipiac.edu
SAT/ACT/GPA: 1070/3.0
Student/Faculty Ratio: 15:1
Undergraduate Enrollment: 3,800
Scholarships/Academic: Yes
Expenses By: Year

Athletic: Yes
In State: $ 24,950

Founded: 1929
Religion: Non-Affiliated
Housing: Yes
Male/Female: 1.25:0.8
Graduate Enrollment: 2,000
Financial Aid: Yes
Out of State: $ 24,950

Degrees Conferred: BA, BS, MS, MBA, MPS, MAT, ID, Associate in Court Education

Programs of Study: Accounting, BioChemistry, Computer Science, Diagnostic Imagery, Economics, English, Finance, Gerontology, Health Administration, History, Legal Studies, Management, Marketing, Mass Communications, Mathematics, Nursing, Occupational and Physical Therapy, Political Science, Psychology, Sociology, Spanish, VetTechnology, etc..

Women's Athletic Profile

New Road
Hamden, CT 06518-1940
Coach: Makeba Davis
Email: mdavis@quinnipiac.edu

NCAA I
Lady Braves, Blue, Gold
Phone: (203) 582-5394
Fax: (203) 281-8716

Did Not Return Profile

Sacred Heart University
Academic Profile

5151 Park Avenue
Fairfield, CT 06432

Phone: (203) 371-7999

Type: Private, 4 Yr., Liberal Arts, Coed
Website: http://www.sacredheart.edu
SAT/ACT/GPA: Competitive
Student/Faculty Ratio: 17:1
Undergraduate Enrollment: 2,350
Scholarships/Academic: Yes
Expenses By: Year

Athletic: Yes
In State: $ 22,000

Founded: 1963
Religion: Catholic
Housing: Yes
Male/Female: 50:50
Graduate Enrollment: N/A
Financial Aid: Yes
Out of State: $ 22,000

Degrees Conferred: AA, AS. BA, BS, MA, MS, MBA

Programs of Study: Business and Management, Business/Office and Marketing/Distribution, Communications, Computer Science, Health Sciences, Law, Letters/Literature, Social Sciences

Men's Athletic Profile

5151 Park Avenue
Fairfield, CT 06432
Coach: Scott Carter
Email:

NCAA II
Pioneers/Red, White
Phone: (203) 365-7647
Fax: (203) 371-7889

Estimated # of Men's Volleyball Scholarships: N/A
Conference: New England Collegiate conference

Women's Athletic Profile

5151 Park Avenue
New Haven, CT 06515
Coach: Scott Carter
Email:

NCAA I
Lady Pioneers, Red, White
Phone: (203) 365-7647
Fax: (203) 365-7696

Did Not Return Profile

Southern Connecticut State University
Academic Profile

125 Wintergreen Avenue
New Haven, CT 06515

Phone: (203) 392-5759

Type: Public, 4 Yr., Liberal Arts, Coed
Website: http://www.fastfeet.com
SAT/ACT/GPA: Required
Student/Faculty Ratio: 15:1
Undergraduate Enrollment: 5,500
Scholarships/Academic: Yes
Expenses By: Year
Degrees Conferred: BA, BS

Athletic: Yes
In State: $ 9,500

Founded: 1893
Religion: Non-Affiliated
Housing: Yes
Male/Female: 1:5
Graduate Enrollment: 2,000
Financial Aid: Yes
Out of State: $ 9,500

Programs of Study: Art Education, Art History, BioChemistry, Biology, Business Administration, Chemistry, Computer Science, Corporate Communication, Earth Science, Economics, Elementary Education, English, Geography, Journalism, Liberal Studies, Mathematics, Nursing, Philosophy, Physical Education, Physics, Political Science, Psychology, Public Health, Social Work, Sociology, Special Education

Women's Athletic Profile

125 Wintergreen Avenue
New Haven, CT 06515
Coach: Patricia Fernandes
Email:

NCAA I
Lady Owls, Navy, White
Phone: (203) 392-6000
Fax: (203) 392-6006

Did Not Return Profile

Teikyo Post University
Academic Profile

800 Country Club Road
Waterburg, CT 06708

Phone: (203) 596-4535

Type: Private, 4 Yr., Liberal Arts, Coed
Website: http://www.teikyopost.edu
SAT/ACT/GPA: 860/18/2.0
Student/Faculty Ratio: 14:1
Undergraduate Enrollment: 1,400
Scholarships/Academic: Yes
Expenses By: Year
Specializes In: International Business and Business Administration
Degrees Conferred: BA, BS, AA, AS

Athletic: Yes
In State: $ 19,900

Founded: 1890
Religion: Non-Affiliated
Housing: Yes
Male/Female: 40:60
Graduate Enrollment: N/A
Financial Aid: Yes
Out of State: $ 19,900

Programs of Study: Accounting, Art (minor), Criminal Justice, Early Childhood Education, English, Equine Management, Finance, General Studies, History, Computer Information Systems, International Business, Legal Assistant, Liberal Arts, Management, Management Information Systems, Marketing, Psychology, Sociology

Women's Athletic Profile

800 Country Club Rd.
Waterbury, CT 06708
Coach: TBA
Email: TBA

NCAA I
Lady Eagles, Green, White
Phone: (203) 596-4535
Fax: (203) 596-4695

Estimated # of Women's Volleyball Scholarships: 8
Conference: NECC (NCAA) CACC (NAIA)
Freshman Receiving Financial Aid/Academic:

		Athletic: 4
Roster In State: 5	**Out of State:** 3	**Out of Country:** 2
Sophomores on Team: 0	**Seniors on Team:** 0	**Graduation %:** Unknown
Most Recent Record: 1-23-0	**Fall Games:** 24	**Spring Games:** 0

Trinity College - Connecticut
Academic Profile

300 Summit St.
Hartford, CT 06106
Type: Private, 4 Yr., Liberal Arts, Coed
Website: http://www.trncoll.edu
SAT/ACT/GPA: 1200
Student/Faculty Ratio: 10:1
Undergraduate Enrollment: 2,088
Scholarships/Academic: Yes
Expenses By: Year
Degrees Conferred: BA, BS, MA, MS

Phone: 860-297-2180

Founded: 1823
Religion: Non-Affiliated
Housing: Yes
Male/Female: 51:49
Graduate Enrollment: 170

Athletic: No
In State: $ 32,130

Financial Aid: Yes
Out of State: $ 32,130

Programs of Study: American Studies, Anthropology, Art History, BioChemistry, Biology, Chemistry, Classics, Comparative Literature, Computer Science, Economics, Educational, Engineering, English, Fine Arts, Guided Studies, History, Interdisciplinary Science, International Studies, Jewish Studies, Legal Studies, Mathematics, Modern Languages, Music, Neuroscience, Political Science, Religion, Studio/Theatre, Women's Studies

Women's Athletic Profile

Summit Street
Hartford, CT 06106
Coach: Renee Najerian
Email: renee.najerian@mail.trincoll.edu

NCAA I
Lady Bantams, Blue, Gold
Phone: (860) 297-2079
Fax: (860) 297-2492

Did Not Return Profile

United States Coast Guard Academy
Academic Profile

15 Mohegan Avenue
New London, CT 06320

Type: Public, 4 Yr., Coed
Website: http://www.cga.edu
SAT/ACT/GPA: None
Student/Faculty Ratio: 1:10
Undergraduate Enrollment: 900
Scholarships/Academic: None
Expenses By: Year
Specializes In: Federal Service Academy
Degrees Conferred: BS

Phone: 800-883-8724

Founded: 1876
Religion: Non-Affiliated
Housing: Yes
Male/Female: 70:30
Graduate Enrollment: N/A

Athletic: None
In State: $ 4,158

Financial Aid: None
Out of State: $ 12,676

Programs of Study: Business and Management, Computer Science, Engineering, Mathematics, Physical Sciences, Social Sciences

Women's Athletic Profile

15 Mohegan Avenue
New London, CT 06320
Coach: Patty Giannattasio
Email: pgiannattasio@exmail.uscga.edu

NCAA I
Lady Cadets, Royal Blue, White
Phone: (860) 444-8589
Fax: (860) 444-8607

Estimated # of Women's Volleyball Scholarships: N/A
Conference: Eastern College Athletic Conference

University of Bridgeport
Academic Profile

120 Waldemere Avenue
Bridgeport, CT 06601

Phone: (203) 576-4727

Type: Private, 4 Yr., Liberal Arts, Engineering, Coed
Website: http://www.bridgeport.edu
SAT/ACT/GPA: 820/18
Student/Faculty Ratio: 13:1
Undergraduate Enrollment: 2,700
Scholarships/Academic: Yes   **Athletic:** Yes
Expenses By: Year   **In State:** $ 20,854
Specializes In: Education, Dental Hygiene
Degrees Conferred: All majors are fully accredited

Founded: 1927
Religion: Non-Affiliated
Housing: Yes
Male/Female: 51:49
Graduate Enrollment: N/A
Financial Aid: Yes
Out of State: $ 20,854

Programs of Study: Accounting, Biology, Business, Computer Engineering, Education, Computer Science, Dental Hygiene, Fashion Merchandising, Finance, Graphic Design, Interior Design, Mass Communications, Social Science, PreVet, Marketing, Advertising, History, Psychology, Political Science, etc...

Women's Athletic Profile

120 Waldermere Avenue
Bridgeport, CT 06601
Coach: Debra Larson
Email:

NCAA I
Purple Knights, Purple, White
Phone: (203) 576-4736
Fax: (203) 475-4057

Did Not Return Profile

University of Connecticut
Academic Profile

2111 Hillside Road, U-78
Storrs, CT 06269

Phone: (860) 486-4204

Type: Public, 4 Yr., Coed
Website: http://www.uconnhuskies.edu
SAT/ACT/GPA: 1100/2.0
Student/Faculty Ratio: 14:1
Undergraduate Enrollment: 11,216
Scholarships/Academic: Yes   **Athletic:** Yes
Expenses By: Year   **In State:** $ 11,216
Degrees Conferred: BA, BFA, BMS, General Studies

Founded: 1881
Religion: Non-Affiliated
Housing: Yes
Male/Female: 48:52
Graduate Enrollment: 19,990
Financial Aid: Yes
Out of State: $ 19,990

Programs of Study: Agriculture and Natural Science, Business Administration, Allied Health, Education, Engineering, Extended and Continuing Education, Family Studies, Fine Arts, General Studies, Honors Program, Liberal Arts & Sciences, Nursing, Pharmacy

Women's Athletic Profile

2111 Hillside Rd. U-78
Storrs, CT 06269-3078
Coach: Keli Myers
Email: kmyers@athletics.ath.ucom.edu

NCAA I
Lady Huskies, Navy, White, Red
Phone: (860) 486-4486
Fax: (860) 486-2197

Estimated # of Women's Volleyball Scholarships: 12
Conference: Big East Conference
Program Profile: In 1998, the Huskies won the regular season championship for the Big East under first year Coach, Kelli Myers. At the University of Connecticut, volleyball games are held in Campbell Pavillion. For the last seven years, the Huskies have posted 20 or more wins.
History: Our program began in 1975 when we joined the Big East Conference. We have won the Big East regular season and have won two Championships. (1991 and 1998).
Achievements: Won regular season Big East Conference Champions in 1994 and 1998. Jenelle Koester and Annette Ryan were voted to the All-District Team for District 1.
Coaching: Kelli Myers, Head Coach, was a two-time All-ACC player at Maryland. She led the Huskies to a 22-10 record and a Big East record of 10-1. Jennifer Kubista and Christy Peters are Assistant Coaches.

Freshman Receiving Financial Aid/Academic: **Athletic:** 1
Roster In State: 1   **Out of State:** 13   **Out of Country:** 0
Sophomores on Team: 4   **Seniors on Team:** 3   **Graduation %:** 91
Most Recent Record: 22-11-0   **Fall Games:** 33   **Spring Games:** 11
Camp of Clinic Dates: July 5-9; August 6-10
Positions Needed: Outside Hitter, Setter, Middle Hitter
Schedule: Michigan, Duke, Indiana, South Carolina, Notre Dame, Georgetown, Duke
Style of Play: We are a middle oriented team. We are defensively sound, so that the middles can run quick in transition. Outsides and right sides also run quick attacks.

University of Hartford
Academic Profile

200 Bloomfield Avenue   **Phone:** 860-768-4296
West Hartford, CT 06117

Type: Private, 4 Yr., Liberal Arts, Coed   **Founded:** 1877
Website: http://www.hartford.edu   **Religion:** Non-Affiliated
SAT/ACT/GPA: 850+   **Housing:** Yes
Student/Faculty Ratio: 11:1   **Male/Female:** 49:50
Undergraduate Enrollment: 5,230   **Graduate Enrollment:** 1,662
Scholarships/Academic: Yes   **Athletic:** Yes   **Financial Aid:** Yes
Expenses By: Year   **In State:** $ 27,218   **Out of State:** $ 27,218
Degrees Conferred: AA, AS, AAS, BA, BS, BFA, MA, MS, MBA, MEd, D
Programs of Study: Accounting, Architecture, Audio Engineering, Business Administration, Business Accounting, BioEngineering, Biology, Chemistry, Communications, Computer Engineering , Dance, Drama, Drawing, Economics, Education, Engineering, History, Mathematics, Music, Nursing, Philosophy, Physics, Psychology, Public Administration, Respiratory Therapy, Women's Studies

Women's Athletic Profile

200 Bloomfield Avenue   **NCAA I**
West Hartford, CT 06117-1599   Lady Hawks, Scarlet, White
Coach: Alexander Ha   **Phone:** (860) 768-5659
Email: **Fax:** (860) 768-5047

Estimated # of Women's Volleyball Scholarships: N/A
Conference: American East Conference
Program Profile: Hartford looks to improve its intensity in the ever improving America East Conference. First Year head Coach Alex Ha leads the team into a 30 game schedule, including two tournaments at Hartford's Sports Center.
History: The program is in its 23rd year starting in 1977 with an All-time mark of 353-359
Achievements: Hartford made its first ever post season appearance in 1990, earning an ECAC tournament bid. In 1993 the Hawks won the North Atlantic Conference title and advanced to the national tournament.
Coaching: Head Coach Alexander Ha first year at Hartford, played at Wesleyan College, graduating in 1994.
Roster In State: 3   **Out of State:** 10
Sophomores on Team: **Seniors on Team:** 3
Most Recent Record: 9-25   **Fall Games:** 30

University of New Haven
Academic Profile

300 Orange Avenue   **Phone:** (203) 932-7027
West Haven, CT 06516
Type: Private, 4 Yr., Liberal Arts, Engineering, Coed   **Founded:** 1920
Website: http://www.newhaven.edu   **Religion:** Non-Affiliated
SAT/ACT/GPA: 820/17   **Housing:** Yes
Student/Faculty Ratio: 14:1   **Male/Female:** 7:5
Undergraduate Enrollment: 1,600   **Graduate Enrollment:** 2,600
Scholarships/Academic: Yes   **Athletic:** Yes   **Financial Aid:** Yes
Expenses By: Year   **In State:** $ 21,000   **Out of State:** $ 21,000
Specializes In: Criminal Justice, Forensic Science
Degrees Conferred: AS, BA, BS, MA, MS, MBA, Ph.D.
Programs of Study: Contact school for programs of study.

Women's Athletic Profile

300 Orange Avenue
West Haven, CT 06516
Coach: Robin Salters
Email: rsalters@charger.newhaven.edu

NCAA I
Lady Chargers, Blue, Gold
Phone: (203) 932-7022
Fax: (203) 932-7470

Estimated # of Women's Volleyball Scholarships: N/A
Conference: New England Collegiate Conference

Wesleyan University
Academic Profile

Freeman Athletic Center
Middletown, CT 06459

Phone: (860) 685-2690

Type: Private, 4 Yr., Liberal Arts, Coed
Website: http://www.wesleyan.edu
SAT/ACT/GPA: 1340
Student/Faculty Ratio: 11:1
Undergraduate Enrollment: 2750
Scholarships/Academic: Yes   **Athletic:** No
Expenses By: Year   **In State:** $ 32,000

Founded: 1831
Religion: Methodist
Housing: Yes
Male/Female: 1:1
Graduate Enrollment: 300
Financial Aid: Yes
Out of State: $ 32,000

Specializes In: Premed, Psychology, Economics, Languages, Arts, Social Sciences
Degrees Conferred: BA, MA, Ph.D.
Programs of Study: Afro-American Studies, American Studies, Anthropology, Archaeological Studies, Art History, Astronomy, Biology, Classical Studies, Classical Civilization, Chemistry, College of Letters, College of Social Studies, Computer Science, Dance, Earth & Environmental Sciences, East Asian Studies, Economics, English, Film Studies, Government, History, Latin American Studies, Mathematics, Medieval Studies, Molecular Biology & BioChemistry, Music, Neuroscience & Behavior, Philosophy, Physics, Psychology, Religion, Romance Languages, Russian & Eastern Studies, Science in Society, Sociology, Studio Art, Theatre, Women's Studies

Women's Athletic Profile

Freeman Athletic Center
Middletown, CT 06457
Coach: Gale Lackey
Email: glackey@wesleyan.edu

NCAA I
Lady Cardinals, Cardinal, Black
Phone: (860) 685-2690
Fax: (860) 685-2691

Estimated # of Women's Volleyball Scholarships: None
Conference: New England Small College Athletic Conference
Program Profile: We have a solid Division III program. We play a competitive schedule that features many ranked regional opponents. The season ends with the NESCAR Tournament. We play about 8 weekend tournaments and 8 weekday matches.
History: Our first varsity season was in 1984. We have a 15 year overall record of 222-212-1.
Achievements: 3 time NESCAR 1st team All-Star-Ashley Chase; Best seasons: 1991(24-11) and 1989 (23-7).
Coaching: Gale Lackey - Head Coach, has been coach for 14 years. Her career record at Wesleyan is 214-215. Joe Rouse has been Assistant for 14 years. Maritza Ubides is Assistant Coach. She was a former Conference All-Star as a setter.
Roster In State: 2   **Out of State:** 11   **Out of Country:** 0
Sophomores on Team: 0   **Seniors on Team:** 3   **Graduation %:** 100
Most Recent Record: 15-19-0   **Fall Games:** 30-35   **Spring Games:** 0
Schedule: Amherst, Williams, Eastern Connecticut, Middlebury, Massachusetts Institute of Technology, Wellesley
Style of Play: 5-1 offense; tough serving team which plays a strong defense behind a big block.

Western Connecticut State University
Academic Profile

181 White Street
Danbury, CT 06810
Type: Public, 4 Yr., Liberal Arts, Coed
Website: http://www.ctstateu.edu
SAT/ACT/GPA: 900/17
Student/Faculty Ratio: 20:1
Undergraduate Enrollment: 1,500
Scholarships/Academic: Yes   **Athletic:** No

Phone: (203) 837-9022

Founded: 1903
Religion: Non-Affiliated
Housing: Yes
Male/Female: 50:50
Graduate Enrollment: 2,950
Financial Aid: Yes

Expenses By: Year   **In State:** $ 9,904   **Out of State:** $ 15,413

Degrees Conferred: AS, BA, BS, MA, MS, MBA

Programs of Study: Accounting, American Studies, Art and Graphic Design, Astronomy, Biology, Business, Chemistry, Communications, Computer Science, Contract Major, Dramatic Arts, Earth Science, Economics, Elementary Education, English, Finance, Government, Health, History, Journalism, Justice and Law Administration, Law, Management, Marketing, Meteorology, Management Information Systems, Mathematics, Media, Music, Music Education, Nursing, Psychology, Political Science, School Professional, Secondary Education, Sociology & Anthropology, Social Work, Theatre

Women's Athletic Profile

181 White Street
Danbury, CT 06810
Coach: Richard Myers
Email: myers@wcsu.ctstateu.edu

NCAA I
Lady Colonials, Blue, White
Phone: (203) 837-9022
Fax: (203) 837-9050

Estimated # of Women's Volleyball Scholarships: 0

Conference: Little East Conference

Program Profile: Feldman Arena has a 2,700 seating capacity. We play on a sport court designed for volleyball only with seats that have back support. There is a weight room and a pool. We have a Fall and a Spring season. We have a conditioning non-traditional program year around.

History: We have been in NCAA since 1981. We have been an independent athletic conference member from 1986 to 1991. We have been a member of the Little East Conference from 1995 to the present.

Achievements: Under the current coach, we won our most recent 1st place in the 1998 ELAC Tournament. We were 2nd in Conference in 1995, 1997 and 1998 (the Conference started in 1995). We were 1st in the Independent Athletic Conference in 1989, 1990 and 1991. We were 2nd in 1988. We left the conference in 1991.

Coaching: Richard Myers, Head Coach, has been here since 1988. Assistant Coach Dan Altro started in 1998. Our overall record is 175-195. The last 6 years we had 18 matches over 500.

Freshman Receiving Financial Aid/Academic: **Athletic:** 0

Roster In State: 7   **Out of State:** 2   **Out of Country:** 0

Sophomores on Team: 4   **Seniors on Team:** 0   **Graduation %:** Unknown

Most Recent Record: 20-16-0   **Fall Games:** 32-36   **Spring Games:** 4-5

Positions Needed: Middle Hitter, Setter

Schedule: Bates College, Amherst College, Williams College, Springfield College, Massachusetts Institute of Technology, Wellesley College

Style of Play: Multiple offense. Establish aggressive first tempo sets along 2/3 of net to open up both combination plays and second tempo attacks. Defense-four blocking scheme with flexible back row read.

Yale University
Academic Profile

Box 208216
New Haven, CT 06520

Phone: 203-432-9300

Type: Private, 4 Yr., Liberal Arts, Coed
Website: http://www.yale.edu
SAT/ACT/GPA: Open
Student/Faculty Ratio: 5:1
Undergraduate Enrollment: 5,200
Scholarships/Academic: Yes   **Athletic:** No
Expenses By: Year   **In State:** $ 30,830

Founded: 1701
Religion: Non-Affiliated
Housing: Yes
Male/Female: 1:1
Graduate Enrollment: 5,200
Financial Aid: Yes
Out of State: $ 30,830

Degrees Conferred: BA, MA, Ph.D.., JD, M.Div, MD, BS, BLS

Programs of Study: African & African - American Studies, Anthropology, Astronomy & Physics, Chemistry, Chinese, Classics, Comparative Literature, Economics, Engineering, English, History, Judaic Studies, Latin American Studies, Mathematics, Organism Biology, Philosophy, Physics, Psychology, Religious Studies, Russian, Sociology, Theatre Studies, Women's Studies

Women's Athletic Profile

P.O. Box 208216
New Haven, CT 06520-7398
Coach: Peg Scofield
Email: peg.scofield@yale.edu

NCAA I
Bulldogs, Eli, Yale Blue, White
Phone: (203) 432-1408
Fax: (203) 432-1417

Estimated # of Women's Volleyball Scholarships: N/A
Conference: Ivy League
Achievements: We were 3rd in Conference Tournament.
Coaching: Peg Scofield, Head Coach, graduated from Rutgers in 1984. She has been at Yale for 13 years and has a record of 249-139. Shawn Monahan is our Assistant Coach.
Most Recent Record: 21-10-0
Schedule: Princeton, Harvard

DELAWARE

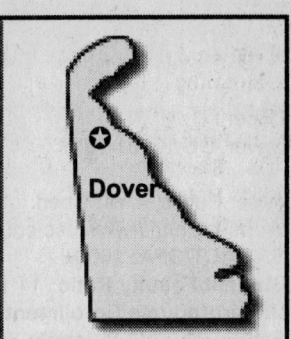

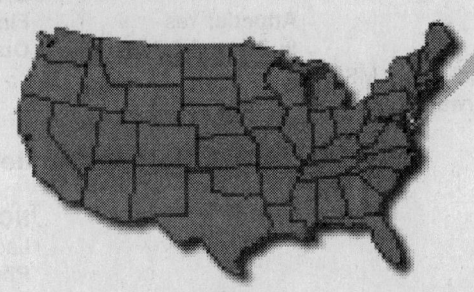

Dover

SCHOOL	CITY	AFFILIATION	PAGE
Delaware State University	Dover	NCAA I	145
Goldey-Beacom College	Wilmington	NAIA	145
University of Delaware	Newark	NCAA I	145
Wilmington College	New Castle	NCAA II/NAIA	146

Delaware State University
Academic Profile

Dupont Hwy.
Dover, DE 19901-2277

Phone: 800-845-2544

Type: Public, 4 Yr., Coed
Website: http://www.dsc.edu
SAT/ACT/GPA: 1000+
Student/Faculty Ratio: 14:1
Undergraduate Enrollment: 3,030
Scholarships/Academic: Yes
Expenses By: Year
Degrees Conferred: BA, BS, MA, MS, MBA, MSW, BT
Programs of Study: Accounting, Airway Science

Founded: 1891
Religion: Non-Affiliated
Housing: Yes
Male/Female: 47:53
Graduate Enrollment: 200
Athletic: Yes   **Financial Aid:** Yes
In State: $ 5,776   **Out of State:** $ 8,808

Women's Athletic Profile

Dupont Hwy.
Dover, DE 19901
Coach: Jane Hicks
Email: jfoster@dsc.edu

NCAA I
Lady Hornets, Blue, Red
Phone: (302) 857-6033
Fax: (302) 739-3553

Goldey - Beacom College
Academic Profile

4701 Limestone Rd
Wilmington, DE 19808

Phone: (302) 998-8814

Type: Private, 4 Yr., Coed
Website: http://www.goldey.edu
SAT/ACT/GPA: 973
Student/Faculty Ratio: 26:1
Undergraduate Enrollment: 1,400
Scholarships/Academic: Yes
Expenses By: Year
Specializes In: Business
Degrees Conferred: AS, BS, MBA
Programs of Study: Accounting, Accounting & Information Systems, Computer Information Systems, Business Administration, Management, Marketing Management, Human Resources Management, Finance Management and International Business

Founded: 1886
Religion: Non-Affiliated
Housing: Yes
Male/Female: 40:60
Graduate Enrollment: 150
Athletic: Yes   **Financial Aid:** Yes
In State: $ 13,370   **Out of State:** $ 13,370

Women's Athletic Profile

4701 Limeston Rd.
Wilmington, DE 19808
Coach: Gerry Szabo
Email:

NCAA I
Lady Braves, Blue, Gold
Phone: (302) 998-8814
Fax: (302) 998-3467

Did Not Return Profile

University of Delaware
Academic Profile

Delaware Field House
Newark, DE 19716-2001
Type: Public, 4 Yr., Liberal Arts, Engineering, Coed
Website: http://www.udel.edu
SAT/ACT/GPA: 1000/3.01
Student/Faculty Ratio: 15:1
Undergraduate Enrollment: 15,000
Scholarships/Academic: Yes
Expenses By: Year
Degrees Conferred: BA, BS, BMAS, Engineering

Phone: (302) 831-2000

Founded: 1743
Religion: Non-Affiliated
Housing: Yes
Male/Female: 45:55
Graduate Enrollment: 3,200
Athletic: Yes   **Financial Aid:** Yes
In State: $ 14,403   **Out of State:** $ 18,765

Programs of Study: Agriculture, Anthropology, Apparel Design, Art, Athletics and Recreation, BioChemistry, Biology, BioTechnology, Business and Economics Accounting, Business Management, Chemistry, Communications, Computer Science, Criminal Justice, Dietetics, Economics, Education, Elementary Education, Engineering (Chemical, Civil, Electrical, Computer, Mechanical, Environmental), English, Entomology, Family and Consumer Services, Finance, Human Resources, Literature, Management, Marketing, Medical Technology, Nursing, Nutrition, Physical Education, Recreation/Park, Textiles and Clothing Merchandising

Women's Athletic Profile

Carpenter Sports Building
Newark, DE 19716
Coach: Barbara Viera
Email: viera@udel.edu

NCAA I
Fighting Blue Hens, Blue, Gold
Phone: (302) 831-8606
Fax: (302) 831-4261

Estimated # of Women's Volleyball Scholarships: 4
Conference: American East Conference
Program Profile: Delaware will enter the 1999 season with a newly renovated gym, a new volleyball locker-room, new volleyball offices and a new training room. The program and facilities are excellent.
History: Program began in 1972, has had a winning record in 22 of 26 seasons under Coach Viera.
Achievements: Coach of the Year three times, 2 Conference Titles. Have been above .500 22 of 26 season under Coach Viera.
Coaching: Barbara Viera, Head Coach, is entering her 26th year with the program. She compiled an overall record of 615-413. Eriis Andrejev and Lorie Miller are the Assistant Coaches.

Freshman Receiving Financial Aid/Academic: **Athletic:** 3
Roster In State: 2   **Out of State:** 13   **Out of Country:** 0
Sophomores on Team: 3   **Seniors on Team:** 4   **Graduation %:** 97
Most Recent Record: 15-21-0   **Fall Games:** 36   **Spring Games:** 4
Camp of Clinic Dates: Last two weeks of July
Positions Needed: Middle Hitter, Setter, Outside Hitter
Schedule: San Diego, Georgetown, Loyola-Chicago, University of Connecticut, Syracuse, New Hampshire
Style of Play: We enjoy playing a quick offense and strong defense.

Wilmington College
Academic Profile

DuPont Hwy.
New Castle, DE 19720

Phone: 877-967-5464

Type: 4 Yr., Coed
Website: http://www.wilmcoll.edu
SAT/ACT/GPA: Open
Student/Faculty Ratio: 22:1
Undergraduate Enrollment: 5,500
Scholarships/Academic:
Expenses By: Year

Founded: 1967
Religion: Non-Affiliated
Housing: No
Male/Female: Not Available
Graduate Enrollment: N/A
Athletic: **Financial Aid:**
In State: $ 6,080+   **Out of State:** $ 6,008+

Degrees Conferred: Bachelors, Masters, Doctoral
Programs of Study: Accounting, Aircraft and Missile Maintenance, Air Traffic Control, Aviation Administration, Aviation Technology, Behavioral Science, Broadcasting, Business Administration, Commerce, Management, Communications, Criminal Justice, Early Childhood Education, Elementary Education, Finance/Banking, Human Resources, Liberal Arts, General Studies, Nursing, Sports Administration, Theatre Arts/Drama

Women's Athletic Profile

320 Dupont Highway
New Castle, DE 19720
Coach: Steve Lenderman
Email: volleyball@wilmcoll.edu

NCAA I
Wildcats, Dark Green, White
Phone: 302-328-9435
Fax: 302-328-8045

Estimated # of Women's Volleyball Scholarships: 2
Conference: Central Atlantic Athletic Conference
Program Profile: Wilmington College is a NAIA and NCAA II (Provisional) member. Play both NAIA and NCAA II schedule. Our home contests are played in Pratt Gymnasium which seats 1000. 1999 NAIA National Tournament 19th seed.
History: Volleyball began at Wilmington College in 1978. The college was a member of the National Small College Athletics Association and has grown to NCAA II. The program is fully supported by the college and has produced some of the college's finest graduates.

Achievements: We have had 14 All-Americans and 5 Academic All-Americans. 1999 Conference Champions, Region X Champions, 3 All Conference selections, and 2 All Region Selections.

Coaching: Second year Head Coach Steve Lenderman is back after completing the most successful season in Wilmington College Volleyball. In addition to coaching, Coach Lenderman is very active in USA Volleyball and has completed Coaches Accreditation Program Level II.

Freshman Receiving Financial Aid/Academic: **Athletic:** 8

Roster In State: 10   **Out of State:** 2   **Out of Country:** 0

Seniors on Team: 1   **Graduation %:** 100

Most Recent Record: 22-11

Camp of Clinic Dates: July 30-August3, August 6-10

Positions Needed: Middle Hitters, Opposite, Outsides

Schedule: West Chester, Millersville, Bloomfield, East Stroudssburg, Kutztown, Goldey Beacom

Style of Play: Variable quick offense utilizing a 5-1. Big blockers and great defense.

DISTRICT OF COLUMBIA

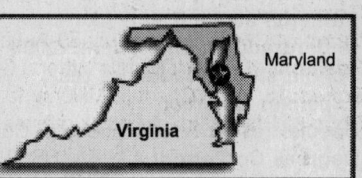

SCHOOL	CITY	AFFILIATION	PAGE
American University	Washington D.C.	NCAA I	149
Catholic University of America	Washington D.C	NCAA III	149
Gallaudet University	Washington D.C	NCAA III	150
George Washington University	Washington D.C	NCAA I	150
Georgetown University	Washington D.C	NCAA I	151
Howard University	Washington D.C	NCAA I	151
University of District of Columbia	Washington D.C	NCAA II	152

American University
Academic Profile

4400 Massachusetts Avenue, NW
Washington, DC 20016

Phone: (202) 885-3031

Type: Private, 4 Yr., Liberal Arts, Coed
Website: http://www.aueagles.edu
SAT/ACT/GPA: 1200/3.4
Student/Faculty Ratio: 15:1
Undergraduate Enrollment: 6,000
Scholarships/Academic: Yes   **Athletic:** Yes
Expenses By: Year   **In State:** $ 29,500

Founded: 1893
Religion: Methodist
Housing: Yes
Male/Female: 2:3
Graduate Enrollment: 5,000
Financial Aid: Yes
Out of State: $ 29,500

Specializes In: Arts & Sciences, Communications, Public Affairs
Degrees Conferred: AA, BA, BS, BFA, MA, MS, MBA, MFA, Ph.D., JD, EdD
Programs of Study: Accounting, American Studies, Anthropology, Art History, Audio Technology, Biological Science, Business Administration, Chemistry, Communications, Computer Science, Economics, Education, Environmental Science, Fine Arts, Foreign Languages & Media, General Studies, Health, History, Interdisciplinary Studies, International Studies, Justice, Law, Liberal, Literature, Mathematics, Music, Performance Arts, Theater, Philosophy, Physics, Political Science, Psychology, Russian Studies, Secondary Education, Sociology, Spanish, Statistics, Studio Art

Women's Athletic Profile

4400 Massachusetts Ave., NW
Washington, DC 20016
Coach: Barry Goldberg
Email: bgoldbe@american.edu

NCAA I
Lady Eagles, Red, Blue, White
Phone: (202) 885-1127
Fax: (202) 885-3033

Estimated # of Women's Volleyball Scholarships: 10
Conference: Colonial Athletic Association
Program Profile: We have a beautiful Washington, D. C. campus. We are a small Division I university with excellent academic reputation and international outreach.
History: Our volleyball program was reinstated in 1985. We had three post-season appearances in the past 5 years including two Colonial Championships in 1997 and 1998.
Achievements: 2 Colonial Conference Champions in 1997-1998; 2 Coach of the Year in the Colonial Conference.
Coaching: Barry Goldberg - Head Coach. His ten year overall record is 249-113. Kim Kumfer is Assistant Coach.
Freshman Receiving Financial Aid/Academic: **Athletic:** 3
Roster In State: 0   **Out of State:** 13   **Out of Country:** 7
Sophomores on Team: 4   **Seniors on Team:** 3   **Graduation %:** 100
Most Recent Record: 29-6-0   **Fall Games:** 33   **Spring Games:** 0
Positions Needed: None
Schedule: James Madison, George Mason, William & Mary, Virginia Commonwealth, East Carolina, UNC Wilmington
Style of Play: Hard and fast.

Catholic University of America
Academic Profile

620 Michigan Avenue
Washington, DC 20064

Phone: 202-319-5305

Type: Private, 4 Yr., Liberal Arts, Engineering, Coed
Website: http://www.cua.edu
SAT/ACT/GPA: 1100
Student/Faculty Ratio: 10:1
Undergraduate Enrollment: 2,400
Scholarships/Academic: Yes   **Athletic:** No
Expenses By: Year   **In State:** $ 28,000

Founded: 1887
Religion: Catholic
Housing: Yes
Male/Female: 47:53
Graduate Enrollment: 2,800
Financial Aid: Yes
Out of State: $ 28,000

Degrees Conferred: BA, BS, BArch, MA, MS, MFA, Ph.D., EdD, JD, Mdiv
Programs of Study: Architecture and Planning, Arts and Sciences, Engineering, Music, Nursing and Philosophy

Women's Athletic Profile

620 Michigan Avenue, NE
Washington, DC 20064
Coach: TBA
Email:

NCAA I
Lady Cardinals, Red, Black
Phone: (202) 319-5286
Fax: (202) 319-6199

Estimated # of Women's Volleyball Scholarships: N/A
Conference: Capital Athletic Conference
History: 1984 was the first year of volleyball at CUA. Member of the Capital Athletic Conference since 1989.
Achievements: Nagy Aledecazer was named 1994 Coach of the year, 1994 CAC champions, Cris Waterhousew was 1994 #1 in the nation in Digs, 1994 Cris Waterhouse was named Woman of the Year in DC, 1996 Kristen Bufka was named Player of the Year.

Roster In State: 0	**Out of State:** 13	**Out of Country:** 0
Sophomores on Team: 5	**Seniors on Team:** 1	**Graduation %:** 100
Most Recent Record: 13-20-0	**Fall Games:** 30	**Spring Games:** 4

Camp of Clinic Dates: August 20-25
Positions Needed: Setter, Middle Hitter
Schedule: Washington & Lee, Gallaudet, Salisbury State, Lycoming, York College, Goucher
Style of Play: We play 5-1 formation and quick attack.

Gallaudet University
Academic Profile

800 Florida Avenue, NE
Washington, DC 20002

Phone: (202)651-5603

Type: Private, 4 Yr., Liberal Arts, Coed
Website: http://www.gallaudet.edu
SAT/ACT/GPA: None
Student/Faculty Ratio: 1/3
Undergraduate Enrollment: 1,300
Scholarships/Academic: Yes   **Athletic:** No
Expenses By: Year   **In State:** $15,000

Founded: 1864
Religion: Non-Affiliated
Housing: Yes
Male/Female: 7/10
Graduate Enrollment: 650
Financial Aid: Yes
Out of State: $15,000

Specializes In: Deaf Education, Business, Computers, Biology, Mathematics
Degrees Conferred: AAS, BA, BS,MA, MS, MBA, M.Ed., Ph.D., EdD
Programs of Study: Accounting, Art History, BioChemistry, Biology, Business, Communications, Computer, Engineering, English, International Studies, Management, Math, Philosophy, Recreation, Deaf Studies, Social Science ***Contact school for more information

Women's Athletic Profile

800 Florida Avenue, NE
Washington, DC 20002
Coach: Patrick O'Brien
Email: ptobrien@gallua.gallaudet.edu

NCAA I
Lady Bison, Buff, Blue
Phone: (202) 651-5712
Fax: (202) 651-5274

Estimated # of Women's Volleyball Scholarships: N/A
Conference: Capital Athletic Conference

George Washington University
Academic Profile

600 22nd Street, NW
Washington, DC 20052

Phone: (202) 994-6650

Type: Private, 4 Yr., Liberal Arts, Engineering, Coed
Website: http://www.gwu.edu
SAT/ACT/GPA: 1100/3.0
Student/Faculty Ratio: 17:1
Undergraduate Enrollment: 5,800
Scholarships/Academic: Yes   **Athletic:** Yes
Expenses By: Year   **In State:** $31,000

Founded: 1776
Religion: Non-Affiliated
Housing: Yes
Male/Female: 2:3
Graduate Enrollment: 10,000
Financial Aid: Yes
Out of State: $31,000

Specializes In: Business, Engineering, Government
Degrees Conferred: 1184 Bachelors Degree conferred 1995-1996 foggy bottom campus.
Programs of Study: Accounting, Anthropology, Applied Mathematics, Archaeology, Arts, Biology, Business, Chemistry, Computer Science, Criminal Justice, Economics, Engineering, Psychology, General Studies

Women's Athletic Profile

600 22nd Street, NW
Washington, DC 20052
Coach: Jojit Coronel
Email: jojitc@yahoo.com

NCAA I
Lady Colonials, Buff, Blue
Phone: (202) 994-5777
Fax: (202) 994-7399

Estimated # of Women's Volleyball Scholarships: N/A
Conference: Atlantic 10 Conference
Achievements: 4 Atlantic 10 Championships; 3 NCAA Appearances; 2 Atlantic 10 Conference Coach of the Year.
Coaching: Susie Homan has been Head Coach here for 10 years. She has directed the Colonials to four consecutive Atlantic 10 Championships and three NCAA Appearances. She is a two-time recipient of the Atlantic 10 Conference Coach of the Year award.
Camp of Clinic Dates: High Potential: August 1-5

Georgetown University
Academic Profile

Athletic Department
Washington, DC 20057

Phone: (202) 687-5414

Type: Private, 4 Yr., Coed
Website: http://www.georgetown.ecu
SAT/ACT/GPA: 1200+
Student/Faculty Ratio: 12:1
Undergraduate Enrollment: 6,000
Scholarships/Academic: No   **Athletic:** Yes
Expenses By: Year   **In State:** $ 31,816
Degrees Conferred: BA, BS, MA, MBA, Ph.D., MD, JD

Founded: 1789
Religion: Jesuit
Housing: Yes
Male/Female: 49:51
Graduate Enrollment: 6,000
Financial Aid: Yes
Out of State: $ 31,816

Programs of Study: Accounting, Anthropology, Archeology, Arts, Biology, Business & Management, Communications, Computer Science, Criminal Justice, Geography, Engineering, Mathematics, Philosophy, Human Resources, Religion, Political Science, Medical Technology, Psychology

Women's Athletic Profile

McDonough Arena
Washington, DC 20057
Coach: Li Liu
Email: liul1@gunet.georgetown.edu

NCAA I
Lady Hoyas, Blue, Grey
Phone: (202) 687-5414
Fax: (202) 687-2491

Estimated # of Women's Volleyball Scholarships: N/A
Conference: Big East Conference

Howard University
Academic Profile

6th & Girards St., NW
Washington, DC 20059

Phone: 800-822-6363

Type: Private, 4 Yr., Engineering, Coed
Website: http://www.howard.edu
SAT/ACT/GPA: 820/18
Student/Faculty Ratio: Not Avai
Undergraduate Enrollment: 7,650
Scholarships/Academic: Yes   **Athletic:** Yes
Expenses By: Year   **In State:** $ 12,000
Specializes In: Business

Founded: 1867
Religion: Non-Affiliated
Housing: No
Male/Female: 40:60
Graduate Enrollment: 3,050
Financial Aid: Yes
Out of State: $ 12,000

Degrees Conferred: BA, BS, BFA, BArch, BBA, BFA, BSW, MA, MS, ,BA, MFA, M.Ed., Ph.D., JD
Programs of Study: Accounting, Actuarial Science, Anthropology, Arabic, Architecture, Banking/Finance, Botany, Business Administration, Chemistry, Criminal Justice, Economics, Education, Engineering, History, Insurance, International Business & Relations, Marketing, MicroBiology, Occupational Therapy

Women's Athletic Profile

6th & Girard Street, NW
Washington, DC 20059
Coach: Linda Spencer
Email: lspencer@howard.edu
Estimated # of Women's Volleyball Scholarships: 12
Conference: Mid-Eastern Athletic Conference
Program Profile: NCAA Division I program. Main Gym is the Burr Gymnasium and has a seating capacity of 3,500. Playing season September-November and have 12 full scholarships.
History: Program began in 1974. Conference affiliation since 1983. Won the Conference Championships 8 times, 5 championships under current coach. NCAA post season play in 1994.
Achievements: 5 Coach of the Year Honors (MEAC), 100 Tachikara Victory Club-1991, 200 Tachikara Victory Club 1997, AVCA-member.

NCAA I
Lady Bison, Navy Blue, White
Phone: (202) 806-5204
Fax: (202) 806-7004

Freshman Receiving Financial Aid/Academic: **Athletic:** 2

Roster In State: 0	**Out of State:** 12	**Out of Country:** 1
Sophomores on Team: 3	**Seniors on Team:** 2	**Graduation %:** 100
Most Recent Record: 14-19-0	**Fall Games:** 33	**Spring Games:** 0

University of the District of Columbia
Academic Profile

4200 Connecticut Ave.
Washington, DC 20008
Type: Public, 4 Yr., Liberal Arts, Engineering, Coed
Website: http://www.udc.edu
SAT/ACT/GPA: Open
Student/Faculty Ratio: 14:1
Undergraduate Enrollment: 10,000
Scholarships/Academic: Yes   **Athletic:** Yes
Expenses By: Year   **In State:** $ 6,500

Phone: 202-274-6110

Founded: 1976
Religion: Non-Affiliated
Housing: No
Male/Female: 42:58
Graduate Enrollment: 595
Financial Aid: Yes
Out of State: $ 9,000

Degrees Conferred: BA, BS, MA, MS, MBA
Programs of Study: Accounting, Administration of Justice, Anthropology, Biology, Business Education & Management, Chemistry, Computer Science, Economics, Emergency Medical Services, Engineering, Environmental Science, Fire Science Administration, Marketing, Physical Education, Physics, Political Science, Sociology, Speech Pathology, Urban Studies

Women's Athletic Profile

4200 Connecticut Avenue, NW
Washington, DC 20008
Coach: Bessie A. Stockard
Email:

NCAA I
Lady Firebirds, Red, Gold
Phone: (202) 274-5076
Fax: (202) 274-5065

Did Not Return Profile

FLORIDA

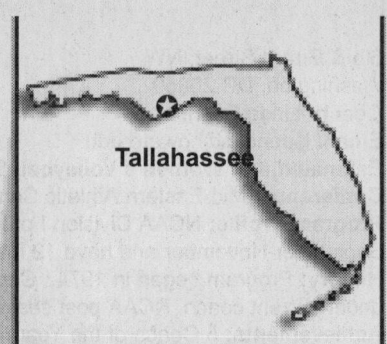

Tallahassee

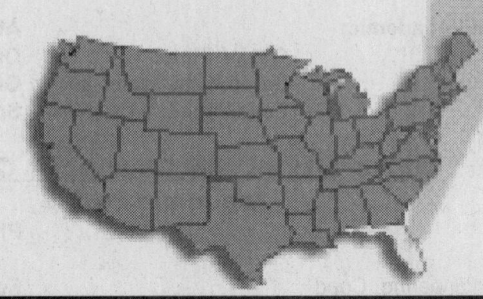

SCHOOL	CITY	AFFILIATION	PAGE
Barry University	Miami Shores	NCAA II	154
Bethune-Cookman College	Daytona Beach	NCAA I	154
Eckerd College	St. Petersburg	NCAA II	155
Embry-Riddle Aeronautical Univ.	Daytona Beach	NAIA	155
Flagler University	St. Augustine	NCAA I	156
Florida A&M University	Tallahassee	NCAA I	157
Florida Atlantic University	Boca Raton	NCAA I	157
Florida Community College	Jacksonville	NJCAA	158
Florida Institute of Technology	Melbourne	NCAA II	158
Florida International University	Miami	NCAA I	159
Florida Memorial College	Miami	NAIA	159
Florida Southern College	Lakeland	NCAA II	160
Florida State University	Tallahassee	NCAA I	160
Jacksonville University	Jacksonville	NCAA I	161
Lynn University	Boca Raton	NCAA II	161
Miami-Dade Community College	Miami	NJCAA	162
Nova Southeastern University	Fort Lauderdale	NCAA II/NAIA	163
Palm Beach Atlantic College	West Palm Beach	NAIA	163
Rollins College	Winter Park	NCAA II	164
Saint Leo College	St. Leo	NCAA II	165
Saint Thomas University	Miami	NAIA	165
Stetson University	De Land	NCAA I	166
University of Central Florida	Orlando	NCAA I	166
University of Florida	Gainesville	NCAA I	167
University of North Florida	Jacksonville	NCAA II	168
University of South Florida	Tampa	NCAA I	169
University of Tampa	Tampa	NCAA II	169
Warner Southern College	Lake Wales	NAIA	170
Webber College	Babson Park	NAIA	171

Barry University
Academic Profile

11300 NE 2nd Avenue
Miami Shores, FL 33161

Phone: 800-695-2279

Type: Private, 4 Yr., Coed
Website: http://www.2.barry.edu
SAT/ACT/GPA: 820
Student/Faculty Ratio: 12:1
Undergraduate Enrollment: 1,750
Scholarships/Academic: Yes   **Athletic:** Yes
Expenses By: Year   **In State:** $ 21,280

Founded: 1941
Religion: Catholic
Housing: Yes
Male/Female: 1:2
Graduate Enrollment: 5,500
Financial Aid: Yes
Out of State: $ 21,280

Specializes In: Health Sciences, Business, Computer Science, Sports
Degrees Conferred: BA, BS, BFA, MA, MS, MBA, Ph.D., DPM
Programs of Study: Accounting, Biology, Business, Communications, Computer Science, Economics, Education, English, Exercise Science, Foreign Languages, History, Marketing, Mathematics, MedTech, Nuclear Medicine, Nursing, Occupational Therapy, Philosophy, Physical Education, Podiatry, Political Science, PreMed, PreVet, Psychology, Social Work, Sociology, Sports Management, Theology

Women's Athletic Profile

11300 NE 2nd Avenue
Miami Shores, FL 33161
Coach: Dave Nichols
Email: fbatteufield@mail.barry.edu

NCAA I
Buccaneers, Black, Red, Silver
Phone: (305) 899-3550
Fax: (305) 899-3556

Estimated # of Women's Volleyball Scholarships: N/A
Conference: Sunshine State Conference
Program Profile: We have been one of the top Division II programs nationally the last five years. We ranked in the top 10 all five seasons. We were 1995 National Champs and 1997 National Runner-Up. We play in the 1,000-seat Health Sports Center, site of the 1995 Elite Eight.
History: Our volleyball program began in 1988 and has won 1 National title and three SSC Championships. Barry has been in the Elite Eight three of the last four years.
Achievements: Leonid Yelin is Division National Coach of the Year; Leonid Yelin and Dave Nichols were named South Region Coach of the Year; has 6 All-Americans in its short history; Former player Mikisha Hurley now starts for USA National Teams; 1997 South Region Coach of the Year.
Coaching: Dave Nichols, Head Coach, started in 1996. He won 5 National Men's Club Championships at California-Berkeley. He played on 3 NCAA title teams at UCLA. Cody Hein is Assistant Coach.
Roster In State: 5   **Out of State:** 7   **Out of Country:** 2
Sophomores on Team: 5   **Seniors on Team:** 3   **Graduation %:** Unknown
Camp of Clinic Dates: General Skills: July 12-16
Positions Needed: Middle Blocker, Setter
Style of Play: Fast tempo offense with a complex 5-1 offense. Coach Nichols stresses defense and blocking. He is renowned as one of the best trainers of middle blockers in the USA.

Bethune - Cookman College
Academic Profile

640 M. McLeod Bethune Blvd.
Daytona Beach, FL 32114

Phone: 800-448-0228

Type: Private, 4 Yr., Liberal Arts, Coed
Website: http://www.bethune.cookman.edu
SAT/ACT/GPA: 500/21/2.25
Student/Faculty Ratio: 25:1
Undergraduate Enrollment: 2,335
Scholarships/Academic: Yes   **Athletic:** Yes
Expenses By: Year   **In State:** $ 13,469

Founded: 1872
Religion: Methodist
Housing: Yes
Male/Female: 47:53
Graduate Enrollment: N/A
Financial Aid: Yes
Out of State: $ 13,469

Specializes In: Business Administration, Education, Nursing, Criminal Justice
Degrees Conferred: Bachelors
Programs of Study: Church Music, English, History, International Studies, Liberal Studies, Mass Communications, Modern Languages, Music, Political Science, Religion & Philosophy, Social Science, Sociology, Accounting, Biology, Business Administration, Chemistry, Computer Science, Criminal Justice, Elementary Education, Gerontology, Mathematics, Nursing, Physics, Psychology, Special Learning Disabilities

Women's Athletic Profile

640 M. McLeod Bethune Blvd.
Daytona Beach, FL 32114-3099
Coach: Paula Thompson
Email: varytima@cookman.edu

NCAA I
Lady Wildcats, Maroon, Gold
Phone: (904) 255-1401
Fax: (904) 253-4231

Estimated # of Women's Volleyball Scholarships: 4
Conference: Mid-Eastern Athletic Conference
Coaching: Paula Thompson, Head Coach, is entering her first season with the program. She coached 15 years in high school. Rebecca Haus, Assistant Coach, is entering her first season with the program.

Roster In State: 4	**Out of State:** 4	**Out of Country:** 1
Sophomores on Team: 1	**Seniors on Team:** 4	**Graduation %:**

Positions Needed: Setters
Schedule: St. Johns, Rice, North Carolina A&T

Eckerd College
Academic Profile

4200 54th Avenue South
St. Petersburg, FL 33711

Phone: 800-456-9009

Type: Private, 4 Yr., Liberal Arts, Coed
Website: http://www.eckerd.edu
SAT/ACT/GPA: 1100/24/3.0
Student/Faculty Ratio: 14:1
Undergraduate Enrollment: 1,500
Scholarships/Academic: Yes   **Athletic:** Yes
Expenses By: Year   **In State:** $ 22,500

Founded: 1958
Religion: Presbyterian
Housing: Yes
Male/Female: 45:55
Graduate Enrollment: N/A
Financial Aid: Yes
Out of State: $ 22,500

Specializes In: Business, Science, Medical
Degrees Conferred: BA, BS
Programs of Study: All areas of study (except physical education) including: Management, International Business, Marine Science/Biology, Political Science, Psychology, Human Resources, Chemistry, PreMed, PreLaw, PreVet

Women's Athletic Profile

4200 54th Avenue. S
St. Petersburg, FL 33733
Coach: Hollie Miller
Email:

NCAA I
Lady Tritons, Red, White, Black
Phone: (727) 864-7875
Fax: (813) 864-8968

Did Not Return Profile

Embry - Riddle Aeronautical University
Academic Profile

600 S Clyde Morris Blvd.
Daytona Beach, FL 32114

Phone: 800-862-2416

Type: Private, 4 Yr., Engineering, Coed
Website: http://www.erau.edu
SAT/ACT/GPA: 1000/20/3.0
Student/Faculty Ratio: 14:1
Undergraduate Enrollment: 4,400
Scholarships/Academic: Yes   **Athletic:** Yes
Expenses By: Year   **In State:** $ 16,000

Founded: 1925
Religion: Non-Affiliated
Housing: Yes
Male/Female: 3:1
Graduate Enrollment: N/A
Financial Aid: Yes
Out of State: $ 16,000

Specializes In: Engineering
Degrees Conferred: Associate, Baccalaureate, Masters
Programs of Study: Aircraft Maintenance, Airway Science, Aviation Business Administration, Aviation Maintenance Technology, Professional Aeronautics, Aerospace Engineering, Aerospace Studies, Aviation Computer Science, Civil Engineering, Electrical Engineering, Engineering Physics

Women's Athletic Profile

600 S. Clyde Morris Boulevard
Daytona Beach, FL 32114
Coach: Trina Keeton
Email: keetont@db.erau.edu

NCAA I
Lady Eagles, Royal Blue, Gold
Phone: (904) 323-5005
Fax: (904) 323-5002

Estimated # of Women's Volleyball Scholarships: 3 3/4 partials
Conference: Florida Sun Conference
Program Profile: Program is starting its 6th year. The facility houses 4 full courts and seats 2200. The Eagles compete all year around with fall being the busy season. Our season runs from Mid-August to early December, and we also compete in the Spring. The main court is regulation size, wooden, and has a spring loaded surface. The University Fieldhouse has 51,511 sq. ft. and has 2 128 sq. ft. Daktronics message scoreboards.
History: Program began September in 1995. The first two years the program was ran by Ellen Bible. Her overall record was 29-31. Trina Keeton is currently our Head Coach, her record is currently 111-43.
Achievements: Trina Keeton is the Head Coach. She was voted Coach of the Year in 1999 for the Florida Sun Conference. The program has a Florida Sun Conference Tournament Title (1998) under their belt. We have had 1 All-American Honorable Mention Moriah Cain (2000). Coach Keeton captained the 1993 Olympic Festival and lead her team to a Silver Medal.
Coaching: Head Coach Trina Keeton. Assistant Coaches Nina Turchon and Angela Patrick. Graduate Assistant Dmitry Fokin.
Freshman Receiving Financial Aid/Academic: **Athletic:** 3
Roster In State: 3   **Out of State:** 7   **Out of Country:** 1
Seniors on Team: 2   **Graduation %:** 95
Most Recent Record: 28-12
Camp of Clinic Dates: 6/4/01-6/7/01, 6/25/01-6/28/01. 7/25/01-1/27
Positions Needed: MB, OH, DS
Schedule: Univ. of Tampa, Fresno Pacific, Palm Beach Atlantic, FIU, Stetson University, Florida Tech, Concoridia, Lynn University.
Style of Play: Extremely competitive defensively and offensively. The Eagles pride themselves on being a "classy" program. They are extremely solid on and off the court.

Flagler University
Academic Profile

74 King Street
St. Augustine, FL 32085
Type: Private, 4 Yr., Liberal Arts, Coed
Website: http://www.flagler.edu
SAT/ACT/GPA: 1010/21/2.5
Student/Faculty Ratio: 20:1
Undergraduate Enrollment: 1,650
Scholarships/Academic: Yes
Expenses By: Year
Specializes In: Education, Business, Arts
Degrees Conferred: BA

Phone: (904) 829-6481x252

Founded: 1968
Religion: Non-Affiliated
Housing: Yes
Male/Female: 55:45
Graduate Enrollment: N/A
Financial Aid: Yes
Athletic: Yes   **In State:** $ 9,960   **Out of State:** $ 9,960

Programs of Study: Accounting, Art, Art Education, Business Communications, Deaf Education, Drama, Elementary Education, English, History, Literature, Mathematics, Philosophy, Psychology, Secondary Education, Social Sciences, Spanish, Sport Management

Women's Athletic Profile

P.O. Box 1027
St. Augustine, FL 32085
Coach: Taylor Mott
Email:

NCAA I
Lady Saints, Red, Gold
Phone: (904) 829-6481x352
Fax: (904) 810-2369

Estimated # of Women's Volleyball Scholarships: 4
Conference: Florida Sun Conference
Program Profile: Volleyball is an important part of the recreational activities on campus. The aim of the program is to develop physical fitness, good sportsmanship, self-reliance and the appreciation of teamwork.
History: We began in 1990 and we are an up and coming program.
Achievements: 1997 All-Conference-Julia Kline and Alicia Liphard; 1998 MVP-Julia Kline; 1998 Coach's Team Award- Kim Morton
Coaching: Taylor Mott became Head Coach in 1999. His previous overall record is 70-9. He was 1998 Mississippi H.S. Coach of the Year. He played at Ole Miss from 1992-1996. He was a 4 year starter and outside hitter. There is no Assistant Coach at this time.

Freshman Receiving Financial Aid/Academic: | **Athletic: 4**

Roster In State: 8 | **Out of State:** 6 | **Out of Country:** 0
Sophomores on Team: 5 | **Seniors on Team:** 2 | **Graduation %:** Unknown
Most Recent Record: 30-8-0 | **Fall Games:** 30 | **Spring Games:** 8
Camp of Clinic Dates: Summer of 2000
Positions Needed: Setter, Middle Blocker
Schedule: Embry-Riddle, Northwood, St. Thomas, Webber, Florida Memorial College, Warner Southern, Nova Southeastern, Eckerd, Palm Beach Atlantic
Style of Play: Excellent defense and a variety of offensive attacks.

Florida A & M University
Academic Profile

Martin Luther King, Jr. Blvd.
Tallahassee, FL 32307

Phone: 850-599-3796

Type: 4 Yr., Coed | **Founded:** 1887
Website: http://www.famu.edu | **Religion:** Non-Affiliated
SAT/ACT/GPA: Open | **Housing:** Yes
Student/Faculty Ratio: 16:1 | **Male/Female:** Not Available
Undergraduate Enrollment: 9,251 | **Graduate Enrollment:** 1,197
Scholarships/Academic: | **Athletic:** | **Financial Aid:** Yes
Expenses By: Year | **In State:** $ 1,863 | **Out of State:** $ 7,108
Degrees Conferred: Bachelors, Master's
Programs of Study: Accounting, Actuarial Science, Agricultural Business, Agricultural Science, Animal Science, Architectural Technologies, Architecture, Art Education, Art/Fine Arts, Biology, Biological Science, Business Administration, Commerce, Management, Business Education, Chemical Engineering, Chemistry, Civil Engineering Technology, Communications, Computer Information Technology, Construction Technology, Criminal Justice, Molecular Biology, Cell Biology, Music, Music Education, Mechanical Engineering, Occupational Therapy, Pest Control Technology

Women's Athletic Profile

South Boulevards Street
Tallahassee, FL 32307
Coach: Tony Trifonov
Email:

NCAA I
Lady Rattlers, Orange, Green
Phone: (850) 561-2194
Fax: (850) 599-3810

Did Not Return Profile

Florida Atlantic University
Academic Profile

777 Glades Rd., P.O. Box 3091
Boca Raton, FL 33431-0991

Phone: (561) 297-3743

Type: Public, 4 Yr., Liberal Arts, Engineering, Coed | **Founded:** 1961
Website: http://www.fau.edu | **Religion:** Non-Affiliated
SAT/ACT/GPA: Sliding Scale | **Housing:** Yes
Student/Faculty Ratio: 20:1 | **Male/Female:** 60:40
Undergraduate Enrollment: 14,280 | **Graduate Enrollment:** 5,419
Scholarships/Academic: Yes | **Athletic:** Yes | **Financial Aid:** Yes
Expenses By: Year | **In State:** $ 7,524 | **Out of State:** $ 14,149
Specializes In: Business, Education
Degrees Conferred: Bachelors, Masters, Specialist, Doctorate
Programs of Study: Accounting, Architecture, Art, Biology, Chemistry, Communications, Computer Engineering, Computer Information System, Computer Science, Counselor Education, Criminal Justice, Early Childhood Education, Economics, Electrical Engineering, English, Elementary Education, Exercise Science, Marketing, Mathematics, Music, Nursing, Ocean Engineering, Physical Therapy, Psychology, Social Work, Social Science, Women's Studies

Women's Athletic Profile

777 Glades Road
Boca Raton, FL 33431-0991
Coach: Jody Brown
Email:

NCAA I
Lady Owls, Atlantic Blue, Grey
Phone: (561) 297-3595
Fax: (561) 297-3963

Estimated # of Women's Volleyball Scholarships: 6
Conference: Trans America Athletic Conference
Program Profile: DI train year around, 6,000 seat gym.
History: 98-99 NCAA Qualifies.
Achievements: Jody Brown Coach of the Year 1998-99, 1998 conference champions
Coaching: Jody Brown, 4 years, 58-44
Freshman Receiving Financial Aid/Academic: **Athletic:** 4
Roster In State: 8   **Out of State:** 3   **Out of Country:**
Seniors on Team: 4   **Graduation %:** 95
Most Recent Record: 18-4   **Fall Games:** 22   **Spring Games:** 4 Dates
Schedule: U.S. Florida, Central Florida, UCONN, Florida State, Georgia State
Style of Play: Aggressive defense and quick offense.

Florida Community College - Jacksonville
Academic Profile

11901 Beach Blvd.   **Phone:** (904) 646-2220
Jacksonville, FL 32246

Type: Public, 2 Yr., Coed   **Founded:** 1969
Website: http://www.fccj.cc.fl.us   **Religion:** Non-Affiliated
SAT/ACT/GPA: Open   **Housing:** No
Student/Faculty Ratio: Low   **Male/Female:** 49:51
Undergraduate Enrollment: 35,000   **Graduate Enrollment:** N/A
Scholarships/Academic: Yes   **Athletic:** Yes   **Financial Aid:** Yes
Expenses By: Year   **In State:** $ 5,700   **Out of State:** $ 9,500
Specializes In: Associate of Arts Degree
Degrees Conferred: AA, AS
Programs of Study: Anything you want!!

Women's Athletic Profile

11901 Beach Blvd.   **NCAA I**
Jacksonville, FL 32246   Stars, Red,White,Blue
Coach: Mary F. Andrew   **Phone:** 904-646-2220
Email: mandrew@fccj.org.cc.fl.us   **Fax:** 904-646-2204

Estimated # of Women's Volleyball Scholarships: 14
Conference: Mid Florida Conference
Program Profile: We have a 3 court air-conditioned facility. It is 10 minutes form the beach. We play a Fall season. We are a Division I NJCAA program that is fully funded.
History: We started in 1989 as a club program. Next year, we will be a full athletic team. We grow stronger every year. We have been in the Top Ten three times.
Achievements: Iskra Perez-1998 Second Team All-American; Jill Lefile-1997 Academic All-American
Coaching: Mary F. Andrew became Head Coach in 1989. Her overall record is 214-133. She was Mid-Florida Conference Coach of the Year in 1998. Her teams have won many honors: 10 Conference Titles, 5 Top 20 National Rankings, 36 All-Conference Players and 16 All-Regional Players.
Freshman Receiving Financial Aid/Academic: **Athletic:** 9
Roster In State: 13   **Out of State:** 1   **Out of Country:** 0
Sophomores on Team: 0   **Seniors on Team:** 8   **Graduation %:** 95
Most Recent Record: 28-4-0   **Fall Games:** 32   **Spring Games:** 3
Camp of Clinic Dates: July 19-26
Positions Needed: Middle Hitter
Schedule: Pasco Hernando C C, South Florida CC, Wallace State CC, Indian River CC, Manatee CC, Miami-Dade CC
Style of Play: We have strong fundamentals and a varied attack style.

Florida Institute of Technology
Academic Profile

150 West University Blvd.   **Phone:** 800-888-4348
Melbourne, FL 32901
Type: Private, 4 Yr., Engineering, Coed   **Founded:** 1958
Website: http://www.fit.edu   **Religion:** Non-Affiliated

SAT/ACT/GPA: 1050+
Student/Faculty Ratio: 14:1
Undergraduate Enrollment: 3,865
Scholarships/Academic: Yes   **Athletic:** Yes
Expenses By: Year   **In State:** $ 18,500
Housing: Yes
Male/Female: 67:33
Graduate Enrollment: 2,082
Financial Aid: Yes
Out of State: $ 18,500
Degrees Conferred: BA, BS, MS, MBA, M.Ed., Ph.D.
Programs of Study: Accounting, Aeronautical Engineering, Aeronautical Science, BioChemistry, Biological Science, Business Administration, Computer Science, Economics, Electrical Engineering, Fisheries, Management, Marine Biology, Marketing, Mathematics, Mechanical Engineering, MicroBiology, Physics, PreProfessional Courses, Science Education, Technical & Business Writing

Women's Athletic Profile

150 West University Boulevard
Melbourne, FL 32901
Coach: Cody Hein
Email:

NCAA I
Lady Panthers, Crimson, Grey
Phone: (321) 674-7333
Fax: (407) 674-7502

Estimated # of Women's Volleyball Scholarships: N/A
Conference: Sunshine State Conference

Florida International University
Academic Profile

University Park Campus
Miami, FL 33199

Phone: (305) 348-6155

Type: Public, 4 Yr., Coed
Website: http://www.fiu.edu
SAT/ACT/GPA: 1100
Student/Faculty Ratio: 18:1
Undergraduate Enrollment: 30,000
Scholarships/Academic: Yes   **Athletic:** Yes
Expenses By: Year   **In State:** $ 5,553
Specializes In: Education, Hospitality
Degrees Conferred: BA, BS, MS, Ph.D.
Founded: 1972
Religion: Non-Affiliated
Housing: Yes
Male/Female: 43:57
Graduate Enrollment: 6,677
Financial Aid: Yes
Out of State: $ 12,207
Programs of Study: School of Architect, College of Arts & Sciences, School of Music, School of Computer Science, College of Business Administration, School of Accounting, College of Education, College of Engineering, College of Health Sciences, School of Hospitality Management, School of Journalism & Mass Communications, College of Urban and Public Affairs, School of Policy and Management, School of Social Work, PreProfessional Programs

Women's Athletic Profile

Tamiami Trail & SW 107 Avenue
Miami, FL 33199
Coach: John Trojaniak
Email:

NCAA I
Golden Panthers, Blue, Yellow
Phone: (305) 348-2759
Fax: (305) 348-2963

Did Not Return Profile

Florida Memorial College
Academic Profile

15800 Northwest 42nd Avenue
Miami, FL 33054

Phone: 305-626-3750

Type: Private, 4 Yr., Coed
Website: http://www.fmc.edu
SAT/ACT/GPA: 840/18
Student/Faculty Ratio: 15:1
Undergraduate Enrollment: 1,600
Scholarships/Academic: No   **Athletic:** Yes
Expenses By: Year   **In State:** $ 8,700
Founded: 1879
Religion: Non-Affiliated
Housing: Yes
Male/Female: 45:55
Graduate Enrollment: N/A
Financial Aid: Yes
Out of State: $ 8,700

Degrees Conferred: BA, BS
Programs of Study: Accounting, Air Traffic Control, Airway Computer Science, Airway Science Management, Aviation, Biological Business, Chemistry, Computer, Criminal Justice, Education, English, Fine Arts, Management, Philosophy, Public, Religion, Transportation Management

Women's Athletic Profile

15800 NW 42nd Avenue
Miami, FL 33054
Coach: Sophie J. Hall
Email:

NCAA I
Lady Lions, Royal Blue, Orange
Phone: (305) 626-3166
Fax: (305) 626-3691

Did Not Return Profile

Florida Southern College
Academic Profile

111 lake Hollingsworth Drive
Lakeland, FL 33801-5698

Phone: 800-274-4131

Type: Private, 4 Yr., Liberal Arts, Coed
Website: http://www.flsouthern.edu
SAT/ACT/GPA: 1000/23
Student/Faculty Ratio: 17:1
Undergraduate Enrollment: 1,800
Scholarships/Academic: Yes
Expenses By: Year

Athletic: Yes
In State: $ 17,930

Founded: 1885
Religion: Methodist
Housing: Yes
Male/Female: 42:58
Graduate Enrollment: 100
Financial Aid: Yes
Out of State: $ 17,930

Degrees Conferred: BA, BS, MBA, Nursing
Programs of Study: Accounting, Art, Biology, Business, Chemistry, Citrus/Horticulture, Communications, Criminology, Economics, Education, English, History, Mathematics, Music, Natural Sciences, Physical Education, Physics, Political Science, Religion

Women's Athletic Profile

111 Lake Hollinsworth Drive
Lakeland, FL 33801
Coach: Jill Stephens
Email: jstephens@flsouthern.edu

NCAA I
Lady Moccasins, Scarlet, White
Phone: (863)680-4474
Fax: (941) 680-4122

Florida State University
Academic Profile

PO Box 2195 Moore Athletic Ctr.
Tallahassee, FL 32316

Phone: 850-644-6200

Type: 4 Yr., Coed
Website: http://www.fsu.edu
SAT/ACT/GPA: 500/21
Student/Faculty Ratio: 20:1
Undergraduate Enrollment: 22,408
Scholarships/Academic:
Expenses By: Year

Athletic:
In State: $ 1,882+

Founded: 1857
Religion: Non-Affiliated
Housing: Yes
Male/Female: Not Available
Graduate Enrollment: 7,856
Financial Aid: Yes
Out of State: $ 7,127+

Degrees Conferred: Bachelors Masters
Programs of Study: Accounting, Actuarial Science, Advertising, American Studies, Anthropology, Applied Mathematics, Archaeology, Art Education, Art/Fine Arts, Art History, BioChemistry, BioEngineering, Civil Engineering, Cell Biology, Clinical Psychology, Communications, Comparative Literature, Computer Science, Corrections, Creative Writing, Criminal Justice, Criminology, Dance, PreDentistry, Ecology, Economics, Education, Electrical Engineering Technology, Elementary Education, English, Environmental Engineering, Environmental Science, Environmental Studies, Fashion Design and Technology, Fashion Merchandising, Food Science, Health Education, History, Home Economics, Hotel and Restaurant Management, Humanities, Human Resources, Insurance, Interior Design, International Business, International Relations, Latin American, Law Enforcement, Police Science, Marine Biology, Liberal Arts, General Science, Molecular Biology, Music, Music Education

Women's Athletic Profile

P.O. Box 2195, Moore Athletic Center
Tallahassee, FL 32306
Coach: Dr. Cecile Reynaud
Email: breynaud@mailer.fsu.edu

NCAA I
Lady Seminoles, Garnet, Gold
Phone: (850) 644-3796
Fax: (941) 680-4122

Estimated # of Women's Volleyball Scholarships: N/A
Conference: Atlantic Coast Conference
Achievements: 2 time Metro Conference Coach of the Year; 1985 Metro Tournament 1st place; 1986 1st in Metro Conference and 1st in Metro Tournament; 1989 1st in Metro Conference and Metro Tournament 1st Place; 1997 2nd in ACC and ACC Tournament
Coaching: Dr. Cecile Reynaud has been Head Coach here for 23 years. Her career record is 564-269. She ranks 11th nationally in career victories among Division I coaches. She was Deputy Competition Manager for the 1996 Centennial Olympic Games.
Most Recent Record: 25-9-0   **Fall Games:** 34   **Spring Games:** 0
Camp of Clinic Dates: High Potential: July 15-18.
Style of Play: We have good height, good ball control, both of our setters are outstanding. Potentially, his team is a group that can go as far as they want to.

Jacksonville University
Academic Profile

2800 University Boulevard N
Jacksonville, FL 32211

Phone: 800-225-2027

Type: Private, 4 Yr., Liberal Arts, Coed
Website: http://www.junix.ju.edu
SAT/ACT/GPA: 1080/23
Student/Faculty Ratio: 14:1
Undergraduate Enrollment: 2,064
Scholarships/Academic: Yes   **Athletic:** Yes
Expenses By: Year   **In State:** $ 17,660
Specializes In: Business, Education
Degrees Conferred: BA, BS, MAT

Founded: 1934
Religion: Non-Affiliated
Housing: Yes
Male/Female: 47:53
Graduate Enrollment: 352
Financial Aid: Yes
Out of State: $ 17,660

Programs of Study: Accounting, Art, Aviation Administration, Biology, Business, Chemistry, Computer, Economics, English, Finance, International Business, Geography, Management, Medical, Philosophy, PreProfessional Programs

Women's Athletic Profile

University Boulevard N
Jacksonville, FL 32211
Coach: Robin Mignerey
Email: rkibben@ju.edu

NCAA I
Lady Dolphins, Green, White
Phone: (904) 745-7405
Fax: (904) 745-7566

Estimated # of Women's Volleyball Scholarships: 4.5
Conference: TAAC
Program Profile: Swisher Gym, capacity 1,500. Fully funded D. I Liberal arts College
History: Program started in 1972. Changed to Div. I status in 1985. Moved to TAAC in 1998
Achievements: 1 All-American, 2 TAAC Conference Player of the Year.
Coaching: Robin Mignerey went to Clemson Univ. She was 1st team ACC in 92, 93, 94, and All-Region in 93, 94.
Freshman Receiving Financial Aid/Academic: **Athletic:** 4.5
Roster In State: 4   **Out of State:** 5   **Out of Country:** 1
Sophomores on Team: **Seniors on Team:** 4   **Graduation %:**
Most Recent Record: 17-11   **Fall Games:** 28   **Spring Games:** 3
Positions Needed: ALL
Schedule: Florida State, Univ. of S. Florida, Princeton, Georgia State.
Style of Play: Aggressive team that wants to win (maybe too aggressive sometimes).

Lynn University
Academic Profile

3601 No Military
Boca Raton, FL 33431
Type: Private, 4 Yr., Liberal Arts, Coed
Website: http://www.lynn.edu
SAT/ACT/GPA: 800/17
Student/Faculty Ratio: 12:1
Undergraduate Enrollment: 2,000
Scholarships/Academic: Yes   **Athletic:** Yes
Expenses By: Year   **In State:** $ 24,000
Specializes In: Business

Phone: 800-544-8035

Founded: 1962
Religion: Non-Affiliated
Housing: Yes
Male/Female: 50:50
Graduate Enrollment: ?
Financial Aid: Yes
Out of State: $ 24,000

Degrees Conferred: AA, AS, BA, BS, MA, MPS
Programs of Study: Accounting, Aviation Management, Behavioral Science, Business & Management, Communications, Computer Science, Design, Education, Engineering, Fashion Marketing, Finance, Fine Arts, Health & Human Services, History, International Business, Management, Marketing, Parks/Recreation, Political Science, Protective Services, Psychology, Public Affairs, Social Sciences & more

Women's Athletic Profile

3601 N. Military Trail
Boca Raton, FL 33431
Coach: Lindy Binns
Email:

NCAA I
Fighting Knights, Blue, White
Phone: (561) 994-0770x315
Fax: (561) 995-8135

Did Not Return Profile

Miami - Dade North Community College
Academic Profile

11380 NW 27th Avenue
Miami, FL 33167
Type: Public, 2 Yr., Liberal Arts, Engineering, Coed
Website: http://www.mdcc.edu
SAT/ACT/GPA: Open
Student/Faculty Ratio: 24:1
Undergraduate Enrollment: 48,000
Scholarships/Academic: Yes   **Athletic:** Yes
Expenses By: Year   **In State:** $ 1,220
Degrees Conferred: AA, AS, Certified Programs

Phone: (305) 237-2000

Founded: 1960
Religion: Non-Affiliated
Housing: No
Male/Female: 30:1
Graduate Enrollment: N/A
Financial Aid: Yes
Out of State: $ 6,000

Programs of Study: Accounting, Aerospace Sciences, Agricultural Science, American Studies, Anthropology, Architectural Technologies, Art Education, Art/Fine Arts, American Studies, Asian/Oriental Studies, Aviation, Business Administration, Commerce, Management, Commercial Art, Computer Programming, Computer Science, Communications, Commercial Art, Computer Graphics, Computer Information Systems, Drafting and Design, Education, Electrical and Electronics Technology, ElectroMechanical Technology, Emergency Medical Technology, Engineering Design, Film Studies, Forestry, Medical Assistant Technology, Natural Science, Music Education, Nursing, Oceanography, Medical Technology, Ornamental Horticulture, Paralegal Studies, Physical Education, Physical Science Public Administration, Respiratory Therapy, Science Education, Veterinary Science

Women's Athletic Profile

300 NE 2nd AVE
Miami, FL 33132
Coach: Ilida Medero
Email:

NCAA I
Sharks, Blue, White, Silver
Phone: 305-237-2000
Fax: 305-237-7582

Estimated # of Women's Volleyball Scholarships: 12
Conference: FCCAA Southern
Program Profile: One of the top Junior College Programs in America, top-10 NJCAA ranked annually, NJCAA Runner up 95-96-97-98, 9 consecutive Southern Conference & FCCAA State Titles-
History: Programs at MDCC have won every FCCAA State Title since inception of FCCAA Volleyball title in 1972 (except 1988).
Achievements: Coach Medero- NJCAA Coach of the Year 90 & 92, FCCAA Coach of the Year 1990-98. Program has produced 26 NJCAA All-Americans.
Coaching: Coach Medero - 1988-98 362 wins, 59 losses, .859 win percentage. 2 NJCAA National Titles, 9 consecutive FCCAA Southern Conference and State Titles.
Freshman Receiving Financial Aid/Academic: **Athletic:** 6
Roster In State: 4   **Out of State:** 2   **Out of Country:** 6
Sophomores on Team: 6   **Seniors on Team:**   **Graduation %:** 90
Most Recent Record: 34-3   **Fall Games:** ALL   **Spring Games:**
Camp of Clinic Dates: June/July
Positions Needed: Setter, Outside hitters
Schedule: Pasco Hernando, Jefferson College, Belleville Area, UT-Brownsville, SW Missouri, Barry College
Style of Play: Aggressive, smart, determined, BUMP, SET, KILL!

Nova Southeastern University
Academic Profile

3301 College Avenue
Fort Lauderdale, FL 33314

Phone: (954) 262-8264

Type: Private, 4 Yr., Coed
Website: http://www.nova.edu
SAT/ACT/GPA: Open enrollment
Student/Faculty Ratio: 13:1
Undergraduate Enrollment: 4,207
Scholarships/Academic: Yes   **Athletic:** Yes
Expenses By: Year   **In State:** $ 17,660

Founded: 1964
Religion: Non-Affiliated
Housing: Yes
Male/Female: 1:2
Graduate Enrollment: 9,714
Financial Aid: Yes
Out of State: $ 17,660

Degrees Conferred: BA, BS, MS, Ph.D., MBA, ID, DMD, DO
Programs of Study: Accounting, Administrative Studies, Applied Professional Studies, Business Administration, Computer Information Systems, Computer Science, Education, Elementary Education, Environmental Science, Business, Exceptional Legal Studies (PreLaw), General Studies, Hospitality Management, Humanities, Liberal Arts, Life Sciences (PreMedical), Ocean Studies, Physician's Assistant, Professional Management, Psychology, Science, Sports Wellness Business

Women's Athletic Profile

3301 College Avenue
Fort Lauderdale, FL 33314
Coach: Lori Rembe
Email: cmorgan@poaris

NCAA I
Lady Knights, Navy, Blue, Gold
Phone: (954) 262-8264
Fax: (954) 262-3926

Estimated # of Women's Volleyball Scholarships: 3 1/2 - 4
Conference: Florida Sun Conference
Program Profile: We play our games at Broward Community George Mayer Gymnasium, which seats 1,000. The program has been one of the most successful in the NAIA SE Region this decade.
History: Our first year was 1985-86. We have five district titles from 1985 to 1989. We won 3 Florida Sun Conference titles in 1993, 1994 and 1995. We also won the NAIA SE Region championship in 1993.
Coaching: Lori Rembe, Head Coach, started in March of 1999. She is the former assistant coach from Jacksonville State University. She is a Memphis State graduate and played professionally in France from 1993 to 1994.

Freshman Receiving Financial Aid/Academic: **Athletic:** 2
Roster In State: 12   **Out of State:** 0   **Out of Country:** 0
Sophomores on Team: 0   **Seniors on Team:** 1   **Graduation %:** Unknown
Most Recent Record: 16-15-0   **Fall Games:** 31   **Spring Games:** 4
Positions Needed: All positions
Schedule: Embry-Riddle, Palm Beach Atlantic, St. Thomas University
Style of Play: New coach— this will be our first season under a new system.

Palm Beach Atlantic College
Academic Profile

P. O. Box 24708
West Palm Beach, FL 33416-4708

Phone: 888-468-6722

Type: Private, 4 Yr., Liberal Arts, Coed
Website: http://www.pbac.edu
SAT/ACT/GPA: 1000/24/3.0
Student/Faculty Ratio: 18:1
Undergraduate Enrollment: 1,800
Scholarships/Academic: Yes   **Athletic:** Yes
Expenses By: Year   **In State:** $ 15,000

Founded: 1968
Religion: Multi-denominational
Housing: Yes
Male/Female: 60:40
Graduate Enrollment: 400
Financial Aid: Yes
Out of State: $ 15,000

Specializes In: Business, Education, Psychology, Music
Degrees Conferred: BA, BS, MS
Programs of Study: Accounting, Art, Biology, Business and Management, Communications, Computer Information System, Economics, Education, Elementary Education, English, Finance, International Business, Marine Biology, Marketing, Mathematics, Music, Physical Science, Political Science, PreDentistry, PreLaw, PreMed, Psychology, Religion

Women's Athletic Profile

901 S. Flagler Drive
West Palm Beach, FL 33416
Coach: Terri Kaiser
Email: kaisert@pbac.edu

NCAA I
Lady Sailfish, Blue, White
Phone: (561) 803-2000
Fax: (561) 803-0345

Estimated # of Women's Volleyball Scholarships: 12
Conference: Florida Sun Conference
Program Profile: We play at the Greene Complex for Sports and Recreation, which seats 2,800. Our season is from August 28th to December 4th. We play in NAIA Division II.
Achievements: Coach of the Year in 1997 and 1999; 1999 Conference Runner-up; 1999 Regional Champ; 1999 All-American Honorable Mentions.
Coaching: Terri Kaiser, Head Coach, started here in 1994 and her overall record is 147-105. She was Coach of the Year in 1999 (Conference, Mikasa & Tachikara). Laura Munsterteiger is Assistant Coach.

Freshman Receiving Financial Aid/Academic:

		Athletic: 10
Roster In State: 6	**Out of State:** 6	**Out of Country:** 0
Sophomores on Team:	**Seniors on Team:** 4	**Graduation %:** 100
Most Recent Record: 42-16-0	**Fall Games:** 50	**Spring Games:** TBA

Camp of Clinic Dates: July 26-August 5
Positions Needed: Middle, Blocker
Schedule: Columbia College, Taylor University, Georgetown College, Florida International University, Lubbock Christian, Northeastern
Style of Play: Fast-paced and intense.

Rollins College
Academic Profile

1000 Holt Avenue
Winter Park, FL 32789

Phone: 407-646-2161

Type: Private, 4 Yr., Liberal Arts, Coed
Website: http://www.rollins.edu
SAT/ACT/GPA: No minimum, 3.0
Student/Faculty Ratio: 12:1
Undergraduate Enrollment: 1,480
Scholarships/Academic: Yes
Expenses By: Year

Athletic: Yes
In State: $ 28,042

Founded: 1885
Religion: Non-Affiliated
Housing: Yes
Male/Female: 40:60
Graduate Enrollment: 686
Financial Aid: Yes
Out of State: $ 28,042

Degrees Conferred: BA, BS
Programs of Study: Anthropology, Art History, Art Studio, Biology, Chemistry, Classical Studies, Computer Science, Economics, Elementary Education, English, Environmental Studies, Foreign Languages, French, German, History, International Studies, International Relations, Latin American Affairs, Mathematics, Music, Philosophy, Physics, Politics, Psychology, Religious Studies, Sociology, Spanish, Theatre Arts

Women's Athletic Profile

Box 2730. 100 Holt Avenue
Winter Park, FL 32789
Coach: Meg Fitzgerald
Email: mlubbers@rollins.edu

NCAA I
Lady Tars, Blue, Gold
Phone: (407) 646-2631
Fax: (407) 646-4499

Estimated # of Women's Volleyball Scholarships: 5
Conference: Sunshine State Conference
Program Profile: The school has 19 varsity sports. Our volleyball season has 31 matches at Alumni Field house. It will be remodeled soon.
History: We began competing at NCAA Division III level in 1977. In 1990 Rollins awarded its first volleyball athletic scholarship. Finishing our 22nd varsity season, the volleyball team has posted 18 winning campaigns culminating with an appearance in the NCAA Championships in 1995.
Coaching: Meg Fitzgerald - Head Coach.

Freshman Receiving Financial Aid/Academic:

		Athletic: 1
Roster In State: 4	**Out of State:** 4	**Out of Country:** 1
Sophomores on Team: 2	**Seniors on Team:** 0	**Graduation %:** Unknown
Most Recent Record: 15-16-0	**Fall Games:** 31	**Spring Games:** 0

Positions Needed: Setter, Middle & Outside Hitter (2)
Schedule: Tampa, Barry, Florida Southern

Saint Leo College
Academic Profile

P.O. Box 6665 MC 2038
Saint Leo, FL 33574

Phone: (352) 588-8221

Type: Private, 4 Yr., Liberal Arts, Coed
Website: http://www.saintleo.edu
SAT/ACT/GPA: 950/2.5
Student/Faculty Ratio: 16:1
Undergraduate Enrollment: 8,555
Scholarships/Academic: Yes   **Athletic:** Yes
Expenses By: Year   **In State:** $ 18,100
Specializes In: Liberal Arts
Degrees Conferred: BA, Masters

Founded: 1889
Religion: Catholic
Housing: Yes
Male/Female: 1:1
Graduate Enrollment: 500
Financial Aid: Yes
Out of State: $ 18,100

Programs of Study: Accounting, American Studies, Banking & Finance, Biology, Business Administration, Business, Law, Chemistry, Communications, Computer Science, Criminology, Economics, Elementary Education, English, History, Hotel Restaurant, Human Resources, International Business, Management, Marketing, Political Science, PreDentistry, PreLaw, PreMed, Psychology, Public Administration, Religion, Social Science, Sports Management

Women's Athletic Profile

MC 2038 Box 6665
St. Leo, FL 33574
Coach: Bill Lent
Email: bill.lent@saintleo.edu

NCAA I
Lady Monarchs, Green, White
Phone: (352) 588-8448
Fax: (352) 588-8290

Estimated # of Women's Volleyball Scholarships: N/A
Conference: Sunshine State Conference

Saint Thomas University
Academic Profile

16400 NW 32nd Avenue
Miami, FL 33054

Phone: (305) 628-6678

Type: Private, 4 Yr., Liberal Arts, Coed
Website: http://www.stu.edu
SAT/ACT/GPA: 950/18/2.5
Student/Faculty Ratio: 15:1
Undergraduate Enrollment: 1,100
Scholarships/Academic: Yes   **Athletic:** Yes
Expenses By: Year   **In State:** $ 17,160
Specializes In: Business Administration, Sports Administration
Degrees Conferred: BA, MA, MS, MBA

Founded: 1961
Religion: Catholic
Housing: Yes
Male/Female: 53:47
Graduate Enrollment: 2,500
Financial Aid: Yes
Out of State: $ 17,160

Programs of Study: Accounting, American Studies, Banking & Finance, Biology, Business Administration, Economics, Business Law, Chemistry, Communications, Computer Science, Criminal Justice, Elementary Education, History, Management, Marketing, Political Science, PreDentistry, PreLaw, PreMed, Psychology, Public Administration, Religion, Social Science, Sport Administration

Women's Athletic Profile

16400 NW 32nd Avenue
Miami, FL 33054
Coach: Martin Najarro
Email: dpezzino@stu.edu

NCAA I
Lady Bobcats, Blue, White
Phone: (305) 628-6000
Fax: (305) 628-6591

Estimated # of Women's Volleyball Scholarships: 5
Conference: Florida Sun Conference
Program Profile: STU is a full scale NAIA collegiate volleyball program.
History: The program started in 1994 and has rapidly grown into a successful and powerful team with trips to the national Tournament in 1996 & 1997.
Achievements: Coach Najarro has been named Conference Coach of the Year 3 consecutive years (in 1996, 1997 & 1998) and Regional Coach of the Year in 1997; Conference Titles in 1996 & 1997; Regional Titles in 1996 & 1997I; All-Americans—Amanda

Villarreal in 1996, 1997 and Rita Gallo in 1996.

Coaching: Martin Najarro started at STU in 1995 and became Head Coach in 1996 with an overall record of 82-23. Luis Guido and Frank Blaze are Assistant Coaches.

Freshman Receiving Financial Aid/Academic:

		Athletic: 3
Roster In State: 10	**Out of State:** 2	**Out of Country:** 1
Sophomores on Team: 4	**Seniors on Team:** 0	**Graduation %:** 74
Most Recent Record: 18-10-0	**Fall Games:** 28	**Spring Games:** 0

Positions Needed: All positions

Schedule: Barry University, Florida International University, Palm Beach Atlantic College, Embry-Riddle University, Florida Tech, Florida Southern University

Style of Play: Counter attacking team that relies heartily on defensive pressure.

Stetson University
Academic Profile

421 N. Woodland Blvd. Unit 8359
Deland, FL 32720

Phone: (904) 822-8117

Type: Private, 4 Yr., Liberal Arts, Coed	**Founded:** 1883
Website: http://www.stetson.edu	**Religion:** Non-Affiliated
SAT/ACT/GPA: 1120/26/3.48	**Housing:** Yes
Student/Faculty Ratio: 11:1	**Male/Female:** 43:57
Undergraduate Enrollment: 2,000	**Graduate Enrollment:** 300
Scholarships/Academic: Yes	**Athletic:** Yes	**Financial Aid:** Yes
Expenses By: Year	**In State:** $ 24,000	**Out of State:** $ 24,000

Specializes In: Business, Liberal Arts, Music, Pre-Med, Pre-Law

Degrees Conferred: BA, BS, BEd, BM, MA, MS, MBA, M.Ed., Ph.D.

Programs of Study: Accounting, American Studies, Art, Biology, Business Administration, Chemistry, Communication Studies, Computer Science, Counseling, Economics, Education, English, Environmental Studies, Finance, Foreign Language, Geography, Geology, History, Humanities, Information Systems, Latin American Studies, Management, Marketing, Mathematics, Military Sciences, Philosophy, Physics, Political Science, Psychology, Religious Studies, Russian Studies, Sociology, Sports & Exercise Science, Sport Administration, Theatre

Women's Athletic Profile

421 N. Woodland Blvd. Unit 8359
De Land, FL 32720
Coach: Janiece Holder
Email: aholder@stetson.edu
Estimated # of Women's Volleyball Scholarships: 5

NCAA I
Lady Hatters, Green, White
Phone: (904) 822-8117
Fax: (904) 822-8148

Conference: Trans America Athletic Conference

Program Profile: We have a mid-level Division I program with limited scholarships. We play at Edmund Center which was built in 1974 and has 5,000 seats.

History: The program began in 1974. We won conference in 1985 and were a runner-up in 1986, 1987 and 1991.

Coaching: Janiece Holder, Head Coach, started with the program in 1988 and has an overall record of 133-217. Deborah Hughes is Assistant Coach.

Freshman Receiving Financial Aid/Academic:

		Athletic: 4
Roster In State: 13	**Out of State:** 2	**Out of Country:** 0
Sophomores on Team: 6	**Seniors on Team:** 1	**Graduation %:** 100
Most Recent Record: 12-15-0	**Fall Games:** 27	**Spring Games:** 4

Camp of Clinic Dates: July 11-17, 1999

Positions Needed: Middle Blocker, Outside Hitter

Schedule: Georgia State

Style of Play: Quick transition scoring, defensively strong.

University of Central Florida
Academic Profile

P.O. Box 160000
Orlando, FL 32816

Phone: 407-823-3000

Type: Public, 4 Yr., Liberal Arts, Engineering, Coed	**Founded:** 1963
Website: http://www.ucf.edu	**Religion:** Non-Affiliated

SAT/ACT/GPA: 1050-2000/22-26/3.1-3.9
Student/Faculty Ratio: 16:1
Undergraduate Enrollment: 23,729
Scholarships/Academic: Yes   **Athletic:** Yes
Expenses By: Year   **In State:** $ 7,627
Housing: Yes
Male/Female: 77:33
Graduate Enrollment: 4,271
Financial Aid: Yes
Out of State: $ 14,283
Specializes In: Engineering, Business, Computer Science
Degrees Conferred: 73 Bachelors, 51 Masters, 3 Advanced Masters, 15 Doctorates
Programs of Study: Education, Health and Public Affairs, Biology, Communications, Visual Performing Arts, Psychology, Physical Therapy, Forensic Science, Social Work, Political Science, Criminal Justice, Public Administration.

Women's Athletic Profile

P.O. Box 163555
Orlando, FL 32816-0002
Coach: Meg Colado
Email: mfitzger@mail.ucf.edu

NCAA I
Golden Knights, Gold, Black
Phone: (407) 823-2025
Fax: (407) 823-2737

Estimated # of Women's Volleyball Scholarships: N/A
Conference: Trans America Athletic Conference
Program Profile: UCF volleyball is an NCAA D. I program in the Trans America Athletic Conference. Home matches are played in the 5,100 seat UCF Arena.
History: The program began as a Div. II team in 1975, and joined the Sunshine State Conference in 1982. It became Div. I in 1984 and joined the New South Conference Athletic Conference in 1985, and in 1992 became a part of the TAAC. UCF won the 1978 AIAW National Championship (we were known as Fla. Tech. University.)
Achievements: Meg Colado 1999 TAAC Coach of the Year, TAAC Champions (1992-97), 50 All-Conference Selections since 1985, 4 NCAA Tournament Appearances.
Freshman Receiving Financial Aid/Academic: **Athletic:** 10
Roster In State: 4   **Out of State:** 5   **Out of Country:** 1
Sophomores on Team: 2   **Seniors on Team:** 0   **Graduation %:**
Most Recent Record: 19-12-0   **Fall Games:** 31   **Spring Games:**
Camp of Clinic Dates: TBA
Schedule: Univ of Wisconsin, Georgia State
Style of Play: Well balanced and quick offense.

University of Florida
Academic Profile

Box 14485
Gainesville, FL 32604

Phone: (352) 375-4683

Type: Public, 4 Yr., Coed
Website: http://www.uaa.ufl.edu
SAT/ACT/GPA: 970/20/2.9
Student/Faculty Ratio: 17:1
Undergraduate Enrollment: 31,329
Scholarships/Academic: Yes   **Athletic:** Yes
Expenses By: Year   **In State:** $ 9,372
Founded: 1906
Religion: Non-Affiliated
Housing: Yes
Male/Female: 49:51
Graduate Enrollment: 8,043
Financial Aid: Yes
Out of State: $ 16,028
Specializes In: Business, Journalism, Architecture, Engineering, Education
Degrees Conferred: Bachelors, Master's, Doctoral
Programs of Study: Accounting, Advertising, Aerospace Engineering, Agricultural Business, Agricultural Economics, Agricultural Education, Agricultural Engineering, Agronomy, Soil and Crop Science, American Studies, Animal Science, Anthropology, Architecture, Art Education, Art/Fine Arts, Art History, Astronomy, Botany/Plant Science, Business Administration, Commerce, Management, Chemical Engineering, Chemistry, Civil Engineering, Classic, Computer Engineering, Computer Science, Conservation, Construction Management, Criminal Justice, Dairy Science, Dance, East Asian Studies, Ecology, Economics, Construction Management, English, Entomology, Health Science, Horticulture, Industrial Engineering, Insurance, Interior Design, Journalism, Management Information Systems, Mechanical Engineering, Microbiology, Music, Music Education, Natural Resources Management, Nuclear Engineering, Nursing, Nutrition, Occupational Therapy, Physician's Assistant Studies, Physics, Political Science, Psychology, Studio Art, Sociology

Women's Athletic Profile

Box 14485
Gainesville, FL 32604
Coach: Mary Wise
Email: mary@gators.uaa.ufl.edu

NCAA I
Lady Gators, Orange, Blue
Phone: (352) 375-4683
Fax: (352) 375-7807

Estimated # of Women's Volleyball Scholarships: 3
Conference: Southeastern Conference
Program Profile: We have new dorms, a dining facility and a 3-court athletic practice facility. These facilities are dedicated solely to volleyball.
History: We began in 1991. We have won 8 SEC Conference Championships. We have made 8 trips to the NCAA Tournaments, 7 trips to the NCAA Regional Finals and 5 trips to the NCAA Final Four.
Achievements: 1992 & 1993 NCAA Coach of the Year; 5 time SEC Coach of the Year; 11 AVCA All-Americans; 7 SEC Players of the Year; 3 Academic First Team All-Americans.
Coaching: Mary Wise, Head Coach, her overall record is 271-28 and her SEC record is 110-2. She has made 5 trips to the NCAA Final Four. Nick Cheronis is Assistant Coach.

Freshman Receiving Financial Aid/Academic: **Athletic:** 3
Roster In State: 1   **Out of State:** 11   **Out of Country:** 0
Sophomores on Team: 0   **Seniors on Team:** 2   **Graduation %:** 97
Most Recent Record: 35-3-0   **Fall Games:** 38   **Spring Games:** 4
Camp of Clinic Dates: July 11-14; July 19-22
Positions Needed: Middle Hitters, Setter
Schedule: Nebraska, Wisconsin, University of California-Santa Barbara, Arkansas, Penn State, Pacific
Style of Play: Work hard, have fun and compete.

University of North Florida
Academic Profile

4567 St. Johns Bluff Road S.
Jacksonville, FL 32224

Phone: (904) 620-2897

Type: Public, 4 Yr., Coed
Website: http://www.unf.edu
SAT/ACT/GPA: 1000/21/3.0
Student/Faculty Ratio: 17:1
Undergraduate Enrollment: 12,000
Scholarships/Academic: Yes   **Athletic:** Yes
Expenses By: Year   **In State:** $ 7,500

Founded: 1972
Religion: Non-Affiliated
Housing: Yes
Male/Female: 58:32
Graduate Enrollment: 2,000
Financial Aid: Yes
Out of State: $ 13,500

Specializes In: Education, Health Sciences, Business
Degrees Conferred: BA, BFA, BS, BBA, BAE, MA, MS, MBA, MED, EdD
Programs of Study: College of Arts & Sciences, Business Administration, Computing Science & Engineering, College of Health, College of Education & Human Services

Women's Athletic Profile

4567 St. John Bluff Rd.
Jacksonville, FL 32224
Coach: Mike Welch
Email: mwelch@unf.edu

NCAA I
Lady Ospreys, Blue, Grey
Phone: (904) 620-2897
Fax: (904) 620-2836

Estimated # of Women's Volleyball Scholarships: 12
Conference: Peach Belt Athletic Conference
Program Profile: We play at UNF Arena, which seats 5,800. Our volleyball team room has oak lockers, couches, a TV/VCR and private showers.
History: The program began in 1991. The team has been nationally ranked eight consecutive years. We advanced to the NCAA Tournament 4 times. We advanced to the NAIA National Tournament two times and won three consecutive Conference Championships.
Achievements: 2 All-American players and 14 All-Region selections in the past five years.
Coaching: Mike Welch, Head Coach, is entering his fifth year with the program. He compiled a record of 108-60 and has been the Head Coach for the USA Youth National Team twice and coached at the US Olympic Festival twice. Ed Garrett is Assistant Coach and is entering his 2nd year. Rich Hall is Assistant Coach and is entering his 4th year.

Freshman Receiving Financial Aid/Academic: **Athletic:** 4
Roster In State: 11   **Out of State:** 3   **Out of Country:** 0
Sophomores on Team: 2   **Seniors on Team:** 3   **Graduation %:** 100
Most Recent Record: 26-8-0   **Fall Games:** 34   **Spring Games:** 4
Camp of Clinic Dates: July 12-15, 1999; July 16-18, 1999
Positions Needed: All
Schedule: Tampa, Barry, Florida Southern, North Dakota State, Augustana, Northern Kentucky
Style of Play: No team will out hustle us, out talk us or out play us. We have a tenacious and tall defense. We are a good communicating team.

University of South Florida
Academic Profile

4202 E. Fowler Avenue, SUNY 141
Tampa, FL 33620

Phone: (813) 947-4149

Type: Public, 4 Yr., Liberal Arts, Coed
Website: http://www.usf.edu
SAT/ACT/GPA: 980/20/3.25
Student/Faculty Ratio: 13:1
Undergraduate Enrollment: 34,000
Scholarships/Academic: Yes   **Athletic:** Yes
Expenses By: Year   **In State:** $ 7,792
Specializes In: Education, Accounting, Engineering

Founded: 1956
Religion: Christian
Housing: Yes
Male/Female: 43:57
Graduate Enrollment: 5,849
Financial Aid: Yes
Out of State: $ 19,785

Degrees Conferred: BA, BS, BFA, MA, MS, MBA, MFA, M.Ed., Ph.D., EdD, MD
Programs of Study: College of Arts & Science, College of Business Administration, College of Education, College of Engineering, Fine Arts, New College and College of Nursing

Women's Athletic Profile

4202 E. Fowler Avenue
Tampa, FL 33620
Coach: Nancy Mueller
Email: muller@admin.usf.edu

NCAA I
Lady Bulls, Green, Gold
Phone: (813) 974-4130
Fax: (813) 974-0837

Estimated # of Women's Volleyball Scholarships: 12
Conference: Conference USA
Program Profile: Our USF Volleyball facility, the Corral, opened to near-capacity four seasons ago. We hosted the Bulls in the Final METRO Conference Tournament at the close of the 1995 season.
History: The program began in 1972.
Achievements: 1995-1996 Conference - USA Champions; 1993-METRO Conference Title; 1995-1996-1997 and 1998 NCAA Tournaments
Coaching: Nancy Mueller is our new Head Coach this year. Katiane Simonetti is Assistant Coach.
Freshman Receiving Financial Aid/Academic: **Athletic:** 4
Roster In State: 3   **Out of State:** 5   **Out of Country:** 3
Sophomores on Team: 2   **Seniors on Team:** 3   **Graduation %:** 100
Most Recent Record: 25-8-0   **Fall Games:** 29   **Spring Games:** 4 Tournaments
Camp of Clinic Dates: July 17, 18, 19-22 and August 2-5
Positions Needed: 2 Middle Defense, 3 Outside Hitters, 1 Right Side Hitter
Schedule: University of Florida, University of Nebraska, University of Arizona, University of Louisville, University of Houston, American University

University of Tampa
Academic Profile

401 W. Kennedy St.
Tampa, FL 33606

Phone: 800-733-4773

Type: Private, 4 Yr., Liberal Arts, Coed
Website: http://www.utspartans@aol.com
SAT/ACT/GPA: 950/21/2.8
Student/Faculty Ratio: 8:1
Undergraduate Enrollment: 2,000
Scholarships/Academic: Yes   **Athletic:** Yes
Expenses By: Year   **In State:** $ 20,000

Founded: 1931
Religion: Non-Affiliated
Housing: Yes
Male/Female: 45:55
Graduate Enrollment: 450
Financial Aid: Yes
Out of State: $ 20,000

Degrees Conferred: BA, BS, BFA, BMus, MBA
Programs of Study: Accounting, Biology, Banking/Finance, Biological Science, Chemistry, Communications, Creative Writing, Criminal Justice, Economics, Education, Fine Arts, Marketing, Mathematics, Medical Laboratory Technology, Nursing, Philosophy, Physics, Psychology, Social Science, Political Science

Women's Athletic Profile

401 W. Kennedy Blvd.
Tampa, FL 33606
Coach: Chris Catanach
Email: ccatanach@aol.com

NCAA I
Spartans, Red, Black, Gold
Phone: (813) 253-6240x3406
Fax: (813) 253-6288

Estimated # of Women's Volleyball Scholarships: 7
Conference: Sunshine State Conference
Program Profile: We have an outstanding training facility. We offer a strength trainer and a traditional and non-traditional season. We have 30-32 matches in a traditional segment.
History: We began in 1975 and won 9 SSC Championships. We made 14 NCAA Appearances. We made 4 Championships round appearances. We were 1996 National Runner-Up. In 1998, we got 3rd place. Our highest ranking (#1) was for six weeks in 1997.
Achievements: 1991 National Coach of the Year; 5 time Regional Coach of the Year; 8 times SSC Coach of the Year.
Coaching: Chris Catanach, Head Coach, began coaching at Tampa in 1984. He compiled a record of 486-108 in 15 seasons. Jeff Reavis is Assistant Coach.
Freshman Receiving Financial Aid/Academic:

		Athletic: 1
Roster In State: 6	**Out of State:** 8	**Out of Country:** 1
Sophomores on Team: 2	**Seniors on Team:** 4	**Graduation %:** 100
Most Recent Record: 31-3-0	**Fall Games:** 31	**Spring Games:** 18

Camp of Clinic Dates: June 27-30; July 5-9; July 10-14 (Team Only)
Positions Needed: Middle, Setter, Outside
Schedule: Barry University, North Dakota State, Florida Southern, North Florida, Augustana, North Alabama
Style of Play: 5-1 offense; perimeter defense. Offensive speed is fast, unless personnel is not adequate.

Warner Southern College
Academic Profile

5301 Highway 27 South
Lake Wales, FL 33853

Phone: 800-949-7248

Type: Private, 4 Yr., Liberal Arts, Coed
Website: http://www.warner.edu
SAT/ACT/GPA: 875/18/2.25
Student/Faculty Ratio: 14:1
Undergraduate Enrollment: 760
Scholarships/Academic: Yes　　**Athletic:** Yes
Expenses By: Year　　**In State:** $12,800
Degrees Conferred: AA, BA

Founded: 1968
Religion: Non-Affiliated
Housing: Yes
Male/Female: 2:3
Graduate Enrollment: N/A
Financial Aid: Yes
Out of State: $12,800

Programs of Study: Accounting, Biblical Studies, Biology, Business Administration, Church Ministry, Communications, Elementary Education, English, English Education, Exceptional Student-Education, Exercise Science, General Studies, History & Political Science, Middle School, Science Education, Music Education, Music Ministry, Physical Education, Teacher Education, Psychology, Sports and Leisure Management

Women's Athletic Profile

5301 US 27 Hwy. South
Lake Wales, FL 33853
Coach: Gary Smith-Wallace
Email: admission@warner.edu

NCAA I
Lady Royals, Royal Blue, Gold
Phone: (941) 638-7212
Fax: (941) 638-1472

Estimated # of Women's Volleyball Scholarships: 4
Conference: Florida Sun Conference
Program Profile: Warner Southern is building a solid program with dedicated recruits. Our Turner Athletic Center seats 2,000. We have dual courts for practices and matches. We average a 30 game schedule not including tournaments.
History: The program began in 1990. One of the best seasons in the history of the program was in 1998. The team won 50% more games than previous seasons. With new recruits and solid returns, the team should finish well above the .500 mark this year.
Coaching: Gary Smith-Wallace is in his second year as a Head Coach.
Freshman Receiving Financial Aid/Academic: N/A

		Athletic: N/A
Roster In State: 7	**Out of State:** 2	**Out of Country:** 0
Sophomores on Team: 0	**Seniors on Team:** 5	**Graduation %:** 100
Most Recent Record: 12-17-0	**Fall Games:** 29	**Spring Games:** 0

Positions Needed: Right side Hitters, Middle Hitters, Defensive Specialist
Schedule: Embry Riddle University, Palm Beach Atlantic College, Eckerd College, Nova Southeastern University, Clearwater Christian College, St. Leo College
Style of Play: We play aggressive defense and work very hard to pass and dig to our target allowing us to run a strong offense. We will utilize a 6-2 offense, but have the capabilities to run a 5-1.

Webber College
Academic Profile

P. O. Box 96
Babson Park, FL 33827

Phone: 941-638-1431

Type: Private, 4 Yr., Coed
Website: http://www.webber.edu
SAT/ACT/GPA: 850/19
Student/Faculty Ratio: 17:1
Undergraduate Enrollment: 437
Scholarships/Academic: Yes   **Athletic:** Yes
Expenses By: Year   **In State:** $ 9,607
Specializes In: Business

Founded: 1922
Religion: Non-Affiliated
Housing: Yes
Male/Female: 50:50
Graduate Enrollment: N/A
Financial Aid: Yes
Out of State: $ 9,607

Degrees Conferred: AA, BA in Business Administration
Programs of Study: Management, Marketing, Finance, Accounting, International Travel and Tourism, Hotel and Restaurant Management, Sports and Club Management

Women's Athletic Profile

P.O. Box 96, 1201 N. Scenic Hwy.
Babson Park, FL 33827
Coach: Michelle Saxon
Email: webbercollege@hotmail.com

NCAA I
Warriors, Gold Green, White
Phone: (941) 638-1431
Fax: (941) 638-2823

Did Not Return Profile

GEORGIA

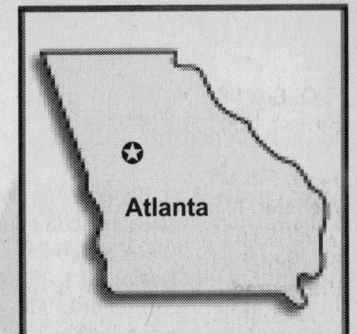

Atlanta

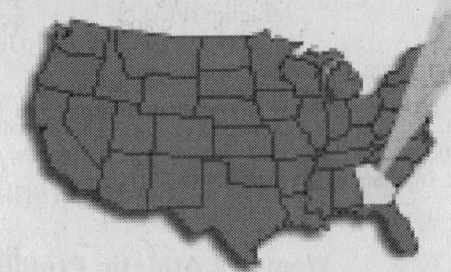

SCHOOL	CITY	AFFILIATION	PAGE
Agnes Scott College	Atlanta	NCAA III	173
Albany State University	Albany	NCAA II	173
Atlanta Christian College	East Point	NCAA II	174
Augusta State University	Augusta	NCAA II	174
Brenau University	Gainesville	NAIA	175
Brewton Parker	Mt. Vernon	NAIA	176
Clark Atlanta University	Atlanta	NCAA II	176
Covenant College	Lookout Mountain	NAIA	177
Emory University	Atlanta	NCAA III	177
Fort Valley State University	Fort Valley	NCAA II	178
Georgia Southern University	Statesboro	NCAA I	178
Georgia Southwestern College	Americus	NCAA II/NAIA	179
Georgia State University	Atlanta	NCAA I	179
Georgia Tech	Atlanta	NCAA I	180
La Grange College	La Grange	NCAA III	181
Mercer University	Macon	NCAA	181
Morris Brown College	Atlanta	NCAA II	182
Oglethorpe University	Atlanta	NCAA III	182
Paine College	Augusta	NCAA II	183
Piedmont College	Demorest	NCAA III	183
Savannah College of Art & Design	Savannah	NCAA III	184
Savannah State University	Savannah	NCAA II	185
University of Georgia	Athens	NCAA I	185
Valdosta State University	Valdosta	NCAA II	186
Wesleyan College	Macon	NCAA III	187

Agnes Scott College
Academic Profile

141 E College Avenue
Decatur, GA 30030

Phone: (404)471-6285

Type: Private, 4 Yr., Liberal Arts, Women
Website: http://www.agnesscott.edu
SAT/ACT/GPA: 1090-130026-28
Student/Faculty Ratio: 10:1
Undergraduate Enrollment: 900
Scholarships/Academic: Yes   **Athletic:** No
Expenses By: Year   **In State:** $24,245.00
Specializes In: Women's college - Liberal Arts, Sciences
Degrees Conferred: BA, Master of Arts in Teaching English

Founded: 1889
Religion: Presbyterian
Housing: Yes
Male/Female: Women
Graduate Enrollment: 25
Financial Aid: Yes
Out of State: $24,245.00

Programs of Study: Art, Astrophysics, BioChemistry, Biology, Chemistry, Classical Civilization, Classical Languages & Literature, Economics, Economics & Business, English, Literature & Creative Writing, French, German Studies, History, International Relations, Mathematics, Mathematics-Economics, Mathematics-Physics, Music, Philosophy, Physics, Theatre, Women's Studies. 28 Majors and 26 Minors.

Women's Athletic Profile

141 E. College Avenue
Atlanta, GA 30030
Coach: Lori Brown
Email: lkbrown@agnesscott.edu

NCAA I
Lady Scotties, Purple, White
Phone: (404) 471-6358
Fax: (404) 638-6099

Estimated # of Women's Volleyball Scholarships: N/A
Conference: Independent
Program Profile: ASC Volleyball is played at the Woodruff Building on campus. The gym is large enough to play on 2 court set up and we have one court as our main court at the center of the gym. The hard wood floor was just redone over this past summer. We play a full 22 date schedule starting the 1st of Sept- end of Oct.
History: Volleyball became a varsity sport in 1995. The program is young and growing. We carry only a varsity squad, but we are looking to expand the program in the next 2 years. The team has strengthened it's schedule and increased the number of tournaments. ASC has improved its record with most wins in a season with 14 this year.
Achievements: 4 All-Tournament Team in several different tournaments.
Coaching: Coach Brown has been coaching at the level for 5 seasons. The last two were with Agnes Scott College. While Head Coach the team has made steady progress in all categories of play, setting new records for the school in number of wins in a season, kill percentage etc..
Roster In State: 5   **Out of State:** 5   **Out of Country:** 2
Seniors on Team: 2   **Graduation %:** 100
Most Recent Record: 14-16-0
Positions Needed: MH, OH, Setter
Schedule: Maryville College, Piedmont College, Centre College
Style of Play: This season the team worked to move from a second tempo to a first tempo game. Serving and defense was the key to our wins. Fundamentals are stressed and play system are incorporated into every match.

Albany State University
Academic Profile

504 College Drive
Albany, GA 31705-2796

Phone: 912-430-4650

Type: 4 Yr., Coed
Website: http://www.asurams.edu
SAT/ACT/GPA: Open
Student/Faculty Ratio:
Undergraduate Enrollment: N/A
Scholarships/Academic: **Athletic:**
Expenses By: Year   **In State:**
Degrees Conferred:

Founded:
Religion: Non-Affiliated
Housing: No
Male/Female:
Graduate Enrollment: N/A
Financial Aid:
Out of State:

Programs of Study: Accounting, Arts, Fine Arts, Biology, Biological Science, Business Administration, Commerce, Management, Business Education, Chemistry, Computer Science, Criminal Justice, Early Childhood Education, English, French, Health Science, History, Marketing, Psychology, Social Work, Sociology, Spanish

Women's Athletic Profile

504 College Drive
Albany, GA 31705
Coach: Robert Skinner
Email:

NCAA I
Lady Rams, Blue, Old Gold
Phone: (912) 430-3817
Fax: (912) 430-3020

Estimated # of Women's Volleyball Scholarships: N/A
Conference: Southern Intercollegiate Conference

Atlanta Christian College
Academic Profile

2605 Ben Hill Road
East Point, GA 30344

Phone: 800-776-1222

Type: Private, 4 Yr., Coed
Website: http://www.acc.edu
SAT/ACT/GPA: 870/1.8
Student/Faculty Ratio: 15:1
Undergraduate Enrollment: 350
Scholarships/Academic: Yes   **Athletic:** No
Expenses By: Year   **In State:** $ 10,500

Founded: 1937
Religion: Christian
Housing: Yes
Male/Female: 1:2
Graduate Enrollment: N/A
Financial Aid: Yes
Out of State: $ 10,500

Programs of Study: Business, Business Administration, Biblical Studies, Bachelor of Theology, Early Childhood Education, Humanities, Human Relations, Music

Women's Athletic Profile

11935 Abercorn Expr.
Savannah, GA 31419
Coach: Alan Segal
Email:

NCAA I
Lady Pirates, Maroon, Gold
Phone: (912) 921-5842
Fax: (912) 921-5571

Estimated # of Women's Volleyball Scholarships: N/A
Conference: Peach Belt Athletic Conference
Program Profile: Rebuilding with a new coach and new players. We will have our own playing facility, used for volleyball only.
Coaching: Alan Segan is our Head Coach, is entering his first season with the program. Kelly Stewartz Assistant Coach.
Freshman Receiving Financial Aid/Academic: **Athletic:** 7
Roster In State: 1   **Out of State:** 10   **Out of Country:** 1
Sophomores on Team: 2   **Seniors on Team:** 1   **Graduation %:**
Most Recent Record: 9-23-0   **Fall Games:** 37   **Spring Games:** 4 Dates
Positions Needed: Setter, Middle, Outside
Schedule: North Florida, Francis Marion, University of California-PA, Florida Tech, St. Leo, SCAD
Style of Play: We play an up-tempo style.

Augusta State University
Academic Profile

2500 Walton Way
Augusta, GA 30904-2200

Phone: 800-341-4373

Type: Public, 4 Yr., Coed
Website: http://www.aug.edu
SAT/ACT/GPA: Open
Student/Faculty Ratio: 19:1
Undergraduate Enrollment: 5,510
Scholarships/Academic: Yes   **Athletic:** Yes
Expenses By: Year   **In State:** $ 6,390

Founded: 1783
Religion: Non-Affiliated
Housing: No
Male/Female: 1:3
Graduate Enrollment: N/A
Financial Aid: Yes
Out of State: $ 11,610

Specializes In: Member of the University System of Georgia
Degrees Conferred: Associate, Bachelor, Master, Specialist
Programs of Study: More than 50 programs of study.

Women's Athletic Profile

2500 Walton Way
Augusta, GA 30904
Coach: Tess Lott
Email: tlott@aug.edu

NCAA I
Lady Jaguars, Blue, White
Phone: (706) 667-4766
Fax: (706) 737-1782

Estimated # of Women's Volleyball Scholarships: 3
Conference: Peach Belt Athletic Conference
Program Profile: The Lady Jaguars play all of their home matches at the 2,216 seat ASU Athletic complex, considered one of the finest facilities in Division II.
History: ASU began Volleyball in 1985 and has a record of 140-259
Achievements: Peach Belt Conference Honors
Seven All- Conference selections
One Coach of the year (Tabetha Stephens, 1995)
Coaching: Tess Lott, a standout for ASU from 1993-96, was named ASU'S sixth volleyball coach prior to the 2000 season.
Roster In State: 5   **Out of State:** 6   **Out of Country:** 0
Seniors on Team: 3
Most Recent Record: 20-17-0
Positions Needed: Setter, Middle Hitter, Outside Hitter
Schedule: Armstrong Atlantic, Francis Marion, USC Aiken, Gardner Webb, North Florida, West Alabama, USC Spartanburg, Lander.
Style of Play: Aggressive on serves and defense.

Brenau University
Academic Profile

1 Centennial Circle
Gainesville, GA 30501

Phone: 800-252-5119

Type: Private, 4 Yr., Liberal Arts, Coed
Website: http://www.brenau.edu
SAT/ACT/GPA: 900/21
Student/Faculty Ratio: 13:1
Undergraduate Enrollment: 650
Scholarships/Academic: Yes   **Athletic:** Yes
Expenses By: Year   **In State:** $ 18,500
Specializes In: The "Arts"
Degrees Conferred: BA, BS, BFA, BM, BSN

Founded: 1878
Religion: Non-sectarian
Housing: Yes
Male/Female: 100% w
Graduate Enrollment: 1,700
Financial Aid: Yes
Out of State: $ 18,500

Programs of Study: Art, Business Administration, Dance, Education , Mass Communications, Environmental Studies, Fashion Merchandising, Interior Design, International Studies, Music, Nursing

Women's Athletic Profile

One Centennial Circle
Gainesville, GA 30501
Coach: Sid Feldman
Email: jupchurch@lib.brenau.edu

NCAA I
Lady Tigers, Black, Gold
Phone: (770) 534-6100
Fax: (770) 538-4306

Estimated # of Women's Volleyball Scholarships: 12 at $2,500 each
Conference: Georgia Athletic Conference
Program Profile: Low level program but play in good conference.
History: The program is three years old and just in its infancy. We did serious recruiting this year. We hope to qualify.
Achievements: SEC Coach of the Year; AUCA Southern Region Coach of the Year.
Coaching: Sid Feldman, Head Coach, compiled a record of 312-190. He coached at the University of Georgia and led the team to two SEC Championships.
Freshman Receiving Financial Aid/Academic: N/A   **Athletic:** N/A
Roster In State: 9   **Out of State:** 1   **Out of Country:** 1
Sophomores on Team: 0   **Seniors on Team:** 1   **Graduation %:** Unknown
Most Recent Record: 3-15-0   **Fall Games:** 21   **Spring Games:** 0
Positions Needed: Has 8 positions open
Style of Play: International 4-2 with some strong hitting and solid defense.

Brewton - Parker College
Academic Profile

Highway 280
Mt. Vernon, GA 30445

Phone: (912) 583-3277

Type: Private, 4 Yr., Liberal Arts, Coed
Website: http://www.bpc.edu
SAT/ACT/GPA: 860/18
Student/Faculty Ratio: 12:1
Undergraduate Enrollment: 1,600
Scholarships/Academic: Yes
Expenses By: Year
Degrees Conferred: BA, BS, Associates

Athletic: Yes
In State: $ 9,310

Founded: 1904
Religion: Baptist
Housing: Yes
Male/Female: 2:3
Graduate Enrollment: N/A
Financial Aid: Yes
Out of State: $ 9,310

Programs of Study: Accounting, Agricultural Business, Applied Art, Art, Biology, Business & Management, Chemistry, Computer Information System, Dental Services, Economics, Education, English, History, Marketing, Mathematics, Medical Assistant Technology, Music, Nursing, Political Science, Ministries, Physical Science, PreProfessionals, Psychology, Social Science

Women's Athletic Profile

Hwy. 280
Mt. Vernon, GA 30445
Coach: Jason Bryant
Email: chbryantpreach99@aol.com

NCAA I
Lady Wildcats, Orange, Blue
Phone: (912) 583-3273
Fax: (912) 583-4498

Estimated # of Women's Volleyball Scholarships: N/A
Conference: GIAC

Clark Atlanta University
Academic Profile

James P Brawley Drive
Atlanta, GA 30314

Phone: 404-880-6605

Type: Private, 4 Yr., Coed
Website: http://www.cau.edu
SAT/ACT/GPA: 900+
Student/Faculty Ratio: 15:1
Undergraduate Enrollment: 2,392
Scholarships/Academic: Yes
Expenses By: Year
Degrees Conferred: BA, BS, MA, MBA, Ph.D., EdD

Athletic: Yes
In State: $ 12,252

Founded: 1869
Religion: Non-Affiliated
Housing: Yes
Male/Female: 31:69
Graduate Enrollment: 1,064
Financial Aid: Yes
Out of State: $ 12,252

Programs of Study: Philosophy, Psychology, Social Science, Math, Engineering, Business and Management, Communications, Computer Science, Languages

Men's Athletic Profile

J.P. Brawley Dr.@ Fair St. SW
Atlanta, GA 30314
Coach:
Email:

NCAA II
Panthers/Red, Black, Grey
Phone: (404) 880-8126
Fax: (404) 880-8397

Estimated # of Men's Volleyball Scholarships: N/A
Conference: Independent

Women's Athletic Profile

240 Chestnut Street, SW
Atlanta, GA 30314
Coach: Larry Nolley
Email:

NCAA I
Panthers, Red, Black, Grey
Phone: (404) 880-8123
Fax: (404) 880-8397

Estimated # of Women's Volleyball Scholarships: N/A
Conference: Southern Intercollegiate Conference

Covenant College
Academic Profile

14049 Scenic Highway
Lookout Mountain, GA 30750

Phone: 888-451-2683

Type: 4 Yr., Coed
Website: http://www.covenant.edu
SAT/ACT/GPA: Open
Student/Faculty Ratio:
Undergraduate Enrollment: N/A
Scholarships/Academic: **Athletic:**
Expenses By: Year **In State:**
Degrees Conferred:
Programs of Study: Contact school for programs of study.

Founded:
Religion: Non-Affiliated
Housing: No
Male/Female:
Graduate Enrollment: N/A
Financial Aid:
Out of State:

Women's Athletic Profile

1500 Scenic Hwy.
Lookout Mountain, GA 30750
Coach: D. Franklin
Email: dfranklin@covenant.edu

NCAA I
Lady Scots, Blue, Gold
Phone: (706) 820-1560
Fax: (706) 820-2165

Estimated # of Women's Volleyball Scholarships: N/A
Conference: TVAC
Coaching: D. Franklin - Head Coach.
Style of Play: Cooperation, teamwork, sacrifice and commitment are the biblical principles we seek to instill in our student athletes

Emory University
Academic Profile

600 Asbury Circle
Atlanta, GA 30322

Phone: 404-727-6036

Type: Private, 4 Yr., Coed
Website: http://www.emory.edu
SAT/ACT/GPA: 1350/28/3.75
Student/Faculty Ratio: 24:1
Undergraduate Enrollment: 5,000
Scholarships/Academic: Yes **Athletic:** No
Expenses By: Year **In State:** $ 32,000
Specializes In: PreLaw, PreMed, Business, Theology, Psychology
Degrees Conferred: BA, BS, MA, MS, MBA, MEd, Ph.D., MD, JD, Mdiv.
Programs of Study: African - American Studies, Anthropology, Art History, Asian Studies, Biology, Chemistry, Classical Civilization, Classical Studies, Classics, Computer Science, Creative Writing, Economics, Education Studies, English, Film Studies, French, French Cultural & Studies, German Studies, Greek History, International Studies, Judaic Languages & Literature, Latin, Literature, Mathematics, Medieval & Renaissance Studies, Music, Philosophy, Sociology, Spanish, Theatre Studies

Founded: 1836
Religion: Methodist
Housing: Yes
Male/Female: 42:58
Graduate Enrollment: 6,000
Financial Aid: Yes
Out of State: $ 32,000

Women's Athletic Profile

600 Asbury Circle
Atlanta, GA 30322
Coach: Jenny McDowell
Email: jmcdowe@emory.edu

NCAA I
Lady Eagles, Blue, Gold
Phone: (404) 727-4693
Fax: (404) 727-4989

Estimated # of Women's Volleyball Scholarships: N/A
Conference: University Athletic Association
Program Profile: We have a tradition of being among the nation's best volleyball teams in the NCAA Division III. We have a state of the art arena.
History: The Lady Eagles were ranked in the top 20 nationally for the entire 1998 season. Five consecutive NCAA Tournament Appearances. Ranked in the Top 10 Nationally for the past 4 years.
Achievements: 3 All-Americans in 1998, 1999, 2000. UAA Coaching staff of the Year 1996-2000.
Coaching: Jenny McDowell - Head Coach. Amber Davis Assistant Coach.

Roster In State: 0
Seniors on Team: 2
Most Recent Record: 32-4-0
Camp of Clinic Dates: July 6-8, July 9-13, July 16-20, July 23-26
Positions Needed: Setter, Outside Hitters, Middle Hitters
Style of Play: Fast, disciplined and aggressive.

Out of State: 12   **Out of Country:** 0
Graduation %: 100

Fort Valley State University
Academic Profile

Fort Valley University
Fort Valley, GA 31030
Type: Public, 4 Yr., Coed
Website: http://www.fvsc.peachnet.edu
SAT/ACT/GPA: Open
Student/Faculty Ratio: 21:1
Undergraduate Enrollment: 2,061
Scholarships/Academic: Yes   **Athletic:** Yes
Expenses By: Year   **In State:** $ 6,012
Degrees Conferred: AA, AS, BA, BS, MA, MS
Programs of Study: Contact school for programs of study.

Phone: 912-825-6307

Founded: 1895
Religion: Non-Affiliated
Housing: No
Male/Female: 51:49
Graduate Enrollment: 307
Financial Aid: Yes
Out of State: $ 7,353

Women's Athletic Profile

State College Drive
Fort Valley, GA 31030
Coach: Lonnie Bartley
Email:

NCAA I
Lady Wildcats, Blue, Gold
Phone: (912) 825-6208
Fax: (912) 825-6394

Estimated # of Women's Volleyball Scholarships: N/A
Conference: Southern Intercollegiate Conference

Georgia Southern University
Academic Profile

P. O. Box 8082
Statesboro, GA 30460-8082

Type: Public, 4 Yr., Coed
Website: http://www.gasou.edu
SAT/ACT/GPA: 1000/2.5
Student/Faculty Ratio: 25:1
Undergraduate Enrollment: 12,000
Scholarships/Academic: Yes   **Athletic:** Yes
Expenses By: Year   **In State:** $ 7,200
Specializes In: Business, Education, Technology
Degrees Conferred: BA, BS, BBA, BSEd, MA, MS, MEd, EdS, EdD
Programs of Study: Accounting, Biology, Broadcasting, Business, Chemistry, Civil Engineering, Communications, Computer Science, Counseling, Economics, Education, Electrical Engineering, English, Exercise Science, Food-Nutrition, Geology, German, Health, Physical Education, History, Industrial, International Studies, Journalism, Kinesiology, Marketing, Mathematics, Nursing, Physics, Political Science, Public Relations, Recreation, Speech, Science, Sports Management, Sports Medicine, Sports Psychology

Phone: (912) 681-5391

Founded: 1906
Religion: Non-Affiliated
Housing: Yes
Male/Female: 45:55
Graduate Enrollment: 2,000
Financial Aid: Yes
Out of State: $ 12,560

Women's Athletic Profile

Landrum Box 8082
Statesboro, GA 30460-8033
Coach: Eddie Matthews
Email: edmatt@gsvms2.cc.gasou.edu

NCAA I
Lady Eagles, Blue, White
Phone: (912) 871-1502
Fax: (912) 681-0046

Estimated # of Women's Volleyball Scholarships: 7 1/2
Conference: Southern Conference
Program Profile: Our home court is Hanner Field house with a record of 4,378. Iron works has a measurement of 5,000 sq. ft. strength facility exclusively for athletes.

History: Our program began in 1985 and has only had 5 head coaches. The overall school record is 144-251.
Achievements: Alexis Dankulic was named Player of the Year in 1993.
Coaching: Eddie Matthews,Head Coach, begins his fourth year at the helm . His overall three-year record at GSU is 24-15. His alma mater is University of North Carolina at Chapel Hill, where he was an assistant coach for ten years. Wendy Schott is our Assistant Coach.

Freshman Receiving Financial Aid/Academic:		**Athletic:** 1
Roster In State: 3	**Out of State:** 7	**Out of Country:** 0
Graduation %: 100		
Most Recent Record: 17-19-0	**Fall Games:** 30	**Spring Games:** 0

Positions Needed: Outside Hitter
Schedule: University of Georgia, Wake Forest University, Indian State, University of Tennessee-Chattanooga, Coastal Carolina
Style of Play: Aggressive serve-receive, strong offensive serving, 5-1 with tactical offensive strategy.

Georgia Southwestern State University
Academic Profile

800 Wheatley St.
American, GA 31709

Phone: 800-338-0082

Type: 4 Yr., Coed
Website: http://www.gswr6k.gsw.peachnet
SAT/ACT/GPA: 500/21
Student/Faculty Ratio: 15:1
Undergraduate Enrollment: 2,066
Scholarships/Academic:
Expenses By: Year
Degrees Conferred: Masters, Bachelors

Founded: 1906
Religion: Non-Affiliated
Housing: Yes
Male/Female: Not Available
Graduate Enrollment: 456
Financial Aid: Yes

Athletic:
In State: $ 1,584

Out of State: $ 5,463

Programs of Study: Accounting, Applied Art, Art Education, Art/Fine Arts, Automotive Technology, Aviation Technology, Behavioral Science, Biology, Biological Science, Botany Plant, Business Administration, Commerce, Management, Business Education, Ceramic Art and Design, Chemistry, Commercial Art, Computer Information System, Computer Programming, Computer Science, Computer Technology, Data Processing, Drafting and Design, Early Childhood Education, Earth Science, Education, Electrical and Electronics /Technology, Elementary Education, English, Environmental Technology, Marketing, Retailing, Merchandising, Mathematics, Middle School Education, Music, Music Education, Nursing, Painting, Drawing, Physical Education, Physical Sciences, Physics, Political Science, Psychology, Studio Art

Women's Athletic Profile

800 Wheatley Street
Americus, GA 31709
Coach: Michelle Haywood
Email: mrh@canes.gsw.peacnet.edu

NCAA I
Lady Hurricanes, Navy, Gold
Phone: (912) 931-2230
Fax: (912) 931-2143

Estimated # of Women's Volleyball Scholarships: N/A
Conference: GAC

Georgia State University
Academic Profile

1 Park Place South
Atlanta, GA 30303

Phone: (404) 651-3183

Type: Public, 4 Yr., Liberal Arts, Coed
Website: http://www.gsu.com
SAT/ACT/GPA: 830/18
Student/Faculty Ratio: 16:1
Undergraduate Enrollment: 24,300
Scholarships/Academic: Yes
Expenses By: Year
Specializes In: Business, Education

Founded: 1913
Religion: Non-Affiliated
Housing: Yes
Male/Female: 40:60
Graduate Enrollment: 24,300
Financial Aid: Yes

Athletic: Yes
In State: $ 11,207

Out of State: $ 18,449

Degrees Conferred: AA, AS, BA, BBA, BFA, BIS, BM, BS, BSEd, BSW, MAS, MAEd, MA, MAT, MBA, MBEd, M.Ed., MFA, MHA, MHP, MLM, MM, MPA
Programs of Study: Accounting, Actuarial Science, Anthropology, Arts, Business Administration, Biological Science, Chemistry, Computer Information Systems, Economics, Education, Exercise Science, Fine Arts, Geography, Health Nutrition, Interdisciplinary Studies, Music, Science, Science in Education, Social Work

Women's Athletic Profile

University Plaza
Atlanta, GA 30303-3038
Coach: Dr. Richard Leonard
Email: admljs@langate.gsu.edu

NCAA I
Panthers, Blue, White, Red
Phone: (404) 651-3183
Fax: (404) 651-0842

Estimated # of Women's Volleyball Scholarships: 8
Conference: Trans America Athletic Conference
Program Profile: We are improving our team with a new head coach and upgraded recruiting. We have a 4,500-seats sports arena (tournament quality). The quality of the schedule will be upgraded in 1999. Our goal is to become a top tier program in the next few years.
History: We began in 1975 (We were dormant 1979-1984). Our all-time record is 291-2. We had four coaches and 11 winning seasons in our program's history.
Achievements: 3 Conference Titles in 1988, 1989 & 1991; 4 straight Division Titles in 1995, 1996, 1997 & 1998.
Coaching: Dr. Richard Leonard, Head Coach, started with the program in 1998 and compiled a record of 26-9. He was a former associate coach at St. Louis where he was AA rated and got 4 USVB Regional Championships. Stephanie Feulner, Assistant Coach, started in 1998. She was a 2-year letter-winner at St. Louis and a 2-time first team All-Conference USA.

Freshman Receiving Financial Aid/Academic:

		Athletic: 3
Roster In State: 3	**Out of State:** 6	**Out of Country:** 2
Sophomores on Team: 3	**Seniors on Team:** 2	**Graduation %:** 90
Most Recent Record: 26-9-0	**Fall Games:** 35	**Spring Games:** 0

Positions Needed: RS, Middle Blocker, Outside Hitter
Schedule: Florida State, Clemson, Georgia, Georgia Tech, Auburn, Alabama
Style of Play: Play a 5-1 alignment, aggressive serving and attacking team. Focus on ball placement, sophisticated blocking schemes.

Georgia Tech
Academic Profile

150 Bobby Dodd Way, NW
Atlanta, GA 30332

Phone: 404-894-4154

Type: Public, 4 Yr., Engineering, Coed
Website: http://www.ramblingwreck.com
SAT/ACT/GPA: Open
Student/Faculty Ratio: Not Avai
Undergraduate Enrollment: N/A
Scholarships/Academic: Yes
Expenses By: Sem
Specializes In: Engineering
Degrees Conferred:

Founded: 1885
Religion: Non-Affiliated
Housing: Yes
Male/Female: 3:1
Graduate Enrollment: N/A
Financial Aid: Yes
In State: $ 4,604   **Out of State:** $ 8,225

Programs of Study: Engineering, Architecture, Business, Biology, Computer Science

Women's Athletic Profile

150 Bobby Dodd Way, NW
Atlanta, GA 30332-0325
Coach: Shelton Collier
Email: scollier@at.gtaa.gatech.edu

NCAA I
Yellow Jackets, Gold, White
Phone: (404) 894-5453
Fax: (404) 894-1248

Estimated # of Women's Volleyball Scholarships: 5
Conference: Atlantic Coast Conference
History: Our program began in 1980.
Coaching: Shelton Collier, Head Coach, started coaching the program in 1990 with the record of 206-84.

Freshman Receiving Financial Aid/Academic:

		Athletic: 11
Roster In State: 1	**Out of State:** 10	**Out of Country:** 2
Sophomores on Team: 6	**Seniors on Team:** 3	**Graduation %:** 100
Most Recent Record: 22-13-0	**Fall Games:** 30	**Spring Games:** 0

Positions Needed: 5
Schedule: Santa Barbara, North Carolina, Florida State, Illinois State, South Carolina, Clemson

LaGrange College
Academic Profile

601 Broad St.
La Grange, GA 30240

Phone: (706) 812-7330

Type: Private, 4 Yr., Liberal Arts, Coed
Website: http://www.lgc.edu
SAT/ACT/GPA: 860/16/2.0
Student/Faculty Ratio: 15:1
Undergraduate Enrollment: 1,000
Scholarships/Academic: Yes   **Athletic:** No
Expenses By: Year   **In State:** $ 15,500

Founded: 1861
Religion: Methodist
Housing: Yes
Male/Female: 1:3
Graduate Enrollment: N/A
Financial Aid: Yes
Out of State: $ 15,500

Degrees Conferred: AA, BA, BS, BBA. MBA, M.Ed.
Programs of Study: Accounting, Arts, Biology, Business Administration, Chemistry, Computer Science, Criminal Justice, Economics, Education, English, History, International Business, Management, Mathematics, Nursing, Philosophy, Physical Education, Physical Science, Physics, PreProfessional Courses, Psychology, Radiological Technology, Religion, Social Work, Theatre

Women's Athletic Profile

601 Broad Street
La Grange, GA 30240
Coach: Kelly Britsky
Email: kbrisky@lgc.edu

NCAA I
Lady Panthers, Red, Black
Phone: (706) 812-7330
Fax: (706) 812-7350

Estimated # of Women's Volleyball Scholarships: 0
Conference: Georgia Alabama Carolina Conference
Program Profile: We play 30 matches in the CEB gym on Callaway Campus. We have a long tradition of winning and excellence.
Achievements: Several conference championships and regional finishes.
Coaching: Kelly Britsky has been Head Coach for 3 years. Her record is 54-24.
Freshman Receiving Financial Aid/Academic: **Athletic:** 0
Roster In State: 6   **Out of State:** 5   **Out of Country:** 0
Sophomores on Team: 0   **Seniors on Team:** 5   **Graduation %:** 100
Most Recent Record: 25-13-0   **Fall Games:** 38   **Spring Games:** 0
Positions Needed: All

Mercer University
Academic Profile

1400 Coleman Avenue
Macon, GA 31207

Phone: (912) 752-2994

Type: Private, 4 Yr., Liberal Arts, Coed
Website: http://www.mercer.peachnet.edu
SAT/ACT/GPA: 980/20
Student/Faculty Ratio: 12:1
Undergraduate Enrollment: 2,800
Scholarships/Academic: Yes   **Athletic:** Yes
Expenses By: Year   **In State:** $ 21,000

Founded: 1833
Religion: Baptist
Housing: Yes
Male/Female: 40:60
Graduate Enrollment: 4,200
Financial Aid: Yes
Out of State: $ 21,000

Specializes In: Liberal Arts, Business, Economics, Engineering, Medical, Pharmacy
Degrees Conferred: BA, BS, BBA, BSEng, BM, BMEd, M.Ed., MBA, MTM, MSEng, MSM, MD
Programs of Study: Accounting, Art, Biology, Biomedical, Business, Chemistry, Communications, Computer Science, Economics, Education, Electrical and Mechanical Engineering, English, Environmental Science, Industrial, Management, Marketing, Medicine, Music, Natural Science, Philosophy, Physics, Political Science, Psychology, Special Education, Sociology, Spanish, Etc.

Women's Athletic Profile

1400 Coleman Avenue
Macon, GA 31207
Coach: Tami Darwin
Email: darwin_tp@mercer.edu

NCAA I
Lady Bears, Orange, Black
Phone: (912) 752-2994
Fax: (912) 752-2061

Estimated # of Women's Volleyball Scholarships: N/A
Conference: Trans America Athletic Conference
Program Profile: The season is in the fall and it lasts approximately 4 months. We play in Porter Gym. We are awaiting a new Convocation Center which should be completed in the next couple of years.
Coaching: Tami Darwin, Head Coach, is in her first year at Mercer. Her 1998 season record is 3-23. Coach Darwin played at one of the top schools in the nation: Duke University. While at Duke, she went to the NCAA Tournaments 4 times including the NCAA "Sweet 16".

Freshman Receiving Financial Aid/Academic:		**Athletic:** 4
Roster In State: 1	**Out of State:** 7	**Out of Country:** 1
Sophomores on Team: 0	**Seniors on Team:** 2	**Graduation %:** 100
Most Recent Record: 3-23-0	**Fall Games:** 26	**Spring Games:** 2 tournaments

Camp of Clinic Dates: N/A
Positions Needed: Middle Blocker, Outside Hitter
Schedule: Duke University, University of Connecticut, Indiana, Florida Atlantic, University of New Orleans, Georgia State

Morris Brown College
Academic Profile

643 M. Luther King. Jr Dr NW
Atlanta, GA 30314

Phone: 404-739-1560

Type: Public, 4 Yr., Liberal Arts, Coed
Website: Not Available
SAT/ACT/GPA: 620+
Student/Faculty Ratio: 15:1
Undergraduate Enrollment: 2,000
Scholarships/Academic: Yes
Expenses By: Year
Degrees Conferred: BA, BS
Programs of Study: Contact school for programs of study.

Founded: 1881
Religion: African Methodist Episcopal
Housing: No
Male/Female: 43:57
Graduate Enrollment: N/A
Athletic: Yes   **Financial Aid:** Yes
In State: $ 12,432   **Out of State:** $ 12,432

Women's Athletic Profile

643 M. Luther King, Jr. Dr NW
Atlanta, GA 30314
Coach: Phillip Wallace
Email:

NCAA I
Wolverettes, Purple, Black
Phone: (404) 220-3625
Fax: (404) 220-0114

Estimated # of Women's Volleyball Scholarships: N/A
Conference: Southern Intercollegiate Conference

Oglethorpe University
Academic Profile

4484 Peachtree Road, NE
Atlanta, GA 30319

Phone: (404) 364-8414

Type: Private, 4 Yr., Liberal Arts, Engineering, Coed
Website: http://www.oglethorpe.edu
SAT/ACT/GPA: 1050/27/3.5
Student/Faculty Ratio: 17:1
Undergraduate Enrollment: 1059
Scholarships/Academic: Yes
Expenses By: Year
Specializes In: Accounting, Education, Premed
Degrees Conferred: BA, BS, MA, MBA
Programs of Study: Biology, Business Administration, Communications, Education, Engineering, Political Science, PreLaw, PreMed, Psychology, Social Sciences

Founded: 1835
Religion: Presbyterian
Housing: Yes
Male/Female: 40:60
Graduate Enrollment: 122
Athletic: No   **Financial Aid:** Yes
In State: $ 21,810   **Out of State:** $ 21,810

Women's Athletic Profile

4484 Peachtree Rd. NE
Atlanta, GA 30319

NCAA I
Stormy Petrels, Gold, Black

Coach: Pam McNaull
Email:

Phone: (404) 364-8487
Fax: (404) 364-8445

Estimated # of Women's Volleyball Scholarships: N/A
Conference: Southern Collegiate Athletic Conference
Program Profile: We play in a strong NCAA Division III program. We play in good facilities. We have a normal playing season. Our conference stretches from Georgia to Texas to Indiana.
History: We were the first women's athletic program offered at Oglethorpe. We have a history of competitive teams.
Achievements: We have a first year coach.
Coaching: Pam McNaull is in her first year as Head Coach. She is a former outstanding player at Tennessee Tech.
Freshman Receiving Financial Aid/Academic: N/A   **Athletic:** N/A
Roster In State: 6   **Out of State:** 6   **Out of Country:** 0
Sophomores on Team: 5   **Seniors on Team:** 1   **Graduation %:** 100
Most Recent Record: 21-23-0
Positions Needed: All
Schedule: Trinity, Southwestern University-Texas, De Paul-Indiana, Rhodes College, Center College, University of the South
Style of Play: Aggressive, up and working.

Paine College
Academic Profile

1235 15th Street
Augusta, GA 30901

Phone: 800-476-7703

Type: Private, 4 Yr., Liberal Arts, Coed
Website: http://www.painecollege.com
SAT/ACT/GPA: 700avg/17avg/2.0
Student/Faculty Ratio: 11:1
Undergraduate Enrollment: 1,000
Scholarships/Academic: Yes   **Athletic:** Yes
Expenses By: Year   **In State:** $ 9,800
Degrees Conferred: BA, BS

Founded: 1882
Religion: CME Church Affiliated
Housing: Yes
Male/Female: 33:67
Graduate Enrollment: N/A
Financial Aid: Yes
Out of State: $ 9,800

Programs of Study: Accounting, Art, Biblical Studies, Biological Science, Business, Communicative Disorder, Computer, Criminal Justice, Drama, Economics, English, Finance, Geology, Health, History, Management, Marketing, Medical, Political Science, Recreation/Parks, Secondary Education, Sociology, Special Education, Speech

Women's Athletic Profile

1235 15th Street
Augusta, GA 30901
Coach: Carol Washington
Email:

NCAA I
Lady Lions, Purple, White
Phone: (706) 821-8353
Fax: (706) 821-8376

Estimated # of Women's Volleyball Scholarships: N/A
Conference: Southern Intercollegiate Conference

Piedmont College
Academic Profile

P.O. Box 10
Demorest, GA 30535

Phone: 800-277-7020

Type: Private, 4 Yr., Liberal Arts, Coed
Website: http://www.piedmont.edu
SAT/ACT/GPA: 850/21+
Student/Faculty Ratio: 15:1
Undergraduate Enrollment: 700
Scholarships/Academic: Yes   **Athletic:** Yes
Expenses By: Year   **In State:** $ 9,800
Degrees Conferred: BA, BS

Founded: 1897
Religion: Congregationalist
Housing: Yes
Male/Female: 40:60
Graduate Enrollment: N/A
Financial Aid: Yes
Out of State: $ 9,800

Programs of Study: Accounting, Art, Art Administration, Biology, Business Administration, Chemistry, Computer Information System, Economics, Education, English, History, Management, Mathematics, Music, Psychology, Social Science, Theatre

Women's Athletic Profile

P.O. Box 10
Demorest, GA 30535
Coach: Terry Martin
Email: wtmartin@piedmont.edu

NCAA I
Lady Lions, Green, Gold
Phone: (706) 778-8500x288
Fax: (706) 776-2811

Estimated # of Women's Volleyball Scholarships: N/A
Conference: Georgia Alabama Carolina Conference (GACC)
Program Profile: In process of building a $3.5 million athletic complex, capable of seating 1,200 spectators. In addition to the new gym the new athletic center will also house a fitness center, elevated running track, locker rooms.
History: The year 2000 will be the 4th year of the Volleyball program. Getting more competive every year.
Coaching: Terry Martin is volleyball and softball coach since 1998. Assistant Katie O'Brien was middle blocker for U of Iowa (94-98) played for Rita "The Rocket" Crokket

Roster In State: 8	**Out of State:** 4	**Out of Country:** 0
Seniors on Team: 0	**Graduation %:** 100	
Most Recent Record: 7-15	**Fall Games:** 20	**Spring Games:** Club season

Positions Needed: Outside, Middle, Right hitter and Setter
Schedule: Faulkner, Georgia South Western
Style of Play: Every year more competive, like to run 5-1 but will run a 4-2. 3 person serve receive, box rotation defense with read.

Savannah College of Art & Design
Academic Profile

PO Box 3146
Savannah, GA 31401

Phone: (912) 238-2401

Type: Private, 4 Yr., Coed
Website: http://www.scad.edu
SAT/ACT/GPA: Varies/2.0
Student/Faculty Ratio: 20:1
Undergraduate Enrollment: 4,000
Scholarships/Academic: Yes
Expenses By: Year
Specializes In: Art & Design

Athletic: No
In State: $ 17,450

Founded: 1978
Religion: Non-Affiliated
Housing: Yes
Male/Female: 50:50
Graduate Enrollment: 1,000
Financial Aid: Yes
Out of State: $ 17,450

Degrees Conferred: BFA, BArch, MArch, MFA, MA
Programs of Study: Architectural History, Architecture, Art History, Computer Art, Fashion, Fibers, Furniture, Graphic Design, Historic Preservation, Illustration, Industrial Design, Interior Design, Metal and Jewelry, Painting, Sequential Art, Photography, Video/Film

Men's Athletic Profile

235 Habersham Street
Savannah, GA 31410
Coach: Karen Ryan
Email: kryan@scad.edu

NCAA III
Bees/Black, White, Gold
Phone: (912) 238-2401
Fax: (912) 231-2367

Estimated # of Men's Volleyball Scholarships: 0
Conference: Independent
Program Profile: We start pre-season 2 1/2 weeks before the school starts. We have four days of try-outs. The fall season ends at the end of November while spring training starts in March and goes to the end of April.
History: The program has gone from 1990 to the present. We had four consecutive 20+ wins seasons. We have made three consecutive trips to the NCAA Regional Championships.
Achievements: 3 time AVCA All-Academic Team award in 1998; 3.68 was highest GPA of any college or university.
Coaching: Karen Ryan, Head Coach, started with the program in 1990. She compiled a record of 153-111.

Freshman Receiving Financial Aid/Academic: 100%
Athletic: 0

Roster In State: 1	**Out of State:** 11	**Out of Country:** 1
Sophomores on Team: 5	**Seniors on Team:** 3	**Graduation %:** 100%
Most Recent Record: 22-12-0	**Fall Games:** 34	**Spring Games:** 2

Positions Needed: All
Schedule: Juniata, Washington University, Hope College, Rochester Institute of Technology, Ithaca, Pomona-Pitzer College
Style of Play: We have fun and work hard.

Women's Athletic Profile

235 Habersham Street
Savannah, GA 31401
Coach: Karen Ryan
Email: kryan@scad.edu

NCAA I
Lady Bees, Black, White, Gold
Phone: (912) 238-2401
Fax: (912) 231-2367

Estimated # of Women's Volleyball Scholarships: 0
Conference: Independent
Program Profile: We start pre-season two and a half weeks before school starts. We have four days of try-outs. Our season ends at the end of November. Spring training is from March to the end of April.
History: The program started in 1990. We are in our 4th 20+ consecutive win season. We took 3 consecutive trips to the NCAA Regional Championships.
Achievements: 3 time AVCA All-Academic Team Award in 1998; 3.68 highest GPA of any college or university.
Coaching: Karen Ryan, Head Coach, joined the team in 1990. To the present, her record is 153-111. There is no assistant coach listed.
Freshman Receiving Financial Aid/Academic: **Athletic:** 0
Roster In State: 1   **Out of State:** 12   **Out of Country:** 1
Sophomores on Team: 5   **Seniors on Team:** 3   **Graduation %:** 100
Most Recent Record: 22-12-0   **Fall Games:** 34   **Spring Games:** 2
Positions Needed: All
Schedule: U of Alaska-Anchorage, U of Alaska-Fairbanks, Washington University, Simpson, Emory University, Ohio Northern
Style of Play: We enjoy the game of volleyball. I believe students learn more when they have fun playing. We are very competitive and enjoy traveling.

Savannah State University
Academic Profile

State College Branch
Savannah, GA 31404

Phone: 912-525-5100

Type: Public, 4 Yr., Coed
Website: http://www.savstate.edu
SAT/ACT/GPA: 800/18
Student/Faculty Ratio: 19:1
Undergraduate Enrollment: 1,750
Scholarships/Academic: Yes   **Athletic:** Yes
Expenses By: Year   **In State:** $ 5,100
Degrees Conferred: AS, BA, BS, BBA, BSW

Founded: 1890
Religion: Non-Affiliated
Housing: Yes
Male/Female: 48:52
Graduate Enrollment: N/A
Financial Aid: Yes
Out of State: $ 6,450

Programs of Study: Accounting, Biology, Business, Chemistry, Engineering, Computer, Criminal Justice, Economics, English, Languages/Literature, Environmental Science, Finance, History, Information Systems, Marine Biology, Marketing, Mathematics, Music

Women's Athletic Profile

State College Branch
Savannah, GA 31404
Coach: Anita Walsh
Email:

NCAA I
Lady Tigers, Blue, Orange
Phone: (912) 353-5274
Fax: (912) 353-5287

Estimated # of Women's Volleyball Scholarships: N/A
Conference: Southern Intercollegiate Conference

University of Georgia
Academic Profile

PO Box 1472
Athens, GA 30603

Phone: 706-542-2112

Type: Public, 4 Yr., Coed
Website: http://www.sports.uga.edu
SAT/ACT/GPA: 1180/3.5
Student/Faculty Ratio: 20:1
Undergraduate Enrollment: 25,000
Scholarships/Academic: Yes   **Athletic:** Yes

Founded: 1785
Religion: Non-Affiliated
Housing: Yes
Male/Female: 49:51
Graduate Enrollment: 5,000
Financial Aid: Yes

Expenses By: Year   **In State:** $ 8,062   **Out of State:** $ 15,304

Programs of Study: Agricultural Environmental Science, Art & Science, PreProfessional Programs, Business Administration, Education, Environmental Design, Family & Consumer Sciences, Forest Resources, Journalism and Mass Communications, Pharmacy, Social work, Veterinary Medicine

Women's Athletic Profile

P.O. Box 1472   **NCAA I**
Athens, GA 30602   Lady Bulldogs, Red, Black
Coach: Jim Iams   **Phone:** (706) 542-7915
Email: jiams@sports.uga.edu   **Fax:** (706) 542-9339
Estimated # of Women's Volleyball Scholarships: N/A
Conference: Southeastern Conference
Program Profile: Ramsey Center where the team plays is hailed as one of the best volleyball-only facilities in the nation holds a capacity of 2,000. Playing season goes Sept-Dec.
History: Program began in 1978. 1985 squad won the SEC championships and advanced to the Sweet 16, 87 squad advanced to Sweet 16 as well. Under Coach Iams the Lady Bulldogs have made five NCAA Appearances
Achievements: 1985 team won SEC Championship. School has two All-Americans in its history.
Coaching: Jim Iams, began in 1989, enters 11th year at Georgia, 232-103, also coached at Oregon State 1982-83. Melinda Claiborne played at University of Washington where she was named an All-America and All-Pac 10

Roster In State: 3   **Out of State:** 9   **Out of Country:**
Sophomores on Team: 1   **Seniors on Team:** 1   **Graduation %:** N/A
Most Recent Record: 14-14

Valdosta State College
Academic Profile

1500 N. Patterson St.   **Phone:** 800-618-1878
Valdosta, GA 31698

Type: Public, 4 Yr., Coed   **Founded:** 1906
Website: http://www.valdosta.peachnet.edu   **Religion:** Non-Affiliated
SAT/ACT/GPA: 700   **Housing:** Yes
Student/Faculty Ratio: 21:1   **Male/Female:** 40:60
Undergraduate Enrollment: 8,000   **Graduate Enrollment:** 1,500
Scholarships/Academic: Yes   **Athletic:** Yes   **Financial Aid:** Yes
Expenses By: Year   **In State:** $ 6,644   **Out of State:** $ 12,068
Specializes In: State Regional University
Degrees Conferred: Ph.D., M Ed, MS, MA, BS, BA, AB, AA
Programs of Study: Accounting, Anthropology, Art, Astronomy, Biology, Business, Business Management, Chemistry, Communications, Computer Science, Criminal Justice, Economics, Education, English, Exercise Fitness, Finance, Fine Arts, Geology, Languages, Management, Marketing, Nursing, Political Science, PreProfessional Programs, Public Relations, Sociology, Speech Pathology, Sport Medicine, Telecommunications

Women's Athletic Profile

Department of Athletics/1500 N.Patterson Str.   **NCAA I**
Valdosta, GA 31698   Lady Blazers, Red, Black
Coach: Paul Cantrell   **Phone:** (912) 333-5894
Email: pcantrel@Valdosta.edu   **Fax:** (912) 333-5972

Estimated # of Women's Volleyball Scholarships: 5.5
Conference: Gulf South Conference
Program Profile: VSU plays in a 5,500 seat arena called "The Complex". We are a Division II South Central Region program. We play in the fall.
History: In 1995, the program was reinstalled after 15 years with a record of 13-17. Our 1996 record was 15-16. Our 1997 record was 21-15. Our 1998 record was 33-9, including votes for top 25. In 1998, we received our first ever Regional ranking of 7th place.
Achievements: 1998 team placed 3rd in GSC; 5 All-Conference Awards; 3rd team Academic All-American GTE; 1997 AVCA Team Academic Award.
Coaching: Paul Cantrell, Head Coach, started coaching the program in 1995. His present record is 82-57. He previously coached at Morehead State University in Kentucky. Glenn Cox and Josh Brannan are Assistant Coaches.
Freshman Receiving Financial Aid/Academic: **Athletic:** 12

Roster In State: 6   **Out of State:** 6   **Out of Country:** 2
Sophomores on Team: 3   **Seniors on Team:** 4   **Graduation %:** 80
Most Recent Record: 33-9-0   **Fall Games:** 40   **Spring Games:** 12
Camp of Clinic Dates: N/A
Positions Needed: Outside Hitter (left & right), Middle
Schedule: Florida Tech, North Florida, Drury, Alabama-Huntsville, North Alabama
Style of Play: Swing offense with a heavy emphasis on serving and blocking.

Wesleyan College
Academic Profile

4760 Forsyth Rd.   **Phone:** (912) 757-5260
Macon, GA 31210

Type: Private, 4 Yr., Liberal Arts, Women Only   **Founded:** 1836
Website: Not Available   **Religion:** Methodist
SAT/ACT/GPA: 1000 + above/21/2.8+   **Housing:** Yes
Student/Faculty Ratio: 12:1   **Male/Female:** Women
Undergraduate Enrollment: 600   **Graduate Enrollment:** N/A
Scholarships/Academic: Yes   **Athletic:** No   **Financial Aid:** Yes
Expenses By: Year   **In State:** $ 22,900   **Out of State:** $ 22,900
Degrees Conferred: BS, AB
Programs of Study: American Studies, Art History, Biology, Business Administration, Chemistry, Communications, Early Childhood Education, English, History, Interdisciplinary Studies, International Business , International Relations, Mathematics, Middle Grades Education, Philosophy, Political Science, Pre-Professional Courses, Psychology, Religion, Secondary Education, Sociology, Spanish, Studio Art

Women's Athletic Profile

4760 Fortsyth Rd.   **NCAA I**
Macon, GA 31210   Lady Pioneers, Purple, White
Coach: William Carter   **Phone:** (912) 757-5255
Email: **Fax:** (912) 757-4030

Estimated # of Women's Volleyball Scholarships: N/A
Conference: Independent
Achievements: Ashley Chace- 1999 NESCAC All-Star; Leslie Pao-1999 NESCAC Academic All-Star; Alex DeToth-1999 NESCAC Academic All-Star;
Coaching: Gale Lackey, Head Coach, is completing her 21st year at Wesleyan. She has 227 wins. She is Senior Woman Athletic Administrator and Assistant Athletic Director, Joe Rouse, has been assistant coach for 14 years here. Maritza Ubides and Joe Rouse are assistant coaches. Martiza has earned all-NESCAC accolades twice.
Roster In State: 0   **Out of State:** 13   **Out of Country:** 0
Sophomores on Team: 3   **Seniors on Team:** 3   **Graduation %:** 100
Most Recent Record: 25-6-0   **Fall Games:** 31   **Spring Games:** 0
Schedule: University of England, Skidmore, Amherst, Trinity, Williams, Colby-Swayer, Union, Springfield, MIT, Skidmore, SUNY, Trinity

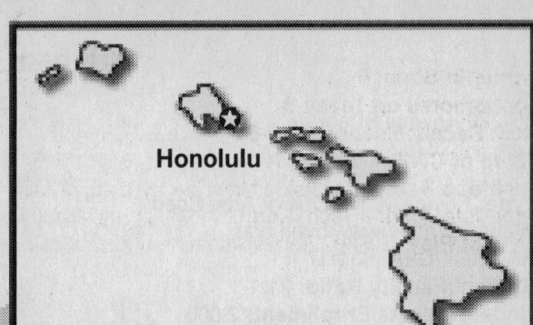

Honolulu

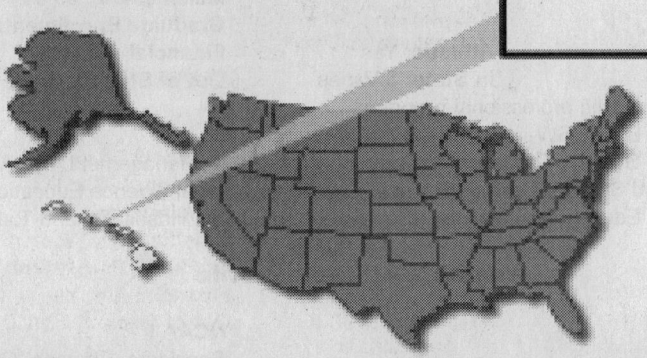

SCHOOL	CITY	AFFILIATION	PAGE
Brigham Young University - Hawaii	Laie	NCAA II	189
Chaminade University	Honolulu	NCAA II	189
Hawaii Pacific University	Honolulu	NCAA II	189
University of Hawaii - Hilo	Hilo	NCAA II	190
University of Hawaii - Manoa	Honolulu	NCAA I	191

Brigham Young University - Hawaii
Academic Profile

55-220 Kulanui Street
Laie, HI 96762

Phone: 808-293-3738

Type: Private, 4 Yr., Liberal Arts, Coed
Website: http://www.byuh.edu
SAT/ACT/GPA: 830/17
Student/Faculty Ratio: 21:1
Undergraduate Enrollment: 2,000
Scholarships/Academic: Yes   **Athletic:** Yes
Expenses By: Year   **In State:** $ Varies

Founded: 1955
Religion: Latter Day Saints (Mormon)
Housing: Yes
Male/Female: 39:61
Graduate Enrollment: N/A
Financial Aid: Yes
Out of State: $ Varies

Specializes In: Emphasizes Liberal Arts with professional programs
Degrees Conferred: AA, AS, BA, BS, BFA, BSW
Programs of Study: Communications Studies, Theatre, Computer Science, Travel Management, Art, Art Education, English, English, Education, History, Music, Pacific Island Studies, Political Science, Psychology, Social Science Education, Accounting, Biological Science, Biology, Education, Business Education, Chemistry, Elementary Education, Hospitality and Tourism

Women's Athletic Profile

55-220 Kulani Street
Laie, HI 96762
Coach: Wilfred Navalta
Email: navaltaw@byu.edu

NCAA I
Seasiders, Crimson, Gold, Grey
Phone: (808) 293-3756
Fax: (808) 293-3763

Estimated # of Women's Volleyball Scholarships: N/A
Conference: Pacific West Conference

Chaminade University
Academic Profile

3140 Waialae Avenue
Honolulu, HI 96816

Phone: 808-735-4735

Type: Private, 4 Yr., Coed
Website: http://www.pixi.com/~chaminad
SAT/ACT/GPA: 950+
Student/Faculty Ratio: 16:1
Undergraduate Enrollment: 2,342
Scholarships/Academic: Yes   **Athletic:** Yes
Expenses By: Year   **In State:** $ 14,080

Founded: 1955
Religion: Catholic
Housing: No
Male/Female: 58:42
Graduate Enrollment: 282
Financial Aid: Yes
Out of State: $ 14,080

Degrees Conferred: AA, AS, BA, BS, BFA, MS, MBA
Programs of Study: Contact school for program of study.

Women's Athletic Profile

3140 Waialae Avenue
Honolulu, HI 96816-1578
Coach: Glennie Adams
Email:

NCAA I
Lady Silverswords, Blue, White
Phone: (808) 735-4790
Fax: (808) 739-4695

Estimated # of Women's Volleyball Scholarships: N/A
Conference: Independent

Hawaii Pacific University
Academic Profile

1060 Bishop St. Ph
Honolulu, HI 96813

Phone: 800-669-4724

Type: Private, 4 Yr., Liberal Arts, Coed
Website: http://www.hpu.edu
SAT/ACT/GPA: 1000/22
Student/Faculty Ratio: 20:1
Undergraduate Enrollment: 7,000

Founded: 1965
Religion: Non-Affiliated
Housing: Yes
Male/Female: 55:45
Graduate Enrollment: 1,000

Scholarships/Academic: Yes   **Athletic:** Yes   **Financial Aid:** Yes
Expenses By: Year   **In State:**   **Out of State:** $ 12,800
Degrees Conferred: AS, BA, BS, BSBA, BSCSci, MBA
Programs of Study: Accounting, American Studies, Anthropology, Applied Mathematics, Business Administration, Communications, Computer Information System, Computer Science, Criminal Justice, Economics, English, History, Humanities, Human Development, Human Resources, Management, Marketing, Nursing, Political Science, Psychology, Social Science, Tourism

Women's Athletic Profile

1060 Bishop St
Honolulu, HI 96813
Coach: Tita Ahuna
Email: tgarman@hpu.edu

NCAA I
Sea Warriors, Blue, Green
Phone: (808) 544-0221
Fax: (808) 566-2405

Estimated # of Women's Volleyball Scholarships: N/A
Conference: Pacific West Conference
Program Profile: The 1999 Lady Sea Warrior volleyball team posted the best record in school history, became the 1st HPU program to be ranked #1 in the nation at the NCAA II level, and captured the team's 1st Pacific West Conference championship.
History: HPU volleyball began in 1980. HPU's 1st intercollegiate team opened their season in Laie with a win over BYU-Hawaii.
Achievements: 1998 NCAA II National Championship. 1998 NCAA II Pacific Region Championship. 1999 Pacific West Conference Championship.
Coaching: Head Coach Tita Ahuna enters her 5th year at HPU and is 83-29 overall.
Roster In State: 4   **Out of State:** 3   **Out of Country:** 4
Sophomores on Team: 2   **Seniors on Team:** 3   **Graduation %:**
Most Recent Record: 25-3-0   **Fall Games:** 25   **Spring Games:**
Schedule: BYU-Hawaii, Chaminade University, University of Alaska-Anchorage, University of Hawaii-Hilo, Central Washington University
Style of Play: The mental aspect of the game is very important. I played with a lot of emotion, and I've found that when our team plays with that same kind of emotion, we play better.

University of Hawaii at Hilo
Academic Profile

200 W. Kawili St.
Hilo, HI 96720

Phone: (808) 974-7520

Type: Public, 4 Yr., Liberal Arts, Coed   **Founded:** 1947
Website: http://www.uhh.hawaii.edu   **Religion:** Non-Affiliated
SAT/ACT/GPA: 900/19/2.5   **Housing:** Yes
Student/Faculty Ratio: 13:1   **Male/Female:** 2:3
Undergraduate Enrollment: 2,668   **Graduate Enrollment:** 9
Scholarships/Academic: Yes   **Athletic:** Yes   **Financial Aid:** Yes
Expenses By: Year   **In State:** $ 5,473   **Out of State:** $ 11,041
Degrees Conferred: BA, BBA, BS, MA
Programs of Study: AgriBusiness, AgroEcology & Environmental Quality, Animal Science, Anthropology, Art, Astronomy, Aquaculture, Biology, Business Administration, Chemistry, Communication, Computer Science, Crop Protection, Economics, English, General Agriculture, Geography, Geology, Hawaiian Studies, History, Japanese Studies, Liberal Studies, Linguistics, Marine Science, Mathematics, Music, Natural Science, Nursing, Philosophy, Physics, Political Science, Psychology, Sociology

Women's Athletic Profile

200 W. Kawili Street
Hilo, HI 96720
Coach: Sharon Peterson
Email: trumbo@hawaii.edu

NCAA I
Lady Vulcans, Red, White, Blue
Phone: (808) 974-7520
Fax: (808) 974-7711

Estimated # of Women's Volleyball Scholarships: N/A
Conference: Pacific West Conference
Program Profile: Our games are played in a 1,000 seat facility that is located on campus. Our matches run from the end of August to the beginning of November.
History: The program began with the 1978 season and was the first program to win four consecutive National Championships. We have won seven Championships and participated in 10 Championship matches.

Achievements: 24 All-Americans; 2 National Players of the Year; 2 AIAW Championships; 5 NAIA Championships

Coaching: Sharon Preston - Head Coach. She has been a coach for 20 seasons and her overall record is 473-176. She played for the Denver Comets in 1975 and 1977. She is a five time USVBA All-American from the University of California at Long Beach. She was a U.S.Olympic member in 1964 and 1968 and was in the World Games in 1966.

Roster In State: 7	**Out of State:** 5	**Out of Country:** 0
Sophomores on Team: 1	**Seniors on Team:** 6	**Graduation %:** Unknown
Most Recent Record: 14-17-0	**Fall Games:** 31	**Spring Games:** 0

Positions Needed: All

Schedule: Brigham Young University-Hawaii, Hawaii Pacific University, Western Washington University

Style of Play: Runs a 6-2 offensive set.

University of Hawaii - Manoa
Academic Profile

1337 Lower Campus Rd.
Honolulu, HI 96822

Phone: 800-897-4456

Type: Public, 4 Yr., Coed	**Founded:** 1907
Website: http://www.hawaii.edu	**Religion:** Non-Affiliated
SAT/ACT/GPA: 430/20	**Housing:** Yes
Student/Faculty Ratio: 14:1	**Male/Female:** 43:57
Undergraduate Enrollment: 13,000	**Graduate Enrollment:** 5,500

Scholarships/Academic: Yes   **Athletic:** Yes   **Financial Aid:** Yes

Expenses By: Year   **In State:** $ 4,607   **Out of State:** $ 7,847

Degrees Conferred: Bachelors, Masters, Doctorate

Programs of Study: Accounting, Agricultural, Animal Anthropology, Architecture, Art, American Studies, Asian, Atmospheric, Biological, Botany, Business, Chemistry, Dental, Design, Economics, Entomology, Mathematics, Real Estate, Religion, Women's Studies

Men's Athletic Profile

1337 Lower Campus Rd.
Honolulu, HI 96822-2370
Coach: Mike Welton
Email:

NCAA I
Rainbows/Green, White
Phone: (808) 956-4505
Fax: (808) 956-4470

Estimated # of Men's Volleyball Scholarships: N/A
Conference: Mountain Pacific Sports Federation

Women's Athletic Profile

1337 Lower Campus Rd.
Honolulu, HI 96822-2370
Coach: Dave Shoji
Email: wvball@hawaii.edu

NCAA I
Rainbows, Green, White
Phone: (808) 956-6229
Fax: (808) 956-4637

Estimated # of Women's Volleyball Scholarships: N/A
Conference: Western Athletic Conference

IDAHO

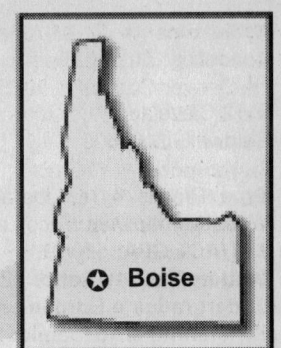

Boise

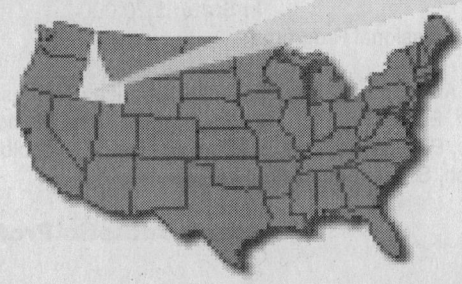

SCHOOL	CITY	AFFILIATION	PAGE
Albertson College of Idaho	Caldwell	NAIA II	193
Boise State University	Boise	NCAA I	193
Idaho State University	Pocatello	NCAA I	194
Lewis - Clarke State University	Lewiston	NCAA II/NAIA	194
Northwest Nazarene College	Nampa	NCAA II/NAIA	195
University of Idaho	Moscow	NCAA I	196

Albertson College - Idaho
Academic Profile

2112 Cleveland
Caldwell, ID 83605

Phone: 800-224-3246

Type: Private, 4 Yr., Liberal Arts, Coed
Website: http://www.acofi.edu
SAT/ACT/GPA: 510/21
Student/Faculty Ratio: 12:1
Undergraduate Enrollment: 681
Scholarships/Academic: Yes
Expenses By: Year
Specializes In: Liberal Arts, Preprofessional Programs
Degrees Conferred: BA, BS

Founded: 1891
Religion: Non-Affiliated
Housing: Yes
Male/Female: 55:45
Graduate Enrollment: N/A
Athletic: Yes   **Financial Aid:** Yes
In State: $ 20,000   **Out of State:** $ 14,100

Programs of Study: Accounting, Anthropology, Art, Biological Science, Business Administration, Chemistry, Computer Science, Economics, Elementary Education, English, French, History, Mathematics, Music, Philosophy, Physical Education, Physical Fitness/Exercise Science, Physics, Political Science, PreLaw, PreMed, Psychology, Religion, Science Education, Secondary Education, Social Science, Spanish, Sports Administration, Theatre

Women's Athletic Profile

2112 Cleveland Boulevard
Caldwell, ID 83605
Coach: Derek Soderblom
Email: dsoderblom@albertson.edu

NCAA I
Lady Coyotes, Purple, Gold
Phone: (208) 459-5858
Fax: (208) 459-5854

Estimated # of Women's Volleyball Scholarships: 5
Conference: Cascade Collegiate
Program Profile: State of the Art Gymnasium 75,000 sq. foot which seats 3,500. It also includes full cybex weight room, lockers, 25 meter swimming pool, athletic coaches offices and classrooms.
History: Program began in 1976.
Achievements: First NAIA Nation Tournament Appearance in 2000 season. Final National ranking # 13 in 2000. Runner up finish Region I tournament in 2000, 1 3rd Team All-American.
Coaching: Derek Soderblom, Head Coach, graduated from Boise State University 1990. Assistant Coach Liz Mendiola graduated from Albertson College in 1994.
Freshman Receiving Financial Aid/Academic: **Athletic:** 3
Roster In State: 8   **Out of State:** 4   **Out of Country:** 0
Sophomores on Team: **Seniors on Team:** 0   **Graduation %:** 100
Most Recent Record: 24-14-0
Camp of Clinic Dates: Aug 6-10
Schedule: Concordia University, Point Loma Nazarene, St. Mary's, Southern Oregon, Northwest Nazarene, Houston Baptist
Style of Play: Very solid ball control team with exceptional defense. Run a quick attack and fast offense.

Boise State University
Academic Profile

1910 University Dr.
Boise, ID 83725

Phone: 800-824-7017

Type: Public, 4 Yr., Coed
Website: http://www.broncosports.com
SAT/ACT/GPA: 750+
Student/Faculty Ratio: 19:1
Undergraduate Enrollment: 12,810
Scholarships/Academic: Yes
Expenses By: Year
Degrees Conferred: AA, AS, BA, BS, BFA, MA, MS, MBA, MFA, AAS
Programs of Study: Contact school for programs of study.

Founded: 1932
Religion: Non-Affiliated
Housing: No
Male/Female: 46:54
Graduate Enrollment: 1,444
Athletic: Yes   **Financial Aid:** Yes
In State: $ 5,753   **Out of State:** $ 8,403

Women's Athletic Profile

1910 University Drive
Boise, ID 83725-1000
Coach: Fred Sturm
Email: fstrum@boisestate.edu

NCAA I
Lady Broncos, Blue, Orange
Phone: (208) 385-1656
Fax: (208) 385-3361

Estimated # of Women's Volleyball Scholarships: N/A
Conference: Big West Conference
Program Profile: Team took second in Eastern Division of the Big West in 1998 and won the league eastern Division in 1997. Play in The Pavilion (12,380).
History: Program began in 1970. Solid program in a great VB conference, with lots of community support
Achievements: Big West East Division Champions 1997, Big Sky Regular season Champions 1998.
Coaching: Fred Sturm- Head Coach 1st year (former USA men's National coach), Keith Rubio (Cal State Northridge graduate) and Jaine penfield (Colorado Sate graduate).
Freshman Receiving Financial Aid/Academic:

		Athletic: 3
Roster In State: 2	**Out of State:** 11	**Out of Country:**
Sophomores on Team: 1	**Seniors on Team:** 3	**Graduation %:** 80
Most Recent Record: 18-9	**Fall Games:** 27	**Spring Games:** 10

Camp of Clinic Dates: July 1999, July 2000
Positions Needed: 3-2
Schedule: Long Beach State, UC Santa Barbara, Fresno State, Washington State, Ohio State.
Style of Play: Runs a 5-1.

Idaho State University
Academic Profile

Box 8270
Pocatello, ID 83209

Phone: 208-282-2475

Type: Public, 4 Yr., Coed
Website: http://www.isu.edu
SAT/ACT/GPA: Open
Student/Faculty Ratio: 16:1
Undergraduate Enrollment: 9,000
Scholarships/Academic: Yes
Expenses By: Year

Athletic: Yes
In State: $ 6,047

Founded: 1901
Religion: Non-Affiliated
Housing: No
Male/Female: 48:52
Graduate Enrollment: 2,000
Financial Aid: Yes
Out of State: $ 8,697

Degrees Conferred: AA, AS, BA, BS, BFA, MA, MS, MBA, MFA, M.Ed., Ph.D.
Programs of Study: Contact school for programs of study.

Women's Athletic Profile

Box 8173
Pocatello, ID 83209
Coach: Mike Welch
Email: welcmike@isu.edu

NCAA I
Lady Bengals, Black, Orange
Phone: (208) 236-4065
Fax: (208) 236-4063

Estimated # of Women's Volleyball Scholarships: 12
Conference: Big Sky Conference
Program Profile: Reed Gym (seats 3,600). Attendance has been above 2000 four times, above 1000 nineteen times.
New coaching staff as of January 2000. Head coach has led collegiate teams to 5 conference championships, 4 NCAA Tournaments and an NIVC Tournament bid.
Achievements: NCAA Tournament participants 1986, 1987 and 1990. NIVC participants in 1994. Conference champions 1986, 1987, and 1990.
Melissa Lucas was a 1999 GTE Academic All-American.
Freshman Receiving Financial Aid/Academic:

		Athletic: 4
Roster In State: 5	**Out of State:** 8	**Out of Country:** 0
Seniors on Team: 3	**Graduation %:** 100	

Camp of Clinic Dates: July 26-28, 2001
Positions Needed: Middle Blocker, outside hitter, right side hitter
Schedule: Washington, Utah, Alabama, Nevada-Las Vegas, San Jose State, Sacramento State Northern Arizona, Eastern Washington, Montana, Montana State
Style of Play: Fast, intense, competitive. Focus on defense.

Lewis-Clark State University
Academic Profile

500 8th Avenue
Lewiston, ID 83501

Phone: 800-933-5272

Type: Public, 4 Yr., Coed
Website: http://www.lcsc.edu

Founded: 1893
Religion: Non-Affiliated

SAT/ACT/GPA: Open
Student/Faculty Ratio: 17:1
Undergraduate Enrollment: 8,200
Scholarships/Academic: Yes **Athletic:** Yes
Expenses By: Year **In State:** $ 5,935
Degrees Conferred: AA, AS, AAS, BA, BS

Housing: Yes
Male/Female: 38:62
Graduate Enrollment: N/A
Financial Aid: Yes
Out of State: $ 9,644

Programs of Study: Accounting, Biological Science, Business Administration, Chemistry, Communications, Criminal Justice, Earth Science, Education, English, Geology, History, Liberal Arts, Management, Mathematics, Natural Science, Nursing, Personnel Management, Secondary Education, Social Science, Special Education

Women's Athletic Profile

500 8th Avenue
Lewiston, ID 83501
Coach: Kip Yoshimura
Email: kyoshimu@lcsc.edu

NCAA I
Warriors, Navy, White, Red
Phone: (208) 799-2309
Fax: (208) 799-2801

Estimated # of Women's Volleyball Scholarships: 8
Conference: Frontier Conference
Program Profile: NAIA Championship caliber program. Play in the Warrior gymnasium (1,450). Surface is a wood-floored basketball court. Part of a very successful athletic program.
History: Program was initiated in 1979. Have had only two losing seasons since 1979. Have made seven NAIA Tournament appearance.
Achievements: Yoshimura has been named Region Coach of the Year five times, including the last four years in a row. Has also been named Section Coach of the Year and Frontier Conference Coach of the Year. LC has won the Pacific Northwest Athletic Conference Title three times ('94, '96, '97), the Pacific West Conference West Division Title ('98), the Pacific Northwest Independent Section ('98) and the Frontier Conference Title ('99). All-Americas at LC are: Janice Fletcher ('88), Maite Castro ('88), Lorrie Holmes ('94), Kelli Harris ('94, '95, '96), Kymm Lingnaw ('96, '97), Angela Igoe ('98, '99), Joy Dunn ('98, '99), Marci Pascua ('98, '99).
Roster In State: 3 **Out of State:** 11 **Out of Country:** 0
Seniors on Team: 2 **Graduation %:** 98
Most Recent Record: 32-6-0
Camp of Clinic Dates: All Summer
Positions Needed: Team Setter, Middle Blocker, Outside Hitter

Northwest Nazarene College
Academic Profile

623 Holly Street
Nampa, ID 83686

Phone: 877-668-4968

Type: Public, 4 Yr., Liberal Arts, Coed
Website: http://www.nnc.edu
SAT/ACT/GPA: 870/18
Student/Faculty Ratio: 14:1
Undergraduate Enrollment: 1096
Scholarships/Academic: Yes **Athletic:** Yes
Expenses By: Year **In State:** $ 16,725

Founded: 1913
Religion: Nazarene
Housing: Yes
Male/Female: 1:1.3
Graduate Enrollment: 147
Financial Aid: Yes
Out of State: $ 16,725

Specializes In: Education, Liberal Arts, Physical Therapy
Degrees Conferred: 3 Associate of Arts, 119 Bachelor of Arts, 39 Masters
Programs of Study: Accounting, Biology, Business Administration, Chemistry, Communications, Computer Information Systems, Computer Science, Elementary Education, Engineering, English, Finance, Fine Arts, History, Humanities, International Relations, Mathematics, Music, Philosophy, Physical Education, Physics, Political Science, PreDentistry, PreLaw, PreMed, PrePharmacy, Psychology, Recreation, Social Science, Social Work, Sociology, Sport Medicine

Women's Athletic Profile

623 Holly Street
Nampa, ID 83686
Coach: Darlene Brasch
Email: dlbrash@wiler.nnc.edu

NCAA I
Lady Crusaders, Red, Black
Phone: (800) NNC-4-YOU
Fax: (208) 462-8645

Estimated # of Women's Volleyball Scholarships: 4
Conference: Independent
Program Profile: We have a dual membership: NAIA and NCAA Division II. Montgomery Field house holds 3,550. Our season is from August to December.

History: The program began in 1973. Our current coach came in 1989. We had the highest average attendance for NAIA schools in 1994,1995 and 1996. We got 4th place in the highest home season total attendance in 1997.
Achievements: Darlene Brasch was Conference Volleyball Coach of the Year in 1994,1995,1998; Conference Women's Coach of the Year in 1997; National Runner-up (NAIA) - 1998; three 1st team All-Americans; three 2nd team All-Americans; one 3rd team 4-Honorable Mention
Coaching: Darlene Brasch started as Head Coach in 1989. Patty Nottingham is Assistant Coach since 1998. She played for Coach Brasch from 1994 to 1997 and was 2nd team All-American. She was NAIA National Tournament Team Selection and MVP of Regional Tournament. She was #5 in the nation for kills per game (51) and holds the school record for most kills in the 1989 season. She has a career 2,129 kills and got most digs in a season, 724.
Freshman Receiving Financial Aid/Academic: **Athletic:** 4
Roster In State: 2   **Out of State:** 10   **Out of Country:** 0
Sophomores on Team: 2   **Seniors on Team:** 2   **Graduation %:** 98
Most Recent Record: 34-7-0   **Fall Games:** 41   **Spring Games:** 14
Positions Needed: Middle Blocker, Back-up Setter (for senior setter)
Schedule: Palm Beach Atlantic Tournament (St. Edward's University, Georgetown, Lee Taylor University, Lubbock Christian) Lewis-Clark State University, Southern Oregon University, Carroll College, Western Baptist
Style of Play: Strong, aggressive offense with tenacious defense.

University of Idaho
Academic Profile

Kibbie -Asui Activity Center
Moscow, ID 83844

Phone: (208) 885-0238

Type: Public, 4 Yr., Coed
Website: http://www.uidaho.edu
SAT/ACT/GPA: 1070/23/2.0
Student/Faculty Ratio: 17:1
Undergraduate Enrollment: 8,128
Scholarships/Academic: Yes   **Athletic:** Yes
Expenses By: Year   **In State:** $ 9,750

Founded: 1887
Religion: Non-Affiliated
Housing: Yes
Male/Female: 7:5
Graduate Enrollment: 2,447
Financial Aid: Yes
Out of State: $ 15,750

Specializes In: Agriculture, Art, Architecture, Business, Education, Engineering
Degrees Conferred: BA, BS, B of Dance, BFA, BGS, B of Land Arch., B of Music, BNS
Programs of Study: A wide variety of undergraduate programs and master's programs in 67 areas.

Women's Athletic Profile

Kibbie ASUI Activity Center
Moscow, ID 83843
Coach: Carl Ferreira
Email: volleyball@uidaho.edu

NCAA I
Lady Vandals, Silver, Idaho
Phone: (208) 885-0238
Fax: (208) 885-2862

Estimated # of Women's Volleyball Scholarships: 3
Conference: Big West Conference
Program Profile: Our program is creating an identity in the Big West and on the national scene. We play our home matches at War Memorial Gymnasium which seats 2,300.
History: Our volleyball program began in 1974. Since that time, there have been 6 Conference Championships and 5 NCAA Tournament Appearances. At one time, we held a 49 match home wining streak (4th longest in NCAA history).
Achievements: 5 Coach of the Year awards for Big Sky Conference; 6 Conference Titles (5 Big Sky and 1 Big West/Eastern Division); 1 All-American.
Coaching: Carl Ferreira, Head Coach, has a 31-28 record. He coached at California State-Bakersfield for three years and his record there was 100-13. He coached 7 All-Americans and the Division II Player of the Year. Ellen Ferreira is Assistant Coach.
Freshman Receiving Financial Aid/Academic: **Athletic:** 3
Roster In State: 1   **Out of State:** 10   **Out of Country:** 1
Sophomores on Team: 2   **Seniors on Team:** 2   **Graduation %:** 80
Most Recent Record: 15-14-0   **Fall Games:** 29   **Spring Games:** 3
Camp of Clinic Dates: Attack/Setters - July 24-28; Team- July 28-31
Positions Needed: Middle Blockers
Schedule: Long Beach State, University of California- Santa Barbara, University of the Pacific, California-Polytechnic, Nevada, Washington State
Style of Play: Fast paced ball control with an aggressive middle blocking system.

ILLINOIS

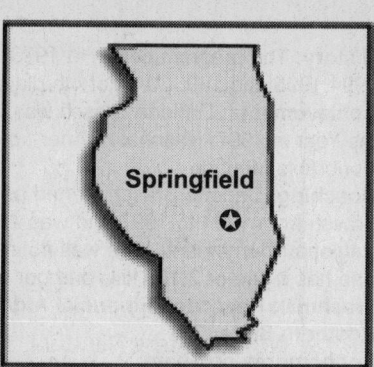

Springfield

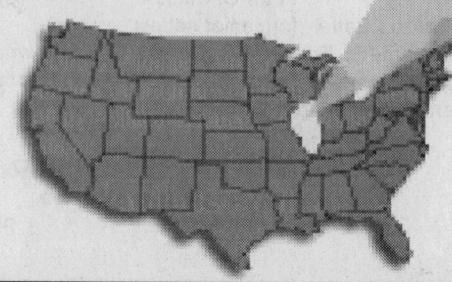

SCHOOL	CITY	AFFILIATION	PAGE
McKendree College	Lebanon	NAIA	216
Millikin University	Decatur	NCAA III	217
Monmouth College	Monmouth	NCAA III	218
North Central College	Naperville	NCAA III	218
North Park University	Chicago	NCAA III	219
Northeastern Illinois University	Chicago	NCAA I	219
Northern Illinois University	De Kalb	NCAA I	220
Northwestern University	Evanston	NCAA I	220
Olivet Nazarene University	Kankakee	NAIA	221
Parkland College	Champaign	NJCAA	222
Principia College	Elsah	NCAA III	222
Quincy University - Illinois	Quincy	NCAA II	223
Robert Morris College	Chicago	NAIA	224
Rockford College	Rockford	NCAA III	224
Saint Xavier University	Chicago	NAIA	225
Southern Illinois Univ- Carbondale	Carbondale	NCAA I	225
Southern Illinois Univ-Edwardsville	Edwardsville	NCAA II	226
Trinity Christian College	Palos Heights	NAIA	227
Trinity International University	Deerfield	NAIA	228
University of Chicago	Chicago	NCAA III	228
University of Illinois - Chicago	Chicago	NCAA I	229
Sangamon State	Springfield	NAIA	229
University of Illinois - Champaign	Champaign	NCAA I	230
Western Illinois University	Macomb	NCAA I	230
Wheaton College	Wheaton	NCAA III	231

Augustana College
Academic Profile

639 - 38th Street
Rock Island, IL 61201

Phone: 309-794-7341

Type: Private, 4 Yr., Liberal Arts, Coed
Website: http://www.augustana.edu
SAT/ACT/GPA: 24/3.2
Student/Faculty Ratio: 14:1
Undergraduate Enrollment: 1,150
Scholarships/Academic: Yes
Expenses By: Year
Specializes In: Business, Sciences
Degrees Conferred: BA, B.Mus., BME

Founded: 1860
Religion: Non-Affiliated
Housing: Yes
Male/Female: 45:55
Graduate Enrollment: N/A
Athletic: No
Financial Aid: Yes
In State: $ 22,224
Out of State: $ 22,224

Programs of Study: Business and Management, Education, Health Science, Letters/Literature, Life Sciences, Psychology, Social Sciences

Women's Athletic Profile

3500 5th Avenue
Rock Island, IL 61201
Coach: Lisle Fowler
Email: pefowler@augustana.edu

NCAA I
Lady Vikings, Blue, Gold
Phone: (309) 794-7432
Fax: (309) 794-7256

Estimated # of Women's Volleyball Scholarships: N/A
Conference: College Conference of Illinois & Wisconsin
Program Profile: Augustana has recorded five straight 20 victory seasons, home court is Carver PE Center.
History: Program began in 1977 with All-time record of 335-359-15 (1985)
Achievements: CCIW Conference champions in 1996
Coaching: Lisle Fowler 148-107 in seven years
Roster In State: 21
Seniors on Team: 4
Most Recent Record: 20-17

Out of State: 11
Graduation %: 100
Fall Games: 36

Out of Country:

Spring Games:

Aurora University
Academic Profile

347 S Gladstone Avenue
Aurora, IL 60506

Phone: (630) 844- 4207

Type: Private, 4 Yr., Liberal Arts, Coed
Website: http://www.aurora.edu
SAT/ACT/GPA: 900/19/2.0
Student/Faculty Ratio: 15:1
Undergraduate Enrollment: 2,700
Scholarships/Academic: Yes
Expenses By: Year
Specializes In: Business, Education, Criminal Justice, Computer Science, Sports
Degrees Conferred: BA, BS, Masters

Founded: 1893
Religion: Non-Denominational
Housing: Yes
Male/Female: 55:45
Graduate Enrollment: 1,000
Athletic: No
Financial Aid: Yes
In State: $ 17,200
Out of State: $ 17,200

Programs of Study: Contact school for programs of study.

Women's Athletic Profile

347 Gladstone
Aurora, IL 60506
Coach: Cindy Schendel
Email:

NCAA I
Lady Spartans, Royal, White
Phone: (630) 892-6431
Fax: (630) 844-7809

Estimated # of Women's Volleyball Scholarships: N/A
Conference: Northern Illinois-Iowa Conference

Barat College
Academic Profile

700 East Westleigh Road
Lake Forest, IL 60045

Phone: 847-234-3000

Type: Private, 4 Yr., Coed
Website: http://www.barat.edu
SAT/ACT/GPA: Open
Student/Faculty Ratio: 12:1
Undergraduate Enrollment: 710
Scholarships/Academic: Yes   **Athletic:** Yes
Expenses By: Year   **In State:** $ 14,200
Degrees Conferred: BA, BS
Programs of Study: Contact school for programs of study.

Founded: 1858
Religion: Roman Catholic
Housing: No
Male/Female: 29:71
Graduate Enrollment: N/A
Financial Aid: Yes
Out of State: $ 14,200

Women's Athletic Profile

700 E. Westleigh Rd.
Lake Forest, IL 60045
Coach: Laura Konieczny
Email:

NCAA I
Lady Bulldogs, Navy, Gold
Phone: (847) 604-6237x6237
Fax: (847) 615-5000

Estimated # of Women's Volleyball Scholarships: N/A
Conference: CCAC

Benedictine University
Academic Profile

5700 College Road
Lisle, IL 60532

Phone: 630-829-6300

Type: Private, 4 Yr., Coed
Website: http://www.ben.edu
SAT/ACT/GPA: 21/2.0
Student/Faculty Ratio: 10:1
Undergraduate Enrollment: 1,750
Scholarships/Academic: Yes   **Athletic:** No
Expenses By: Year   **In State:** $ 18,580
Specializes In: Sciences, Business, Education
Degrees Conferred: 38 Undergraduates majors; 12 Graduate programs
Programs of Study: Accounting, Arts Administration, Biochemistry, Biology, Business and Economics, Chemistry, Clinical Laboratory Science, Communications Arts, Computer Science, Economics, Elementary Education, Engineering Science, English Languages & Literature, Environmental Science, Finance, Health Science, History, International Studies, Management & Organizational Behavior, Marketing, Mathematics, Molecular Biology, Music, Nutrition, Philosophy, Physics, Political Science, Sociology, Spanish, Special Education, Writing and Publishing

Founded: 1887
Religion: Roman Catholic
Housing: Yes
Male/Female: 48:52
Graduate Enrollment: 900
Financial Aid: Yes
Out of State: $ 18,580

Women's Athletic Profile

5700 College Road
Lisle, IL 60532
Coach: Jerry Angle
Email: jangle@ben.edu

NCAA I
Lady Eagles, White, Cardinal
Phone: (630) 829-6154
Fax: (630) 960-0899

Estimated # of Women's Volleyball Scholarships: 0
Conference: Northern Illinois-Iowa Conference
Program Profile: We play at the Ralph Nolan Gymnasium, built in 1997, featurring two full-size game courts.
History: Conference Champions 18 out of 23 seasons and NCAA Apperances.
Achievements: 1998: Academic All-Americans- Libby Nielsen, Becky Jeffers; All-Conference-Kelly Walsh, Jodi Rense, Karen Kutis; MVP-Karen Kurtis; Avila All-Tournament Team- Kelly Walsh, Karen Kurtis
Coaching: 15 Years of Division I experience Coach of the Year 6 times, former member of the USA Volleyball Coaching Cadre, assistant coach for USA Men's Volleyball Team.
Roster In State: 10   **Out of State:** 0   **Out of Country:** 0
Sophomores on Team: **Seniors on Team:** 5   **Graduation %:** 100
Most Recent Record: 26-12-0

Blackburn College
Academic Profile

700 College Avenue
Carlinville, IL 62626

Phone: 800-233-3550

Type: Private, 4 Yr., Liberal Arts, Coed
Website: http://www.blackburn.edu
SAT/ACT/GPA: 1000/21/3.0-4.0
Student/Faculty Ratio: 15:1
Undergraduate Enrollment: 561
Scholarships/Academic: Yes   **Athletic:** No
Expenses By: Year   **In State:** $ 11,120
Specializes In: Education, Sciences

Founded: 1837
Religion: Presbyterian
Housing: Yes
Male/Female: 1:1
Graduate Enrollment: N/A
Financial Aid: Yes
Out of State: $ 11,120

Degrees Conferred: BA, BS in Engineering & Applied Science, Preprofessional Programs
Programs of Study: Accounting, Art, Biology, Business Administration & Management, Chemistry, Computer Science, Elementary Education, Political Science, Psychology, Spanish, PreDentistry, PreEngineering, PreLaw, PreNursing, PreMedicine, PrePhysical Therapy, PreVet

Women's Athletic Profile

700 College Avenue
Carlinville, IL 62626
Coach: Carl Clayton
Email: cclay@mail.blackburn.edu

NCAA I
Battling Beavers, Scarlet, Black
Phone: (217) 854-3231x4333
Fax: (217) 854-5520

Estimated # of Women's Volleyball Scholarships: N/A
Conference: St. Louis Intercollegiate Athletic Conference
Coaching: Carl Clayton-Head Coach year #2
Roster In State: 15   **Out of State:** 2   **Out of Country:** 0
Sophomores on Team: **Seniors on Team:** 4   **Graduation %:** 100
Most Recent Record: 5-11
Positions Needed: 2 Middle Hitters, 2 Outside Hitters, 1 DS
Schedule: Westminster College, Maryville University
Style of Play: Quick offense with a lot of fun plays, 6-2 system offense, and defense pride. Team built on being a student, believing in yourself, the team and the coach. Also all year around training.

Bradley University
Academic Profile

1501 W. Bradley Avenue
Peoria, IL 61625

Phone: (309) 677-3626

Type: Private, 4 Yr., Liberal Arts, Coed
Website: http://www.bradley.edu
SAT/ACT/GPA: 1140/25
Student/Faculty Ratio: 15:1
Undergraduate Enrollment: 5,000
Scholarships/Academic: Yes   **Athletic:** Yes
Expenses By: Year   **In State:** $ 19,552

Founded: 1897
Religion: Non-Affiliated
Housing: Yes
Male/Female: 45:55
Graduate Enrollment: 1,000
Financial Aid: Yes
Out of State: $ 19,552

Degrees Conferred: BA, BS, MA, MS, MBA, MFA
Programs of Study: Business Administration, Communications and Fine Arts, Educational and Sciences, Engineering and Technology, Liberal Arts and Sciences

Women's Athletic Profile

1501 W. Bradley
Peoria, IL 61625
Coach: Scott Luster
Email: lustler@bradley.edu

NCAA I
Lady Braves, Red, White
Phone: (309) 677-2649
Fax: (309) 677-3626

Estimated # of Women's Volleyball Scholarships: N/A
Conference: Missouri Valley Conference

Program Profile: Our program needs to improve from last year's 15-15 season. Our team has some real talent this year. We have a new coach, Scott Luster who is focused on revitalizing our program.

Achievements: Samantha Darwick 1998 MVC Newcomer; Tegan Catlin 1998 member of Missouri Valley Conference Scholar-Athlete team;

Coaching: Scott Luster is our new Head Coach. He came with a career record of 448-251 and a .641 winning percentage. Leanne Kling, Assistant Coach, was a 2-time All-American. She also got the 1992 Big Ten Player of the Year award.

Roster In State: 3	**Out of State:** 9	**Out of Country:** 0
Sophomores on Team: 2	**Seniors on Team:** 4	**Graduation %:** 100

Most Recent Record: 9-19-0

Schedule: Northeast Louisiana, Western Kentucky, Missouri, Hawaii, Arizona State, Baylor, Wichita State, SW Missouri State, Drake

Style of Play: Physically strong, goal-oriented and team-oriented; make the game challenging and fun

Chicago State University
Academic Profile

9501 S King Dr.
Chicago, IL 60628

Phone: 773-995-2513

Type: Public, 4 Yr., Coed
Website: http://www.csu.edu
SAT/ACT/GPA: 16
Student/Faculty Ratio: 9:1
Undergraduate Enrollment: 9,412
Scholarships/Academic: Yes   **Athletic:** Yes
Expenses By: Year   **In State:** $ 6,508

Founded: 1867
Religion: Non-Affiliated
Housing: Yes
Male/Female: 5:1
Graduate Enrollment: 2,436
Financial Aid: Yes
Out of State: $ 8,476

Degrees Conferred: BA, BS, MA, MS, MED

Programs of Study: Accounting, Art, Banking/Finance, BioChemistry, Biological Science, Broadcasting, Business, Chemistry, Computer, Criminal Justice, Data Processing, Dietetics, Early Childhood Education, English, Geography, History, Hotel/Restaurant Management, Information Science, Management, Marketing, Mathematics, Medical, Music, Nursing, Occupation, Political Science, Psychology, Social Science, PreProfessional Programs

Women's Athletic Profile

95t01 S & King Drive
Chicago, IL 60628
Coach: Steve Houghton
Email: s-houghton@csu.edu

NCAA I
Lady Cougars, White, Green
Phone: (773) 995-3653
Fax: (773) 995-3656

Estimated # of Women's Volleyball Scholarships: 6
Conference: Mid-Continent Conference
Program Profile: Developing program small high school gym (new 10,500 seat gym planned break ground in 2000). Travel to 2 tournaments, host 1 tournament in 2000 and conference schedule of 14 matches and 4 non-conference.
History: 1988 moved from NAIA to Divison I winning record in NAIA, poor record in D-I.
Achievements: Coach Houghton was NJCAA Region four Coach of the Year- 6 times, NJCAA district 7 Coach of the Year-6 times, and 1995 AVCA Midwest Region Coach of the Year.
Coaching: Steve Houghton was named Head Coach in 1997. He coached at Kankakee Community College. His volleyball teams won the Region IV Championships in each of his six years there. His career record is 411-158. At NJCAA his record was 293-48 where he also had 16 NJCAA All-Americans

Freshman Receiving Financial Aid/Academic:

		Athletic: 1
Roster In State: 7	**Out of State:** 2	**Out of Country:** 1
Sophomores on Team:	**Seniors on Team:** 5	**Graduation %:** 71
Most Recent Record: 0-28	**Fall Games:** 28	**Spring Games:** 4 tournament

Positions Needed: OH/MH

Schedule: Oral Roberts, Kansas, TCU, Southern Illinois, Auburn

Style of Play: Quick, aggressive, and smart. Teams have been very inexperienced with inconsistent skills. Recruits for 1999 season are major upgrade in talent.

Truman College
Academic Profile

1145 West Wilson Avenue
Chicago, IL 60640

Phone: (773) 878-1700

Type: Public, 2 Yr., Coed
Website: http://www.truman.edu

Founded: 1956
Religion: Non-Affiliated

SAT/ACT/GPA: Open
Student/Faculty Ratio: 22:1
Undergraduate Enrollment: N/A
Scholarships/Academic: No   **Athletic:** No
Expenses By: Year   **In State:** $
Specializes In: Liberal Arts and Sciences
Degrees Conferred: Associate
Programs of Study: Contact school for programs of study.

Housing: No
Male/Female: 48:52
Graduate Enrollment: N/A
Financial Aid: Yes
Out of State: $

Women's Athletic Profile

1145 W, Wilson Ave.
Chicago, IL 60640-5616
Coach:
Email:

NCAA I
Lady Falcons, Green, White
Phone: (773) 878-1700
Fax: (773) 989-6135

Estimated # of Women's Volleyball Scholarships: N/A
Conference: Skyway

College of DuPage
Academic Profile

425 22nd Street
Glen Ellyn, IL 60137

Phone: (630) 942-2365

Type: Public, 2 Yr., Coed
Website: http://www.cod.edu
SAT/ACT/GPA: None
Student/Faculty Ratio: 15:1
Undergraduate Enrollment: 34,000
Scholarships/Academic: Yes   **Athletic:** No
Expenses By: Quarter   **In State:** $32 quarter hr.
Specializes In: 2 year community college
Degrees Conferred: AA, AS, AAS, AGS, AES

Founded: 1967
Religion: Non-Affiliated
Housing: No
Male/Female: .7:1
Graduate Enrollment: N/A
Financial Aid: Yes
Out of State: $94 quarter hr.

Programs of Study: 85 areas of study: Accounting, Anthropology, Art, Advertising, Design and Illustration, Architectural Drafting, Design and Technology, Automotive Service Technology, Biology, Botany, Business, Chemistry, Computer Science, Criminal Justice, Certified Nursing Assistant, Child Care and Development, Communication Arts and Sciences, Computer Information Systems, Criminal Justice, Earth Science, Economics, Education, Engineering, English, Geography, History, Home Economics, Humanities, Journalism, Languages, Marketing, Management, Mathematics, Music, Philosophy, Physical Education, Physics, Political Science, Psychology, Speech, Theatre, Zoology

Women's Athletic Profile

425 22nd Street
Glen Ellyn, IL 60137
Coach: LuAnn Zimmick
Email: zimmick@cdnet.cod.edu

NCAA I
Lady Chaparrals, Green, Gold
Phone: (630) 942-2365
Fax: (630) 858-5404

Estimated # of Women's Volleyball Scholarships: 0
Conference: North Central Community College
Program Profile: We are top ranked in the Conference, Region and the nation. We have a 129,000 square-foot arena. It has 700 seats, an 8-lane indoor track, an 8-lane pool with diving board, a strength complex, a fitness lab and a training room.
Achievements: 1992 Conference Champions; 1992 Conference Tournament Champions; 1993 Conference Tournament Champions 1994,1995,1996,1998 Conference and Conference Tournament Champions; 1998 NJCAA Division III National Champions.
Coaching: LuAnn Zimmick has been Head Coach from 1989 to the present. Her overall record is 309-185. She was Conference Coach if the Year in 1992,1994, 1995,1997, 1998. She was 1998 Region and NJCAA Division III Coach of the Year. She was 1998 AVCA/Techikara Midwest Region Coach of the Year. She coached the 1998 NJCAA Division National Champions.
Freshman Receiving Financial Aid/Academic: **Athletic:** 0
Roster In State: 12   **Out of State:** 0   **Out of Country:** 0
Sophomores on Team: 0   **Seniors on Team:** 3   **Graduation %:** 98
Most Recent Record: 33-16-0   **Fall Games:** 43   **Spring Games:** 0
Positions Needed: 4

Schedule: Kankakee Community College, Elgin Community College, Parkland College, McHenry Community College, Ridgewater Community College, Owens Community College

Concordia University
Academic Profile

7400 Augusta St.
River Forest, IL 60305

Phone: 800-285-2668

Type: Private, 4 Yr., Coed
Website: http://www.curf.edu
SAT/ACT/GPA: 22avg
Student/Faculty Ratio: 16:1
Undergraduate Enrollment: 1,300
Scholarships/Academic: No
Expenses By: Year

Athletic: Yes
In State: $ 14,100

Founded: 1864
Religion: Non-Affiliated
Housing: Yes
Male/Female: 33:67
Graduate Enrollment: 950
Financial Aid: Yes
Out of State: $ 14,100

Programs of Study: Biological Science, Business, Chemistry, Communications, Computer, Early Childhood Education, Earth Science, English, Geography, History, Management, Mathematics, Music, Nursing, Philosophy, Physical Fitness/Movement, Political Science, PreProfessional Programs, Psychology, Religion, Science Education, Secondary Education, Social Science

Women's Athletic Profile

7400 Augusta Street
River Forest, IL 60305
Coach: Rick Pruett
Email:
Estimated # of Women's Volleyball Scholarships: N/A
Conference: Northern Illinois-Iowa Conference

NCAA I
Lady Cougars, Maroon, Gold
Phone: (708) 209-3116
Fax: (708) 209-3176

De Paul University
Academic Profile

1011 W. Belden Ave.
Chicago, IL 60604

Phone: 800-433-7285

Type: Private, 4 Yr., Coed
Website: http://www.depaul.edu
SAT/ACT/GPA: 1200/27
Student/Faculty Ratio: 16:1
Undergraduate Enrollment: 6,839
Scholarships/Academic: Yes
Expenses By: Year

Athletic: Yes
In State: $ 18,000

Founded: 1898
Religion: Catholic
Housing: No
Male/Female: 1:1
Graduate Enrollment: 6,683
Financial Aid: Yes
Out of State: $ 18,000

Degrees Conferred: BA, BS, BFA, BM, BSC, MA, MS, MBA, MFA, M.Ed., Ph.D., JD
Programs of Study: Accounting, Banking/Finance, Biology, Business Administration, Chemistry, Communications, Computer Science, Economics, Education, English, Environmental Science, French, Geography, International Relations, Management, Marketing, Mathematics, Medical Laboratory Technology, Music, Performing Arts, Philosophy, Physical Education, Physics, Political Science, Psychology, Religion, Social Science

Women's Athletic Profile

2323 N. Sheffield
Chicago, IL 60614
Coach: Dawn Dockstader
Email: ddocksta@wppost.depaul.edu

NCAA I
Blue Demons, Scarlet, Blue
Phone: (773) 325-7250
Fax: (773) 325-7212

Estimated # of Women's Volleyball Scholarships: 2
Conference: Conference USA
Program Profile: De Paul Athletic Center, capacity 3,000, was just completed in May 2000, playing surface wooden basketball floor. DePaul is a program on the rise, The Blue Demons advanced to the semifinals of the C-USA tournament before falling in 5 games to NCAA qualifier Cincinnati. 1993 Great Midwest Conference Champs, 1985 North Star Conference Champs.
History: 1st year of the program 1967, W-L since 1984 255-313. 449 accurate records prior to 1984 are not available. School wins record 1991-32-7.
Achievements: 1993 Great Midwest Conference Champs, GMC Player of the Year in 91,93. 1985 North Star Conference Champs,

NSC Player of the Year in 83, Coach of the Year, GMC Coach of the Year 91.

Coaching: Dockstader was 1999 Conference USA Coach of The Year. 2000 is Dockstader's 4th season. In 1999 she guide the team to first 20 win season since 1993. Team's 12-3 start in 2000 was best in school history.

Freshman Receiving Financial Aid/Academic:

		Athletic: 2
Roster In State: 6	**Out of State:** 5	**Out of Country:** 0
Sophomores on Team: 1	**Seniors on Team:** 1	**Graduation %:** 95-100
Most Recent Record: 21-12-0	**Fall Games:** 33	**Spring Games:**

Camp of Clinic Dates: TBA

Positions Needed: Setter, Right Side

Schedule: Illinois, Louisville, Houston, Cincinnati, Illinois State, Loyola and South Florida.

Style of Play: Athletic, doesn't run a position type offense instead uses a "swing" offense where everyone hits from anywhere.

Dominican University
Academic Profile

7900 W Division Street
River Forest, IL 60305

Phone: (708) 366-2490

Type: Private, 4 Yr., Liberal Arts, Coed

Founded: 1901

Website: http;//www.dom.edu

Religion: Catholic

SAT/ACT/GPA: 950/20/2.5-4.0

Housing: Yes

Student/Faculty Ratio: 11:1

Male/Female: 37:63

Undergraduate Enrollment: 1,100

Graduate Enrollment: 900

Scholarships/Academic: Yes   **Athletic:** No   **Financial Aid:** Yes

Expenses By: Year   **In State:** $ 19,260   **Out of State:** $ 19,260

Specializes In: Psychology, Business, Accounting, Communications, English

Degrees Conferred: BA, BS, MA, MS

Programs of Study: Accounting, American Studies, Art, Arts & Media Management, Biology, Biology-Chemistry, Business Administration, Business-Writing, Chemistry, Communication Arts & Sciences, Computer Graphics, Computer Information Systems, Computer Science, Corporate Communications, Criminology, Economics, Education, Environmental Management, Environmental Science, Fashion, Fine & Performing Arts, Food Science, Food Service Management, French, German, Geography, Greek, Hebrew, History, International Business, International Relations and Diplomacy, International Studies, Italian, Latin, Linguistic, Mathematics, Math & Computer Science, Medical Technology, Modern Languages, Spanish, Music, Natural Science, Nursing, Nutrition Sciences, Pastoral Ministry, Philosophy, Health and Physical Education, Physics, Political Science, Psychology, Religious Studies, Sociology

Men's Athletic Profile

7900 Division Street
River Forest, IL 60305
Coach: Paul Lawson
Email: mharty@email.dom.edu

NCAA III
Stars/Royal Blue, Black, White
Phone: (708) 488-5053
Fax: (708) 488-5095

Estimated # of Men's Volleyball Scholarships: N/A
Conference: Independent

Women's Athletic Profile

7900 W. Division Street
River Forest, IL 60305
Coach: Marcia Kartch
Email: mkartch@email.dom.edu
Estimated # of Women's Volleyball Scholarships: N/A
Conference: Independent

NCAA I
Lady Stars, I Blue, Black, White
Phone: (708) 524-6232
Fax: (708) 488-5095

Eastern Illinois University
Academic Profile

600 Lincoln Avenue
Charleston, IL 61920

Phone: 217-252-5711

Type: Public, 4 Yr., Liberal Arts, Coed

Website: http://www.eiu.edu

Founded: 1895

SAT/ACT/GPA: 860/18

Religion: Non-Affiliated

Student/Faculty Ratio: 17:1

Housing: Yes

Undergraduate Enrollment: 10,000

Male/Female: 40:60

Graduate Enrollment: 1,700

Scholarships/Academic: Yes **Athletic:** Yes **Financial Aid:** Yes
Expenses By: Year **In State:** $ 7,433 **Out of State:** $ 11,951
Specializes In: Liberal Arts
Degrees Conferred: BA, BS, BM, BSR, BSEd, MA, MS, MBA
Programs of Study: Accounting, Administrative Information Systems, African-American Studies, Art, Anthropology, Biological Studies, Botany, Business Education, Career Occupations, Chemistry, Communication Disorders and Sciences, Computer Management

Women's Athletic Profile

600 Lincoln Ave NCAA I
Charleston, IL 61920-3099 Lady Panthers, Blue, Grey
Coach: Betty Ralston **Phone:** (217) 581-2924
Email: cfer@eiu.edu **Fax:** (217) 581-7001

Estimated # of Women's Volleyball Scholarships: 3
Conference: Ohio Valley Conference
Program Profile: Recruit only academically viable student athletes who have a desire to excel on the court but also in the classroom. Play regional opponents with emphasis on winning conference.
History: Has been DI since 1982. Overall DI record vs. DI opponents 319-253.
Achievements: Won OVC (17-1) in 1998, OVC player of the year 1998, AVCA National Player of week 1998, OVC District 6 Coach of the year 1998, National Division I Team Dig. Champion 1997-98, 3 academic All-Americans.
Coaching: Betty Ralston Head Coach since 1983, EIU record 306-242 (391-287 overall) Andrew Epperly Asst. Coach 1st year.
Freshman Receiving Financial Aid/Academic: **Athletic:** 4
Roster In State: 26 **Out of State:** **Out of Country:**
Sophomores on Team: 5 **Seniors on Team:** 2 **Graduation %:** 100
Most Recent Record: 24-7 **Fall Games:** 32 **Spring Games:** 4 tournaments
Camp of Clinic Dates: July 11-18
Positions Needed: Middle Hitter (2)
Style of Play: Tenacious defense, understand that VB still has to be fun and not a chore, Goal is to win!

Elmhurst College
Academic Profile

190 Prospect Ave **Phone:** (630) 617-3740
Elmhurst, IL 60126

Type: Private, 4 Yr., Liberal Arts, Coed **Founded:** 1871
Website: http://www.elmhurts.edu **Religion:** United Church of Christ
SAT/ACT/GPA: 1000/21/2.75 **Housing:** Yes
Student/Faculty Ratio: 14:1 **Male/Female:** 1:2
Undergraduate Enrollment: 3,000 **Graduate Enrollment:** 52
Scholarships/Academic: Yes **Athletic:** No **Financial Aid:** Yes
Expenses By: Year **In State:** $ 19,100 **Out of State:** $ 19,100
Specializes In: Nursing, Education, Business (45 Majors)
Degrees Conferred: BA, BS
Programs of Study: Art, Biology, Business, Chemistry, Communications Arts, Computer Science & Information Systems, Economics, Education, English, Environmental Planning, Foreign Languages, Geography, History, Literature, Mathematics, Music, Nursing, Philosophy, Physical Education, Physics, Political Science, PreProfessional Programs, Psychology, Religion, Sociology, Theology, Urban Studies

Women's Athletic Profile

190 Prospect NCAA I
Elmhurst, IL 60126 Lady Blue Jays, Blue, White
Coach: Julie Hall **Phone:** (630) 617-3145
Email: JulieH@Elmhurst.edu **Fax:** (630) 617-3726

Estimated # of Women's Volleyball Scholarships: N/A
Conference: College Conference of Illinois & Wisconsin (CCIW)
Program Profile: We were National Champions in 1983 and 1985. We recently won Conference and garnered an NCAA 1998 berth. We have a junior varsity team which also won Conference. Our record for the past two years is 64-14.

History: We started our program in 1972. Our overall school record is 579-391-4. Our best record (57-4) was in 1983 when we were National Champions.
Achievements: CCIW Coach of the Year in 1998; 6 All-Conference Players; Sarah Hawkins CCIW Player of the Year in 1997 and 1998 and Regional All-American Player in 1998.
Coaching: Julie Hall, Head Coach, took over in 1993 with a program that was 9-32. After 5 seasons, her overall record is 118-78. Our team went from 7th in conference to 4th, 3rd, 2nd and 1st.

Roster In State: 12	**Out of State:** 16	**Out of Country:** 0
Sophomores on Team: 7	**Seniors on Team:** 6	**Graduation %:** 100
Most Recent Record: 31-8-0	**Fall Games:** 39	**Spring Games:** 16

Positions Needed: Middle Hitters, Outside Hitters
Schedule: Washington University, Central Iowa, University of Wisconsin -Whitewater, University of Wisconsin River Falls, Nebraska Wesleyan, Illinois Wesleyan
Style of Play: Fast offense generated from middle; very "team" oriented group of players; although highly offensive emphasis, more recent focus is on defensive end.

Eureka College
Academic Profile

300 College Avenue
Eureka, IL 61530

Phone: (309) 467-6350

Type: Private, 4 Yr., Coed
Website: http://www.eureka.edu
SAT/ACT/GPA: 21avg
Student/Faculty Ratio: 12:1
Undergraduate Enrollment: 460
Scholarships/Academic: No
Expenses By: Year
Degrees Conferred: BA, BS

Founded: 1855
Religion: Disciples of Christ
Housing: Yes
Male/Female: 49:51
Graduate Enrollment: N/A
Athletic: Yes   **Financial Aid:** Yes
In State: $ 19,000   **Out of State:** $ 19,000

Programs of Study: Accounting, Biological, Business, Chemistry, Communications, Computer, Dramatics Arts, Economics, Education, English, Fine Arts, History, Management, Mathematics, Medical, Music, Philosophy, Physical Education, Physical Science, Psychology, Religion, Science Education, Social Science, Speech

Women's Athletic Profile

300 College Avenue
Eureka, IL 61530
Coach: Molly Logan
Email:

NCAA I
Lady Red Devils, Maroon, Gold
Phone: (309) 467-6376
Fax: (309) 467-6402

Estimated # of Women's Volleyball Scholarships: N/A
Conference: Northern Illinois-Iowa Conference
Program Profile: We work to promote academic success and leadership abilities as well as physical abilities.
History: Eureka College is a member of the National Collegiate Athletic Association Division III and the Northern Illinois and Iowa Conference. We also compete with other NCAA Division III schools around the mid-west.
Coaching: Dennis Dighton - Head Coach.
Most Recent Record: 13-21-0
Schedule: Wesleyan, Millikin, Augustana, Knox, Monmouth, Wheaton, Clarke, MacMurray, Concordia, Benedictine, Rockford, Aurora

Greenville College
Academic Profile

315 E College Street
Greenville, IL 62246

Phone: 618-664-2800

Type: Private, 4 Yr., Liberal Arts, Coed
Website: http://www.greenville.edu
SAT/ACT/GPA: 20/2.0
Student/Faculty Ratio: 17:1
Undergraduate Enrollment: 1,100
Scholarships/Academic: Yes
Expenses By: Year
Specializes In: Christian Liberal Arts

Founded: 1892
Religion: Free Methodist
Housing: Yes
Male/Female: 40:60
Graduate Enrollment: 100
Athletic: No   **Financial Aid:** Yes
In State: $ 17,400   **Out of State:** $ 17,400

Degrees Conferred: BA, BS, MA
Programs of Study: Education, Christian Contemporary Music, PreMed, Business, Marketing, Management Information Systems, Computers, History, Political Science, Psychology, Sociology, Social Work, etc..

Women's Athletic Profile

PO Box 59, 315 E. College Ave.
Greenville, IL 62246
Coach: Pam Craig
Email:

NCAA I
Lady Panthers, Orange, Black
Phone: (618) 664-2800x4371
Fax: (618) 664-1060

Estimated # of Women's Volleyball Scholarships: N/A
Conference: St. Louis Intercollegiate Athletic Conference

Illinois Central College
Academic Profile

One College Drive
East Peoria, IL 61635

Phone: (309) 694-5426

Type: Public, 2 Yr., Coed
Website: http://www.icc.cc.il.us
SAT/ACT/GPA: Open door policy
Student/Faculty Ratio: 21:1
Undergraduate Enrollment: 11,750
Scholarships/Academic: Yes
Expenses By: Year

Founded: 1966
Religion: Non-Affiliated
Housing: No
Male/Female: Not Available
Graduate Enrollment: N/A
Athletic: Yes
Financial Aid: Yes
In State: $ 1,500
Out of State: $ 4,000

Degrees Conferred: AA, AS, Applied Science, Engineering Science, General Education
Programs of Study: Have 93 degree programs and 55 certified programs.

Women's Athletic Profile

One College Drive
East Peoria, IL 61635
Coach: Sue Sinclair
Email: iccathletics@jcc.cc.il.us

NCAA I
Cougars, Royal Blue, Gold
Phone: (309) 964-5426
Fax: (309) 699-5579

Estimated # of Women's Volleyball Scholarships: 10
Conference: None
Program Profile: Please go to our website.
History: Our program began in 1973. We have been to 17 National Tournament Appearances. We have 25 All-Americans and over 70 scholarship winners out of our program on to 4 year schools.
Achievements: We won 5 times District NJCAA Coach of the Year, 1 time AVCA Regional Coach of the Year, past NJCAA Volleyball Coaches Association President.
Coaching: Sue Sinclair, Head Coach, started with the program in 1990. She has an overall record of 359-127, she has taken team to nationals 5 times finishing as high as fifth and has coached 28 players that moved on to play for four year schools and coached 9 All-Americans.

Freshman Receiving Financial Aid/Academic:
Roster In State: 8
Sophomores on Team: 5
Most Recent Record: 36-20-0

Out of State: 2
Seniors on Team: 0
Fall Games: 50

Athletic: 5
Out of Country: 0
Graduation %: Unknown
Spring Games: 5 dates

Positions Needed: Setter, Middle Hitter, Outside Hitter
Schedule: Barton County, Miami Dade, Jefferson, Kirkwood, Kellogg, Southwest Missouri
Style of Play: We play a 5-1 offense with quick tempo and play a set of combinations.

Illinois College
Academic Profile

1101 W. College Avenue
Jacksonville, IL 62650

Phone: (217) 245-3000

Type: Private, 4 Yr., Liberal Arts, Coed
Website: http://www.ic.edu

Founded: 1829
Religion: Presbyterian/United Church of Christ

SAT/ACT/GPA: 20
Student/Faculty Ratio: 15:1
Undergraduate Enrollment: 883
Scholarships/Academic: Yes   **Athletic:** No
Expenses By: Year   **In State:** $ 15,300
Degrees Conferred: BA, BS

Housing: Yes
Male/Female: 55:45
Graduate Enrollment: N/A
Financial Aid: Yes
Out of State: $ 15,300

Programs of Study: Accounting, Art, Art Management, Biology, Chemistry, Communications and Theatre, Computer Science, CytoTechnology and Medical Technology, Economics, Education, English, Fine Arts, French, German, History, Interdisciplinary Studies, International Studies, Management Information Systems, Music, Philosophy, Physical Education, Political Science, PreDental, PreEngineering, PreLegal, PreMedical, PreMinisterial, PreNursing, PreOccupational Therapy, PreOptometry, PrePharmacy, PrePhysical Therapy, PreVeterinary Medicine, Psychology, Religious Studies, Sociology, Special Education

Women's Athletic Profile

1101 W. College Avenue
Jacksonville, IL 62650
Coach: Brenna Kelly
Email: admissions@hilltop.ic.edu

NCAA I
Lady Blues, Blue, White
Phone: (217) 245-3000
Fax: (217) 245-3034

Estimated # of Women's Volleyball Scholarships: 0
Conference: Midwest Conference
Program Profile: Illinois College opens practice in late August and typically plays a schedule that includes contests against other NCAA Division III colleges and universities throughout September and October. The Lady Blues participate in several prestigious tournaments and play each South Division opponent before concluding the season at the Midwest Conference Championship Tournament in early November. Home matches are played in Memorial Gymnasium, which will be replaced in approximately 2002 by a new, multi-purpose building designed to provide enhanced facilities for practice as well as match play.
History: With five championship trophies in the past eight seasons, Illinois College has secured a dominant position among volleyball teams in the Midwest Conference. The Lady Blues own an impressive record of 208-70 this decade and perennially rank as one of the top teams in the Midwest region. Illinois College fielded its first NCAA Division III volleyball team in 1976 and the program developed at a modest pace over its first 14 seasons. With the appointment of Brenna Kelly as Head Coach in 1990, tremendous gains have been made. Today, the Lady Blues are highly regarded for their competitive excellence and winning attitude.
Achievements: 5 MWC Championships, National Tournament Qualifier 1993; Brenna Kelly Coach of the Year 3 Times; 8 South Division Championships, 4 All-Region Players, 3 Academic All-Region Players.
Coaching: Brenna Kelly started as Head Coach in 1990. She was in the College Sports Hall of Fame in 1996. Her overall record is 208-70. Assistant coach Joanna Ramsey started in 1996. She is a 3-time MWC All-Conference, a 2-time All-Region and a 2-time MVP. She was MWC Player of the Year. She held the Illinois state record for points served. She holds the school records for top serving aces (163 career) and assists (3588 career).
Freshman Receiving Financial Aid/Academic: **Athletic:** 0
Roster In State: 18   **Out of State:** 0   **Out of Country:** 0
Sophomores on Team: 0   **Seniors on Team:** 5   **Graduation %:** 100
Most Recent Record: 20-11-0   **Fall Games:** 30   **Spring Games:** 0
Camp of Clinic Dates: July 5-7, 1999
Positions Needed: Middle Hitter, Outside Hitter
Schedule: Washington University, University of Wisconsin-Whitewater, University of Wisconsin-Osh Kosh, Central College, Nebraska Wesleyan, Wittenburg
Style of Play: Quick offense with man options; 5-1; aggressive serves and serve receive; "Never say die" defense.

Illinois Institute of Technology
Academic Profile

3040 S. Wabash
Chicago, IL 60616

Phone: (312) 567-7127

Type: Private, 4 Yr., Engineering, Coed
Website: http://www.iit.edu
SAT/ACT/GPA: 24
Student/Faculty Ratio: 9:1
Undergraduate Enrollment: 2,546
Scholarships/Academic: Yes   **Athletic:** Yes
Expenses By: Year   **In State:** $ 22,500

Founded: 1940
Religion: Non-Affiliated
Housing: Yes
Male/Female: 75:25
Graduate Enrollment: 3,262
Financial Aid: Yes
Out of State: $ 22,500

Specializes In: Engineering, Architecture, Sciences
Degrees Conferred: BA, BS, MBA, MS, JD
Programs of Study: All fields of Engineering, Computer Science, Architecture, Biology, Chemistry, Physics, Math, Psychology, Political Science, PreMed, PreLaw, Information Systems Management

Women's Athletic Profile

3040 South Wabash
Chicago, IL 60616
Coach: Chris Meyer
Email:

NCAA I
Scarlet Hawks, Scarlet, Grey
Phone: (312) 567-7127
Fax: (312) 567-7133

Estimated # of Women's Volleyball Scholarships: 8
Conference: Chicagoland Collegiate Athletic Conference
Program Profile: We have a top Midwest program that combines an Engineering degree with NAIA volleyball. Our Arena is Keating Sports Center which includes the following: 1,200 seats, a workout room, a 25 yard swimming pool, four racquetball courts, an outdoor running track. Homecoming at our college is a volleyball match.
History: Our program started in 1979. Total won-loss record is 506-198. We have 20 consecutive winning seasons. We have 17 consecutive seasons with 20 or more wins.
Achievements: 12 NAIA Academic All-Americans in the last 9 years including 3 in 1998 ; coach Chris Meyer was District 20 NAIA Coach of the Year in 1992.
Coaching: Chris Meyer, Head Coach, started coaching the program in 1979. He compiled an overall record of 506-198. He is one of only 9 NAIA coaches with 500 or more wins. He received the USAV Award of National Clinician of the Year in 1996. He has 17 years as an All-American rated player (1975-1992). Mike Vivona is Assistant Coach.

Freshman Receiving Financial Aid/Academic:		**Athletic:** 4
Roster In State: 12	**Out of State:** 3	**Out of Country:** 0
Sophomores on Team: 0	**Seniors on Team:** 3	**Graduation %:** 91
Most Recent Record: 28-10-0	**Fall Games:** 38	**Spring Games:** 8

Camp of Clinic Dates: July 12-15
Positions Needed: All, especially Setter & Middle
Schedule: St. Francis, University of Wisconsin-Whitewater, Michigan, Bethel, St. Xavier, Dominican
Style of Play: Fast, intelligent, tactical and fun.

Illinois State University
Academic Profile

Office of Admissions, Chovey Hall 201
Normal, IL 61790-2200

Phone: (309) 438-2181

Type: Public, 4 Yr., Yes Coed
Website: http://www.infosys.ilstu.edu
SAT/ACT/GPA: 86018
Student/Faculty Ratio: 19-1
Undergraduate Enrollment: 17,703
Scholarships/Academic: Yes
Expenses By: Year

Founded: 1857
Religion: Non-Affiliated
Housing: Yes
Male/Female: 59:41
Graduate Enrollment: 2,578

Athletic: Yes
In State: $9437

Financial Aid: Yes
Out of State: $ 15,876

Specializes In: Education, Business, Applied Science & Technology
Degrees Conferred: BA, BS, BM, B.Ed., BFA, BME, MS, MA
Programs of Study: Accounting, Business Information Systems, Agriculture Science, Computer Science, Graphic Design, Art, Business, Education, Chemistry, Biology, Criminal Justice, Economics, English, Dietetics, Fashion Merchandising, Foreign Languages, International Business, Broadcasting, Journalism, Math, Music, Physical Education, Philosophy, Nursing

Women's Athletic Profile

234 Redbird Arena Campus Box 2660
Normal, IL 61790-2660
Coach: Julie Morgan
Email: jqmorga@ilstu.edu

NCAA I
Redbirds, Red, White, Black
Phone: (309) 438-2567
Fax: (309) 438-3596

Estimated # of Women's Volleyball Scholarships: 12
Conference: Midwestern Collegiate Conference
Program Profile: We have a strong tradition. We play in Redbird Arena which seats 10,000 people. We average 2,600 fans a match. We are the 3rd largest average attendance in the country. Our season is from August to December.

History: The program began in 1993. We have made 11 trips to the NCAA Tournament since 1982. We are traditionally one of the top two teams in the Missouri Valley Conference.

Achievements: 5 Coach of the Year; 9 Regular Season Conference Titles; 8 Conference Tournament Championships; 2 All-Americans; 2 went on to play internationally.

Coaching: Julie Morgan became Head Coach in 1987. Her overall record is 277-129. Her team won the National Championship at USC. Kalani Mahi and Christi started as Assistant Coaches in 1998.

Freshman Receiving Financial Aid/Academic:

		Athletic: 4
Roster In State: 10	**Out of State:** 4	**Out of Country:** 0
Sophomores on Team: 0	**Seniors on Team:** 4	**Graduation %:** 84
Most Recent Record: 22-10-0	**Fall Games:** 32	**Spring Games:** 13

Camp of Clinic Dates: Individual Skills: July 9-11; Hitter/Setter: July 16-18

Positions Needed: Middle Hitter, Outside Hitter

Schedule: Wisconsin, Washington, Illinois, Georgia Tech, Clemson, Notre Dame

Style of Play: We are big and physical at the net, fast on offense and strong on defense. The team is intense and competitive.

Illinois Wesleyan University
Academic Profile

PO Box 2900
Bloomington, IL 61702-2900

Phone: (309) 556-3031

Type: Private, 4 Yr., Liberal Arts, Coed
Website: http://www.iwu.edu
SAT/ACT/GPA: 126027.8
Student/Faculty Ratio: 13:1
Undergraduate Enrollment: 2,000
Scholarships/Academic: Yes
Expenses By: Year

Athletic: No
In State: $ 25,560

Founded: 1850
Religion: Methodist
Housing: Yes
Male/Female: 43/57
Graduate Enrollment: N/A
Financial Aid: Yes
Out of State: $ 25,560

Specializes In: PreMed, Business, Fine Arts, Nursing, Natural Science

Degrees Conferred: BA, BS, BFA, BSCompSci

Programs of Study: Accounting, Art, Biology, Business Administration, Chemistry, Computer Science, Economics, Political Science, Psychology, Religion, Risk Management & Financial Services, Sociology, Spanish, Theatre Arts

Women's Athletic Profile

P.O. Box 2900
Bloomington, IL 61702-2900
Coach: Kim Nelson-Brown
Email: knbrown@titan.iwu.edu

NCAA I
Lady Titans, Green, White
Phone: (309) 556-3349
Fax: (309) 556-3484

Estimated # of Women's Volleyball Scholarships: 0

Conference: College Conference of Illinois & Wisconsin

Program Profile: Season: Sept-Nov. Facility: Sotack Center, Wood Floor. 18 Conference games, seats 2680

History: 1974 program began, 3 NCAA III Appearances, 8 -20win seasons in the 1990's

Achievements: 1997- Kim Nelson-Brown Selected Coach of the Year (CCIW), 1991-97 Conference Champions

Coaching: Kim Nelson-Brown, Krista Ridder, Pat Hawn

Freshman Receiving Financial Aid/Academic:

		Athletic: 0
Roster In State: 20	**Out of State:** 0	**Out of Country:** 0
Seniors on Team: 4	**Graduation %:** 100	

Most Recent Record: 3-2

Camp of Clinic Dates: TBA

Positions Needed: Middles

Style of Play: 5-1 Offense, quick offense

Judson College
Academic Profile

1151 North State Street
Elgin, IL 60123

Phone: (847) 695-2500

Type: Private, 4 Yr., Coed
Website: http://www.judson-il.edu
SAT/ACT/GPA: Open
Student/Faculty Ratio: 12:1

Founded: 1963
Religion: Baptist
Housing: Yes
Male/Female: 1:4

Undergraduate Enrollment: 900

Graduate Enrollment: N/A

Scholarships/Academic: Yes   **Athletic:** Yes   **Financial Aid:** Yes

Expenses By: Semester   **In State:** $ 9,000   **Out of State:** $ 9,000

Degrees Conferred: BA, BS

Programs of Study: Anthropology, Architecture, Art, Biblical Studies, Biology, Business, Chemistry, Communication Arts, Communications, Computer Science, Education, English, Graphic Design, History, International Business, Mathematics, Music, Physics, Political Science, PreNursing, Psychology, Science, Sociology, Sport Management, Teacher Education, Theatre, Youth Ministry

Women's Athletic Profile

1151 N. State

Elgin, IL 60123

Coach: Jennifer Salazar

Email:

NCAA I

Lady Eagles, Royal Blue, White

Phone: (847) 695-2500

Fax: (847) 695-9252

Estimated # of Women's Volleyball Scholarships: 6

Conference: CCAC

Program Profile: We have 3 full courts, an indoor track, a nautilus and a weight room. Our season goes from August to November. We have a 12 roster varsity and a 10 roster junior varsity program.

History: Karen Swanson was Head Coach from 1992 to 1996. She was NHIH Coach of the Year and took the team to the NCCAA Nationals 3 times .

Coaching: Jennifer Salazar became Head Coach in 1997. Her overall record in her 3rd season is 51-24. She played at Judson from 1992-1994. She was MVP for 2 years. She was CCAC Freshman of the Year, All-Region Conference and All-American NCCAA. She played Division II at Cal State University at Bakersfield from 1994-1996.

Freshman Receiving Financial Aid/Academic: **Athletic:** 4

Roster In State: 4   **Out of State:** 6   **Out of Country:** 0

Sophomores on Team: 4   **Seniors on Team:** 1   **Graduation %:** 100

Most Recent Record: 18-18-0   **Fall Games:** 36   **Spring Games:** 5

Camp of Clinic Dates: August 9-12

Positions Needed: Middle Hitter, Defensive Specialist

Schedule: Fresno State, University of St. Francis, Bethel, Lewis & Clark, Huntington College, Cornerstone

Style of Play: 100% all-out, teamwork, play together, well-disciplined, well structured, good sportsmanship. Out to play with no regrets all the time. Run 5:1 with quick offense, not afraid to try new things.

Kendall College
Academic Profile

2408 Orrington Avenue

Evanston, IL 60201

Phone: 877-588-8860

Type: Private, 4 Yr., Liberal Arts, Coed

Website: http://www.kendall.edu

SAT/ACT/GPA: 18/2.7

Student/Faculty Ratio: 12:1

Undergraduate Enrollment: 500

Founded: 1934

Religion: Methodist

Housing: Y

Male/Female: 50:50

Graduate Enrollment: N/A

Scholarships/Academic: Yes   **Athletic:** Yes   **Financial Aid:** Yes

Expenses By: Year   **In State:** $ 16,500   **Out of State:** $ 16,500

Specializes In: Liberal Arts, Business, Human Services

Degrees Conferred: BA, BS, AA, AAS

Programs of Study: American Studies, Literature, History, Political Science, Sociology, Psychology, Business, International Business, Marketing, CIS, Hotel & Restaurant Management, Human Resources Management, Early Childhood Education, Culinary Arts, Culinary Management

Women's Athletic Profile

2408 Orrington Avenue

Evanston, IL 60201

Coach: Wendy Fahlstrom

Email: scout9@megsinet.net

NCAA I

Lady Vikings, Red, Black, White

Phone: (847) 869-6660

Fax: (847) 866-1320

Did Not Return Profile

Knox College
Academic Profile

2 E. South Street
Galesburg, IL 61401

Phone: (309) 341-7000

Type: Private, 4 Yr., Liberal Arts, Coed
Website: http://www.knox.edu
SAT/ACT/GPA: 1100/24
Student/Faculty Ratio: 12:1
Undergraduate Enrollment: 1,195
Scholarships/Academic: Yes   **Athletic:** No
Expenses By: Year   **In State:** $ 24,150
Specializes In: Liberal Arts
Degrees Conferred: BA, Bachelors Degree

Founded: 1837
Religion: Non-Affiliated
Housing: Yes
Male/Female: 46:54
Graduate Enrollment: N/A
Financial Aid: Yes
Out of State: $ 24,150

Programs of Study: Accounting, American Studies, Anthropology, Art, Biology, Business, Chemistry, Classics, Computer Science, Economics, Education, English, French, German, History, Humanities, International Languages, Literature, Nursing/Medical Technology, Philosophy, Physics, PreProfessional Programs, Psychology, Social Science, Spanish, Studio Art, Theatre, Women's Studies

Women's Athletic Profile

2 E. South Street
Galesburg, IL 61401
Coach: Kathy Wagoner
Email: hknosher@knox.edu

NCAA I
Lady Prairie Fire, Purple, Gold
Phone: (309) 341-7000
Fax: (309) 341-7090

Estimated # of Women's Volleyball Scholarships: N/A
Conference: Midwest Atlantic Conference
Program Profile: We are a member of Division III. Our 2 court facility includes a hard wood floor, a tartan surface court and a weight facility. We play approximately 40 matches from September through November.
History: Our program began in the early 1970's. We have an average program which is usually in the middle of the conference. We were Conference Champions in 1980 and received 2nd place in 1990.
Achievements: Conference Champions in 1980; second place in 1990; top 10 academic team in the country in 1993.
Coaching: Kathryn Wagoner, Head Coach, is entering her ninth year at Knox . She has 18 years of collegiate coaching and has compiled over 200 wins. Darcy Earley is Assistant Coach.
Freshman Receiving Financial Aid/Academic: **Athletic:** 0
Roster In State: 2/3   **Out of State:** 1/3   **Out of Country:** 0
Sophomores on Team: 5   **Seniors on Team:** 4   **Graduation %:** 100
Most Recent Record: 1-31-0   **Fall Games:** 32   **Spring Games:** 0
Positions Needed: Setter, Middle Blockers
Schedule: University of Illinois-Springfield, Illinois College, Illinois Wesleyan University, Augustana College, St. Norbert, Millikin University
Style of Play: We are usually shorter than our opponents but we play a fast offense, scrappy on defense. We are usually an excellent passing team.

Lake Forest College
Academic Profile

555 N. Sheridan Road
Lake Forest, IL 60045

Phone: 800-828-4751

Type: Private, 4 Yr., Liberal Arts, Coed
Website: http://www.lfc.edu
SAT/ACT/GPA: None/25
Student/Faculty Ratio: 11:1
Undergraduate Enrollment: 1,000
Scholarships/Academic: Yes   **Athletic:** No
Expenses By: Year   **In State:** $ 23,600
Degrees Conferred: Bachelor of Arts/Science

Founded: 1857
Religion: Non-Affiliated
Housing: Yes
Male/Female: 50:50
Graduate Enrollment: 200
Financial Aid: Yes
Out of State: $ 23,600

Programs of Study: Art, Biology, Chemistry, German, History, Philosophy, Business, Spanish, French, Educational, Mathematics, Politics, PreMed, Sociology and Anthropology, Sciences, English, Computer Science, Communications

Women's Athletic Profile

555 N. Sheridan Rd.
Lake Forest, IL 60045
Coach: Beth Pier
Email: pier@lakeforest.edu

NCAA I
Lady Foresters, Red, Black
Phone: (847) 735-5295
Fax: (847) 735-6290

Estimated # of Women's Volleyball Scholarships: N/A
Conference: Midwest Conference
Program Profile: Gym seats 1200 fans, wood floor, fall season only. In contention for conference championship yearly. Also a very beautiful campus 30 miles north of Chicago.
History: Began in 1976. 392-303 overall record. 128-60 record under current Head coach Beth Pier seven seasons. 2 trips to NCAA Tournament (1999, 2000). Advanced to 2nd round in 1999.
Achievements: Midwest Conference Championship ttiles: 1997,99,2000. Midwest Conference Coach of the Year: Beth Pier 97, 99, 00. 3 Midwest Conference Player of the Year 97,99,00
Coaching: Beth Pier Head Coach, 7 seasons, has a BA from St. Norbert College. Wendy Zwiefelhofer, Assistant Coach, 2 seasons, BA from Lake Forest College.
Roster In State: 5   **Out of State:** 9   **Out of Country:** 0
Seniors on Team: 3
Most Recent Record: 23-6-0
Camp of Clinic Dates: Last week in June
Positions Needed: Setter, MD, Opposite, OH
Schedule: Wisconsin- Whitewater, Elmhurst College, Illinois Wesleyan Univ. Augustana College, St. Norbert College
Style of Play: We serve aggressively and run a quick offense. We emphasize making the opponent defend the entire court by running a balanced attack and hitting a variety of shots.

Lewis University
Academic Profile

Rt. 53
Romeoville, IL 60446

Phone: 800-897-9000

Type: Private, 4 Yr., Liberal Arts, Coed
Website: http://www.lewisu.edu
SAT/ACT/GPA: 700+/17+
Student/Faculty Ratio: 15:1
Undergraduate Enrollment: 4,000
Scholarships/Academic: Yes   **Athletic:** Yes
Expenses By: Year   **In State:** $ 19,296

Founded: 1933
Religion: Catholic (Christian Brothers)
Housing: Yes
Male/Female: 50:50
Graduate Enrollment: 1,000
Financial Aid: Yes
Out of State: $ 19,296

Specializes In: Accounting, Aviation, Education, Nursing
Degrees Conferred: BA, BS, MBA, MSN, M Ed
Programs of Study: Accounting, Airway Science, Applied Science, Art, Athletic Training, Avionics, Biology, Broadcasting, Business Administration, Chemistry, Communications, Computer Science, Criminal Justice, Economics, Education, English, Finance, History, Journalism, Liberal Arts, Marketing, Mathematics, Music, Nursing, Philosophy, Physics, Political Science, Psychology, Religion, Sociology

Men's Athletic Profile

Route 53
Romeoville, IL 60446
Coach: Dave Deuser
Email:

NCAA II
Flyers/Red, White
Phone: (815) 838-0500
Fax: (815) 836-5853

Estimated # of Men's Volleyball Scholarships: N/A
Conference: Midwestern Intercollegiate Volleyball Association

Women's Athletic Profile

Route 53
Romeoville, IL 60446
Coach: Karen Kerner Lockyer
Email:

NCAA I
Lady Flyers, Red, White
Phone: (815) 838-0500x5454
Fax: (815) 836-5835

Estimated # of Women's Volleyball Scholarships: 3
Conference: Great Lakes Valley Conference
Program Profile: Regionally competitive program. Home court is Neil Carev Arena. Play a fall season of approximately 32 match-es. Spring season is 4 tournaments with Division 1 mix.
History: Program started in 1974. Best finish 2nd in NCAA Championship in 1981. 7 NCAA Tournament appearances. Finished 3rd in AIAW Championship in 1979.
Achievements: Conference coach of the year 3x. Regional coach of year once. 600 career wins. Conference Champion-4 All-Americans, 3 players
Freshman Receiving Financial Aid/Academic: **Athletic:** 6

Roster In State: 10	**Out of State:** 4	**Out of Country:**
Sophomores on Team: 2	**Seniors on Team:** 4	**Graduation %:** 100
Most Recent Record: 16-10	**Fall Games:** 32	**Spring Games:** 12

Positions Needed: MH, Setter
Schedule: Florida Southern, Tampa, Edinboro, Northern Kentucky, IPFW, St. Cloud State
Style of Play: Strong net play game with quick movement of hitters. Emphasis on middle hitter-with effective use of right side court with MH or PH.

Loyola University
Academic Profile

6525 N Sheridan Road   **Phone:** (773) 508-2560
Chicago, IL 60626

Type: Private, 4 Yr., Liberal Arts, Coed   **Founded:** 1870
Website: http://www.loyolaramblers.com   **Religion:** Non-Affiliated
SAT/ACT/GPA: Open   **Housing:** Yes
Student/Faculty Ratio: 13:1   **Male/Female:** 40:60
Undergraduate Enrollment: N/A   **Graduate Enrollment:** N/A
Scholarships/Academic: Yes   **Athletic:** Yes   **Financial Aid:** Yes
Expenses By: Year   **In State:** $ 25,000   **Out of State:** $ 25,000
Specializes In: Jesuit Education, Law, Medical, Philosophy
Degrees Conferred: BA, BS, BSEd, BA (Classics), BBA, BSN, MA, MS, MBA, M.Ed., Ph.D., JD, MDiv, EdD, DMD
Programs of Study: Accounting, Anthropology, Art, Biology, Business & Management, Chemistry, Classics, Communications, Computer Information Systems, Computer Science, Criminal Justice, Economics, Elementary Education, English, French, German, Greek, History, Italian, Latin, Linguistics, Management Information Systems, Marketing, Mathematics, Music, Nursing, Philosophy, Physics, Political Science, PreDentistry, PreLaw, PreMed, PreVet, Psychology, Social Work, Sociology, Spanish, Special Education, Speech, Statistics, Theatre, Theology

Men's Athletic Profile

6525 N. Sheridan Rd.   **NCAA I**
Chicago, IL 60611   Ramblers/Maroon, Gold
Coach: Gordon Mayforth   **Phone:** (773) 508-8897
Email: cschwar@luc.edu   **Fax:** (773) 508-3884

Estimated # of Men's Volleyball Scholarships: N/A
Conference: Independent

Women's Athletic Profile

6525 N. Sheridan Rd.   **NCAA I**
Chicago, IL 60626   Lady Ramblers, Maroon, Gold
Coach: Liz Tortorello   **Phone:** (773) 508-2560
Email: **Fax:** (773) 508-3884

Estimated # of Women's Volleyball Scholarships: 4
Conference: Midwestern Collegiate Conference
Program Profile: We play a national schedule. We play at Alumni Gym which seats 3,000.
History: Our program started in 1978. We were in the top 2 in the Conference in 1995.
Achievements: Conference Championship in 1995. All-American in 1992.
Coaching: Liz Nelson, Head Coach, was a player at the University of Wisconsin from 1989 to 1992. She was a two-time All Big Ten and a two-time Sports Festival participant. Ray Gorden is Assistant Coach.
Freshman Receiving Financial Aid/Academic: **Athletic:** 11

Roster In State: 8
Sophomores on Team: 0
Most Recent Record: 20-14-0
Camp of Clinic Dates: July
Positions Needed: None
Schedule: Houston, LSU, Tulane, Western Michigan, Central Michigan, South Florida,
Style of Play: Athletic, not mechanical.

Out of State: 4
Seniors on Team: 1
Fall Games: All

Out of Country: 0
Graduation %: Unknown
Spring Games: 0

McMurray College
Academic Profile

447 E. College Avenue
Jacksonville, IL 62650

Phone: (217) 479-7211

Type: Private, 4 Yr., Liberal Arts, Coed
Website: http://www.mac.edu
SAT/ACT/GPA: 16/2.0
Student/Faculty Ratio: 12:1
Undergraduate Enrollment: 650
Scholarships/Academic: Yes
Expenses By: Year
Specializes In: Preprofessional Programs
Degrees Conferred: BA, BS

Athletic: No
In State: $ 8,500

Founded: 1846
Religion: Methodist
Housing: Yes
Male/Female: 1:1
Graduate Enrollment: N/A
Financial Aid: Yes
Out of State: $ 8,500

Programs of Study: Accounting, Art, Biology, Business Administration, Chemistry, Computer Electronics, Computer Science, Criminal Justice, Deaf Studies: Teacher Education, Elementary Education, English, French, History, International Studies, Journalism, Learning Disabilities and Social Emotional Disorders, Management Information Systems, Marketing, Mathematics, Music, Nursing, PreMedicine, PreOccupation Therapy, PrePhysical Therapy, PreVet, Psychology, Religion, Secondary Education, Social Work, Spanish, Sports Management

Women's Athletic Profile

447 E. College Avenue
Jacksonville, IL 62650
Coach: Juile Manker
Email: jumanker@mac.edu

NCAA I
Lady Highlanders, Navy, Scarlet
Phone: (217) 479-7156
Fax: (217) 479-7174

Estimated # of Women's Volleyball Scholarships: N/A
Conference: St. Louis Intercollegiate Athletic Conference

McKendree College
Academic Profile

701 College Rd.
Lebanon, IL 62254

Phone: 800-232-7228

Type: Private, 4 Yr., Liberal Arts, Coed
Website: http://www.mckendree.edu
SAT/ACT/GPA: 20/2.5
Student/Faculty Ratio: 14:1
Undergraduate Enrollment: 1,883
Scholarships/Academic: Yes
Expenses By: Year
Specializes In: Business, Education, Computer Science
Degrees Conferred: BA, BS, BBA, BFA, BSEd, BSN

Athletic: Yes
In State: $ 16,100

Founded: 1828
Religion: United Methodist
Housing: Yes
Male/Female: 40:60
Graduate Enrollment: N/A
Financial Aid: Yes
Out of State: $ 16,100

Programs of Study: Accounting, Art, Athletic Training, Biology, Business, Chemistry, Computer Science, Education, Economics/Finance, History, International Relations, Mathematics, Music, Management, Marketing, Medicine, Occupational Therapy, PreDentistry, PreLaw, PreMed, PreOptometry, PreVet, Sociology, Religious Studies, Speech Communications

Women's Athletic Profile

701 College Rd
Lebanon, IL 62254
Coach: Evelyn Bean
Email: scordon@atlas.mckendree.edu

NCAA I
Lady Bearcats, Purple, White
Phone: (618) 537-6831
Fax: (618) 537-6876

Estimated # of Women's Volleyball Scholarships: 6
Conference: American Midwest Conference
Program Profile: We have two squads, junior and varsity. We try to have 12 players on each squad. We have a gymnasium which seats 1,000 people. Varsity plays approximately 40 matches and junior plays approximately 25 matches.
History: The program began in 1972. We have participated in two National Tournaments. For the first time, we qualified for Regional Playoffs in 1998.
Achievements: Coach of the Year, 1998.
Coaching: Evelyn Bean, Head Coach, since 1997, has compiled a record of 49-27. Sharon Kampwerth is assistant coach.
Freshman Receiving Financial Aid/Academic: **Athletic:** 6
Roster In State: 23 **Out of State:** 1 **Out of Country:** 0
Sophomores on Team: 3 **Seniors on Team:** 7 **Graduation %:** 100
Most Recent Record: 30-10-0 **Fall Games:** 40 **Spring Games:** 10
Positions Needed: Setter, Middle, Power Defense Specialist
Schedule: Columbia College, Culver Stockton, Rockhurst
Style of Play: We have a very quick offensive with explosive power. Our defense is above average. Our serving is an offensive weapon.

Millikin University
Academic Profile

1184 W. Main Street
Decatur, IL 62522

Phone: 800-373-7733

Type: Private, 4 Yr., Coed
Website: http://www.millikin.edu
SAT/ACT/GPA: 880+/21+
Student/Faculty Ratio: 15:1
Undergraduate Enrollment: 1,840
Scholarships/Academic: Yes **Athletic:** No
Expenses By: Year **In State:** $ 15,800
Specializes In: Nursing

Founded: 1901
Religion: Presbyterian
Housing: No
Male/Female: 45:55
Graduate Enrollment: N/A
Financial Aid: Yes
Out of State: $ 15,800

Degrees Conferred: BA, BFA, BS, BSN, BMus
Programs of Study: Accounting, Agricultural Business, Automotive Technologies, Business Administration/Commerce/Management, Child Care, Criminal Justice, Drafting and Design, Legal Secretarial Studies, Liberal Arts, General Studies, Science

Women's Athletic Profile

1184 W. Main
Decatur, IL 62511
Coach: Linda Slagell
Email: lslagell@mail.millikin.edu

NCAA I
Lady Big Blue, Blue, White
Phone: (217) 420-6622
Fax: (217) 362-6414

Estimated # of Women's Volleyball Scholarships: 0
Conference: College Conference of Illinois & Wisconsin
History: Began in 1975 and have an overall record of 484-324.
Coaching: Slagell-1987-present 269-172 (.609)
Freshman Receiving Financial Aid/Academic: **Athletic:** 0
Roster In State: 21 **Out of State:** 3 **Out of Country:**
Seniors on Team: 9 **Graduation %:** 92
Most Recent Record: 22-17 **Fall Games:** 35-40 **Spring Games:** 0
Positions Needed: Setter
Schedule: University of Wis. Whitewater, Kalamazoo, University of Wis. Oshkosh, DePauw, Elmhurst

Monmouth College
Academic Profile

700 East Broadway
Monmouth, IL 61462

Phone: (309)456-2322

Type: Private, 4 Yr., Liberal Arts, Coed
Website: http://www.monm.edu
SAT/ACT/GPA: 18/2.5
Student/Faculty Ratio: 14:1
Undergraduate Enrollment: 1060
Scholarships/Academic: Yes   **Athletic:** No
Expenses By: Year   **In State:** $26,550
Specializes In: Liberal Arts
Degrees Conferred: BA

Founded: 1853
Religion: Presbyterian
Housing: Yes
Male/Female: 47:53
Graduate Enrollment: N/A
Financial Aid: Yes
Out of State:

Programs of Study: Art, Biology, Chemistry, Classics, Communication/Theatre Arts, Education, English, Environmental Science, Government, History, Math/Computer Science, Modern Languages, Music, Philosophy, Physical Education, Physics, Political Economy & Commerce, Psychology, Sociology, Women's Studies

Women's Athletic Profile

700 E. Broadway
Monmouth, IL 61462
Coach: TBA
Email: kathy@monm.edu

NCAA I
Lady Fighting Scots, Red, White
Phone: (309) 457-2176
Fax: (309) 457-2168

Estimated # of Women's Volleyball Scholarships: N/A
Conference: Midwest Conference
Program Profile: Matches are played in the 2000-seat Glennie Gymnasium.
History: First year of competition 1974
Achievements: Conference titles 1981,1982. 18 All-Conference members
Roster In State: 18
Seniors on Team: 2
Most Recent Record: 19-19-0

North Central College
Academic Profile

30 North Brainard
Naperville, IL 60566

Phone: 630-637-5800

Type: Private, 4 Yr., Liberal Arts, Coed
Website: http://www.noctrl.edu
SAT/ACT/GPA: 820/20
Student/Faculty Ratio: 14:1
Undergraduate Enrollment: 1,300
Scholarships/Academic: Yes   **Athletic:** No
Expenses By: Year   **In State:** $ 16,326
Degrees Conferred: BA, BS, MA, MS, MBA

Founded: 1861
Religion: Methodist
Housing: Yes
Male/Female: 52:48
Graduate Enrollment: 1,200
Financial Aid: Yes
Out of State: $ 16,326

Programs of Study: 36 Academic Majors, 6 Graduate Degrees; Business Management, Communications, Computer Sciences, Physical Sciences, Psychology, Social Sciences

Women's Athletic Profile

30 N. Brainard
Naperville, IL 60566
Coach: Karen Seremet
Email: kasereme@noctrl.edu

NCAA I
Lady Cardinals, Red, White
Phone: (630) 637-5531
Fax: (630) 637-5521

Estimated # of Women's Volleyball Scholarships: N/A
Conference: College Conference of Illinois & Wisconsin

North Park University
Academic Profile

3225 W Foster Avenue
Chicago, IL 60625

Phone: 800-888-6728

Type: Private, 4 Yr., Liberal Arts, Coed
Website: http://www.northpark.com
SAT/ACT/GPA: 860/18/Upper 1/2
Student/Faculty Ratio: 15:1
Undergraduate Enrollment: 1,700
Scholarships/Academic: Yes   **Athletic:** No
Expenses By: Year   **In State:** $ 20,200
Degrees Conferred: 35

Founded: 1891
Religion: Evangelical Covenant
Housing: Yes
Male/Female: 45:55
Graduate Enrollment: 500
Financial Aid: Yes
Out of State:

Programs of Study: Accounting, Anthropology, Art, Biblical Studies, Biology, Business Administration, Chemistry, Clinical Laboratory, Science, Communication Arts, Constructed Majors, Economics, Education, English, Finance, General Science, History, International Business, Marketing, Math, Music, Nursing, Philosophy, PE, Physics, Politics and Government, Psychology, Social Studies, Sociology, Spanish, Sports Medicine, Swedish, Youth Ministry

Women's Athletic Profile

3225 W. Foster Avenue
Chicago, IL 60625
Coach: Susan Zimmer
Email:

NCAA I
Lady Vikings, Royal Blue, Gold
Phone: (773) 244-5673
Fax: (773) 244-4952

Estimated # of Women's Volleyball Scholarships: N/A
Conference: College Conference of Illinois & Wisconsin
Program Profile: North Park University competes in the CCIW, one of the toughest Division II Conference in the nation. We have both a junior and varsity program. We have a fall season.
History: North Park University joined the CCIW Conference in 1962.
Achievements: We have 1998-1999 All-Conference player.
Coaching: Susan Zimmer is entering her third season Head Coach of the Vikings. She competed at Illinois Wesleyan University. She earned All-Conference and MVP honors as a player. Brian Mallo, Assistant Coach.

Roster In State: 10   **Out of State:** 5   **Out of Country:** 0
Sophomores on Team: 3   **Seniors on Team:** 2   **Graduation %:** 94
Most Recent Record: 17-17-0   **Fall Games:** 34   **Spring Games:** 0
Positions Needed: 5
Schedule: Elmhurst, Illinois Wesleyan
Style of Play: We run an aggressive offense that relies predominantly.

Northeastern Illinois University
Academic Profile

Department of Athletics, Soccer
Chicago, IL 60625-4099
Type: Public, 4 Yr., Coed
Website: http://www.ECNet.Net/users/uneiuweb/
SAT/ACT/GPA: 890/19
Student/Faculty Ratio: 20:1
Undergraduate Enrollment: 8,000
Scholarships/Academic: Yes   **Athletic:** Yes
Expenses By: Year   **In State:** $ 2,000
Specializes In: Education, Business
Degrees Conferred: BA, BS, MA, MS, MBA

Phone: 773-583-4050

Founded: 1961
Religion: Non-Affiliated
Housing: Yes
Male/Female: 40:60
Graduate Enrollment: 3,000
Financial Aid: Yes
Out of State: $ 6,000

Programs of Study: Anthropology, Art, Biology, Chemistry, Computer Science, Criminal Justice, Economics, Geography, History, Mathematics, Music, Philosophy, Physics, Political Science, Sociology, Business Administration, Elementary Education, Earth Science, Management, Marketing, Accounting, Social Work, Human Resources, Psychology

Women's Athletic Profile

5500 N. St. Louis Avenue
Chicago, IL 60625
Coach: Dorinda Von Tersh
Email:

NCAA I
Golden Eagles, Blue, Gold
Phone: (773) 794-2991
Fax: (773) 794-6128

Estimated # of Women's Volleyball Scholarships: N/A
Conference: Mid-Continent Conference

Northern Illinois University
Academic Profile

224 Evans FieldHouse
DeKalb, IL 60115

Phone: 815-753-0446

Type: Public, 4 Yr., Coed
Website: http://www.niu.edu
SAT/ACT/GPA: 22/3.0
Student/Faculty Ratio: 17:1
Undergraduate Enrollment: 15,781
Scholarships/Academic: Yes   **Athletic:** Yes
Expenses By: Year   **In State:** $ 11,300
Specializes In: Business, Education
Degrees Conferred: BA, BS, BSBA
Programs of Study: College of Business, College of Education, College of Engineering and Engineering Technology, College of Liberal Arts and Sciences, College of Professional Studies, College of Visual and Performing Arts

Founded: 1895
Religion: Non-Denominational
Housing: Yes
Male/Female: 45:55
Graduate Enrollment: 6,471
Financial Aid: Yes
Out of State: $ 13,730

Women's Athletic Profile

139 Evans Field House
De Kalb, IL 60115-2854
Coach: Todd kress
Email: tkress@niu.edu

NCAA I
Lady Huskies, Cardinal, Black
Phone: (815) 753-9533
Fax: (815) 753-7700

Estimated # of Women's Volleyball Scholarships: walk on's only.
Conference: Mid-American Conference
Program Profile: We play in Evans Field House and are building a new convocation center set to open in the spring of 2002. The Convocation Center will be state of the art and will seat 10,000 people.
History: The volleyball program began in 1970. Since then it has won 6 conference championships and has been an NCAA Tournament participant 4 years advancing to the second round twice.
Achievements: Todd Kress- District II Coach of the Year honors in 1998, conference titles in 88,91,92,93,96,97.
Coaching: Dani Kress Graduated from University of Cincinnati 1994-Four year letter winner and one of the only 3 members of 1,000 kill-1,000 Dig Club at UC. Was outside hitter all four years. Married to Head Coach Todd Kress.
Jenny Fette-Graduated from Toledo in 98. Four year letter winner.
Freshman Receiving Financial Aid/Academic: **Athletic:** 4
Roster In State: 4   **Out of State:** 8   **Out of Country:** 0
Seniors on Team: 1
Most Recent Record: 14-3
Camp of Clinic Dates: June 3-6, June 6-9, July 15-19
Positions Needed: Middle Blocker
Schedule: Florida, Illinois, Arkansas, Michigan, Ball State, Western Michigan
Style of Play: Fast paced offense and hard-nosed aggressive defense. "Leave it all on the court" attitude.

Northwestern University
Academic Profile

1501 Central Street
Evanston, IL 60208

Phone: 847-491-7271

Type: Private, 4 Yr., Liberal Arts, Engineering, Coed
Website: http://www.nusports.com
SAT/ACT/GPA: Depends on school
Student/Faculty Ratio: 10:1
Undergraduate Enrollment: 7,600
Scholarships/Academic: No   **Athletic:** Yes
Expenses By: Year   **In State:** $ 30,000

Founded: 1851
Religion: Non-Affiliated
Housing: Yes
Male/Female: 49:51
Graduate Enrollment: 6,100
Financial Aid: Yes
Out of State: $ 30,000

Degrees Conferred: BA, BS, MS, MA, Ph.D.
Programs of Study: African-American Studies, Anthropology, Applied Mathematics, Art, Art History, Asian Studies, Astronomy, Biological Science, Chemistry, Classic, English, Environmental Science, Computer Science, Dance, Economics, Engineering, Geography, Geological Science, History, International Studies, Italian, Journalism, Music, Music Education, Neuroscience, Philosophy, Physics, Political Science, Psychology, Religion, Secondary Education, Sociology, Theatre

Women's Athletic Profile

1501 Central Street
Evanston, IL 60208
Coach: Keylor Chan
Email:

NCAA I
Lady Wildcats, Purple, White
Phone: (847) 491-4683
Fax: (847) 491-8818

Did Not Return Profile

Olivet Nazarene University
Academic Profile

240 East Marsile
Kankakee, IL 60901

Phone: 800-648-1463

Type: Private, 4 Yr., Liberal Arts, Coed
Website: http://www.olivet.edu
SAT/ACT/GPA: 18/2.0
Student/Faculty Ratio: 17:1
Undergraduate Enrollment: 1,800
Scholarships/Academic: Yes
Expenses By: Year
Specializes In: Business, Education
Degrees Conferred: BA, BS, MBA

Athletic: Yes
In State: $ 16,424

Founded: 1907
Religion: Church of the Nazarene
Housing: Yes
Male/Female: 43:57
Graduate Enrollment: 600
Financial Aid: Yes
Out of State: $ 16,424

Programs of Study: Accounting, Art, Athletic Training, Biblical Studies, Biology, Botany, Business Administration, Chemistry, Child Education, Christian Education, Church Music, Computer Science, Dietetics, Economics and Finance, Education, Engineering, English, Environmental Science, French, Fashion Merchandising, Geology, History, Mathematics, Medical Technology, Music, Nursing, Philosophy and Religion, Physical Education, Physical Science, Psychology, Religion, Romance Languages, Social Justice, Social Science, Social Work, Sociology, Spanish, Speech Communication, Theology, Zoology

Women's Athletic Profile

240 E. Marsile
Kankakee, IL 60901
Coach: Brenda Williams
Email: bwillia1@olivet.edu

NCAA I
Lady Tigers, Purple, Gold
Phone: (815) 939-5372
Fax: (815) 939-7933

Estimated # of Women's Volleyball Scholarships: 8
Conference: Chicagoland Collegiate Conference
Program Profile: McHie Arena was the Home of the 1997 and 1998 NAIA National Tournament and Birchard Gymnasium gave ONU up to courts. Our fall playing season begins August 15 and runs through December. Our program is in a growth process. We are a very competitive program that is getting stronger.
History: Our volleyball program began intercollegiate play in 1978 under the direction of Brenda Patterson.
Achievements: Brenda Patterson 1984 NCAA District Coach of the Year; 2 NCCAA All-Americans; 5 NCAA Academic All-Americans; 2 NAIA Academic All-Americans; Brenda Villiams-1996/CCAC Coach of the Year in 1997; 2 NCCAA All-Americans; 9 All-CCAC Players; 2 NAIA Academic All-Americans.
Coaching: Brenda Williams became Head Coach in 1996. Her overall record is 353-298. Her record here at ONU is 63-71. The team played a strong regional and national ranked schedule. She was NCAA I head coach at the University of Alabama-Birmingham from 1980 to 1992, Sunbelt Conference Coach of the Year in 1989, Chicagoland Collegiate Coach of the Year in 1997. Kerri Hudson is Assistant Coach.
Freshman Receiving Financial Aid/Academic:

		Athletic: 4
Roster In State: 9	**Out of State:** 4	**Out of Country:** 0
Sophomores on Team: 2	**Seniors on Team:** 3	**Graduation %:** 100
Most Recent Record: 17-24-0	**Fall Games:** 30	**Spring Games:** 2

Camp of Clinic Dates: July 25-29 (Overnight/All skills); July 29-30 (Youth Camp)
Positions Needed: Middle Hitter, Setter (have already signed)
Schedule: Bethel College-IN, Lee University-TN, Palm Beach Atlantic-FL, Taylor University-IN, St. Xavier University-IL, St. Ambrose

University-IA.
Style of Play: We have a power style of play but depend heavily on a quick middle transition game. We have run 5-1 offense but can put in 6-2 when needed. We will vary defenses according to our opponents. We have a well-rounded offense with many options to choose from.

Parkland College
Academic Profile

2400 W Bradley Ave.
Champaign, IL 61822

Phone: 800-346-8089

Type: Public, 2 Yr., Coed
Website: http://www.parkland.cc.il.us
SAT/ACT/GPA: None
Student/Faculty Ratio: 20:1
Undergraduate Enrollment: 9,000
Scholarships/Academic: Yes   **Athletic:** Yes
Expenses By: Year   **In State:** $ 6,202

Founded: 1966
Religion: Non-Affiliated
Housing: Yes
Male/Female: 40:60
Graduate Enrollment: N/A
Financial Aid: Yes
Out of State: $ 8,312

Specializes In: Agriculture, Biology, Education, Computers
Degrees Conferred: AA, AS
Programs of Study: Agriculture, Business Administration, Communications, Criminal Justice, Education, Engineering, Liberal Arts, Life Sciences, Math, Physical Education, Physical Science, PreProfessional Medicine

Women's Athletic Profile

2400 Bradley Ave.
Champaign, IL 61822
Coach: Joana Ramsey
Email: jramsey@parkland.ceil.us

NCAA I
Lady Cobras, Green, Gold
Phone: (217) 373-3758
Fax: (217) 373-3897

Estimated # of Women's Volleyball Scholarships: 3
Conference: Collegiate Conference of Illinois
Program Profile: Pre-season starts August 6, season starts at August 6-Nov. 14. Gymnasium has three courts.
History: 1999- National Champions NJCAA Div.11
Achievements: 4 All-Region Players; 5 All-Conference Players; 7 All-Americans; CCCI Conference Champions in 1995,1996,1997 and 1998. 7th in the Nation in 1991; 3rd in Region 24 in 1989,1992,1993, 1996,1997, and 1998. Conference Coach of the Year in 2000.
Freshman Receiving Financial Aid/Academic: **Athletic:** 10
Roster In State: 11
Graduation %: 98
Most Recent Record: 37-17-0
Positions Needed: Middle Hitter, Outside, Setter
Schedule: Kellogg CC, Kalamazoo, Kirkwood, Kishwaukee, Danville
Style of Play: Run a quick offense.

Principia College
Academic Profile

1 Maybeck Place
Elsah, IL 62028

Phone: (618) 374-2131

Type: Private, 4 Yr., Liberal Arts, Coed
Website: http://www.prin.edu
SAT/ACT/GPA: 910/2.0
Student/Faculty Ratio: 8:1
Undergraduate Enrollment: 550
Scholarships/Academic: Yes   **Athletic:** No
Expenses By: Year   **In State:** $ 21,500

Founded: 1898
Religion: Christian Science
Housing: Yes
Male/Female: 40:60
Graduate Enrollment: N/A
Financial Aid: Yes
Out of State: $ 21,500

Specializes In: Liberal Arts
Degrees Conferred: BA, BS

Programs of Study: Liberal Arts and Sciences, Business and Education, Computer Science, Communications, Earth Science, Economics, Education, Engineering Science, Environmental Studies, Mass Communications, Philosophy, Physics, Religion, Political Science

Women's Athletic Profile

1 Maybeck Place
Elsah, IL 62068
Coach: Lee Suarez
Email:

NCAA I
Lady Panthers, Navy Blue, Gold
Phone: (618) 374-5026
Fax: (618) 374-5221

Estimated # of Women's Volleyball Scholarships: N/A
Conference: St. Louis Intercollegiate Athletic Conference
Program Profile: 8 week fall season at Liberal Arts school of SSO
Achievements: Brand New Coach-coached University of Mississippi-Asst. Junior Volleyball for 10 years, and high school for 5 years. Played through college and adult A/AA ball

Roster In State: 2
Seniors on Team: 4
Most Recent Record: 8-16

Out of State: 8
Graduation %: 100
Fall Games: 24

Schedule: Anderson, Earlham, Augustana, DePauw
Style of Play: Scrappy defensive, play the percentages offensive. Tough serving.

Quincy University
Academic Profile

1800 College Avenue
Quincy, IL 62301

Phone: 217-228-5210

Type: Private, 4 Yr., Liberal Arts, Coed
Website: http://www.quincy.edu
SAT/ACT/GPA: 950/20/2.0
Student/Faculty Ratio: 12:1
Undergraduate Enrollment: 1,300
Scholarships/Academic: Yes
Expenses By: Year
Specializes In: Business, Education

Founded: 1860
Religion: Catholic - Franciscan
Housing: Yes
Male/Female: 50:50
Graduate Enrollment: 150
Athletic: Yes
In State: $ 18,300

Financial Aid: No
Out of State: $ 18,300

Degrees Conferred: BA, BS, MA, MBA
Programs of Study: Accounting, Art Biology, Business Administration, Chemistry, Communications, Computer Science, Education, English, Finance, History, Humanities, Human Resources, Information Science, International Studies, Management, Marketing, Mathematics, Medical Technology, Music, Music Business, Philosophy, Political Science, Psychology, Religious Education, Social Science, Special Education, Sports Management, Theology

Men's Athletic Profile

1800 College Avenue
Quincy, IL 62301
Coach: Tim Koth
Email:

NCAA II
Hawks/Brown, White, Gold
Phone: (217) 228-5293
Fax: (217) 228-5034

Estimated # of Men's Volleyball Scholarships: N/A
Conference: Midwestern Intercollegiate Volleyball Association

Women's Athletic Profile

1800 College Avenue
Quincy, IL 62301-2699
Coach: Tim Koth
Email: volleyball@quincy.edu

NCAA I
Hawks, Brown, White, Gold
Phone: (217) 228-5293
Fax: (217) 228-5034

Estimated # of Women's Volleyball Scholarships: N/A
Conference: MIVA
Program Profile: In the year 2000, our new Health and Fitness Center will be completed.
History: Our program is in its third year as a scholarship program.

Coaching: Tim Koth - Head Coach. Rob Beam is assistant coach.

Roster In State: 2   **Out of State:** 6   **Out of Country:** 3
Sophomores on Team: 0   **Seniors on Team:** 0   **Graduation %:** 100
Most Recent Record: 7-12-0   **Fall Games:** 4   **Spring Games:** 25
Positions Needed: Setter, Outside Hitter
Schedule: Indiana Purdue-Fort Wayne, Ohio State, Lewis, Ball State, Cal State Northridge, University of California-Santa Barbara

Robert Morris College - Chicago Campus
Academic Profile

401 South State
Chicago, IL 60605

Phone: (312) 935-6815

Type: Private, 4 Yr., Coed
Website: http://www.RMCIL.EDU
SAT/ACT/GPA: 18/2.0-4.0
Student/Faculty Ratio: 14:1
Undergraduate Enrollment: 3,600
Scholarships/Academic: Yes
Expenses By: Year
Specializes In: Business, Computer, Health Care, Graphic Design
Degrees Conferred: BBA, AAS
Programs of Study: Please call admissions.

Athletic: Yes
In State: $ 14,000

Founded: 1913
Religion: Non-Affiliated
Housing: Yes
Male/Female: 1:1
Graduate Enrollment: 120
Financial Aid: Yes
Out of State: $ 14,000

Women's Athletic Profile

180 N. La Salle
Chicago, IL 60601
Coach: Chris Pruitt
Email:

NCAA I
Lady Eagles, Maroon, Gold
Phone: (312) 733-9008
Fax: (312) 836-6270

Estimated # of Women's Volleyball Scholarships: N/A
Conference: CCAC

Rockford College
Academic Profile

5050 E. State St.
Rockford, IL 61108

Phone: (815) 226-4085

Type: Private, 4 Yr., Coed
Website: http://www.rockford.edu
SAT/ACT/GPA: 18/2.0, 2.5 (Transfers)
Student/Faculty Ratio: 14:1
Undergraduate Enrollment: 775
Scholarships/Academic: Yes
Expenses By: Year
Specializes In: General Education
Degrees Conferred: BA, BS, BSN, BFA, MBA, MAT
Programs of Study: Anthropology, Art, Biology, Business, Chemistry, Computer Science, Dance, Economics, English, French, German, History, Mathematics, Philosophy, Political Science, Psychology, Sociology, Spanish, Education, Physical Education, Athletic Training

Athletic: No
In State: $ 23,000

Founded: 1847
Religion: Non-Affiliated
Housing: Yes
Male/Female: 60:40
Graduate Enrollment: 40
Financial Aid: Yes
Out of State: $ 23,000

Women's Athletic Profile

5050 E. State Street
Rockford, IL 61108
Coach: Joan Mosher
Email:

NCAA I
Lady Regents, Purple, White
Phone: (815) 394-5067
Fax: (815) 226-4085

Estimated # of Women's Volleyball Scholarships: N/A
Conference: Northern Illinois-Iowa Conference
Program Profile: Varsity Program, Seaver Gymnasium, Seating 800, Season August 28-November 6

History: First Year of Volleyball 1972
Coaching: Joan Mosher-Casazza-1996-1998
Roster In State: 10   **Out of State:** 4
Seniors on Team: 1   **Graduation %:** 100
Most Recent Record: 4-24   **Fall Games:** 28
Positions Needed: Middle Hitter, Outside Hitters
Schedule: Augustana, Dubuque, Cornell, Knox, Trinity, North Central

Saint Xavier University
Academic Profile

3700 W. 103rd St.   **Phone:** 800-462-9288
Chicago, IL 60655

Type: Private, 4 Yr., Liberal Arts, Coed   **Founded:** 1846
Website: http://www.sxu.edu   **Religion:** Roman Catholic
SAT/ACT/GPA: Required   **Housing:** No
Student/Faculty Ratio: 15:1   **Male/Female:** 25:75
Undergraduate Enrollment: 2,400   **Graduate Enrollment:** 1,400
Scholarships/Academic: Yes   **Athletic:** Yes   **Financial Aid:** Yes
Expenses By: Year   **In State:** $ 15,000   **Out of State:** $15,000
Degrees Conferred: BA, BS, MA, MS, MBA
Programs of Study: Accounting, Aeronautical Engineering, Banking & Finance, Biology, Chemical Engineering, Chemistry, Communications, Computer Science, Criminal Justice, Education, English, Fine Arts, French, History, International Business, Management, Philosophy, Political Science, International Business, Mathematics, PreDentistry, PreMed, PreLaw, PrePharmacy, Religion, Social Science, Spanish, Speech Pathology

Women's Athletic Profile

3700 W. 103rd Street   **NCAA I**
Chicago, IL 60655   Cougars, Scarlet, Grey, White
Coach: Bob Heersema   **Phone:** (773) 298-3105
Email: sxuvbise@aol.com   **Fax:** (773) 298-3111

Estimated # of Women's Volleyball Scholarships: 6 Partical
Conference: CCAC
Program Profile: New 11.5 Million CAC which seats 2, 500.
History: The St. Xavier Lady Cougars have been an imposing force in the NAIA and NCAA Division II and III.
Achievements: Coach of the Year 3 times, tournament champs 86, 2000, 1 2000 3rd team All-American
Coaching: Bob Heersema, Head Coach, has led our team be one of the Top Ten teams in the Great Lakes Region.
Freshman Receiving Financial Aid/Academic: **Athletic:** 2
Roster In State: 15   **Out of State:** 0   **Out of Country:** 0
Seniors on Team: 5   **Graduation %:** 100
Most Recent Record: 36-14
Camp of Clinic Dates: Nike Camp middle of July
Positions Needed: OSH, MB, OH, Setters

Southern Illinois University - Carbondale
Academic Profile

Lingle Hall Room 118   **Phone:** 618-536-4405
Carbondale, IL 62901

Type: Public, 4 Yr., Coed   **Founded:** 1869
Website: http://www.siu.edu   **Religion:** Non-Affiliated
SAT/ACT/GPA: 20avg   **Housing:** Yes
Student/Faculty Ratio: 16:1   **Male/Female:** 40:60
Undergraduate Enrollment: 18,700   **Graduate Enrollment:** 4,4500
Scholarships/Academic: Yes   **Athletic:** Yes   **Financial Aid:** Yes
Expenses By: Year   **In State:** $ 7,991   **Out of State:** $ 10,800
Degrees Conferred: AAS, BA, BS, BFA, MA, MS, MBA, MFA, MPA, MD, DBA, JD
Programs of Study: Accounting, Advertising, Agriculture, Animal, Anthropology, Architectural, Banking/Finance, Biological Science,

Botany, Broadcasting, Business, Dental, Design, Dietetics, English, Forestry, Geology, Horticulture, Hotel/Restaurant, Journalism, Languages, Management, Optometry, Parks/Recreation, Paralegal, Photography, PreProfessional Programs, etc..

Women's Athletic Profile

Lingle Hall Rm. 118
Carbondale, IL 62901
Coach: Sonya Locke
Email: siuvb@siu.edu

NCAA I
Lady Salukis, Maroon, White
Phone: (618) 453-5473
Fax: (618) 453-3255

Estimated # of Women's Volleyball Scholarships: 2
Conference: Missouri Valley
Program Profile: Davies Gym Seats 1500 people, wood floor, personal team locker room.
History: Volleyball program has been in existence since 1961. Winning percentage of .564
Achievements: Olympians- Janet Baer Howes, All-American- Sonya Locke, Conference MVP- Lori Simpson
Coaching: Sonya Locke has been the Head Coach for 10 seasons. Misher has assisted for 7 years, Steele is in her first year. We are dedicated and hard working, we are determined to take this program into the NCAA tournament.
Freshman Receiving Financial Aid/Academic: | | **Athletic:** 2
Roster In State: 8 | **Out of State:** 6 | **Out of Country:** 1
Seniors on Team: 2 | **Graduation %:** 95
Most Recent Record: 8-22
Camp of Clinic Dates: June 10, July 5-8, July 9-12, July 19-22
Positions Needed: MB, Setter
Schedule: Oregon State, San Jose State, Cal State Sacramento, Southeast Missouri, Northern Iowa, Illinois State
Style of Play: Fast, crisp, free flowing, not stagnant.

Southern Illinois University - Edwardsville
Academic Profile

Box 1129
Edwardsville, IL 62026
Type: Public, 4 Yr., Coed
Website: http://www.siue.edu
SAT/ACT/GPA: Call for info.
Student/Faculty Ratio: 16/1
Undergraduate Enrollment: 9,313
Scholarships/Academic: Yes
Expenses By: Varies

Phone: (618) 650-2000

Founded: 1957
Religion: Non-Affiliated
Housing: Yes
Male/Female: 1/1.44
Graduate Enrollment: 2,564
Athletic: Yes | **Financial Aid:** Yes
In State: $3,771.55 | **Out of State:** $4,908.55

Degrees Conferred: Bachelor, Master's and professional
Programs of Study: Anthropology, Art and Design, Biological Sciences, Computer Management and Information Systems, Chemistry, Economics, Education, English, Geography, Health, Mass Communications, Mathematics, Music, Nursing, Psychology, Physics, Political Science, Social Work, Sociology, Speech, Theatre

Men's Athletic Profile

Box 1129
Edwardsville, IL 62026-1129
Coach: Joe Fisher
Email: josfish@siue.edu

NCAA II
Cougars/Red/White
Phone: 618-650-5923
Fax: 618-650-3369

Estimated # of Men's Volleyball Scholarships: N/A
Conference: Great Lakes Valley Conference
Program Profile: We have a nationally and regionally ranked Division II program. Our Vadalabene Center is air-conditioned and has 4,000 seats.
History: We began in 1995. In 1998, we finished 29-7 and advanced to the Regional Championship match.
Achievements: 1998- two All-Region players
Coaching: Joe Fisher took over as Head Coach in the beginning of the 1999 season.
Roster In State: 12 | **Out of State:** 0 | **Out of Country:** 0
Seniors on Team: 4 | **Graduation %:** 100%
Most Recent Record: 29-7 | **Fall Games:** 36 | **Spring Games:** 10
Camp or Clinic Dates: Skills Camp July 26/27; Team Camp: July 29/31
Schedule: Northern Kentucky, Indiana University Purdue-Fort Wayne, North Alabama, Central Missouri State, Alabama Huntsville, Rockhurst, Northwood
Style of Play: Aggressive, fast-offense oriented.

Women's Athletic Profile

SIUE Box 1129
Edwardsville, IL 62026
Coach: Joe Fisher
Email: josfish@siue.edu

NCAA I
Lady Cougars, Red, White
Phone: (618) 650-2870
Fax: (618) 650-3369

Estimated # of Women's Volleyball Scholarships: N/A
Conference: Great Lakes Valley Conference
Program Profile: We play in Vadalabene Center with a seating capacity of 4,000.
History: Our volleyball program initiated in 1995. We advanced to four GLVC Tournament Appearances. We made our first NCAA Appearance during the 1998 season.
Achievements: Michele Gilman was named GLVC Player of the Year in 1996 & 1998, All-Region in 1996 & 1998. Lindsey Rust was named First Team All-Region, First Team All-GLVC. Michele Gilman signed professional contract to play in Europe.
Coaching: Joe Fisher, Head Coach, is entering his first season with the program. He was an assistant at SIUE since 1995. He helped coach 4 consecutive GLVC Tournament Appearances with an NCAA Appearances last year. Nikki Renniger, Assistant Coach, was a former coach at Bucknell University to NCAA Appearances in 1998.

Roster In State: 13 **Out of State:** 1 **Out of Country:** 0
Sophomores on Team: 3 **Seniors on Team:** 3 **Graduation %:**
Most Recent Record: 29-7-0 **Fall Games:** 32 **Spring Games:** 0
Schedule: IUOU-Fort Wayne, Northern Kentucky, Central Missouri, Northern Alabama, Alabama Huntsville

Trinity Christian College
Academic Profile

6601 W College Drive
Palos Heights, IL 60463

Phone: (800) 748-0085

Type: Private, 4 Yr., Liberal Arts, Coed
Website: http://www.trnty.edu
SAT/ACT/GPA: 1030/22/2.0
Student/Faculty Ratio: 12:1
Undergraduate Enrollment: 630
Scholarships/Academic: Yes **Athletic:** Yes
Expenses By: Year **In State:** $ 18,240
Specializes In: Business, Education, Nursing
Degrees Conferred: BA, BS

Founded: 1959
Religion: Non-Affiliated
Housing: No
Male/Female: 37:63
Graduate Enrollment: N/A
Financial Aid: Yes
Out of State: $ 18,240

Programs of Study: Accounting, Banking & Finance, Biology, Chemistry, Communications, Computer Science, Education, English, Fine Arts, History, Marketing, Music, Nursing, Philosophy, PreDentistry, PreLaw, PreMed, Psychology, Religion, Social Science, Special Education

Men's Athletic Profile

6601 W. College Drive
Palos Heights, IL 60463
Coach: David L. Ribbens
Email: dave.ribbens@trnty.edu
Estimated # of Men's Volleyball Scholarships: 1.0
Conference: MCVA

NAIA
Trolls/Navy, Columbia Blue
Phone: (708) 239-4781
Fax: (708) 396-7460

Program Profile: We play at Mitchell Memorial Gymnasium, which seats 1,800. Our season goes from January to March.
Freshman Receiving Financial Aid/Academic: 40% **Athletic:** 60%
Roster In State: 4 **Out of State:** 6 **Out of Country:** 0
Seniors on Team: 5 **Graduation %:** 100%
Most Recent Record: 19-12-0 **Fall Games:** 0 **Spring Games:** 30
Positions Needed: Setter, Outside Hitter

Women's Athletic Profile

6601 W. College Drive
Palos Heights, IL 60463
Coach: Sue Gasparec
Email:

NCAA I
Lady Trolls, Navy, Blue, White
Phone: (708) 239-4805
Fax: (708) 396-7460

Estimated # of Women's Volleyball Scholarships: 1.5
Conference: Chicagoland Collegiate Athletic Conference
Freshman Receiving Financial Aid/Academic:
Roster In State: 4
Sophomores on Team: 0
Most Recent Record: 22-22-0
Positions Needed: Outside Hitters
Schedule: Columbia, Lubbock Christian, Taylor, Madonna, Bethel, Palm Beach Atlantic

Out of State: 7
Seniors on Team: 3
Fall Games: 40-50

Athletic: 4
Out of Country: 1
Graduation %:
Spring Games: 6

Trinity International University
Academic Profile

2065 Half Day Road
Deerfield, IL 60015

Phone: 800-822-3225

Type: Private, 4 Yr., Liberal Arts, Coed
Website: http://www.trin.edu
SAT/ACT/GPA: 900/20
Student/Faculty Ratio: 17:1
Undergraduate Enrollment: 850
Scholarships/Academic: Yes
Expenses By: Year
Specializes In: Business, Sports Medicine, Athletic Training, Education
Degrees Conferred: BA
Programs of Study: Biblical Studies, Biology, PreMed, Business Administration, Chemistry, Communications, Education, History, Music, English, Mathematics, Psychology, Sports and Wellness Management, Youth Ministry, Sports Medicine, Athletic Training

Athletic: Yes
In State: $ 17,800

Founded: 1897
Religion: Evangelical Free Church
Housing: Yes
Male/Female: 50:50
Graduate Enrollment: 1,500
Financial Aid: Yes
Out of State: $ 17,800

Women's Athletic Profile

2065 Half Day
Deerfield, IL 60015
Coach: Nathan Brand
Email:

NCAA I
Lady Trojans, Blue, White
Phone: (847) 317-7095
Fax: (847) 317-8056

Did Not Return Profile

University of Chicago
Academic Profile

5640 South University Ave.
Chicago, IL 60637

Phone: (773) 702-7684

Type: Private, 4 Yr., Liberal Arts, Coed
Website: http://www.uchicago.edu
SAT/ACT/GPA: 1100/25/3.5
Student/Faculty Ratio: 6:1
Undergraduate Enrollment: 3,400
Scholarships/Academic: Yes
Expenses By: Year
Specializes In: Economics, PreProfessional Programs, Social Sciences
Degrees Conferred: BA, BS, MA, MS, MBA, MFA, Ph.D., MD, JD
Programs of Study: Astronomy, Biology, Chemistry, Physics, Geology, Computer Science, Anthropology, English, History, Languages, Physical Science, Sociology, Law, Literature, Economics, PreMed, PreLaw

Athletic: No
In State: $ 33,200

Founded: 1892
Religion: Non-Affiliated
Housing: Yes
Male/Female: 56:44
Graduate Enrollment: 6,000
Financial Aid: Yes
Out of State: $ 33,200

Women's Athletic Profile

5640 S. University Avenue
Chicago, IL 60637
Coach: Christine Masel
Email: cmasel@midway.uchicago.edu

NCAA I
Lady Maroons, Maroon, White
Phone: (773) 702-7684
Fax: (773) 702-6517

Estimated # of Women's Volleyball Scholarships: N/A

Conference: University Athletic Association
Program Profile: We are a growing program within Division III and have national recognition. Our fall season is from August to November. Our spring season is from March to May. We play at Henry Crown Field House which has four stand alone courts, an indoor track and a varsity weight room. In 2001, a new facility will open that will accommodate basketball, volleyball and swimming.
History: Our program has over 45 years of varsity volleyball. We are traditionally in the top third of the conference. Coach Masel is the third volleyball coach in UC history.
Coaching: Christine Masel, Head Coach, started in 1998 at UC. Her record is 12-22. She was a player in 3 NCAA Division III National Championships. She won 4 UAA Conference Titles and All-Conference.
Roster In State: 5   **Out of State:** 7   **Out of Country:** 0
Seniors on Team: 5   **Graduation %:** 100
Positions Needed: Middle, Outside, Setter
Schedule: Washington University in St. Louis, Emory University, University of Wisconsin-La Crosse, University of Wisconsin-Oshkosh, Illinois, Wesleyan, Elmhurst
Style of Play: Competitive, fast, controlled, flowing and poised.

University of Illinois - Chicago
Academic Profile

901 West Roosevelt Road
Chicago, IL 60607

Phone: 312-996-4350

Type: Public, 4 Yr., Liberal Arts, Engineering, Coed   **Founded:** 1982
Website: http://www.uic.edu   **Religion:** Non-Affiliated
SAT/ACT/GPA: 21/3.0-3.5   **Housing:** Yes
Student/Faculty Ratio: 11:1   **Male/Female:** 46:54
Undergraduate Enrollment: 16,500   **Graduate Enrollment:** 6,000
Scholarships/Academic: Yes   **Athletic:** Yes   **Financial Aid:** Yes
Expenses By: Year   **In State:** $ 12,145   **Out of State:** $ 18,421
Specializes In: Medicine, Dentistry, Pharmacy, Kinesiology
Degrees Conferred: Bachelors, Masters, Doctoral
Programs of Study: Architecture, Medical, Business, Education, PreProfessional Programs

Women's Athletic Profile

901 W. Roosevelt Rd.
Chicago, IL 60607
Coach: Don August
Email:

NCAA I
Lady Flames, Blue, Red
Phone: (312) 996-2056
Fax: (312) 996-8349

Estimated # of Women's Volleyball Scholarships: 12
Conference: Midwestern Collegiate Conference
Program Profile: UIC Pavilion Seating 6500
Achievements: Conf Reg season Champs 1988, Conf Tournament Champion 1989, Coach of the Year 1988.
Coaching: Don August Head Coach 1981, Chers Cooper Asst. Coach 1998 -Three Time All- American.
Freshman Receiving Financial Aid/Academic: **Athletic:** 2
Roster In State: 12   **Out of State:** 2
Sophomores on Team: 2   **Seniors on Team:** 4   **Graduation %:** 99
Most Recent Record: 15-16   **Fall Games:** Approx. 30
Positions Needed: MH, OH, S
Schedule: University of Washington, University of Tennessee, North Carolina State, Butler University, Loyola-Chicago, University of Wisconsin-Mil
Style of Play: Solid defensive team with good serving and relatively quick. We utilize a middle offense.

Sangamon St. University
Academic Profile

Shepherd Road
Springfield, IL 62794-9243

Phone:

Type: Public, 2 Yr., Liberal Arts, Coed   **Founded:** 1969
Website: http://www.uis.edu   **Religion:** Non-Affiliated
SAT/ACT/GPA: Open   **Housing:** Yes
Student/Faculty Ratio: 17:1   **Male/Female:** 40:60

Undergraduate Enrollment: 2,388
Scholarships/Academic: Yes
Expenses By: Year
Graduate Enrollment: 1,861
Financial Aid: Yes
Athletic: Yes
In State: $ 5,500
Out of State: $ 10,500

Specializes In: Upper Division (some sophomores)
Degrees Conferred: BA, BBA, BSN, BSW, BS, MA, MBA, MPA
Programs of Study: Accounting, Biology, Business Administration, Chemistry, Clinical Laboratory Science, Communication, Computer Science, Criminal Justice, Economics, English, Health Services Administration, History, Labor Relations, Legal Studies, Management, Mathematics, Nursing, Political Science, Psychology, Sociology/Anthropology, Visual Arts

Women's Athletic Profile

Did Not Return Profile

University of Illinois - Urbana/Champaign
Academic Profile

901 W. Illinois Street
Urbana, IL 61801

Phone: (217) 333-0302

Type: Public, 4 Yr., Coed
Website: http://www.uiuc.edu
SAT/ACT/GPA: 1150avg/25-29avg
Student/Faculty Ratio: 19:1
Undergraduate Enrollment: 27,452
Scholarships/Academic: Yes
Expenses By: Year
Founded: 1867
Religion: Non-Affiliated
Housing: Yes
Male/Female: 1:1
Graduate Enrollment: 8,851
Financial Aid: Yes
Athletic: Yes
In State: $ 10,186
Out of State: $ 17,002

Specializes In: 8 Colleges and One Institution offer over 4,000 courses
Degrees Conferred: Undergraduate, Graduate and Professional Degrees available
Programs of Study: College of Agricultural, Consumer and Environmental Sciences, Applied Life Studies, College of Commerce and Business Administration, College of Communications, College of Education, College of Engineering, College of Fine and Applied Arts, College of Liberal Arts and Sciences. The University of Illinois has over 150 programs of study.

Women's Athletic Profile

1700 S. South Street
Champaign, IL 61820
Coach: Don Hardin
Email:

NCAA I
Fighting Illinois, Orange, Blue
Phone: (217) 333-8606
Fax: (217) 244-9753

Estimated # of Women's Volleyball Scholarships: 2
Conference: Big Ten Conference
Program Profile: The Fighting Illinois Volleyball team plays in Huff Hall, an historic tradition in the University of Illinois athletics. This multi-use facility holds 4,500 and is currently in the middle of step-by-step upgrades. The team plays in Europe every fourth summer.
History: The Volleyball program began in 1974, the same year that the University of Illinois recognized women's athletics as part of the Athletic Association. This past season, the team advanced to the NCAA Mountain Regional Semi-Final and ended the season with a number 14 ranking.
Achievements: 4 Big Ten Titles; 11 NCAA tournaments with a 15-11 marking; 3 former first-team All-Americans; 3 second-team All-Americans; 1 former third-team All-American
Coaching: Don Hardin, Head Coach, is in his 4th year with a school record of 52-39. Jeff Hulsmeyer and Denise Baez are Assistant Coaches.
Freshman Receiving Financial Aid/Academic:
Athletic: 3

Roster In State: 11
Sophomores on Team: 0
Most Recent Record: 22-11-0
Out of State: 3
Seniors on Team: 5
Fall Games: 33
Out of Country: 1
Graduation %: 100
Spring Games: 0

Schedule: Penn State, Wisconsin, Louisville, Michigan State, Ohio State, Indiana

Western Illinois University
Academic Profile

203 Western Hall
Macomb, IL 61455

Phone: (309) 298-1190

Type: Public, 4 Yr., Coed
Website: http://www.wiu.edu
SAT/ACT/GPA: 1010/18
Student/Faculty Ratio: 14:1
Undergraduate Enrollment: 9,606
Scholarships/Academic: Yes   **Athletic:** Yes
Expenses By: Year   **In State:** $ 7,789
Specializes In: Education, Criminal Justice, Business
Degrees Conferred: BA, BFA, BB, BS, BSEd, MS, MA

Founded: 1899
Religion: Non-Affiliated
Housing: Yes
Male/Female: 51:49
Graduate Enrollment: 2,509
Financial Aid: Yes
Out of State: $ 9,974

Programs of Study: Accounting, Agriculture, Art, BioChemistry, Communications, Computer Science, Education, Economics, Foreign Languages, Geography, Geology, Health Education, Physical Education, Industrial, Math, Marketing, Music, Philosophy, Physics, Political Science, Psychology, Recreation/Parks, Tourism, Sociology, Speech, Theatre

Women's Athletic Profile

Western Hall
Macomb, IL 61455
Coach: Michelle Gomez
Email:

NCAA I
Lady Westerwinds, Purple, Gold
Phone: (309) 298-1190
Fax: (309) 298-2009

Estimated # of Women's Volleyball Scholarships: N/A
Conference: Mid-Continent Conference
Program Profile: New program and new coach.
History: New program and new coach.
Achievements: New program and new coach.
Coaching: Michelle Gomez, Head Coach.
Camp of Clinic Dates: June 9-13, 1999
Schedule: TBA
Style of Play: New program and new coach.

Wheaton College - Illinois
Academic Profile

501 E. College Avenue
Wheaton, IL 60187

Phone: (630) 752-5047

Type: Private, 4 Yr., Liberal Arts, Coed
Website: http://www.wheaton.edu
SAT/ACT/GPA: 1340/30
Student/Faculty Ratio: 16:1
Undergraduate Enrollment: 2,300
Scholarships/Academic: Yes   **Athletic:** Yes
Expenses By: Year   **In State:** $ 20,000
Degrees Conferred: BA, BS, BM, BMEd, MA, Ph.D.

Founded: 1860
Religion: Interdenominational
Housing: Yes
Male/Female: 1:1
Graduate Enrollment: 350
Financial Aid: Yes
Out of State: $ 20,000

Programs of Study: Ancient Languages, Archeology, Art, Biblical Studies, Biology, Business/Economics, Chemistry, Christian Education, Communications, Computer Science/Mathematics, Economics, Education, Environmental Science, French, Geological Studies, German, History, History/Social Science, Interdisciplinary Studies, Liberal Arts, Engineering,Nursing, Literature, Mathematics, Music (6 majors), Philosophy, Physical Education, Physical Science, Physics, Political Science, Psychology, Religious Studies, Sociology, Spanish

Women's Athletic Profile

501 College Avenue
Wheaton, IL 60187
Coach: Jennifer King Soderquist
Email: jennifer.k.soderquist@wheaton.edu

NCAA I
Lady Crusaders, Orange, Blue
Phone: (630) 752-5125
Fax: (630) 752-7007

Estimated # of Women's Volleyball Scholarships: N/A
Conference: College Conference of Illinois & Wisconsin
Program Profile: Competition Gym being renovated into arena. We will continue to have three courts. August through November is our playing season. Spring practice season in mid-February to late April.
Achievements: 1989 Conference Title, 1987 & 1989 NCAA II National Tournament participant, 2 All-Americans 2nd Team, 7 All-Midwest player.
Coaching: Jennifer King Soderquist, Head Coach, started with the program in 1986. She compiled a record of 330-271 and was

named Conference Coach of the Year in 1989.

Roster In State: 0   **Out of State:** 13   **Out of Country:** 0

Sophomores on Team: 0   **Seniors on Team:** 1   **Graduation %:** 94

Most Recent Record: 24-19-0

Positions Needed: Setters, Outside Hitters, Middle Hitters

Schedule: Calvin College, Elmhurst College, Kalamazoo College, Illinois Wesleyan, Millikin College

Style of Play: Fast offense; strong attack and aggressive defense.

INDIANA

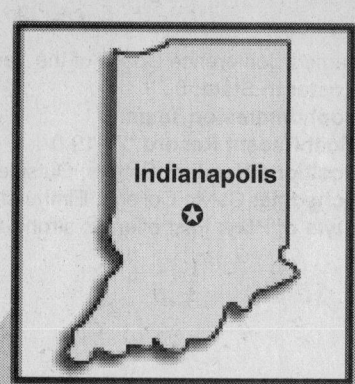

Indianapolis

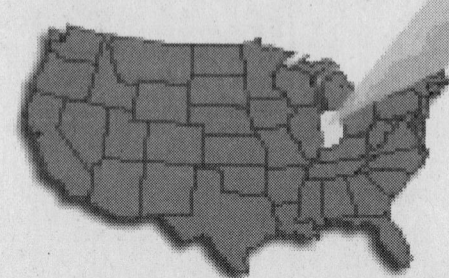

SCHOOL	CITY	AFFILIATION	PAGE
Anderson University	Anderson	NCAA III	235
Ball State University	Muncie	NCAA I	235
Bethel College	Mishawaka	NCCAA/NAIA	236
Butler University	Indianapolis	NCAA I	236
DePauw University	Greencastle	NCAA III	237
Earlham College	Richmond	NCAA III	238
Franklin College	Franklin	NCAA III	238
Goshen College	Goshen	NAIA	239
Grace College	Winona Lake	NCCAA I/NAIA	239
Hanover College	Hanover	NCAA III	240
Huntington College	Huntington	NAIA	241
Indiana State University	Terre Haute	NCAA I	241
Indiana University - Bloomington	Bloomington	NCAA I	242
Indiana University-PU-Fort Wayne	Fort Wayne	NCAA II	242
Indiana University - Purdue	Indianapolis	NCAA I	243
Indiana University Southeast	New Albany	NAIA	244
Indiana Wesleyan University	Marion	NAIA	244
Manchester College	North Manchester	NCAA III	245
Marian College	Indianapolis	NAIA	246
Oakland City University	Oakland City	NCAA II	246
Purdue University	West Lafayette	NCAA I	247
Purdue University - Calumet	Calumet	NAIA	247
Rose-Hulman Institute of Tech.	Terre Haute	NCAA III	248
Saint Joseph's College - Indiana	Rensselaer	NCAA II	249
Saint Mary's College - Indiana	Notre Dame	NCAA III	249
Taylor University	Upland	NCCAA/NAIA	250
Tri-State University	Angola	NAIA	250
University of Evansville	Evansville	NCAA I	251

SCHOOL	CITY	AFFILIATION	PAGE
University of Indianapolis	Indianapolis	NCAA II	251
University of Notre Dame	Notre Dame	NCAA I	252
University of St. Francis	Ft. Wayne	NAIA	252
University of Southern Indiana	Evansville	NCAA II	253
Valparaiso University	Valparaiso	NCAA I	254

Anderson University
Academic Profile

1100 E. 5th Street
Anderson, IN 46012-3462

Phone: 765-641-3043

Type: Private, 4 Yr., Liberal Arts, Coed
Website: http://www.anderson.edu
SAT/ACT/GPA: 975+/21+
Student/Faculty Ratio: 15:1
Undergraduate Enrollment: 2,240
Scholarships/Academic: Yes
Expenses By: Year
Specializes In: Education, Liberal Arts, Theology
Degrees Conferred: AA, BA, BSN, MBA, MA, MDiv
Programs of Study: Athletic Training, Business/Marketing, Finance, Management, Accounting, Computer Science, Education, Health Sciences, Psychology, Social Sciences, Philosophy, Theology, Visual & Performing Arts, Music and Communications

Athletic: No
n State: $ 16,000

Founded: 1917
Religion: Church of God
Housing: Yes
Male/Female: 42:58
Graduate Enrollment: 400
Financial Aid: Yes
Out of State: $ 16,00

Women's Athletic Profile

1100 E. Fifth Street
Anderson, IN 46012
Coach: Ed Allen
Email: edallen@anderson.edu

NCAA I
Lady Ravens, Orange, Black
Phone: (765) 641-4478
Fax: (765) 641-3857

Estimated # of Women's Volleyball Scholarships: 0
Conference: Heartland Collegiate Athletic Conference
History: The program has compiled five consecutive 20+ win seasons. We have been in existence 25 years.
Achievements: 1998 Academic All-American; 1998 HCAC Player of the Week; 1994 ICAC Coach of the Year; Chandra Backes a two-time All-American in 1997 and 1998.
Coaching: Ed Allen enters his seventh year as Head Volleyball Coach. His overall record is 157-88. He was named the Indiana Collegiate Athletic Conference Coach of the Year in 1994. Beth Stewart-Etchison started her first year as Assistant Coach. She graduated from Anderson in 1992. She was MVP and captain of the volleyball team in 1992.
Freshman Receiving Financial Aid/Academic:
Sophomores on Team: 6
Most Recent Record:
Positions Needed: Middle Hitter, Outside Hitter
Schedule: Mt. St. Joseph-Ohio, Kalamazoo, Allegheny, Millikin, John Carrol-Ohio, Benedictine

Athletic: 0
Seniors on Team: 2
Fall Games: 27 **Spring Games:** 0

Ball State University
Academic Profile

2000 University Drive
Muncie, IN 47306-0949

Phone: (765) 285-1671

Type: Public, 4 Yr., Coed
Website: http://www.bsu.edu
SAT/ACT/GPA: 1150/24/3.0
Student/Faculty Ratio: 13:1
Undergraduate Enrollment: 18,000
Scholarships/Academic: Yes
Expenses By: Year
Specializes In: Broad Liberal Arts & Sciences Curriculum
Degrees Conferred: BA, BS, BFA, MA, MS, Ph.D.
Programs of Study: Education, Exercise Science, Architecture, Business, Telecommunications, Arts, Psychology, etc..

Athletic: Yes
In State: $ 8,700

Founded: 1910
Religion: Non-Affiliated
Housing: Yes
Male/Female: 50:50
Graduate Enrollment: 2,000
Financial Aid: Yes
Out of State: $ 14,700

Men's Athletic Profile

2000 W. University Avenue
Muncie, IN 47306
Coach: Joel Walton
Email: aseger@wp.bsu.edu

NCAA I
Cardinals/Cardinal, White
Phone: (765) 285-8151
Fax: (765) 285-5123

Estimated # of Men's Volleyball Scholarships: N/A
Conference: Midwestern Intercollegiate Volleyball Association

Women's Athletic Profile

200 University Avenue
Muncie, IN 47306
Coach: Randy Litchfield
Email: litch@sprynet.com

NCAA I
Lady Cardinals, Cardinal, White
Phone: (765) 285-1465
Fax: (765) 285-5123

Estimated # of Women's Volleyball Scholarships: N/A
Conference: Mid-American Conference
Achievements: 4 Players in the 1998 Pepsi All-Mid-American Conference Team; 31 All-Mid-American Conference selections; 27 Academic All-MAC honorees.
Coaching: Randy Litchfield took over in 1989 as Head Coach. He has had 31 All-Mid-American Conference selections and 27 Academic All-MAC honorees. This is more than any other league institution. Chad Weyenberg is in his 10th season as Assistant Coach. He graduated from Ball State in 1985. He was All-Midwest Intercollegiate Volleyball Association First-Team. Stephanie Decker is Graduate Assistant. She graduated from Ball State in 1992. She was an All-Mid-American Conference First Team member and an Academic All-MAC First Team member.
Most Recent Record: 21-10-0   **Fall Games:** 31   **Spring Games:** 0
Schedule: Tennessee Tech, Austin Peay, Dayton, Texas Tech, Oregon State, Alaska-Fairbanks, Boise State, Indiana State, Duke

Bethel College
Academic Profile

1001 W McKinley Avenue
Mishawaka, IN 46545

Phone: 219-257-3339

Type: Private, 4 Yr., Liberal Arts, Engineering, Coed
Website: http://www.bethel-in.edu
SAT/ACT/GPA: 900/Open/2.0
Student/Faculty Ratio: 18:1
Undergraduate Enrollment: 1,627
Scholarships/Academic: Yes   **Athletic:** Yes
Expenses By: Year   **In State:** $ 17,050
Specializes In: Education, Engineering, ASL
Degrees Conferred: AA, AND, BA, BSN, BS, MM, MBA

Founded: 1947
Religion: Missionary Church
Housing: Yes
Male/Female: 34:66
Graduate Enrollment: N/A
Financial Aid: Yes
Out of State: $ 17,050

Programs of Study: Accounting, American Sign Languages, Art, Biblical Studies, Biology, Business Administration, Business Education, Chemistry, Christian Ministries, Communications, Drama, Elementary Education, PreDentistry, PreLaw, PreMedicine, Engineering, English, English Education, History, Interior Design, Liberal Arts, Mathematics, Music Education, Nursing, Psychology, Recreation Administration, Secondary Education, Science Education, Social Science, Sociology, Visual Communications

Women's Athletic Profile

1001 McKinley Avenue
Mishawaka, IN 46545
Coach: Julia Reininga
Email: reininj@bethel-in.edu

NCAA I
Lady Pilots, Blue, White
Phone: (219) 257-2573
Fax: (219) 257-3385

Did Not Return Profile

Butler University
Academic Profile

4600 Sunset Ave.
Indianapolis, IN 46208

Phone: (800) 368-6852

Type: Private, 4 Yr., Liberal Arts, Engineering, Coed
Website: http://www.butleruniversity.edu
SAT/ACT/GPA: 1000/3.0
Student/Faculty Ratio: 12:1
Undergraduate Enrollment: 3,200
Scholarships/Academic: Yes   **Athletic:** Yes
Expenses By: Year   **In State:** $ 23,000
Specializes In: Pharmacy, Physician's Assistant, TV & Radio
Degrees Conferred: AA, AS, BA, BS, BFA, BM, BSHS, MA, MS, MBA, MM

Founded: 1855
Religion: Independent
Housing: Yes
Male/Female: 40:60
Graduate Enrollment: 800
Financial Aid: Yes
Out of State: $ 23,000

Programs of Study: Accounting, Art, Biology, Business Administration, Chemistry, Composition, Computer Science, Dance, Economics, Education, Elementary Education, German, Journalism, History, Marketing, Management, Music, Mathematics, Philosophy, Religion, Political Science, Telecommunications, Sociology, Pharmacy, Psychology

Women's Athletic Profile

4600 Sunset Avenue
Indianapolis, IN 46208-3485
Coach: Sharon Dingman
Email: sdingman@butler.edu

NCAA I
Lady Bulldogs, Blue, White
Phone: (317) 940-9211
Fax: (317) 940-9808

Estimated # of Women's Volleyball Scholarships: 3
Conference: Midwestern Collegiate Conference
Program Profile: We play at Hinkle Field House. It has 11,043 seats. The center of Butler's strength and conditioning program is the new 3,500 square foot weight training room. The weight room has free weights, weight machines, stationary bikes, stairmasters and related apparatus.
History: We started Division I play in 1982. We have 3 Conference Championships and 3 UAS Post-Season (NIVE & NCAA)
Achievements: 1997 MCC Coach of the Year; 1997 Regular Season & Tournament MCC Champions; All-District Selections; 20+ All-Conference Players; 1997 Player of the Year
Coaching: Sharon Dingman has been head coach at Butler for 7 years. Her overall record is 174-99. Michelle Gurban has been assistant coach for 3 years. Jennifer Kintzel has been assistant coach for 2 years.

Freshman Receiving Financial Aid/Academic:		Athletic: 3
Roster In State: 8	Out of State: 7	Out of Country: 0
Sophomores on Team: 0	Seniors on Team: 3	Graduation %: 80
Most Recent Record: 15-15-0	Fall Games:	Spring Games: 4

Camp of Clinic Dates: July 11-14, July 15-18, July 20-30; Coaches clinic in August
Positions Needed: Setter, Middle Hitter, Outside Hitter
Schedule: Arkansas, University of California-Santa Barbara, Florida, Oral Roberts
Style of Play: Ball control team. Very steady physically and emotionally. Strong academically.

De Pauw University
Academic Profile

Women's Soccer Office
Greencastle, IN 46135

Phone: (800) 446-5295

Type: Private, 4 Yr., Liberal Arts,Coed
Website: http://www.depauw.edu
SAT/ACT/GPA: 1180/25/3.3
Student/Faculty Ratio: 11:1
Undergraduate Enrollment: 2,100
Scholarships/Academic: Yes
Expenses By: Year

Athletic: No
In State: $ 25,810

Founded: 1837
Religion: Methodist
Housing: Yes
Male/Female: 45:55
Graduate Enrollment: N/A
Financial Aid: Yes
Out of State: $ 25,810

Specializes In: Business, Media, Music, Sciences; Honors and Fellows Programs
Degrees Conferred: Bachelor of Arts, Bachelor of Science, Bachelor of Music
Programs of Study: College of Liberal Arts, with a choice of 41 majors including: Biological Sciences, Chemistry, Communications, Economics, Education, Health and Physical Performance, International Studies, Management, Political Science, Psychology, etc. ; Also offers a School of Music with a choice of 5 majors.

Women's Athletic Profile

Lily Center 702 S. College
Greencastle, IN 46135
Coach: Deb Zellers
Email: dzellers@depauw.edu

NCAA I
Lady Tigers, Old Gold, Black
Phone: (765) 658-4969
Fax: (765) 658-4625

Estimated # of Women's Volleyball Scholarships: N/A
Conference: Southern California Athletic Conference
History: We were ranked 8th in the South Region in 1997.
Achievements: 1991 NCAA Division III Championship; Janie Hodgkinson SCAC Player of the Week; Third place at 1997 Calvin Midwest Invitational;
Coaching: Deb Zellers - Head Coach.

Most Recent Record: 28-8-0   **Fall Games:** 36   **Spring Games:** 0
Schedule: Earlham, Hanover, Albion, Olivet, Ohio Wesleyan, Center, Mount St. Joseph, Trinity, Illinois Wesleyan, Hope, St. Mary's, Southwestern

Earlham College
Academic Profile

801 National Road West
Richmond, IN 47374

Phone: 800-327-5426

Type: Private, 4 Yr., Liberal Arts, Coed
Website: http://www.earlham.edu
SAT/ACT/GPA: 1210
Student/Faculty Ratio: 11:1
Undergraduate Enrollment: 1,100
Scholarships/Academic: Yes
Expenses By: Year
Specializes In: Liberal Arts, Education
Degrees Conferred: Bachelors

Athletic: No
In State: $ 25,066

Founded: 1847
Religion: Society of Friends (Quakers)
Housing: Yes
Male/Female: 46:54
Graduate Enrollment: N/A
Financial Aid: Yes
Out of State: $ 25,066

Programs of Study: Art, African-American Studies, Biology, Chemistry, Classics, Computer Science, Economics, Education, English, French, Geology, German, History, Human Development & Social Relations, International Studies, Japanese Studies, Philosophy, Physics, Astronomy, Politics, Psychology, Religion, Sociology, Anthropology, Spanish, Theatre Arts, Women's Studies

Women's Athletic Profile

801 National Road W.
Richmond, IN 47374
Coach: Beth Politi
Email: politbe@earlham.edu

NCAA I
Lady Quakers, Maroon, White
Phone: (765) 983-1490
Fax: (765) 983-1446

Estimated # of Women's Volleyball Scholarships: N/A
Conference: North Coast Athletic Conference
Program Profile: We practice, play and train in the new $13-million Athletic & Wellness Center. The state-of-the-art facility includes outstanding performance and multi-purpose gymnasiums, a large and well-equipped weight training area and spacious locker rooms.
History: Belonging to the NCAA Division III, Earlham offers academic scholarships to qualifying students as well as need-based financial aid.
Achievements: Jenny Maure and Salena Coletta 1998 Quaker Co-MVP's
Coaching: Beth Politi, Head Coach, attended Gettysburg College where she was co-captain and earned All-Centennial Conference first-team honors. Samantha Wolinski is in her first year as assistant coach.
Roster In State: 4   **Out of State:** 5   **Out of Country:** 0
Sophomores on Team: 6   **Seniors on Team:** 0   **Graduation %:** Unknown
Most Recent Record: 11-21-0   **Fall Games:** 32   **Spring Games:** 0
Schedule: Anderson, Indiana Wesleyan, Wittenberg, Franklin, Ohio Wesleyan, Thomas More, Wilmington, DePauw, Kentucky Wesleyan, Kalamazoo, Olivet, Bethany, Saint Francis
Style of Play: We work on essential skills and build confidence. I am a coach who believes in fundamentals.

Franklin College
Academic Profile

501 E Monroe Street
Franklin, IN 46131

Phone: 800-852-0232

Type: Private, 4 Yr., Liberal Arts, Coed
Website: http://www.franklincoll.edu
SAT/ACT/GPA: 1000
Student/Faculty Ratio: 13:1
Undergraduate Enrollment: 900
Scholarships/Academic: Yes
Expenses By: Year
Specializes In: Education, Business, Preprofessional, Athletic Training, Journalism
Degrees Conferred: BA, BS

Athletic: No
In State: $ 18,000

Founded: 1834
Religion: Baptist
Housing: Yes
Male/Female: 45:55
Graduate Enrollment: N/A
Financial Aid: Yes
Out of State: $ 18,000

Programs of Study: Franklin College offers majors in a variety of traditional programs, academic discipline as well as fields which uniquely blend the study of traditional liberal arts and sciences with PreProfessional preparation; 26 majors.

Women's Athletic Profile

501 East Monroe Street
Franklin, IN 46131
Coach: Lori Wilkerson
Email: mwilkerson@iquest.net

NCAA I
Lady Grizzlies, Blue, Gold
Phone: (317) 738-8130
Fax: (317) 738-8248

Estimated # of Women's Volleyball Scholarships: N/A
Conference: Heartland Collegiate Athletic Conference

Goshen College
Academic Profile

1700 S. Main Street
Goshen, IN 46526

Phone: 800-348-7422

Type: Private, 4 Yr., Liberal Arts,Coed
Website: http://www.goshen.edu
SAT/ACT/GPA: 920/19/2.0
Student/Faculty Ratio: 13:1
Undergraduate Enrollment: 1,000
Scholarships/Academic: Yes   **Athletic:** Yes
Expenses By: Year   **In State:** $ 16,920
Degrees Conferred: BA, BS

Founded: 1894
Religion: Mennonite
Housing: Yes
Male/Female: 45:55
Graduate Enrollment: N/A
Financial Aid: Yes
Out of State: $ 16,920

Programs of Study: Accounting, Anthropology, Architecture, Art, Art Therapy, Bible & Religion, Biblical Studies, Business, Business Administration, Chemical Engineering, Chemistry, Church Music, Coaching, Communications, Computer Science, Computer Systems, Data Processing, Early Childhood Education, Economics, Education, Elementary Education, English, Environmental Studies, Family Life, French, German, Graphics Design, Health & Safety, History, International Studies, Journalism, Mathematics, Medical Technology, Music, Music Performance, Music Research, Natural Science, Nursing, Physical Studies, Physics, Political Science, PreEngineering, PreLaw, PreMed, PrePhysical Therapy, PreSeminary, PreVeterinary, Productions Crafts, Psychology, Recreational Leadership, Science, Social Studies, Social Work, Sociology, Spanish, Speech Communication, Sport Communication, Sport Management, Studio Art, TESOL, Theatre, Tropical Agriculture, Visual Arts, Women's Studies.

Women's Athletic Profile

1700 Main Street
Goshen, IN 46526
Coach: Valerie Hershberger
Email:

NCAA I
Maple Leafs, Purple, White
Phone: (219) 535-7494
Fax: (219) 535-7531

Estimated # of Women's Volleyball Scholarships: N/A
Conference: Mid-Central Conference

Grace College
Academic Profile

200 Seminary Drive
Winona, IN 46590

Phone: 800-544-7223

Type: Private, 4 Yr., Liberal Arts, Coed
Website: http://www.grace.edu
SAT/ACT/GPA: 920/19/2.0
Student/Faculty Ratio: 16:1
Undergraduate Enrollment: 777
Scholarships/Academic: Yes   **Athletic:** Yes
Expenses By: Year   **In State:** $ 14,988
Specializes In: Education
Degrees Conferred: BA, BS, BM, MS, AS

Founded: 1948
Religion: Grace Brethren
Housing: Yes
Male/Female: 2:3
Graduate Enrollment: 35
Financial Aid: Yes
Out of State: $ 14,988

Programs of Study: Accounting, Art, Art Education, Biblical Studies, Biology, Biology Education, Business Administration, Business Education, Christian Ministries, Communication, Counseling, Criminal Justice, Education (Elementary, Secondary), English, English Education, French, French Education, General Science, German, German Education, Graphic Arts, International Business, Management Information Systems, Mathematics, Mathematics Education, Music Education, Music Management, Physical Education,

Sports Broadcasting, Sport Journalism, Sports Management, Sports Medicine, Sports Psychology, Teaching Major, PreDentistry, PreLaw, PreMed, PrePharmacy, PrePhysical Therapy, Psychology, Russian, Science Education, Sociology, Spanish, PreVeterinary Medicine

Women's Athletic Profile

200 Seminary Drive
Winona Lake, IN 46590
Coach: Candace Moats
Email: HAUNRE@grace.edu

NCAA I
Lady Lancers, Red, White
Phone: (219) 372-5217
Fax: (219) 372-5677

Estimated # of Women's Volleyball Scholarships: N/A
Conference: Mid-Central Conference (MCC)
Program Profile: Grace plays in Lancer Gym, which seats 15,000 people. The Lancers play approximately 40 matches in the Fall season, competing in one of the toughest conference in the country at the NAIA level.
Coaching: Candace Moats, Head Coach, began coaching in 1985 with a record of 262-122. She started coaching at Grace in 1995 with a record of 138-47. She has been named NCCAA Coach of the Year three times in the 1990's. Cindy Younis is assistant coach.

Roster In State: 3	**Out of State:** 9	**Out of Country:** 0
Sophomores on Team: 0	**Seniors on Team:**	**Graduation %:** Unknown
Most Recent Record: 19-16-0	**Fall Games:** 35-45	**Spring Games:** 0
Schedule: Bethel, Taylor		

Hanover College
Academic Profile

P. O. Box 809
Hanover, IN 47243

Phone: (812) 866-7388

Type: Private, 4 Yr., Liberal Arts, Coed
Website: http://www.hanover.edu
SAT/ACT/GPA: 1145/25/3.0
Student/Faculty Ratio: 11:1
Undergraduate Enrollment: 1,050
Scholarships/Academic: Yes
Expenses By: Year
Specializes In: Not Available
Degrees Conferred: BA

Athletic: No
In State: $ 15,000

Founded: 1827
Religion: Presbyterian
Housing: Yes
Male/Female: 48:52
Graduate Enrollment: N/A
Financial Aid: Yes
Out of State: $ 15,000

Programs of Study: Anthropology, Biology, Broadcasting, Business Administration, Chemistry, Communications, Dramatic Arts, Economics, Education, English, Film Arts, French, Geology, German, History, International Relations, Management, Mathematics, Music, Philosophy, Physics, Political Science, PreDentistry, PreLaw, PreMed, Psychology, Religion, Social Science, Sociology, Spanish, Speech Pathology, Telecommunications, Theatre

Women's Athletic Profile

P.O. Box Main Street
Hanover, IN 47243
Coach: Peter Preocanin
Email: hall@hanover.edu

NCAA I
Lady Panthers, Red, Blue
Phone: (812) 866-7385
Fax: (812) 866-2164

Estimated # of Women's Volleyball Scholarships: N/A
Conference: Heartland Collegiate Athletic Conference
Program Profile: Panthers play in the 2,000-seat air conditioned Collier Arena in the Horner Center, which was completed in 1995.
History: Our program began in 1971 and were Conference Champions in 1992, 1993 & 1997. Winning seasons 10 out of the past 11 seasons.
Achievements: Lynn Hall was named Coach of the Year in 1992, 1993 & 1997, same years won Conference Titles.
Coaching: Peter Preocanin is entering his first season with the program. He spent previous three years as the Hanover's assistant coach. He played on National Canadian Teams in the late 1980's.
Freshman Receiving Financial Aid/Academic:

		Athletic: 0
Roster In State: 8	**Out of State:** 4	**Out of Country:** 0
Sophomores on Team: 1	**Seniors on Team:** 2	**Graduation %:** 98
Most Recent Record: 18-13-0	**Fall Games:** 36	**Spring Games:** 0
Positions Needed: Setter, Middle Hitters		

Huntington College
Academic Profile

2303 College Avenue
Huntington, IN 46750

Phone: 219-356-6000

Type: Private, 4 Yr., Liberal Arts, Coed
Website: http://www.huntcol.edu
SAT/ACT/GPA: 800/18
Student/Faculty Ratio: 12:1
Undergraduate Enrollment: 700
Scholarships/Academic: Yes
Expenses By: Year
Degrees Conferred: AA, BA, BS, Masters

Athletic: Yes
In State: $ 14,900

Founded: 1897
Religion: United Brethren
Housing: Yes
Male/Female: 49:51
Graduate Enrollment: 50
Financial Aid: Yes
Out of State: $ 14,900

Programs of Study: Accounting, Arts, Biblical Studies, Biology, Broadcasting, Business Administration, Chemistry, Communications, Computer Science, Economics, Education, Elementary Education, English, Graphic Art, History, Management, Mathematics, Medical Technology, Ministries, Music, Natural Resources, Philosophy, Physical Education, Physical Fitness/Exercise Science, PreDentistry, PreEngineering, PreLaw, PreMed, PreVet, Psychology, Recreation & Leisure, Religion, Science, Secondary Education, Sociology, Special Education, Theatre, Theology.

Women's Athletic Profile

2303 College Avenue
Huntington, IN 46750
Coach: Dave Schroeder
Email:

NCAA I
Lady Foresters, Green, Red
Phone: (219) 359-4212x4289
Fax: (219) 356-4090

Estimated # of Women's Volleyball Scholarships: N/A
Conference: Mid-Central Conference

Indiana State University
Academic Profile

200 N. 6th Street
Terre Haute, IN 47809

Phone: 800-742-0891

Type: Public, 4 Yr., Coed
Website: http://www.indstate.edu
SAT/ACT/GPA: 820/20
Student/Faculty Ratio: 20:1
Undergraduate Enrollment: 11,870
Scholarships/Academic: Yes
Expenses By: Year

Athletic: Yes
In State: $ 7,050

Founded: 1865
Religion: Non-Affiliated
Housing: Yes
Male/Female: 49:1
Graduate Enrollment: 1,500
Financial Aid: Yes
Out of State: $ 11,346

Degrees Conferred: AA, AS, AAS, BA, BS, BFA, MA, MS, MBA, MFA
Programs of Study: Accounting, Anthropology, Athletic, Banking/Finance, Biology, Business, Chemistry, Communications, Computer, Dietetics, Economics, Education, Engineering, English, Medical, Nursing, Office, Parks/Recreation, PreProfessional Programs, Religion, Safety, Textiles/Clothing, Urban Studies

Women's Athletic Profile

200 N. 6th Street
Terre Haute, IN 47809
Coach: Jim Bertoli
Email: athberto@scifac.instate.edu

NCAA I
Lady Sycamores, Blue, White
Phone: (812) 237-4171
Fax: (812) 237-4157

Estimated # of Women's Volleyball Scholarships: N/A
Conference: Midwestern Collegiate Conference

Indiana University
Academic Profile

Assembly Hall 1001 El 17th Street
Bloomington, IN 47408-1590

Phone: (812) 855-3989

Type: Public, 4 Yr., Coed
Website: http://www.athletics.indiana.edu
SAT/ACT/GPA: 800/19
Student/Faculty Ratio: Not Avai
Undergraduate Enrollment: 27,000
Scholarships/Academic: Yes   **Athletic:** Yes
Expenses By: Year   **In State:** $ 12,332

Founded: 1820
Religion: Non-Affiliated
Housing: Yes
Male/Female: 1:3
Graduate Enrollment: 6,500
Financial Aid: Yes
Out of State: $ 20,948

Specializes In: Business, Music, Journalism, Health, Physical Education and Recreation
Degrees Conferred: BA, BS, BFA, MBE, BSGS, AA, MA, MFA, MED, PH.D, OD, JD
Programs of Study: Over 850 degree programs offered including: Business, Criminal Justice, Education, Exercise Science, Music, Political Science, Psychology, Sports Marketing

Women's Athletic Profile

Assembly Hall
Bloomington, IN 47405
Coach: Katie Weismiller
Email: kueismil@indiana.edu

NCAA I
Lady Hoosiers, Red, White
Phone: (812) 855-3989
Fax: (812) 855-9401

Estimated # of Women's Volleyball Scholarships: 12
Conference: Big Ten Conference
Program Profile: We play at a volleyball/wrestling arena which seats 2,500 people. A new 2,000 seat arena will be built for women's basketball and women's volleyball in a few years.
History: In 1975, we became a varsity sport. We joined the Big 10 in 1985. We were in the NCAA playoffs in 1995 and 1998.
Achievements: Julie Fickley- All-District 1997; Ryann Connors - NCAA Player of the Week.
Coaching: Katie Weismiller became head coach in 1993. Her record is 142-143. She was All-Southern Conference Selection in 1983-1986 at UTA. Elaine Oden became assistant coach in 1998. She was a 1992 and 1996 Olympian. She was also 1985-86 National Champion at UDP. Anne Kordes started as assistant coach in 1999. She was an All-American at the University of Louisville.
Freshman Receiving Financial Aid/Academic: **Athletic:** 2
Roster In State: 6   **Out of State:** 10   **Out of Country:** 0
Sophomores on Team: 3   **Seniors on Team:** 5   **Graduation %:** 100
Most Recent Record: 20-12-0   **Fall Games:** 31   **Spring Games:** 14
Camp of Clinic Dates: Resident Camps: July 10-13, (Advanced) July 14-17; Commuter Camp
Positions Needed: 5 scholarships - need every position
Schedule: Penn State, Wisconsin, Illinois, Michigan State, Ohio State, Florida State, Duke
Style of Play: A 5-1 offense that is a traditionally good passing and defensive team. A quick offense that outsmarts its opponents rather that over power them.

Indiana University - PU/Fort Wayne
Academic Profile

2101 Coliseum Blvd.
Fort Wayne, IN 46805

Phone: (219) 481-6643

Type: Public, 4 Yr., Liberal Arts, Engineering, Coed
Website: http://www.ipfw.indiana.edu
SAT/ACT/GPA: 820/2.0
Student/Faculty Ratio: 22:1
Undergraduate Enrollment: 11,000
Scholarships/Academic: Yes   **Athletic:** Yes
Expenses By: Year   **In State:** $ 6,100

Founded: 1973
Religion: Non-Affiliated
Housing: No
Male/Female: 1:1
Graduate Enrollment: N/A
Financial Aid: Yes
Out of State: $ 12,100

Degrees Conferred: Associates, Bachelors, Masters
Programs of Study: We offer over 140 degrees.

Men's Athletic Profile

2101 E. Coliseum Blvd.
Fort Wayne, IN 46805-1499
Coach: Arnie Ball
Email:

NCAA II
Mastadons/Blue, White
Phone: (219) 481-6643
Fax: (219) 481-6002

Estimated # of Men's Volleyball Scholarships: 4.5
Conference: Midwestern Intercollegiate Volleyball Association
Program Profile: Will be playing an NCAA Division II in a 3,000 seat arena with an average attendance of 1,400. Playing season is in the spring which starts January through March.
History: The program began in 1981; has participated in four NCAa Finals (1991, 1992, 1994 & 1999); This year's record is 23-4.
Achievements: Has 4 Coach of the Year; 5 Conference Titles, 5 all-Americans; USA MW's Team starting setter.
Coaching: Arnie Ball, Head Coach, started with the program in 1981 with a record of 324-229. He was named Conference Coach of the Year when he was at Ball State. He was a former player at Ball State in 1964-1967.
Freshman Receiving Financial Aid/Academic: 1   **Athletic:** 2
Roster In State: 2   **Out of State:** 11   **Out of Country:** 1
Sophomores on Team: 2   **Seniors on Team:** 5   **Graduation %:** 90%
Fall Games: 4   **Spring Games:** 28
Camp or Clinic Dates: July 12-15; July 19-22
Positions Needed: Setter, Middle, Outside
Schedule: USC, Penn State, Ohio State, Long Beach, Hawaii, UCLA
Style of Play: Play a strong defense (Big team) offensive with many options.

Women's Athletic Profile

2101 Coliseum Boulevard E
Fort Wayne, IN 46805
Coach: Kelley Hartley
Email: hartleyk@ipfw.edu

NCAA I
Lady Mastadons, Blue, White
Phone: (219) 481-6021
Fax: (219) 481-6002

Estimated # of Women's Volleyball Scholarships: N/A
Conference: GLVC

Indiana University - Purdue University at Indianapolis
Academic Profile

901 W New York St.
Indianapolis, IN 46202

Phone: (317) 278-1823

Type: Public, 4 Yr., Liberal Arts, Engineering, Coed
Website: http://www.iupui.edu
SAT/ACT/GPA: 840/18/2.0
Student/Faculty Ratio: 8:1
Undergraduate Enrollment: 21,000
Scholarships/Academic: Yes   **Athletic:** Yes
Expenses By: Year   **In State:** $ 6,952

Founded: 1969
Religion: Non-Affiliated
Housing: Yes
Male/Female: 55:45
Graduate Enrollment: 7,200
Financial Aid: Yes
Out of State: $ 12,438

Specializes In: Liberal Arts, Engineering, Medical, Law, Education, Business
Degrees Conferred: AA, AS, AAS, BA, BS, BAE, BGS, BSE, BSEE, BSME, BSW, MA, MS, MBA
Programs of Study: Accounting, Anthropology, Art History, Banking and Finance, Biology, Business, Chemistry, City Planning, Communications, Computer Science & Technology, Economics, Education, Engineering, Engineering Technology, Marketing, Mathematics, Nursing, Philosophy, Physics, Political Science, Psychology, Telecommunications, Public Administration

Women's Athletic Profile

901 W. New York Street, ste. 105
Indianapolis, IN 46202
Coach: Steve Payne
Email: scpayne@iupui.edu
Estimated # of Women's Volleyball Scholarships: 12
Conference: Mid-Continent Conference
Program Profile: We play at IUPUI Gymnasium with a seating capacity 1,800.
History: 1998 was first season as a Division I program.

NCAA I
Jaguars, Red, Gold
Phone: (317) 274-0620
Fax: (317) 274-0609

Coaching: Steve Payne, Head Coach with a record of 30-35. Jill Bakle is our Assistant Coach.
Freshman Receiving Financial Aid/Academic: **Athletic:** 2
Roster In State: 12 **Out of State:** 1 **Out of Country:** 0
Sophomores on Team: 6 **Seniors on Team:** 1 **Graduation %:** 100
Most Recent Record: 13-17-0 **Fall Games:** 30 **Spring Games:** 0
Schedule: Southern Mississippi, Oral Roberts, Arkansas State, Butler, Ball State, Loyola University-Chicago
Style of Play: Very aggressive and a fast offense.

Indiana University Southeast
Academic Profile

4201 Grantline Rd. **Phone:** 800-852-8835
New Albany, IN 47150

Type: Public, 4 Yr., Coed **Founded:**
Website: http://www.ius.indiana.edu **Religion:** Non-Affiliated
SAT/ACT/GPA: Open **Housing:** No
Student/Faculty Ratio: **Male/Female:**
Undergraduate Enrollment: 5,500 **Graduate Enrollment:** N/A
Scholarships/Academic: **Athletic:** **Financial Aid:**
Expenses By: Year **In State:** $ 2,500+ **Out of State:** $ 7,000+
Degrees Conferred:
Programs of Study: Accounting, Biological, Business, Chemistry, Computer, Communications, Early Childhood Education, Economics, Education, English, Geography, History, Management, Marketing, Math, Music, Nursing, Political Science, Psychology, Secondary Education, Social Science

Women's Athletic Profile

4201 Grantline Road **NCAA I**
New Albany, IN 47150 Grenadiers, Red, White, Navy
Coach: Robin Farris **Phone:** (812) 941-2438
Email: **Fax:** (812) 941-2434

Estimated # of Women's Volleyball Scholarships: 2
Conference: Kentucky Intercollegiate Athletic Conference
Program Profile: Our facility is good and has a seating capacity of 1,500. The playing season is from August 15th through December 1.
History: Our program has been in existence for almost 20 years.
Achievements: Robin Farris was named Coach of the Year in 1998; Conference titles in 1998 and 1997.
Coaching: Robin Farris, Head Coach, compiled a record of 156-130 in nine years. Bernie Merkel is assistant coach.
Roster In State: 12 **Out of State:** 1 **Out of Country:** 0
Sophomores on Team: 0 **Seniors on Team:** 2 **Graduation %:** Unknown
Most Recent Record: 24-3-0 **Fall Games:** 30 **Spring Games:** 0
Positions Needed: 5
Style of Play: Based upon talent and athlete's ability of current team.

Indiana Wesleyan University
Academic Profile

4201 South Washington St. **Phone:** (765) 677-2318
Marion, IN 46953
Type: Private, 4 Yr., Liberal Arts, Coed **Founded:** 1920
Website: http://www.indwes.edu **Religion:** Wesleyan
SAT/ACT/GPA: 840/17/2.3 **Housing:** Yes
Student/Faculty Ratio: 17:1 **Male/Female:** 2:3
Undergraduate Enrollment: 1,800 **Graduate Enrollment:** 125
Scholarships/Academic: Yes **Athletic:** Yes **Financial Aid:** Yes
Expenses By: Year **In State:** $ 16,340 **Out of State:** $ 16,340
Specializes In: Education, Nursing, Psychology, Athletic Training, Sports Management
Degrees Conferred: AA, AS, BA, BS, MA, Master of Education, Master in Counseling and Ministerial Education, Master in Business Management and Community Health, MS, MBA
Programs of Study: Accounting, Art, Art Education, Athletic Training, Biology, Chemistry, Business Administration, Commercial Arts, Criminal Justice, Mathematics, Economics, Education, Physical Education, Social Science, Political Science, Nursing Education,

Management, Marketing, Psychology, Social Studies, Sociology, Christian Ministry

Women's Athletic Profile

4201 W. Washington
Marion, IN 46953
Coach: Deane Webb
Email: dwebb@indwes.edu

NCAA I
Lady Wildcats, Red, Grey
Phone: (765) 677-2322
Fax: (765) 677-2328

Estimated # of Women's Volleyball Scholarships: 3
Conference: Mid-Central Conference
Program Profile: Our facilities include 5 courts and the Lucky Center Gymnasium has a seating capacity of 2,500. The season starts August 15 and goes through December 5.
History: We began in 1978. We were strong in the early mid-1980's. We were fair in the late 1980's. We were weak in the early mid-1990's, but we are strong in the late 1990's.
Achievements: MCC Coach of the Year in 1998; Great Lakes Region Coach of the Year in 1998; AVCA Tachikara nominee for National Coach of the Year.
Coaching: Deane Webb is our Head Coach. Alyne Thoman, Ken Carver and Jessica Keller are assistant coaches.
Freshman Receiving Financial Aid/Academic: **Athletic:** 4
Roster In State: 6   **Out of State:** 5   **Out of Country:** 0
Sophomores on Team: 0   **Seniors on Team:** 1   **Graduation %:** 100
Most Recent Record: 35-16-0   **Fall Games:** 50   **Spring Games:** 10
Camp of Clinic Dates: June 17-19
Positions Needed: 2 Middle, Outside, 1 Setter
Schedule: Columbia, Bethel, Taylor, Cornerstone College
Style of Play: Fast, multiple attack offense; led the nation (NAIA) in digs per game; defense centered.

Manchester College
Academic Profile

4015 Wedgewood
North Manchester, IN 46962

Phone: (219) 982-5000

Type: Private, 4 Yr., Liberal Arts, Coed
Website: http://www.manchester.edu
SAT/ACT/GPA: Open
Student/Faculty Ratio: 14:1
Undergraduate Enrollment: 1,100
Scholarships/Academic: Yes   **Athletic:** No
Expenses By: Year   **In State:** $ 18,140+
Founded: 1889
Religion: Church of the Brethren
Housing: Yes
Male/Female: 50:50
Graduate Enrollment: N/A
Financial Aid: Yes
Out of State: $ 18,140+
Specializes In: Accounting, Education, Social Work
Degrees Conferred: BA, BS, Masters in Accounting
Programs of Study: Accounting, Art, Biology, Business, Chemistry, Computer Science, Economics, Communications, PreEngineering, Education-Elementary & Secondary, PreLaw, Music, Math, Physical Education, Political Science, History, PreMed, Psychology, Physics, Sociology, Social Work, Athletic Training, Peace Studies, Philosophy, English, Modern Languages, Criminal Justice

Women's Athletic Profile

604 College Avenue
North Manchester, IN 46962
Coach: Eric Field
Email:

NCAA I
Lady Spartans, Black, Gold
Phone: (219) 982-5000
Fax: (219) 982-6868

Estimated # of Women's Volleyball Scholarships: N/A
Conference: Heartland Collegiate Athletic Conference
Program Profile: We play in the Fall and practice in the Spring. We use our main arena for practice and game, which seats 1,200. We are a growing program.
History: . We won Conference Titles in the middle 1980's. Our first 20 win season was in 1997.

Coaching: Eric Field has been head coach for two years. His overall record is 28-37.

Roster In State: 15   **Out of State:** 2   **Out of Country:** 0

Sophomores on Team: 4   **Seniors on Team:** 3   **Graduation %:** Unknown

Most Recent Record: 8-23-0   **Fall Games:** 35   **Spring Games:** 0

Positions Needed: Middle Hitter, Setter, Outside Hitter

Schedule: Ohio Northern, Kalamazoo, Hope, Calvin, Wittenberg, Mount Saint Joseph

Style of Play: We have a quick attack with concentration on serve and serve reception.

Marian College
Academic Profile

3200 Cold Spring Road
Indianapolis, IN 46222

Phone: (317) 955-6116

Type: Private, 4 Yr., Liberal Arts, Coed   **Founded:** 1936

Website: http://www.marian.edu   **Religion:** Catholic

SAT/ACT/GPA: 860/18/2.3   **Housing:** Yes

Student/Faculty Ratio: 13:1   **Male/Female:** 2:3

Undergraduate Enrollment: 1,400   **Graduate Enrollment:** N/A

Scholarships/Academic: Yes   **Athletic:** Yes   **Financial Aid:** Yes

Expenses By: Year   **In State:** $ 19,892   **Out of State:** $ 19,892

Specializes In: Nursing, Education, Business & Finance

Degrees Conferred: AA, AS, BA, BS, BSN, AN

Programs of Study: Accounting, Art, Art History, Athletic Training, Biology, Business Administration, Chemistry, Coaching Endorsement, Computer Study, Economics, Elementary Education, Finance, Health & Safety, Interior Design, Liberal Arts, Nursing, Psychology, Philosophy, Religion, Sport Management, Sociology, Theatre, Theology

Women's Athletic Profile

3200 Cold Spring Rd.
Indianapolis, IN 46222
Coach: Dan Findley
Email:

NCAA I
Lady Knights, Blue, Gold
Phone: (317) 955-6119
Fax: (317) 955-6448

Estimated # of Women's Volleyball Scholarships: 2

Conference: Mid-Central Conference

Program Profile: We have one gymnasium that seats 1,500. Our program on upswing since 1997-1998 season. Our record is 25-6 set school record also have 20 consecutive match wins.

Achievements: 1988 Conference Champs, 1998-1999 we were 3rd place in conference.

Coaching: Dan Findley, Head Coach, compiled a record of 20-11 in 1998. Marsha Shoemaker is the Assistant Coach, started with the program in 1999.

Freshman Receiving Financial Aid/Academic: **Athletic:** 4

Roster In State: 15   **Out of State:** 0   **Out of Country:** 0

Sophomores on Team: 0   **Seniors on Team:** 1   **Graduation %:** 100

Most Recent Record: 20-11-0   **Fall Games:** 35   **Spring Games:** 6

Positions Needed: Setter

Schedule: Mount Vernon, Taylor, Bethel, Olivet Nazarene, St. Francis, University of Indianapolis

Style of Play: We are currently running a 6-1 system. We use multiple options and quick options.

Oakland City University
Academic Profile

143 Lucretia St.
Oakland City, IN 47660

Phone: 800-737-5125

Type: Private, 4 Yr., Coed   **Founded:** 1885

Website: Not Available   **Religion:** Non-Affiliated

SAT/ACT/GPA: 800/21   **Housing:** Yes

Student/Faculty Ratio: 15:1   **Male/Female:** 49:51

Undergraduate Enrollment: 742   **Graduate Enrollment:** 10

Scholarships/Academic: Yes   **Athletic:** Yes   **Financial Aid:** Yes

Expenses By: Year   **In State:** $ 11,250   **Out of State:** $ 11,250

Degrees Conferred: AA, AS, AAS, BA, BS, M
Programs of Study: Accounting, Biology, Business Administration, Business Education, Elementary Education, English, Humanities, Mathematics, Music, Physical Education, Religion, Science, Visual Arts

Women's Athletic Profile

143 Lucretia Street
Oakland City, IN 47660-1099
Coach: Patti Buchta
Email:

NCAA I
Lady Oaks, Navy, White
Phone: (812) 749-1265
Fax: (812) 749-1291

Estimated # of Women's Volleyball Scholarships: N/A
Conference: Independent

Purdue University
Academic Profile

1080 Schleman Hall
W. Lafayette, IN 47907

Phone: 765-494-1776

Type: Public, 4 Yr., Coed
Website: http://www.purdue.edu
SAT/ACT/GPA: Open
Student/Faculty Ratio: 13:1
Undergraduate Enrollment: 28,000
Scholarships/Academic: Yes
Expenses By: Year
Degrees Conferred: BA, BS, Preprofessional programs
Programs of Study: All

Founded: 1869
Religion: Non-Affiliated
Housing: Yes
Male/Female: 55:45
Graduate Enrollment: 9,000
Athletic: Yes **Financial Aid:** Yes
In State: $ 10,984 **Out of State:** $ 19,334

Women's Athletic Profile

1790 Mackey Arena
West Lafayette, IN 47907
Coach: Jeff Hulsmeyer
Email: lleaton@purdue.edu

NCAA I
Boilermakers, Old Gold, Black
Phone: (765) 494-0605
Fax: (765) 496-1280

Estimated # of Women's Volleyball Scholarships: 4
Conference: Big Ten Conference
Program Profile: Program is building. Have new coaches, Entering second season. Compete in Intercollegiate Athletic facility that seats up to 2000.
History: Purde Volleyball started in the fall of 1975 and was coached by Carol Dewey. They have won 4 big Ten Championships
Achievements: 4 times as Big Ten Champions
Coaching: Jeff Hulsmeyer- summer 1999, Laura Leaton summer 1999
Freshman Receiving Financial Aid/Academic: **Athletic:** 2
Roster In State: 3 **Out of State:** 8 **Out of Country:** 1
Sophomores on Team: 2 **Seniors on Team:** 2 **Graduation %:** 100
Most Recent Record: 14-15 **Fall Games:** 29
Positions Needed: All positions
Schedule: American Univ., George Washington Univ., Kansas, Penn State, Illinois, Wisconsin, Minnesota, Ohio State, W.Michigan, Boston College
Style of Play: Dynamic and flexible

Purdue University - Calumet
Academic Profile

2200 - 169th Street
Hammond, IN 46323

Phone: 219-989-2213

Type: Public, 4 Yr., Liberal Arts, Coed
Website: http://www.calumet.purdue.edu
SAT/ACT/GPA: 830+

Founded: 1946
Religion: Non-Affiliated
Housing: Yes

Student/Faculty Ratio: 30:1
Undergraduate Enrollment: 7,500
Scholarships/Academic: Yes   **Athletic:** Yes
Expenses By: Year   **In State:** $ 4,000
Specializes In: Engineering, Professional Studies
Degrees Conferred: AA, AS, BA, BS, BSCh, BSE, MA, MS

Male/Female: 50:50
Graduate Enrollment: 800
Financial Aid: Yes
Out of State: $ 7,000

Programs of Study: Accounting, Banking & Finance, Biology, BioTechnology, Broadcasting, Chemistry, Communications, Computer Science, Computer Technology, Criminal Justice, Economics, Education, Electrical Engineering & Technology, English, French, German, History, Hotel/Restaurant Management, Industrial Engineering, Information Science, International Relations, Marketing, Mathematics, Mechanical Engineering & Technology, Medical Technology, MicroBiology, Nursing, Optometry, Philosophy, Physical Therapy, Physics, Political Science, PreDentistry, PreLaw, PreMed, PrePharmacy, PreVeterinary, Psychology, Social Science, Spanish, Zoology.

Women's Athletic Profile

2200 169th Street
Calumet, IN 46323
Coach: Sallee Malinich
Email:

NCAA I
Lady Lakers, Gold, Black
Phone: (219) 989-2556
Fax: (219) 989-2766

Estimated # of Women's Volleyball Scholarships: N/A
Conference: CCAC

Rose - Hulman Institute of Technology
Academic Profile

5500 Wabash Avenue
Terre Haute, IN 47803

Phone: 800-248-7448

Type: Private, 4 Yr., Engineering, Coed
Website: http://www.rose-hulman.edu
SAT/ACT/GPA: 550 M/ 500V SAT
Student/Faculty Ratio: 12:1
Undergraduate Enrollment: 1,500
Scholarships/Academic: Yes   **Athletic:** No
Expenses By: Year   **In State:** $ 29,200
Specializes In: Math, Science, Engineering
Degrees Conferred: BS, MS

Founded: 1874
Religion: Non-Affiliated
Housing: Yes
Male/Female: 4:1
Graduate Enrollment: 100
Financial Aid: Yes
Out of State: $ 29,200

Programs of Study: Civil Engineering, Computer Engineering, Electrical Engineering, Mechanical Engineering, Applied Optics, Chemistry, Computer Science, Economics, Mathematics, Physics

Women's Athletic Profile

5500 Wabash Avenue
Terre Haute, IN 47803
Coach: Brenda Davis
Email: brenda.davis@rose-hulman.edu
Estimated # of Women's Volleyball Scholarships: N/A
Conference: Southern Collegiate Athletic Conference

NCAA I
Fighting Engineers, Rose, White
Phone: (812) 877-8017
Fax: (912) 877-8407

Program Profile: Facilities- Hulbert Arena (Stadium size 2000) Sports and Recreation Center Built in 1997 Volleyball program is in its 4th year, 2nd year in the SCAC
History: total overall record 20-64, Hosted Conference Championship in 1997-1998
Achievements: 2 players 3rd team All-Conference 1998
Freshman Receiving Financial Aid/Academic: **Athletic:** 0
Roster In State: 6   **Out of State:** 4   **Out of Country:** 0
Sophomores on Team: 4   **Seniors on Team:** 1   **Graduation %:** 100
Most Recent Record: 6-13   **Fall Games:** 41   **Spring Games:** 0
Camp of Clinic Dates: June of 2000
Positions Needed: Setter, Middle and Outside Hitters, Defensive Specialist
Schedule: Washington University, Illinois Wesleyan University, Trinity University, University of Wisconsin-Platteville, Mount St. Joseph, DePauw, Averett
Style of Play: We have hard working student athletes, with good attitudes and are wonderful to work with. They are a very excitable and scrappy team.

Saint Joseph's College - Indiana
Academic Profile

P.O. Box 875
Rensselaer, IN 47978

Phone: 800-447-8781

Type: Private, 4 Yr., Liberal Arts, Coed
Website: http://www.saintjoe.edu
SAT/ACT/GPA: Open
Student/Faculty Ratio: 14:1
Undergraduate Enrollment: 900-1000
Scholarships/Academic: Yes   **Athletic:** Yes
Expenses By: Year   **In State:** $ 18,380

Founded: 1891
Religion: Catholic
Housing: Yes
Male/Female: 50:50
Graduate Enrollment: N/A
Financial Aid: Yes
Out of State: $ 18,380

Specializes In: Business, Preprofessional Programs, Elementary Education
Degrees Conferred: AA, AS, BA, BS, BSN, MA
Programs of Study: Accounting, BioChemistry, Biology, Business Administration, Chemistry, Communications, Computer Information System, Computer Science, Economics, Education, Elementary Education, English, Human Services, Management, Music, Nursing, Philosophy, Physical Education, Social Science, Physics, Political Science, Humanities, Human Services, GeoPhysics, Psychology, Social Science

Women's Athletic Profile

P.O. Box 875
Rensselaer, IN 47978
Coach: Kevin Furnish
Email: kevinf@saintjoe.edu

NCAA I
Pumas, Maroon, Purple, Black
Phone: (219) 866-6120
Fax: (219) 866-6140

Estimated # of Women's Volleyball Scholarships: 5
Conference: Great Lakes Valley Conference
Program Profile: We are a member of Division II. Our field house has a 5,000 seating capacity. It has a fully equipped weight room. The team plays a fall and spring season.
Coaching: Kevin Furnish, Head Coach, started coaching the program in 1996 with an overall record of 33-54. He graduated from Ball State University. He played 3 years and went to two NCAA Final Fours. Linda Deno is assistant coach.

Freshman Receiving Financial Aid/Academic: **Athletic:** 3
Roster In State: 5   **Out of State:** 5   **Out of Country:** 0
Sophomores on Team: 2   **Seniors on Team:** 1   **Graduation %:** 100
Most Recent Record: 11-18-0   **Fall Games:** 29   **Spring Games:** 4
Positions Needed: Setter, Outside, Middle
Schedule: Northern Kentucky, Indiana University - Purdue/Fort Wayne, Southern Illinois-Edwardsville, Northwood, Quincy University, Lewis University
Style of Play: Aggressive, scrappy, and defensively- oriented team.

Saint Mary's College - Indiana
Academic Profile

Angela Athletic Facility
Notre Dame, IN 46556

Phone: 800-551-7621

Type: Private, 4 Yr., Liberal Arts, Women Only
Website: http://www.saintmarys.edu
SAT/ACT/GPA: 900+
Student/Faculty Ratio: 11:1
Undergraduate Enrollment: 1,550
Scholarships/Academic: No   **Athletic:** No
Expenses By: Year   **In State:** $ 18,000

Founded: 1844
Religion: Catholic
Housing: No
Male/Female: Women
Graduate Enrollment: N/A
Financial Aid: Yes
Out of State: $ 18,000

Degrees Conferred: BA, BS, BFA, BBA, BMus
Programs of Study: Accounting, Anthropology, Art, Art Education, Biology, Business & Management, Chemistry Communications, Creative Writing, Economics, Elementary Education, English, Finance, French, History, Humanities, International Business, Literature, Marketing, Mathematics, Music, Education, Nursing, Philosophy, Political Science, Psychology, Religion, Social Science, Spanish, Theatre

Women's Athletic Profile

Angela Athletic Facility
Notre Dame, IN 46556
Coach: Julie Schroeder-Biek
Email:

NCAA I
Lady Belles, Blue, White
Phone: (219) 284-4908
Fax: (219) 284-4797

Estimated # of Women's Volleyball Scholarships: N/A
Conference: Michigan Intercollegiate Athletic Association

Taylor University
Academic Profile

500 W Read Avenue
Upland, IN 46989

Phone: (765) 998-5376

Type: Private, 4 Yr., Liberal Arts, Coed
Website: http://www.tayloru.edu
SAT/ACT/GPA: 1183/26/3.7
Student/Faculty Ratio: 17:1
Undergraduate Enrollment: 1,880+
Scholarships/Academic: Yes
Expenses By: Year
Specializes In: Liberal Arts
Degrees Conferred: AA, BA, BS, BMEd
Programs of Study: 44 majors available plus PreProfessional programs in Medicine, Engineering, Law & Medical Technology

Athletic: Yes
In State: $ 19,748

Founded: 1846
Religion: Interdenominational
Housing: Yes
Male/Female: 47:53
Graduate Enrollment: N/A
Financial Aid: Yes
Out of State: $ 19,748

Women's Athletic Profile

500 W. Reade Avenue
Upland, IN 46989
Coach: Angie Fincannon
Email: anfincann@tu.edu

NCAA I
Lady Trojans, Purple, Gold
Phone: (765) 998-5317
Fax: (765) 998-4920

Estimated # of Women's Volleyball Scholarships: N/A
Conference: MCC

Tri-State University
Academic Profile

1 University Avenue
Angola, IN 46703

Phone: 800-347-4878

Type: Private, 4 Yr., Coed
Website: http://www.tristate.edu
SAT/ACT/GPA: 800/19
Student/Faculty Ratio: 15:1
Undergraduate Enrollment: 1,200
Scholarships/Academic: Yes
Expenses By: Year
Specializes In: Arts & Science, Engineering, Business
Degrees Conferred: AA, AS, BA, BS
Programs of Study: Arts and Sciences (Biology, Chemistry, Communications, Computer Science, Corporate English, Criminal Justice, Elementary Education, English, Environmental Science, General Studies, History, Individual Studies, Legal Administration, Mathematics, Physical Education, Physical Science, PreMedical, Psychology, Secondary Education, Social Science); Business (Accounting, Applied Management, Business and Arts, Computer Information Systems, General Studies, Management, Marketing, Office Administration); Engineering (Aerospace, Chemical, Civil, Computer Aided Drafting and Design, Electrical and Computer, Engineering Administration, General Studies, Mechanical)

Athletic: Yes
In State: $ 9,000

Founded: 1884
Religion: Non-Affiliated
Housing: Yes
Male/Female: 3:3
Graduate Enrollment: N/A
Financial Aid: Yes
Out of State: $ 9,000

Women's Athletic Profile

1 University Avenue
Angola, IN 46703
Coach: John Wilder
Email: wilderj@tristate.edu

NCAA I
Lady Thunders, Blue, White
Phone: (219) 665-4842
Fax: (219) 665-4839

Estimated # of Women's Volleyball Scholarships: N/A
Conference: Wolverine-Hoosier Conference

University of Evansville
Academic Profile

1800 Lincoln Avenue
Evansville, IN 47722

Phone: 800-423-8633

Type: Private, 4 Yr., Liberal Arts, Engineering, Coed
Website: http://www.evansville.edu
SAT/ACT/GPA: No minimum
Student/Faculty Ratio: 13:1
Undergraduate Enrollment: 2,600
Scholarships/Academic: Yes   **Athletic:** Yes
Expenses By: Year   **In State:** $ 10,600
Specializes In: Physical Therapy, Theatre
Degrees Conferred: BA, BS, BFA, MSPT, MSHCM
Programs of Study: Over 80 degree programs - please visit our website.

Founded: 1854
Religion: Methodist
Housing: Yes
Male/Female: 45:55
Graduate Enrollment: 100
Financial Aid: Yes
Out of State: $ 10,600

Women's Athletic Profile

1800 Lincoln Avenue
Evansville, IN 47722
Coach: Mark Hardaway
Email: mh59@evansville.edu

NCAA I
Aces, Purple, White, Orange
Phone: (812) 479-2755
Fax: (812) 479-2199

Estimated # of Women's Volleyball Scholarships: 3
Conference: Missouri Valley
Freshman Receiving Financial Aid/Academic: **Athletic:** 3
Roster In State: 7   **Out of State:** 4   **Out of Country:** 1
Sophomores on Team: **Seniors on Team:** 3   **Graduation %:** 100%
Most Recent Record: 19-15
Camp of Clinic Dates: 6\11\01 - 6\15\01 Instructional   7\8\01 - 7\13\01 Elite\Specialty   7\23\01 - 7\27\01 Instructional
Positions Needed: All Positions filled (except walk-on)
Schedule: Northern Iowa, Ohio State, South Florida, Loyola-Chicago, Western Kentucky, Illinois State, Southwest Missouri State, Southeast Missouri State.

University of Indianapolis
Academic Profile

1400 E Hanna Avenue
Indianapolis, IN 46227

Phone: 800-232-8634

Type: Private, 4 Yr., Liberal Arts, Coed
Website: http://www.uindy.edu
SAT/ACT/GPA: 900/18/2.5
Student/Faculty Ratio: 14:1
Undergraduate Enrollment: 2,000
Scholarships/Academic: Yes   **Athletic:** Yes
Expenses By: Year   **In State:** $ 19,000
Specializes In: Physical Therapy, Occupational Therapy, Education
Degrees Conferred: AA, AS, BA, BS, MA, MS, MBA
Programs of Study: Business, Education (Elementary & Secondary), Criminal Justice, Music, Art, Drama, Communications, Athletic Training, Health Science

Founded: 1902
Religion: Methodist
Housing: Yes
Male/Female: 45:55
Graduate Enrollment: 1,500
Financial Aid: Yes
Out of State: $ 19,000

Women's Athletic Profile

1400 E. Hanna Avenue
Indianapolis, IN 46227-3697
Coach: Jody Rogers
Email:

NCAA I
Greyhounds, Crimson, Grey
Phone: (317) 788-3578
Fax: (317) 788-3472

Estimated # of Women's Volleyball Scholarships: N/A
Conference: Great Lakes Valley Conference
Program Profile: NCAA II program which competes in the Ruth Litty Center seats 1,000. Our fall season runs from August to November, with a non-traditional season in the spring. Our University is an excellent private institution located 10min from downtown Indianapolis
History: The University of Indianapolis women's volleyball program began in 1978 under current UI Associate Director of Athletics Dr. Sue Willey. Willey guided the Greyhounds to three straight 20 win in 1980-82, with the Hounds posting a 27-11 record in 1981. Current UI head coach Jody Rogers is the fifth coach in program history.
Coaching: Jody Rogers, head coach, started at UI 1998, 9-22 record in one season, Matt Botsford Asst. coach.

Roster In State: 10	**Out of State:** 1	**Out of Country:** 0
Sophomores on Team:	**Seniors on Team:** 1	**Graduation %:**
Most Recent Record: 9-22	**Fall Games:** 31	**Spring Games:**

University of Notre Dame
Academic Profile

Phone: 219-631-7505

Notre Dame, IN 46556

Type: Private, 4 Yr., Liberal Arts, Engineering, Coed
Website: http://www.und.com
SAT/ACT/GPA: 1240 avg/3.5
Student/Faculty Ratio: 12:1
Undergraduate Enrollment: 7,500
Scholarships/Academic: Yes   **Athletic:** Yes
Expenses By: Year   **In State:** $ 27,000
Specializes In: Business, Science

Founded: 1842
Religion: Catholic
Housing: Yes
Male/Female: 53:47
Graduate Enrollment: 3,000
Financial Aid: Yes
Out of State: $ 27,000

Degrees Conferred: BA, BS, BFA, MA, MS, MBA, MFA, Ph.D., JD
Programs of Study: Accounting, American Studies, Architecture, BioChemistry, Biological Sciences, Economics, Engineering (Aerospace, Civil, Computer, Electrical, Environmental, Mechanical) Finance, Government, History, Management Information Systems, Marketing, Mathematics, Philosophy, Physics, PreDental, PreMed, Theatre, Theology

Women's Athletic Profile

Joyce Arena
Notre Dame, IN 46556
Coach: Debbie Brown
Email: Hendrick.2@nd.edu

NCAA I
Lady Fighting Irish, Gold, Blue
Phone: (219) 631-5987
Fax: (219) 631-9690

Estimated # of Women's Volleyball Scholarships: 12
Conference: Big East Conference
Program Profile: We are a member of the Big East Conference. Our home arena is called Joyce Center with a seating capacity of 11,500. National play is scheduled to start from August through December.
History: The program began in 1980. We had 8 straight NCAA Appearances and 3 Sweet Sixteen Appearances.
Achievements: Debbie Brown was named Conference Coach of the Year in 1991 and 1995; 6 All-Americans; 8 Conference Titles; several international players.
Coaching: Debbie Brown, Head Coach, entered her 13th season with a record of 307-141. As a player, she was named two-time all-time All-American at USC. She was National and Olympic team captain in 1980. Steve Hendrick and Jessica Kerr are assistant coaches.

Freshman Receiving Financial Aid/Academic: **Athletic:** All

Roster In State: 2	**Out of State:** 13	**Out of Country:** 0
Sophomores on Team: 0	**Seniors on Team:** 4	**Graduation %:** 100
Most Recent Record: 19-13-0	**Fall Games:** 30-35	**Spring Games:** 4

Camp of Clinic Dates: July 6-10; July 11-15
Positions Needed: Setter, 2 Middle, Outside
Schedule: Pacific, Louisville, BYU, Colorado State, Georgetown, Illinois State
Style of Play: High energy and fun. A very positive environment where work ethic and team chemistry is a priority.

University of Saint Francis (St. Francis College)
Academic Profile

2701 Spring Street
Fort Wayne, IN 46808

Phone: (219) 434-7476

Type: Private, 4 Yr., Liberal Arts, Coed

Founded: 1890

Website: http://www.sf.edu
SAT/ACT/GPA: 920/19/2.0
Student/Faculty Ratio: 18:1
Undergraduate Enrollment: 1560
Scholarships/Academic: Yes   **Athletic:** Yes
Expenses By: Year   **In State:** $ 15,000
Specializes In: Arts, Business, Education, Nursing, Psychology, Social Work
Degrees Conferred: AA, AS, BA, BBA, BS in Education, BS in Nursing, MBA, MSEd, MS
Programs of Study: Accounting, Allied Health, American Studies, Art, Biology, Business Administration, Chemistry, Commercial Art, Communications, Education, English, Environmental Science, Fine Arts, Health and Safety, History, Human Resources, General Science, Medical Technology, Ministry, Nursing, PreLaw, PreMed, PreVet, Protective Services, Psychology, Radiography, Religious Studies, Social Science, Special Education

Religion: Catholic
Housing: Yes
Male/Female: 34:66
Graduate Enrollment: 420
Financial Aid: Yes
Out of State: $ 15,000

Women's Athletic Profile

2701 Spring Street
Ft. Wayne, IN 46808
Coach: Patti Martin
Email: sf.edu/pmartin@sf.edu

NCAA I
Lady Cougars, Blue, White
Phone: (219) 434-7476
Fax: (219) 434-7441

Estimated # of Women's Volleyball Scholarships: 3
Conference: Mid-Central Conference
Program Profile: We participate in the strongest Conference for volleyball in NAIA. We play indoors at Hutzell Athletic Center. Our facilities are five years old. The weight room is one year old. Our season begins at the end of August and the play-offs are in December. Spring season is from March to April.
History: Our program has been in existence for eight years. We won the Conference Title in 1997 and have been ranked as high as 5th in the region.
Achievements: Won Conference in 1997; Had 2 Academic All-Americans this past season; Theresa Shenkel -All-Conference Setter; Jenny Zund and Jody Bradford : All-Conference Honorable Mention
Coaching: Patti Martin - Head Coach. This fall season was the best volleyball season at Saint Francis. We finished 4th in the conference with a 17-17 overall record. Felipe Ralat is assistant coach. He plays on the Puerto Rican National Team. Theresa Schenkel is our other assistant coach.

Roster In State: 18   **Out of State:** 2   **Out of Country:** 0
Sophomores on Team: 0   **Seniors on Team:** 2   **Graduation %:** 100
Most Recent Record: 18-17-0   **Fall Games:** 34   **Spring Games:** 12
Camp of Clinic Dates: None
Positions Needed: Middle Hitter, Outside Hitter
Schedule: Taylor, Olivet Nazarene, Walsh, Bethel, Grace, Indiana Wesleyan
Style of Play: Quick transition offense; hardcore in your-face ball!!!

University of Southern Indiana
Academic Profile

8600 University Blvd.
Evansville, IN 47712

Phone: 800-467-1965

Type: Public, 4 Yr., Coed
Website: http://www.usi.edu
SAT/ACT/GPA: 17/2.0
Student/Faculty Ratio: 26:1
Undergraduate Enrollment: 8,500
Scholarships/Academic: Yes   **Athletic:** Yes
Expenses By: Year   **In State:** $ 6,000
Specializes In: Education
Degrees Conferred: AA, BS, AS, BA, MA, MS, MBA
Programs of Study: Accounting, Business and Management, Science and Technology, PreMed, Allied Health, Communications, Education, Psychology, Social Science

Founded: 1967
Religion: Non-Affiliated
Housing: Yes
Male/Female: 1:5
Graduate Enrollment: N/A
Financial Aid: Yes
Out of State: $ 12,000

Women's Athletic Profile

8600 University Boulevard
Evansville, IN 47712-3534
Coach: Chrissy Smith
Email: smith@usi.edu

NCAA I
Screaming Eagles, Red, White
Phone: (812) 464-1846
Fax: (812) 465-7094

Estimated # of Women's Volleyball Scholarships: N/A
Conference: Great Lakes Valley Conference

Valparaiso University
Academic Profile

Kretzmann Hall
Valparaiso, IN 46383

Phone: (219) 464-5011

Type: Private, 4 Yr., Liberal Arts, Engineering, Coed
Website: http://www.valpo.edu
SAT/ACT/GPA: 1100+/21+/2.85
Student/Faculty Ratio: 12:1
Undergraduate Enrollment: 2,900
Scholarships/Academic: Yes   **Athletic:** Yes
Expenses By: Year   **In State:** $ 22,025

Founded: 1859
Religion: Independent Lutheran
Housing: Yes
Male/Female: 46:54
Graduate Enrollment: 730
Financial Aid: Yes
Out of State: $ 22,025

Specializes In: Engineering, Business, Law School
Degrees Conferred: AS, BA, BS, BSW, MA, M Ed, MM, MS, JD, ML
Programs of Study: Accounting, Art, Biology, Chemistry, Chinese & Japanese Studies, Civil Engineering, Communication, Computer Science, Criminology, Decision Science, Economics, Education, Electrical Engineering, English, Environmental Science, Finance, French, Geography, Geology, German, History, International Economics & Cultural Affairs, International Business, International Service, Management, Marketing, Mathematics, Mechanical Engineering, Meteorology, Music, Nursing, Philosophy, Physical Education, Athletic Training, Sports Management, Physics, Political Science, Psychology, Sociology, Spanish, Theatre/Television Arts, Theology

Women's Athletic Profile

182 Athletics Recreation Center
Valparaiso, IN 46383-6493
Coach: Becky Madden
Email: becky.madden@valpo.edu

NCAA I
Lady Crusaders, Brown, Gold
Phone: (219) 464-5791
Fax: (219) 464-5762

Estimated # of Women's Volleyball Scholarships: 3
Conference: Mid-Continent Conference
Program Profile: Div. I program, we train year-round. Our playing season is Aug-Dec, we play in a 4,200 arena wood floor.
History: Won conference in 1994, 95, 96. 2000 season we went to conference tournament.
Achievements: In my second season at Valparaiso. We are in a rebuilding phase.
Freshman Receiving Financial Aid/Academic: **Athletic:** 5
Roster In State: 1   **Out of State:** 11   **Out of Country:**
Seniors on Team: 3   **Graduation %:** 100
Most Recent Record: 9-26
Camp of Clinic Dates: Overnight-July 8-11, hitters & Setters Clinic July 14, 2001, Day camp July 16-20, 2001
Positions Needed: Outside, RS, Middle
Schedule: Notre Dame, Purdue, Loyola, Indiana State, Milwaukee, Oral Roberts.
Style of Play: Quick tempo, moves the ball around, Variety of play sets, good defensive team

Des Moines

SCHOOL	CITY	AFFILIATION	PAGE
Briar Cliff College	Sioux City	NAIA	256
Buena Vista University	Storm Lake	NCAA III	256
Central College - Iowa	Pella	NCAA III	257
Clarke College	Dubuque	NCAA III	257
Coe College	Cedar Rapids	NCAA III	258
Cornell College	Mt. Vernon	NCAA III	259
Dordt College	Sioux Center	NAIA	260
Drake University	Des Moines	NCAA I	260
Graceland College	Lamoni	NAIA	261
Grand View College	Des Moines	NAIA	261
Grinnell College	Grinnell	NCAA III	262
Indian Hills Community College	Ottumwa	NJCAA	262
Iowa State University	Ames	NCAA I	263
Iowa Wesleyan College	Mt. Pleasant	NAIA	264
Loras College	Dubuque	NCAA III	264
Luther College	Decorah	NCAA III	265
Marycrest International University	Davenport	NAIA	265
Morningside College	Sioux City	NCAA II	266
Mount Mercy College	Cedar Rapids	NAIA	267
Mount Saint Clare College	Clinton	NAIA	267
Northwestern College	Orange City	NAIA	268
Saint Ambrose University	Davenport	NAIA	269
Simpson College	Indianola	NCAA III	270
Southwestern Community College	Creston	NJCAA	271
University of Dubuque	Dubuque	NCAA III	271
University of Iowa	Iowa City	NCAA I	272
University of Northern Iowa	Cedar Falls	NCAA I	273
Upper Iowa University	Fayette	NCAA III	273
William Penn University	Oskaloosa	NCAA III	274

Briar Cliff College
Academic Profile

3303 Rebecca St.
Sioux City, IA 51104-2100

Phone: 800-662-3303

Type: Private, 4 Yr., Liberal Arts, Coed
Website: http://www.briar-cliff.edu
SAT/ACT/GPA: 890/19/2.25
Student/Faculty Ratio: 12:1
Undergraduate Enrollment: 1,150
Scholarships/Academic: Yes
Expenses By: Year
Specializes In: Liberal Arts
Degrees Conferred: BA, BS

Founded: 1930
Religion: Catholic
Housing: Yes
Male/Female: 1:3
Graduate Enrollment: 600

Athletic: Yes
In State: $ 16,578

Financial Aid: Yes
Out of State: $ 16,578

Programs of Study: Majors: Accounting, Art, Biology, Business Administration, Chemistry, Computer Information Systems, Criminal Justice, Elementary Education, English, HPER, History, Human Resource Management, Mass Communications, Photography, Mathematics, Music, Nursing, Psychology, Secondary Education, Social Work, Sociology, Spanish, Theatre, Theology, Writing, PreProfessional Programs: Chiropractic, Church Ministry, Dentistry, Engineering, Law, Medical Technology, Medicine/Physician's Assistant, Occupational Therapy, Optometry, Pharmacy, Physical Therapy, Radiological Technology, Veterinary Medicine

Women's Athletic Profile

3303 Rebecca
Sioux City, IA 51104
Coach: Mary Schroeder
Email: admissions@briarcliff.edu

NCAA I
Lady Chargers, Blue, Gold
Phone: (800) 662-3303
Fax: (712) 279-5410

Estimated # of Women's Volleyball Scholarships: 4.5
Conference: Independent
Program Profile: Briar Cliff's volleyball program is making great strides to become a national contender. We play a great schedule of nationally ranked teams and our goal is to become one of those teams. Our season runs from August to December with a five week spring season. Our facility holds 2,100 people.
History: Marian Pesky began the volleyball program in 1970. She coached the team for 25 seasons accumulating over 600 wins and a national tournament berth in 1979. Briar Cliff continues to be very competitive into next millennium.
Coaching: Mary Schroeder, Head Coach, started in 1996 and compiled a record of 66-61. Denise Burhoop is assistant coach.
Freshman Receiving Financial Aid/Academic:

		Athletic: 9
Roster In State: 7	**Out of State:** 12	**Out of Country:** 0
Sophomores on Team: 0	**Seniors on Team:**	**Graduation %:** 100
Most Recent Record: 23-18-0	**Fall Games:** 28	**Spring Games:** 3

Camp of Clinic Dates: July 19-23; July 26-30; July 30-31
Positions Needed: 7
Schedule: Dordt, BYU, Hawaii Pacific, Northwestern, Graceland, CSM
Style of Play: We run a 5-1 offense and try to keep the tempo quick. We are an excellent defensive team leading our region in digs per game at 22.5.

Buena Vista University
Academic Profile

610 W. 4th Street
Storm Lake, IA 50588

Phone: 712-749-2235

Type: Private, 4 Yr., Liberal Arts, Coed
Website: http://www.bvu.edu
SAT/ACT/GPA: 1075/24
Student/Faculty Ratio: 15:1
Undergraduate Enrollment: 1,250
Scholarships/Academic: Yes
Expenses By: Year
Degrees Conferred: BA, BS

Founded: 1891
Religion: Presbyterian
Housing: Yes
Male/Female: 49:51
Graduate Enrollment: 140

Athletic: No
In State: $ 20,393

Financial Aid: Yes
Out of State: $ 20,393

Programs of Study: 35 majors in the following schools: Communications & Arts, Business, Education, Science, Social Science, Philosophy & Religions

Women's Athletic Profile

610 w. 4th Street
Storm Lake, IA 50588
Coach: Andrea Brinton
Email: brinton@ngw.bvu.edu

NCAA I
Lady Beavers, Navy Blue, Gold
Phone: (712) 749-2253
Fax: (712) 749-1460

Estimated # of Women's Volleyball Scholarships: N/A
Conference: Iowa Intercollegiate Athletic Conference

Central College
Academic Profile

812 University Street
Pella, IA 50219

Phone: (515) 678-5139

Type: Private, 4 Yr., Liberal Arts, Coed
Website: http://www.central.edu
SAT/ACT/GPA: Combination of test scores and class rank & activities
Student/Faculty Ratio: 13:1
Undergraduate Enrollment: 1,300
Scholarships/Academic: Yes   **Athletic:** No
Expenses By: Year   **In State:** $ 17,980
Specializes In: Liberal Arts, Business, Education
Degrees Conferred: Many

Founded: 1853
Religion: Reformed Church
Housing: Yes
Male/Female: 45:55
Graduate Enrollment: N/A
Financial Aid: Yes
Out of State: $ 17,980

Programs of Study: Accounting, Art, Biology, Business Management, Chemistry, Communications, Theatre, Computer Science, Economics, Elementary Education, French, English, German, History, International Management, Mathematics, Science, Music, Music Education, Philosophy, Anthropology, Spanish, Athletic Training

Women's Athletic Profile

812 University Street
Pella, IA 50219
Coach: Megan Clayberg
Email: claybergm@central.edu

NCAA I
Lady Dutch, Red, White
Phone: (641) 628-5139
Fax: 641) 628-5356

Estimated # of Women's Volleyball Scholarships: N/A
Conference: Iowa Intercollegiate Athletic Conference
Program Profile: Kuyper Gymnasium holds 2,500. New fitness center and weightroom addition in 1999. Team typically travels to tournaments throughout the mid-west. JV program typically plays 20-25 matches a season.
History: Program began in 1973. Have won 10 Conference titles, won the NCAA D III National Title in 1998-99. Set NCAA All-Division record for most consecutive wins with 60 matches (2000), 2 time National Player of the Year, Led D III in attendance in 98,99. Record in 1999 41-0
Achievements: 10 Conference titles, 3 All-Americans, National Coach of the Year (98), 2 time National Player of the Year (Abbie Brown)
Coaching: Megan Clayberg (Wayne State Univ), Kent Clayberg (Central, 1990) Doug Frazell (Central, 1999)
Freshman Receiving Financial Aid/Academic: **Athletic:** 0
Roster In State: 33   **Out of State:** 3   **Out of Country:** 0
Sophomores on Team: **Seniors on Team:** 2   **Graduation %:** 100
Most Recent Record: 37-2-0
Positions Needed: ALL
Style of Play: Quick Offense

Clarke College
Academic Profile

1550 Clarke Drive
Dubuque, IA 52001

Phone: (319) 588-6300

Type: Private, 4 Yr., Liberal Arts, Coed
Website: http://www.clarke.edu
SAT/ACT/GPA: 1000 +/21+/2.0-4.0
Student/Faculty Ratio: 12:1

Founded: 1843
Religion: Catholic
Housing: Yes
Male/Female: 35:65

Undergraduate Enrollment: 1,279

Scholarships/Academic: Yes   **Athletic:** No

Expenses By: Year   **In State:** $ 18,668

Graduate Enrollment: 162

Financial Aid: Yes

Out of State: $ 18,668

Degrees Conferred: AA, BA, BS, BFA, MA, BSN, MED, MS

Programs of Study: Accounting, Art, BioChemistry, Business and Management, Chemistry, Communications, Computer Information Systems, Computer Science, Economics, Education, Music, English, French, German, Journalism, Liberal Arts, Marketing, Mathematics, Medical Technology, Nursing, Philosophy, Physical Therapy, Political Science, PreLaw, PreMed, PreVet, Psychology, Public Relations, Religion, Social Science, Theatre

Men's Athletic Profile

1550 Clarke Drive

Dubuque, IA 52001

Coach: Al Ronek

Email: lboike@keller.clarke.edu

NCAA III

Crusaders/Gold, Navy

Phone: (319) 588-6657

Fax: (319) 588-6666

Estimated # of Men's Volleyball Scholarships: 0

Conference: Midwestern Intercollegiate Volleyball Association

History: The men's volleyball program was established as a club in 1994. Our team has ranked sixth nationally in the American Volleyball Coaches Association Division III Top 10 poll as of March 23. Clarke is a Division III team in the MIVA which was formed in the early 1960's. Our program follows the guidelines of the NCAA and the NAIA.

Achievements: Coach Ronek was named Mississippi Valley Conference Coach of the Year in 1986 and 1993.

Coaching: Al Ronek was named head coach in 1995. He is a member of the American Volleyball Coaches Association.

Schedule: La Verne, Juniata, SUNY New Paltz, Mount St. Vincent, Lehman, Medaille

Women's Athletic Profile

1550 Clarke Drive

Dubuque, IA 52001

Coach: Amy Hawkins

Email:

NCAA I

Lady Crusaders, Gold, Blue

Phone: (319) 588-6300

Fax: (319) 588-6666

Estimated # of Women's Volleyball Scholarships: 0

Conference: Northern Illinois-Iowa Conference

Program Profile: We play 22 matches per season. We host 3 tournaments per season. We compete in a 6 team Conference. Our home matches are played at the Kehl Center, which holds about 1,000 fans.

Coaching: Amy Hawkins became head coach in 1998. Jeremy Hawkins became our assistant coach in 1999.

Freshman Receiving Financial Aid/Academic: **Athletic:** 0

Roster In State: 4   **Out of State:** 13   **Out of Country:** 0

Sophomores on Team: 6   **Seniors on Team:** 3   **Graduation %:** 100

Most Recent Record: 19-20-0   **Fall Games:** 22   **Spring Games:** 0

Positions Needed: Middle, Back row Specialist, Utility

Schedule: Benedictine, Dominican, Luther, University of Chicago, University of Dubuque

Style of Play: Up tempo, enthusiastic.

Coe College
Academic Profile

1220 1st Avenue, NE

Cedar Rapids, IA 52402

Phone: 319-399-8500

Type: Private, 4 Yr., Liberal Arts, Coed

Website: http://www.coe.edu

SAT/ACT/GPA: 950/20/3.0

Student/Faculty Ratio: 12:1

Undergraduate Enrollment: 1,100

Scholarships/Academic: Yes   **Athletic:** No

Expenses By: Year   **In State:** $ 23,060

Founded: 1851

Religion: Presbyterian U.S.A.

Housing: Yes

Male/Female: 40:60

Graduate Enrollment: 200

Financial Aid: Yes

Out of State: $ 23,060

Degrees Conferred: BA, BS, Nursing

Programs of Study: Accounting, American Studies, Asian Studies, Biological Sciences, African-American Studies, Business

Administration, Education, English, Environmental Science, French, German, History, Interdisciplinary Studies, Liberal Arts, Literature, Mathematics, Medical Technology, Molecular Biology, Music, Nursing, Philosophy, Physical Education, Physical Sciences, Physics, Political Science, PreLaw, PreVeterinary, Psychology, Religious Studies, Sciences, Social Science, Spanish, Speech, Theatre

Women's Athletic Profile

1220 1st Avenue, NE
Cedar Rapids, IA 52402
Coach: Michelle Woodard
Email: mwoodard@coe.edu

NCAA I
Lady Kohawks, Red, Gold
Phone: (319) 399-8233
Fax: (319) 399-8721

Estimated # of Women's Volleyball Scholarships: N/A
Conference: Iowa Intercollegiate Athletic Conference
Program Profile: We play in one of the toughest Volleyball Conferences in the nation. We just joined this conference two years ago. We play in Eby Gymnasium which has 3 practice floors and a main court with 2,600 seats. The facilities also include a swimming pool, a rock climbing wall and a large weight room. Our fall season starts in the middle of August .
History: We used to play in the Midwest Conference
Achievements: Jean Pregler COSIDA 1987 GTE Academic All-American; 1979 MACW Conference Champions; 1994 Division III Statistical Champions in Team Kills; 1985 MACW Conference Champions.
Coaching: Michelle Woodard became head coach in 1996. Her record here is 27-58. No assistant coach listed.
Freshman Receiving Financial Aid/Academic: **Athletic:** 0
Roster In State: 12   **Out of State:** 3   **Out of Country:** 0
Sophomores on Team: 5   **Seniors on Team:** 2   **Graduation %:** 98
Most Recent Record: 5-24-0
Positions Needed: Middle Hitters
Schedule: Central College, Simpson College, University of Dubuque, UW-La Crosse, Illinois College
Style of Play: Blue collar: work hard on both sides of the play.

Cornell College
Academic Profile

600 First St. West
Mt. Vernon, IA 52314-1098

Phone: 800-747-1112

Type: Private, 4 Yr., Liberal Arts, Coed
Website: http://www.cornell-iowa.edu
SAT/ACT/GPA: 1010/20/3.0-4.0
Student/Faculty Ratio: 14:1
Undergraduate Enrollment: 1,050
Scholarships/Academic: Yes
Expenses By: Year
Specializes In: One Course -at-a -Time Curriculum
Degrees Conferred: BA, BSS, BM, BP
Programs of Study: Biology, Education, English, International Business, Politics, Psychology, Economics, PreProfessional Programs

Founded: 1853
Religion: Non-Affiliated
Housing: Yes
Male/Female: 45:55
Graduate Enrollment: N/A
Financial Aid: Yes

Athletic: No
In State: $ 24,135

Out of State: $ 24,135

Women's Athletic Profile

600 First Street, W
Mt. Vernon, IA 52314
Coach: Shannon Staton
Email: Sstaton@cornell-iowa.edu

NCAA I
Rams, Purple, White
Phone: (319) 895-4257
Fax: (319) 895-5895

Estimated # of Women's Volleyball Scholarships: N/A
Conference: Iowa Intercollegiate Athletic Conference
Program Profile: This prestigious university offers excellent athletic facilities and a wonderful environment for volleyball athletes.
Coaching: Shannon Staton beings her first season as head coach after serving as an assistant for the past two years.
Freshman Receiving Financial Aid/Academic: **Athletic:** 0
Roster In State: 6   **Out of State:** 12   **Out of Country:**
Sophomores on Team: 0   **Seniors on Team:** 2   **Graduation %:** 99
Most Recent Record: 7-0-0
Camp of Clinic Dates: July 2000 - call for more details 319-895-4005

Positions Needed: 8 - 10
Schedule: Central College, Loras College, University of Dubuque, William Penn, Wartburg College, Coe College, Simpson College, Buena Vista University, Lurther College, Upper Iowa University
Style of Play: The team right now is very young but very aggressive and ambitious. The women work hard at maintaining a fast and diverse offense while continuing to push themselves to be relentless defenders.

Dordt College
Academic Profile

498 - 4th Avenue NE
Sioux Center, IA 51250

Phone: (712) 722-2273

Type: Private, 4 Yr., Liberal Arts, Coed
Website: http://www.dordt.edu
SAT/ACT/GPA: 910/19/2.0 to 2.25
Student/Faculty Ratio: 14:1
Undergraduate Enrollment: 1,400
Scholarships/Academic: Yes   **Athletic:** Yes
Expenses By: Year   **In State:** $ 16,500

Founded: 1955
Religion: Christian Reformed
Housing: Yes
Male/Female: 45:54
Graduate Enrollment: 15
Financial Aid: Yes
Out of State: $ 16,500

Specializes In: Elementary/Secondary Education, Social Work, Engineering, Business
Degrees Conferred: AA, BA, BS (Engineering), BSW (Social Work), MA
Programs of Study: Agriculture, Business/Office and Marketing/Distribution, Business and Management, Communications, Education, Letters/Literature, Life Sciences, Multi/Interdisciplinary Studies, Psychology, Social Sciences

Women's Athletic Profile

498 4th Avenue NE
Sioux Center, IA 51250
Coach: Tom Van Don Bosch
Email: tomvb@dordt.edu

NCAA I
Lady Defenders, Black, White
Phone: (712) 722-2273
Fax: (712) 722-1967

Estimated # of Women's Volleyball Scholarships: N/A
Conference: SDIC
Program Profile: We have a new facility that opened in 1997.
History: We competed in the "Elite Eight " in 1998.
Achievements: 1998 Regional Coach of the Year; 4th Straight Conference Championships; National Sportsmanship Award 1998.
Coaching: Tom Van Don Bosch, Head Coach, has a high school coaching career record of 709-71. His college coaching record is 68-19.
Freshman Receiving Financial Aid/Academic: **Athletic:** 8
Roster In State: 10   **Out of State:** 4   **Out of Country:** 0
Sophomores on Team: 2   **Seniors on Team:** 2   **Graduation %:** Unknown
Most Recent Record: 46-5-0   **Fall Games:** 51   **Spring Games:** 10
Positions Needed: Setter
Style of Play: Great team chemistry. Consistently aggressive, no matter what the score is . Play because it is fun.

Drake University
Academic Profile

1421 27th St.
Des Moines, IA 50311

Phone: (800) 44-DRAKE

Type: Private, 4 Yr., Liberal Arts, Coed
Website: http://www.drake.edu
SAT/ACT/GPA: 970
Student/Faculty Ratio: 12:1
Undergraduate Enrollment: 3,000
Scholarships/Academic: Yes   **Athletic:** Yes
Expenses By: Year   **In State:** $ 20,970

Founded: 1881
Religion: Non-Affiliated
Housing: Yes
Male/Female: 42:58
Graduate Enrollment: 2,000
Financial Aid: Yes
Out of State: $ 20,950

Specializes In: Business, Journalism, Law School, Pharmacy
Degrees Conferred: BA, BS, BFA, BMus, BSBA, BSEd, BSN, BSPharm, MA, MS, MBA, MFA, M.Ed., EdD, PharmD
Programs of Study: Accounting, Advertising, Art, Art Education, Art History, Astronomy, Biology, Business Studies, Chemistry, Church Music, Computer Science, Cultural Studies, Early Childhood Education, English, Economics, Business Administration, Electronic Media, Elementary Education, German, Graphic Design, History, International Relations, Journalism, Latin American & Caribbean Area Studies, Military Science, Marine Science, Music, Music Education, Nursing, Painting, Pharmacy, Philosophy, Physics, Political Science, Psychology, Religion, Sociology, Spanish, Theatre Arts, Theatre Education, PreProfessional Programs

Women's Athletic Profile

25th & University
Des Moines, IA 50311-4505
Coach: Blaine Tendler
Email: admitinfo@acad.drake.edu

NCAA I
Lady Bulldogs, Blue, White
Phone: (515) 271-2760
Fax: (515) 271-3015

Estimated # of Women's Volleyball Scholarships: 2
Conference: Missouri Valley
Program Profile: We play in the beautiful Knapp Center, which was built in 1992. It has a capacity for 7,002 seats. The Missouri Valley Conference is very competitive and receives an automatic bid to the NCAA tournament.
History: Our program began in 1978. The best finishes in Conference play have been in 1994, 1995 and 1996. In each of those years, Drake has finished second in the MVC tournament. Drake finished second in the regular season in 1995 and 1996.
Achievements: Drake has had 6 first team All-Conference players, 5 MVC All-Tournament selections, 7 MVC Scholar athletes, 1 All-Newcomer Team player and 1 MVC Player of the Year.
Coaching: Blaine Tendler became head coach in 1998. His record that year was 13-14. He coached 4 years at the Division I level and has also coached internationally in Canada, Germany and France. Mary Tendler started as assistant coach in 1998. She coached 6 years at the Division I level and was a 3 time All-American at Illinois.
Freshman Receiving Financial Aid/Academic: **Athletic:** 2
Roster In State: 5   **Out of State:** 8   **Out of Country:** 0
Sophomores on Team: 0   **Seniors on Team:** 2   **Graduation %:** Unknown
Most Recent Record: 13-14-0   **Fall Games:** 29   **Spring Games:** 14
Camp of Clinic Dates: July 23-29
Positions Needed: Positions are all filled
Schedule: Nebraska, Arkansas, Oral Roberts, Minnesota, Northern Iowa, Illinois State
Style of Play: Our team is very versatile, with each player hitting from many different areas on the net. We have an aggressive style of play that takes advantage of each player's strengths.

Graceland College
Academic Profile

700 College Avenue
Lamoni, IA 50140

Phone: 800-346-9208

Type: Private, 4 Yr., Liberal Arts, Coed
Website: http://www.graceland.edu
SAT/ACT/GPA: 960/22/2.0
Student/Faculty Ratio: 13:1
Undergraduate Enrollment: 1,100
Scholarships/Academic: Yes   **Athletic:** Yes
Expenses By: Year   **In State:** $ 16,340
Degrees Conferred: BA, BSN, BS

Founded: 1895
Religion: Latter Day Saints
Housing: Yes
Male/Female: 50:50
Graduate Enrollment: N/A
Financial Aid: Yes
Out of State: $ 16,340

Programs of Study: Accounting, Art, Athletic Training, Basic Science, Biology, Business Administration, Chemistry, Commercial Design, Communications, Computer Science, Economics, Education, English, French, German, Health, History, Human Services, Information Technology, International Studies, Liberal Studies, Literature, Mathematics, Music, Music Education, Nursing, Philosophy and Religion, Physical Education, PreDentistry, PreEngineering, PreLaw, PreMedicine, PreOptometry, Psychology, Publications Design, Recreation, Social Science, Sociology, Spanish, Speech, Theatre, Wellness Program Management,

Women's Athletic Profile

700 College Avenue
Lamoni, IA 50140
Coach: Stew McDole
Email: mcdole@graceland.edu

NCAA I
Lady Yellow Jackets, Blue, Gold
Phone: (515) 784-5315
Fax: (515) 784-5472

Estimated # of Women's Volleyball Scholarships: N/A
Conference: HAAC

Grand View College
Academic Profile

1200 Grand View Avenue
Des Moines, IA 50316
Type: Private, 4 Yr., Liberal Arts, Coed
Website: http://www.gvc.edu

Phone: (800) 444-6083

Founded: 1896
Religion: Lutheran

SAT/ACT/GPA: Open/2.0
Student/Faculty Ratio: 15:1
Undergraduate Enrollment: 1,400
Scholarships/Academic: Yes   **Athletic:** Yes
Expenses By: Year   **In State:** $ 16,352
Specializes In: Art, Education, Nursing
Degrees Conferred: AA, BA, BS

Housing: Yes
Male/Female: 1:3
Graduate Enrollment: N/A
Financial Aid: Yes
Out of State: $ 16,352

Programs of Study: Accounting, Applied Mathematics, Arts, Biology, Broadcasting, Business Administration, Chemistry, Commercial Art, Computer Information Systems, Computer Science, Creative and Performing Arts, Criminal Justice, Economics, Education, Elementary Education, English, History, International Business, Journalism, Music, Nursing, Philosophy, Physics, Political Science, PreLaw, PreMed, PreVet, Psychology, Radio and Television, Religion, Special Education, Visual Arts

Women's Athletic Profile

1200 Grandview Avenue
Des Moines, IA 50316
Coach: LeAnn Stefani
Email:

NCAA I
Lady Vikings, Red, White
Phone: (515) 263-2965
Fax: (515) 263-2882

Estimated # of Women's Volleyball Scholarships: N/A
Conference: MCC

Grinnell College
Academic Profile

P.O. Box 805, PEC
Grinnell, IA 50112

Phone: 800-247-0113

Type: Private, 4 Yr., Liberal Arts, Coed
Website: http://www.grinnell.edu
SAT/ACT/GPA: 1250+/25+/3.5
Student/Faculty Ratio: 10:1
Undergraduate Enrollment: 1,300
Scholarships/Academic: Yes   **Athletic:** No
Expenses By: Year   **In State:** $ 23,860
Specializes In: PreProfessional Programs
Degrees Conferred: BA

Founded: 1846
Religion: Non-Affiliated
Housing: Yes
Male/Female: 40:60
Graduate Enrollment: N/A
Financial Aid: Yes
Out of State: $ 23,860

Programs of Study: American Studies, Anthropology, Arts, Biology, Chemistry, Chinese, Classic, Computer Science, Economics, English, Education, French, General Science, German, History, Math, Music, Philosophy, Physical Education, Physics, Political Science, Psychology, Religious Studies, Russian, Sociology, Spanish, Theatre

Women's Athletic Profile

P.O. Box 805
Grinnell, IA 50112
Coach: Tom Sonnichsen
Email: sonnichs@ac.grin.edu

NCAA I
Lady Pioneers, Scarlet, Black
Phone: (515) 269-3814
Fax: (515) 269-3818

Estimated # of Women's Volleyball Scholarships: N/A
Conference: Midwest Conference
Program Profile: Our school was founded in 1846. Grinnell is located 60 miles from both Des Moines and Cedar Rapids.
Achievements: South Division Championship in 1998; Second in 1998 Midwest Conference;
Coaching: Tom Sonnichsen, Head Coach, started his second year with the Pioneers in 1998. At Baylor, he coached the most successful volleyball program in the school's history and was Southwest Conference Coach of the Year in 1991.
Most Recent Record: 23-9-0   **Fall Games:** 32   **Spring Games:** 0
Camp of Clinic Dates: General Skills: July 11-15

Indian Hills Community College
Academic Profile

608 Indian Hills Drive, Bldg. #11
Ottumwa, IA 52501
Type: Public, 2 Yr., Jr. College, Coed
Website: http://www.ihcc.cc.ia.us

Phone: (515) 683-5243

Founded: 1966
Religion: Non-Affiliated

SAT/ACT/GPA: Open
Student/Faculty Ratio: 23:1
Undergraduate Enrollment: 3,424
Scholarships/Academic: Yes
Expenses By: Year
Degrees Conferred: AAS

Athletic: Yes
In State: $ 4,470

Housing: Yes
Male/Female: Not Available
Graduate Enrollment: N/A
Financial Aid: Yes
Out of State: $ 5,220

Programs of Study: 38 Technical Programs including: Agricultural Technologies, Automotive Technology, Business Administration, Commerce, Management, Criminal Justice, Drafting/Design, Flight Training, Food Services Technology, Health Services Administration, Laser Technology, Marine and Tool Technology, Nursing, Physical Therapy, General Studies, Practical Nursing

Women's Athletic Profile

608 Indian Hills Drive Bldg. #11
Ottumwa, IA 52501
Coach: Terry Carlson
Email:

NCAA I
Lady Warriors, Maroon, Gold
Phone: 515-683-5243
Fax: 515-683-5222

Estimated # of Women's Volleyball Scholarships: 15
Program Profile: We have a new Division I NJCAA program. We have our own volleyball facility, Sport Court, which was built in 1998.
History: The program began in 1997. Our record in 1998 was 32-16 and in 1999 it was 34-13.
Achievements: Irina Polikarpova -All-American Honorable Mention.
Coaching: Terry Carlson started as head coach in 1998. She was a former coach for the Iowa Blizzard of the National Volleyball Association. Lorenzo Wadkins is assistant coach.
Freshman Receiving Financial Aid/Academic:
Roster In State: 11
Sophomores on Team: 0
Most Recent Record: 34-13-0
Positions Needed: Setter, Left Side Hitter

Out of State: 0
Seniors on Team: 7
Fall Games: 18

Athletic: 6
Out of Country: 3
Graduation %: 100
Spring Games: 14

Schedule: Kirkwood CC, South Western CC, Iowa Western CC, Bellview CC, Elgin CC, Illinois Central CC
Style of Play: Fast and quick.

Iowa State University
Academic Profile

Women's Athletic Office
Ames, IA 50014

Phone: 800-262-3810

Type: Public, 4 Yr., Coed
Website: http://www.iastate.edu
SAT/ACT/GPA: Open/3.0
Student/Faculty Ratio: 19:1
Undergraduate Enrollment: 24,726
Scholarships/Academic: Yes
Expenses By: Year
Specializes In: Science, Technology
Degrees Conferred: BA, BS, MS, MA, MFA, MEd, Ph.D.

Athletic: Yes
In State: $ 10,000

Founded: 1858
Religion: Non-Affiliated
Housing: Yes
Male/Female: Not Available
Graduate Enrollment: N/A
Financial Aid: Yes
Out of State: $ 16,280

Programs of Study: Accounting, Agriculture, Anthropology, Applied Art, Architecture, Arts, BioChemistry, BioPhysics, Botany, Broadcasting, Business and Management, Computer Science, Dietetics, Communications, City/Community/Regional Planning, Linguistics, Meteorology, MicroBiology, Russian, Sociology, Religion, Biology, Zoology, Social Work

Women's Athletic Profile

1800 So. 4th Street
Ames, IA 50011
Coach: Linda Grensing
Email: jmccall@instate.edu

NCAA I
Lady Cyclones, Cardinal, Gold
Phone: (515) 294-3395
Fax: (515) 294-6046

Estimated # of Women's Volleyball Scholarships: N/A
Conference: Big 12 Conference
Program Profile: Compete in a strong conference, season August-December, home matches held in Hilton Coliseum, wood suspendend floor and 1,400 seating capacity.

History: 1973 program began. 1995 NCAA Tournament 2nd round.
Freshman Receiving Financial Aid/Academic:
Roster In State: 8   **Out of State:** 5   **Athletic:** 5   **Out of Country:** 0
Seniors on Team: 2
Most Recent Record: 2-27
Camp of Clinic Dates: TBA
Positions Needed: OH, MB, Setter
Schedule: Nebraska, Texas A & M, Kansas State, Missouri, Texas Tech, Colorado

Iowa Wesleyan College
Academic Profile

601 N. Main
Mt. Pleasant, IA 52641

Phone: (319) 385-6301

Type: Private, 4 Yr., Liberal Arts, Coed
Website: http://www.iwc.edu
SAT/ACT/GPA: 980/18/2.0
Student/Faculty Ratio: 14:1
Undergraduate Enrollment: 800
Scholarships/Academic: Yes   **Athletic:** Yes
Expenses By: Year   **In State:** $ 16,950

Founded: 1842
Religion: United Methodist
Housing: Yes
Male/Female: 50:50
Graduate Enrollment: N/A
Financial Aid: Yes
Out of State: $ 16,950

Specializes In: Real World Learning
Degrees Conferred: BA, BME, BSN, BS, BGS
Programs of Study: Accounting, Art, Biology, Business Administration, Business Computer Information Systems, Chemistry, Communications, Computer Science, Criminal Justice, Early Childhood Education, Elementary Education, English, Environmental Health, History, Political Science, International Business, Life Science, Mathematics, Music, Nursing, Physical Education, Psychology, Sociology, Sport Management

Women's Athletic Profile

601 N. Main
Mt. Pleasant, IA 52641
Coach: Brian Meeter
Email:

NCAA I
Lady Tigers, Black, Purple
Phone: (319) 385-6305
Fax: (319) 385-6384

Estimated # of Women's Volleyball Scholarships: 3
Conference: Midwest Classic Conference
Program Profile: The Tigers play home matches in the field house. Although small in size, the facility has the best atmosphere in the Conference. The season starts in late August and runs through November.
Achievements: 1997 MCC Coach of the Year Jeff Meeker retired after the 1998 season.
Coaching: Brian Meeter, Head Coach, began his first year with the program. There is no assistant coach listed.
Freshman Receiving Financial Aid/Academic:
Roster In State: 12   **Out of State:** 3   **Athletic:** 2   **Out of Country:** 0
Sophomores on Team: 0   **Seniors on Team:** 2   **Graduation %:** 0
Most Recent Record: 20-17-0   **Fall Games:** 37   **Spring Games:** 0
Positions Needed: Outside Hitter, 1 Middle Hitter, Setter
Schedule: St. Ambrose, Central, Culver-Stockton, Briar Cliff, Northwestern, Wartburg
Style of Play: We have an aggressive team that plays with emotion. We are a team that can physically play with the best in the country.

Loras College
Academic Profile

1450 Alta Vista
Dubuque, IA 52004-0178

Phone: (319) 588-4975

Type: Private, 4 Yr., Liberal Arts, Coed
Website: http://www.loras.edu
SAT/ACT/GPA: Open
Student/Faculty Ratio: 13:1
Undergraduate Enrollment: 1,800
Scholarships/Academic: Yes   **Athletic:** No

Founded: 1839
Religion: Catholic
Housing: Yes
Male/Female: 50:50
Graduate Enrollment: 200
Financial Aid: Yes

Expenses By: Year   **In State:** $ 18,000   **Out of State:** $ 18,000
Specializes In: Liberal Arts
Degrees Conferred: BA, BS, Masters
Programs of Study: Accounting, Art Education, Biology, Biological Research, Business, Chemistry, Classical Studies, Criminal Justice, Computer Science, Early Childhood Education, Economics, Elementary Education, Engineering, Physics, Finance, French, German, History, International Business, Journalism, Literature, Management, Management Information Systems, Marketing, Mathematics, Medicine Studies, Music, Parish Ministry, Philosophy, Physics, Physical Education, Sports Science, Sports Management, Psychology

Women's Athletic Profile

1450 Alta Vista
Dubuque, IA 52004
Coach: Brian Lamppa
Email:

NCAA I
Lady Hawks, Purple, Gold
Phone: (319) 588-7742
Fax: (319) 588-7983

Estimated # of Women's Volleyball Scholarships: N/A
Conference: Iowa Intercollegiate Athletic Conference
Program Profile: Team plays in the 1,000 seat Graber Center. Plays in 6 tournaments, including its own River City classic.
History: Began in 1975.
Achievements: 16 All-Conference players in past 11 years, won IIAC tournament 1990, A.I.A.W. State Champs in 1976,77,78. 3 Academic All-District and 1 Academic All-American.
Coaching: Brian Lamppa first season and David Jackson 2nd season as Asst. Coach
Roster In State: 10   **Out of State:** 8
Most Recent Record: 19-11   **Fall Games:** 30
Schedule: Central, St. Olaf, St. Mary's
Style of Play: Aggressive, quick attack offense with solid defense

Luther College
Academic Profile

700 College Drive
Decorah, IA 52101

Phone: (319) 387-2000

Type: Private, 4 Yr., Liberal Arts, Coed
Website: http://www.Luther.edu
SAT/ACT/GPA: Open
Student/Faculty Ratio: 14:1
Undergraduate Enrollment: 2,500
Scholarships/Academic: Yes   **Athletic:** No
Expenses By: Year   **In State:** $ 21,100
Degrees Conferred: BA, BS

Founded: 1861
Religion: Lutheran
Housing: Yes
Male/Female: 40:60
Graduate Enrollment: N/A
Financial Aid: Yes
Out of State: $ 21,100

Programs of Study: Accounting, Anthropology, Art, Biblical Languages, Biology, English, Chemistry, Communications, Computer Science, Economics, Elementary Education, History, Management, Mathematics, Music, Nursing, Philosophy, Physical Education, Physics, Political Science, Psychology, Religion, Social Work, Sociology, Spanish, Speech, Sports Management

Women's Athletic Profile

700 College Drive
Decorah, IA 52101
Coach: Ellen Drewes-Stoen
Email: drewesel@martin.luther.edu

NCAA I
Lady Norse, Blue, White
Phone: (319) 387-1587
Fax: (319) 387-1228

Estimated # of Women's Volleyball Scholarships: N/A
Conference: Iowa Intercollegiate Athletic Conference

Marycrest International U(Teikyo)
Academic Profile

1607 W 12th Street
Davenport, IA 52804
Type: Private, 4 Yr., Liberal Arts, Coed
Website: http://www.mcrest.edu

Phone: 800-728-9705

Founded: 1039
Religion: Non-Affiliated

SAT/ACT/GPA: 840/20/2.3
Student/Faculty Ratio: 14:1
Undergraduate Enrollment: 1,150
Scholarships/Academic: Yes   **Athletic:** Yes
Expenses By: Year   **In State:** $ 14,700
Specializes In: Multi-media, Nursing, Education, Business
Degrees Conferred: BA, BS, BSN, BSW, MA, MS, BIB

Housing: Yes
Male/Female: 1:1
Graduate Enrollment: 100
Financial Aid: Yes
Out of State: $ 14,700

Programs of Study: Accounting, American Language & Culture, Agriculture, Art, Biology, Business Administration, Chemistry/Biology, Communications, Computer Graphics, Computer Science, Early Childhood Education, Elementary Education, English, Environmental Management, Environmental Science, Food & Nutrition, Global Studies, Government, History, International Business, Mathematics, Liberal Arts, Multimedia, Musical Theatre, Nursing, PreLaw, PreMed, Psychology, Social Work, Spanish, Speech Communications/Theatre Education, Special Studies, Theatre Arts

Women's Athletic Profile

1607 West 12th Street
Davenport, IA 52804-4096
Coach: Paul Lawson
Email: plawson@mcrest.edu

NCAA I
Marauding Eagles, Blue, White
Phone: (312) 326-9512
Fax: (319) 326-9375

Estimated # of Women's Volleyball Scholarships: 14
Conference: Midwest Classic Conference
History: Our program is being brought back for the Fall 2000.
Achievements: In 1994 women's program won the MCC Conference title under Coach Bruce Billingsley.

Morningside College
Academic Profile

1501 Morningside Avenue
Sioux City, IA 51106-1751

Phone: (712) 274-5000

Type: Private, 4 Yr., Liberal Arts, Coed
Website: http://www.morningside.edu
SAT/ACT/GPA: Open
Student/Faculty Ratio: 1:15
Undergraduate Enrollment: 1,100
Scholarships/Academic: Yes   **Athletic:** Yes
Expenses By: Year   **In State:** $ 16,500
Degrees Conferred: BA, BS, M

Founded: 1894
Religion: Methodist
Housing: Yes
Male/Female: 1:3
Graduate Enrollment: 300
Financial Aid: Yes
Out of State: $ 16,500

Programs of Study: Accounting, Art, Biology, Business, Chemistry, Communications, Criminal Justice, Computer, Dramatic Arts, Economics, Education, Engineering, Graphic Arts, History, Humanities, Indian Studies, Industrial, Psychology, Mass Communications, Mathematics, Music, Natural Science, Nursing, Philosophy, Photography, PreProfessional Programs, Recreation, Religious Studies, Sociology, Spanish, Special Education, Speech, Theatre

Women's Athletic Profile

1501 Morningside Avenue
Sioux City, IA 51106
Coach: Theresa Kathman-Trees
Email:

NCAA I
Mustangs, Maroon, White, Black
Phone: (712) 274-5000
Fax: (712) 274-5578

Estimated # of Women's Volleyball Scholarships: 2
Conference: North Central Conference
Program Profile: Last year was our rebuilding year. We look for great things in this coming season. We hope to be back in the Top 25. We practice where we compete. Our gym has 4,000 seats.
History: Our program began in 1972. We have been a member of the North Central Conference since 1989. It is considered one of the most elite volleyball Division II conferences in the nation. In the past 8 years we have finished in the top half of the Conference all but one year. We were Regional qualifiers in 1991 and 1995.
Achievements: We have been ranked as high as 7th in the nation from 1994 to 1996. We have almost always been ranked in the top 25.
Coaching: Theresa Trees, Head Coach, started here in 1998. Her first year record is 8-23. Assistant Coach Steph Baddeley started in 1998. Both coaches were All-Conference players and All-Region. Both coaches were alumni of Morningside.
Freshman Receiving Financial Aid/Academic: **Athletic:** 4
Roster In State: 6   **Out of State:** 5   **Out of Country:** 0

Sophomores on Team: 0   **Seniors on Team:** 1   **Graduation %:** 98
Most Recent Record: 8-23-0   **Fall Games:** 31   **Spring Games:** 10
Positions Needed: Middle Hitters, Outside Hitters
Schedule: North Dakota State, Augustana, Rockhurst, South Dakota State, Hawaii Pacific, St. Cloud State
Style of Play: Fast-tempo offense. Defense is the key to the team's success. The fast-paced game we play is played by almost every team in our conference. Hitters run many options and we focus on consistent play.

Mount Mercy College
Academic Profile

1330 Elmhurst Drive
Cedar Rapids, IA 52402

Phone: (319) 363-1323

Type: Private, 4 Yr., Liberal Arts, Coed
Website: http://www.mtmercy.edu
SAT/ACT/GPA: Open/18/2.5
Student/Faculty Ratio: 14/1
Undergraduate Enrollment: 1350
Scholarships/Academic: Yes   **Athletic:** No
Expenses By: Year   **In State:** $ 17,500
Specializes In: Education, Criminal Justice, Health Careers
Degrees Conferred: BA, BS, BBA

Founded: 1928
Religion: Roman Catholic
Housing: Yes
Male/Female: 1/3
Graduate Enrollment: N/A
Financial Aid: Yes
Out of State: $ 17,500

Programs of Study: Art, Biology, Business Administration, Computer Information Systems, Computer Science, Criminal Justice Administration, Education, English, Health Services Administration, History, International Studies , Mathematics, Marketing, Medical Technician, Music, Nursing, Political Science, Psychology, Public Relations, Religion, Social Studies, Sociology, Speech Drama, Urban Studies

Women's Athletic Profile

1330 Elmhurst Dr. NE
Cedar Rapids, IA 52402
Coach: JoAnn Jennings
Email:

NCAA I
Lady Mustangs, Blue, Gold
Phone: (319) 363-1323
Fax: (319) 363-6341

Estimated # of Women's Volleyball Scholarships: N/A
Conference: Midwest Classic Conference
Program Profile: We have both a JV and Varsity team with a "no cut" policy. The 2 teams compete separate schedules. Our season begins late August and runs through mid November. Our home matches are played in our Hennessey Rec. Center on wooden floors.
History: Our program began in 1985. We won three conference championships in 1991,1992 and 1993. We had two All-Americans in 1994 and 1997. We have a win/loss record of 297/287 for a .508 average.
Achievements: Conference titles in 1991, 1992 and 1993, Coach of the Year Doug Van Ort 1991, 1992, 1993, each year we have had several Academic All-Conference Selections as well as Academic All-Region Selections.
Coaching: JoAnn Jennings Head Coach. Tori Riha Assistant Coach
Roster In State: 12   **Out of State:** 4   **Out of Country:** 0
Sophomores on Team: 0   **Seniors on Team:** 5   **Graduation %:** 100
Most Recent Record: 12-16-0
Positions Needed: Middle, Left Side
Schedule: Dordt, Northwestern, Iowa Wesleyan, St. Ambrose, Worthburg, Culver-Stockton, Kirkwood CC
Style of Play: After graduation 4 starting seniors we are looking for 2 middle and 2 left side players. We want to become a very quick and agile team.

Mount Saint Clare College
Academic Profile

400 North Bluff Blvd.
Clinton, IA 52732

Phone: 800-242-4153

Type: Private, 4 Yr., Liberal Arts, Coed
Website: www.clare.edu
SAT/ACT/GPA: 860/18/2.0
Student/Faculty Ratio: 12:1
Undergraduate Enrollment: 625
Scholarships/Academic: Yes   **Athletic:** Yes

Founded: 1918
Religion: Franciscan/Catholic
Housing: Yes
Male/Female: 1/1.5
Graduate Enrollment: N/A
Financial Aid: Yes

Expenses By: Year   **In State:** $18,620   **Out of State:** $18,620

Specializes In: Education, Business, Accounting

Degrees Conferred: AA, AAS, BA, BGS

Programs of Study: Accounting, Business Administration, Clinical CytoTechnology, Computer Information Systems, Elementary Education, Social Science, Liberal Arts, Fine Arts, Journalism, Music, Science, Social Science, PreLaw, PreMed, Precounseling, Arts, Biology, Chemistry, Computer Science, Early Childhood Education, Mathematics, Music, Philosophy, PreDentistry, Sociology, Speech Therapy, English as a second language

Women's Athletic Profile

400 N. Bluff
Clinton, IA 52732
Coach: Selena Eggers
Email:

NCAA I
Lady Mounties, Purple, Gold
Phone: (319) 242-4023
Fax: (319) 243-8580

Estimated # of Women's Volleyball Scholarships: 1

Conference: Midwest Classics Conference

Program Profile: Play in a six team conference (MCC) play approx. 35-40 matches each year including tournaments and non-conference games. Gym holds 2,000 and it opened 1998

Coaching: Started in 1998. Was 3rd team All-American, 2 time All-Region, 3 time 1st team All-Conference, MCC Conference player of the Year, St. Ambrsose MVP

Freshman Receiving Financial Aid/Academic: **Athletic:** 5

Roster In State: 8   **Out of State:** 7   **Out of Country:**

Sophomores on Team: 4   **Seniors on Team:** 2   **Graduation %:** 100

Most Recent Record: **Fall Games:** 30   **Spring Games:**

Positions Needed: Setter, Middle hitter, Defense specialist

Schedule: Graceland, Northwestern, St. Ambrose, St. Xavier

Style of Play: Aggressive defense, quick offense

Northwestern College - Iowa
Academic Profile

101 7th St. SW
Orange City, IA 51041

Phone: (712) 737-7130

Type: Private, 4 Yr., Liberal Arts, Coed

Website: http://www.nwciowa.edu

SAT/ACT/GPA: 18/2.2

Student/Faculty Ratio: 16:1

Undergraduate Enrollment: 1,177

Scholarships/Academic: Yes   **Athletic:** Yes

Expenses By: Year   **In State:** $ 15,770

Specializes In: Liberal Arts Curriculum

Degrees Conferred: BA

Founded: 1882

Religion: Reformed Church of America

Housing: Yes

Male/Female: 55:45

Graduate Enrollment: N/A

Financial Aid: Yes

Out of State: $ 15,770

Programs of Study: Art, Accounting, Biology, Business Administration, Business Education, Chemistry, Christian Education, Communications, Computer Science, Economics, Elementary Education, English, Exercise Science, History, Humanities, Mathematics, Medical Technology, Music, Philosophy, Physical Education, Political Science, Psychology, Religion, Social Work, Sociology, Spanish, Theatre, Theatre/Speech

Women's Athletic Profile

101 7th Street, SW
Orange City, IA 51041
Coach: Mike Meyer
Email: meyer@nwciowa.edu

NCAA I
Lady Red Raiders, Red, White
Phone: (712) 737-7285
Fax: (712) 737-7290

Estimated # of Women's Volleyball Scholarships: N/A

Conference: NIAC

Saint Ambrose University
Academic Profile

518 W. Locust
Davenport, IA 52803

Phone: 319-333-6000

Type: Private, 4 Yr., Liberal Arts, Coed
Website: http://www.sau.edu
SAT/ACT/GPA: 950/21/2.4
Student/Faculty Ratio: 15:1
Undergraduate Enrollment: 2114
Scholarships/Academic: Yes   **Athletic:** Yes
Expenses By: Year   **In State:** $ 20,000

Founded: 1882
Religion: Catholic
Housing: Yes
Male/Female: 42/58
Graduate Enrollment: 897
Financial Aid: Yes
Out of State: $ 20,000

Specializes In: Liberal Arts and Pre-Professional Career preparation
Degrees Conferred: BS, BA, MBA, MPT
Programs of Study: Business, Computer Science, Education, Social Work, Criminal Justice, History, Physical Therapy, Biology, Psychology, Accounting, Industrial Engineering, Mass Communications, Radio & TV, Special Education, Computer Networking

Men's Athletic Profile

518 West Locust Street
Davenport, IA 52803
Coach: Bruce Billingsley
Email: bbiliny@sau.edu

NAIA
Fighting Bees/Navy, White
Phone: 319-333-6452
Fax: 319-333-6239

Estimated # of Men's Volleyball Scholarships: Partial Scholarships
Conference: MIVA
Program Profile: Second year program, all freshman and sophomores. 28 playing dates, January-April. Home court is Lee Lohman Arena, capacity 2500.
History: Program started in 1999-2000 school year. This is the second men's collegiate program started by Coach Billingsley. Last spring is the first year the team featured ten freshmen and no upperclassmen.
Achievements:
Coaching: Bruce Billingsley, head coach, has three MIVA Championships (1996-98). He holds 2 MIVA Coach of the Year awards. Alexei Bibik is a graduate assistant and was a two-time MIVA Player of the Year.
Freshman Receiving Financial Aid/Academic: 5   **Athletic:** 5
Roster In State: 0   **Out of State:** 14   **Out of Country:** 1
Most Recent Record: 4-20-0
Camp or Clinic Dates: TBA
Positions Needed: All
Schedule: California Baptist, Marycrest International, Park, Lindenwood, La Verne
Style of Play: Average to above average quickness, wide variety of offensive options.

Women's Athletic Profile

518 W. Locust Street
Davenport, IA 52803
Coach: Bruce Billingsley
Email: bbiliny@sau.edu

NCAA I
Queen Bees, Navy, White
Phone: (319) 333-6452
Fax: (319) 333-6239

Estimated # of Women's Volleyball Scholarships: Partial scholarships
Conference: Midwest Classics Conference
Program Profile: Solid program, regionally and nationally competitive program. JV program in place. In rebuilding stages started five freshman in 2000. Home court is Lee Lohman Arena, capacity 2000.
History: Our program started in 1975. Overall record is 636-334. We won consecutive Midwest Classic Conference Championships in 1995 and 1998. We made 4 National Tournament appearances. Five conference championships in last six years.
Achievements: Midwest Classic Conference Champions 1994, 97, 98, 99. MCC Coach of the Year 1994, 98, 99 NAIA Region VII Coach of the Year 1999, Midwestern Intercollegiate Volleyball Association Champions 1995, 96, 97, MIVA Coach of the Year 1995, 97. 7 Conference Players, 8 All-Americans, and four top 20 finishes.
Coaching: Bruce Billingsley, Head Coach, has 246 career wins, six conference titles and 4 Coach of the Year Awards. Molly Schurr, Graduate Assistant Coach, was two-time All-American and Academic All-American. She also received Player of the Year twice. Shannon Nicklas is assistant coach.
Freshman Receiving Financial Aid/Academic: **Athletic:** 9

Roster In State: 6   **Out of State:** 15   **Out of Country:** 0
Sophomores on Team: 0   **Seniors on Team:** 2   **Graduation %:** 100
Most Recent Record: 16-19-0
Camp of Clinic Dates: TBA
Positions Needed: All
Schedule: St. Xavier, Graceland, Olivet Nazarene, UW-Platteville, North Western
Style of Play: Strong defensively, run a quick tempo offense with the ball distributed all along the net.

Simpson College
Academic Profile

701 North C St.   **Phone:** (800) 362-2454
Indianola, IA 50125

Type: Private, 4 Yr., Liberal Arts, Coed   **Founded:** 1860
Website: http://www.simpson.edu   **Religion:** Methodist
SAT/ACT/GPA: Contact Simpson Admissions Office at admiss@simpson.edu   **Housing:** Yes
Student/Faculty Ratio: 14:1   **Male/Female:** 1:1
Undergraduate Enrollment: 1,992   **Graduate Enrollment:** N/A
Scholarships/Academic: Yes   **Athletic:** No   **Financial Aid:** Yes
Expenses By: Year   **n State:** $ 16,710   **Out of State:** $ 16,710
Specializes In: Education, Music
Degrees Conferred: BA, BS
Programs of Study: Accounting, Art, Art with Commercial Design, Biology, Chemistry, Communication Studies, Computer Science, Computer Information Systems, Criminal Justice, Early Childhood Education, Economics, Elementary and Secondary Education, English, Environmental Science, French, German, History, International Management, Management, Mathematics, Medical Technology, Music, Music Education, Music Performance, Physical Education, Philosophy, Political Science, PreDentistry, PreEngineering, PreLaw, PreMed, PreNursing, PreOptometry, PrePhysical Therapy, PreTheology, PreVeterinary Medicine, Psychology, Russian Studies

Women's Athletic Profile

701 North C Street   **NCAA I**
Indianola, IA 50125   Lady Storms, Red, Gold
Coach: Lana Smith   **Phone:** (800) 362-2454
Email: info@simpson.edu   **Fax:** (515) 961-1498

Estimated # of Women's Volleyball Scholarships: 0
Conference: Iowa Intercollegiate Athletic Conference
Program Profile: Simpson is a traditional power in the Iowa Conference. With the addition of the Carse Fitness Hall and revamped Cowles Field House, the Storm play in one of the most modern facilities throughout the Midwest. The Carse Fitness Hall has a 5,000 square foot weight room, where the Storm train all year long. Cowles now seats 3,000, but in volleyball trim, a cozy 11,500 can pack the gym.
History: Since 1976, the Storm have fielded a varsity squad. Simpson was the first NCAA Division III school to earn a spot in the NCAA Tournament in 1990. Simpson has won six Iowa Conference titles and has earned four NCAA Tournament spots. Simpson has had over 60 All-Conference players, 15 All-Region players and 5 All-American players in the program
Achievements: Shelley O'Meara-IIAC Coach of the Year in 1985,1987, 1991, 1994,1998; Region Coach of the Year-1987; All-Americans-Rosie Michels, 1990,1991,1992; Megan Amelse-1991, Kris Michels-1994, Amy Trowbridge-1997.
Coaching: Lana Smith is in her first year as head coach. She served as an assistant coach in 1998. She was head coach at Indianola H.S. from 1988 to 1997, where she compiled a 243-89 record. Indianola H. S. won five Conference Titles (1990-92,1996 and 1997) and appeared in four State Tournaments under Smith. Smith played at Iowa from 1983 to 1986 and was 11th in career kills. Barb Overton and Joel Van Roekel are assistant coaches.
Roster In State: 18   **Out of State:** 1   **Out of Country:** 0
Sophomores on Team: 3   **Seniors on Team:** 3   **Graduation %:** 90-95
Most Recent Record: 17-17-0   **Fall Games:** 34   **Spring Games:** 0
Camp of Clinic Dates: August 9-10 (Team); August 11-13 (Individual)
Positions Needed: Outside Hitter, Middle Hitter
Schedule: Central, Washington, St. Benedict, University of Wisconsin-Whitewater, University of Wisconsin-Platteville, Wartburg
Style of Play: Fundamentally sound, strong, quick and fun to watch.

Southwestern Community College
Academic Profile

1501 Townline Road
Creston, IA 50801

Phone: (515) cc.ia.us

Type: Public, 2 Yr., \ Coed
Website: http://www.swcc.cc.ia.us
SAT/ACT/GPA: Open
Student/Faculty Ratio: 1:24
Undergraduate Enrollment: N/A
Scholarships/Academic: Yes   **Athletic:** Yes
Expenses By: Year   **In State:** $ 5,800

Founded: 1966
Religion: Non-Affiliated
Housing: Yes
Male/Female: Not Available
Graduate Enrollment: N/A
Financial Aid: Yes
Out of State: $ 6,700

Specializes In: Transferable general education degree
Degrees Conferred: AA, AS, AAA, AGS, Diploma & Teaching Certificates
Programs of Study: Arts & Sciences, Accounting, AgriBusiness, Business Administration, Computer Programming, Office System Specialist, Sales Marketing, Auto Collision, Electronics, Carpentry, MicroComputer, LPN, RN, Professional Music, Office Associate, Structional Drafting

Women's Athletic Profile

1501 W. Townline
Creston, IA 50801
Coach: Rita Schroeder
Email:

NCAA I
Spartans, Red, White, Blue
Phone: (515) 782-7081
Fax: (515) 782-3312

Estimated # of Women's Volleyball Scholarships: 12
Conference: Iowa
Program Profile: Home matches are played in the Student Center located on campus. There is seating for 2,000 people. We have a two court facility, a weight room, locker rooms and a team chat room.
History: Volleyball started here in 1983. Coach Schroeder began coaching in 1985 and her teams have won 4 State Titles, 4 NJCAA Academic Awards, numerous All-Regional players and 7 All-Americans. Our team continually ranks in the Top 2 in the state.
Achievements: District Coach of the Year 4 times.
Coaching: Rita Schroeder, Head Coach, began coaching in 1985 and has a career record of 442-159.
Freshman Receiving Financial Aid/Academic: **Athletic:** 12
Roster In State: 11   **Out of State:** 1   **Out of Country:** 0
Sophomores on Team: 0   **Seniors on Team:** 4   **Graduation %:** 100
Most Recent Record: 46-9-0   **Fall Games:** 55   **Spring Games:** 0
Camp of Clinic Dates: July 5-8, July 12-15, August 6
Positions Needed: Outside Hitter, Middle Hitter, Defensive Setter
Schedule: Barton College, Kirkwood, Indian Hills, Indiana Wesleyan Community College, Illinois Central
Style of Play: We have a strong blocking and hitting team. We have aggressive setting and are strong fundamentally.

University of Dubuque
Academic Profile

2000 University Avenue
Dubuque, IA 52001

Phone: 319-589-3200

Type: Private, 4 Yr., Liberal Arts, Coed
Website: http://www.duq.edu
SAT/ACT/GPA: 18/2.5
Student/Faculty Ratio: 13:1
Undergraduate Enrollment: 800
Scholarships/Academic: Yes   **Athletic:** No
Expenses By: Year   **In State:** $ 17,770

Founded: 1852
Religion: Presbyterian
Housing: Yes
Male/Female: 1:1
Graduate Enrollment: 200
Financial Aid: Yes
Out of State: $ 17,770

Specializes In: Environmental Science, Aviation, Business, Education
Degrees Conferred: BA, MA, BS
Programs of Study: Accounting, Aviation, Business, Computer Science, English, History, Environmental Science, Education, Physical Education, Biology, Communications, Math, Chemistry, Economics, Music, Political Science, Psychology, Sociology, Religious Studies, Spanish

Women's Athletic Profile

2000 University Avenue
Dubuque, IA 52001
Coach: Randy Dolson
Email: admission@univ.dbq.edu

NCAA I
Lady Spartans, Blue, White
Phone: (800) 722-5583
Fax: (319) 589-3690

Estimated # of Women's Volleyball Scholarships: None
Conference: Iowa Intercollegiate Athletic Conference
Program Profile: We play in McCormick Gymnasium which seats 2,500. Our playing season runs from September through Mid November. In 3 out of the 4 past seasons, we have ranked in the Top 10 nationwide for attendance.
History: The program began in 1980. We got two Conference titles in 1982 and 1995. We made 3 NCAA appearances in 1994, 1995 and 1998. Our overall record since 1980 is 463-380.
Achievements: NCAA Division III playoffs in 1994, 1995 and 1998; 37 All-Conference players; 4 All-American players; 5 All-Region players.
Coaching: Randy Dolson, Head Coach, has coached the team from 1996 to the present. He was a former assistant coach of the team. He compiled a record of 59-48 as a head coach. Dave Thielen and Stacy Ruff are assistant coaches

Freshman Receiving Financial Aid/Academic:		**Athletic:** 0
Roster In State: 14	**Out of State:** 8	**Out of Country:** 0
Sophomores on Team: 3	**Seniors on Team:** 3	**Graduation %:** 100
Most Recent Record: 23-12-0	**Fall Games:** 35	**Spring Games:** 0

Camp of Clinic Dates: June 21-25; July 6-8; July 12-16 (Hitting, Setting, Defensive, All-Skills)
Positions Needed: Outside Hitter, Middle Blocker, Setter
Schedule: University of Wisconsin-Whitewater, Central, Wartburg, St. Olaf, St. Benedict, University of Wisconsin-Oshkosh
Style of Play: Up-tempo, quick, slides, combinations. Great defensive team.

University of Iowa
Academic Profile

107 Calvin Hall
Iowa City, IA 52242
Type: Public, 4 Yr., Coed
Website: http://www.uiowa.edu
SAT/ACT/GPA: 700/17
Student/Faculty Ratio: 17:1
Undergraduate Enrollment: 19,337
Scholarships/Academic: Yes
Expenses By: Year

Phone: (800) 553-4692

Founded: 1847
Religion: Non-Affiliated
Housing: Yes
Male/Female: 45:55
Graduate Enrollment: 9,368

Athletic: Yes	**Financial Aid:** Yes
In State: $ 7,368	**Out of State:** $ 14,810

Degrees Conferred: BA, BS, BFA, BLS, BM, BSN, MA, MBA, MFA, MD
Programs of Study: Accounting, Arts, Business Administration, Computer Science, Education, Engineering, Fine Arts, Health Administration, Jurisprudence, Law, Music, Nursing, Philosophy, Pharmacy, Physician Assistant, Science

Women's Athletic Profile

1 Elliott Drive
Iowa City, IA 52242
Coach: Rita Buck-Crockett
Email: rita-crockett@uiowa.edu

NCAA I
Lady Hawkeyes, Gold, Black
Phone: (319) 335-9259
Fax: (319) 335-9417

Estimated # of Women's Volleyball Scholarships: 4
Conference: Big Ten Conference
Program Profile: International Flare-Corver Hawkeye Arena with a seating capacity of 16,000. Our playing season is in September through December.
Coaching: Rita Buck-Crockett, Head Coach, started coaching the program in 1998 with a record of 9-22. She holds a 1984 Olympic Medal, Silver. She played professionally in Japan and coached and played in Italy and Switzerland, where team was World Champion in 1989 and WPVA Beach Tours. Sylvie Monnett and Lonise Norfleet are the Assistant Coaches.

Freshman Receiving Financial Aid/Academic:		**Athletic:** 5
Roster In State: 5-7	**Out of State:** 7	**Out of Country:** 3-4
Sophomores on Team: 4	**Seniors on Team:** 4	**Graduation %:** N/A
Most Recent Record:	**Fall Games:** 26	**Spring Games:** 0

Camp of Clinic Dates: June 21-24, July 23-25, Tentative

Positions Needed: 4
Schedule: Nebraska, Florida, Texas A&M, Santa Clara, Penn State, Wisconsin
Style of Play: Dynamic quick attack with professional and international flare.

University of Northern Iowa
Academic Profile

1222 West 27th Street
Cedar Falls, IA 50614

Phone: 800-772-2037

Type: Public, 4 Yr., Liberal Arts, Coed
Website: http://www.uni.edu
SAT/ACT/GPA: 21
Student/Faculty Ratio: 17:1
Undergraduate Enrollment: 11,858
Scholarships/Academic: Yes **Athletic:** Yes
Expenses By: Year **In State:** $ 6,914
Specializes In: Business, Education

Founded: 1876
Religion: Non-Affiliated
Housing: Yes
Male/Female: 1:1.3
Graduate Enrollment: 1,687
Financial Aid: Yes
Out of State: $ 11,674

Degrees Conferred: BA, BS, BFA, MS, MBA, MED, EDD, DIT
Programs of Study: Accounting, American Studies, Anthropology, Art, Asian Studies, Biology, BioTechnology, Business Management, Chemistry, Communications, Computer Science, Criminology, Earth Science, Education, English, Environmental Science, Finance, Foreign Languages, General Studies, Geology, Humanities, Journalism, Management, Mathematics, Natural History, Nutrition/Food, Physics, Psychology, Religion, Science, Sociology, Textile/Apparel, Theatre

Women's Athletic Profile

23rd & College
Cedar Falls, IA 50614
Coach: Dr. Iradge Ahrabi-Fard
Email: Bobbi.petersen@uni.edu

NCAA I
Lady Panthers, Purple, Old Gold
Phone: (319) 273-7170
Fax: (319) 273-6112

Estimated # of Women's Volleyball Scholarships: N/A
Conference: Midwestern Collegiate Conference

Upper Iowa University
Academic Profile

P.O. Box 1857
Fayette, IA 52142

Phone: (319) 425-5285

Type: Private, 4 Yr., Liberal Arts, Coed
Website: http://www.uiu.edu
SAT/ACT/GPA: 760/17/2.0
Student/Faculty Ratio: 18:1
Undergraduate Enrollment: 760
Scholarships/Academic: Yes **Athletic:** No
Expenses By: Year **In State:** $ 15,000
Specializes In: Conservation Management, Science, Business, Education

Founded: 1857
Religion: Non-Affiliated
Housing: Yes
Male/Female: 3:1
Graduate Enrollment: 17
Financial Aid: Yes
Out of State: $ 15,000

Degrees Conferred: BA, BS, Master of Business Leadership
Programs of Study: Accounting, American Studies, Applied Plant Science, Art, Art Administration, Athletic Training, Biology, Business Administration, Chemistry, Communications, Computer Conservation Management, Construction Management, Criminology, Education, Elementary Education, English, Financial Management, Fine Arts, Graphic Design, Health Care, Human Services, Life Science, Management Information Systems, Marketing, Mathematics, Music, Psychology, Physical Education, Reading, Recreation, Science, Social Science, Sociology, Spanish, Sports Science, Wellness

Women's Athletic Profile

Box 1857
Fayette, IA 52142
Coach: Clem Messerli
Email: messerlic@uiu.edu

NCAA I
Lady Peacocks, Blue, White
Phone: (319) 425-5258
Fax: (319) 425-5334

Estimated # of Women's Volleyball Scholarships: 0
Conference: Iowa Intercollegiate Athletic Conference
Program Profile: Our team size is 12-15 players. We play at Dorman Gym, which has a wooden floor and seats 1,000. We have a Fall season that goes from September to November.

History: Our program started in 1974. We had early success in the late 1970's and 1980's. We have had limited success since then.
Achievements: None
Coaching: Clem Messerli is in his second year as head coach, with a record of 2-29.
Freshman Receiving Financial Aid/Academic: **Athletic:** 0
Roster In State: 6   **Out of State:** 9   **Out of Country:** 0
Sophomores on Team: 0   **Seniors on Team:** 1   **Graduation %:** 95
Most Recent Record: 2-29-0   **Fall Games:** 31-35   **Spring Games:** 0
Positions Needed: Setters, Outside Hitters, Middle Hitters
Schedule: Central College, Simpson College, St. Mary's-Minnesota, Coe College, Mt. Mercy College, Warburg College
Style of Play: Quick swing offense, aggressive serves. our setters call offense and the coach calls serves.

William Penn University
Academic Profile

201 Trueblood Avenue   **Phone:** 800-779-7366
Oskaloosa, IA 52577

Type: Private, 4 Yr., Liberal Arts, Coed   **Founded:** 1873
Website: http://www.wmpenn.edu   **Religion:** Quaker
SAT/ACT/GPA: Open   **Housing:** Yes
Student/Faculty Ratio: 14:1   **Male/Female:** 2:1.5
Undergraduate Enrollment: 1,300   **Graduate Enrollment:** N/A
Scholarships/Academic: Yes   **Athletic:** No   **Financial Aid:** Yes
Expenses By: Year   **In State:** $ 16,150   **Out of State:** $ 16,150
Specializes In: Teacher Education, Industrial Technology
Degrees Conferred: BA, BS
Programs of Study: Industrial Technology, Teacher Education, Business, Computer Science, Physical Education, Communications, Accounting, Business Management, Biology, History, Psychology, Sociology, PreProfessional

Women's Athletic Profile

201 Trueblood Avenue   **NCAA I**
Oskaloosa, IA 52577   Lady Statesmen, Blue, Gold
Coach: Jim Overturf   **Phone:** (515) 673-1018
Email: overturfj@wmpenn.edu   **Fax:** (515) 673-1373

Estimated # of Women's Volleyball Scholarships: N/A
Conference: Iowa Intercollegiate Athletic Conference
Program Profile: Our facilities include: 3 volleyball courts, 2 gyms and a stadium which seats 2,000. We have a fall playing season.
History: We began in 1976 . Our conference was organized for women in 1983 .
Achievements: Coach of the Year in 1983; 2 Conference titles in 1983 and 1985; 2 All-Regional; several All-Conference players.
Coaching: Jim Overturf, Head Coach, started in 1997, with an overall record of 238-255. He has 2 conference titles. He was named Coach of the Year in 1983. Michelle Smith is assistant coach.
Freshman Receiving Financial Aid/Academic: **Athletic:** 0
Roster In State: 10   **Out of State:** 8   **Out of Country:** 0
Sophomores on Team: 0   **Seniors on Team:** 3   **Graduation %:** 100
Most Recent Record: 8-25-0   **Fall Games:** 33   **Spring Games:** 0
Positions Needed: Middle Hitter, Blocker
Schedule: Central, Simpson, Wartburg, Dubuque
Style of Play: Like to run, quick sets on transition. Will run options accordingly to athlete's ability.

KANSAS

Topeka

SCHOOL	CITY	AFFILIATION	PAGE
Baker University	Baldwin City	NAIA	276
Benedictine College	Atchison	NAIA	276
Bethany College	Lindsborg	NAIA	277
Bethel College	North Newton	NAIA	277
Emporia State University	Emporia	NCAA II	278
Friends University	Hays	NAIA	279
Fort Hays State University	Wichita	NCAA II	279
Kansas State University	Manhattan	NCAA I	280
Kansas Wesleyan University	Salina	NAIA	281
McPherson College	McPherson	NAIA	281
Mid-America Nazarene	Olathe	NAIA	282
Newman University	Wichita	NAIA	282
Ottawa University	Ottawa	NAIA	283
Pittsburgh State University	Pittsburg	NCAA II	283
Saint Mary College	Leavenworth	NAIA	284
Southwestern College	Winfield	NAIA	284
Sterling College	Sterling	NAIA	285
Tabor College	Hillsboro	NAIA	286
University of Kansas	Lawrence	NCAA I	286
Washburn University	Topeka	NCAA II	287
Wichita State University	Wichita	NCAA I	287

Baker University
Academic Profile

P. O. Box 65
Baldwin City, KS 66006-0065

Phone: 800-873-4282

Type: Private, 4 Yr., Liberal Arts, Engineering, Coed
Website: http://www.bakeru.edu
SAT/ACT/GPA: 1000/21/3.0
Student/Faculty Ratio: 14:1
Undergraduate Enrollment: 850
Scholarships/Academic: Yes   **Athletic:** Yes
Expenses By: Year   **In State:** $ 16,530
Specializes In: Business, Liberal Arts

Founded: 1858
Religion: Non-Affiliated
Housing: Yes
Male/Female: 1:2
Graduate Enrollment: 1,800
Financial Aid: Yes
Out of State: $ 16,530

Degrees Conferred: BA, BS, BFA, BM, BE, BME, MS, MBA
Programs of Study: Accounting, Banking and Finance, Biology, Business, Chemistry, Communications, Computer Science, Economics, Education, English, Fine Arts, French, German, History, Languages, Life Science, Mathematics, Music, Philosophy, Physics, Political Science, PreDentistry, PreLaw, PreMed, Psychology, Religion, Sociology, Spanish, Physical Education

Women's Athletic Profile

P.O. Box 65
Baldwin City, KS 66006-0065
Coach: Kathy Allen
Email: allen@harvey.bakeru.edu

NCAA I
Lady Wildcats, Orange
Phone: (785) 594-8316
Fax: (785) 594-8377

Estimated # of Women's Volleyball Scholarships: N/A
Conference: HAAC

Benedictine College
Academic Profile

1020 North Second St.
Atchison, KS 66002

Phone: (913) 376-5340

Type: Private, 4 Yr., Liberal Arts, Coed
Website: http://www.benedictine.edu
SAT/ACT/GPA: 18/2.0/2.2
Student/Faculty Ratio: 14:1
Undergraduate Enrollment: 1,200
Scholarships/Academic: Yes   **Athletic:** Yes
Expenses By: Year   **In State:** $ 16,200
Degrees Conferred: BA, BS

Founded: 1858
Religion: Catholic
Housing: Yes
Male/Female: 53:47
Graduate Enrollment: N/A
Financial Aid: Yes
Out of State: $ 16,200

Programs of Study: Accounting, Astronomy, BioChemistry, Biology, Business, Chemistry, Computer Science, Economics, Education, English, French, Journalism, Physics, Natural Science, Sociology, Political Science, Religion, Philosophy, Technical Marketing

Women's Athletic Profile

1020 N. 2nd
Atchison, KS 66002
Coach: Chris Herron
Email: cherron@benedictine.edu

NCAA I
Lady Ravens, Black, White, Red
Phone: (913) 367-5340x2377
Fax: (913) 367-2564

Estimated # of Women's Volleyball Scholarships: 5
Conference: Heart of America Conference
Program Profile: Ralph Nolan gymnasium was built in 1997. It has a seating capacity 1800, wood floors and 3 courts.
Achievements: This season Benedictine won its first ever HAAC Championship. Finishing with a record of 30-8. This season outside hitter Jodi Renze was All-American Honorable Mention. Head Coach Chris Herron was selected HAAC Coach of the Year.
Coaching: Head Coach Chris Herron finished 2nd year at Benedictine. In his first season at B.C he had a 13-15 record and this season a 30-8 record. Shawn Schneikart also finished his 2nd year with the Raven program.
Freshman Receiving Financial Aid/Academic: **Athletic:** 4
Roster In State: 14   **Out of State:** 6   **Out of Country:** 0
Sophomores on Team: **Seniors on Team:** 5   **Graduation %:** 90

Most Recent Record: 30-8-0
Schedule: Graceland University, Lindenwood University, Baker University, Northwest Missouri State University, Mid-America Nazarene University, Doane College.

Bethany College
Academic Profile

421 N First St.
Lindsborg, KS 67456

Phone: 800-826-2281

Type: Private, 4 Yr., Liberal Arts, Engineering, Coed
Website: http://www.bethany.bethanylb.edu
SAT/ACT/GPA: 910/19/2.5
Student/Faculty Ratio: 13:1
Undergraduate Enrollment: 650
Scholarships/Academic: Yes   **Athletic:** Yes
Expenses By: Year   **In State:** $ 15,105+
Specializes In: All Majors
Degrees Conferred: Bachelors

Founded: 1881
Religion: Lutheran
Housing: Yes
Male/Female: 1:1
Graduate Enrollment: N/A
Financial Aid: Yes
Out of State: $ 15,105+

Programs of Study: Art, Communications, English, Music, Religion, Natural Science, Social Science, Biology, Chemistry, Computer Information Systems, Mathematics, Engineering, Economics, Elementary Education, Political Science, Psychology, Recreation, Sociology, Social Work, Physical Education

Women's Athletic Profile

421 N. 1st St.
Lindsborg, KS 67456
Coach: Deb Johnson
Email: johnsond@bethany.bethanylb.edu

NCAA I
Lady Swedes, Blue, Gold
Phone: (785) 227-3311
Fax: (785) 227-2021

Estimated # of Women's Volleyball Scholarships: N/A
Conference: KCAC

Bethel College
Academic Profile

300 E 27th Street
North Newton, KS 67117

Phone: 800-522-1887

Type: Private, 4 Yr., Liberal Arts, Coed
Website: http://www.bethelks.edu
SAT/ACT/GPA: 19
Student/Faculty Ratio: 10:1
Undergraduate Enrollment: 600
Scholarships/Academic: Yes   **Athletic:** Yes
Expenses By: Year   **In State:** $ 15,870
Specializes In: Strong in many areas: Liberal Arts, Education, Biology, Business
Degrees Conferred: BA, BS

Founded: 1887
Religion: Mennonite Church
Housing: Yes
Male/Female: 50:50
Graduate Enrollment: N/A
Financial Aid: Yes
Out of State: $ 15,870

Programs of Study: Accounting, Art, Bible and Religion, Biology, Business Administration, Chemistry, Communication Arts, Elementary Education, English, Fine Arts, German, Global Peace and Justice, Health Management and Human Ecology, History, History and Social Sciences, Mathematical Sciences, Music, Natural Sciences, Nursing, Physics, Psychology, Social Science, Social Work, Spanish, Political Science, International Development, Sociology, Special Education, Speech Communications, Theatre Arts

Women's Athletic Profile

300 E. 27th Street
North Newton, KS 67117
Coach: Bev Mayer
Email: bmayer@bethelks.edu

NCAA I
Lady Threshers, Maroon, Grey
Phone: (316) 284-5298
Fax: (316) 284-5830

Estimated # of Women's Volleyball Scholarships: partials
Conference: KCAC
Program Profile: Thresher Gymnasium seats 2,500 and has four locker rooms and a training room. Memorial Hall provides a sec-

ond gym for practices and off season workouts. Housed in the basement of Mem Hall is a Wellness Center which consists of weight room and aerobic fitness room. Also located in Memorial Hall is a Sports Medicine Center with state of the art athletic training facility.

History: Program began in 1973 with the KCAC coming into existence in 1975. Since that time, Bethel College has won the conference in volleyball 15 out of the past 24 years. The highest finish in history was in 1981 with a 3rd place finish and 1983 a 9th place finish in the nation. Region IV has been in existence for 6 years and Bethel has qualified to compete in regionals five of the six years of its existence.

Achievements: Bev Mayer-Current Coach has been named Coach of the Year 3 times in the past 6 yrs with most recent coming in 1999. Bethel has won the conference 3 of Coach Mayer's six years. Coach Mayer has coached 2 All-Americans, 8 Academic All-Americans, 6 All-Region Selection, 20 All-conference selections, 26 Academic All-Conference Selections.

Coaching: Bev Mayer-Head coach since 1994, Assistant Coach at Glendale Community College, Phoenix Arizona 1988-1994, Chad Schilling-Assistant Coach since 1993

Freshman Receiving Financial Aid/Academic: **Athletic:** 8

Roster In State: 12   **Out of State:** 3   **Out of Country:** 0

Sophomores on Team: **Seniors on Team:** 6   **Graduation %:** 99

Most Recent Record: 17-2

Camp of Clinic Dates: July 30,31 Aug 1,2001

Positions Needed: Setter and Outside Hitters

Schedule: Univ of Puerto Rico-Cayan, Concordia College, Minnesota

Style of Play: Fast Pace Offense, usually run a 5-1 offense, strong defensive teams.

Emporia State University
Academic Profile

1200 Commercial   **Phone:** (316) 341-1200
Emporia, KS 66801-5599

Type: Public, 4 Yr., Coed   **Founded:** 1863
Website: http://www.emporia.edu   **Religion:** Non-Affiliated
SAT/ACT/GPA: 21/2.0 res.2.5 non-resident   **Housing:** Yes
Student/Faculty Ratio: 18:1   **Male/Female:** 38:62
Undergraduate Enrollment: 3,787   **Graduate Enrollment:** 1,361
Scholarships/Academic: Yes   **Athletic:** Yes   **Financial Aid:** Yes
Expenses By: Semester   **In State:** $ 3,171   **Out of State:** $ 3,578
Specializes In: Education
Degrees Conferred: BS, BA, MS, MA

Programs of Study: Art, Biology, Business, Chemistry, Communications, Dramatic Arts, Earth Science, Education, English, Foreign Languages, General Studies, History, Mathematics, Music, Nursing, Physical Sciences, Physics, Political Science, Psychology, Recreation, Social Sciences and Sociology

Women's Athletic Profile

1200 Commercial   **NCAA I**
Emporia, KS 66801   Lady Hornets, Black, Gold
Coach: Maxine Mehus   **Phone:** (316) 341-1200
Email: go2esu.emporia.edu   **Fax:** (316) 341-5599

Estimated # of Women's Volleyball Scholarships: 2-3

Conference: Mid-America Intercollegiate Athletics Association

Program Profile: ESU has been a steady force in volleyball. The traditional season runs from August to November followed by the non-traditional season in the spring. The non-traditional season allows for four dates of competition. All home games are played at William Allen White Auditorium, which seats 3,700 and is located one-half mile south of the campus.

History: The ESU Hornet Volleyball program was started in the early 1970's. Emporia State was initially affiliated with the AIAW, then the NAIA and most recently the NCAA.

Achievements: Coach Mehus ranked 7th in the Active Division Coaches; Former Hornet Lena Rusche still holds the NCAA II record for most service aces in a single match when she tallied 19 against Friends University in 1991; Kristi Wetjen is 10th all-time in most kills (three game match) as she recorded 26 against Northwest Missouri State in 1996; 10 All-Americans; 1994 National Invitational Tournament Champions; Coach Mehus named NAIA District volleyball Coach of the Year 1988,1989, 1990 and 1991.

Coaching: Maxine Mehus, Head Coach, is in her 12th season at Emporia State. She received her bachelor's degree from Mayville State in 1972 and her maser's degree from South Dakota State University in 1977. Will Condon has been assistant coach for the past 3 seasons. Andrea Peak is beginning her fifth year as graduate assistant coach.

Freshman Receiving Financial Aid/Academic: **Athletic:** 13

Roster In State: 13   **Out of State:** 4   **Out of Country:** 0
Sophomores on Team: 0   **Seniors on Team:** 4   **Graduation %:** 80
Most Recent Record: 27-8-0   **Fall Games:** 35   **Spring Games:** 4
Camp of Clinic Dates: 1999-July 17-19; 20-22; 23-24
Positions Needed: Middle Hitters (1-2), Outside Hitters (1-2) Setter/RS (1)
Schedule: North Alabama, Central Missouri, Alabama-Huntsville, Rockhurst, Henderson State, Nebraska-Kearney
Style of Play: A 5-1 offense; 'swing hitting" into their offense; "hard nosed" volleyball. Aggressive play can be expected and is the style of the Hornets. The Hornets go after their opponents and play an up-tempo game.

Friends University
Academic Profile

2100 University
Wichita, KS 67213

Phone: 800-577-2233

Type: Private, 4 Yr., Liberal Arts, Coed   **Founded:** 1898
Website: http://www.friends.edu   **Religion:** Non-Affiliated
SAT/ACT/GPA: N/A/18   **Housing:** yes
Student/Faculty Ratio: 15:1   **Male/Female:** 48:52
Undergraduate Enrollment: 800   **Graduate Enrollment:** 800
Scholarships/Academic: Yes   **Athletic:** Yes   **Financial Aid:** Yes
Expenses By: Year   **In State:** $ 13,000   **Out of State:** $ 13,000
Degrees Conferred: BA, BS, BFA, MA, MS, MBA
Programs of Study: Fine Arts & Business are strong areas of study. Management, Education, Psychology

Women's Athletic Profile

2100 University
Wichita, KS 67213
Coach: Tina Schremmer-Prince
Email: tprince@friends.edu

NCAA I
Lady Falcons, Scarlet, Grey
Phone: (316) 295-5763
Fax: (316) 269-3818

Estimated # of Women's Volleyball Scholarships: 8
Conference: KCAC
Program Profile: Varsity and JV program with a facility that seats three thousand, three volleyball courts.
Freshman Receiving Financial Aid/Academic: **Athletic:** All
Roster In State: 10   **Out of State:** 3   **Out of Country:** 1
Sophomores on Team: **Seniors on Team:** 2   **Graduation %:** 90
Most Recent Record: 6-19
Positions Needed: All-5'9-5'10 setter
Style of Play: I would like to run a 5-1

Fort Hays State University
Academic Profile

600 Park St.
Hays, KS 67601

Phone: (785) 628-4392

Type: Public, 4 Yr., Liberal Arts,Coed   **Founded:** 1902
Website: http://www.fhsu.edu   **Religion:** Non-Affiliated
SAT/ACT/GPA: 68/2.0   **Housing:** Yes
Student/Faculty Ratio: 18:1   **Male/Female:** 46:54
Undergraduate Enrollment: 4,200   **Graduate Enrollment:** 1,200
Scholarships/Academic: Yes   **Athletic:** Yes   **Financial Aid:** Yes
Expenses By: Year   **In State:** $ 5,200   **Out of State:** $ 8,150
Specializes In: Education, Art, Business Wears
Degrees Conferred: AS, BA, BS, BBA, BFA, BGS, BM, BSAF, MA, MS, MBA, MFA
Programs of Study: Accounting, Art, Biological, Business, Chemistry, Communications, Computer, Earth Science, Economics, Education, English, Fine Arts, Languages, History, Management, Marketing, Music, Nursing, Philosophy, Political Science, Psychology, Social Science, Speech Pathology

Women's Athletic Profile

600 Park Street
Hays, KS 67601
Coach: Dixie E. Wescott
Email: dwescott@fhus.edu

NCAA I
Lady Tigers, Black, Gold
Phone: (785) 628-4392
Fax: (785) 628-4383

Estimated # of Women's Volleyball Scholarships: 7
Conference: Rocky Mountain Athletic Conference
Program Profile: Our first winning season was in 1999 since going NCAA in 1992. Gross Memorial Colliseum is a large, beautiful facility with 7,000 seats. The season runs from August to November.
History: We began in 1969. The program has had much success when we became a member of the NAIA. We had a National Tournament Appearance.
Achievements: 2 All-Americans; 5 Academic All-Americans
Coaching: Dixie E. Wescott, Head Coach, became head coach in 1991. Her overall record is 197-148. Harvey Sanders is assistant coach.
Freshman Receiving Financial Aid/Academic: | | **Athletic:** 1

Roster In State: 8	**Out of State:** 6	**Out of Country:** 0
Sophomores on Team: 3	**Seniors on Team:** 5	**Graduation %:** 90
Most Recent Record: 21-11-0	**Fall Games:** 32	**Spring Games:** 6

Camp of Clinic Dates: July 30-31; August 2-5
Positions Needed: Setter, Middle Hitter, Middle Blocker
Schedule: Regis, Metro State, University of Nebraska-Kearney, University of Nebraska-Omaha, Colorado Christian
Style of Play: We are defensively oriented. We have quick plays both offensively and defensively. Three persons are primarily passers allowing one setter to run the show.

Kansas State University
Academic Profile

1800 College Ave.
Manhattan, KS 66502

Phone: 785-532-6250

Type: Public, 4 Yr., Coed
Website: http://www.ksu.edu
SAT/ACT/GPA: 21avg
Student/Faculty Ratio: 16:1
Undergraduate Enrollment: 16,990
Scholarships/Academic: Yes
Expenses By: Year

Founded: 1863
Religion: Non-Affiliated
Housing: Yes
Male/Female: 54:46
Graduate Enrollment: 3,675
Athletic: Yes **Financial Aid:** Yes
In State: $ 6,000 **Out of State:** $ 11,700

Degrees Conferred: AA, AS, BA, BS, BFA, MA, MS, MFA
Programs of Study: Contact school for programs of study.

Women's Athletic Profile

Ahearn Field house
Manhattan, KS 66506
Coach: Jim McLaughlin
Email: ksuvbal@ksu.edu

NCAA I
Lady Wildcats, Purple, White
Phone: (785) 532-5935
Fax: (785) 532-2340

Estimated # of Women's Volleyball Scholarships: 3
Conference: Big 12 Conference
Program Profile: Kansas State volleyball has advanced to the NCAA tournament three consecutive years. We finished ranked #23 in the country . We were ranked among the top 12 in attendance in the legendary Ahearn Field house.
History: We began in 1973. In 1998 we marked the 25th Anniversary of Kansas State Volleyball.
Achievements: Numerous All-Big 12, All-District players; 90 NCAA Coach of the Year.
Coaching: Jim McLaughlin, Head Coach, is in his third year with the program. He coached the World University Games in 1991, 1993 & 1995, and was a US Olympic Team Consultant in 1992, & 1996. Suzie Wiemers and Jeff Grove are assistant coaches.
Freshman Receiving Financial Aid/Academic: | | **Athletic:** 4

Roster In State: 2	**Out of State:** 12	**Out of Country:** 0
Sophomores on Team: 3	**Seniors on Team:** 2	**Graduation %:** 95
Most Recent Record: 19-13-0	**Fall Games:** 32	**Spring Games:** 0

Camp of Clinic Dates: July 18-21; July 22-25; June 14-16 (Clinic)

Positions Needed: Middle Blocker, Outside Hitter
Schedule: Long Beach State, Penn State, Nebraska, Texas, Colorado, Texas A & M
Style of Play: Our primary philosophy is to teach both the technical and tactical aspects of the game of volleyball and develop athletes to learn the demands of the task involved. Our secondary philosophy is to prepare for life after volleyball and college.

Kansas Wesleyan University
Academic Profile

100 E Claflin
Salina, KS 67401

Phone: 800-874-1154

Type: Private, 4 Yr., Coed
Website: http://www.kwu.edu
SAT/ACT/GPA: 22avg
Student/Faculty Ratio: 14:1
Undergraduate Enrollment: 500
Scholarships/Academic: Yes
Expenses By: Year
Degrees Conferred: AA, AAS, BA, BS

Founded: 1886
Religion: Non-Affiliated
Housing: Yes
Male/Female: 54:46
Graduate Enrollment: N/A
Athletic: Yes
Financial Aid: Yes
In State: $ 12,100
Out of State: $ 12,100

Programs of Study: Accounting, Art, Biology, Chemistry, Communications, Computer, Criminal Justice, Dramatic Arts, Economics, History, Mathematics, Music, Physics, PreLaw, Psychology, Religion, Secondary Education, Social Science, Spanish, Special Education, Speech, Studio Art

Women's Athletic Profile

100 E. Claflin
Salina, KS 67401
Coach: Jennifer Head
Email: kjennyh@acck.edu

NCAA I
Lady Coyotes, Purple, Gold
Phone: (785) 827-3120
Fax: (785) 827-0927

Estimated # of Women's Volleyball Scholarships: N/A
Conference: KCAC

McPherson College
Academic Profile

1600 E. Euclid
McPherson, KS 67460

Phone: (316)241-0731

Type: Private, 4 Yr., Liberal Arts, Coed
Website: http://www.mcpherson.edu
SAT/ACT/GPA: 860182.25
Student/Faculty Ratio: 11.5/1
Undergraduate Enrollment: 465
Scholarships/Academic: Yes
Expenses By: Year
Specializes In: Liberal Arts (General)
Degrees Conferred: BA, BS, AT (Associates degree of Technology)

Founded: 1887
Religion: Church of the Brethren
Housing: Yes
Male/Female: 1/1
Graduate Enrollment: N/A
Athletic: No
Financial Aid: Yes
In State: $ 18,360
Out of State: $ 18,360

Programs of Study: Nearly everything, especially since we have an interdisciplinary major where if we do not have specific major, you can combine classes from different areas to form that major. Contact admissions for complete list of majors….

Women's Athletic Profile

1600 E. Euclid
McPherson, KS 67460
Coach: Jennifer Williams
Email:

NCAA I
Lady Bulldogs, Cardinal, White
Phone: (316) 241-0731
Fax: (316) 241-8443

Estimated # of Women's Volleyball Scholarships: N/A
Conference: KCAC
Program Profile: One of the only air conditioned facilities in the conference, wooden playing surface
History: Second year as head coach 3-21 first season.
Freshman Receiving Financial Aid/Academic: **Athletic:** 5

Roster In State: 4

Seniors on Team: 2

Most Recent Record: 3-21

Positions Needed: OH, MB

Schedule: Bethel College, Sterling College, Kansas Wesleyan College, Ottawa University, Mid-America Nazarene

Out of State: 10

Mid-America Nazarene University
Academic Profile

2030 E. College Way
Olathe, KS 66062

Phone: 913-782-3750

Type: Private, 4 Yr., Liberal Arts, Coed
Website: http://www.mnu.edu
SAT/ACT/GPA: 700+/18+
Student/Faculty Ratio: 20:1
Undergraduate Enrollment: 1,300
Scholarships/Academic: Yes   Athletic: Yes
Expenses By: Year   In State: $ 16,892
Degrees Conferred: AA, BA, BSN, MBA, MEd

Founded: 1966
Religion: Nazarene
Housing: Yes
Male/Female: 5:7
Graduate Enrollment: 150
Financial Aid: Yes
Out of State: $ 16,892

Programs of Study: Accounting, AgriBusiness, Biological Science, Business, Chemistry, Christian Education, Church Music, Communications, Computer Science, History, International, Management, Mathematics, Languages, Music, Physics, Psychology, Religion, Secondary Education, Spanish

Women's Athletic Profile

2030 E. College Way
Olathe, KS 66062
Coach: Lanette Sessnick
Email: rhill@mnu.edu

NCAA I
Pioneers, Red, Blue, White
Phone: (913) 791-3278
Fax: (913) 791-3456

Estimated # of Women's Volleyball Scholarships: N/A
Conference: Heart of America Athletic Conference
Program Profile: We will be in our new gymnasium next year which will seat approximately 3,500. Our season goes from September through November. We have both a varsity and a junior varsity program.
History: Our program began in the mid 1970's.
Achievements: Erin Nekvinda - NCCAA All-American 2nd team (Freshman of the Year).
Coaching: Lanette Sessink, Head Coach, began coaching in the fall of 1995, with an overall record of 64 wins and 75 losses. She was MVP for four years in volleyball at Olivet Nazarene University. She was All-American at Olivet, and was inducted into Olivet's Hall of Fame in 1992. Krystal Kennard is assistant coach.

Freshman Receiving Financial Aid/Academic: Athletic: 9
Roster In State: 10   Out of State: 12   Out of Country: 0
Sophomores on Team: 0   Seniors on Team: 4   Graduation %: 95
Most Recent Record: 18-13-0   Fall Games: 31   Spring Games: 0
Positions Needed: Setter, Middle Blocker
Schedule: Graceland College, Lindenwood University, Culver-Stockton, Pittsburgh State, Washburn University
Style of Play: Team work! team work! team work!

Newman University
Academic Profile

3100 McCormick
Wichita, KS 67213

Phone: 316-942-4291

Type: Private, 4 Yr., Liberal Arts, Coed
Website: http://www.newmanu.edu
SAT/ACT/GPA: Open182.0
Student/Faculty Ratio: N/A
Undergraduate Enrollment: 1967
Scholarships/Academic: Yes   Athletic: Yes
Expenses By: Year   In State: $14,098
Specializes In: Nursing, Pre-med, Education, Business
Degrees Conferred: AS, BA, BS

Founded: 1933
Religion: Catholic
Housing: Yes
Male/Female: 1/2
Graduate Enrollment: N/A
Financial Aid: Yes
Out of State: $14,098

Programs of Study: Accounting, Biology, Business Administration, Chemistry, Communications, Computer Science, CytoTechnology, Education, English, Fine Arts, Graphic Design, Health Science, History, Management, Marketing, Mathematics, Medical Laboratory Technology, Nursing, PreLaw, PreMed, Psychology, Religion, Social Science

Women's Athletic Profile

3100 McCormick Avenue
Wichita, KS 67213
Coach: Gary Loop
Email: loopg@newman.edu

NCAA I
Lady Jets, Scarlet, Royal
Phone: (316) 942-4291
Fax: (316) 942-4483

Estimated # of Women's Volleyball Scholarships: N/A
Conference: Midlands Collegiate Athletic College

Ottawa University
Academic Profile

1001 S. Cedar, Box #7
Ottawa, KS 66067

Phone: 785-242-5200

Type: Private, 4 Yr., Liberal Arts, Coed
Website: http://www.ottawa.edu
SAT/ACT/GPA: 18/2.5
Student/Faculty Ratio: 15:1
Undergraduate Enrollment: 500
Scholarships/Academic: Yes   **Athletic:** Yes
Expenses By: Year   **In State:** $ 14,100
Degrees Conferred: BA

Founded: 1865
Religion: American Baptist
Housing: Yes
Male/Female: 60:40
Graduate Enrollment: N/A
Financial Aid: Yes
Out of State: $ 14,100

Programs of Study: Art, Business Administration, Biology, PreMed, PreVet, PreDentistry, PreNursing, Chemistry, Communications, Education, English, History, Human Services, Management of Information Systems, Mathematics, Music, Physical Education, Political Science, Psychology, Religion, Sociology, Speech, Theatre

Women's Athletic Profile

1001 S. Cedar
Ottawa, KS 66067
Coach: Kendra Kahler
Email: kahler@ottawa.edu

NCAA I
Lady Braves, Black, Gold
Phone: (913) 242-5469
Fax: (913) 242-4393

Estimated # of Women's Volleyball Scholarships: N/A
Conference: KCAC

Pittsburgh State University
Academic Profile

1701 S. Broadway
Pittsburgh, KS 66762

Phone: (316) 235-4646

Type: Public, 4 Yr., Liberal Arts, Coed
Website: http://www.pittstate.edu
SAT/ACT/GPA: 840/18/2.0
Student/Faculty Ratio: 23:1
Undergraduate Enrollment: 5,000+
Scholarships/Academic: Yes   **Athletic:** Yes
Expenses By: Year   **In State:** $ 3,106
Specializes In: Education, Business, Engineering
Degrees Conferred: BA, BS, BBA, BSEd, BFA, BGS, BET, BSN

Founded: 1903
Religion: Non-Affiliated
Housing: Yes
Male/Female: 49:51
Graduate Enrollment: 600+
Financial Aid: Yes
Out of State: $ 5,339

Programs of Study: Art, Biology, Chemistry, Education, Communications, English, Foreign Languages, History, Math, Music, Nursing, Physics, Social Sciences, Accounting, Computer Science, Economics & Finance, Engineering, Graphics, Psychology

Women's Athletic Profile

1701 S. Broadway
Pittsburg, KS 66762
Coach: Ibraheem Suberu
Email: isuberu@pittstate.edu

NCAA I
Lady Gorillas, Crimson, Gold
Phone: 316-235-4674
Fax: (316) 235-4661

Estimated # of Women's Volleyball Scholarships: N/A
Conference: Mid-America Intercollegiate Athletics Association

Saint Mary College
Academic Profile

4100 South 4th St.
Leavenworth, KS 66048

Phone: (800) 752-7043

Type: Private, 4 Yr., Liberal Arts, Coed
Website: http://www.smcks.edu
SAT/ACT/GPA: 19/2.5
Student/Faculty Ratio: 11:1
Undergraduate Enrollment: 860
Scholarships/Academic: Yes
Expenses By: Year
Specializes In: Pre-Med, Education, Fine Arts, Theatre
Degrees Conferred: AA, BA, BS, BMus, BSN

Founded: 1858
Religion: Roman Catholic
Housing: Yes
Male/Female: 1:2
Graduate Enrollment: 400 +
Athletic: Yes   **Financial Aid:** Yes
In State: $ 15,900   **Out of State:** $ 15,900

Programs of Study: Accounting, Biology, Business Administration, Chemistry, Computer Science, Criminal Justice, Dramatic Arts, Elementary Education, English, Fine Arts, History, Human Services, Languages, Management, Mathematics, Medical Technology, Music, Nursing, Performing Arts, Psychology, Public Affairs, Social Science, Spanish, Theology, Voice

Women's Athletic Profile

4100 South 4 Trafficway
Leavenworth, KS 66048
Coach: Ibraheen Suberu
Email: admiss@lwb.smacks.edu

NCAA I
Lady Spires, Royal Blue, Gold
Phone: (913) 758-6127
Fax: (913) 758-6140

Estimated # of Women's Volleyball Scholarships: Varied
Conference: Midlands Collegiate Athletic Conference
Program Profile: We are competitive among Midwest NAIA programs.
History: Our program began in 1987.
Achievements: Several All-Conference selections and Academic All-Americans.
Coaching: Ibraheem Suberu, Head Coach, is in his second year. His overall record is 30-35.
Freshman Receiving Financial Aid/Academic: **Athletic:** 10
Roster In State: 6   **Out of State:** 6   **Out of Country:** 0
Sophomores on Team: 3   **Seniors on Team:** 3   **Graduation %:** 100
Most Recent Record: 19-18-0   **Fall Games:** 37   **Spring Games:** 2
Camp of Clinic Dates: June 2-4, June 6-10, July 26-30
Positions Needed: Middle Blocker, Outside Hitter, Setter
Schedule: Rockhurst College (NCAA II), College of St. Mary, St. Ambrose
Style of Play: Aggressive defense to attack style.

Southwestern College
Academic Profile

100 College St.
Winfield, KS 67156-2499

Phone: (316) 221-4150

Type: Private, 4 Yr., Liberal Arts, Coed
Website: http://www.sckans.edu
SAT/ACT/GPA: 889/18/2.5
Student/Faculty Ratio: 13:1
Undergraduate Enrollment: 983
Scholarships/Academic: Yes

Founded: 1885
Religion: Methodist
Housing: Yes
Male/Female: 50:50
Graduate Enrollment: 5
Athletic: Yes   **Financial Aid:** Yes

Expenses By: Year   **In State:** $ 15,924   **Out of State:** $ 15,924
Specializes In: Liberal Arts
Degrees Conferred: BA, BS, MA, M.Ed.
Programs of Study: Biology, Business Administration, Business and Computer Information Systems, Business Quality Management, Chemistry, Computer Science, Criminal Justice, Education, Elementary Education, English, Health and Physical Education, Sports Management, History, Human Resource Development, Modern Languages, Liberal Studies, Manufacturing Technology, Marine Biology, Mass Communication and Film, Mathematics, Music, Nursing, Philosophy & Religious Studies, Physics, Psychology, Theatre

Women's Athletic Profile

100 College Street
Winfield, KS 67156
Coach: Julie Murphy
Email: scadmit@jinx.sckns.edu

NCAA I
Moundbuilders, Purple, White
Phone: (316) 221-4150
Fax: (316) 221-2762

Estimated # of Women's Volleyball Scholarships: 12
Conference: KCAC
Program Profile: Stewart Fieldhouse was renovated in 1998 and seats 1,500.
History: Our program began in 1974. We won the Conference Tournament in 1994.
Achievements: We had 2 Academic All-Americans on our 1998 team.
Coaching: Julie Murphy is our head coach and Lori Wedel is our assistant coach. This year will be the coaching staff's second year with the program.

Freshman Receiving Financial Aid/Academic:		**Athletic:** 2
Roster In State: 10	**Out of State:** 1	**Out of Country:** 0
Sophomores on Team: 4	**Seniors on Team:** 2	**Graduation %:** Unknown
Most Recent Record: 9-20-0	**Fall Games:** 24	**Spring Games:** 0

Positions Needed: Middle Hitter, Setter
Schedule: William Woods, Sterling, Bethel, Peru State, Hastings
Style of Play: Very intense team; run a quick offense; very scrappy on defense

Sterling College
Academic Profile

P.O. Box 98
Sterling, KS 67579

Phone: 1-800-346-1017

Type: Private, 4 Yr., Liberal Arts, Coed
Website: http://www.sterling.edu
SAT/ACT/GPA: 860/18/2.2
Student/Faculty Ratio: 14:1
Undergraduate Enrollment: 450
Scholarships/Academic: Yes   **Athletic:** Yes
Expenses By: Year   **In State:** $ 16,522

Founded: 1887
Religion: Presbyterian
Housing: Yes
Male/Female: 2.1:25
Graduate Enrollment: N/A
Financial Aid: Yes
Out of State: $ 16,522

Specializes In: PreMed, Education, Business, Computers
Degrees Conferred: BA, BS
Programs of Study: Art, Behavioral Science, Biology, Business Administration, Christian Education, Communications and Theatre Arts, Computer Information Technology, Elementary Education, English, History and Government, Mathematics, Music, Music Education, Physical Education and Health, Religion and Philosophy, Secondary Education Certification

Women's Athletic Profile

Gleason Center Po Box 98
Sterling, KS 67579-0098
Coach: Mary Ver Steeg
Email: mversteeg@sterling.edu

NCAA I
Lady Warriors, Blue, Silver
Phone: (316) 278-4257
Fax: (316) 278-4319

Estimated # of Women's Volleyball Scholarships: Varies
Conference: KCAC-Kansas Collegiate Athletic Conference
Program Profile: Our season is in the fall and we play in the Gleason Physical Education Center, which seats 2, 500. We get strong support from our campus and local communities. We stress a year-round conditioning program. This past season we ran a 6-2 offense and would like to do so again if we can recruit the personnel to effectively run it.
History: Program began in 1975

Achievements: SC has won 2 KCAC Championships during Coach Ver Steeg's tenure. Coach Ver Steeg has twice been named KCAC Coach of the Year. In 1997 the Lady Warriors finished with a perfect KCAC record of 18-0 and qualified for the Great Plains Regional in Minnesota.

Coaching: Mary Versteeg, in her 13th season as Head Volleyball Coach at Sterling, was two time KCAC Coach of the Year in 1993, 1997.

Freshman Receiving Financial Aid/Academic: **Athletic:** 10

Roster In State: 12   **Out of State:** 5   **Out of Country:** 0

Sophomores on Team: **Seniors on Team:** 3   **Graduation %:** 94

Most Recent Record: 15-17

Positions Needed: Setter, Outside Hitters, MB

Schedule: John Brown Univ., Univ of Puerto Rico Cayey, Lyon College, Southern Naz. Univ., Benedictine College, Conoroia College, Williams Baptist, Bethel College.

Style of Play: Aggressive and efficient.

Tabor College
Academic Profile

400 S. Jefferson   **Phone:** 800-822-6799
Hillsboro, KS 67063

Type: Private, 4 Yr., Liberal Arts, Coed   **Founded:** 1908

Website: http://www.tabor.edu   **Religion:** Mennonite Brethren

SAT/ACT/GPA: 860/18   **Housing:** Yes

Student/Faculty Ratio: 14:1   **Male/Female:** 1.4:1

Undergraduate Enrollment: 500   **Graduate Enrollment:** N/A

Scholarships/Academic: Yes   **Athletic:** Yes   **Financial Aid:** Yes

Expenses By: Year   **In State:** $ 16,090 **Out of State:** $ 16,090

Degrees Conferred: AA, BA, BS

Programs of Study: Accounting, Biology, Botany, Business Law, Business Administration, Chemistry, Communication, Computer Science, Economics, Education, History, Management, Marketing, Mathematics, Medical Technology, Philosophy, Physics, Religion, Psychology, Social Science

Women's Athletic Profile

400 S. Jefferson   **NCAA I**
Hillsboro, KS 67063   Lady Bluejays, Royal Blue, Gold

Coach: Ann Leppke   **Phone:** (316) 947-3121x1312

Email: **Fax:** (316) 947-3789

Estimated # of Women's Volleyball Scholarships: N/A

Conference: KCAC

University of Kansas
Academic Profile

275 Parrott   **Phone:** (785) 864-3556
Lawrence, KS 66045

Type: Public, 4 Yr., Coed   **Founded:** 1866

Website: http://www.ukas.edu   **Religion:** Non-Affiliated

SAT/ACT/GPA: 1000+/20+/3.5   **Housing:** Yes

Student/Faculty Ratio: 20:1   **Male/Female:** 45:55

Undergraduate Enrollment: 18,892   **Graduate Enrollment:** N/A

Scholarships/Academic: Yes   **Athletic:** Yes   **Financial Aid:** Yes

Expenses By: Year   **In State:** $ 6,859 **Out of State:** $ 13,462

Specializes In: Law and Medicine

Degrees Conferred: BA, BGS, MA, MBA, MS

Programs of Study: Aerospace, Anthropology, Architecture, Art, Astronomy, Broadcasting, Business, Cellular Biology, Economics, Education, Engineering, Humanities, Illustration, Journalism, Languages, Linguistics, Mass Communications, Nursing, Pharmacy, Social Welfare, Theatre, Urban Design, Voice, Women's Studies

Women's Athletic Profile

Allen Field House
Lawrence, KS 66045-8881
Coach: Ray Bechand
Email: rayb@falcon.cc.ukans.edu
Estimated # of Women's Volleyball Scholarships: 4
Conference: Big 12 Conference

NCAA I
Lady Jayhawks, Crimson, Blue
Phone: (785) 864-3921
Fax: (785) 864-5035

Program Profile: Just moved into a brand new volleyball facility, 3 practice courts. Competition court and new VB locker room. Seats 2000. Also play some matches in Allen Field house 16,500 capacity.

History: Volleyball program has been in existence since 1960's. Very strong in the 70's. Average team in the Big 8 Conference. Now building phase, looking to get into the NCAA tournament in the next year

Achievements: Coach Bechand was Jr. College Coach of the Year 90 and 1993. Completed his career at BCCC with highest all-time winning record among Jr. College Coaches.

Roster In State: 2   **Out of State:** 10   **Out of Country:**
Sophomores on Team: **Seniors on Team:** 5   **Graduation %:** 100
Most Recent Record: 13-15   **Fall Games:** 30   **Spring Games:** 3-4 tournament
Positions Needed: 2 OH, 1 MB, 1RS
Schedule: Nebraska, Texas, Colorado
Style of Play: Good blocking team, good mix of experience and talent for fall season. Lots of middle attacking

Washburn University
Academic Profile

1700 SW College Ave.
Topeka, KS 66621

Phone: 800-332-0291

Type: Public, 4 Yr., Coed
Website: hhtp://www.washburn.edu
SAT/ACT/GPA: Sliding Scale
Student/Faculty Ratio: 18:1
Undergraduate Enrollment: 5,500
Scholarships/Academic: Yes   **Athletic:** Yes
Expenses By: Year   **In State:** $ 7,455

Founded: 1865
Religion: Non-Affiliated
Housing: Yes
Male/Female: 1:1
Graduate Enrollment: 7
Financial Aid: Yes
Out of State: $ 11,325

Degrees Conferred: AA, AS, AAS, BA, BS, BFA, BM, MA
Programs of Study: Accounting, Anthropology, Art, Banking and Finance, Biological Science, Business, Chemistry, Communications, Computer Science, Criminal, Dramatic Arts, Early Childhood Education, Economics, Education, English, History, Information Management, Marketing, Mathematics, Medical, Music, Philosophy, Physics, Political Science, Psychology, Secondary Education, Social Science

Women's Athletic Profile

1700 College
Topeka, KS 66621
Coach: Allison Jones
Email: zzjones@washburn.edu
Estimated # of Women's Volleyball Scholarships: N/A
Conference: Mid-America Intercollegiate Athletics Association

NCAA I
Lady Blues, Yale Blue, White
Phone: 785-231-1010
Fax: (785) 231-1091

Wichita State University
Academic Profile

1845 Fairmount
Wichita, KS 67260-0018

Phone: (316) 978-3257

Type: Public, 4 Yr., Coed
Website: http://www.twsu.edu
SAT/ACT/GPA: Variable between colleges
Student/Faculty Ratio: 20:1
Undergraduate Enrollment: 11,515
Scholarships/Academic: Yes   **Athletic:** Yes
Expenses By: Year   **In State:** $ 7,382

Founded: 1895
Religion: Non-Affiliated
Housing: Yes
Male/Female: 49:51
Graduate Enrollment: 3.154
Financial Aid: Yes
Out of State: $ 14,103

Specializes In: Engineering (including Aeronautical), Business (Entrepreneurship)

Degrees Conferred: BA, BS, MA, MS, MBA
Programs of Study: Accounting, Advertising, Anthropology, Art Education, Art History, BioChemistry, Biology, Business Administration, Communications, Dental Hygiene, Economics, Exercises, Finance, Fine Arts, French, German, Gerontology, Graphic Design, Health Professions, Health Science, History, International Marketing, Liberal Arts, Mathematics, Nursing, Physical Education, Real Estate, Music Education, Public Health, Secondary Education, Social Studies, Spanish

Women's Athletic Profile

1845 Fairmount
Wichita, KS 67260
Coach: Phil Shoemaker
Email: dudley@twsuvm.uc.twsu.edu

NCAA I
Lady Shockers, Black, Yellow
Phone: (316) 978-3257
Fax: (316) 978-3388

Estimated # of Women's Volleyball Scholarships: 3
Conference: Missouri Valley Conference
Program Profile: We are a NCAA Division I team with full compliment of 12 scholarships. We had 6 playoff appearances in the 1990's. We have excellent facilities and a home arena that seats 10,500. We were in the Nation's top 10 academically , 4 times in the 1990's.
History: We were reinstated in 1983 and have since established ourselves as one of the top teams in the Missouri Valley Conference. We are competitive regionally and nationally.
Achievements: We have had 16 All-conference selections. We've received the AVCA Coaches Academic Team Award four times. Michele Hallagrin, a senior setter was a selection on the 3rd team Academic All-American Team.
Coaching: Phil Shoemaker became head coach of the program in 1983. He is the winningest coach in WSU's history. His overall record is 234-280. He served as a coach and administrator for the USA Junior National Program. He has coached 20 All-Americans at the junior boys level. Chris dudley, Assistant Coach, started with the program in 1997. Jodi Harmsen, Graduate Assistant, started in 1998.
Freshman Receiving Financial Aid/Academic: **Athletic:** 2
Roster In State: 3   **Out of State:** 10   **Out of Country:** 0
Sophomores on Team: 3   **Seniors on Team:** 3   **Graduation %:** 100
Most Recent Record: 17-17-0   **Fall Games:** 31   **Spring Games:** 12
Camp of Clinic Dates: June 6-10,June 14-17,July 12-15, July 19-22
Positions Needed: Setter, Middle Hitter, Outside Hitter
Schedule: University of Arkansas, Oral Roberts University, University of Kansas, Northern Iowa University, Illinois State University, University of Oklahoma
Style of Play: We have an aggressive, fun-loving, hard-working open style of play.

KENTUCKY

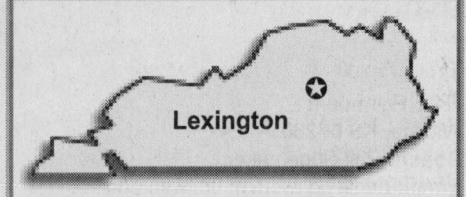

Lexington

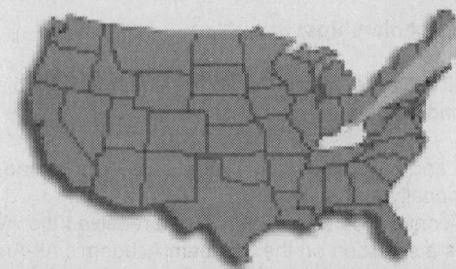

SCHOOL	CITY	AFFILIATION	PAGE
Asbury College	Wilmore	NAIA	290
Bellarmine College	Louisville	NCAA II	290
Berea College	Berea	NAIA	291
Brescia University	Owensboro	NAIA	291
Campbellsville University	Campbellsville	NCCAA/NAIA	292
Centre College	Danville	NCAA III	292
Cumberland College	Williamsburg	NAIA	293
Eastern Kentucky University	Richmond	NCAA I	293
Georgetown College	Georgetown	NAIA	294
Kentucky Christian College	Grayson	NCCAA	295
Kentucky State University	Frankfort	NCAA II	295
Kentucky Wesleyan College	Owensboro	NCAA II	295
Lindsey Wilson College	Columbia	NAIA	296
Midway College	Midway	NAIA	296
Morehead State University	Morehead	NCAA I	297
Murray State University	Murray	NCAA I	297
Northern Kentucky University	Highland Heights	NCAA II	298
Pikeville College	Pikeville	NAIA	299
Spalding University	Louisville	NAIA I	299
Thomas More College	Crestview Hills	NCAA III	300
Union College	Barbourville	NAIA	300
University of Kentucky	Lexington	NCAA I	301
University of Louisville	Louisville	NCAA I	301
Western Kentucky University	Bowling Green	NCAA I	302

Asbury College
Academic Profile

1 Macklem Drive
Wilmore, KY 40390

Phone: 800-888-1818

Type: Private, 4 Yr., Liberal Arts, Coed
Website: http://www.asbury.edu
SAT/ACT/GPA: 1000/21/2.5
Student/Faculty Ratio: 13.3:1
Undergraduate Enrollment: 1,300
Scholarships/Academic: Yes
Expenses By: Year
Specializes In: Communication, Education
Degrees Conferred: BA, BS

Athletic: Yes
In State: $ 16,410

Founded: 1890
Religion: Christian
Housing: Yes
Male/Female: 43:57
Graduate Enrollment: N/A
Financial Aid: Yes
Out of State: $ 16,410

Programs of Study: Accounting, Art, Athletic Training, Bible, BioChemistry, Business, Chemistry, Christian Ministries and Mission, Languages, Communication, Economics, Education, Engineering, English, Exercise Science, History, Journalism, Math, Music, Philosophy, Physical Education, PreMed, Psychology, Recreation, Social Work, Sociology, Theatre, Urban Studies

Women's Athletic Profile

1 Macklem Drive
Wilmore, KY 40390
Coach: David A. Baillie
Email: david.baillie@asbury.edu

NCAA I
Lady Eagles, Purple, White
Phone: (800)888-1818
Fax: (606) 858-3921

Estimated # of Women's Volleyball Scholarships: N/A
Conference: KIAC

Bellarmine College
Academic Profile

Newburg Rd.
Louisville, KY 40205

Phone: 800-274-4723

Type: Private, 4 Yr., Liberal Arts, Coed
Website: http://www.bellarmine.edu
SAT/ACT/GPA: 950/21/2.5
Student/Faculty Ratio: 14:1
Undergraduate Enrollment: 1,250
Scholarships/Academic: Yes
Expenses By: Year
Degrees Conferred: BA, BS, BSN, MA, M.Ed., MAT, MBA, MLS

Athletic: Yes
In State: $ 15,050

Founded: 1950
Religion: Catholic
Housing: Yes
Male/Female: 41:59
Graduate Enrollment: 950
Financial Aid: Yes
Out of State: $ 15,050

Programs of Study: Accounting, Art, Art Administration, Biology, Business Administration, Chemistry, Communication, Computer Engineering, Computer Science, Economics, Education, English, History, Mathematics, Music, Nursing, Philosophy, Political Science, Psychology, Sociology, Theology

Women's Athletic Profile

Newburg Rd.
Louisville, KY 40205
Coach: Kevin Payne
Email: kpayne@bellarmine.edu

NCAA I
Lady Knights, Scarlet, Silver
Phone: (502) 452-8380
Fax: (502) 452-8450

Estimated # of Women's Volleyball Scholarships: N/A
Conference: Great Lakes Valley Conference
History: Bellarmine began volleyball in 1972, where it was a club sport. In 1975, volleyball became a collegiate sport.
Achievements: Over the past few years, Bellarmine has had numerous players achieve all conference honors. Also freshman of the year and all-academic teams.
Coaching: Kevin Payne, 1983 graduate from Univ. of Louisville, has been the head coach for the past 14 seasons. His record at Bellarmine is 208-232 (not including this year)

Roster In State: 8
Sophomores on Team:
Most Recent Record: 5-14
Schedule: Northern Kentucky

Out of State: 3
Seniors on Team: 2

Out of Country: 0
Graduation %:

Berea College
Academic Profile

CPO 2287
Berea, KY 40404

Phone: 800-326-5948

Type: Private, 4 Yr., Liberal Arts, Coed
Website: http://www.berea.edu
SAT/ACT/GPA: 950/21
Student/Faculty Ratio: 14:1
Undergraduate Enrollment: N/A
Scholarships/Academic: No   **Athletic:** No
Expenses By: Year   **In State:** $ 7,000
Degrees Conferred: BA, BS
Programs of Study: Biblical Studies, Guidance, Ministries, Religious Education, Theology

Founded: 1855
Religion: Nonsectarian Christian
Housing: No
Male/Female: 45:55
Graduate Enrollment: N/A
Financial Aid: Yes
Out of State: $ 7,000

Women's Athletic Profile

CPO 2287
Berea, KY 40404
Coach: Jim Larkin
Email:

NCAA I
Lady Mountaineers, Blue, White
Phone: (606) 986-9341x5433
Fax: (606) 986-7505

Estimated # of Women's Volleyball Scholarships: N/A
Conference: KIAC

Brescia College
Academic Profile

717 Frederica Street
Owensboro, KY 42301-3023

Phone: 877-273-7242

Type: Private, 4 Yr., Liberal Arts, Coed
Website: http://www.brescia.edu
SAT/ACT/GPA: Open
Student/Faculty Ratio: 15:1
Undergraduate Enrollment: 760
Scholarships/Academic: Yes   **Athletic:** Yes
Expenses By: Year   **In State:** $ 11,849
Degrees Conferred: AA, AS, BA, BS, MS in Management
Programs of Study: Accounting, Art, Art Education, Biology, Business, Chemistry, English, General Studies, Graphic Design, History, Mathematics, PreProfessional Courses, Psychology, Social Studies, Sociology

Founded: 1950
Religion: Catholic
Housing: Yes
Male/Female: 38:62
Graduate Enrollment: 9
Financial Aid: Yes
Out of State: $ 11,849

Women's Athletic Profile

717 Frederica
Owensboro, KY 42301
Coach: Kelly Lewis-Kiplinger
Email:

NCAA I
Lady Bearcats, Blue, White
Phone: (502) 688-4207
Fax: (502) 686-4317

Estimated # of Women's Volleyball Scholarships: N/A
Coaching: Kelly Lewis-Kiplinger is beginning her first season as head coach. She is a certified personal trainer with the National Strength and Conditioning Association. Heather Heister is assistant coach. She was a two year letter winner and 1997 MVP from Brescia.
Roster In State: 4   **Out of State:** 4   **Out of Country:** 0
Sophomores on Team: 1   **Seniors on Team:** 3   **Graduation %:** 100
Most Recent Record: 15-12-0
Schedule: Madonna, Michigan, St. Xavier, Central St., Oakland City University, Indiana University Southeast, Lindsey Wilson College, Asbury College, Bethel College, Spalding, McKendree, Pikeville, Kentucky Wesleyan College

Campbellsville University
Academic Profile

1 University Drive
Campbellsville, KY 42718

Phone: 800-264-6014

Type: Private, 4 Yr., Liberal Arts,Coed
Website: http://www.campbellsvil.edu
SAT/ACT/GPA: 890/19
Student/Faculty Ratio: 16:1
Undergraduate Enrollment: 1,530
Scholarships/Academic: Yes   **Athletic:** Yes
Expenses By: Year   **In State:** $ 11,700
Degrees Conferred: BA, BS, AA

Founded: 1906
Religion: Baptist
Housing: Yes
Male/Female: 1:9
Graduate Enrollment: 37
Financial Aid: Yes
Out of State: $ 11,700

Programs of Study: Accounting, Art, Athletic Training, Biology, Business Administration, Economics, Office Management, Chemistry, English, History, Journalism, Mathematics, PreProfessional Courses, Psychology, Social Work, Sociology, Sports Medicine/Exercise Science

Women's Athletic Profile

1 University Drive
Campbellsville, KY 42718
Coach: Shannon Wathen
Email: swathen@campbellsvil.edu

NCAA I
Tigers, Maroon, Grey, White
Phone: (207)789-5261
Fax: (502) 789-5095

Did Not Return Profile

Centre College
Academic Profile

600 West Walnut St.
Danville, KY 40422

Phone: 859-238-5493

Type: Private, 4 Yr., Liberal Arts, Coed
Website: http://www.centre.edu
SAT/ACT/GPA: 1150/25/3.0
Student/Faculty Ratio: 10/1
Undergraduate Enrollment: 1,150
Scholarships/Academic: Yes   **Athletic:** No
Expenses By: Year   **In State:** $ 22,400
Specializes In: Biology, Chemistry, Education, Pre Med, Pre Law
Degrees Conferred: BA, BS

Founded: 1819
Religion: Presbyterian
Housing: Yes
Male/Female: 1:1
Graduate Enrollment: N/A
Financial Aid: Yes
Out of State: $ 22,400

Programs of Study: Art, Anthropology, BioChemistry, Molecular Biology, Biology, Chemistry, Chemical Physics, Classics, Economics, Elementary Education, English, French, German, Government, History, Mathematics, Music, Philosophy, Physics, PsychoBiology, Psychology, Religion, PreLaw, PreMed, Secondary Education

Women's Athletic Profile

600 W. Walnut Street
Danville, KY 40422
Coach: Stephanie Dragan
Email: dragon@centre.edu

NCAA I
Lady Colonels, Gold, White
Phone: 800-423-6236
Fax: 606-236-6081

Estimated # of Women's Volleyball Scholarships: N/A
Conference: Southern California Athletic Conference
Program Profile: We have a strong tradition in Region and Conference averaging 26 wins per season. We have a significant increase in our operating budget and the expansion of our two facilitates. Our playing season begins in September and ends in November.
History: Volleyball became varsity in 1986. In 1996, the school record was 32-9. We have been averaging 23 victories per season.
Coaching: Stephanie Dragan, Head Coach, first season at Centre. Her overall record is 15-17. She was a Standout Player at Shawnee State University.
Freshman Receiving Financial Aid/Academic: **Athletic:** 0
Roster In State: 2   **Out of State:** 7   **Out of Country:** 0

Sophomores on Team: 3
Most Recent Record: 15-17-0
Camp of Clinic Dates: June 21-26
Positions Needed: Middle Hitters, Outside Hitters
Schedule: Trinity-Texas, Emory, Southwestern-Texas, DePauw, Ohio Northern, Washington & Lee
Style of Play: Quick tempo, large emphasis on blocking, big heart defense.

Seniors on Team: 1
Fall Games: 32

Graduation %: 99
Spring Games: TBA

Cumberland College
Academic Profile

6178 College Station Drive.
Williamsburg, KY 40769

Phone: (606) 539-4241

Type: Private, 4 Yr., Liberal Arts, Coed
Website: http://www.cumber.edu
SAT/ACT/GPA: Sliding Scale/18/2.0
Student/Faculty Ratio: 16:1
Undergraduate Enrollment: 1,416
Scholarships/Academic: Yes
Expenses By: Year
Specializes In: Liberal Arts, Preprofessional Programs
Degrees Conferred: Bachelor - Arts, Science, Music, General Studies, M.Ed.
Programs of Study: Biological Sciences/Life Sciences, Computer and Information Sciences, Education, English Languages and Literature/Letters, Law and Legal Studies, Mathematics, Philosophy and Religion, Physical Sciences, Psychology, Social Sciences and History, Theological Studies and Religion Vocations, Visual and Performing Arts

Founded: 1889
Religion: Baptist
Housing: Yes
Male/Female: 45:55
Graduate Enrollment: 180

Athletic: Yes
In State: $ 14,106

Financial Aid: Yes
Out of State: $ 14,106

Women's Athletic Profile

7526 College Station Drive
Williamsburg, KY 40769
Coach: Dale Walker
Email:

NCAA I
Lady Indians, Maroon, White
Phone: (606) 539-4155
Fax: (606) 539-4459

Estimated # of Women's Volleyball Scholarships: 4 1/2
Conference: Mid-South Conference
Program Profile: Our games are played in our new 2,000 seat arena. We have practice facilities in I.M.Gynmasium that allows for double courts to be used. Our program includes varsity and junior varsity schedules.
History: Our program began in 1992. Our teams have struggled in the early years. In our past seasons under Coach Walker, school records in wins were set. This past season we recorded a school record of 14 wins.
Achievements: 5 All-Conference players; one NAIA Academic All-American; 1998-99 third place in the Conference - the highest rank in our history
Coaching: Dale Walker, Head Coach, took over a team that recorded only 4 wins in 1996-97. In his first season, the team went 10-22. This past season, the record was 14-19. With everyone returning and the addition of key recruits, the team should be strong.
Freshman Receiving Financial Aid/Academic:
Roster In State: 0
Sophomores on Team: 5
Most Recent Record: 14-19-0
Camp of Clinic Dates: Team Camp July 18 - July 23 1999
Positions Needed: Would like to carry 20 athletes on roster
Schedule: Georgetown, Lincoln Memorial University, Cumberland University, Campbellsville, Union College, Brevard
Style of Play: Use quick hit offense mostly 5-1 sets.

Athletic: 5
Out of State: 12
Seniors on Team: 2
Fall Games: 33

Out of Country: 1
Graduation %: 100
Spring Games: 5

Eastern Kentucky University
Academic Profile

129 Alumni Coliseum
Richmond, KY 40475

Phone: 800-465-9191

Type: Public, 4 Yr., Coed
Website: http://www.eku.edu
SAT/ACT/GPA: Open
Student/Faculty Ratio: 16:1

Founded: 1909
Religion: Non-Affiliated
Housing: Yes
Male/Female: 1:2

Undergraduate Enrollment: 15,000

Graduate Enrollment: 2,000

Scholarships/Academic: Yes **Athletic:** Yes **Financial Aid:** Yes

Expenses By: Year **In State:** $ 5,190 **Out of State:** $ 12,030

Specializes In: Education, Police Administration, Nursing

Degrees Conferred: AA, BA, BS, BFA, BBA, BM, BSN, MA, MS

Programs of Study: Anthropology, Banking/Finance, Chemistry, Construction, Corrections, Dietetics, Economics, English, Environmental, Fashion, History, Insurance, Interior Design, Industrial, Law, Management, Marketing, Philosophy, Real Estate, Religion, Wildlife

Women's Athletic Profile

521 Lancaster Avenue
Richmond, KY 40475-3101
Coach: Lori Duncan
Email: athduncl@acs.eku.edu

NCAA I
Lady Colonels, Maroon, White
Phone: (606) 622-3654
Fax: (606) 622-5108

Estimated # of Women's Volleyball Scholarships: 12
Conference: Ohio Valley Conference
Program Profile: We play in McBrayer Arena with 6,000 seats. Our playing season is in the fall.
History: We have been Perennial Conference Champions through 1995. We are currently rebuilding and have a new coach.
Coaching: Lori Duncan is our new head coach.
Freshman Receiving Financial Aid/Academic: **Athletic:** 4
Roster In State: 8 **Out of State:** 8 **Out of Country:** 0
Sophomores on Team: 0 **Seniors on Team:** 1 **Graduation %:** 100
Most Recent Record: 3-17-0 **Fall Games:** 28 **Spring Games:** 4
Camp of Clinic Dates: Summer 1999
Positions Needed: All
Schedule: Tennessee, Kentucky, Louisville

Georgetown College
Academic Profile

400 East College St.
Georgetown, KY 40324

Phone: 800-788-9985

Type: Private, 4 Yr., Liberal Arts, Coed
Website: http://www.gtc.georgetown.ky.us
SAT/ACT/GPA: 930/20
Student/Faculty Ratio: 10:1
Undergraduate Enrollment: 1,200
Scholarships/Academic: Yes **Athletic:** Yes
Expenses By: Year **In State:** $ 5,432

Founded: 1829
Religion: Baptist
Housing: Yes
Male/Female: 50:50
Graduate Enrollment: 200
Financial Aid: Yes
Out of State: $ 5,432

Degrees Conferred: BA, BS, MA

Programs of Study: Accounting, American Studies, Biological Sciences, Business Administration, Chemistry, Economics, Elementary Education, Environmental Science, History, Marketing/Finance, Mathematics, Medical Technology, Philosophy, Physical Education, Physics, Political Science, PreProfessional Courses, Psychology, Sociology

Women's Athletic Profile

400 East College Street
Georgetown, KY 40324
Coach: Donna Hawkins
Email: dhawkins@georgetowncollege.edu

NCAA I
Lady Tigers, Black, Orange
Phone: (502) 863-8061
Fax: (502) 868-8892

Estimated # of Women's Volleyball Scholarships: Variable
Conference: Mid-South Conference
Program Profile: Top-20 NAIA Program. Multiple appearances in NAIA tournament. Season from August through November. 1,500-seat gymnasium.
History: 583-213 Record over last 19 years. 1980-1st year recommended.
Achievements: Five consecutive Conference Titles. Six-Time Coach of the Year-Donna Hawkins. Hawkins was conference and region Coach of the Year in 1998.
Coaching: Hawkins (Georgetown '65) 583-213 career record
Doneva Bays (Milligan '97) All-American at Milligan

Roster In State: 7   **Out of State:** 5   **Out of Country:** 0
Most Recent Record: 25-8   **Fall Games:** All   **Spring Games:**

Kentucky Christian College
Academic Profile

100 Academic Parkway
Grayson, KY 41143-2005
Type: Private, 4 Yr., Coed
Website: http://www.kcc.edu
SAT/ACT/GPA: 830/17/2.0
Student/Faculty Ratio: 48:52
Undergraduate Enrollment: 550
Scholarships/Academic: Yes   **Athletic:** No
Expenses By: Year   **In State:** $ 11,500
Degrees Conferred: AA, BA, BS, BSW

Phone: 800-522-3181

Founded: 1919
Religion: Church of Christ
Housing: Yes
Male/Female: 16:1
Graduate Enrollment: N/A
Financial Aid: Yes
Out of State: $ 11,500

Programs of Study: History, PreLaw, Christian Ministry, Psychology, Counseling, Social Work, Business Administration, Music, Music Education, Teacher Education, Elementary, Church Music, Bible

Women's Athletic Profile

100 Academic Parkway
Grayson, KY 41143
Coach: Bruce W. Dixon
Email: bdixon@email.kcc.edu

NCAA I
Lady Knights, Black, Red, White
Phone: (606) 474-3215
Fax: (606) 474-3159

Did Not Return Profile

Kentucky State University
Academic Profile

E. Main St.
Frankford, KY 40601

Type: Public, 4 Yr., Coed
Website: http://www.kysu.edu
SAT/ACT/GPA: 800/19
Student/Faculty Ratio: 14:1
Undergraduate Enrollment: 800
Scholarships/Academic: Yes   **Athletic:** Yes
Expenses By: Year   **In State:** $ 13,250
Degrees Conferred: Associate in Nursing, BA, BS

Phone: 502-227-6813

Founded: 1858
Religion: Non-Affiliated
Housing: No
Male/Female: 50:50
Graduate Enrollment: N/A
Financial Aid: Yes
Out of State: $ 13,250

Programs of Study: Business and Management, Communications, Education, Health Science, Life Science, Psychology, Social Science

Women's Athletic Profile

E. Main street
Frankfort, KY 40601
Coach: Carol J. Washington Clark
Email:

NCAA I
Lady Thorobrettes, Green, Gold
Phone: (502) 597-5974
Fax: (502) 227-6466

Estimated # of Women's Volleyball Scholarships: N/A
Conference: Southern Intercollegiate Conference

Kentucky Wesleyan College
Academic Profile

PO Box 1039
Owensboro, KY 42301

Type: Private, 4 Yr., Liberal Arts, Coed
Website: http://www.kwc.edu

Phone: 800-999-0592

Founded: 1858
Religion: United Methodist

SAT/ACT/GPA: 800/19
Student/Faculty Ratio: 14:1
Undergraduate Enrollment: 800
Scholarships/Academic: Yes
Expenses By: Year
Degrees Conferred: Associate in Nursing, BA, BS
Programs of Study: Business & Management, Communications, Education, Health Sciences, Life Sciences, Psychology, Social Sciences

Athletic: Yes
In State: $ 13,250

Housing: No
Male/Female: 50:50
Graduate Enrollment: N/A
Financial Aid: Yes
Out of State: $ 13,250

Women's Athletic Profile

P.O. Box 1039, 3000 Frederica St.
Owensboro, KY 42302-1039
Coach: Kelly Bennett
Email:

NCAA I
Lady Panthers, Purple, White
Phone: (502) 683-4795x483
Fax: (502) 684-5028

Lindsey Wilson College
Academic Profile

210 Lindsey Wilson St.
Columbia, KY 42728

Phone: 270-384-2126

Type: Private, 4 Yr., Liberal Arts, Coed
Website: http://www.lindsey.edu
SAT/ACT/GPA: 860/18
Student/Faculty Ratio: 20:1
Undergraduate Enrollment: 1,320
Scholarships/Academic: Yes
Expenses By: Year
Degrees Conferred: AA, BA, BS, MA
Programs of Study: All Liberal Art types including: Business and Management, Computer Science, Education, and all Preprofessional Programs

Athletic: Yes
In State: $ 12,510

Founded: 1903
Religion: Methodist
Housing: Yes
Male/Female: 60:40
Graduate Enrollment: 50
Financial Aid: Yes
Out of State: $ 12,510

Women's Athletic Profile

210 Lindsey Wilson Street
Columbia, KY 42728
Coach: Holly Sheilley
Email: sheilley@lindsey.edu

NCAA I
Lady Blue Raiders, Blue, White
Phone: (502) 384-8058
Fax: (502) 384-8070

Midway College
Academic Profile

512 E Stephens Street
Midway, KY 40347-1120
Type: Private, 4 Yr., Liberal Arts, Women Only
Website: Not Available
SAT/ACT/GPA: 860/18
Student/Faculty Ratio: 13:1
Undergraduate Enrollment: 1,000
Scholarships/Academic: Yes
Expenses By: Year
Specializes In: Nursing, Equestrian Studies
Degrees Conferred: 12 Degreed Programs
Programs of Study: Accounting, Biology, Business, Computer Information System, Early Childhood Education, Equine Studies, Liberal Studies, Nursing, Paralegal, Physical Therapy Assistant, Psychology, Teacher Education

Phone: 800-755-0031

Athletic: Yes
In State: $ 12,260

Founded: 1847
Religion: Disciples of Christ
Housing: Yes
Male/Female: Women
Graduate Enrollment: N/A
Financial Aid: Yes
Out of State: $ 12,260

Women's Athletic Profile

512 E. Stephen Street
Midway, KY 40347
Coach: Walter Pauly
Email: jmcdannold@midway.edu

NCAA I
Lady Eagles, Royal, White, Gold
Phone: (606) 846-5761
Fax: (606) 846-5754

Estimated # of Women's Volleyball Scholarships: 4
Conference: Kentucky Intercollegiate Conference
Freshman Receiving Financial Aid/Academic: **Athletic:** 3
Roster In State: 6   **Out of State:** 3   **Out of Country:** 0
Sophomores on Team: **Seniors on Team:** 1   **Graduation %:** 89
Positions Needed: Setter
Schedule: Georgetown, Indian Southwest, Spartanburg

Morehead State University
Academic Profile

UPO Box 1004   **Phone:** (606) 783-2089
Morehead, KY 40351

Type: Public, 4 Yr., Coed   **Founded:** 1923
Website: http://www.morehead-st.edu   **Religion:** Non-Affiliated
SAT/ACT/GPA: 14+   **Housing:** Yes
Student/Faculty Ratio: 18:1   **Male/Female:** 1:2
Undergraduate Enrollment: 6,734   **Graduate Enrollment:** 1,520
Scholarships/Academic: Yes   **Athletic:** Yes   **Financial Aid:** Yes
Expenses By: Year   **In State:** $ 4,858+ **Out of State:** $ 8,698+
Specializes In: Education, Business, Communications, Nursing, PreLaw, PreVet
Degrees Conferred: AA, BA, BS,MA
Programs of Study: MSU offers 72 Undergraduate degree programs, including 15 Associate level degrees and 10 PreProfessional programs in four colleges-Business, Education, Behavioral Sciences, Humanities and Science and Technology and 21 academic departments. There are 24 graduate degree programs plus 2 graduate level non-degree programs designed especially for professional educators.

Women's Athletic Profile

University Boulevard   **NCAA I**
Morehead, KY 40351-1689   Lady Eagles, Royal Blue, Gold
Coach: Mike Swan   **Phone:** (606) 783-2089
Email: mswan@morehead-st.edu   **Fax:** (606) 783-5035

Estimated # of Women's Volleyball Scholarships: 2
Conference: Ohio Valley Conference
Program Profile: The Eagle team trains and competes in Wetherby Gymnasium, which seats 5,000. In 1999-2000, the Eagles will compete in 27 regular season appearances and attend four spring tournaments.
History: The women's volleyball program began in 1971 and has seen four coaches prior to Mike Swan. The total record is 612-344-7(.561). The program has had six regular season Championship Titles and two Conference Tournament Titles.
Achievements: Mid-East Region Coach of the Year 1993; Conference Coach of the Year 1986 and 1993; 7 Conference Championships; 1 All-American, 1998 team ranked 2nd in nation for team G.P.A.
Coaching: Mike Swan is in his 2nd year as head coach. His career record is 320-170. Amy Dettmer is in her 2nd year as assistant coach. She was All-Conference setter for 2 seasons.
Freshman Receiving Financial Aid/Academic: **Athletic:** 1
Roster In State: 4   **Out of State:** 10   **Out of Country:** 0
Sophomores on Team: 4   **Seniors on Team:** 6   **Graduation %:** Unknown
Most Recent Record: 15-18-0   **Fall Games:** 33   **Spring Games:** 4
Positions Needed: Middle, Left Side Hitter
Schedule: Miami of Ohio, Ball State, Southeast Missouri, North Carolina State, Eastern Illinois, West Virginia University
Style of Play: Aggressive on defense; up-tempo offense; disciplined; use many players.

Murray State University
Academic Profile

Athletic Dept. Stewart Stadium   **Phone:** 800-272-4678
Murray, KY 42071

Type: Public, 4 Yr., Coed   **Founded:** 1922
Website: http://www.murraystate.edu   **Religion:** Non-Affiliated
SAT/ACT/GPA: 18   **Housing:** Yes
Student/Faculty Ratio: 16:1   **Male/Female:** 46:54

Undergraduate Enrollment: 7,350
Scholarships/Academic: Yes **Athletic:** Yes
Expenses By: Year **In State:** $ 6,450
Degrees Conferred: AA, AS, BA, BS, BFA, BSN, BSA, MA, MS

Graduate Enrollment: 1,550
Financial Aid: Yes
Out of State: $ 6,450

Programs of Study: Accounting, Art, Biology, Business, Chemistry, Engineering, Construction, Consumer Affairs, Dietetics, Earth Science, Finance, Manufacturing, Marketing, Music, Medical, Middle School, Occupational, Parks/Recreation Management, Education, Speech, Theatre, Vocational

Women's Athletic Profile

Athletic Dept. Stewart Stadium
Murray, KY 42071-0009
Coach: Dave Schwepker
Email: David.Schwepker@Murraystate.edu

NCAA I
Lady Racers, Navy Blue, Gold
Phone: (502) 762-6800
Fax: (502) 762-6814

Estimated # of Women's Volleyball Scholarships: 12
Conference: Ohio Valley Conference
Program Profile: The team plays at Cutchin Fieldhouse which is the second largest volleyball-only facility in Division I in the nation. It has a seating capacity of 5,500. A hardwood playing surface was installed in 1987.
History: The program began in 1983. Our overall record is 232-293-1 (.442) in 16 seasons.
Achievements: OVC Tournament Championships in 1989 and 1992; 2 NIVC Tournament Appearances.
Coaching: David Schwepker, Head Coach, started with the program in February, 1998. Marlene Metti, Assistant Coach, started with the program in July, 1998.

Freshman Receiving Financial Aid/Academic: **Athletic:** 4
Roster In State: 1 **Out of State:** 11 **Out of Country:** 0
Sophomores on Team: 0 **Seniors on Team:** **Graduation %:** Unknown
Most Recent Record: 13-19-0 **Fall Games:** 32 **Spring Games:** 12
Camp of Clinic Dates: N/A
Positions Needed: Middle Blockers, Outside Hitter (left side) Defensive Setter
Schedule: University of Connecticut, Delaware, Cleveland State, Southeast Missouri State University, St. Louis University, Ohio Univ.
Style of Play: Fast offense & great defense.

Northern Kentucky University
Academic Profile

Nunn Drive
Highland Heights, KY 41099-7500

Phone: (606) 572-6372

Type: Public, 4 Yr., Coed
Website: http://www.nku.edu
SAT/ACT/GPA: 18
Student/Faculty Ratio: 12.5:1
Undergraduate Enrollment: 12,489
Scholarships/Academic: Yes **Athletic:** Yes
Expenses By: Year **In State:** $ 6,432
Specializes In: Broad scope of programs

Founded: 1968
Religion: Non-Affiliated
Housing: Yes
Male/Female: 58:42
Graduate Enrollment: 897
Financial Aid: Yes
Out of State: $ 10,272

Degrees Conferred: BA, BS, BFA, BMus, BMus Ed, BSN, BSW, MA, MBA, JD
Programs of Study: Accounting, Anthropology, Art Education, Biological Science, Business Education, Chemistry, English, Finance, Geology, Geography, Graphic Design, History, Journalism, Justice Studies, Management, Marketing, Mathematics, Philosophy, Physical Education, Physics, Psychology, Social Studies, Social Work, Sociology

Women's Athletic Profile

Nunn Drive
Highland Heights, KY 41099
Coach: Mary Biermann
Email: biermann@nku.edu

NCAA I
Lady Norse, Gold, Black
Phone: (606) 572-6372
Fax: (606) 572-6089

Estimated # of Women's Volleyball Scholarships: 4
Conference: Great Lakes Valley Conference
Program Profile: We are a top 20 program. We made a National Tournament appearance in 1998.
History: Our overall record from 1975-1998 is 583-289.

Achievements: 1998 Regional Coach of the year; 1992, 1994, 1995 and 1997 GLUC Coach of the Year.
Coaching: Mary Biermann - Head Coach. The 1989-98 overall record is 438-243. It is 226-97 at NKU. Her team won the Conference Championship in 1995,1997 and 1998. They were Regional Champions in 1998 and made a National Tournament appearance in 1998.
Freshman Receiving Financial Aid/Academic: **Athletic:** 2
Roster In State: 4   **Out of State:** 9   **Out of Country:** 1
Sophomores on Team: 0   **Seniors on Team:** 5   **Graduation %:** 90
Most Recent Record: 29-4-0   **Fall Games:** 35   **Spring Games:** 12
Camp of Clinic Dates: June 21-21; July 5-9
Positions Needed: Outside Hitters
Schedule: Central Missouri, North Dakota State, Tampa, Northern Michigan, Northwood, North Florida, Grand Valley
Style of Play: 5-1 offense, emphasis on defense and speed.

Pikeville College
Academic Profile

214 Syracuse St.
Pikeville, KY 41501

Phone: 606-432-9322

Type: Private, 4 Yr., Coed
Website: http://www.pc.edu
SAT/ACT/GPA: 18avg
Student/Faculty Ratio: 14:1
Undergraduate Enrollment: 775
Scholarships/Academic: Yes
Expenses By: Year
Degrees Conferred: AS, BA, BS, BBA

Founded: 1889
Religion: Non-Affiliated
Housing: Yes
Male/Female: 31:69
Graduate Enrollment: N/A

Athletic: Yes   **Financial Aid:** Yes
In State: $ 10,000   **Out of State:** $ 10,000

Programs of Study: Accounting, Biological, Business Administration, Education, Chemistry, Computer Science, Early Childhood Education, Elementary Education, English, History, Management, Mathematics, Nursing, Religion, Science, Secondary Education, Social Science, Special Education

Women's Athletic Profile

214 Sycamore
Pikeville, KY 41501
Coach: TBA
Email:

NCAA I
Lady Bears, Black, Orange
Phone: (606) 432-9319
Fax: (606) 432-9624

Estimated # of Women's Volleyball Scholarships: N/A
Conference: KIAC

Spalding University
Academic Profile

851 South Fourth St.
Louisville, KY 40203

Phone: (800) 896-8941

Type: 4 Yr., Coed
Website: http://www.spalding.edu
SAT/ACT/GPA: 930/20+/3.0
Student/Faculty Ratio:
Undergraduate Enrollment: N/A
Scholarships/Academic:
Expenses By: Year
Degrees Conferred:

Founded:
Religion: Non-Affiliated
Housing: No
Male/Female:
Graduate Enrollment: N/A

Athletic: **Financial Aid:**
In State: **Out of State:**

Programs of Study: Contact school for programs of study.

Women's Athletic Profile

851 S 4th St.
Louisville, KY 40203-2115
Coach: Bridget Yates
Email:

NCAA I
Lady Pelicans, Blue, Gold
Phone: (502) 585-9911
Fax: (502) 585-7158

Estimated # of Women's Volleyball Scholarships: Yes
Conference: KIAC
Program Profile: Our team plays a wide array of teams in Indiana, Kentucky and Tennessee. Our home matches are played in the University Center Building on Spalding University's campus in downtown Louisville.
History: Our program began in 1996.
Achievements: 1996 KWIC Championship; 1997 & 1998 KAIC Runners-up; 1998 KWIC Championship
Coaching: Bridget Yates, Head Coach, has a 27-11 record . At Hanover College, she played middle hitter from 1993 to 1996. She began as head coach in 1998. She previously was an assistant coach at Spalding University.
Freshman Receiving Financial Aid/Academic: **Athletic:** 11
Roster In State: 9   **Out of State:** 2   **Out of Country:** 0
Sophomores on Team: 0   **Seniors on Team:**   **Graduation %:**
Most Recent Record: 27-11-0   **Fall Games:** 38   **Spring Games:** 0
Positions Needed: Setter
Schedule: Mt. Vernon, Georgetown, Madonna
Style of Play: Our team has a very quick game at the net accompanied by stellar blocking and defense.

Thomas More College
Academic Profile

333 Thomas More Parkway
Crestview Hills, KY 41017

Phone: (606) 344-3332

Type: Private, 4 Yr., Liberal Arts, Coed
Website: http://www.thomasmore.edu
SAT/ACT/GPA: 1010/20/80%
Student/Faculty Ratio: 12:1
Undergraduate Enrollment: 1,350
Scholarships/Academic: Yes   **Athletic:** No
Expenses By: Year   **In State:** $ 15,456
Founded: 1921
Religion: Roman Catholic
Housing: Yes
Male/Female: 47:53
Graduate Enrollment: 250
Financial Aid: Yes
Out of State: $ 15,456
Degrees Conferred: BA, BS, BSN, BES, AA, AES
Programs of Study: Accountancy, Art, Art History, Biology, Business Administration, Chemistry, Computer Information Systems, Criminal Justice, Drama, Economics, Education, English, Exercise Science, Gerontology, History, International Studies, Mathematics, Medical Technology, Nursing, Philosophy, Physics, Political Sciences, PreLegal Studies, Psychology, Sociology, Spanish, Speech Communications, Theology, PreDental, PreEngineering, PreLaw, PreMedical, PreOccupational, Physical Therapy, PrePharmacy, PreVeterinary

Women's Athletic Profile

333 Thomas Parkway
Crestview Hills, KY 41017
Coach: Phil Nickel
Email:

NCAA I
Lady Saints, Royal Blue, White
Phone: (606) 344-3634
Fax: (606) 344-3632

Estimated # of Women's Volleyball Scholarships: N/A
Conference: Independent

Union College
Academic Profile

310 College St.
Barbouville, KY 40906

Phone: 800-489-8646

Type: Private, 4 Yr., Liberal Arts, Pre-Engineering, Coed
Website: http://www.unionky.edu
SAT/ACT/GPA: 860/18/2.0
Student/Faculty Ratio: 13:1
Undergraduate Enrollment: 700
Scholarships/Academic: Yes   **Athletic:** Yes
Expenses By: Year   **In State:** $ 14,840
Founded: 1879
Religion: Methodist
Housing: Yes
Male/Female: 51:49
Graduate Enrollment: 200
Financial Aid: Yes
Out of State: $ 14,840
Specializes In: Business, Education, Science Majors
Degrees Conferred: Bachelors, Masters
Programs of Study: Accounting, Athletic Training, Biology, Business, Business Education, Chemistry, Christian Education, Church Music, Criminal Justice, Drama, Early Elementary Education, English, Journalism, History, History & Political Science, Math, Middle Grades Education, Music, Music Education, Philosophy, Religion, Physical Education, Physics, Psychology, Religion, Science Education, Secondary Education, Sociology, Special Education, Sports Management

Women's Athletic Profile

310 College Street
Barbourville, KY 40926
Coach: Margo Gander
Email:

NCAA I
Lady Bulldogs, Orange, Black
Phone: (606) 546-1365
Fax: (606) 546-1286

Estimated # of Women's Volleyball Scholarships: N/A
Conference: MSC

University of Kentucky
Academic Profile

100 Funkhouser Building
Lexington, KY 40506

Phone: 606-257-2000

Type: Public, 4 Yr., Coed
Website: http://www.uky.edu
SAT/ACT/GPA: NCAA Minimums
Student/Faculty Ratio: 20:1
Undergraduate Enrollment: 30,000
Scholarships/Academic: Yes
Expenses By: Year
Degrees Conferred: BA, BS, BFA, MA, MS, MBA, MFA, M.Ed., Ph.D., EdD, JD
Programs of Study: Business/Office & Marketing/Distribution, Business & Management, Communications, Education, Engineering, Health Sciences, Social Sciences

Founded: 1865
Religion: Non-Affiliated
Housing: Yes
Male/Female: 49:51
Graduate Enrollment: N/A
Athletic: Yes
Financial Aid: Yes
In State: $ Varies
Out of State: $ Varies

Women's Athletic Profile

Memorial Coliseum
Lexington, KY 40506-0032
Coach: Jona Braden
Email: jbrad1@pop.uky.edu

NCAA I
Lady Wildcats, Blue, White
Phone: (606) 257-6800
Fax: (606) 323-8570

Estimated # of Women's Volleyball Scholarships: 4
Conference: Southeastern Conference
Program Profile: Kentucky begins its second season under Coach Jona braden, who is working hard to return the program to national prominence. The season begins September 1 with Kentucky playing all home matches in Memorial Coliseum with a seating capacity of 8,700.
History: Kentucky began playing varsity women's volleyball in 1979. They were SEC Champions in their first two seasons and won five of the first ten SEC Championships.
Achievements: Kentucky won the SEC Conference in 1979, 1980, 1983, 1987 & 1988. They were SEC Tournament Runner-Up in 1984 and 1989.
Coaching: Jona Braden, Head Coach, was a former coach at Butler University from 1983-1990. She was named Coach of the Year in 1985, 1986 & 1987 for the conference while at Butler University. She was a varsity player for Ball state. Reita Clanton, Assistant Coach, graduated from Auburn University in 1974 and member of 4th place in1984 US Olympic Handball Team. In 1998 was her first year as a volleyball coach. Jamie Gordon is our Assistant Coach, was a West Virginia Wesley Head Coach in 1996-1998.
Freshman Receiving Financial Aid/Academic:
Roster In State: 1
Sophomores on Team: 2
Most Recent Record: 16-14-0
Camp of Clinic Dates: 2 Developing Camps, 1 Elite Camp, etc
Positions Needed: 4

Out of State: 11
Seniors on Team: 4
Fall Games: 29

Athletic: 2
Out of Country: 0
Graduation %: 100
Spring Games: 4

Schedule: University of Florida, Notre Dame, Arkansas, Clemson, University of Louisville, South Carolina
Style of Play: Scrappy defensive with fast transition to execute offense. The offense will start with the middle and the right to the outside with backcourt attack incorporate on transition. Ball control is a high priority. Blocking is a strength and a part of defensive mindset.

University of Louisville
Academic Profile

Student Activities Center
Louisville, KY 40292

Phone: (800) 334-3635

Type: Public, 4 Yr., Liberal Arts, Engineering, Coed

Founded: 1798

Website: http://www.louisville.edu
SAT/ACT/GPA: 820/17/2.5
Student/Faculty Ratio: 19:1
Undergraduate Enrollment: 20,857
Scholarships/Academic: Yes
Expenses By: Year
Specializes In: Business, Research

Athletic: Yes
In State: $ 13,322

Religion: Non-Affiliated
Housing: Yes
Male/Female: 48:52
Graduate Enrollment: 4,000
Financial Aid: Yes
Out of State: $ 19,342

Degrees Conferred: More than 17 Degrees in each of 11 colleges/schools
Programs of Study: Speed Scientific School, College of Arts & Sciences (Biology, Chemistry, English, ect..), College of Business and Public Administration, School of Allied Health Sciences, School of Dentistry, School of Education, Law & Medical School, Kent School of Social Work, School of Music, School of Nursing

Women's Athletic Profile

Student Activities Center
Louisville, KY 40292
Coach: Leonid Yelin
Email: LOYELIO1@athena.louisville.edu

NCAA I
Cardinals, Red, White, Black
Phone: (800) 334-8635
Fax: (502) 852-0815

Estimated # of Women's Volleyball Scholarships: 12
Conference: Conference USA
Program Profile: We play in Cardinal Arena which is a state-of-the art facility. It is a 894 arena theater style and can seat an average of 817 people. We play on Sport Court and our record is 81-13 in Cardinal Arena.
History: We began in 1977. Susan Johns coached from 1977 to 1979. Her overall record was 28-60-2 (.311). Scott Luster coached from 1980 to 1984. His overall record was 138-90-60 . Bob McCarthy coached from 1985-1987. His overall record was 98-49 (.454). Don Hardin coached from 1988 to 1995. His overall record was 192-74 (.722). Leonid Yelin started in 1996. His overall record is 42-17.
Achievements: 1990-94 Metro Champions; 1995,1996,1998 CUSA Champions; 1990-96 NCAA First Round; 1995, 1996 NCAA Second Round; 1996, 1998 NCAA Sweet Sixteen
Coaching: Leonid Yelin started as head coach in 1996. He was a 1970-75 member of the Uzbekistan National Team. He was 1995 AVCA Coach of the Year. In 1995, his team was Division II National Champions at Barry University. Rick Nold and Beth Kuhnell are assistant coaches.
Freshman Receiving Financial Aid/Academic:
Roster In State: 7
Sophomores on Team: 2
Most Recent Record: 29-5-0

Out of State: 3
Seniors on Team: 2
Fall Games: 35

Athletic: 1
Out of Country: 3
Graduation %: Unknown
Spring Games: 15

Camp of Clinic Dates: July 5-7, July 12-14, July 16-18, July 19-21
Positions Needed: Middle Blocker, Middle Hitter
Schedule: Pacific, Notre Dame, Colorado State, Illinois, Maryland, South Florida, Houston
Style of Play: We will be regarded by our opponents as an aggressive, explosive and offensive unit.

Western Kentucky University
Academic Profile

Departments of Athletics
Bowling Green, KY 42101

Phone: 270-745-2551

Type: Public, 4 Yr., Coed
Website: http://www.wku.edu
SAT/ACT/GPA: 890/21
Student/Faculty Ratio: 20:1
Undergraduate Enrollment: 15,087
Scholarships/Academic: Yes
Expenses By: Year
Specializes In: Arts and Sciences

Athletic: Yes
In State: $ 6,140

Founded: 1906
Religion: Non-Affiliated
Housing: Yes
Male/Female: 44:56
Graduate Enrollment: 2,067
Financial Aid: Yes
Out of State: $ 10,180

Degrees Conferred: BA, BS, BFA, MS, MA
Programs of Study: Accounting, Advertising, Anthropology, BioChemistry, Biology, Botany, Communications, Computer Science, Creative Writing, Economics, Education, Engineering, Environmental Science, Finance, Fine Arts, Journalism, Liberal Arts, Library Science, Mathematics, Medical Technology, Physical Science, Religion, Social Science

Women's Athletic Profile

1 Big Red Way
Bowling Green, KY 42101-3576
Coach: Travis Hudson
Email: travis.hudson@wku.edu

NCAA I
Lady Toppers, Red, White
Phone: (502) 745-6496
Fax: (270) 745-3444

Estimated # of Women's Volleyball Scholarships: 3
Conference: Sun Belt Conference
Program Profile: Our program is in its 18th season with a lifetime record of 338-340 (.499). We have a fall season and play our matches in E.A.Duddle Arena which has 11,300 seats. We have spacious locker room facilities with a weight room. There are also study accommodations on site.
History: Our program began in 1981. We have had 10 winning years in the first 17 seasons. We had 3 runner-up finishes at Sun Belt Conference Tournament in 1998. We posted best improvement of any team in the nation (+17 wins, +14.5 overall).
Achievements: 3 Academic All-Americans (District IV); 1 AVCA All-American (District IV); 1998 Sun Belt Player of the Year; 1990 SBC Regular Season Champions; 1991 SBC West Champions.
Coaching: Travis Hudson has been head coach since 1995. His overall record is 60-75 (.444). He guided WKU to the "most improved " team in the nation in 1998 (9-22 to 26-10). The team was a Sun Belt Tournament Runner-Up. Ken Marshall and Dianna Marshall are assistant coaches.
Freshman Receiving Financial Aid/Academic: **Athletic:** 1

Roster In State: 8	**Out of State:** 3	**Out of Country:** 0
Sophomores on Team: 0	**Seniors on Team:** 3	**Graduation %:** 100
Most Recent Record: 26-10-0	**Fall Games:** 31	**Spring Games:** 0

Camp of Clinic Dates: None
Positions Needed: Middle Hitter, Outside Hitter
Schedule: Miami-Ohio, Ball State, Kentucky, Arkansas-Little Rock, Cincinnati, Duke
Style of Play: Fast, transition offense (middle-oriented); ball- control oriented

LOUISIANA

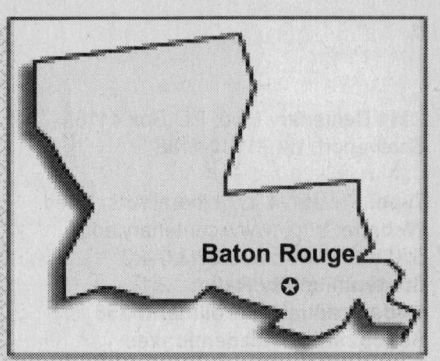

Baton Rouge ☆

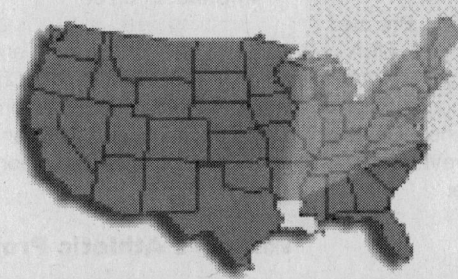

SCHOOL	CITY	AFFILIATION	PAGE
Centenary College - Louisiana	Shreveport	NCAA I	305
Grambling State University	Grambling	NCAA I	305
Louisiana State University	Baton Rouge	NCAA I	306
Louisiana Tech University	Ruston	NCAA I	306
Loyola University	New Orleans	NAIA	307
McNeese State University	Lake Charles	NCAA I	307
Nicholls State University	Thibodaux	NCAA I	308
Northeast Louisiana University	Monroe	NCAA I	308
Northwestern State University	Natchitoches	NCAA I	309
Southern University A & M	Baton Rouge	NCAA I	310
Southeastern Louisiana University	Hammond	NCAA I	310
Tulane University	New Orleans	NCAA I	311
University of New Orleans	New Orleans	NCAA I	312
Univ. of Southwestern Louisiana	Lafayette	NCAA I	312

Centenary College of Louisiana
Academic Profile

2911 Centenary Blvd, PO Box 4118
Shreveport, LA 71134-1188

Phone: (318) 869-5165

Type: Private, 4 Yr., Liberal Arts, Coed
Website: http://www.centenary.edu
SAT/ACT/GPA: 900/22/3.0-4.0
Student/Faculty Ratio: 12:1
Undergraduate Enrollment: 858
Scholarships/Academic: Yes   **Athletic:** Yes
Expenses By: Year   **In State:** $18,700
Specializes In: Business, Education, Pre-med

Founded: 1825
Religion: Methodist
Housing: Yes
Male/Female: 1/3
Graduate Enrollment: 175
Financial Aid: Yes
Out of State: $18,700

Degrees Conferred: BA, BS, MA, MS, MBA
Programs of Study: Accounting, Art, Art Administration, Biblical Studies, BioChemistry, Biology, BioPhysics, Business Administration, Chemistry, Communications, Computer Science, Dance, Earth Science, Economics, Education, Elementary Education, Engineering and Applied Science, English, French, Geology, Health Education, Health Science, Physical Therapy, Physics, Political Science, PreDentistry, PreLaw, PreMed, PreVet, Psychology, Religion, Science Education, Secondary Education, Social Science, Spanish, Speech Pathology, Theatre, Voice

Women's Athletic Profile

Box 41188
Shreveport, LA 71134-1188
Coach: Francis Kinnison
Email: fkinniso@centenary.edu

NCAA I
Ladies, Maroon, White
Phone: (318) 869-5717
Fax: (318) 869-5145

Estimated # of Women's Volleyball Scholarships: 4
Conference: Independent
Program Profile: Our home arena is the Gold Dome and it seats 3,000.
History: In 1985, we began with NAIA. In 1992, we became a member of NCAA Division I. Frances Kinnison's first year as head coach was 1997-98.
Achievements: In the past two years, under new head coach Frances Kinnison, the Ladies have set 32 team and individual school records.
Coaching: Francis Kinnison began as head coach in 1997-1998. She is a 1990 graduate of Angelo State. She served as assistant at the U.S.Naval Academy and later as head coach at Bowie State. In 1992, she became a restricted earnings coach at Texas Tech and spent two years playing professional volleyball in Brazil. Julie Baldwin is the graduate assistant coach.
Freshman Receiving Financial Aid/Academic: **Athletic:** 4
Roster In State: 2   **Out of State:** 8   **Out of Country:** 1
Sophomores on Team: 12   **Seniors on Team:** 4   **Graduation %:** 100
Most Recent Record: 16-22-0   **Fall Games:** 38   **Spring Games:** 3
Camp of Clinic Dates: Clinics: Jan. 31th, Feb.7th, Feb.14th, Feb.21st. Feb.28th Camp:7/23/
Positions Needed: Middle Blockers; Outside Hitters
Schedule: St.Johns, Rutgers, USL, McNeese, Nicholls St., Lamar
Style of Play: Fast-paced, competitive Division I. Multi-oriented offense & defense.

Grambling State University
Academic Profile

Box 868
Grambling, LA 71245

Phone: 318-274-6183

Type: Public, 4 Yr., Coed
Website: http://www.gram.edu
SAT/ACT/GPA: 700avg/17avg
Student/Faculty Ratio: 21:1
Undergraduate Enrollment: 8,150
Scholarships/Academic: Yes   **Athletic:** Yes
Expenses By: Year   **In State:** $ 5,600

Founded: 1901
Religion: Non-Affiliated
Housing: Yes
Male/Female: 42:58
Graduate Enrollment: 575
Financial Aid: Yes
Out of State: $ 7,600

Degrees Conferred: AS, BA, BS, MA, MS
Programs of Study: Accounting, Anthropology, Art, Automotive, Biological Science, Business Administration, Computer, Construction, Criminal Justice, Cardiopulmonary, CytoTechnology, Drafting, Economics, Education, Geography, History, Journalism, Mathematics, Medical, Music, Political Science, Psychology, Radio/Television, Recreation, Secondary/Special Education, Speech/Languages, Hearing Specialist, Theatre, Urban Studies

Women's Athletic Profile

Box 868
Grambling, LA 71245
Coach: Fredrick Payne
Email:

NCAA I
Lady Tigers, Black, Gold
Phone: (318) 274-3216
Fax: (318) 274-2761

Estimated # of Women's Volleyball Scholarships: N/A
Conference: Southwestern Athletic Conference

Louisiana State University - Baton Rouge
Academic Profile

P.O. Box 25095
Baton Rouge, LA 70894-5095

Phone: 225-388-1175

Type: Public, 4 Yr., Coed
Website: http://www.sports.lsu.edu
SAT/ACT/GPA: 990/21/2.3
Student/Faculty Ratio: 40:1
Undergraduate Enrollment: 24,773
Scholarships/Academic: Yes   **Athletic:** Yes
Expenses By: Year   **In State:** $ 4,584
Specializes In: Agricultural & Mechanical

Founded: 1860
Religion: All Denominations
Housing: Yes
Male/Female: 1:1.5
Graduate Enrollment: 5,108
Financial Aid: Yes
Out of State: $ 8,784

Degrees Conferred: BA, BS, BFA, B.Arch, BM, BME, MBA, M.Ed., Ph.D., JD
Programs of Study: Agriculture, Arts & Science, Basic Science, Business, Engineering, Mass Communications, Music, History, Physics, Political Science, Psychology, Criminology

Women's Athletic Profile

P.O. Box 25095
Baton Rouge, LA 70803
Coach: Fran Flory-Ansley
Email: frflory@lsu.edu

NCAA I
Lady Tigers, Purple, Gold
Phone: (225) 388-5050
Fax: (225) 388-1861

Estimated # of Women's Volleyball Scholarships: N/A
Conference: Southeastern Conference

Louisiana Tech University
Academic Profile

PO Box 3178
Ruston, LA 71272
Type: Public, 2 Yr., Coed
Website: http://www.latech.edu
SAT/ACT/GPA: 1010/21/2.00-4.00
Student/Faculty Ratio: 26:1
Undergraduate Enrollment: 6,697
Scholarships/Academic: Yes   **Athletic:** Yes
Expenses By: Year   **In State:** $ 5,382
Specializes In: Business, Education, Engineering, Liberal Arts, Natural Sciences

Phone: 800-528-3241

Founded: 1894
Religion: Non-Affiliated
Housing: Yes
Male/Female: 49:51
Graduate Enrollment: 1,550
Financial Aid: Yes
Out of State: $ 8,697

Degrees Conferred: AS, BA, BS, BLFA, MA, MS, MBA, MFA
Programs of Study: Accounting, Agricultural, Animal, Architecture, Banking and Finance, Botany, Business, Computer, Dietetics, Engineering, Fashion, Forestry, Languages, Geography, Geology, Horticulture, Journalism, Management, Medical, Photography, Physics, PreProfessional Programs, Psychology, Special Education, Speech, Writing, Wildlife, Zoology

Women's Athletic Profile

P.O. Box 3046
Ruston, LA 71272
Coach: Lisa Huntley
Email: lhuntley@latech.edu

NCAA I
Lady Techsters, Red, Blue
Phone: (318) 257-4111
Fax: (318) 257-4437

Estimated # of Women's Volleyball Scholarships: 2
Conference: Sun Belt Conference
Program Profile: Thomas Assembly Center-(8,000)
History: Started in 1987. Eight winning seasons in 17 years. Best record was 29-10 in 1992. Have finished second in the SBC Twice. Overall record of 200-190.
No NCAA appearances
Achievements: none as of yet
Coaching: Lisa Huntley-started 2/98-record 12-21 All SEC player, MVP for 2 years at Univ. of Tenn.- Played International competition with International Ambassadors. Experience: NAIA=1 year asst and 3 years coach NCAA Division I= 2 years asst. and 1 1/2 years coach.

Freshman Receiving Financial Aid/Academic:
Roster In State: 3
Sophomores on Team: 3
Most Recent Record: 12-21
Positions Needed: Setter and Middle Blocker
Schedule: Arkansas-Little Rock, Baylor, Rice University

Out of State: 4
Seniors on Team: 2
Fall Games: 24

Athletic: 12
Out of Country: 1
Graduation %:
Spring Games: 7

Loyola University - New Orleans
Academic Profile

6363 St. Charles Ave.
New Orleans, LA 70148-2135

Phone: (800) 4-LOYOLA

Type: Private, 4 Yr., Liberal Arts, Coed
Website: http://www.loyno.edu
SAT/ACT/GPA: 1270/28/3.55
Student/Faculty Ratio: 12:1
Undergraduate Enrollment: 3,500
Scholarships/Academic: Yes
Expenses By: Year
Degrees Conferred: BA, BS, BFA, BM, BAM, BME, BMT
Programs of Study: College of Arts & Sciences, College of Business Administration, College of Music

Founded: 1912
Religion: Catholic (Jesuit)
Housing: Yes
Male/Female: 2:3
Graduate Enrollment: 2,000
Athletic: No
In State: $ 21,577

Financial Aid: Yes
Out of State: $ 21,577

Women's Athletic Profile

6363 St. Charles Avenue
New Orleans, LA 70118-6143
Coach: Greg Castillo
Email: ninonggreg@aol.com

NCAA I
Lady Wolfpack, Maroon, Gold
Phone: (504) 865-3137
Fax: (504) 865-3081

Estimated # of Women's Volleyball Scholarships: N/A
Conference: Gulf Coast Conference

McNeese State University
Academic Profile

P.O. Box 91535
Lake Charles, LA 70609

Phone: 337-475-5000

Type: Public, 4 Yr., Coed
Website: http://www.mcneese.edu
SAT/ACT/GPA: 820/18
Student/Faculty Ratio: 24:1
Undergraduate Enrollment: 6,000
Scholarships/Academic: Yes
Expenses By: Year

Founded: 1939
Religion: Non-Affiliated
Housing: Yes
Male/Female: 48:52
Graduate Enrollment: 2,000
Athletic: Yes
In State: $ 4,800

Financial Aid: Yes
Out of State: $ 9,800

Degrees Conferred: AA, AS, BA, BS, BM, BMEd, BSN, MS, MA
Programs of Study: College of Business, College of Engineering, College of Education, College of Science, College of Liberal Arts and the College of Nursing

Women's Athletic Profile

Ryan Street
Lake Charles, LA 70609
Coach: Lee McBride
Email: lmcbride@acc.mcneese.edu

NCAA I
Cowgirls, Blue, Gold
Phone: (318) 437-5476
Fax: (318) 475-5202

Estimated # of Women's Volleyball Scholarships: N/A
Conference: Southland Conference

Nicholls State University
Academic Profile

PO Box 2032
Thibodaux, LA 70310

Phone: 877-642-4655

Type: Public, 4 Yr., Coed
Website: http://www.server.nich.edu
SAT/ACT/GPA: None
Student/Faculty Ratio: 22:1
Undergraduate Enrollment: 6,627
Scholarships/Academic: Yes
Expenses By: Year

Athletic: Yes

In State: $ 6,277

Founded: 1948
Religion: Non-Affiliated
Housing: Yes
Male/Female: 1:1.66
Graduate Enrollment: 791
Financial Aid: Yes
Out of State: $10,549

Degrees Conferred: AA, AS, BA, BS, MA, MBA
Programs of Study: Accounting, Agriculture, Arts, Biology, Business Administration, CardioPulmonary Care Science, Chemistry, Computer Science, Communicative Disorders, Computer Information Systems, Criminal Justice, Culinary Arts, CytoTechnology, Dietetics, Education, Finance, French, Government, History, Legal Assistant Studies, Management, Marketing, Mass Communication, Mathematics, Nursing, Psychology, Respiratory Therapy Science, Safety Technology, Sociology, Special Education

Women's Athletic Profile

P.O. Box 2032
Thibodaux, LA 70310
Coach: Alycia Martin-Varytimidis
Email:

NCAA I
Lady Colonels, Red, Grey
Phone: (504) 448-4283
Fax: (504) 448-4924

Estimated # of Women's Volleyball Scholarships: 11
Conference: Southland Conference
Program Profile: All home matches are played in the Stopher Gymnasium which seats 3,800 fans. Our Fall season goes from September through November. Our Spring season goes from March through May.
History: Our program started in 1975.
Achievements: 1998 was the first season in school history that Nicholls State won a Southland Conference Tournament match. The Lady Colonels also made an appearance in the finals in 1998
Coaching: Alycia Martin-Varytimidis is in her first year as head coach. She spent two seasons at Bethune-Cookman College where she had a 13-40 record. She played at Georgia and graduated from Northeast Louisiana in 1994. Jennifer Fulkerson, assistant coach, began coaching here in 1998. She played at NSU.
Freshman Receiving Financial Aid/Academic:
Roster In State: 6
Sophomores on Team: 5
Most Recent Record: 5-25-0
Positions Needed: Middle Blockers (3)

Out of State: 8
Seniors on Team: 0
Fall Games: 30

Athletic: 4
Out of Country: 0
Graduation %: Unknown
Spring Games: 0

Schedule: Southern Mississippi, Southwest Texas State, Stephen F. Austin State, University of Texas-Arlington, McNeose State University, Lamar University

Northeast Louisiana University
Academic Profile

Department of Athletics, Stadium Drive
Monroe, LA 71209

Phone: (318) 342-5090

Type: Public, 4 Yr., Liberal Arts, Coed
Website: http://www.nlu.edu

Founded: 1931
Religion: Non-Affiliated

SAT/ACT/GPA: Open Admission
Student/Faculty Ratio: 20:1
Undergraduate Enrollment: 9,411
Scholarships/Academic: Yes   **Athletic:** Yes
Expenses By: Year   **In State:** $ 2,805
Specializes In: Health, Sciences, Business
Degrees Conferred: AA, AS, AGS, BA, BS, BFA, BM, BME, MA, MS, MBA
Programs of Study: Over 100 programs in five colleges - Business, Education, Liberal Arts, Pharmacy & Health Sciences, Pure & Applied Sciences

Housing: Yes
Male/Female: 1:1.5
Graduate Enrollment: 1,116
Financial Aid: Yes
Out of State: $ 5,217

Women's Athletic Profile

106 Ewing Coliseum
Monroe, LA 71209-3000
Coach: Leanne Zeek
Email: zeekl@linknet.net

NCAA I
Lady Indians, Cardinal, Gold
Phone: (318) 342-5411
Fax: (318) 342-5464

Estimated # of Women's Volleyball Scholarships: 12
Conference: Southland Conference
Program Profile: We are a mid-level Division I program on the rise. We compete in our 5,000 seat arena with renovation currently occurring. Our four gyms will become the competition site for volleyball.
History: Volleyball in Louisiana has never had a successful conference season and NLU is the same. We are coming off of our most successful Conference season ever and are building from there. We hope to also continue 1st team All-Conference honors for at least one player per year.
Achievements: 1998 Best Conference record in school history
1998 1st team All-Conference player for the first time in 10 years
Coaching: Leanne Zeek, Head Coach, started with the program in 1996 and compiled a record of 19-77. She is a three-time All-Conference player and school record holder from Lamar University. Jenny Wilson , Assistant Coach, is in her first year. She played at the University of Denver.
Freshman Receiving Financial Aid/Academic: **Athletic:** 4
Roster In State: 1   **Out of State:** 9   **Out of Country:** 0
Sophomores on Team: 3   **Seniors on Team:** 3   **Graduation %:** 100
Most Recent Record: 8-23-0   **Fall Games:** 31   **Spring Games:** 0
Schedule: Louisiana State University, Arkansas State, Southwest Texas State, University of Texas-Arlington, University of New Orleans
Style of Play: Emphasis on ball control and defense. Offensively we run a quick offense with main attack through the middles.

Northwestern State University - Louisiana
Academic Profile

Prather Coliseum
Natchitoches, LA 71497

Phone: (318) 357-4337

Type: Public, 4 Yr., Coed
Website: http://www.nsudemons.com
SAT/ACT/GPA: 17
Student/Faculty Ratio: 17:1
Undergraduate Enrollment: 9,000
Scholarships/Academic: Yes   **Athletic:** Yes
Expenses By: Year   **In State:** $ 6,003
Specializes In: Most majors and programs
Degrees Conferred: AA, AS, BA, BM, BS, MS, MFA
Programs of Study: Accounting, Advertising, Animal, Anthropology, Art, Biological Science, Botany, Broadcasting, Business, Dance, Early Childhood Education, Engineering, English, Fine Arts, History, Information, Journalism, Marketing, Management, Math, Medical, Music, Nursing, Personnel Management, Photography, Political Science, Physics, Psychology, Speech

Founded: 1922
Religion: Non-Affiliated
Housing: Yes
Male/Female: 45:55
Graduate Enrollment: 1,000
Financial Aid: Yes
Out of State: $ 10,413

Women's Athletic Profile

College Avenue
Natchitoches, LA 71497-0003
Coach: James Onikeku
Email: dejutem@ALPHA.NSULA.EDU

NCAA I
Lady Demons, Purple, White
Phone: (318) 357-4227
Fax: (318) 357-4515

Estimated # of Women's Volleyball Scholarships: 3
Conference: Southland Conference
Program Profile: Coach James Onikeku led 1999 season as the Demons' head coach. With five returning players and 8 new players recruited by Onikeku, the Demons expect to have a successful season, although it will be a beginning for many. The Demons call Prather Coliseum a 3,900 capacity multi-purpose coliseum home. They share the facilities with men and women's basketball as well as house sports information and compliance offices.
History: The Demon Volleyball began in 1983, holding an overall record to date of 141-298. It was started by Former Head Coach Ari-Iwan Waworuntu and James Onikeku was the 7th head coach at Northwestern.

Freshman Receiving Financial Aid/Academic:		Athletic: 4
Roster In State: 5	Out of State: 9	Out of Country: 0
Sophomores on Team: 0	Seniors on Team: 2	Graduation %:
Most Recent Record: 6-26-0	Fall Games: 32	Spring Games: 4

Positions Needed: Setter, Middle, Outside
Schedule: University of Tulsa, University of Texas-Arlington, University of Texas-San Antonio, Troy State University, University of Missouri-Kansas City, University of New Orleans

Southern University & A&M
Academic Profile

P.O. Box 10850
Baton Rouge, LA 70813

Phone: 225-771-2430

Type: Public, 4 Yr., Coed	**Founded:** 1880
Website: Not Available	**Religion:** Non-Affiliated
SAT/ACT/GPA: 700avg/17avg	**Housing:** Yes
Student/Faculty Ratio: 20:1	**Male/Female:** 1:1
Undergraduate Enrollment: 10,000	**Graduate Enrollment:** 1,200
Scholarships/Academic: Yes	**Athletic:** Yes	**Financial Aid:** Yes
Expenses By: Year	**In State:** $ 5,110	**Out of State:** $ 7,600

Degrees Conferred: AA, AS, AAS, BA, BS, BM, BME, MA, MS
Programs of Study: Accounting, Agricultural, Animal, Art, Biological Science, Broadcasting, Business, CardioPulmonary, Chemistry, Clothing/Textiles, Communications, Computer, CytoTechnology, Dietetics, Economics, Education, Health, History, Journalism, Marketing, Math, Occupational, Physical, Physics, Political Science, Plant, Rehabilitation, Soil, Zoology

Women's Athletic Profile

P.O. Box 9942
Baton Rouge, LA 70813
Coach: Nathaniel Denu
Email: denu@engr.subr.edu

NCAA I
Lady Jaguars, Blue, Gold
Phone: (225) 771-5115
Fax: (504) 771-4400

Estimated # of Women's Volleyball Scholarships: N/A
Conference: Southwestern Athletic Conference

Southeastern Louisiana University
Academic Profile

SLU 10309
Hammond, LA 70402

Phone: (504) 549-2253

Type: Public, 4 Yr., Coed	**Founded:** 1925
Website: http://www.selu.edu/athletics	**Religion:** Non-Affiliated
SAT/ACT/GPA: 830/17	**Housing:** Yes
Student/Faculty Ratio: 25:1	**Male/Female:** 38:62
Undergraduate Enrollment: 15,500	**Graduate Enrollment:** N/A
Scholarships/Academic: Yes	**Athletic:** Yes	**Financial Aid:** Yes
Expenses By: Year	**In State:** $ 4,758	**Out of State:** $ 10,086

Specializes In: Liberal Arts, Sciences, Professional Fields
Degrees Conferred: BA, BS, MA, MS
Programs of Study: Accounting, Biology, Business, Chemistry, Communication and Theatre, Computer Science, Counseling, Criminal Justice, Design Drafted Technology, Education, English, Finance, Foreign Languages, History, Industry Technology, Kinesiology, Literature, Management, Marketing, Mathematics, Music, Nursing, Physics, Political Science, Psychology, Sociology, Visual Arts

Women's Athletic Profile

P.O. Box 10309
Hammond, LA 70402
Coach: Roni Armeda
Email: armeda4@yahoo.com

NCAA I
Lady Lions, Green, Gold
Phone: (504) 549-2253
Fax: (504) 549-3495

Estimated # of Women's Volleyball Scholarships: 11
Conference: Southland Conference
Program Profile: The Lady Lions have been playing in the University Center for 16 years. The $16 million multi-purpose arena seats 7,500 fans. We have a new weight room that recently opened this past spring in the Strawberry Stadium with lights, bleachers and machines.
History: We began in 1974. We were first in West Division of the TAAC for 4 years in a row (1993-1996). In 1997, we switched to the Southland Conference from Trans America Athletic Conference. We led Southland in digs per games in 1997. We were 4th in best digs per game in the country.
Achievements: 1995 and 1996 Coach of the Year in TAAC; 1996 RPI ranking in Louisiana; 1st place in West Division of TAAC in 1993,1994,1995 and 1996; 25 game win streak with .824 winning percentage in 1996.
Coaching: Roni Armeda became head coach in 1993 and his overall record is 129-87. He was TAAC Coach of the Year in 1995 and 1996. His winning percentage in 1996 was .824. He was a four year starter at University of Florida (1986-89). He was an All-Southeastern Conference Selection in 1989. Anne Bauer is assistant coach.
Freshman Receiving Financial Aid/Academic:

		Athletic: 3
Roster In State: 3	**Out of State:** 9	**Out of Country:** 1
Sophomores on Team: 4	**Seniors on Team:** 1	**Graduation %:** 50
Most Recent Record: 12-18-0	**Fall Games:** 29	**Spring Games:** 3

Camp of Clinic Dates: July 5-8
Positions Needed: None
Schedule: Georgetown, Northern Arizona, Southwest Texas, Stephen F. Austin, McNeese, University of Texas-San Antonio
Style of Play: Defensive.

Tulane University
Academic Profile

James W. Wilson Ctr.
New Orleans, LA 70118-5681

Phone: (504) 865-5574

Type: Private, 4 Yr., Coed
Website: http://www.tulane.edu
SAT/ACT/GPA: 1200/27/Top 10%
Student/Faculty Ratio: 12:1
Undergraduate Enrollment: 6,500
Scholarships/Academic: Yes
Expenses By: Year

Athletic: Yes
In State: $ 31,343

Founded: 1834
Religion: Non-denominational
Housing: Yes
Male/Female: 50:50
Graduate Enrollment: 4,800
Financial Aid: Yes
Out of State: $ 31,343

Specializes In: Architecture, Business, Engineering, Liberal Arts, Sciences
Degrees Conferred: BA, BS, Maters, Ph.D.
Programs of Study: School of Law, Medicine, Public Health, Tropical Medicine, Social Work, Engineering, Business, Architecture, Liberal Arts.

Women's Athletic Profile

James Wilson, Jr. Center
New Orleans, LA 70118-0000
Coach: Betsy Becker Ferrer
Email: ebecker@mailhost.tcs.tulane.edu

NCAA I
Wave, Green, Blue
Phone: (504) 865-5570
Fax: (504) 865-5512

Estimated # of Women's Volleyball Scholarships: 4
Conference: Conference USA
Program Profile: We are an up and coming volleyball program. We play at a state-of-the-art facility called Fogelman Arena, which has a capacity of 3,600.
History: We just took over 5 months ago and we want to turn the fortunes around.
Achievements: Betsy Becker Ferrer was 1998 Louisiana Coach of the Year.
Coaching: Betsy Becker Ferrer, is in her first year as head coach. She came from UNO where she had back to back 20 winning seasons. (1997:27-5 and 1998: 20-12). Cappy Myer and Roy Martin are in their first year as assistant coaches.

Freshman Receiving Financial Aid/Academic: **Athletic:** 12
Roster In State: 5   **Out of State:** 4   **Out of Country:** 2
Sophomores on Team: 3   **Seniors on Team:** 4   **Graduation %:** 100
Most Recent Record: 6-26-0   **Fall Games:** 28   **Spring Games:** 4
Camp of Clinic Dates: July 12-15, July 19-22
Positions Needed: Setter, 2 Middles, 1 Leftside
Schedule: Stanford, Louisville, South Florida, Houston, University of North Carolina, Northern Illinois
Style of Play: We are small, feisty and scrappy. The game is played high and won down low.

University of New Orleans
Academic Profile

Lakefront Arena - Athletic Dept.   **Phone:** 800-256-5866
New Orleans, LA 70148

Type: Public, 4 Yr., Coed   **Founded:** 1958
Website: http://www.uno.edu   **Religion:** Non-Affiliated
SAT/ACT/GPA: 950/20   **Housing:** Yes
Student/Faculty Ratio: 16:1   **Male/Female:** 43:57
Undergraduate Enrollment: 10,999   **Graduate Enrollment:** 3,738
Scholarships/Academic: Yes   **Athletic:** Yes   **Financial Aid:** Yes
Expenses By: Year   **In State:** $ 8,145   **Out of State:** $ 10,937
Degrees Conferred: BA, BS, BGS, MA, MS, MBA, Ph.D.
Programs of Study: Accounting, Anthropology, Banking/Finance, Biological, Business, Communications, Computer, Dental, Economics, Education

Women's Athletic Profile

Lakefront Arena   **NCAA I**
New Orleans, LA 70148   Lady Privateers, Blue, Silver
Coach: TBA   **Phone:** (504) 280-7055
Email: **Fax:** (504) 280-7240

Estimated # of Women's Volleyball Scholarships: N/A
Conference: Sun Belt Conference

University of Southwestern Louisiana
Academic Profile

201 Reihardt Dr.   **Phone:** (337) 482-6391
Lafayette, LA 70506

Type: Public, 4 Yr., Coed   **Founded:** 1900
Website: http://www.ragincajuns.com   **Religion:** Non-Affiliated
SAT/ACT/GPA: Open Admission   **Housing:** Yes
Student/Faculty Ratio: 15:1   **Male/Female:** 48:52
Undergraduate Enrollment: 14,500   **Graduate Enrollment:** 2,500
Scholarships/Academic: Yes   **Athletic:** Yes   **Financial Aid:** Yes
Expenses By: Year   **In State:** $ 4,536   **Out of State:** $ 8,136
Specializes In: Computer Science
Degrees Conferred: BS, BA
Programs of Study: Accounting, Advertising, Agricultural, Animal, Anthropology, Banking/Finance, Broadcasting, Business, Chemistry, Communications, Community Services, Computer, Criminal Justice, Dance, Dietetics, Dramatics Arts, Economics, Education, English, Fashion Design, Fine Arts, French, Geography, Horticulture, Industrial, Journalism, Land Use, Nursing, Office, PreProfessional Programs, Special Education, Speech, Statistics, Telecommunications, Urban Studies, Wildlife Management

Women's Athletic Profile

Earl K. Long Gym, St. Mary Blvd.   **NCAA I**
Lafayette, LA 70504-1008   Cajuns, Red, White
Coach: Chris Campbell   **Phone:** (318) 482-6327
Email: **Fax:** (318) 482-6649

Estimated # of Women's Volleyball Scholarships: 17
Conference: Sun Belt Conference
Program Profile: We play at E.K. Long Gymnasium with a seating capacity of 1,000.
History: Our program began in 1976. Conference Appearances in 1997 & 1998 and reached semi-final in 1997.
Achievements: 6 Conference All-Stars in 1990's.
Coaching: Chris Campbell is our Head Coach. His alma mater is University of British Columbia. Eduardo Fiallos is our Assistant Coach.
Freshman Receiving Financial Aid/Academic: **Athletic:** 3
Roster In State: 4   **Out of State:** 5   **Out of Country:** 2
Sophomores on Team: 0   **Seniors on Team:** 3   **Graduation %:**
Most Recent Record: 16-19-0   **Fall Games:** 35   **Spring Games:** 0
Positions Needed: 3
Schedule: University of Arkansas-Little Rock, Louisiana State University, Mississippi State, Oral Roberts
Style of Play: Strong blocking, precise passing and fast offense.

MAINE

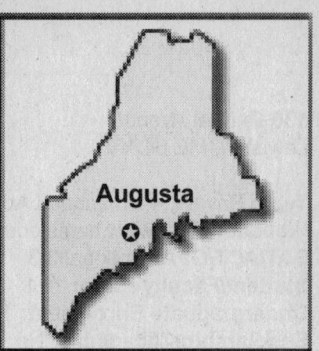

Augusta

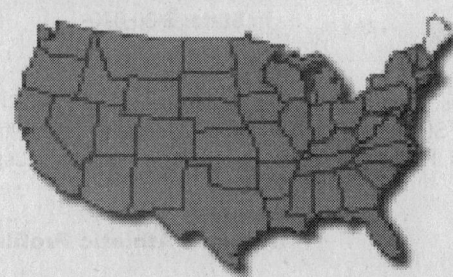

SCHOOL	CITY	AFFILIATION	PAGE
Bates College	Lewiston	NCAA III	315
Bowdoin College	Brunswick	NCAA III	315
Colby College	Waterville	NCAA III	316
Husson College	Bangor	NCAA III/NAIA	316
Saint Joseph College - Maine	Standish	NCAA III	317
Thomas College	Waterville	NCAA III	317
University of Maine	Orono	NCAA I	317
University of Maine - Farmington	Farmington	NCAA III/NAIA	318
University of Maine - Fort Kent	Fort Kent		319
University of Maine - Machias	Machias	NAIA	319
University of Maine - Presque Isle	Presque Isle	NAIA	319
University of New England	Biddeford	NCAA III	320
University of Southern Maine	Gorham	NCAA III	320

Bates College
Academic Profile

130 Central Avenue
Lewiston, ME 04240

Phone: 207-786-6000

Type: Private, 4 Yr., Liberal Arts, Coed
Website: http://www.bates.edu
SAT/ACT/GPA: Optional/3.3
Student/Faculty Ratio: 11:1
Undergraduate Enrollment: 1,600
Scholarships/Academic: No
Expenses By: Year
Specializes In: Liberal Arts
Degrees Conferred: BA, BS

Athletic: No
In State: $ 30,070

Founded: 1855
Religion: Non-Affiliated
Housing: Yes
Male/Female: 51:49
Graduate Enrollment: N/A
Financial Aid: Yes
Out of State: $ 31,070

Programs of Study: African Studies, American Studies, Anthropology, Art, BioChemistry, Biology, Chemistry, Chinese, Classics, Economics, English, Environmental Studies, French, Geology, German, History, Interdisciplinary Studies, Mathematics, Medieval Studies, Music, Philosophy, Physics, Political Science, Psychology, Religion, Russian, Social Science, Spanish, Speech, Theatre, Women's Studies

Women's Athletic Profile

141 Nichols St.
Lewiston, ME 04240-6414
Coach: Sandie Shollenberger
Email: admissions@bates.edu

NCAA I
Lady Bobcats, Maroon, White
Phone: (207) 786-6000
Fax: (207) 786-6025

Estimated # of Women's Volleyball Scholarships: N/A
Conference: NESCAC
Program Profile: We have four courts in the Alumni Gymnasium and the Gray Cage in use simultaneously. Bates offers one of the finest volleyball facilities in Division III of New England. We host two volleyball tournaments each year and enjoy strong fan support. We have had a winning program over the past 14 years with a 73.9 % winning percentage.
History: We began in 1967. Over the course of 32 seasons we comprised a record of 647-252-1 (71.4%) . We have played in 7 post-seasons, comprising a record of 10-4. We won one NCAA tournament berth and 3 ECAC Championship titles in Division III North.
Achievements: 4 post-season berths; 2 ECAC Championships;1989,1990 & 1998 ECAC Division III North Champions; Kate Hagstrom - All-New England/All-NESCAC-Set record with 144 service aces; Amanda Colby-Division III National Player of the Week; Among the top 10 in the nation in hitting percentage.
Coaching: Sandie Shollenberger, Head Coach, is in her first season at Bates. She was an assistant at Ithaca for the past two years, where the team compiled a 50-26 record and went to two NCAA Tournaments. She is a 1995 graduate of Ithaca. She was twice named Division III All-Region Setter. Gwen Lexow is Assistant Coach.

Roster In State: 0
Sophomores on Team: 5
Most Recent Record: 25-12-0

Out of State: 14
Seniors on Team: 0
Fall Games: 37

Out of Country: 0
Graduation %: 100
Spring Games: 0

Schedule: Williams, Wellesley, Eastern Connecticut, Middlebury, Coast Guard, Amherst

Bowdoin College
Academic Profile

Morrell gymnasium
Brunswick, ME 04011

Phone: 207-725-3100

Type: Private, 4 Yr., Liberal Arts, Coed
Website: http://www.bowdoin.edu
SAT/ACT/GPA: No standarized tests required
Student/Faculty Ratio: 11:1
Undergraduate Enrollment: 1,605
Scholarships/Academic: No
Expenses By: Year
Degrees Conferred: BA

Athletic: No
In State: $ 31,950

Founded: 1795
Religion: Non-Affiliated
Housing: Yes
Male/Female: 50:50
Graduate Enrollment: N/A
Financial Aid: Yes
Out of State: $ 31,950

Programs of Study: Fine Arts, Archeology, Art History, Classics, English, French, German, History, Music, Philosophy, Religion, Romance, Russian, Spanish, Studio Art, Biology, Mathematics, BioChemistry, Chemistry, Physics, Natural Sciences, Geology, Computer Science, Chemical Physics, Physics, Sociology, African Studies, Asian Studies, Environmental Studies, Latin American

Women's Athletic Profile

Morrell Gymnasium
Brunswick, ME 04011
Coach: Lynn Ruddy
Email: ruddy@henry.bowdoin.edu

NCAA I
Lady Polar Bears, White
Phone: (207) 725-3623
Fax: (207) 725-3019

Estimated # of Women's Volleyball Scholarships: N/A
Conference: Eastern College Athletic Conference

Colby College
Academic Profile

Mayflower Hill
Waterville, ME 04901

Phone: 800-723-3032

Type: Private, 4 Yr., Liberal Arts, Coed
Website: http://www.colby.edu
SAT/ACT/GPA: Open
Student/Faculty Ratio: 11:1
Undergraduate Enrollment: 1,800
Scholarships/Academic: No
Expenses By: Year
Degrees Conferred: BA

Athletic: No
In State: $ 30,420

Founded: 1813
Religion: Non-Affiliated
Housing: Yes
Male/Female: 50:50
Graduate Enrollment: N/A
Financial Aid: Yes
Out of State: $ 30,420

Programs of Study: 45 Majors- largest English, Economics, Psychology, Government, Biology

Women's Athletic Profile

4900 Mayflower Hill
Waterville, ME 04901
Coach: Candice Parent
Email:

NCAA I
Lady White Mules, Blue, Grey
Phone: (207) 872-3545
Fax: (207) 872-3420

Estimated # of Women's Volleyball Scholarships: N/A
Conference: Independent

Husson College
Academic Profile

One College Circle
Bangor, ME 04401
Type: Private, 4 Yr., Coed
Website: http://www.husson.edu
SAT/ACT/GPA: 740+
Student/Faculty Ratio: 15:1
Undergraduate Enrollment: 1,000
Scholarships/Academic: Yes
Expenses By: Year
Specializes In: Business, Health
Degrees Conferred: AS, BS, MS

Phone: 800-448-7766

Athletic: No
In State: $ 14,000

Founded: 1898
Religion: Non-Affiliated
Housing: Yes
Male/Female: 40:60
Graduate Enrollment: 200
Financial Aid: Yes
Out of State: $ 14,000

Programs of Study: Accounting, Banking & Finance, Business Administration, Computer Science, Court Reporting, Education, Management Information Systems, Marketing, Nursing, Physical Therapy, Personnel Management, Professional Studies, Secretarial Studies, Sport Management

Women's Athletic Profile

One College Circle
Bangor, ME 04401
Coach: Patrick DeBeck
Email:

NCAA I
Lady Braves, Green, White
Phone: (207) 941-7026
Fax: (207) 941-7028

Estimated # of Women's Volleyball Scholarships: N/A
Conference: Independent

Saint Joseph's College - Maine
Academic Profile

278 White's Bridge Road
Standish, ME 04084

Phone: 800-338-7057

Type: Private, 4 Yr., Liberal Arts, Coed
Website: http://www.sjcme.edu
SAT/ACT/GPA: Open
Student/Faculty Ratio: 16:1
Undergraduate Enrollment: 750
Scholarships/Academic: Yes
Expenses By: Year
Specializes In: Business Administration, Communications, Physical Education
Degrees Conferred: AS, BA,BS

Athletic: No
In State: $ 20,285

Founded: 1912
Religion: Roman Catholic
Housing: No
Male/Female: 60:40
Graduate Enrollment: N/A
Financial Aid: Yes
Out of State: $ 20,285

Programs of Study: BioChemistry, Biology, Business Administration, Communications, Elementary Education, English, Environmental Science, History, Human Development, Mathematics, Natural Science, Nursing, Philosophy, Physical Education, Psychology, Radiology Technology, Theology, Sociology, PreProfessional (PreDental, PreLaw, PreMed, PreVet), Secondary Education. Honors Programs. Study Abroad.

Women's Athletic Profile

278 Whites Bridge Road
Standish, ME 04084
Coach: Dan Fourneir
Email:

NCAA I
Lady Monks, Royal Blue, White
Phone: (207) 893-6665
Fax: (207) 893-7860

Estimated # of Women's Volleyball Scholarships: N/A
Conference: Independent

Thomas College
Academic Profile

180 West River Road
Waterville, ME 04901

Phone: 800-339-7001

Type: Private, 4 Yr., Coed
Website: http://www.thomas.edu
SAT/ACT/GPA: For traditional students only - Freshmen
Student/Faculty Ratio: 16:1
Undergraduate Enrollment: 775
Scholarships/Academic: Yes
Expenses By: Year
Specializes In: Business
Degrees Conferred: BS, MBA, MS

Athletic:
In State: $ 16,800

Founded: 1894
Religion: Non-Affiliated
Housing: Yes
Male/Female: 45:55
Graduate Enrollment: 150
Financial Aid: Yes
Out of State: $ 16,800

Programs of Study: Accounting, Accounting Information Systems, Business Teacher Education, Computer Information Systems, Banking & Investments, Environmental Management, International Business Studies, Management, Management Information System, Marketing Information Systems, Math/Computer Teacher Education, Retail Management, Sport Management

Women's Athletic Profile

West River Rd.
Waterville, ME 04901
Coach: Michele Collins
Email: acaddean@thomas.edu

NCAA I
Lady Nighthawks, Green, White
Phone: (207) 873-0771
Fax: (207) 877-0114

Estimated # of Women's Volleyball Scholarships: N/A
Conference: WMAC

University of Maine
Academic Profile

5747 Memorial Gym
Orono, ME 04469-5747

Phone: 877-486-2364

Type: Public, 4 Yr., Liberal Arts, Engineering, Coed

Founded: 1865

Website: http://www.maine.edu
SAT/ACT/GPA: Varies
Student/Faculty Ratio: 14:1
Undergraduate Enrollment: 7,500
Scholarships/Academic: Yes   **Athletic:** Yes
Expenses By: Year   **In State:** $ 9,681
Specializes In: Various

Religion: Non-Affiliated
Housing: Yes
Male/Female: 50:50
Graduate Enrollment: 2,000
Financial Aid: Yes
Out of State: $ 16,551

Degrees Conferred: BA, BS, MA, MS, MBA, MEd, Ph.D., EdD, JD
Programs of Study: College of Arts & Humanities, College of Business Administration, College of Education, College of Engineering, College of Sciences, College of Social Behavioral Sciences, College of Natural Resources, Forestry & Agriculture

Women's Athletic Profile

5747 Memorial Gym
Orono, ME 04469
Coach: Sue Medley
Email: christopher.dudley@umit.maine.edu

NCAA I
Black Bears, Blue, White
Phone: 207-581-1048
Fax: 207-581-3070

Estimated # of Women's Volleyball Scholarships: 3
Conference: American East
Program Profile: NCAA I program in the America East Conference. Only in their second ever season. Compete in Memorial Gymnasium Known as "The Pit" which seats 1, 000 spectators and has a brand new wood floor. Weight training occurs in the 6, 000 sq. foot Lahi Fitness Center. Currently under construction is our new volleyball team and locker room.
History: University of Maine volleyball is currently in their second year of "existence". Maine had volleyball until it was disbanded in 1983. Last fall the team finished 12-18 overall and 5-11 in conference play. Good enough for a 6th place finish in the America East.
Achievements: 1 player was first team All-Conference, 1 player Honorable Mention All-Conference and first team newcomer.
Coaching: Head Coach Sue Medley finished last season with an overall record of 126-149 over 10 seasons. Prior to the Univ. of Maine she was the Head Coach at Cornell University, where she had 20 win seasons.
Freshman Receiving Financial Aid/Academic: **Athletic:** 5
Roster In State: 3   **Out of State:** 6   **Out of Country:** 3
Seniors on Team: 1   **Graduation %:** 100
Most Recent Record: 12-18
Camp of Clinic Dates: June 18-22, July 15-19, July 19-Aug 5, Aug 17-19
Positions Needed: OH, MH
Schedule: Hofstra, New Hampshire, Dartmouth, Boston College, Eastern Washington, Delaware, Northeastern.

University of Maine - Farmington
Academic Profile

86 Main St.
Farmington, ME 04938

Phone: 207-778-7050

Type: Public, 4 Yr., Coed
Website: http://www.umf.maine.edu
SAT/ACT/GPA: Open
Student/Faculty Ratio: 15:1
Undergraduate Enrollment: 2,000
Scholarships/Academic: Yes   **Athletic:** No
Expenses By: Year   **In State:** $ 8,160
Specializes In: Liberal Arts, Education, Human Services
Degrees Conferred: BA, BS

Founded: 1863
Religion: Non-Affiliated
Housing: Yes
Male/Female: 1:4
Graduate Enrollment: N/A
Financial Aid: Yes
Out of State: $ 12,930

Programs of Study: Education, Liberal Arts, Business and Economics, Health and Rehabilitation, Psychology, Social Sciences, Letters/Literature, Multi/Interdisciplinary Studies

Women's Athletic Profile

86 Main Street
Farmington, ME 04938
Coach: Krista Nigels-Gin
Email: krista@maine.maine.edu

NCAA I
Beaverettes, Maroon, White
Phone: (207) 778-7139
Fax: (207) 778-8177

Estimated # of Women's Volleyball Scholarships: N/A
Conference: Eastern College Athletic Conference

University of Maine - Fort Kent
Academic Profile

25 Pleasant Street
Fort Kent, ME 04743-1292

Phone: (888) 879-8635

Type: Public, 4 Yr., Liberal Arts, Coed
Website: http://www.umfk.maine.edu
SAT/ACT/GPA: Open
Student/Faculty Ratio: 15:1
Undergraduate Enrollment: 800
Scholarships/Academic: Yes   **Athletic:** No
Expenses By: Year   **In State:** $ 8,160
Specializes In: Education, Environmental Studies, Nursing, Biology
Degrees Conferred: BS, AA

Founded: 1878
Religion: Non-Affiliated
Housing: Yes
Male/Female: 1:3
Graduate Enrollment: N/A
Financial Aid: Yes
Out of State: $ 12,630

Programs of Study: Behavioral Science, Biology, Business, Computer Science, Education, English, French, Environmental Science, Nursing, Social Sciences, Agricultural Studies, Business Management, Computer Science, Bi-Cultural Studies, Business Management, Computer Science, Criminal Justice, Forest Technology, Human Services

Women's Athletic Profile

Did Not Return Profile

University of Maine - Machias
Academic Profile

9 O'Brien Avenue
Machias, ME 04654

Phone: 888-468-6866

Type: Public, 4 Yr., Liberal Arts, Coed
Website: http://www.umm.maine.edu
SAT/ACT/GPA: 860/18/2.0
Student/Faculty Ratio: 16:1
Undergraduate Enrollment: 1,000
Scholarships/Academic: Yes   **Athletic:** No
Expenses By: Year   **In State:** $ 7,460
Specializes In: Marine Biology, Environmental Science, Business, Outdoor Recreation
Degrees Conferred: BA, BS, AA

Founded: 1909
Religion: Non-Affiliated
Housing: Yes
Male/Female: 2:3
Graduate Enrollment: N/A
Financial Aid: Yes
Out of State: $ 11,760

Programs of Study: Elementary Education, Secondary Education, Business Education, Business Administration, English, Fine Arts, History, Behavioral Science, Recreation Management, Environmental Studies, Biology, Marine Biology

Women's Athletic Profile

9 O'Brien
Machias, ME 04654
Coach: Sharon Bonaventure
Email:

NCAA I
Lady Clippers, Green, White
Phone: (207) 255-1348
Fax: (207) 255-4864

Estimated # of Women's Volleyball Scholarships: N/A
Conference: Maine Athletic Conference

University of Maine - Presque Isle
Academic Profile

181 Main St.
Presque Isle, ME 04769

Phone: 207-768-9532

Type: Public, 4 Yr., Liberal Arts, Coed
Website: http://www.umpi.maine.edu
SAT/ACT/GPA: 760
Student/Faculty Ratio: 12:1
Undergraduate Enrollment: 1,500
Scholarships/Academic: Yes   **Athletic:** No

Founded: 1903
Religion: Non-Affiliated
Housing: Yes
Male/Female: 1:4
Graduate Enrollment: N/A
Financial Aid: Yes

Expenses By: Year　　　　　　**In State:** $ 7,274　　　　**Out of State:** $ 11,324
Specializes In: Education, Physical Education, Teaching, Criminal Justice
Degrees Conferred: AA, AS, BA, BFA, BLS, BSW, Masters
Programs of Study: Accounting, Athletic Training, Art, Psychology, Sociology, Biology, Business, Communications, Criminal Justice, Elementary Education, English, Environmental Studies, Fine Arts, Fitness & Wellness, International Studies, Political Science, Liberal Studies, Mathematics, Physical Education, PreLaw, PreMed, Recreation & Leisure Services, Social Work

Women's Athletic Profile

181 Main Street
Presque Isle, ME 04769
Coach: John McCrea
Email: umpi_vball@yahoo.com

NCAA I
Lady Owls, Blue, Gold
Phone: (207) 764-2102
Fax: (207) 768-9476

Estimated # of Women's Volleyball Scholarships: N/A
Conference: Maine Athletic Conference

University of New England
Academic Profile

11 Hills Beach Road
Biddeford, ME 04005

Phone: 800-477-4863

Type: Private, 4 Yr., Liberal Arts, Coed
Website: http://www.une.edu
SAT/ACT/GPA: 900
Student/Faculty Ratio: 14:1
Undergraduate Enrollment: 850
Scholarships/Academic: Yes　　**Athletic:** Yes
Expenses By: Year　　　　**In State:** $ 16,800
Specializes In: Education

Founded: 1953
Religion: Non-Affiliated
Housing: No
Male/Female: 15:85
Graduate Enrollment: 550
Financial Aid: Yes
Out of State: $ 16,800

Degrees Conferred: AS, BA, BS, MS, Ph.D.
Programs of Study: Biology, BioMedical Science, Business Administration, Education, Environmental Science, Health Care Administration, Management, Marine Biology, Medical Laboratory Technology, Nursing, Occupational Therapy, Physical Therapy, PreDentistry, PreLaw, PreMed, PrePharmacy, Psychology, Sport Management

Women's Athletic Profile

11 Hills Beach Rd.
Biddeford, ME 04005
Coach: Karol L'Heureux
Email:

NCAA I
Blue, Grey
Phone: (207) 283-0170
Fax: (207) 294-5403

Estimated # of Women's Volleyball Scholarships: N/A
Conference: Commonwealth Coast
Roster In State: 0　　　　**Out of State:** 12　　　**Out of Country:** 0
Sophomores on Team:　　　　**Seniors on Team:** 3　　**Graduation %:** 100
Most Recent Record: 12-12
Positions Needed: All
Schedule: Gordon, Bates.

University of Southern Maine
Academic Profile

37 College Avenue
Gorham, ME 04038

Phone: (207) 780-5430

Type: Public, 4 Yr., Coed
Website: http://www.usm.maine.edu
SAT/ACT/GPA: 950 & up
Student/Faculty Ratio: 13/1
Undergraduate Enrollment: 4,000
Scholarships/Academic: Yes　　**Athletic:** No

Founded: 1970
Religion: Non-Affiliated
Housing: Yes
Male/Female: 40/60
Graduate Enrollment: 1,800
Financial Aid: Yes

Expenses By: Semester In State: **$4461+** Out of State: **$7806+**
Degrees Conferred: AA, AS, BA, BS, MA, M.Ed.
Programs of Study: Applied Chemistry, Art, Biology, PreMed, PreVet, PreDental, Communications, Criminology, Economics, English, Environmental Science & Policy, French, Geography, Anthropology, Geology, History, Mathematics, Music, Philosophy, Physics, Political Science, Psychology, Social Work, Social Science, Sociology, Management, Computer Science, Engineering, Nursing

Women's Athletic Profile

37 College Avenue
Gorham, ME 04038
Coach: Hobson Jandebeur
Email: hobsonj@usm.maine.edu

NCAA I
Huskies, Crimson, Blue, White
Phone: (207) 780-5430
Fax: (207) 780-5182

Estimated # of Women's Volleyball Scholarships: None
Conference: Little East Conference
History: The Southern Maine program began in 1967 and ran through the 1986 season before being disbanded. The program was reinstated in 1996.
Coaching: Hobson Jandebeur - Head Coach. Andrea Jandebeur is our Assistant Coach.
Sophomores on Team: 2 **Seniors on Team:** 3 **Graduation %:**
Most Recent Record: 5-27-0 **Fall Games:** 22 **Spring Games:** 0
Positions Needed: All
Schedule: Eastern Connecticut

Annapolis

SCHOOL	CITY	AFFILIATION	PAGE
Bowie State University	Bowie	NCAA II	323
Cantonsville Community College	Baltimore	NJCAA II	323
College of Notre Dame	Baltimore	NCAA III	324
Columbia Union College	Takoma Park	NCAA II	324
Coppin State College	Baltimore	NCAA I	325
Frostburg State University	Forstburg	NCAA III	325
Goucher College	Towson	NCAA III	326
Hagerstown Junior College	Hagerstown	NJCAA	326
Hood College	Frederick	NCAA III	327
John Hopkins University	Baltimore	NCAA III	328
Loyola College	Baltimore	NCAA I	328
Morgan State University	Baltimore	NCAA I	329
Saint Mary's College - Maryland	St. Mary's City	NCAA III	329
Salisbury State University	Salisbury	NCAA III	330
Towson University	Towson	NCAA I	331
US Naval Academy	Annapolis	NCAA I	331
Univ. of Maryland - College Park	College Park	NCAA I	332
Univ. of Maryland-Baltimore County	Baltimore	NCAA I	332
Univ. of Maryland-Eastern Shore	Princess Anne	NCAA I	333
Villa Julie College	Stevenson	NCAA III	333
Washington College - Maryland	Chestertown	NCAA III	334
Western Maryland College	Westminster	NCAA III	335

Bowie State University
Academic Profile

14000 Jericho Park
Bowie, MD 20715

Phone: 301-464-6570

Type: Public, 4 Yr., Liberal Arts, Coed
Website: http://www.bowiestate.edu
SAT/ACT/GPA: 950/18/2.2
Student/Faculty Ratio: 15.5:1
Undergraduate Enrollment: 2,330
Scholarships/Academic: Yes
Expenses By: Year
Specializes In: Teacher Education, Computer Science
Degrees Conferred: BA, BS, MA, MS, MED

Athletic: Yes
In State: $ 3,557+

Founded: 1865
Religion: Non-Affiliated
Housing: Yes
Male/Female: 1:2
Graduate Enrollment: 1,629
Financial Aid: Yes
Out of State: $ 5,968+

Programs of Study: Air Traffic Control, Architecture, Automotive, Aviation, Business, Commercial Art, Computer, Corrections, Criminal Justice, Deaf Interpreter Training, Engineering, International, Law, Legal Studies, Manufacturing, Medical, Photography, Real, Estate, Recreation, Science, Zoology

Women's Athletic Profile

1400 Jericho Park Rd.
Bowie, MD 20715-9465
Coach: Paulette Gabourel
Email: PGABOURE@email.usps.gov

NCAA I
Lady Bulldogs, Black, Gold
Phone: (301) 860-3583
Fax: (301) 464-7524

Estimated # of Women's Volleyball Scholarships: N/A
Conference: Central Intercollegiate Athletic Association

Catonsville Community College
Academic Profile

800 South Rolling Road
Cantonsville, MD 21228

Phone: (410) 455-4197

Type: 2 Yr., Jr. College, Coed
Website: http://www.cat.cc.md.us
SAT/ACT/GPA: None
Student/Faculty Ratio: Not Avai
Undergraduate Enrollment: 4,312
Scholarships/Academic:
Expenses By: Year
Specializes In: Technology and Nursing
Degrees Conferred: AA,AAS

Athletic:
In State: $113 /credit

Founded: 1956
Religion: Non-Affiliated
Housing: No
Male/Female: 43:57
Graduate Enrollment: N/A
Financial Aid:
Out of State: $166 per credit

Programs of Study: Contact admissions office at 410-455-4304

Women's Athletic Profile

800 South Rolling Road
Baltimore, MD 21228
Coach: Jerry Hulla
Email: jhulla@neors.cat.cc.md.us

NCAA I
Lady Cardinals, Red, Black
Phone: (410) 455-4197
Fax: (410) 455-4998

Estimated # of Women's Volleyball Scholarships: 4-6
Conference: Maryland Junior College Conference
Program Profile: We have a 5 court facility with new $30,000 floor and 2 newly renovated state-of-the-art fitness and lifeline facilities. Our campus cable station broadcasts matches on local cable. Our playing season is in the fall from August to November and it includes the post-season. Our spring season is from February to May with competitions in April.
History: We began qualifying for the National Tournament in 1974 when we finished 2nd at the Region XX Tournament. (The qualifying tournament for Nationals). We were first in the Region and undefeated. We were first in the Conference and undefeated. We were Conference Champions. We were also ranked as high as 19th by the NJCAA National Poll.
Achievements: Coach Hulla: Tachikara/AVCA JC/CC Northeast-Southeast Region Coach of the Year in 1998; Maryland JuCo Conference Coach of the Year in 1981; CCBC-Cantonsville Coach of the Year 1998-99; Players: 3- 1st and 2 -2nd team; All-Conference (1 Honorable Mention); 3 -1st and 2- 2nd Team All-Region (I Honorable Mention); 2 All-Americans; 1 All-Tournament Team; 4 All-Region Tournament, 1 Player of the Year; 3 Players Nationally Ranked; Conference Championship 1981.

Coaching: Jerry Hulla, Head Coach, just completed his third year and has an overall record of 48-29. He was Coach of the Year four times. He got a silver medal at the Pan-American Championships. He played pro-beach volleyball in the east and west coast for 8 years. He has 45 Club Awards. Charlene Diamond and Chris Harman are assistant coaches.

Freshman Receiving Financial Aid/Academic: | | **Athletic:** 8

Roster In State: 8   **Out of State:** 4   **Out of Country:** 0

Sophomores on Team: 0   **Seniors on Team:** 2   **Graduation %:** 100

Most Recent Record: 27-10-0   **Fall Games:** 37   **Spring Games:** varies

Camp of Clinic Dates: August 9-13 (Grades 6-12, Girls)

Positions Needed: Setter, Outside Hitter, Middle Hitter, Defensive Specialist

Schedule: Lee College, Jamestown CC, College of DuPage, Owens CC, Parkland, Kirkwood

Style of Play: Fast-paced offense, based on: strong right-side, back row & combination attacks; strong defensive philosophy with attention to blocking. Team motto: "Bigger, Stronger, Faster". We take pride in our academic accomplishments as well as our strength & conditioning improvements. We are known as "hardest working team in the Region." "Family style approach to team chemistry."

College of Notre Dame - Maryland
Academic Profile

4701 N Charles Street
Baltimore, MD 21210-2476

Phone: 800-435-0300

Type: Private, 4 Yr., Liberal Arts, Women Only
Website: http://www.ndm.edu
SAT/ACT/GPA: 950
Student/Faculty Ratio: 15:1
Undergraduate Enrollment: 650
Scholarships/Academic: Yes   **Athletic:** No
Expenses By: Year   **In State:** $ 16,000
Specializes In: Education, Sciences
Degrees Conferred: BA, BS

Founded: 1896
Religion: Catholic
Housing: Yes
Male/Female: Women Only
Graduate Enrollment: N/A
Financial Aid: Yes
Out of State: $ 16,000

Programs of Study: Art, Biology, Business, Chemistry, Classical Studies, Communication Arts, Computer Information Systems, Computer Science, Economics, Education, Engineering, English, History, Interdisciplinary Studies, Liberal Arts, Mathematics, PreProfessional Programs

Women's Athletic Profile

Did Not Return Profile

Columbia Union College
Academic Profile

7600 Flower Avenue
Takoma Park, MD 20912

Phone: 800-835-4212

Type: Private, 4 Yr., Liberal Arts, Coed
Website: http://www.cuc.edu
SAT/ACT/GPA: Open
Student/Faculty Ratio: 14:1
Undergraduate Enrollment: 950
Scholarships/Academic: Yes   **Athletic:** Yes
Expenses By: Year   **In State:** $ 13,500
Specializes In: Business
Degrees Conferred: AA, BA, BS

Founded: 1904
Religion: Seventh Day Adventist
Housing: No
Male/Female: 40:60
Graduate Enrollment: N/A
Financial Aid: Yes
Out of State: $ 13,500

Programs of Study: Accounting, Banking/Finance, BioChemistry, Broadcasting, Business Administration, Chemistry, Communications, Computer Science, Education, English, Health Science, History, Information Science, Journalism, Management, Mathematics, Medical Laboratory Technology, Music, Nursing, Personnel/Management, Physics, PreDentistry, PreLaw, PreMed, Psychology, Religion

Men's Athletic Profile

7600 Flower Avenue
Takoma park, MD 20912
Coach: Terri Kerley
Email:

NCAA II
Pioneers/Gold, White
Phone: (301) 891-4540
Fax: (301) 891-4026

Estimated # of Men's Volleyball Scholarships: N/A
Conference: Independent

Women's Athletic Profile

7600 Flower Avenue
Takoma Park, MD 20912
Coach: Brenda Stephens
Email:

NCAA I
Lady Pioneers, Blue, Gold
Phone: (301) 891-4540
Fax: (301) 891-4026

Estimated # of Women's Volleyball Scholarships: N/A
Conference: Independent

Coppin State College
Academic Profile

2500 W. North Ave.
Baltimore, MD 21216

Phone: 410-383-5995

Type: Public, 4 Yr., Coed
Website: http://www.coppin.umd.edu
SAT/ACT/GPA: 820/68
Student/Faculty Ratio: 25:1
Undergraduate Enrollment: 2,925
Scholarships/Academic: Yes
Expenses By: Year
Degrees Conferred: BA, BS, BN, MA, MS

Founded: 1900
Religion: Non-Affiliated
Housing: Yes
Male/Female: 1:3
Graduate Enrollment: 350
Athletic: Yes   **Financial Aid:** Yes
In State: $ 7,967   **Out of State:** $ 11,972

Programs of Study: Adapted Physical Education, Biology, Chemistry, Computer Science, Criminal Justice, General Studies, Engineering, Nursing, Philosophy, PreProfessional Programs, Concentrations, Special Education

Women's Athletic Profile

2500 W. North Avenue
Baltimore, MD 21216
Coach: Stephanie Ready
Email:
Estimated # of Women's Volleyball Scholarships: N/A
Conference: Mid-Eastern Athletic Conference

NCAA I
Lady Eagles, Royal Blue, Gold
Phone: (410) 383-5972
Fax: (410) 383-2511

Frostburg State University
Academic Profile

112 Pullen Hall
Frostburg, MD 21532

Phone: 301-687-4201

Type: Public, 4 Yr., Liberal Arts, Engineering, Coed
Website: http://www.fsu.umd.edu
SAT/ACT/GPA: Open
Student/Faculty Ratio: 17:1
Undergraduate Enrollment: 4,600
Scholarships/Academic: Yes
Expenses By: Year
Specializes In: Education, Engineering, Environmental Sciences & Business

Founded: 1898
Religion: Non-Affiliated
Housing: Yes
Male/Female: 48:52
Graduate Enrollment: 800
Athletic: No   **Financial Aid:** Yes
In State: $ 9,454   **Out of State:** $ 14, 012

Degrees Conferred: BA, BS, BFA, B Ed , MA, MS, M Ed, MBA
Programs of Study: Art & Design, English, Foreign Languages and Literature, History, Mass Communications, Music, Philosophy, Speech Communications and Theatre, Business Administration, Accounting, Economics, Actuarial Science, Biology, Chemistry, PreMed, Computer Science, Earth Science, Electrical Engineering, Physics, Political Science, Psychology, Social Science, Social Work, Education, Early Childhood Education, Liberal Studies, Physical Education & Recreation

Women's Athletic Profile

P.E. Center
Frostburg, MD 21532
Coach: John Teetzel
Email:

NCAA I
Bobcats, Red, White, Black
Phone: (301) 687-7014
Fax: (301) 687-4780

Estimated # of Women's Volleyball Scholarships: N/A
Conference: Eastern College Athletic Conference

Goucher College
Academic Profile

1021 Dulaney Valley Rd
Baltimore, MD 21204

Phone: 410-337-6385

Type: Private, 4 Yr., Liberal Arts, Coed
Website: http://www.goucher.edu
SAT/ACT/GPA: 1170/3.0
Student/Faculty Ratio: 11/1
Undergraduate Enrollment: 1,150
Scholarships/Academic: Yes
Expenses By: Year
Specializes In: Liberal Arts
Degrees Conferred: BS, BA, M.Ed.

Athletic: No
In State: $29,140

Founded: 1885
Religion: Non-Denominational
Housing: Yes
Male/Female: 31/69
Graduate Enrollment: 725
Financial Aid: Yes
Out of State: $29,140

Programs of Study: American Studies, Art, Business, Interdisciplinary, Chemistry, Cognitive Studies, Communications, Computer Science, Dance, Economics, Education, English, French, German, Historic Preservation, History, Interdisciplinary Studies, International and Intercultural Studies, International Relations, Management, Mathematics, Music, Peace Studies, Philosophy, Physics, Political Science, Psychology, Religion, Russian, Sociology, Sociology and Anthropology, Spanish, Special Education, Theatre, Women's Studies

Women's Athletic Profile

Dulaney Valley Road
Towson, MD 21204
Coach: Charleata Beale
Email: cbeale@gaucher.edu

NCAA I
Lady Gophers, Blue, Gold
Phone: (410) 337-6386
Fax: (410) 337-6576

Estimated # of Women's Volleyball Scholarships: 0
Conference: Independent
Program Profile: Sports and recreational center/capacity 1200, Average-40 matches per year since 1990
History: Began:1983, Cumulative Record: 253-276
Achievements: Over .500, 6 of past 7 years 179-113, since '92 1993 Team: 44-4, capital Athletic Conference Champs
Coaching: Charleata Beale, 1998, 21-16, 1 year
Roster In State: 5
Sophomores on Team:
Most Recent Record: 21-16
Camp of Clinic Dates: Camp-1st week of August
Positions Needed: approx. 5
Schedule: Rowan, Gettysburg, Oneonta, Gallowplat, St. Mary's-MD, Franklin and Marshall

Out of State: 7
Seniors on Team: 1

Out of Country: 1
Graduation %: 90

Hagerstown Junior College
Academic Profile

11400 Robinwood Drive
Hagerstown, MD 21742

Phone: (301) 790-2800

Type: Public, 2 Yr., Jr. College, Coed
Website: http://www.western-md.com
SAT/ACT/GPA: None for Admission
Student/Faculty Ratio: 18:1
Undergraduate Enrollment: 3,000
Scholarships/Academic: Yes
Expenses By: Year
Specializes In: Transfer Programs
Degrees Conferred: AA and Certificates

Athletic: Yes
In State: $ 2,400+

Founded: 1946
Religion: Non-Affiliated
Housing: No
Male/Female: 53:49
Graduate Enrollment: N/A
Financial Aid: Yes
Out of State: $ 4,400+

Programs of Study: Biology, Education, Engineering, Nursing, Radiology, Human Services, General Studies, Computer Science, Business, Psychology

Women's Athletic Profile

11400 Robinwood Drive
Hagerstown, MD 21742
Coach: Marleys Palmer
Email:

NCAA I
Lady Hawks, Green, White
Phone: (301) 790-2800
Fax: (301) 733-0097

Estimated # of Women's Volleyball Scholarships: 6
Conference: MD Juco Region 20 NJCAA
Program Profile: We have a fieldhouse that has 5,000 seats, 3 courts and 2 weight rooms.
History: We started in 1978. We have 9 National Tournament Appearances and 9 Regional Championships.
Achievements: Coach of the Year 9 times; record number of transfers to 4 year institutions; 7 All-Americans; 9 Conference Titles
Coaching: Marlys Palmer, Head Coach, became Head Coach in 1998. She has an overall record of 598-144. She is 2 time AVCA Coach of the Year
Freshman Receiving Financial Aid/Academic: | **Athletic:** 2
Roster In State: 8 | **Out of State:** 4 | **Out of Country:** 0
Sophomores on Team: 0 | **Seniors on Team:** 6 | **Graduation %:** 98
Most Recent Record: 28-13-0 | **Fall Games:** | **Spring Games:** 0
Camp of Clinic Dates: July 26-30
Positions Needed: All
Schedule: Catonsville, Jamestown, Spartanburg, Genesee, Delaware Tech
Style of Play: Aggressive, with tough offense, serving, and smart hitting.

Hood College
Academic Profile

401 Rosemont Avenue
Frederick, MD 21701

Phone: 800-922-1599

Type: Private, 4 Yr., Liberal Arts, Women Only
Website: http://www.hood.edu
SAT/ACT/GPA: 1090-1230/A or B Average
Student/Faculty Ratio: 10:1
Undergraduate Enrollment: 1,200
Scholarships/Academic: Yes
Expenses By: Year
Degrees Conferred: BA, BS, MA, MS, MBA

Founded: 1893
Religion: Church of Christ
Housing: Yes
Male/Female: Women Only
Graduate Enrollment: 1,000
Athletic: No | **Financial Aid:** Yes
In State: $ 23,910 | **Out of State:** $ 23,910

Programs of Study: Art, BioChemistry, Biology, Chemistry, English, Education - Early Childhood, Special and Secondary, History, French, Management, Music, Political Science, Psychology, Sociology, Spanish

Women's Athletic Profile

401 Rosemont Avenue
Frederick, MD 21701
Coach: Joe Mahan
Email: mahan@hood.edu

NCAA I
Lady Blazers, Navy, Grey
Phone: (301) 696-3998
Fax: (301) 696-3488

Estimated # of Women's Volleyball Scholarships: N/A
Conference: AWCC
Program Profile: We play at Gambrill Gym with a seating capacity of 200. We have a locker room, weight room and pool. Volleyball competes in NCAA Championship. We play a fall season.
History: Our program is in its fifth year as a varsity team.
Coaching: Joe Mahan is our Head Coach. He started with the program in 1998. He compiled a record of 4-17 and overall coaching career is 48-91. He was named All-Conference Middle Blocker at George Washington University in 1989-1992.
Roster In State: 11 | **Out of State:** 3 | **Out of Country:** 0
Sophomores on Team: 0 | **Seniors on Team:** 1 | **Graduation %:** 100
Most Recent Record: 4-17-0 | **Fall Games:** 21 | **Spring Games:** 0
Positions Needed: Setter, Middle Blocker
Style of Play: Up-tempo with quick offense and scrappy defense. Consistent serving team.

Johns Hopkins University
Academic Profile

3400 Worth Charles Street
Baltimore, MD 21218-2684

Phone: 410-516-8171

Type: Private, 4 Yr., Liberal Arts, Engineering, Coed
Website: http://www.jhu.edu
SAT/ACT/GPA: 1100avg/2.5
Student/Faculty Ratio: 10:1
Undergraduate Enrollment: 3,600
Scholarships/Academic: Yes   **Athletic:** No
Expenses By: Year   **In State:** $ 32,000

Founded: 1876
Religion: Non-Affiliated
Housing: Yes
Male/Female: 60:40
Graduate Enrollment: 1,400
Financial Aid: Yes
Out of State: $ 32,000

Specializes In: Natural Science, Engineering, English, History
Degrees Conferred: BA, BS, MA, MS, Ph.D., MD
Programs of Study: Arts and Sciences, Engineering (Biomedical, Chemical, Civil, Computer Science, Electrical, Computer, Mechanics, Geography, Environmental, Materials Science, Math, Mechanical), Anthropology, Behavioral Biology, Biology, BioPhysics, Chemistry, Classics, Cognitive Science, Comparative American Cultures, Earth and Planetary Science, East Asian Studies, Economics, English, Environmental Earth Sciences, History, Humanistic Studies, Math, Music, Natural Sciences, Neuroscience, Philosophy, Physics and Astronomy, Political Science, Psychology, Public Health, Social and Behavioral Sciences, Sociology, Writing Seminars

Women's Athletic Profile

3400 N. Charles Street
Baltimore, MD 21218
Coach: Chris Weidenborner
Email: hopkinsvolleyball@hotmail.com

NCAA I
Lady Blue Jays, Blue, Black
Phone: (410) 516-7968
Fax: (410) 516-7482

Estimated # of Women's Volleyball Scholarships: N/A
Conference: Centennial Conference

Loyola College - Baltimore
Academic Profile

4501 N Charles Street
Baltimore, MD 21210-2699

Phone: 800-221-9107

Type: Private, 4 Yr., Liberal Arts, Engineering, Coed
Website: http://www.loyola.edu
SAT/ACT/GPA: 1200
Student/Faculty Ratio: 14:1
Undergraduate Enrollment: N/A
Scholarships/Academic: Yes   **Athletic:** Yes
Expenses By: Year   **In State:** $ 26,700

Founded: 1852
Religion: Catholic
Housing: Yes
Male/Female: 43:57
Graduate Enrollment: N/A
Financial Aid: Yes
Out of State: $ 26,700

Specializes In: Business, Science, Computer, Engineering
Degrees Conferred: BA, BS, BBA
Programs of Study: Accounting, Biology, Business Administration, Chemistry, Communications, Computer Science, Creative Writing, Economics, Electrical Engineering, Elementary Education, English, Finance, Fine Arts, French, Latin, Management, Marketing, Mathematics, Philosophy, Physics, Political Science, Psychology, Sociology, Pathology, Theology

Women's Athletic Profile

4501 N. Charles Street
Baltimore, MD 21210
Coach: Angie Ruthledge
Email: aruthledge1@juno.com

NCAA I
Lady Greyhounds, Grey, Green
Phone: (410) 617-2772
Fax: (410) 617-2008

Estimated # of Women's Volleyball Scholarships: 3
Conference: Metro Atlantic Athletic Conference
Program Profile: We play at Reitz Arena, which is named for Emil G. "Lefty" Reitz, an extraordinary man who served Loyola College for 36 years. Mr. Reitz died in April 1992. He is remembered fondly by the college, not only for his phenomenal accomplishments as a coach of any number of the school's athletic programs, but also for his efforts in making Loyola a more enjoyable place for students, faculty, administration and other staff members.

History: Loyola wins their most matches in four seasons, participating in the Metro Athletic Conference Tournament for the second consecutive season. Loyola Volleyball team ended its 1997 season at the MAAC Championships, the Greyhounds couldn't boast of winning the title.

Achievements: Loyola was qualified for the MAAC's post-season tournament for the second straight season, also for the first time since 1993. Loyola former Coach Katha Scheeler was named the MAAC's Co-Coach of the Year along with Fairfield's Todd Kress. Jaci Knight was named to the Academic All-MAAC Team and Shauna Lagatol was selected to the MAAC All-Tournament Team.

Coaching: Angie Rutledge in her first year as the Head Coach. Prior to her appointment, Rutledge served as an assistant Coach with the Greyhounds for two seasons. She is a native of the State of Tennessee, but grew up in Bristol, Virginia. She was a four-year letter-winner at Radford University, twice earning recognition as the team's top defensive player. She graduated from Radford in 1991 after serving her Bachelor Degree in Physical Education. she went on to earn her Master's Degree in Physical Education and Wellness in 1994.

Roster In State: 2   **Out of State:** 9   **Out of Country:** 0
Sophomores on Team: 1   **Seniors on Team:** 2   **Graduation %:**
Schedule: Rutgers, Coppin, George Washington, La Salle, Delaware, Americans, Bucknells, Rider, Yale

Morgan State University
Academic Profile

1700 E. Coldsprings Ln.
Baltimore, MD 21239

Phone: 800-332-6674

Type: Public, 4 Yr., Coed
Website: http://www.morgan.edu
SAT/ACT/GPA: 900+
Student/Faculty Ratio: 18:1
Undergraduate Enrollment: 4,542
Scholarships/Academic: Yes   **Athletic:** Yes
Expenses By: Year   **In State:** $ 9,378
Degrees Conferred: BA, BS, MA, MS, MBA, EdD
Programs of Study: Contact school for program of study.

Founded: 1867
Religion: Non-Affiliated
Housing: No
Male/Female: 43:57
Graduate Enrollment: 492
Financial Aid: Yes
Out of State: $ 11,446

Women's Athletic Profile

1700 E. Coldspring Lane
Baltimore, MD 21251
Coach: Ramona Riley-Bozier
Email: lgermany@moac.morgan.edu

NCAA I
Lady Bears, Orange, Blue
Phone: 443-885-3887
Fax: 410-319-3221

Estimated # of Women's Volleyball Scholarships: 3
Conference: Mid-Eastern Athletic Conference
Achievements: Ramona Riley-Bozier is four time MEAC Coach of the Year; Morgan State won MEAC titles in 97 and 98;
Coaching: Ramona Riley-Bozier is Head Coach and Sherita Hall assistant.
Freshman Receiving Financial Aid/Academic: **Athletic:** 3
Roster In State: 0   **Out of State:** 15   **Out of Country:**
Sophomores on Team: **Seniors on Team:** 1   **Graduation %:** 85
Most Recent Record: 21-9
Positions Needed: Outside hitter, Setter
Style of Play: Aggressive, attacking style with emphasis on fundamentals

St. Mary's College - Maryland
Academic Profile

18952 E. Fisher Rd.
St. Mary's City, MD 20686

Phone: 800-492-7181

Type: Public, 4 Yr., Liberal Arts, Coed
Website: http://www.smcm.edu
SAT/ACT/GPA: 1100/21/3.0
Student/Faculty Ratio: 14:1
Undergraduate Enrollment: 1,500
Scholarships/Academic: Yes   **Athletic:** No
Expenses By: Year   **In State:** $ 13,144

Founded: 1840
Religion: Non-Affiliated
Housing: Yes
Male/Female: 40:60
Graduate Enrollment: N/A
Financial Aid: Yes
Out of State: $ 17,844

Specializes In: 31 Different majors
Degrees Conferred: BA
Programs of Study: Art, Dramatic Arts, English, Foreign Languages, Music, Anthropology, Sociology, Economics, History, Political Science, Education, Philosophy, Psychology, Religion, Biology, Chemistry, Mathematics, Computer Science, Physics, Interdisciplinary Majors, Cross Studies Majors

Women's Athletic Profile

18952 E. Fisher Rd.
St. Mary's City, MD 20686
Coach: Bryan Snyder
Email: brSnyder@osprey.smcm.edu

NCAA I
Lady Seahawks, Navy, Old Gold
Phone: (301) 862-0320
Fax: (301) 862-0480

Estimated # of Women's Volleyball Scholarships: N/A
Conference: Capital Athletic Conference
Program Profile: We are a Division III program. We have a fall season from late August to early November and a six weeks spring season with 2-3 practices a week and approximately 2 USAU Tournaments. Somerset Gymnasium has 750 seats.
History: SMC joined the NCAA Division III prior to the 1977-1978 academic year. Our volleyball team has had 20+ wins in 4 out of the last 5 seasons.
Coaching: Bryan Snyder, Head Coach, started this year with the program. He compiled a record of 20-11 in his first season. Corinne Marino is Assistant Coach.

Freshman Receiving Financial Aid/Academic:		**Athletic:** 0
Roster In State: 10	**Out of State:** 1	**Out of Country:** 0
Sophomores on Team: 0	**Seniors on Team:** 3	**Graduation %:** Unknown
Most Recent Record: 20-11-0	**Fall Games:** 31	**Spring Games:** 6

Positions Needed: Middle Hitter, Outside Hitter, Setter
Schedule: Franklin & Marshall, Salisbury State, Washington & Lee, York, Gallaudet, Marymount
Style of Play: Currently, we run a 5-1 offense and a perimeter-oriented defense. We are aggressive on defense and offense. Six to nine players play each match. We have a very efficient use of back row attacks.

Salisbury State University
Academic Profile

1101 Camden Avenue
Salisbury, MD 21801

Phone: 888-543-0148

Type: Public, 4 Yr., Liberal Arts, Coed
Website: http://www.ssu.umd.edu
SAT/ACT/GPA: 980-1050
Student/Faculty Ratio: 17:1
Undergraduate Enrollment: 6,000
Scholarships/Academic: Yes
Expenses By: Year
Specializes In: Business, Education

Founded: 1925
Religion: Non-Affiliated
Housing: Yes
Male/Female: 50:50
Graduate Enrollment: N/A
Athletic: No   **Financial Aid:** Yes
In State: $ 8,500   **Out of State:** $ 13,000

Degrees Conferred: BA, BS, BFA, BSN, BSW, MA, MS, MBA, MED
Programs of Study: Accounting, Biology, Broadcasting, Business Administration, Chemistry, Communications, Dramatic Arts, Earth Science, Economics, Education, English, Environmental Science, Fine Arts, French, History, Management, Marine Science, Marketing, Mathematics, PreLaw, PreMed, Psychology, Recreation, Social Science, Respiratory Therapy

Women's Athletic Profile

1101 Camden Avenue
Salisbury, MD 21801
Coach: Margie Knight
Email:

NCAA I
Lady Sea Gulls, Maroon, Gold
Phone: (410) 543-6357
Fax: (410) 546-2639

Estimated # of Women's Volleyball Scholarships: 9
Conference: Capital Athletic Conference
Program Profile: Our playing season lasts from September through November or longer in case of a NCAA Tournament. We have excellent facilities. We travel in buses, have an equipment manager and several uniforms.
History: Our program started in the early 1970's. We participated in an NCAA Tournament for the first time in 1998. We have won several ECAC Tournaments in the early 1990's.

Achievements: 1998 Conference Coach of the Year; Conference Champions in 1998; Conference Player of the Year in 1998; All-Region Selection in 1994-5; 1998 led NCAA Division III in Digs.

Coaching: Margie Knight started as Head Coach in 1997 and has an overall record of 45-30. She was inducted into the SSU's Hall of Fame in 1995. Dean Shuttleworth is Assistant Coach.

Roster In State: 11	**Out of State:** 1	**Out of Country:** 0
Sophomores on Team: 0	**Seniors on Team:** 3	**Graduation %:** 95
Most Recent Record: 25-14-0	**Fall Games:** 35	**Spring Games:** 0

Camp of Clinic Dates: August 4-9

Positions Needed: Outside Hitter, Back-up Setter

Schedule: Gettysburg, York, Mary Washington, St.Mary's

Style of Play: Varies with personnel, but always aggressive.

Towson University
Academic Profile

8000 York Rd.
Towson, MD 21252-0001

Phone: (410) 830-3165

Type: Public, 4 Yr., Liberal Arts, Coed
Website: http://www.towson.edu
SAT/ACT/GPA: 1000/3.0
Student/Faculty Ratio: 17:1
Undergraduate Enrollment: 12,614
Scholarships/Academic: Yes **Athletic:** Yes
Expenses By: Year **In State:** $ 9,164
Specializes In: Liberal Arts

Founded: 1866
Religion: Non-Affiliated
Housing: Yes
Male/Female: 45:55
Graduate Enrollment: 2,382
Financial Aid: Yes
Out of State: $ 14,242

Degrees Conferred: BA, BS, BFA, BM, MA, MS, MAT, MFA, M.Ed., MM

Programs of Study: Accounting, Art, Art Education, Biology, Business Administration, Chemistry, Communications, Computer Science, Dance, Early Childhood Education, Economics, Elementary Education, English, French, General Education, Geography, German, Health Science, Mass Communications, Physical Education, Physics, Political Science, Psychology, Social Science, Sociology

Women's Athletic Profile

8000 York Rd.
Towson, MD 21252-0001
Coach: Chris Riley
Email: criley@towson.edu

NCAA I
Lady Tigers, White, Gold, Black
Phone: (410) 704-4028
Fax: (410) 830-4322

Estimated # of Women's Volleyball Scholarships: N/A
Conference: American East Conference

United States Naval Academy
Academic Profile

566 Brownson Road
Annapolis, MD 21402

Phone: 410-293-4361

Type: Public, 4 Yr., Engineering, Coed
Website: http://www.nadn.navy.mil
SAT/ACT/GPA: 1200/3.2
Student/Faculty Ratio: 20:1
Undergraduate Enrollment: 4,000
Scholarships/Academic: Yes **Athletic:** No
Expenses By: Year **In State:** Free if Appointed
Specializes In: Engineering, Math

Founded: 1845
Religion: Non-Affiliated
Housing: Yes
Male/Female: 87:13
Graduate Enrollment: N/A
Financial Aid: No
Out of State: Free if Appointed

Degrees Conferred: BS

Programs of Study: 9 Engineering majors, Math, Political Science, History, Economics, Oceanography, English, Chemistry, Physics

Women's Athletic Profile

566 Brownson Rd
Annapolis, MD 21402-500
Coach: Mike Schwob
Email: schwob@nadn.navy.mil

NCAA I
Lady Midshipmen, Blue, Gold
Phone: (410) 293-5546
Fax: (410) 263-7390

Estimated # of Women's Volleyball Scholarships: N/A
Conference: The Patriot League

University of Maryland
Academic Profile

P. O. Box 295
College Park, MD 20741-0295

Phone: 800-422-5867

Type: Public, 4 Yr., Liberal Arts, Coed
Website: http://www.umd.edu
SAT/ACT/GPA: 1200/23/3.6
Student/Faculty Ratio: 13:1
Undergraduate Enrollment: 21,224
Scholarships/Academic: Yes
Expenses By: Year
Specializes In: Everything
Degrees Conferred: BA, BS, BFS, MA, MS, MFA

Founded: 1856
Religion: Non-Affiliated
Housing: Yes
Male/Female: 1:1
Graduate Enrollment: 13,776
Athletic: Yes **Financial Aid:** Yes
In State: $ 11,349 **Out of State:** $ 17,871

Programs of Study: Within college of Agriculture & Natural Resources, School of Architecture, College of Arts & Humanities, College of Behavioral & Social Sciences, Smith School of Business, College of Computer, Mathematical & Physical Science, College of Education, Clark School of Engineering, College of Health and Human Performance, College of Journalism, College of Life Sciences, more...

Women's Athletic Profile

P.O. Box 295
College Park, MD 20740
Coach: Janice Kruger
Email: VB-paul_dscheel@umail.umd.edu

NCAA I
Terrapins, Red, White, Black
Phone: (301) 314-7114
Fax: (301) 314-9826

Estimated # of Women's Volleyball Scholarships: 3
Conference: Atlantic Coast Conference
Program Profile: Ritchie Coliseum seats 1,850. We have a fall playing season.
History: We began in 1971and in 27 years we have had 2 coaches. Our overall record is 66-336. We have a record in the ACC of 95-54 since 1981. We have 3 ACC Titles and 4 NCAA appearances.
Achievements: Janice Kryger was named 3 ACC Coach of the Year. She has 2 District 3 Coach of the Year honors. She ranks 14th among coaches in career wins (579). She is the winningest active ACC Coach and got 2 NCAA Division II Coach of the Year honors. She was UMD Sears Director Cup ranking - 1995-57th, 1996-36th, 1997-32th and 1998-19th.
Coaching: Janice Kruger - Head Coach. Paul Scheel is Assistant Coach and graduated from St. Cloud State in 1991. He joined Terps in 1994. He was a three year letterman at St. Cloud State and earned All-Conference all three years. He led St. Cloud State to a 60-12 record and a 2nd place finish at the 1989 NIVC Tournament. When he was a senior at Eastern Montana College, he led the team to its best Division I record in school history of 20-8. He is a recruiter, signing some of the nation's best prep players. Felix Hou, Assistant Coach, graduated from Shanghai Physical Education Institute in 1986. He started with the program in 1994. He started playing volleyball in 1971 until 1993 in Asia and Europe. He started coaching in 1984 in Asia, Europe and USA. He is a former Chinese National player, 5th in the world. He was former Chinese Youth National Team Coach. He was on the Iceland National team and an Iceland University team coach. He was Yohan women's pro volleyball coach in Asia. He has a BA in Coaching Management from Shanghai Physical Education Institute.
Freshman Receiving Financial Aid/Academic: **Athletic:** 2
Roster In State: 4 **Out of State:** 9 **Out of Country:** 1
Sophomores on Team: 3 **Seniors on Team:** 2 **Graduation %:** 100
Most Recent Record: 13-16-0 **Fall Games:** 25 **Spring Games:** 4
Camp of Clinic Dates: July 11-24; August 7-9
Positions Needed: Setter, 2 Middle Hitters
Schedule: Penn State, University of San Diego, Colorado State, Louisville, Florida State, North Carolina
Style of Play: Fast offense with a combination attack system. Defense - different systems according to opponent's strengths and weaknesses.

University of Maryland-Baltimore County
Academic Profile

5401 Wilkins Avenue
Baltimore, MD 21228

Phone: (410) 455-3003

Type: Public, 4 Yr., Liberal Arts, Engineering, Coed
Website: http://www.ab.umd.edu
SAT/ACT/GPA: 1100/2.5

Founded: 1966
Religion: Non-Affiliated
Housing: Yes

Student/Faculty Ratio: 20:1		**Male/Female:** 45:55
Undergraduate Enrollment: 10,000		**Graduate Enrollment:** 2,000
Scholarships/Academic: Yes	**Athletic:** Yes	**Financial Aid:** Yes
Expenses By: Year	**In State:** $ 10,000	**Out of State:** $ 14,000

Specializes In: Sciences

Degrees Conferred: BA, BS, MA, MS, MFA, Ph.D.

Programs of Study: Art, BioChemistry, Biological Science, Chemistry, Computer Science, Economics, Engineering, Geography, Mathematics, Nursing, Philosophy, Physics, Political Science, Psychology, Social Work, Sociology, Theatre

Women's Athletic Profile

1000 Hilltop Circle	**NCAA I**
Baltimore, MD 21250-0000	Retrievers, Black, Gold, Red
Coach: Catherine Lavery	**Phone:** (410) 455-3241
Email: lavery@gl.wmbc.edu	**Fax:** (410) 455-3994

Estimated # of Women's Volleyball Scholarships: 3

Conference: Big South Conference

Achievements: Coach of the Year 1990, 1991, 1992 and 1994; NCAA first appearance; 3 Conference Titles

Coaching: Catherine Lavery, Head Coach, began with our program in 1990.

Freshman Receiving Financial Aid/Academic:		**Athletic:** 4
Roster In State: 2	**Out of State:** 10	**Out of Country:** 0
Sophomores on Team: 0	**Seniors on Team:** 0	**Graduation %:** 75
Most Recent Record:	**Fall Games:** 26	**Spring Games:** 0

Camp of Clinic Dates: July 1-15

Positions Needed: Three

Schedule: Georgetown, Syracuse, West Virginia University, University of North Carolina State

University of Maryland - Eastern Shore
Academic Profile

P.O. Box 1060 UMES	**Phone:** 410-651-8410
Princess Ann, MD 21853	

Type: Public, 4 Yr., Coed	**Founded:** 1886
Website: http://www.umes.umd.edu	**Religion:** Non-Affiliated
SAT/ACT/GPA: Open	**Housing:** Yes
Student/Faculty Ratio: 25:1	**Male/Female:** 2:1
Undergraduate Enrollment: 2,200	**Graduate Enrollment:** 300
Scholarships/Academic: Yes	**Financial Aid:** Yes
Expenses By: Year	**Out of State:** $ 12,107

Athletic: Yes **In State:** $ 7,570

Degrees Conferred: BA, BS, MA, MS, Ph.D.

Programs of Study: Accounting, Agriculture, Air Traffic Control, Biology, Business & Management, Chemistry, Communications, Computer Science, Criminal Science, Ecology, Education, Engineering, Environmental Science, Fashion Merchandise, History, Liberal Arts, Marine Biology, Mathematics, Medical Laboratory Technology, Music, Physical Education, Physical Therapy, PreDentistry, PreLaw, PreMed, Radiological Technology, Social Sciences, Special Education

Women's Athletic Profile

Tawes Gymnasium	**NCAA I**
Princess Anne, MD 21853-1299	Lady Hawks, Maroon, Gray
Coach: Eric Carlson	**Phone:** (410) 651-6538
Email:	**Fax:** (410) 651-7600

Estimated # of Women's Volleyball Scholarships: N/A

Conference: Mid-Eastern Athletic Conference

Villa Julie College
Academic Profile

1525 Greenspring Valley Road	**Phone:** 877-468-6852
Stevenson, MD 21153-0641	

Type: Private, 2/4YR Liberal Arts, Coed	**Founded:** 1947
Website: http://www.vjc.edu	**Religion:** Non-Affiliated
SAT/ACT/GPA: 900	**Housing:** No

Student/Faculty Ratio: 12:1
Undergraduate Enrollment: 2,000
Scholarships/Academic: Yes   **Athletic:** No
Expenses By: Year   **In State:** $ 15,530
Specializes In: Off campus college-owned apartments available
Degrees Conferred: AA,AAS, BS,BA,MSATT

Male/Female: 30:70
Graduate Enrollment: 80
Financial Aid: Yes
Out of State: $ 15,530

Programs of Study: Accounting, Administrative Science, Applied Mathematics, Art, Biology, BioTechnology, Business, Business Communication, Business Information Systems, Chemistry, Child Development, Computer Accounting, Computer Information Systems, Court Reporting, Early Childhood Education, Economics, Elementary Education, English Language and Literature, Environmental Technology, Finance, History, Interdisciplinary Studies, Liberal Arts & Technology: Computer, Liberal Arts & Technology: Science, Marketing, Medical Laboratory Technology, MicroBiology, Nursing, Paralegal Studies, PreDental, PreLaw, PreMedicine, PrePharmacy, PrePhysical Therapy, PreVeterinary, Psychology, Video/Film/Theater, Visual Communication Design, Writing

Women's Athletic Profile

1525 Greenspring Valley Rd.
Stevenson, MD 21153
Coach: Madge Ferreira
Email:

NCAA I
Lady Mustangs, Green, White
Phone: (410) 602-7183
Fax: (410) 602-6564

Estimated # of Women's Volleyball Scholarships: N/A
Conference: Independent
Program Profile: We have an NCAA Division III program and we are attempting to get into ECAC Conference. Games are played during the fall season.
History: Last year was the first year for our program. Our record was 4-10. For our 2000 season, we are looking to play tough teams and 3-5 all day tournaments to help us play more as a team.
Achievements: New program.
Coaching: Madge Ferreira is Head Coach, her record last year was 4-10. This is admirable for a school that had never played volleyball before. Geoffrely Koger is Assistant Coach.
Roster In State: 14   **Out of State:** 0   **Out of Country:** 0
Most Recent Record: 4-10-0   **Fall Games:** 14   **Spring Games:** 0
Camp of Clinic Dates: N/A
Positions Needed: Setter, Middle Blocker
Schedule: Gettysburg, Catholic University, Mary Washington, York College, St.Mary's
Style of Play: Quick middle offense, middle back with slide defense, 6 x 2 attack scheme. (1998 season).

Washington College
Academic Profile

300 Washington Avenue
Chestertown, MD 21620

Phone: (410) 778-7700

Type: Private, 4 Yr., Liberal Arts, Engineering, Coed
Website: http://www.washcoll.edu
SAT/ACT/GPA: 1100
Student/Faculty Ratio: 12:1
Undergraduate Enrollment: 1,100
Scholarships/Academic: Yes   **Athletic:** No
Expenses By: Year   **In State:** $ 24,940
Degrees Conferred: BA, BS, MA

Founded: 1782
Religion: Non-Affiliated
Housing: Yes
Male/Female: 40:60
Graduate Enrollment: 100
Financial Aid: Yes
Out of State: $ 24,940

Programs of Study: American Studies, Anthropology, Art, Behavioral NeuroScience, Biology, Business Management, Chemistry, Creative Writing, Drama, Economics, English, Environmental Studies, French, German, History, Humanities, International Studies, Mathematics, Music, Philosophy, Physics, Political Science, Psychology, Sociology, Spanish, PreMed, PreLaw, Computer Science, Teacher Education

Women's Athletic Profile

300 Washington Avenue
Chestertown, MD 21620
Coach: Jennifer MIller
Email: Jennifer.R.Miller@washcoll.edu
Estimated # of Women's Volleyball Scholarships: N/A
Conference: Centennial Conference

NCAA I
Lady Sho'Men, Maroon, Black
Phone: (410) 778-7227
Fax: (410) 778-7741

Western Maryland College
Academic Profile

2 College Hill
Westminster, MD 21784

Phone: (800) 638-5005

Type: Private, 4 Yr., Liberal Arts, Coed
Website: http://www.wmdc.edu
SAT/ACT/GPA: 1140/25/3.3
Student/Faculty Ratio: 13:1
Undergraduate Enrollment: 1,500
Scholarships/Academic: Yes   **Athletic:** No
Expenses By: Year   **In State:** $ 24,000
Specializes In: Liberal Arts
Degrees Conferred: BA, BS, MA, MS

Founded: 1867
Religion: Non-Affiliated
Housing: Yes
Male/Female: 1:1
Graduate Enrollment: 1,500
Financial Aid: Yes
Out of State: $ 24,000

Programs of Study: Art, Art History, Biology, Business Administration, Chemistry, Communications, Economics, English, Exercise Science, Physical Education, French, German, History, Math, Music, Philosophy, Physics, Political Science, Psychology, Religious Studies, Social Work, Sociology, Spanish, Theatre Arts

Women's Athletic Profile

2 College Hill
Westminster, MD 21784
Coach: Carole Molloy
Email: cmolloy@wmdc.edu

NCAA I
Lady Green Terror, Green, Gold
Phone: (800) 638-5005
Fax: (410) 857-2757

Estimated # of Women's Volleyball Scholarships: N/A
Conference: Centennial Conference
Program Profile: Our season begins late August and runs through early November. The teams play on a hardwood practice surface and a competition surface. They have 3 full size courts to host tournaments and 2 courts in the auxiliary gym and a complete life fitness center for conditioning. We have a maximum 22 date on schedule and 4 tournaments.
History: Our program began in 1968. The overall record since 1968 is 734-252 with 7 National Tournament Appearances: one was AIAW and six were NCAA Division III.
Achievements: Numerous All-Conference, All-Region and All-American athletes throughout the years, 6 Conference titles, 5 Mid-Atlantic Conference and 1 Centennial Conference.
Coaching: Carole Molloy as Head Coach in 1993. Her overall record is 211-161. She has 100 and 200 career victory awards from Tachikara. Tina Houck is Assistant Coach.
Roster In State: 10   **Out of State:** 3   **Out of Country:** 0
Sophomores on Team: 6   **Seniors on Team:** 2   **Graduation %:** 100
Most Recent Record: 18-15-0   **Fall Games:** 30   **Spring Games:** 6
Camp of Clinic Dates: July 19-23
Positions Needed: Setter, Outside Hitter
Schedule: Gettysburg, Lycoming, Franklin & Marshall, Moravian, Juniata, Frostburg
Style of Play: Simple yet effective offense, dominantly using the outside hitter combined with a quick middle. Many strategies fall into place based upon personnel each season. Desire to increase back row attack and use of slide into offense with new personnel.

MASSACHUSETTS

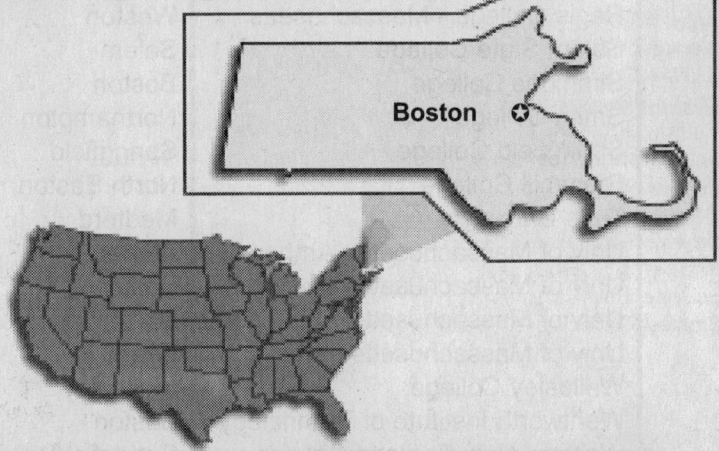

Boston

SCHOOL	CITY	AFFILIATION	PAGE
American International College	Springfield	NCAA II	338
Amherst College	Amherst	NCAA III	338
Anna Maria College	Paxton	NCAA III	338
Assumption College	Worcester	NCAA II	339
Atlantic Union College	Lancaster	NAIA	339
Babson College	Babson Park	NCAA III	340
Becker College	Leicester	NCAA III	341
Bentley College	Waltham	NCAA II	341
Boston College	Chestnut	NCAA I	342
Brandeis University	Waltham	NCAA III	342
Bridgewater State College	Bridgewater	NCAA III	343
Clark University	Worcester	NCAA III	343
College of the Holy Cross	Worcester	NCAA I	344
Eastern Nazarene College	Quincy	NCAA III	345
Emerson College	Boston	NCAA III	345
Emmanuel College	Boston	NCAA III	346
Endicott College	Beverly	NCAA III	346
Fitchburg State College	Fitchburg	NCAA III	347
Framingham State College	Framingham	NCAA III	348
Gordon College	Wenham	NCAA III	349
Harvard University	Cambridge	NCAA I	349
Lasell College	Newton	NCAA III	350
Massachusetts Institute of Tech	Cambridge	NCAA III	351
Massachusetts Maritime Academy	Buzzards Bay	NCAA III	351
Merrimack College	North Andover	NCAA II	352
Mount Holyoke college	South Hadley	NCAA III	353
Massachusetts College-Liberal Arts	North Adams	NCAA III	353
Northeastern University	Boston	NCAA I	354

SCHOOL	CITY	AFFILIATION	PAGE
Pine Manor College	Chestnut Hill	NCAA III	354
Regis College - Massachusetts	Weston	NCAA III	355
Salem State College	Salem	NCAA III	355
Simmons College	Boston	NCAA III	356
Smith College	Northampton	NCAA III	356
Springfield College	Springfield	NCAA III	357
Stonehill College	North Easton	NCAA II	358
Tufts University	Medford	NCAA III	358
Univ of Massachusetts- Amherst	Amherst	NCAA I	359
Univ of Massachusetts- Boston	Boston	NCAA III	359
Univ of Massachusetts- Dartmouth	North Dartmouth	NCAA III	360
Univ of Massachusetts- Lowell	Lowell	NCAA II	360
Wellesley College	Wellesley	NCAA III	361
Wentworth Institute of Technology	Boston	NCAA III	361
Western New England College	Springfield	NCAA III	362
Westfield State College	Westfield	NCAA III	362
Wheaton College	Norton	NCAA III	363
Williams College	Williamstown	NCAA III	363
Worcester Polytechnic Institute	Worcester	NCAA III	364
Worcester State College	Worcester	NCAA III	365

American International College
Academic Profile

1000 State St.
Springfield, MA 01109

Phone: (413) 747-6546

Type: Private, 4 Yr., Liberal Arts, Coed
Website: http://www.aic.edu
SAT/ACT/GPA: 900/20
Student/Faculty Ratio: 15:1
Undergraduate Enrollment: 1,100
Scholarships/Academic: Yes   **Athletic:** Yes
Expenses By: Year   **In State:** $ 20,206
Founded: 1885
Religion: Non-Affiliated
Housing: Yes
Male/Female: 55:45
Graduate Enrollment: 900
Financial Aid: Yes
Out of State: $ 20,206
Specializes In: Education, International Business, Liberal Arts, Physical Therapy
Degrees Conferred: BA, BS, BSN, BSE, MBA
Programs of Study: Biology, Business, Chemistry, Communications, Criminal Justice, Education, Human Services, International Business, Nursing, Occupational Therapy, Psychology, Physical Therapy

Women's Athletic Profile

100 State Street
Springfield, MA 01109
Coach: Amy Perkins
Email:

NCAA I
Yellow Jackets, Gold, White
Phone: (413) 747-6540
Fax: (413) 731-5710

Estimated # of Women's Volleyball Scholarships: N/A
Conference: Northeast-10 Conference

Amherst College
Academic Profile

Box 2230, P.O. 5000
Amherst, MA 01002-5000

Phone: 413-542-2328

Type: Private, 4 Yr., Liberal Arts, Coed
Website: http://www.amherst.edu
SAT/ACT/GPA: 1200+
Student/Faculty Ratio: 10:1
Undergraduate Enrollment: 1,600
Scholarships/Academic: No   **Athletic:** No
Expenses By: Year   **In State:** $ 30,000
Founded: 1835
Religion: Non-Affiliated
Housing: Yes
Male/Female: 55:45
Graduate Enrollment: N/A
Financial Aid: Yes
Out of State: $ 30,000
Degrees Conferred: BA
Programs of Study: American Studies, Anthropology & Sociology, Asian Languages & Civilization, Astronomy, Biology, Black Studies, Chemistry Classics, Economics, English, European Studies, Fine Arts, Geology, German, History, LJST, Mathematics & Computer Science, Music, Neuroscience, Philosophy, Physics, Political Science, Psychology, Religion, Romance

Women's Athletic Profile

Box 2230
Amherst, MA 01002
Coach: Suzanne Everden
Email: sjeverden@amherst.edu

NCAA I
Lady Jeffs, Purple, White, Black
Phone: (413) 542-7939
Fax: (413) 542-2527

Estimated # of Women's Volleyball Scholarships: N/A
Conference: Eastern College Athletic Conference

Anna Maria College
Academic Profile

Sunset Lane
Paxton, MA 01612

Phone: 800-344-4586

Type: Private, 4 Yr., Liberal Arts, Coed
Website: http://www.anna-maria.edu
SAT/ACT/GPA: 1000/2.8
Founded: 1946
Religion: Roman Catholic
Housing: Yes

Student/Faculty Ratio: 16:1
Undergraduate Enrollment: 500
Scholarships/Academic: Yes   **Athletic:** No
Expenses By: Year   **In State:** $ 18,250
Specializes In: Criminal Justice, Education, Music Therapy, Art Therapy
Degrees Conferred: AA, AS, BA, BFA, BM, BBA, MA, MS, MBA
Programs of Study: Art, Biology, Natural Sciences, Business Administration, Criminal Justice, Education, Music, Music Therapy, Art Therapy, Psychology, Social Work, Paralegal Studies, English, History, Political Science

Male/Female: 60:40
Graduate Enrollment: 1,100
Financial Aid: Yes
Out of State: $ 17,000

Women's Athletic Profile

Sunset Lane
Paxton, MA 01612
Coach: Nancy Pedersen-Gac
Email: gacna01@svh-worc.com

NCAA I
Lady Amcats, Royal Blue, White
Phone: (508) 849-3446
Fax: (508) 849-3449

Estimated # of Women's Volleyball Scholarships: N/A
Conference: Eastern College Athletic Conference
Roster In State: 11   **Out of State:** 1   **Out of Country:** 1
Sophomores on Team: 2   **Seniors on Team:** 2   **Graduation %:** Unknown
Most Recent Record: 8-18-0   **Fall Games:** 26   **Spring Games:** 0
Schedule: Atlantic Union, Roger Williams, Wentworth, Framingham State, Worcester State, LaSalle, Westfield State, Johnson & Wales, Plymouth State, Becker, Regis, Colby-Sawyer, Fitchburg State

Assumption College
Academic Profile

500 Salisbury Street
Worcester, MA 01615-0005

Phone: 800-882-7786

Type: Private, 4 Yr., Liberal Arts, Engineering, Coed
Website: http://www.assumption.edu
SAT/ACT/GPA: 1000/26/3.0
Student/Faculty Ratio: 18:1
Undergraduate Enrollment: 1,900
Scholarships/Academic: Yes   **Athletic:** No
Expenses By: Year   **In State:** $ 22,000
Specializes In: Liberal Arts, Communications
Degrees Conferred: BA, BS, MA, CAGS
Programs of Study: Accounting, Biology, Business, Management, Chemistry, Communications, Computer Science, Education English, Languages, Liberal Arts, Medical, Natural Science, Philosophy, Political Science, Rehabilitation Therapy, Religion, Romance Language

Founded: 1904
Religion: Catholic
Housing: Yes
Male/Female: 1:4
Graduate Enrollment: 450
Financial Aid: Yes
Out of State: $ 22,000

Women's Athletic Profile

500 Salisbury St.
Worcester, MA 01615
Coach: Christian Franklin
Email:

NCAA I
Lady Hounds, Royal Blue, White
Phone: (888)882-7786
Fax: (508) 798-2568

Estimated # of Women's Volleyball Scholarships: N/A
Conference: Northeast-10 Conference

Atlantic Union College
Academic Profile

Main Street
South Lancaster, MA 01561

Phone: 800-282-2030

Type: Private, 4 Yr., Coed
Website: http://www.atlanticuc.edu
SAT/ACT/GPA: Open
Student/Faculty Ratio: 10:1
Undergraduate Enrollment: 1,411
Scholarships/Academic: Yes   **Athletic:** Yes

Founded: 1882
Religion: Seventh-day Adventist
Housing: No
Male/Female: 57:43
Graduate Enrollment: N/A
Financial Aid: Yes

Expenses By: Year   **In State:** $ 14,600   **Out of State:** $ 14,600
Degrees Conferred: AS, BA, BS, BM
Programs of Study: Contact school for programs of study.

Women's Athletic Profile

Main Street   **NCAA I**
Lancaster, MA 01561   Lady Flames, Maroon, Gold
Coach: Rob Thomas   **Phone:** (508) 368-2142
Email: rthomas@atlanticuc.edu   **Fax:** (508) 368-2017

Estimated # of Women's Volleyball Scholarships: 3
Conference: May Flower
History: 1988 AUC added women's Volleyball
Achievements: 91, Coach of The Year for district 5 in NAIA. 92 Champion of District 5
Roster In State: 3   **Out of State:** 4   **Out of Country:** 2
Sophomores on Team: **Seniors on Team:** 1   **Graduation %:** 82
Most Recent Record: 9-10
Positions Needed: Setter, Middle Hitter, 2 Outside hitters.

Babson College
Academic Profile

Webster Center   **Phone:** 800-488-3696
Babson Park, MA 02157

Type: Private, 4 Yr., Liberal Arts, Coed   **Founded:** 1919
Website: http://www.babson.edu   **Religion:** Non-Affiliated
SAT/ACT/GPA: Open   **Housing:** Yes
Student/Faculty Ratio: 20:1   **Male/Female:** 60:40
Undergraduate Enrollment: 1,600   **Graduate Enrollment:** 300
Scholarships/Academic: Yes   **Athletic:** No   **Financial Aid:** 60%
Expenses By: Year   **In State:** $ 27,000   **Out of State:** $ 27,000
Specializes In: Business
Degrees Conferred: BS, MBA
Programs of Study: Contact school for program of study.

Women's Athletic Profile

Webster Center   **NCAA I**
Babson Park, MA 02157   Lady Beavers, Green, White
Coach: Bob Bennett   **Phone:** (781) 239-4250
Email: bbennett@babson.edu   **Fax:** (781) 239-5218

Estimated # of Women's Volleyball Scholarships: 0
Conference: New England Women's & Men's Athletic Conference
Program Profile: Play home contests in Webster Center (capacity 800). Team participates in NEWMAC conference tournament at the conclusion of the regular season.
Coaching: a 1992 graduate of the University of Scranton, Bob Bennett enters his first season as head coach of the women's volleyball team. Bennett, began his coaching career as a senior at Scranton, where he led the Royals to their first winning record in several years, most recently served as the assistant men's volleyball coach at MIT. Prior to that, he was an assistant coach for the women's team at the University of Vermont, where he earned his Master's degree in Chemistry in 1998. Still an active competitor, Bennett has played club volleyball since 1988, helping his team reach the NISRA Club Nationals on three different occasions. He currently plays for the Newton Mavericks club team.
In addition to coaching and playing volleyball, Bennett has spent the last three years working as a scientist in Medicinal Chemistry for Millennium Pharmaceuticals Inc. A native of Clarks Summit, Pennsylvania, he now resides, with his wife Tara, in Holliston, Massachusetts.
Freshman Receiving Financial Aid/Academic: **Athletic:** 0
Roster In State: 8   **Out of State:** 5   **Out of Country:** 1
Sophomores on Team: **Seniors on Team:** 2   **Graduation %:** 100
Most Recent Record: 10-20
Positions Needed: MN, OH, DS
Schedule: Wheaton, Springfield, Wellesley, Smith, Clark, MIT, Mt. Holyoke, WPI, Coast Guard

Becker College
Academic Profile

3 Paxton St.
Leicester, MA 01524

Phone: 877-523-2537

Type: Private, 4 Yr., Coed
Website: http://www.beckercollege.edu
SAT/ACT/GPA: Open/2.0
Student/Faculty Ratio: 15:1
Undergraduate Enrollment: 1,030
Scholarships/Academic: Yes
Expenses By: Year
Degrees Conferred: BS

Founded: 1887
Religion: Non-Affiliated
Housing: Yes
Male/Female: 1:4
Graduate Enrollment: N/A
Athletic: No **Financial Aid:** Yes
In State: $ 18,000 **Out of State:** $ 18,000

Programs of Study: Accounting, Business Administration, Veterinary Science, Early Childhood Education, Elementary Education, Human Resources, Kinesiology, Legal Studies, Marketing, Psychology, Paralegal

Women's Athletic Profile

3 Paxton Street
Leicester, MA 01524
Coach: Christian Franklin
Email:

NCAA I
Hawks, White, Scarlet, Royal
Phone: (508) 791-9241x464
Fax: (508) 892-8131

Estimated # of Women's Volleyball Scholarships: N/A
Conference: Independent
History: From 1979 to 1997, we played as a junior college. Our program has a .582 lifetime winning percentage.
Roster In State: 6 **Out of State:** 2 **Out of Country:** 0
Most Recent Record: 1-18-0 **Fall Games:** 19 **Spring Games:** 0
Positions Needed: Hitter, Setter
Schedule: Western New England, Westfield State, St. Anselm, Green Mountain, Framingham State, Lasell College

Bentley College
Academic Profile

175 Forest Street
Waltham, MA 02154-4705

Phone: (781) 891-2256

Type: Private, 4 Yr., Coed
Website: http://www.bentley.edu
SAT/ACT/GPA: 1100/3.0
Student/Faculty Ratio: 17:1
Undergraduate Enrollment: 3,293
Scholarships/Academic: Yes
Expenses By: Year
Specializes In: Business, Computer Technology
Degrees Conferred: BA, BS, MBA, MS

Founded: 1917
Religion: Non-Affiliated
Housing: Yes
Male/Female: 53:47
Graduate Enrollment: 1,589
Athletic: Yes **Financial Aid:** Yes
In State: $ 25,855 **Out of State:** $ 25,855

Programs of Study: Accounting, Accounting Information Systems, Business Communications, Business Economics, Computer Information Systems, Economics-Finance, English, Finance-Bank Management, Global Financial Analysis, History, International Business, International Culture and Economy, Liberal Arts, Management Information Systems, Managerial Economics, Marketing, Mathematical Sciences, Paralegal Studies, Philosophy, Self Design

Women's Athletic Profile

175 Forest Street
Waltham, MA 02452
Coach: Sandy Hoffman
Email: shoffman@bentley.edu

NCAA I
Lady Falcons, Blue, Gold
Phone: (781) 891-2780
Fax: (781) 891-2282

Estimated # of Women's Volleyball Scholarships: 2
Conference: Northeast-10 Conference
Program Profile: The program has consistently ranked among the top 4 Division II programs in the Northeast.
History: We began in 1981. Our overall record is 445-199 (.69%) . We have an average of over 24 match wins per season.

Achievements: NCAA Tournaments in 1993, 1995, & 1998; Northeast 10 Conference Champions 10 of 17 years; 14 All-Northeast Region players.

Coaching: Sandy Hoffman, Head Coach, started in 1982. Her record is 443-185 (.705). She was five times Conference Coach of the Year.

Freshman Receiving Financial Aid/Academic: **Athletic:** 4

Roster In State: 5   **Out of State:** 11   **Out of Country:** 0

Sophomores on Team: 0   **Seniors on Team:** 2   **Graduation %:** 100

Most Recent Record: 27-8-0   **Fall Games:** 35   **Spring Games:** 4

Camp of Clinic Dates: July 18-24, 1999; July 25-29, 1999

Positions Needed: Setter

Schedule: Florida Southern, New Haven, Alaska-Anchorage, Alaska-Fairbanks, Pace University

Style of Play: Play a 5-1 offense, fast paced-multiple attack options.

Boston College
Academic Profile

140 Commonwealth Avenue   **Phone:** 800-360-2522
Chestnut Hill, MA 02167

Type: Private, 4 Yr., Liberal Arts, Coed   **Founded:** 1863
Website: http://www.bc.edu   **Religion:** Catholic
SAT/ACT/GPA: 1200/28/3.5   **Housing:** Yes
Student/Faculty Ratio: 15:1   **Male/Female:** 48:52
Undergraduate Enrollment: 8,958   **Graduate Enrollment:** 5,500
Scholarships/Academic: Yes   **Athletic:** Yes   **Financial Aid:** Yes
Expenses By: Year   **In State:** $ 31, 010   **Out of State:** $ 31,010
Degrees Conferred: BA, BS, MA, MS, Ph.D.
Programs of Study: Arts & Sciences, Management, Nursing, Engineering

Women's Athletic Profile

140 Commonwealth Drive   **NCAA I**
Chestnut, MA 02467-3934   Lady Eagles, Maroon, Gold
Coach: Jackie Hadel   **Phone:** (617) 552-4639
Email: hadel@bc.edu   **Fax:** (617) 552-4903

Estimated # of Women's Volleyball Scholarships: N/A

Conference: Big East Conference

Program Profile: Our volleyball season goes through May 2, 1999. We host two tournaments in the Spring.

Achievements: Won 1999 Volleyball Spring Tournament; won against Manhattan in a four-game match; El Hag won Big East Volleyball honors.

Coaching: Jackie Hadel - Head Coach. Sean McMorrow started in 1999 as Assistant Coach. Coach McMorrow has been coaching for 15 years.

Most Recent Record: 11-19-0

Schedule: Boston College, Hartford, Indiana University, Harvard, St.John's, Georgetown, Rutgers, Seton Hall, Notre Dame, Syracuse, Providence, Sacred Heart, West Virginia, Pittsburgh

Style of Play: Style depends on the type of players on our team that year.

Brandeis University
Academic Profile

415 South Street   **Phone:** 800-622-0622
Waltham, MA 02254-9110

Type: Private, 4 Yr., Liberal Arts, Coed   **Founded:** 1948
Website: http://www.logos.cc.brandies.edu   **Religion:** Non-Sectarian
SAT/ACT/GPA: 1100+   **Housing:** Yes
Student/Faculty Ratio: 9:1   **Male/Female:** 50:50
Undergraduate Enrollment: 3,700   **Graduate Enrollment:** 973
Scholarships/Academic: Yes   **Athletic:** No   **Financial Aid:** Yes
Expenses By: Year   **In State:** $ 33,000   **Out of State:** $ 33,000
Specializes In: Liberal Arts
Degrees Conferred: BA, MA, MFA, Ph.D.

Programs of Study: Anthropology, Art, Aviation Science, Biology, Business, Chemistry, Professional Chemistry, Communications Arts & Science, Computer Science, Early Childhood Education, Earth Science, Education, Economics, English, French, Geography, History, Management, Science, Mathematics, Music, Philosophy, Physical Education, Physics, Political Science, Psychology, Secondary Science, Social Work, Spanish, Special Education

Women's Athletic Profile

415 South Street
Waltham, MA 02454
Coach: Sheryl Sousa
Email: sousa@brandeis.edu

NCAA I
Lady Judges, Blue, White
Phone: (781) 736-3663
Fax: (781) 736-3656

Estimated # of Women's Volleyball Scholarships: N/A
Conference: University Athletic Association

Bridgewater State College
Academic Profile

Room 021
Bridgewater, MA 02325

Phone: 508-697-1237

Type: Public, 4 Yr., Liberal Arts, Coed
Website: http://www.bridgew.edu
SAT/ACT/GPA: 850
Student/Faculty Ratio: 17:1
Undergraduate Enrollment: 5,700
Scholarships/Academic: Yes
Expenses By: Year
Degrees Conferred: BA, BB, BSE, MA, MS, M.Ed. (31 degrees)

Founded: 1840
Religion: Non-Affiliated
Housing: yes
Male/Female: 33:67
Graduate Enrollment: 750

Athletic: No
In State: $ 7,983

Financial Aid: Yes
Out of State: $ 12,077

Programs of Study: Anthropology, Art, Aviation Science, Biology, Business, Chemistry, Professional Chemistry, Communications Art & Science, Early Childhood Education, Earth Science, Economics, Elementary Education, English, French, Geography, History, Management, Science, Mathematics, Music, Philosophy, Physical Education, Physics, Political Science, Psychology, Secondary Education

Women's Athletic Profile

Room 012
Bridgewater, MA 02325
Coach: Kenneth Duarte
Email:

NCAA I
Lady Bears, Red, White
Phone: (508) 697-1352
Fax: (508) 697-1356

Estimated # of Women's Volleyball Scholarships: N/A
Conference: Massachusetts State College Athletic Conference
Program Profile: We play 22 matches during the season.
History: Our program began approximately1976. We won Conference 8 times.
Achievements: 1997 Coach of the Year; Undefeated Conference Champions, 1995-1998.
Coaching: Kenneth Duarte, Head Coach, began with BSC in 1994. He has led the team to 4 titles. He has over 20 years playing experience, including 5 National Championships. Cathie Karl and Dodi Herk are Assistant Coaches.
Freshman Receiving Financial Aid/Academic: | | **Athletic:** 0
Roster In State: 13 | **Out of State:** 1 | **Out of Country:** 0
Sophomores on Team: 0 | **Seniors on Team:** 1 | **Graduation %:** 100
Most Recent Record: 16-22-0 | **Fall Games:** 20 | **Spring Games:** 5
Camp of Clinic Dates: August
Positions Needed: Outside & Rightside Hitters
Schedule: Wellesley College, Eastern Connecticut, Susquehanna, Scranton, Tufts, Wheaton
Style of Play: Aggressive and fun.

Clark University
Academic Profile

950 Main Street
Worcester, MA 01610

Phone: 1-800-GO-CLARK

Type: Private, 4 Yr., Liberal Arts,Coed
Website: http://www.clarku.edu

Founded: 1887
Religion: Non-Affiliated

SAT/ACT/GPA: 1150avg/25/3.2
Student/Faculty Ratio: 12/1
Undergraduate Enrollment: 1925
Scholarships/Academic: Yes   **Athletic:** No
Expenses By: Year   **In State:** $28,500
Specializes In: Geography, Psychology, Government, International Development
Degrees Conferred: BA, MA, Ph.D.

Housing: Yes
Male/Female: 41:59
Graduate Enrollment: 600
Financial Aid: Yes
Out of State: $28,500

Programs of Study: Ancient Civilization, BioChemistry, Biology, Chemistry, Communication & Culture, Comparative Literature, Computer Science, Economics, Education, Engineering, English, Environmental Science & Policy, Foreign Languages, Geography, Government, History, International Development, Management, Mathematics & Computer Science, Philosophy, Physics, Psychology, Sociology, Visual & Performing Arts

Women's Athletic Profile

950 Main Street
Worcester, MA 01610
Coach: Jennifer Herbert
Email: rball@clarku.edu

NCAA I
Lady Cougars, Scarlet, White
Phone: (508) 793-7161
Fax: (508) 793-8819

Estimated # of Women's Volleyball Scholarships: N/A
Conference: New England Women's & Men's Athletic Conference

Roster In State: 3	**Out of State:** 4	**Out of Country:** 1
Sophomores on Team: 3	**Seniors on Team:** 0	**Graduation %:** Unknown
Most Recent Record: 12-20-0	**Fall Games:** 32	**Spring Games:** 0

College of the Holy Cross
Academic Profile

One College St.
Worcester, MA 01610-2395

Phone: (508) 793-2000

Type: Private, 4 Yr., Liberal Arts, Coed
Website: http://www.holycross.edu
SAT/ACT/GPA: 1250/3.5
Student/Faculty Ratio: 13:1
Undergraduate Enrollment: 2,700
Scholarships/Academic: No   **Athletic:** No
Expenses By: Year   **In State:** $ 31,930
Specializes In: Liberal Arts
Degrees Conferred: BA, BS

Founded: 1843
Religion: Catholic-Jesuit
Housing: Yes
Male/Female: 50:50
Graduate Enrollment: N/A
Financial Aid: Yes
Out of State: $ 31,930

Programs of Study: Accounting, Biology, Chemistry, Classics, Computer, Economics, English, Education, Gerontology, History, International, Math, Peace Studies, PreProfessional Programs, Religious, Sociology, Theatre

Women's Athletic Profile

College Street
Worcester, MA 01610-2395
Coach: Peter Viteritti
Email: pviteritti@holycross.edu

NCAA I
Lady Crusaders, Purple, White
Phone: (508) 793-2000
Fax: (508) 793-2309

Estimated # of Women's Volleyball Scholarships: 4
Conference: The Patriot League
Program Profile: Our facility is Hart Center and seats 3,700. We are looking to strengthen our schedule as we start to bring in Division I volleyball players.
Achievements: Sophomore, Kathryn Lynch, was recently named Patriot Defensive player of the Year. Holy Cross led the PL with most digs (16.93 a game).
Coaching: Peter Viteritti, Head Coach, has an overall record is 6-49 .He walked into a program that finished last in Conference for 9 years in a row. He finished 5th last year. The year 1999 will be our first recruiting year.
Freshman Receiving Financial Aid/Academic: **Athletic:** 4

Roster In State: 0	**Out of State:** 12	**Out of Country:** 0
Sophomores on Team: 3	**Seniors on Team:** 1	**Graduation %:** 95
Most Recent Record: 4-27-0	**Fall Games:** 28	**Spring Games:** 4 tournaments

Positions Needed: Outside Hitter, Right Setter, Middle
Schedule: University of New Hampshire, Rutgers, Oregon, Harvard, Providence, Siena
Style of Play: Aggressive style of defense. Focus on movement, ball control, and good hitting. Rally positioning.

Eastern Nazarene College
Academic Profile

23 East Elm Avenue
Quincy, MA 02170

Phone: 1-617-745-3639

Type: Private, 4 Yr., Liberal Arts, Coed
Website: http://www.enc.edu
SAT/ACT/GPA: 960
Student/Faculty Ratio: 12:1
Undergraduate Enrollment: 646
Scholarships/Academic: Yes   **Athletic:** No
Expenses By: Year   **In State:** $18,612
Degrees Conferred: BA, BS, MA, MS
Programs of Study: For more information go to www.enc.edu

Founded: 1900
Religion: Church of the Nazarene
Housing: Yes
Male/Female: 45:55
Graduate Enrollment: 119
Financial Aid: Yes
Out of State: $18,612

Women's Athletic Profile

23 E. Elm Avenue
Quincy, MA 02170
Coach: Heather Patch
Email: calhounj@enc.edu

NCAA I
Lady Crusaders, Red, White
Phone: (617) 745-3597
Fax: (617) 745-3938

Estimated # of Women's Volleyball Scholarships: 0
Conference: Commonwealth Coast
Program Profile: We play at Lahue Center which seats 1,600. We have a Fall season.
History: Nancy Detwiler was Head Coach from 1970 to 91. She had 506 wins and 180 losses. Janet Calhoun was Head Coach from 1992 to 1999. She had 134 wins and 90 losses. Heather Patch started Head Coach in the Fall of 1999.
Achievements: Dr. Nancy Detwiller was 3 times 3 NAIA District Coach of the Year; 6 NAIA National Tournaments; Dr. Nancy was inducted into the NAIA Hall of Fame on December 4, 1997; Janet Calhoun was 2 Commonwealth Coast Conference Coach of the Year; 2 CCC Titles
Coaching: Heather Patch, Head Coach, will start as head coach in the Fall of 1999.
Roster In State: 3   **Out of State:** 9   **Out of Country:** 0
Sophomores on Team: 0   **Seniors on Team:** 4   **Graduation %:** 98
Most Recent Record: 13-17-0   **Fall Games:** 22   **Spring Games:** 0
Positions Needed: Outside Hitter, Middle Hitter
Schedule: Wellesley College, Tufts University, Bates College

Emerson College
Academic Profile

100 Bacon St.
Boston, MA 02116

Phone: 617-824-8600

Type: Private, 4 Yr., Liberal Arts, Coed
Website: http://www.emerson.edu
SAT/ACT/GPA: 1040-1240
Student/Faculty Ratio: 17:1
Undergraduate Enrollment: 2,600
Scholarships/Academic: Yes   **Athletic:** No
Expenses By: Year   **In State:** $ 27,620
Specializes In: Communications, Performing Arts
Degrees Conferred: BA, BS, BFA, BLI, BM, BSSP, MA, MS, MFA, Ph.D.
Programs of Study: Advertising, Broadcasting, Communication Disorders, Communications, Creative Writing, Dance, Film Arts, Literature, PreLaw, Public Relations, Publishing, Radio & Television, Speech, Speech Pathology, Theatre

Founded: 1880
Religion: Independent
Housing: Yes
Male/Female: 45:55
Graduate Enrollment: 1,000
Financial Aid: Yes
Out of State:

Women's Athletic Profile

100 Beacon Street
Boston, MA 02116
Coach: Vicki Lawrence
Email:

NCAA I
Lady Lions, Purple, Gold
Phone: (617) 824-8930
Fax: (617) 824-8529

Estimated # of Women's Volleyball Scholarships: N/A

Conference: The Great Northeast Athletic Conference

History: The Lions finished 1998 with a record of 8-8 in Lawrence's first ear at the helm. Emerson looks forward to improving on that mark next season and making some noise in the Great Northeast Athletic Conference Tournament.

Achievements: Holly Anderson was named GNAC-first team All-Conference.

Coaching: Vicki Lawrence, Head Coach, made an immediate impact on the women's volleyball program since her arrival on the Emerson campus. After inheriting a struggling three year program that had a record of 5-14 in 1997, Lawrence raised expectations and performance with her aggressive coaching style. She was a former player, having played at the University of Massachusetts-Lowell. Prior to that, Lawrence developed her skills as a captain of the Medway High School team.

Schedule: Albertus Magnus, St. Joseph-CT, Framingham State, Daniel Webster, Endicott, Lasell, Emmanuel

Emmanuel College
Academic Profile

400 The Fenway
Boston, MA 02115

Phone: (617) 735-9715

Type: Private, 4 Yr., Liberal Arts, Women Only
Website: http://www.emmanuel.edu
SAT/ACT/GPA: 1000/3.0-avg
Student/Faculty Ratio: 13:1
Undergraduate Enrollment: 1,500
Scholarships/Academic: Yes   **Athletic:** No
Expenses By: Year   **In State:** $ 22,968

Founded: 1919
Religion: Catholic
Housing: Yes
Male/Female: Women Only
Graduate Enrollment: 173
Financial Aid: Yes
Out of State: $ 22,968

Specializes In: Biology, Education, Psychology, Management

Degrees Conferred: BA, BS, BFA, MA, MS, M.Ed.

Programs of Study: Art, Biology, Chemistry, Economics & Management, Mathematics, Physics, English, Foreign Languages, History, Mathematics, Physics, Political Science, Psychology, Sociology, Arts, English, Literature, Music, Speech, Communications, Theatre Arts, Art Therapy, Organization, Psychology, Philosophy

Women's Athletic Profile

400 The Fenway
Boston, MA 02115
Coach: Joseph Seid
Email:

NCAA I
Lady Saints, Royal, Gold
Phone: (617) 735-9985
Fax: (617) 735-9885

Estimated # of Women's Volleyball Scholarships: N/A

Conference: The Great Northeast Athletic Conference

Endicott College
Academic Profile

376 Hale Street
Beverly, MA 01915

Phone: (978) 232-2305

Type: Private, 4 Yr., Coed
Website: http://www.endicott.edu
SAT/ACT/GPA: Required for Admission
Student/Faculty Ratio: 13:1
Undergraduate Enrollment: 1,200
Scholarships/Academic: Yes   **Athletic:** No
Expenses By: Year   **In State:** $ 21,966

Founded: 1939
Religion: Non-Affiliated
Housing: Yes
Male/Female: 30:70
Graduate Enrollment: 100
Financial Aid: Yes
Out of State: $ 21,966

Specializes In: Liberal & Preprofessional Programs, Required Internship

Degrees Conferred: BA, BS, M.Ed.

Programs of Study: Advertising, American Studies, Athletic Training, Business Administration, Communications, Creative Arts Therapy, Criminal Justice, Early Childhood Education, Elementary Education, Entrepreneurial Studies, Fine Arts, Visual Communications, Hotel/Restaurant/Travel/Administration, Interior Design, International Business, Liberal Studies, Management, Marketing, Nursing, Physical Education, Psychology, Sport Management, Physical Therapy Assistant

Men's Athletic Profile

376 Hale Street
Beverly, MA 01915
Coach: Andrew R. Viselli
Email:

NCAA III
Power Gulls/Royal, Kelly, White
Phone: (978) 927-0585
Fax: (978) 232-2600

Estimated # of Men's Volleyball Scholarships: N/A
Conference: Independent

Roster In State: 6	**Out of State:** 5	**Out of Country:** 0
Sophomores on Team: 4	**Seniors on Team:** 0	**Graduation %:** 100%
Most Recent Record: 5-8	**Spring Games:** 13	

Schedule: Rivier, Johnson & Wales, Medaille, Daniel Webster, Roger Williams, D'Youville, Rampo College, Wentworth

Women's Athletic Profile

376 Hale Street
Beverly, MA 01915
Coach: Tim Byram
Email: tbyram@endicott.edu

NCAA I
Power Gulls, Royal, Green
Phone: (978) 232-2443
Fax: (978) 232-2600

Estimated # of Women's Volleyball Scholarships: N/A
Conference: The Great Northeast Athletic Conference
History: The 1998 Power Gulls finished with the best record in the school's history: 18-11.
Achievements: Appearance in the 1998 MAIAW Tournament
Coaching: Tim Byram Head Coach.

Most Recent Record: 18-11-0	**Fall Games:** 29	**Spring Games:** 0

Schedule: Gordon, Plymouth State, Daniel Webster, Regis, Simmons, Salem State, Suffolk, Pine Manor, Emerson, Rhode Island, Emmanuel

Fitchburg State College
Academic Profile

160 Pearl St.
Fitchburg, MA 01420

Phone: 800-705-9692

Type: Public, 4 Yr., Liberal Arts, Coed
Website: http://www.fsc.edu
SAT/ACT/GPA: 1090/2.0
Student/Faculty Ratio: 13:1
Undergraduate Enrollment: 2,700
Scholarships/Academic: Yes
Expenses By: Year

Founded: 1894
Religion: Non-Affiliated
Housing: Yes
Male/Female: 45:55
Graduate Enrollment: 3,000

Athletic: No
In State: $ 8,400

Financial Aid: Yes
Out of State: $ 14,450

Specializes In: Communications, Nursing, Education, Business
Degrees Conferred: BA, BS, BSEd, MA, MS, M.Ed.
Programs of Study: Biology, Business Administration, Clinical Laboratory Science, Communications, Computer Information Systems, Computer Science, Criminal Justice, Economics, Education, Secondary Education, English, Environmental Science, Fitness Management, General Studies, Geography, History, Human Services, Industrial Technology, Mathematics, Nursing, Political Science, Psychology, Sociology, Theatre, Undeclared

Women's Athletic Profile

160 Pearl Street
Fitchburg, MA 01420
Coach: Lisa Paciorek
Email: FSCVB@AOL.COM

NCAA I
Falcons, Green, White, Gold
Phone: (978) 345-2151
Fax: (978) 665-4540

Estimated # of Women's Volleyball Scholarships: N/A
Conference: Massachusetts State College Athletic Conference
Program Profile: The FSC Volleyball program is a smaller program, but it is rapidly growing and fully supported by the administration. A new sports complex is being built and it will be completed in the year 2000. It will house three volleyball courts, as well as many other courts. Fitchburg looks to host the MASCAC Volleyball Championships for the first time when the sports complex is finished. The team is starting Spring practices this year and looks to add dedicated and enthusiastic players. We want to be regionally ranked as soon as possible.
History: The FSC Volleyball program started in 1978 within the NCAA, but was actually running years before the NCAA took over the women's intercollegiate sports arena. Since 1978, we have amassed an overall winning percentage of 0.385 (217-362). We have won MASCAC Championships a couple of years and have had several players make the All-MASCAC Conference Team. In fact, we even got Player of the Year for our Conference in 1997.

Achievements: Two All-MASCAC Teams Players yearly; MASCAC Champions; One MASCAC Player of the Week; Conference Player of the Year.

Coaching: Lisa Paciorek, Head Coach, started at FSC in the fall of 1997, and has an overall percentage at FSC of 0.318. She has coached all levels from high school to college level. She has an extensive knowledge about conditioning, sports psychology, team dynamics, offensive and defensive systems and tactics, proper form for the greatest efficiency in movement on the court, and even knows joint angles to use for the best vertical leap possible. She has her bachelor's of Science Degree in Exercise Science. She has worked with some of the nation's top players and coaches (Pat Powers, Deb Richardson, Brian Rofer and more). She has learned the art of coaching from coaches, such as Doug Beal, Bob Bertucci and Brian Gimmillaro. There is no assistant coach listed.

Freshman Receiving Financial Aid/Academic: **Athletic:** 100%

Roster In State: 8   **Out of State:** 1   **Out of Country:** 1
Sophomores on Team: 0   **Seniors on Team:** 2   **Graduation %:** Unknown
Most Recent Record: 6-18-0   **Fall Games:** 20-30   **Spring Games:** 0
Camp of Clinic Dates: One week before classes starts
Positions Needed: Setter, 2 Middle Hitters, 2 Outside Hitters
Schedule: Worcester Polytechnic Institute, Brandeis, Mt. Holyoke, Simmons, Endicott, Keene State, Westfield State, Salem State, Bridgewater State
Style of Play: We are a young team with lots of heart and spunk. Excellent defense and passing have kept us competitive, even though we did not have any real hitters on the team. We play a tough schedule and will keep it that way because we are learning rapidly from it. We look to have some serious height coming next year and look forward to having our first real Spring season next Spring. At FSC, academics are the first priority, so I personally monitor the class' progress for all my players.

Framingham State College
Academic Profile

100 State Street
Framingham, MA 01701-9101

Phone: 508-626-4500

Type: Public, 4 Yr., Liberal Arts, Coed   **Founded:** 1839
Website: http://www.framingham.edu   **Religion:** Non-Affiliated
SAT/ACT/GPA: 900   **Housing:** No
Student/Faculty Ratio: 17:1   **Male/Female:** 1:3
Undergraduate Enrollment: 3,000   **Graduate Enrollment:** 600
Scholarships/Academic: Yes   **Athletic:** No   **Financial Aid:** Yes
Expenses By: Year   **In State:** $ 5,364   **Out of State:** $ 9,412
Specializes In: Education
Degrees Conferred: BA, BS, MA, MS
Programs of Study: Accounting, Art, Biology, Business Administration, Chemistry, Communications, Computer Science, Construction Technology, Economics, Education, English, Environmental Science, Film Studies, Geography, Graphic Art, History, Human Services, Industrial Engineering, Literature, Management, Manufacturing Technology, Marketing, Mathematics, Medical Technology, Nursing, Photography, PreLaw, PreMed, Psychology, Sociology, Radio & Television, Special Education

Women's Athletic Profile

100 State Street
Framingham, MA 01701
Coach: Jan Stannard
Email:

NCAA I
Lady Rams, Black, Gold
Phone: (508) 626-4614
Fax: (508) 626-4069

Estimated # of Women's Volleyball Scholarships: N/A
Conference: Massachusetts State College Athletic Conference
Program Profile: We play in Dwight Gym which has 1,500 seats. We are building a new 3,500 seats facility that will be completed in the fall of 2000. We play a fall season.
History: Our program started in 1975. Carol Fishman was our first coach. Our best record is 25-6 in 1991.
Achievements: 1991 and 1992 MASCAC regular season champions; 1992 MASCAC post-season champions
Coaching: Jan Stannard has been Head Coach since 1996. Her record is 23-34. Robert Stannard started as Assistant Coach in 1996.
Roster In State: 6   **Out of State:** 1   **Out of Country:** 1
Sophomores on Team: 3   **Seniors on Team:** 0   **Graduation %:** 100
Most Recent Record: 12-12-0   **Fall Games:** 24   **Spring Games:** 0
Positions Needed: Hitters, Setters
Schedule: Bridgewater St., Westfield St., Brandeis, University of Massachusetts-Dartmouth

Gordon College
Academic Profile

255 Grapevine Road
Wenham, MA 01984
Type: Private, 4 Yr., Liberal Arts, Coed
Website: http://www.gordonc.edu
SAT/ACT/GPA: 1300
Student/Faculty Ratio: 14:1
Undergraduate Enrollment: 1,500
Scholarships/Academic: Yes
Expenses By: Year
Degrees Conferred: BA, BM, MEd

Phone: 800-343-1379

Founded: 1889
Religion: Non-Denominational
Housing: Yes
Male/Female: 40:60
Graduate Enrollment: N/A
Athletic: No   **Financial Aid:** No
In State: $ 21,000   **Out of State:** $ 21,000

Programs of Study: Accounting, Allied Health, Biology, Business Administration, Chemistry, Communication Arts, Computer Science, Early Childhood Education, Economics, Elementary Education, English, French, International Affairs, Mathematics, Philosophy, Physics, Political Science, Psychology, Sociology, Social Work

Women's Athletic Profile

255 Grapevine Rd.
Wenham, MA 01984
Coach: Valerie Gin
Email: gin@faith.gordonc.edu

NCAA I
Fighting Scots, Blue, White
Phone: (978) 927-2306x4337
Fax: (978) 524-3000

Estimated # of Women's Volleyball Scholarships: N/A
Conference: Commonwealth Coast Conference

Harvard University
Academic Profile

8 Garden Street
Cambridge, MA 02138

Phone: 617-495-1551

Type: Private, 4 Yr., Liberal Arts, Coed
Website: http://www.harvard.edu
SAT/ACT/GPA: Competitive
Student/Faculty Ratio: 11:1
Undergraduate Enrollment: 6,400
Scholarships/Academic: Yes
Expenses By: Year
Specializes In: Liberal Arts, PreMed
Degrees Conferred: All

Founded: 1636
Religion: Non-Affiliated
Housing: Yes
Male/Female: 48:52
Graduate Enrollment: N/A
Athletic: No   **Financial Aid:** Yes
In State: $ 33,000   **Out of State:** $ 33,000

Programs of Study: Biology, Economics, Government, BioChemistry, Computer Science, English, Psychology, Sociology, Anthropology, Philosophy, Social Studies, Chemistry, African American Studies, History and Literature, History of Science

Men's Athletic Profile

65 North Harvard Street/Murr ctr.
Cambridge, MA 02138-3800
Coach: Ihsan Gurdal
Email:

NCAA I
Crimson/Crimson
Phone: (617) 495-4848
Fax: (617) 496-9950

Estimated # of Men's Volleyball Scholarships: N/A
Conference: Independent

Women's Athletic Profile

60 John F. Kennedy Street
Cambridge, MA 02138-3800
Coach: Jennifer Weiss
Email: jbates@fas.harvard.edu

NCAA I
Lady Crimson, Crimson
Phone: (617) 496-7390
Fax: (617) 495-2130

Estimated # of Women's Volleyball Scholarships: N/A
Conference: Ivy Group

Coaching: Jennifer Weiss graduated from Bentley in 1988. She is entering her sixth year as a Head Coach. She served as Harvard's Assistant Coach for one year prior to her appointment as a head coach in 1993. She has a Bachelor's degree in Finance. She had a successful career as a four-year starter for the Lady Falcons. As a freshman she was named Rookie of the Year in the Northeast 10 Conference and was an All-Conference player. In two of her four seasons, she helped lead the Falcons to the Northeast 10 Title. She earned her Master's of Education from Springfield College in 1992. Chris Ridolfi, Assistant Coach, joined the staff this season after a two-year stint as an assistant coach at Boston College. He is also the club director and head coach for boy's volleyball team at Milford high School since 1991.

Lasell College
Academic Profile

1844 Commonwealth Avenue
Newton, MA 02466

Phone: 888-527-3554

Type: Private, 4 Yr., Coed
Website: http://www.lasell.edu
SAT/ACT/GPA: 900-1000/2.5-3.0
Student/Faculty Ratio: 17:1
Undergraduate Enrollment: 635
Scholarships/Academic: Yes   **Athletic:** No
Expenses By: Year   **In State:** $ 22,100
Degrees Conferred: AA, AS, BA, BS

Founded: 1851
Religion: Non-Affiliated
Housing: Yes
Male/Female: 20:80
Graduate Enrollment: N/A
Financial Aid: Yes
Out of State: $ 22,100

Programs of Study: Accounting, Athletic Training, Business Administration, Business Management, Criminal Justice, Daycare Administration, Elementary Education, Exercise, Physiology, Fashion Design, Finance, General Studies, Health Care Administration, Hotel & Travel Administration, Human Services, Legal Studies, Liberal Arts, Marketing, Non-Profit Management, Paralegal Studies, Physical Therapy Assistant, Psychology, Sociology, Special Education

Men's Athletic Profile

1844 Commonwealth
Newton, MA 02466
Coach: Rich Hereau
Email: kwateen@lasell.edu

NCAA III
Lasses/Sky Blue, Navy, White
Phone: (617) 243-2147
Fax: (617) 796-4019

Estimated # of Men's Volleyball Scholarships: NCAA III
Conference: Northeastern College Volleyball Association
Program Profile: Has a regulation field, 2 courts, weight room, overhead track with a seating capacity of 200. Playing season starts late January through April.
History: First year of the program in the year 2000.
Coaching: Rich Hereau is Head Coach.
Spring Games: 12-14
Positions Needed: All
Schedule: D'Youville, Western New England, Endicott, Johnson-Wales, Rivier, Wentworth

Women's Athletic Profile

1844 Commonwealth Avenue
Newton, MA 02466
Coach: Mary Tom
Email: k.walter@lasell.edu

NCAA I
Lady Lasers, Blue, White
Phone: (617) 243-2147
Fax: (617) 796-4019

Estimated # of Women's Volleyball Scholarships: N/A
Conference: North Atlantic Conference
Program Profile: We are a young program that is still in its building phase. We play in a regulation gym that has 2 courts, a weight room, an overhead track and a seating capacity of 200. We play a traditional season. We have a fall and a non-traditional spring season.
History: Our program began in the late 1980's. We became a member of the NCAA in September 1998. We are increasing our squad size and the number of contests consistently.
Coaching: Mary Tom became Head Coach in 1997. Her records are: 17-18 in 1997 and 5-12 in 1998. Kamn Shue is Assistant Coach.

Roster In State: 13   **Out of State:** 4   **Out of Country:** 0
Sophomores on Team: 1   **Seniors on Team:** 2   **Graduation %:** 95

Most Recent Record: 12-6-0   **Fall Games:** 25   **Spring Games:** 3
Positions Needed: Setter, Outside Hitter, Outside Setter
Schedule: Connecticut College, Clark University, Regis, Wentworth, Suffolk

Massachusetts Institute of Technology (MIT)
Academic Profile

MIT Branch P. O. Box D
Cambridge, MA 02139

Phone: 617-253-4791

Type: Private, 4 Yr., Liberal Arts, Engineering, Coed
Website: http://www.web.mit.edu
SAT/ACT/GPA:
Student/Faculty Ratio: 4:1
Undergraduate Enrollment: 5,500
Scholarships/Academic: No   **Athletic:** No
Expenses By: Year   **In State:** $ 36,600

Founded: 1861
Religion: Non-Affiliated
Housing: Yes
Male/Female: 56:44
Graduate Enrollment: 4,000
Financial Aid: Yes
Out of State: $ 36,600

Specializes In: Engineering, Science, Humanities, Social Sciences, Architecture
Degrees Conferred: BA, BS, MBA, MS, PhD
Programs of Study: Aero/Astro Engineering, Chemical Engineering, Civil Engineering, Environmental Engineering, Electrical Engineering, Mechanical Engineering, Nuclear Engineering, Computer Science, Biology, Chemistry, Mathematics, Physics, Anthropology, Asian Studies, Economics, Film, Foreign Languages, History, Literature, Music, Philosophy Political, Latin American Studies, Woman's Studies, Writing, Architectural Design, Building Technology, Visual Arts, Management, Information Technology, Operations Research, Finance and Marketing Research

Women's Athletic Profile

Office of Admissions-Room 3-108
Cambridge, MA 02139
Coach: Paul Dill
Email: pdill@mit.edu

NCAA I
Lady Engineers, Maroon, Grey
Phone: (617) 253-4791
Fax: (617) 258-7343

Estimated # of Women's Volleyball Scholarships: 0
Conference: New England Women's & Men's Athletic Conference. ECAC
Program Profile: Our playing season runs from late August to mid November. We strive to provide an environment where the students can grow both as players and as people. The team acts as a support group for each member as they move through their academic career. We promote leadership, teamwork and high self esteem as part of the program's mission. We teach life skills that will compliment classroom experience to help prepare students for life after MIT.
History: Our first season was 1975. As the program enters its 25th season, MIT has enjoyed 20 winning seasons, an overall record of 522 wins 210 losses and an overall winning percentage of .71. Our conference consists of Boston College, Clark University, U. S. Coast Guard Academy, Mount Holyoke College, Smith College, Springfield College, Wellesley College and Wheaton College.
Achievements: MIT has taken 13 tries to the NCAA tournament and has finished as high as second in the country. The program has also won several conference titles and has produced several All-Americans
Coaching: Paul Dill, Head Coach, was MIT assistant coach of the men's and women's teams for three years. He has been head coach since 1996. His record is 66-33-2. He had 2 NCAA tournament bids in 1997 and 1998. He coached the University of Connecticut men's team for one year. He played for Bates College where he was captain. He currently coaches England Jr. National Women's Team in the off-season. Sutoshi Asari and Bob Moser are assistant coaches.
Roster In State: 3   **Out of State:** 9   **Out of Country:** 1
Sophomores on Team: 0   **Seniors on Team:** 5   **Graduation %:** 100
Most Recent Record: 26-10-0   **Fall Games:** 36   **Spring Games:** 3
Positions Needed: Middle, Outside Hitters
Schedule: Wellesley College, Williams College, Eastern CT State University, Amherst College, Springfiled College, University of Rochester
Style of Play: The team plays with a very scrappy determination. Although many times we are outsized or out powered by a team's personnel, we more often than not find a way to win through defense and relentless pursuit of winning.

Massachusetts Maritime Academy
Academic Profile

101 Academy Drive
Buzzards Bay, MA 02532

Phone: 800-544-3411

Type: Public, 4 Yr., Engineering, Coed

Founded: 1891

Website: Not Available
SAT/ACT/GPA: Open
Student/Faculty Ratio: 14:1
Undergraduate Enrollment: 750
Scholarships/Academic: Yes   **Athletic:** No
Expenses By: Year   **In State:** $ 7,253
Specializes In: Marine Engineering, Environmental Protection, Marine transportation
Degrees Conferred: BS
Programs of Study: Environment Protection, Facilities Engineering, Marine Engineering, Marine Safety, Marine Trans

Religion: Non-Affiliated
Housing: Yes
Male/Female: 7:1
Graduate Enrollment: N/A
Financial Aid: Yes
Out of State: $ 12,763

Women's Athletic Profile

101 Academy Drive
Buzzards Bay, MA 02532
Coach: Dianne Bunker
Email:

NCAA I
Lady Buccaneers, Blue, Gold
Phone: (508) 830-5053
Fax: (508) 830-5056

Estimated # of Women's Volleyball Scholarships: N/A
Conference: Massachusetts State College Athletic Conference

Merrimack College
Academic Profile

315 Turnpike St.
North Andover, MA 01845

Phone: (978) 837-5345

Type: Private, 4 Yr., Liberal Arts, Coed
Website: http://www.merrimack.edu
SAT/ACT/GPA: 820/17
Student/Faculty Ratio: 14/1
Undergraduate Enrollment: 2,200
Scholarships/Academic: Yes   **Athletic:** Yes
Expenses By: Year   **In State:** $ 22,050
Specializes In: Business, Science, Liberal Arts
Degrees Conferred: BA, BS, M.Ed.

Founded: 1947
Religion: Catholic
Housing: Yes
Male/Female: 40/60
Graduate Enrollment: N/A
Financial Aid: Yes
Out of State: $ 22,050

Programs of Study: Liberal Arts (Communications, Economics, English, Fine Arts, French, History, Philosophy, Political Science, Psychology, Religion, Sociology, Spanish), Business Administration (Accounting, Finance, Business Economics, International Business, Management, Marketing), Sciences & Engineering (BioChemistry, Biology, Chemistry, Civil Engineering, Computer Science, Electrical Engineering, Environmental Science, Health Science, Math, Physics, Sport Medicine, Athletic Training, Exercise Physiology, PrePhysical Therapy)

Women's Athletic Profile

315 Turnpike St.
North Andover, MA 01845
Coach: Keith Schoonover
Email:

NCAA I
Lady Warriors, Navy Blue, Gold
Phone: (508) 837-5341
Fax: (978) 837-5079

Estimated # of Women's Volleyball Scholarships: N/A
Conference: Northeast-10 Conference
Program Profile: Competitive Division II program with a balanced philosophy of participation on the court as well as in the classroom. Play home games on campus in the Volpe Center (Capacity 1,500).
History: The school was founded in 1947. Since Keith Schoonover took over in 1996, the Warriors are 66-86.
Achievements: ECAC Tournament Finalist 1999.
Coaching: Head Coach- Keith Schoonover, five seasons, 66-86. Deb Finnigan and Joey Pacis are the Assistant Coaches.
Roster In State: 4   **Out of State:** 6   **Out of Country:** 0
Seniors on Team: 2
Most Recent Record: 13-13
Schedule: Binghamton, Pace, New Haven, Lock Haven, Mercy, C.W. Post, American International, Bryant.

Mount Holyoke College
Academic Profile

Kendall Hall
South Hadley, MA 01075

Phone: 413-538-2023

Type: Private, 4 Yr., Liberal Arts, Women Only
Website: http://www.mtholyoke.edu/athletics
SAT/ACT/GPA: 1200/Top 10-15%
Student/Faculty Ratio: 10:1
Undergraduate Enrollment: 1,980
Scholarships/Academic: Yes   **Athletic:** No
Expenses By: Year   **In State:** $ 33,589

Founded: 1837
Religion: Non-Affiliated
Housing: Yes
Male/Female: Women Only
Graduate Enrollment: N/A
Financial Aid: Yes
Out of State: $ 33,589

Specializes In: Education, Liberal Arts, Pre-Law, Pre-Med
Degrees Conferred: BA
Programs of Study: African-American Studies, African Studies, Anthropology, Art History, Asian Studies, Astronomy, BioChemistry, Biology, Chemistry, Classical Languages, Computer Science, Dance, Economics, Education, English, European Studies, French, Geography, Geology, German, Greek, International Relations, Italian, Latin American Studies, Mathematics, Music, Philosophy, Physics, Political Science, PsychoBiology, Psychology, Religion, Romance, Social Science, Sociology & Anthropology

Women's Athletic Profile

Kendall Hall
South Hadley, MA 01075
Coach: Penny Curtis
Email: pcurtis@mtholyoke.edu

NCAA I
Lady Lyons, Blue, White
Phone: (413) 538-2850
Fax: (413) 538-2183

Estimated # of Women's Volleyball Scholarships: 0
Conference: Eastern College Athletic Conference
Program Profile: We have a competitive program with a strong New England Conference. We have two courts and a weight room. Our season is from late August to early November.
History: We began in 1974. We went to Nationals two times in the 1980's. We won seven SIS and 6 Tournaments. We are usually in the top third of our conference.
Coaching: Penny Curtis has been Head Coach since 1981. Her overall record is 262-228. She was the Athlete of the Year at Ithaca College where she graduated in 1970 with a BS degree. The assistant coach is to be announced.
Roster In State: 3   **Out of State:** 9   **Out of Country:** 2
Sophomores on Team: 0   **Seniors on Team:** 1   **Graduation %:** 100
Most Recent Record: 9-16-0   **Fall Games:** 25   **Spring Games:** Varies
Positions Needed: Setter, Outside Hitters
Schedule: Wellesley, MIT, Springfield College, Wheaton, Smith
Style of Play: Aggressive service game, quick attack, aggressive offensive game.

Massachusetts College
Academic Profile

375 Church Street
North Adams, MA 01247

Phone: 800-292-6632

Type: Public, 4 Yr., Liberal Arts, Coed
Website: http://www.mcla.mass.edu
SAT/ACT/GPA: 1000/2.7
Student/Faculty Ratio: 14:1
Undergraduate Enrollment: 1,500
Scholarships/Academic: Yes   **Athletic:** No
Expenses By: Year   **In State:** $ 8,258

Founded: 1894
Religion: Non-Affiliated
Housing: Yes
Male/Female: 1:1
Graduate Enrollment: 150
Financial Aid: Yes
Out of State: $ 13,498

Specializes In: Liberal Arts with professional program
Degrees Conferred: BA, BS, MEd
Programs of Study: Biology, Business Administration, Computer Science, Education, English, Communications, Fine and Performing Arts, History, Math, Philosophy, Physics, Psychology, Sociology

Women's Athletic Profile

375 Church Street
North Adams, MA 01247
Coach: TBA
Email: cferris@mcla.mass.edu

NCAA I
Lady Mohawks, Blue, Gold
Phone: (413) 662-5411
Fax: (413) 662-5357

Estimated # of Women's Volleyball Scholarships: N/A
Conference: MASCAC

Northeastern University
Academic Profile

219 Cabot Center
Boston, MA 02115

Phone: (617) 373-3556

Type: Private, 4 Yr., Liberal Arts, Coed
Website: http://www.northeastern.edu
SAT/ACT/GPA: 1080/24/3.0
Student/Faculty Ratio: 14:1
Undergraduate Enrollment: 11,978
Scholarships/Academic: Yes   **Athletic:** Yes
Expenses By: Year   **In State:** $ Varies

Founded: 1898
Religion: Non-Affiliated
Housing: Yes
Male/Female: 49:51
Graduate Enrollment: 2,696
Financial Aid: Yes
Out of State: $ Varies

Specializes In: Physical Therapy, Engineering, Political Science, History
Degrees Conferred: Associate, Bachelor, Master, Doctoral Level
Programs of Study: Accounting, Anthropology, Art, Banking/Finance, Computer Technology, Biology, Broadcasting, Business, Chemistry, Communications, Computer Science, Criminal Justice, Economics, Education, Engineering, History, Human Services, Journalism, Marketing, Mathematics, Philosophy, Political Science, Public Administration, Physical Therapy

Women's Athletic Profile

219 Cabot Ctr.
Boston, MA 02115-5096
Coach: Mary Kaminski
Email: mkaminski@lynx.neu.edu

NCAA I
Lady Huskies, Red, Black
Phone: (617) 373-3556
Fax: (617) 373-8988

Estimated # of Women's Volleyball Scholarships: 12
Conference: American East Conference
Program Profile: We are in a competitive program. We finished 3rd in the Conference (28-10). We play teams from other regions. We have a 2,500 seat facility that will be renovated this summer.
History: In 1974, we became a Division II program. In 1991, we became a Division I program.
Achievements: AVCA Tachikara Division II Coach of the Year in 1994; GLIAC Champions in 1994; Coach of the Year in 1993 and 1994. Region Coach of the Year in 1994; 7 All-Americans; 2 professional players; Conference Player of the Year in 1998.
Coaching: Mary Kaminski became Head Coach in 1984. Her overall record is 300-235. She is a former Academic All-American and All-Region. Phuong Luong is Assistant Coach.
Freshman Receiving Financial Aid/Academic: **Athletic:** 2
Roster In State: 2   **Out of State:** 8   **Out of Country:** 2
Sophomores on Team: 5   **Seniors on Team:** 2   **Graduation %:** 100
Most Recent Record: 28-10-0   **Fall Games:** 30   **Spring Games:** 4
Positions Needed: Middle Hitters, Setter
Schedule: Georgetown, University of Connecticut, Rutgers, University of New Hampshire, Hostra
Style of Play: Swing offense; 5-1; Read/rotate defense

Pine Manor College
Academic Profile

400 Heath Street
Chestnut Hill, MA 02467

Phone: 617-731-7104

Type: Private, 4 Yr., Liberal Arts, Women Only
Website: http://www.pmc.edu
SAT/ACT/GPA: 800-900
Student/Faculty Ratio: 10:1

Founded: 1911
Religion: Non-Affiliated
Housing: Yes
Male/Female: Women Only

Undergraduate Enrollment: 320
Scholarships/Academic: Yes   **Athletic:** No
Expenses By: Year   **In State:** $ 10,000
Specializes In: 1007 Students participate in internships
Degrees Conferred: AA, AS, BA, M.Ed.

Graduate Enrollment: N/A
Financial Aid: Yes
Out of State: $ 16,000

Programs of Study: Accounting, Allied Health, American Studies, Art History, Biology, BioTechnology, Broadcast, Business Management, Communications, Criminal Justice, Early Childhood Education, Economics, Elementary Education, English, Environmental Science, European Studies, International Business, International Systems, Liberal Arts, Management, Marine Studies, Marketing, Mass Communications, Museum Studies, Psychology, Social & Political Systems, Sociology, Visual Arts

Women's Athletic Profile

400 Health Street
Chestnut Hill, MA 02167
Coach: Katie Haik
Email: haikkatr@pmc.edu

NCAA I
Lady Gators, Dark Green, White
Phone: (617) 731-5058
Fax: (617) 731-7035

Estimated # of Women's Volleyball Scholarships: N/A
Conference: Eastern College Athletic Conference

Regis College
Academic Profile

235 Wellesley Street
Weston, MA 02193-1571

Phone: 800-456-1820

Type: Private, 4 Yr., Liberal Arts, Women Only
Website: http://www.regiscollege.edu
SAT/ACT/GPA: 1000
Student/Faculty Ratio: 11:1
Undergraduate Enrollment: 850
Scholarships/Academic: Yes   **Athletic:** No
Expenses By: Year   **In State:** $ 23,600
Specializes In: Sciences, Communication, Education, Fine Arts
Degrees Conferred: BA, BS, MS

Founded: 1927
Religion: Catholic
Housing: No
Male/Female: Women Only
Graduate Enrollment: 450
Financial Aid: Yes
Out of State: $ 23,600

Programs of Study: Art, Biology, BioChemistry, Business Administration, Chemistry, Classics, Communications, Education, Economics, English, French, German, History, Management, Mathematics, Political Science, Psychology, Social Science, Spanish, Women's Studies, Graphic Design

Women's Athletic Profile

235 Wellesley Street
Weston, MA 02193
Coach: Wayne Lem
Email:

NCAA I
Lady Beacons, Cardinal, Gold
Phone: (781) 768-7141
Fax: (781) 768-8339

Estimated # of Women's Volleyball Scholarships: N/A
Conference: Commonwealth Coast Conference

Salem State College
Academic Profile

352 Lafayette St.
Salem, MA 01970-5353

Phone: 978-542-6200

Type: Public, 4 Yr., Liberal Arts, Coed
Website: Not Available
SAT/ACT/GPA: 980/2.7
Student/Faculty Ratio: 20:1
Undergraduate Enrollment: 6,000
Scholarships/Academic: Yes   **Athletic:** No
Expenses By: Year   **In State:** $ 4,800
Specializes In: Business, Nursing

Founded: 1854
Religion: Non-Affiliated
Housing: Yes
Male/Female: 45:55
Graduate Enrollment: 4,000
Financial Aid: Yes
Out of State: $ 4,800

Degrees Conferred: BA, BS, BFA, MS, MBA, M.Ed.
Programs of Study: Art, Aviation Science, Biology, Business Administration, Business Technology & Education, Cartography, Chemistry, Education, Communications, Computer & Information Studies, Criminal Justice, Economics, Educational Studies, English, Fire Science, General Studies, Geography, Geological Science, History, Mathematics, Music, Nursing, Office Management, Political Science, PreEngineering, Psychology, Social Work, Sociology, Sport/Fitness/Leisure Studies, Theatre Arts, Undeclared

Women's Athletic Profile

352 Lafayette Street
Salem, MA 01970
Coach: Bette Bailey
Email:

NCAA I
Lady Vikings, Orange, Blue
Phone: (978) 542-6586
Fax: (978) 741-2926

Estimated # of Women's Volleyball Scholarships: N/A
Conference: Massachusetts State College Athletic Conference

Simmons College
Academic Profile

300 The Fenway
Boston, MA 02115

Phone: (800) 345-8486

Type: Private, 4 Yr., Liberal Arts, Women
Website: http://www.simmons.edu
SAT/ACT/GPA: 480-570m, 510-610v
Student/Faculty Ratio: 10:1
Undergraduate Enrollment: 1,210
Scholarships/Academic: Yes
Expenses By: Year
Specializes In: Physical Therapy
Degrees Conferred: BA, BS, MA, MS, MBA, Ph.D.

Founded: 1899
Religion: Nonsectarian
Housing: Yes
Male/Female: Women Only
Graduate Enrollment: 2,191
Athletic: No **Financial Aid:** Yes
In State: $ 28,680 **Out of State:** $ 28,680

Programs of Study: Accounting, Arts, Arts Administration, Applied Music, BioChemistry, Chemistry, Chemistry/Pharmacy, Communications, Computer Science, East Asian Studies, Economics, Education, English, Environmental Science, Finance, Foreign Languages, Graphic Design, History, International Management, Management Information Systems, Mathematics, Music History, Nutrition, Nursing, Philosophy, Physical Therapy, Physics, Political Science, PreLaw, PsychoBiology, Psychology, Pubic Relations, Retail Management, Sociology, Women's Studies

Women's Athletic Profile

300 The Fenway
Boston, MA 02115
Coach: Charles Smith
Email: csmith@simmons.edu

NCAA I
Lady Sharks, Blue, Yellow
Phone: (617) 521-1042
Fax: (617) 521-1026

Estimated # of Women's Volleyball Scholarships: N/A
Conference: The Great Northeast Athletic Conference

Smith College
Academic Profile

Ainsworth Gym
Northampton, MA 01063

Phone: (413) 585-2713

Type: Private, 4 Yr., Liberal Arts, Women Only
Website: http://www.pmc.edu
SAT/ACT/GPA: 1200+/3.5
Student/Faculty Ratio: 10:1
Undergraduate Enrollment: 2,800
Scholarships/Academic: Yes
Expenses By: Year
Specializes In: Liberal Arts
Degrees Conferred: BA, MA, MS
Programs of Study: Almost everything available; Liberal Arts

Founded: 1880
Religion: Non-Affiliated
Housing: Yes
Male/Female: Women Only
Graduate Enrollment: 100
Athletic: No **Financial Aid:** Yes
In State: $ 30,000 **Out of State:** $ 30,000

Women's Athletic Profile

Ainsworth Gymnasium
Northampton, MA 01063
Coach: Bonnie May
Email: bmay@ais.smith. edu

NCAA I
Pioneers, Gold, White, Blue
Phone: (413) 585-2713
Fax: (413) 585-2712

Estimated # of Women's Volleyball Scholarships: 0
Conference: New England Women's & Men's Athletic Conference
Program Profile: We play from late August until the middle of November. We have two competition courts with seating for 600 spectators.
History: Our program began in the early 1970's. We are a traditionally strong program usually ranking among the Top 10 teams in New England. We have had 2 NCAA Appearances and numerous regional post season appearances.
Achievements: NEWMAC Coach of the Year in 1988, 1994, 1995; Conference Titles in 1988, 2nd in 1987, 1989, 1994, 1995, 1996; ECAC Champions in 1997; All-American: Kelly Bates in 1988, 1989; Academic All-Americans: Kelly Bates -1988, Rachel Beck -1993.
Coaching: Bonnie May became Head Coach in 1980. Her overall record is 424-291. She was New England Coach of the Year in 1988 and Conference Coach of the Year in 1988, 1994 and 1995. She is a member of the Division III National NCAA Volleyball Committee. Bardee Sadlier is Assistant Coach.

Roster In State: 0
Sophomores on Team: 0
Most Recent Record: 15-15-0

Out of State: 13
Seniors on Team: 2
Fall Games: 30-40

Out of Country: 1
Graduation %: 100
Spring Games: 0

Positions Needed: Setter, Middle Blockers, Defense Specialist
Schedule: Wellesley College, Amherst College, Williams College, Massachusetts Institute of Technology, Eastern Connecticut State University, Wheaton College
Style of Play: We are a very strong defensive team. We run a multiple offense.

Springfield College
Academic Profile

263 Alden Street
Springfield, MA 01109-3797

Phone: (413) 748-3850

Type: Private, 4 Yr., Coed
Website: http://www.spfldrol.edu
SAT/ACT/GPA: Varies
Student/Faculty Ratio: 18:1
Undergraduate Enrollment: 2,000
Scholarships/Academic: No
Expenses By: Year
Specializes In: PE Athletics Related
Degrees Conferred: BA, BS

Athletic: No
In State: $ 23,400

Founded: 1885
Religion: Non-Affiliated
Housing: Yes
Male/Female: 50:50
Graduate Enrollment: 600
Financial Aid: Yes
Out of State: $ 23,400

Programs of Study: Art, Art Therapy, Training, Biology, Business, Chemistry, Computer Systems Management, Early Childhood Education, English, Environmental Studies, Gerontology, Health Service Administration, History, Human Services, Laboratory Science, Management, Mathematics, Medical Technology, Physical Education, Physical Therapy, Political Science, Psychology, Sociology

Women's Athletic Profile

263 Alden Street
Springfield, MA 01109
Coach: Joel Dearing
Email: jbdearing@aol.com

NCAA I
Lady Pride, Maroon, White
Phone: (413) 748-3351
Fax: (413) 748-3855

Estimated # of Women's Volleyball Scholarships: 0
Conference: Eastern College Athletic Conference
Program Profile: 6 Indoor courts, traditional and non traditional seasons. Full-time coach. Support staff: athletic trainer assigned to our team, strength coach, sports information.
History: Program started in 1971-has had 28 consecutive winning seasons. Springfield has appeared in 4 of the last 5 NCAA Tournaments. Elite 8 in 1995 and 1996.
Achievements: All-Americans: Kerri Camuso (1st team-1995) 2nd team (1996) Julie Frahm (2nd team-1995)
Coach Dearing was selected as NE-10 Coach of the Year in 90,93 ,94, and AVCA Regional Coach of the Year in 94, and 96. He is also a USA Volleyball CAP CADRE
Coaching: Coach Dearing: Overall Women's coaching record 392-216 Overall men's coaching record.

Roster In State: 1   **Out of State:** 9   **Out of Country:**
Sophomores on Team: 3   **Seniors on Team:** 5   **Graduation %:** 100
Most Recent Record: 22-14
Positions Needed: Recruit strong athletes for all positions
Schedule: Wellesley, RIT, Eastern CT, Williams, Ithaca, MIT
Style of Play: Springfield players compete with confidence and focus. Strong defensively, quick offensively. Must have Championship mentality.

Stonehill College
Academic Profile

320 Washington Street   **Phone:** 508-565-1373
North Easton, MA 02356

Type: Private, 4 Yr., Liberal Arts, Coed   **Founded:** 1948
Website: http://www.stonehill.edu   **Religion:** Non-Affiliated
SAT/ACT/GPA: Open   **Housing:** Yes
Student/Faculty Ratio: 16:1   **Male/Female:** 42:58
Undergraduate Enrollment: 2,000   **Graduate Enrollment:** N/A
Scholarships/Academic: Yes   **Athletic:** No   **Financial Aid:** Yes
Expenses By: Year   **In State:** $ 24,000   **Out of State:** $ 24,000
Degrees Conferred: BA, BS, BSBA
Programs of Study: American Studies, Communications, Criminal Justice, Economics, Education, Health Care Administration, History, International Studies, English, Mathematics, Philosophy, Political Science, Psychology, Public Administration, Religious, Sociology, Philosophy, Chemistry, Computer Science, Math-Computer, Medical Technology, Business Administration, Accounting, Finance, Marketing

Women's Athletic Profile

320 Washington Street   **NCAA I**
North Easton, MA 02357   Lady Chieftains, Purple, White
Coach: Dan Kiley   **Phone:** (508) 565-1529
Email: dkiley@stonehill.edu   **Fax:** (508) 565-1460

Estimated # of Women's Volleyball Scholarships: N/A
Conference: Northeast-10 Conference

Tufts University
Academic Profile

Athletics Department, Cousens Gym   **Phone:** (617) 627-3232
Medford, MA 02155

Type: Private, 4 Yr., Liberal Arts, Engineering, Coed   **Founded:** 1852
Website: http://www.tufts.edu   **Religion:** Non-Affiliated
SAT/ACT/GPA: 1100+/30+   **Housing:** Yes
Student/Faculty Ratio: 12:1   **Male/Female:** 48:52
Undergraduate Enrollment: 4,500   **Graduate Enrollment:** 500
Scholarships/Academic: No   **Athletic:** No   **Financial Aid:** Yes
Expenses By: Year   **In State:** $ 31,000   **Out of State:** $ 31,000
Specializes In: International Relations, PreMed, Engineering
Degrees Conferred: BA, BS, BSL, MA, ME, MS
Programs of Study: Biological and Physical Sciences, Education, Engineering, International Relations, Languages, Letters/Literature, Mathematics, Nutrition, PreLaw, PreMed, Psychology, Social Sciences, Visual and Performing Arts

Women's Athletic Profile

College Avenue   **NCAA I**
Medford, MA 02155   Lady Jumbos, Brown, Blue
Coach: Kris Talon   **Phone:** (617) 627-5241
Email: kris.talon@tufts.edu   **Fax:** (617) 627-3614

Estimated # of Women's Volleyball Scholarships: 0
Conference: NESCAC

Program Profile: We are a top 10 program in a strong New England region. We play 35 matches from September 10th through December 15th. We have 3 courts and 2 gyms.

History: We started in 1985 and have a .500. We are winning more percentage every year.

Achievements: NESCAC Coach of the Year in 1996; NESCAC Champions in 1996; Conference Rookie of the Year in 1998.

Coaching: Kris Talon is our Head Coach. Cora Thompson is our Assistant Coach.

Freshman Receiving Financial Aid/Academic: **Athletic:** Need based

Roster In State: 2	**Out of State:** 9	**Out of Country:** 0
Sophomores on Team: 11	**Seniors on Team:** 3	**Graduation %:** 100
Most Recent Record: 20-15-0	**Fall Games:**	**Spring Games:** 35

Positions Needed: Middle Hitter, Setter

Schedule: Wellesley, Williams, Middleburg , Amhurst , Wheaton, Coast Guard Academy

Style of Play: Defensive play team strength. 5-1 fully specialized offense. Aggressive.

University of Massachusetts - Amherst
Academic Profile

219 Boyden Bldg.
Amherst, MA 01003

Phone: (413) 545-4343

Type: Public, 4 Yr., Liberal Arts, Engineering, Coed

Website: http://www.umass.edu

SAT/ACT/GPA: 950+

Student/Faculty Ratio: 18:1

Undergraduate Enrollment: 18,000

Scholarships/Academic: Yes   **Athletic:** Yes

Expenses By: Year   **In State:** $ 9,749

Founded: 1863

Religion: Non-Affiliated

Housing: Yes

Male/Female: 1:1

Graduate Enrollment: 6,000

Financial Aid: Yes

Out of State: $ 16,970

Specializes In: Sport Management, Engineering, Business

Degrees Conferred: 6 Associates, 89 Bachelors, 68 Masters, Doctoral

Programs of Study: College of Natural Science & Mathematics, College of Humanities & Fine Arts, College of Social Behavioral Sciences, Education, College of Engineering, College of Food and Natural Resources, School of Nursing, Isenberg School of Management, School of Public Health Sciences

Women's Athletic Profile

220 Boyden Building
Amherst, MA 01003
Coach: Bonnie Kenny
Email: bjkenny@admin.umass.edu

NCAA I
Minutewomen, Maroon, Black
Phone: (413) 545-3153
Fax: (413) 545-1752

Estimated # of Women's Volleyball Scholarships: 3-4

Conference: Atlantic 10 Conference

Achievements: Jill Meyers named GTE Academic All-District 1 and AVCA All-District 1 these are just a few of many awards.

Coaching: Head Coach Bonnie Kenny is going into her 8th season and has an overall record of 140-91.

Freshman Receiving Financial Aid/Academic: **Athletic:** 2

Roster In State: 0	**Out of State:** 13	**Out of Country:** 1
Sophomores on Team:	**Seniors on Team:** 2	**Graduation %:** 100

Camp of Clinic Dates: July 15-19

Positions Needed: OH, MH, RS

Schedule: Cal Berkley, Florida State, UConn, Temple, Xavier, George Washington

Style of Play: Versatility, depth and pure athleticism is the recipe for success.

University of Massachusetts - Boston
Academic Profile

100 Morrisey Boulevard
Boston, MA 02125

Phone: (617) 287-7000

Type: Public, 4 Yr., Coed

Website: http://www.umb.edu

SAT/ACT/GPA: 1130/25/2.0

Student/Faculty Ratio: 15:1

Undergraduate Enrollment: 9,482

Scholarships/Academic: Yes   **Athletic:** No

Founded: 1964

Religion: Non-Affiliated

Housing: Yes

Male/Female: 43:57

Graduate Enrollment: 3,071

Financial Aid: Yes

Expenses By: Year   **In State:** $ 6,994   **Out of State:** $ 6,994
Specializes In: Multiple
Degrees Conferred: BA, BS, MA, MS, MBA, Doctorals
Programs of Study: Anthropology, Biology, Chemistry, Classics, Community Services, Computer Science, Criminal Justice, Dramatic Arts, Economics, Engineering, Physics, English, Fine Arts, French, Geography, German, Gerontology, Human Services, Law, Management, Mathematics, Music, Nursing, Philosophy, Physical Education, Political Science, Psychology, Social Science

Women's Athletic Profile

100 Morrissey Blvd.
Boston, MA 02125
Coach: Derek Schmitt
Email: derek.schmitt@umb.edu

NCAA I
Lady Beacons, Blue, White
Phone: (617) 287-7859
Fax: (617) 287-7840

Estimated # of Women's Volleyball Scholarships: N/A
Conference: Little East Conference, ECAC, MAIW
Program Profile: We are a young team and have excellent facilities. We offer outstanding support in terms of academic advising. We include strength and conditioning and Sports Medicine.
History: Our program began in 1983. In 1995, our team went 15-5 and qualified for MAIAW Tourney.

Roster In State: 8	**Out of State:** 1	**Out of Country:** 1
Sophomores on Team: 5	**Seniors on Team:** 0	**Graduation %:** Unknown
Most Recent Record: 4-20-0	**Fall Games:** 24	**Spring Games:** 0

Positions Needed: 5 Middle Hitters
Schedule: Eastern Connecticut State, Western Connecticut State, Plymouth State

University of Massachusetts - Dartmouth
Academic Profile

285 Old Westport Rd.
North Dartmouth, MA 02747-2300

Phone: 508-999-8605

Type: Public, 4 Yr., Engineering, Coed
Website: http://www.umassd.edu
SAT/ACT/GPA: Required/2.0
Student/Faculty Ratio: 13:1
Undergraduate Enrollment: 6,000
Scholarships/Academic: Yes   **Athletic:** No
Expenses By: Year   **In State:** $ 9,943

Founded: 1895
Religion: Non-Affiliated
Housing: Yes
Male/Female: 52:48
Graduate Enrollment: 725
Financial Aid: Yes
Out of State: $ 16,805

Specializes In: Business, Nursing, Arts & Sciences, Visual & Performing Arts
Degrees Conferred: 893 undergraduates, 169 graduates, 1 doctorate
Programs of Study: College of Art & Sciences: Biology, Chemistry, Computer Science, Economics, Education, English, French, German, History, Humanities & Social Sciences, Mathematics, Medical Laboratory, Psychology, Sociology, Political Science, Spanish, Accounting, Business Information, Engineering, Computer Engineering, Art History, Music, Painting

Women's Athletic Profile

285 Old Wesport Rd.
North Dartmouth, MA 02747
Coach: Kristy Tripp
Email: rquintin@gnbvoc.mec.edu

NCAA I
Corsairs, Blue, Gold, White
Phone: (508) 999-8717
Fax: (508) 999-8730

Estimated # of Women's Volleyball Scholarships: N/A
Conference: Independent

University of Massachusetts - Lowell
Academic Profile

One University Avenue
Lowell, MA 01854
Type: Public, 4 Yr., Liberal Arts, Engineering, Coed
Website: http://www.uml.edu
SAT/ACT/GPA: 960/3.0
Student/Faculty Ratio: 17:1
Undergraduate Enrollment: 6,000

Phone: 800-410-4607

Founded: 1975
Religion: Non-Affiliated
Housing: Yes
Male/Female: 42:58
Graduate Enrollment: 2,700

Scholarships/Academic: Yes
Expenses By: Year
Specializes In: Arts, Sciences, Engineering, Health Professions
Degrees Conferred: Bachelors, Masters, Doctorate
Programs of Study: Health Professions, Engineering, Management, Fine Arts, Arts and Sciences, Business, Communications, Computer Sciences, Education (graduate level only), Letters/Literature, Liberal Arts, Parks/Recreation, Psychology, Protective Services, Public Affairs, Social Sciences, Visual and Performing Arts

Athletic: Yes
In State: $ 9,500

Financial Aid: Yes
Out of State: $ 16,000

Women's Athletic Profile

1 University Avenue
Lowell, MA 01854
Coach: Karen McNutty
Email:

NCAA I
River Hawks, Red, White, Blue
Phone: (978) 934-2319
Fax: (978) 934-2313

Estimated # of Women's Volleyball Scholarships: N/A
Conference: Independent

Wellesley College
Academic Profile

106 Central St.
Wellesley, MA 02481

Phone: (781) 283-2010

Type: Private, 4 Yr., Liberal Arts, Women Only
Website: http://www.wellesley.edu
SAT/ACT/GPA: 1350 Average
Student/Faculty Ratio: 15:1
Undergraduate Enrollment: 2,500
Scholarships/Academic: No
Expenses By: Year
Specializes In: Liberal Arts
Degrees Conferred: BA
Programs of Study: American Studies, Anthropology, Architecture, Art, Astronomy, Biological Science, Chemistry, Chinese, Computer Science, Economics, English, French, Geology, German, Greek, History, International Relations, Mathematics, Music, Philosophy, Physics, Political Science, Psychology, Religion, Russian, Sociology, Theatre

Founded: 1870
Religion: Non-Affiliated
Housing: Yes
Male/Female: Women Only
Graduate Enrollment: N/A
Financial Aid: need basis
Out of State: $ 30,000

Athletic: No
In State: $ 30,000

Women's Athletic Profile

Keohane Sport Ct, 106 Central St.
Wellesley, MA 02481
Coach: Dorothy Hert-Webb
Email: dwebb1@wellesley.edu

NCAA I
Blue, Royal Blue, White
Phone: (781) 283-2010
Fax: (781) 283-3641

Estimated # of Women's Volleyball Scholarships: N/A
Conference: New England Women's & Men's Athletic Conference
History: Our program started in 1998. We finished third nationally in Division 3.
Achievements: Dorothy Webb was 4 times Conference Coach of the Year and 2 times Regional AUCA Coach of the Year. 2 National All-Americans in 1998; 3 Regional All-Americans in 1998.
Coaching: Dorothy Hert-Webb, Head Coach, led the team twice to win the Division I National Championship. She was USUBA All-American . She was also a Bud Light 4-Person Professional and an athlete of Team Nike.
Sophomores on Team:
Most Recent Record: 38-1-0
Camp of Clinic Dates: August 9-12, 16-19
Positions Needed: 3
Schedule: Juniata, Springfield, Cortland State, Ithaca, Massachusetts Institute of Technology

Seniors on Team: 3
Fall Games: 39

Graduation %: 100
Spring Games: 10

Wentworth Institute of Technology
Academic Profile

550 Huntingdon Avenue
Boston, MA 02115

Phone: 800-556-0610

Type: Private, 4 Yr., Engineering, Coed
Website: http://www.wit.edu

Founded: 1925
Religion: Non-Affiliated

SAT/ACT/GPA: 820
Student/Faculty Ratio: 19:1
Undergraduate Enrollment: 2,800
Scholarships/Academic: Yes
Expenses By: Year
Specializes In: Architecture, Engineering, Construction Management
Degrees Conferred: AAS, BS, BArch
Programs of Study: Airway Science, Architecture, Building Construction Technology, Engineering, Computer Science, Construction Management, Interior Design, Mechanical Engineering, Technical Management

Housing: Yes
Male/Female: 3:1
Graduate Enrollment: N/A
Athletic: No
Financial Aid: Yes
In State: $ 16,000
Out of State: $ 16,000

Women's Athletic Profile

550 Huntington Avenue
Boston, MA 02115
Coach: Jason Jeffers
Email: athletics@wit.edu

NCAA I
Lady Leopards, Black, Gold
Phone: (617) 989-4655
Fax: (617) 989-4150

Estimated # of Women's Volleyball Scholarships: N/A
Conference: Commonwealth Coast Conference
Program Profile: We are a very young program.
History: Our program began in 1988.
Coaching: Jason Jeffers, Head Coach, is entering his first season with the program.
Roster In State: 8   Out of State: 4   Out of Country: 0
Sophomores on Team: 3   Seniors on Team: 3   Graduation %: 100
Most Recent Record: 8-13-0 Fall Games: 24   Spring Games: 0
Positions Needed: All
Schedule: Eastern Nazarene, Gordon, Colby Sawyer, Endicott, Roger Williams

Western New England College
Academic Profile

1215 Wilbraham Rd.
Springfield, MA 01119

Phone: (413) 782-1377

Type: Private, 4 Yr., Liberal Arts, Engineering, Coed
Website: http://www.wnec.edu
SAT/ACT/GPA: Varies by program of study
Student/Faculty Ratio: 17:1
Undergraduate Enrollment: 1950 fulltime
Scholarships/Academic: Yes
Expenses By: Year
Specializes In: Professional and Pre-Professional
Degrees Conferred: AA,BA, BS, MS, MBA, JD

Founded: 1919
Religion: Non-Affiliated
Housing: Yes
Male/Female: 56/44
Graduate Enrollment: 1,700
Athletic: No
Financial Aid: Yes
In State: $23,154
Out of State: $23,154

Programs of Study: Accounting, American Studies, Biology, BioMedical Engineering, Chemistry, Computer Science, Criminal Justice, Economics, Electrical Engineering, English, Environmental Science, Finance, General Business, Government, History, International Business, Liberal Studies, Law and Conflict Resolution & Leadership, Management Studies & Manufacturing Management, Marketing, Marketing Communication Advertising, Mathematical Sciences, Mechanical Engineering, PrePharmacy, PrePhysician's Assistant, PreVeterinary, Social Work, Sociology, Sport Management

Women's Athletic Profile

1215 Willbraham Rd
Springfield, MA 01119
Coach: Gregg Poole
Email:
Estimated # of Women's Volleyball Scholarships: N/A
Conference: Independent

NCAA I
Lady Golden Bears, Blue, Gold
Phone: (413) 782-1550
Fax: (413) 796-2121

Westfield State College
Academic Profile

577 Western Avenue
Westfield, MA 01086-1630

Phone: (413) 572-5405

Type: Public, 4 Yr., Liberal Arts, Coed

Founded: 1839

Website: http://www.wsc.mass.edu
SAT/ACT/GPA: 800/2.7
Student/Faculty Ratio: 18:1
Undergraduate Enrollment: 3,100
Scholarships/Academic: Yes   **Athletic:** No
Expenses By: Year   **In State:** $ 7,148
Specializes In: Business, Criminal Justice, Education, Mass Communications
Degrees Conferred: BA, BS, BSE, MA, MS, M.Ed.
Religion: Non-Affiliated
Housing: No
Male/Female: 47:53
Graduate Enrollment: 1,800
Financial Aid: Yes
Out of State: $ 13,468

Programs of Study: Biology, Business Administration, Chemistry, Communications, Computer Science, Criminal Justice, Economics, Education, English, Fine Arts, French, Geology, Geography, History, Information Science, Management, Mathematics, Music, Political Science, Psychology, Social Science, Spanish, Special Education, Urban Studies

Women's Athletic Profile

Western Avenue
Westfield, MA 01086
Coach: Hilary Ducharme
Email:

NCAA I
Lady Owls, Royal Blue, White
Phone: (413) 572-5417
Fax: (413) 572-5477

Estimated # of Women's Volleyball Scholarships: N/A
Conference: Independent

Wheaton College - Massachusetts
Academic Profile

E Main Street
Norton, MA 02766

Phone: 800-394-6003

Type: Private, 4 Yr., Liberal Arts, Coed
Website: http://www.weatonma.edu
SAT/ACT/GPA: None/2.5
Student/Faculty Ratio: 13:1
Undergraduate Enrollment: 1,400
Scholarships/Academic: Yes   **Athletic:** No
Expenses By: Year   **In State:** $ 28,460
Degrees Conferred: BA, BS
Founded: 1834
Religion: Non-Affiliated
Housing: Yes
Male/Female: 1:2
Graduate Enrollment: N/A
Financial Aid: Yes
Out of State: $ 28,460

Programs of Study: American Studies, Anthropology, Art History, BioChemistry, Biology, Chemistry, Economics, Mathematics, Music, Philosophy, Physics, Social Psychology, Sociology, International Relations, Political Science, Computer Science, Religion

Women's Athletic Profile

Evelyn D. Haas Athletic Ctr.
Norton, MA 02766
Coach:
Email:

NCAA I
Lady Warriors, Blue, White
Phone: (508) 286-3994
Fax: (508) 286-8273

Estimated # of Women's Volleyball Scholarships: N/A
Conference: New England Women's & Men's Athletic Conference
Program Profile: Top 15 in New England Region, 35 matches against some of the regions best. State of the art athletic facility.
History: from 1990 to 2000 have 244-153 record. 3 conference titles 92, 93, 94. Sweet 16 NCAA 1997, 6 appearances in the ECAC post season tournament.
Achievements: Coach of the Year 92, 91. 10 Regional All-Americans, 17 All-Conference Players, 15 All-Academic Awards.
Roster In State: 3   **Out of State:** 10   **Out of Country:** 0
Sophomores on Team: **Seniors on Team:** 2   **Graduation %:** 100
Most Recent Record: 13-17
Camp of Clinic Dates: Aug. 5-9
Positions Needed: All
Schedule: Springfield, Wellesley, Amherst, Williams, Tufts, Smith, MIT, Gordon, Western Connecticut State

Williams College
Academic Profile

Lasell Gym
Williamstown, MA 01267

Phone: 413-597-2211

Type: Private, 4 Yr., Liberal Arts, Coed

Founded: 1793

Website: http://www.williams.edu
SAT/ACT/GPA: Open
Student/Faculty Ratio: 11:1
Undergraduate Enrollment: 2,000
Scholarships/Academic: Yes   **Athletic:** No
Expenses By: Sem   **In State:** $ 16,000
Degrees Conferred: BA, MA

Religion: Non-Affiliated
Housing: Yes
Male/Female: 51:49
Graduate Enrollment: N/A
Financial Aid: Yes
Out of State: $ 16,000

Programs of Study: African & Middle Eastern Studies, Afro-American Studies, American Studies, Anthropology & Sociology, Art History, Art Studio, Asian Studies, Astronomy, AstroPhysics, BioChemistry, Biology, Chemistry, Classics, Computer Science, Economics, English, Environmental Studies, GeoScience, German History, History of Science, Linguistic, Literacy Studies, Mathematics, Music, NeuroScience, Philosophy, Physics, Political Science, Political Economy, Psychology, Religion, Russian, Science & Technology Studies, Theatre, Women's Studies

Women's Athletic Profile

Spring Street
Williamstown, MA 01267
Coach: Frances.D.Vandermeer
Email:

NCAA I
Lady Ephs, Purple, Gold
Phone: (413) 458-9094
Fax: (413) 597-4272

Estimated # of Women's Volleyball Scholarships: N/A
Conference: Eastern College Athletic Conference
Achievements: 1995 NEWVA Coach of the Year; 3 NCAA Appearances in 1994, 1995 and 1998.
Coaching: Pat Manning, has been Head Coach at Williams since 1990. She led the Ephs to the ECAC Tournament Championship in 1996. Our team was ranked #2 in New England throughout the season.
Most Recent Record: 28-6-0   **Fall Games:** 34   **Spring Games:** 0
Camp of Clinic Dates: General Skills: July 25-29

Worcester Polytechnic Institute
Academic Profile

486 Chandler State
Worcester, MA 01602

Phone: 508-831-5286

Type: Private, 4 Yr., Liberal Arts, Coed
Website: http://www.wpi.edu
SAT/ACT/GPA: 890/2.7
Student/Faculty Ratio: 12:1
Undergraduate Enrollment: 2,600
Scholarships/Academic: Yes   **Athletic:** No
Expenses By: Year   **In State:** $ 27,592
Specializes In: Liberal Arts
Degrees Conferred: BS, BA, BS in Education

Founded: 1874
Religion: Non-Affiliated
Housing: Yes
Male/Female: 80:20
Graduate Enrollment: 800
Financial Aid: Yes
Out of State: $ 27,592

Programs of Study: Engineering: BioMedical, Civil, Chemical, Electrical, Fire Protection, Industrial, Mechanical, Manufacturing, Materials, Sciences, BioChemistry, Chemistry, Computer Science, Math, Physics, Humanities, Management, Interdisciplinary Studies

Women's Athletic Profile

100 Institute Rd.
Worcester, MA 01609
Coach: Nancy Vaskas
Email:

NCAA I
Lady Engineers, Crimson, Grey
Phone: (508) 831-5243
Fax: (508) 831-5775

Estimated # of Women's Volleyball Scholarships: N/A
Conference: New England Women's & Men's Athletic Conference
Program Profile: We are a member of the NCAA Division III program. The Harrington Auditorium has a seating capacity of 3,000. We play a Fall season and a casual Spring volleyball.
History: The program began in 1979 and has a record of 291-300.
Achievements: 6 Division III State Titles in 1987, 1990, 1991, 1992, 1996 & 1998; 1998 City Champions; 12 Academic All-Americans; 3 All-Conference players; 1998 Conference Rookie of the Year; 2 All-New England players.
Coaching: Nancy Vaskas, Head Coach, has been in charge of our program from 1980 to the present and has a record of 285-289.
Freshman Receiving Financial Aid/Academic:

Athletic: 0
Roster In State: 3   **Out of State:** 9   **Out of Country:** 0
Sophomores on Team: 3   **Seniors on Team:** 2   **Graduation %:** 100

Most Recent Record: 21-9-0   **Fall Games:** 30   **Spring Games:** 0
Positions Needed: Defense, Middle Hitter, Setter, Weakside Hitter
Schedule: Wellesley, MIT, Springfield, Wheaton, Smith, Brandeis
Style of Play: Prefer 6-2, but also play a modified 6-2 or 5-1. Recently initiated quick offense and back row attack, with some multiple offense. Setter back perimeter defense.

Worcester State College
Academic Profile

486 Chandler Street
Worcester, MA 01602-2597

Phone: 508-929-8040

Type: Public, 4 Yr., Coed
Website: http://www.mass.edu
SAT/ACT/GPA: 820/2.7
Student/Faculty Ratio: 16:1
Undergraduate Enrollment: 4,800
Scholarships/Academic: Yes   **Athletic:** No
Expenses By: Year   **In State:** $ 6,900
Specializes In: Business, Education, Physics
Degrees Conferred: BA, BS

Founded: 1874
Religion: Non-Affiliated
Housing: Yes
Male/Female: 1:3
Graduate Enrollment: 3,200
Financial Aid: Yes
Out of State: $ 6,900

Programs of Study: Biology, BioTechnology, Business Administration, Chemistry, Communications, Communications Disorders, Computer Science, Economics, Early Childhood Education, Elementary Education, English, Engineering Transfer Program, French, Geography, Health Studies, History, Mathematics, Nursing, Natural Science, Occupational Therapy, Physics, Psychology, Sociology, Spanish, Urban Studies

Women's Athletic Profile

486 Chandler Street
Worcester, MA 01602
Coach: Pam Grady
Email:

NCAA I
Lady Lancers, Royal Blue, Gold
Phone: (508) 929-8034
Fax: (508) 929-8128

Estimated # of Women's Volleyball Scholarships: N/A
Conference: Massachusetts State College Athletic Conference

MICHIGAN

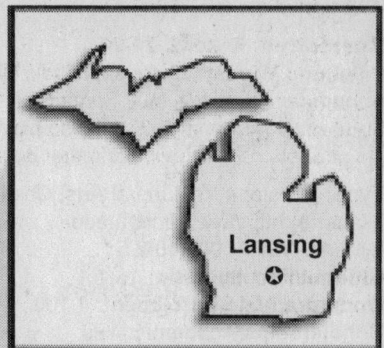

Lansing ✪

SCHOOL	CITY	AFFILIATION	PAGE
Adrian College	Adrian	NCAA III	367
Albion College	Albion	NCAA III	367
Alma College	Alma	NCAA III	368
Aquinas College	Grand Rapids	NAIA	368
Calvin College	Grand Rapids	NCAA III	369
Central Michigan University	Mt. Pleasant	NCAA I	369
Concordia College	Ann Arbor	NAIA/NCCAA I	370
Cornerstone College	Grand Rapids	NAIA	370
Eastern Michigan University	Ypsilanti	NCAA I	371
Ferris State University	Big Rapids	NCAA II	372
Grand Valley State University	Allendale	NCAA II	372
Hillsdale College	Hillsdale	NCAA II	373
Hope College	Holland	NCAA III	374
Kalamazoo College	Kalamazoo	NCAA III	374
Lake Superior State University	Sault Ste. Marie	NCAA II	375
Madonna University	Livonia	NAIA	375
Michigan State University	East Lansing	NCAA I	376
Northern Michigan University	Marquette	NCAA II	377
Northwood University	Midland	NCAA II	377
Oakland University	Rochester	NCAA I	378
Olivet College	Olivet	NCAA III	379
Saginaw Valley State University	University Center	NCAA II	379
Siena Heights University	Adrian	NAIA	380
Spring Arbor College	Spring Arbor	NAIA	380
University of Michigan- Ann Arbor	Ann Arbor	NCAA I	381
University of Michigan - Dearborn	Dearborn	NAIA	381
Wayne State University - Michigan	Detroit	NCAA II	382
Western Michigan University	Kalamazoo	NCAA I	382

Adrian College
Academic Profile

110 S. Madison St.
Adrian, MI 49221-2575

Phone: 800-877-2246

Type: Private, 4 Yr., Liberal Arts, Coed
Website: http://www.adrian.edu
SAT/ACT/GPA: 900/18/2.5
Student/Faculty Ratio: 16:1
Undergraduate Enrollment: 1,100
Scholarships/Academic: Yes   **Athletic:** No
Expenses By: Year   **In State:** $ 17,950

Founded: 1859
Religion: United Methodist
Housing: Yes
Male/Female: 50:50
Graduate Enrollment: N/A
Financial Aid: Yes
Out of State: $ 17,950

Specializes In: Accounting, Criminal Justice, Teacher Education
Degrees Conferred: AA, BS, BA, BFA, BMus, BMEd, BB
Programs of Study: Accounting, Art, Biology, Business Administration, Chemistry, Criminal Justice, Communication Arts, Earth Science, Economics, English, French, German, Health/Physical Education, International Business, Math, Music, Philosophy, Religion, Sociology, Teacher Education, Medical Technology, Political Science, PreLaw, PreMed, PreDentistry

Women's Athletic Profile

110 S. Madison Street
Adrian, MI 49221
Coach: Mike Watkins
Email: mwatkins@adrian.edu

NCAA I
Lady Bulldogs, Black, Gold
Phone: (517) 265-5161x3968
Fax: (517) 264-3802

Estimated # of Women's Volleyball Scholarships: N/A
Conference: Michigan Intercollegiates Athletic Association
Achievements: Kris Griffith 1996 First Team All-MIAA pick; Linda Risner 1998 MVP and Second Team All-MIAA;
Coaching: Norma Gladu is in her 23rd season as Head Coach. She has more than 300 wins. Her teams have finished with at least 20 wins nine times and guided the Bulldogs to four consecutive MIAA titles from 1978-81. Cannon Sanford and Jeannie Rainey are Assistant Coaches.
Roster In State: 14   **Out of State:** 1   **Out of Country:** 0
Sophomores on Team: 4   **Seniors on Team:** 1   **Graduation %:** 100
Most Recent Record: 16-5-0   **Fall Games:** 25   **Spring Games:** 0
Schedule: Bluffton, Purdue, Goshen, Indiana Wesleyan, Hope, St.Mary's, Albion, Alma, Calvin, Olivet, Kalamazoo, Concordia, Tiffin
Style of Play: Fierce and optimistic

Albion College
Academic Profile

611 E. Porter Street
Albion, MI 49224

Phone: (517) 629-1000

Type: Private, 4 Yr., Liberal Arts, Coed
Website: http://www.albion.edu
SAT/ACT/GPA: V-540-640, Math-530-640/22-283.0
Student/Faculty Ratio: 19:1
Undergraduate Enrollment: 1,450
Scholarships/Academic: Yes   **Athletic:** No
Expenses By: Year   **In State:** $ 23,000
Specializes In: Business, PreMed
Degrees Conferred: BA, BFA

Founded: 1835
Religion: United Methodist
Housing: Yes
Male/Female: 1:1
Graduate Enrollment: N/A
Financial Aid: Yes
Out of State: $ 23,000

Programs of Study: Accounting, Anthropology, Art, Biology, Business and Management, Chemistry, Communications, Economics, Education, English, Geology, history, Letters/Literature, Life Sciences, Mathematics, Music, Philosophy, Physical Education, Physics, Political Science, Psychology, Religious Studies, Social Science, Speech, Theatre

Women's Athletic Profile

4830 Kellogg Ctr.
Albion, MI 49224
Coach: Darrell Sedersten
Email: Dsedersten@Albion.edu

NCAA I
Lady Britons, Purple, Gold
Phone: (517) 629-0518
Fax: (517) 629-1648

Estimated # of Women's Volleyball Scholarships: N/A
Conference: Michigan Intercollegiate Athletic Association

Alma College
Academic Profile

614 W. Superior
Alma, MI 48801

Phone: (517) 463-7017

Type: Private, 4 Yr., Liberal Arts, Coed
Website: http://www.alma.edu
SAT/ACT/GPA: 1030/22/3.0
Student/Faculty Ratio: 14:1
Undergraduate Enrollment: 1,400
Scholarships/Academic: Yes   **Athletic:** No
Expenses By: Year   **In State:** $ 21,000
Founded: 1888
Religion: Presbyterian
Housing: Yes
Male/Female: 45:55
Graduate Enrollment: N/A
Financial Aid: Yes
Out of State: $ 21,000
Specializes In: Business, Education, Exercise & Health Science, Pre-Med
Degrees Conferred: BA, BS, Bachelor of Fine Arts, Bachelor of Music
Programs of Study: Accounting, Art, BioChemistry, Business Management, Chemistry, Communications, Computer Science, Corporate Fitness, Ecology, Economics, Elementary Education, English, Environmental Studies, Exercise Science, Foreign Languages, Graphic Design, Health Science, History, Humanities, International Business, Journalism, Liberal Arts, Literature, Mathematics, Modern Languages, Music, Philosophy, Physics, Political Science, PreDensity, PreEngineering, PreLaw, PreMed, Psychology, Public Health, Religion, Sociology, Sport Medicine, Theater

Women's Athletic Profile

614 W. Superior St.
Alma, MI 48801
Coach: Penny Allen-Cook
Email: cook@alma.edu

NCAA I
Lady Scots, Maroon, White
Phone: (517) 463-7017
Fax: (517) 463-7018

Estimated # of Women's Volleyball Scholarships: N/A
Conference: Michigan Intercollegiate Athletic Association
Program Profile: Cappaert Gymnasium is home to men's and women's volleyball. It was renovated in 1993. The Tartan surface was replaced with a maple hardwood floor. Facilities include team practice areas, classrooms and weight rooms.
History: The Scots completed their 1998 home season with a dramatic five-game win over Albion. Alma finished their season by going 1-3 at the competitive Spike-It-Up Classic hosted by Colorado College.
Coaching: Penny Allen-Cook has been Head Coach since 1996. She also serves as Alma's women's athletic director and is an Assistant Coach on the Scots track and field team. Lisa Arnold has been Assistant Coach since 1995.
Roster In State: 13   **Out of State:** 0   **Out of Country:** 0
Sophomores on Team: 0   **Seniors on Team:** 2   **Graduation %:** 100
Most Recent Record: 12-17-0   **Fall Games:** 39   **Spring Games:** 0
Positions Needed: Setter, Middle, Outside Hitter
Schedule: Hope College, Calvin College, Rochester Institute of Technology, University of Wisconsin-River Falls, University of Wisconsin-Whitewater
Style of Play: We are a defense oriented team, with middle dominated offense.

Aquinas College
Academic Profile

1607 Robinson Rd.
Grand Rapids, MI 49506

Phone: 616-459-8281x3101

Type: Private, 4 Yr., Liberal Arts, Coed
Website: http://www.aquinas.edu
SAT/ACT/GPA: Open/18Top 1/2 of class
Student/Faculty Ratio: 14/1
Undergraduate Enrollment: 2100
Scholarships/Academic: Yes   **Athletic:** Yes
Expenses By: Year   **In State:** $14,034
Founded: 1922
Religion: Catholic-Dominican
Housing: Yes
Male/Female: 37/63
Graduate Enrollment: 600
Financial Aid: Yes
Out of State: $14,034
Specializes In: Liberal Arts
Degrees Conferred: AA, AS, BA, BS, BFA, M
Programs of Study: Accounting, Art, Art History, Athletic Training, Biology, Business, Chemistry, Commercial Art, Communications, Computer Information Systems, Ecology, Economics, Education, English, Environmental Science, French, Geography, German, Gerontology, Graphic Art, History, Interior Design, International Business, Liberal Arts, Mathematics, Medical Laboratory Technology, Music, Nuclear Medical Technology, Philosophy, Science, PreDentistry, PreEngineering, PreLaw, PreMed, PreVet, Psychology, Religion, Science, Social Science, Spanish

Women's Athletic Profile

1607 Robinson Rd. SE
Grand Rapids, MI 49506
Coach: Marc Schultz
Email: schulmar@aquinas.edu

NCAA I
Lady Saints, Red, White
Phone: (616) 459-3102
Fax: (616) 732-4548

Estimated # of Women's Volleyball Scholarships: N/A
Conference: WHAC

Calvin College
Academic Profile

3201 Burton SE
Grand Rapids, MI 49546

Phone: (616) 957-6606

Type: Private, 4 Yr., Liberal Arts, Coed
Website: http://www.calvin.edu
SAT/ACT/GPA: 470v 470m/ 2020/2.5
Student/Faculty Ratio: 17:1
Undergraduate Enrollment: 4,086
Scholarships/Academic: Yes
Expenses By: Year

Founded: 1876
Religion: Christian Reformed Church
Housing: Yes
Male/Female: 44:56
Graduate Enrollment: 42

Athletic: No
In State: $ 18,500

Financial Aid: Yes
Out of State: $ 18,500

Specializes In: Business, Communications, Education, Engineering, Sciences
Degrees Conferred: BA, BS, BSA, M Ed
Programs of Study: Accounting, BioChemistry, Biology, Business Administration, Christian Ministry, Communications, Computer Science, Criminal Justice, Economics, Education, Film Studies, French, Geography, Geology, German, History, Mathematics, Medical Technology, Music, Natural Science, Nursing, Sociology, Social Science, Telecommunications

Women's Athletic Profile

3201 Burton SE
Grand Rapids, MI 49546
Coach: Dr. Mary Schutten
Email: schutn@calvin.edu

NCAA I
Lady Knights, Maroon, Gold
Phone: (616) 957-6181
Fax: (616) 957-6060

Estimated # of Women's Volleyball Scholarships: N/A
Conference: Michigan Intercollegiate Athletic Association
Program Profile: Play in 4,500 seat Calvin Field house
History: Varsity program since 1978 has claimed 9 MIAA titles. Has also made 12 NCAA III tournament appearances including three berths in the final four. National runner-up in 1988.
Achievements: Six NCAA Division III All-Americans.
Coaching: Mary Schutten, Head Coach, is in her 15th year of collegiate coaching with a record of 366-158 overall. Her record at Calvin is 241-98.
Roster In State: 7
Sophomores on Team: 0
Most Recent Record: 27-8-0
Positions Needed: Setter

Out of State: 6
Seniors on Team: 3

Out of Country: 0
Graduation %: 100

Schedule: Ithaca, John Carroll, Cornerstone, Hope, Wisconsin-Oshkosh, Case Wester Reserve.

Central Michigan University
Academic Profile

Rose Center 111
Mount Pleasant, MI 48859

Phone: 517-774-3076

Type: Public, 4 Yr., Coed
Website: http://www.cmichi.edu
SAT/ACT/GPA: NCAA minimums
Student/Faculty Ratio: 17:1
Undergraduate Enrollment: 17,000
Scholarships/Academic: Yes
Expenses By: Year

Founded: 1892
Religion: Non-Affiliated
Housing: Yes
Male/Female: 1:1
Graduate Enrollment: 4,000

Athletic: Yes
In State: $ 21,500

Financial Aid: Yes
Out of State: $ 21,500

Specializes In: Education, Business
Degrees Conferred: BA, BS, BFA, BAA, BSBA, MA, MS
Programs of Study: Numerous Majors offered in each of these areas: Business Administration, Communications, Health-Related Programs, Human Services, Liberal Arts, Fine Arts, PreProfessional Programs, Science and Technology, Elementary Education, Secondary Education, Special Education

Women's Athletic Profile

Rose Center
Mt. Pleasant, MI 48859-0001
Coach: Elaine Piha
Email: elaine.a.phia@cmich.edu

NCAA I
Lady Chippewas, Maroon, Gold
Phone: (517) 774-7452
Fax: (517) 774-7324

Estimated # of Women's Volleyball Scholarships: 12
Conference: Mid-American Conference
Program Profile: Rose Arena, 5200 capacity, wood court
History: began in 1997, only 3 coaches since existence, first coach is now SWA.
Achievements: Academic All-MAC (last year-3 players), Academic All-American (4 previous Winners),Numerous All-MAC performers, top 1/2 of conference-every year but 2.
Freshman Receiving Financial Aid/Academic: **Athletic:** 2
Roster In State: 11   **Out of State:** 4   **Out of Country:** 0
Sophomores on Team: **Seniors on Team:** 2   **Graduation %:** 85
Most Recent Record: 14-18
Camp of Clinic Dates: July 9-16th
Positions Needed: OH-Setter
Schedule: Loyola Marymont, Fresno State, Miami-Ohio, Ball State, Western MI, Auron
Style of Play: fast-aggressive-powerful

Concordia College - Ann Arbor
Academic Profile

4090 Geddes Rd.
Ann Harbor, MI 48105

Phone: (734)995-7342

Type: Private, 4 Yr., Liberal Arts,Coed
Website: http://www.ccaa.edu
SAT/ACT/GPA: 20/2.5
Student/Faculty Ratio: 12:1
Undergraduate Enrollment: 550
Scholarships/Academic: Yes   **Athletic:** Yes
Expenses By: Year   **In State:** $ 20,200
Specializes In: Education, Business, Art, Music, Psychology, English
Degrees Conferred: BA

Founded: 1963
Religion: Lutheran
Housing: Yes
Male/Female: 60:40
Graduate Enrollment: N/A
Financial Aid: Yes
Out of State: $ 20,200

Programs of Study: Art, Biblical Languages, Biology, Business Administration, Communications, Elementary Education, English, General Science, History, Political Science, Mathematics, Music, Church Music, Physical Education, Psychology, Religious Studies, Social Studies, Sociology, Sports Management

Women's Athletic Profile

4090 Geddes Road
Ann Arbor, MI 48105
Coach: John Groves
Email: grovej@ccaa.edu

NCAA I
Lady Cardinals, Red, White
Phone: (313) 995-7406
Fax: (313) 995-4883

Estimated # of Women's Volleyball Scholarships: N/A
Conference: Wolverine-Hoosier Conference

Cornerstone College
Academic Profile

1001 E. Beltline NE
Grand Rapids, MI 49505

Phone: 616-222-1426

Type: 4 Year
Website: http://www.cornerstone.edu

Founded: 1941
Religion: Non-Affiliated

SAT/ACT/GPA: Open
Student/Faculty Ratio: 20:1
Undergraduate Enrollment: 9,418
Scholarships/Academic: **Athletic:**
Expenses By: **In State:**
Degrees Conferred:
Programs of Study: Contact school for programs of study.

Housing: No
Male/Female: Not Available
Graduate Enrollment: N/A
Financial Aid:
Out of State:

Women's Athletic Profile

1001 E. Beltline NE
Grand Rapids, MI 49505
Coach: Amy Settle
Email: Amy_L_Settle@Cornerstone.edu

NAIA
Golden Eagles, Navy, Gold
Phone: (616) 831-1356
Fax: (616) 222-1542

Estimated # of Women's Volleyball Scholarships: N/A
Conference: Wolverine-Hoosier Conference
Program Profile: The season begins with a trip to California and matches against three NAIA teams ranked in the Top 10 in the nation.
Coaching: Scott Caulk, Head Coach, returns for his third season. The team made huge improvements and earned the first ever WHAC Championship for any women's team at Cornerstone. Felicia Fortosis is Assistant Coach. She has been here 3 years. Dave Shumaker is Assistant Coach. He just started here this year.

Roster In State: 6   **Out of State:** 4   **Out of Country:** 0
Sophomores on Team: 2   **Seniors on Team:** 1   **Graduation %:** Unknown
Schedule: Westmont, Concordia, Christian Heritage, Biola University, University of Michigan -Dearborn, Indiana Wesleyan, Ferris State

Eastern Michigan University
Academic Profile

200 Bowen Field House
Ypsilanti, MI 48197

Phone: (734) 487-0291

Type: Public, 4 Yr., Coed
Website: http://www.emich.edu
SAT/ACT/GPA: Sliding Scale/21/3.0
Student/Faculty Ratio: 20:1
Undergraduate Enrollment: 25,000
Scholarships/Academic: Yes   **Athletic:** Yes
Expenses By: Year   **In State:** $ 8,825
Specializes In: Education, Business

Founded: 1849
Religion: Non-Affiliated
Housing: Yes
Male/Female: 1:4
Graduate Enrollment: 10,000
Financial Aid: Yes
Out of State: $ 13,878

Degrees Conferred: BA, BS, BFA, BAE, BBA, BBE, BMP, MA, MS, MBA, MFA
Programs of Study: Accounting, Advertising, Anthropology, Aviation, Banking/Finance, BioChemistry, Biology, Chemistry, Broadcasting, Communications, Computer Science, Criminal Justice, Design, Dramatic Arts, Earth Science, Economics, Education, English, Geography, Geology, Management, Marketing, MicroBiology, Music, Nursing, Physics, Political Science, Psychology, Social Science

Women's Athletic Profile

301 Convocation Center
Ypsilanti, MI 48197
Coach: Kim Berrington
Email: kim.berrington@emich.edu

NCAA I
Lady Eagles, Dark Green, White
Phone: (734) 487-0291
Fax: (734) 487-6898

Estimated # of Women's Volleyball Scholarships: 3
Conference: Mid-American Conference
Program Profile: Our 10,000 seat Convocation Center opened in November 1998.
History: Our program began in 1976 as a club. We have competed in the Mid-American Conference since 1980. We earned the only post-season berth to the National Invitation Volleyball Championship in 1990 when we finished the year with a 30-5 record.
Achievements: Kim Berrington has 3 Coach of the Year Honors; 2 All-Americans; 2 Conference titles.
Coaching: Kim Berrington, Head Coach, played at the University of South Carolina. She has 12 years of collegiate coaching experience. Her overall record is 129-120.

Freshman Receiving Financial Aid/Academic:

		Athletic: 3
Roster In State: 7	**Out of State:** 3	**Out of Country:** 5
Sophomores on Team: 2	**Seniors on Team:** 2	**Graduation %:** 100
Most Recent Record: 11-18-0	**Fall Games:** 29	**Spring Games:** 4 dates

Camp of Clinic Dates: July 5-8, 8-10, 11-15
Positions Needed: 2
Schedule: University of Tennessee, University of Kansas, Miami University, Ball State University, Northern Illinois, Georgia Southern
Style of Play: Wide full-open. We play hard and have a lot of fun doing it! We pride ourselves on our defense and run a varied multiple offense.

Ferris State University
Academic Profile

901 S. State Street
Big Rapids, MI 49307-2295

Phone: (616) 592-2000

Type: Public, 4 Yr., Liberal Arts, Coed
Website: http:www.ferris.edu
SAT/ACT/GPA: 700 Min/2.0 or better 4.0 scale
Student/Faculty Ratio: 17:1
Undergraduate Enrollment: 10,919
Scholarships/Academic: Yes
Expenses By: Year
Specializes In: Technical Career Oriented
Degrees Conferred: AA, AS, AAS, BS, MS, OD, PharmD
Programs of Study: Applied Health Science, Arts and Sciences, Business, Education, Optometry, Pharmacy, Technology

Founded: 1884
Religion: Non-Affiliated
Housing: Yes
Male/Female: 3:2
Graduate Enrollment: 269
Athletic: Yes — **Financial Aid:** Yes
In State: $ 10,163 — **Out of State:** $ 14,711

Women's Athletic Profile

901 South State Street
Big Rapids, MI 49307-2295
Coach: Tia Brandel
Email: brandelt@ferris.edu

NCAA I
Lady Bulldogs, Crimson, Gold
Phone: (616) 592-3821
Fax: (616) 592-3775

Estimated # of Women's Volleyball Scholarships: 8
Conference: Great Lakes Intercollegiate Athletic Conference
Program Profile: Our program has increased scholarship dollars. Our facilities have been renovated
History: Ferris State led the nation in NCAA Division II volleyball attendance in 1989 and ranked seventh nationally in 1990.
Achievements: GLIAC Champions in 1982,1983,1984,1985,1986,1987,1989 and 1990.
Coaching: Tia Brandel, is in her third season as Head Coach. The record for her first two seasons was 33-10. She directed FSU to a 19-12 record and a top national ranking in 1996. Mr. J. J. O'Connell, Assistant Coach, is beginning his first season.
Freshman Receiving Financial Aid/Academic:

		Athletic: 3
Roster In State: 8	**Out of State:** 3	**Out of Country:** 0
Sophomores on Team: 5	**Seniors on Team:** 3	**Graduation %:** 100
Most Recent Record: 25-10-0	**Fall Games:** 35	**Spring Games:** 15

Camp of Clinic Dates: Individual Skills:7/6 -7/9;Team:7/9-7/11; Specialty:7/13-7/14; Advanced: 7/14 - 7/17
Positions Needed: 1/2
Schedule: Fairmont State, Indiana-Purdue, Lake Superior State, Aquinas, Hope, Cornerstone, Northern Michigan, Mercyhurst, Gannon
Style of Play: Fun, fast and aggressive.

Grand Valley State University
Academic Profile

1 Campus Dr.
Allendale, MI 49401

Phone: 800-748-0246

Type: Public, 4 Yr., Coed
Website: http://www.gvsu.edu
SAT/ACT/GPA: 19/2.8
Student/Faculty Ratio: 15:1
Undergraduate Enrollment: 12,000
Scholarships/Academic: Yes

Founded: 1963
Religion: Non-Affiliated
Housing: Yes
Male/Female: Not Available
Graduate Enrollment: 3,000
Athletic: Yes — **Financial Aid:** Yes

Expenses By: Year   **In State:** $ 8,362   **Out of State:** $ 12,346
Degrees Conferred: BA, BS, MED, MBA
Programs of Study: Contact school for program of study.

Women's Athletic Profile

1 Campus Drive
Allendale, MI 49401
Coach: Deanne Scanlon
Email: scanlond@gvsu.edu

NCAA I
Lady Lakers, Blue, Black, White
Phone: (616) 895-3339
Fax: (616) 895-3232

Estimated # of Women's Volleyball Scholarships: N/A
Conference: Great Lakes Intercollegiate Athletic Conference
Program Profile: The Arena has a wooden floor with a seating capacity of 4,100.
History: Program began in 1969. Deanne Scanlon (Head Coach Six Seasons) has an overall record of 144-61 (.702).
Achievements: 2000 GLIAC Conference Champions, 2000 NCAA Regional Champion, 2000 NCAA Elite Eight, Kathy Vis 1st Team All-American, Kristy Kale 2nd Team All-American, Deanne Scanlon Great Lakes NCAA Region Coach of the Year.
Coaching: Head Coach Deanne Scanlon played for the U.S. National Team and was an All-American at NCAA D I. She is only the second coach in the history of Laker Volleyball. Assistant Coaches
Jason Johnson and Lori Janssen.
Freshman Receiving Financial Aid/Academic: **Athletic:** 3
Roster In State: 15   **Out of State:** 1   **Out of Country:** 0
Sophomores on Team: **Seniors on Team:** 4   **Graduation %:** 100
Most Recent Record: 31-4
Camp of Clinic Dates: June 15-16, July 13-16, June 29-30, July 22-25
Schedule: Northern Kentucky, Northwood, Northern Michigan, Ferris State, Central MO.

Hillsdale College
Academic Profile

201 Oak St.
Hillsdale, MI 49242

Phone: (517) 437-7341

Type: Private, 4 Yr., Liberal Arts, Coed
Website: http://www.hillsdale.edu
SAT/ACT/GPA: 1200/26/3.5
Student/Faculty Ratio: 11:1
Undergraduate Enrollment: 1,200
Scholarships/Academic: Yes   **Athletic:** Yes
Expenses By: Year   **In State:** $ 19,090

Founded: 1844
Religion: Non-Affiliated
Housing: Yes
Male/Female: 1:1
Graduate Enrollment: N/A
Financial Aid: Yes
Out of State: $ 19,090

Degrees Conferred: BA, BS
Programs of Study: Accounting, Art, Biology, Business Administration, Chemistry, Classical Studies, Early Childhood Education, Economics, Education, Elementary Education, English, French, German, History, Mathematics, Music, Philosophy, Physical Education, Physics, Political Science, Psychology, Religion, Sociology, Spanish, Theatre and Speech

Women's Athletic Profile

201 Oak St.
Hillsdale, MI 49242-1298
Coach: Chris Gravel
Email: chris.gravel@ac.hillsdale.edu

NCAA I
Lady Chargers, Blue, White
Phone: (517) 437-7341x3162
Fax: (517) 437-0014

Estimated # of Women's Volleyball Scholarships: 6
Conference: Great Lakes Intercollegiate Athletic Conference
Program Profile: All competitions are held at the Jesse Phillips Arena. We have a 3 court layout. The season begins in early August and goes through November. Spring volleyball begins at the end of January and goes until the end of April. We have a brand new weight room, aerobic dance room and a pool.
Achievements: Coach Gravel started in 1996 as Head Coach at Hillside College. He and his teams broke several school records. His best overall record is 23-11. He got his first regional ranking ever and most conference wins ever. This was the first time ever to qualify for post-season play.
Coaching: Chris Gravel, Head Coach, has been coaching for 9 years in the GLIAC conference. He started his career in 1990 as an assistant at Wayne State University. In 1993, he became Grand Valley State University assistant volleyball coach. He then became head volleyball coach for Hillsdale College. Stephanie Gravel, Assistant Coach.

Roster In State: 8   **Out of State:** 6   **Out of Country:** 0
Sophomores on Team: 8   **Seniors on Team:** 2   **Graduation %:** 78
Most Recent Record: 14-17-0   **Fall Games:** 31   **Spring Games:** 15
Positions Needed: Setter, Outside Hitter Middle Hitter, Defensive Specialist
Schedule: Northern Michigan, IPFW, Grand Valley State University, Ferns, Northwood, Wayne State
Style of Play: When you commit to this team, you are entering into something which is much larger than yourself. Time, effort and complying with team rules and regulation are just a few areas in which great discipline is required. I have a broad understanding of the game, its rules and its style of play. My approach to styles of play tends to be adaptable and selective with many options. I take pains to ensure that the athletes understand not just the techniques involved but the 'whys" underlying their use. My ultimate goal is the same for all players, namely developing physical and mental skills that will render them effective in a wide range of game situations and strategies.

Hope College
Academic Profile

PO Box 9000
Holland, MI 49422

Phone: 800-968-7850

Type: Private, 4 Yr., Liberal Arts, Coed
Website: http://www.hope.edu
SAT/ACT/GPA: Open
Student/Faculty Ratio: 13:1
Undergraduate Enrollment: 2,900
Scholarships/Academic: Yes   **Athletic:** No
Expenses By: Year   **In State:** $ 19,874
Specializes In: Sciences
Degrees Conferred: BA, BS

Founded: 1866
Religion: Christian
Housing: Yes
Male/Female: 45:55
Graduate Enrollment: N/A
Financial Aid: Yes
Out of State: $ 19,874

Programs of Study: Liberal Arts with concentrated study in 39 academic areas including Business and Management, Letters/Literature, Life Sciences, Physical Sciences, Psychology, Social Sciences

Women's Athletic Profile

P.O. Box 9000
Holland, MI 49422
Coach: Maureen Dunn
Email: dunnm@hope.edu

NCAA I
Dutchwomen, Blue, Orange
Phone: (616) 396-7695
Fax: (616) 395-7175

Estimated # of Women's Volleyball Scholarships: N/A
Conference: Michigan Intercollegiate Athletic Association

Kalamazoo College
Academic Profile

1200 Academy St.
Kalamazoo, MI 49006

Phone: (616) 337-7000

Type: Private, 4 Yr., Liberal Arts, Coed
Website: http://www.kzoo.edu
SAT/ACT/GPA: 1280/
Student/Faculty Ratio: 13/1
Undergraduate Enrollment: 1,322
Scholarships/Academic: Yes   **Athletic:** No
Expenses By: Year   **In State:** $25,725
Degrees Conferred: BA

Founded: 1833
Religion:
Housing: Yes
Male/Female: 43/57
Graduate Enrollment: N/A
Financial Aid: Yes
Out of State: $25,725

Programs of Study: 24 Majors, 30 concentrations & special programs including Anthropology, Biology, Business Administration, Chemistry, Computer Science, Dramatic Arts, Economics, English, Fine Arts, French, German, Health Science, History, Management, Mathematics, Music, Philosophy, Physics, Political Science, PreDental, PreLaw, PreMed, Psychology, Religion, Secondary Education, Social Science, Spanish

Women's Athletic Profile

1200 Academy Street
Kalamazoo, MI 49006
Coach: Jeanne Hess
Email: jhess@k200.edu

NCAA I
Lady Hornets, Orange, Black
Phone: (616) 337-7086
Fax: (616) 337-7401

Estimated # of Women's Volleyball Scholarships: 0

Conference: Michigan Intercollegiate Athletic Association
Program Profile: The team competes in the fall. Anderson Athletic Center is on campus, has three courts and 2,000 seats.
History: The program began in 1970's, perhaps in 1976.
Achievements: MIAA Champions in 1990, 1991, 1993, 1994, & 1995; NCAA Participants in 1990, 1991, 1993, 1994, & 1996; AVCA Midwest Coach of the Year in 1990 & 1991; Regional Coach of the Year in 1990 and 1991.
Coaching: Jeanne Hess, Head Coach, BS from the University of Michigan 1980, began at Kalamazoo College in 1984, with an overall record is 320-194. Cathy Holmes Galloway, Assistant Coach, graduated from Northern Illinois in 1988 . She began coaching the team in 1997.

Roster In State: 20	**Out of State:** 2	**Out of Country:** 0
Sophomores on Team: 0	**Seniors on Team:** 4	**Graduation %:** 95
Most Recent Record: 24-10-0	**Fall Games:** 35	**Spring Games:** 0

Camp of Clinic Dates: June 28-July 2
Positions Needed: Setter, Outside
Schedule: Wittenberg, Ithaca, De Pauw, Hope, Calvin College, Wheaton
Style of Play: Upbeat, enthusiastic, defense oriented, high percentage of points on transition. We will know how to create points.

Lake Superior State University
Academic Profile

650 W. Easterday Ave.
Sault Ste.. Marie, MI 49783

Phone: 888-800-5778

Type: Public, 4 Yr., Engineering, Coed
Website: http://www.lssu.edu
SAT/ACT/GPA: 20
Student/Faculty Ratio: 19:1
Undergraduate Enrollment: 3,200
Scholarships/Academic: Yes   **Athletic:** Yes
Expenses By: Year   **In State:** $ 8,800

Founded: 1946
Religion: Non-Affiliated
Housing: Yes
Male/Female: 54:46
Graduate Enrollment: 200
Financial Aid: Yes
Out of State: $ 11,000

Specializes In: Engineering, Business Administration, PreMed, Nursing
Degrees Conferred: AA, BA, BS, MBA
Programs of Study: All Bachelors, Exercise Science, Natural Resources Technology, Fisheries, Wildlife

Women's Athletic Profile

650 W. Easterday Avenue
Sault Ste. Marie, MI 49783
Coach: Mark Engle
Email:

NCAA I
Lady Lakers, Blue, Gold
Phone: (906) 635-2627
Fax: (906) 635-2753

Estimated # of Women's Volleyball Scholarships: 8
Conference: Great Lakes Intercollegiate Athletic Conference
Program Profile: We were the most improved team in the Conference in 1998. We have a large facility with a new playing surface for the 1999 season.
History: We joined GLIAC volleyball in 1972.
Achievements: Our team won more Conference matches in 1998 than the prior five years combined.
Coaching: Mark Engle, Head Coach, has an overall record of 35-90. Joe Susi is Assistant Coach.
Freshman Receiving Financial Aid/Academic: **Athletic:** 4

Roster In State: 12	**Out of State:** 0	**Out of Country:** 0
Sophomores on Team: 2	**Seniors on Team:** 3	**Graduation %:** 80
Most Recent Record: 13-18-0	**Fall Games:** 31	**Spring Games:** 3

Style of Play: Good ball control and variety attack.

Madonna University
Academic Profile

36600 Schoolcraft Road
Livonia, MI 48150

Phone: 734-432-5339

Type: Private, 4 Yr., Liberal Arts, Coed
Website: http://www.munet.edu
SAT/ACT/GPA: 18/2.8

Founded: 1947
Religion: Catholic
Housing: Yes

Student/Faculty Ratio: 18:1

Male/Female: 1:4

Undergraduate Enrollment: 4,000

Graduate Enrollment: Varies

Scholarships/Academic: Yes   **Athletic:** Yes

Financial Aid: Yes

Expenses By: Year   **In State:** $ 9,500

Out of State: $ 9,500

Specializes In: Education, Nursing, Criminal Justice, Business

Degrees Conferred: Bachelors, Master

Programs of Study: Criminal Justice, Sign Languages Studies, Nursing, Business & Education, Social Work, Sociology, Fire Science, Athletic Training, Art, Applied Science, Chemistry, English, Journalism, Hospice Care, History, Mental Health, Communications

Women's Athletic Profile

36600 Schoolcraft

Livonia, MI 48150

Coach: Jeny Abraham

Email:

NCAA I

Lady Crusaders, Blue, Gold

Phone: (734) 432-5612

Fax: (734) 432-5611

Estimated # of Women's Volleyball Scholarships: 1.5

Conference: Independent

Program Profile: Ranked to 25 in the country past 8 years, top NAIA program

History: 1987-Present .757 winning %, Never have had a losing season

Avg. 40 wins per season

Achievements: 2 Regional Coach of Year, 2 Conference Coach of Year, 2 WHAC Titles

10 All-Americans, 7 Academic All-Americans

Coaching: Tim Debelliso 3rd Season Brian McClain 9th Season

Freshman Receiving Financial Aid/Academic: **Athletic:** 2

Roster In State: 10   **Out of State:** 1   **Out of Country:**

Sophomores on Team: **Seniors on Team:** 2   **Graduation %:** 99

Most Recent Record: 44-7   **Fall Games:** 50-55   **Spring Games:**

Positions Needed: Outside Hitter/ Middle Hitter

Schedule: Columbia College, MO, Mesa State College, CO, Taylor University, Bethel College, IN Dordt College, ID, Palm Beach Atlantic, FL

Style of Play: MH Domination Quick Offense

Michigan State University
Academic Profile

404 Jenison Field House

East Lansing, MI 48824

Phone: 517-355-1855

Type: Public, 4 Yr., Coed

Founded: 1855

Website: http://www.msu.edu

Religion: Non-Affiliated

SAT/ACT/GPA: 1120/24

Housing: Yes

Student/Faculty Ratio: 25:1

Male/Female: 48:52

Undergraduate Enrollment: 31,000

Graduate Enrollment: 9,000

Scholarships/Academic: Yes   **Athletic:** Yes

Financial Aid: Yes

Expenses By: Year   **In State:** $ 17,320

Out of State: $ 31,450

Degrees Conferred: AA, BA, BS, MS, Ph.D., AAS

Programs of Study: Agriculture and Natural Resources, Arts and Letters, Business, Communication, Arts and Science, Education, Engineering, Human Ecology/Medicine, Natural Science, Nursing, Osteophathic Medicine, Social Science, Veterinary Medicine

Women's Athletic Profile

248 Jenison Field House

East Lansing, MI 48824

Coach: Chuck Erbe

Email: erbe@msu.edu

NCAA I

Lady Spartans, Green, White

Phone: (517) 355-4750

Fax: (517) 432-1047

Estimated # of Women's Volleyball Scholarships: N/A

Conference: Big Ten Conference

Northern Michigan University
Academic Profile

1401 Presque Isle Avenue
Marquette, MI 49855

Phone: (906) 227-2105

Type: Public, 4 Yr., Liberal Arts, Coed
Website: http://www.nmu.edu
SAT/ACT/GPA: 900/19/2.25
Student/Faculty Ratio: 20:1
Undergraduate Enrollment: 8,186
Scholarships/Academic: Yes   **Athletic:** Yes
Expenses By: Year   **In State:** $ 8,186
Specializes In: Education

Founded: 1899
Religion: Non-Affiliated
Housing: Yes
Male/Female: 1:1
Graduate Enrollment: 1,200
Financial Aid: Yes
Out of State: $ 10,622

Degrees Conferred: Baccalaureate, Associate, Certificate, Diploma
Programs of Study: Accounting, Art, Biology, Broadcasting, Business, Chemistry, Computer Programming, Criminal Justice, Elementary Education, English, French, Geography, Health, Liberal Arts, Math, Nursing, Physical Education, Psychology, Public Relations, Social Work, Sociology, Sport Medicine, Theatre, Water Science, Zoology, and many others.

Women's Athletic Profile

Presque Isle Avenue
Marquette, MI 49855
Coach: Toby Rens
Email: trens@nmu.edu

NCAA I
Lady Wildcats, Green, Gold
Phone: (906) 227-2105
Fax: (906) 227-2492

Estimated # of Women's Volleyball Scholarships: 8
Conference: Great Lakes Intercollegiate Athletic Conference
Program Profile: Our facilities are volleyball only. We have one of the best facilities in the country with 3 practice courts. We average over 400 attendance per match.
History: Our program started in 1974. From 1991 to the present, we made eight NCAA Tournament Appearances, were in the Final Eight 7 times and were National Champions in 1993 and 1994.
Achievements: Eight straight Conference Championships; 18 All-Americans
Coaching: Toby Rens started as Head Coach in 1998. His overall record here is 30-6. Tracy Seiler and Brian Blindt started as Assistant Coaches in 1999.
Freshman Receiving Financial Aid/Academic: **Athletic:** 5
Roster In State: 2   **Out of State:** 9   **Out of Country:** 2
Sophomores on Team: 2   **Seniors on Team:** 2   **Graduation %:** 94
Most Recent Record: 30-6-0   **Fall Games:** 36   **Spring Games:** 12
Camp of Clinic Dates: June 14-19
Positions Needed: Outside Hitter, Right Side Hitter
Schedule: North Dakota State, Augustana, Minnesota State, St. Cloud State, Regis, Metro State
Style of Play: We are very up-tempo, strong at net play and very high risk.

Northwood University
Academic Profile

3225 Cook Road
Midland, MI 48460-2398

Phone: (800) 457-7878

Type: Private, 4 Yr., Coed
Website: http://www.northwood.edu
SAT/ACT/GPA: 820/68/2.0
Student/Faculty Ratio: 24:1
Undergraduate Enrollment: 1,700
Scholarships/Academic: Yes   **Athletic:** Yes
Expenses By: Year   **In State:** $ 17,659
Specializes In: Business, Computer, Computer Science

Founded: 1960
Religion: Non-Affiliated
Housing: Yes
Male/Female: 55:45
Graduate Enrollment: 207
Financial Aid: Yes
Out of State: $ 17,659

Degrees Conferred: AA, BBA, MBA
Programs of Study: Accounting, Advertising, Automotive After-Market Management, Automotive Marketing and Management, Banking and Finance Management, Business Management, Computer Information Management, Economics & Management, Fashion Marketing & Merchandising, Health Care Management, Hotel Restaurant and Resort Management, International Business and Management

Women's Athletic Profile

3225 Cook Rd.
Midland, MI 48640
Coach: Jeff Williams
Email: admissions@northwood.edu

NCAA I
Timberwolves, Red, Blue
Phone: (800) 457-7878
Fax: (517) 837-4484

Estimated # of Women's Volleyball Scholarships: N/A
Conference: Great Lakes Intercollegiate Athletic Conference
Program Profile: We have a Top 20 Division II program. We play in a very strong volleyball conference (GLIAC). Our home matches are played in Bennett Sports Center which has 1,200 seats.
History: We had sixteen winning seasons in 17 years.
Achievements: 9 NAIA District Championships; 9 NAIA National Appearances; 3rd place in 1991; Finished 3rd (3 times); 2nd and 1st in GLIAC in the past 5 years; NCAC Regional Runner-up in 1996 and 1997; 12 players have received 29 All-American awards.
Coaching: Jeff Williams, Head Coach, started the volleyball program in 1982 and coached for 5 seasons. He returned to the program in 1996 and has a career record of 176-89 . Gary Stangleqicz is Assistant Coach.

Freshman Receiving Financial Aid/Academic:		**Athletic:** 5

Roster In State: 8 | **Out of State:** 0 | **Out of Country:** 4
Sophomores on Team: 1 | **Seniors on Team:** 5 | **Graduation %:** 91
Most Recent Record: 19-14-0 | **Fall Games:** 32 | **Spring Games:** 0

Camp of Clinic Dates: Individual Skills-July 6-8; Setter-July 9-11; Hitters: July 10-11
Positions Needed: Setter, 2 Middle Hitters, 2 Outside Hitters
Schedule: Northern Michigan, Northern Kentucky, West Texas A & M, Colorado Christian, SIU Edwardsville, IP Fort Wayne
Style of Play: 5-1 offensive system with multiple plays and audible.

Oakland University
Academic Profile

Lepley Sport Center
Rochester, MI 48309-4401

Phone: (248) 370-3190

Type: Public, 4 Yr., Liberal Arts, Engineering, Coed
Website: http://www.acs.oakland.edu
SAT/ACT/GPA: 23/2.5
Student/Faculty Ratio: 19:1
Undergraduate Enrollment: 14,000
Scholarships/Academic: Yes
Expenses By: Year

Athletic: Yes
In State: $ 8,000

Founded: 1957
Religion: Non-Affiliated
Housing: Yes
Male/Female: 35:65
Graduate Enrollment: N/A
Financial Aid: Yes
Out of State: $ 14,000

Specializes In: Broad base academic offering
Degrees Conferred: Bachelors, Master, Doctorate
Programs of Study: Accounting, Anatomy, Anthropology, Art, History, BioChemistry, Biology, Business, Chemistry, Communications, Computer Science, CytoTechnology, Economics, Education, Engineering, Environmental Science, Finance, French, German, Journalism, Mathematics, Marketing, Medical Laboratory, Music, Nursing, Philosophy, Physical Therapy, Physics, Political Science, Psychology, Toxicology, PreLaw, PreMed, PreDentistry

Women's Athletic Profile

Athletic Department
Rochester, MI 48309
Coach: TBA
Email:

NCAA I
Golden Grizzlies, Gold, Black
Phone: (248) 370-4057
Fax: (248) 370-4056

Estimated # of Women's Volleyball Scholarships: N/A
Conference: Mid-Continent Conference
Program Profile: OU just completed a new $31 million Recreation and Athletic Center in 1998. The 250,000 square foot facility houses an indoor arena, a gymnasium, a weight training/fitness area, a running track, a wellness center and a host of athletic courts. We play in the indoor arena that holds 3,000 fans.
History: The women's volleyball program began in 1976 as a Division II program in the GLIAC Conference. Oakland made the move to Division I in 1997 and will be a full-fledged Division I program in the fall of 1999.
Achievements: 3 All-Americans in 1995.
Coaching: The position for Head Coach is open.
Style of Play: No coach at the moment

Olivet College
Academic Profile

300 South Main Street
Olivet, MI 49076

Phone: 248-341-2200

Type: 4 year
Website: http://www.olivetnet.edu
SAT/ACT/GPA: Open
Student/Faculty Ratio:
Undergraduate Enrollment: 24,941
Scholarships/Academic:
Expenses By:
Degrees Conferred:
Programs of Study: Contact school for programs of study.

Founded: 1844
Religion: Non-Affiliated
Housing: No
Male/Female: Not Available
Graduate Enrollment: N/A
Athletic: **Financial Aid:**
In State: **Out of State:**

Women's Athletic Profile

300 South Main Street
Olivet, MI 49076
Coach: Dennis Richardson
Email:

NCAA I
Lady Comets, Scarlet, White
Phone: (616) 749-6604
Fax: (616) 749-7229

Estimated # of Women's Volleyball Scholarships: N/A
Conference: Michigan Intercollegiate Athletic Association

Saginaw Valley State University
Academic Profile

7400 Bay Rd.
University Center, MI 48710
Type: Public, 4 Yr., Liberal Arts, Engineering, Coed
Website: http://www.su.su.edu
SAT/ACT/GPA: 17/2.5
Student/Faculty Ratio: 25:1
Undergraduate Enrollment: 6,701
Scholarships/Academic: Yes
Expenses By: Year

Phone: (517) 790-4000

Founded: 1963
Religion: Non-Affiliated
Housing: Yes
Male/Female: 1:1.5
Graduate Enrollment: 1,353
Athletic: Yes **Financial Aid:** Yes
In State: $ 8,536 **Out of State:** $11,801
Degrees Conferred: BAS, BA, BFA, BS, BBA, BSEE, BSME, BSN, BSW, MAT, MEd, MBA, MSN
Programs of Study: Accounting, Art, Banking/Finance, Biology, Business, Chemistry, Communications, Computer, Criminal Justice, Design, Dramatic Arts, Economics, Political Science, PreProfessional Programs, Psychology, Secondary Education

Women's Athletic Profile

7400 Bay Road
University Center, MI 48710-0001
Coach: Robert L. Sells, Jr.
Email: wasket@tardis.svsu.edu

NCAA I
Cardinals, Red, White, Blue
Phone: (517) 790-4000
Fax: (517) 790-0545

Estimated # of Women's Volleyball Scholarships: 3
Conference: Great Lakes Intercollegiate Athletic Conference
Program Profile: We play a fall season. We have a progressive and improving program. We play in a small gym that has 500 seats.
History: In 1980, we had a below .500 program. We are now becoming more competitive.
Achievements: Our coach has been here 3 years. He got 33 wins in the past two years. He has the best overall record than all the other 5 previous coaches.
Coaching: Robert L. Sells, Jr. has been Head Coach from 1997 to the present. His overall record is 33-30.
Freshman Receiving Financial Aid/Academic: **Athletic:** 4
Roster In State: 14 **Out of State:** **Out of Country:**
Sophomores on Team: 3 **Seniors on Team:** 2 **Graduation %:** 100
Most Recent Record: 18-13-0 **Fall Games:** 32 **Spring Games:** 0
Camp of Clinic Dates: June 27-29 (9-12 grades); July 5-7 (team); August 1-3 (6-8 grades)
Positions Needed: Middle Hitters
Schedule: Northern Michigan, West Texas A & M, Northern Kentucky, Northwood, Ferris State, Grand Valley
Style of Play: We play an aggressive style of defense with a quick offense. A group of solid athletes who strive to over achieve.

Siena Heights University
Academic Profile

1247 E. Siena Heights Dr.
Adrian, MI 49221

Phone: (517) 264-7873

Type: Private, 4 Yr., Liberal Arts, Coed
Website: http://www.sienahts.com
SAT/ACT/GPA: 22/2.5
Student/Faculty Ratio: 14:1
Undergraduate Enrollment: 1,100
Scholarships/Academic: Yes   **Athletic:** Yes
Expenses By: Year   **In State:** $ 16,190
Specializes In: A wide variety of academic majors
Degrees Conferred: AA, BA, AFA, BFA, BS, BAS, AS

Founded: 1919
Religion: Dominican
Housing: Yes
Male/Female: 55:45
Graduate Enrollment: 200
Financial Aid: Yes
Out of State: $ 16,190

Programs of Study: Accounting, American Studies, Art, Biology, Business Administration, Management, Marketing, Chemistry, Child Development, Computer Information Systems, Hospitality Management, Human Services, Criminal Justice, Gerontology, Psychology, Public Administration, Music, PreLaw, Philosophy, PreEngineering, PreDentistry

Women's Athletic Profile

1247 E. Siena Hights Drive
Adrian, MI 49211
Coach: Craig Vlietstra
Email: cvlietst@sienahts.edu

NCAA I
Lady Saints, Blue, Gold
Phone: (517) 264-7875
Fax: (517) 264-7737

Estimated # of Women's Volleyball Scholarships: N/A
Conference: WHAC

Spring Arbor College
Academic Profile

106 Main Street
Spring Arbor, MI 49283

Phone: (517) 750-1200

Type: Private, 4 Yr., Liberal Arts, Coed
Website: http://www.admin.arbor.edu
SAT/ACT/GPA: 20
Student/Faculty Ratio: 25:1
Undergraduate Enrollment: 1,900
Scholarships/Academic: Yes   **Athletic:** Yes
Expenses By: Year   **In State:** $ 15,310
Specializes In: Education, Communication
Degrees Conferred: Bachelors, Associate

Founded: 1873
Religion: Free Methodist
Housing: Yes
Male/Female: 1:3
Graduate Enrollment: 800
Financial Aid: Yes
Out of State: $ 15,310

Programs of Study: Exercise Sports, PreMed, Communications, Education, Christian Ministries, Psychology, Biology, Music, Arts, Chemistry, English, BioChemistry, French, Spanish, Geography, History, Greek, Math, Philosophy, Political Science, Religion, Social Work, Sociology, Speech, Urban Studies, Accounting, Business

Women's Athletic Profile

Main Street
Spring Arbor, MI 49283
Coach: Bill Brenton
Email:
Estimated # of Women's Volleyball Scholarships: N/A
Conference: WHAC

NCAA I
Lady Cougars, Blue, Gold
Phone: (517) 750-6502
Fax: (517) 750-2745

University of Michigan - Ann Arbor
Academic Profile

1000 S. State Street
Ann Arbor, MI 48109-2201

Phone: (734) 764-7433

Type: Public, 4 Yr., Liberal Arts, Engineering, Coed
Website: http://www.mgoblue.com

Founded: 1817
Religion: Non-Affiliated

SAT/ACT/GPA: 1030+
Student/Faculty Ratio: 15:1
Undergraduate Enrollment: 36,450
Scholarships/Academic: Yes
Expenses By: Year
Specializes In: Architecture, Nursing

Athletic: Yes
In State: $ 9,559

Housing: Yes
Male/Female: 1.2:1
Graduate Enrollment: 14,000
Financial Aid: Yes
Out of State: $ 19,881

Degrees Conferred: AB, BS, BFA, BBA, BMus, BSN, MA, MS, MBA, MFA, Ph.D., MD, JD
Programs of Study: Accounting, Anthropology, Art, Architecture, Astronomy, Atmospheric/Oceanic Studies, Biblical, Biology, Botany, Business, Chemistry, Computer, Dentistry, Design, Economics, Education, Engineering, Geology, History, Kinesiology, Literature, Management, Mathematics, Medieval, Movement, Music, Natural Resources, Nursing, Oceanography, Pharmacy, Philosophy

Women's Athletic Profile

1000 S. State Street
Ann Arbor, MI 48109-2201
Coach: Gregory Giovanazzi
Email: rosenma@umich.edu

NCAA I
Lady Wolverines, Maize, Blue
Phone: (734) 647-3035
Fax: (734) 647-3221

Estimated # of Women's Volleyball Scholarships: 3
Conference: Big Ten Conference
Program Profile: We are an up and coming program in the best conference in the country. We play in Cliff Keen Arena, a volleyball only facility, which seats 2, 200 people. We are a large university with a very rich tradition in academics and athletics.
History: Our program began in 1973 and we went to post season play in 1995 (NIVC) and 1997 (NCAA second round).
Coaching: We have a new staff in 1999. Head coach Mark Rosen has a career record of 209-37. He won the 1994 NCAA Division II National Championship at Northern Michigan University. In 1994, he was Asics/Volleyball Coach of the Year. Leisa rosen and Jun Liu are the assistant coaches.
Freshman Receiving Financial Aid/Academic:
Roster In State: 7
Sophomores on Team: 6
Most Recent Record: 12-18-0
Camp of Clinic Dates: July 25-29, August 1-5
Positions Needed: Middle Blocker (1), Outside Hitter (1), MB/OH (1)

Out of State: 12
Seniors on Team: 5
Fall Games: 30

Athletic: 3
Out of Country: 0
Graduation %: 100
Spring Games: 4

Schedule: Penn State, Wisconsin, Ohio State, Michigan State, Illinois, Brigham Young University, Arkansas, Pepperdine
Style of Play: Pursuit mentality on defense with up tempo transition style offense. A team that plays hard every point.

University of Michigan - Dearborn
Academic Profile

4901 Evergreen
Dearborn, MI 48128

Phone: 313-593-5100

Type: 4 Yr., Coed
Website: http://www.umd.umich.edu
SAT/ACT/GPA: Open
Student/Faculty Ratio:
Undergraduate Enrollment: N/A
Scholarships/Academic:
Expenses By: Year

Athletic:
In State:

Founded:
Religion: Non-Affiliated
Housing: No
Male/Female:
Graduate Enrollment: N/A
Financial Aid:
Out of State:

Programs of Study: Accounting, Anthropology, Art, Architecture, Astronomy, Atmospheric/Oceanic Studies, Biblical, Biology, Botany, Business, Chemistry, Computer, Dentistry, Design, Economics, Education, Engineering, Geology, History, Literature, Management, Math, Medieval, Movement, Music, Natural Resources, Nursing, Oceanography, Pharmacy, Philosophy, etc.

Women's Athletic Profile

4901 Evergreen Rd.
Dearborn, MI 48128
Coach: Mike Gibson
Email:

NCAA I
Lady Wolves, Blue, Gold
Phone: (313) 593-5673
Fax: (313) 593-5436

Did Not Return Profile

Wayne State University
Academic Profile

101 Matthaei Bldg.
Detroit, MI 48202

Phone:

Type: Public, 4 Yr., Liberal Arts, Coed
Website: http://www.wayne.edu
SAT/ACT/GPA: 20avg
Student/Faculty Ratio: 9:1
Undergraduate Enrollment: 20,230
Scholarships/Academic: Yes   **Athletic:** Yes
Expenses By: Year   **In State:** $ 3,800

Founded: 1868
Religion: Non-Affiliated
Housing: No
Male/Female: 43:57
Graduate Enrollment: 14,000+
Financial Aid: Yes
Out of State: $ 7,900

Degrees Conferred: BA, BS, BFA, BGS, BM, BPA, BSMS, BSW, MA, MS, MBA, MFA, Ph.D.
Programs of Study: Accounting, Ancient Civilization, Anthropology, Art, Banking/Finance, Biological, Broadcasting, Chemistry, Classics, Communications, Computer, Criminal, Dance, Design, Dietetics, Geography, Geology, History, Humanities, International, Journalism, Linguistics, etc..

Women's Athletic Profile

101 Matthaei Blgd., 5101 John Lodge Dr.
Detroit, MI 48202-3489
Coach: Loretta Vogel
Email:

NCAA I
Lady Tartars, Green, Gold
Phone: (313) 577-7541
Fax: (313) 577-5997

Estimated # of Women's Volleyball Scholarships: N/A
Conference: Great Lakes Intercollegiate Athletic Conference

Western Michigan University
Academic Profile

217 Read Fieldhouse
Kalamazoo, MI 49008

Phone: 800-400-4968

Type: Public, 4 Yr., Coed
Website: http://www.wmich.edu
SAT/ACT/GPA: 900/18/2.5
Student/Faculty Ratio: Not Avai
Undergraduate Enrollment: 23,000
Scholarships/Academic: Yes   **Athletic:** Yes
Expenses By: Year   **In State:** $ Varies

Founded: 1903
Religion: Non-Affiliated
Housing: Yes
Male/Female: 60:40
Graduate Enrollment: 5,000
Financial Aid: Yes
Out of State: $ Varies

Specializes In: Business, Engineering, Education
Degrees Conferred: BA, BS, BFA, MA, MS, MFA, Ph.D.
Programs of Study: Business and Management, Business/Office and Marketing/Distribution, Communications, Education, Engineering, Parks/Recreation, Protective Services, Public Affairs, Fine Arts, Health & Human Services

Women's Athletic Profile

Read Fieldhouse
Kalamazoo, MI 49008-5134
Coach: Cathy George
Email: cathy.george@wmich.edu

NCAA I
Lady Broncos, Brown, Gold
Phone: (616) 387-3940
Fax: (616) 387-3668

Estimated # of Women's Volleyball Scholarships: N/A
Conference: Mid-American Conference

MINNESOTA

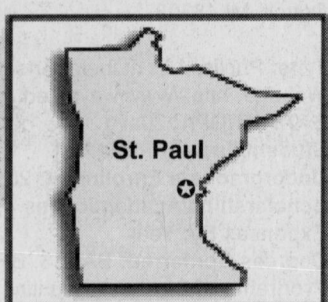

St. Paul

SCHOOL	CITY	AFFILIATION	PAGE
Augsburg College	Minneapolis	NCAA III	384
Bemidji State University	Bemidji	NCAA II	384
Bethel College	St. Paul	NCAA III	385
Carleton College	Northfield	NCAA III	386
College of St. Benedict	St. Joseph	NCAA III	386
College of St. Catherine	St. Paul	NCAA III	387
College of Saint Scholastica	Duluth	NCAA III/NAIA	387
Concordia College - Moorhead	Moorhead	NCAA III	388
Concordia University - Saint Paul	St. Paul	NAIA	388
Gustavus Adolphus College	St. Peter	NCAA III	389
Hamline University	St. Paul	NCAA III	390
Macalester College	St. Paul	NCAA III	390
Minnesota State University	Mankato	NCAA II	391
Martin Luther College	New Ulm	NCAA III, NAIA	392
Moorhead State University	Moorhead	NCAA II	392
Northwestern College	Roseville	NCCAA/NAIA	393
Saint Cloud State University	St. Cloud	NCAA II	393
Saint Mary's University	Winona	NCAA III	394
Saint Olaf College	Northfield	NCAA III	395
Southwest State University	Marshall	NCAA II	395
Univ of Minnesota-Twin Cities	Minneapolis	NCAA I	396
Univ of Minnesota - Crookston	Crookston	NCAA I	397
Univ of Minnesota - Duluth	Duluth	NCAA II	397
Univ of Minnesota - Morris	Morris	NCAA II	398
University of Saint Thomas	St. Paul	NCAA III	399
Winona State University	Winona	NCAA II	399

Augsburg College
Academic Profile

2211 Riverside Avenue
Minneapolis, MN 55454

Phone: (800) 788-5678

Type: Private, 4 Yr., Liberal Arts, Coed
Website: http://www.augsburg.edu
SAT/ACT/GPA: 950/20
Student/Faculty Ratio: 14:1
Undergraduate Enrollment: 1,550
Scholarships/Academic: Yes   **Athletic:** No
Expenses By: Year   **In State:** $ 20,490
Specializes In: Business, Education, Music Therapy
Degrees Conferred: BA, BS, MA, MSW, BM

Founded: 1869
Religion: ELCA Lutheran
Housing: Yes
Male/Female: 49:51
Graduate Enrollment: 1,292
Financial Aid: Yes
Out of State: $ 20,490.

Programs of Study: Accounting, Art, Biology, Business Administration, Central and East European Studies, Chemistry, Communications, Computer Science, East Asian Studies, Economics, Education, Engineering, English, Health Education, History, International Relations, Management Information Systems, Mathematics, Metro-Urban Studies, Modern Languages, Music, Nordic Area Studies, Nursing, Philosophy, Physical Education, Physician's Assistant, Physics, Political Science, Psychology, Religion, Russian, Social Work, Sociology, Theatre Arts, Trans-Disciplinary Women's Studies

Women's Athletic Profile

2211 Riverside, Campus Box 313 (Athletics) 145 SID
Minneapolis, MN 55454
Coach: Than Pham
Email: floridan@augsburg.edu

NCAA I
Lady Auggies, Maroon, Grey
Phone: (612) 330-1249
Fax: (612) 330-1372

Estimated # of Women's Volleyball Scholarships: N/A
Conference: Minnesota Intercollegiate Athletic Conference
Program Profile: We have a new Si Melby Hall fitness center rebuilt in 1993. It houses a gymnasium that has 2,800 seats, a health and fitness education program and the athletic department offices. We play on a hardwood floor surface.
History: The varsity program began in 1973. Our highest finishes in MIAC have been second (three times). Our overall record since 1973 is 438-476-10. Last year's 17-11 finish was our program's best since the 1985 school record of 32-16 campaign.
Achievements: Tasha Hamann: All-Minnesota Intercollegiate Athletic Conference Volleyball Team in 1998
Coaching: Than Pham is in his first year as Head Coach. He served as an Assistant Coach at Augsburg from 1994-1996. Marilyn Floridan is assistant coach. She was head coach from 1981-1998. Her career record is 271-366. Lisa Nos is Assistant Coach. She was a player here from 1994-1998.
Freshman Receiving Financial Aid/Academic: **Athletic:** 0
Roster In State: 15   **Out of State:** 2   **Out of Country:** 1
Sophomores on Team: 7   **Seniors on Team:** 2   **Graduation %:** 100
Most Recent Record: 17-11-0   **Fall Games:** 28   **Spring Games:** 0
Camp of Clinic Dates: None
Positions Needed: Setter, Middle Hitter
Schedule: St.Olaf, St.Benedict, Gustavus Adolphus, Bethel, St.Thomas, St. Mary's
Style of Play: Depends on the type of players we have on the team that year.

Bemidji State University
Academic Profile

1500 Birchmont Dr. NW
Bemidji, MN 56601

Phone: 800-475-2001

Type: Public, 4 Yr., Liberal Arts, Coed
Website: http://www.bemidji.msus.edu
SAT/ACT/GPA: 700/17
Student/Faculty Ratio: 11:1
Undergraduate Enrollment: 4,900
Scholarships/Academic: Yes   **Athletic:** Yes
Expenses By: Year   **In State:** $ 5,200
Degrees Conferred: AA, AS, BA, BS, BFA, MA, MS

Founded: 1919
Religion: Non-Affiliated
Housing: No
Male/Female: 1:2
Graduate Enrollment: 550
Financial Aid: Yes
Out of State: $ 7,600

Programs of Study: Accounting, Anthropology, Art, Biological, Broadcasting, Business, Chemistry, Communications, Community Services, Computer, Criminal Justice, Early Childhood, Earth Science, Economics, Education, English, Languages, Geography, Geology, Health, Journalism, Management, Medical, PreProfessional Programs, etc..

Women's Athletic Profile

1500 Birchmont Dr. NW
Bemidj, MN 56601
Coach: Donna Palivec
Email: dpalivec@bji.net

NCAA I
Lady Beavers, Green, White
Phone: (218) 755-2074
Fax: (218) 755-3898

Estimated # of Women's Volleyball Scholarships: equivalent to 3 full
Conference: Northern Sun Intercollegiate Conference
Program Profile: Preseason begins in mid-August, prior to the start of classes. When classes begin, practices are daily 3:30-6:00 pm in the fall. Fall season runs late August- Division II championships. Weight training begins after Thanksgiving and spring season is late February- May with 4 tournaments in the spring. Facility has a wood floor, main court for matches, 3 courts for practices.
History: Extramural program offered in 1967 & 1968. Women's intercollegiate volleyball program began in 1969. The program began as a part of the Minn-Kota conference then moved to the Northern Sun conference in 1979, and is presently a member of the 10 team conference. AIAW affiliation from 1971-1990 and then NAIA from 1982-1990 and from 1991 to the present, a member of NCAA Division II. Nine Minn-Kota conference championships and two 2nd place finishes in the Northern Sun conference.
Achievements: Past records have not been kept completely. Donna Palivec earned NSIC Coach of the Year in 1995.
Freshman Receiving Financial Aid/Academic: **Athletic:** 12
Roster In State: 12   **Out of State:** 0   **Out of Country:** 0
Sophomores on Team: **Seniors on Team:** 5   **Graduation %:**
Most Recent Record: 25-7
Positions Needed: Setter, Outside, Middle, Defensive Specialist
Schedule: Augustana, West Texas A & M, Nebraska-Omaha, Minnesota-Duluth all nationally ranked.
Style of Play: Team currently plays a 5-1 system with 3 person receive and defensive variations of the read and rotation defense. Philosophy of "Team" is a strong element of the program. Players support one another on and off the court and are expected to uphold the reputation, integrity, and responsibility of their commitment to Bemidji State University and the volleyball program.

Bethel College
Academic Profile

3900 Bethel Drive
St. Paul, MN 55112

Phone: (651) 638-6400

Type: Private, 4 Yr., Liberal Arts, Coed
Website: http://www.bethel.edu
SAT/ACT/GPA:
Student/Faculty Ratio:
Undergraduate Enrollment: 2,456
Scholarships/Academic: Yes   **Athletic:** No
Expenses By: Year   **In State:** $21,560

Founded: 1947
Religion: Baptist General Conference
Housing: Yes
Male/Female:
Graduate Enrollment: N/A
Financial Aid: Yes
Out of State: $21,560

Specializes In: Education, Sciences, Business
Degrees Conferred: BA, BS, BAEd, M.Ed.
Programs of Study: Has 67 different areas of study within 58 majors.

Women's Athletic Profile

3900 Bethel Drive
St. Paul, MN 55112
Coach: Andrew Palileo
Email: klodav@bethel.edu

NCAA I
Lady Royals, Royal Blue, Gold
Phone: (612) 638-6780
Fax: (612) 635-8645

Estimated # of Women's Volleyball Scholarships: N/A
Conference: Minnesota Intercollegiate Athletic Conference
Coaching: Andrew Palileo, Head Coach, is in his second year. He has coached volleyball for 10 years. He has developed and directed the Junior Olympic Programs at Waconia and Edina. Dave Johnson is Assistant Coach. He is also the head coach for Club Nike in Junior Olympic Volleyball.
Sophomores on Team: **Seniors on Team:**   **Graduation %:** 100
Most Recent Record: 15-6-1
Schedule: Wisconsin-Eau Claire, St. Olaf, St. Benedict, Hamline

Carleton College
Academic Profile

One North College Street
Northfield, MN 55057

Phone: 800-995-2275

Type: Private, 4 Yr., Liberal Arts, Coed
Website: http://www.carleton.edu
SAT/ACT/GPA: 25
Student/Faculty Ratio: 11:1
Undergraduate Enrollment: 1,800
Scholarships/Academic: N/A
Expenses By: Year
Specializes In: Liberal Arts
Degrees Conferred: BA

Founded: 1866
Religion: Non-Affiliated
Housing: Yes
Male/Female: 50:50
Graduate Enrollment: N/A
Athletic: No
Financial Aid: Yes
In State: $ 26,950
Out of State: $ 26,950

Programs of Study: African/African-American Studies, American Studies, Art & Art History, Asian Languages, Asian Studies, Biology, Chemistry, Classical Languages, Studies in Dance, East Asian Studies, Economics, Educational, Studies, English, ENTS, French, Geology, German, History, Latin American Studies, Math and Computer Science, Medieval Studies, Music, Philosophy, Physics and Astronomy, Political Science, Psychology, Religion, Russian, Sociology, Anthropology, Spanish, Theatre Arts, Women's Studies

Women's Athletic Profile

One N. College Street
Northfield, MN 55057
Coach: Elizabeth Jarnigan
Email: hluehman@carleton.edu

NCAA I
Lady Carls, Maize, Blue
Phone: (507) 646-4489
Fax: (507) 646-5550

Estimated # of Women's Volleyball Scholarships: N/A
Conference: Minnesota Intercollegiate Athletic Conference

College of Saint Benedict
Academic Profile

37 S. College Avenue
St. Joseph, MN 56374

Phone: (320) 363-5873

Type: Public, 4 Yr., Liberal Arts, Women Only
Website: http://www.csbsju.edu
SAT/ACT/GPA: Open
Student/Faculty Ratio: 13:1
Undergraduate Enrollment: 1,940
Scholarships/Academic: Yes
Expenses By: Year
Specializes In: Nursing, Medical Technology
Degrees Conferred: BA, BS in Nursing and Medical Technology

Founded: 1913
Religion: Catholic
Housing: Yes
Male/Female: All Female
Graduate Enrollment: N/A
Athletic: No
Financial Aid: Yes
In State: $ 21,466
Out of State: $21,466

Programs of Study: Accounting, Allied Health, Art, Biology, Business and Management, Chemistry, Classics, Communications, Computer Science, Dietetics, Economics, Elementary Education, English, Forestry, French, German, Government, History, Humanities, Latin, Liberal Studies, Management, Math, Medical Technology, Ministries, Music, Natural Science, Nursing, Nutrition, Occupational Therapy, Peace Studies, Pharmacy, Philosophy, Physical Therapy, Physics, Political Science, PreDentistry, PreEngineering, PreLaw, PreMed, PreVet, Psychology, Religion, Social Science, Social Work, Sociology, Spanish, Theatre, Theology, Teacher Education

Women's Athletic Profile

37 S. College Avenue
St. Joseph, MN 56374
Coach: Carol Howe-Veenstra
Email:

NCAA I
Lady Blazers, Red, White
Phone: (320) 363-5201
Fax: (320) 363-6098

Estimated # of Women's Volleyball Scholarships: N/A
Conference: Minnesota Intercollegiate Athletic Conference
History: Prior to 1997, few players on the CSB volleyball roster had ever experienced an NCAA tournament berth. None had been a part of a Conference title but all that has changed as the 1998 squad took to the floor in the fall.

Coaching: Carol Howe-Veenstra - Head Coach. She is a two-time Central Region Coach of the Year (1986 and 1990). She was MIAC Coach of the Year in 1989 and 1997 She is a member of the Minnesota High School League Coach Hall of Fame. Michelle Blaser is assistant coach. Michelle is the owner of the Play Hard Sports Camp, Inc. which conducts summer youth volleyball camps. Jill Beyer is assistant coach. She played volleyball at Saint Benedict.

Roster In State: 19	**Out of State:** 4	**Out of Country:** 0
Sophomores on Team: 8	**Seniors on Team:** 1	**Graduation %:** 100
Most Recent Record:	**Fall Games:** 30	**Spring Games:** 0

Schedule: University of California-San Diego, Emory-Georgia, St.Olaf, Central College-Iowa, Trinity-Texas
Style of Play: Team play. Stress communication skills and be aggressive.

College of Saint Catherine
Academic Profile

2004 Randolph Avenue
St. Paul, MN 55105

Phone: (651) 690-8850

Type: Private, 4 Yr., Liberal Arts, Women Only
Website: http://www.stkate.edu
SAT/ACT/GPA: 820+/19/2.0
Student/Faculty Ratio: 14:1
Undergraduate Enrollment: 2,470
Scholarships/Academic: Yes   **Athletic:** No
Expenses By: Year   **In State:** $ 19,000
Specializes In: Health Care

Founded: 1905
Religion: Catholic
Housing: Yes
Male/Female: Women Only
Graduate Enrollment: 589
Financial Aid: Yes
Out of State: $ 19,000

Degrees Conferred: Associate Degree and certificate programs in Health care
Programs of Study: Accounting, Art, Biology, Business Administration, Chemistry, Communications, Computer Science, Economics, Education, English, History, Hotel/Restaurant Management, International Business, Journalism, Management, Marketing, Mathematics, Medical Laboratory Technology, Music, Nursing, Pharmacy

Women's Athletic Profile

2004 Randolp Avenue
St. Paul, MN 55105
Coach: Richelle Wahi Reiff
Email: rmwahireiff@stkate.edu

NCAA I
Lady Wildcats, Purple, Gold
Phone: (612) 690-6082
Fax: (612) 690-8790

Estimated # of Women's Volleyball Scholarships: N/A
Conference: Minnesota Intercollegiate Athletic Conference

College of Saint Scholastica
Academic Profile

1200 Kenwood Avenue
Duluth, MN 55811

Phone: (218) 723-6000

Type: Private, 4 Yr., Liberal Arts, Coed
Website: http://www.css.edu
SAT/ACT/GPA: Open
Student/Faculty Ratio: 16:1
Undergraduate Enrollment: 1,200
Scholarships/Academic: Yes   **Athletic:** No
Expenses By: Year   **In State:** $ 15,420
Specializes In: Health Sciences

Founded: 1912
Religion: Roman Catholic
Housing: Yes
Male/Female: 30:70
Graduate Enrollment: 720
Financial Aid: Yes
Out of State: $ 15,420

Degrees Conferred: BA, BS, BSN, MSN, MA, MS
Programs of Study: Accounting, American Indian Studies, Art, Biology, Broadcasting, Business Administration, Chemistry, Communications, Computer Science, Clinical Laboratory Science, Economics, Education, English, History, Hotel/Restaurant Management, International Business, Journalism, Management, Marketing, Mathematics, Medical Laboratory Technology, Music, Nursing, Pharmacy, Photography, Physical Therapy, PreDentistry, PreLaw, PreMed, Psychology, Religion, Social Science, Theatre Art

Women's Athletic Profile

1200 Kenwood Avenue
Duluth, MN 55811
Coach: Dana Moore
Email: dmoore@css.edu

NCAA I
Lady Saints, Blue, Gold
Phone: (218) 723-6721
Fax: (218) 723-5958

Estimated # of Women's Volleyball Scholarships: N/A
Conference: Upper Midwest Athletic Conference
Program Profile: 2001-2002 will bring my Head Coaching into the 5th year. Finally feel established. Single gym with 3 hardwood courts, seating approx.1000. We play a fall traditional, as well as spring segment. Played most matches (43) in 2000 in NAIA Region III. Try to attend tournaments for more weekend play.
History: 1980's NJCAA Champs in 1983, 84, 88.
Achievements: Coach of the Year 1998, UMAC Conference title 1998, UMAC Conference tournament title 2000.
Roster In State: 12   **Out of State:** 1   **Out of Country:** 0
Sophomores on Team: **Seniors on Team:** 2   **Graduation %:** 100
Most Recent Record: 22-21
Camp of Clinic Dates: July 2,3,5,6
Schedule: Graceland University Tournament, Michigan Tech, Augustana, Univ. of WI Eau Claire.
Style of Play: Defensive oriented, want middle hitters to close a block, very fundamental and perimeter defense.

Concordia College - Moorhead
Academic Profile

901 South 8th Street
Moorhead, MN 56562

Phone: (218) 299-4434

Type: Private, 4 Yr., Liberal Arts, Coed
Website: http://www.cord.edu
SAT/ACT/GPA: 900+/20+
Student/Faculty Ratio: 15:1
Undergraduate Enrollment: 2,800
Scholarships/Academic: Yes   **Athletic:** No
Expenses By: Year   **In State:** $ 17,100
Specializes In: Education, Music, Sciences
Degrees Conferred: BA, BS

Founded: 1891
Religion: Lutheran
Housing: Yes
Male/Female: 1:2
Graduate Enrollment: N/A
Financial Aid: Yes
Out of State: $ 17,100

Programs of Study: Accounting, Advertising, Art, Biology, Broadcasting, Business & Management, Chemistry, Classics, Communications, Computer Science, Creative Writing, Criminal Justice, Music, History, Humanities, Physical Education, Mathematics, Nursing, Political Science, Philosophy, Political Science, Religion, Social Work, Sociology

Women's Athletic Profile

901 South 8th Street
Moorhead, MN 56562
Coach: Tim Mosser
Email: mosser@cord.edu

NCAA I
Lady Cobbers, Maroon, Gold
Phone: (218) 299-3520
Fax: (218) 299-4189

Estimated # of Women's Volleyball Scholarships: N/A
Conference: Minnesota Intercollegiate Athletic Conference

Concordia University - Saint Paul
Academic Profile

275 N. Syndicate
St. Paul, MN 55104

Phone: 800-656-5283

Type: Private, 4 Yr., Liberal Arts, Coed
Website: http://www.csp.edu
SAT/ACT/GPA: 17+
Student/Faculty Ratio: 17:1
Undergraduate Enrollment: 1,200
Scholarships/Academic: Yes   **Athletic:** No
Expenses By: Year   **In State:** $ 13,700
Degrees Conferred: AA, BA, MA

Founded: 1893
Religion: Lutheran
Housing: No
Male/Female: 45:55
Graduate Enrollment: 4
Financial Aid: Yes
Out of State: $ 13,700

Programs of Study: Accounting, Banking & Finance, Biblical Languages, Biology, Business Administration, Economics, Education, English, Environmental Science, Fine Arts, History, Languages, Literature, Management, Marketing, Mathematics, Music, Natural Science, Physical Science, PreLaw, PreMed, Psychology, Religion, Religious Education, Social Science, Speech Science

Women's Athletic Profile

275 N. Syndicate
St. Paul, MN 55104
Coach: Geoff Carlston
Email: carlston@csp.edu

NCAA I
Lady Comets, Navy, White
Phone: (651)603-6173
Fax: (612) 641-8787

Estimated # of Women's Volleyball Scholarships: N/A
Conference: UMAC

Gustavus Adolphus College
Academic Profile

800 W. College Avenue
St. Peter, MN 56083

Phone: 800-487-8288

Type: Private, 4 Yr., Liberal Arts, Coed
Website: http://www.gac.edu
SAT/ACT/GPA: 1100/27/3.6
Student/Faculty Ratio: 13:1
Undergraduate Enrollment: 2,300
Scholarships/Academic: Yes   **Athletic:** No
Expenses By: Year   **In State:** $ 21,800
Specializes In: Bachelor of Arts in 40 majors, Liberal Arts, PreProfessional Programs

Founded: 1862
Religion: ELCA (Lutheran)
Housing: Yes
Male/Female: 45:55
Graduate Enrollment: N/A
Financial Aid: Yes
Out of State: $ 21,800

Degrees Conferred: BA
Programs of Study: Accounting, Art, Athletic Training, Biology, Chemistry, Classics, Communications, Computer Science, Criminal Justice, Economics, Education, English, Environmental Studies, General Sciences, Geography, Geology, Health and Fitness, History, International Management, Management, Mathematics, Music, Nursing, Philosophy, Physical Education and Health, Physics, Physical Science, Political Science, Psychology, Religion, Sociology/Anthropology, Speech, Theatre. PreProfessional Programs: Actuarial Science, Architecture, Arts Administration, Church Vocations, Dentistry, Engineering, Law, Medicine, Ministry, Occupational Therapy, Optometry, Pharmacy, Physical Therapy, Veterinary Medicine

Women's Athletic Profile

800 College Avenue
St. Peter, MN 56082
Coach: Kari Eckheart
Email: keckheart@gac.edu

NCAA I
Lady Gusties, Black, Gold
Phone: (507) 933-7617
Fax: (507) 933-8412

Estimated # of Women's Volleyball Scholarships: N/A
Conference: Minnesota Intercollegiate Athletic Conference
Program Profile: The team arrives late August and we end sometime in November depending on how we do. We play at Lund Center which is a state-of-the-art athletic facility located on campus.
History: Our program began in 1968 under Head Coach Gretchen Koehler. Hoelhler was the head coach until 1996 and finished her career as the eighth winningest coach in the Division III history with a record of 548-353-0.
Achievements: 4 MIAC Titles; 4 NCAA Tournament Appearances in 16 years; Won 1984 MIAC Title to advance to the NCAA Elite Eight.
Coaching: Gretchen Koehler, was Head Coach, from 1968-1996. Her all-time record is 548-353-10. Kari Eckheart became our Head Coach in 1997. Her record here is 35-27. Shanda Ness is Assistant Coach.
Freshman Receiving Financial Aid/Academic: **Athletic:** 0
Roster In State: 15   **Out of State:** 3   **Out of Country:** 0
Sophomores on Team: 4   **Seniors on Team:** 3   **Graduation %:** 100
Most Recent Record: 15-13-0   **Fall Games:** 28   **Spring Games:** 0
Camp of Clinic Dates: August 2-3; August 4-5; Team Camp: August 6
Positions Needed: Defensive Specialist, Outside Hitter, Right Side Hitter
Schedule: Central, Saint Olaf, Saint Benedict, Saint Thomas, Macalester, River Falls
Style of Play: We are an up tempo type of team. We stress low passes on serve receive and during defense along with lower sets and a quick offense.

Hamline University
Academic Profile

1536 Hewitt Avenue
St. Paul, MN 55104

Phone: 800-753-9753

Type: Private, 4 Yr., Liberal Arts, Coed
Website: http://www.hamlin.edu
SAT/ACT/GPA: Open
Student/Faculty Ratio: 13:1
Undergraduate Enrollment: 1,709
Scholarships/Academic: Yes
Expenses By: Year
Specializes In: Preprofessional Programs

Athletic: No
In State: $ 21,941

Founded: 1854
Religion: Methodist
Housing: Yes
Male/Female: 37:63
Graduate Enrollment: 1,282
Financial Aid: Yes
Out of State: $ 21,941

Degrees Conferred: BA, MAPA, MFA, MAEd, JD, LLM, DPA, EdD
Programs of Study: Anthropology, Art, Art History, Biology, Chemistry, Communication Studies, Criminal Justice, East Asian Studies, Economics, Environmental Studies, International Studies, Latin American Studies, Legal Studies, Management, Mathematics, Musical Studies, Philosophy, Physical Education, Physics, Political Science, Psychology, Religion, Russian, Social Studies, Sociology, Spanish, Theater Arts, Urban Studies, Woman's Studies

Women's Athletic Profile

1536 Hewitt Ave
St. Paul, MN 55104-1284
Coach: Katharine Romme
Email: kromme@gw.hamline.edu

NCAA I
Lady Pipers, Scarlet, White
Phone: (651) 523-2331
Fax: (651) 523-2390

Estimated # of Women's Volleyball Scholarships: 0
Conference: Minnesota Intercollegiate Athletic Conference
Program Profile: Pre-season starts late August and our competitive season runs to the first weekend in November. We have a brand new floor for the 1999 season in Hutton Arena. There are three practice courts and a great match court.
History: Our program started in the 1980's. We have finished in the MIAC twice and just missed qualifying for regional both times.
Achievements: Coach of the Year in 1991 and 1994; 2 All-Region selection; 1 All-American Selections; numerous Academic Awards; rank nationally in team GPA many times.
Coaching: Katharine Romme, Head Coach, started at Hamline in 1991 and had seven years prior head coaching experience at the college level. Her overall coaching record is 295-300. Pam Aufderhar, Assistant Coach, was named All-Region and two-time All-Conference player.
Freshman Receiving Financial Aid/Academic:
Roster In State: 15
Sophomores on Team: 5
Most Recent Record: 12-24-0
Positions Needed: Setter, Middle Hitter

Out of State: 9
Seniors on Team: 3
Fall Games: 32

Athletic: 0
Out of Country: 0
Graduation %: 99
Spring Games: 0

Schedule: St. Benedict, University of Wisconsin-River Falls, St. Olaf, University of Wisconsin-Eau Claire
Style of Play: We play a scrappy and intense defense and work hard to run audible and quick tempo offense.

Macalester College
Academic Profile

1600 Grand Avenue
St. Paul, MN 55102

Phone: (651) 696-6467

Type: Private, 4 Yr., Liberal Arts, Coed
Website: http://www.macalester.edu
SAT/ACT/GPA: 1000/26/3.4
Student/Faculty Ratio: 10:1
Undergraduate Enrollment: 1,700
Scholarships/Academic: Yes
Expenses By: Year
Specializes In: Liberal Arts

Athletic: No
In State: $ 25,394

Founded: 1885
Religion: Presbyterian
Housing: Yes
Male/Female: 45:55
Graduate Enrollment: N/A
Financial Aid: Yes
Out of State: $ 25,394

Degrees Conferred: BA, BS
Programs of Study: Anthropology, Art, Biology, Chemistry, Classics, Communication Studies, Computer Science, Dance, Dramatic Arts, East Asian Studies, Economics, Education, English, Environmental Studies, French, Geography, Geology, German, History, Humanities, Individually Designed Major, International Studies, Japan Studies, Latin American Studies, Legal Studies, Linguistics, Mathematics, Music, NeuroScience, Philosophy, Physics, Political Science, Psychology, Religious Studies, Russian, Russian/Central and Eastern European Studies, Sociology, Spanish, Urban Studies, Women's Studies

Women's Athletic Profile

1600 Grand Avenue
St. Paul, MN 55105
Coach: Stephanie Schleuder
Email: schleuder@macalester.edu

NCAA I
Lady Scots, Blue, Orange
Phone: (651) 696-6467
Fax: (651) 696-6328

Estimated # of Women's Volleyball Scholarships: 0
Conference: Minnesota Intercollegiate Athletic Conference
Program Profile: We are members of the nationally recognized MIAC-one of the strongest Division III Conferences in the country. There are 12 women's teams in the Conference. We play in a newly remodeled gym, which has a 1,000 seating capacity. Our season runs from August 20 to the middle of November. We have a short off-season.
History: Our program began in the mid 1960's. We have won one Conference Championship. The program has been steadily improving in the past 3 years after it hit on several poor Conference finishes. In 1997, we finished 5th in the Conference. In 1998, we were 3rd in the Conference and ranked 7th in the NCAA Region.
Achievements: 1998-MIAC Conference Coach of the Year; 1998-2 All-Conference Players.
Coaching: Stephanie Schleuder started as head coach in 1998 and compiled a record of 19-10. From 1981 to 1995, she was Head Coach at the University of Minnesota. Her Division I career record is 580-295. She is in the Top 10 of Division III Coaches.
Freshman Receiving Financial Aid/Academic: **Athletic:** 0
Roster In State: 2 **Out of State:** 12 **Out of Country:** 1
Sophomores on Team: 0 **Seniors on Team:** 4 **Graduation %:** 99
Most Recent Record: 19-10-0 **Fall Games:** 28 **Spring Games:** 0
Camp of Clinic Dates: 3 weeks in July
Positions Needed: Middle Hitters, Setter
Schedule: Trinity-San Antonio, St. Ben's, St.Olaf, Wisconsin-La Crosse, Wisconsin-River Falls, Grinnell-Iowa
Style of Play: We have an aggressive offensive system, which is redesigned each year to take advantage of team strengths. Last year, we relied heavily on our quick middle attack. This year we will focus more on a swing offense designed for our strong outside hitters. The team has a strong net game and aggressive serving game.

Minnesota State University
Academic Profile

PO Box 8400
Mankato, MN 56002

Phone: (507) 389-2673

Type: Public, 4 Yr., Liberal Arts, Coed
Website: http://www.makato.msus.edu
SAT/ACT/GPA: 960/23
Student/Faculty Ratio: 20:1
Undergraduate Enrollment: 12,000
Scholarships/Academic: Yes **Athletic:** Yes
Expenses By: Year **In State:** $ 6,119
Founded: 1868
Religion: Non-Affiliated
Housing: Yes
Male/Female: 50:50
Graduate Enrollment: 3,000
Financial Aid: Yes
Out of State: $ 9,319
Specializes In: Accredited Business Program, top Nursing program, Elementary Education
Degrees Conferred: BA, BS, MS
Programs of Study: Over 150 degree programs: Business College including Marketing, Management, Accounting, Insurance; Education College including both Elementary and Secondary Education; Speech Pathology, Accredited undergraduates Athletic Training Program, PreMed, PreDental, PrePhysical Therapy, as well as all common Liberal Arts degree as English, History, Psychology, Sociology, etc.

Women's Athletic Profile

123 Highland Center
Mankato, MN 56001
Coach: Doug Tully
Email: douglas.twly@mankato.msus

NCAA I
Lady Mavericks, Purple, Gold
Phone: (507) 389-5570
Fax: (507) 389-2904

Estimated # of Women's Volleyball Scholarships: 8
Conference: North Central Collegiate Athletic Conference
Program Profile: We play in a top Conference. A new stadium will be completed in 2000. We have great community support. We are a broad based athletic department with 23 sports.
Achievements: In 1998, the team was ranked in the Top 25 National Rankings.

Coaching: Doug Tully, Head Coach, has just completed his first year. He had a very successful recruiting class for 1999. He was an assistant coach with Michigan State for 4 years. Carlene Pariseau is Assistant Coach.

Freshman Receiving Financial Aid/Academic: **Athletic:** 3

Roster In State: 6   **Out of State:** 6   **Out of Country:** 0

Sophomores on Team: **Seniors on Team:**   **Graduation %:** 95

Most Recent Record: 16-13-0   **Fall Games:** 30   **Spring Games:** 4

Camp of Clinic Dates: July 8-22

Style of Play: Very fast; movement style of offense.

Martin Luther College
Academic Profile

1995 Luther Ct.   **Phone:** (507) 354-8221
New Ulm, MN 56073

Type: Private, 4 year, Coed   **Founded:** 1995

Website: http://www.mlc.wels.edu   **Religion:** Wels Lutheran

SAT/ACT/GPA: Open   **Housing:** Yes

Student/Faculty Ratio: 10:1   **Male/Female:** 1:2

Undergraduate Enrollment: 600   **Graduate Enrollment:** 200

Scholarships/Academic: **Athletic:** No   **Financial Aid:** Yes

Expenses By: **In State:**   **Out of State:**

Specializes In: Wels Lutheran Teachers and Pastors

Degrees Conferred: BA

Programs of Study: Contact school for programs of study.

Women's Athletic Profile

1995 Luther Ct.   **NCAA I**

New Ulm, MN 56073   Lady Knights, Black, Red, White

Coach: Drew Buck   **Phone:** (507) 354-8221

Email: buckdm@mlc_wels.edu   **Fax:** (507) 354-2172

Estimated # of Women's Volleyball Scholarships: 0

Conference: Upper Midwest Athletic Conference

Coaching: Drew Buck, Head Coach, began coaching in 1983. He has an overall record of 311-26.

Freshman Receiving Financial Aid/Academic: **Athletic:** 0

Roster In State: 4   **Out of State:** 10   **Out of Country:** 0

Sophomores on Team: 0   **Seniors on Team:** 1   **Graduation %:** 100

Most Recent Record: 17-13-0

Moorhead State University
Academic Profile

1107 17th Street   **Phone:** 800-593-7246
Moorhead, MN 56563

Type: Public, 4 Yr., Liberal Arts, Coed   **Founded:** 1889

Website: http://www.moorhead.msus.edu   **Religion:** Non-Affiliated

SAT/ACT/GPA: 21   **Housing:** Yes

Student/Faculty Ratio: 18:1   **Male/Female:** 40:60

Undergraduate Enrollment: 6,000   **Graduate Enrollment:** 800

Scholarships/Academic: Yes   **Athletic:** Yes   **Financial Aid:** Yes

Expenses By: Year   **In State:** $ 5,800   **Out of State:** $ 8,500

Specializes In: Business, Education, Biology, Communications

Degrees Conferred: AA, AS, BA, BS, BFA, MA, MS, MBA

Programs of Study: Accounting, Anthropology, Advertising, Arts, Biology, Broadcasting, Chemistry, Communications, Computer Information Systems, Computer Science, Criminal Justice, Earth Science, Education, Economics, Finance, Fine Arts, Journalism, Marketing, Mathematics, Nursing, Physical Education, Political Science, Social Science, Physics, PreLaw, PreMed, Psychology, Therapy, Social Science

Women's Athletic Profile

17th St & 9th Avenue St.
Moorhead, MN 56563
Coach: Tammy Blake
Email: blake@mnstate.edu

NCAA I
Dragons, Red, Black, White
Phone: (218) 236-2321
Fax: (218) 299-5825

Estimated # of Women's Volleyball Scholarships: N/A
Conference: Northern Sun Intercollegiate Conference
Program Profile: Facility has been remodeled, brand new locker rooms.
History: We won the Conference this year 28-4 record. We were 3 games away from going to Nationals, in my 6 years here at MSUM we have been 2nd place 3 times in conference and 1 time conference champs.
Achievements: 2000 Coach of the Year, 2000 Jessica Bruns was Player of the Year.

Roster In State: 11   **Out of State:** 5   **Out of Country:**
Sophomores on Team: **Seniors on Team:** 5   **Graduation %:** 99
Most Recent Record: 28-4-0
Positions Needed: Outside, Setter, MB, RS
Schedule: North Dakota State, Nebraska Omaha, South Dakota State, Minnesota Duluth, Augustana, Lewis Chicago, University of North Dakota, St. Cloud State, South West State
Style of Play: Aggressive defense and strong middle attack.

Northwestern College
Academic Profile

3003 Snelling Avenue N.
St. Paul, MN 55113

Phone: 800-827-6827

Type: Private, 4 Yr., Liberal Arts, Coed
Website: http://www.nwc.edu
SAT/ACT/GPA: Open enrollment
Student/Faculty Ratio: 15:1
Undergraduate Enrollment: 1,350
Scholarships/Academic: Yes   **Athletic:** No
Expenses By: Year   **In State:** $ 18,690
Degrees Conferred: BA, BS, AA

Founded: 1902
Religion: Non-Denominational Christian
Housing: Yes
Male/Female: 1:3
Graduate Enrollment: N/A
Financial Aid: Yes
Out of State: $ 18,690

Programs of Study: Accounting, Adult/Continuing Education, Agriculture, Art, Bible Studies, Broadcasting, Business & Management, Communications, Computer Information Systems, Education, Elementary Education, English, Finance, Fine Arts, Graphic Arts, Human Resources, International Business, Journalism, Liberal Arts, Literature, Marketing, Mathematics, Ministries, Music, Physical Education, PreEngineering, Psychology, Science, Social Science, Theatre, Theology

Women's Athletic Profile

3003 N. Snelling Avenue
Roseville, MN 55113
Coach: Jill Peterson
Email:

NCAA I
Lady Eagles, Purple, Gold
Phone: (651) 631-5219
Fax: (651) 628-3350

Did Not Return Profile

Saint Cloud State University
Academic Profile

701 4th Avenue South
St. Cloud, MN 56301

Phone: (320) 255-3041

Type: Public, 4 Yr., Liberal Arts, Coed
Website: http://www.stcloudstate.edu
SAT/ACT/GPA: 1000/25
Student/Faculty Ratio: 15:1
Undergraduate Enrollment: 1500
Scholarships/Academic: Yes   **Athletic:** Yes
Expenses By: Year   **In State:** $ 6,000

Founded: 1869
Religion: Non-Affiliated
Housing: Yes
Male/Female: 46:53
Graduate Enrollment: 2500
Financial Aid: Yes
Out of State: $ 8.400

Degrees Conferred: BA, BS
Programs of Study: Accounting, Advertising, Anthropology, Arts, Banking/Finance, Biological Science, Broadcasting, Business Administration, Chemistry, Earth Science, Elective Studies, Geography, International Business & Relations, Journalism, PreProfessional Programs, Psychology, *** contact school for more information.

Women's Athletic Profile

701 4th St. South
St. Cloud, MN 56301
Coach: Dianne Glowatzke
Email:

NCAA I
Lady Huskies, Red, Black
Phone: (320) 255-3141
Fax: (320) 255-9442

Estimated # of Women's Volleyball Scholarships: 2
Conference: North Central Collegiate Athletic Conference
Program Profile: Our facilities contain 3 wooden courts.
History: We started in 1969. Our overall record is 589-381.
Achievements: Diane Glowatzke-North Central Region Coach of the Year; 1995 North Central Coach of the Year in 1985. Four NCAA Regional.
Coaching: Dianne Glowatzke, Head Coach, has been a coach for 22 years. She has over 500 wins.
Freshman Receiving Financial Aid/Academic: **Athletic:** 2
Roster In State: 12   **Out of State:** 0   **Out of Country:** 0
Sophomores on Team: 4   **Seniors on Team:** 1   **Graduation %:** 98
Most Recent Record: 16-13-0   **Fall Games:** 29   **Spring Games:** 4 tournaments
Camp of Clinic Dates: June 13-17
Positions Needed: Setter, Middle
Schedule: North Dakota State, Augustana, South Dakota State, Northern Michigan, Northern Colorado, Univ of Minnesota-Duluth
Style of Play: 5-1, 1 and 2 tempo.

Saint Mary's University - Minnesota
Academic Profile

700 Terrace Ht.. #49
Winona, MN 55987

Phone: (507) 457-1583

Type: Private, 4 Yr., Liberal Arts, Coed
Website: http://www.smumn.edu
SAT/ACT/GPA: 21/3.1
Student/Faculty Ratio: 13:1
Undergraduate Enrollment: 1,300
Scholarships/Academic: Yes   **Athletic:** No
Expenses By: Year   **In State:** $ 18,000
Specializes In: Education, Business, Psychology
Degrees Conferred: BA, BS

Founded: 1912
Religion: Catholic
Housing: Yes
Male/Female: 50:50
Graduate Enrollment: 100
Financial Aid: Yes
Out of State: $ 18,000

Programs of Study: Accounting, Art, Graphic Design, Art Studio, Biology, Chemistry, Computer Science, Criminal Justice, Electronic Publishing, Elementary Education, English Education, French, History, Life Science, Marketing, Mathematics, Mathematics Education, Music Merchandising, Philosophy, Physics, Political Science, Social Science, Sociology, Theatre, Theatre Education, Theology, PreProfessional Programs

Women's Athletic Profile

700 Terrace Heights #62
Winona, MN 55987
Coach: Mike Lester
Email:

NCAA I
Lady Cardinals, Red, White
Phone: (507) 457-6954
Fax: (507) 457-1439

Estimated # of Women's Volleyball Scholarships: N/A
Conference: MIAC
Program Profile: Matches are played in the SNU Fieldhouse, which seats about 1,000 fans. Our playing season runs approximately 2 1/2 months.
History: St. Mary's Volleyball program has been on the move in the MIAC and NCAA over the last three years and should continue this improvement.

Coaching: Mike Lester, Head Coach, compiled a record in 1999 of 17-16. He played at University of Nebraska-Kearney in 1996, where team went to first ever NCAA II elite Eight. He was named 2-time All-American at Graceland College in 1992,1994. Corey Phelps is our Assistant Coach.

Roster In State: 17   **Out of State:** 10   **Out of Country:** 0

Sophomores on Team: 0   **Seniors on Team:** 1   **Graduation %:** 99.9

Most Recent Record: 17-16-0

Camp of Clinic Dates: August

Positions Needed: Outside Hitters, Middle Hitters

Schedule: St. Olaf, St. Benedict, UW-Lacrosse, Winona State University, UW-Oshkosh, UW-River Falls

Style of Play: Our style of play is one of quickness and aggressiveness. The offense is reliant on our exceptional serve-receive, which leads to our quick attacking offense. We focused on our middle attack. This leads to the isolation of our outside hitters.

Saint Olaf College
Academic Profile

1520 St. Olaf Avenue
Northfield, MN 55057

Phone: 800-800-3025

Type: Private, 4 Yr., Coed   **Founded:** 1874

Website: http://www.stolaf.edu   **Religion:** Lutheran

SAT/ACT/GPA: 25   **Housing:** Yes

Student/Faculty Ratio: 11:1   **Male/Female:** 2.4:3

Undergraduate Enrollment: 2,888   **Graduate Enrollment:** N/A

Scholarships/Academic: Yes   **Athletic:** No   **Financial Aid:** Yes

Expenses By: year   **In State:** $ 15,000   **Out of State:** $ 15,000

Degrees Conferred: BA, BS, BM

Programs of Study: Art, Art History, Asian Studies, Biology, Chemistry, Classic, Dance, Economics, English, Fine Arts, French, Mathematics, Music, Nursing, Physical Education, Physics, Political Science, Philosophy, PreLaw, PreMed, PreDentistry, Religion, Psychology, Social Studies, Social Work

Women's Athletic Profile

1520 Street Avenue
Northfield, MN 55057
Coach: Cindy Brook
Email:

NCAA I
Oles, Black, Gold
Phone: (507) 646-3255
Fax: (507) 646-3572

Estimated # of Women's Volleyball Scholarships: N/A

Conference: Minnesota Intercollegiate Athletic Conference

Program Profile: We play in gymnasium at Skoglund Center on St. Olaf campus. It has a seating capacity of 3,500. Our season runs from early September to mid-November.

History: Program began in 1973 and has reached a point of conference dominance here in the 1990's.

Achievements: We were 1993, 1994, 1995 & 1996 MIAC Champions; 6 consecutive years NCAA Playoffs; Central Region Champs in 1994, 1995 & 1996; 6 consecutive years MIAC Player of the Year, 3rd place NCAA Champions in 1996.

Coaching: Cindy Brook, Head Coach, started coaching the program in 1991. She compiled a record of 231-67 at St. Olaf. Previously had been at Kent State and Bethel College. Lori Littleton and Kathy Thompson are the Assistant Coaches.

Freshman Receiving Financial Aid/Academic: **Athletic:** 0

Roster In State: 9   **Out of State:** 4   **Out of Country:** 0

Sophomores on Team: 0   **Seniors on Team:** 1   **Graduation %:** 100

Most Recent Record: 25-8-0   **Fall Games:** 25+   **Spring Games:** 0

Camp of Clinic Dates: Summer

Schedule: Central College, Nebraska Wesleyan, Trinity-TX, St. Ben's, UW-Eau Claire, Wartburg, UW-River Falls

Style of Play: Fast paced attack with rock-solid defense.

Southwest State University
Academic Profile

1501 State Street
Marshall, MN 56258

Phone: (507) 537-7021

Type: Public, 4 Yr., Liberal Arts, Coed   **Founded:** 1967

Website: http://www.southwest.com   **Religion:** Non-Affiliated

SAT/ACT/GPA: 21/2.5   **Housing:** Yes

Student/Faculty Ratio: 18:1
Undergraduate Enrollment: 3,000
Scholarships/Academic: Yes   **Athletic:** Yes
Expenses By: Year   **In State:** $ 6,966
Specializes In: Liberal Arts
Male/Female: 40:60
Graduate Enrollment: 300
Financial Aid: Yes
Out of State: $ 10,284

Degrees Conferred: BA, BS, AS, MA, M.Ed.
Programs of Study: Accounting, AgriBusiness Management, Agronomy, Anthropology, Applied Technology, Art, Art Education, Art Graphic, Biology, Biology Education, Business Administration, International Business, Management, Chemistry, Chemistry Education, Computer Science, Criminal Justice, Early Childhood Education, Elementary Education, English Education, History, Literature, Marketing, Mathematics, Teaching, Music, Music Education, Philosophy, Physical Education, Physical Science, Political Science, Psychology, Radio & TV, Restaurant Administration, Sociology, Spanish, Speech Communications, Secondary Education, Theatre Arts, Graduate Programs (Master of Science in Education, Master of Science in Business Management), PreProfessional Programs

Women's Athletic Profile

1501 State Street
Marshall, MN 56258
Coach: Deb Denbeck
Email: KC06@a1.swt.edu

NCAA I
Golden Mustangs, Gold, Brown
Phone: (507) 537-7271
Fax: (507) 537-6578

Estimated # of Women's Volleyball Scholarships: 6
Conference: Northern Sun Intercollegiate Conference
Program Profile: Our team plays in two campus facilities. R/A facility has 4,000 seats. The P.E Gym has 2,000 seats.
History: We started in 1971. Our all-time record is 489-496-9.
Achievements: Named 1983 Nebraska College Coach of the Year while at College of St. Mary's.
Coaching: Deb Denbeck started as Head Coach in 1986. Her record in 13 years here is 235-292. Her career record of 17 years at SSU and St.Mary's (NE) is 336-352.
Freshman Receiving Financial Aid/Academic: N/A   **Athletic:** N/A
Roster In State: 10   **Out of State:** 7   **Out of Country:** 0
Sophomores on Team: 0   **Seniors on Team:** 3   **Graduation %:** Unknown
Most Recent Record: 13-19-0
Schedule: North Dakota State, Nebraska-Omaha, Augustana-SD, Minnesota-Duluth, South Dakota State, Minnesota State-Mankato

University of Minnesota - Twin Cities
Academic Profile

516 15th Avenue S.E.
Minneapolis, MN 55455-0101

Phone: 800-752-1000

Type: Public, 4 Yr., Coed
Website: http://www.umn.edu
SAT/ACT/GPA: Sliding Scale
Student/Faculty Ratio: 25:1
Undergraduate Enrollment: 24,000
Scholarships/Academic: Yes   **Athletic:** Yes
Expenses By: Year   **In State:** $ 9,719
Founded: 1851
Religion: Non-Affiliated
Housing: Yes
Male/Female: 1:1
Graduate Enrollment: 14,000
Financial Aid: Yes
Out of State: $ 17,680

Degrees Conferred: BA, BS, MA, MS, MBA, DMD, JD
Programs of Study: Liberal Arts, PreMed, Medical/Dental, Veterinary Med., Agriculture, Management, Engineering, Forestry, Teaching, Pharmacy, Physical Therapy, Kinesiology, Housing Design, Social Work, Nutrition, Biology, and over 200 undergraduates.

Women's Athletic Profile

516 15th Ave SE
Minneapolis, MN 55455
Coach: Dr. Mike Hebert
Email: batie001@tc.umn.edu

NCAA I
Lady Gophers, Maroon, Gold
Phone: 612-624-6533
Fax: 612-626-0020

Estimated # of Women's Volleyball Scholarships: 2
Conference: Big 10 Conference
Program Profile: We play at the Sports Pavilion which is known throughout the volleyball community as the "Taj Mahal" of volleyball. When the $41 million dollar renovation was completed, the Sports Pavilion will set a precedent for women's facilities around the nation. In only the third year for the current staff, the attendance figures continue to hold among the nation's best in response to the winning ways and style of the Gopher team.

History: Minnesota has won 65% of its volleyball matches since the program began in 1972. The Gophers have qualified for four NCAA tournaments including two in the past three years. Minnesota has advanced to the "Sweet 16" twice in school history and has a 5-4 record in NCAA tournament play.

Achievements: Minnesota's first first-team NCAA All-American in 1996: Katrien DeDecker; 14 All-District awards; 1 All-Big Ten Selection: Nicole Branagh in 1998.

Coaching: Dr. Mike Hebert, Head Coach, enters his fourth season at Minnesota with a record of 64-35 (.646). Dr. Mike Hebert has a career record of 636-292 (.685) making him one of the winningest volleyball coaches in the nation. He has also coached in 14 NCAA Tournaments, two NCAA Final Fours, and four Big Ten titles. Nuarice Batie and Nao Ikeda are Assistant Coaches.

Freshman Receiving Financial Aid/Academic: **Athletic:** 1

Roster In State: 7   **Out of State:** 7   **Out of Country:** 2

Sophomores on Team: 0   **Seniors on Team:** 2   **Graduation %:** Unknown

Most Recent Record: 17-14-0   **Fall Games:** 31   **Spring Games:** 11

Camp of Clinic Dates: General Skills, Setter, Middle Blocker: 7/20-7/23; General Skills, High Potential:7/24-7/27

Positions Needed: Setter, Outside Hitters, Middle

Schedule: Penn State, Hawaii, UCLA, Wisconsin, Ohio State, Michigan State, Illinois

Style of Play: Coach Hebert's teams are always known for their high level of ball control and ability to play defense. Hebert is one of the most innovative and technically sound coaches in the collegiate game.

University of Minnesota - Crookston
Academic Profile

Sport Center
Crookston, MN 56716

Phone: 218-281-8569

Type: 4 Yr., Coed   **Founded:** 1966

Website: http://www.crk.umn.edu   **Religion:** Non-Affiliated

SAT/ACT/GPA: Open   **Housing:** Yes

Student/Faculty Ratio: 11:1   **Male/Female:** Not Available

Undergraduate Enrollment: 937   **Graduate Enrollment:** 937

Scholarships/Academic: **Athletic:**   **Financial Aid:** Yes

Expenses By: Year   **In State:** $ 3,114+   **Out of State:** $ 8,835+

Degrees Conferred: Bachelors

Programs of Study: Accounting, Agriculture, Animal Science, Aviation, Business Administration, Biology, Computer Information Systems, Environmental Studies, Liberal Arts, General Studies, Food Services, Management, Natural Sciences, Flight Training, Retail Management, Soil Conservation

Women's Athletic Profile

2900 University Avenue
Crookston, MN 56716
Coach: Kelly Hollands
Email: kholland@mail.crk.umn.edu

NCAA I
Lady Golden Eagles,
Phone: (218) 281-6510
Fax: (218) 281-8430

Estimated # of Women's Volleyball Scholarships: N/A

Program Profile: Our program is in a rebuilding period. We are working on a foundation from which we can build a solid competitive program

History: Kelly Hollands is the sixth coach in the University of Minnesota volleyball 20 year history.

Achievements: Jody Lundbohm was one of the top setters in the NDCAC in 1998.

Coaching: Kelly Hollands, Head Coach, has been coaching here since 1994. Larry Woodbridge is Assistant Coach.

Style of Play: We appeal to the athlete's senses and blend the physical skills with the mental aspects of the game.

University of Minnesota - Duluth
Academic Profile

10 University Drive
Duluth, MN 55812

Phone: (218) 726-8000

Type: Public, 4 Yr., Liberal Arts, Coed   **Founded:** 1947

Website: http://www.umn.edu   **Religion:** Non-Affiliated

SAT/ACT/GPA: 820/19   **Housing:** Yes

Student/Faculty Ratio: 19:1   **Male/Female:** 52:48

Undergraduate Enrollment: 7,100   **Graduate Enrollment:** 310

Scholarships/Academic: Yes   **Athletic:** Yes   **Financial Aid:** Yes

Expenses By: Year   **In State:** $ 9,868   **Out of State:** $ 17,848
Specializes In: Business, Education, Engineering
Degrees Conferred: AA, AS, BA, BS, BAA, BAS, BM, MA, MS, MBA
Programs of Study: Accounting, American Studies, Anthropology, Applied Sciences, Biological Science, Business Administration, Chemistry, Communications, Computer, Criminology, Dramatic Arts, Early Childhood Education, Earth Science, Economics, Education, Engineering, English, Fine Arts, Geography, Geology, History, Liberal Arts, Mathematics, Music, Philosophy, Physics, Political Science, Psychology, Speech, Women's Studies

Women's Athletic Profile

10 University Drive
Duluth, MN 55812-2496
Coach: Patti Rolf
Email: prolf2@d.umn.edu

NCAA I
Lady Bulldogs, Maroon, Gold
Phone: (218) 726-8000
Fax: (218) 726-7146

Estimated # of Women's Volleyball Scholarships: 4
Conference: Northern Sun Intercollegiate Conference
Program Profile: We play at Romano Gymnasium, which seats 2,759. The University of Minnesota is a Division II School which plays a 20-25 game schedule.
History: Records before 1976 are unavailable. The program was led by former Head Coach and current UMD Women's Athletic Coordinator, Linda Larson. Larson led the team from 1976 to 1981. Her overall record was 278-57. She led the Bulldogs to 3 AIAW National Tournament appearances. In 1980, UMD placed 5th at the A IAW Division II National Championships. Larson helped the Bulldogs to 3 Northern Sun Intercollegiate Conference Championships and had 3 Bulldogs named to the NSIC All-Conference Team.
Achievements: 10 NSIC Championships; 3 NCAA Division II playoff appearances; 9 AVCA All-North Central Region players, 22 All-NSIC selections; 6 NSIC Most Valuable Players; Middle Hitter, Jodi Jose was AVCA All-American; NSIC Coach of the Year 4 times.
Coaching: Patti Rolf, Head Coach, started here in 1988 after playing at North Dakota State where she was a 4 year letter winner. She was All-Region and All-NCC while at North Dakota State. Her overall record is 249-146. Her teams have 10 NSIC Titles, 3 Appearances in NCAA Division II and went to three Regional Tournaments (1991,1994,1998). Anita Hanson is Assistant Coach.
Freshman Receiving Financial Aid/Academic: **Athletic:** 1
Roster In State: 12   **Out of State:** 1   **Out of Country:** 0
Sophomores on Team: 0   **Seniors on Team:** 4   **Graduation %:** 100
Most Recent Record: 21-7-0   **Fall Games:** 27   **Spring Games:** 4
Camp of Clinic Dates: Grades 7-9, July 11-14; Grades 9-12, July 25-28; Team Camp July 16-18
Positions Needed: Middle Hitters
Schedule: North Dakota State, Northern Michigan, University of Nebraska-Omaha, Barry, Minnesota State-Mankato
Style of Play: UMD Volleyball is known for its emphasis on the fundamentals of consistent ball control, solid defense and strong play at the net. The offense revolves around an athletic setter who can set all attacks from any position on the court.

University of Minnesota - Morris
Academic Profile

E. 2nd St.
Morris, MN 56267

Phone: 320-589-6035

Type: Public, 4 Yr., Liberal Arts, Coed
Website: http://www.mrs.umn.edu
SAT/ACT/GPA: 820/17min
Student/Faculty Ratio: 15:1
Undergraduate Enrollment: 1,933
Scholarships/Academic: Yes
Expenses By: Year
Degrees Conferred: BA
Programs of Study: Contact school for program of study.

Founded: 1959
Religion: Non-Affiliated
Housing: No
Male/Female: 45:55
Graduate Enrollment: N/A
Financial Aid: Yes
Out of State: $ 15,000

Athletic: No
In State: $ 8,000

Women's Athletic Profile

E. 2nd Street
Morris, MN 56267
Coach: Heather Pennie
Email: penniehl@mrs.umn.edu

NCAA I
Lady Cougars, Maroon, Gold
Phone: (320) 589-64291
Fax: (320) 589-6428

Estimated # of Women's Volleyball Scholarships: N/A
Conference: Northern Sun Intercollegiate Conference

University of Saint Thomas
Academic Profile

2115 Summit Avenue
St. Paul, MN 55105

Phone: 800-752-1000

Type: Private, 4 Yr., Liberal Arts, Coed
Website: http://www.stthomas.edu
SAT/ACT/GPA: 800/20
Student/Faculty Ratio: 17:1
Undergraduate Enrollment: 5,000
Scholarships/Academic: Yes   **Athletic:** No
Expenses By: Year   **In State:** $ 16,800
Degrees Conferred: BA, MA, MS, MBA, EdD, Mdiv

Founded: 1885
Religion: Catholic
Housing: No
Male/Female: 50:50
Graduate Enrollment: 5,000
Financial Aid: Yes
Out of State: $ 16,800

Programs of Study: Accounting, Advertising, Art History, Asian Studies, Banking & Finance, Biology, Broadcasting, Business Administration, Chemistry, Communications, Computer Science, Criminal Justice, Dramatic Arts, Education, English, French, Geography, Geology, German, History, International Business, Journalism, Latin, Literature, Management, Marketing, Mathematics, Music, Philosophy, Psychology, Public Relations, Public Administration, Russian, Social Science, Spanish, Speech, Telecommunications, Theology, Urban Studies

Women's Athletic Profile

2115 Summit Avenue
St. Paul, MN 55105
Coach: Penny Thompson
Email: cvtallmann@st.thomas University

NCAA I
Lady Tommies, Purple, Grey
Phone: (612) 962-5912
Fax: (612) 962-5910

Estimated # of Women's Volleyball Scholarships: N/A
Conference: Minnesota Intercollegiate Athletic Conference
Program Profile: Integral part of one of the nation's most successful NCAA Division III athletic programs in the country. On campus facilities include 2 swimming pools, a fieldhouse, and gymnasium space for 10 indoor volleyball courts. Intercollegiate matches are played in the 2,500 seat Shoenecker Arena.
History: St. Thomas Volleyball has enjoyed 21 years of success. with an overall record of 408-270 and six NCAA tournament playoff appearances since 1978, has had an impact on both the regional and national levels. Since joining the Minnesota Intercollegiate Athletic Conference in 1984, St. Thomas has finished either first or second eight times.
Achievements: See history.
Coaching: Cole Tallman, Head Coach, have generated an overall collegiate record of 474-141 prior to coming to St. Thomas in 1999. In 1998 ranked 9th among NCAA Division I coaches in career winning percentage and 18th in total career wins. During that time, he coached nine volleyball All-Americans and 2 Academic All-Americans including a GTE first team member in 1996. Other honors produced by his teams included 13 conference, regional or district Coach of the Year awards.
Roster In State: 60%   **Out of State:** 40%   **Out of Country:** 0
Sophomores on Team: 0   **Seniors on Team:** 5   **Graduation %:** 100
Most Recent Record: 16-14-0
Camp of Clinic Dates: July 13-16, 27-30; August 2-6, 2000
Style of Play: St. Thomas Volleyball's success will continue to be based a coaching philosophy with a premium on solid preparation, multi faceted players, intimidating defense and blocking schemes, and a share the wealth multiple offense run at a tempo faster than all but a few teams in the country. Nine previous All-Americans have ranged from 6 "3" to 5 "4" in height. Backgrounds have included multi sports stars, athletes with limited volleyball experience, and club volleyball "lifers" tired of having an adult with maturity problems telling them they cannot go to Prom and/or have realized the benefits of playing in college for someone who cares about their academic success more than their ability to side out.

Winona State University
Academic Profile

PO Box 5838
Winona, MN 55987

Phone: 800-342-5978

Type: Public, 4 Yr., Liberal Arts, Coed
Website: http://www.winona.msus.edu
SAT/ACT/GPA: 700/21/2.50
Student/Faculty Ratio: 21:1
Undergraduate Enrollment: 6,500
Scholarships/Academic: Yes   **Athletic:** Yes
Expenses By: Year   **In State:** $ 6,500

Founded: 1858
Religion: Non-Affiliated
Housing: No
Male/Female: 42:58
Graduate Enrollment: 500
Financial Aid: Yes
Out of State: $ 9,800

Specializes In: 80 Different undergraduate programs
Degrees Conferred: BA, BS
Programs of Study: Accounting, Administrative Information Systems, Advertising, Art, Athletic Training, Biology, Broadcasting, Business Administration, Chemistry, Communication Studies, Comparative Material Engineering, Computer Science, Criminal Justice, CytoTechnology, Early Childhood Education, Economics, Elementary Education, English, Exercise Science, Finance, French, GeoScience, German, Health Care Management, History, Human Resource Management, Journalism, Management Information Systems, Marketing, Mass Communications, Cardiac Rehab, Mathematics, Medical Technology, Middle School Education, Music, Nursing, Paralegal, Physical Education, Physics, Political Science, Psychology, Recreation & Leisure Studies, Sociology, Spanish, Special Education, Speech/Theatre, Statistics, PreDentistry, Pre-Engineering, PreLaw, PreMed.

Women's Athletic Profile

P.O. Box 5838
Winona, MN 55987
Coach: Amy Fisher
Email: afisher@winona.msus.edu

NCAA I
Lady Warriors, Purple, White
Phone: (507) 457-5204
Fax: (507) 457-5479

Estimated # of Women's Volleyball Scholarships: Partials
Conference: Northern Sun Intercollegiate Conference
Program Profile: We compete in NCAA II in the prestigious North Central Region. Our gym has a seating capacity of 5, 000 and wooden floors. We have a new Wellness Fitness Center, and a strength training coach. Full year program with spring practices.
History: Program began in mid 70's. Started in the NAIA and then made transition to NCAA in 1995.
Achievements: 15 All-Conference Players, 25 All-Academic, 1 All-Region
Coaching: Head Coach Amy Fisher. Assistant Coach Christa Matter
Freshman Receiving Financial Aid/Academic: **Athletic:** 5
Roster In State: 7   **Out of State:** 7   **Out of Country:** 0
Sophomores on Team: **Seniors on Team:** 2   **Graduation %:** 90-100
Most Recent Record: 6-27-0
Camp of Clinic Dates: In June
Positions Needed: Middle Hitters, Outside Hitters
Schedule: Augustana, North Dakota State, Nebraska-Omaha, Rockhurst, UM-Duluth, South Dakota State, Moorhead State, Southwest State, Wayne State, North Dakota
Style of Play: Typically run a 5-1. Like to play a quick offense with middle hitters dominating, audible offense hitters can hit any type of set and good blocking.

MISSISSIPPI

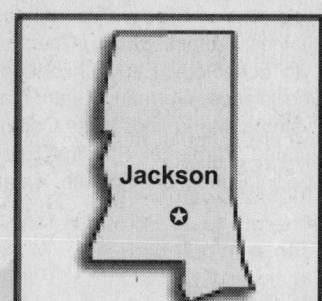

Jackson

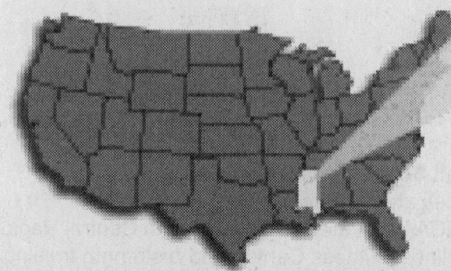

SCHOOL	CITY	AFFILIATION	PAGE
Alcorn State University	Lorman	NCAA I	402
Belhaven College	Jackson	NAIA	402
Jackson State University	Jackson	NCAA I	402
Millsaps College	Jackson	NCAA III	403
Mississippi College	Clinton	NCAA III	404
Mississippi State University	Mississippi State	NCAA I	404
Mississippi University for Women	Columbus	NCAA II	405
Mississippi Valley State University	Itta Bena	NCAA I	405
Rust College	Holly Springs	NCAA III	406
University of Mississippi	University	NCAA I	406
University of Southern Mississippi	Hattiesburg	NCAA I	407

Alcorn State University
Academic Profile

1000 ASU Dr., #510
Lorman, MS 39096

Phone: 800-222-6790

Type: 4 Yr., Coed
Website: http://www.alcorn.edu
SAT/ACT/GPA: Open
Student/Faculty Ratio:
Undergraduate Enrollment: N/A
Scholarships/Academic:
Expenses By: Year
Degrees Conferred:
Programs of Study: General Studies

Athletic:
In State:

Founded:
Religion: Non-Affiliated
Housing: No
Male/Female:
Graduate Enrollment: N/A
Financial Aid:
Out of State:

Women's Athletic Profile

100 ASU Drive, #510
Lorman, MS 39096-9402
Coach: Nate Kilbert
Email:

NCAA I
Lady Braves, Purple, Old Gold
Phone: (601) 877-6667
Fax: (601) 877-3821

Did Not Return Profile

Belhaven College
Academic Profile

1500 Peachtree St.
Jackson, MS 39202

Phone: 800-960-5940

Type: Private, 4 Yr., Liberal Arts, Coed
Website: http://www.belhaven.edu
SAT/ACT/GPA: 960/20/2.0
Student/Faculty Ratio: 18:1
Undergraduate Enrollment: 1,300
Scholarships/Academic: Yes
Expenses By: Year
Degrees Conferred: BA, BS, BM
Programs of Study: Accounting, Art, Biblical Studies, Biology, Business Administration, Chemistry, Combined Science, Computer Information Systems, Computer Science, Dance, Elementary Education, English, History, Humanities, Mathematics, Music, Philosophy, Sports Administration, Sports Medicine, Sports Ministry, PreLaw, PreMed, Psychology

Athletic: Yes
In State: $ 7,025

Founded: 1883
Religion: Presbyterian
Housing: Yes
Male/Female: 1:2.5
Graduate Enrollment: 100
Financial Aid: Yes
Out of State: $ 7,025

Women's Athletic Profile

1500 Peachtree Street
Jackson, MS 39202
Coach: Judy Chance
Email: jchance@belhaven.edu

NCAA I
Lady Blazers, Green, Gold
Phone: (601) 968-8842
Fax: (601) 968-5953

Did Not Return Profile

Jackson State University
Academic Profile

1325 W Lynch Street
Jackson, MS 39217

Phone: 800-848-6817

Type: Public, 4 Yr., Coed
Website: http://www.jsums.edu
SAT/ACT/GPA: 700avg/17avg
Student/Faculty Ratio: 17:1
Undergraduate Enrollment: 5,455
Scholarships/Academic: Yes
Expenses By: Year

Athletic: Yes
In State: $ 5,400

Founded: 1877
Religion: Non-Affiliated
Housing: Yes
Male/Female: 43:57
Graduate Enrollment: 890
Financial Aid: Yes
Out of State: $ 7,600

Degrees Conferred: BA, BS, BBA, BM, BME, BSE, BSW, MA, MS, MBA

Programs of Study: Accounting, Art/Fine Arts, Biology, Biological Science, Business Administration, Commerce, Management, Business Economics, Business Education, Chemistry, Child Care/Child and Family Studies, Communications, Computer Science, Criminal Justice, PreDentistry, Journalism, Economics, Electrical and Electronics Technology, Fire Science, Health Education, Law Enforcement, Police Science, Political Science

Women's Athletic Profile

1325 W. Lynch Street
Jackson, MS 39217
Coach: Dwaine Powe
Email:

NCAA I
Lady Tigerettes, Blue, White
Phone: (601) 968-2421
Fax: (601) 968-7008

Did Not Return Profile

Millsaps College
Academic Profile

1701 North State Street
Jackson, MS 39210

Phone: (601) 974-1198

Type: Private, 4 Yr., Liberal Arts, Coed
Website: http://www.millsaps.edu
SAT/ACT/GPA: 1100/21/2.5
Student/Faculty Ratio: 15:1
Undergraduate Enrollment: 1,200
Scholarships/Academic: Yes
Expenses By: Year
Athletic: No
In State: $21,000

Founded: 1890
Religion: United Methodist
Housing: Yes
Male/Female: 49:51
Graduate Enrollment: 250
Financial Aid: Yes
Out of State: $21,000

Specializes In: Business, Education, Liberal Arts, Premed

Degrees Conferred: BA, BS, BBA, BMus, MBA, MA, MLS, BLS

Programs of Study: Accounting, Biology, Business Administration, Chemistry, Classics, Computer Science, Dramatic Arts, Economics, Elementary Education, English, Fine Arts, French, Geology, History, Management, Mathematics, Music, Philosophy, Physics, Political Science, Psychology, Religion, Science Education, Social Science, Spanish

Women's Athletic Profile

1701 N. State
Jackson, MS 39210
Coach: Peter Cosmiano
Email: Cosmopc@millsaps.edu

NCAA I
Lady Majors, Purple, White
Phone: (601) 974-1197
Fax: (601) 974-1209

Estimated # of Women's Volleyball Scholarships: 0

Conference: Southern Collegiate Athletic Conference

Program Profile: The Millsaps Varsity Volleyball Gym holds 3,000. Millsaps has a brand new state of the art athletic complex, the Maurice Hall Activities Center, which houses workout facilities, racquetball and squash courts intramural basketball and volleyball courts, and much more.

History: Millsaps Volleyball began in 1992, and they have already become a conference powerhouse and spent time in NCAA III national rankings. This year they are picked to finish 3rd in the SCAC. Head Coach Peter Cosmiano has compiled a career record of 51-20 in two years.

Achievements: 1 SCAC Coach of the Year, 1 first Team All-SCAC, 3 Second Team All-SCAC, 1 Third Team All-SCAC, 8 All-SCAC Honorable Mention.

Coaching: Peter Cosmiano guided the Majors to a 26-9 record and number eight ranking in the NCAA South Regional poll in his rookies season as a Head Coach. Prior to coming to Millsaps, Cosmiano was an assistant coach at New Mexico Highlands University, A NCAA Division II. After three years, he served as the interim head coach for a year. He has also formed several volleyball clubs, including a men's club while in school at Union University. In addition to his experience as a player and coach, he has worked with the Atlanta Committee for Olympic games and with USA volleyball and served as a staff coach at Lambuth University Volleyball camps.

Roster In State: 0
Sophomores on Team:
Most Recent Record: 25-11

Out of State: 14
Seniors on Team: 2

Out of Country: 0
Graduation %: 100

Mississippi College
Academic Profile

P.O. Box 4203
Clinton, MS 39058

Phone: (601) 925-3000

Type: Private, 4 Yr., Liberal Arts, Coed
Website: http://www.mc.edu
SAT/ACT/GPA: 870/18
Student/Faculty Ratio: 20:1
Undergraduate Enrollment: 2,500
Scholarships/Academic: Yes   **Athletic:** No
Expenses By: Year   **In State:** $12,998
Degrees Conferred: BS, BA, MA

Founded: 1826
Religion: Southern Baptist
Housing: No
Male/Female: Not Available
Graduate Enrollment: 1,000
Financial Aid: Yes
Out of State: $12,998

Programs of Study: Accounting, Administration of Justice, Art, Biology, Business Administration, Chemistry, Christian Studies, Communications, Computer Science, Counseling, English, Foreign Languages, Geography, Paralegal, Mathematics, Music, Nursing, Physics, PreMed, Psychology, Sociology, Teacher Education

Women's Athletic Profile

P.O. Box 4245
Clinton, MS 39058
Coach: Jenny Hazelwood
Email: hazelwoo@mc.edu

NCAA I
Lady Choctaws, Old Gold, Blue
Phone: (601) 925-3357
Fax: (601) 924-6517

Did Not Return Profile

Mississippi State University
Academic Profile

PO Box 6334
Mississippi State, MS 39762
Type: Public, 4 Yr., Liberal Arts, Engineering, Coed
Website: http://www.msstate.edu
SAT/ACT/GPA: Call for information
Student/Faculty Ratio: 15/1
Undergraduate Enrollment: 10,818
Scholarships/Academic: Yes   **Athletic:** Yes
Expenses By: Year   **In State:** $4,358
Specializes In: Engineering, Veterinarian Medicine

Phone: 662-325-3076

Founded: 1878
Religion: Non-Affiliated
Housing: Yes
Male/Female: 55:45
Graduate Enrollment: 2,946
Financial Aid: Yes
Out of State: $6,332

Degrees Conferred: BA, BBA, BFA, BGS, BS, BLA, BPA, MA, MS, MAM, MBA
Programs of Study: Accounting, Agriculture, Anthropology, Biology, Business and Management, Chemistry, Communications, Computer, Education, Engineering, English, Finance, Management, Sciences, Technology, etc..

Women's Athletic Profile

P.O. Drawer 5327
Mississippi State, MS 39762-5509
Coach: Brenda Bowlin
Email: bbowlin@athletics.msstate.edu

NCAA I
Lady Bulldogs, Maroon, White
Phone: (601) 325-2722
Fax: (601) 325-9051

Estimated # of Women's Volleyball Scholarships: N/A
Conference: South Eastern Conference
Program Profile: MSU is a member of the 12 school Southeastern Conference, competing in the SEC Western Division. MSU's Fall volleyball season features home competition at the Newell-Grisson Building (3,500) and Humphrey Coliseum (9, 600). The Bulldogs have appeared in FOX-Sports Net TV games the last three years.
History: We started in 1975 and are continuing to improve our team athletically and academically. 128-150 Record in 8 seasons at MSU.
Achievements: 3rd place finish in Western Division of SEC Conference. MSU athletes have earned academic All-Conference honors 56 times since 1984, 25 of them during the past 4 years.
Coaching: Brenda Bowlin started as Head Coach in 1997 along with Craig Bere as an Assistant Coach. In 1998, Rani Whitson joined the coaching staff as an Assistant Coach.

Freshman Receiving Financial Aid/Academic: **Athletic:** 2-3
Roster In State: 0   **Out of State:** 12   **Out of Country:** 0
Sophomores on Team: 0   **Seniors on Team:** 2   **Graduation %:** 100
Most Recent Record: 16-14-0   **Fall Games:** 29   **Spring Games:** 3 tournaments
Positions Needed: Setter, MB, OH
Schedule: Florida, University of Arkansas, Fresno, Auburn University, University of South Carolina, University of Georgia.
Style of Play: A defense focused team.

Mississippi University for Women
Academic Profile

Box W-1636, c/o Dale Star   **Phone:** (601) 329-7228
Columbus, MS 39701

Type: Public, 4 Yr., Liberal Arts,Coed   **Founded:** 1884
Website: http://www.muw.edu   **Religion:** Non-Affiliated
SAT/ACT/GPA: 850/18/2.0   **Housing:** Yes
Student/Faculty Ratio: 16:1   **Male/Female:** 17:82
Undergraduate Enrollment: 3,300   **Graduate Enrollment:** 400
Scholarships/Academic: Yes   **Athletic:** Yes   **Financial Aid:** Yes
Expenses By: Year   **In State:** $ 5,513   **Out of State:** $ 8,503
Specializes In: Education, Nursing
Degrees Conferred: BS, MS, BA
Programs of Study: Accounting, Art/Fine Art, Biology/Biological Sciences, Business Administration/Commerce/Management, Criminal Justice, Elementary Education, English, Mathematics, Physical Education, Secretarial Studies/Office Management, Sociology

Women's Athletic Profile

Box 1636   **NCAA I**
Columbus, MS 39701   Lady Blues, Light/Dark Blue
Coach: Dale Starr   **Phone:** (601) 329-7228
Email: dalestarr@hotmail.com   **Fax:** (601) 329-8554

Estimated # of Women's Volleyball Scholarships: 8
Conference: Gulf South Conference
Program Profile: We play at Ody-Pohl Gymnasium which has a capacity of 2,000. Our season lasts from August 31 to November 11.
History: The program started in 1970. Our all time record is 436-230. We had 2 NCAA Tournament appearances with our last appearance in 1986. In 1994, we had one NIVT appearance.
Achievements: 1985 NCAA Regional Championship; 1986 NCAA Regional Championship; #9 in NCAA Division II in 1986; 1993 GSC Championship
Coaching: Dale Starr,started in 1999 as our head coach. He was in the Northern Colorado Men's Club Team and was 5th at the 1996 NIRSH National Tournament as a setter. He got an Honorable Mention and an All-American. There is no assistant coach listed.
Roster In State: 0   **Out of State:** 10   **Out of Country:** 1
Sophomores on Team: 4   **Seniors on Team:** 1   **Graduation %:** 95
Camp of Clinic Dates: N/A
Schedule: University of N. Alabama, Arkansas Tech University, Henderson State University, Drury College, University of South Alabama, Valdosta State University
Style of Play: Aggressive, scrappy, intense.

Mississippi Valley State University
Academic Profile

Highway 82   **Phone:** 601-254-9041
Itta Benna, MS 38941

Type: Public, 4 Yr., Coed   **Founded:** 1950
Website: Not Available   **Religion:** Non-Affiliated
SAT/ACT/GPA: 700avg/17avg   **Housing:** Yes
Student/Faculty Ratio: **Male/Female:**
Undergraduate Enrollment: 2,170   **Graduate Enrollment:** 15
Scholarships/Academic: Yes   **Athletic:** Yes   **Financial Aid:** Yes
Expenses By: Year   **In State:** $ 5,200   **Out of State:** $ 7,350

Degrees Conferred: BA, BS, BME, BSW, MA, MS
Programs of Study: Accounting, Art/Fine Arts, Administration, Commerce, Management, Chemistry, Communications, Computer Science, Criminal Justice, Education, Elementary Education, Engineering, Physical Education, Political Science, Public Administration, Secondary Education, Office Management, Social Work

Women's Athletic Profile

Highway 82
Itta Bena, MS 38941-1400
Coach: Jessie Harris
Email:

NCAA I
Lady Delta Devils, Green, White
Phone: 662-254-3550
Fax: (601) 254-3639

Did Not Return Profile

Rust College
Academic Profile

150 Rust Avenue
Holly Springs, MS 38365

Phone: 662-252-8000

Type: Private, 4 Yr., Liberal Arts, Coed
Website: http://www.centuryinter.net/rust
SAT/ACT/GPA: Preferred
Student/Faculty Ratio: 15:1
Undergraduate Enrollment: 852
Scholarships/Academic: Yes
Expenses By: Year

Athletic: No
In State: $ 7,300

Founded: 1866
Religion: United Methodist
Housing: Yes
Male/Female: 1:1
Graduate Enrollment: N/A
Financial Aid: Yes
Out of State: $ 7,300

Specializes In: Science & Math, Mass Communications, Teacher Education
Degrees Conferred: AS, BA, BS
Programs of Study: Accounting, Biology, Biological Science, Business Administration, Commerce, Management, Chemistry, Communications, Computer Science, Early Childhood Education, Economics, Education, Elementary Education, English, History, Physics, Political Science, Science, Education, Social Work, Sociology

Women's Athletic Profile

150 Rust Avenue
Holly Springs, MS 38635
Coach: Nancy Binion
Email:

NCAA I
Lady Bearcats, Blue, White
Phone: (601) 252-4661x4418
Fax: (601) 252-6107

Estimated # of Women's Volleyball Scholarships: N/A
Conference: Independent

University of Mississippi (Ole Mississippi)
Academic Profile

PO Box 217
University, MS 38677

Phone: (601) 232-7541

Type: Public, 4 Yr., Coed
Website: http://www.olemiss.edu
SAT/ACT/GPA: 18/2.0
Student/Faculty Ratio:
Undergraduate Enrollment: 9,000
Scholarships/Academic: Yes
Expenses By: Year

Athletic: Yes
In State: $ 10,364

Founded: 1844
Religion: Non-Affiliated
Housing: Yes
Male/Female:
Graduate Enrollment: 3,000
Financial Aid: Yes
Out of State: $ 13,466

Degrees Conferred: BA, BS, BFA, BAc, BAE, BALM, BBA, BE, BM, BPA, BSCE, BSChE, BSCS, BSE, BSES, BSEE, BSG, BSHE, BSME, BSPharm, BSW, MA, MS, MBA, MFA, M.Ed., Ph.D., EdD, JD
Programs of Study: Over 100 - College of Liberal Arts, School of Law, School of Engineering, School of Education, School of Business, School of Accounting, School of Medicine, School of Pharmacy, School of Dentistry, School of Health, Related Professions, etc.

Women's Athletic Profile

Athletic Department
University, MS 38677
Coach: John Blair
Email: jmecks@olemiss.edu

NCAA I
Lady Rebels, Red, Navy Blue
Phone: (601) 232-7541
Fax: (601) 232-5648

Estimated # of Women's Volleyball Scholarships: 3
Conference: Southeastern Conference
Coaching: John Blair - Head Coach. Jenny Meeks is Assistant Coach.
Freshman Receiving Financial Aid/Academic: **Athletic:** 2
Roster In State: 0   **Out of State:** 13   **Out of Country:** 1
Sophomores on Team: 0   **Seniors on Team:** 1   **Graduation %:** 98
Camp of Clinic Dates: June 10-13 Skills July 29-Aug.1

University of Southern Mississippi
Academic Profile

Box 5017
Hattiesburg, MS 39406-5017

Phone: (601) 266-6220

Type: Public, 4 Yr., Liberal Arts, Coed
Website: http://www.usm.edu
SAT/ACT/GPA: 870/18/2.0-2.5
Student/Faculty Ratio: 18:1
Undergraduate Enrollment: 11,000
Scholarships/Academic: No   **Athletic:** Yes
Expenses By: Year   **In State:** $ 5,580
Specializes In: Education, Technology, Liberal Arts
Degrees Conferred: Bachelors, Masters, Doctoral

Founded: 1910
Religion: Non-Affiliated
Housing: Yes
Male/Female: Not Available
Graduate Enrollment: 2,000
Financial Aid: No
Out of State: $ 8,475

Programs of Study: Accounting, Advertising, American Studies, Anthropology, Architecture, Art, Biology, Business Administration, Chemistry, Community Services, Computer Engineering, Computer Science, Computer Technologies, Economics, Education, Film Studies, Management, Music, Music Education, Nursing, Pathology, Physical Education, Real Estate, Science Education, Speech

Women's Athletic Profile

Fairchild Fieldhouse, University Blvd.
Hattiesburg, MS 39406
Coach: Steve Sykes
Email: steve.sykes@usm.edu

NCAA I
Golden Eagles, Black, Gold
Phone: (601) 266-6220
Fax: (601) 266-6690

Conference: Conference USA
Program Profile: The University of Southern Mississippi has a very competitive volleyball program. We play our matches in Green Coliseum which has 8,600 seats.
History: Our first year was 1979.
Coaching: Steve Sykes, Head Coach, started in 1997. He was assistant coach for four years here. He lead the team to its first back to back winning seasons in 1997 and 1998. Chris Laird is Assistant Coach.
Freshman Receiving Financial Aid/Academic: **Athletic:** 3
Roster In State: **Out of State:** 12   **Out of Country:** 2
Sophomores on Team: 4   **Seniors on Team:** 3   **Graduation %:** 100
Most Recent Record: 21-10-0   **Fall Games:** 31   **Spring Games:** 0
Camp of Clinic Dates: June 6-9, 1999
Positions Needed: 1
Schedule: Michigan State, Louisville, Houston, S.Florida, St. Louis, Cincinnati
Style of Play: Quick offense, multiple defense.

MISSOURI

Jefferson City

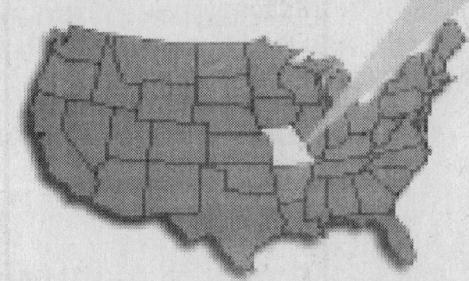

SCHOOL	CITY	AFFILIATION	PAGE
Avila College	Kansas City	NAIA	410
Central Methodist College	Fayette	NAIA	410
Central Missouri State University	Warrenburg	NCAA II	411
College of the Ozarks	Point Lookout	NAIA	411
Columbia College	Columbia	NAIA	411
Culver - Stockton College	Canton	NAIA	412
Drury University	Springfield	NCAA II	413
Evangel College	Springfield	NAIA	413
Fontbonne College	St. Louis	NCAA III	414
Hannibal-LaGrange College	Hannibal	NCCAA I/NAIA	415
Harris-Stowe State College	St. Louis	NAIA	415
Jefferson College	Hillsboro	NJCAA	415
Lindenwood College	St. Charles	NCAA III/NAIA	416
Maryville University of Saint Louis	St. Louis	NCAA III	417
Missouri Baptist College	St. Louis	NAIA	417
Missouri Southern State College	Joplin	NCAA II	418
Missouri Valley College	Marshall	NAIA	418
Missouri Western State College	St. Joseph	NCAA II	419
Northwest Missouri State Univ	Maryville	NCAA II	420
Park University	Parkville	NAIA	420
Rockhurst University	Kansas City	NCAA II	421
Saint Louis College of Pharmacy	St. Louis	NAIA	421
Saint Louis University	St. Louis	NCAA I	422
Southeast Missouri State Univ	Cape Girardeau	NCAA I	423
Southwest Baptist University	Bolivar	NCAA II	423
Southwest Missouri State Univ	West Plains	NCAA I	424
Stephens College	Columbia	NCAA III/NAIA	424
Truman State University	Kirksville	NCAA II	425

SCHOOL	CITY	AFFILIATION	PAGE
University of Missouri - Columbia	Columbia	NCAA I	425
University of Missouri - K.C.	Kansas City	NCAA I	426
University of Missouri - St. Louis	St. Louis	NCAA II	427
Washington University	St. Louis	NCAA III	427
Webster University	Webster Groves	NCAA III	428
Westminster College	Fulton	NCAA III	429
William Jewell College	Liberty	NAIA	429
William Woods University	Fulton	NAIA	430

Avila College
Academic Profile

11901 Wornall Rd.
Kansas City, MO 64145

Phone: (816) 942-8400

Type: Private, 4 Yr., Liberal Arts, Coed
Website: http://www.avila.edu
SAT/ACT/GPA: 22/3.2
Student/Faculty Ratio: 13:1
Undergraduate Enrollment: 1,200
Scholarships/Academic: Yes   **Athletic:** Yes
Expenses By: Year   **In State:** $ 16,010
Specializes In: Nursing, Education, Radiological Technology, Communications
Degrees Conferred: BA, BS, BSBA, BSN, BSMT, BSW, BFA, MS, MBA
Programs of Study: Art, Communication, English, General Studies, History, Mathematics, Music, Natural Sciences, Political Sciences, Psychology, Sociology, Theatre, Theology, Etc.

Founded: 1916
Religion: Catholic
Housing: Yes
Male/Female: 40:60
Graduate Enrollment: 200
Financial Aid: Yes
Out of State: $ 16,010

Women's Athletic Profile

11901 Wornall Rd.
Kansas City, MO 64145
Coach: Jim McMurray
Email: freemanca@mail.avila.edu

NCAA I
Lady Eagles, Purple, Gold
Phone: (816) 942-8400x2418
Fax: (816) 942-3362

Did Not Return Profile

Central Methodist College
Academic Profile

411 Central Methodist Square
Fayette, MO 65248

Phone: (660) 248-6348

Type: Private, 4 Yr., Liberal Arts, Coed
Website: http://www.cmc.edu
SAT/ACT/GPA: 1840/18/2.0
Student/Faculty Ratio: 14:1
Undergraduate Enrollment: 1161
Scholarships/Academic: Yes   **Athletic:** Yes
Expenses By: Year   **In State:** $ 15,490
Specializes In: Education, Nursing, Pre-professional (Law and Medicine)
Degrees Conferred: AA, AS, BA, BS, BSEd, BSN, BM, BMEd, B Music
Programs of Study: Accounting, Athletic Training, Biology, Business Administration, Chemistry, Communications, Community Services, Computer Science, Criminal Justice, Dramatic Arts, Economics, Education, English, Environmental Science, French, German, History, Languages, Management, Mathematics, Music, Music History, Nursing, Philosophy, Physical Science, Political Science, PreLaw, Psychology, Recreation Administration Management, Religion, Social Science

Founded: 1852
Religion: Methodist
Housing: Yes
Male/Female: 2:1
Graduate Enrollment: 30
Financial Aid: Yes
Out of State: $ 15,490

Women's Athletic Profile

411 CMC Square
Fayette, MO 654248
Coach: Tamara Turner
Email: vb@cmc.edu

NCAA I
Eagles, Green, Black, White
Phone: (660) 248-6353
Fax: (660) 248-1632

Estimated # of Women's Volleyball Scholarships: N/A
Conference: HAAC
Program Profile: We play at the Philips Recreation Center. The Clingenpeel Physical Education Building has a weight room staffed with coaches to make certain your physical activities are safe.
Roster In State: 13   **Out of State:** 0   **Out of Country:** 0
Sophomores on Team: 3   **Seniors on Team:** 2   **Graduation %:** Unknown
Schedule: Missouri Valley, Lindenwood, Hannibal LaGrange, Culver-Stockton, Evangel, Westminster, Benedictine, Nazarene, Graceland, Baker

Central Missouri State University
Academic Profile

500 Washington Street
Warrensburg, MO 64093

Phone: 660-7292678

Type: Public, 4 Yr., Liberal Arts, Coed
Website: http://www.cmsu.edu
SAT/ACT/GPA: 20
Student/Faculty Ratio: 20:1
Undergraduate Enrollment: 9,500
Scholarships/Academic: Yes   **Athletic:** Yes
Expenses By: Year   **In State:** $ 7,200
Specializes In: Education, Criminal Justice, State Mission in Technology

Founded: 1871
Religion: Non-Affiliated
Housing: Yes
Male/Female: 47:53
Graduate Enrollment: 1,500
Financial Aid: Yes
Out of State: $ 10,050

Degrees Conferred: AS, AA, BA, BS, BFA, BM, BME, BSBA, MA, MS, MBA, MEd
Programs of Study: Accounting, Actuarial Science and Mathematics, Agriculture, Art, Anthropology, Asian Studies, Power Technology, Biology, Broadcasting, Business, Chemistry, Coaching, Computer Information Systems, Criminal Justice, Education, Engineering, English, Fashion, Fitness/Wellness, Languages, Graphic Arts, History, Hotel Administration, International Studies, Music, Nursing, Medical Technology, Photography, Political Science, etc, Also, Law, Medicine, Physical Therapy, etc..Please call for more

Women's Athletic Profile

500 Washington Street
Warrenburg, MO 64093
Coach: Peggy Martin
Email: pmartin@cmsu1.cmsu.edu

NCAA I
Lady Jennies, Cardinal, Black
Phone: (660) 543-4011
Fax: (660) 543-8034

Estimated # of Women's Volleyball Scholarships: N/A
Conference: Mid-America Intercollegiate Athletics Association

College of the Ozarks
Academic Profile

College Avenue
Point Lookout, MO 65726

Phone: 800-222-0525

Type: Private, 4 Yr., Liberal Arts, Coed
Website: http://www.cofo.edu
SAT/ACT/GPA: 19
Student/Faculty Ratio: 14:1
Undergraduate Enrollment: 1,500
Scholarships/Academic: Yes   **Athletic:** Yes
Expenses By: Year   **In State:** $ 3,350

Founded: 1906
Religion: Presbyterian Founding
Housing: Yes
Male/Female: 1:1.5
Graduate Enrollment: N/A
Financial Aid: Yes
Out of State: $ 3,350

Degrees Conferred: BA, BS
Programs of Study: Accounting, Administration of Justice, Agriculture, Art, Aviation, Biology, Business, Chemistry, Computer, Education, English, Family & Consumer Science, Graphic Arts, History, Hotel & Restaurant Management, Mass, Media, Mathematics, Military Science, Music, Nursing, Philosophy, Physical Education, Political Science, Psychology, Religion, Sociology, Theatre, Technology

Women's Athletic Profile

Opportunity Avenue
Point Lookout, MO 65726
Coach: Jo Beth Elfrink
Email:

NCAA I
Lady Eagles, Purple, Gold
Phone: (417)334-6411
Fax: (501) 979-1330

Estimated # of Women's Volleyball Scholarships: N/A
Conference: MCAC

Columbia College
Academic Profile

1001 Rogers
Columbia, MO 65216

Phone: (573) 875-7414

Type: Private, 4 Yr., Liberal Arts, Coed
Website: http://www.ccis.edu
SAT/ACT/GPA: 18/2.0
Student/Faculty Ratio: 14:1
Undergraduate Enrollment: 1,500
Scholarships/Academic: Yes   **Athletic:** Yes
Expenses By: Year   **In State:** $ 14,394
Specializes In: Business Administration, Criminal Justice, Education
Degrees Conferred: AA, BA, BS, MBA

Founded: 1851
Religion: Disciples of Christ
Housing: Yes
Male/Female: 1:3
Graduate Enrollment: 50
Financial Aid: Yes
Out of State: $ 14,394

Programs of Study: Accounting, Art History, Biology, Business Administration, Ceramics, Chemistry, Computer Science, Criminal Justice, Education, English, Environmental Studies, Finance, Geology, Graphic Design, Sports Medicine, Social Work, All-Pre-Areas, Political Science

Women's Athletic Profile

1001 Rogers
Columbia, MO 65216
Coach: Melinda Wrye-Washington
Email: mwwashington@email.ccis.edu

NCAA I
Lady Cougars, Silver, Navy
Phone: (573) 875-7409
Fax: (573) 875-7415

Estimated # of Women's Volleyball Scholarships: 8
Conference: American Midwest
Program Profile: The Southwell complex gymnasium has been the home for Columbia College volleyball and basketball since 1988, and it seats 800 people. Plans have been finalized for the expansion of Southwell complex gymnasium.
History: Over the past several years, the Cougar volleyball program has become a national powerhouse and established itself as the one of the top programs in the history of the sport at any level. The team entered the 1998 season rated number one in the NAIA preseason poll, since that time, the Cougars have claimed two NAIA National Championships.
Achievements: Cougar have participated in six consecutive NAIA national tournaments, finishing fifth in 1995,1997, third in1996, and as national champions 1998,1999. Also have had five consecutive regional championships, seven consecutive American Midwest conference championships. Cougars have been named All-American Midwest Conference 27 times. 2 NAIA national Players of the Year.
Coaching: Coach Melinda Wrye-Washington was a former player who became the first NAIA first team All-American in Cougar volleyball history. Assist. Mariuska Hamilton who played for the Cougars in 1998-1999 enters her first season. K.C. Trimble begins his third year as an assistant to the women's volleyball program
Freshman Receiving Financial Aid/Academic: **Athletic:** 8
Roster In State: 8   **Out of State:** 1   **Out of Country:** 4
Sophomores on Team: **Seniors on Team:** 0   **Graduation %:**
Most Recent Record: 26-1
Positions Needed: Middle hitter, Setter, Outside hitter
Schedule: William Woods University, Park University, Williams Baptist College, Washington University.
Style of Play: Aggressive offense with focus on middles as primary hitters. Audible transition with quick pace. Discipline on defensive drops and focus on putting up a fundamental block.

<u>Culver - Stockton College</u>
Academic Profile

1 College Hill
Canton, MO 63435

Phone: 800-537-1883

Type: Private, 4 Yr., Liberal Arts, Coed
Website: http://www.culver.edu
SAT/ACT/GPA: 23/3.0
Student/Faculty Ratio: 1:16
Undergraduate Enrollment: 908
Scholarships/Academic: Yes   **Athletic:** Yes
Expenses By: Year   **In State:** $ 14,670
Specializes In: Business, Education
Degrees Conferred: BA, BS, BFA, BME, BSN

Founded: 1853
Religion: Non-Affiliated
Housing: Yes
Male/Female: 1:3
Graduate Enrollment: N/A
Financial Aid: Yes
Out of State: $ 14,670

Programs of Study: Art, Biology, Accounting, Business & Management, Chemistry, Communications, Computer Information Systems, Computer Science, Criminal Justice, Education, Foreign Languages, Health Science, History, Marketing, Mathematics, Music, Nursing, Philosophy, Political Science, Engineering, PreProfessional Programs, Psychology, Religion, Psychology, Religion, Social Science, Theatre & Drama

Women's Athletic Profile

1 College Hill
Canton, MO 63435
Coach: TBA
Email:

Did Not Return Profile

NCAA I
Lady Wildcats, Blue, White
Phone: (217) 231-6379
Fax: (217) 231-6611

Drury University
Academic Profile

900 N. Benton
Springfield, MO 65802

Phone: (417) 873-7449

Type: Private, 4 Yr., Liberal Arts, Coed
Website: http://www.drury.edu
SAT/ACT/GPA: 21
Student/Faculty Ratio: 12:1
Undergraduate Enrollment: 1,400
Scholarships/Academic: Yes
Expenses By: Year
Specializes In: Liberal Arts

Athletic: Yes
In State: $ 15,500

Founded: 1873
Religion: United Church of Christ
Housing: Yes
Male/Female: 53:47
Graduate Enrollment: 300
Financial Aid: Yes
Out of State: $ 15,500

Degrees Conferred: BA, BS BArch, BM, BME, BSN, AS, MBA, M.Ed.
Programs of Study: Liberal Arts, Business, Education, Architecture, Communications, PreLaw, PreMedicine, Accounting, Environmental Studies, Criminology, Exercise and Sports Science, English, Political Science, Art

Women's Athletic Profile

900 North Benton
Springfield, MO 65802
Coach: Barbara Cowherd
Email: druryad@lib.drury.edu

NCAA I
Panthers, Red, Black, Grey
Phone: (417) 873-7363
Fax: (417) 873-7510

Estimated # of Women's Volleyball Scholarships: 7.75
Conference: Independent
Program Profile: For an NCAA Division II school, our facilities are very nice. We have a volleyball locker room that is only 3 years old. Our gymnasium has 2,200 seats.
History: The volleyball program began in 1973 with NAIA. We joined NCAA II in 1990. The South Central Regional Conference is in the works before the fall semester. We were nationally ranked from 1986 to 1992. We were ranked in the Top Ten in Region most of the season.
Achievements: 1998 NAIA District Champions; Paula Wohnhas-NAIA All-American in 1997-1998; Stephanie Bates-NAIA All-American in 1990; Sandy Rippee NAIA H.M All-American in 1993.
Coaching: Barbara Cowherd, Head Coach, started at Drury in 1980. She has an overall career record of 469-333-16. She graduated from Missouri Southern State in 1978. She was named 1988 District 16 Coach of the Year. Lawrence Anderson is Assistant Coach and is in his 4th season.
Freshman Receiving Financial Aid/Academic:
Roster In State: 8
Sophomores on Team: 5
Most Recent Record: 19-20-0
Positions Needed: Setter, Hitter, Middle Blocker

Out of State: 4
Seniors on Team: 2
Fall Games: 41

Athletic: 3
Out of Country: 0
Graduation %: 98
Spring Games: 0

Schedule: Central Missouri State University, Rockhurst, North Alabama, Missouri Western, Valdosta State University, Alabama-Huntsville
Style of Play: We run a swing offense right now. All of our hitters have this ability to hit a variety of sets regardless of their position.

Evangel College
Academic Profile

1111 N. Glenstone
Springfield, MO 65802

Phone: (417) 865-2811

Type: Private, 4 Yr., Liberal Arts, Coed
Website: http://www.evangel.edu

Founded: 1955
Religion: Assemblies of God

SAT/ACT/GPA: 16/2.0
Student/Faculty Ratio: 18:1
Undergraduate Enrollment: 1,604
Scholarships/Academic: Yes   **Athletic:** Yes
Expenses By: Year   **In State:** $ 12,815
Degrees Conferred: BA, BS, BBA, BFA, B.Mus.

Housing: Yes
Male/Female: 1:1.5
Graduate Enrollment: N/A
Financial Aid: Yes
Out of State: $ 12,815

Programs of Study: Majors offered are Behavioral Sciences, Biblical Studies, Business & Economics, Communications, Education, Humanities, Music, Physical Education, Science & Technology, Social Sciences, Professional Programs

Women's Athletic Profile

1111 N. Glenstone
Springfield, MO 65802
Coach: Mary Penrodl
Email: fillmored@evangel.edu

NCAA I
Lady Crusaders, Maroon, White
Phone: (417) 865-2811x7421
Fax: (417) 865-6906

Estimated # of Women's Volleyball Scholarships: N/A
Conference: Heart of America
Achievements: We won the 1998 Mid America Conference Tournament Quarterfinals
Coaching: Leon Neal - Head Coach. Dawn Neal is Assistant Coach. Student coaches are Angela Brown and Jenne Eklund.
Most Recent Record: 14-20-0   **Fall Games:** 34   **Spring Games:** 0
Schedule: William Jewell, Missouri Valley, Culver-Stockton, Benedictine, Bethel, Baker, Graceland, Friends, Central Methodist, St.Mary's

Fontbonne College
Academic Profile

6800 Wydown Blvd.
St. Louis, MO 63108

Phone: (314) 889-1444

Type: Private, 4 Yr., Liberal Arts, Coed
Website: http://www.fontbonne.edu
SAT/ACT/GPA: 21/2.5 or above
Student/Faculty Ratio: 14:1
Undergraduate Enrollment: 1,400
Scholarships/Academic: Yes   **Athletic:** No
Expenses By: Year   **In State:** $ 16,000
Specializes In: Deaf Education
Degrees Conferred: BS, BA, Masters, Ph.D.

Founded: 1914
Religion: Catholic
Housing: Yes
Male/Female: 1:2
Graduate Enrollment: 600
Financial Aid: Yes
Out of State: $ 16,000

Programs of Study: Applied Mathematics, Art, Biology, Broadcasting, Business, Communication Disorders, Computer Science, Deaf Education, Dietetics, Drawing, English, Fashion, Painting, Sculpture, Special Education, Studio Major, Mathematics, Human Services

Women's Athletic Profile

6800 Wydown Street
St. Louis, MO 63105
Coach: Kim Kutis-Hantak
Email:

NCAA I
Griffins, Purple, Gold, Black
Phone: (314) 889-1453
Fax: (314) 889-4507

Estimated # of Women's Volleyball Scholarships: N/A
Conference: St. Louis Intercollegiate Athletic Conference
Program Profile: Up and coming program, young nucleus. Our playing season is in September 1 through October 31.
History: We became a Division III program in 1999. Women's sports date back about seventy years ago.
Coaching: Kim Kutis-Hantak, Head Coach, started with the program in 1998. She compiled a record of 12-7 and was Fontbonne College Hall of Fame Inductee. Rebecca Lind is our Assistant Coach.
Roster In State: 11   **Out of State:** 3   **Out of Country:** 0
Sophomores on Team: 0   **Seniors on Team:** 3   **Graduation %:** 95
Most Recent Record: 12-7-0   **Fall Games:** 28   **Spring Games:** 0
Positions Needed: Middle Hitter, Outside Hitter
Schedule: Eckerd College, Southeastern College, Westminster College, Lindenwood University, University of Chicago, Muhlenberg
Style of Play: Strong defensive core with a quick offensive set.

Hannibal - LaGrange College
Academic Profile

2800 Palmyra Rd.
Hannibal, MO 63401

Phone: 573-221-3113

Type: Private, 4 Yr., Liberal Arts, Coed
Website: http://www.hlg.edu
SAT/ACT/GPA: 18
Student/Faculty Ratio: 14:1
Undergraduate Enrollment: 900
Scholarships/Academic: Yes   **Athletic:** Yes
Expenses By: Year   **In State:** $ 9,400

Founded: 1858
Religion: Southern Baptist
Housing: No
Male/Female: 37:63
Graduate Enrollment: N/A
Financial Aid: Yes
Out of State: $ 9,400

Degrees Conferred: AA, AS, AAS, BA, BS, BCE, BRS, BSEd, BSN
Programs of Study: Accounting, Banking/Finance, Biological, Business, Christian Studies, Communications, Computer, Criminal, Early Childhood Education, Education, English, Fine Arts, Humanities, Management, Marketing, Mathematics, Music, Nursing and Allied Health, Personnel Management, Sciences, Secondary Education

Women's Athletic Profile

2800 palmyra Rd.
Hannibal, MO 63401
Coach: Trish Meadors
Email:

NCAA I
Trojans, Scarlet, White, Blue
Phone: (573) 221-0411x287
Fax: (573) 221-9424

Estimated # of Women's Volleyball Scholarships: N/A
Conference: American Midwest Conference

Harris - Stowe State College
Academic Profile

3026 Laclede Avenue
St. Louis, MO 63103

Phone: (314) 340-3530

Type: Public, 4 Yr., Coed
Website: http://www.hssc.edu
SAT/ACT/GPA: 21
Student/Faculty Ratio: 15:1
Undergraduate Enrollment: 1,700
Scholarships/Academic: Yes   **Athletic:** Yes
Expenses By: Year   **In State:**

Founded: 1857
Religion: Non-Affiliated
Housing: N
Male/Female: 2:3
Graduate Enrollment: N/A
Financial Aid: Yes
Out of State:

Specializes In: Education and Business
Degrees Conferred: BS, BA, CJ, Urban Education
Programs of Study: Business Administration, Criminal Justice, Early Childhood, Elementary Education, Secondary Education, Urban Education, Interdisciplinary Study.

Women's Athletic Profile

3026 Laclede
St. Louis, MO 63103
Coach: Barb Krushibbeler
Email:

NCAA I
Lady Hornets, Brown, Gold
Phone: (314) 340-3530
Fax: (314) 340-5762

Estimated # of Women's Volleyball Scholarships: 8
Conference: American Midwest Conference
Program Profile: We are members of the NAIA and the American Midwest Conference.

Jefferson College
Academic Profile

1000 Viking Dr.
Hillsboro, MO 63103
Type: Public, 4 Yr., Coed

Phone: (636) 789-3000

Founded: 1963

Website: http://www.jeffco.edu
SAT/ACT/GPA: ASSET- Math & English Placement
Student/Faculty Ratio: 19:1
Undergraduate Enrollment: 4,220
Scholarships/Academic: Yes
Expenses By: Year
Degrees Conferred: Associate

Athletic: Yes
In State: $ Varies

Religion: Non-Affiliated
Housing: No
Male/Female: 43:57
Graduate Enrollment: N/A
Financial Aid: Yes
Out of State: $ Varies

Programs of Study: Accounting, Architectural, Art, Automotive, Business, Computer, Criminal Justice, Data Processing, Drafting/Design Technology, Education, Electronics/Electrical Technology, Medical Laboratory, History, Law, Laser, Liberal Arts, Machine/Tool Technology, Marketing, Math, Mechanical, Nursing, Psychology, Public, Retail, Robotics, Science, Spanish, Speech

Women's Athletic Profile

1000 Viking Drive
Hillsboro, MO 63050-2421
Coach: Jo Ellen Stringer
Email: jstring@gateway.jeffco.edu

NCAA I
Lady Vikings, Red, Blue, White
Phone: (314) 797-3000
Fax: (314) 789-2419

Estimated # of Women's Volleyball Scholarships: 10
Conference: Missouri Community College Athletic Association
Program Profile: We have one of the top community college programs in the nation. Jefferson has participated in more National Championships and accumulated more victories than any community college in the NJCAA. The schedule is one of the most competitive with an annual out-of-state trip.
History: Our program began in 1975. Coach Stringer has been the head coach throughout its history. The school record is 917-267. There are 19 Conference Championships, 19 Regional Championships and 21 trips to the NCAA National Championships. There are more All-Americans than any other athletic program.
Achievements: 9 Conference Coach of the Year Awards, 8 Region 16 Coach of the Year; 19 District 12 Coach of the Year Awards; Stringer-NJCAA Coach of the Year; NJCAA Hall of Fame inductee; 15 All-Americans.
Coaching: Joe Ellen Stringer has been Head Coach for 24 years and her record is 955-281. She has the most victories of any coach in the NJCAA. She is in the AVCA Victory Club for 900 victories and others that are mentioned under achievements.
Freshman Receiving Financial Aid/Academic:
Roster In State: 8
Sophomores on Team: 0
Most Recent Record: 38-1-4
Out of State: 2
Seniors on Team: 6
Fall Games: 42
Athletic: 10
Out of Country: 1
Graduation %: 95
Spring Games: 5
Camp of Clinic Dates: Regular camp: June 21-24; Super Camp: June 28-July 1; Regular Camp July 5-8
Positions Needed: 5 various
Schedule: Miami-Dade Wolfson, Barton County, Utah Valley, Pasco-Hernado, Belleville Area, SMSU-West Plains
Style of Play: We usually do a 5-1 offense and we like to balance offense and defense. We usually have a fast tempo middle. We run as quick an offense as passing allows. Basics are important!

Lindenwood College
Academic Profile

209 S. Kings Highway
St. Charles, MO 63301
Type: Private, 4 Yr., Liberal Arts, Coed
Website: http://www.lindenwood.edu
SAT/ACT/GPA: 860/18/2.0
Student/Faculty Ratio: 18:1
Undergraduate Enrollment: 4,168
Scholarships/Academic: Yes
Expenses By: Year
Degrees Conferred: BA, BS, MA, MS, MBA, MPA

Athletic: Yes
In State: $ 16,850

Phone: 636-949-2000

Founded: 1827
Religion: Non-Affiliated
Housing: Yes
Male/Female: 44:56
Graduate Enrollment: 2,426
Financial Aid: Yes
Out of State: $ 16,850

Programs of Study: Accounting, Art, Art History, Biology, Business, Chemistry, Computer Science, Corporate Communications, Criminal Justice, Early Childhood Education, Elementary Education, Fashion Marketing, French, History, Human Resources, Management, Marketing, Mass Communications, Mathematics, Physical Education, Political Science, Psychology, Public Administration, Secondary Education, Sociology, Special Education, Theatre, PreLaw, PreMed, PreVet

Women's Athletic Profile

209 S. Kings Highway
St. Charles, MO 63301
Coach: Dave Witter
Email:

NCAA I
Lady Lions, Black, Gold
Phone: (636) 916-1932
Fax: (314) 949-4910

Estimated # of Women's Volleyball Scholarships: N/A
Conference: Independent

Maryville University - Saint Louis
Academic Profile

13550 Conway Road
St. Louis, MO 63141

Phone: 800-627-9855

Type: Private, 4 Yr., Coed
Website: http://www.maryvillestl.edu
SAT/ACT/GPA: 950/20
Student/Faculty Ratio: 17:1
Undergraduate Enrollment: 1,300
Scholarships/Academic: Yes   **Athletic:** No
Expenses By: Year   **In State:** $ 16,300
Degrees Conferred: BA, BS, BFA

Founded: 1872
Religion: Non-Affiliated
Housing: Yes
Male/Female: 1:3
Graduate Enrollment: 400
Financial Aid: Yes
Out of State: $ 16,300

Programs of Study: Art (Studio & International Design), Business, Communications, Education, History, English, Nursing, Physical Therapy, Occ. Therapy, Music, Psychology, Accounting, Management, Business Administration, Biology, Chemistry, Science

Women's Athletic Profile

13550 Conway Road
St. Louis, MO 63141
Coach: Rebecca Czuppon
Email:

NCAA I
Lady Saints, Red, White
Phone: (314) 529-9313
Fax: (314) 529-9947

Estimated # of Women's Volleyball Scholarships: N/A
Conference: St. Louis Intercollegiate Athletic Conference

Missouri Baptist College
Academic Profile

1 College Park Dr.
St. Louis, MO 63141

Phone: 877-434-1115

Type: Private, 4 Yr., Liberal Arts, Coed
Website: http://www.mobap.edu
SAT/ACT/GPA: 840/18/2.0
Student/Faculty Ratio: 18:1
Undergraduate Enrollment: 2,300
Scholarships/Academic: Yes   **Athletic:** Yes
Expenses By: Year   **In State:** $ 13,590
Specializes In: Business, Education, Music
Degrees Conferred: AA, AS, BA, BS, BSEd, BSN

Founded: 1950
Religion: Southern Baptist
Housing: Yes
Male/Female: 40:60
Graduate Enrollment: 500
Financial Aid: Yes
Out of State: $ 13,590

Programs of Study: Accounting, Behavioral Science, Biblical Studies, Biology, Business Administration, Chemistry, Communications, Computer Information Systems, Computer Science, Management, Mathematics, Military Science, Music, Natural Science, Nursing, Philosophy, Physical Education, PreDental, PreLaw, PreMed, PreVet, Psychology, Religion, Secondary Education, Social Science, Theology

Women's Athletic Profile

One College Park Drive
St. Louis, MO 63141
Coach: Jay Potter
Email: athletics@mobap.edu

NCAA I
Lady Spartans, Blue, White
Phone: (314) 434-1115
Fax: (314) 434-7596

Estimated # of Women's Volleyball Scholarships: V-8; JV-3
Conference: American Midwest Conference
Program Profile: We are a competitive program pushing for a high conference finish with regional and national ranking. We place individuals on all-academic teams.
History: Our records go back to 1994. Our first year record was 22-18 (2nd in the conference). In 1995, our record was 30-7. In 1996, our record was 33-8. In 1997, our record was 24-9 (second tie). In 1998, our record was 17-17 (3rd in the conference, 11th in the region).

Achievements: Ranked 11th in the region; 4 All-Conference players; 4 Academic All-Conference; 2 Academic All-Region.

Coaching: Jay Potter, Head Coach, was four years at Colorado Christian University. He was four years at University of Nebraska with a record of 114-18. He was five years at University of Illinois with a record of 147-51. He was two years at Indiana State with a record of 25-35. He was one year Missouri Baptist with a record of 17-17. He has coached 15 All-Americans and several national team members and two-time Olympian Setter, Lori Endicott, who was recruited out of Willard Missouri. He was on the 1990 Gold Medal Olympic Festival Team Staff. Carrie Steele is Assistant Coach.

Freshman Receiving Financial Aid/Academic: **Athletic:** 5

Roster In State: 10   **Out of State:** 2   **Out of Country:** 0

Sophomores on Team: 0   **Seniors on Team:** 5   **Graduation %:** 100

Most Recent Record: 17-17-0   **Fall Games:** 34   **Spring Games:** 3-4

Positions Needed: Outside Hitter, MH, TR, Setter, DS

Schedule: Columbia, St. Ambrose, Graceland College, Culver Stockton, Rockhurst, William Woods

Style of Play: Fast & Furious: Move the ball to setter as fast as possible. Run swing and multiple offense using opposing motion. Intensive work on team systems and tactics.

Missouri Southern State College
Academic Profile

3950 Newman Road
Joplin, MO 64801

Phone: (417) 625-9573

Type: Public, 4 Yr., Coed   **Founded:** 1937

Website: http://www.mssc.ecu   **Religion:** Non-Affiliated

SAT/ACT/GPA: 18   **Housing:** Yes

Student/Faculty Ratio: 25:1   **Male/Female:** 4:5

Undergraduate Enrollment: 5,400   **Graduate Enrollment:** N/A

Scholarships/Academic: Yes   **Athletic:** Yes   **Financial Aid:** Yes

Expenses By: Year   **In State:** $ 6,427   **Out of State:** $ 8,843

Degrees Conferred: AA, AS, AAS, BA, BS, BSBA, BSE, BGS

Programs of Study: Accounting, Biology, Broadcasting, Business Administration, Chemistry, Computer Science, Criminal Justice, Dramatic Arts, Economics, Education, Fine Arts, History, Management, Mathematics, Music, Nursing, Physics, PreDentistry, PreMed, Social Science

Women's Athletic Profile

3950 E. Newman Rd.
Joplin, MO 64801
Coach: Debbie Traywick
Email:

NCAA I
Lady Lions, Green, Gold
Phone: (417) 625-9705
Fax: (417) 625-9773

Estimated # of Women's Volleyball Scholarships: 2

Conference: Mid-America Intercollegiate Athletics Association

Program Profile: Own facility with wood floor.

Freshman Receiving Financial Aid/Academic: **Athletic:** 2

Roster In State: 8   **Out of State:** 6   **Out of Country:** 0

Sophomores on Team: **Seniors on Team:** 4   **Graduation %:**

Positions Needed: Middle Hitters, Outside Hitter

Schedule: Central Missouri, Truman State, Henderson State, Missouri Western, West Florida

Missouri Valley College
Academic Profile

500 East College St.
Marshall, MO 65340

Phone: (660) 831-4000

Type: Private, 4 Yr., Liberal Arts, Coed   **Founded:** 1889

Website: http://www.murlin.com/~webfx/mvc/   **Religion:** Presbyterian

SAT/ACT/GPA: 800/18/2.0   **Housing:** Yes

Student/Faculty Ratio: 10:1   **Male/Female:** 3:1

Undergraduate Enrollment: 1,300   **Graduate Enrollment:** 50

Scholarships/Academic: Yes   **Athletic:** Yes   **Financial Aid:** Yes

Expenses By: Year   **In State:** $ 17,000   **Out of State:** $ 17,000

Degrees Conferred: AA, BA, BS, Master of Arts

Programs of Study: Accounting, Actuarial Sciences, Agribusiness, Alcohol & Drug Studies, Art, Biology, Business Administration, Computer Information Systems, Criminal Justice, Economics, Elementary Education, English, Exercise Science, General Studies, History, Human Services Agency Management, Mass Communications, Mathematics, Physical Education, Political Science, Public Administration, Psychology, Recreation Administration, Religious, Social Studies Education, Sociology, Speech Communications, Theatre, PreProfessional Programs

Women's Athletic Profile

500 E. College
Marshall, MO 65340
Coach: Kenny Holstine
Email: holstinek@moval.edu

NCAA I
Lady Vikings, Purple, Orange
Phone: (660) 831-4201
Fax: (660) 831-4038

Estimated # of Women's Volleyball Scholarships: 8
Conference: Heart of America Athletic Conference
Program Profile: Varsity and Junior Varsity program. Highly competitive conference. Three court facility, 2 wood courts, one with rubber surface. Team plays from end of August to the 1st of December and the facility seats 2000.
History: The Lady Vikings have qualified for post-season in each of the past 4 seasons.
Achievements: 1993 District Coach of the Year. Have coached 5 All-American Players.
Freshman Receiving Financial Aid/Academic: | | **Athletic:** All
Roster In State: 10 | **Out of State:** 14 | **Out of Country:** 0
Sophomores on Team: | **Seniors on Team:** 2 | **Graduation %:** 85-90
Most Recent Record: 5-22
Positions Needed: 3 Middle, 1 Rightside, 2 Outside
Schedule: Graceland, Culver-Stockton, Lindenwood, Benedictine
Style of Play: Fast-paced with multiple options.

Missouri Western State College
Academic Profile

4525 Downs Dr.
St. Joseph, MO 64507

Phone: 816-271-4200

Type: Public, 4 Yr., Liberal Arts, Coed
Website: http://www.mwsc.edu
SAT/ACT/GPA: 18avg
Student/Faculty Ratio: 19:1
Undergraduate Enrollment: 5,230
Scholarships/Academic: Yes
Expenses By: Year
Specializes In: Liberal Arts & Sciences
Degrees Conferred: AS, BA, BSBA, BSE, BSN, BSW

Founded: 1969
Religion: Non-Affiliated
Housing: Yes
Male/Female: 42:58
Graduate Enrollment: N/A
Athletic: Yes | **Financial Aid:** Yes
In State: $ 6,250 | **Out of State:** $ 8,150

Programs of Study: Accounting, Art, Biology, Chemistry, Computer Science, Criminal Justice, Economics, Electronics Engineering Tech, Elementary Education, English, French, History, Management, Marketing, Mathematics, Music, Psychology, Physical Education, Physical Therapy Assistant, Spanish, Speech and Theatre, Speech Communications

Women's Athletic Profile

4525 Downs Drive
St. Joseph, MO 64507
Coach: Cindy Brauck
Email: admission@griffon.mwsc.edu

NCAA I
Lady Griffons, Black, Gold
Phone: (816) 271-4266
Fax: (816) 271-5833

Estimated # of Women's Volleyball Scholarships: 4
Conference: Mid-America Intercollegiate Athletics Association
Program Profile: We have a successful volleyball tradition. MWSC Arena holds 4,000. We have a year-round training program with a high commitment level.
History: We began in 1975 with an overall record of 797-374-14. We had 5 NAIA National Championship Appearances. We had one 4th place finish at Nationals in 1982 and one NCAA All-American - Shelby Lowry in 1995.
Achievements: Nebraska Independent League Conference Champions in 1990.
Coaching: Cindy Brauck, Head Coach, started from 1996 to the present. She was a former assistant coach at Southwest Missouri in 1986-1989. She was head coach at Peru State College from 1989 to 1991. She was Head Coach at Wisconsin-Green Bay from 1991 to 1996. Her current record is 47-22. Monica Peck is Assistant Coach.

Freshman Receiving Financial Aid/Academic:

Roster In State: 6	**Out of State:** 6	**Athletic:** 4
Sophomores on Team: 0	**Seniors on Team:** 5	**Out of Country:** 0
Most Recent Record: 22-16-0	**Fall Games:** 38	**Graduation %:** 80
		Spring Games: 16

Positions Needed: Outside Hitter, Middle Hitter
Schedule: Central Missouri State, Rockhurst, North Alabama, Emporia State, Henderson State, Wayne State
Style of Play: Aggressive serve and block, low error offense, finesse shots for high percent and kills.

Northwest Missouri State University
Academic Profile

800 University Drive
Maryville, MO 64468

Phone: (660) 562-1562

Type: Public, 4 Yr., Coed
Website: http://www.nwmissouri.edu
SAT/ACT/GPA: 860/21/2.0
Student/Faculty Ratio: 27:1
Undergraduate Enrollment: 5,300
Scholarships/Academic: Yes
Expenses By: Year
Specializes In: Education

Athletic: Yes
In State: $ 7,077

Founded: 1905
Religion: Non-Affiliated
Housing: Yes
Male/Female: 45:55
Graduate Enrollment: 700
Financial Aid: Yes
Out of State: $ 9,207

Degrees Conferred: BS, BA, MA, MS, BFA, MFA, BMT, BSF, MBA
Programs of Study: Accounting, Agricultural, Banking/Finance, Botany, Broadcasting, Early Childhood, Computer Earth Science, Economics, History, Horticulture, Humanities, Journalism, Philosophy, PreProfessional Programs, Science, Special Education, Speech, Zoology

Women's Athletic Profile

800 University Drive
Maryville, MO 64468
Coach: Sarah Pelster
Email: sipelster@hotmail.com

NCAA I
Lady Bearcats, Green, White
Phone: (660) 562-1297
Fax: (660) 562-1483

Estimated # of Women's Volleyball Scholarships: 7-8
Conference: Mid-America Intercollegiate Athletics Association
Coaching: Sarah Pelster, Head Coach
Freshman Receiving Financial Aid/Academic:

Roster In State: 5	**Out of State:** 11	**Athletic:** 3
Sophomores on Team: 5	**Seniors on Team:** 2	**Out of Country:** 0
Most Recent Record: 21-12-0	**Fall Games:** 38	**Graduation %:** 100
		Spring Games: 4

Positions Needed: Outside, Middle Hitter
Schedule: Central Missouri State University, Seattle Pacific, Rockhurst, Emporia, University of Atlanta-Huntsville, Grand Valley, Truman

Park University
Academic Profile

8700 NW River Park Drive
Parkville, MO 64152

Phone: 816-741-2000

Type: Private, 4 Yr., Liberal Arts, Coed
Website: http://www.park.edu
SAT/ACT/GPA: 840/20/2.0
Student/Faculty Ratio: 9:1
Undergraduate Enrollment: 17,000
Scholarships/Academic: Yes
Expenses By: Year
Specializes In: Liberal Arts, Sports Medicine

Athletic: Yes
In State: $ 9,400

Founded: 1875
Religion: Non-Affiliated
Housing: Yes
Male/Female: 60:40
Graduate Enrollment: 1,000
Financial Aid: Yes
Out of State: $ 9,400

Degrees Conferred: BA, BS, AA, AS, MBA, M.Ed., M.Rel
Programs of Study: Physical Therapy, Sports Medicine, Management, Elementary Education, Secondary Education, International Business, Accounting, Math, English, Art

Women's Athletic Profile

Box 66, 8700 NW River Park
Parkville, MO 64152
Coach: Ronda Miles
Email:

NCAA I
Lady Pirates, Canary, Wine
Phone: (816) 741-6493
Fax: (816) 741-4911

Estimated # of Women's Volleyball Scholarships: N/A
Conference: American Midwest Conference

Rockhurst University
Academic Profile

1100 Rockhurst Rd
Kansas City, MO 64110

Phone: (816) 501-4141

Type: Private, 4 Yr., Liberal Arts, Coed
Website: http://www.rockhurst.edu
SAT/ACT/GPA: 20+/2.5
Student/Faculty Ratio: 14:1
Undergraduate Enrollment: 1,000
Scholarships/Academic: Yes   **Athletic:** Yes
Expenses By: Year   **In State:** $ 18,650
Specializes In: Business

Founded: 1910
Religion: Catholic/Jesuit
Housing: Yes
Male/Female: 45:55
Graduate Enrollment: 1,400
Financial Aid: Yes
Out of State: $ 18,650

Degrees Conferred: BA, BS, BA Elem. Ed, BSBA, BSN, MS, MBA
Programs of Study: Business, Communications, Computer Science, Chemistry, Education, English, Human Relations, Marketing, Mathematics, Nursing, Occupational Therapy, Physical Therapy, PreDental, PreLaw, PreMedical, Psychology, Science, Spanish

Women's Athletic Profile

1100 Rockhurst Road
Kansas City, MO 64110
Coach: Tracy Rietzke
Email: athletics@Rockhurst.com

NCAA I
Lady Hawks, Blue, White
Phone: (816) 501-4141
Fax: (816) 501-4119

Estimated # of Women's Volleyball Scholarships: 4
Conference: Independent
Program Profile: As an NAIA program, Rockhurst made six trips to the Nationals finishing 2nd twice and 5th once. In the first year of NCAA Division II (1998-99), we finished 42-5 and made it to the round of the Final Sixteen. Our fieldhouse has 1,500 seats.
History: Our first year was 1974. Our overall record for the last eleven years is 500-65.
Achievements: Two time AVCA Region Coach of the Year (NAIA); Five time District Coach of the Year (NAIA); 8 All-Americans (NAIA).
Coaching: Tracy Rietzke, Head Coach, became head coach in 1988. His overall record in 17 years of coaching is 678-121.
Freshman Receiving Financial Aid/Academic: **Athletic:** 3
Roster In State: 6   **Out of State:** 9   **Out of Country:** 0
Sophomores on Team: 2   **Seniors on Team:** 4   **Graduation %:** Unknown
Most Recent Record: 42-3-0   **Fall Games:** 40   **Spring Games:** 12
Positions Needed: 0
Schedule: University of North Alabama, Central Michigan State, Southern Illinois University-Edwardsville, Alabama Huntsville, Henderson State, Truman State

St. Louis College of Pharmacy
Academic Profile

4588 Parkview Place
St. Louis, MO 63110

Phone: 314-367-8700

Type: Private, 4 Yr., Coed
Website: Not Available
SAT/ACT/GPA: 18
Student/Faculty Ratio: 13:1
Undergraduate Enrollment: 800
Scholarships/Academic: Yes   **Athletic:** No

Founded: 1864
Religion: Non-Affiliated
Housing: Yes
Male/Female: 40:60
Graduate Enrollment: N/A
Financial Aid: Yes

In State: $ 18,295   Out of State: $ 18,295

Expenses By: Year
Specializes In: Pharmacy
Degrees Conferred: BS, ParmD
Programs of Study: Pharmacy

Women's Athletic Profile

4588 Parkview Place
St. Louis, MO 63110
Coach: Merry Graf
Email: bhepfinger@stlcop.edu

NCAA I
Lady Eutectics, Purple, Gold
Phone: (314) 367-8700
Fax: (314) 367-2784

Estimated # of Women's Volleyball Scholarships: N/A
Program Profile: Pre-season begins in August with a week of training before classes begin. The schedule runs through the end of October and averages 2 games per week.
History: St. Louis College of Pharmacy Volleyball began in 1993 as a response to the growing demand for more student activities and a higher level of competition.
Coaching: Merry Graf, Head Coach, started in 1996 at St. Louis College of Pharmacy. She also coaches the St. Louis Volleyball Club team. She broke Monmouth College record (as a player) for most solo blocks and receives "Best Block Award". Julie Scheller, Assistant Coach, started in 1996. She also coaches at the Volleyball Training Network. She earned All-Conference as a player at St. Louis University.

Roster In State: 3 | **Out of State:** 10 | **Out of Country:** 0
Sophomores on Team: 2 | **Seniors on Team:** 2 | **Graduation %:** Unknown
Most Recent Record: 9-20-0 | **Fall Games:** 29 | **Spring Games:** 0
Schedule: Webster, Fontbonne, Hannibal-LaGrange, Principia, Greenville, Baptist Bible

Saint Louis University
Academic Profile

221 N. Grand Blvd.
St. Louis, MO 63103

Phone: 314-977-3266

Type: Private, 4 Yr., Coed
Website: http://www.slu.edu
SAT/ACT/GPA: 1165/20-27/average last year
Student/Faculty Ratio: 15/1
Undergraduate Enrollment: 6,889
Scholarships/Academic: Yes
Expenses By: Year
Founded: 1818
Religion: Jesuit
Housing: Yes
Male/Female: 44/56
Graduate Enrollment: 3,111
Athletic: Yes | **Financial Aid:** Yes
In State: $ 17,000+ | **Out of State:** $ 17,000+
Specializes In: Business, Law, Medicine, and Aeronautics
Degrees Conferred: BA, BS, MA, MS, MBA, Ph.D., Ed, JD
Programs of Study: Arts & Sciences, Law, Medicine, Philosophy & Letters, Business and Administration, Nursing, Social Services, Engineering & Aviation, Allied Health Professions, Public Health, Professional Studies, 23 Doctoral Degrees, 40 Master Degrees

Women's Athletic Profile

3672 W. Pine
St. Louis, MO 63108
Coach: Marilyn McReavy Nolen
Email:

NCAA I
Lady Billikens, Blue, White
Phone: (314) 977-3266
Fax: (314) 977-3178

Estimated # of Women's Volleyball Scholarships: N/A
Conference: Conference USA
Program Profile: Strong conference with usually top 3 going on to NCAA tournament. Great backing for program on the rise. Great education. Graduates are sought for employment and get good jobs. Several players have played professionally.
History: Program began in 1975. Has posted record of 464-387 in 24 seasons of play.
Achievements: Marily Nolen named the 1998 Conference USA Coach of the Year. 3 players NCAA All District. Three players named to the All-C-USA team in 1998. Setter of the Year 1998 in Lelia Roberts.
Coaching: Marilyn Nolen is the most winning coach in SLU history. Record of 111-66 over five seasons. Coach Nolen is eight on the all-time NCAA coaching victories list with 730 wins.

Freshman Receiving Financial Aid/Academic: | **Athletic:** 5
Roster In State: 3 | **Out of State:** 7 | **Out of Country:** 2
Sophomores on Team: 3 | **Seniors on Team:** 1 | **Graduation %:** 100

Most Recent Record: 21-7   **Fall Games:** 28   **Spring Games:** 4
Camp of Clinic Dates: July 10-22, 2000
Positions Needed: All positions
Schedule: Clemson, Louisville, Kansas, South Florida, Houston,Cincinnati, Western Kentucky
Style of Play: '98 team was very skilled, defensively apt, and experienced with 5 seniors. Fought hard to win and had great record. Won lots of tight matches. Team gets along well and loves to play volleyball.

Southeast Missouri State University
Academic Profile

#1 University Plaza
Cape Girardeau, MO 63701

Phone: 573-651-2255

Type: Public, 4 Yr., Coed
Website: http://www.semo.edu
SAT/ACT/GPA: 990/21
Student/Faculty Ratio: 17:1
Undergraduate Enrollment: 6,409
Scholarships/Academic: Yes   **Athletic:** Yes
Expenses By: Year   **In State:** $ 4,704+
Degrees Conferred: AA, AAS, BA, BS, BGS, BSBA, BSEd, BSM, MA, MS
Programs of Study: Accounting, Advertising, Art, Banking/Finance, Biological, Business, Chemistry, Computer, Dietetics, Earth Science, Engineering, Nursing, Parks/Recreation, etc..

Founded: 1873
Religion: Non-Affiliated
Housing: No
Male/Female: 44:56
Graduate Enrollment: 721
Financial Aid: Yes
Out of State: $ 6,552

Women's Athletic Profile

#1 University Plaza
Cape Girardeau, MO 63701
Coach: Cindy Gannon
Email: cmgannon@semovm.semo.edu

NCAA I
Lady Otahkians, Red, White
Phone: (573) 651-2997
Fax:

Estimated # of Women's Volleyball Scholarships: N/A
Conference: Ohio Valley Conference

Southwest Baptist University
Academic Profile

1600 University Avenue
Bolivar, MO 65613

Phone: 417-328-1739

Type: Private, 4 Yr., Coed
Website: http://www.sbuniv.edu
SAT/ACT/GPA: Not Available
Student/Faculty Ratio: 17/1
Undergraduate Enrollment: 2,000
Scholarships/Academic: Yes   **Athletic:** Yes
Expenses By: Year   **In State:** $13,000
Specializes In: Education, Business and Physical Therapy
Degrees Conferred: BA, BBA, BS, MED, MBA, MS
Programs of Study: College of Education & Social Sciences, College of Science & Mathematics, College of Business, College of Music, Arts & Letters, College of Christian Studies

Founded: 1878
Religion: Southern Baptist
Housing: Yes
Male/Female: N/A
Graduate Enrollment: 1,000
Financial Aid: Yes
Out of State: $13,000

Women's Athletic Profile

1600 University Avenue
Bolivar, MO 65613
Coach: Cindy Rear
Email: crear@sbuniv.edu
Estimated # of Women's Volleyball Scholarships: N/A
Conference: Mid-America Intercollegiate Athletics Association

NCAA I
Lady Bearcats, Purple, White
Phone: (417) 328-1709
Fax: (417) 326-0966

Southwest Missouri State University
Academic Profile

128 Garfield
West Plains, MO 65775

Phone: 877-311-7322

Type: 4 year
Website:
SAT/ACT/GPA: Open
Student/Faculty Ratio:
Undergraduate Enrollment: N/A
Scholarships/Academic:
Expenses By:
Degrees Conferred:

Athletic:
In State:

Founded:
Religion: Non-Affiliated
Housing:
Male/Female:
Graduate Enrollment: N/A
Financial Aid:
Out of State:

Programs of Study: Contact school for programs of study.

Women's Athletic Profile

128 Garfield
West Plains, MO 65775
Coach: Trish Kissiar-Knight
Email: Tknight@wp.smsu.edu

NCAA I
Lady Bears, Maroon, White
Phone: (417) 257-2404
Fax: (417) 256-8482

Estimated # of Women's Volleyball Scholarships: N/A
Conference: Missouri Valley
Program Profile: Our program has fast developed into one of the top junior college programs. We are well-funded and benefit from a great deal of community support. We have a great season schedule. We strive to go out and get the best competition. Our stadium is one of the nicest around for junior colleges. It seats 3,000 and is a great place to play.
History: Our program will be on its seventh year in 1999. It began in 1993. The program's record is 252-70-2. We have been ranked in the Top Ten of the National Poll for the past three seasons.
Achievements: Trish Kissiar-Knight has been named Region XVI Coach of the Year four times; program has produced four All-Americans
Coaching: Trish Kissiar Knight, Head Coach, played at Southwest Missouri State Division I program. She is a member of the SMSI Women's Athletics Hall of Fame. She coached high school for 14 years and won 4 consecutive Championships.
Freshman Receiving Financial Aid/Academic:

		Athletic: All
Roster In State: 5	**Out of State:** 7	**Out of Country:** 0
Sophomores on Team: 1	**Seniors on Team:** 5	**Graduation %:** 98
Most Recent Record: 46-11-0	**Fall Games:** 60	**Spring Games:** 30

Camp of Clinic Dates: Basic Skills Camp: July 6-8; Elite Hitter Setter Camp July 9-11; JV: July13-16; Varsity: July 19/22
Positions Needed: Setter, Middle Hitter, Outside Hitter
Schedule: Miami-Dade Community College, Illinois Central, Belleville Area College, Utah Valley, Brownsville Community College, Jefferson College, College of Southern Idaho, Gendale Community College
Style of Play: We play a very high level of volleyball. Our style of play incorporates a very creative offense. Our players really enjoy the offensive system we use. Defensively, we have always been strong. We like to play read defense and teach pursuit.

Stephens College
Academic Profile

1200 East Broadway Street
Columbia, MO 65215

Phone: 800-876-7207

Type: Private, 4 Yr., Liberal Arts, Women
Website: http://www.stephens.edu
SAT/ACT/GPA: Open
Student/Faculty Ratio: 11:1
Undergraduate Enrollment: 550
Scholarships/Academic: Yes
Expenses By: Year

Athletic: No
In State: $ 19,000

Founded: 1833
Religion: Non-Affiliated
Housing: Yes
Male/Female: 1:34
Graduate Enrollment: 36
Financial Aid: Yes
Out of State: $ 19,000

Specializes In: Education, Sciences, Theatre, Dance
Degrees Conferred: AA, AS, BA, BS
Programs of Study: Biology, Business Administration, English, International Studies, Mathematical Sciences, Philosophy, Social Sciences, Psychology, Creative Writing, Dance, Fashion Design, Theatre Arts, Accounting, Health Sciences, Early Childhood Education, Elementary Education, Environmental Science, Equestrian, Business Management, Marketing, Mass Communications, Student-initiated Majors

Women's Athletic Profile

1200 East Broadway
Columbia, MO 65215
Coach: Lori Towle
Email: ltowle@wc.stephens.edu

NCAA I
Lady Stars, Burgundy, Gold
Phone: (573) 876-7212
Fax:

Did Not Return Profile

Truman State U (Northeast MO St. U)
Academic Profile

Pershing Blvd.
Kirksville, MO 63501-4221

Phone: (660) 785-4468

Type: Public, 4 Yr., Liberal Arts, Coed
Website: http://www.truman.edu
SAT/ACT/GPA: 1000/22/3.0
Student/Faculty Ratio: 16:1
Undergraduate Enrollment: 6,300
Scholarships/Academic: Yes   **Athletic:** Yes
Expenses By: Year   **In State:** $ 8,400
Specializes In: Liberal Arts and Sciences

Founded: 1867
Religion: Non-Affiliated
Housing: Yes
Male/Female: 45:55
Graduate Enrollment: 250
Financial Aid: Yes
Out of State: $ 11,016

Degrees Conferred: BA, BS, BFA, MAE, MA, MS, MBA
Programs of Study: Accounting, Agricultural Science, Anthropology, Art, Art History, Business, Biology, Chemistry, Communication, Computer Science, Economics, Education, English, French, German, Health and Exercise Science, History, Journalism, Justice Systems, Mathematics, Music, Nursing, Performance, Philosophy, Physics, Political Science, PreDental

Women's Athletic Profile

100 E. Normal St.
Kirksville, MO 63501
Coach: Becky Eggering
Email: eggering@truman.edu

NCAA I
Lady Bulldogs, Purple, White
Phone: (660) 785-4236
Fax: (660) 785-4189

Estimated # of Women's Volleyball Scholarships: N/A
Conference: MIAA
Program Profile: We are a NCAA Division II school. The MIAA Conference includes ten schools. Pershing Building has 4,000 seats. We play a Fall season.
History: We started in 1973. Coach Eggering is the 6th coach at Truman. She has an overall record of 43-28.
Achievements: 3rd of the Conference in 1998; Four All-Region Players since 1995.
Coaching: Becky Eggering, Head Coach, compiled a record of 43-28. Qi Wang is Associate Coach. They both began coaching here in 1997.
Freshman Receiving Financial Aid/Academic: **Athletic:** 3
Roster In State: 3   **Out of State:** 10   **Out of Country:** 0
Sophomores on Team: 0   **Seniors on Team:** 1   **Graduation %:** Unknown
Most Recent Record: 22-13-0   **Fall Games:** 35   **Spring Games:** 2
Camp of Clinic Dates: July 14-18
Positions Needed: Outside Setter
Schedule: North Alabama, Rockhurst, Central Missouri, Northern Kentucky
Style of Play: All around, with offensive and defensive balance.

University of Missouri - Columbia
Academic Profile

374 Hearnes Center
Columbia, MO 65211

Phone: (573) 882-3894

Type: Public, 4 Yr., Liberal Arts, Coed
Website: http://www.mutigers.edu
SAT/ACT/GPA: 700 Min/25.8/2.0
Student/Faculty Ratio: 19:1
Undergraduate Enrollment: 17,346

Founded: 1839
Religion: Non-Affiliated
Housing: Yes
Male/Female: 47:53
Graduate Enrollment: 5,154

Scholarships/Academic: Yes   **Athletic:** Yes   **Financial Aid:** Yes
Expenses By: Year   **In State:** $ 9,368   **Out of State:** $ 16,524
Degrees Conferred: BA, BS, BFA, AB, BSEd, BGS, BSN, BJ, BM, MA, MS, MFA, BSW, MBA, BES
Programs of Study: College of Agriculture, Food and Natural Resources, School of Natural Resources, College of Arts & Sciences, School of Fine Arts, College of Business and Public Administration, School of Accounting, College of Education, College of Engineering, College of Human Environmental Sciences, School of Social Work, School of Nursing, School of Journalism, School of Law, School of Medicine, School of Health Related Problems

Women's Athletic Profile

355 Hearnes Center
Columbia, MO 65211-1050
Coach: Disa Johnson
Email: vossc@missouri.edu

NCAA I
Lady Tigers, Old Gold, Black
Phone: (573) 882-3894
Fax: (573) 884-7577

Estimated # of Women's Volleyball Scholarships: 12
Conference: Big 12 Conference
Program Profile: We are a young program that is growing quickly. We play at Hearnes Center with a seating capacity of 15,000. We have practice courts at Hearnes Center also. Our season begins in August and ends in late November.
History: Our program began in 1974. The team will begin to play in its 26th season in 1999. We were a part of the Big 8 until 1996 when the Big 12 was formed. We finished better each year in the Big 12.
Coaching: Disa Johnson - Head Coach. She was a former All Big-Ten setter for the University of Illinois. Chuck Voss and Andy Nedgel are assistant coaches.
Freshman Receiving Financial Aid/Academic: **Athletic:** 3
Roster In State: 3   **Out of State:** 10   **Out of Country:** 0
Sophomores on Team: 0   **Seniors on Team:** 0   **Graduation %:** 100
Most Recent Record: 14-19-0   **Fall Games:** 33   **Spring Games:** 4
Camp of Clinic Dates: Individual Skills: July 9-11; General Skills: July 19-22, July 26-29
Positions Needed: 2
Schedule: Nebraska, Colorado, Texas, Texas A & M, Arkansas, Oregon State
Style of Play: We play a fast attack that is dictated by good passes and solid defense. Tough serving and aggressive blocking are stressed. We are a very disciplined program that does not quit anytime in the match.

University of Missouri - Kansas City
Academic Profile

5100 Rock Hill Road
Kansas City, MO 64110

Phone: (816) 235-1036

Type: Public, 4 Yr., Liberal Arts, Coed
Website: http://www.umkc.edu
SAT/ACT/GPA: 850/24
Student/Faculty Ratio: 14:1
Undergraduate Enrollment: 6,108
Scholarships/Academic: Yes
Expenses By: Year

Founded: 1963
Religion: Non-Affiliated
Housing: Yes
Male/Female: 2:3
Graduate Enrollment: 4,502
Athletic: Yes   **Financial Aid:** Yes
In State: $ 11,000   **Out of State:** $ 16,000
Specializes In: Medicine, Dentistry
Degrees Conferred: BA, BS, BFA, MA, MS, MBA, Ph.D., JD, PharmD, MD, DMD
Programs of Study: Accounting, Arts & Science, Business Administration & Management, Communications, Dentistry, Education, Engineering, English, Law, Law Enforcement & Correction, Mathematics, Medicine, Music, Nursing, Performing Arts, Pharmacy, Psychology, Social Sciences

Women's Athletic Profile

5100 Rockhill Rd.
Kansas City, MO 64110-2499
Coach: Steve Dallman
Email: geem@smtpgate.umkc.edu

NCAA I
Lady Kangaroos, Blue, Gold
Phone: (816) 235-1036
Fax: (816) 235-1035

Estimated # of Women's Volleyball Scholarships: 11
Conference: Mid-Continent Conference
Program Profile: Our playing season runs from August to December. The team plays at Swinney Recreation Center, with a maximum 1,600 capacity.
History: In 1987, we began as a NCAA Division I program. The #8 Jersey of Catalina Suarez was retired - one of two student-athletes at UMKC to have had their number retired.

Achievements: 1996 & 1998 John Mckenna Academic Award (highest GPA in conference); 1997 first team All-Conference was Katy Kempschroeder and Julie Mohrfeld; 1997 second team was named Courtney Cella; 1998 second team - Julie Mohrfeld; 1998 USA National Team Try-outs and 1997 Setter of the Year was Katy Kamschroeder.
Coaching: Steve Dallman, Head Coach, began coaching our program this year. He is a former assistant coach at Louisville in 1997, with a record of 16-2. He coached at Mississippi for three seasons with a record of 32-68. He was an assistant coach at St. Francis for two seasons with a record of 35-6. Maggie Mohrfeld, Assistant Coach, also has entered her first year with the program.
Freshman Receiving Financial Aid/Academic: **Athletic:** 2
Roster In State: 3   **Out of State:** 6   **Out of Country:** 0
Sophomores on Team: 2   **Seniors on Team:** 0   **Graduation %:** 100
Most Recent Record: 13-18-0
Camp of Clinic Dates: Individual Skills: July 12-14; Setter/Middle Hitters - July 14-16
Positions Needed: Middle, Right side
Schedule: Oral Roberts, Tulsa, Kansas, UNLV, St. Louis, Iowa State
Style of Play: Quick offense and tenacious defense.

University of Missouri - Saint Louis
Academic Profile

8001 Natural Bridge Rd.
St. Louis, MO 63121

Phone: 314-516-5451

Type: Public, 4 Yr., Coed
Website: http://www.umsl.edu
SAT/ACT/GPA: 24
Student/Faculty Ratio: 14:1
Undergraduate Enrollment: 12,844
Scholarships/Academic: Yes   **Athletic:** Yes
Expenses By: Year   **In State:** $ 7,545

Founded: 1963
Religion: Non-Affiliated
Housing: Yes
Male/Female: 50:50
Graduate Enrollment: 2,732
Financial Aid: Yes
Out of State: $ 13,500

Degrees Conferred: BA, NS, MA, MS, MEd, MBA, Ph.D., BFA, BGS, BM, BSBA, BSEd, BSN, BSPA, BSW,, MPPA, MSN, EdD, OD
Programs of Study: Anthropology, Art History, Biology, Business Administration, Chemistry, Communication, Computer Science, Criminal Justice, Economics, Education, English, French, German, History, Management, Mathematics, Music, Nursing, Philosophy, Physics, Political Science, Psychology, Public Administration, Social Science, Spanish, Special Education

Women's Athletic Profile

8001 Natural Bridge Rd.
St. Louis, MO 63121-4499
Coach: Denise Silvester
Email: denise_silvester@umsl.edu

NCAA I
Riverwomen, Red, Gold
Phone: (314) 516-5643
Fax: (314) 516-5503

Estimated # of Women's Volleyball Scholarships: N/A
Conference: Great Lakes Valley Conference

Washington University-St. Louis
Academic Profile

Campus Box 1067, One Brookings Drive
St. Louis, MO 63130-4899

Phone: (314) 935-4713

Type: Private, 4 Yr., Liberal Arts, Engineering, Coed
Website: http://www.bearsports.wustl.edu
SAT/ACT/GPA: 1300+/27+
Student/Faculty Ratio: 1:15-17
Undergraduate Enrollment: 5,452
Scholarships/Academic: Yes   **Athletic:** No
Expenses By: Year   **In State:** $ 33,000

Founded: 1853
Religion: Non-Affiliated
Housing: Yes
Male/Female: 1:1
Graduate Enrollment: 5,700
Financial Aid: Yes
Out of State: $ 33,000

Specializes In: 3,100 undergraduates in Arts & Sciences, 1,030 undergrad Engineering
Degrees Conferred: BS, BA, MS
Programs of Study: Consistently ranked in the top 20 universities in America. Business, Engineering, Biological Sciences, PreMed, PreLaw, Education

Women's Athletic Profile

One Brooking Drive, Box 1067
St. Louis, MO 63130
Coach: Rich Luenemann
Email: luenemann@athletics.wustl.edu

NCAA I
Lady Bears, Red, Green
Phone: (314) 935-4713
Fax: (314) 935-5545

Estimated # of Women's Volleyball Scholarships: 0
Conference: University Athletic Association
Program Profile: We play at Washington University Fieldhouse which has 3,000 seats. There are 3 gyms available for multiple competition.
History: Teri Clemens was head coach from 1985 to 1998. Rich Luenemann became head coach in 1999. We have an NCAA Record 59 match win streak from November 9, 1991 to September 18, 1993.
Achievements: Teri Clemens-National Coach of the Year 5 times; 8 National Players of the Year; 36 AVCA All-Americans; 10 Conference Titles
Coaching: Rich Luenemann, became Head Coach in 1999. He was head coach at University of St.Francis. His overall record there was 590-262 with a wining percentage of .692. He is a member of the NAIA Hall of Fame. The assistant coach position is to be announced.
Freshman Receiving Financial Aid/Academic: | | **Athletic:** 7
Roster In State: 8 | **Out of State:** 7 | **Out of Country:** 0
Sophomores on Team: 0 | **Seniors on Team:** 3 | **Graduation %:** 100
Most Recent Record: 37-4-0 | **Fall Games:** 21 | **Spring Games:** 4
Camp of Clinic Dates: June 20 to July 2
Positions Needed: Middle Blocker, Setter, Defensive Specialist
Schedule: Central Iowa, Juniata, Southern Illinois-Edwardsville, University of Missouri at St.Louis, San Diego, Emory
Style of Play: We have a fast paced offense (5-1) and sophisticated systems of play.

Webster University
Academic Profile

470 East Lockwood
St. Louis, MO 63119

Phone: (314) 968-7191

Type: Private, 4 Yr., Liberal Arts, Coed
Website: http://www.websteruniv.edu
SAT/ACT/GPA: 1000/22/2.5
Student/Faculty Ratio: 15:1
Undergraduate Enrollment: 1,800
Scholarships/Academic: Yes
Expenses By: Year

Athletic: No
In State: $ 18,460

Founded: 1915
Religion: Non-Affiliated
Housing: Yes
Male/Female: 40:60
Graduate Enrollment: 2,500
Financial Aid: Yes
Out of State: $ 18,460

Specializes In: Business, Communication, Education
Degrees Conferred: BA, BFA, BS, BM, MA, MBA, MM, MT
Programs of Study: Accounting, Advertising, Art, Behavioral & Social Science, Biology, Business, Business Administration, Computer Science, Dance, Education, English, Film, Foreign Languages, History, Journalism, Marketing, Mathematics, Media Communications, Music, Political Science, Public Relations, Science

Women's Athletic Profile

470 E. Lockwood
Webster Groves, MO 63119
Coach: Heather Husek
Email: hhusek@pulitzer.net

NCAA I
Gorloks, Gold, White, Navy
Phone: (314) 968-6984
Fax: (314) 963-6092

Estimated # of Women's Volleyball Scholarships: N/A
Conference: St. Louis Intercollegiate Athletic Conference
Program Profile: Play home matches in air-conditioned Grant Gymnasium. Season begins middle of August and ends the 1st week in November.
History: Started 1984, 1990's 158 wins 112 losses, Overall Record 1990's 44 wins 23 losses
Achievements: Coach of the Year 1995, 97 Conference Title 1995-97
Coaching: Heather Husek('95) Overall record 76-50 (.603) Conference Record; 37-5 (.881)
Roster In State: 12 | **Out of State:** | **Out of Country:**
Sophomores on Team: | **Seniors on Team:** 11 | **Graduation %:** 100

Most Recent Record: **Fall Games:** 32 **Spring Games:**
Positions Needed: S, OH, MH
Schedule: Illinois College, Westminster College, Maryville University, Augustana College
Style of Play: Play an aggressive, attacking style of play. Use our speed and quickness to one advantage

Westminster College
Academic Profile

501 Westminster Avenue **Phone:** 800-475-3361
Fulton, MO 65251

Type: Private, 4 Yr., Liberal Arts, Coed **Founded:** 1851
Website: http://www.westminster-mo.edu **Religion:** Historically Presbyterian
SAT/ACT/GPA: Yes **Housing:** Yes
Student/Faculty Ratio: 12:1 **Male/Female:** 6:4
Undergraduate Enrollment: 700 **Graduate Enrollment:** N/A
Scholarships/Academic: Yes **Athletic:** No **Financial Aid:** Yes
Expenses By: Year **In State:** $ 17,190 **Out of State:** $ 17,190
Degrees Conferred: BS, BA
Programs of Study: Accounting, Advertising, Art, Biology, Business Administration, Business Communications, Chemistry, Classic, Economics, Education, English, French, History, Mathematics, Philosophy, Physical Education, Physics, Political Science, PreLaw, PreMed, Psychology, Religion, Sport Medicine

Women's Athletic Profile

501 Westminster Avenue **NCAA I**
Fulton, MO 65251 Lady Blue Jays, Blue, White
Coach: Melinda Washington **Phone:** (573) 592-5302
Email: **Fax:** (573) 592-5366

Estimated # of Women's Volleyball Scholarships: N/A
Conference: St. Louis Intercollegiate Athletic Conference
History: Our program started in 1981. During the past 18 seasons, the Blue Jays have compiled a 278-320-1 record. We won Conference Titles in 1996 and 1998.
Achievements: Coach Melinda Washington named Conference Coach of the Year in 1998.
Coaching: Melinda Washington, Head Coach, in her two seasons here, her record is 47-13.
Most Recent Record: 25-6-0

William Jewell College
Academic Profile

500 College Hill **Phone:** 800-753-7009
Liberty, MO 64068

Type: Private, 4 Yr., Liberal Arts, Coed **Founded:** 1849
Website: http://www.jewell.edu **Religion:** Baptist
SAT/ACT/GPA: Open **Housing:** Yes
Student/Faculty Ratio: 15:1 **Male/Female:** 1:3
Undergraduate Enrollment: 1,200 **Graduate Enrollment:** N/A
Scholarships/Academic: Yes **Athletic:** Yes **Financial Aid:** Yes
Expenses By: Year **In State:** $ 17,400 **Out of State:** $ 17,400
Degrees Conferred: BA, BS
Programs of Study: Art, Biology, British Studies, Business Administration & Economics, Accounting, Chemistry, Communications, Speech/Theatre, Education, English, History, Languages, Mathematics, Computer Science, Music, Nursing, Oxbridge Honors Program, Philosophy, Physics, Political Science, Psychology, Religion, Sociology

Women's Athletic Profile

500 College Hill **NCAA I**
Liberty, MO 64068 Cardinals, Red, Black
Coach: Frankie Albitz **Phone:** (816) 781-5285
Email: albitzf@william.jewell.edu **Fax:** (816) 415-5029

Estimated # of Women's Volleyball Scholarships: Varies
Conference: Heart of America Athletic Conference
Program Profile: Great facility, we have varsity & junior varsity teams and play on tartan playing surface. We are also a strong academic school.
History: Improving each year. First full-time Coach hired in 1997.
Coaching: Head Coach Frankie Albitz.

Roster In State: 12	**Out of State:** 12	**Out of Country:** 0
Sophomores on Team:	**Seniors on Team:** 1	**Graduation %:** 100

Most Recent Record: 16-19
Camp of Clinic Dates: June 3-7
Positions Needed: Setter, RS, LS
Schedule: Graceland, Benedictine, Culver-Stockton, Rockhurst, Mid-America Nazarene, Lindenwood
Style of Play: Fast offense and aggressive defense.

William Woods University
Academic Profile

200 W 12th Street
Fulton, MO 65251

Phone: (573) 592-4340

Type: Private, 4 Yr., Liberal Arts, Women Only
Website: http://www.wmwoods.edu
SAT/ACT/GPA: Open
Student/Faculty Ratio: 13:1
Undergraduate Enrollment: 700
Scholarships/Academic: Yes
Expenses By: Year
Founded: 1870
Religion: Disciples of Christ
Housing: Yes
Male/Female: Women Only
Graduate Enrollment: 300
Athletic: Yes
Financial Aid: Yes
In State: $ 16,000
Out of State: $ 16,000
Programs of Study: Accounting, Biology, Business Administration, Chemistry, Commercial Art, Communications, Computer Science, Deaf Interpreter, Design, Early Childhood Education, Economics, English, Equestrian Science, Fashion Merchandising, Fine Arts, French, Geography, German, History, Interior Design, Management, Marketing, Mathematics, Military Science, Music, Philosophy, Physics, Political Science, PreLaw, PreMed, Psychology, Religion, Secondary Education, Social Science, Spanish, Special Education, Speech, Visual & Performing Arts

Women's Athletic Profile

200 W. Twelfth St.
Fulton, MO 65251-10983.5
Coach: Roger Worsley
Email: rworsley@iris.wmwoods.edu

NCAA I
Lady Owls, Green, White
Phone: (573) 592-4340
Fax: (573) 592-4386

Estimated # of Women's Volleyball Scholarships: 3.5
Conference: American Midwest Conference
Program Profile: We play at Helen Stephens Sports Complex which has 800 seats. Our season is from August to November.
History: We started in 1974. We have done very well in both district play and more recently in regional play. We consistently are in the Top Ten at the regional level. Our overall program record is 612-359.
Achievements: 1997 AMC Coach of the Year; AMC Conference Coaches Chair; Laurin Rehkop-All-American Scholar Athlete in 1996.
Coaching: Roger Worsley, has been Head Coach for 3 years. His overall record is 68-60. Mark Jones has been Assistant Coach for 1 year.

Roster In State: 11	**Out of State:** 3	**Out of Country:** 0
Sophomores on Team: 3	**Seniors on Team:** 4	**Graduation %:** 100
Most Recent Record: 28-19-0	**Fall Games:** 47	**Spring Games:** 0

Schedule: Washington University, Columbia College, Rockhurst College, Peru State, Truman State
Style of Play: Fast-paced offense and multi-faceted defense. When we step on the court-whether for practice or a game-it is all business. Strong fundamentals. Swing offense and perimeter defense.

MONTANA

Helena

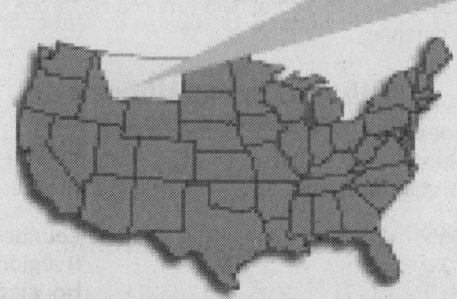

SCHOOL	CITY	AFFILIATION	PAGE
Carroll College	Helena	NAIA	432
Montana State Univ- Bozeman	Bozeman	NCAA I	432
Montana State Univ- Billings	Billings	NCAA II	433
Montana Tech	Butte	NAIA	434
University of Montana	Missoula	NCAA I	434

Carroll College
Academic Profile

North Benton Avenue
Helena, MT 59625

Phone: 800-992-3648

Type: Private, 4 Yr., Liberal Arts, Coed
Website: http://www.carroll.edu
SAT/ACT/GPA: Open
Student/Faculty Ratio: 14:1
Undergraduate Enrollment: 1,400
Scholarships/Academic: Yes
Expenses By: Year
Specializes In: Science
Degrees Conferred: AA, BA

Athletic: Yes
In State: $ 12,750

Founded: 1909
Religion: Catholic
Housing: No
Male/Female: 45:55
Graduate Enrollment: N/A
Financial Aid: Yes
Out of State: $ 12,750

Programs of Study: Accounting, Biology, Business Administration, Classical Languages, Combined Science, Communications Arts, Computer Science, Computer Software Engineering, Economics, Elementary Education, Engineering, English, English/Writing, French, Mathematics, Medical Technology, Nursing, Occupational Therapy, Philosophy, Physical Therapy, Physical Education, Political Science, Psychology, Public Administration, Public Relations, Social Science, Social Work, Sociology, Spanish

Women's Athletic Profile

1601N.Benton Ave.
Helena, MT 59601
Coach: Amy Heuiser
Email: awilliam@carroll.edu

NCAA I
Lady Fighting Saints, Blue, Gold
Phone: (406) 447-4480
Fax: (406) 477-4955

Estimated # of Women's Volleyball Scholarships: 8
Conference: UMAC
Program Profile: Our facility, called Carroll PE Center, has a seating capacity of 2,800. Our conference just increased from 5 members to 7 members. The 1999-2000 schedule includes 4 competitive tournaments and 12 conference games. Regular season is from late August to the beginning of November.
History: Our season began in the early 1980's. We have won several conference titles in the mid-1980's. We got conference titles from 1991 to 1996. We had one appearance at the National Tournament in 1992.
Achievements: Frontier Conference Champions in 1996-97,1995-96,1994-95,1993-94,1992 All-American-Triara Ainuu; 1994 All-American-Amy Williams; 1995 & 1996 All-American-Tiffany Hofer; 1998 All American- Stacy Phillipe
Coaching: Amy Heuiser, Head Coach, started here in 1997. Her record is 29-29. As a player, she was All-Conference, All-Region, Honorable Mention All-American, District MVP and Conference MVP. Her team won 4 Conference Titles and got 5th place at Nationals in 1992. Jill Jenneskens and Tiffany Hofer are Assistant Coaches.

Freshman Receiving Financial Aid/Academic:
Roster In State: 12
Sophomores on Team: 4
Most Recent Record: 13-13-0
Camp of Clinic Dates: July 18-22
Positions Needed: None

Out of State: 5
Seniors on Team: 3
Fall Games: 26

Athletic: 2
Out of Country: 0
Graduation %: 85
Spring Games: 3

Schedule: Montana State University-Bozeman, Point Loma Nazarene, Dickinson State University, Lewis-Clark State, Fresno Pacific, Northwest Nazarene
Style of Play: Offensively aggressive with a quick offense. Defense reads opponents' offense around a strong block.

Montana State University
Academic Profile

Office of New Student Services
Bozeman, MT 59717

Phone: 800-678-2287

Type: Public, 4 Yr., Coed
Website: http://www.montana.edu
SAT/ACT/GPA: 1030/22/2.50
Student/Faculty Ratio: 19.5:1
Undergraduate Enrollment: 10,254
Scholarships/Academic: Yes
Expenses By: Year

Athletic: Yes
In State: $ 10,626

Founded: 1893
Religion: Non-Affiliated
Housing: Yes
Male/Female: 60:40
Graduate Enrollment: 1,492
Financial Aid: Yes
Out of State: $ 16,375

Specializes In: Education, Engineering, Nursing, Sciences
Degrees Conferred: Bachelors, Masters, Doctors
Programs of Study: Accounting, Agriculture, Architecture, Art, Biology, Chemistry, Earth Sciences, Education, Engineering, Exercise and Wellness, History, Mathematics, Media and Theatre Arts, Modern Languages, Music, Nursing, Physics, Psychology, Sociology

Women's Athletic Profile

Office of New Student Services
Bozeman, MT 59717-3380
Coach: Dave Gantt
Email: rondar@Montana.edu

NCAA I
Lady Bobcats, Blue, Gold
Phone: (406) 994-2452
Fax: (406) 994-1923

Estimated # of Women's Volleyball Scholarships: 4
Conference: Big Sky Conference
Program Profile: We are a Top 60 program at NCAA Division I level that competes in the Big Sky Conference. We are consistently among the Top 40 in attendance. We play in the volleyball-only Shroyer Gym which has 1,800 seats.
History: Montana State had a strong start in 1977 under the leadership of Bill Neville. After 4 winning seasons, Neville left to coach the USA Men's Olympic Team. After some down years in the 1980's, Dave Gantt took over in 1994 and will look to guide the team to its fifth wining season.
Achievements: Kim Steffel (1989-1992) AVCA NW All-Region; 53 All-Big Sky Conference Academic Selections.
Coaching: Dave Gantt, Head Coach, started coaching the program in 1994 and compiled a record of 136-125 in 9 years. Jerry Wagner is Assistant Coach. He was Assistant Coach at MSU, Oregon State, and Montana. Mya Malauuw is Assistant Coach. She played at Oregon State. She was ranked 3rd on the All-Time PAC-10 Assists Chart.
Freshman Receiving Financial Aid/Academic: | | **Athletic:** 3
Roster In State: 6 | **Out of State:** 8 | **Out of Country:** 2
Sophomores on Team: 3 | **Seniors on Team:** 5 | **Graduation %:** 99
Most Recent Record: 21-6-0 | **Fall Games:** 27 | **Spring Games:** 10
Camp of Clinic Dates: call 406-994-3066
Positions Needed: All
Schedule: Minnesota, Wyoming, Wake Forest, North Carolina State, Cal State-Sacramento, Eastern Washington
Style of Play: Competitive, quick, upbeat, dynamic and positive.

Montana State University-Billings
Academic Profile

1500 North 30th
Billings, MT 59101

Phone: 800-656-6782

Type: 4 Yr., Coed
Website: http://www.msubillings.edu
SAT/ACT/GPA: Open
Student/Faculty Ratio: 20:1
Undergraduate Enrollment: 3,624
Scholarships/Academic: | **Athletic:** | **Financial Aid:**
Expenses By: | **In State:** | **Out of State:**
Specializes In:
Degrees Conferred: Masters, Bachelors

Founded: 1927
Religion: Non-Affiliated
Housing: No
Male/Female: Not Available
Graduate Enrollment: N/A

Programs of Study: Accounting, Art Education, Art/Fine Arts, Automotive Technology, Biology, Biological Science, Computer Information Systems, Human Services, Practical Nursing, Reading, Education, Music, Sociology

Women's Athletic Profile

1500 N. 30th
Billings, MT 59101
Coach: Pa'ulasi Matavao
Email: pmatavao@msubillings.edu

NCAA I
Lady Yellow Jackets, Blue, Gold
Phone: (406) 657-2603
Fax: (406) 657-2366

Estimated # of Women's Volleyball Scholarships: N/A
Conference: Pacific West Conference

Montana Tech of the University of Montana
Academic Profile

West Park Street
Butte, MT 59701

Phone: 800-445-8324

Type: Public, 4 Yr., Engineering, Coed
Website: http://www.mtech.edu
SAT/ACT/GPA: 20/2.5
Student/Faculty Ratio: 16:1
Undergraduate Enrollment: 1,731
Scholarships/Academic: Yes   **Athletic:** Yes
Expenses By: Year   **In State:** $ 7,104
Specializes In: Engineering

Founded: 1900
Religion: Non-Affiliated
Housing: Yes
Male/Female: 2:1.5
Graduate Enrollment: 92
Financial Aid: Yes
Out of State: $ 12,183

Degrees Conferred: Bachelors, Masters
Programs of Study: Engineering Science, Environmental Engineering, Petroleum Engineering, Mining Engineering, Metallurgical Engineering, Geological Engineering, Geophysical Engineering, Biology, Business, Chemistry, Computer Science, Liberal Science, Mathematics, Occupational Safety and Health, Professional and Technical Communications

Women's Athletic Profile

West Park Street
Butte, MT 59701
Coach: Marilyn Tobin
Email: athletics@mtech.edu

NCAA I
Lady Orediggers, Forest Green
Phone: (406) 496-4292
Fax: (406) 496-4711

Estimated # of Women's Volleyball Scholarships: 3
Conference: Frontier Conference
Program Profile: We have 12 players returning, 1 senior setter is graduating. We started 4 freshmen and were 2nd in Conference. We play at HPER complex, which has 3 full volleyball courts. We play mid-August to mid-November.
History: The volleyball program began in 1975.
Achievements: 1998 Coach of the Year; 1 Conference Title in 1990; 2nd in Conference 5 out of nine years; made Conference play-offs (only top 3 go) 8 out of nine years.
Coaching: Marilyn Tobin, Head Coach, started with the program in 1990. She compiled a record of 155-145. She attended Montana Tech as a first team and was named All-Conference, All-District, team MVP and Academic All-Conference. She graduated with honors. Stacey McCauley is Assistant Coach.
Freshman Receiving Financial Aid/Academic: **Athletic:** 3
Roster In State: 12   **Out of State:** 0   **Out of Country:** 1
Sophomores on Team: 2   **Seniors on Team:** 1   **Graduation %:** 100
Most Recent Record: 17-11-0   **Fall Games:** 28   **Spring Games:** 3 Tourneys
Positions Needed: Setter, Outside Hitter
Schedule: Lewis Clark State, Northwest Nazarene, Western Montana, Albertsons
Style of Play: Great passing and defense. Freshmen learning to terminate ball. One player (setter) away from being a great team.

University of Montana
Academic Profile

Adams Field House
Missoula, MT 59812-1291

Phone: (406) 243-2760

Type: Public, 4 Yr., Liberal Arts, Coed
Website: http://www.umt.edu
SAT/ACT/GPA: 1030/22/2.5
Student/Faculty Ratio: 19:1
Undergraduate Enrollment: 9,000
Scholarships/Academic: Yes   **Athletic:** Yes
Expenses By: Year   **In State:** $ 8,500
Specializes In: Business, Education, Forestry, Physical Therapy, Sports Medicine

Founded: 1892
Religion: Non-Affiliated
Housing: Yes
Male/Female: 50:50
Graduate Enrollment: 2,000
Financial Aid: Yes
Out of State: $ 13,500

Degrees Conferred: BA, BS
Programs of Study: Arts & Sciences, Business Administration, Education, Fine Arts, Forestry, Honors College, Journalism, Law, Pharmacy

P.O. Box 173380
Missoula, MT 59812-1291
Coach: Dick Scott
Email: grizvb@selway.umt.edu

NCAA I
Grizzlies, Silver, Gold, Maroon
Phone: (406) 243-5411
Fax: (406) 243-6859

Estimated # of Women's Volleyball Scholarships: 3
Conference: Big Sky Conference
Program Profile: We have been Conference Champion contenders every year. We have a brand new 1,200 seat Volleyball Center . We have weight rooms and great facilities. We play a traditional fall schedule from August to December, with a non-traditional spring season from January to May.
History: In 1978, we had a 20 win season. We were Conference Champions three times. We were conference tournament participants 15 of the17 times. We got second place in conference 10 times.
Achievements: Conference Coach of the Year once; Northwest Region Coach of the Year twice; three Conference titles.
Coaching: Dick Scott, Head Coach, started here in 1958. He has an overall record of 399-307. His coaching career overall record is 510-327. He coached at UCLA and at Santa Monica College. Colleen Frohlich and Sam Rogers are Assistant Coaches.
Freshman Receiving Financial Aid/Academic: | | **Athletic:** 1

Roster In State: 4	**Out of State:** 11	**Out of Country:** 0
Sophomores on Team: 0	**Seniors on Team:** 3	**Graduation %:** 100
Most Recent Record: 9-18-0	**Fall Games:** 30	**Spring Games:** 4

Camp of Clinic Dates: July 5-9-10-11-13
Positions Needed: 3 Setters, Middle Hitter, Outside Hitter
Schedule: Boise State University, Northwestern, Idaho, Central Florida, Cal State Sacramento, Cal State Northridge
Style of Play: Aggressive defensively. Quick tempo offensively. 5-1 modified swing

NEBRASKA

Omaha ✪

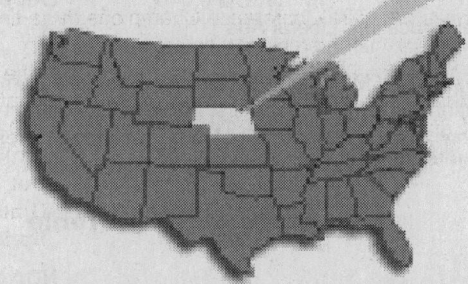

SCHOOL	CITY	AFFILIATION	PAGE
Bellevue University	Bellevue	NAIA	437
Chadron State College	Chadron	NCAA II	437
Creighton University	Omaha	NCAA I	438
Concordia University	Seward	NAIA	439
Dana College	Blair	NAIA	439
Doane College	Crete	NAIA	440
Hasting College	Hasting	NAIA	440
Midland Lutheran College	Freemont	NAIA	441
Nebraska Wesleyan University	Lincoln	NCAA III	441
Peru State College	Peru	NAIA	442
University of Nebraska - Lincoln	Lincoln	NCAA I	442
University of Nebraska - Kearney	Kearney	NCAA II	443
University of Nebraska - Omaha	Omaha	NCAA II	444
Wayne State College - Nebraska	Wayne	NCAA II	444

Bellevue University
Academic Profile

1000 Galvin Rd. South
Bellevue, NE 68005

Phone: (402) 293-3783

Type: Private, 4 Yr., Liberal Arts, Coed
Website: http://www.bellevue.edu
SAT/ACT/GPA: 870/18/2.0
Student/Faculty Ratio: 13:1
Undergraduate Enrollment: 3,000
Scholarships/Academic: Yes   **Athletic:** Yes
Expenses By: Year   **In State:** $ 6,640

Founded: 1966
Religion: Non-Affiliated
Housing: Yes
Male/Female: 54:46
Graduate Enrollment: 1,100
Financial Aid: Yes
Out of State: $ 6,640

Specializes In: Business & Professional Education, Liberal Arts
Degrees Conferred: BA,BS,MA,MS
Programs of Study: Accounting, Art History, Art Management, Biology, Business Administration, Chemical Dependency, Communication Arts, Computer Information Systems, Economics, English, Environmental Science, Geology, History, International Studies, Mathematics, Physical Education, Political Science, PreMed, PreNursing, PrePhysical Therapy, Psychology, Social Science, Sociology, Spanish, Sports Management, Studio Art, Urban Studies, Women's Studies

Women's Athletic Profile

1000 S. Galvin Rd.
Bellevue, NE 68005-3098
Coach: Joel McCartney
Email: joel@scholars.bellevue.edu

NCAA I
Lady Bruins, Purple, Gold
Phone: (402) 293-3783
Fax: (402) 293-2020

Estimated # of Women's Volleyball Scholarships: N/A
Conference: Midlands Collegiate Athletic Conference
Program Profile: The Bruins compete in the Gordon Lozier Physical Health Center with a seating capacity of 500. The season begins the first week in August and continues through November or December.
History: The volleyball program started in 1990. Coach McCartney began in 1996. In three years, the team has finished each year among the Top Ten teams in the Great Plains Region and within the Top Four teams in the Conference.
Achievements: 1996 MCAC Runner-Up, 1997 MCAC Runner-Up, 12 athletes recognized as All-Conference Athletes; 2 All-Region Athletes; 1 player continued on to play in the women's professional league (NVA-National Volleyball Association); Kia Jarvis Academic All-American
Coaching: Joel McCartney, Head Coach, started in 1996. His overall record is 84-43. He is a 1987 graduate of Graceland College where he was a Collegiate All-American and Academic All-American. Andrea Viviano is Assistant Coach.
Freshman Receiving Financial Aid/Academic: **Athletic:** 3
Roster In State: 14   **Out of State:** 0   **Out of Country:** 2
Sophomores on Team: 5   **Seniors on Team:** 2   **Graduation %:** 100
Most Recent Record: 28-16-0   **Fall Games:** 44   **Spring Games:** 4
Camp of Clinic Dates: Recruit Camp: July 9-11
Positions Needed: Setter, Outside Hitter, Middle Hitter
Schedule: Concordia, College of St. Mary, Dickinson State, Northwestern College, Hastings College, Fresno Pacific
Style of Play: We have up-tempo offensive system with multiple attack routes. The team is getting bigger every year, so emphasis is changing to team blocking on defense.

Chadron State College
Academic Profile

1000 Main Street
Chadron, NE 69337

Phone: (308) 432-6000

Type: Public, 4 Yr., Coed
Website: http://www.csc.edu
SAT/ACT/GPA: Open Admission
Student/Faculty Ratio: 18:1
Undergraduate Enrollment: 2,443
Scholarships/Academic: Yes   **Athletic:** Yes
Expenses By: Year   **In State:** $ 5,963

Founded: 1911
Religion: Non-Affiliated
Housing: No
Male/Female: 3.4:5
Graduate Enrollment: 366
Financial Aid: Yes
Out of State: $ 7,838

Specializes In: Business Administration, Criminal Justice, Teacher Education
Degrees Conferred: BA, BSE, MBA, MA, MSE, Specialist
Programs of Study: Art, Biology, Business Administration, Chemistry, Counseling, Elementary & Secondary Education, Family & Consumer Science, Health Professions, Industrial Technology, Mathematics, Music, Physics, Psychology, Speech & Theatre

Women's Athletic Profile

1000 Main Street
Chadron, NE 69337
Coach: Dawn Brammer
Email: dbrammer@csc1.csc.edu

NCAA I
Lady Eagles, Cardinal, White
Phone: (308) 432-6000
Fax: (308) 432-6464

Estimated # of Women's Volleyball Scholarships: 6
Conference: Rocky Mountain Athletic Conference
Program Profile: We play at Armstrong Gymnasium which has 2,500 seats.
Achievements: RMAC Honorable Mention in Volleyball; 3-time All-American (NAIA) Shot-putter
Coaching: Dawn Brammer, Head Coach, has been here 2 years and her overall record is 6-20.
Freshman Receiving Financial Aid/Academic: **Athletic:** 2
Roster In State: 8   **Out of State:** 9   **Out of Country:** 1
Sophomores on Team: 0   **Seniors on Team:** 6   **Graduation %:** 100
Most Recent Record: 6-20-0   **Fall Games:** 26   **Spring Games:** 0
Camp of Clinic Dates: July 16-23
Positions Needed: None
Schedule: Regis, Metro State, Colorado Christian, University of Nebraska-Kearney
Style of Play: Play hard and together.

Creighton University
Academic Profile

2500 California Plaza
Omaha, NE 68178

Phone: (402) 280-2703

Type: Private, 4 Yr., Liberal Arts, Coed
Website: http://www.creighton.edu
SAT/ACT/GPA: 700/17/2.0
Student/Faculty Ratio: 14:1
Undergraduate Enrollment: 4,000
Scholarships/Academic: Yes
Expenses By: Year
Specializes In: Preprofessional School, Business

Founded: 1878
Religion: Catholic Jesuit
Housing: Yes
Male/Female: 1:1.08
Graduate Enrollment: 2,000
Athletic: Yes   **Financial Aid:** Yes
In State: $ 18,584   **Out of State:** $ 18,584

Degrees Conferred: AA, AS, BA, BS, BFA, MA, MS, MBA, Ph.D., DMD, MD
Programs of Study: American Studies, Art Administration, Applied Computer Studies, Atmospheric Science, Biology, Chemistry, Classical Civilization, Communication, Computer Science, Economics, Education, English, Environmental Science, Exercise Science, French, German, Graphic Design, Greek, Health Administration, History, International Studies, Journalism, Medical Physics, Ministry, Music, Pharmacy, Philosophy, Political Science, Theatre, Theology, Physics, Political Science, Psychology, Secondary Education, Social Work, Sociology, Spanish, Theology

Women's Athletic Profile

2500 California Plaza
Omaha, NE 68178-0001
Coach: Howard Wallace
Email:

NCAA I
Lady Bluejays, Blue, White
Phone: (402) 280-2703
Fax: (402) 280-2685

Estimated # of Women's Volleyball Scholarships: 2
Conference: Missouri Valley Conference
Program Profile: We have a new Academic Learning Center and a newly renovated Sports Medicine Center with a weight room. We play games at Omaha South High School with a seating capacity of 2,000. We will be going to a Hawaii Tournament in 2000.
History: The program began in 1994. Coach Wallace arrived in 1997 and led us to our first winning season and a third place finish in the MVC Tournament. This was Creighton's first appearance and they placed several players on the All-Conference team.
Achievements: Coach Wallace was designated Conference Coach of the Year for MVC in 1997.
Coaching: Howard Wallace, Head Coach, began his coaching career in 1983 at University of Hawaii. He was an assistant coach from 1988 to 1996. He started coaching at Creighton in 1997. He was named Conference Coach of the Year. Julie Krofcheck Strong is Assistant Coach.
Freshman Receiving Financial Aid/Academic: **Athletic:** 4
Roster In State: 5   **Out of State:** 10   **Out of Country:** 0
Sophomores on Team: 3   **Seniors on Team:** 2   **Graduation %:** 80
Most Recent Record: 7-18-0   **Fall Games:** 23   **Spring Games:** 4
Camp of Clinic Dates: June 10-11; July 10-12; July 19-23
Positions Needed: Middle Hitters, Setter

Concordia University - Nebraska
Academic Profile

800 North Columbia
Seward, NE 68434

Phone: (402) 643-7328

Type: Private, 4 Yr., Liberal Arts, Coed
Website: http://www.cune.edu
SAT/ACT/GPA: 890/18/2.0
Student/Faculty Ratio: 13:1
Undergraduate Enrollment: 1,110
Scholarships/Academic: Yes
Expenses By: Semester
Specializes In: Education, Liberal Arts
Degrees Conferred: BA, BSEd, MAEd

Athletic: Yes
In State: $ 7,898

Founded: 1894
Religion: Lutheran Church - Missouri Synod
Housing: Yes
Male/Female: 44:56
Graduate Enrollment: 90
Financial Aid: Yes
Out of State: $ 7,898

Programs of Study: Business, Commercial Art, Computer Science, Director of Christian Education, Law, Medicine and other Health Careers, PreProfessional Programs in Engineering, Social Work, PreSeminary, Teacher Education, other Liberal Arts Fields

Women's Athletic Profile

800 N. Columbia
Seward, NE 68434
Coach: Diane Mendenhall
Email: dmendenhall@seward.cune.edu

NCAA I
Lady Bulldogs, Navy, White
Phone: (402) 643-7328
Fax: (402) 643-3966

Estimated # of Women's Volleyball Scholarships: 2.6 full
Conference: NIAC
Program Profile: We have a Varsity and a Junior Varsity program that consists of 20 players.
Achievements: 1 Drafted player ; 1 All-American.
Coaching: Diane Mendenhall, Head Coach, was a former coach at the high school level. In 1985, she was named Jefferson County Conference Coach of the Year. She started with the program in 1996 and has a record of 65-43. When she was a player here in 1980, she became a captain . Wendy Hall is Assistant Coach.

Freshman Receiving Financial Aid/Academic:
Roster In State: 13
Sophomores on Team: 0
Most Recent Record: 19-15-0

Out of State: 7
Seniors on Team: 3
Fall Games: 34

Athletic: 7
Out of Country: 0
Graduation %: 100
Spring Games: 10

Camp of Clinic Dates: June 27-30; July 1-2; July 7-9
Positions Needed: 2-Outside Hitters, Setter, Middle Hitter
Schedule: Hasting College, College of St. Mary

Dana College
Academic Profile

2848 College Drive
Blair, NE 68008

Phone: (402) 426-7272

Type: Private, 4 Yr., Liberal Arts, Coed
Website: http://www.acad2.dana.edu
SAT/ACT/GPA: 18/2.5
Student/Faculty Ratio: 13:1
Undergraduate Enrollment: 600
Scholarships/Academic: Yes
Expenses By: Year
Degrees Conferred: BA, BS

Athletic: Yes
In State: $ 16,800

Founded: 1884
Religion: Lutheran
Housing: Yes
Male/Female: 60:40
Graduate Enrollment: N/A
Financial Aid: Yes
Out of State: $ 16,800

Programs of Study: Contact school for program of study.

Women's Athletic Profile

2848 College Drive
Blair, NE 68008
Coach: Julie Strong
Email:

NCAA I
Lady Vikings, Scarlet, White
Phone: (402) 426-7298
Fax: (402) 426-7299

Estimated # of Women's Volleyball Scholarships: N/A
Conference: NIAC

Doane College
Academic Profile

1014 Boswell Avenue
Crete, NE 68333

Phone: 800-333-6263

Type: Private, 4 Yr., Liberal Arts, Coed
Website: http://www.doane.edu
SAT/ACT/GPA: NAIA eligibility required/2.0
Student/Faculty Ratio: 15:1
Undergraduate Enrollment: 915
Scholarships/Academic: Yes   **Athletic:** Yes
Expenses By: Year   **In State:** $ 14,420
Specializes In: Education, Business
Degrees Conferred: BA, BS, M
Programs of Study: Accounting, Biological Science, Business Administration, Chemistry, Communications, Computer Science, Elementary Education, English, Environmental Science, German, Human Services, International Studies, Management, Philosophy, Physical Science, Political Science, Psychology, Public Administration, Science, Social Science, Special Education

Founded: 1872
Religion: Church of Christ
Housing: Yes
Male/Female: 1:1
Graduate Enrollment: 200
Financial Aid: Yes
Out of State: $ 14,420

Women's Athletic Profile

Boswell Avenue
Crete, NE 68333
Coach: Cindy Meyer
Email:

NCAA I
Lady Tigers, Orange, Black
Phone: (402) 826-8202
Fax: (402) 826-8202

Estimated # of Women's Volleyball Scholarships: N/A
Conference: NIAC

Hasting College
Academic Profile

800 Turner Avenue
Hasting, NE 68901

Phone: 800-532-7642

Type: Private, 4 Yr., Liberal Arts, Coed
Website: http://www.hasting.com
SAT/ACT/GPA: 20/2.0
Student/Faculty Ratio: 13:1
Undergraduate Enrollment: 1,100
Scholarships/Academic: Yes   **Athletic:** Yes
Expenses By: Year   **In State:** $ 17,004
Degrees Conferred: BA, MA, BM, MAT
Programs of Study: Contact school for program of study.

Founded: 1882
Religion: Presbyterian
Housing: Yes
Male/Female: 1.5:1
Graduate Enrollment: N/A
Financial Aid: No
Out of State: $ 17,004

Women's Athletic Profile

7th & Turner
Hasting, NE 68902
Coach: Rick Squiers
Email:

NCAA I
Lady Broncos, Crimson, White
Phone: (402) 461-7335
Fax: (402) 461-7489

Estimated # of Women's Volleyball Scholarships: 8
Conference: NIAC
Program Profile: NAIA Nebraska-Iowas Athletic Conference
Play in Kiewit Gymnasium seats 1700
History: 1975 program began
Achievements: 1st year coach
Coaching: Crystal Bejarano-1st year/2 time NAIA All-American
Freshman Receiving Financial Aid/Academic: **Athletic:** 4
Roster In State: 11   **Out of State:** 3   **Out of Country:** 0
Sophomores on Team: 3   **Seniors on Team:** 4   **Graduation %:** 80
Most Recent Record: 35-4   **Fall Games:** 27   **Spring Games:**

Positions Needed: 4

Schedule: Cal Poly Pomona, Fresno Pacific, Doane, Nebraska Wesleyan, Peru State, Northwestern

Style of Play: Aggressive hitters and defense

Midland Lutheran College
Academic Profile

900 N. Clarkson
Fremont, NE 68025

Phone: 402-721-0250

Type: Private, 4 Yr., Liberal Arts, Coed
Website: http://www.mlc.edu
SAT/ACT/GPA: Top half
Student/Faculty Ratio: 18:1
Undergraduate Enrollment: 1,025
Scholarships/Academic: Yes   **Athletic:** Yes
Expenses By: Year   **In State:** $ 14,000
Degrees Conferred: AA, BA, BS, BBA, BSN
Programs of Study: Contact school for program of study.

Founded: 1883
Religion: Lutheran
Housing: No
Male/Female: 2:3
Graduate Enrollment: N/A
Financial Aid: Yes
Out of State: $ 14,000

Women's Athletic Profile

900 n. Clarkson
Freemont, NE 68025
Coach: Rick Pruett
Email: pruett@admin.mlc.edu

NCAA I
Lady Warriors, Orange, Black
Phone: (402) 721-5480x6512
Fax: (402) 721-9406

Estimated # of Women's Volleyball Scholarships: N/A
Conference: NIAC

Nebraska Wesleyan University
Academic Profile

5000 St. Paul Avenue
Lincoln, NE 68504

Phone: (402)466-2371

Type: Private, 4 Yr., Liberal Arts, Coed
Website: http://www.nebwesleyan.edu
SAT/ACT/GPA:
Student/Faculty Ratio: 14:1
Undergraduate Enrollment: 1,682
Scholarships/Academic: Yes   **Athletic:** No
Expenses By: Year   **In State:** $16,716
Degrees Conferred: BA, BS

Founded: 1887
Religion: United Methodist
Housing: Yes
Male/Female: 41/59
Graduate Enrollment: N/A
Financial Aid: Yes
Out of State: $16,716

Programs of Study: Full Liberal Arts and PreProfessional Curriculum; Applied Music, Art, Biology, BioChemistry, Business Administration, Business Psychology, Business, Sociology, Chemistry, Communications, Computer Science, Economics, Elementary Education, English, French, German, Health/Physical Science, History, International Business, Mathematics, Music, Physics, Political Science, Psychology, Physical Education, Philosophy, Sport Management

Women's Athletic Profile

5000 St. Paul
Lincoln, NE 68504
Coach: Carrie Broomfield
Email: cbs@nebrwesleyan.edu

NCAA I
Plainswomen, Brown, Gold
Phone: (402) 465-2373
Fax: (402) 465-2179

Estimated # of Women's Volleyball Scholarships: N/A
Conference: Nebraska-Iowa Athletic Conference
Program Profile: Nebraska Wesleyan's athletics facilities are among the finest in the NCAA Division III. Our facilities include: Weary Center, Snyder Arena and Knight Fieldhouse. The $9.6 million Marion and Marian Weary Center for Health and Fitness was the largest single construction project in Wesleyan history. The state-of-the-art facility, which opened in 1995, includes the 2,350 seats Snyder Arena. There are locker rooms and training rooms and laboratories for the Department of Health and Human Performance. Included are : racquetball courts, a cardiovascular exercise area, an aerobics/dance exercise room and a swimming pool. Knight

Fieldhouse was originally constructed in 1976 and is connected to the Weary Center. Knight Fieldhouse, which features an indoor track and can be used for tennis and volleyball play, was also remodeled as part of the Weary Center project.

History: The program began in 1974 with an all-time winning percentage above .500. During the 1997-1998 season, nine teams finished or earned ranking among the top 20 nationally, and 24 athletes earned All-American recognition. We have also won the Nebraska-Iowa Athletic Conference All-Sports Trophy for the past 15 years. We rank fifth nationally in the number of prestigious GTE/COSIDA Academic All-Americans in all sports in the 1990's.

Achievements: 1998 Conference Runner-Up; 3 consecutive NCAA Tournament Appearances; 3 All-Americans in the past three years and 6 All-Region players; made Sweet 16 round in NCAA 2-time in the past three years.

Coaching: Carrie Broomfield, Head Coach, is entering her first season with the program. Her coaching career record is 27-9 and her team has a #3 national ranking. She made Sweet 16 Round of ACAA National Tourney. She is a former Wesleyan All-American Volleyball player and graduated in 1997.

Roster In State: 17	**Out of State:** 1	**Out of Country:** 0
Sophomores on Team: 0	**Seniors on Team:** 2	**Graduation %:** 100
Most Recent Record: 27-9-0	**Fall Games:** 36	**Spring Games:** 14-17

Positions Needed: Middle Blockers, Defensive Specialist

Schedule: Juniata College, Central college, UC-San Diego, Hasting College, UW-Whitewater, Wartburg University

Style of Play: We play a 5-1 multiple option offense with man back rotation defense. Our team runs a very quick offense as well.

Peru State College
Academic Profile

PO Box 10
Peru, NE 68421

Phone: 800-742-4412

Type: Public, 4 Yr., Coed	**Founded:** 1867
Website: http://www.peru.edu	**Religion:** Non-Affiliated
SAT/ACT/GPA: 18	**Housing:** No
Student/Faculty Ratio: 18:1	**Male/Female:** 47:53
Undergraduate Enrollment: 1,600	**Graduate Enrollment:** 200

Scholarships/Academic: Yes	**Athletic:** Yes	**Financial Aid:** Yes
Expenses By: Year	**In State:** $ 4,950	**Out of State:** $ 6,600

Degrees Conferred: AA, BA, BS, BT

Programs of Study: Business and Management, Computer Science, Education, Mathematics, Psychology, Social Science, Trade & Industry

Women's Athletic Profile

600 Hoyt Street PO Box 10
Peru, NE 68421
Coach: Becki Deisley
Email: bdeisley@oakmail.peru.edu

NCAA I
Lady Bobcats, Blue, White
Phone: (402) 872-2297
Fax: (402) 872-2302

Estimated # of Women's Volleyball Scholarships: 1

Conference: Midlands Collegiate Athletic Conference

Program Profile: Al Wheeler Activity Center is host for all in house sports. Activity Center has four courts and is on rubberized gym floor.

History: 1995, 1996 National Volleyball Tournament appearances.

Achievements: Janelle Findlay 2000 All-American Honorable Mention

Freshman Receiving Financial Aid/Academic:		**Athletic:** 2
Roster In State: 11	**Out of State:** 1	**Out of Country:** 0
Sophomores on Team:	**Seniors on Team:** 4	**Graduation %:** 90
Most Recent Record: 21-12		

Positions Needed: RS, MB, Setter

Schedule: University of Nebraska at Kearney, College of St. Mary, Bellevue University, Wayne State College, Concordia University.

Style of Play: Great blocking team with impressive speed and quickness at net and backcourt.

University of Nebraska - Lincoln
Academic Profile

1024 Avery Avenue
Lincoln, NE 68588-0243

Phone: 800-742-8800

Type: Public, 4 Yr., Liberal Arts, Engineering, Coed	**Founded:** 1869

Website: http://www.huskerwebcast.com
SAT/ACT/GPA: 850/20/2.0
Student/Faculty Ratio: 17:1
Undergraduate Enrollment: 25,000
Scholarships/Academic: Yes   **Athletic:** Yes
Expenses By: Year   **In State:** $ 6,812
Specializes In: Agriculture, Education, Journalism
Degrees Conferred: AS, BA, BFA, BS, BBA, BJ, BSAE, BSBSE, MBA

Religion: Non-Affiliated
Housing: Yes
Male/Female: 54:46
Graduate Enrollment: 5,100
Financial Aid: Yes
Out of State: $ 10,585

Women's Athletic Profile

103 S. Stadium
Lincoln, NE 68588
Coach: Terry Pettit
Email: nuhuskers@unl.edu

NCAA I
Cornhuskers, Scarlet, Cream
Phone: (402) 472-3011
Fax: (402) 472-9675

Estimated # of Women's Volleyball Scholarships: N/A
Conference: Big 12 Conference
Program Profile: NV plays in Nebraska Coliseum with 4,200 capacity, second in Division I in attendance (3,866 per match), one of nation's largest weight rooms (32,000 square feet). Newly remodeled locker-rooms "ready room".
History: Our program began in 1975; averaged 30 wins through last 22 seasons; 15 NCAA Regional Appearances; finished in top 10 14 straight seasons, Nebraska holds record for academic All-Americans (all sports).
Achievements: We have 17 straight NCAA Tournament Appearances, 6 Final Four Appearances, 21 Conference Titles in 23 years; NCAA record 31 All-Americans - 3 in 1998, 1995 National Champions, Terry Pettit was named National Coach of the Year in 1986 & 1994.
Coaching: Terry Pettit, is in her 23rd season as a Head Coach and has an all-time record of 667-142-11at Nebraska also leading Wisconsin to two top 10 national finish.
Freshman Receiving Financial Aid/Academic:

Roster In State: 9	**Out of State:** 5	**Athletic:** 4
Sophomores on Team: 1	**Seniors on Team:** 4	**Out of Country:** 1
Most Recent Record: 32-2-0	**Fall Games:** 29	**Graduation %:**
		Spring Games: 0

Camp of Clinic Dates: Call for information
Schedule: Florida, Pacific, Wisconsin, Texas, Texas A&M, Arizona

University of Nebraska - Kearney
Academic Profile

Hwy. 30 & 15th Avenue
Kearney, NE 68849

Phone: 800-532-7639

Type: Public, 4 Yr., Liberal Arts, Coed
Website: http://www.unk.edu
SAT/ACT/GPA: 20avg
Student/Faculty Ratio: 21:1
Undergraduate Enrollment: 6,450
Scholarships/Academic: Yes   **Athletic:** Yes
Expenses By: Year   **In State:** $ 4,500
Degrees Conferred: BA, BS, BFA, MA, MS, MEd, SPED
Programs of Study: Contact school for program of study.

Founded: 1903
Religion: Non-Affiliated
Housing: No
Male/Female: 45:55
Graduate Enrollment: 1,130
Financial Aid: Yes
Out of State: $ 5,950

Women's Athletic Profile

Health & Sports Ctr., Hwy 30 & 15th Avenue
Kearney, NE 68849
Coach: Rick Squires
Email: squiresr@unk.edu

NCAA I
Antelopes (Loper), Blue, Gold
Phone: (308) 865-8031
Fax: (306) 865-8187

Estimated # of Women's Volleyball Scholarships: 3
Conference: Rocky Mountain Athletic Conference
Program Profile: Play matches in the Health and Sports center which seats 5500. NCAA II Attendance Leader.
History: In the history of the University of Nebraska at Kearney, athletic success has always been a constant. UNK has won countless conference championship, several national championships and had many All-Americans.
Achievements: 2000 RMAC Coach of the Year, 1999, 2000 RMAC Champs, NCAA Qualifier.
Coaching: Head Coach Rick Squiers enters his third year at the helm for the Lopers. Squiers is just the third head coach in school

history. Overall record at UNK is 30-4. Aisstant Coaches are Kerry Beidleman and Peggy Meyer.

Freshman Receiving Financial Aid/Academic: **Athletic:** 2
Roster In State: 13   **Out of State:** 3   **Out of Country:** 0
Sophomores on Team: **Seniors on Team:** 2   **Graduation %:**
Most Recent Record: 29-6-0
Camp of Clinic Dates: July 17-21, July 24-28
Positions Needed: Setter, LH, RH
Schedule: Nebraska-Omaha, Northern Colorado, Regis University, Metro State, Western State
Style of Play: Power game with intense defense.

University of Nebraska - Omaha
Academic Profile

103 S. Stadium   **Phone:** 402-554-2393
Lincoln, NE 68588

Type: Public, 4 Yr., Coed   **Founded:** 1908
Website: http://www.unomaha.edu   **Religion:** Non-Affiliated
SAT/ACT/GPA: 21avg   **Housing:** No
Student/Faculty Ratio: 30:1   **Male/Female:** 48:52
Undergraduate Enrollment: 13,300   **Graduate Enrollment:** 2,588
Scholarships/Academic: Yes   **Athletic:** Yes   **Financial Aid:** Yes
Expenses By: Year   **In State:** $ 2,500   **Out of State:** $ 5,500
Degrees Conferred: AS, BA, BS, BFA, BBA, BGS
Programs of Study: Contact school for program of study.

Women's Athletic Profile

60th and Dodge   **NCAA I**
Omaha, NE 68182   Lady Mavericks, Red, Black
Coach: Rose Shires   **Phone:** (402) 554-3407
Email: rose_shires@uwomaha.edu   **Fax:** (402) 554-2555

Estimated # of Women's Volleyball Scholarships: 3
Conference: North Central Conference
Profile: Extremely competitive top Division II program. Playing fall season in the toughest D-II conference in the Nation. New suspended wood floor in a 4,000 seat arena. $11 million renovation project just completed on fieldhouse, including $1.5 million weight room.
History: Program began in 1979.
Achievements: 1996 D-II National Champs, 6 Elite Eight Appearances, 8 NCC titles. 18 AVCA All-Americans, 31 AVCA All-Region Members, 62 All-Conference selections.
Roster In State: 10   **Out of State:** 2
Seniors on Team: 3   **Graduation %:** 90%
Positions Needed: Middle Hitter and Setters
Camp Dates: July 9-22
Schedule: Augustana, South Dakota State, North Dakota State, Northern Colorado, Metro State, Regis, Tampa
Style of Play: Fast pace offense, strong defensive emphasis. Our team has a strong work ethic with a proud tradition of exellence.

Wayne State College
Academic Profile

1111 Main Street   **Phone:** 800-228-9972
Wayne, NE 68787

Type: Public, 4 Yr., Coed   **Founded:** 1910
Website: http://www.wsc.edu   **Religion:** Non-Affiliated
SAT/ACT/GPA: Open Admission2.0   **Housing:** Yes
Student/Faculty Ratio: 17:1   **Male/Female:** 44:56
Undergraduate Enrollment: 13,300   **Graduate Enrollment:** 725
Scholarships/Academic: Yes   **Athletic:** Yes   **Financial Aid:** Yes
Expenses By: Year   **In State:** $ 5,733   **Out of State:** $ 7,518
Degrees Conferred: BA, BS, BFA, MA, MS, MBA

Programs of Study: Art, Business, Chemistry, Computers, Computer Science, Criminal Justice, Early Childhood, English, Exercise Science, Family & Consumer Sciences, Food Services, Geography, History, Counseling, Industrial Tech, Life Sciences, Mass Communications, Math, Modern Languages, Music, Political Science, Psychology, Social Sciences, Sociology, Speech Communications, Sports Management, Technology, Theatre and many major inside of these broad subject.

Women's Athletic Profile

1111 Main Street
Wayne, NE 68787
Coach: Sharon Vanis
Email: svanis@wscgate.wsc.edu

NCAA I
Wildcats, Black, Gold
Phone: (402) 375-7303
Fax: (402) 375-7120

Estimated # of Women's Volleyball Scholarships: 8
Conference: Northern Sun Conference
Program Profile: We play at Rice Auditorium with a seating capacity of 2,5000. Varsity women's has locker-room, varsity weight room, training staff, and rehabilitation facilities.
History: Our program began in 1971. We moved to NCAA II in 1992.
Achievements: Coach of the Year - JUCO level in 1989, Region IX, NCCAC, District 13 2nd team All-American in 1989.
Coaching: Sharon Vanis, Head Coach, is entering her seventh season with the program. Jon Misfeldt is our Assistant Coach.

Roster In State: 11	**Out of State:** 2	**Out of Country:** 0
Sophomores on Team: 4	**Seniors on Team:** 3	**Graduation %:** 97
Most Recent Record: 18-20-0	**Fall Games:** 6	**Spring Games:** 4

Camp of Clinic Dates: June, July
Positions Needed: Outside Hitter, Middle Hitter
Schedule: UNO, UNK, SDSU, Duluth
Style of Play: Quick offense style of play.

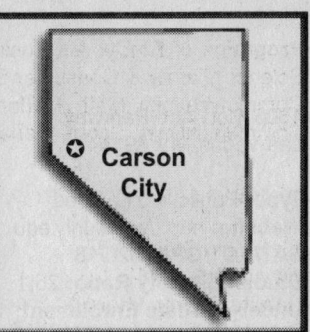

Carson City

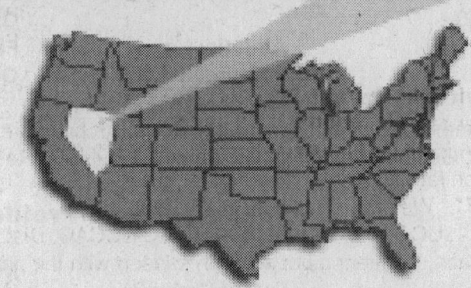

SCHOOL	CITY	AFFILIATION	PAGE
University of Nevada - Las Vegas	Las Vegas	NCAA I	447
University of Nevada - Reno	Reno	NCAA I	447

University of Nevada - Las Vegas
Academic Profile

4505 Maryland Parkway
Las Vegas, NV 89154

Phone: 702-895-3443

Type: Public, 4 Yr., Coed
Website: http://www.unly.edu
SAT/ACT/GPA: 820/18
Student/Faculty Ratio: 25;1
Undergraduate Enrollment: 14,350
Scholarships/Academic: Yes   **Athletic:** Yes
Expenses By: Year   **In State:** $ 7,000

Founded: 1957
Religion: Non-Affiliated
Housing: No
Male/Female: 46:54
Graduate Enrollment: 5,350
Financial Aid: Yes
Out of State: $ 12,000

Degrees Conferred: BA, BS, BFA, BArch, MA, MS, MBA, MFA, M.Ed., Ph.D.
Programs of Study: Accounting, Anthropology, Applied Mathematics, Architecture, Art, Biochemistry, Biology, Botany, Management, Comparative Literature, Geography, Geology, Industrial, Insurance, Linguistics, Recreation, Romance Languages, Travel, Zoology

Women's Athletic Profile

Box 450001
Las Vegas, NV 89154
Coach: Dietre Collins
Email: Dcollins@ccmail.nevada.edu

NCAA I
Lady Rebels, Scarlet, Grey
Phone: (702) 895-1507
Fax: (702) 895-4468

Estimated # of Women's Volleyball Scholarships: N/A
Conference: Western Athletic Conference

University of Nevada - Reno
Academic Profile

Legacy Hall/MS 264
Reno, NV 89557

Phone: (775)784-6900

Type: Public, 4 Yr., Coed
Website: http://www.wolfpack.edu
SAT/ACT/GPA: Open2.5
Student/Faculty Ratio: 21:1
Undergraduate Enrollment: 9,644
Scholarships/Academic: Yes   **Athletic:** Yes
Expenses By: Year   **In State:** $ 8,288

Founded: 1874
Religion: Non-Affiliated
Housing: Yes
Male/Female: 44/56
Graduate Enrollment: 2,807
Financial Aid: Yes
Out of State: $ 14,098

Specializes In: Business, Engineering, Education, Medicine, Journalism, Agriculture
Degrees Conferred: BA, BS, Masters, Ph.D.
Programs of Study: Engineering, Education, Mining, Agricultural, Journalism, Home Economics, Business, Nursing, School of Medicine, Arts & Science, Community & Health Sciences

Women's Athletic Profile

Old Gym 265
Reno, NV 89557
Coach: Devin Scruggs
Email: dscruggs@unr.edu

NCAA I
Lady Wolf Packs, Silver, Blue
Phone: (702) 784-4698
Fax: (702) 784-4386

Estimated # of Women's Volleyball Scholarships: N/A
Conference: Big West Conference
Program Profile: Division I. Our playing season is in the fall. Our team plays in the University of Nevada's old gym with a seating capacity of 1,800.
Achievements: First Nevada women's team to post 20 wins in a season in 1998. Team won Big West Eastern Division crown in 1998. First NCAA Appearance in 1998.
Coaching: Devin Scruggs, Head Coach, started coaching the program in 1997 with a record of 34-26 in two years. He graduated from Pacific in 1991. Sue Peters is our Assistant Coach. Lee Nelson, Assistant Coach, is entering his first season with the program.
Roster In State: 1   **Out of State:** 12   **Out of Country:** 0
Sophomores on Team: 6   **Seniors on Team:** 1   **Graduation %:**
Most Recent Record: 22-7-0   **Fall Games:** 29   **Spring Games:** 0
Schedule: Hawaii, USC, Long Beach St, Pacific, UC-Santa Barbara, Fresno State

NEW HAMPSHIRE

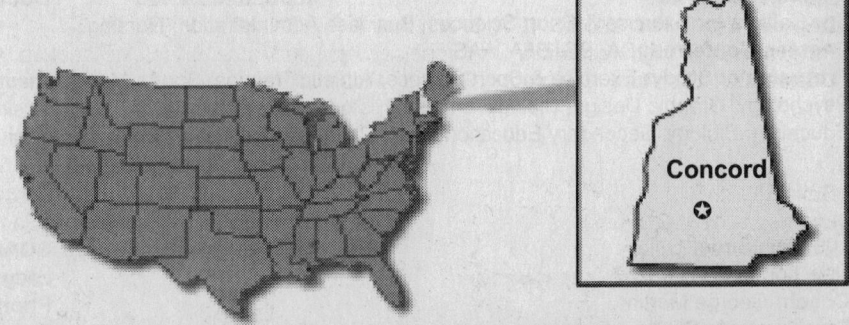

Concord

SCHOOL	CITY	AFFILIATION	PAGE
Colby-Sawyer College	New London	NCAA III	449
Daniel Webster College	Nashua	NCAA III	449
Dartmouth College	Hanover	NCAA I	450
Franklin Pierce College	Rindge	NCAA II	450
Keene State College	Keene	NCAA III	451
New Hampshire College	Manchester	NCAA II	451
Plymouth State College	Plymouth	NCAA III	452
Rivier College	Nashua	NCAA III	453
Saint Anselm College	Manchester	NCAA II	453
University of New Hampshire	Durham	NCAA I	454

Colby - Sawyer College
Academic Profile

100 Main Street
New London, NH 03257

Phone: 800-272-1015

Type: Private, 4 Yr., Liberal Arts, Coed
Website: http://www.colby-sawyer.edu
SAT/ACT/GPA: 1100/2.0
Student/Faculty Ratio: 12:1
Undergraduate Enrollment: 793
Scholarships/Academic: Yes   **Athletic:** No
Expenses By: Year   **In State:** $ 24,400

Founded: 1837
Religion: Non-Affiliated
Housing: Yes
Male/Female: 1:2
Graduate Enrollment: N/A
Financial Aid: Yes
Out of State: $ 24,400

Specializes In: Exercise & Sport Sciences, Business Administration, Nursing
Degrees Conferred: BA, BS, BFA, AAS
Programs of Study: Exercise & Sport Science, Athletic Training, Sports Management, Exercise Science, Communications Study, Psychology, Graphic Design, Biology, English, History, Society and Culture, Art, Nursing, Child Development, Teacher Certificate, Art Education, Biology, Secondary Education, Early Childhood Education, English, Social Science,

Women's Athletic Profile

100 Main Street
New London, NH 03257
Coach: George Martin
Email: gmartin@colby-sawyer.edu

NCAA I
Lady Chargers, Blue, White
Phone: (603) 526-3604
Fax: (603) 526-3452

Estimated # of Women's Volleyball Scholarships: N/A
Conference: Commonwealth Coast Conference
Program Profile: Our team plays a fall season. Matches are played in Hogan Center with a seating capacity of 600.
History: Our records date back to 1976. Our team won four consecutive New Hampshire Women's Athletic Conference Championships from 1985-1988.
Achievements: 1998 Commonwealth Coach Conference Coach of the Year; 1996-1998 Commonwealth Coast Conf Runner-Up.
Coaching: George Martin, Head Coach, compiled a record of 90-43. He was named Commonwealth Coast Conference Coach of the Year. Marian Hunter and Courtney Diamond are Assistant Coaches.
Freshman Receiving Financial Aid/Academic: **Athletic:** 16
Roster In State: 11   **Out of State:** 5   **Out of Country:** 0
Sophomores on Team: 0   **Seniors on Team:** 7   **Graduation %:** Unknown
Most Recent Record: 26-5-0   **Fall Games:** 31   **Spring Games:** 0
Schedule: Middlebury, St. Anselms, Bridgewater State, Eastern Nazarene, Gordon

Daniel Webster College
Academic Profile

20 University Dr.
Nashua, NH 06063-1300

Phone: (800) 325-6876

Type: Private, 4 Yr., Coed
Website: http://www.dwc.edu
SAT/ACT/GPA: 1050
Student/Faculty Ratio: 14:1
Undergraduate Enrollment: 450
Scholarships/Academic: Yes   **Athletic:** No
Expenses By: Year   **In State:** $ 22,083

Founded: 1965
Religion: Non-Affiliated
Housing: Yes
Male/Female: 4:1
Graduate Enrollment: N/A
Financial Aid: Yes
Out of State: $ 22,083

Specializes In: Aviation, Business, Computer Science, Engineering
Programs of Study: Air Traffic Control, Aviation Management, Aviation Flight Operations, Business and Management, Computer Science, Computer Systems, Engineering, Engineering Science, Flight Operations, Sports Management

Men's Athletic Profile

20 University Drive
Nashua, NH 03063
Coach: TBA
Email:

NCAA III
Eagles/Navy, Red, White
Phone: (603) 577-6493
Fax: (603) 577-6001

Estimated # of Men's Volleyball Scholarships: N/A
Conference: Independent

Women's Athletic Profile

20 University Drive
Nashua, NH 03063
Coach: Donna Ruseckas
Email: ruseckas@dwc.edu

NCAA I
Lady Eagles, Royal, White
Phone: (603) 577-6495
Fax: (603) 577-6001

Estimated # of Women's Volleyball Scholarships: N/A
Conference: The Great Northeast Athletic Conference

Dartmouth College
Academic Profile

6083 Alumni Gym
Hanover, NH 03755

Phone: (603) 646-3529

Type: Private, 4 Yr., Liberal Arts, Engineering, Coed
Website: http://www.dartmouth.edu
SAT/ACT/GPA: 1100+
Student/Faculty Ratio: 12:1
Undergraduate Enrollment: 4,200
Scholarships/Academic: No
Expenses By: Year
Degrees Conferred: BA, MA, MS, MBA, Ph.D., MD

Athletic: No
In State: $ 31,722

Founded: 1769
Religion: Non-Affiliated
Housing: Yes
Male/Female: 50:50
Graduate Enrollment: 1,260
Financial Aid: Yes
Out of State: $ 31,722

Programs of Study: Anthropology, Art, Asian, BioChemistry and Molecular Biology, Biology, BioPhysical, Chemistry, Classical Archaeology, Classics, Cognitive, Comparative Literature, Computer Science, Drama, Economics, Engineering, English, Earth Science, Environmental, Genetics, Geography, Government, Mathematics, Music, Philosophy, Physics, Psychology, Religion, Sociology, Spanish, Women's Studies

Women's Athletic Profile

6083 Alumni Gym
Hanover, NH 03755
Coach: Ann Marie Larese
Email: larese@dartmouth.edu

NCAA I
Big Green, Green, White
Phone: (603) 646-3529
Fax: (603) 646-3348

Conference: Ivy League
Program Profile: We are a competitive program. Our Conference is loaded with potential contenders for the championship. We play at Leede Arena which has 2,100 seats and will host the Ivy Championships in 1999.
History: Larese was hired as Darmouth's first full-time head coach in June of 1994. She has led the team to three straight record setting seasons since a 2-18 campaign in her first year. The 1995 team set a school record with 17 wins. In 1996, the team improved the record to a 18-10 mark. In 1997, we had 24 wins and played for the championship at the Conference Tournament. In 1998, we had a 14-game winning streak and were undefeated at home. We had the highest mark of any Ivy team in the region.
Achievements: 2nd in Conference in 1997; All-Ivy Players: Anne Murray, Felicity Kolp, Janna Merryfield, Amy Shortridge; GTE Academic All-American: Felicity Kolp.
Coaching: Ann Marie Laresse, Head Coach, began here in 1994. She is a graduate of UMUSS Amherst and received an MBA from Bentley. She coached at Clarion, Bucknell, Bently and Dana Hall. Maria Stutsman y Marquez is Assistant Coach.

Roster In State: 0
Sophomores on Team: 0
Most Recent Record:
Camp of Clinic Dates: General Skills: July 18-22
Positions Needed: Setter, Middle Hitter, Right Side Hitter

Out of State: 15
Seniors on Team: 4
Fall Games: 27

Out of Country: 0
Graduation %: 100
Spring Games: 0

Franklin Pierce College
Academic Profile

PO Box 60, College Rd.
Rindge, NH 03461

Phone: 800-437-0048

Type: Private, 4 Yr., Liberal Arts,Coed
Website: http://www.fpc.edu

Founded: 1962
Religion: Non-Affiliated

SAT/ACT/GPA: 900
Student/Faculty Ratio: 20:1
Undergraduate Enrollment: 1,495
Scholarships/Academic: Yes
Expenses By: Year
Specializes In: Liberal Arts
Degrees Conferred: BA, BS, MBA

Athletic: Yes
In State: $ 23,875

Housing: Yes
Male/Female: 50:50
Graduate Enrollment: 150
Financial Aid: Yes
Out of State: $ 23,875

Programs of Study: 28 majors - 5 Divisions: Humanities, Behavioral Sciences, Natural Science, Business Administration, Visual and Performing Arts

Women's Athletic Profile

P.O. Box 60, College Rd.
Rindge, NH 03461
Coach: Andy Calisewski
Email:

NCAA I
Lady Raven, Crimson, Grey
Phone: (603) 899-4084
Fax: (603) 899-4328

Estimated # of Women's Volleyball Scholarships: N/A
Conference: New England Collegiate Conference

Keene State College
Academic Profile

229 Main Street
Keene, NH 03435-0002

Phone: 800-572-1909

Type: Public, 4 Yr., Liberal Arts,Coed
Website: http://www.keene.edu
SAT/ACT/GPA: 1000/2.5
Student/Faculty Ratio: 21:1
Undergraduate Enrollment: 3,900
Scholarships/Academic: Yes
Expenses By: Year

Athletic: No
In State: $ 10,434

Founded: 1909
Religion: Non-Affiliated
Housing: Yes
Male/Female: 2:3
Graduate Enrollment: 500
Financial Aid: Yes
Out of State: $ 15,744

Degrees Conferred: Associates, Bachelors, Masters
Programs of Study: American Studies, Biology, Chemistry, Computer Science, Dietetics, Dramatic Arts, Education, English, Environmental Science, Fine Arts, Geography, History, Industrial Technology, Journalism, Mathematics, Music, Music Performance, Political Science, Psychology, Safety Management, Social Science, Spanish, Special Education, Sports Management, Sports Med

Women's Athletic Profile

229 Main Street
Keene, NH 03435
Coach: Scott Price
Email: scprice@keene.edu

NCAA I
Lady Owls, Red, White
Phone: 603-358-2835
Fax: (603) 358-2888

Estimated # of Women's Volleyball Scholarships: N/A
Conference: Little East Conference

New Hampshire College
Academic Profile

2500 River Rd.
Manchester, NH 03106

Phone: 800-642-4968

Type: Private, 4 Yr., Liberal Arts, Coed
Website: http://www.nhc.edu
SAT/ACT/GPA: 820/20/2.8
Student/Faculty Ratio: 15:1
Undergraduate Enrollment: 1,500
Scholarships/Academic: Yes
Expenses By: Year
Specializes In: Business
Degrees Conferred: AS, AAS, BS, MS, MBA

Athletic: Yes
In State: $ 19,500

Founded: 1932
Religion: Non-Affiliated
Housing: Yes
Male/Female: 1:1
Graduate Enrollment: 300
Financial Aid: Yes
Out of State: $ 19,500

Programs of Study: Business Administration, Business Studies, Communications, Computer Science, Economics, English, Finance, Hotel/Restaurant Management, Liberal Arts, Marketing, PreLaw, Psychology, Social Science, Sports Management, System Analysis, Teacher Education

Women's Athletic Profile

2500 River Rd.
Manchester, NH 03106-1045
Coach: John Vaughn
Email: auburnvaughns@aol.com

NCAA I
Lady Penmen, Blue, Gold
Phone: (603) 645-9764
Fax: (603) 645-9686

Estimated # of Women's Volleyball Scholarships: N/A
Conference: Northeast 10
Program Profile: We are a competitive Division II program. The season runs from September to early November. We will be entering our first season in the Northeast 10 conference.
Roster In State: 5   **Out of State:** 7
Seniors on Team: 2
Most Recent Record: 6-16
Positions Needed: all positions
Schedule: University of Mass. Lowell, Pace, Bryant, Merrimack, American International, Bentley, Le Moyne, Saint Anselm, Stonehill, Saint Rose

Plymouth State College
Academic Profile

MSC #32
Plymouth, NH 03264

Phone: (603) 535-2778

Type: Public, 4 Yr., Liberal Arts, Coed
Website: http://www.plymouth.edu
SAT/ACT/GPA: 850/2.0
Student/Faculty Ratio: 19:1
Undergraduate Enrollment: 3,500
Scholarships/Academic: Yes
Expenses By: Year

Athletic: No
In State: $ 9,554

Founded: 1871
Religion: Non-Affiliated
Housing: Yes
Male/Female: 50:50
Graduate Enrollment: 500
Financial Aid: Yes
Out of State: $ 14,854

Degrees Conferred: 80 academic majors & 50 minors offered
Programs of Study: Actuarial Science, Athletic Training, Business and Management, Computer Science, Education, Health & Physical Education, Liberal Arts, Meteorology, Parks/Recreations, Protective Sciences, Psychology, Public Affairs, Social Sciences, Visual & Performing Arts

Women's Athletic Profile

MSC #32
Plymouth, NH 03264
Coach: Moira Long
Email: Mlong@mail.plymouth.edu

NCAA I
Lady Panthers, Green, White
Phone: (603) 535-2778
Fax: (603) 535-2758

Estimated # of Women's Volleyball Scholarships: N/A
Conference: Independent
Program Profile: We have a gymnasium with three courts that can hold 3,000 people. Our fieldhouse is Holland Union Building and it has 2 courts and 2 fitness rooms.
History: We started in 1996. We had three 20 win seasons.
Coaching: Moira Long, Head Coach, compiled a record of 22-11. She was assistant coach at Springfield College, where her team made 2 NCAA Final 8 Appearances. She was also a coach at Western New England College and Dickinson College.
Roster In State: 6   **Out of State:** 6   **Out of Country:** 0
Sophomores on Team: 0   **Seniors on Team:** 5   **Graduation %:** 100
Most Recent Record: 22-11-0   **Fall Games:** 33-35   **Spring Games:** 5
Camp of Clinic Dates: July 12-15
Positions Needed: Middle Hitter, Outside Hitter
Schedule: Bates, Middlebury, Eastern Connecticut State, Western Connecticut State University, Massachusetts Institute of Tech
Style of Play: Quick offense and great defense.

Rivier College
Academic Profile

420 Main Street
Nashua, NH 03060-5086

Phone: (800) 44-RIVIER

Type: Private, 4 Yr., Liberal Arts, Coed
Website: http://www.rivier.edu
SAT/ACT/GPA: Required/B-avg..
Student/Faculty Ratio: 18:1
Undergraduate Enrollment: 1,600
Scholarships/Academic: Yes
Expenses By: Year
Specializes In: Comprehensive

Founded: 1933
Religion: Roman Catholic
Housing: Yes
Male/Female: 1:4
Graduate Enrollment: 1,100

Athletic: No
In State: $ 20,680

Financial Aid: Yes
Out of State: $ 20,680

Degrees Conferred: AA, AS, BA, BS, BFA, MA, MAT, MSN
Programs of Study: Art, Accounting, Art Education, Athletic Training, Biology, Biology Education, Business Administration, Business Information Systems, Chemistry, Chemistry Education, Communications, Computer Science, Early Childhood Education, Elementary and Secondary Education, Special Education, English, English Education, Exercise Physiology, French, Graphic Design, History, Human Development, Illustration, Law & Government, Liberal Arts, Management, Mathematics, Math Education, Modern Languages, Nursing, Photography & Digital Imaging

Men's Athletic Profile

420 Main Street
Nashua, NH 03060
Coach: Craig Kolek
Email:

NCAA III
Raiders/Blue, Grey
Phone: (603) 888-1311
Fax: (603) 888-3975

Estimated # of Men's Volleyball Scholarships: N/A
Conference: Eastern College Athletic Conference

Women's Athletic Profile

420 Main Street
Nashua, NH 03060
Coach: Craig Koleh
Email: ckoleh@river.edu

NCAA I
Lady Raiders, Navy, Silver
Phone: (603)-897-8467
Fax: (603) 897-8886

Estimated # of Women's Volleyball Scholarships: 0
Conference: The Great Northeast Athletic Conference
Roster In State: 4 | **Out of State:** 9 | **Out of Country:** 0
Sophomores on Team: | **Seniors on Team:** 0 | **Graduation %:** 80
Most Recent Record: 15-10
Positions Needed: OH, MH, Setter
Schedule: Colby-Sawyer, St. Anselms, Roger Williams, Framingham State, Johnson & Wales University, Western New England
Style of Play: Defensive.

Saint Anselm College
Academic Profile

100 St. Anselm Drive
Manchester, NH 03102-1310

Phone: (603) 656-6014

Type: Private, 4 Yr., Liberal Arts, Coed
Website: http://www.anselm.edu
SAT/ACT/GPA: 1000
Student/Faculty Ratio: 17:1
Undergraduate Enrollment: 2,000
Scholarships/Academic: Yes
Expenses By: Year
Specializes In: Nursing, Business, Criminal Justice

Founded: 1889
Religion: Catholic-Benedictine
Housing: Yes
Male/Female: 40:60
Graduate Enrollment: N/A

Athletic: No
In State: $ 22,530

Financial Aid: Yes
Out of State: $ 22,530

Programs of Study: Biology, Business & Management, Chemistry, Computers, Criminal Justice, Economics, Education, Engineering, English, Health Sciences, History, Languages, Liberal Arts, Life Sciences, Mathematics, Nursing, Parks/Recreation, Political Science, Protective Services, Psychology, Public Affairs, Social Sciences and many others.

Women's Athletic Profile

100 St. Anselm Drive
Manchester, NH 03102-1310
Coach: Paul Bucheshe
Email: pduchesne@prodigy,net
Estimated # of Women's Volleyball Scholarships: 0
Conference: NE-10

NCAA I
Lady Hawks, Navy Blue, White
Phone: (603) 656-6014
Fax: (603) 641-7172

Program Profile: We have a dedicated varsity gym that has 800 seats. Our season runs from the last week in August to the middle of November. We a play 30+ match season.
History: Our program existed from 1976-1981. It was reinstated in 1993. In 1978, we had a 19+ win season which existed for three years.
Coaching: Paul Duchesne, became Head Coach in 1998. He was assistant coach here from 1993-98. Peter Julia is Assistant Coach.
Freshman Receiving Financial Aid/Academic:

		Athletic: 0
Roster In State: 3	**Out of State:** 10	**Out of Country:** 0
Sophomores on Team: 0	**Seniors on Team:**	**Graduation %:** 100
Most Recent Record: 20-12-0	**Fall Games:** 32	**Spring Games:** 5

Positions Needed: Outside Hitter, Setter
Schedule: Bentley College, Bryant College, Pace University, Williams College, Merrimack College, University of Mass- Lowell
Style of Play: Aggressive, low passing, quick offense

University of New Hampshire
Academic Profile

UNH Fieldhouse Room 161
Durham, NH 03824

Phone: (603) 862-3822

Type: Public, 4 Yr., Coed
Website: http://www.geocities.com
SAT/ACT/GPA: 1150
Student/Faculty Ratio: 14:1
Undergraduate Enrollment: 10,000
Scholarships/Academic: Yes
Expenses By: Year

Athletic: Yes
In State: $ 11,400

Founded: 1923
Religion: Non-Affiliated
Housing: Yes
Male/Female: 43:57
Graduate Enrollment: 1,500
Financial Aid: Yes
Out of State: $ 20,900

Specializes In: Business, Engineering, Athletic Training, Environmental Sciences
Degrees Conferred: AA, Bachelors, Masters, Doctorate Degree
Programs of Study: Business Administration, Psychology, Biology, Communications, Criminal Justice, Engineering, English, Kinesiology, Liberal Arts, Life Science, Music and Arts, Nursing, Occupational Therapy, Political Science

Women's Athletic Profile

145 Main Street
Durham, NH 03824
Coach: Jill Hirschinger
Email: aleonard@hopper.unh

NCAA I
Lady Wildcats, Blue, White
Phone: (603) 862-4664
Fax: (603) 862-0159

Estimated # of Women's Volleyball Scholarships: 12
Conference: American East Conference
Program Profile: UNH volleyball is a competitive program on the rise. We are a nationally known program that competes with the top 15 teams. UNH facilities are located right on campus with the volleyball arena seating 3,000 fans.
History: UNH volleyball is relatively new. Induction of Volleyball was 1995 In that short span, we have taken UNH volleyball to the NCAA tournament in 1998. We were undefeated in the regular season.
Achievements: Jill Hirschinger has been at UNH 3 years. She has been Coach of the Year for 2 years. We have had a Conference Player of the Year and 6 All-Conference players. 1 All-District player.
Coaching: Jill Hirschinger, Head Coach, has been a coach for 20 years. She has been to the NCAA's for 8 appearances. She has 18 winning seasons as a head coach. She was a member of NCAA II National Volleyball Committee. She served as Assistant Athletic Director. She was a member of the Utah State National Championship Team.

Roster In State: 5 | **Out of State:** 10 | **Out of Country:** 0
Sophomores on Team: 5 | **Seniors on Team:** 4 | **Graduation %:** 100
Most Recent Record: 24-11-0
Camp of Clinic Dates: July 11-15, 1999; August 13-15

Positions Needed: Middle Hitters, Setters
Schedule: Oregon, Michigan State, Arkansas, Kansas State, New Mexico, U Conn
Style of Play: Competitive style, challenging teammates. Team is close and has fun on the court. Coaches encourage the players to be intense, competitive and have fun. They play for the love of the game.

NEW JERSEY

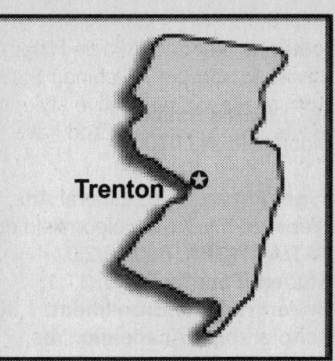

Trenton

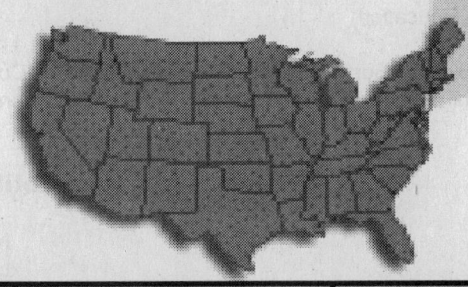

SCHOOL	CITY	AFFILIATION	PAGE
Bloomfield College	Bloomfield	NCAA II/NAIA	457
Centenary College - New Jersey	Hackettstown	NCAA III	457
College of Saint Elizabeth	Morristown	NCAA III	458
Fairleigh Dickinson Univ- Madison	Madison	NCAA III	458
Fairleigh Dickinson Univ- Teaneck	Teaneck	NCAA I	459
Kean University	Union	NCAA III	459
Montclair State University	Upper Montclair	NCAA III	460
New Jersey City University	Jersey City	NCAA III	460
New Jersey Institute of Tech	Newark	NCAA II	461
Princeton University	Princeton	NCAA I	462
Ramapo College of New Jersey	Mahwah	NCAA III	463
Richard Stockton State College	Pomona	NCAA III	463
Rider University	Lawrenceville	NCAA I	464
Rowan University	Glassboro	NCAA III	465
Rutgers State Univ of New Jersey	New Brunswick	NCAA I	465
Rutgers State Univ of NJ/Camden	Camden	NCAA III	466
Rutgers State Univ-Newark	Newark	NCAA III	467
Saint Peter's College	Jersey City	NCAA I	467
Seton Hall University	South Orange	NCAA I	468
Stevens Institute of Technology	Hoboken	NCAA III	468
William Paterson University	Wayne	NCAA III	469

Bloomfield College
Academic Profile

467 Franklin Street
Bloomfield, NJ 07003

Phone: (973) 748-9000

Type: Private, 4 Yr., Liberal Arts, Coed
Website: http://www.bloomfield.edu
SAT/ACT/GPA: 860/18/2.0
Student/Faculty Ratio: 17:1
Undergraduate Enrollment: 1,900
Scholarships/Academic: Yes   **Athletic:** Yes
Expenses By: Year   **In State:** $ 15,500
Specializes In: Business, Nursing, Education
Degrees Conferred: BA, BS

Founded: 1868
Religion: Presbyterian
Housing: Yes
Male/Female: 35:65
Graduate Enrollment: N/A
Financial Aid: Yes
Out of State: $ 15,500

Programs of Study: Accounting, Biology, Business Administration, Chemistry, Communications, Computer Information Systems, Creative Arts & Technology, Criminal Justice, Economics, English, History, Humanities, Philosophy, Political Science, Psychology, Religion, Sociology

Women's Athletic Profile

467 Franklin Street
Bloomfield, NJ 07003
Coach: Sheila Wooten
Email:

NCAA I
Lady Deacons, Maroon, Gold
Phone: (973) 748-9000x364
Fax: (973) 743-3998

Estimated # of Women's Volleyball Scholarships: N/A
Conference: Independent
Program Profile: The season began with three losses against the Rutgers Newark Invitational.
Achievements: Teresa Dweera : 1997 MVP and Freshman of the Year. Semi-finals of the Rowan Tournament and Appeared at the Conference Tournament finals.
Coaching: Sheila Wooten, Head Coach, her record this year was 19-6. Her record last year was 26-9. Dan Rogers is the trainer.
Roster In State: 10   **Out of State:** 1   **Out of Country:** 0
Sophomores on Team: 5   **Seniors on Team:** 1   **Graduation %:** 100
Most Recent Record: 19-6-0
Schedule: Montclair University, Molloy, St. Elizabeth, Rutgers, Centenary, Jersey City State, City College of New York, St. Thomas Aquinas, Teikyo Post University
Style of Play: We have the strongest team in our history.

Centenary College - New Jersey
Academic Profile

400 Jefferson Street
Hackettstown, NJ 07840

Phone: (908) 852-1400

Type: Private, 4 Yr., Liberal Arts, Coed
Website: http://www.centenarycollege.edu
SAT/ACT/GPA: 850/18/2.3
Student/Faculty Ratio: 13:1
Undergraduate Enrollment: 750
Scholarships/Academic: Yes   **Athletic:** No
Expenses By: Year   **In State:** $ 19,870
Specializes In: Business, Education, Equine Studies
Degrees Conferred: AA, AS, BA, BS

Founded: 1867
Religion: United Methodist
Housing: Yes
Male/Female: 40:60
Graduate Enrollment: 40
Financial Aid: Yes
Out of State: $ 19,870

Programs of Study: Accounting, Applied Mathematics, Art, Business Administration, Commercial Art, Communication, Computer Information Systems, Early Childhood Education, Education, Elementary Education, English, Equestrian Studies, Fashion Design/Technology, Fashion Merchandising, Graphical & Art Design, History, Interior Design, International Studies, Liberal Arts, Marketing, Merchandising, Mathematics, Political Science, Psychology, Radio/Television, Secondary Education, Special Education, Social & Behavioral Sciences, Sports Management, Teacher Aide, Textile/Clothing

Women's Athletic Profile

400 Jefferson Street
Hackettstown, NJ 07840
Coach: Jeremy Sands
Email:

NCAA I
Lady Cyclones, Blue, White
Phone: (908) 852-1400x2297
Fax: (908) 813-8295

Estimated # of Women's Volleyball Scholarships: N/A
Conference: Eastern College Athletic Conference
History: The 1998 Record at Centenary College was 8-20.

Roster In State: 9	**Out of State:** 1	**Out of Country:** 1
Sophomores on Team: 0	**Seniors on Team:** 1	**Graduation %:** Unknown
Most Recent Record:	**Fall Games:** 21	**Spring Games:** 4

Schedule: Misericordia, William Patterson, Maywood
Style of Play: Fundamentally basic volleyball, we use a 5-1 set which includes 3 passers and focus on the defensive schemes.

College of Saint Elizabeth
Academic Profile

2 Convent Road
Morristown, NJ 07960-6989

Phone: 800-210-7900

Type: Private, 4 Yr., Liberal Arts
Website: Not Available
SAT/ACT/GPA: 750+
Student/Faculty Ratio: 10:1
Undergraduate Enrollment: 1,202
Scholarships/Academic: Yes   **Athletic:** No
Expenses By: Year   **In State:** $ 15,900
Degrees Conferred: BA, BS

Founded: 1899
Religion: Catholic
Housing: No
Male/Female: 8:92 Women Only
Graduate Enrollment: N/A
Financial Aid: Yes
Out of State: $ 15,900

Programs of Study: Contact school for program of study.

Women's Athletic Profile

2 Convent Road
Morristown, NJ 07960
Coach: Mike Tully
Email:

NCAA I
Lady Eagles, Blue, Gold
Phone: (973) 290-4207
Fax: (973) 290-4207

Estimated # of Women's Volleyball Scholarships: None
Conference: Independent
Program Profile: The season games are played in Saint Joseph Hall which seats approx. 425 fans. The season begins on Sept. 13th and ends October 25.
History: Has been in existence for over 30 years. We are reaching gain through rebuilding years.
Roster In State: 12

Sophomores on Team: 4	**Seniors on Team:** 3	**Graduation %:** 92
Most Recent Record: 1-18	**Fall Games:** 20	**Spring Games:**

Schedule: Stevens Tech, Kean University, Marymont, Ramapo, New Jersey City University, St. Joseph
Style of Play: Aggressive-Small but quick-new defense this year.

Fairleigh Dickinson University - Madison
Academic Profile

285 Madison Avenue
Madison, NJ 07940

Phone: (973) 443-8500

Type: Private, 4 Yr., Liberal Arts, Coed
Website: http://www.fdu.edu
SAT/ACT/GPA: 1000
Student/Faculty Ratio: 30:1
Undergraduate Enrollment: 2,200
Scholarships/Academic: Yes   **Athletic:** No
Expenses By: Year   **In State:** $ 21,110
Specializes In: Business, Education, Psychology, 5-year quest program
Degrees Conferred: BA, BS, MA, MAT, MBA, MS, MPA, DMD

Founded: 1958
Religion: Non-Affiliated
Housing: Yes
Male/Female: 1:3
Graduate Enrollment: 1,200
Financial Aid: Yes
Out of State: $ 21,110

Programs of Study: Accounting, Biology, Business Management, Chemistry, Clinical Laboratory Science, Computer Science, Economics, Electronic Filmmaking & Digital Video Design, English Languages & Literature, Finance, Fine Arts, French Languages & Literature, History, Hotel/Restaurant Management, Humanities, Marine Biology, Marketing, Mathematics, Medical Technology, Philosophy, Political Science, Psychology, Radiological Technology, Sociology

Women's Athletic Profile

285 Madison Avenue
Madison, NJ 07940
Coach: Bill Shaw
Email:

NCAA I
Lady Devils, Black, Blue, White
Phone: (973) 443-8829
Fax: (973) 443-8796

Conference: Middle Atlantic States Conference
Program Profile: Our gymnasium has three multipurpose courts for volleyball, basketball and badminton. It also has a 2,300 seat spectator facility for varsity contests. We have fully carpeted women's locker rooms and private showers. Our fitness center has the latest state-of-the-art weight machines.
History: Our teams are in Division III of the National Collegiate Athletic Association and the Eastern College Athletic Conference. Our team is regularly ranked among the best in our division, both regionally and nationally.

Fairleigh Dickinson University - Teaneck
Academic Profile

1000 River Road
Teaneck, NJ 07666

Phone: (201) 692-2000

Type: Private, 4 Yr., Liberal Arts, Coed
Website: http://www.fdu.edu
SAT/ACT/GPA: 900+
Student/Faculty Ratio: 15:1
Undergraduate Enrollment: 4,000
Scholarships/Academic: Yes   **Athletic:** Yes
Expenses By: Year   **In State:** $ 19,858
Degrees Conferred: BS, BA

Founded: 1942
Religion: Non-Affiliated
Housing: Yes
Male/Female: 50:50
Graduate Enrollment: N/A
Financial Aid: Yes
Out of State: $ 19,858

Programs of Study: Accounting, Arts, Biology, Business Management, Chemistry, Economics, English Language & Literature, Finance, History, International Studies, Marine Biology, Marketing, Mathematics, Philosophy, Psychology, Science, Sociology, PreProfessional Courses

Women's Athletic Profile

1000 River Road
Teaneck, NJ 07666
Coach: Stacy Recanati
Email:

NCAA I
Knights, Blue, Black, White
Phone: (201) 692-2254
Fax: (201) 692-9361

Estimated # of Women's Volleyball Scholarships: N/A
Conference: Northeast Conference

Kean University
Academic Profile

1000 Morris Avenue
Union, NJ 07083

Phone: 908-527-2195

Type: Public, 4 Yr., Liberal Arts, Coed
Website: http://www.kean.edu
SAT/ACT/GPA: 950+/2.0
Student/Faculty Ratio: 18:1
Undergraduate Enrollment: 4,000
Scholarships/Academic: Yes   **Athletic:** No
Expenses By: Year   **In State:** $ 10,908
Degrees Conferred: BA, BS, BFA, BSN, BSW, MA, MS

Founded: 1855
Religion: Non-Affiliated
Housing: Yes
Male/Female: 1:4
Graduate Enrollment: 5,000
Financial Aid: Yes
Out of State: $ 12,090

Programs of Study: School of Business, Government & Technology, School of Liberal Arts, School of Natural Science, Nursing, Mathematics, School of Education

Women's Athletic Profile

Morris Avenue
Union, NJ 07083
Coach: Bridget White
Email: mwhite@turbo.kean.edu

NCAA I
Lady Cougars, Blue, Silver
Phone: (908) 527-2937
Fax: (908) 354-9423

Estimated # of Women's Volleyball Scholarships: 0
Conference: New Jersey Athletic Conference
Program Profile: We have a traditional and non-traditional competitive Division III volleyball program. We offer year-round training. We have a five year plan for a new indoor facility
History: The program started in 1973.
Achievements: Coach of the Year in 1989, 1992, 1993 & 1994; NJCA Champs in 1993, 1994 & 1995.
Coaching: Bridget White, Head Coach, has coached here from 1988 to the present and has a record of 209-105. In 1983 & 1984, she was a National Championships Participant as a student-athlete.

Roster In State: 12	**Out of State:** 1	**Out of Country:** 0
Sophomores on Team: 8	**Seniors on Team:** 0	**Graduation %:** Unknown
Most Recent Record: 9-21-0	**Fall Games:** 30	**Spring Games:** 16

Camp of Clinic Dates: August 21 - September 1
Positions Needed: 2 Middle Blockers, 2 Outside Hitters, Setter
Style of Play: Aggressive defense - relentless. Put team goals above individual differences. Synergy "We strive for excellence through integrity, respect, enthusiasm and team work", -The Kean Volleyball Ethos.

Montclair State University
Academic Profile

1 Normal Avenue
Upper Montclair, NJ 07043

Phone: (973) 655-7830

Type: Public, 4 Yr., Coed
Website: http://www.montclair.edu
SAT/ACT/GPA: 1200
Student/Faculty Ratio: 30:1
Undergraduate Enrollment: 10,000
Scholarships/Academic: Yes
Expenses By: Year

Athletic: No
In State: $ 5,000

Founded: 1908
Religion: Non-Affiliated
Housing: Yes
Male/Female: 14:1
Graduate Enrollment: 3,500
Financial Aid: Yes
Out of State: $ 5,000

Specializes In: Teaching University
Degrees Conferred: School of Business, School of Arts, College of Humanities, Social Sciences
Programs of Study: Has 43 undergraduate majors, 30 graduate majors, Aging Doctor Program, all school of Business, Arts, Humanities, Sciences, and Math Education

Women's Athletic Profile

Normal Avenue
Upper Montclair, NJ 07043
Coach: Sandra Sanchez
Email:

NCAA I
Lady Red Hawks, Redt, White
Phone: (973) 655-7830
Fax: (973) 655-5390

Estimated # of Women's Volleyball Scholarships: N/A
Conference: New Jersey Athletic Conference
History: Our program has been going on from 1989 to the present.
Achievements: 1997-1998 NJAC Championship and Coach of the Year; 1998-1999 2nd place in Conference.
Coaching: Sandra E. Sanchez-Lombeyda became Head Coach in 1999. She was assistant coach from 1989-1999. Her record is 19-7. She was 1997-1998 Coach of the Year.
Freshman Receiving Financial Aid/Academic:

		Athletic: 4
Roster In State: 15	**Out of State:** 1	**Out of Country:** 0
Sophomores on Team: 4	**Seniors on Team:** 1	**Graduation %:** 100
Most Recent Record: 19-7-0	**Fall Games:** 26	**Spring Games:** 4

Camp of Clinic Dates: Still working on setting a camp
Positions Needed: (2) Setters, Defensive Position
Schedule: WPC, Kean, Stockton, USMMA, Vassar, Elmira
Style of Play: 5-1, 3 man receive reception

New Jersey City University
Academic Profile

2039 Kennedy Boulevard
Jersey City, NJ 07305-1597
Type: Public, 4 Yr., Liberal Arts, Coed
Website: http://www.njcu.edu
SAT/ACT/GPA: 480-V, 480-M

Phone: (201) 200-3317

Founded: 1929
Religion: Non-Affiliated
Housing: Yes

Student/Faculty Ratio: 17:1
Undergraduate Enrollment: 5,200
Scholarships/Academic: Yes   **Athletic:** No
Expenses By: Year   **In State:** $ 8,042
Specializes In: Comprehensive college with liberal arts and professional programs
Degrees Conferred: BA, BS, BFA, BSN, MA, MS

Male/Female: 48:52
Graduate Enrollment: 1,800
Financial Aid: Yes
Out of State: $ 9,332

Programs of Study: Accounting, Biology, Chemistry, Communications, Computer Science, CIS, Economics, English, History, Justice Studies, Management, Marketing, Music, Elementary Education, Music Education, Special Education, Social Work, Sociology, Art History, Art Education, Psychology, Film Studies, and more

Men's Athletic Profile

2039 Kennedy Boulevard
Jersey City, NJ 07305
Coach: Frank Cella
Email: webmaster@mail.nju.edu

NCAA III
Gothic Knights/Green, Gold
Phone: (201) 200-3317
Fax: (201) 200-2365

Estimated # of Men's Volleyball Scholarships: N/A
Conference: NECVA
Program Profile: We are a competitive NCAA Division III program. New Jersey City University plays approximately 35 matches in a 12-week season. All home matches are played in the 2,000 seats athletic and fitness center built in 1994.
History: The men's volleyball program began in 1990. Our program has recorded three straight 20-win seasons since 1996. Our team advanced to the semi-finals of the 12 team NECVA Tournament last season.
Achievements: Satsay Thongvichith (1995-1998) was selected Metro Conference Player of the Year in 1996; team went 13-3 in conference and advanced to the semi-finals of the NECVA Tournament in 1998.
Coaching: Frank Cella, Head Coach, is entering his fourth season as NJCU men's volleyball coach. He has a three year record of 74-37 (66.7 win percentage). He coached the NJCU women from 1995 to 1998 and was also the head women's coach at Fordham.
Freshman Receiving Financial Aid/Academic: 4   **Athletic:** 0
Roster In State: 11   **Out of State:** 0   **Out of Country:** 0
Graduation %: 75%
Most Recent Record: 20-14-0   **Fall Games:** 0   **Spring Games:** 30-35
Positions Needed: Outside Hitter, Setter
Schedule: New York City, Mt. St. Vincent, Ramapo, Queens, US Merchant Marine, Clarke
Style of Play: Focus on defense, using two blockers. Quick back row players must keep the ball alive and pass to the setter. Offensive style is up tempo utilizing quickness since the squad does not traditionally have tall players.

Women's Athletic Profile

2039 Kennedy Boulevard
Jersey City, NJ 07305
Coach: TBA
Email: webmaster@mail.njcu.edu

NCAA I
Gothic Knights, Green, Gold
Phone: (201) 200-3317
Fax: (201) 200-2365

Estimated # of Women's Volleyball Scholarships: No
Conference: New Jersey Athletic Conference
Program Profile: We are a competitive NCAA Division III program. New Jersey City University plays approximately 30 matches in a nine-week season. All home matches are played in the 2,000 seat Athletic & Fitness Center built in 1994.
History: The first year of varsity competition was 1983. The 1997 team set a school record for wins in a season with 26. The program has recorded two 20-win seasons in the last four years.
Achievements: Last appearance in the six-team conference tournament was 1997.
Roster In State: 10   **Out of State:** 0   **Out of Country:** 0
Sophomores on Team: 0   **Seniors on Team:**   **Graduation %:** 80
Most Recent Record: 8-18-0   **Fall Games:** 25-30   **Spring Games:** 0
Positions Needed: OH,MB
Schedule: Richard Stockton, Rutgers-Newark, Montclair State, Rowan, U.S. Merchant Marine, FDU-Madison

New Jersey Institute of Technology
Academic Profile

80 Lock St.
Newark, NJ 07102

Phone: 800-925-6548

Type: Public, 4 Yr., Engineering, Coed
Website: http://www.njit.edu
SAT/ACT/GPA: required

Founded: 1881
Religion: Non-Affiliated
Housing: Yes

Student/Faculty Ratio: 14;1
Undergraduate Enrollment: 3,400
Scholarships/Academic: Yes
Expenses By: Year
Athletic: No
In State: $ 11,200
Male/Female: 82:18
Graduate Enrollment: 2,500
Financial Aid: Yes
Out of State: $ 15,800
Degrees Conferred: BA, BS, BArch, BSCE, BSChemE, BSEE, BSET, BSME, MA, MArch, MS, Ph.D.
Programs of Study: Actuarial Sciences, Architecture, Chemical Engineering, Chemistry, Civil Engineering, Computer Science, Mathematics, Physics, Science, Technology & Society, Statistics

Men's Athletic Profile

80 Lock Street
Newark, NJ 07102
Coach: Dave DeNure
Email: catalano@adm.njit.edu

NCAA II
Highlanders/Scarlet, White
Phone: (973) 596-3634
Fax: (973) 596-8295

Estimated # of Men's Volleyball Scholarships: N/A
Conference: New York Collegiate Conference

Women's Athletic Profile

80 Lock St.
Newark, NJ 07102
Coach: Manny Del Rio
Email:

NCAA I

Phone: (201) 596-3636
Fax:

Did Not Return Profile

Princeton University
Academic Profile

Dillon Gym
Princeton, NJ 08544

Phone: 609-258-3060

Type: Private, 4 Yr., Liberal Arts, Engineering, Coed
Website: http://www.princeton.edu
SAT/ACT/GPA: 1260+/27+
Student/Faculty Ratio: 5:1
Undergraduate Enrollment: 4,524
Scholarships/Academic: Yes
Expenses By: Year
Athletic: No
In State: $ 30,000
Founded: 1746
Religion: Non-Affiliated
Housing: Yes
Male/Female: 58:42
Graduate Enrollment: 1,770
Financial Aid: Yes
Out of State: $ 30,000
Degrees Conferred: BA, BS, MA, Ph.D.
Programs of Study: Aeronautical Engineering, Anthropology, Archeology, Architectural Engineering, Computer Engineering, Asian Studies, AstroPhysics, Biology, Chemistry, Computer Science, Economics, Fine Arts, Geology, History, International Relations, Math, Music, Philosophy, Physics, Political Science, Psychology, Religion, Social Science

Men's Athletic Profile

P.O. Box 71
Princeton, NJ 08544
Coach: Glenn Nelson
Email:

NCAA I
Tigers/Orange, Black
Phone: (609) 258-3532
Fax: (609) 258-4477

Estimated # of Men's Volleyball Scholarships: N/A
Conference: Eastern College Athletic Conference

Women's Athletic Profile

P.O. Box 71
Princeton, NJ 08544
Coach: Glenn Nelson
Email:

NCAA I
Lady Tigers, Orange, Black
Phone: (609) 258-3532
Fax: (609) 258-4477

Estimated # of Women's Volleyball Scholarships: N/A
Conference: Ivy Group

Ramapo College of New Jersey
Academic Profile

505 Ramapo Valley rd.
Mahwah, NJ 07430

Phone: 800-972-6276

Type: Public, 4 Yr., Liberal Arts, Coed
Website: http://www.ramapo.edu
SAT/ACT/GPA: 1150/85
Student/Faculty Ratio: 15:1
Undergraduate Enrollment: 4,533
Scholarships/Academic: Yes   **Athletic:** No
Expenses By: Year   **In State:** $ 7,658
Degrees Conferred: BA, BS

Founded: 1969
Religion: Non-Affiliated
Housing: Yes
Male/Female: 49:51
Graduate Enrollment: N/A
Financial Aid: Yes
Out of State: $ 9,658

Programs of Study: Accounting, American Studies, BioChemistry, Biology, Business Administration, Management, Marketing, Chemistry, Clinical Laboratory Science, Communications, Arts, Graphic Design, Journalism, Public Communications, Radio/Television, Writing, Computer Science, Contemporary Arts, Economics, Environmental Science, Environmental Studies, History, Fine Arts, Information Systems, Literature, Law and Society, Mathematics, Metropolitan Studies, Nursing, Physics, Political Science, Social Work, Sociology, Anthropology, Philosophy, Psychology, Elementary Education, Women's Studies, Sociology

Men's Athletic Profile

505 Ramapo Valley Rd
Mahwah, NJ 07430
Coach: Don Vandebeck
Email:

NCAA III
Roadrunners/Scarlet, Gold
Phone: (201) 529-7674
Fax: (201) 529-6708

Estimated # of Men's Volleyball Scholarships: N/A
Conference: Independent

Women's Athletic Profile

505 Ramapo Valley Rd.
Mahwah, NJ 07430
Coach: Reggie Pantophlet
Email: rtpantophlet@att.net

NCAA I
Lady Roadrunners, Red, Black
Phone: (201) 684-7068
Fax: (201) 684-7958

Estimated # of Women's Volleyball Scholarships: N/A
Conference: New Jersey Athletic Conference
History: Under Coach Pantophelt 1997 3-21, 1998 14-11, 1999 20-11.
Achievements: 1998 Coach of the Year WIAC, 1998 WIAC Champion undefeated, 1999 WIAC Champion undefeated.
Coaching: Head Coach Reggie Pantophlet, Statistician Kristin Eammasams
Roster In State: 11
Seniors on Team: 1
Most Recent Record: 20-11
Camp of Clinic Dates: 3rd week in August
Positions Needed: Setters

Richard Stockton State College
Academic Profile

P. O. Box 195
Pomona, NJ 08240
Type: Public, 4 Yr., Liberal Arts, Coed
Website: http://www.stockton.edu
SAT/ACT/GPA: 1140/24/top 20%
Student/Faculty Ratio: 20:1
Undergraduate Enrollment: 6,000
Scholarships/Academic: Yes   **Athletic:** No
Expenses By: Year   **In State:** $ 9,300
Degrees Conferred: BA, BS, Master's in Business, Nursing, Physical Therapy

Phone: (609) 652-4875

Founded: 1969
Religion: Non-Affiliated
Housing: Yes
Male/Female: 43:57
Graduate Enrollment: 200
Financial Aid: Yes
Out of State: $ 11,200

Programs of Study: Business, Marine Biology, Computer Science, Nursing, Public Health, Speech, Pathology/Audiology, Criminal Justice, Economics, Political Science, Psychology, Social Work, Sociology, Anthropology, Art, Latin, English, French, Biological Science, Earth Science, Elementary, Mathematics, Music, Physical Science, Social Studies, Spanish

Women's Athletic Profile

Jim Leeds Rd.
Pomona, NJ 08240
Coach: Eric Illjes
Email: iaprod433@stockton.edu

NCAA I
Lady Ospreys, Black, Red
Phone: (609) 652-4875
Fax: (609) 748-5510

Estimated # of Women's Volleyball Scholarships: 0
Conference: New Jersey Athletic Conference
Program Profile: We have 30-40 games per season that go from September to November. We have a new $17 million 3,000 seat athletic facility.
History: Our program started in 1973.
Achievements: ECAC Champions (south) in 1996; Conference Champions in 1996, Undefeated in regular season conference play for the last three years.
Coaching: Eric Illjes, started as Head Coach in 1999. He was assistant coach for six years. His record is 152-75.

Roster In State: 5	**Out of State:** 7	**Out of Country:** 1
Sophomores on Team: 0	**Seniors on Team:** 1	**Graduation %:** 97
Most Recent Record: 23-11-0	**Fall Games:** 35	**Spring Games:** 1

Positions Needed: Middle Hitter, Outside Hitter, Setter
Schedule: Gettysburg, Moravion, Franklin & Marshall, Salisbury, Rutgers, Elizabethtown
Style of Play: 6-2 offense utilizing quick and slide middle attacks, powerful outside and weak side hitting ; 3-1, shoot. Stress no mistakes.

Rider University
Academic Profile

2083 Lawrenceville Rd.
Lawrenceville, NJ 08648

Phone: 800-257-9026

Type: Private, 4 Yr., Liberal Arts, Coed
Website: http://www.rider.edu
SAT/ACT/GPA: 960/18/2.4
Student/Faculty Ratio: 1:19
Undergraduate Enrollment: 2,900
Scholarships/Academic: Yes
Expenses By: Year

Athletic: Yes
In State: $ 23,000

Founded: 1865
Religion: Non-Affiliated
Housing: Yes
Male/Female: 1:1
Graduate Enrollment: 750
Financial Aid: Yes
Out of State: $ 23,000

Specializes In: Business, Education, Liberal Arts
Degrees Conferred: BA, BS, MA, MBA
Programs of Study: Business (11 majors), Communications, Computer Sciences, Liberal Arts, PreLaw, PreMed, Psychology, Sociology, Teacher Education

Women's Athletic Profile

2083 Lawrenceville Rd.
Lawrenceville, NJ 08648-3099
Coach: Emily Ahlquist
Email: eahlquist@rider.edu

NCAA I
Lady Broncs, Cranberry, White
Phone: (609) 896-5239
Fax: (609) 896-5744

Estimated # of Women's Volleyball Scholarships: 3
Conference: Metro Atlantic Athletic Conference
Program Profile: Fall season- we play in Alumni Gym, hardwood floor and seats about 3,500
History: New Coach
Coaching: Emily Ahlquist played at the University of Minnesota, before coaching at Rider. There she still holds many records.
Freshman Receiving Financial Aid/Academic:

Athletic: 3

Roster In State: 5	**Out of State:** 9	**Out of Country:**
Seniors on Team: 2	**Graduation %:** 100	

Most Recent Record: 1-16
Positions Needed: OH/MB

Schedule: American, Akron, Fairfield, Brown, Yale.
Style of Play: Fast offense and scrappy defense.

Rowan University
Academic Profile

201 Mullica Hill Road
Glassboro, NJ 08028
Type: Public, 4 Yr., Liberal Arts, Coed
Website: http://www.rowan.edu
SAT/ACT/GPA: Average:1,000-1,300
Student/Faculty Ratio: 16:1
Undergraduate Enrollment: 9,480
Scholarships/Academic: Yes
Expenses By: Year
Degrees Conferred: BA, BS, MA, MS, MBA

Phone: (609) 256-4684

Founded: 1923
Religion: Non-Affiliated
Housing: Yes
Male/Female: 40:60
Graduate Enrollment: N/A
Athletic: No   **Financial Aid:** Yes
In State: $ 5,021   **Out of State:** $ 6,731

Programs of Study: Art, Biological Science, Chemistry, Communications, Computer Science, Economics, Elementary Education, English, Engineering, Geography, Health & Physical Education, History, Law/Justice, Liberal Studies, Mathematics, Music, Physical Science, Physics, Political Science, Psychology, School Nursing, Sociology, Spanish, Theatre

Women's Athletic Profile

201 Mullica Hill Road
Glassboro, NJ 08028
Coach: Ed Weems
Email: weems@rowan.edu

NCAA I
Lady Profs, Brown, Gold
Phone: (609) 256-4693
Fax: (609) 256-4916

Estimated # of Women's Volleyball Scholarships: 0
Conference: New Jersey Athletic Conference
Program Profile: This is only the fifth year for the Women's Volleyball program at Rowan after a seven year hiatus. The Profs play in Esby gymnasium which seats 1,500. Rowan plays a fall season and is in the New Jersey Athletic Conference. The NJAC Champion receives a bid to the NCAA Division III Championship Tournament.
History: From 1978-80, the women's volleyball programs was a club at Rowan University. In 1981 the team was made varsity and competed until the sports was discontinued after the 1987 season. The volleyball programs reinstated in 1995. The Profs received a bid to the NCAA championship Tournament in 1985. Rowan won the conference championship from 1984-87. Last year, the women's volleyball team made their fourth straight appearance in the conference tournament.
Achievements: Coach of the year honors, Conference titles, All-Americans, Olympians, etc. New Jersey Athletic Conference All-Conference. Jane Gheilerman 1996, first team, 1997 first team. Blair Stockwell 1996, Second team. Kristy Mackiewicz 1999, first team.
Coaching: Ed Weems is in his second season as Head Coach at Rowan. Weems is the fourth coach in the history of the program. At Rowan, Weems was the assistant women's volleyball coach under Libby Ranero since 1996. A member of the U.S. Volleyball Association, Weems has over 10 years of experience playing and coaching volleyball.
Freshman Receiving Financial Aid/Academic: **Athletic:** 0
Roster In State: 12   **Out of State:** 3   **Out of Country:** 0
Seniors on Team: 4   **Graduation %:** 100
Most Recent Record: 9-18
Style of Play: 5-1 offense , rotation defense and moderate speed.

Rutgers State University of New Jersey
Academic Profile

130 College Ave.
New Brunswick, NJ 08903

Phone: (732) 932-6501

Type: Public, 4 Year, Coed
Website: http://www.rutgers.edu
SAT/ACT/GPA: All
Student/Faculty Ratio: 1:15
Undergraduate Enrollment: 35,712
Scholarships/Academic: Yes
Expenses By: Year

Founded: 1766
Religion: Non-Affiliated
Housing: Yes
Male/Female: 46:54
Graduate Enrollment: 12,000
Athletic: Yes   **Financial Aid:** Yes
In State: $ 12,178   **Out of State:** $ 16,902

Programs of Study: Accounting, Administration of Justice, African Studies, Agricultural Science, Animal Science, Anthropology, Art History, BioChemistry, Biological Science, Chemical Engineering, Chemistry, Civil Engineering, Communication, Computer Science,

Dance, Economics, Electrical Engineering, Environmental Sciences, Exercise Sciences and Sports Studies, Finance, Food Science, Geography, Geological Sciences, History and Political Science, Human Ecology, Industrial Engineering, Journalism and Mass Media, Linguistics, Management, Marketing, Mechanical Engineering, Medical Technology, Music, Natural Resources Management, Nursing, Nutritional Sciences, Pharmacy, Philosophy, Physics, Psychology, Public Health, Religion, Social Work, Sociology, Statistics-Mathematics, Theater Arts, Visual Arts, Women's Studies

Women's Athletic Profile

P.O. Box 5061
New Brunswick, NJ 08903
Coach: Ann Leonard-House
Email: ruwvb@rci.rutgers.edu

NCAA I
Lady Knights, Scarlet
Phone: (732) 932-6501
Fax: (732) 932-1363

Estimated # of Women's Volleyball Scholarships: 3
Conference: Big East Conference
Program Profile: For the first time since Rutgers joined the Big East Conference in 1994, the Scarlet Knights advanced to the Big East Tournament with a 6-5 conference record. The No. 4 seed, RU defeated fifth seed West Virginia 3-0 in the first round, but fell to No 1 G-town 4-1 in the semifinals.
History: The program started in 1977. The Knights were coached by Socrates "Scott" Mose from 1977 to 1982 recording a 214-60 team record.
Coaching: Ann Leonard-House, Head Coach, attended the University of Massachusetts-Lowell from 1986 to 1993. Her record there was 181-88. She has been at Rutgers from 1994 to 1998. Her record here is 71-84. Assistant Coach, Carrie McCaw, has been at Rutgers from 1998-99. She graduated from Syracuse in 1997.
Roster In State: **Out of State:** 8   **Out of Country:** 3
Graduation %: 100
Most Recent Record: 18-16-0   **Fall Games:** 34   **Spring Games:** 4 day competition
Camp of Clinic Dates: Summer Day Camp. August 2-5 and August 9-12
Positions Needed: Outside, Middle,Rightside
Schedule: Fairfield, Louisville, Notre Dame, Colorado State, Georgetown,Temple
Style of Play: 5-1 aggressive and exciting

Rutgers University - Camden
Academic Profile

3rd & Linden Street
Camden, NJ 08102

Phone: 856-225-6104

Type: Public, 4 Yr., Liberal Arts, Coed
Website: http://www.camden-www.rutgers.edu/
SAT/ACT/GPA: 1030
Student/Faculty Ratio: 15:1
Undergraduate Enrollment: 3,455
Scholarships/Academic: Yes   **Athletic:** No
Expenses By: Year   **In State:** $ 6,105
Specializes In: Liberal Arts
Degrees Conferred: BA, BS, MA, MS, MSW

Founded: 1927
Religion: Non-Affiliated
Housing: Yes
Male/Female: 1:1
Graduate Enrollment: 1,587
Financial Aid: Yes
Out of State: $ 10,986

Programs of Study: Bachelor of Arts: Afro-American Studies, Art, Biology, Chemistry, Computer Science, Criminal Justice, Economics, English, French, German, History, Student-Proposed Major, Mathematics, Music, Philosophy, Political Science, Psychology, General Studies, Social Work, Sociology, Spanish, Theatre Arts, Urban Studies; Bachelor of Science: BioMedical Technology, Nursing

Women's Athletic Profile

3rd & Street
Camden, NJ 08102
Coach: Joe Gillespie
Email:

NCAA I
Scarlet Raptors, Scarlet, Black
Phone: (609) 225-6195
Fax: (609) 225-6024

Estimated # of Women's Volleyball Scholarships: N/A
Conference: Independent

Rutgers University - Newark
Academic Profile

Golden Dome Athletic Center
Newark, NJ 07102

Phone: 973-353-5205

Type: Public, 4 Yr., Liberal Arts, Engineering, Coed
Website: http://www.rutger.edu/newark
SAT/ACT/GPA: Open
Student/Faculty Ratio: 12:1
Undergraduate Enrollment: 6,000
Scholarships/Academic: Yes   **Athletic:** No
Expenses By: Year   **In State:** $ 7,500
Degrees Conferred: BA, BS

Founded: 1766
Religion: Non-Affiliated
Housing: Yes
Male/Female: 46:54
Graduate Enrollment: 3,500
Financial Aid: Yes
Out of State: $ 11,000

Programs of Study: Business, Marketing, Management, Computer Science, Literature, Education, Criminal Justice, Mathematics, PreLaw, Engineering, Psychology, PreMed, Social Sciences

Men's Athletic Profile

42 Warren St.
Newark, NJ 07102
Coach: Ron Larsen
Email:

NCAA III
Scarlet Raiders/Scarlet
Phone: (973) 353-5474
Fax: (973) 353-1431

Estimated # of Men's Volleyball Scholarships: N/A
Conference: Eastern Intercollegiate Volleyball Association

Women's Athletic Profile

42 Warren Street
Newark, NJ 07102
Coach:
Email:

NCAA I
Lady Raiders, Scarlet
Phone:
Fax:

Estimated # of Women's Volleyball Scholarships: N/A
Conference: Eastern College Athletic Conference

Saint Peter's College
Academic Profile

2641 Kennedy Boulevard
Jersey City, NJ 07306

Phone: 201-915-9213

Type: Private, 4 Yr., Liberal Arts, Coed
Website: http://www.spc.edu
SAT/ACT/GPA: Varies
Student/Faculty Ratio: 12:1
Undergraduate Enrollment: 2,900
Scholarships/Academic: Yes   **Athletic:** Yes
Expenses By: Sem   **In State:** $ 10,500
Specializes In: Business, Education, Sociology, Accounting, Communications
Degrees Conferred: MBA, MA, MS, BA, BS, AA, AAS

Founded: 1872
Religion: Roman Catholic
Housing: Yes
Male/Female: 55:45
Graduate Enrollment: 800
Financial Aid: Yes
Out of State: $ 10,500

Programs of Study: Accounting, American Studies, Art History, Biological, Chemistry, Biology, Business Management, Chemistry, Clinical Laboratory, Medical Technology, Toxicology, Computer Science, Economics, Mathematics, Elementary Education, English, History, Marketing, Management, Political Science, Philosophy, Physics, Psychology, Sociology, Theology

Women's Athletic Profile

2641 Kennedy Blvd.
Jersey City, NJ 07306
Coach: Mikhail Sigalov
Email: m_sigalov@hotmail.com

NCAA I
Peahens, Blue, White
Phone: (201) 413-7280
Fax: (201) 915-9102

Estimated # of Women's Volleyball Scholarships: 6
Conference: Metro Atlantic Athletic Conference
Achievements: 1999 Coach of the Year.

Roster In State: 0	**Out of State:** 5	**Out of Country:** 2
Sophomores on Team:	**Seniors on Team:** 2	**Graduation %:** 100

Most Recent Record: 15-14
Positions Needed: MB, Setter
Schedule: Virginia Tech, St. John's, Setton Hall, Rutgers, Hofstra, Princeton, Fairfield

Seton Hall University
Academic Profile

400 South Orange Avenue
South Orange, NJ 07079

Phone: (973) 275-9498

Type: Private, 4 Yr., Liberal Arts, Coed
Website: http://www.shu.edu
SAT/ACT/GPA: All factors are considered
Student/Faculty Ratio: 14/1
Undergraduate Enrollment: 4,700

Founded: 1856
Religion: Catholic
Housing: Yes
Male/Female: 46/54
Graduate Enrollment: 6,000

Scholarships/Academic: Yes	**Athletic:** Yes	**Financial Aid:** Yes
Expenses By: Year	**In State:** $26,187	**Out of State:** $26,187

Degrees Conferred: BA, BS, MS, MA, Ph.D., EdD
Programs of Study: 40 majors at the undergraduate level, as well as many minors, certificates and special programs that includes: Business, Arts, Sciences, Nursing, Education, Theology, Law, Medical Education

Women's Athletic Profile

400 S. Orange Avenue
South Orange, NJ 07079
Coach: Stephanie Mose'
Email: thehall@shu.edu

NCAA I
Pirates, Blue, White
Phone: (973) 761-9332
Fax: (973) 275-2040

Estimated # of Women's Volleyball Scholarships: 10
Conference: Big East Conference
Program Profile: We have a well-rounded program; on & off. We continued to strive for excellence and play in Walsh Gym that seats 2,500. Our players involved with Life Skills program and volunteer efforts.
History: We started with losing records and program turned-around in 1989. Made great strides in conference and in region where level of program jumped.
Achievements: In 1992 & 1994, we were Regular Season Champions, Academic All-Americans in 1996 & 1997, All-Region in 1994, NJ-NCAA Women of the Year in 1996.
Coaching: Stephanie Mose', Head Coach, started in 1972 as a part-time staff and went full-time in 1989. She compiled an overall record of 224-168. She played professionally in France in 1985-1987 as a player and a starting member of Rutgers-Atlantic 10 Champions in 1982.

Freshman Receiving Financial Aid/Academic:		**Athletic:** 2
Roster In State: 1	**Out of State:** 8	**Out of Country:** 2
Sophomores on Team: 1	**Seniors on Team:** 4	**Graduation %:** 97
Most Recent Record: 11-16-0	**Fall Games:** 27	**Spring Games:** 4

Camp of Clinic Dates: July 30-August 1; August 9-12th
Positions Needed: Setters, Middle Blocker, Outside Hitter
Schedule: UCLA, Michigan State, Notre Dame, Cincinnati, Georgetown, Connecticut
Style of Play: We play fast paced, quick transitioning and like to dominate the net.

Stevens Institute of Technology
Academic Profile

Castle Point Station
Hoboken, NJ 07030

Phone: (201) 216-5691

Type: Private, 4 Yr., Engineering, Coed
Website: http://www.stevens.tech
SAT/ACT/GPA: Required

Founded: 1870
Religion: Non-affiliated
Housing: Yes

Student/Faculty Ratio: 9:1

Undergraduate Enrollment: 1,533

Scholarships/Academic: Yes   **Athletic:** No

Expenses By: Year   **In State:** $ 29,400

Male/Female: 78:22

Graduate Enrollment: 1,934

Financial Aid: Yes

Out of State: $ 29,400

Specializes In: Engineering, Applied Science, Computer Science, Preprofessional

Degrees Conferred: BA, BE, BS, M Eng, MS, ME, MIM, MTM, Ph D

Programs of Study: B.A. in English, and American Literature, History, Philosophy; B.E. in Chemical, Civil, Computer, Electrical, Environmental Materials and Mechanical Engineering, Engineering Management and Engineering Physics; B.S. in Applied Physics, Chemical Biology, Chemistry, Computer Science and Mathematical Sciences; Pre-Professional Programs in Pre-Dental, Pre-Law and Pre-Med. Accelerated programs, too.

Men's Athletic Profile

Castle Point Station

Hoboken, NJ 07030

Coach: Patrick Dorywalski

Email: pdorywal@stevens.Tech

NCAA III

Ducks/Red, Grey

Phone: (201) 216-5691

Fax: (201) 216-8244

Estimated # of Men's Volleyball Scholarships: 0

Conference: Eastern College Athletic Conference

Program Profile: Our program started in 1989. We play between 25 and 75 matches. We play at 13.5 million dollar complex that is ideal for volleyball.

History: Our best year was 19-8.

Achievements: Coach of the Year 3 times. Numerous All-Conference players every year.

Coaching: Patrick Dorywalski has been Head Coach for 25 years. His overall record for men's is 100-92. P. Nugyen and J. Vilardo are Assistant Coaches.

Freshman Receiving Financial Aid/Academic: 100%   **Athletic:** 0

Roster In State: 22   **Out of State:** 13   **Out of Country:** 1

Seniors on Team: 7   **Graduation %:** 95%

Most Recent Record: 10-5

Positions Needed: Middle Hitter, Blocker

Schedule: D'Youville, Clarke College - Iowa, Mount State Vincent, USMMA-Kings Point, Sacred Heart-D II, Columbia Union - D II

Style of Play: Kinetic, energetic, scrappy and a pleasure to watch.

Women's Athletic Profile

Castle on Hudson

Hoboken, NJ 07030

Coach: Pat Dorywalski

Email:

NCAA I

Lady Ducks, Red, Grey

Phone: (201) 216-5691

Fax: (201) 216-8244

Estimated # of Women's Volleyball Scholarships: N/A

Conference: Eastern College Athletic Conference

Program Profile: We have a women 20-25 match program, which started in 1983. We play at a 13.5 million dollar complex which is ideal for volleyball.

History: The women's volleyball has won 3 conference championships. They have played in San Diego, Hawaii and Germany.

Achievements: Coach of the year 3 times. Numerous all conference players every year.

Coaching: Pat Dorywalski, Head Coach, his 25 year overall record is:

women: 126-136. Men: 100-92. P. Nugyen and J. Vilardo are Assistant Coaches.

Freshman Receiving Financial Aid/Academic: **Athletic:** 0

Roster In State: 22   **Out of State:** 13   **Out of Country:** 1

Sophomores on Team: 0   **Seniors on Team:** 7   **Graduation %:** 95

Most Recent Record: 10-5-0   **Fall Games:** 20   **Spring Games:** 0

Positions Needed: Middle Hitter, Blocker

Schedule: D'Youville, Clarke College - Iowa, Mt. St. Vincent, University of Massachusetts-King's Point, Sacred Heart

Style of Play: Kinetic, energetic, scrappy and a pleasure to watch.

William Paterson University
Academic Profile

300 Pompton Road

Wayne, NJ 07470

Phone: 877-978-3935

Type: Public, 4 Yr., Coed

Website: http://www.wpunj.edu

Founded: 1855

Religion: Non-Affiliated

SAT/ACT/GPA: 1100
Student/Faculty Ratio: 1:28
Undergraduate Enrollment: 9,800
Scholarships/Academic: Yes   **Athletic:** No
Expenses By: Year   **In State:** $ 9,200
Specializes In: Business, Biology, Athletic Training, Education, Music
Degrees Conferred: BA, BS, BFA, MA, MS, MBA, MEd
Programs of Study: Business and Management, Communications, Health Sciences, Psychology, Social Sciences, Teacher Education, Visual and Performing Arts

Housing: Yes
Male/Female: 45:55
Graduate Enrollment: 2,400
Financial Aid: Yes
Out of State: $ 10,800

Women's Athletic Profile

300 Pompton Road
Wayne, NJ 07470
Coach: Sandra Ferrarella
Email: Ferrarellas@wpunj.edu
Estimated # of Women's Volleyball Scholarships: 0
Conference: New Jersey Athletic Conference
Program Profile: Rec center seats 4000 fans, wood floor, 3 court facility. Playing season from Sept- 1st week in November main games on Tue/Thurs/Sat (tournaments) 23-30 game schedule.
History: Volleyball program began in 1969.
Achievements: Coach of Year 1991. NJAC Conference champs 1982, 1983, 1991. 9 times in 2nd place in NJAC. Head coach for past 22 years, 4 years J.V. coach ECAC appearance 1985
Coaching: Head Coach Sandy Ferrarella, Assistant Susan Paskas

NCAA I
Lady Pioneers, Black, Orange
Phone: (973) 720-3012
Fax: (973) 720-3017

NEW MEXICO

☆ Santa Fe

SCHOOL	CITY	AFFILIATION	PAGE
College of the Southwest	Hobbs	NAIA	472
Eastern New Mexico University	Portales	NCAA II	472
New Mexico Higlands University	Las Vegas	NCAA II	473
New Mexico State University	Las Cruces	NCAA I	473
University of New Mexico	Albuquerque	NCAA I	474
Western New Mexico University	Silver City	NCAA II	474

College of the Southwest
Academic Profile

6610 Lovington Highway
Hobbs, NM 88240

Phone: 800-530-4400

Type: Private, 4 Yr., Liberal Arts, Coed
Website: http://www.csw.edu
SAT/ACT/GPA: 910/19/2.5
Student/Faculty Ratio: 13:1
Undergraduate Enrollment: 577
Scholarships/Academic: Yes   **Athletic:** Yes
Expenses By: Year   **In State:** $ 4,338
Specializes In: Teacher Education, Business
Degrees Conferred: BA, BS, BBA, MSE

Founded: 1962
Religion: Non-Denominational
Housing: Yes
Male/Female: 1:2
Graduate Enrollment: 108
Financial Aid: Yes
Out of State: $ 4,338

Programs of Study: Accounting, Athletic Training, Biology, Business, Education, English, Fine Arts, History, Human Relations, Mathematics, Natural Science, Psychology, Social Science, Counseling

Women's Athletic Profile

6610 Lovington Hwy.
Hobbs, NM 88240
Coach: Bert Luallen
Email: cswlibr@wtaccess.com

NCAA I
Mustangs, Red, White, Blue
Phone: (505) 392-6561
Fax: (505) 392-6006

Estimated # of Women's Volleyball Scholarships: 3.5
Conference: Red River Athletic Conference
History: Our program began in 1994. Our all-time record is 91-99. Qualified for post-season tournament play past four consecutive seasons. Finished 2nd in conference in 1998.
Achievements: June Smith Academic All-American in 1996 & 1997.
Coaching: Bert Luallen, Head Coach, started in 1994 to the present with a record of 91-99.
Freshman Receiving Financial Aid/Academic: **Athletic:** 7
Roster In State: 10   **Out of State:** 4   **Out of Country:** 0
Sophomores on Team: 0   **Seniors on Team:** 2   **Graduation %:** 60
Most Recent Record: 16-24-0
Positions Needed: Middle Hitter, Setter
Schedule: Lubbock Christian University, Houston Baptist University, University of Central Oklahoma, Adams State University, University of Colorado-Colorado Springs, Wayland Baptist University
Style of Play: Up-tempo offensively.

Eastern New Mexico University
Academic Profile

Greyhound Arena
Portales, NM 88130

Phone: 800-367-3668

Type: Public, 4 Yr., Liberal Arts, Coed
Website: http://www.enmu.edu
SAT/ACT/GPA: 700/17
Student/Faculty Ratio: 22:1
Undergraduate Enrollment: 4,000
Scholarships/Academic: Yes   **Athletic:** Yes
Expenses By: Year   **In State:** $ 4,840
Degrees Conferred: AA, AS, BS, BFA, BAE, BBA, BM, BSE, MA, MS, MBA

Founded: 1934
Religion: Non-Affiliated
Housing: Yes
Male/Female: 40:60
Graduate Enrollment: 500
Financial Aid: Yes
Out of State: $ 9,106

Programs of Study: Accounting, Agricultural, Business Management, Anthropology, Biological Science, Business Administration, Chemistry, Communications, Computer Science, Economics, Education, French, Geology, History, Information Science, Journalism, Marketing, Mathematics, Personnel Management, Physics, Political Science, Psychology, Social Science, Statistics, Wildlife Management

Women's Athletic Profile

Greyhound Arena
Portales, NM 88130
Coach: Mike Maguire
Email: mike.maguire@enm.edu

NCAA I
Lady Zia, Green, Silver
Phone: (505) 562-2275
Fax: (505) 562-2822

Estimated # of Women's Volleyball Scholarships: N/A
Conference: Lone Star Conference

New Mexico Highlands University
Academic Profile

Athletic Department Fieldhouse
Las Vegas, NM 87701

Phone: 505-454-3233

Type: Public, 4 Yr., Liberal Arts, Coed
Website: Not Available
SAT/ACT/GPA: NCAA Minimum
Student/Faculty Ratio: 17:1
Undergraduate Enrollment: 2,250
Scholarships/Academic: Yes
Expenses By: Year

Founded: 1893
Religion: Non-Affiliated
Housing: No
Male/Female: 42:58
Graduate Enrollment: 821
Athletic: Yes　**Financial Aid:** Yes
In State: $ 4,776　**Out of State:** $ 9,474

Degrees Conferred: BA, BS, MA, MS, MBA, MEd, MSW
Programs of Study: Accounting, Biological Sciences, Business Administration, Computer Technology, Environmental Sciences, History, Journalism, Management Information Systems, Marketing, Mathematics, Physical Fitness & Movements, Political Science, PreProfessional Programs, Psychology, Radio & Television Technology, Recreation & Leisure Service, Social Science, Technical Education, Travel & Tourism

Women's Athletic Profile

Athletic Department Fieldhouse
Las Vegas, NM 87701
Coach: Venese Hiapo
Email: Hiapo@trail.com

NCAA I
Cowgirls, Purple, White
Phone: (505) 454-3206
Fax: (505) 454-3368

Estimated # of Women's Volleyball Scholarships: N/A
Conference: Rocky Mountain Athletic Conference

New Mexico State University
Academic Profile

Box 30001 MSC 3145
Las Cruces, NM 88003

Phone: 800-662-6678

Type: Public, 4 Yr., Engineering, Coed
Website: http://www.nmsu.edu
SAT/ACT/GPA: 1000/20/2.5
Student/Faculty Ratio: 18.2:1
Undergraduate Enrollment: 15,000
Scholarships/Academic: Yes
Expenses By: Year

Founded: 1888
Religion: Non-Affiliated
Housing: Yes
Male/Female: 50:50
Graduate Enrollment: N/A
Athletic: Yes　**Financial Aid:** Yes
In State: $ 7,288　**Out of State:** $ 12,592

Specializes In: Business, Education, Engineering
Degrees Conferred: AA, AS, AAS, BA, BS, BFA, BSA, BSN, BM, BSPE, BSW, MA, MS, MBA, MFA, Ph.D., EdD
Programs of Study: Agricultural Business Management, Agricultural Engineering, Agriculture, Banking/Finance, BioChemistry, City/Community/Regional Planning, Civil Engineering, Communications, Computer Science, Fisheries, Geological Science, Engineering, Geology, Horticulture, Latin American Studies, Mexican-American Studies, MicroBiology, Range Management

Women's Athletic Profile

Box 30001
Las Cruces, NM 88003
Coach: Michael Jordan
Email: micjorda@nmsu.edu

NCAA I
Roadrunners, Crimson, White
Phone: (505) 646-4921
Fax: (505) 646-5221

Estimated # of Women's Volleyball Scholarships: N/A
Conference: Big West Conference

University of New Mexico
Academic Profile

Johnson Center
Albuquerque, NM 87131

Phone: 800-225-5866

Type: Public, 4 Yr., Engineering, Coed
Website: http://www.unm.edu
SAT/ACT/GPA: 850/2.25
Student/Faculty Ratio: 19:1
Undergraduate Enrollment: 23,700
Scholarships/Academic: Yes   **Athletic:** Yes
Expenses By: Year   **In State:** $ 6,945
Degrees Conferred: BS, MS, MS, Ph.D.

Founded: 1887
Religion: Non-Affiliated
Housing: Yes
Male/Female: 45:55
Graduate Enrollment: 3,500
Financial Aid: Yes
Out of State: $ 13,165

Programs of Study: Over 170 accredited disciplines; Accounting, Anthropology, Architecture, Art, Art Education, Art History, BioChemistry, Biology, Business Computer Systems, Business Education, Engineering, Communications, Computer Science, Creative Writing, Criminology, Dance, Earth Science, Elementary Education, Economics, Music, Nursing, Pharmacy, Philosophy, Physical Education, Physical Therapy, Sociology

Women's Athletic Profile

South Campus
Albuquerque, NM 87131
Coach: Laurel Brassey Iversen
Email: iversen@unm.edu

NCAA I
Lady Lobos, Cherry, Silver
Phone: (505) 277-3804
Fax: (505) 925-5509

Estimated # of Women's Volleyball Scholarships: 3
Conference: Mountain West Conference
Program Profile: Facility is called Johnson Center with a seating capacity of 5,000. We have a fall schedule with a post-season conference championships. Facilities include state of the art and weight training.
History: Our program started in 1975 with an overall record of 365-321, celebrating 25th anniversary.
Achievements: Two Conference Titles (HCAC in 1998), WAC in 1991; 4 All-Americans: Karen Saavedra Warmick, Maria Guerreri, Pauline Manser and Sharon Browning.
Coaching: Laurel Brassey Iversen is entering 15 years as a Head Coach with an overall record at University of New Mexico of 244-166. She was a former US National Team Member, Olympic Member (1980 Boycott Team and 1988 Team). Matt McShane is our Assistant Coach.
Freshman Receiving Financial Aid/Academic: **Athletic:** 5
Roster In State: 5   **Out of State:** 8   **Out of Country:** 2
Sophomores on Team: 4   **Seniors on Team:** 3   **Graduation %:**
Most Recent Record: 9-18-0   **Fall Games:** 31   **Spring Games:** 0
Camp of Clinic Dates: Early June
Positions Needed: 1 Middle Blocker
Schedule: BYU, SDSU, CSU

Western New Mexico University
Academic Profile

1000 College Ave.
Silver City, NM 88061

Phone: (505) 538-6163

Type: Public, 4 Yr., Liberal Arts, Coed
Website: http://www.wnmu.edu
SAT/ACT/GPA: 17/2.0
Student/Faculty Ratio: 18:1
Undergraduate Enrollment: 1,500
Scholarships/Academic: Yes   **Athletic:** Yes
Expenses By: Year   **In State:** $ 5,100
Specializes In: Education

Founded: 1893
Religion: Non-Affiliated
Housing: Yes
Male/Female: 46:54
Graduate Enrollment: 3,000
Financial Aid: Yes
Out of State: $ 9,800

Degrees Conferred: AA, AS, AAS, BA, BS, MA, MBA, M.Ed., MD, PharmD, JD
Programs of Study: Art, Biology, Criminal Justice, Botany, Business, Accounting, Marketing, Chemistry, Computer Science, Education, Forestry, Wildlife, Nursing, Early Childhood Care, Law Enforcement

Women's Athletic Profile

1000 College Avenue
Silver City, NM 88061
Coach: James Callender
Email: callenderj@iron.wnmu.edu

NCAA I
Lady Mustangs, Purple, Gold
Phone: (505) 538-6225
Fax: (505) 538-6163

Estimated # of Women's Volleyball Scholarships: 4
Conference: Pacific West Conference
Program Profile: Athletic participation at Western New Mexico is considered part of a students education. Those who compete on the University's athletic teams develop leadership skills, discipline, and the ability to work in harmony with others. We want to help the players consummate their dreams.
History: The 1998 Mustangs season schedule was intense and tough. With wins over conference opponents Western Washington Regionally ranked Seattle Pacific ect. The Mustangs qualified for their first PAC West Conference Championship. Finished with a 15-15 record
Achievements: PAC West Conference Championships Qualifier. ACVA Molton team, Academic award (1999), Prod ivied 10 Academic all-conference, 1 All-American
Coaching: Coach Jim Callender has an overall record of 409-263 including 35-28 in his first two years at WNMU. Callender has been named NAIA coach of the Year in 1995. He has coached at Memphis State, Western Oregon State, Saint Mary's University, University-Minnesota and Brigham Young, as well as USA Olympic volleyball campus clinics. He is presently the AVCA/NCAA II # 24 All-Time winning coach and #16 active winning coach.
Freshman Receiving Financial Aid/Academic: **Athletic:** 5
Roster In State: 4   **Out of State:** 11   **Out of Country:** 1
Seniors on Team: 5   **Graduation %:** 80
Most Recent Record: 15-6   **Fall Games:** 30   **Spring Games:** 4
Camp of Clinic Dates: June 19-23 2000
Positions Needed: Setters, middle, outside
Schedule: Hawaii Pacific University, BYU,Hawaii, CAL State Bakersfield, CAL State LA
Style of Play: Up tempo, swing offense, aggressive serving, a good passing and defensive team. Philosophy is give 110% and have fun all the time, and the rest will take care of it self.

NEW YORK

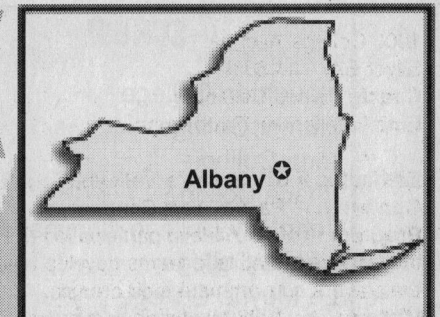

Albany ⭐

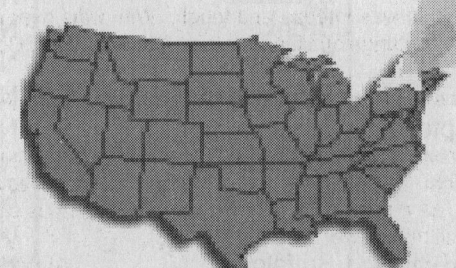

SCHOOL	CITY	AFFILIATION	PAGE
Adelphi University	Garden City	NCAA II	479
Alfred University	Alfred	NCAA III	479
Bard College	Annandale-On-Hudson	NCAA III	480
Baruch College	New York	NCAA III	480
Binghamton University	Binghamton	NCAA I	480
Brooklyn College	Brooklyn	NCAA III	481
Canisius College	Buffalo	NCAA I	482
Cazenovia College	Cazanovia	NCAA III	482
City College of New York	New York	NCAA III	483
Clarkson University	Potsdam	NCAA III	483
Colgate University	Hamilton	NCAA I	486
College of Mount St. Vincent	Riverdale	NCAA III	486
College of New Rochelle	New Rochelle	NCAA III	487
College of Saint Rose	Albany	NCAA II	488
College of Staten Island	Staten Island	NCAA III	489
Columbia Univ-Barnard College	New York	NCAA I	489
Concordia College - New York	Bronxville	NCAA II	489
Cornell University	Ithaca	NCAA I	490
Daemen College	Amherst	NAIA	491
Dominican College	Orangeburg	NCAA II	492
Dowling College	Oakdale	NCAA II	492
D'youville College	Buffalo	NCAA III	493
Elmira College	Elmira	NCAA III	494
Fordham University	Bronx	NCAA I	494
Hamilton College	Clinton	NCAA III	495
Hartwick College	Oneonta	NCAA III	496
Hilbert College	Hamburg	NCAA III	496
Hofstra University	Hempstead	NCAA I	497

SCHOOL	CITY	AFFILIATION	PAGE
Houghton College	Houghton	NAIA	498
Hunter College	New York	NCAA III	498
Iona College	New Rochelle	NCAA I	499
Ithaca College	Ithaca	NCAA III	499
John Jay College-Criminal Justice	New York	NCAA III	484
Keuka College	Keuka Park	NCAA III	500
Le Moyne College	Syracuse	NCAA II	500
Lehman College	Bronx	NCAA III	484
Long Island Univ-Brooklyn	Brooklyn	NCAA I	501
Long Island Univ- CW Post	Brookville	NCAA II	501
Long Island Univ- Southampton	Southampton	NCAA II	502
Manhattan College	Riverdale	NCAA I	502
Manhattanville College	Purchase	NCAA III	503
Marist College	Poughkeepsie	NCAA I	503
Medaille College	Buffalo	NCAA III, NSCAA	504
Medgars Evers College	Brooklyn	NCAA III	505
Mercy College	Dobbs Ferry	NCAA II	505
Molloy College	Rockville Centre	NCAA II	506
Mount St. Mary College	Newgurgh	NCAA III	506
Nassau Community College	Garden City	NJCAA	507
Nazareth College	Rochester	NCAA III	507
New York Institute of Technology	Old Westbury	NCAA II	508
New York University	New York	NCAA III	508
Niagara University	Niagara University	NCAA I	510
Nyack College	Nyack	NCAA II/NAIA	510
Pace University	Pleasantville	NCAA II	510
Polytechnic University	Brooklyn	NCAA III	511
Queens College - New York	Flushing	NCAA II	485
Robert Wesleyan College	Rochester	NAIA	511
Rochester Institute of Technology	Rochester	NCAA III	512
Russell Sage College	Troy	NCAA III	513
Saint Bonaventure University	St. Bonaventure	NCAA I	513
Saint Francis College	Brooklyn Heights	NCAA I	514
Saint John Fisher College	Rochester	NCAA III	514
Saint John's University	Jamaica	NCAA I	515
Saint Joseph's College	Patchogue	NCAA III	516
Saint Lawrence University	Canton	NCAA III	516
Saint Thomas Aquinas College	Sparkill	NCAA II	517
Siena College	Loudonville	NCAA I	517
Skidmore College	Saratoga Springs	NCAA III	518
State Univ College-Fredonia	Fredonia	NCAA III	522
State Univ College-New Paltz	New Paltz	NCAA III	522
State Univ College - Oneonta	Oneonta	NCAA I	524
State Univ of NY-Binghamton	Binghamton	NCAA II	519
State Univ of NY - Brockport	Brockport	NCAA III	519
State Univ of NY - Buffalo	Buffalo	NCAA I	520

SCHOOL	CITY	AFFILIATION	PAGE
State Univ of New York - Cortland	Cortland	NCAA III	521
State Univ of New York - Geneseo	Geneseo	NCAA III	522
State Univ of NY - Old Westbury	Old Westbury	NCAA III	523
State Univ of New York - Oswego	Oswego	NCAA III	524
State Univ of New York - Potsdam	Potsdam	NCAA III	525
State Univ of NY - Stony Brook	Stony Brook	NCAA II	526
State Univ of New York -Cobleskill	Cobleskill	NJCAA	520
SUNY Martime College	Bronx	NCAA I	526
SUNY-Plattsburgh	Plattsburgh	NCAA III	525
Syracuse University	Syracuse	NCAA I	527
Union College	Schenectady	NCAA III	529
University of Albany	Albany	NCAA I	527
University of Rochester	Rochester	NCAA III	528
US Merchant Marine Academy	Kings Point	NCAA III	530
US Military Academy	West Point	NCAA I	530
Utica College	Utica	NCAA III	529
Vassar College	Poughkeepsie	NCAA III	531
Wagner College	Staten Island	NCAA I	532

Adelphi University
Academic Profile

South Avenue
Garden City, NY 11530

Phone: 800-233-5744

Type: Private, 4 Yr., Liberal Arts, Coed
Website: http://www.adelphi.edu
SAT/ACT/GPA: 900
Student/Faculty Ratio: 12:1
Undergraduate Enrollment: 4,100
Scholarships/Academic: Yes   **Athletic:** Yes
Expenses By: Year   **In State:** $ 19,200
Degrees Conferred: Varied

Founded: 1896
Religion: Non-Affiliated
Housing: Yes
Male/Female: 1:1.3
Graduate Enrollment: 2,000
Financial Aid: Yes
Out of State: $ 19,200

Programs of Study: Business and Management, Communications, Education, Health Sciences, Life Sciences, Multi/Interdisciplinary Studies, Nursing, Physical Education, Psychology, Social Sciences

Women's Athletic Profile

Woodruff Hall, 1 South Avenue
Garden City, NY 11530
Coach: Jeffrey Lipton
Email: lipton@adelphi.edu

NCAA I
Lady Panthers, Gold, Brown
Phone: (516) 877-4240
Fax: (516) 877-4237

Estimated # of Women's Volleyball Scholarships: 2
Conference: New York Collegiate Athletic Conference
Program Profile: The Panthers play in Woodruff Hall with a capacity of 600. The playing season is from September to November. The top 8 teams in the NYCAC make the postseason tournament.
History: The program began in 1992 and since been competitive in the conference each year, usually in the upper half.
Roster In State: 10   **Out of State:** 3   **Out of Country:** 1
Seniors on Team: 2   **Graduation %:** 95
Most Recent Record: 5-13
Positions Needed: Setter, MH
Schedule: Dowling, Mercy, New Haven, Pace, Queens, C.W. Post

Alfred University
Academic Profile

Saxon Drive-McLane Center
Alfred, NY 14802

Phone: (607) 871-2115

Type: Public, 4 Yr., Liberal Arts, Engineering, Coed
Website: http://www.alfred.edu
SAT/ACT/GPA: v500-600, m510-620/24-28
Student/Faculty Ratio: 12:1
Undergraduate Enrollment: 2,000
Scholarships/Academic: Yes   **Athletic:** No
Expenses By: Year   **In State:** $ 26,248

Founded: 1836
Religion: Non-Affiliated
Housing: Yes
Male/Female: 49:51
Graduate Enrollment: 500
Financial Aid: Yes
Out of State: $ 26,248

Specializes In: Art, Athletics Training, Business, Education, Engineering, Sciences
Degrees Conferred: BA, BS, BFA, MA, MBA, MPS,MS, MFA, MSE, Ph.D., DPsy
Programs of Study: Engineering & Professionals Studies, Business, Art & Science, Ceramics, Art & Design, Environmental Studies, Performing Arts, Computer Science, Criminal Justice, Sport Medicine, Mechanical Engineering, Chemistry, Accounting

Women's Athletic Profile

McLane Center
Alfred, NY 14802
Coach: Gene Doorley
Email: doorley@big.vax.alfred.edu

NCAA I
Lady Saxons, Purple, Gold
Phone: (607) 871-2901
Fax: (607) 871-2373

Estimated # of Women's Volleyball Scholarships: N/A
Conference: Independent
Program Profile: Our gymnasium has a seating capacity of 1,500. Our playing season runs from September through November.
History: Our program started in 1996 and had 4 appearances. We were NYS Champs Tournament 2 in the past two years (1997 & 1998).

Achievements: Jennifer McLaughlin was named GTE All-American in 1997 & 1998.
Coaching: Gene Doorley, Head Coach, started coaching the program in 1995 to the present with an overall coaching record of 53-49. Best in school record history was 27-12 in 1996.

Roster In State: 2 | **Out of State:** 13 | **Out of Country:** 0
Sophomores on Team: 7 | **Seniors on Team:** 2 | **Graduation %:** 100
Most Recent Record: 17-17-0
Positions Needed: Middle Hitter, Outside Hitter
Schedule: Rochester Institute of Technology, Ithaca, Cortland, St. John Fisher, Elmira, Fredonia
Style of Play: Power volleyball with multi-tempo offense.

Bard College
Academic Profile

Department of Athletics
Annandale-on-Hudson, NY 12504-5000

Phone: (914) 758-7531

Type: Private, 4 Yr., Liberal Arts, Coed
Website: http://www.bard.edu
SAT/ACT/GPA: Not required, but very competitive
Student/Faculty Ratio: 9:1
Undergraduate Enrollment: 1,100
Scholarships/Academic: Yes | **Athletic:** No
Expenses By: Year | **In State:** $ 31,220
Specializes In: Film, Arts, Social Sciences, Prelaw
Degrees Conferred: BA, MA, MFA

Founded: 1860
Religion: Independent, Nonsectarian
Housing: Yes
Male/Female: 48:52
Graduate Enrollment: 200
Financial Aid: Yes
Out of State: $ 31,220

Programs of Study: Anthropology, Economics, History, Philosophy, Political Studies, Psychology, Religion, Sociology, Arts, Photography, Environmental Science, Biochemistry, Biology, Ecology, Mathematics, Chemistry, Natural Science, Studio Art

Women's Athletic Profile

Stevenson Gymnasium
Annandale-On-Hudson, NY 12504
Coach: Kris Hall
Email: hall@bard.edu

NCAA I
Lady Raptors, White, Black
Phone: (914) 758-7531
Fax: (914) 758-7647

Estimated # of Women's Volleyball Scholarships: 0
Conference: Hudson Valley Women's Athletic Conference
Program Profile: We are a small Division III program. We are successful in the Conference. We play a regional schedule at Stevenson Gym which has 700 seats.
Achievements: IAC Champions, HVWAC Champions; Conference Player of the Year; Various All-Conference Selections.
Coaching: Kris Hall, Head Coach, started in 1991. She has been Coach of the Year in Conference four times.
Freshman Receiving Financial Aid/Academic: | | **Athletic:** 0
Roster In State: 3 | **Out of State:** 7 | **Out of Country:** 0
Sophomores on Team: 0 | **Seniors on Team:** 2 | **Graduation %:** 97
Most Recent Record: 16-13-0 | **Fall Games:** 29 | **Spring Games:** 2
Positions Needed: Setter, Outside Hitter
Schedule: Haverford, Vassar
Style of Play: We have an upbeat offensive style and a quick tempo on the court.

Baruch College - CUNY
Academic Profile

17 Lexington Avenue
New York City, NY 10010

Phone: 212-802-2300

Type: Public, 4 Yr., Coed
Website: Not Available
SAT/ACT/GPA: 990+/23+
Student/Faculty Ratio: 30:1
Undergraduate Enrollment: 12,300
Scholarships/Academic: Yes | **Athletic:** No
Expenses By: Year | **In State:** $ 5,152
Degrees Conferred: BA, BS, MBA, BBA

Founded: 1968
Religion: Non-Affiliated
Housing: Yes
Male/Female: 43:57
Graduate Enrollment: 2,450
Financial Aid: Yes
Out of State: $ 7,752

Programs of Study: Accounting, Actuarial Science, Advertising, Communications, Computer Science, Consumer Research, Economics, Education, English, Finance, Hebrew, History, Industrial, Psychology, Journalism, Management, Marketing, Mathematics, Office Administration, Operation Research, Personnel Management

Men's Athletic Profile

17 Lexington Avenue
New York, NY 10010
Coach: Frances Lee
Email:

NCAA III
Statesmen/White, Gold
Phone: (212) 387-1270
Fax: (212) 387-1277

Estimated # of Men's Volleyball Scholarships: N/A
Conference: Eastern College Athletic Conference

Women's Athletic Profile

17Lexington
New York, NY 10010
Coach: Jimmy Lam
Email:

NCAA I
Statesmen, Blue, White, Gold
Phone: (212) 802-3065
Fax: (212) 387-1277

Estimated # of Women's Volleyball Scholarships: N/A
Conference: ECAC

Binghamton University
Academic Profile

Box 6000 East Gym
Binghamton, NY 13902

Phone: (607) 777-4802

Type: Public, 4 Yr., Coed
Website: http://www.binghamton.edu
SAT/ACT/GPA: Open
Student/Faculty Ratio: 13:1
Undergraduate Enrollment: 9,460
Scholarships/Academic: Yes   **Athletic:** Yes
Expenses By: Year   **In State:** $ 10,337
Specializes In: School of Management, Engineering, Nursing

Founded: 1946
Religion: Non-Affiliated
Housing: yes
Male/Female: 48:52
Graduate Enrollment: 2,696
Financial Aid: Yes
Out of State: $ 15,237

Degrees Conferred: BA, BFA, BS, BM, MA, ME, MM, MSED, PhD, MS
Programs of Study: Accounting, African Studies, American Studies, Anthropology, Arabic, Art, Art History, BioChemestry, Chemistry, Cinema, Classical Studies, Comparative Literature, Computer Science, Economics, Electrical Engineering, English, Environmental Studies, French, Geography, Geology, History, Human Development, Linguistics, Management, Math, Mechanical Engineering, Medieval Studies, Music, Nursing, Philosophy, Physics, Political Sciences, Psychology, PsychoBiology

Women's Athletic Profile

P. O. Box 6000 East Gym
Binghamton, NY 13902
Coach: Glenn Kiriyama
Email: kiriyama@binghamton.edu

NCAA I
Bearcats, Dark Green, White
Phone: (607) 772-2842
Fax: (607) 777-4467

Estimated # of Women's Volleyball Scholarships: 3
Conference: Independent
Program Profile: We are moving to Division I in 2001 and will play a full Division I schedule beginning in 2001. We play in the east Gym, which has a wood floor and seats up to 1800.
History: 1971 was the first year of the program and we began at the Division III level. In 1998 we moved to Division II and 2001 will be our first year at Division I.
Achievements: 1995 Conference Champions; NCAA participant in 1995 and 1997; 1999 ECAC Champions; 5 All-Region Selections Since 1986; Region and State Coach of the Year in 1995.
Coaching: Glenn Kiriyama, started as Head Coach in 1999. He has previously been an assistant coach at Division I schools the past 9 years. He played at Brigham Young University. Overall record for 2 years is 49-20.
Freshman Receiving Financial Aid/Academic: **Athletic:** 3

Roster In State: 9
Sophomores on Team:
Most Recent Record: 20-11-0
Positions Needed: Setter, Middle Hitter, Outside Hitter
Out of State: 3
Seniors on Team: 1
Out of Country: 0
Graduation %: 98

Style of Play: We do not have height on the team so we must be fundamentally sound and utilize a quick offense along with scrappy defense. Currently run a 5-1 offense.

Brooklyn College
Academic Profile

602 James Hall
Brooklyn, NY 11210

Phone: (718) 951-50011

Type: 4 Yr., Coed
Website: http://www.brooklyn.cuny.edu
SAT/ACT/GPA: Open
Student/Faculty Ratio: 16:1
Undergraduate Enrollment: 10,504
Degrees Conferred: Masters, Bachelors

Founded: 1930
Religion: Non-Affiliated
Housing: No
Male/Female: Not Available
Graduate Enrollment: 2,763

Programs of Study: Accounting, African Studies, American Studies, Anthropology, Art Education, Broadcasting, Arts, Fine Arts, Computer Science, Creative Writing, Dance, Early Childhood Education, Home Economics Education, Biology, Biological Science, Business Administration, Journalism, Psychology, Music Education, Philosophy, Spanish, Special Education

Women's Athletic Profile

Did Not Return Profile

Canisius College
Academic Profile

2001 Main St.
Buffalo, NY 14208

Phone: 800-843-1517

Type: Private, 4 Yr., Liberal Arts, Coed
Website: http://www.canisius.edu
SAT/ACT/GPA: 950/2.5
Student/Faculty Ratio: 17:1
Undergraduate Enrollment: 3,000
Scholarships/Academic: Yes
Expenses By: Year
Specializes In: Business, Education
Degrees Conferred: BS, BA, MBA, PA, MPA, MS, MSEd

Athletic: Yes
In State: $ 21,000

Founded: 1870
Religion: Jesuit
Housing: Yes
Male/Female: 1:1
Graduate Enrollment: 500
Financial Aid: Yes
Out of State: $ 21,000

Programs of Study: Accounting, Anthropology, Art, Athletic, Banking/Finance, Biology, Business, Chemistry, Economics, International, Languages, Management, Marketing, Medical, Religion, Social Science, Urban, Women's Studies

Women's Athletic Profile

2001 Main Street
Buffalo, NY 14208-1098
Coach: Pam Vogel
Email: pam@wesand.com

NCAA I
Lady Golden Griffins, Blue, Gold
Phone: (716) 888-2970x2940
Fax:

Estimated # of Women's Volleyball Scholarships: N/A
Conference: Metro Atlantic Athletic Conference
Achievements: 1984 Region III Player of the Year
Coaching: Pam Vogel, is entering her fifth season as Head Coach. Her overall record is 11-21. She coached the Buffalo State College team before she came here. She took the Lady Bengals to the State University of New York Athletic Conference Championships all four years and compiled an overall mark of 71-61. Rebecca Orsi is Assistant Coach.
Most Recent Record: 11-21-0
Fall Games: 32
Spring Games: 0
Schedule: St.Francis, Duquesne, Drexel, Lehigh, Navy, Robert Morris, Columbia, Youngstown State, Niagara, Siena, Fairfield, Princeton, Iona, St. Bonaventure, St. Peter's

Cazenovia College
Academic Profile

Lincklaen Street
Cazenovia, NY 13035

Phone: 315-655-8005

Type: Private, 4 Yr., Coed
Website: http://www.cazenova.edu
SAT/ACT/GPA: Open
Student/Faculty Ratio: 14:1
Undergraduate Enrollment: 750
Scholarships/Academic: Yes
Expenses By: Year
Specializes In: Graphic Design, Sports Management, Human Service

Founded: 1824
Religion: Non-Affiliated
Housing: Yes
Male/Female: 60:40
Graduate Enrollment: N/A
Athletic: No
Financial Aid: Yes
In State: $ 12,658
Out of State: $ 12,658

Programs of Study: Bachelors Liberal Arts, Human Services, Management, Accounting, Advertising, Business Management, Criminal Justice, Early Childhood Education, Social Services, Elementary Education

Women's Athletic Profile

Lincklaen Street
Cazanovia, NY 13035
Coach: Heather Burnet
Email:

NCAA I
Lady Wildcats, Blue, Gold
Phone: (315) 655-7142
Fax: (315) 655-1099

Estimated # of Women's Volleyball Scholarships: N/A
Conference: Eastern College Athletic Conference

City College of New York
Academic Profile

138th Street at Convent Avenue
New York, NY 10031

Phone: 212-650-6977

Type: Public, 4 Yr., Engineering, Coed
Website: http://www.cuny.edu
SAT/ACT/GPA: 1020/80
Student/Faculty Ratio: 16:1
Undergraduate Enrollment: 5,000
Scholarships/Academic: No
Expenses By: Year
Specializes In: Engineering, Liberal Arts, Education, Social Sciences
Degrees Conferred: BA, BS

Founded: 1847
Religion: Non-Affiliated
Housing: No
Male/Female: 45:55
Graduate Enrollment: 2,000
Athletic: No
Financial Aid: Yes
In State: $c3,200
Out of State: $ 6,800

Programs of Study: Atmospheric Sciences, Computer Engineering, Electrical Engineering, Humanities, Marine Engineering, Marine Transportation & Business, Mechanical Engineering, Meteorology, Naval Architecture, Oceanography

Men's Athletic Profile

138th & Convent Street
New York, NY 10031
Coach: William Savary
Email:

NCAA III
Beavers/White, Purple
Phone: (212) 650-8228
Fax: (214) 650-8230

Estimated # of Men's Volleyball Scholarships: N/A
Conference: City University of New York Athletic Conference
Program Profile: We play at Holman Gymnasium with a seating capacity of 2,700.
History: The men's volleyball program started approximately 10 years ago.
Achievements: Various Conference Championships.
Coaching: William Savary, is entering his first year as a Head Coach of the men's volleyball program.
Roster In State: 10
Out of State: 0
Out of Country: 0
Sophomores on Team:
Seniors on Team: 3
Graduation %: 80%
Most Recent Record: 5-13-0
Fall Games: 18
Spring Games: 18
Positions Needed: All
Schedule: New Paltz, New Jersey City University, Bloomfield, Mt. St. Vincent, Hunter

Women's Athletic Profile

138 St. & Convent Avenue
New York, NY 10031
Coach: William Savary
Email:

NCAA I
Lady Beavers, White, Purple
Phone: (212) 650-8228
Fax: (212) 650-8230

Estimated # of Women's Volleyball Scholarships: N/A
Conference: City University of New York Athletic Conference
Program Profile: The team plays at Holman Gymnasium with a seating capacity of 2,700.
History: The program is approximately 30 years old.
Achievements: Various Conference Championships.
Coaching: William Savary, Head Coach, is entering his first year with the program.

Roster In State: 10	**Out of State:** 0	**Out of Country:** 0
Sophomores on Team: 0	**Seniors on Team:** 3	**Graduation %:** 80
Most Recent Record: 5-13-0	**Fall Games:** 18	**Spring Games:** 18

Positions Needed: All
Schedule: New Paltz, New Jersey City University, Bloomfield, Mt. St. Vincent, Hunter

CUNY - John Jay College of Criminal Justice
Academic Profile

899 Tenth Avenue
New York, NY 10019
Type: Private, 4 Yr., Liberal Arts, Coed
Website: Not Available
SAT/ACT/GPA: None
Student/Faculty Ratio: 20:1
Undergraduate Enrollment: 10,500
Scholarships/Academic: Yes
Expenses By: Year
Specializes In: Criminal Justice
Degrees Conferred: BA, BS, AA

Phone: 212-237-8865

Founded: 1964
Religion: Non-Affiliated
Housing: No
Male/Female: Even
Graduate Enrollment: 2,000
Financial Aid: Yes
Out of State: $ 5,000

Athletic: No
In State: $ 1,700

Programs of Study: Behavioral Science, Computer Information Systems, Corrections, Criminal Justice, Criminology, Fire Science, Forensic Studies, Law Enforcement, PreLaw, Psychology, Public Administration, Safety and Security Technology, Toxicology

Men's Athletic Profile

899 10th Ave
New York, NY 10019
Coach: Mamdouh Hassan
Email:

NCAA III
Bloodhounds/Royal Blue, Gold
Phone: (212) 237-8431
Fax: (212) 237-8474

Estimated # of Men's Volleyball Scholarships: N/A
Conference: City University of New York Athletic Conference

Women's Athletic Profile

899 10th Avenue
New York, NY 10019
Coach: Sonia Galarza
Email:

NCAA I
Lady Bloodhounds, Blue, Gold
Phone: (212) 237-8322
Fax: (212) 237-8474

Estimated # of Women's Volleyball Scholarships: N/A
Conference: City University of New York Athletic Conference

CUNY - Lehman College
Academic Profile

250 Bedford Park Blvd. W
Bronx, NY 10475

Phone: 718-960-8706

Type: Public, 4 Yr., Coed

Founded: 1968

Website: Not Available
SAT/ACT/GPA: 900+/20+
Student/Faculty Ratio: 18:1
Undergraduate Enrollment: 8,300
Scholarships/Academic: Yes   **Athletic:** No
Expenses By: **In State:** $ 5,200
Degrees Conferred: AA, AS, BA, BS, MBA

Religion: Non-Affiliated
Housing: No
Male/Female: 4:9
Graduate Enrollment: 1,553
Financial Aid: Yes
Out of State: $ 1,553

Programs of Study: Accounting, Afro-American Studies, American Studies, Ancient Civilization, Anthropology, Biology, Business, Chemistry, Communications, Computer Science, Criminal Justice, Dance, Dietetics, Economics, Education, English, Family/Consumer Studies, Fine Arts, French, Geography, Geology, German, Greek, Health Care, Hebrew, History, International Relations, Italian, Languages, Latin American Studies, Management, Mathematics, Music, Nursing, Philosophy, Physics, Political Science, PreDentistry, PreLaw, PreMed, Psychology, Public Health, Russian

Men's Athletic Profile

250 Bedford Park Blvd. W
Bronx, NY 10468
Coach: Junior Garcia
Email:

NCAA III
Lightning/Blue, Green, White
Phone: (718) 960-7176
Fax: (718) 960-1140

Estimated # of Men's Volleyball Scholarships: N/A
Conference: Independent

Women's Athletic Profile

250 Bedford Park Boulevard W
Bronx, NY 10468
Coach: Iris Alonso
Email:

NCAA I
Lightning, Blue, Green, White
Phone: (718) 960-7176
Fax: (718) 960-1140

Estimated # of Women's Volleyball Scholarships: N/A
Conference: City University of New York Athletic Conference

CUNY - Queens College
Academic Profile

65-30 Kissena Blvd.
Flushing, NY 11367

Phone: 718-997-5600

Type: Public, 2 Yr., Liberal Arts, Coed
Website: Not Available
SAT/ACT/GPA: 900 avg.
Student/Faculty Ratio: 18:1
Undergraduate Enrollment: 14,460
Scholarships/Academic: Yes   **Athletic:** Yes
Expenses By: Year   **In State:** $ 3,150
Degrees Conferred: AA, AS, BA, BS, MA, MS, MBA, Ph.D., JD

Founded: 1937
Religion: Non-Affiliated
Housing: No
Male/Female: 40:60
Graduate Enrollment: 3,290
Financial Aid: Yes
Out of State: $ 5, 750

Programs of Study: Business and Management, Communications, Computer Science, Education, Letters/Literature, Psychology, Social Science, Visual & Performing Arts

Women's Athletic Profile

65-30 Kissena Blvd.
Flushing, NY 11367
Coach: Pascale Lubin
Email:

NCAA I
Lady Knights, Silver, Blue
Phone: (718) 997-2761
Fax: (718) 997-2793

Estimated # of Women's Volleyball Scholarships: N/A
Conference: New York Collegiate Athletic Conference

Clarkson University
Academic Profile

Box 5830 Alumni Gym
Potsdam, NY 13699-5830

Phone: 315-268-6622

Type: Private, 4 Yr., Engineering, Coed
Website: http://www.clarkson.edu
SAT/ACT/GPA: Not available
Student/Faculty Ratio: 16/1
Undergraduate Enrollment: 2,581
Scholarships/Academic: Yes   **Athletic:** No
Expenses By: Year   **In State:** $28,781
Specializes In: Engineering and Management
Degrees Conferred: BS, MBA, MA

Founded: 1896
Religion: Non-Affiliated
Housing: Yes
Male/Female: 3/2
Graduate Enrollment: 321
Financial Aid: Yes
Out of State: $28,781

Programs of Study: Biological Science, Business, Communications and the Arts, Computer and Physical Science, Engineering & Environmental Design, Health Professions, Social Sciences, Physical Therapy

Women's Athletic Profile

Box 5830
Potsdam, NY 13699
Coach: Laura Habacker
Email: habacker@clarkson.edu

NCAA I
Lady Knights, Green, Gold
Phone: (315) 268-3757
Fax: (315) 268-7613

Estimated # of Women's Volleyball Scholarships: N/A
Conference: Upstate Collegiate Athletic Association
Program Profile: Clarkson is entering this season with a bright future. The Lady Knights posted the second best record ever in the program's history compiling a 23-16 overall mark.
History: Clarkson has been competing at the varsity level since 1975. Under the direction of long-time coach Marilyn Johnson, the Lady Knights enjoyed tremendous success in the mid-1980's reaching the highly competitive New York State Tournament in 1986 and 1987.
Achievements: UCAA 1998 All-Tournament Team;
Coaching: Laura Habacker, is in her second year as Head Coach. She guided the Lady Knights to their second best record last fall.
Roster In State: 10   **Out of State:** 4   **Out of Country:** 0
Sophomores on Team: 3   **Seniors on Team:** 1   **Graduation %:** Unknown
Schedule: St. Lawrence, Cortland, Nazareth, Plattsburgh, Colby Sawyer, Potsdam, Hartwick, Cazenovia, Oneonta, New Platz

Colgate University
Academic Profile

13 Oak Drive
Hamilton, NY 13346

Phone: (315) 228-7969

Type: Private, 4 Yr., Liberal Arts, Coed
Website: http://www.colgate.edu
SAT/ACT/GPA: 1250/27/3.5
Student/Faculty Ratio: 11:1
Undergraduate Enrollment: 2,750
Scholarships/Academic: Yes   **Athletic:** No
Expenses By: Year   **In State:** $ 31,000
Specializes In: Liberal Arts, Business, English, Political Science, Science
Degrees Conferred: BA, MA

Founded: 1819
Religion: Non-Affiliated
Housing: Yes
Male/Female: 49:51
Graduate Enrollment: N/A
Financial Aid: Yes
Out of State: $ 31,000

Programs of Study: 49 majors and opportunities for individualized majors; 24 faculty led off-campus study groups. Student/faculty collaborative research projects.

Women's Athletic Profile

13 Oak Drive
Hamilton, NY 13346-1304
Coach: TBA
Email: dvontersch@mail.colgate.edu

NCAA I
Raiders, Maroon, White
Phone: (315) 228-7969
Fax: (315) 228-7925

Estimated # of Women's Volleyball Scholarships: N/A
Conference: The Patriot League
Freshman Receiving Financial Aid/Academic:
Roster In State: 3
Sophomores on Team: 7
Most Recent Record: 14-15-0
Positions Needed: All

Athletic: 2
Out of State: 9 | **Out of Country:** 0
Seniors on Team: 1 | **Graduation %:** 100
Fall Games: 29 | **Spring Games:** 0

Schedule: Long Beach State, University of California - Santa Barbara, University of Cincinnati, Steven F. Austin, Villanova, Syracuse

College of Mount Saint Vincent
Academic Profile

6301 Riverdale Avenue
Riverdale, NY 10471

Phone: (718) 405-3200

Type: Private, 4 Yr., Liberal Arts, Coed
Website: http://www.cmsv.edu
SAT/ACT/GPA: 1000/2.75
Student/Faculty Ratio: 12:1
Undergraduate Enrollment: 1,350
Scholarships/Academic: Yes
Expenses By: Year
Degrees Conferred: AA, BA, BS, MS, AAS

Founded: 1847
Religion: Catholic
Housing: No
Male/Female: 1:4
Graduate Enrollment: 150

Athletic: No
In State: $ 17,100

Financial Aid: Yes
Out of State: $ 21,950

Programs of Study: Allied Health Studies, Biology, Business Administration, Chemistry, Computer Science, Economics, Education, English, Exercise and Athletic Training, Fine Arts, French, Health Education, History, International Studies, Liberal Arts, Management, Mathematics, Nursing, Peace Studies, Philosophy, Physics, PreDentistry, PreLaw, PreMed, Psychology, Religious Studies, Social Science, Spanish, Urban Studies

Men's Athletic Profile

6301 Riverdale Ave.
Riverdale, NY 10471
Coach: Karl France
Email: kef702@ad.com

NCAA III
Dolphins/Gold, Navy, White
Phone: (718) 405-3410
Fax: (718) 405-3765

Estimated # of Men's Volleyball Scholarships: N/A
Conference: North Eastern Collegiate Volleyball Association
Program Profile: We are less than 10 years old and have a tradition of being a winning program. We are looking to expand our profile from a local power to a regional power, then nationally to the top 5 schools. Our home court seats 700 above the court very close to the action. We have great acoustics and a great advantage at home.
History: We started as a club in 1990 and ascended to varsity status at the Division III level in 1992. Since 1995, we have not failed to win 19 matches in a season.
Achievements: All-American David Milton 1997; Conference Coach of the Year Jeff Adams 1997; 2 Conference Titles: 1997 (Metro) 1998 (NECVA); 3 Division Titles 1997, 1998 and 1999 Metro East.
Coaching: Karl France became Head Coach in 1999. He has a record of 22-11. He led Marymount H.S. (NY) to the state quarterfinals in 1998. Jeff Adams became Assistant Coach in 1996. He was 1997 Metro Coach of the Year, starting setter and MVP for Yale University. Erik Loefem became Assistant Coach in 1997. He was head coach for SUNY women 's volleyball.
Freshman Receiving Financial Aid/Academic:
Roster In State: 9
Sophomores on Team: 1
Most Recent Record: 22-11
Positions Needed: Setter, Middle Blocker

Athletic: 2
Out of State: 1 | **Out of Country:** 0
Seniors on Team: 1 | **Graduation %:** 100%
Fall Games: 0 | **Spring Games:** 33

Schedule: New York University, SUNY - New Paltz, D'Youville College, Vassar College, Hunter College, Queens College
Style of Play: Fast or quick tempo, swing hitter offense with athletic middle blockers. Also attacking from back row with a 5-1 setting system.

Women's Athletic Profile

Riverdale Avenue & 263rd Street
Riverdale, NY 10471
Coach: Lisa Verrastro
Email:
Estimated # of Women's Volleyball Scholarships: N/A
Conference: New York State Women's Collegiate Athletic Association

NCAA I
Lady Dolphins, Gold, White
Phone: (718) 405-3411
Fax: (718) 405-3765

College of New Rochelle
Academic Profile

Castle Place
New Rochelle, NY 10805

Phone: 914-654-5452

Type: Private, 4 Yr.,
Website: http://www.cnr.edu
SAT/ACT/GPA: 810+
Student/Faculty Ratio: 18:1
Undergraduate Enrollment: 3,248
Scholarships/Academic: Yes
Expenses By: Year
Degrees Conferred: BA, BS, BFA, MA, MS
Programs of Study: Contact school for program of study.

Athletic: No
In State: $ 15,650

Founded: 1904
Religion: Catholic
Housing: No
Male/Female: 10:90 Women Only
Graduate Enrollment: N/A
Financial Aid: Yes
Out of State: $ 15,650

Women's Athletic Profile

Castle Place
New Rochelle, NY 10805
Coach: Susan Kimmel
Email:

NCAA I
Lady Blue Angels, Blue, White
Phone: (914) 654-5315
Fax: (914) 654-5866

Estimated # of Women's Volleyball Scholarships: N/A
Conference: New York State Women's Collegiate Athletic Association

College of Saint Rose
Academic Profile

432 Western Avenue
Albany, NY 12203

Phone: 800-637-8556

Type: Private, 4 Yr., Liberal Arts, Coed
Website: http://www.strose.edu
SAT/ACT/GPA: 920+/3.0
Student/Faculty Ratio: 17:1
Undergraduate Enrollment: 1,950
Scholarships/Academic: Yes
Expenses By: Year

Athletic: Yes
In State: $ 11,968

Founded: 1920
Religion: Independent
Housing: Yes
Male/Female: 27:73
Graduate Enrollment: 1,400
Financial Aid: Yes
Out of State: $ 11,968

Degrees Conferred: Numerous undergraduate and graduate
Programs of Study: Accounting, American Studies, Art Education, BioChemistry, Biology, Business Administration, Chemistry, Communication Disorders, Communications, Computer Information Systems, Elementary Education, English, Graphic Design, History, Political Science, Religious Studies, Mathematics, Medical Technology, Music, Music Education, Psychology, Religious Studies, Secondary Education, Social Work, Sociology, Sociology/Criminal Justice, Spanish, Special Education, Studio Arts, Studio Music

Women's Athletic Profile

432 Western Avenue
Albany, NY 12203
Coach: Jaerk Lasek
Email:

NCAA I
Golden Knights, Gold, Brown
Phone: (518) 454-5158
Fax: (518) 458-5457

Estimated # of Women's Volleyball Scholarships: N/A
Conference: New York Collegiate Athletic Conference
Coaching: Jaerk Lasek - Head Coach.   We have a new coaching staff for the 1999 season.

Roster In State: 14
Sophomores on Team: 0
Most Recent Record: 2-22-0

Out of State: 0
Seniors on Team: 1
Fall Games: 24

Out of Country: 0
Graduation %: 100
Spring Games: 0

Positions Needed: Setter (1), Outside Hitter (2), Middle Hitter (1)
Schedule: Adelphi, Dowling, LeMoyne, Ithaca, Albany State, Mercy
Style of Play: Strong emphasis on defense and playing smart, quick and moderately complex offense.

College of Staten Island
Academic Profile

2800 Victory Rd.
Staten Island, NY 10314

Phone: 718-982-2000

Type: Public, 4 Yr., Coed
Website: http://www.csi.cuny.eud
SAT/ACT/GPA: 1020 up/80 and better
Student/Faculty Ratio: 19:1
Undergraduate Enrollment: 10,674
Scholarships/Academic: Yes   **Athletic:** No
Expenses By: Year   **In State:** $ Varies
Specializes In: All fields

Founded: 1976
Religion: Non-Affiliated
Housing: None
Male/Female: 1:1.5
Graduate Enrollment: 1,522
Financial Aid: Yes
Out of State: $ Varies

Degrees Conferred: Associates, Bachelor's in Arts and Science, Master's
Programs of Study: Accounting, American Studies, Anthropology, BioChemistry, Biology, Business Administration, Chemistry, Communications, Computer Science, Dramatic Arts, Economics, Education, Engineering, English, Film Arts, Fine Arts, History, International Studies, Languages, Political Science, Psychology, Social Science, Spanish

Women's Athletic Profile

Willowbrook
Staten Island, NY 10314
Coach: Gina Battista
Email:

NCAA I
Lady Dolphins, Maroon, Blue
Phone: (718) 982-3163
Fax: (718) 982-3138

Estimated # of Women's Volleyball Scholarships: N/A
Conference: New York State Women's Collegiate Athletic Association

Columbia University
Academic Profile

3030 Broadway, MC 1930
New York, NY 10027

Phone: (212) 854-7772

Type: Private, 4 Yr., Liberal Arts, Engineering, Coed
Website: http://www.columbia.edu
SAT/ACT/GPA: 1100/26/Top 20%
Student/Faculty Ratio: 7:1
Undergraduate Enrollment: 4,500
Scholarships/Academic: No   **Athletic:** No
Expenses By: Year   **In State:** $ 31,000
Degrees Conferred: BA, BS, BE

Founded: 1754
Religion: Non-Affiliated
Housing: Yes
Male/Female: 49:51
Graduate Enrollment: 17,000
Financial Aid: Yes
Out of State: $ 31,000

Programs of Study: Just about everything.

Women's Athletic Profile

Dodge Physical, Fitness Center
New York, NY 10027
Coach: Carolyn Elwood
Email:

NCAA I
Lady Lions, Blue, White
Phone: (212) 854-8864
Fax: (212) 854-8168

Estimated # of Women's Volleyball Scholarships: N/A
Conference: Ivy Group

Concordia College - New York
Academic Profile

171 White Plains Road
Bronxville, NY 10708

Phone: 800-937-2655

Type: Private, 4 Yr., Liberal Arts, Coed
Website: http://www.ccri.cc.ri.us

Founded: 1881
Religion: Lutheran

SAT/ACT/GPA: No minimum
Student/Faculty Ratio: 10:1
Undergraduate Enrollment: 600
Scholarships/Academic: Yes   **Athletic:** Yes
Expenses By: Year   **In State:** $ 18,340
Specializes In: Education, Business, Music, Social Work
Degrees Conferred: BA, BS, B.Mus.

Housing: Yes
Male/Female: 41:58
Graduate Enrollment: N/A
Financial Aid: Yes
Out of State: $ 18,340

Programs of Study: Behavioral Science, Biology, Business Administration, Church Music, Education, English, Environmental Science, History, Interdisciplinary Studies, Mathematics, Music Education, Social Work

Men's Athletic Profile

171 White Plains Rd.
Bronxville, NY 10708
Coach: Ivan Marquez
Email: ISM@concordia-ny.edu

NCAA II
Clippers/Royal Blue, Gold
Phone: (914) 337-9300
Fax: (914) 395-4515

Estimated # of Men's Volleyball Scholarships: 4.5
Conference: Eastern Intercollegiate Volleyball Association
Program Profile: We have a relatively young program that in its third year is competing against top teams in the East, Midwest and West. We take a yearly spring trip to San Juan Puerto Rico.
Freshman Receiving Financial Aid/Academic: 0   **Athletic:** 2
Roster In State: 3   **Out of State:** 0   **Out of Country:** 6
Sophomores on Team: 2   **Seniors on Team:** 0   **Graduation %:** 100%
Most Recent Record: 5-15-0   **Fall Games:** 4   **Spring Games:** 30
Positions Needed: 1 Middle, 2-Outside Hitters
Schedule: UCLA, Brigham Young, Rutgers, Penn State, George Mason, Indiana Univ Purdue-Fort Wayne

Women's Athletic Profile

171 White Plains Road
Bronxville, NY 10708
Coach: Ivan Marquez
Email: ism@concordia-ny.edu

NCAA I
Lady Clippers, Blue, Gold
Phone: (914) 337-9300x2443
Fax: (914) 395-4515

Estimated # of Women's Volleyball Scholarships: 4.5 Full
Conference: Eastern Intercollege Volleyball Association
Program Profile: Concordia competes for the NCAA Division I National Title. We play a challenging schedule against only the top teams in the country. Concordia participates in the EIUA and plays for their conference automatic bid to the NCAA Final Four. Concordia travels yearly to play top teams from MPSF and MIVI.
History: Concordia has participated at the D.I level since 1996. In 1999 were elevated to the top level of the EIVA Conference and have since amassed a record of 40-19.
Achievements: 1999 Oteneal Conference Champions, 2000 EIVA Final Four Finalist, 5 All-EIVA Honorees.
Coaching: Ivan Marquez started in 1995 and a record of 71-109. Asst. Coach Kris Zuiter started in 1999 was a former player.
Freshman Receiving Financial Aid/Academic: **Athletic:** 1
Roster In State: 3   **Out of State:** 1   **Out of Country:** 6
Sophomores on Team: 3   **Seniors on Team:** 5   **Graduation %:** 94
Most Recent Record: 21-9-0   **Fall Games:**   **Spring Games:** 28
Positions Needed: Setter, MB
Schedule: UCLA, IPFW, Penn State, BYU, Ball State, UC-Irvine, Cal State-Northridge, Rutger-Newark
Style of Play: Athletic players, powerful sideout, heavy emphasis on blocking.

Cornell University
Academic Profile

Teagle Hall, Campus Road
Ithaca, NY 14853

Phone: (607) 255-4762

Type: Private, 4 Yr., Liberal Arts, Engineering, Coed
Website: http://www.cornell.edu
SAT/ACT/GPA: Varies around 1300; Top 10%
Student/Faculty Ratio: 12:1

Founded: 1865
Religion: Non-Affiliated
Housing: Yes
Male/Female: 52:48

Undergraduate Enrollment: 13,300

Scholarships/Academic: No   **Athletic:** No

Graduate Enrollment: 5,134

Financial Aid: Yes

Expenses By: Year   **In State:** $ 19,000   **Out of State:** $ 30,000

Specializes In: 7 Specialized diverse colleges on campus

Degrees Conferred: BA, BS, BFA, BA in Architecture, MA, MS, MFA

Programs of Study: Major programs in seven undergraduate colleges: Agriculture & Life Sciences; Art & Architecture Planning ; Arts & Sciences; Engineering; Hotel Administration; Human Ecology; Industrial and Labor Relations

Women's Athletic Profile

Teagle Hall, Campus Rd.
Ithaca, NY 14853
Coach: Christie Jackson
Email: cj32@cornell.edu

NCAA I
Lady Big Red, Red, White
Phone: (607) 255-3813
Fax: (607) 255-2969

Estimated # of Women's Volleyball Scholarships: 0

Conference: Ivy League

Program Profile: We play at Newman Arena which has 4,473 seats. We have our own strength and conditioning center just for varsity athletes. We have new equipment and state-of-the-art nets, poles, balls, clothing and shoes. We have rigorous practice and our game schedule is during the fall season. We also have a brief spring season with practices and 2 tournaments.

History: The program began in 1972 and our overall record is 524-291-7.   We have won the Ivy League Championships in 1990, 1991 & 1993. We won 6 New York State Championships and 2 Eastern Championships.

Coaching: Christie Jackson, Head Coach, is entering her first year with the program. She was the starting setter for University of Idaho. Steve Loeswick is assistant coach. He was a four year starter at USC.

Roster In State: 2	**Out of State:** 14	**Out of Country:** 0
Sophomores on Team: 0	**Seniors on Team:** 3	**Graduation %:** 98
Most Recent Record: 8-18-0	**Fall Games:** 26	**Spring Games:** 2

Camp of Clinic Dates: July 18-29

Positions Needed: Outside Hitters, Middle Blockers, Setter

Schedule: UC-Irvine, UC-Fullerton, UC-Northridge, Villanova, Brown, Harvard

Style of Play: We are hard workers, a very young team right now, but dedicated to improvement. We probably will be at the top of the Ivy League next fall. We play quick, aggressive and smart.

Daemen College
Academic Profile

4380 Main Street
Amherst, NY 14226-3592

Phone: (716) 839-8346

Type: Private, 4 Yr., Coed

Website: http://www.daemen.edu

SAT/ACT/GPA: 900/16/18% admittance

Student/Faculty Ratio: Not Avai

Undergraduate Enrollment: 1,850

Scholarships/Academic: Yes   **Athletic:** Yes

Expenses By: Year   **In State:** $ 19,120

Founded: 1947

Religion: Non-Affiliated

Housing: Yes

Male/Female: 1:3

Graduate Enrollment: 50

Financial Aid: Yes

Out of State: $ 19,120

Specializes In: Physical Therapy, Education, Physician's Assistant, Business

Degrees Conferred: BA, BS, MS

Programs of Study: Contact school for programs of study.

Women's Athletic Profile

4380 Main St.
Amherst, NY 14226-3592
Coach: Sally Kus
Email: skus@shs.k12.ny.us

NCAA I
Lady Warriors, Blue, White
Phone: (716) 839-8346
Fax: (716) 839-8516

Estimated # of Women's Volleyball Scholarships: 8

Conference: ISCAC

Program Profile: Daemen volleyball begins its second year of existence with new coaching leadership.

History: Our volleyball program is only two years old, we started in 1997.

Achievements: Coach Kus was 1993 Coach of the Year for the Women's Sports Foundation; Coach Kus was inducted into the National Volleyball Hall of Fame in 1996; 1997-two All-Conference Players; 1998-Freshaman Player of the Year and 3 All-Conference Players.

Coaching: Sally Kus, Head Coach, is entering her first year here. She was a high school coach for 23 years at Sweet Home High. Her overall record is 790-29. Her team got 6 N.Y.State Titles, 21 Conference and 20 Sectional Titles. She was 1997 National Coach of the Year. She got the National Record for Consecutive Wins at 292 Any Sport Male or Female. Gretchen Gegenfurtner is Assistant Coach.

Freshman Receiving Financial Aid/Academic:

Athletic: 4

Roster In State: 13	**Out of State:** 1	**Out of Country:** 0
Sophomores on Team: 4	**Seniors on Team:** 0	**Graduation %:** Unknown
Most Recent Record: 15-19-0	**Fall Games:** 36	**Spring Games:** 2

Positions Needed: Middle Hitter, Setter, Utility

Schedule: Mercyhurst, Mt.Vernon of Nazarene, Roberts Wesleyan, Houghton College, Le Moyne College

Style of Play: Looking for dedication, aggressiveness and great attitudes in our players. Aggressive and scrappy.

Dominican College
Academic Profile

470 Western Highway
Orangeburg, NY 10962-1299

Phone: (914) 398-3008

Type: Private, 4 Yr., Liberal Arts, Coed
Website: http://www.dc.edu
SAT/ACT/GPA: 1000 Average
Student/Faculty Ratio: 12:1
Undergraduate Enrollment: 1,850
Scholarships/Academic: Yes
Expenses By: Semester

Athletic: Yes
In State: $ 20,000

Founded: 1952
Religion: Catholic
Housing: Yes
Male/Female: 1:3
Graduate Enrollment: 1,000
Financial Aid: Yes
Out of State: $ 20,000

Specializes In: Athletic Training, Business Administration, Computers, Education, Etc.

Degrees Conferred: AA, BA, BS, BSN, BSW

Programs of Study: Athletic Training, Biology, Business Administration, Computers, Elementary Education, English, Financial Management, History, Humanities, Nursing, Occupational Therapy, Physical Therapy, Psychology, Special Education

Women's Athletic Profile

470 Western Hwy.
Orangeburg, NY 10962-1299
Coach: Colleen Killen
Email:

NCAA I
Chargers, Black, White, Red
Phone: (845) 359-7800
Fax: (914) 398-3042

Estimated # of Women's Volleyball Scholarships: N/A
Conference: Independent

Dowling College
Academic Profile

150 Idle Hour Boulevard
Oakdale, NY 11769

Phone: (800) Dowling

Type: Private, 4 Yr., Liberal Arts, Coed
Website: http://www.dowling.edu
SAT/ACT/GPA: NCAA Div II Requirements
Student/Faculty Ratio: 15:1
Undergraduate Enrollment: 4,000
Scholarships/Academic: Yes
Expenses By: Semester

Athletic: Yes
In State: $ 5,000

Founded: 1955
Religion: Non-Affiliated
Housing: Yes
Male/Female: 1:3
Graduate Enrollment: 1,000
Financial Aid: Yes
Out of State: $ 5,000

Specializes In: Aviation, Business, Education

Degrees Conferred: BA, BS, MBA, MS, Ph D in Education

Programs of Study: Accounting, Aero, Airway Science, Arts, Biology, Computer Information Systems, Computer Science, Economics, Education, Elementary Education, English, Finance, History, Humanities, Management, Marketing, Mathematics, Music, Natural Science, Political Science, Psychology, Languages, Social Science, Special Education, Speech, Drama Arts, Travel and Tourism, Visual Arts

Women's Athletic Profile

150 Idle Hour Boulevard
Oakdale, NY 11769
Coach: Bruce Grandin
Email: desantij@dowling.edu

NCAA I
Lady Golden Lions, Blue, Gold
Phone: (516) 244-3019
Fax: (516) 244-3317

Estimated # of Women's Volleyball Scholarships: 8-Partial
Conference: New York Collegiate Athletic Conference
Program Profile: Very successful program in region, going to NCAA tournament 4 straight years. Extensive regional schedule, play reduced spring schedule. We have a new facility planned for Fall of 2000.
History: One of the top programs in history of Dowling athletics. One of original sports sponsored by the college, dates back to 1979.
Achievements: We have seven out of eight NYCAC Titles, 4 consecutive NCAA Appearances.
Coaching: Bruce Grandin, Head Coach, compiled an overall record at Dowling of 271-76 in eight years.
Freshman Receiving Financial Aid/Academic: | | **Athletic:** 3
Roster In State: 6 | **Out of State:** 4 | **Out of Country:** 2
Graduation %: 100
Most Recent Record: 30-12-0 | **Fall Games:** 42 | **Spring Games:** 4
Schedule: Florida Southern, University of New Heaven, Millersville
Style of Play: We play a 5-1 formation offense with multiple attack formations. emphasis on court defense, accurate passing and fun.

D'youville College
Academic Profile

320 Porter Avenue
Buffalo, NY 14201

Phone: 800-777-3921

Type: Private, 4 Yr.
Website: http://www.dyouville.edu
SAT/ACT/GPA: Open
Student/Faculty Ratio:
Undergraduate Enrollment: N/A
Scholarships/Academic: Yes | **Athletic:** No
Expenses By: | **In State:** $ 15,650

Founded: 1908
Religion: Non-Affiliated
Housing: Yes
Male/Female:
Graduate Enrollment: N/A
Financial Aid: Yes
Out of State: $ 15,650

Specializes In: Health Sciences, Education, Business
Programs of Study: Contact school for programs of study.

Men's Athletic Profile

320 Porter Avenue
Buffalo, NY 14201
Coach: John Hutton
Email: tuckert@dyc.edu

NCAA II
Spartans/Red, White, Grey
Phone: (716) 881-7789
Fax: (716) 881-7788

Estimated # of Men's Volleyball Scholarships: N/A
Conference: Northeast Collegiate Volleyball Association
Program Profile: D'Youville College Center features a pool, a weight training facility and a volleyball gym that seats 1000 spectators.
History: D'Youville men's volleyball went from a club to a varsity in 1996. The first varsity season was in 1997. The team played local clubs and Canadian Varsity teams, finishing with a 12-8 record. In the 1998 season, D'Youville competed with NCAA, NAIA, clubs and Canadian Squads. The team finished 35-6. The 1999 campaign will be the team's first season as an NCAA member.
Achievements: 1998 National Small College National Champions; 2 National Small College All-American Selections; 10 National Small college Academic All-Americans.
Freshman Receiving Financial Aid/Academic: 1 | **Athletic:** 0
Roster In State: 7 | **Out of State:** 4 | **Out of Country:** 0
Sophomores on Team: 3 | **Seniors on Team:** 5 | **Graduation %:** 78%
Positions Needed: Middle Blocker, Swing Hitters, Outside Hitter
Schedule: Mercyhurst, Sacred Heart, Mt. St. Vincent, Roger Williams, United States Merchant, Stevens Institute of Technology
Style of Play: Up-tempo, multiple offense featuring middle and right side hitting. All players in the school are interchangeable and are required to learn two or three different positions.

Women's Athletic Profile

College Ctr., Porter Avenue
Buffalo, NY 14201
Coach: John Hutton
Email:

NCAA I
Spartans, Red, White, Black
Phone: (716) 881-7687
Fax: (716) 881-7788

Estimated # of Women's Volleyball Scholarships: N/A
Conference: Independent

Elmira College
Academic Profile

One Park Place
Elmira, NY 14901
Type: Private, 4 Yr., Liberal Arts, Coed
Website: http://www.elmira.edu.com
SAT/ACT/GPA: Open
Student/Faculty Ratio: 12:1
Undergraduate Enrollment: 1,150
Scholarships/Academic: Yes
Expenses By: Year
Specializes In: Liberal Arts Education
Degrees Conferred: AA, AS,BA, BS, MSE

Phone: (607) 735-1800

Founded: 1855
Religion: Non-Affiliated
Housing: Yes
Male/Female: 2:3
Graduate Enrollment: 400
Athletic: No   **Financial Aid:** Yes
In State: $ 26,956   **Out of State:** $ 26,956

Programs of Study: Accounting, American Studies, Anthropology, Art, Art History, Biology, BioChemistry, Business Administration, Chemistry, Classical Studies, Computer Information Systems, Criminal Justice, Economics, Elementary Education, English Literature, Environmental Studies, Foreign Languages, History, Human Services, Liberal Arts, Marketing, Mathematics, Medical Technology, Music, Nursing, Philosophy & Religion, Political Science, PreDentistry, PreLaw, Psychology, Social Science, Sociology

Women's Athletic Profile

One Park Place
Elmira, NY 14901
Coach: Rhonda Faunce
Email: rfaunce@elmira.edu

NCAA I
Soaring Eagles, Purple, Gold
Phone: (607) 735-1800
Fax: (607) 735-1717

Estimated # of Women's Volleyball Scholarships: N/A
Conference: Independent
Program Profile: Our season runs from the end of August to the beginning of November. Our gymnasium seats 500 people. We have newly constructed facilities as of 1994.
History: Our season's first appearance at the NCAA Tournament was in 1998. Our program started in 1973.
Achievements: 1986 GTE All-American Kathie Beebe; 1998 All-Region Leah Mullins
Coaching: Rhonda Faunce, Head Coach, started coaching here in 1989. Her overall record is 243-180. She was All-American in Volleyball in 1983 at Ithaca College

Roster In State: 8   **Out of State:** 3   **Out of Country:** 1
Sophomores on Team: 0   **Seniors on Team:** 0   **Graduation %:** 100
Most Recent Record: 32-8-0 **Fall Games:** 40   **Spring Games:** TBA

Positions Needed: Setter, Outside Hitter, Defensive Specialist
Schedule: Ithaca College, New York University, SUNY Geneseo, SUNY New Paltz, York College, Vassar College
Style of Play: 5-1 offense, quick defense and strong middle attack

Fordham University
Academic Profile

441 E. Fordham Road
Bronx, NY 10458

Type: Private, 4 Yr., Liberal Arts, Coed
Website: http://www.fordham.edu
SAT/ACT/GPA: 1000/3.0
Student/Faculty Ratio: 27:1
Undergraduate Enrollment: 6,275
Scholarships/Academic: Yes

Phone: (718) 817-4412

Founded: 1841
Religion: Jesuit
Housing: Yes
Male/Female: 45:55
Graduate Enrollment: 5,000
Athletic: Yes   **Financial Aid:** Yes

Expenses By: Year   **In State:** $ 28,200   **Out of State:** $ 28,200
Specializes In: PreLaw, PreMed, Business, Theatre, Arts, Sciences
Degrees Conferred: Bachelors, Masters, Doctoral, Professional
Programs of Study: American Studies, Anthropology, Art, Biology, Broadcasting, Business, Chemistry, Economics, Journalism, Medieval, Peace, Public, Theology, Urban, Women's Studies

Women's Athletic Profile

441 East Fordham Road
Bronx, NY 10458-5155
Coach: Megan Gamble
Email: mgamble@Murray.Fordham.edu

NCAA I
Lady Rams, Cardinal, White
Phone: (718) 817-4297
Fax: (718) 817-5588

Estimated # of Women's Volleyball Scholarships: 9
Conference: Atlantic 10 Conference
Program Profile: Fordham is entering its 5th year in the Atlantic 10. Facilities include the historic Rose Hill Gymnasium, the oldest Division I gym in use, and the Walsh Training Facility. We have a weight room that is for Fordham athletes only.
History: Our program began in 1974. The Ram Volleyball program has competed in the MAAC, the Patriot League and the Atlantic 10 Conference. Our overall program record is 298-423-10.
Coaching: Megan Gamble, became Head Coach in April 1999. In the 1998 season, she was assistant coach at Valparaiso. During the 1996 and 1997 seasons, she was assistant coach at Drake University. From 1994 to 1995, she was assistant coach at Creighton. From 1992 to 1993, she was assistant at Andrew College (NAIA). Shen Sheng Jiang had been assistant coach for 4 years.
Freshman Receiving Financial Aid/Academic: **Athletic:** 3
Roster In State: 1   **Out of State:** 10   **Out of Country:** 1
Sophomores on Team: 2   **Seniors on Team:** 3   **Graduation %:** Unknown
Most Recent Record: 10-0-0   **Fall Games:** 32   **Spring Games:** 10
Schedule: Eastern Illinois Univ, University of Dayton, Temple Univ, Xavier University, Virginia Tech, University of New Jersey, Rutgers
Style of Play: We play a very fast transition offense. We are a solid blocking team with good ball control.

Hamilton College
Academic Profile

198 College Hill Road
Clinton, NY 13323

Phone: (315) 859-4421

Type: Private, 4 Yr., Liberal Arts, Coed
Website: http://www.hamilton.edu
SAT/ACT/GPA: 1220/30
Student/Faculty Ratio: 10:1
Undergraduate Enrollment: 1,700
Scholarships/Academic: Yes   **Athletic:** No
Expenses By: Year   **In State:** $ 32,000
Specializes In: Liberal Arts
Degrees Conferred: BA

Founded: 1812
Religion: Non-Affiliated
Housing: Yes
Male/Female: 51:48
Graduate Enrollment: N/A
Financial Aid: Yes
Out of State: $ 32,000

Programs of Study: Anthropology, Arts, Biochemistry, Biology, Chemistry, Classics, Comparative Literature, Computer Science, Creative Writing, Economics, English, French, Geology, German, Greek, History, International Studies, Latin, Linguistic, Literature, Mathematics, Modern Languages, Molecular Biology, Music, Philosophy, Physics, Political Science, Psychology, Public Affairs, Religion, Sociology, Spanish, Theatre

Women's Athletic Profile

198 College Hill Rd
Clinton, NY 13323
Coach: Susan Keller
Email: sekeller@hamilton.edu

NCAA I
Lady Continentals, Buff, Blue
Phone: (315) 859-4806
Fax: (315) 859-4535

Estimated # of Women's Volleyball Scholarships: 0
Conference: NESCAC, ECAC
Program Profile: The Volleyball team participates in the New England Small College Athletic Conference for the first time in 2000-01. The Continentals host a number of tournaments each year at the 2000 seat Margaret Bundy Scott Field House located on Hamilton's campus. Players have access to Hamilton's newly renovated fitness center as well as swimming pool, free weight room.
Achievements: In 1999-00 the Continentals finished the year ranked 10th in NCAA III in hitting percentage. Katelyn Clark, a middle-hitter, finished the year 12th in Division III in hitting percentage. Korey O'Malley and Clark were NESAC All-Academic selections.

Coaching: Susan Keller begins her second year as the Head Coach of Hamilton's volleyball team. She led Hamilton to a second place finish at the NCAA tournament last year and a 17-14 overall record. Julie Dieht is a 1991 graduate of Hamilton College. While at Hamilton she played volleyball and basketball. She is currently Hamilton's head women's basketball coach.

Roster In State: 13   **Out of State:** 4   **Out of Country:** 0
Sophomores on Team: **Seniors on Team:** 2   **Graduation %:** 100
Most Recent Record: 17-14-0
Schedule: Williams, Trinity, Colby, Ithaca, Middlebury, Bowdoin
Style of Play: The Continentals play an attack style with solid play from the middle and outside hitters.

Hartwick College
Academic Profile

Binder P. E. Center
Oneonta, NY 13820

Phone: 888-427-8942

Type: Private, 4 Yr., Liberal Arts, Coed
Website: http://www.hartwick.edu
SAT/ACT/GPA: Open
Student/Faculty Ratio: 13:1
Undergraduate Enrollment: 1,200
Scholarships/Academic: Yes   **Athletic:** Yes
Expenses By: Sem   **In State:** $ 14,000
Specializes In: Business, Liberal Arts
Degrees Conferred: BA, BS

Founded: 1797
Religion: Non-Affiliated
Housing: Yes
Male/Female: 50:50
Graduate Enrollment: N/A
Financial Aid: Yes
Out of State: $ 14,000

Programs of Study: Accounting, Anthropology, Arts, BioChemistry, Biology, Business Administration, Chemistry, Computer Science, Economics, English, French, Geology, German, History, Information Science, Management, Mathematics, Medical Technology, Music, Nursing, Philosophy, Physics, Political Science, PreLaw, PreMed, PreVet, Psychology, Religion, Sociology, Spanish, Theatre

Women's Athletic Profile

Binder PE Center
Oneonta, NY 13820
Coach: Louise Lansing
Email: llansingl@hartwick.edu

NCAA I
Lady Hawks, Royal Blue, White
Phone: (607)431-4722
Fax: (607) 431-4720

Estimated # of Women's Volleyball Scholarships: 0
Conference: Empire Eight
Program Profile: The volleyball program competes in the Binder gym. The playing season begins the 1st week of September and ends the last week of October. State tournament begins in the 1st week & 2nd week in November.
History: The program began in 1991. In 1997 the program qualified for the state tournament with a record of 24-19.
Coaching: Head Coach Louise Lansing, 8th year.
Roster In State: 12   **Out of State:** 1   **Out of Country:** 0
Seniors on Team: 2
Most Recent Record: 10-27
Camp of Clinic Dates: July 22-26, 2001
Schedule: Alfred, St. John Fisher, NIT
Style of Play: 6-2 offense, works hard defensively, using tall blockers to take away the visibility of the court. We rely on our outsider hitters to generate our offense.

Hilbert College
Academic Profile

5200 South Park Avenue
Hamburg, NY 14075

Phone: (716) 649-7900

Type: Private, 4 Yr., Liberal Arts, Coed
Website: http://www.hilbert.edu
SAT/ACT/GPA: Open
Student/Faculty Ratio: 10:1
Undergraduate Enrollment: 950
Scholarships/Academic: Yes   **Athletic:** No
Expenses By: Year   **In State:** $ 10,000
Specializes In: Criminal Justice, Economics, Crime Investigation

Founded: 1957
Religion: Franciscan
Housing: Yes
Male/Female: 306:345
Graduate Enrollment: N/A
Financial Aid: Yes
Out of State: $ 10,000

Degrees Conferred: BA, BS, AAS, AA, AS
Programs of Study: Accounting, Business Administration, Criminal Justice, English, Human Services, Paralegal Studies, Psychology, Banking, Liberal Arts, Management Information Systems, Economics

Women's Athletic Profile

5200 South Park Avenue
Hamburg, NY 14075
Coach: Chad Ahren
Email:

NCAA I
Lady Hawks, Royal Blue, White
Phone: (716) 649-7900x243
Fax: (716) 649-6429

Estimated # of Women's Volleyball Scholarships: N/A
Conference: Eastern College Athletic Conference
Program Profile: We play home games in Brad Hofner Gymnasium
History: Hilbert was a Junior College and became a four-year school in 1994.

Roster In State: 10	**Out of State:** 0	**Out of Country:** 0
Most Recent Record: 0-21-0	**Fall Games:** 18	**Spring Games:** 0

Positions Needed: All
Schedule: Alfred, Buffalo State, Daemen, Keuka, Theil, Medaille
Style of Play: We are scrappy and intense.

Hofstra University
Academic Profile

100 Heampstead Turnpike
Heampstead, NY 11550

Phone: (516) 463-6750

Type: Private, 4 Yr., Coed
Website: http://www.hofstra.edu
SAT/ACT/GPA: 1/3 of class, SAT combined score of 1050
Student/Faculty Ratio: 13:1
Undergraduate Enrollment: 9,346
Scholarships/Academic: Yes   **Athletic:** Yes
Expenses By: Year   **In State:** $ 22,282

Founded: 1935
Religion: Non-Affiliated
Housing: Yes
Male/Female: 1:1
Graduate Enrollment: 2,978
Financial Aid: Yes
Out of State: $ 22,282

Specializes In: Education, Business
Degrees Conferred: AAS, BA, BS, BFA, BBA, BE, BSE, Ph.D., JD, MS, MA, MBA
Programs of Study: American Studies, Anthropology, Art History, Asian Studies, Biology, Chemistry, Communications, Comparative Literature & Languages, Computer Science, Drama & Dance, Economics, Engineering, English, Fine Arts, French, Geology, History, Humanities, International Affairs, Mathematics, Military Science, Music, Philosophy, Physics, Political Science, Psychology, Religious Studies, Sociology

Women's Athletic Profile

230 PFC Volleyball Office
Hempstead, NY 11550
Coach: Fran Kalafer
Email: athmzh@hofstra.edu

NCAA I
Flying Dutchmen, Blue, Gold
Phone: (516) 463-6758
Fax: (516) 463-7514

Estimated # of Women's Volleyball Scholarships: 4
Conference: American East Conference
Program Profile: We have a competitive Division I program. We have locker rooms and a large gym. We play a fall season.
Achievements: American East Champs 1997,1996,1995. North Atlantic champions 1993.
Coaching: Fran Kalafer, Head Coach, started coaching our team in 1981. He has been here 18 years and his overall record is 454-244. Elaine Roque is in her first year as Assistant Coach. She was WPVA and FIVB National Team. Monica Holms has been here 2 years as Assistant Coach.
Freshman Receiving Financial Aid/Academic: **Athletic:** 5

Roster In State: 1	**Out of State:** 10	**Out of Country:** 2
Sophomores on Team: 0	**Seniors on Team:** 3	**Graduation %:** 88
Most Recent Record: 21-13-0	**Fall Games:** 34	**Spring Games:** 10

Camp of Clinic Dates: 6/29 to 7/3/99
Positions Needed: Middle Hitter, Setter, Right Setter, Outside Hitter
Schedule: UC Irvine, Southeast Missouri State University, Kentucky
Style of Play: Swing offense.

Houghton College
Academic Profile

1 Willard Ave.
Houghton, NY 14744-0128

Phone: 800-777-2556

Type: Private, 4 Yr., Liberal Arts, Coed
Website: http://www.houghton.edu
SAT/ACT/GPA: 1170/3.4
Student/Faculty Ratio: 15:1
Undergraduate Enrollment: 1,250
Scholarships/Academic: Yes
Expenses By: Year
Specializes In: Liberal Arts
Degrees Conferred: BA, BS

Athletic: Yes
In State: $19,000

Founded: 1886
Religion: Non-Affiliated
Housing: Yes
Male/Female: 1:1.8
Graduate Enrollment: N/A
Financial Aid: Yes
Out of State: $19,000

Programs of Study: Accounting, Art, Bible, Biology, Business, Chemistry, Christian Ministry, Communications, Computer Science, Elementary Education, English, French, History, International Studies, Mathematics, Music, Philosophy, Physical Education, Physics, Political Science, PreMental, PreMed , PreVet, Psychology, Recreation, Religion, Sociology, Spanish,

Women's Athletic Profile

1 Willard Avenue
Houghton, NY 14744
Coach: Nancy Cole
Email: ncole@houghton.edu

NCAA I
Lady Highlanders, Purple, Gold
Phone: (716) 567-9292
Fax: (716) 567-9365

Estimated # of Women's Volleyball Scholarships: N/A
Conference: North Atlantic Conference
Achievements: 1998 Conference Regional Champions and qualified for the National Tournament.
Coaching: Nancy Cole, has been Head Coach for 3 years. Her record is 65-25. Rigel MeKee is assistant.
Freshman Receiving Financial Aid/Academic:
Roster In State: 7
Sophomores on Team: 0
Most Recent Record: 27-9-0
Camp of Clinic Dates: July 11-16

Out of State: 7
Seniors on Team: 2
Fall Games: 30

Athletic: 3
Out of Country: 2
Graduation %: 12
Spring Games: 1

Schedule: SUNY-Cortland, Malone, Walsh, Gannon, Siena Heights, Ohio Dominican

Hunter College
Academic Profile

695 Park Avenue
New York, NY 10021

Phone: 212-772-4490

Type: Public, 4 Yr., Liberal Arts,Coed
Website: http://www.hunter.cuny.edu
SAT/ACT/GPA: Open
Student/Faculty Ratio: 17:1
Undergraduate Enrollment: 14,100
Scholarships/Academic: Yes
Expenses By: Year
Specializes In: Education, Nursing, Liberal Arts
Degrees Conferred: BA, BS, BFA, MA, MS, MFA, M.Ed.
Programs of Study: Numerous fields of study.

Athletic: No
In State: $ 5,672

Founded: 1870
Religion: Non-Affiliated
Housing: Yes
Male/Female: 3:1
Graduate Enrollment: 4,300
Financial Aid: Yes
Out of State: $ 9,272

Men's Athletic Profile

695 Park Avenue
New York, NY 10021
Coach: Lauren Caiaccia
Email:

NCAA III
Hawks/Purple, White, Gold
Phone: (212) 772-4783
Fax: (212) 772-4739

Estimated # of Men's Volleyball Scholarships: N/A
Conference: City University of New York Athletic Conference
Program Profile: Primary playing season begins in January and continue through April. We have two gyms with one main count and two practice courts.

Roster In State: 3
Fall Games: 0
Positions Needed: Middle Hitter

Out of State: 2   **Out of Country:** 4
Spring Games: 32

Women's Athletic Profile

695 Park Avenue
New York, NY 10021
Coach: Jeffrey Lipton
Email:
Estimated # of Women's Volleyball Scholarships: 0
Conference: Skyline Conference

NCAA I
Hawks, Purple, White, Gold
Phone: (212) 772-4783
Fax: (212) 772-4739

Iona College
Academic Profile

715 North Avenue
New Rochelle, NY 10801

Phone: (914) 633-2315

Type: Private, 4 Yr., Liberal Arts, Coed
Website: http://www.iona.edu
SAT/ACT/GPA: 820
Student/Faculty Ratio: 12:1
Undergraduate Enrollment: 6,000
Scholarships/Academic: Yes   **Athletic:** Yes
Expenses By: Year   **In State:** $ 23,000
Specializes In: Liberal Arts, Business

Founded: 1940
Religion: Catholic
Housing: Yes
Male/Female: 1:1
Graduate Enrollment: 1,000
Financial Aid: Yes
Out of State: $ 23,000

Degrees Conferred: AA, AAS, BA, BS, MA, MS, MBA, M.Ed.
Programs of Study: Accounting, BioChemistry, Biology, Chemistry, Computer and Information Science, Business, Education, PrePhysical Therapy, Communications, Psychology, Teacher Education, Computer Science, Law, Math, Health Science

Women's Athletic Profile

715 North Avenue
New Rochelle, NY 10801
Coach: Bob Weiner
Email: bweiner@iona.edu

NCAA I
Lady Gaels, Maroon, Gold
Phone: (914) 633-2317
Fax: (914) 633-2662

Estimated # of Women's Volleyball Scholarships: N/A
Conference: Metro Atlantic Athletic Conference
Program Profile: home court-Mulcahy Center, fall playing season, spring "unofficial season, wood playing surface
Roster In State: 7   **Out of State:** 5   **Out of Country:** 2
Sophomores on Team: **Seniors on Team:** 5   **Graduation %:** 100
Most Recent Record: 12-18
Positions Needed: S, OH, MB

Ithaca College
Academic Profile

953 Danby Road
Ithaca, NY 14850

Phone: 800-429-4274

Type: Private, 4 Yr., Liberal Arts, Coed
Website: http://www.ithaca.edu
SAT/ACT/GPA: None
Student/Faculty Ratio: 12:1
Undergraduate Enrollment: 5,600
Scholarships/Academic: Yes   **Athletic:** No
Expenses By: Year   **In State:** $ 19,849
Degrees Conferred: BA, BS, BFA, BM, MS, MM

Founded: 1892
Religion: Non-Affiliated
Housing: Yes
Male/Female: 47:53
Graduate Enrollment: 200
Financial Aid: Yes
Out of State: $ 19,849

Programs of Study: Accounting, Finance, Human Resources Management, International Business, Management and Marketing, Corporate Communications, Film, Photography, Arts, Journalism, Media Studies, Telecommunications, Health Services, Athletic Training, Exercise Science, Clinical Science, Physical Therapy, Community Health Education, Health & Physical Education, Health Information Management, Physical Education Teacher, Recreation, Anthropology, Applied Psychology, Musical Theatre, Computer Science, Sociology, Spanish, Music, Religion

Women's Athletic Profile

Hill Athletic Center
Ithaca, NY 14850
Coach: Janet Donovan
Email: jdonovan@ithaca.edu

NCAA I
Lady Bombers, Blue, Gold
Phone: (607) 274-1269
Fax: (607) 274-1671

Estimated # of Women's Volleyball Scholarships: N/A
Conference: Independent

Keuka College
Academic Profile

Weed Physical Arts Center
Keuka Park, NY 14478

Phone: 800-335-3852

Type: Private, 4 Yr., Liberal Arts, Coed
Website: http://www.keuka.edu
SAT/ACT/GPA: 1040
Student/Faculty Ratio: 11:1
Undergraduate Enrollment: 1,000
Scholarships/Academic: Yes　　**Athletic:** No
Expenses By: Year　　**In State:** $ 19,063
Specializes In: Occupational Therapy, Education, Business, Nursing
Degrees Conferred: BA, BS, Pre-Professional

Founded: 1890
Religion: American Baptist
Housing: Yes
Male/Female: 1:5
Graduate Enrollment: N/A
Financial Aid: Yes
Out of State: $ 19,063

Programs of Study: Occupational Therapy, Unified Education, Special Education, Secondary Education, Elementary Education, Business, Marketing, Nursing, Advertising, Hotel Resource Management: We are a liberal arts school.

Women's Athletic Profile

Weed Physical Arts
Keuka Park, NY 14478
Coach: David Sweet
Email: kmcmahon@mail.keuka.edu

NCAA I
Lady Warriors, Green, Gold
Phone: (315) 536-5249
Fax: (315) 536-5380

Estimated # of Women's Volleyball Scholarships: N/A
Conference: Eastern College Athletic Conference

Le Moyne College
Academic Profile

Springfield Road
Syracuse, NY 13214

Phone: 800-333-4733

Type: Private, 4 Yr., Liberal Arts, Coed
Website: http://www.lemoyne.edu
SAT/ACT/GPA: 1000+
Student/Faculty Ratio: 13:1
Undergraduate Enrollment: 1,800
Scholarships/Academic: Yes　　**Athletic:** Yes
Expenses By: Year　　**In State:** $ 11,700
Degrees Conferred: BA, BS, MBA

Founded: 1946
Religion: Jesuit
Housing: Yes
Male/Female: 47:53
Graduate Enrollment: N/A
Financial Aid: Yes
Out of State: $ 11,700

Programs of Study: Business and Management, Education, Letters/Literature, Life Science, Psychology, Social Science, Accounting, Biology, Chemistry, Computer Science, Economics, History, Industrial Relations, Mathematics, Physics, Philosophy, Political Science, Psychology

Women's Athletic Profile

1419 Split Springs Rd.
Syracuse, NY 13214
Coach: Ken King
Email: kingk@mail.lemoyne.edu

NCAA I
Lady Dolphins, Green, Gold
Phone: (315) 445-4420
Fax: (315) 445-4678

Estimated # of Women's Volleyball Scholarships: Varies
Conference: Northeast-10 Conference
Program Profile: Pre-season from mid-August to Sept-Nov. Matches are played at Hennings Athletic Center on wooden surface and with a seating capacity of 2500.
History: Program began in the 1980's. Record over the last 10 years is 186-140. Finished 4th in NE-10 in 2000 and advanced to conference semi-finals.

Freshman Receiving Financial Aid/Academic: N/A		**Athletic:** 2
Roster In State: 8	**Out of State:** 4	**Out of Country:** 0
Sophomores on Team:	**Seniors on Team:** 2	**Graduation %:** 100

Most Recent Record: 20-11
Camp of Clinic Dates: Day Camp
Positions Needed: Middle, Setter, OH
Schedule: Bryant College, Poce University, U. Mass Lowell, American International, Wheeling Jesuit Tournament Opponents, Bentley College, Roberts Wesleyan
Style of Play: Up tempo offense, use of the whole team as 2000 stats indicate.

Long Island University - Brooklyn Campus
Academic Profile

1 University Plaza
Brooklyn, NY 11201

Phone: 718-488-1011

Type: Private, 4 Yr., Liberal Arts, Coed
Website: http://www.liu.edu
SAT/ACT/GPA: 820/17
Student/Faculty Ratio: 14:1
Undergraduate Enrollment: 6,300
Scholarships/Academic: Yes   **Athletic:** Yes
Expenses By: Year   **In State:** $ 23,100

Founded: 1926
Religion: Non-Sectarian
Housing: No
Male/Female: 45:55
Graduate Enrollment: 2,800
Financial Aid: Yes
Out of State: $ 23,100

Specializes In: Health Professions, Media Arts, Education
Degrees Conferred: BA, BS, AA, MBA, Ph.D.
Programs of Study: Biology, Communications, Journalism, Art, Jazz Studies, Dance, Nursing, Physical Therapy, Respiratory Therapy, Occupational Therapy, Athletic Training, Physician's Assistant, Pharmacy, Elementary Education, Secondary Education, Physical Education, Modern Languages, English, Speech, Social Work, Anthropology, Accounting, Business Management, Computer Science, United Nations, PreLaw, Political Science

Women's Athletic Profile

University Plaza
Brooklyn, NY 11201
Coach: Mike Massone
Email:

NCAA I
Lady Blackbirds, Blue, White
Phone: (718) 488-1532
Fax: (718) 488-3302

Estimated # of Women's Volleyball Scholarships: N/A
Conference: Northeast Conference

Long Island University - CW Post Campus
Academic Profile

Northern Boulevard
Brookville, NY 11548

Phone: (516)299-3856

Type: Private, 4 Yr., Liberal Arts, Coed
Website: http://www.cwpost.liunet.edu
SAT/ACT/GPA: 840/2.0
Student/Faculty Ratio: 16:1
Undergraduate Enrollment: 4,500
Scholarships/Academic: Yes   **Athletic:** Yes
Expenses By: Year   **In State:** $ 21,000

Founded: 1954
Religion: Non-Affiliated
Housing: Yes
Male/Female: 38:62
Graduate Enrollment: 3,600
Financial Aid: Yes
Out of State: $ 21,000

Specializes In: Business, Criminal Justice, Education
Degrees Conferred: AA, BA, Bs, BFA, Ma, MS, MBA, MFA, D
Programs of Study: Acting, Art, Biology, Broadcasting, Business, Chemistry, English, Environmental, Interdisciplinary, International, Mathematics, Molecular Bio, PreProfessional Programs, Radiological, Teachers of Special Ed/Speech/Hearing Handicapped

Women's Athletic Profile

Northern Boulevard
Brookville, NY 11548
Coach: Susan Cassidy
Email: athletic@titan.liu.edu

NCAA I
Lady Pioneers, Green, White
Phone: (516) 299-3854
Fax: (516) 299-3155

Estimated # of Women's Volleyball Scholarships: N/A
Conference: New York Collegiate Athletic Conference

Long Island University - Southampton College
Academic Profile

239 Montauk Hwy.
Southampton, NY 11968

Phone: 800-548-7562

Type: Private, 4 Yr., Coed
Website: http://www.southampton.liunet.edu
SAT/ACT/GPA: 900+/80+
Student/Faculty Ratio: 20:1
Undergraduate Enrollment: 1,350
Scholarships/Academic: Yes
Expenses By: Year
Specializes In: Marine Science
Degrees Conferred: BA, BS, MS
Programs of Study: Marine Biology, Education, Business, Communications, Arts

Athletic: Yes
In State: $ 23,000

Founded: 1962
Religion: Non-Affiliated
Housing: Yes
Male/Female: 4:6
Graduate Enrollment: 300
Financial Aid: Yes
Out of State: $ 23,000

Men's Athletic Profile

239 Montauk Hwy.
Southampton, NY 11968
Coach: Scott Gleason
Email: mtopping@southampton.liunet.edu

NCAA II
Colonials/Blue, Gold
Phone: (516) 287-8386
Fax: (516) 287-8188

Estimated # of Men's Volleyball Scholarships: N/A
Conference: New York Collegiate Athletic Conference

Women's Athletic Profile

Montauk Hwy
Southampton, NY 11968
Coach: Ray MacLean
Email:

NCAA I
Lady Colonials, Blue, Gold
Phone: (516) 287-8386
Fax: (516) 287-8188

Estimated # of Women's Volleyball Scholarships: N/A
Conference: New York Collegiate Athletic Conference

Manhattan College
Academic Profile

1513 Manhattan College Parkway
Riverdale, NY 10471

Phone: (718) 862-7227

Type: Private, 4 Yr., Liberal Arts, Engineering, Coed
Website: http://www.mancol.edu
SAT/ACT/GPA: 1000/23
Student/Faculty Ratio: 13:1
Undergraduate Enrollment: 3,200
Scholarships/Academic: Yes
Expenses By: Year
Specializes In: Business, Education, Science
Degrees Conferred: BA, BS, MA, MBA, Ph.D.
Programs of Study: Liberal Arts with freshman Perceptional and portfolio systems.

Athletic: No
In State: $ 23,450

Founded: 1853
Religion: Roman Catholic
Housing: Yes
Male/Female: 55:45
Graduate Enrollment: 1,000
Financial Aid: Yes
Out of State: $ 23,450

Women's Athletic Profile

Manhattan College Parkway
Riverdale, NY 10471
Coach: Pete Volkert
Email: jbernste@manhattan.edu

NCAA I
Lady Jaspers, Green, White
Phone: (718) 862-7839
Fax: (718) 543-8020

Estimated # of Women's Volleyball Scholarships: N/A
Conference: Metro Atlantic Athletic Conference

Manhattanville College
Academic Profile

2900 Purchase Street
Purchase, NY 10577

Phone: 914-323-5464

Type: Private, 4 Yr., Liberal Arts, Coed
Website: http://www.mville.edu
SAT/ACT/GPA: 1000
Student/Faculty Ratio: 10:1
Undergraduate Enrollment: 1,100
Scholarships/Academic: Yes   **Athletic:** No
Expenses By: Year   **In State:** $ 25,000
Specializes In: Business
Degrees Conferred: BA, BS, MA, MAT, MFA

Founded: 1841
Religion: Sacred Heart
Housing: Yes
Male/Female: 1:2
Graduate Enrollment: 800
Financial Aid: Yes
Out of State: $ 25,000

Programs of Study: Business Management, Chemistry, Computer Science, Design, Dramatic Arts, Economics, Education, English, Environmental Science, Finance, Philosophy, Photography, Physics, Political Science, PreDentistry, PreLaw, PreMed, Psychology, Sociology

Women's Athletic Profile

2900 Purchase Street
Purchase, NY 10577
Coach: Ann Bonner
Email: athletics@mville.edu

NCAA I
Lady Valiants, Red, White
Phone: (914) 323-5280
Fax: (914) 323-5130

Estimated # of Women's Volleyball Scholarships: N/A
Conference: Hudson Valley Women's Athletic Conference
Program Profile: We play in Kennedy Gym which is on campus and has 400 seats. We play a fall season. "Hoosiers" feel to it.
History: Began in 1978. After nine straight losing seasons, the team rebounded back with 7 consecutive 19 win years in 98 and 99.
Achievements: Won HVWAC Conference Playoffs last Fall season; had 2 All-Conference players in 1998.
Coaching: Ann Bonner, Head Coach, has compiled a record of 19-7 in her first year here. She played four years Division I at Iona.
Roster In State: 9   **Out of State:** 2   **Out of Country:** 2
Sophomores on Team: 0   **Seniors on Team:** 1   **Graduation %:** 100
Most Recent Record: 10-7-0
Schedule: USMMA, Mt. St.Mary, Connecticut College, Cazenovia

Marist College
Academic Profile

290 North Road
Poughkeepsie, NY 12601

Phone: 800-436-5483

Type: Private, 4 Yr., Liberal Arts, Coed
Website: http://www.marist.edu
SAT/ACT/GPA: 1000+/23/85%
Student/Faculty Ratio: 15:1
Undergraduate Enrollment: 3,200
Scholarships/Academic: Yes   **Athletic:** Yes
Expenses By: Year   **In State:** $ 19,000
Specializes In: Education, Communications, Business, Fashion
Degrees Conferred: BA, BS, MA, MS, MFA, MBA

Founded: 1946
Religion: Catholic
Housing: Yes
Male/Female: 55:45
Graduate Enrollment: 500
Financial Aid: Yes
Out of State: $ 19,000

Programs of Study: Accounting, American Studies, BioChemistry, Biology, Business Administration, Chemistry, Communications, Computer Science, Criminal Justice, Economics, Education, Fashion Design, Film Arts, History, Journalism, Management, Mathematics, Medical Laboratory Technology, Political Science, Psychology, Social Science

Women's Athletic Profile

290 North Rd
Poughkeepsie, NY 12601-1387
Coach: Elizabeth Herzner
Email: liz.herzner@marist.edu

NCAA I
Lady Red Foxes, Red, White
Phone: (914) 575-3000
Fax: (914) 575-3322

Estimated # of Women's Volleyball Scholarships: N/A
Conference: Metro Atlantic Athletic Conference
Program Profile: McCann Center (3,944), 20,000 sq foot fitness center. Traditional fall season, spring post season includes 2-3 tournaments, weight-lifting and conditioning programs with a strength coach.
History: 1997-98 1 st year in MAAC. NEC Member 1987-1997
Achievements: Athletic department honored with MAAC Commissioner's cup in 1998-99 and 1999-2000, 4 All-MAAC Academic team winners in 3 years.
Coaching: 6-46 overall record , 2 yrs (school record same), Quinnipiac asst 2 yrs. 4 year letter winner at Marist College.
Freshman Receiving Financial Aid/Academic: | | **Athletic:** 2
Roster In State: 6 | **Out of State:** 7 | **Out of Country:** 1
Sophomores on Team: 5 | **Seniors on Team:** 4 | **Graduation %:** 100
Most Recent Record: 1-24-0 | **Fall Games:** 25 | **Spring Games:** TBA
Positions Needed: Middle, Setter, RS, OH
Schedule: Fairfield, Dartmouth, Harvard, Bucknell, Yale, Seton Hall
Style of Play: 5-1

Medaille College
Academic Profile

18 Agassiz Circle
Buffalo, NY 14214

Phone: 716-884-3281

Type: Private, 4 Yr., Coed
Website: http://www.medaille.edu
SAT/ACT/GPA: Open
Student/Faculty Ratio: 14:1
Undergraduate Enrollment: 1,000
Scholarships/Academic: Yes **Athletic:** No
Specializes In: Elementary Education, Sports Management
Degrees Conferred: BA, BS
Programs of Study: Art, Accounting, Biology, Chemistry, Computer Science, Education, English, Foreign Languages, Marketing, Philosophy, Physics, Speech, Sports Management, Theatre

Founded: 1875
Religion: Non-Affiliated
Housing: Yes
Male/Female: 7:1
Graduate Enrollment: N/A
Financial Aid: Yes

Women's Athletic Profile

18 Agassiz Circle
Buffalo, NY 14214
Coach: Laura Edholm
Email: ledholm@medaille.edu

NCAA I
Mavericks, Navy, White, Scarlet
Phone: (716) 884-3281
Fax: (716) 884-0291

Estimated # of Women's Volleyball Scholarships: N/A
Conference: TBA
Coaching: Laura Edholm, became Head Coach in 1999. Traci Illig is Assistant Coach and she has been here 2 previous seasons. She played NCAA Division I Volleyball at Coastal Carolina College.
Roster In State: 10 | **Out of State:** 0 | **Out of Country:** 0
Most Recent Record: 9-13-0 | **Fall Games:** 18 | **Spring Games:** 0
Positions Needed: Setter, Middle Hitter

Medgar Evers College
Academic Profile

1150 Carolyn Street
Brooklyn, NY 11225-2201

Phone: 718-270-6449

Type: Public, 4 Yr., Coed
Website: Not Available
SAT/ACT/GPA: Not Required
Student/Faculty Ratio: 21:1
Undergraduate Enrollment: 5,200
Scholarships/Academic: No   **Athletic:** No
Expenses By: Year   **In State:** $ 2,200
Programs of Study: Contact school for program of study.

Founded: 1969
Religion: Non-Affiliated
Housing: No
Male/Female: 25:75
Graduate Enrollment: N/A
Financial Aid: Yes
Out of State: $ 2,800

Men's Athletic Profile

1150 Carroll Street
Brooklyn, NY 11225
Coach: Avril O'Neal
Email: roy@mec.cuny.edu

NCAA III
Cougars/Black, Gold
Phone: 718-270-6071
Fax: 718-270-6198

Estimated # of Men's Volleyball Scholarships: N/A
Conference: City University of New York
History: First Year of Varsity Men's Volleyball

Women's Athletic Profile

1150 Carroll Street
Brooklyn, NY 11225
Coach: Tina Salak
Email:

NCAA I
Lady Cougars, Gold, Black
Phone: (718) 270-6071
Fax: (718) 270-6496

Estimated # of Women's Volleyball Scholarships: N/A
Conference: New York State Women's Collegiate Athletic Association

Mercy College
Academic Profile

555 Broadway
Dobbs Ferry, NY 10522

Phone: 914-693-7324

Type: Private, 4 Yr., Liberal Arts, Coed
Website: http://www.mercynet.edu
SAT/ACT/GPA: 700+
Student/Faculty Ratio: 15:1
Undergraduate Enrollment: 6,500
Scholarships/Academic: Yes   **Athletic:** Yes
Expenses By: Year   **In State:** $ 10,000
Degrees Conferred: BA, BS, MS

Founded: 1950
Religion: Non-Affiliated
Housing: No
Male/Female: 3:1
Graduate Enrollment: 1,000
Financial Aid: Yes
Out of State: $ 10,000

Programs of Study: Accounting, Actuarial Sciences, Animal Science, Banking & Finance, Behavioral Science, Biology, Broadcasting, Business Administration, Chiropractic, Communications, Computer Science, Criminal Justice, Education, English, French, Graphic Design, History, Italian, Journalism, Management, Marketing, Mathematics, Medical Laboratory Technology, Music, Nursing, Political Science, PreDentistry, PreLaw, PreMed, PrePharmacy, Psychology, Social Science, Spanish, Speech, Speech Pathology

Women's Athletic Profile

555 Broadway
Dobbs Ferry, NY 10522
Coach: Garvey Pierre
Email:

NCAA I
Lady Flyers, Blue, White
Phone: (914) 674-7220
Fax: (914) 674-7281

Estimated # of Women's Volleyball Scholarships: N/A
Conference: New York Collegiate Athletic Conference

Molloy College
Academic Profile

1000 Hempstead Avenue
Rockville center, NY 11570

Phone: 888-466-5569

Type: Private, 4 Yr., Liberal Arts, Coed
Website: http://www.molloy.edu
SAT/ACT/GPA: 900
Student/Faculty Ratio: 11:1
Undergraduate Enrollment: 2,000
Scholarships/Academic: Yes   **Athletic:** Yes
Expenses By: Year   **In State:** $ 10,600

Founded: 1955
Religion: Catholic
Housing: Yes
Male/Female: 23:77
Graduate Enrollment: 300
Financial Aid: Yes
Out of State: $ 10,600

Specializes In: Medical, Education
Degrees Conferred: AA, BA, MS, MA, AS, BS
Programs of Study: Accounting, Art, Biology, Business Management, Cardio-Respiratory Sciences, Communications, Computer Science, English, French, Gerontology, History, Interdisciplinary Studies, International Peace & Justice, Mathematics, Music, Nursing, Philosophy, Political Science, Psychology, Social Work, Sociology, Theology, Preparation for Teaching Certification in Secondary, Elementary and Special Education

Women's Athletic Profile

1000 Hempstead
Rockville Centre, NY 11570
Coach: Kara Buffolino
Email: athletics@molloy.edu

NCAA I
Lady Lions, Maroon, White
Phone: (516) 256-2207
Fax: (516) 256-2210

Estimated # of Women's Volleyball Scholarships: 2
Conference: New York Collegiate Athletic Conference
Program Profile: Our volleyball court is located at Quely Hall (gymnasium). Our games and practices are in the fall.
History: The program is 25 years old.
Achievements: Numerous All-Conference; 2 Academic All-Americans.
Coaching: Kara Buffolino, Head Coach, started two years ago with a record of 38-30.
Freshman Receiving Financial Aid/Academic: **Athletic:** 3
Roster In State: 12   **Out of State:** 0   **Out of Country:** 0
Sophomores on Team: 4   **Seniors on Team:** 3   **Graduation %:** 100
Most Recent Record: 19-15-0   **Fall Games:** 40   **Spring Games:** 0
Positions Needed: Setter, Outside Hitter, Catcher
Schedule: Dowling, Stony Brook, New Haven
Style of Play: A great defense.

Mount Saint Mary College - New York
Academic Profile

330 Powell Avenue
Newburgh, NY 12550

Phone: 888-937-6762

Type: Private, 4 Yr., Liberal Arts, Coed
Website: http://www.msmc.edu
SAT/ACT/GPA: 950/18
Student/Faculty Ratio: 16:1
Undergraduate Enrollment: 1,900
Scholarships/Academic: Yes   **Athletic:** No
Expenses By: Year   **In State:** $ 14,730

Founded: 1960
Religion: Catholic
Housing: Yes
Male/Female: 1:2.5
Graduate Enrollment: 400
Financial Aid: Yes
Out of State: $ 14,730

Degrees Conferred: BA, BS, BSN, MBA, MSEd, MSM
Programs of Study: Accounting, Biology, Business Management/Administration, Chemistry, Communications, Computer Science, Elementary Education, English, Political Science, International Studies, Mathematics, Medical Technology, Nursing, PreDentistry, Social Science, Sociology, Theatre

Women's Athletic Profile

330 Powell Avenue
Newgurgh, NY 12550
Coach: Gary Bice
Email: bice@msmc.edu

NCAA I
Lady Knights, Royal, Gold
Phone: (914) 569-3111
Fax: (914) 569-3584

Estimated # of Women's Volleyball Scholarships: N/A
Conference: Skyline Conference (NYSWCAA)
Program Profile: An established program that has been improving its competitive level due to being in an automatic bid conference for the NCAA tournament. Committed players who have a positive attitude and the will to improve. They push each other to stay focused and play as a unified team.
History: Started in the Mid-1980's not a huge commitment to volleyball until the mid-1990's. The continuity of having the same coach for the past 6 seasons has allowed the program to grow and become as competitive as any point in its history. The team is now made up of players with high school and club experience which allows for the creativity within the offense to happen. Within the next two season this team will be in the NCAA tournament.
Achievements: WIAC Champions 1995, HVWAC Champions 1998, 1999. HVWAC Coach of the Year in 1998.
Coaching: Gary Bice, Head Coach since 1995, overall record 83-56, three conference championships, One Coach of the Year.

Roster In State: 11	**Out of State:** 2	**Out of Country:** 0
Sophomores on Team:	**Seniors on Team:** 1	**Graduation %:** 98
Most Recent Record: 12-9-0	**Fall Games:** 21	**Spring Games:** 0

Positions Needed: OH, MH, S
Schedule: King's Point, Alfred College, Hunter College, Manhattanville College, JUNY-Oreonta
Style of Play: 6-2, good defense and serving, strong OH. Young team who gained a lot of confidence this year. Close group who really care about each other and have the shared goal of reaching the NCAA Finals.

Nassau Community College
Academic Profile

1 Education Drive
Garden City, NY 11530-6793

Phone: (516) 572-7522

Type: Public, 2 Yr., Jr. College,Coed
Website: http://www.sunynassau.edu
SAT/ACT/GPA: Open
Student/Faculty Ratio: 13:1
Undergraduate Enrollment: 20,620
Degrees Conferred: Associates

Founded: 1959
Religion: Non-Affiliated
Housing: No
Male/Female: Not Available
Graduate Enrollment: N/A

Programs of Study: Accounting, Applied Arts, Banking/Finance, Business, Civil Engineering Technology, Engineering Science, Humanities, Law Enforcement, Liberal Arts, Marketing, Mathematics, Operating Room Technology, Paralegal Studies, Contact school admission office for more information on academic and admission.

Women's Athletic Profile

One Education Drive
Garden City, NY 11530-6793
Coach: Chuck Schilling
Email: coachlibanccvb@aol.com

NCAA I
Lady Lions, Blue, Orange
Phone: (516) 572-7522
Fax: (516) 228-3531

Estimated # of Women's Volleyball Scholarships: 0
Conference: Region XV
Program Profile: We have a 192,000 square foot Physical Education Complex that includes a swimming/diving pool, a gymnasium, a fieldhouse, a dance room and a weight room.
History: Our program started in 1978. We had National Tournament Appearances in 1978, 1981, 1982, 1983, 1992, 1993 and 1998. We were Region XV Champions in 1978, 1981, 1982, 1983, 1991, 1992, 1993, 1995 and 1998.
Achievements: Region XV Coach of the Year 1992, 1993, 1995, 1998; District II Coach of the Year 1992, 1993, 1998; 5 Honorable Mention All-Americans; 1 Academic All-American; 4 Region MVP, currently 10th in all-time coaching winning % (.754) 169-55. 19 All-Region Players.
Coaching: Chuck Schilling, became Head Coach in 1991. His overall record is 169-55. Debbie Drew is in her first year as Assistant Coach.

Roster In State: 9	**Out of State:** 0	**Out of Country:** 0
Sophomores on Team: 0	**Seniors on Team:** 4	**Graduation %:** 95
Most Recent Record: 24-7-0	**Fall Games:** 30	**Spring Games:** 0

Schedule: Suffolk CC, Hagerstown J C, Bronx CC, Sullivan CC, Westchester CC, Lehigh Corbon CC

Nazareth College - Rochester
Academic Profile

4245 East Avenue
Rochester, NY 14618-3790

Phone: 800-462-3944

Type: Private, 4 Yr., Liberal Arts, Coed
Website: http://www.nax.edu

Founded: 1924
Religion: Non-Affiliated

SAT/ACT/GPA: 1120/24/85
Student/Faculty Ratio: 13:1
Undergraduate Enrollment: 1,800
Scholarships/Academic: Yes   **Athletic:** No
Expenses By: Year   **In State:** $ 21,500
Specializes In: Physical Therapy, Business, Education
Degrees Conferred: BA, BS, BSE, MBA, MS Education, MS
Programs of Study: Business Administration, Accounting, Physical Therapy, Education, Speech & Languages, Pathology, Political Science, Environmental Science, Social Work, PreMed, PreVet, PreDental

Housing: No
Male/Female: 1:3
Graduate Enrollment: 1,000
Financial Aid: Yes
Out of State: $ 21,500

Women's Athletic Profile

4245 East Avenue
Rochester, NY 14618
Coach: Tony Zostant
Email:

NCAA I
Golden Flyers, Purple, Gold
Phone: (716) 389-2195
Fax: (716) 389-2839

Estimated # of Women's Volleyball Scholarships: N/A
Conference: New York State Women's Collegiate Athletic Association

New York Institute of Technology
Academic Profile

Northern Boulevard
Old Westbury, NY 11568-800

Phone: 800-345-6948

Type: Private, 4 Yr., Liberal Arts, Engineering, Coed
Website: http://www.nyit.edu
SAT/ACT/GPA: NCAA Requirements
Student/Faculty Ratio: 18:1
Undergraduate Enrollment: 6,000
Scholarships/Academic: Yes   **Athletic:** Yes
Expenses By: Year   **In State:** $ 21,000
Specializes In: Liberal Arts & Science
Degrees Conferred: AAS, BA, BS, BFA, BArch, MA, MS, MFA, DO
Programs of Study: Accounting, Advertising, Architectural Technology, Architecture, Art, Biology, Business & Management, Chemistry, Communications, Computer Information Systems, Computer Science, Economics, Education, Electrical Engineering & Technology, Mathematics, Political Science

Founded: 1955
Religion: Non-Affiliated
Housing: No
Male/Female: 6:4
Graduate Enrollment: 4,000
Financial Aid: Yes
Out of State: $ 21,000

Women's Athletic Profile

P.O. Box 8000
Old Westbury, NY 11568
Coach: Gail Wasmus
Email:

NCAA I
Lady Bears, Blue, Gold, White
Phone: (516) 686-7447
Fax: (516) 626-0750

Estimated # of Women's Volleyball Scholarships: N/A
Conference: New York Collegiate Athletic Conference

New York University
Academic Profile

181 Mercer Street
New York, NY 10012

Phone: (212) 998-1212

Type: Private, 4 Yr., Liberal Arts, Coed
Website: http://www.nyu.edu
SAT/ACT/GPA: Required/3.6
Student/Faculty Ratio: 13:1
Undergraduate Enrollment: 17,673
Scholarships/Academic: Yes   **Athletic:** No
Expenses By: Year   **In State:** $ 33,582
Specializes In: Business, Law, Performing Arts, PreMed

Founded: 1831
Religion: Non-Affiliated
Housing: Yes
Male/Female: Not Available
Graduate Enrollment: 19,406
Financial Aid: Yes
Out of State: $ 33,582

Degrees Conferred: Associate, Bachelor's, Certificate, Diploma, Doctoral, First Pre-Professional, Master's, Post-Doctoral Certificate, Post-Master's Certificate

Programs of Study: Accounting, Acting, Africans Studies, Anthropology, Biology, Chemistry, Cinema Studies, Classical Civilization, Communication Studies, Comparative Literature, Computer Science, Dance, Dramatic Literature, Dramatic Writing, Early Childhood Education, East Asian Studies, Economics, English Literature, English Education, European Studies, Film/Television, Finance, Fine Arts, French, History, Hotel/Tourism Management, Individualized Major, Information Systems, Journalism/Mass Communication, Latin American Studies, Linguistics and Languages, Management and Organizational Behavior, Marketing, Mathematics, Metropolitan Studies, Music Education, Music/Business/Technology, Neural Science, Nursing, Nutrition and Food Studies, Philosophy, Politics, Psychology, Religious Studies, Social Work, Sociology, Special Education, Speech and Hearing Handicap Education, Sports Management and Marketing, Recreation and Leisure Studies, Studio Art

Men's Athletic Profile

70 Washington Square South
New York, NY 10012
Coach: Jose A. Pina, II
Email:

NCAA III
Violets/Purple, White
Phone: (212) 998-1212
Fax: (212) 995-4105

Estimated # of Men's Volleyball Scholarships: N/A
Conference: ELVA
Program Profile: The program is varsity since 1989. Play matches at the Coles Sport Center. Has a spring playing season. Facility can hold up to 2,000 fans.
History: The program began as a club sport in 1983, became a varsity program in 1989. Has made it to the NCAA playoffs three times (1992, 1993 & 1999).
Achievements: 1999 ELVI Division III Coach of the Year; 1992 ELVA Coach of the Year with a 23-10; no conference yet, has 2 Division III All-Americans (Rob Scharz in 1998 & Mitch Kallick in 1999).
Coaching: Jose A. Pina, II, Head Coach, has compiled a record of 61-80. EIVA Division III Coach of the Year in 1999. Edward Ceasar, Assistant Coach.

Freshman Receiving Financial Aid/Academic: 15 | **Athletic:** 0
Roster In State: 7 | **Out of State:** 9 | **Out of Country:** 0
Sophomores on Team: 1 | **Seniors on Team:** 3 | **Graduation %:** 90%
Most Recent Record: 20-8-0 | **Fall Games:** 4 | **Spring Games:** 28
Positions Needed: 2001-4
Schedule: Penn State, Rutgers-Newark, La Verne University, George Mason University, Juniata College, Princeton University
Style of Play: Play a quick paced offense, aggressive, serving and blocking.

Women's Athletic Profile

181 Mercer Street
New York, NY 10012
Coach: Kelly Stosik
Email: kas5@is4.nyu.edu

NCAA I
Bobcats, Purple, White
Phone: (212) 998-2068
Fax: (212) 995-4105

Estimated # of Women's Volleyball Scholarships: N/A
Conference: University Athletic Association
Program Profile: We are fully funded. We use charter buses for trips less than four hours and the longer trips. We have state-of-the-art facilities and play an aggressive schedule. We do a spring practice.
History: The program started in 1985, and a major commitment was made in 1997 when we hired a full-time coach. In 1997, we had a winning record and improved our play. In 1998, we finished in the 2nd round of the NCAA tournament. Our strength and schedule have increased dramatically.
Achievements: 1998 UAA Coach of the Year, 4 players were All-Conference, 2 players were All-Region
Coaching: Kelly Stosik - Head Coach. Allison Lind and Jari Jonas are the Assistant Coaches.
Roster In State: 0 | **Out of State:** 13 | **Out of Country:** 0
Sophomores on Team: 4 | **Seniors on Team:** 1 | **Graduation %:** 98
Most Recent Record: 26-10-0 | **Fall Games:** 35-4o | **Spring Games:** 8-10
Positions Needed: Middles, Setter
Schedule: Washington University, Emory, SUNY Courtland, Rochester Institute of Technology, John Hopkins, Rutgers
Style of Play: Quick and aggressive

Niagara University
Academic Profile

P. O. Box 2009
Niagara, NY 14109-2009

Phone: (716) 286-8600

Type: Private, 4 Yr., Liberal Arts, Coed
Website: http://www.niagara.edu
SAT/ACT/GPA: 1000
Student/Faculty Ratio: 16:1
Undergraduate Enrollment: 2,400+
Scholarships/Academic: Yes
Expenses By: Year
Specializes In: Travel & Tourism

Athletic: Yes
In State: $19,290

Founded: 1856
Religion: Catholic/Vincentian
Housing: Yes
Male/Female: 42:58
Graduate Enrollment: 600
Financial Aid: Yes
Out of State: $19,290

Programs of Study: Accounting, Biology, Business, Chemistry, Commerce, Criminal Justice, Education, English, French, History, Hotel/Restaurant Administration, Inclusion Elementary & Special Education, Mathematics, Nursing, Philosophy, Social Work, Travel/Tourism

Women's Athletic Profile

P.O. Box 2009
Niagara University, NY 14109
Coach: Rocco Lucci, Jr.
Email:

NCAA I
Lady Eagles, Purple, White
Phone: (716) 286-8662
Fax: (716) 286-8609

Estimated # of Women's Volleyball Scholarships: N/A
Conference: Metro Atlantic Athletic Conference

Nyack College
Academic Profile

1 South Boulevard
Nyack, NY 10960

Phone: 800-336-9225

Type: Private, 4 Yr., Liberal Arts, Coed
Website: http://www.nyackcollege.du
SAT/ACT/GPA: 860/18/2.0
Student/Faculty Ratio: 10:1
Undergraduate Enrollment: 790
Scholarships/Academic: Yes
Expenses By: Year
Degrees Conferred: BA, BS

Athletic: Yes
In State: $ 18,440

Founded: 1886
Religion: Christian
Housing: Yes
Male/Female: 3.5:5
Graduate Enrollment: 300
Financial Aid: Yes
Out of State: $ 18,440

Programs of Study: Biblical Studies, Business & Economics, Christian Studies, Communication, Education, English, History, Humanities, Management, Math, Ministries, Missions, Music, Music Theory & Composition, Natural Science, Performing Arts, Philosophy, Psychology, Religion, Religious Education, Religious Music, Secondary Education, Social Science, Voice, Youth Ministry

Women's Athletic Profile

1 South Boulevard
Nyack, NY 10960
Coach: Madaline Toliver
Email: mtoliver@jhha.org
Estimated # of Women's Volleyball Scholarships: N/A
Conference: Independent

NCAA I
Purple Pride, Purple, White
Phone: (914) 358-1710
Fax: (914) 353-2147

Pace University
Academic Profile

861 Bedford Rd.
Pleasantville, NY 10570

Phone: 800-874-7223

Type: Private, 4 Yr., Coed
Website: http://www.pace.edu
SAT/ACT/GPA: 900
Student/Faculty Ratio: 21:1
Undergraduate Enrollment: 3,500

Founded: 1963
Religion: Non-Affiliated
Housing: Yes
Male/Female: 1:2
Graduate Enrollment: N/A

Scholarships/Academic: Yes   **Athletic:** Yes   **Financial Aid:** Yes
Expenses By: Year   **In State:** $ 21,000   **Out of State:** $ 21,000
Specializes In: Business
Degrees Conferred: AA, AS, AAS, BA, BS, BBA, BFA, LLM, MBA, MSN
Programs of Study: Business and Management, Equestrian Science, Communications, BioEngineering and BioMedical, Engineering, International Studies, Psychology, Social Sciences

Women's Athletic Profile

861 Bedford Rd.
Pleasantville, NY 10570
Coach: Dinu Dan
Email: ddan@pace.edu

NCAA I
Lady Setters, Navy Blue, Gold
Phone: (914) 773-3650
Fax: (914) 773-3441

Estimated # of Women's Volleyball Scholarships: N/A
Conference: Northeast-10 Conference

Polytechnic University
Academic Profile

6 Metrotech Center
Brooklyn, NY 11201

Phone: 800-765-9832

Type: Private, 4 Yr.,Engineering, Coed   **Founded:** 1854
Website: http://www.poly.edu   **Religion:** All
SAT/ACT/GPA: Open   **Housing:** Yes
Student/Faculty Ratio: 18:1   **Male/Female:** 7:1
Undergraduate Enrollment: 1,200   **Graduate Enrollment:** 1,000
Scholarships/Academic: Yes   **Athletic:** No   **Financial Aid:** Yes
Expenses By: Year   **In State:** $ 18,000   **Out of State:** $ 18,000
Specializes In: Engineering, Computer Science & Engineering, Humanities
Degrees Conferred: BS, Masters, Ph.D.
Programs of Study: Mechanical Engineering, Electrical Engineering, Civil Engineering, Computer Science, Computer Engineering, Technical Writing, Chemical Engineering, Pure Science, Humanities

Men's Athletic Profile

333 Jay Street
Brooklyn, NY 11201
Coach: William Brooks
Email:

NCAA III
Blue Jays/Blue, Grey
Phone: (718) 637-5910
Fax: (718) 637-5959

Estimated # of Men's Volleyball Scholarships: N/A
Conference: Independent

Women's Athletic Profile

333 Jay Street
Brooklyn, NY 11201
Coach: James Zeng
Email:

NCAA I
Lady Blue Jays, Blue, Grey
Phone: (917) 826-4294
Fax: (718) 637-5959

Estimated # of Women's Volleyball Scholarships: N/A
Conference: Eastern College Athletic Conference

Roberts Wesleyan College
Academic Profile

2301 Westside Drive
Rochester, NY 14624
Type: Private, 4 Yr., Liberal Arts, Coed
Website: http://www.roberts.edu
SAT/ACT/GPA: 860/18/2.0

Phone: 716-594-6371

Founded: 1866
Religion: Free Methodist Church of N America
Housing: Yes

Student/Faculty Ratio: 14:1
Undergraduate Enrollment: 1,200
Scholarships/Academic: Yes   **Athletic:** Yes
Expenses By: Year   **In State:** $ 17,458
Specializes In: Christian Liberal Arts Education

Male/Female: 1:2
Graduate Enrollment: 300
Financial Aid: Yes
Out of State: $ 17,458

Degrees Conferred: AS, BA, BS, M.Ed., MSW
Programs of Study: Accounting, Art, Biology, Business Administration, Chemistry, Computer Science, Criminal Justice, Chemistry, Communications, Education, Engineering, Fine Arts, Gerontology, Mathematics, Music, Physical Science, Physics, PreMed, Psychology, Religion, Philosophy, Social Work, Sociology, Contemporary Ministries, History, Humanities, Math, Music, Nursing, Physics, Religion, Sociology

Women's Athletic Profile

2301 Westside Drive
Rochester, NY 14624
Coach: Jim Vanderhoof
Email: VBALLHOOF@AOL.com

NCAA I
Lady Raiders, Red, White, Black
Phone: (716) 594-6130
Fax: (716) 594-6580

Estimated # of Women's Volleyball Scholarships: 4
Conference: North Atlantic Conference
Program Profile: We are a small school with four volleyball courts and one sand court. Our facility has a seating capacity of 3,500. We also have weight rooms, aqua-training and plyometric training.
History: Our program began in 1995-1996 as a NAIA Division I team. We have made post-season play in every year of existence. We have a very strong reputation for good athletes and tremendous academics.
Achievements: Conference Coach of the Year in 1998/1999; Northwest Region Coach of the Year in 1998/1999; 3 All-American players in 4 seasons; Conference Runner-UP Champions in 1997/1998 and 1998/1999.
Coaching: Jim Vanderhoof, Head Coach, started the program in the 1995-1996 season.
Freshman Receiving Financial Aid/Academic: **Athletic:** 6
Roster In State: 7   **Out of State:** 5   **Out of Country:** 0
Sophomores on Team: 5   **Seniors on Team:** 1   **Graduation %:** 100
Most Recent Record: 36-8-0   **Fall Games:** 44   **Spring Games:** 20
Camp of Clinic Dates: July 26-30; August 2-6
Positions Needed: Setter, Middle, Outside
Schedule: Cortland, Ithaca, RIT, Southampton College, Mercy College, Mount Vernon
Style of Play: Quick offense and very defensive. Offensive serving (jump serves); very strong middle attack with middles moving around/across the net. Team unity, traveling to tournaments and very fun to be part of RWC Volleyball.

Rochester Institute of Technology
Academic Profile

51 Lomb Memorial Drive
Rochester, NY 14623

Phone: 716-475-6700

Type: Private, 4 Yr., Coed
Website: http://www.rit.edu
SAT/ACT/GPA: Open
Student/Faculty Ratio: 12/1
Undergraduate Enrollment: 11,300
Scholarships/Academic: Yes   **Athletic:** No
Expenses By: Year   **In State:** $25,989

Founded: 1829
Religion: Non-Affiliated
Housing: Yes
Male/Female: N/A
Graduate Enrollment: 2200
Financial Aid: Yes
Out of State: $25,989

Degrees Conferred: AAS, AS, BS, BA, BFA, MS, MA, MGA, MST, Ph.D.
Programs of Study: Applied Science & Technology (Computer Science, Food, Hotel & Travel Management, Packing Science, Engineering Technology, Industrial Technology), Business, Engineering, Imaging Arts & Sciences (School for American Craftsmen, School of Arts and Design, School of Printing Management Services, Center for Imaging Science), Liberal Arts, Science and the National Technical Institute for the Deaf

Women's Athletic Profile

51 Lomb Memorial Drive
Rochester, NY 14623-5603
Coach: Mary Powell
Email:

NCAA I
Tigers, Orange, White
Phone: (716) 475-5295
Fax: (716) 475-2617

Estimated # of Women's Volleyball Scholarships: N/A
Conference: New York State Women's Collegiate Athletic Association
History: Women' volleyball began in 1974.
Achievements: Went to Empire Eight Championships (1999) lost in the final against Ithaca, NCAA (1999) lost in third round.
Coaching: This is Mary Powells first season here at RIT. She was the assistant coach at Division I Morehead State University in Kentucky for one year. Prior to that Mary was the head coach at Freaonia from 1995-99.

Roster In State: 6	**Out of State:** 5	**Out of Country:** 0

Seniors on Team: 2
Most Recent Record: 17-8
Schedule: Cortland, Nazareth, Brockport, Ithaca

Russell Sage College
Academic Profile

45 Ferry Street
Troy, NY 12180

Phone: 888-837-9724

Type: Private, 4 Yr., Liberal Arts, Women Only
Website: http://www.sage.edu
SAT/ACT/GPA: 1050/2.75
Student/Faculty Ratio: 12:1
Undergraduate Enrollment: 1,038
Scholarships/Academic: Yes   **Athletic:** No
Expenses By: Year   **In State:** $ 21,580

Founded: 1916
Religion: Non-Affiliated
Housing: Yes
Male/Female: Women Only
Graduate Enrollment: N/A
Financial Aid: Yes
Out of State: $ 21,580

Specializes In: Physical, Creative Arts & Occupational Therapy, Theatre
Degrees Conferred: BA, BS, MS
Programs of Study: Offers more than 30 Bachelor's Degrees to women. Art Management, Communications, Biology, Computer Science, Computer Information Systems, Math, Medical Technology, Economics, Criminal Justice, Marketing, Political Science, Psychology

Women's Athletic Profile

45 Ferry Street
Troy, NY 12180
Coach: Tina Phillips
Email: phill@sage.edu

NCAA I
Lady Gators, Green, White
Phone: (518) 244-2417
Fax: (518) 244-3107

Estimated # of Women's Volleyball Scholarships: N/A
Conference: New York State Women's Collegiate Athletic Association
Program Profile: Our team plays a tournament based schedule in the fall. The team practices and plays in the Robison Athletic and Recreation Center Gymnasium.
History: Our program began in 1971-1972.
Achievements: Team captures Russell Sage Family Weekend Classic, place third at Hunter College Invitational and Hamilton College Tournament.
Coaching: Tina Phillips, Head Coach, began coaching here this year with a record of 7-21. She played starter on high school and junior college level and played USVBA for four years. She coached at Thomas A. Edison High School for four years. She was a 1995 Metro-Elmira Coach of the Year.
Freshman Receiving Financial Aid/Academic: **Athletic:** 0

Roster In State: 9	**Out of State:** 3	**Out of Country:** 0
Sophomores on Team: 0	**Seniors on Team:** 1	**Graduation %:** 100
Most Recent Record: 7-21-0	**Fall Games:** 28	**Spring Games:** TBA

Positions Needed: Setter, Middle Hitter
Schedule: Elmira College, Skidmore, SUNY-Plattsburg, SUNY-Potsdam, Union, Hartwick
Style of Play: We use both 6-2 and 5-1 offense. On defense uses middle deep and rotation alignments.

Saint Bonaventure University
Academic Profile

P. O. Box 6
St. Bonaventure, NY 14778

Phone: 800-462-5050

Type: Private, 4 Yr., Liberal Arts, Coed
Website: http://www.cs.sbu.edu
SAT/ACT/GPA: Open

Founded: 1858
Religion: Catholic
Housing: Yes

Student/Faculty Ratio: 16:1
Undergraduate Enrollment: N/A
Scholarships/Academic: Yes   **Athletic:** Yes
Expenses By: Year   **In State:** $ 19,600
Degrees Conferred: BA, BS, BSEd, MA, MBA, MS, MSEd

Male/Female: 50:50
Graduate Enrollment: N/A
Financial Aid: Yes
Out of State: $ 19,600

Programs of Study: Biology, BioChemistry, Environmental Science, Accounting, Finance, Management Science, Marketing, Economics, Math & Business Administration, JMC, Computer Science, Elementary Education, Physical Education, French, Spanish, Latin, Medical Technology, English, Philosophy, Math, Physics, Chemistry, Political Science, Psychology, Social Science, Social Studies, History, Sociology, Visual Arts, Art Teacher, Interdisciplinary Studies

Women's Athletic Profile

P.O. Box G
St. Bonaventure, NY 14778
Coach: John Wasielewski
Email:

NCAA I
Lady Bonnies, Brown, White
Phone: (716) 375-2640
Fax: (716) 375-2280

Estimated # of Women's Volleyball Scholarships: N/A
Conference: Atlantic 10 Conference

Saint Francis College - New York
Academic Profile

180 Remson Street
Brooklyn, NY 11201

Phone: 718-522-2300

Type: Private, 4 Yr., Liberal Arts, Coed
Website: http://www.stfranciscollege.edu
SAT/ACT/GPA: 820/18
Student/Faculty Ratio: 24:1
Undergraduate Enrollment: 2,300
Scholarships/Academic: Yes   **Athletic:** Yes
Expenses By: Year   **In State:** $ 8,000
Degrees Conferred: AS, AAS, BA, Bs

Founded: 1884
Religion: Franciscan Brothers
Housing: No
Male/Female: 45:55
Graduate Enrollment: N/A
Financial Aid: Yes
Out of State: $ 8,000

Programs of Study: Accounting, Aviation Management, Biology, BioMedical Science, Broadcasting, Business Administration, Communications, Computer Information Systems, Computer Science, Criminal Justice, Economics, Elementary Education, English, Film Studies, Finance, Health Services, History, Interdisciplinary Studies, Liberal Arts, Management, Marketing, Mathematics, Medical Technology Physical Education, Political Science, PreDentistry, PreLaw, PreMed, Psychology, Secondary Education, Social Science, Special Education

Women's Athletic Profile

180 Remsen Street
Brooklyn Heights, NY 11201-4398
Coach: Steve Hagenlocher
Email:

NCAA I
Lady Terriers, Red, Blue
Phone: (718) 489-5490
Fax: (718) 797-2140

Estimated # of Women's Volleyball Scholarships: N/A
Conference: Northeast Conference

Saint John Fisher College
Academic Profile

3690 East Avenue
Rochester, NY 14618

Phone: (716) 385-8309

Type: Private, 4 Yr., Liberal Arts, Coed
Website: http://www.sjfc.edu
SAT/ACT/GPA: 1050/22/8.5
Student/Faculty Ratio: 15:1
Undergraduate Enrollment: 1,500
Scholarships/Academic: Yes   **Athletic:** No
Expenses By: Year   **In State:** $ 19,290
Specializes In: Liberal Arts, Accounting, Education, Business

Founded: 1948
Religion: Roman Catholic
Housing: Yes
Male/Female: 45:55
Graduate Enrollment: 386
Financial Aid: Yes
Out of State: $ 19,290

Degrees Conferred: BA, BS, MBA
Programs of Study: Accounting, Biology, Chemistry, Communications, Computer Science, Economics, English, French, German, History, Interdisciplinary Studies, International Studies, Italian, Mathematics, Philosophy, Physics, Political Science, Psychology, Sociology, Spanish

Women's Athletic Profile

3690 E. Avenue
Rochester, NY 14618
Coach: Darrell Schoenl
Email: schoenl@sjfc.edu

NCAA I
Lady Cardinals, Red, Gold
Phone: (716) 385-8309
Fax: (716) 385-7308

Estimated # of Women's Volleyball Scholarships: No
Conference: Eastern College Athletic Conference, New York State Women's Collegiate Athletic Association
Program Profile: The program is in its 25th season.
Achievements: 1998-99 second place State Champions, NCAA Tournament Appearances 1997-98; 1st place State Championships, NCAA Tournament Appearance.
Coaching: Darrell Schoenl, Head Coach, has a 179-120 overall record. Laurie Schoenl is Assistant Coach.
Freshman Receiving Financial Aid/Academic: **Athletic:** 0
Roster In State: 8   **Out of State:** 0   **Out of Country:** 0
Sophomores on Team: 0   **Seniors on Team:** 1   **Graduation %:** 100
Most Recent Record: 26-18-0
Positions Needed: 6/4
Schedule: Juniata College, SUNY Cortland, Ithica College, Rochester Institute of Technology

Saint John's University - New York
Academic Profile

8000 Utopia Parkway
Jamaica, NY 11439

Phone: (718) 990-6161

Type: Private, 4 Yr., Liberal Arts, Coed
Website: http://www.stjohns.edu
SAT/ACT/GPA: 1000/21/80
Student/Faculty Ratio: 15:1
Undergraduate Enrollment: 12,000
Scholarships/Academic: Yes   **Athletic:** Yes
Expenses By: Year   **In State:** $ 23,000
Specializes In: Business, Law, Pharmacy, Health, Sports Medicine
Degrees Conferred: BA, BS, BFA, MA, MBA, MS

Founded: 1875
Religion: Vincentian
Housing: Yes
Male/Female: 45:55
Graduate Enrollment: 3,000
Financial Aid: Yes
Out of State: $ 23,000

Programs of Study: Accounting, American Studies, Anthropology, Banking and Finance, Biology, Broadcasting, Business, Chemistry, Communications, Computer Science, Criminal Justice, Economics, Education, English, Environmental Science, Fine Arts, Journalism, Management, Marketing, Mathematics, Nursing, Pharmacy, Philosophy, Physical Education Physics, Political Science, Psychology, Religion, Social Science, Toxicology

Women's Athletic Profile

8000 Utopia Parkway
Jamaica, NY 11439
Coach: Joanne Persico-Smith
Email: persicoj@st.johns.edu

NCAA I
Lady Storms, Red, White
Phone: (718) 990-1872
Fax: (718) 990-1988

Estimated # of Women's Volleyball Scholarships: 12
Conference: Big East Conference
Program Profile: We are members of Division I Big East Conference. We practice and play at Alumni Hall which has 6,000 seats. It is perfect for volleyball. We have newly built dorms.
History: In 1994, we began our Volleyball Division I program. We were in the playoffs in 1995 and 1996. We missed the Big East Playoffs in 1998 by one game. We were ECAC defending champions. We have an AVCA Academic Team GPA of 3.54 which is ranked 3rd in the country.
Achievements: Big East Academic All-Americans each year; Big East All-Rookie Team - Staiha Levi; Big East Second Team - Connie Chafe
Coaching: Joanne Persico-Smith, Head Coach, is entering her fifth season as volleyball coach at St. John's University. She brings a wealth of knowledge to the sport as a player, coach and official. She is a 1987 graduate of Syracuse University and was inducted into

the Orange Plus Hall of Fame in 1988. In her senior year, she was named Big-East Player of the Year, Most Valuable Player and team captain. She was named GTE/COSIDA Academic All-American Team. Chris Riler, Assistant Coach, begins his fifth season with the program as a full-time assistant.

Freshman Receiving Financial Aid/Academic:

		Athletic: 3
Roster In State: 3	**Out of State:** 9	**Out of Country:** 0
Sophomores on Team: 0	**Seniors on Team:** 4	**Graduation %:** 100
Most Recent Record: 19-14-0	**Fall Games:** 30	**Spring Games:** 0

Positions Needed: Outside Hitter
Schedule: Notre Dame, Fairfield, Georgetown, University of Connecticut, James Madison, Pittsburgh
Style of Play: Players' coach. Defense oriented. Team oriented. 5-1. Setters call the plays. Aggressive blocking.

Saint Joseph's College - New York
Academic Profile

155 Roe Boulevard
Patchogue, NY 11772-2603

Phone: 631-447-3219

Type: Private, 4 Yr., Liberal Arts,Coed
Website: Not Available
SAT/ACT/GPA: 980/80
Student/Faculty Ratio: 20:1
Undergraduate Enrollment: 2,400
Scholarships/Academic: Yes   **Athletic:** No
Expenses By: Sem   **In State:** $ 4,300
Specializes In: Liberal Arts
Degrees Conferred: BA, BS

Founded: 1916
Religion: Catholic
Housing: No
Male/Female: 40:60
Graduate Enrollment: 100
Financial Aid: Yes
Out of State: $ 4,300

Programs of Study: Accounting, Biology, Business Administration, Child Study, Classics, Computer Science, Education, English, Fine Arts, History, Human Relations, Mathematics, Modern Languages, Philosophy, Physical Education, Physical Sciences, Recreation, Religious Studies, Social Science, Psychology, Religious Studies, Social Science, Speech Communications, Interdisciplinary Courses, Sociology

Women's Athletic Profile

155 Roe Boulevard
Patchogue, NY 11772
Coach: Cynthia Krejei
Email:

NCAA I
Golden Eagles, Blue, White
Phone: (516) 447-3292
Fax: (516) 447-3347

Estimated # of Women's Volleyball Scholarships: N/A
Conference: Eastern College Athletic Conference

Saint Lawrence University
Academic Profile

Augsbury P.E. Center
Canton, NY 13617

Phone: 800-285-1856

Type: Private, 4 Yr., Liberal Arts, Coed
Website: http://www.stlawu.edu
SAT/ACT/GPA: Open
Student/Faculty Ratio: 12:1
Undergraduate Enrollment: 1,950
Scholarships/Academic: Yes   **Athletic:** No
Expenses By: Year   **In State:** $ 28,815
Degrees Conferred: BA, BS, MA, MS, MEd

Founded: 1856
Religion: Non-Affiliated
Housing: Yes
Male/Female: 1:1
Graduate Enrollment: 100
Financial Aid: Yes
Out of State: $ 28,815

Programs of Study: African Studies, Anthropology, Art, Asian Studies, Biology, BioPhysics, Canadian Studies, Chemistry, Computer Science, Creative Writing, Ecology, Economics, Engineering, English, Environmental Science, Fine Arts, French, Geology, Geophysics, German, Government, History, Literature, Mathematics, Modern Languages, Music, Philosophy, Physical Education, Physics, Political Science, Psychology, Recreation & Leisure, Religion, Romance Languages, Speech, Social Sciences, Spanish

Women's Athletic Profile

Park Street
Canton, NY 13617
Coach: Kristenne Robison
Email: krobison@stlawu.edu

NCAA I
Lady Saints, Scarlet, Brown
Phone: (315) 229-5875
Fax: (315) 229-5589

Estimated # of Women's Volleyball Scholarships: N/A
Conference: Upstate Collegiate Athletic Association
Program Profile: Main season is fall August-November. Non-traditional season late March-late April. Play in Burkman Gymnasium with seating capacity of 1500. There are two playing courts.
History: Program began in 1982. Program on the rise 1998 1-19, 1999 13-23, 2000 18-17.
Achievements: Numerous All-Conference Players.
Coaching: Kristenne Robison overall record since 1999 31-40. She played at Baldwin-Wallace College.

Roster In State: 5	**Out of State:** 5	**Out of Country:** 0
Sophomores on Team:	**Seniors on Team:** 0	**Graduation %:** 100
Most Recent Record: 18-17	**Fall Games:** 35	**Spring Games:**
Camp of Clinic Dates: TBA		

Positions Needed: Middle Hitters
Schedule: Skidmore, Nazareth, Vassar, Union, Middlebury
Style of Play: Run a 5-1, excellent passing and defensive skills, run an aggressive and quick offense.

Saint Thomas Aquinas College
Academic Profile

125 Route 340
Sparkill, NY 10976-1050

Phone: 914-398-4100

Type: Private, 4 Yr., Coed	**Founded:** 1952
Website: http://www.stac.edu	**Religion:** Non-Affiliated
SAT/ACT/GPA: 830+	**Housing:** No
Student/Faculty Ratio: 18;1	**Male/Female:** 50;50
Undergraduate Enrollment: 1,400	**Graduate Enrollment:** 40

Scholarships/Academic: Yes   **Athletic:** Yes   **Financial Aid:** Yes
Expenses By: Year   **In State:** $ 15,000   **Out of State:** $ 15,000
Degrees Conferred: BA, BS, MEd
Programs of Study: Accounting, Applied Art, Applied Mathematics, Business Administration, Communications, Computer Information Systems, Criminal Justice, Education, Engineering, English, Finance, Fine Arts, History, Humanities, Journalism, Mathematics, Medical Laboratory Technology, Modern Languages, Natural Science, PreMed, Psychology, Recreation & Leisure, Religion, Romance, Social Science, Spanish, Speech Education

Women's Athletic Profile

125 Route 340
Sparkill, NY 10976
Coach: Debbie Metz
Email:

NCAA I
Lady Spartans, Maroon, Gold
Phone: (914) 398-4053
Fax: (914) 359-8136

Estimated # of Women's Volleyball Scholarships: N/A
Conference: Independent

Siena College
Academic Profile

515 Loudon Road
Loudonville, NY 12211-1462

Phone: (518) 583-2450

Type: Private, 4 Yr., Liberal Arts, Coed	**Founded:** 1937
Website: http://www.siena.edu	**Religion:** Franciscan
SAT/ACT/GPA: 1000/80	**Housing:** Yes
Student/Faculty Ratio: 16:1	**Male/Female:** 47:53
Undergraduate Enrollment: 2,700	**Graduate Enrollment:** N/A

Scholarships/Academic: Yes   **Athletic:** Yes   **Financial Aid:** Yes
Expenses By: Year   **In State:** $ 21,100   **Out of State:** $ 21,100
Specializes In: Biology, Business
Degrees Conferred: BA, BS, MBA
Programs of Study: Accounting, American Studies, Biology, Chemistry, Computer Science, Economics, English, Environmental Studies, Finance, French, History, Marketing/Management, Mathematics, Physics, Political Science, Religious Studies, Social Work, Sociology, Spanish, Undecided Arts

Women's Athletic Profile

515 Loudon Rd.
Loudonville, NY 12211-1462
Coach: Hank Wysocki
Email: volleyball@siena.edu

NCAA I
Lady Saints, Green, Gold
Phone: (518) 783-2450
Fax: (518) 783-2992

Estimated # of Women's Volleyball Scholarships: 4
Conference: Metro Atlantic Athletic Conference
Program Profile: We play at the 4,500-seat Alumni Recreation Center. We won the MAAC 4 years in a row . We never finished below 3rd place in 6 years. We play both fall and spring.
History: The program began in 1977. We were Division III until 1989. went Division I in 1991. We will have 12 full scholarships and a fully funded program this year.
Achievements: 3-time Siena College Coach of the Year; 2-time Metro Atlantic Conference Coach of the Year; 2nd all time Siena College coaching record; 4 straight MAAC Conference Titles; NIVC tournament berth; NCAA tournament berth (10-20 win seasons).
Coaching: Hank Wysocki, Head Coach, started with the program in 1983. Ron Racey, Assistant Coach, started in 1992. Steve Goodyear, Assistant Coach, started in 1995.

Freshman Receiving Financial Aid/Academic: | | **Athletic:** 1
Roster In State: 12 | **Out of State:** 3 | **Out of Country:** 0
Sophomores on Team: 4 | **Seniors on Team:** 4 | **Graduation %:** 100
Most Recent Record: 15-20-0 | **Fall Games:** 35 | **Spring Games:** 3
Camp of Clinic Dates: July 9-13; July 16-20
Positions Needed: Outside Hitter, Middle Hitter, Setter
Schedule: Purdue, University of Arkansas-Little Rock, McNeese State, Syracuse, Fairfield, Harvard
Style of Play: Aggressive , middle attack oriented team.

Skidmore College
Academic Profile

North Broadway
Saratoga Springs, NY 12866

Phone: (518) 580-5000

Type: Private, 4 Yr., Liberal Arts, Coed
Website: http://www.skidmore.edu
SAT/ACT/GPA: Median combined SAT 1100+
Student/Faculty Ratio: 10:1
Undergraduate Enrollment: 2,200
Scholarships/Academic: Yes
Expenses By: Year
Degrees Conferred: BA, BS

Athletic: No
In State: $ 28243+

Founded: 1911
Religion: Presbyterian
Housing: Yes
Male/Female: 2:3
Graduate Enrollment: N/A
Financial Aid: Yes
Out of State: $ 28243+

Programs of Study: All traditional Liberal Arts majors and Business, Social Work, Exercise Science, and Elementary Education

Women's Athletic Profile

815 N. Broadway
Saratoga Springs, NY 12866
Coach: Hilda Arrechea
Email: harreche@skidmore.edu

NCAA I
Thoroughbreds, Green, White
Phone: (518) 580-5367
Fax: (518) 580-5396

Estimated # of Women's Volleyball Scholarships: N/A
Conference: Upstate Collegiate Athletic Association
Achievements: 2000, 99, 98, 96 UCAA Coaching staff, AU Regional Players in 2000, 3 Conference Titles (2000, 99,98) 2 NCAA Appearances.
Coaching: Overall record of 140-67.

Roster In State: 4 | **Out of State:** 9 | **Out of Country:** 0
Sophomores on Team: 2 | **Seniors on Team:** 3 | **Graduation %:** 100
Most Recent Record: 35-5-0 | **Fall Games:** 40 | **Spring Games:**
Camp of Clinic Dates: July 16-20, 2001
Positions Needed: Setter

SUNY - Binghamton University
Academic Profile

P. O. Box 6000
Binghamton, NY 13904

Phone: (607) 777-6838

Type: Public, 4 Yr., Coed
Website: http://www.binghamton.edu
SAT/ACT/GPA: 1207/92.2
Student/Faculty Ratio: 13:1
Undergraduate Enrollment: 9,460
Scholarships/Academic: Yes   **Athletic:** Yes
Expenses By: Year   **In State:** $ 9,637

Founded: 1946
Religion: Non-Affiliated
Housing: Yes
Male/Female: 1:1.2
Graduate Enrollment: 2,696
Financial Aid: Yes
Out of State: $ 14,537

Degrees Conferred: BA, BS, BFA, MA, MS, MFA, M.Ed., Ph.D.
Programs of Study: Accounting, American Studies, Anthropology, Art, Art History, BioChemistry, Biology, Business & Management, Chemistry, Classics, Comparative Literature, Computer Science, Creative Writing, Ecology, Economics, Engineering, English, Environmental Studies, Film Studies, French, Geography, Geology, Geophysics, German, History, Liberal Arts, Life Sciences, Literature, Mathematics, Nursing, Philosophy, Physical Education, Political Science, PreDentistry, PreLaw, PreMed, PreVet, Psychology, Social Science, Theatre

Women's Athletic Profile

P.O. Box 6000
Binghamton, NY 13902-6000
Coach: Glenn Kiriyama
Email: kiriyama@binghamton.edu

NCAA I
Colonials, Dark Green, White
Phone: (607) 777-2842
Fax: (607) 777-4597

Estimated # of Women's Volleyball Scholarships: N/A
Conference: Independent

State University of New York College - Brockport
Academic Profile

350 New Campus Drive
Brockport, NY 14420-2915

Phone: 800-382-8447

Type: Public, 4 Yr., Coed
Website: http://www.brockport.edu
SAT/ACT/GPA: 1000/20/3.0
Student/Faculty Ratio: 21:1
Undergraduate Enrollment: 7,691
Scholarships/Academic: No   **Athletic:** No
Expenses By: Year   **In State:** $ 9,840
Specializes In: Physical Education

Founded: 1840
Religion: Non-Affiliated
Housing: Yes
Male/Female: 44:56
Graduate Enrollment: 1,890
Financial Aid: Yes
Out of State: $ 14,740

Degrees Conferred: All
Programs of Study: Accounting, African-American Studies, Anthropology, Art History, Art Studio, Art for Children, Biological Science, Business Administration, Chemistry, Communications, Computer Science, Criminal Justice, Dance, Earth Science, Engineering, Economics, English, Environment & Forest, French, Geology, Health Science, History, International Business & Economics, International Studies, Journalism, Liberal Studies, Mathematics, Medical Technology, Meteorology, Nursing, Philosophy, Physical Education, Physics, Political Science, Psychology, Social Work, Sociology, Spanish, Theatre, Water Resources

Women's Athletic Profile

350 New Campus Drive
Brockport, NY 14420
Coach: John Tuttle
Email: jtuttle@brockport.edu

NCAA I
Golden Eagles, Gold, Green
Phone: (716) 395-5841
Fax: (716) 395-2160

Estimated # of Women's Volleyball Scholarships: N/A
Conference: State University of New York Athletic Conference
Program Profile: Games played at the Tuttle south Gymnasium which holds 1,000 fans.
Achievements: 7 NCAA Tournament appearances, SUNYAC Champions 1990-1994, 4 All-Americans.
Coaching: Head Coach, John Tuttle, is in his first year at Brockport along with his Assistant JJ O'Connell. Our student Assistant is

Nikky Klingler.
Roster In State: 15
Graduation %: 98
Most Recent Record: 21-18
Schedule: Cortland, Itchaca, Geneseo, RIT, Nazareth, Oswego

State University of New York College - Buffalo
Academic Profile

1300 Elmwood Ave.
Buffalo, NY 14222-1095

Phone: (716) 878-5420

Type: Public, 4 Yr., Liberal Arts, Engineering, Coed
Website: http://www.ubathletics.buffalo.edu
SAT/ACT/GPA: 900/20/2.0
Student/Faculty Ratio: 12:1
Undergraduate Enrollment: 11,000
Scholarships/Academic: Yes
Expenses By: Semester

Founded: 1871
Religion: Non-Affiliated
Housing: Yes
Male/Female: 3:5
Graduate Enrollment: 4,000

Athletic: No
In State: $ 3,550

Financial Aid: Yes
Out of State: $ 6,000

Specializes In: Art-related Fields, Broadcasting, Education
Degrees Conferred: BA, BS
Programs of Study: Anthropology, Art, Biology, Broadcasting, Business, Chemistry, Communications, Computer Information Systems, Criminal Justice, Design, Dietetics, Earth Sciences, Economics, Engineering, Education, English, Fashion, Forensic Chemistry, Geography Health & Wellness, History, Hospitality, Humanities, Journalism, Mathematics, Music, Philosophy, Photography, Physics, Political Science, Psychology, Social Work, Speech Language, Pathology, Theatre, Urban Regional Analysis & Planning

Women's Athletic Profile

Box 605000
Buffalo, NY 14260
Coach: TBA
Email:

NCAA I
Lady Bulls, Royal Blue, White
Phone: (716) 645-3149
Fax: (716) 645-3756

Estimated # of Women's Volleyball Scholarships: 12 full
Conference: Mid-American Conference
Program Profile: We have a fast growing program. We practice and play at Alumni Arena which has 8,000 seats. FB Stadium has 30,000 seats.
History: We started in 1966 and became Division I in 1991. We joined the Mid American Conference in 1998.
Achievements: Mid-Continent Conference Final 4 in 1996-1997. Bob Maxwell was Coach of the Year in 1997. We hosted the Championship in 1997 by winning the Eastern Division.
Freshman Receiving Financial Aid/Academic:
Roster In State: 13
Sophomores on Team: 2
Most Recent Record: 10-23-0

Out of State: 0
Seniors on Team: 6
Fall Games: 30-34

Athletic: 3
Out of Country: 2
Graduation %: 40% (6 of 15)
Spring Games: 4

Positions Needed: Middle (2), Outside (1)
Schedule: Northern Illinois, Miami, Ball State, Montana State, San Diego State, Western Michigan, Marshall, Syracuse, Villanova
Style of Play: To be determined by the new coach.

State University of New York College - Cobleskill
Academic Profile

Athletics Department/ Bouck Hall
Cobleskill, NY 12043

Phone: (518) 255-5127

Type: Public, 2 Yr., Coed
Website: http://www.cobleskill.edu
SAT/ACT/GPA: Not Required
Student/Faculty Ratio: 19:1
Undergraduate Enrollment: 2,350
Scholarships/Academic: Yes
Expenses By: Year

Founded: 1911
Religion: Non-Affiliated
Housing: Yes
Male/Female: 1:1
Graduate Enrollment: N/A

Athletic: No
In State: $ 9,275

Financial Aid: Yes
Out of State: $ 11,075

Specializes In: Agriculture, Business, Culinary Arts, Early Childhood
Degrees Conferred: AA, AS, AAS, AOS
Programs of Study: 40+ majors in the following areas: Agriculture and Natural Resources, Business and Computer Technologies, Culinary Arts, Hospitality and Tourism, Early Childhood, Liberal Arts and Sciences

Women's Athletic Profile

Route 7
Cobleskill, NY 12043
Coach: TBA
Email: sitterly@snycorva.cortland.edu

NCAA I
Fighting Tigers, Orange, Black
Phone: (518) 255-5127
Fax: (518) 255-5828

Estimated # of Women's Volleyball Scholarships: 0
Conference: Mountain Valley
History: Our program is about 15 years old. We have multiple Conference Championships. We have some All-Regional players.
Achievements: 1998 Season: Nationally ranked; Regional Final Four; 20-6 record; co-Conference Champions; 1 All-American (1st team); 3 All-Region team members; Conference Coach of the Year
Coaching: TBA

Roster In State: 100%	**Out of State:** 0	**Out of Country:** 0
Sophomores on Team: 0	**Seniors on Team:** 6	**Graduation %:** Unknown
Most Recent Record: 20-6-0	**Fall Games:** All	**Spring Games:** 0

Positions Needed: Setter, Middle Hitter
Schedule: Jamestown CC, Corning CC, Adirondack CC, Fulerton-Montgomery CC, Broome CC, Mohawk Valley CC
Style of Play: Defense oriented with a moderately complex offense. Athletic ability and smart playing is a priority over height alone.

State University of New York College - Cortland
Academic Profile

P. O. Box 2000
Cortland, NY 13045

Phone: 607-753-4711

Type: Public, 4 Yr., Liberal Arts, Coed
Website: http://www.Cortland.edu
SAT/ACT/GPA: 1000/85
Student/Faculty Ratio: 20:1
Undergraduate Enrollment: 5,500

Founded: 1868
Religion: Non-Affiliated
Housing: Yes
Male/Female: 45:55
Graduate Enrollment: 2,000

Scholarships/Academic: Yes | **Athletic:** No | **Financial Aid:** Yes
Expenses By: Year | **In State:** $ 9,944 | **Out of State:** $ 14,844

Specializes In: Education, Biology, PE, Sports Management
Degrees Conferred: BS, BA, BSE, MA, MSE
Programs of Study: Elementary & Secondary Education, Physical Education, Athletic Training, Art, Biology, Business, Chemistry, Communications, Economics, English, PreEnvironmental Science, Health Science, History, Math, Political Science, Psychology, Recreation, Philosophy, Sociology, Speech & Hearing Science, Sports Management, Exercise Science, Spanish, French, PreDental, PreLaw, PreMedicine

Women's Athletic Profile

P.O. Box 2000
Cortland, NY 13045
Coach: Joan Sitterly
Email: Sitterly@cortland.edu

NCAA I
Lady Red Dragons, Red, White
Phone: (607) 753-4992
Fax: (607) 753-4929

Estimated # of Women's Volleyball Scholarships: N/A
Conference: State University of New York Athletic Conference
Program Profile: Cortland Volleyball plays in the 5,000-seat Corey Gymnasium, located in Park PER Center. Along with four courts in Park Center, our fieldhouse can accommodate six courts and Moffett Gym, which has 2 courts.
History: The program began in 1968 and has a tradition of excellence. We have been a national contender every year since the program's inception. Cortland has been ranked 5th nationally for the past three years. Our overall record is 800-297-9 (.723).
Achievements: Nine of the past twelve years, the SUNYAC Championships, 3 time defending NCAA regional champions, Conference Coach of the Year; All-Region Coach of the Year both six times; 2 All-Americans in 1998.
Coaching: Joan Sitterly, Head Coach, is entering 16 years with the program and he has compiled a record of 612-182 (.771) and is the third coach in history of NCAA Division III to have reached 600 wins. Matt Giufre is Assistant Coach.
Freshman Receiving Financial Aid/Academic: | | **Athletic:** 0

Roster In State: 14	**Out of State:** 1	**Out of Country:** 0
Sophomores on Team: 5	**Seniors on Team:** 3	**Graduation %:** 100
Most Recent Record: 39-3-0	**Fall Games:** 42	**Spring Games:** 4

Camp of Clinic Dates: July 19-22; August 9-13
Positions Needed: Setter, Middle Hitter
Schedule: Juniata College, Hope College, University of Wisconsin-Whitewater, Nebraska Wesleyan, Trinity, Wellesley
Style of Play: Quick, versatile offense with a fundamentally sound defense.

State University of New York College - Fredonia
Academic Profile

178 Central Avenue
Fredonia, NY 14063

Phone: 800-252-1212

Type: Public, 4 Yr., Liberal Arts, Coed
Website: http://www.cs.fredonia.edu
SAT/ACT/GPA: 1000/3.0
Student/Faculty Ratio: 20:1
Undergraduate Enrollment: 4,591
Scholarships/Academic: Yes   **Athletic:** No
Expenses By: Year   **In State:** $ 9,990
Specializes In: Education, Music

Founded: 1826
Religion: Non-Affiliated
Housing: Yes
Male/Female: 42:58
Graduate Enrollment: 218
Financial Aid: Yes
Out of State: $ 14,895

Degrees Conferred: BA, BS, BFA, BM, MA, MS, Post-Master's Certificate
Programs of Study: Accounting, Art, Biology, Business Administration, Chemistry, Communications, Computer Information Science, Cooperative Agriculture, Cooperative Engineering, Earth Science, Economics, (Elementary and Secondary) Education, English, French, GeoSciences, Health Service Administration, History, Industrial Management, Interdisciplinary Studies, Mathematics, Medical Technology, Music, Philosophy, Physics, Political Science, Psychology, Recombinant Gene Technology, Social Work, Sociology, Sound Recording, Spanish, Speech and Hearing Handicapped, Theatre Arts

Women's Athletic Profile

145 Dods Hall
Fredonia, NY 14063
Coach: Geoff Braun
Email:

NCAA I
Blue Devils, Royal Blue, White
Phone: (716) 673-3687
Fax: (716) 673-3136

Estimated # of Women's Volleyball Scholarships: N/A
Conference: SUNYAC, ECAC

State University of New York College - Geneseo
Academic Profile

1 College Circle
Geneseo, NY 14454

Phone: 716-245-5571

Type: Public, 4 Yr., Liberal Arts, Coed
Website: http://www.geneseo.edu
SAT/ACT/GPA: 1200
Student/Faculty Ratio: 20:1
Undergraduate Enrollment: 5,000
Scholarships/Academic: Yes   **Athletic:** No
Expenses By: Year   **In State:** $ 8,500

Founded: 1871
Religion: Non-Affiliated
Housing: Yes
Male/Female: 34:66
Graduate Enrollment: 200
Financial Aid: Yes
Out of State: $ 11,500

Degrees Conferred: BA, BS, BSEd, MA, MS, M.Ed.
Programs of Study: Business, Accounting, Economics, Management, Education, Art & Science, Computer, Pharmacy, Chemistry, Literature, Communication, Sociology, Art Studio, English, French, Optometry, Law, Physics, Biology

Women's Athletic Profile

1 College Circle
Geneseo, NY 14454
Coach: Martha Martin
Email: martinm@geneseo.edu

NCAA I
Lady Knights, Blue, White
Phone: (716) 245-5341
Fax: (716) 245-5344

Estimated # of Women's Volleyball Scholarships: N/A
Conference: State University of New York Athletic Conference

State University of New York College - New Paltz
Academic Profile

755 Manheim Blvd. Suite 1
New Paltz, NY 12561-2499

Phone: (888) 639-7589

Type: Public, 4 Yr., Liberal Arts, Engineering, Coed
Website: http://www.newpaltz.edu

Founded: 1828
Religion: Non-Affiliated

SAT/ACT/GPA: 1000/22/3.0
Student/Faculty Ratio: 19:1
Undergraduate Enrollment: 4,986
Scholarships/Academic: Yes   **Athletic:** No
Expenses By: Year   **In State:** $ 9,914

Housing: Yes
Male/Female: 2:3
Graduate Enrollment: 1,606
Financial Aid: Yes
Out of State: $ 14,814

Degrees Conferred: BA, BS, BFA, BSE, BS Ed., MA, MS, MFA, MS Ed., MAT, MST, CAS
Programs of Study: Accounting, Art, Biology, Business, Chemistry, Communication Disorders, Computer Engineering, Computer Science, Elementary Education, Electrical Engineering, English, Foreign Languages, Geology, History, International Relations, Journalism, Mathematics, Media, Medical Program (7 Year), Music Therapy, Political Science, Physics, Psychology, Sociology, Special Education

Men's Athletic Profile

75 S Manheim Blvd.
New Paltz, NY 12561
Coach: Antonio Bonilla
Email:

NCAA III
Hawks/Burnt Orange, Blue
Phone: (914) 257-3931
Fax: (914) 257-3920

Estimated # of Men's Volleyball Scholarships: N/A
Conference: Eastern College Athletic Conference

Women's Athletic Profile

Elting Gymnasium
New Paltz, NY 12561
Coach: Bob Thorburn
Email:

NCAA I
Hawks, Blue, Burnt Orange
Phone: (888) 639-7589
Fax:

Estimated # of Women's Volleyball Scholarships: N/A
Conference: SUNYAC

State University of New York College - Old Westbury
Academic Profile

RT 107
Old Westbury, NY 11568

Phone: 516-876-3073

Type: Public, 4 Yr., Coed
Website: http://www.oldwestbury.edu
SAT/ACT/GPA: 800
Student/Faculty Ratio: 25:1
Undergraduate Enrollment: 3,800
Scholarships/Academic: No   **Athletic:** No
Expenses By: Year   **In State:** $ 7,600

Founded: 1968
Religion: Non-Affiliated
Housing: No
Male/Female: 45:55
Graduate Enrollment: 800
Financial Aid: Yes
Out of State: $ 11,900

Degrees Conferred: BA, BS
Programs of Study: Business, Accounting, Economics, Management, Education, Arts & Sciences, American Studies, Anthropology, Applied Physics, Art History, Art Studio, BioChemistry, Biology, BioPhysics, Chemistry, Communications, Comparative Literate, Computer

Men's Athletic Profile

P.O. Box 210
Old Westbury, NY 11568
Coach: Harry Weinstein
Email:

NCAA III
Panthers/Green, White
Phone: (516) 876-3244
Fax: (516) 876-3230

Estimated # of Men's Volleyball Scholarships: N/A
Conference: Eastern College Athletic Conference

Women's Athletic Profile

P.O. Box 210
Old Westbury, NY 11568
Coach: Maria Catennacci
Email:

NCAA I
Lady Panthers, Green, White
Phone: (516) 876-3241
Fax: (516) 876-3230

Estimated # of Women's Volleyball Scholarships: N/A
Conference: Eastern College Athletic Conference

State University of New York College - Oneonta
Academic Profile

Upper West Street
Oneonta, NY 13820

Phone: 800-786-9123

Type: Public, 4 Yr., Liberal Arts, Engineering, Coed
Website: http://www.oneonta.edu
SAT/ACT/GPA: 1000/21/85
Student/Faculty Ratio: 21:1
Undergraduate Enrollment: 5,500
Scholarships/Academic: Yes   **Athletic:** No
Expenses By: Year   **In State:** $ 9,600

Founded: 1889
Religion: Non-Affiliated
Housing: Yes
Male/Female: 2:3
Graduate Enrollment: 250
Financial Aid: Yes
Out of State: $ 14,500

Degrees Conferred: BS, BA, BBA, MA, MS, MST
Programs of Study: Accounting, Adulthood and Aging Studies, African and Latino Studies, Anthropology, Art History, Art Studio, Biology, Dietetics, Earth Science, Food & Business, French, Geography, Geology, History, Home Economics, Hospitality Management, Human Ecology, International Studies, Mathematics, Meteorology

Women's Athletic Profile

Chase PE Building
Oneonta, NY 13820
Coach: Colleen Cashman
Email: cashmacm@oneonta.edu

NCAA I
Red Dragons, Red, White
Phone: (607) 436-2145
Fax: (607) 436-3088

Estimated # of Women's Volleyball Scholarships: N/A
Conference: Independent

State University of New York College - Oswego
Academic Profile

Laker Hall
Oswego, NY 13126

Phone: (315) 341-4280

Type: Public, 4 Yr., Liberal Arts, Coed
Website: http://www.oswego.edu
SAT/ACT/GPA: 1050/87
Student/Faculty Ratio: 21:1
Undergraduate Enrollment: 6,100
Scholarships/Academic: Yes   **Athletic:** No
Expenses By: Year   **In State:** $10,300

Founded: 1861
Religion: Non-Affiliated
Housing: Yes
Male/Female: 47:53
Graduate Enrollment: 1,000
Financial Aid: Yes
Out of State: $15,200

Specializes In: Arts & Science, Business, Education
Degrees Conferred: BA, BS, MA, MS, M.Ed., CAS, MBA, MAT, MBA
Programs of Study: Over 40 majors with in 3 schools: School of Education, School of Business, School of Arts and Sciences

Women's Athletic Profile

Route 104
Oswego, NY 13126
Coach: Dani Drews
Email: drews@oswego.edu

NCAA I
Lakers, Green, Black, White
Phone: (315) 341-4280
Fax: (315) 341-6397

Estimated # of Women's Volleyball Scholarships: N/A
Conference: State University of New York Athletic Conference
Program Profile: The Lakers compete in the newly renovated 1,500-seat Laker Hall Gymnasium. We compete in the Fall and have a non-traditional season practice and competition in the Spring.
History: The volleyball program at Oswego is over 30 years old, but it has enjoyed its greatest success in the 1990's. The 1994 team become the first at Oswego to gain a berth in the NCAA Championship tournament and finished the year as NYS Champions with a 42-4 record. The team competes in the highly competitive SUNYAC Conference and has qualified for post-season in 5 of the last 8 seasons.
Achievements: NYS Champions, SUNYAC West Co-Champs, AVCA All-Academic team, Coach of the Year (NYS-SUNYAC) in 1994;

SUNYAC Coach of the Year in 1991; All-Conference players in 7 of the last 8 seasons.

Coaching: Dani Drews, Head Coach, started in 1991 to the present with a record of 158-127. He was named SUNYAC Coach of the Year 2-times. He was 1994 NYS Coach of the Year. His team got NYS Champions Title. He was NYSWCAA Chair, and 1994 AVCA All-Academic Team. Sean Meetze is an Assistant Coach.

Freshman Receiving Financial Aid/Academic:

Roster In State: 10	**Out of State:** 1	**Athletic:** 0
Sophomores on Team: 4	**Seniors on Team:** 0	**Out of Country:** 0
Most Recent Record: 7-21-0	**Fall Games:** 28	**Graduation %:** 99
		Spring Games: 5

Positions Needed: Setter, Middle Hitter, LS

Schedule: Geneseo, Fredonia, Cortland, Skidmore, St. John Fisher, Elmira

Style of Play: Stress quick outside attack in combination with varied middle; aggressive perimeter defense.

State University of New York College - Plattsburgh
Academic Profile

Memorial Hall
Plattsburgh, NY 12901

Phone: 518-564-2040

Type: Public, 4 Yr., Liberal Arts, Coed
Website: http://www.plattsburgh.edu
SAT/ACT/GPA: 1000/22/"B"
Student/Faculty Ratio: 18:1
Undergraduate Enrollment: 5,400
Scholarships/Academic: Yes   **Athletic:** No
Expenses By: Year   **In State:** $ 8,445

Founded: 1889
Religion: Non-Affiliated
Housing: Yes
Male/Female: 43:57
Graduate Enrollment: N/A
Financial Aid: Yes
Out of State: $ 13,345

Specializes In: Liberal Arts & Science, Business, Professional Studies

Degrees Conferred: BA, BS, MEd, MST, Cas, MA, MSEd

Programs of Study: Accounting, Anthropology, Art, Biology, Business Administration, Business Economics, Canadian Studies, Cellular BioChemistry, Chemistry, Child Care Management, Child/Family Services, Communications Disorders, Communications, Radio/TV/Speech, Computer Science, Criminal Justice, Economics, Elementary Education, Engineering, English, Environmental Science, Food-Nutrition, French, Geography, Geology, History, Hotel & Restaurant and Tourism Management, Mathematics, Nursing, Political Science, PreLaw, PreMed, Psychology, Secondary Education, Social Work, Spanish, Theatre

Women's Athletic Profile

101 Broad Street
Plattsburgh, NY 12901
Coach: Dena O'Connell
Email:

NCAA I
Cardinals, Red, White
Phone: (518) 564-4155
Fax: (518) 564-4155

Estimated # of Women's Volleyball Scholarships: N/A
Conference: SUNYAC

State University of New York College - Potsdam
Academic Profile

Pierrepont Ave.
Potsdam, NY 13676-2294

Phone: (315) 267-2313

Type: Public, 4 Yr., Liberal Arts, Coed
Website: http://www.potsdam.edu
SAT/ACT/GPA: 960/20
Student/Faculty Ratio: 18:1
Undergraduate Enrollment: 3,475
Scholarships/Academic: Yes   **Athletic:** No
Expenses By: Year   **In State:** $ 9,700

Founded: 1816
Religion: Non-Affiliated
Housing: No
Male/Female: 2:3
Graduate Enrollment: 525
Financial Aid: Yes
Out of State: $ 9,575

Specializes In: Mathematics, Music Education, Teacher Education

Degrees Conferred: BA, BS, MA, MST

Programs of Study: Art, Anthropology, Biology, Chemistry, Communication, Computer Science, Dance, Dramatic Arts, Education, English, Fine Arts, Geology, History, Mathematics, Music, Physics, Political Science, Photography, Science

Women's Athletic Profile

Maxcy Hall
Potsdam, NY 13676
Coach: Elaine Torda
Email:

NCAA I
Lady Bears, Maroon, Gray
Phone: (315) 267-3132
Fax: (315) 267-2316

Estimated # of Women's Volleyball Scholarships: N/A
Conference: State University of New York Athletic Conference

State University of New York College - Stony Brook
Academic Profile

USB Sports Complex

Stony Brook, NY 11794-3500

Phone: (631) 632-6868

Type: Public, 4 Yr., Liberal Arts, Coed
Website: http://www.sunysb.edu
SAT/ACT/GPA: For athletes 80 avg/900
Student/Faculty Ratio: 20:1
Undergraduate Enrollment: 12,500
Scholarships/Academic: Yes   **Athletic:** Yes
Expenses By: Year   **In State:** $ 12,657
Degrees Conferred: BA, BS

Founded: 1959
Religion: Non-Affiliated
Housing: Yes
Male/Female: 50:50
Graduate Enrollment: 5,500
Financial Aid: Yes
Out of State: $ 17,575

Programs of Study: Biological Science, Communications and the Arts, Computer & Physical Science, Education, Engineering & Environmental Design, Exercise Science, Health Profession, Physical Therapy, Social Science

Women's Athletic Profile

USB Sports Complex
Stony Brook, NY 11794
Coach: Theresa Tiso
Email: ttiso@notes.cc.sunysb.edu

NCAA I
Lady Seawolves, Scarlet, Grey
Phone: (516) 632-7214
Fax: (516) 632-7122

Estimated # of Women's Volleyball Scholarships: 4
Conference: Independent
Program Profile: First year in Division I. We play in 1,400-seats sport arena. We have full fall and spring programs. We have a year-round training program.
History: Stony Brook was a Division III program from 1978-1994; a Division II program in 1994-1998. This is our first season at the Division I level. The program made 5 straight NCAA Tournament Appearances from 1990-1994. The program won the New England Collegiate Conference Title in 1998. In 1992, Stony Brook placed 3rd in the nation in Division II.
Achievements: Stasia Nikas was named All-American in 1991 &1992. She was named Player of the Year in 1992. Hanna Kuhner was named All-Americans in 1992. Linda Wertz-Millman was named Academic All-American.
Coaching: Theresa Tiso, Head Coach, is entering her eighth season with the program. She compiled a record of 515-212 and ranks fifth all-time amongst Division II volleyball coaches.
Freshman Receiving Financial Aid/Academic: **Athletic:** 4
Roster In State: 11   **Out of State:** 1   **Out of Country:** 0
Sophomores on Team: 3   **Seniors on Team:** 3   **Graduation %:** 100
Most Recent Record: 33-8-0   **Fall Games:** 41   **Spring Games:** 4
Camp of Clinic Dates: 6/26-30; 7/5-8, 2000
Positions Needed: 4
Schedule: St. John's, Hofstra, West Virginia, Southwest Missouri State, Princeton, Delaware
Style of Play: We are a scrappy, hard working team. Excellent setting and outside attack. Play tough defense led by three seniors. Almaris Miranda and Sarah Boecckell and Jessica Serrano.

State University of New York Maritime College
Academic Profile

Fort Schuyler
Bronx, NY 10465

Phone: 718-409-7220

Type: Public, 4 Yr., Engineering, Coed
Website: Not Available

Founded: 1874
Religion: Non-Affiliated

SAT/ACT/GPA: 990+
Student/Faculty Ratio: 15:1
Undergraduate Enrollment: 725
Scholarships/Academic: Yes   **Athletic:** No
Expenses By: Year   **In State:** $ 11,000
Degrees Conferred: BS, MS

Housing: No
Male/Female: 90:10
Graduate Enrollment: 190
Financial Aid: Yes
Out of State: $ 11,000

Programs of Study: Afro-American Studies, Anthropology, Architecture, Asian Studies, BioChemistry, Biology, Business Administration, Chemical Engineering, Chemistry, Civil Engineering, Classics, Communications, Computer Science, Creative Writing, Dance, Earth Science, Economics, Education, Electrical Engineering, English, French, Geography, Geology, German, Management, Marine Science, Mathematics, Music, Nursing, Philosophy, Physics, Political Science, PreDentistry, PreLaw, PreMed, Psychology, Social Science, Spanish, Speech, Speech Pathology, Visual & Performing Arts

Women's Athletic Profile

6 Pennyfield Ave.
Bronx, NY 10465
Coach: Meredith Johansson
Email:

NCAA I
Orangemen, Orange, Blue
Phone: (212) 409-7331
Fax:

Estimated # of Women's Volleyball Scholarships: N/A
Conference: Big East Conference

Syracuse University
Academic Profile

Manley Fieldhouse
Syracuse, NY 13244-5020

Phone: (315) 443-5859

Type: Private, 4 Yr., Liberal Arts, Engineering, Coed
Website: http://www.sur/edu
SAT/ACT/GPA: Depends on applicant
Student/Faculty Ratio: 11:1
Undergraduate Enrollment: 10,400
Scholarships/Academic: Yes   **Athletic:** Yes
Expenses By: Year   **In State:** $ 19,360

Founded: 1870
Religion: Non-Affiliated
Housing: Yes
Male/Female: 49:51
Graduate Enrollment: 4,200
Financial Aid: Yes
Out of State:

Specializes In: Liberal Arts, Communications, Education, Engineering, etc.
Degrees Conferred: BA, BS, BFA, BArch, MA, MS, MBA, MFA, Ph.D., JD, EdD
Programs of Study: Architecture, Arts and Sciences, Education, Engineering and Computer Science, Human Development, Information Studies, Management, Public Communications, Nursing, Social Work, Visual and Performing Arts, 200+ Majors

Women's Athletic Profile

Manley Field House
Syracuse, NY 13244
Coach: Jing Pu
Email: jpu@syr.edu

NCAA I
Orangewomen, Orange, Navy
Phone: (315) 443-4149
Fax: (315) 443-2076

Estimated # of Women's Volleyball Scholarships: 3
Conference: Big East Conference
Program Profile: Our home court is called Manley Fieldhouse with a seating capacity of 9,500 and women's building has 7,500.
Achievements: Keri Potts was 1998 GTE Academic All-American 1st team.
Coaching: Jing Pu is our Head Coach. Alexis Dankulic is our Assistant Coach.
Freshman Receiving Financial Aid/Academic: **Athletic:** 2
Roster In State: 3   **Out of State:** 8   **Out of Country:** 1
Most Recent Record: 19-12-0   **Fall Games:** 34   **Spring Games:** 4 Dates
Positions Needed: Hitters
Schedule: Pepperdine, Arkansas, Michigan, Kansas State, San Diego State, Weber State

University at Albany
Academic Profile

1400 Washington Avenue
Albay, NY 12222

Phone: (518) 442-4391

Type: Public, 4 Yr., Liberal Arts, Coed

Founded: 1896

Website: http://www.Albany.edu
SAT/ACT/GPA: 1000/80 or above
Student/Faculty Ratio: 17:1
Undergraduate Enrollment: 10,000
Scholarships/Academic: Yes   **Athletic:** Yes
Expenses By: Year   **In State:** $ 10,681
Specializes In: Business, Criminal Justice, Education
Degrees Conferred: BA, BS, MA, MS, MEd, Ph.D.

Religion: Non-Affiliated
Housing: Yes
Male/Female: 52:48
Graduate Enrollment: N/A
Financial Aid: Yes
Out of State: $ 15,581

Programs of Study: Accounting, Afro-American Studies, Ancient Civilization, Anthropology, Archaeology, Biochemistry, Biology, Business Administration, Caribbean Studies, Chemistry, Chinese, Communications, Computer Science, Criminal Justice, Economics, Education, English, Fine Arts, French, Geography, Geology, German, Greek, History, Human Biology, Music, Philosophy, Physics, Political Science, PreDentistry, PreLaw, PreMed, Psychology, Religion, Russian, Social Science, Spanish

Women's Athletic Profile

1440 Washington Avenue
Albany, NY 12222
Coach: Curtis Strife
Email:

NCAA I
Lady Great Danes, Purple, Gold
Phone: (518) 442-3263
Fax: (518) 442-3031

Estimated # of Women's Volleyball Scholarships: 4
Conference: New England Collegiate Conference
Program Profile: We will be a strong program. We have three courts with a seating capacity of 3,000 people.
History: A new NCAA Division I program for the 1999/2000 year. Volleyball program has been in existence more than 20 years.
Coaching: Curtis Strife, Head Coach, started in February 1999. This is his first year as a head coach. Lisa Griener and Jeff Pole are the Assistant Coaches.
Freshman Receiving Financial Aid/Academic: **Athletic:** 0
Roster In State: 14   **Out of State:** 1   **Out of Country:** 0
Sophomores on Team: 3   **Seniors on Team:** 6   **Graduation %:** 100
Most Recent Record: 18-14-0 **Fall Games:** 25   **Spring Games:** 4
Positions Needed: Middle Hitter, Outside Hitters, Setters
Schedule: Colgate, Holy Cross, Siena, Dartmouth, Stony Brook, University of Pennsylvania
Style of Play: Upbeat with an emphasis on passing and defense. We believe a strong defense cracks an unbeatable offense.

University of Rochester
Academic Profile

Alumni Gym
Rochester, NY 14627
Type: Private, 4 Yr., Liberal Arts, Engineering, Coed
Website: http://www.rochester.edu
SAT/ACT/GPA: 1190
Student/Faculty Ratio: 9:1
Undergraduate Enrollment: 3,000
Scholarships/Academic: Yes   **Athletic:** No
Expenses By: Year   **In State:** $ 30,000
Degrees Conferred: BA, BS, MA, MS, Ph.D., EdD

Phone: 888-822-2256

Founded: 1850
Religion: Non-Affiliated
Housing: Yes
Male/Female: 50:50
Graduate Enrollment: 3,000
Financial Aid: Yes
Out of State: $ 30,000

Programs of Study: Anthropology, Applied Mathematics, Art, Astronomy, BioChemistry, Biology, Chemistry, Classic, Computer Science, Earth Science, Economics, Engineering, English, Environmental Science, French, Geology, German, Health Science, History, Mathematics, Music, Natural Science, Nursing, Philosophy, Physics, Political Science, Psychology, Religion, Science, Spanish

Women's Athletic Profile

Alumni Gym
Rochester, NY 14627
Coach: Dawn Kelly
Email: dkelly@sports.rochester.edu

NCAA I
Yellow Jackets, Blue, Yellow
Phone: (716) 275-9461
Fax: (716) 461-5081

Estimated # of Women's Volleyball Scholarships: N/A
Conference: University Athletic Association

Utica College - Syracuse University
Academic Profile

1600 Burrstone Road
Utica, NY 13502

Phone: 800-782-8884

Type: Private, 4 Yr., Liberal Arts, Coed
Website: http://www.utica.edu
SAT/ACT/GPA: Not required
Student/Faculty Ratio: 10:1
Undergraduate Enrollment: 2,300
Scholarships/Academic: Yes   **Athletic:** No
Expenses By: Year   **In State:** $ 15,414
Specializes In: Physical Therapy & Occupational Therapy
Degrees Conferred: BA, BS

Founded: 1947
Religion: Non-Affiliated
Housing: Yes
Male/Female: 40:60
Graduate Enrollment: N/A
Financial Aid: Yes
Out of State: $ 15,414

Programs of Study: Liberal Arts, specialize in Occupational Therapy, Physical Therapy & Therapeutic Recreation

Women's Athletic Profile

1600 Burrstone Rd.
Utica, NY 13502
Coach: Darin Lynch
Email: athletic@utica.ucso.edu

NCAA I
Lady Pioneers, Navy, Orange
Phone: (315) 792-3791
Fax: (315) 792-3211

Estimated # of Women's Volleyball Scholarships: N/A
Conference: Empire 8 Conference
Program Profile: 6 year program, Clark athletic center. Gymnasium, Basketball court, stadium size 2,200.
History: 6 year program, varsity 1994
Roster In State: 11
Seniors on Team: 2
Most Recent Record: 11-14
Positions Needed: Outside and Middle hitters
Schedule: Nazareth, Ithaca, RIT, Elmira, and Alfred Univ.

Union College - New York
Academic Profile

Alumni Gym
Schenectady, NY 12308

Phone: 888-843-6688

Type: Private, 4 Yr., Liberal Arts, Engineering, Coed
Website: http://www.union.edu
SAT/ACT/GPA: 1260/3.3
Student/Faculty Ratio: 11:1
Undergraduate Enrollment: 2,000
Scholarships/Academic: Yes   **Athletic:** No
Expenses By: Year   **In State:** $ 30,000

Founded: 1795
Religion: Non-Affiliated
Housing: No
Male/Female: 1:1
Graduate Enrollment: 100
Financial Aid: Yes
Out of State: $ 30,000

Programs of Study: Anthropology, Art History, BioChemistry, Biological Science, Chemistry, Engineering, Computer Science, Dance, Economics, English, Environmental Studies, Geology, History, Mathematics, Music, Philosophy, Political Science, Psychology, Sociology, Fine Arts, Theatre

Women's Athletic Profile

Alumni Gym
Schenectady, NY 12308
Coach: Leslie Bogucki
Email:

NCAA I
Dutchwomen, Garnet, Grey
Phone: (518) 388-6284
Fax: (518) 388-6514

Estimated # of Women's Volleyball Scholarships: N/A
Conference: Upstate Collegiate Athletic Association
Program Profile: Our season is from end of August through first week in November. We play our games in Memorial Fieldhouse.
History: Our program began in 1975.
Achievements: UCAA Coaching Staff of the Year in 1997.

Coaching: Leslie Bogucki, Head Coach, started with the program in 1992 as an assistant coach. He took over in 1993 with an over-all record of 106-87 since 1993. We've been to the NYS Division III Championships twice finishing 50th higher. Linda Beualander is the Assistant Coach.

Roster In State: 10   **Out of State:** 0   **Out of Country:** 0
Sophomores on Team: 0   **Seniors on Team:** 2   **Graduation %:** 100
Most Recent Record: 20-14-0   **Fall Games:** 30   **Spring Games:** 0
Camp of Clinic Dates: August 9-15
Positions Needed: Middle Hitter, Outside Hitter, Setter
Schedule: Elmira, Vassar, Middlebury, SUNY-Oswego, SUNY-Oneonta
Style of Play: Aggressive, runs a quick offense with ambitions, solid blocking and middle blocker defense.

United States Merchant Marine Academy
Academic Profile

O'Harra Hall
Kings Point, NY 11024

Phone: 800-732-6267

Type: Public, 4 Yr., Engineering, Coed   **Founded:** 1943
Website: http://www.usmma.edu   **Religion:** Non-Affiliated
SAT/ACT/GPA: 1050/21   **Housing:** Yes
Student/Faculty Ratio: 12:1   **Male/Female:** 9:1
Undergraduate Enrollment: 950   **Graduate Enrollment:** N/A
Scholarships/Academic: No   **Athletic:** No   **Financial Aid:** No
Expenses By: Year   **In State:** $ Free   **Out of State:** $ Free
Programs of Study: Engineering and Business. One of five federal service academics. Students can major in Engineering or Business and may enter any branch of the services as an active duty officer or serve in the naval reserve (2 weeks a year).

Men's Athletic Profile

Steamboat Rd.
Kings Point, NY 11024
Coach: Jeff Lipton
Email:

NCAA III
Mariners/Royal Blue, Grey
Phone: (516) 773-5324
Fax: (516) 773-5469

Estimated # of Men's Volleyball Scholarships: N/A
Conference: Eastern College Athletic Conference

Women's Athletic Profile

O'Hara Hall, Steaboat Rd
Kings Point, NY 11024
Coach: Jamie Strotmeyer
Email: strotmeyerj@usmma.edu

NCAA I
Lady Mariners, Blue, Grey
Phone: (516) 773 - 5394
Fax: (516) 773-5469

Estimated # of Women's Volleyball Scholarships: N/A
Conference: Skyline Conference

United States Military Academy
Academic Profile

ODIA, Building #639
West Point, NY 10996

Phone: (914) 938-6528

Type: Public, 4 Yr., Liberal Arts, Engineering, Coed   **Founded:** 1802
Website: http://www.usma.edu   **Religion:** Non-Affiliated
SAT/ACT/GPA: 1200/Top 10%   **Housing:** Yes
Student/Faculty Ratio: 10:1   **Male/Female:** 4:1
Undergraduate Enrollment: 4,000   **Graduate Enrollment:** N/A
Scholarships/Academic: Yes   **Athletic:** No   **Financial Aid:** Yes
Expenses By: Year   **In State:** $ Free   **Out of State:** $ Free
Specializes In: Military Academy-Engineering, Science, Computer Science
Degrees Conferred: BS
Programs of Study: Behavioral Science, Engineering, Foreign Languages, General Management, Letter/Literature, Life Sciences, Mathematical Science, Military Science, Physical Science, Social Science

Women's Athletic Profile

ODIA Bldg. 639
West Point, NY 10996
Coach: Lynn Fielitz
Email: pl9669@exmail.usma.edu

NCAA I
Cadets, Black, Gold, Grey
Phone: (914) 938-6525
Fax: (914) 938-6524

Estimated # of Women's Volleyball Scholarships: 4
Conference: The Patriot League
Program Profile: We compete at Chryist Arena. We play competitive in the fall and in the spring season. We are now playing in our main arena with an expanded emphasis on our program to again claim the Patriot League Championship.
History: We started in 1977. We were 3 times Patriot League Champions.
Our 1998 record was 20-15.
Achievements: Rookie of the Year the last 2 years; Coach of the Year
Coaching: Lynn Fielitz, is in her 4th year as Head Coach. Her 1998 record is 20-15. She was named Coach of the Year. Payton Fleischer has been Assistant Coach 2 years. He had an outstanding playing career at Virginia Commonwealth University.

Freshman Receiving Financial Aid/Academic:
Athletic: 4

Roster In State: 12	**Out of State:** 0	**Out of Country:** 0
Sophomores on Team: 4	**Seniors on Team:** 1	**Graduation %:** 100
Most Recent Record: 20-15-0	**Fall Games:** 20	**Spring Games:** 5

Camp of Clinic Dates: July 26-31, 1999
Positions Needed: Setter, Middle Blocker
Schedule: Navy, Air-Force, Western Michigan, Buckwell, Lehigh, Colgate
Style of Play: Tenacious defense with 100% effort every play; constant and never-ending improvement. We are aggressive with emphasis on defense.

Vassar College
Academic Profile

124 Raymond Ave
Poughkeepsie, NY 12604

Phone: (845)437-7450

Type: Private, 4 Yr., Liberal Arts, Coed
Website: http://www.vassar.edu
SAT/ACT/GPA: 1200283.5
Student/Faculty Ratio: 11:1
Undergraduate Enrollment: 2,400
Scholarships/Academic: No
Expenses By: Year
Specializes In: Liberal Arts
Degrees Conferred: BA, BS

Founded: 1861
Religion: Non-Affiliated
Housing: Yes
Male/Female: 40:60
Graduate Enrollment: N/A

Athletic: No
Financial Aid: Need Based
In State: $ 30,000
Out of State: $ 30,000

Programs of Study: African Studies, American Studies, Anthropology, Art Education, Asian Studies, BioChemistry, Biology, Chemistry, Computer Science, Dramatic Arts, Economics, Elementary Education, Engineering, English, Film Arts, Fine Arts, Foreign Language, Geography, Geology, International Studies, Mathematics, Music, Philosophy, Physics, Political Science, PreLaw, PreMed, PsychoBiology, Psychology

Men's Athletic Profile

124 Raymond Avenue
Poughkeepsie, NY 12601
Coach: Jonathan Penn
Email:

NCAA III
Brewers/Gray, Burgundy
Phone: (914) 437-7458
Fax: (914) 437-7562

Estimated # of Men's Volleyball Scholarships: 0
Conference: Eastern College Athletic Conference
Coaching: Jonathan Penn, Head Coach, started coaching with the program in 1997 with a record of 17-24. Antonia Sweet, Assistant Coach, is entering her first year.

Freshman Receiving Financial Aid/Academic: 0
Athletic: 2

Roster In State: 4	**Out of State:** 7	**Out of Country:** 1
Sophomores on Team:	**Seniors on Team:** 2	**Graduation %:** 100%
Most Recent Record: 8-16-2	**Fall Games:** 0	**Spring Games:** 20

Positions Needed: Outsides, Hitters

Schedule: Juniata, Springfield, New York University, University of California-San Diego
Style of Play: Based on quickness and ball control, depending on general athleticism.

Women's Athletic Profile

Box 259, 124 Raymond Avenue
Poughkeepsie, NY 12604
Coach: Jonathan Penn
Email: jopenn@vassar.edu

NCAA I
Lady Brewers, Grey, Burgundy
Phone: (914) 437-7458
Fax: (914) 437-7033

Estimated # of Women's Volleyball Scholarships: 0
Conference: Great Lakes Volleyball Athletic, East college Athletic Conference
Coaching: Jonathan Penn, Head Coach, compiled an overall record of 39-48 since 1996. Antonia Sweet, Assistant Coach, compiled a record of 13-16 since 1998.
Freshman Receiving Financial Aid/Academic: **Athletic:** 2
Roster In State: 4   **Out of State:** 7   **Out of Country:** 1
Sophomores on Team: 0   **Seniors on Team:** 2   **Graduation %:** 100
Most Recent Record: 8-12-0   **Fall Games:** 0   **Spring Games:** 20
Positions Needed: Swing Hitter, Middle Hitter
Schedule: Juniata, Springfield, New York University, University of California-San Diego
Style of Play: We are quick and ball control, depending on general athleticism.

Wagner College
Academic Profile

631 Howard Avenue
Staten Island, NY 10301

Phone: 718-390-3411

Type: Private, 4 Yr., Liberal Arts, Coed
Website: http://www.wagner.edu
SAT/ACT/GPA: 1000/18/3.0
Student/Faculty Ratio: 12:1
Undergraduate Enrollment: 1,800
Scholarships/Academic: Yes   **Athletic:** Yes
Expenses By: Year   **In State:** $ 24,000

Founded: 1883
Religion: Lutheran
Housing: No
Male/Female: 50:50
Graduate Enrollment: 400
Financial Aid: Yes
Out of State: $ 24,000

Specializes In: Liberal Arts
Programs of Study: Accounting, Anthropology, Arts Administration, Banking/Finance, Biology, Business Administration, Chemistry, Computer Science, Criminal Justice, Education, English, Mathematics, Music, Physics, Physician's Assistant, Psychology, Theatre

Women's Athletic Profile

631 Howard Avenue
Staten Island, NY 10301-4495
Coach: Lauris Murnieks
Email: Larman65@aol.com

NCAA I
Lady Seahawks, Green, White
Phone: (718) 390-3199
Fax: (718) 390-3347

Estimated # of Women's Volleyball Scholarships: N/A
Conference: Northeast Conference
Program Profile: 2001 will be our tenth season as we continue to rebuild our program after a large graduating class in 1999, 2000 was beginning of the rebuilding with only two seniors on team. Playing season is in the fall, with preseason starting in Mid-August. We have a new 11 million dollar facility with a parquet floor (like the Boston Garden). The Spiro Sports Center holds 3, 500 fans.
History: The volleyball program began in 1992 at the Division I level. Started the program without any scholarship players. In 1994 we start awarding partial scholarships based highly on academics and in 1997 we won the conference championship.
Achievements: 1997 Northeast Conference Champions. Four Rookie of the Year performers. Six First Team All-NEC performers. Two Second Team All-NEC performers. 1997 Coach of the Year honors.
Coaching: Head Coach Lauris Murnieks has been the only coach in the programs history. He will begin his tenth season. He graduated from Wagner College in 1988 and in 1991 received his masters degree. He has been part of Wagner athletics since 1983 both as a student-athlete and coach.
Roster In State: 5   **Out of State:** 8   **Out of Country:** 0
Sophomores on Team: **Seniors on Team:** 2   **Graduation %:** 100
Most Recent Record: 4-27-0
Positions Needed: Middle Hitter, Setter
Schedule: West Virginia, Akron, Boston College, Cornell, St. Peter's
Style of Play: We really stress defense, using multiple defensive sets, with different blocking schemes, while running a quick attack using every possible attacker available, including Back Row.

NORTH CAROLINA

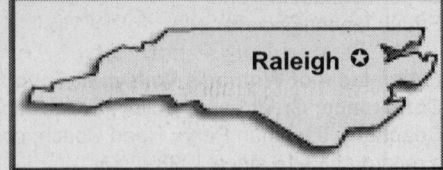

Raleigh ✪

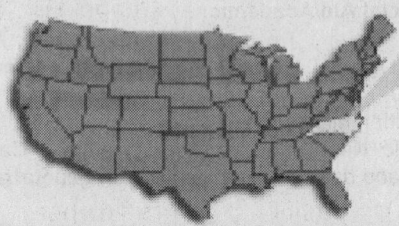

SCHOOL	CITY	AFFILIATION	PAGE
Appalachian State University	Boone	NCAA I	535
Barber - Scotia College	Concord	NAIA	535
Barton College	Wilson	NCAA II	536
Bennett College	Greensboro	NCAA III	536
Campbell University	Buies Creek	NCAA I	537
Catawba College	Salisbury	NCAA II	538
Chowan College	Murfreesboro	NCAA III	538
Davidson College	Davidson	NCAA I	539
Duke University	Durham	NCAA III	539
East Carolina University	Greenville	NCAA I	540
Elizabeth City State University	Elizabeth City	NCAA II	541
Elon College	Elon College	NCAA I	541
Fayetteville State University	Fayetteville	NCAA II	542
Gardner - Webb University	Boling Springs	NCAA II	542
Greensboro College	Greensboro	NCAA III	543
Guilford College	Greensboro	NCAA III	543
High Point University	High Point	NCAA II	544
Johnson C. Smith University	Charlotte	NCAA II	545
Lees - McRae College	Banner Elk	NCAA II	545
Lenoir - Rhyne College	Hickory	NCAA II	546
Livingstone College	Salisbury	NCAA II	546
Mars Hill College	Mars Hill	NCAA II	547
Meredith College	Raleigh	NCAA III	547
Methodist College	Fayetteville	NCAA III	548
Montreat College	Montreat	NAIA	549
Mount Olive College	Mount Olive	NCAA II	549
North Carolina A&T State Univ	Greensboro	NCAA I	550
North Carolina Central University	Durham	NCAA II	550

SCHOOL	CITY	AFFILIATION	PAGE
North Carolina State University	Raleigh	NCAA I	551
North Carolina Wesleyan College	Rocky Mount	NCAA III	551
Peace College	Raleigh	NCAA III	552
Pfeiffer University	Misenheimer	NCAA II	552
Queens College - North Carolina	Charlotte	NCAA II	553
St. Andrews Presbyterian College	Laurinburg	NCAA II	553
Saint Augustine's College	Raleigh	NCAA II	554
Shaw University	Raleigh	NCAA II	554
Univ of North Carolina - Asheville	Asheville	NCAA I	555
Univ of North Carolina	Chapel Hill	NCAA I	555
Univ of North Carolina - Charlotte	Charlotte	NCAA I	556
Univ of North Carolina-Greensboro	Greensboro	NCAA I	557
Univ of North Carolina - Pembroke	Pembroke	NCAA II	557
Univ of North Carolina-Wilmington	Wilmington	NCAA I	558
Wake Forest University	Winston-Salem	NCAA I	559
Western Carolina University	Culluwhee	NCAA I	559
Wingate University	Wingate	NCAA II	559
Winston - Salem State University	Winston - Salem	NCAA II	560

Appalachian State University
Academic Profile

Broome-Kirk Gym
Boone, NC 28608

Phone: (828) 262-2000

Type: Public, 4 Yr., Liberal Arts,Coed
Website: http://www.AppState.edu
SAT/ACT/GPA: 1100/25/3.5
Student/Faculty Ratio: 16:1
Undergraduate Enrollment: 11,300
Scholarships/Academic: Yes
Expenses By: Year
Specializes In: Comprehensive- 5 Colleges
Degrees Conferred: BA, BS, MA, M.Ed., Education Specialist, Doctoral

Founded: 1899
Religion: Non-Affiliated
Housing: Yes
Male/Female: 49:51
Graduate Enrollment: 1,000
Athletic: Yes   **Financial Aid:** Yes
In State: $ 5,313   **Out of State:** $ 12,583

Programs of Study: Over 170 majors to choose from in all areas of study including Arts and Science, Business and Management, Education, Fine and Applied Arts, Music, Natural Sciences, Parks/Recreation, Protective Services, Public Affairs, Psychology, Social Sciences, and over 300 majors

Women's Athletic Profile

Broome-Kirk Gym
Boone, NC 28608
Coach: Chris Redding
Email: Reddingcf@appstate.edu

NCAA I
Lady Mountaineers, Black, Gold
Phone: (828) 262-2000
Fax: (828) 262-6106

Estimated # of Women's Volleyball Scholarships: 4
Conference: Southern Conference
Program Profile: The Convocation Center which will have 8,000 seats, will open in August, 2000. We are annually strong in the Southern Conference. We play a regionally competitive schedule. We are playing in the Varsity Gym currently.
History: We have won 6 Southern Conference regular season Championships. We have won 4 Southern Conference Tournaments and made 2 NCAA Appearances. We have 1 Conference Player of the Year, 3 Conference Tournament MVP's, 24 All-Southern Conference Teams and 23 Southern Conference All-Tournament Teams.
Achievements: First year for the program.
Coaching: Chris Redding, is in his first year as Head Coach. He has coached at University of Florida, University of North Florida, University of the Pacific and Cal State at Bakersfield. No assistant coach is listed.

Roster In State: 5	**Out of State:** 6	**Out of Country:** 0
Sophomores on Team: 3	**Seniors on Team:** 3	**Graduation %:** Unknown
Most Recent Record:	**Fall Games:** 26	**Spring Games:** 4

Camp of Clinic Dates: Team Camp: June 27-30; Individual Camp July 18-21
Positions Needed: Setter, Middle Blocker, Outside Hitter
Schedule: North Carolina-Chapel Hill, South Carolina, Furman, Davidson, Tennessee-Chattanooga, Western Carolina
Style of Play: The style will change due to each coach. The offensive system will be fast and complex. With the offensive pace quickening, the team's defensive aggressiveness will increase.

Barber - Scotia College
Academic Profile

145 Cabarrus Avenue
Concord, NC 28025

Phone: 800-610-0778

Type: Private, 4 Yr., Liberal Arts, Coed
Website: http://www.barber-scotia.edu
SAT/ACT/GPA: 700+
Student/Faculty Ratio: 12:1
Undergraduate Enrollment: 600
Scholarships/Academic: Yes
Expenses By: Year
Degrees Conferred: BA, BS

Founded: 1867
Religion: Presbyterian
Housing: No
Male/Female: 42:58
Graduate Enrollment: N/A
Athletic: Yes   **Financial Aid:** Yes
In State: $ 8,512   **Out of State:** $ 8,512

Programs of Study: Administration of Justice, Anthropology, Biology, Business Administration, Communications, Journalism, Education, English, Mathematics, Medical Technology, Political Science, Recreation Administration, Sociology

Women's Athletic Profile

145 Cabarrus Avenue
Concord, NC 28025
Coach: Tolondo Rose
Email:

NCAA I
Lady Sabers, Royal Blue, Grey
Phone: (704) 789-2960
Fax: (704) 793-4945

Did Not Return Profile

Barton College
Academic Profile

College Station
Wilson, NC 27893

Phone: (252) 399-6552

Type: Private, 4 Yr., Liberal Arts, Coed
Website: http://www.barton.edu
SAT/ACT/GPA: 820/17/2.0
Student/Faculty Ratio: 20:1
Undergraduate Enrollment: 1,500
Scholarships/Academic: Yes   **Athletic:** Yes
Expenses By: Year   **In State:** $ 14,726
Specializes In: Liberal Arts
Degrees Conferred: BA, BS, BFA, BLS

Founded: 1902
Religion: Disciples of Christ
Housing: Yes
Male/Female: 1:2
Graduate Enrollment: N/A
Financial Aid: Yes
Out of State: $ 14,726

Programs of Study: Accounting, Art, Art Education, Biology, Business Administration, Chemistry, Computer Information Systems, Communications, Criminal Justice, Economics, Education, English, Environmental Science, French, Hispanic Studies, History, Management of Human Resources, Music, Nursing, Psychology, Religion, Sports Management, Studio Art, Writing, Sports Medicine

Women's Athletic Profile

Campus Box 5000
Wilson, NC 27893-7000
Coach: Wendee Saintsing
Email:

NCAA I
Lady Bulldogs, Blue, White
Phone: (252) 399-6514
Fax: (252) 399-6516

Estimated # of Women's Volleyball Scholarships: 3
Conference: Carolinas - Virginia Athletic Conference
Program Profile: We play 25 games, including tournaments. We play at Wilson Gym which has a capacity of 1500. We have two side courts and a main court. Our season extends from August to November.
Achievements: Coach of the Year 1993-94.
Coaching: Wendee Saintsing, Head Coach, started here in 1987. Her overall record is 187-142.
Freshman Receiving Financial Aid/Academic: **Athletic:** 100%
Roster In State: 4   **Out of State:** 6   **Out of Country:** 1
Sophomores on Team: 0   **Seniors on Team:** 2   **Graduation %:** 100
Most Recent Record: 16-12-0   **Fall Games:** 28   **Spring Games:** 0
Camp of Clinic Dates: July 26-30
Positions Needed: Middle Hitter, Outside Hitter, Outside Setter
Schedule: Lees McRae, Queens College
Style of Play: Variation of hits using-quick, slides, crosses back row; aggressive blocking and aggressive defense.

Bennett College
Academic Profile

900 East Washington Street
Greensboro, NC 27401-3239

Phone: 336-370-8624

Type: Private, 4 Yr., Liberal Arts, Women Only
Website: http://www.bennett.edu
SAT/ACT/GPA: 950+
Student/Faculty Ratio: 10:1
Undergraduate Enrollment: 568
Scholarships/Academic: Yes   **Athletic:** No

Founded: 1873
Religion: Methodist
Housing: No
Male/Female: Women Only
Graduate Enrollment: N/A
Financial Aid: Yes

Expenses By: Year   **In State:** $ 10,100   **Out of State:** $ 10,100
Degrees Conferred: AA, BA, BS
Programs of Study: Contact school for programs of study.

Women's Athletic Profile

900 E. Washington Street   NCAA I
Greensboro, NC 27401   Bennett Belles, Blue, White
Coach: Joyce Spruill   **Phone:** (336)370-8655
Email: **Fax:**

Did Not Return Profile

Campbell University
Academic Profile

P. O. Box 10   **Phone:** (910) 893-1333
Buies Creek, NC 27506

Type: Private, 4 Yr., Liberal Arts, Coed   **Founded:** 1887
Website: http://www.campbell.edu   **Religion:** Southern Baptist
SAT/ACT/GPA: 850/17/2.5   **Housing:** Yes
Student/Faculty Ratio: 18:1   **Male/Female:** 1:2
Undergraduate Enrollment: 2,100   **Graduate Enrollment:** 900
Scholarships/Academic: Yes   **Athletic:** Yes   **Financial Aid:** Yes
Expenses By: Year   **In State:** $ 14,500 **Out of State:** $ 14,500
Specializes In: Business, Education, Law, Pharmacy
Degrees Conferred: BA, BS, MSC, MBA, Pharmacy, Law, Education
Programs of Study: Accounting, Applied Science, Art, Biology, Business Administration, Chemistry, Computer Information Systems, Drama, Economics, Elementary Education, English, Journalism, Mass Communications, Mathematics, Music, Philosophy, Physical Education, PreLaw, PreMedicine, Psychology, Religion, Social Science, Sports Management

Women's Athletic Profile

P.O. Box 10   NCAA I
Buies Creek, NC 27506   Fighting Camels, Black, Orange
Coach: T.J. Meagher   **Phone:** (910) 893-1343
Email: meagher@mailcenter.campbell.edu   **Fax:** (910) 893-1330

Estimated # of Women's Volleyball Scholarships: 7
Conference: Trans America Athletic Conference
Program Profile: We play in Carter Gym which has a seating capacity of 945.
History: Our program was started in 1985 (152-277) . We recorded 4 winning seasons. The last two years have been the most successful seasons in history with a record of 32-7 and currently 23-7. We were a member of the Big South Conference until 1994 when we joined the Trans American Athletic Conference.
Achievements: Big South Coach of the Year in 1989; 3 players named All-TAAC in 1997, 1 player named All-TAAC in 1995, and 1 player named All-TAAC in 1996; 12 players named TAAC All-Academic; 1 player named All-Big South in 1986, 1 player named in 1987, 1 player named in 1989, 1 player named in 1990, 1 in 1993; 1 player named 1985 NAIA All-District 26.
Coaching: T.J. Meagher, Head Coach, is entering his first year with the program. He compiled a record of 23-7 for Kentucky's Club Team in 1991 that finished in the top 25. Kristine Rogers, Assistant Coach, is entering her first year with the program, she was named three-time All-TAAC. She ranked nationally in digs and got TAAC All-Academic.
Freshman Receiving Financial Aid/Academic: **Athletic:** 3
Roster In State: 2   **Out of State:** 9   **Out of Country:** 0
Sophomores on Team: 0   **Seniors on Team:** 4   **Graduation %:** Unknown
Most Recent Record: 23-7-0   **Fall Games:** 30   **Spring Games:** 6
Camp of Clinic Dates: July 4-9, 1999
Positions Needed: Middle Blockers, Outside Hitters
Schedule: Georgia State, NC State, Central Florida, Florida Atlantic, Liberty, Jacksonville
Style of Play: Solid fundamental training and positive motivation define Coach Meagher's philosophy. Our coach teaches players to use athleticism to have fun playing the game.

Catawba College
Academic Profile

2300 West Innes Street
Salisbury, NC 28144

Phone: 800-228-2922

Type: Private, 4 Yr., Liberal Arts, Coed
Website: http://www.catawba.edu
SAT/ACT/GPA: 800 min/2.8
Student/Faculty Ratio: 15:1
Undergraduate Enrollment: 1,200
Scholarships/Academic: Yes   **Athletic:** Yes
Expenses By: Year   **In State:** $ 16,784
Degrees Conferred: BA, BS, M Ed

Founded: 1851
Religion: United Church of Christ
Housing: Yes
Male/Female: 50:50
Graduate Enrollment: 100
Financial Aid: Yes
Out of State: $ 16,784

Programs of Study: Accounting, Biology, Business and Management, Chemistry, Communications, Computer Science, Education, English, French, History, Law, Mathematics, Medical Technology, Philosophy, Political Science, PreProfessional, Psychology, Religion, Social Sciences, Sport Medicine

Women's Athletic Profile

2300 W. Innes Street
Salisbury, NC 28144-2488
Coach: Ginger Ashley
Email: gcashley@catawba.edu

NCAA I
Lady Indians, Navy Blue, White
Phone: (704) 637-4480
Fax: (704) 637-5705

Estimated # of Women's Volleyball Scholarships: 3
Conference: South Atlantic Conference
Program Profile: We play in Goodman Gymnasium with a seating capacity of 3,500. Our traditional season is August 15 through November 13. We have a spring non-traditional season from January through April.
History: We began in 1971. We went from NAIA to NCAA Division II in 1992. We are the winningest program at Catawba.
Achievements: Conference Tournament Champions in 1990-1991; Coach of the Year Honors in 1994 & 1998.
Coaching: Ginger Ashley, Head Coach, finished her ninth season with a record of 206-109 at the collegiate level. Her high school record was 95-14. She played at Appalachian State. Dean Miller, Assistant Coach, is entering his second year with the program. We play doubles.

Freshman Receiving Financial Aid/Academic: **Athletic:** 2
Roster In State: 10   **Out of State:** 3   **Out of Country:** 0
Sophomores on Team: 5   **Seniors on Team:** 4   **Graduation %:** 100
Most Recent Record: 21-10-0   **Fall Games:** 31   **Spring Games:** 4
Camp of Clinic Dates: S/H Clinic June 5-6, 1999; Team June 6-10, 1999
Positions Needed: 4 positions
Schedule: Tampa, Barry, Florida Southern, North Florida, Francis Marion, Florida Tech
Style of Play: Aggressive serve and defense; quick offense with lots of variety.

Chowan College
Academic Profile

200 Jones Drive
Murfreesboro, NC 27855

Phone: (252) 398-4499

Type: Private, 4 Yr., Liberal Arts, Coed
Website: http://www.chowan.edu
SAT/ACT/GPA: 900192.0
Student/Faculty Ratio: 12:1
Undergraduate Enrollment: 780
Scholarships/Academic: Yes   **Athletic:** No
Expenses By: Year   **In State:** $ 17,000

Founded: 1848
Religion: Baptist
Housing: Yes
Male/Female: 58:42
Graduate Enrollment: N/A
Financial Aid: Yes
Out of State: $17,000

Programs of Study: Art-Graphic Design, Studio Art, Biology Allied Health/Laboratory Technology, Environmental Science, General Biology, Business Administration Accounting, Computer Information Systems, Marketing, Small Business Management, General Business Administration, Communications, Criminal Justice, Drama, Elementary Education, English, Music Church Music, Conducting, Performance, Physical Education, Athletic Training, Sport Management, Sport Science, Teacher Education, Physical Science-Chemistry, Physics, PreProfessional Programs PreNursing, PreOptometry, PrePharmacy, PrePhysical Therapy, PreVet, PreMed Religion

Women's Athletic Profile

P.O. Box 1848
Murfreesboro, NC 27855
Coach: Leslie Simpson
Email:

NCAA I
Lady Braves, Blue, White
Phone: 252-398-6500
Fax: (919) 398-1390

Estimated # of Women's Volleyball Scholarships: N/A
Schedule: Peace, Lynchburg, Ferrum, Methodist, Greensboro, Guilford, Bennett, Salem, Meredith, Barton, College of Notre Dame
Style of Play: Positive team chemistry.

Davidson College
Academic Profile

P. O. Box 1750
Davidson, NC 28036

Phone: 800-768-0380

Type: Private, 4 Yr., Liberal Arts, Coed
Website: http://www.davidson.edu
SAT/ACT/GPA: 1380/28/3.8
Student/Faculty Ratio: 10.7:1
Undergraduate Enrollment: 1,600
Scholarships/Academic: Yes   **Athletic:** Yes
Expenses By: Year   **In State:** $ 28,000
Specializes In: Preprofessional Programs
Degrees Conferred: BA, BS

Founded: 1837
Religion: Presbyterian
Housing: Yes
Male/Female: 1:1
Graduate Enrollment: N/A
Financial Aid: Yes
Out of State: $ 28,000

Programs of Study: Anthropology, Art, Biology, Chemistry, Classical Studies, Economics, English, French, German, Russian, Mathematics, Music, Philosophy, Physics, Political Science, Psychology, Religion, Sociology, Spanish, Theatre

Women's Athletic Profile

P.O. Box 1750
Davidson, NC 28036
Coach: Marston
Email: limarsto@davidson.edu

NCAA I
Lady Wildcats, Red, Black
Phone: (704) 892-2633
Fax: (704) 892-2636

Estimated # of Women's Volleyball Scholarships: 1/2
Conference: Southern Conference
Program Profile: We have a stable program. Our arena has 5 volleyball courts, great training facilities, and an Olympic size pool. Our season runs from mid-August to late November or early December.
History: Our program began in 1986. We joined the Southern Conference in 1992.
Achievements: Coach Marston received Coach of the Year in 1998. She has coached 4 all-conference players. The 1998 conference standing of 2nd place was the best in school history.
Coaching: Marston, will be in her 5th year as Davidson's Head Coach. Her overall record is 54-75. She has taken the team from 7th to 2nd in the Southern Conference.
Freshman Receiving Financial Aid/Academic: **Athletic:** 4
Roster In State: 3   **Out of State:** 11   **Out of Country:** 0
Sophomores on Team: 4   **Seniors on Team:** 2   **Graduation %:** 95-100
Most Recent Record: 21-11-0   **Fall Games:** 31   **Spring Games:** 4
Camp of Clinic Dates: July 11th-14th; July 18th-21st
Positions Needed: Setter, Middle, Right side
Schedule: North Carolina State University, University of North Carolina-Charlotte, University of Tennessee-Chattanooga, Furman University, Georgia State University, Radford University
Style of Play: Modified swing offense. Quick-always great blocking team.

Duke University
Academic Profile

Box 90555
Durham, NC 27708-0555

Phone: 919-684-3214

Type: Private, 4 Yr., Liberal Arts, Coed
Website: http://www.duke.edu
SAT/ACT/GPA: 1200/28/3.5

Founded: 1838
Religion: United Methodist
Housing: Yes

Student/Faculty Ratio: 11:1

Undergraduate Enrollment: 5,800

Scholarships/Academic: Yes   **Athletic:** Yes

Expenses By: Year   **In State:** $ 31,000

Male/Female: 55:45

Graduate Enrollment: 3,000

Financial Aid: Yes

Out of State: $ 31,000

Degrees Conferred: BA, BS, MA, MS, MBA, D, MD, JD, Mdiv

Programs of Study: Engineering, Letters/Literature, Life Sciences, Psychology, Social Science, PreMed, Arts & Art History, Chemistry, Sociology, Philosophy, Economics, International Studies

Women's Athletic Profile

Box 90555

Durham, NC 27708-0555

Coach: Kristen Hall

Email: goduke.com

NCAA I

Lady Raptors, Black, White

Phone: (919) 684-2120

Fax: (919) 681-7866

Estimated # of Women's Volleyball Scholarships: N/A

Conference: HVWAC

Program Profile: We are a small Division III program and we have been successful in our Conference. We play in Stevenson Gym. We have a regional schedule.

Achievements: IAC Champions; HVWAC Champions, Conference Player of the Year; Various All-Conference.

Coaching: Kristen Hall, has been Head Coach from 1991 to the present. She has been Conference Coach of the Year four times.

Freshman Receiving Financial Aid/Academic: **Athletic:** 0

Roster In State: 3   **Out of State:** 7   **Out of Country:** 0

Sophomores on Team: 0   **Seniors on Team:** 2   **Graduation %:** 97

Most Recent Record: 18-4-0   **Fall Games:** 29   **Spring Games:** 1-2

Positions Needed: Setter, Outside Hitter

Schedule: Haverford, Vassar

Style of Play: Upbeat offensive style; quick tempo court.

East Carolina University
Academic Profile

104 Scales Fieldhouse

Greenville, NC 27858

Phone: 252-328-6640

Type: Public, 4 Yr., Coed

Website: http://www.ecu.edu

SAT/ACT/GPA: Varies

Student/Faculty Ratio: 25:1

Undergraduate Enrollment: 15,000

Scholarships/Academic: Yes   **Athletic:** Yes

Expenses By: Year   **In State:** $ 6,200

Founded: 1907

Religion: Non-Affiliated

Housing: Yes

Male/Female: 50:50

Graduate Enrollment: 2,000

Financial Aid: Yes

Out of State: $ 13,200

Specializes In: Education, Business, Exercise Science, Art

Degrees Conferred: BA, BS, BFA, BM, BSA, BSBA, BSBE, MA, MS, MBA, MFA, MEd, Ph.D.

Programs of Study: Offers 106 undergraduate and 92 graduate majors in the Schools of Allied Health Sciences, Art, Arts/Sciences, Business, Education, Health and Human Performance, Human Environ. Sciences, Industry/Technology, Music, Nursing, Social Work

Women's Athletic Profile

Scales Field House

Greenville, NC 27858-4353

Coach: Colleen Farrell

Email: farrellc@mail.ecu.edu

NCAA I

Lady Pirates, Purple, Gold

Phone: (252) 328-4612

Fax: (252) 328-4647

Estimated # of Women's Volleyball Scholarships: 11

Conference: Conference USA

Program Profile: Home Court Minges Coliseum seats 7, 500, wood surface. Season is played in the Fall

History: Began 1977. Only 6 winning season since program began. Started in CAA 1985, 2000 season 1st winning record in CAA. Joining conference USA 2001-2002 season.

Achievements: 9 All-Conference Players.

Freshman Receiving Financial Aid/Academic: **Athletic:** 3

Roster In State: 3   **Out of State:** 10   **Out of Country:** 0

Sophomores on Team: **Seniors on Team:** 4   **Graduation %:** 95
Most Recent Record: 17-13
Positions Needed: Outside, Middle
Schedule: Duke, North Carolina, North Carolina St, Wake Forrest, North Western, Georgetown, Houston, Louisville, Mississippi State.
Style of Play: We are new coaches and are establishing a quick and explosive style of play.

Elizabeth City State University
Academic Profile

1704 Weeksville Rd.   **Phone:** 800-347-3278
Elizabeth, NC 27909

Type: Public, 4 Yr., Liberal Arts, Coed   **Founded:** 1891
Website: http://www.ecsu.edu   **Religion:** Non-Affiliated
SAT/ACT/GPA: 750 avg.   **Housing:** No
Student/Faculty Ratio: 13:1   **Male/Female:** 39:61
Undergraduate Enrollment: 2,130   **Graduate Enrollment:** N/A
Scholarships/Academic: Yes   **Athletic:** Yes   **Financial Aid:** Yes
Expenses By: Year   **In State:** $ 5,150   **Out of State:** $ 10,500
Degrees Conferred: BA, BS, BSEd
Programs of Study: Contact school for program of study.

Women's Athletic Profile

1704 Weeksville Rd.   **NCAA I**
Elizabeth City, NC 27909   Lady Vikings, Royal Blue, White
Coach: Ola Goss   **Phone:** (252) 335-3387
Email: **Fax:** (252) 335-3675

Estimated # of Women's Volleyball Scholarships: N/A
Conference: Central Intercollegiate Athletic Association

Elon College
Academic Profile

2500 Campus Box   **Phone:** 336-584-2370
Elon College, NC 27244

Type: Private, 4 Yr., Liberal Arts, Coed   **Founded:** 1889
Website: http://www.elon.edu   **Religion:** United Church of Christ
SAT/ACT/GPA: 1090/3.2   **Housing:** Yes
Student/Faculty Ratio: 16:1   **Male/Female:** 45:55
Undergraduate Enrollment: 3,800   **Graduate Enrollment:** 300
Scholarships/Academic: Yes   **Athletic:** Yes   **Financial Aid:** Yes
Expenses By: Year   **In State:** $ 17,446   **Out of State:** $ 17,446
Specializes In: Liberal Arts, Career-oriented majors & graduate programs
Degrees Conferred: AB, BFA, BS, MED, MBA, MPT
Programs of Study: Accounting, Art, Biology, Business, Chemistry, Communications, Computer Science, Dance, Economics, Education, English, Sport Medicine, History, Human Services, Math, Medical Technology, Music, Physics, Religion, Social Science, Theatre, Health Education, Environmental Science, Leisure Sport Management, Journalism, Philosophy, Sociology, Political Science

Women's Athletic Profile

2500 Campus Box   **NCAA I**
Elon College, NC 27244   Fighting Christians, Maroon
Coach: Susan Leonard   **Phone:** (336) 584-2420
Email: leonard@numen.elon.edu   **Fax:** (336) 584-2686

Estimated # of Women's Volleyball Scholarships: 5
Conference: Big South Conference
Program Profile: We play in alumni gym in Koury Center, which seats 3,000. We can utilize two courts in alumni and two courts in Jordan (also in alumni gym). We have a separate athletic weight facility.
History: The program began in 1972. Until 1993, we were NAIA, from 1991-1996 we were NCAA Division II. We applied for NCAA

Division I in 1996 and we were accepted into the Big South Conference.

Achievements: We have won the conference (Division II) for four years. In 1992, we won the District and earned a berth to the National Tournament. Coach Leonard has won Coach of the Year in 1996 and East Regional Coach of the Year and District Coach of the Year in 1992.

Coaching: Sue Leonard, Head Coach, has coached the program from 1988 to the present and has compiled an overall record of 278-136. There is no assistant coach listed.

Freshman Receiving Financial Aid/Academic: | | **Athletic:** 1

Roster In State: 1 | **Out of State:** 14 | **Out of Country:** 0
Sophomores on Team: 0 | **Seniors on Team:** 3 | **Graduation %:** 99
Most Recent Record: 13-22-0 | **Fall Games:** 35 | **Spring Games:** 4
Camp of Clinic Dates: July 26-30, 1999
Positions Needed: 3-4
Schedule: Wake Forest University, Liberty University, Virginia Commonwealth, UNC-Wilmington, Radford University, Coastal Carolina
Style of Play: We play a very exciting game with a lot of enthusiasm. The offense is fairly quick and defense is aggressive.

Fayetteville State University
Academic Profile

1200 Murchison Rd.
Fayetteville, NC 2830-4298

Phone: (901) 486-1314

Type: Public, 4 Yr., Coed
Website: http://www.uncfsu.edu
SAT/ACT/GPA: 550+
Student/Faculty Ratio: 20:1
Undergraduate Enrollment: 3,943
Scholarships/Academic: Yes
Expenses By: Year
Specializes In: Education

Athletic: Yes
In State: $ 6,564

Founded: 1867
Religion: Non-Affiliated
Housing: Yes
Male/Female: 1:2
Graduate Enrollment: 775
Financial Aid: Yes
Out of State: $ 12,990

Degrees Conferred: Baccalaureate Degrees, Master Degrees, Doctoral Degree
Programs of Study: Accounting, Biology, Business Administration, Business Education, Chemistry, Computer Science, Criminal Justice, Economics, (Elementary, Middle, Secondary) Education, English Languages, Geography, Health Education, History, Marketing Education, Mathematics, Medical Technology, Music Education, Nursing, Office Administration, Physical Education, Political Science, Psychology, Sociology, Spanish, Speech and Theatre, Visual Arts

Women's Athletic Profile

1200 Murcheson Road
Fayetteville, NC 28301-4298
Coach: Elorine Hill
Email: mcrowe@chiluncfsu.edu

NCAA I
Lady Broncos, Blue, White
Phone: (910) 486-1513
Fax: (910) 486-1241

Did Not Return Profile

Gardner - Webb University
Academic Profile

P.O. Box 877, 100 S Main St.
Boiling Spring, NC 28017

Phone: 800-253-6472

Type: Private, 4 Yr., Liberal Arts, Coed
Website: http://www.gardner-webb.edu
SAT/ACT/GPA: 850/17/2.4
Student/Faculty Ratio: 16:1
Undergraduate Enrollment: 2,369
Scholarships/Academic: Yes
Expenses By: Year

Athletic: Yes
In State: $ 16,010

Founded: 1905
Religion: Baptist
Housing: Yes
Male/Female: 37:62
Graduate Enrollment: 551
Financial Aid: Yes
Out of State: $ 16,010

Degrees Conferred: BA, BS, BSN, AA in Nursing, MA, MD, MBA
Programs of Study: American Sign Languages, Communication Studies, English, French, History, Journalism, Music, Political Science, Religious Studies, Sacred Music, Social Sciences, Sociology, Spanish, Theatre, Accounting, Athletic Training, Biology, Business Administration, Chemistry, Computer Science, Mathematics, Elementary Education, Health Education, International Business, Nursing, Management, Information System, Mathematics, Medical Technology, Middle Grades, Education, Physical Education, Pschology, Sport Management, Agency Counseling, Business, Divinity, Elementary Education, English Education, Middle Grades Eduction, Physical Education, School Counseling and School Administration

Women's Athletic Profile

Main Street
Boling Springs, NC 28017
Coach: Angell Benson
Email: abenson@gardner-webb.edu

NCAA I
Bulldogs, Scarlet, White, Black
Phone: (704) 434-4736
Fax: (704) 434-4739

Conference: South Atlantic Conference
Program Profile: The team plays from August to November. They play in the Rutz-Yelton Convocation Center, which holds five thousand five hundred people. Volleyball has always been a strong sport for the University.
Roster In State: 7 | **Out of State:** 5 | **Out of Country:** 0
Sophomores on Team: 1 | **Seniors on Team:** 3 | **Graduation %:**

Greensboro College
Academic Profile

815 W Market Street
Greensboro, NC 27358

Phone: (336) 272-7102

Type: Private, 4 Yr., Liberal Arts, Coed
Website: http://www.gborocollege.edu
SAT/ACT/GPA: 800/2.0
Student/Faculty Ratio: 15:1
Undergraduate Enrollment: 1,000
Scholarships/Academic: Yes **Athletic:** No
Expenses By: Year **In State:** $ 16,500
Specializes In: Business, Education
Degrees Conferred: BA, BS

Founded: 1838
Religion: Methodist
Housing: Yes
Male/Female: 55:45
Graduate Enrollment: N/A
Financial Aid: Yes
Out of State: $ 16,500

Programs of Study: Accounting, Biological Science, Business Administration, Chemistry, Elementary Education, English, French, History, Interdisciplinary Studies, Liberal Arts, Management, Mathematics, Medical Laboratory Technology, Music, Physical Education, Political Science, PreDentistry, PreLaw, PreMed, PreVet, Psychology, Radiological Technology, Religion, Secondary Education, Spanish, Special Education, Sports Medicine, Theatre

Women's Athletic Profile

815 W. Market Street
Greensboro, NC 27401
Coach: Jean Lojko
Email: lojko@gborocollege.edu

NCAA I
Lady Pride, Green, White, Silver
Phone: (336) 272-7102
Fax: (336) 230-9707 ext.336

Estimated # of Women's Volleyball Scholarships: N/A
Conference: Dixie Intercollegiate Athletic Conference
Program Profile: We play NCAA , Division III and DIAC volleyball. Home games are at Hones Gymnasium which has 850 seats.
History: We played in the NCAA Tournament in 1990. We were ranked 9th in the nation and #1 in the region.
Achievements: Regional Coach of the Year in 1990; DIAC Coach of the Year in 1983, 1986 and 1989. DVAC titles in 1983, 1986, 1989, 1990, 1991 and 1997; All-Americans - 1989, 1990; 13 All-Region Players
Coaching: Jean Lojko, has been Head Coach since 1982. Her overall record is 339-254. There is no assistant coach listed.
Roster In State: 9 | **Out of State:** 3 | **Out of Country:** 0
Sophomores on Team: 3 | **Seniors on Team:** 9 | **Graduation %:** 95
Most Recent Record: 20-14-0 | **Fall Games:** 34 | **Spring Games:** 6
Camp of Clinic Dates: Off Campus
Positions Needed: Middle Hitter, Setter
Schedule: Emory, Washington & Lee, Savannah College of Arts & Design, Carthage College, Centre College, Avertt
Style of Play: 5-1 offense with many play options.

Guilford College
Academic Profile

5800 West Friendly Avenue
Greensboro, NC 27410
Type: Private, 4 Yr., Liberal Arts, Coed
Website: http://www.guilford.edu
SAT/ACT/GPA:

Phone: (336) 316-2190

Founded: 1837
Religion: Quaker
Housing: Yes

Student/Faculty Ratio: 13:1
Undergraduate Enrollment: 1,245
Scholarships/Academic: Yes
Expenses By: Year
Degrees Conferred: AB, BS, BFA, BAS

Athletic: No
In State: $ 22,280

Male/Female: 48:52
Graduate Enrollment: N/A
Financial Aid: Yes
Out of State: $ 22,280

Programs of Study: Biology, Business & Management, Chemistry, Criminal Justice, Dentistry, Education, History, Justice & Policy, Law, Letters/Literature, Liberal Arts, Management, Medicine, Parks/Recreation, Philosophy, Physical Education, Physics, Psychology, Public Affairs, Sport Management, Sport Medicine, Social Sciences

Women's Athletic Profile

5800 W. Friendly Avenue
Greensboro, NC 27410
Coach: Chuck McCracken
Email: mccrackencr@rascal.guilford.edu

NCAA I
Lady Quakers, Crimson, Grey
Phone: (336) 316-2189
Fax: (336) 316-2953

Estimated # of Women's Volleyball Scholarships: None
Conference: Old Dominion Athletic Conference
Program Profile: Playing season is from last August through November. Games are played in Ragean Brow Fieldhouse (seats 2,000). Excellent playing floor, plenty of room.
History: Started in 1974. 478-282 overall record since.
Achievements: Coach of the year in the Old Dominion Athletic Conference 1993
NCAA Tournament Bid 1993; ODAC Conference Champions 1993 and 1991
Coaching: Chuck McCracken. 109-88. Played at Earlham College
Freshman Receiving Financial Aid/Academic:
Roster In State: 4
Sophomores on Team:
Most Recent Record: 5-21
Positions Needed: Setter, middle, Outside

Out of State: 11
Seniors on Team: 2
Fall Games: 30-35

Athletic:0
Out of Country: none
Graduation %: 100
Spring Games:

Schedule: Emory, Savana College of Art and Design, Thomas Moore, Averett, Bridgewater, Washington and Lee
Style of Play: Defensively strong blockin and digging with tough serving and movement with quicker tempo offense.

High Point University
Academic Profile

University Station
High Point, NC 27262

Phone: 800-345-6993

Type: Private, 4 Yr., Liberal Arts, Coed
Website: http://www.highpoint.edu
SAT/ACT/GPA: 1130
Student/Faculty Ratio: 16:1
Undergraduate Enrollment: 2,500
Scholarships/Academic: Yes
Expenses By: Year
Specializes In: Well rounded Liberal Arts
Degrees Conferred: BA, BS, MBA

Athletic: Yes
In State: $ 15,680

Founded: 1924
Religion: United Methodist
Housing: Yes
Male/Female: 45:55
Graduate Enrollment: 300
Financial Aid: Yes
Out of State: $ 17,280

Programs of Study: Art, Elementary Education, English, French, History, Human Relations, International Studies, Special Education, Philosophy, Religion, Sociology, Spanish, Theatre Arts, Political Science, Accounting, Biology, Business Administration, Chemistry, Computer Information Systems, Exercise, Forestry, Business-all areas, Mathematics, Physical Education, Psychology, Sports Management, Sports Medicine, etc..

Women's Athletic Profile

University Station
High Point, NC 27262-3598
Coach: Georgette Crawford
Email: gcrawfor@highpoint.edu

NCAA I
Lady Panthers, Purple, White
Phone: (336) 841-9000
Fax: (336) 841-9182

Estimated # of Women's Volleyball Scholarships: N/A
Conference: Big South Conference

Johnson C. Smith University
Academic Profile

100 Beatties Ford Rd.
Charlotte, NC 28216

Phone: 704-378-1010

Type: Private, 4 Yr., Liberal Arts, Coed
Website: http://www.jcsu.edu
SAT/ACT/GPA: 550+
Student/Faculty Ratio: 17:1
Undergraduate Enrollment: 1,256
Scholarships/Academic: Yes
Expenses By: Year
Degrees Conferred: BA, BS
Programs of Study: Contact school for program of study.

Founded: 1867
Religion: Non-Affiliated
Housing: No
Male/Female: 40:60
Graduate Enrollment: N/A
Athletic: Yes   **Financial Aid:** Yes
In State: $ 10,389   **Out of State:** $ 10,389

Women's Athletic Profile

100 Beatties Ford Road
Charlotte, NC 28216
Coach: Mark Raley
Email:

NCAA I
Lady Golden Bulls, Blue, Gold
Phone: (704) 378-1072
Fax: (704) 378-1073

Estimated # of Women's Volleyball Scholarships: 12
Conference: Central Intercollegiate Athletic Association
Program Profile: On Camp Gym-Brayboy
History: Up and coming team with new coach. Program has come from losing to winning and ranking Nationally in stats.
Achievements: Coach Raley has brought this team to another level in playing volleyball. Coach of the Year 1998-First time in history for school. First time school has made championship in the last two years. Runner-Ups in 1998. Three All-Americans
Coaching: Third year at JCSU, 1 Head Coach-Mark Raley, no assistance.
Freshman Receiving Financial Aid/Academic: **Athletic:** 4
Roster In State: 1   **Out of State:** 11   **Out of Country:** 1
Graduation %: 99
Camp of Clinic Dates: July 28th-30th
Positions Needed: Defense Sp. Outside Hitter/MH
Schedule: NC Central, Mt. Olive College, Lenior Rhyne, Fayetteville St., Shaw , Bowie State, Soelman College, Rockingham-College
Style of Play: Aggressive, loud, die-hard players. Nothing hits the floor on our side.

Lees - McRae College
Academic Profile

P. O. Box 128
Banner Elk, NC 28604

Phone: (828) 898-8725

Type: Private, 4 Yr., Liberal Arts, Coed
Website: http://www.lmc.edu
SAT/ACT/GPA:
Student/Faculty Ratio: 14:1
Undergraduate Enrollment: N/A
Scholarships/Academic: Yes
Expenses By: Year
Degrees Conferred: BA, BS
Programs of Study: Art, Biology, Naturalist, Pre-Health Professional, Science Education, Sports Medicine, Business Administration, Computer Information Systems, Criminal Justice, Dance, Education, English (Communication & Literature), History, Interdisciplinary Studies, International Studies, Mathematics, Military Science, Music, Musical Theatre, Physical Education, Psychology, Reading, Religious Studies, Social Studies, Sociology, Theatre Arts

Founded: 1900
Religion: Presbyterian
Housing: Yes
Male/Female: N/A
Graduate Enrollment: N/A
Athletic: Yes   **Financial Aid:** Yes
In State: $15,400   **Out of State:** $15,400

Women's Athletic Profile

P.O. Box 128
Banner Elk, NC 28604-0128
Coach: Chad Esposito, Jim Lodes
Email: esposito@lmc.edu

NCAA I
Lady Bobcats, Green, Gold
Phone: (828) 898-8891
Fax: (828) 898-8742

Estimated # of Women's Volleyball Scholarships: 2.5
Conference: Carolinas - Virginia Athletic Conference
Program Profile: Williams Gymnasium (seats 1,100), Coach Lodes is in his first season at LMC, but inherits a team that has won the CVAC the past two seasons. His teaching abilities and proven record has everyone excited about the furthered growth of volleyball at Lees-McRae.
History: 1991 was first year of volleyball
Achievements: The Bobcats have won the past three regular season CVAC Championships and two consecutive conference titles. They appeared in the NCAA Division II National Tournament for the first time last year.
Coaching: Jim Lodes begins his 10th year of collegiate volleyball coaching at Lees-McRae College. His overall coaching record in nine seasons is 222-156. Highlights include 1993 NCAA Division III third place finish among 3 overall NCAA Division III appearances. Lodes has coached 3 different All-Americans, 3 different Academic All-Americans and 8 different All-Region student athletes. Lodes was honored with NCAA Region Coach of the Year honors in 1992.
Freshman Receiving Financial Aid/Academic: **Athletic:** 2
Roster In State: 2   **Out of State:** 7   **Out of Country:** 0
Sophomores on Team: 2   **Seniors on Team:** 2   **Graduation %:** 100
Most Recent Record: 35-6-0   **Fall Games:** 39   **Spring Games:** 4
Positions Needed: 2-Setters, 4-Outside Hitters, 4-Middle Blockers, 2-Defensive Specialists
Schedule: Wheeling Jesuit, Lock Haven, Millersville, University of Charleston, Anderson, USC-Aiken, Rollins College
Style of Play: We like to run a fast offense using a 5-1 or 6-2 system. On defense, we use several different systems. We try to be aggressive in our approach to the game.

Lenoire - Rhyne College
Academic Profile

P. O. Box 7356
Hickory, NC 28603

Phone: 828-328-7300

Type: Private, 4 Yr., Liberal Arts, Coed
Website: http://www.lrc.edu
SAT/ACT/GPA: 900/18
Student/Faculty Ratio: 11:1
Undergraduate Enrollment: 1,633
Scholarships/Academic: Yes   **Athletic:** Yes
Expenses By: Year   **In State:** $ 17,000

Founded: 1891
Religion: Lutheran
Housing: Yes
Male/Female: 60:40
Graduate Enrollment: N/A
Financial Aid: Yes
Out of State: $ 18,500

Degrees Conferred: BA, BS, BME, MA, Education & Counseling
Programs of Study: Accounting, Anthropology, Art, Astronomy, Biology, Business, Chemistry, Classics, Computer Science, Dance, Drama, Earth Science, Education, Environmental Studies, Geography, Sport Studies, Mathematics, Military Science, Nursing, Office Science, Sociology, Social Science

Women's Athletic Profile

P.O. Box 7356
Hickory, NC 28603
Coach: Glenda Parrish
Email: parrishg@lrc.edu

NCAA I
Lady Bears, Red, Black
Phone: (828) 328-7215
Fax: (828) 328-7399

Did Not Return Profile

Livingstone College
Academic Profile

701 W. Monroe St.
Salisbury, NC 28144

Phone: 704-638-5500

Type: Private, 4 Yr., Liberal Arts, Coed
Website: Not Available
SAT/ACT/GPA: 500+
Student/Faculty Ratio: 15:1
Undergraduate Enrollment: 683
Scholarships/Academic: Yes   **Athletic:** Yes
Expenses By: Year   **In State:** $ 10,100

Founded: 1879
Religion: African Methodist Episcopal Zion
Housing: No
Male/Female: 62:38
Graduate Enrollment: N/A
Financial Aid: Yes
Out of State: $ 10,100

Degrees Conferred: BA, BS
Programs of Study: Contact school for programs of study.

Women's Athletic Profile

701 W. Monroe Street
Salisbury, NC 28144
Coach: Linda Bell
Email:

NCAA I
Fighting Blue Bears, Blue, Black
Phone: (704) 638-5714
Fax: (704) 638-5712

Did Not Return Profile

Mars Hill College
Academic Profile

Mars Hill College
Mars Hill, NC 28754

Phone: (330) 672-2121

Type: Private, 4 Yr., Liberal Arts, Coed
Website: http://www.mhc.edu
SAT/ACT/GPA: 820/2.5
Student/Faculty Ratio: 13:1
Undergraduate Enrollment: 1,200
Scholarships/Academic: Yes
Expenses By: Year
Specializes In: Numerous Areas
Degrees Conferred: BA, BS, BM, BSM, BFA

Athletic: Yes
In State: $ 12,700

Founded: 1856
Religion: Baptist
Housing: Yes
Male/Female: 52:48
Graduate Enrollment: N/A
Financial Aid: Yes
Out of State: $ 12,700

Programs of Study: Business Administration & Economics, Business/Office and Marketing/Distribution, Education, Fine Arts, Health, Humanities, Life Science, Natural Science & Mathematics, Physical Education & Recreation, Social Behavioral Sciences, Sport Medicine

Women's Athletic Profile

P.O. Box 1881, 1532 W. Claybourn
Mars Hill, NC 28754
Coach: Bill Shook
Email: bshook@mhc.edu

NCAA I
Lady Lions, Blue, Gold
Phone: (828) 689-1497
Fax: (828) 689-1501

Estimated # of Women's Volleyball Scholarships: 3
Conference: South Atlantic Conference
Program Profile: MHC Volleyball plays its home matches in Stanford Arena/Chambers Gym (cap.3,500)
Traditional season-Fall, playing a mixture of tournaments and duel matches
Non-Traditional Season-Spring, playing 2 tournaments and 2 duel matches.
History: MHC VB participated as an NAIA member from 1981-1992. The highlight of this period was the program's 1985 District and zonal Championships and participation in the National championships. All of the SAC Sports became full NCAA Division II Members in 1993. Coach Shook has built hits NCAA Program to Championship level in just four years.
Achievements: 1997 Conference Tournament Finalist
1998 South Atlantic conference Champions (14-0 regular season , 4-0 town) 18-0 conference record. 57-14 overall record for the last two seasons; (24-4 in conference matches)
Coaching: Bill Shook MHC Head Coach '94-present, (111wins-74losses), Various USA/International Coaching Experiences, 4 State championships in Maryland (Centennial HS), and numerous Club Championships. '96 Olympics supervisor of VB Statistics
Freshman Receiving Financial Aid/Academic:
Roster In State: 5
Sophomores on Team:
Most Recent Record: 32-6
Camp of Clinic Dates: TBA

Out of State: 10
Seniors on Team: 5
Fall Games: 35+

Athletic: 3
Out of Country: 2
Graduation %: 95
Spring Games: 10

Positions Needed: 3-5 players (including 1 setter, 1 MB, 1 OH, and 1BCS)
Schedule: Hawaii Pacific U (Division II National Champs), U. of Tampa (#1 South Region, Top 5 country), U. of Hawaii-Hilo, BYU-Hawaii, Cal State-San Bernardino, King College (NAIA)
Style of Play: We have developed a consistent 3 tempo, fast offense with a reliable "read" defense (#1 in country for NCAA-2 team statistical "Digs per game" avg.)

Meredith College
Academic Profile

3800 Hillsborough St.
Raleigh, NC 27607-5298

Phone: 800-637-3348

Type: Private, 4 Yr., Liberal Arts
Website: http://www.meredith.edu

Founded: 1891
Religion: Historically Baptist

SAT/ACT/GPA: 800
Student/Faculty Ratio: 17:1
Undergraduate Enrollment: 2,000
Scholarships/Academic: Yes
Expenses By: Year
Specializes In: Liberal Arts

Housing: Yes
Male/Female: Women Only
Graduate Enrollment: 800
Athletic: No
In State: $ 14,090
Financial Aid: Yes
Out of State: $ 14,090

Degrees Conferred: BA, BS, BMus, MBA, M.Ed., Master of Health Administration
Programs of Study: Accounting, American Civilization, Art, Biology, Business, Chemistry, Communications, Computer Science, Criminal Justice, Dance, Economics, Education, English, Fashion Merchandising, French, Health Science, History, Home Economics, International Business International Studies, Management, Mathematics, Medical Technology, Music, Nutrition, Political Science, PreDentistry, PreLaw, PreMed, PreVet, Psychology, Religion, Social Work, Theatre

Women's Athletic Profile

3800 Hillsborough Street
Raleigh, NC 27607
Coach: Kathy Mayberry
Email:

NCAA I
Lady Angels, Maroon, White
Phone: (919) 829-2374
Fax: (919) 829-2341

Did Not Return Profile

Methodist College
Academic Profile

5400 Ramsey St.
Fayetteville, NC 28311

Phone: (910) 630-7182

Type: Private, 4 Yr., Liberal Arts, Coed
Website: http://www.methodist.edu
SAT/ACT/GPA: 800/2.0
Student/Faculty Ratio: 17:1
Undergraduate Enrollment: 1,700
Scholarships/Academic: Yes
Expenses By: Year
Specializes In: Business

Founded: 1954
Religion: United Methodist
Housing: Yes
Male/Female: 2:1
Graduate Enrollment: N/A
Athletic: No
In State: $ 16,000
Financial Aid: Yes
Out of State: $ 16,000

Degrees Conferred: BS, BA
Programs of Study: Business and Management, Education, Criminal Justice, Sports Medicine, Physician's Assistant, Physical Education, Sports Management, Social Work, Art, Theatre, Communications, Accounting, Professional Golf Management, Professional Tennis Management, Music, Foreign Languages, Marketing, Mathematics

Women's Athletic Profile

5400 Ramsey Street
Fayetteville, NC 28311
Coach: Doug Tabbert
Email:

NCAA I
Lady Monarchs, Green, Yellow
Phone: (910) 630-7182
Fax: (910) 630-1300

Conference: Dixie Intercollegiate Athletic Conference
Program Profile: We are a Division III women's varsity program. We do a full fall season and a partial spring season. We play in a 1,300 seat air-conditioned gymnasium with three courts in a modern athletic facility.
Achievements: 1988 Regular Season Conference Champions; 1986 & 1988 Conference Tournament Champions; 1988 & 1991 Conference Coach of the Year Awards.
Coaching: Doug Tabbert, Head Coach, entered his first year with the program and compiled a record of 14-18. He has Division III National Tournament experience as an assistant coach.
Freshman Receiving Financial Aid/Academic:
Roster In State: 8
Sophomores on Team: 0
Most Recent Record: 14-18-0
Positions Needed: All positions
Schedule: Averett College, Greensboro College
Style of Play: Multiple attack swing offense with verbal audible system.

Out of State: 4
Seniors on Team: 2
Fall Games: 32

Athletic: 0
Out of Country: 1
Graduation %: 90-95
Spring Games: 0

Montreat College
Academic Profile

P. O. Box 1267
Montreat, NC 28757

Phone: (828) 669-8011

Type: Private, 4 Yr., Liberal Arts, Coed
Website: http://www.montreat.edu
SAT/ACT/GPA: 860/18/2-3
Student/Faculty Ratio: 12:1
Undergraduate Enrollment: 500
Scholarships/Academic: Yes
Expenses By: Year
Specializes In: Outdoor Education, Business
Degrees Conferred: BA, BS

Founded: 1916
Religion: Presbyterian
Housing: Yes
Male/Female: 50:50
Graduate Enrollment: N/A
Athletic: Yes **Financial Aid:** Yes
In State: $ 15,272 **Out of State:** $ 15,272

Programs of Study: Accounting, Bible Studies, Business and Management, Ecology, Economics, English, Environmental Studies, History, Human Services, Liberal Arts, Mathematics, Missionary Studies, Religion, Secondary Education, Social Sciences

Women's Athletic Profile

405 Assembly Drive
Montreat, NC 28757
Coach: Toby Brooks
Email: tbrooks@montreat.edu

NCAA I
Lady Cavaliers, Navy, Gold
Phone: (828) 669-8012x3409
Fax: (828) 669-8014

Did Not Return Profile

Mount Olive College
Academic Profile

634 Henderson Street
Mount Olive, NC 28365

Phone: (919) 658-5056

Type: Private, 4 Yr., Liberal Arts, Coed
Website: http://www.mountolivetrojans.com
SAT/ACT/GPA: 820/18/2.5
Student/Faculty Ratio: 15:1
Undergraduate Enrollment: 1,600
Scholarships/Academic: Yes
Expenses By: Year
Specializes In: Liberal Arts, Sciences, Business, Criminal Justice, English, Math
Degrees Conferred: BA, BS, BAS

Founded: 1951
Religion: Free-will Baptist
Housing: Yes
Male/Female: 2:1
Graduate Enrollment: N/A
Athletic: Yes **Financial Aid:** Yes
In State: $ 12,810 **Out of State:** $ 12,810

Programs of Study: Arts, Biology, English, Communications, English with Secondary School Education, Fine Arts, General Studies, History, Music, Psychology, Recreation & Leisure Studies, Business Administration, Church Ministries, Criminal Justice, Math, PreMed, PreVet, PreDental, Pharmacy

Women's Athletic Profile

634 Henderson Street
Mount Olive, NC 28365
Coach: Sharon Gregory
Email: sgregory@exchange.moc.edu

NCAA I
Lady Trojans, Green, White
Phone: (919) 658-5056
Fax: (919) 658-1753

Estimated # of Women's Volleyball Scholarships: 2.75
Conference: Carolinas - Virginia Athletic Conference
Program Profile: Our program is small, yet very competitive. We have a multi-attack offense with a strong net play offensively and defensively. Our facilities are very modern. They are climate-controlled with upper and lower level seating options and 2 courts, with set-up for practices and a center court arrangement for matches. Our playing season extends from mid August to mid November.
Achievements: We were CVAC Tournament Champions in 1997.
Coaching: Sharon Gregory, Head Coach, started here in 1997. Her record is 43-30.
Roster In State: 8 **Out of State:** 6 **Out of Country:** 0
Most Recent Record: 18-17-0 **Fall Games:** 35 **Spring Games:** 5
Camp of Clinic Dates: July 19th through 22nd

Positions Needed: Middle Hitter, Right Side Hitter, Outside Hitter, Outside Setter
Schedule: University of Charleston, Lees McRae, Fairmont State, Alderson-Broddus.
Style of Play: Multi-attack offense with 3-4 hitter options and a dynamic defense. Our team averages 16+ digs/gm.

North Carolina A & T State University
Academic Profile

1601 East Market Street
Greensboro, NC 27411

Phone: 800-443-8964

Type: Public, 4 Yr., Liberal Arts, Engineering, Coed
Website: http://www.ncat.edu
SAT/ACT/GPA: 920
Student/Faculty Ratio: 16:1
Undergraduate Enrollment: 7,050
Scholarships/Academic: Yes   **Athletic:** Yes
Expenses By: Year   **In State:** $ 5,540

Founded: 1890
Religion: Non-Affiliated
Housing: Yes
Male/Female: 50:50
Graduate Enrollment: 1,000
Financial Aid: Yes
Out of State: $ 13,000

Degrees Conferred: BA, BS, BFA, BSN, BSW, MA, MS, Ph.D.
Programs of Study: Accounting, Animal Science, Computer Science, Elementary Education, (Electrical, Industrial, Architectural, Mechanical) Engineering, Finance, Marketing, Nursing, Physical Education, Technology, Transportation

Women's Athletic Profile

Corbett Sports Ctr.
Greensboro, NC 27411
Coach: Kathy Rouhlac
Email:

NCAA I
Lady Aggies, Navy Blue, Gold
Phone: (336) 334-7500
Fax:

Did Not Return Profile

North Carolina Central University
Academic Profile

1801 Fayetteville
Durham, NC 27707

Phone: 919-560-6298

Type: Public, 4 Yr., Coed
Website: http://www.nccu.edu
SAT/ACT/GPA: 650+
Student/Faculty Ratio: 14:1
Undergraduate Enrollment: 4,039
Scholarships/Academic: Yes   **Athletic:** No
Expenses By: Year   **In State:** $ 5,004

Founded: 1910
Religion: Non-Affiliated
Housing: No
Male/Female: 39:61
Graduate Enrollment: 1,346
Financial Aid: Yes
Out of State: $ 10,058

Degrees Conferred: BA, BS, BArch, MA, MS, MBA, M.Ed., JD
Programs of Study: Contact school for program of study.

Women's Athletic Profile

1801 Fayetteville Street
Durham, NC 27707
Coach: Ingrid Wicker
Email:

NCAA I
Lady Eagles, Maroon, Gray
Phone: (919) 530-7053
Fax: (919) 560-5426

Conference: CIAA
Program Profile: McLendon-McDougald Gymnasium & wood floor surface; stadium seats around 3,200; fall playing season; good team program with good number of wins in the past few seasons.
Achievements: 1999 CIAA conference champions..
Coaching: Head Coach Ingrid Wicker; Assistant coach Shannon Gamble
Roster In State: 12   **Out of State:** 2
Seniors on Team: 2
Most Recent Record: 22-15-0
Schedule: UMASS-Lowell, U of Indianapolis, New Haven, Southern Connecticut, Fayetteville State, Clarion, Tiffin, Ashland, St. Joseph's, Winston-Salem

North Carolina State University
Academic Profile

Box 8501
Raleigh, NC 27659

Phone: (919) 515-3013

Type: Public, 4 Yr., Engineering, Coed
Website: http://www.ncsu.edu
SAT/ACT/GPA: Varies
Student/Faculty Ratio: 13:1
Undergraduate Enrollment: 18,700
Scholarships/Academic: Yes
Expenses By: Year
Specializes In: Engineering and Textiles
Degrees Conferred: Various

Athletic: Yes
In State: $ 4,085

Founded: 1887
Religion: Non-Affiliated
Housing: Yes
Male/Female: 58:42
Graduate Enrollment: 8,900
Financial Aid: Yes
Out of State: $ 14,296

Programs of Study: Agriculture & Life Sciences, Design, Education, Engineering, Forest Resources, Humanities, Management, Mathematics, Physical Sciences, Psychology, Social Science, Textiles

Women's Athletic Profile

Box 8501, Case Athletics Ctr.
Raleigh, NC 27695-8501
Coach: Kim Hall
Email: kim_hall@ncsu.edu

NCAA I
Wolfpack, Red, White
Phone: (919) 515-3826
Fax: (919) 515-5443

Estimated # of Women's Volleyball Scholarships: 12
Conference: Atlantic Coast Conference
Program Profile: We are a member of one of top volleyball conference in the country. We play in Reynolds Coliseum and we have great athletic tradition and reputation.
Coaching: Kim Hall - Head Coach. Li Xiou-Feng is our Assistant Coach.
Freshman Receiving Financial Aid/Academic:
Roster In State: 1
Sophomores on Team: 4
Most Recent Record: 14-20-0
Camp of Clinic Dates: Call (919) 858-8751

Athletic: 5
Out of State: 11
Seniors on Team: 2
Fall Games: 24

Out of Country: 0
Graduation %: 100
Spring Games: 4

Schedule: Texas Tech, Utah, Florida State, UNC-Chapel Hill, Duke, Virginia
Style of Play: Athletic!, young!, fast!, disciplined.

North Carolina Wesleyan College
Academic Profile

3400 N. Wesleyan Boulevard
Rocky Mount, NC 27804

Phone: (252) 985-5209

Type: Private, 4 Yr., Liberal Arts, Coed
Website: http://www.ncwc.edu
SAT/ACT/GPA: 850/2.0
Student/Faculty Ratio: 1:13
Undergraduate Enrollment: 1,000
Scholarships/Academic: Yes
Expenses By: Year
Degrees Conferred: BA, BS

Athletic: No
In State: $ 14,000

Founded: 1956
Religion: Methodist
Housing: Yes
Male/Female: 1:1
Graduate Enrollment: N/A
Financial Aid: Yes
Out of State: $ 14,000

Programs of Study: Accounting, Biology, Business Administration, Chemistry, Computer Information Systems, Elementary Education, English, Environmental Science, Food Services and Hotel Management, History, Justice Studies, Mathematics, Middle Grades Education, Philosophy-Religious Studies, Physical Education, Political Science, Psychology, Religious Studies, Secondary Education Certification, Sociology-Anthropology, Theatre

Women's Athletic Profile

3400 Wesleyan Blvd.
Rocky Mount, NC 27804
Coach: Michon Lubbers
Email: mlubbers@ncwc.edu

NCAA I
Battling Bishops, Blue, Gold
Phone: (252) 985-5216
Fax: (252) 985-5252

Estimated # of Women's Volleyball Scholarships: 0
Conference: Dixie Intercollegiate Athletic Conference
Program Profile: Facilities: Everett Hall. Playing Season: Sept-early November
Graduation %: 100
Positions Needed: Middle Hitter, Outside Hitter, Defensive Specialist
Schedule: Emory University, Averett College, Greensboro College, Washington and Lee, Guilford College, Shenandoah College
Style of Play: A quick paced, multi-attack offense of force, characterized by tough serving and defense in addition to fast transition.

Peace College
Academic Profile

15 East Peace Street
Raleigh, NC 27604

Phone: 919-508-2000

Type: Private 4 Yr., Liberal Arts
Website: http://www.peace.edu
SAT/ACT/GPA: 900193.0
Student/Faculty Ratio: 41:1
Undergraduate Enrollment: 604
Scholarships/Academic: Yes
Expenses By: Year
Specializes In: Liberal Arts
Degrees Conferred: B.S., B.A. & Associate Degrees

Athletic: No
In State: $13,177

Founded: 1857
Religion: Presbyterian
Housing: Yes
Male/Female: Women Only
Graduate Enrollment: N/A
Financial Aid: Yes
Out of State: $13,177

Programs of Study: Biology, Business Administration, Communication, English, Human Resources, Leadership Studies, Liberal Studies, Music performance, Psychology, Spanish and Visual Communication

Women's Athletic Profile

15 E. Peace Street
Raleigh, NC 27604
Coach: Debbie Edwards
Email:

NCAA I
Lady Pride, Green, White
Phone: (919) 508-2334
Fax: (919) 508-2326

Did Not Return Profile

Pfieffer University
Academic Profile

P. O. Box 960 Hwy. 52
Misenheimer, NC 28109

Phone: 800-338-2060

Type: Private, 4 Yr., Liberal Arts, Coed
Website: http://www.pfeiffer.edu
SAT/ACT/GPA: 820/17/2.0
Student/Faculty Ratio: 15:1
Undergraduate Enrollment: 800
Scholarships/Academic: Yes
Expenses By: Year
Specializes In: Business, Athletic Training, Sports Medicine
Degrees Conferred: BA, BS, MBA, Masters

Athletic: Yes
In State: $ 15,211

Founded: 1885
Religion: Methodist
Housing: Yes
Male/Female: 1:1
Graduate Enrollment: 600
Financial Aid: Yes
Out of State: $ 15,211

Programs of Study: Accounting, Arts Administration, Biology, Business Administration, Chemistry, Economics, Elementary Education, Law, Journalism, Engineering, Sociology, Sport Management, Sport Medicine, Psychology, Physical Education History, Mathematics

Women's Athletic Profile

Highway 52 p.o box 960
Misenheimer, NC 28109-0960
Coach: Dean Miller
Email: dmiller@pfeiffer.edu

NCAA I
Lady Falcons, Black, Gold
Phone: (704) 463-1360x2421
Fax: (704) 463-5051

Estimated # of Women's Volleyball Scholarships: N/A
Conference: Carolinas - Virginia Athletic Conference

Roster In State: 5   **Out of State:** 9
Seniors on Team: 2
Most Recent Record: 7-21
Positions Needed: Middle hitter, Outside hitters
Schedule: Lees McRae College, Cataza College, Lenoir Rityne College, Queens College

Queens College
Academic Profile

1900 Selwyn Avenue
Charlotte, NC 28274

Phone: 800-849-0202

Type: Private, 4 Yr., Liberal Arts, Coed
Website: Not Available
SAT/ACT/GPA: 970-1160/20-26/3.1
Student/Faculty Ratio: 13:1
Undergraduate Enrollment: 1600
Scholarships/Academic: Yes   **Athletic:** Yes
Expenses By: Year   **In State:** $ 18,580
Degrees Conferred: BS, BA, BM, BSN, MBA, MAT, MA

Founded: 1857
Religion: Presbyterian
Housing: Yes
Male/Female: 1:2
Graduate Enrollment: N/A
Financial Aid: Yes
Out of State: $ 18,580

Programs of Study: Accounting, American Studies, Art, BioChemistry, Biology, Business Administration, Communications, Education, English, Drama, Foreign Languages, History, Mathematics, Music, Nursing, Philosophy, Political Science, Psychology, Religion; Can be combined with over 50 concentrations.

Men's Athletic Profile

65-30 Kissena Blvd.
Flushing, NY 11367
Coach: Karl Pierre
Email:

NCAA II
Knights/Silver, Blue
Phone: (718) 997-2780
Fax: (718) 997-2799

Estimated # of Men's Volleyball Scholarships: N/A
Conference: Eastern College Athletic Conference

Women's Athletic Profile

1900 Selwyn Avenue
Charlotte, NC 28274
Coach: Chrys Baker
Email:

NCAA I
Lady Royals, Light Blue, White
Phone: (704) 337-2360
Fax: (704) 337-2237

Estimated # of Women's Volleyball Scholarships: N/A
Conference: Carolinas - Virginia Athletic Conference

Saint Andrews Presbyterian College
Academic Profile

1700 Dogwood Mile
Laurinburg, NC 28352

Phone: 910-277-5555

Type: Private, 4 Yr., Liberal Arts, Coed
Website: http://www.sapc.edu
SAT/ACT/GPA: 820/17/2.0
Student/Faculty Ratio: 12:1
Undergraduate Enrollment: 600
Scholarships/Academic: Yes   **Athletic:** Yes
Expenses By: Year   **In State:** $ 18,500
Degrees Conferred: BA, BS

Founded: 1958
Religion: Presbyterian
Housing: Yes
Male/Female: 2:1
Graduate Enrollment: N/A
Financial Aid: Yes
Out of State: $ 18,500

Programs of Study: Art, BioChemistry, Biology, Business, Chemistry, Communications, Theatre, Creative Writing, Education, English, Environmental Science, History, International Business, Math, Math Computer Science, Music, Philosophy, Physical Education, Sports Management, Politics, Psychology, Religious Studies, Sports Med, Accounting, Dentistry, Engineering, Law, Medicine, Equine Studies

Women's Athletic Profile

1700 Dogwood Mile
Laurinburg, NC 28352-5598
Coach: Sean J. Dieleman
Email:

NCAA I
Lady Knights, Royal, White
Phone: (910) 277-5429
Fax: (910) 277-5272

Estimated # of Women's Volleyball Scholarships: 2-4
Conference: Carolinas - Virginia Athletic Conference
Program Profile: Quality conference play with emphasis on receiving a quality education. We have 700 student body.
History: Our program has been 20 years in existence.
Coaching: Sean J. Dieleman, Head Coach, is entering first year with the program. She has coached high school, Division I, Division II, & Division III.

Roster In State: 2	**Out of State:** 7	**Out of Country:** 0
Sophomores on Team: 0	**Seniors on Team:** 5	**Graduation %:** 95
Most Recent Record: 14-17-0	**Fall Games:** 21	**Spring Games:** 4

Camp of Clinic Dates: Summer 2000
Positions Needed: Setters, Middles
Schedule: Lees-McRae, Mount Olive, Pembroke-UNC, Queens, Coker
Style of Play: Allow players to have input in game settings. Option offense with emphasis on strong fundamentals.

Saint Agustine College
Academic Profile

1315 Oakwood Avenue
Raleigh, NC 27610

Phone: (919) 516-4131

Type: Private, 4 Yr., Liberal Arts, Coed
Website: http://www.st.aug.
SAT/ACT/GPA: 700/2.0
Student/Faculty Ratio: 15:1
Undergraduate Enrollment: 1,700
Scholarships/Academic: Yes   **Athletic:** Yes
Expenses By: Year   **In State:** $ 12,390

Founded: 1867
Religion: Non-Affiliated
Housing: Yes
Male/Female: 3:7
Graduate Enrollment: N/A
Financial Aid: Yes
Out of State: $ 12,390

Programs of Study: Accounting, Biological, Business, Chemistry, Communications, Computer, Criminal Justice, Early Childhood Education, Economics, Engineering, Education, English, Fine Arts, History, Industrial, Medical, Mathematics, Music, Office, Physical Education/Therapy, Physics, Political Science, PreLaw, PreMed, Psychology, Social Science, Spanish, Urban Studies

Women's Athletic Profile

1315 Oakwood Avenue
Raleigh, NC 27610
Coach: Deborah Dove
Email:

NCAA I
Lady Falcons, Blue, White
Phone: (919) 516-4175
Fax: (919) 516-9731

Estimated # of Women's Volleyball Scholarships: N/A
Conference: Central Intercollegiate Athletic Association

Shaw University
Academic Profile

118 E. South St.
Raleigh, NC 27601

Phone: 800-214-6683

Type: Private, 4 Yr., Liberal Arts, Coed
Website: Not Available
SAT/ACT/GPA: 17avg
Student/Faculty Ratio: 13:1
Undergraduate Enrollment: 4,245
Scholarships/Academic: Yes   **Athletic:** Yes
Expenses By: Year   **In State:** $ 9,600

Founded: 1865
Religion: Baptist
Housing: No
Male/Female: 42:58
Graduate Enrollment: N/A
Financial Aid: Yes
Out of State: $ 9,600

Programs of Study: Accounting, Behavioral Science. Biology, Biological Science, Business, Management, Commercial, Chemistry, Communications, Computer Information Systems, Elementary Education, International Studies, Physical Education, Music, Social Science, Recreation Therapy, Speech Pathology

118 E. South Street
Raleigh, NC 27601
Coach: Dianthia Ford
Email: dford@shawu.edu

NCAA I
Lady Bears, Maroon, White
Phone: (919) 546-8290
Fax: (919) 546-8299

Estimated # of Women's Volleyball Scholarships: N/A
Conference: Central Intercollegiate Athletic Association

University of North Carolina - Asheville
Academic Profile

One University Heights
Asheville, NC 28804

Phone: (828) 251-6386

Type: Public, 4 Yr., Liberal Arts, Coed
Website: http://www.cs.unca.edu
SAT/ACT/GPA: 1000/20/3.0
Student/Faculty Ratio: 19:1
Undergraduate Enrollment: 3,000
Scholarships/Academic: Yes   **Athletic:** Yes
Expenses By: Year   **In State:** $ 6,603
Specializes In: Meteorology, Business, Computer Science, Psychology
Degrees Conferred: BA, BS, BFA, M

Founded: 1927
Religion: Non-Affiliated
Housing: Yes
Male/Female: 47:53
Graduate Enrollment: N/A
Financial Aid: Yes
Out of State: $ 13,086

Programs of Study: Accounting, Actuarial Science, Applied Mathematics, Art, Atmospheric Science, Biology, Business and Management, Chemistry, Classics, Communications, Computer Information Systems, Computer Science, Economics, Education, English, Environmental Science, Finance, French, German, Greek, Health Services, History, Latin, Literature, Marketing, Mathematics, Music, Philosophy, Physics, Political Science, Psychology, Social Science, Spanish, Theatre

Women's Athletic Profile

One University Heights
Asheville, NC 28804-3299
Coach: Julie Torbett
Email: jtorbett@unca.edu

NCAA I
Lady Bulldogs, Blue, White
Phone: (828) 251-6423
Fax: (828) 251-6386

Estimated # of Women's Volleyball Scholarships: 6
Conference: Big South Conference
Program Profile: We play at the Justice Center , which seats 1,200 fans. Our season is from August to November.
History: We are one of the smallest public Division I schools in the country. We have a real family atmosphere.
Achievements: 1991 Conference Champions; 1992 Conference Champions.
Coaching: Julie Torbett- , Head Coach. She is in her 5th year at UNC Ashville. She started here as an assistant coach in 1993. While at Penn State, she was an Atlantic 10 Academic All-Conference performer. Jennifer Reynolds is the Assitant coach.
Freshman Receiving Financial Aid/Academic: **Athletic:** 7
Roster In State: 6   **Out of State:** 6   **Out of Country:** 0
Sophomores on Team: 3   **Seniors on Team:** 1   **Graduation %:** 100
Most Recent Record: 18-13-0   **Fall Games:** 34   **Spring Games:** 4
Camp of Clinic Dates: June 21-24; July 31 Day Clinic; August 1
Positions Needed: Middle Hitters, Outside Hitter
Schedule: Tennessee, Rice, St. John's, Liberty, Radford, Central Florida, Evansville
Style of Play: Our style will depend on how the individual players mesh together and how the chemistry develops on the court.

University of North Carolina - Chapel Hill
Academic Profile

P. O. Box 2126
Chapel Hill, NC 27515

Phone: 919-966-3621

Type: Public, 4 Yr., Liberal Arts, Coed
Website: http://www.ga.unc.edu
SAT/ACT/GPA:
Student/Faculty Ratio: 10:1

Founded: 1792
Religion: Non-Affiliated
Housing: Yes
Male/Female: 40:60

Undergraduate Enrollment: 18,000
Scholarships/Academic: Yes
Expenses By: Year
Specializes In: Liberal Arts
Degrees Conferred: Bachelors, Masters, Doctoral, Professional Degree
Programs of Study: African Studies, American Studies, Art, Astronomy, History, BioStatistics, Biology, Dental, Economics, Engineering, Geology, Geography, Health, Math, Recreation, Political, Physical, Physics, Sociology, Religious

Athletic: Yes
In State: $ 7,000

Graduate Enrollment: 7,000
Financial Aid: Yes
Out of State: $ 17,000

Women's Athletic Profile

P.O. Box 2126
Chapel Hill, NC 27514
Coach: Joe Sagula
Email: jsagula@unc.edu

NCAA I
Lady Tar Heels, Blue, White
Phone: (919) 962-5228
Fax: (919) 843-8543

Estimated # of Women's Volleyball Scholarships: 2
Conference: Atlantic Coast Conference
Program Profile: Home court is the Carmichael Audturium and it seats 10, 000 with wooden floor.
History: Volleyball at UNC started in 1975. UNC has won 7 ACC Tititles most ACC victories in conference. UNC has played in the NCAA tournament 2000, 1999, 1998, 1989, 83, 82.
Achievements: 1998 Atlantic Coast Conference Coach of the Year; AVCA/Tachikara District 3 Coach of the Year; 1998 NCAA Tournament Appearance, ACC Champions in 1998, 1999, 2000.
Coaching: Joe Sagula, has been Head Coach here for 10 years. He is one of the country's most respected coaches. The Tar Heels ended the season with a Top 25 national ranking. Assistant Coaches are Kiran Mistry and Ashley Powers.
Freshman Receiving Financial Aid/Academic:
Roster In State: 3
Sophomores on Team:
Most Recent Record: 28-6
Camp of Clinic Dates: July 15-19, July 22-26, July 27-29
Positions Needed: Setter, MH
Schedule: Pepperdine, UC Santa Barbara, Penn State, Santa Clara, Kansas, Georgia Tech, Duke, Florida State, Wake Forest
Style of Play: Competing with some of the top twenty five programs.

Out of State: 10
Seniors on Team: 3

Athletic: 3
Out of Country:
Graduation %: 100

University of North Carolina - Charlotte
Academic Profile

9201 University City Boulevard
Charlotte, NC 28223

Phone: 704-687-2213

Type: Public, 4 Yr., Liberal Arts, Engineering, Coed
Website: http://www.uncc.edu
SAT/ACT/GPA: 1030/18/3.0
Student/Faculty Ratio: 16:1
Undergraduate Enrollment: 13,770
Scholarships/Academic: Yes
Expenses By: Year
Specializes In: Architecture, Engineering, Business, Education, Nursing
Degrees Conferred: AS, AA, BArch, BSBA, BSEE, BET, BSME, BSN, BSW, MS
Programs of Study: Accounting, African Studies, Anthropology, Architecture, Biological Science, Business Administration, Chemistry, Civil Engineering, Computer Science, Criminal Justice, Dance, Dramatic Arts, Economics, Electrical Engineering, Elementary Education, Engineering Technology, English, Fine Arts, French, Geography, German, History, Human Services, Management, Mathematics, Mechanical Engineering, Music, Nursing, Political Science, Philosophy, Physics, Psychology, Religion, Social Science

Founded: 1946
Religion: Non-Affiliated
Housing: Yes
Male/Female: 45:55
Graduate Enrollment: 2,670
Financial Aid: Yes
Out of State: $ 6,754

Athletic: Yes
In State: $ 3,119

Women's Athletic Profile

9201 University City Blvd.
Charlotte, NC 28223
Coach: Julie Ibieta
Email: pdennison@email.uncc.edu

NCAA I
Lady 49ers, Green, White
Phone: (704) 547-2213
Fax: (704) 547-6483

Estimated # of Women's Volleyball Scholarships: 4
Conference: Conference USA

Program Profile: Our program is currently 7th in the Conference USA. Halton Arena was built in 1997 and has 9,105 seats. Our playing season is from August to December.

History: We began in 1974 and we were a low Division I program. We have now moved to a middle/top 200 program. The program has made significant advances in Conference USA. We have moved from the bottom half of the conference to the middle half.

Achievements: Ozlem Ayture (Soph)-Honorable Mention All-Conference team 1998;All-Freshman Team 1997; Jamie Bielenda (Sr.'97) All-Conference 3rd Team 1997.

Coaching: Julie Ibieta, Head Coach, started in 1997 and has a 25-39 record. As a player at LSU-SEC, she was named Freshman of the Year in 1998. She was in the 1st team SEC in 1989,1990 and 1991. She went to the NCAA Final Four in 1990 and 1991. She was team captain in 1991. Coach Launey started in 1998. As a player at LSU, she went to the NCAA Final Four in 1990 and 1991.

Freshman Receiving Financial Aid/Academic: **Athletic:** 4

Roster In State: 0	**Out of State:** 7	**Out of Country:** 2
Sophomores on Team: 2	**Seniors on Team:** 3	**Graduation %:** 100
Most Recent Record: 14-17-0	**Fall Games:** 31	**Spring Games:** 4

Camp of Clinic Dates: Individual Camp-July 11-14, 1999; Team Camp-July 30-31, 1999

Positions Needed: 2 Outside Hitters and 2 Middle Blockers

Schedule: Penn State, UNC Chapel Hill, Louisville, Wake Forest, South Florida, Houston

University of North Carolina at Greensboro
Academic Profile

1000 Spring Garden St.
Greensboro, NC 27412-0001

Phone: 336-334-5243

Type: Public, 4 Yr., Liberal Arts, Coed
Website: http://www.uncg.edu
SAT/ACT/GPA: Floating scale
Student/Faculty Ratio: 14:1
Undergraduate Enrollment: 12,000
Scholarships/Academic: Yes   **Athletic:** Yes
Expenses By: Year   **In State:** $ 6,000

Founded: 1891
Religion: Non-Affiliated
Housing: Yes
Male/Female: 35:65
Graduate Enrollment: 2,500
Financial Aid: Yes
Out of State: $ 14,500

Degrees Conferred: BA, BS, BFA, MA, MS, MFA, MEd, Ph.D., EdD

Programs of Study: UNCG is organized into the Graduate School, The College of Arts and Sciences and six Professional Schools: The Joseph M. Bryan School of Business and Economics, School of Education, School of Health and Human Performance, School of Human Environmental Sciences, School of Music, School of Nursing

Women's Athletic Profile

337 HHP Building
Greensboro, NC 27402-6170
Coach: Stacy Meadows
Email: sbmeadow@uncg.edu

NCAA I
Spartans, Gold, White, Navy
Phone: (336) 334-5303
Fax: (336) 334-3182

Estimated # of Women's Volleyball Scholarships: N/A
Conference: Southern Conference

University of North Carolina at Pembroke
Academic Profile

P.O. Box 1510-UNCP
Pembroke, NC 28372-1510

Phone: 800-949-8627

Type: Public, 4 Yr., Liberal Arts, Coed
Website: http://www.uncp.edu
SAT/ACT/GPA: 820
Student/Faculty Ratio: 16:1
Undergraduate Enrollment: 2,900
Scholarships/Academic: Yes   **Athletic:** Yes
Expenses By: Year   **In State:** $ 5,000

Founded: 1887
Religion: Non-Affiliated
Housing: Yes
Male/Female: 45:55
Graduate Enrollment: 250
Financial Aid: Yes
Out of State: $ 12,00

Specializes In: More than 50 majors

Degrees Conferred: BA, BS, BSN, BSW, BM, MA, MS, MBA, M.Ed.

Programs of Study: American Indian Studies, Art, Business, Business Administration, Accounting, Chemistry, English, Education, Theatre Arts, Elementary Education, Middle School Education, Special Education, Physical Education, Recruiting Management, Athletic Training, Community Health, History, Social Science Education, Mass Communications, Journalism, Broadcasting, Math, Math Education, Computer Science, Music, Music Education, Philosophy & Religion, Political Science, PreLaw, Public Administration, International Studies, Psychology, Sociology, Criminal Justice, Social Work

Women's Athletic Profile

1 University Drive
Pembroke, NC 28358
Coach: Beverly Justice
Email: justice@sassette.uncp.edu

NCAA I
Lady Braves, Black, Gold
Phone: (910) 521-6273
Fax: (910) 521-6551

Estimated # of Women's Volleyball Scholarships: 5
Conference: Peach Belt Athletic Conference
Program Profile: Volleyball program is the winningest women's team in UNCP school history in terms of all-time winning percentage. Home court is the 3,000-seat Jones Athletic Complex, home of the 2000 Peach Belt Conference Tournament. The complex is undergoing major upgrades, including: installation of permanent seats to replace wooden bleachers, a recently opened new $25,000 weight room and fitness, center, upgrades to locker rooms and additions to the Olympic size pool. Facilities include modern training room, video rooms, booster club and full-sized auxiliary gym in addition to main arena.
Achievements: Four Conference Championships. 1 All-American, 1 Academic All-American, 3 Conference Coach of the Year Awards.
Coaching: Head coach: Beverly Justice
Freshman Receiving Financial Aid/Academic: **Athletic:** 4
Roster In State: 7 **Out of State:** 4
Seniors on Team: 2
Most Recent Record: 9-27
Positions Needed: Middle blocker, Blockers. Also looking for height
Schedule: North Florida, Armstrong Atlantic, Francis Marion.
Style of Play: Excellent hitting team with hitting percentage over.300 through first half of 2000 season.

University of North Carolina - Wilmington
Academic Profile

601 S. College St.
Wilmington, NC 28403-3297

Phone: 800-228-5571

Type: Public, 4 Yr., Liberal Arts, Coed
Website: http://www.uncwil.edu
SAT/ACT/GPA: 1100/3.0
Student/Faculty Ratio: 16:1
Undergraduate Enrollment: 9,000
Scholarships/Academic: Yes **Athletic:** Yes
Expenses By: Year **In State:** $ 7,500
Specializes In: Marine Biology
Degrees Conferred: BA, BS, MA, M.Ed., MAT, MFA

Founded: 1947
Religion: Non-Affiliated
Housing: Yes
Male/Female: 41:59
Graduate Enrollment: 600
Financial Aid: Yes
Out of State: $ 14,600

Programs of Study: Anthropology, Art, Biology, Chemistry, Communications, Criminal Justice, Economics, Elementary Education, English, Environmental Studies, French, Geology, History, Mathematics, Music, Music Education, Parks & Recreation Management, Philosophy & Religion, Physical Education, Physics, Political Science, Psychology, Social Science, Secondary Education, Sociology, Spanish, Special Education, Account, Chemistry, Computer Science, Economics, Finance, Geology, Marine Biology, Marketing, Mathematics, Physics

Women's Athletic Profile

601 S. College Rd
Wilmington, NC 28403-3297
Coach: China Jude
Email: judec@uncwil.edu

NCAA I
Seahawks, Green, Gold, Navy
Phone: (910) 962-3242
Fax: (910) 962-3002

Estimated # of Women's Volleyball Scholarships: N/A
Conference: Colonial Athletic Association

Wake Forest University
Academic Profile

1834 Wake Forest Rd.
Winston - Salem, NC 27109-7265

Phone: 336-758-5201

Type: Private, 4 Yr., Liberal Arts, Coed
Website: http://www.wfu.edu
SAT/ACT/GPA: 1270/29
Student/Faculty Ratio: 11.4:1
Undergraduate Enrollment: 3,841
Scholarships/Academic: Yes
Expenses By: Year
Specializes In: Preparation for graduate and professional education
Degrees Conferred: BA, BS, MA, MS, MBA, MEd, Ph.D., MD, JD.

Athletic: Yes
In State: $ 26,700

Founded: 1834
Religion: Non-Affiliated
Housing: Yes
Male/Female: 1:1
Graduate Enrollment: 2,226
Financial Aid: Yes
Out of State: $ 26,700

Programs of Study: Anthropology, Art History, Studio Art, Chemistry, Classical Studies, Communications, Economics, English, French, German, Greek, History, Latin, Music, Philosophy, Physics, Politics, Psychology, Religion, Russian, Sociology, Spanish, Theatre, Biology, Computer Science, Health & Exercise Science, Mathematical Economics, Mathematics, Elementary Education, Education, Dentistry, Engineering, Forestry, Environmental Studies, Medieval Technology, Physician's Assistant, Business, Analytical Finance, Professional Accountancy

Women's Athletic Profile

P.O. Box 7265
Winston-Salem, NC 27109
Coach: Valorie Baker
Email: bakervg@wful.edu

NCAA I
Demon Deacons, Black, Gold
Phone: (336) 758-6993
Fax: (336) 758-4565

Estimated # of Women's Volleyball Scholarships: N/A
Conference: Atlantic Coast Conference

Western Carolina University
Academic Profile

WCU Athletics Baseball, Ramsey Center
Cullowhee, NC 28723

Phone: 828-227-7317

Type: Public, 4 Yr., Coed
Website: http://www.wcu.edu
SAT/ACT/GPA: 850avg
Student/Faculty Ratio: 17:1
Undergraduate Enrollment: 5,685
Scholarships/Academic: Yes
Expenses By: Year
Degrees Conferred: BA, BFA, BS, BSBA, BSN, MBA, MA, MS

Athletic: Yes
In State: $ 4,250

Founded: 1889
Religion: Non-Affiliated
Housing: Yes
Male/Female: 49:51
Graduate Enrollment: 866
Financial Aid: Yes
Out of State: $ 10,700

Programs of Study: 90 programs leading to Bachelors degree and 70+ programs leading to Masters degree.

Women's Athletic Profile

Ramsey Center
Culluwhee, NC 28723
Coach: Michelle Hansen
Email: mhansen@wpoff.edu

NCAA I
Lady Cats, Purple, Gold
Phone: (828) 227-7338
Fax: (828) 227-7688

Estimated # of Women's Volleyball Scholarships: N/A
Conference: Southern Conference

Wingate University
Academic Profile

Box 2510
Wingate, NC 28174
Type: Private, 4 Yr., Liberal Arts, Coed

Phone: 800-755-5550

Founded: 1895

Website: http://www.wingate.edu
SAT/ACT/GPA: 850+
Student/Faculty Ratio: 15:1
Undergraduate Enrollment: 1,400
Scholarships/Academic: Yes   **Athletic:** Yes
Expenses By: Year   **In State:** $ 16,000
Specializes In: Education, Business, Sports Medicine, Pre-Professional
Degrees Conferred: AA, AS, BA, BS, MBA
Programs of Study: Accounting, Biology, Business & Management, Chemistry, Communications, Computer Information Systems, Economics, Education, English, Fine Arts, Journalism, Liberal Arts, Mathematics, Music, Parks Management, PreEngineering, PreLaw, PreMed, PreVet, Religion, Social Science, Speech, Sports Medicine, Telecommunications

Religion: Baptist
Housing: Yes
Male/Female: 1:3
Graduate Enrollment: 150
Financial Aid: Yes
Out of State: $ 16,000

Women's Athletic Profile

Box 3054
Wingate, NC 28174
Coach; Susan Deaton
Email: sdeaton@wingate.edu
Conference: South Atlantic Conference

NCAA I
Lady Bulldogs, Navy Blue, Gold
Phone: (704) 233-8167
Fax: (704) 233-8170

Winston - Salem State University
Academic Profile

601 ML King Drive
Winston-Salem, NC 27110

Phone: 336-750-2057

Type: Public, 4 Yr., Coed
Website: http://www.cs.wssu.edu
SAT/ACT/GPA: 600+
Student/Faculty Ratio: 15:1
Undergraduate Enrollment: 2,604
Scholarships/Academic: Yes   **Athletic:** Yes
Expenses By: Year   **In State:** $ 6,390
Degrees Conferred: BA, BS
Programs of Study: Contact school for programs of study.

Founded: 1892
Religion: Non-Affiliated
Housing: No
Male/Female: 38:62
Graduate Enrollment: N/A
Financial Aid: Yes
Out of State: $ 10,864

Women's Athletic Profile

601 ML King Drive
Winston - Salem, NC 27110
Coach: Terri Eanes
Email:

NCAA I
Lady Rams, Scarlet, White
Phone: (336) 750-2598
Fax: (336) 750-2141

Estimated # of Women's Volleyball Scholarships: 4 partial
Conference: Central Intercollegiate Athletic Association
Program Profile: small division II program-play in recently renovated Whitaker Gym. Season last August 31-Oct. 31. Limited partial scholarships available.
Coaching: Terri Eames-started 1997, 11-23 overall
Freshman Receiving Financial Aid/Academic: **Athletic:** 0
Roster In State: 11   **Out of State:** 1   **Out of Country:**
Sophomores on Team: **Seniors on Team:** 3   **Graduation %:**
Most Recent Record: 6-11   **Fall Games:** 23   **Spring Games:** 0
Positions Needed: Setter, Middle
Schedule: Fayetteville State University, St. Augustine's College, North Carolina Central, High Point University, Guilford College, Johnson C. Smith University

NORTH DAKOTA

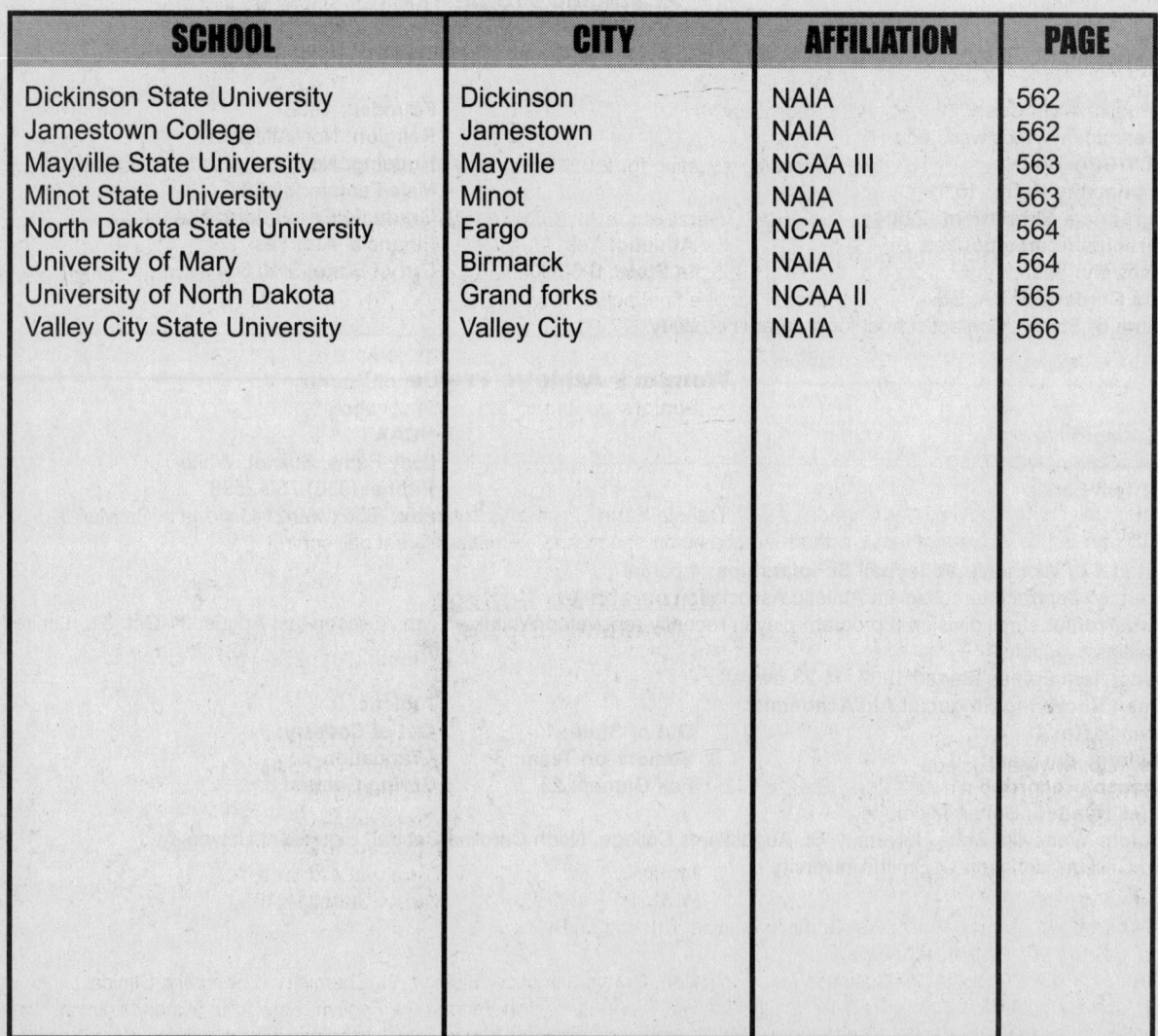

Bismarck ✪

SCHOOL	CITY	AFFILIATION	PAGE
Dickinson State University	Dickinson	NAIA	562
Jamestown College	Jamestown	NAIA	562
Mayville State University	Mayville	NCAA III	563
Minot State University	Minot	NAIA	563
North Dakota State University	Fargo	NCAA II	564
University of Mary	Birmarck	NAIA	564
University of North Dakota	Grand forks	NCAA II	565
Valley City State University	Valley City	NAIA	566

Dickinson State University
Academic Profile

291 Campus Drive
Dickinson, ND 58601

Phone: (800) 279-HAWK

Type: Public, 4 Yr., Liberal Arts, Coed
Website: http://www.dsu.nodak.edu
SAT/ACT/GPA: 19/2.0
Student/Faculty Ratio: 16:1
Undergraduate Enrollment: 1,800
Scholarships/Academic: Yes   **Athletic:** Yes
Expenses By: Year   **In State:** $ 5,296
Specializes In: Agriculture, Business, Education, Nursing
Degrees Conferred: AA, AS, AAS, BA, BS

Founded: 1918
Religion: Non-Affiliated
Housing: Yes
Male/Female: 40:60
Graduate Enrollment: N/A
Financial Aid: Yes
Out of State: $ 6,312

Programs of Study: Accounting, Agricultural, Art, Biology, Business, Chemistry, Communications, Computer, Early Childhood Education, Earth Science, Education, English, Fine Arts, Geography, History, Journalism, Management, Mathematics, Music, Nursing, Political Science, Secondary Education, Social Science, Spanish, Speech

Women's Athletic Profile

291 Campus Drive
Dickinson, ND 58601
Coach: Dave Moody
Email: dave_moody@eagle.dsu.nodak.edu

NCAA I
Lady Blue Hawks, Blue, Grey
Phone: (701) 227-2120
Fax: (701) 227-2025

Estimated # of Women's Volleyball Scholarships: 4
Conference: NDCAC
Program Profile: We play in Scott Gym which has seating for 2,000. We have a spring and a fall season. Pre-season begins in mid-August.
History: Our program began in 1974. We had an overall record of 378-270. We got 6 Conference Championships. We made 2 National Tournament Appearances.
Achievements: Conference Coach of the Year 1995,1997 and 1998. Region Coach of the Year 1997; 8 All-Americans, 2 National Tournament Appearances; Ranked 5th nationally in the final poll.
Coaching: Dave Moody, Head Coach, his overall record is 227-93.
Freshman Receiving Financial Aid/Academic: **Athletic:** 1
Roster In State: 1   **Out of State:** 11   **Out of Country:** 4
Sophomores on Team: 0   **Seniors on Team:** 2   **Graduation %:** 90
Most Recent Record: 31-6-0
Camp of Clinic Dates: July 5 to 9
Positions Needed: 1 Middle, 2 Outsides
Schedule: University of Manitoba (Canada), North Dakota State University, Columbia, St. Edwards, College of St. Mary's
Style of Play: 5-1 west coast offense with an emphasis on speed and deception. Great ball control.

Jamestown College
Academic Profile

6000 College Lane
Jamestown, ND 58402

Phone: (701) 252-3467

Type: Private, 4 Yr., Liberal Arts, Coed
Website: http://www.acc.jc.edu
SAT/ACT/GPA: 850/18/2.5
Student/Faculty Ratio: 17:1
Undergraduate Enrollment: 1,100
Scholarships/Academic: Yes   **Athletic:** Yes
Expenses By: Year   **In State:** $ 11,050
Specializes In: Accounting, Business, Criminal Justice, Education, Biology
Degrees Conferred: Bachelors (4-year)

Founded: 1883
Religion: Presbyterian
Housing: Yes
Male/Female: 1:1
Graduate Enrollment: N/A
Financial Aid: Yes
Out of State: $ 11050

Programs of Study: Accounting, Business Administration, Criminal Justice, Biology, BioChemistry, Chemistry, Clinical Laboratory Science, Communications, Computer Science, Education, Elementary and Secondary, English, Fine Arts, History-Political Sciences, Management Information Science, Mathematics, Music, Nursing, Physical Education, Psychology, Radiological Technology, Religion, Philosophy

Women's Athletic Profile

P.O. Box 6088
Jamestown, ND 58402
Coach: Tom Heck
Email: mahoney@acc.jc.edu

NCAA I
Lady Jimmies, Black, Orange
Phone: (701) 252-3467x2559
Fax: (701) 253-4318

Estimated # of Women's Volleyball Scholarships: N/A
Conference: NDCAC

Mayville State University
Academic Profile

330 3rd St. NE
Mayville, ND 58257

Phone: 800-437-4104

Type: Public, 4 Yr., Coed
Website: http://www.masu.nodak.edu
SAT/ACT/GPA: Open enrollment/2.0
Student/Faculty Ratio: 18:1
Undergraduate Enrollment: 750
Scholarships/Academic: Yes
Expenses By: Year
Degrees Conferred: AA, BA, BS, BGS

Athletic: Yes
In State: $ 5,868

Founded: 1889
Religion: Non-Affiliated
Housing: Yes
Male/Female: 50:50
Graduate Enrollment: N/A
Financial Aid: Yes
Out of State: $ 8,928

Programs of Study: Business and Management, Business/Office and Marketing/Distribution, Computer Studies, Sciences, Social Science, Teacher Education, Child Development, Professional Programs

Women's Athletic Profile

330 3rd Street NE
Mayville, ND 58527
Coach: Patricia Mickow
Email:

NCAA I
Lady Comets, Royal Blue, White
Phone: (701) 786-2301
Fax: (701) 786-4840

Did Not Return Profile

Minot State University
Academic Profile

500 University Avenue, W
Minot, ND 58707

Phone: 800-542-6866

Type:
Website: Not Available
SAT/ACT/GPA: Open
Student/Faculty Ratio: 22:1
Undergraduate Enrollment: 2,277
Scholarships/Academic:
Expenses By:
Degrees Conferred:

Athletic:
In State:

Founded: 1966
Religion: Non-Affiliated
Housing: No
Male/Female: Not Available
Graduate Enrollment: N/A
Financial Aid:
Out of State:

Programs of Study: Contact school for programs of study.

Women's Athletic Profile

500 University Avenue, W
Minot, ND 58707
Coach: Dana Fielder
Email:

NCAA I
Lady Beavers, Red, Green
Phone: (701) 858-3169
Fax: (701) 858-3136

Estimated # of Women's Volleyball Scholarships: 5
Conference: NDCAC
Program Profile: Our program has been in the top of the NDCAC Conference in the last few years. We have the best facilities in the Conference and in the area. Dome Stadium has a seating capacity of 10,000 people. Our season runs from mid-August through the end of November.

History: The program began in 1978. Volleyball has been at MSU for 20 years or so. We have grown into a very competitive program and NDCAC Conference.

Achievements: 1993-1994 NDCAC Coach of the Year; 4 Academic All-American in the last five years; 2 most valuable graduating seniors in NDCAC Conference; All-American Honorable Mention.

Coaching: Dana Fiedler, Head Coach, started with the program in 1993. She was named NDCAC Coach of the Year in 1993 & 1994. Her overall record since starting in 1993 to the present is 127-127.

Freshman Receiving Financial Aid/Academic:

		Athletic: 1
Roster In State: 5	**Out of State:** 1	**Out of Country:** 6
Sophomores on Team: 5	**Seniors on Team:** 2	**Graduation %:** 99
Most Recent Record: 16-16-0	**Fall Games:** 35-40	**Spring Games:** 0

Camp of Clinic Dates: June 21-24 (8-12 graders)

Positions Needed: Power Hitter, Middle Hitter, Blocker, Setter

Schedule: Dickinson State University, Dordt College, Doane College, University of Mary, Northwestern College, Newman University

Style of Play: Aggressive, never say die attitude. Play a very quick and aggressive tempo offense, because of our overall size in the past. A dig or die defensive attitude, nothing hits the floor.

North Dakota State University - Fargo
Academic Profile

1301 Administrative Avenue
Fargo, ND 58105

Phone: 800-488-6378

Type: Public, 4 Yr., Liberal Arts, Coed
Website: http://www.ndsu.nodak.edu
SAT/ACT/GPA: 21/2.5
Student/Faculty Ratio: 19:1
Undergraduate Enrollment: 9,626
Scholarships/Academic: Yes
Expenses By: Year

Athletic: Yes
In State: $ 6,027

Founded: 1890
Religion: Non-Affiliated
Housing: Yes
Male/Female: 60:40
Graduate Enrollment: N/A
Financial Aid: Yes
Out of State: $ 10,003

Specializes In: Agriculture, Liberal Arts, Engineering

Degrees Conferred: BA, BS, MA, MS, Ph.D.

Programs of Study: College of Agriculture, College of Business Administration, College of Engineering & Architecture, College of Human Development & Education, College of Arts, Humanities & Social Sciences, College of Pharmacy, College of Science & Mathematics, College of University Studies

Women's Athletic Profile

Bison Sports Arena
Fargo, ND 58105
Coach: Zaundra Bina
Email: zbina@prairie.nodak.edu

NCAA I
Lady Bison, Green, Gold
Phone: (701) 231-8859
Fax: (701) 231-8022

Estimated # of Women's Volleyball Scholarships: 3

Conference: North Central Collegiate Athletic Conference

Program Profile: We are a traditionally strong, elite program at the Division II level. We have a facility that has 2,500 seats.

History: The program began in 1975.

Achievements: Conference Titles in 1981, 1982, 1988, 1989, 1990, 1991, 1997 7 1998; 1998 Division II Runner-Up; Elite 8 in 1986, 1988, 1989, 1990, 1992, & 1998; All-Americans - NDSU has had volleyball athletes named All-American 25 times.

Coaching: Zaundra Bina, Head Coach, has been here for four years with an overall record of 113-26. She was named Division II Coach of the Year. Bob Jones Assistant Coach. He is in his fifth year with the program.

Freshman Receiving Financial Aid/Academic:

		Athletic: 5
Roster In State: 2	**Out of State:** 11	**Out of Country:** 0
Sophomores on Team: 2	**Seniors on Team:** 3	**Graduation %:** 96
Most Recent Record: 33-4-0	**Fall Games:** 30-38	**Spring Games:** 16

Camp of Clinic Dates: July 5-15

Positions Needed: Setter, Middle, Outside Hitter

Schedule: Tampa, North Florida, North Michigan, North Kentucky, University of Minnesota-Duluth, Edinboro

Style of Play: Fast transition offense; one point take-off by middles and right side players in front of setter and behind setter.

University of Mary
Academic Profile

7500 University Drive
Birmarck, ND 58504

Phone:

Type: 4 Yr.,

Founded:

Website:
SAT/ACT/GPA: Open
Student/Faculty Ratio:
Undergraduate Enrollment: N/A
Scholarships/Academic: **Athletic:**
Expenses By: **In State:**
Degrees Conferred:
Programs of Study: Contact school for programs of study.

Religion: Non-Affiliated
Housing: No
Male/Female:
Graduate Enrollment: N/A
Financial Aid:
Out of State:

Women's Athletic Profile

7500 University Drive
Birmarck, ND 58504
Coach: Annette Sabot
Email: admision@umary.edu

NAIA
Marauders, Blue, Orange, White
Phone: (701) 255-7500
Fax: (701) 255-7687

Estimated # of Women's Volleyball Scholarships: 8
Conference: NDCAC
History: Our program started in 1980.
Achievements: Conference Titles in 1990,1992,1993 and 1994; Coach of the Year in 1992; Academic All-Americans 8 in 8 past years.
Coaching: Annette Sabot, became Head Coach in 1991. Her overall record is 172-102. Cindy Bohn became Assistant Coach in 1998. She has been the junior varsity coach for the past 4 years.
Freshman Receiving Financial Aid/Academic: **Athletic:** All
Roster In State: 18   **Out of State:** 10   **Out of Country:** 0
Sophomores on Team: 3   **Seniors on Team:** 3   **Graduation %:** 98
Most Recent Record: 23-17-0   **Fall Games:** 24   **Spring Games:** 0
Camp of Clinic Dates: None this year
Positions Needed: Outside Hitter (2), Right Setter (1)
Schedule: Dickson State University, Northwestern, Dordt, Rocky Mountain College, Butte
Style of Play: Aggressive and quick.

University of North Dakota
Academic Profile

Box 9013
Grand Forks, ND 58202

Phone: 800-225-5863

Type: Public, 4 Yr., Coed
Website: http://www.nodak.edu
SAT/ACT/GPA: Open/2.0 grade-point
Student/Faculty Ratio: 15:1
Undergraduate Enrollment: 9,500
Scholarships/Academic: Yes   **Athletic:** Yes
Expenses By: Year   **In State:** $ 6,160
Degrees Conferred: BA, BS, BFA, MA, MS, MFA, MD

Founded: 1883
Religion: Non-Affiliated
Housing: Yes
Male/Female: 50:50
Graduate Enrollment: 1,500
Financial Aid: Yes
Out of State: $ 10,000

Programs of Study: There are over 165 different fields of study with 11 academic divisions: Arts & Sciences, Aerospace Sciences, Business & Public Administration, Engineering and Mines, Fine Arts & Communications, Nursing, Education & Human Development, Medicine & Health Sciences, Law; graduate School and Continuing Education

Women's Athletic Profile

Box 9013
Grand forks, ND 58202
Coach: Maria Bruggeman
Email: maria_bruggeman@und.nodak.edu

NCAA I
Fighting Sioux, Green, White
Phone: (701) 777-2508
Fax: (701) 777-4352

Estimated # of Women's Volleyball Scholarships: N/A
Conference: North Central Collegiate Athletic Conference

Valley City State University
Academic Profile

101 College St. SW
Valley City, ND 58072
Type: Public, 4 Yr., Coed
Website: http://www.vcsu.nodak.edu
SAT/ACT/GPA: Students must meet core requirements
Student/Faculty Ratio: 18:1
Undergraduate Enrollment: 1,100
Scholarships/Academic: Yes   **Athletic:** Yes
Expenses By: Year   **In State:** $ 2,461
Specializes In: Liberal Arts
Degrees Conferred: BA, BS, BSEd

Phone: (701) 845-7101

Founded: 1890
Religion: Non-Affiliated
Housing: Yes
Male/Female: 1:1
Graduate Enrollment: N/A
Financial Aid: Yes
Out of State: $ 3,864

Programs of Study: Art, Business, Chemistry, Biology, Computer Science, English, Fine Arts, Health, History, Human Resources, Library Media, Mathematics, Music, Physical Education, Psychology, Social Science, Spanish, Technology Education, University Studies

Women's Athletic Profile

101 College Street, SW
Valley City, ND 58072
Coach: Diane Burr
Email: diane_burr@mail.vcsu.nodak.edu

NCAA I
Vikings, Cardinal, Royal Blue
Phone: (701) 845-7101
Fax: (701) 845-7213

Estimated # of Women's Volleyball Scholarships: 3
Conference: NDCAC
Program Profile: We play at Graichen gym and have a fall season.
History: Our program began in 1970. By 1979, VCSU started first of eight NDCAC Championships. The Vikings, since the 1979 season, have only finished lower than 3rd place in the NDCAC three times.
Achievements: Coach of the Year in NAIA District 12 in 1981; Conference Titles in 1981,1982,1987,1988,1993 and 1996; coached 6 most valuable graduating seniors in the NDCAC
Coaching: Diane Burr, Head Coach, joined the Vikings in 1981. Her career record at VCSU is 325-249.
Freshman Receiving Financial Aid/Academic: **Athletic:** 1
Roster In State: 3   **Out of State:** 1   **Out of Country:** 9
Sophomores on Team: 0   **Seniors on Team:** 5   **Graduation %:** 99
Most Recent Record: 25-12-0
Positions Needed: Setter, Middle Hitter
Schedule: Dickinson State, To be decided in tournament play
Style of Play: High concentration on explosive offense/ persistent floor defense.

OHIO

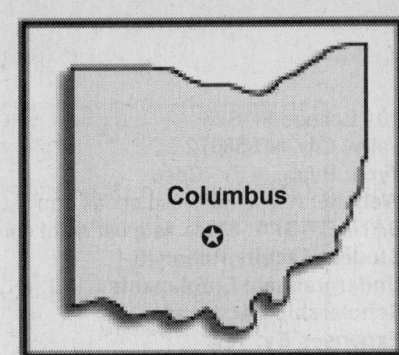

Columbus ★

SCHOOL	CITY	AFFILIATION	PAGE
Ashland University	Ashland	NCAA II	569
Baldwin-Wallace College	Berea	NCAA III	569
Bluffton College	Bluffton	NCAA III	570
Bowling Green State University	Bowling Green	NCAA I	570
Capital University	Columbus	NCAA III	571
Case Western Reserve University	Cleveland	NCAA III	572
Cedarville College	Cedarville	NCCAA/NAIA	572
Central State University	Wilbeforce	NAIA	573
Cleveland State University	Cleveland	NCAA I	574
College of Mount St. Joseph	Cincinnati	NCAA III	574
College of Wooster	Wooster	NCAA III	575
Defiance College	Defiance	NCAA III	576
Denison University	Granville	NCAA III	577
Heidelberg College	Tiffin	NCAA III	577
Hiram College	Hiram	NCAA III	578
John Carroll University	University Heights	NCAA III	578
Kent State University	Kent	NCAA I	579
Kenyon College	Gambier	NCAA III	579
Lake Erie College	Painesville	NCAA III	580
Malone College	Canton	NAIA	581
Marietta College	Marietta	NCAA III	581
Miami University	Miami	NCAA I	581
Mount Union College	Alliance	NCAA III	582
Mount Vernon Nazarene College	Mt. Vernon	NAIA	583
Muskingum College	New Concord	NCAA III	583
Notre Dame College - Ohio	South Euclid	NAIA	584
Oberlin College	Oberlin	NCAA III	585
Ohio Dominican College	Columbus	NAIA	585

SCHOOL	CITY	AFFILIATION	PAGE
Ohio Northern University	Ada	NCAA III	586
Ohio State University	Columbus	NCAA I	587
Ohio University	Athens	NCAA I	588
Ohio Wesleyan University	Delaware	NCAA III	588
Otterbein College	Westerville	NCAA III	589
Shawnee State University	Portsmouth	NAIA	589
Tiffin University	Tiffin	NCAA II/NAIA	590
University of Akron	Akron	NCAA I	591
University of Cincinnati	Cincinnati	NCAA I	591
University of Dayton	Dayton	NCAA I	592
University of Findlay	Findley	NCAA II	593
University of Rio Grande	Rio Grande	NAIA	594
University of Toledo	Toledo	NCAA I	594
Urbana University	Urbana	NAIA	595
Walsh University	North Canton	NAIA	595
Wilmington College	Wilmington	NCAA III	596
Wittenberg University	Springfield	NCAA III	597
Wright State University	Dayton	NCAA I	597
Xavier University	Cincinnati	NCAA I	598
Youngstown State University	Youngstown	NCAA I	598

Ashland University
Academic Profile

401 College Avenue
Ashland, OH 44805

Phone: 800-882-1548

Type: Private, 4 Yr., Liberal Arts, Coed
Website: http://www.ashland.edu
SAT/ACT/GPA: 870/18/2.5
Student/Faculty Ratio: 14:1
Undergraduate Enrollment: 2,000
Scholarships/Academic: Yes
Expenses By: Year
Specializes In: Business, Education
Degrees Conferred: BA, BS, M.Ed., MBA

Athletic: Yes
In State: $ 19,366

Founded: 1878
Religion: Brethren Church
Housing: Yes
Male/Female: 41:59
Graduate Enrollment: 3,000
Financial Aid: Yes
Out of State: $ 19,366

Programs of Study: Art, Biology, Business Administration, Chemistry, Communications, Computer Science, Criminal Justice, Economics, English, Foreign Languages, Geology, History, Journalism, Math, Music, Nursing, Philosophy, Physical Science, Education, Physics, Political Science, Psychology, Radio/Television, Recreation, Religion, Social Work, Sociology, Speech, Theatre, Athletic Administration

Women's Athletic Profile

401 College Avenue
Ashland, OH 44805
Coach: Sue Martensen-Uebel
Email:

NCAA I
Lady Eagles, Purple, Gold
Phone: (419) 289-5454
Fax: (419) 289-5468

Estimated # of Women's Volleyball Scholarships: N/A
Conference: Great Lakes Intercollegiate Athletic Conference
Program Profile: Kates Gymnasium hosts our home volleyball games. It has the capacity to be subdivided to facilitate concurrent practice sessions. Wurster Fitness Center has state-of-the-art weight training equipment.
History: Ashland competes on the NCAA Division II level. We are a member of the newly-formed Great Lakes Intercollegiate Athletic Conference.
Seniors on Team: 1
Most Recent Record: 12-19-0   **Fall Games:** 28   **Spring Games:** 0
Schedule: Saginaw Valley State, Gannon, Mercyhurst, Northwood, Wayne State, Hillsdale, Grand Valley, Ferris State, Michigan Tech, Northern Michigan
Style of Play: The youngsters who went through this season's battles will be a year older and wiser next season and that could pay off in a return to the postseason.

Baldwin - Wallace College
Academic Profile

275 East Land Road
Berea, OH 44017

Phone: 877-292-7759

Type: Private, 4 Yr., Liberal Arts, Coed
Website: http://www.balwinw.edu
SAT/ACT/GPA: 1050/21/3.0
Student/Faculty Ratio: 14:1
Undergraduate Enrollment: 2,800
Scholarships/Academic: Yes
Expenses By: Year

Athletic: No
In State: $ 20,000

Founded: 1845
Religion: Methodist
Housing: Yes
Male/Female: 40:60
Graduate Enrollment: 600
Financial Aid: Yes
Out of State: $ 20,000

Degrees Conferred: BA, BS, BM, BME, MBA, MAEd
Programs of Study: Accounting, Banking/Finance, Biology, Business Administration, Chemistry, Communications, Computer Science, Dance, Earth Science, Education, Geology, Health, Marketing, Mathematics, Medical Laboratory, Physical Education, Psychology, Sports Management, Sociology, Sports Medicine

Women's Athletic Profile

275 Eatland Rd.
Berea, OH 44017
Coach: Victoria Brault
Email: vbrault@bw.edu

NCAA I
Yellow Jackets, Brown, Gold
Phone: (440) 826-3254
Fax: (440) 826-2192

Estimated # of Women's Volleyball Scholarships: N/A

Conference: Ohio Athletic Conference

Program Profile: One of the finest gymnasiums which seats 2, 300 fans, has wooden floors and 2 courts, a complete training facility with a track, racquetball and weight training room.

History: Program began in 1965, joined the Ohio Athletic Conference in 1984. Our overall record is 336-260. We have always had a winning tradition, finishing in the top 3-4 in the conference and in the past 4 years we have had 20 wins in a season. We also have a junior varsity program.

Achievements: OAC Coach of the Year 2000, OAC Tournament Champions, OAC Freshman of the Year 2000, 12 athletes OAC honors, and 1 graduate with regional honors.

Coaching: Victoria Brault Head Coach. In the past 4 years her record is 91-44 and 24-10 in conference. OAC Tournament Champion, NCAA Appearance and Coach of the Year in 2000.

Roster In State: 16

Graduation %: 100

Most Recent Record: 25-10

Positions Needed: 3 Middle Hitters, 2 OH, Setter

Schedule: Juniata, Ohio Northern, Muskingham, Calvin, RIT

Style of Play: 5-1 offense with fast swing and solid defense.

Bluffton College
Academic Profile

280 W. College Avenue
Bluffton, OH 45817

Phone: (419) 358-3000

Type: Private, 4 Yr., Liberal Arts, Coed
Website: http://www.bluffton.edu
SAT/ACT/GPA: 920/19/2.3
Student/Faculty Ratio: 15:1
Undergraduate Enrollment: 981
Scholarships/Academic: Yes
Expenses By: Year
Degrees Conferred: BA, BS, BM, MA

Founded: 1899
Religion: Mennonite
Housing: Yes
Male/Female: 45:55
Graduate Enrollment: 19
Athletic: No　　**Financial Aid:** Yes
In State: $ 17,496　　**Out of State:** $ 17,496

Programs of Study: Accounting, Apparel/Textile Merchandising & Design, Art, Biology, Business, Chemistry, Child Development, Communications, Computer Science, Criminal Justice, Dietetics, Economics, Early Childhood Education, English, Family & Consumer Science, Food & Nutrition, Health, History, Humanities, Mathematics, Middle Childhood Education, Music, Physical Education, Psychology, Recreational Management, Religion, Social Work, Young Adult Education, Youth Ministries

Women's Athletic Profile

280 W. College Avenue
Bluffton, OH 45817
Coach: Sara Wakefield
Email:

NCAA I
Lady Beavers, Purple, White
Phone: (419) 358-3000
Fax: (419) 358-3070

Estimated # of Women's Volleyball Scholarships: N/A

Conference: Heartland Collegiate Athletic Conference

Program Profile: Our volleyball team is consistently ranked nationally and plays a demanding schedule of dual and invitational contests. Having appeared in post-season NCAA Championship competition, the team is recognized as one of the best in the United States. Many of our players have received post-season honors. The team plays both a traditional Fall schedule and an off-season schedule that provides for play into the winter and spring.

History: We started playing in 1982.

Achievements: Kim Fischer was named WBCC Coach of the Year in 1982,1984, 1987 and 1990. In 1982 we had 4 All-Conference Players and in 1983, we had 2 All-Conference Players. In 1984, we had 3 All-Conference Players. In 1991, we had 4 AMC All-Conference Players. IN 1992, we had 3 AMC All-Conference Players. In 1993, we had 5 AMC All-Conference Players. In 1994, we had 6 AMC All-Conference Players. In 1995, we had 4 AMC All-Conference Players.

Coaching: Sara Wakefield, Head Coach, is entering her first year with the program. She is a graduate of Bluffton.

Freshman Receiving Financial Aid/Academic:　　**Athletic:** 0

Roster In State: 10　　**Out of State:** 0　　**Out of Country:** 0

Sophomores on Team: 6　　**Seniors on Team:** 3　　**Graduation %:** Unknown

Bowling Green State University
Academic Profile

Perry Stadium
Bowling Green, OH 43403

Phone: (419) 372-2401

Type: Public, 4 Yr., Coed

Founded: 1910

Website: http://www.bgsu.edu
SAT/ACT/GPA: Varies/Varies
Student/Faculty Ratio: 18:1
Undergraduate Enrollment: 14,000
Scholarships/Academic: Yes
Expenses By: Year
Specializes In: Education & Business along with 16 other majors
Degrees Conferred: AA, Bachelors, Masters

Athletic: Yes
In State: $ 10,600

Religion: Non-Affiliated
Housing: Yes
Male/Female: 40:60
Graduate Enrollment: 4,000
Financial Aid: Yes
Out of State: $ 15,600

Programs of Study: Accounting, Apparel Merchandising & Production Development, Applied Health Science, Art, Biological Sciences, Chemistry, Child & Family Community Service, Computer Science, Criminal Justice, Economics, English, Exercise Specialist, Finance, Hospitality Management, Human Movement Science, Human Resource Management, Information Systems Auditing, International Business, Interpersonal Communications, Journalism, Management Information Systems, Marketing, Mathematics, Music, Nursing, Philosophy, Photography, Physical Therapy, Physics, Political Science, Popular Culture, PreLaw, PreMed, PreOccupational Therapy, Psychology, Recreation & Tourism, Social Work, Sports Management, Teacher Preparation, Early Childhood Education, Special Education, Physical Education, Telecommunications, Visual Communications

Women's Athletic Profile

201 Memorial Hall
Bowling Green, OH 43403
Coach: Denise Van De Walle
Email: denisev@bgnet.bgsu.edu

NCAA I
Lady Falcons, Brown, Orange
Phone: (419) 372-7067
Fax: (419) 372-7676

Estimated # of Women's Volleyball Scholarships: 4.5
Conference: Mid-American Conference
Program Profile: Anderson Arena is the home of the Falcons, seating 5,000 fans. The falcons have a brand new locker room as of September 1998. Bowling Green Volleyball has a history of success at the conference and regional level.
History: Program began in 1976. Bowling Green has three MAC regular season championships and one MAC tournament crown. Played in the 1991 NCAA tournament. Played in two NIVC tournaments (1992-1993). Placing second in 1992, program has over 400 wins all time.
Achievements: Coach Van De Walle is a four time MAC Coach of the Year who has led Bowling Green to over 300 wins and three conference championships. Bowling Green has had four MAC players of the Year winners.
Coaching: Denise Van De Walle has a career mark of 305-208, all at Bowling Green since 1983.
Roster In State: 7   **Out of State:** 6   **Out of Country:** 2
Seniors on Team: 4   **Graduation %:** 100
Most Recent Record: 9-8   **Fall Games:** 32
Camp of Clinic Dates: Mid-July
Positions Needed: Middle, Right side hitter, Setter
Style of Play: Competitive, goal and technique oriented. Disciplined yet fun.

Capital University
Academic Profile

2199 E. Main St.
Columbus, OH 43209

Phone: (614) 236-6918

Type: Private, 4 Yr., Liberal Arts, Coed
Website: http://www.capital.edu
SAT/ACT/GPA: 870/17
Student/Faculty Ratio: 14:1
Undergraduate Enrollment: 1,900
Scholarships/Academic: Yes
Expenses By: Year

Athletic: No
In State: $ 18,500

Founded: 1830
Religion: Lutheran
Housing: Yes
Male/Female: Not Available
Graduate Enrollment: 1,900
Financial Aid: Yes
Out of State: $ 18,500

Programs of Study: Accounting, Art, Art Education, Art Therapy, Biology, Business, Chemistry, Communications, Computer Science, Criminology, Economics, Education, Elementary Education, English, Finance, French, Health Education, Liberal Arts, Management, Marketing, Math, Music, Nursing, Philosophy, Physical Education, Political Science, PreDentistry, PreLaw, PreMed, Psychology, Public Administration, Social Science

Women's Athletic Profile

2199 E. Main Street
Columbus, OH 43209
Coach: Pam Briggs
Email: rbriggs414@aol.com

NCAA I
Lady Crusaders, Purple, White
Phone: (614) 236-6918
Fax: (614) 236-6178

Estimated # of Women's Volleyball Scholarships: N/A
Conference: Ohio Athletic Conference
Program Profile: Alumni gym has 1,200 seats. We will have a new facility in the year 2001. The playing season is from August through November.
Achievements: Coach of the Year in 1995; Conference champs in 1996; All-American was Carrie Ferguson; Academic All-American in 1997
Coaching: Pam Briggs, Head Coach, is entering six years with the program. She compiled a record of 115-79. Pam Wesley, Assistant Coach, compiled a record of 98-99. Greg Peters, Assistant Coach, compiled a record of 98-99.
Roster In State: 12

Sophomores on Team: 5	**Seniors on Team:** 1	**Graduation %:** 100

Most Recent Record: 16-17-0
Camp of Clinic Dates: June 9-12
Positions Needed: 2 Middles, 1 Outside Hitter, 2 Setters
Schedule: Ohio Northern, Muskingum, Baldwin Wallace, Ohio Weselyan, Mt. Union College, Mt. St. Joseph
Style of Play: Aggressive, swing offense; audible attackers and tough defense.

Case Western Reserve University
Academic Profile

10900 Euclid Avenue
Cleveland, OH 44106-7223

Phone: (216) 368-0322

Type: Private, 4 Yr., Engineering, Coed
Website: http://www.cwru.edu
SAT/ACT/GPA: 1250/27
Student/Faculty Ratio: 8:1
Undergraduate Enrollment: 3,600

Founded: 1967
Religion: Non-Affiliated
Housing: Yes
Male/Female: 59:41
Graduate Enrollment: 6,300

Scholarships/Academic: Yes	**Athletic:** No	**Financial Aid:** Yes
Expenses By: Year	**In State:** $ 24,666	**Out of State:** $ 24,666

Specializes In: Engineering, Nursing, PreMed, Biology, Chemistry, Management
Degrees Conferred: BA, BA
Programs of Study: Accounting, Art, BioChemistry, Biology, Chemistry, Communications, Computer Science, Economics, Engineering, English, French, German, History, Literature, Management, Math, Music, Natural Sciences, Nursing, Nutrition, Physics, Political Science, Sociology, Theatre, Women's Studies

Women's Athletic Profile

10900 Euclid Avenue
Cleveland, OH 44106
Coach: Karen Chambers
Email: klc3@po.cwru.edu

NCAA I
Spartans, Blue, Grey, White
Phone: (216) 368-0322
Fax: (216) 368-5475

Estimated # of Women's Volleyball Scholarships: None
Conference: North Coast Athletic Conference
Program Profile: Our season runs from the end of August to the end of November.
History: Our program is 28 years old.
Achievements: 1997 and 1998 NCAC Coach of the Year; 1997 UAA Coaching Staff of the Year.
Coaching: Karen Chambers, Head Coach, started here in 1995. She has an overall record of 88-69. Nelson Wittenmyer is Assistant Coach.

Roster In State: 9	**Out of State:** 3	**Out of Country:** 0
Sophomores on Team: 3	**Seniors on Team:** 3	**Graduation %:** 100
Most Recent Record: 24-16-0	**Fall Games:** 40	**Spring Games:** 0

Positions Needed: All
Schedule: Washington University-St. Louis, Emory University, Calvin College, New York University, Kalamazoo College, Hanover

CedarVille College
Academic Profile

Box 601
Cedarville, OH 45314
Type: 2 Yr.,
Website: http://www.dcccd.edu/cvc
SAT/ACT/GPA: Open
Student/Faculty Ratio:

Phone:

Founded:
Religion: Non-Affiliated
Housing: No
Male/Female:

Undergraduate Enrollment: N/A		Graduate Enrollment: N/A
Scholarships/Academic:	Athletic:	Financial Aid:
Expenses By:	In State:	Out of State:

Degrees Conferred:
Programs of Study: Contact school for programs of study.

Women's Athletic Profile

Box 601
Cedarville, OH 45314
Coach: Teresa Clark
Email: womackm@cedarville.edu

NCAA I
Yellow Jackets, Blue, Yellow
Phone: (937) 766-7763
Fax: (937) 766-5556

Estimated # of Women's Volleyball Scholarships: 2
Conference: American Mideast Conference
Program Profile: Volleyball at Cedarville College combines a competitive experience and atmosphere with opportunity to minister to our opponents, officials and others. Our season runs from September 1st to November 15th. Home matches are held in the athletic center, which was built in 1981.
History: Our program began in 1963. Our overall record for the past 36 years is 629-470 with a winning percentage of .572. June Kearney was coach for 19 years. Elaine Brown was coach for 13 years. Kathy Freese coached for one year. Teresa Clark has been our coach for the last three years.
Achievements: 1989 Western Buckeye Collegiate Conference Champions; 1998 American Mideast Conference Champions; 1998 Teresa Clark was voted American Mideast Conference Coach of the Year
Coaching: Teresa Clark, Head Coach, is a 1975 graduate of the College. She previously coached for seven years at Blackhawk Christian in Fort Wayne, Indiana. Jim Clark is Assistant Coach.

Freshman Receiving Financial Aid/Academic:		**Athletic:** 6
Roster In State: 3	**Out of State:** 10	
Seniors on Team: 3	**Graduation %:** 100	
Most Recent Record: 32-12-0	**Fall Games:** 45	**Spring Games:** 6-8

Camp of Clinic Dates: July 12-16, 1999
Positions Needed: None-recruiting is complete
Schedule: Taylor University, Mt. Vernon Nazarene, Walsh University, Grace College, University of St. Francis, University of Findlay
Style of Play: Cedarville volleyball has a tradition of teams playing in unity with perseverance. The style of play combines powerful front row hitting and blocking with tenacious defense that often frustrates the opponents.

Central State University
Academic Profile

1400 Brush Row Road
Wilberforce, OH 45384-3002

Phone: 937-376-6348

Type: Public, 4 Yr., Coed		**Founded:** 1887
Website: http://www.centralstate.edu		**Religion:** Non-Affiliated
SAT/ACT/GPA: Open		**Housing:** Yes
Student/Faculty Ratio: 15:1		**Male/Female:** 50:50
Undergraduate Enrollment: 2,765		**Graduate Enrollment:** 18
Scholarships/Academic: Yes	**Athletic:** Yes	**Financial Aid:** Yes
Expenses By: Year	**In State:** $ 8,250	**Out of State:** $ 11,750

Degrees Conferred: AAS, BS, BA, M
Programs of Study: Accounting, Advertising, Banking/Finance, Biological Science, Business Administration, Chemistry, Communications, Economics, Education, English, French, History, Journalism, Management, Marketing, Mathematics, Philosophy, Physics, Political Science, Preprofessional Programs, Psychology, Social Science, Telecommunications

Women's Athletic Profile

1400 Brush Row Rd.
Wilbeforce, OH 45384
Coach: Rosie Turner
Email:

NCAA I
Lady Marauders, Maroon, Gold
Phone: (937) 376-6297
Fax: (937) 376-6291

Estimated # of Women's Volleyball Scholarships: N/A
Conference: Independent

Cleveland State University
Academic Profile

2451 Euclid Avenue
Cleveland, OH 44115

Phone: 216-687-3754

Type: Public, 4 Yr., Liberal Arts, Engineering, Coed
Website: http://www.csuohio.edu
SAT/ACT/GPA: 820/68/2.0
Student/Faculty Ratio: 27:1
Undergraduate Enrollment: 11,000+
Scholarships/Academic: Yes   **Athletic:** Yes
Expenses By: Year   **In State:** $ 8,848
Specializes In: Engineering, PreLaw, Business
Degrees Conferred: BA, BS

Founded: 1964
Religion: Non-Affiliated
Housing: Yes
Male/Female: 46:54
Graduate Enrollment: 5,000
Financial Aid: Yes
Out of State: $ 12,448

Programs of Study: College of Arts and Sciences, College of Business Administration, College of Education, College of Engineering, Graduate Degrees, College of Law

Women's Athletic Profile

2415 Euclid Avenue
Cleveland, OH 44115
Coach: Chuck Voss
Email: c.dvoss@popmail.csuohio.edu

NCAA I
Lady Vikings, Green, White
Phone: (216) 687-5112
Fax: (216) 687-9242

Estimated # of Women's Volleyball Scholarships: 2
Conference: Midwestern Collegiate Conference
Roster In State: 12
Seniors on Team: 4
Most Recent Record: 12-17
Positions Needed: OH, MH

College of Mount Saint Joseph
Academic Profile

5701 Delhi Rd.
Cincinnati, OH 45233

Phone: 800-654-9314

Type: Private, 4 Yr., Liberal Arts, Coed
Website: http://www.msj.edu
SAT/ACT/GPA: 400/19
Student/Faculty Ratio: 15:1
Undergraduate Enrollment: 2,500
Scholarships/Academic: Yes   **Athletic:** No
Expenses By: Year   **In State:** $ 15,130
Degrees Conferred: BA, BS, MA, AA, AS

Founded: 1920
Religion: Catholic
Housing: No
Male/Female: 32:68
Graduate Enrollment: 200
Financial Aid: Yes
Out of State: $ 15,130

Programs of Study: Art, Behavioral Science, Biology, Business, Chemistry, Education, Humanities, Liberal Arts, Mathematics, Music, Nursing, Physical Therapy, Religious and Pastoral Studies, PreProfessional Programs

Women's Athletic Profile

5701 Delhi Rd.
Cincinnati, OH 45233
Coach: Michele Benoit
Email: michelle_benoit@mail.msj.edu
Estimated # of Women's Volleyball Scholarships: N/A
Conference: Heartland Collegiate Athletic Conference

NCAA I
Lady Lions, Royal Blue, Gold
Phone: (513) 244-4311
Fax: (513) 244-4928

Program Profile: Final AVCA ranking in 1998 was #15 (Division III). Our 1998 record was 32-5, won ACAC Title. New in 1998 was the 2,000-seat arena called Harrington Student Center, which include weight room with Hammer strengths, free weight and aux gym. We play from mid-August through November (February through April is our non-traditional season).
History: Our program began in 1968 with a .760 winning percentage.
Achievements: We were HCAC Champions in 1998 and won Coach of the Year in 1998.
Coaching: Michele Benoit, Head Coach, started with the program in 1995 and has an overall record of 100-53.

Freshman Receiving Financial Aid/Academic: **Athletic:** 0
Roster In State: 11   **Out of State:** 2   **Out of Country:** 0
Seniors on Team: 2   **Graduation %:** 98
Most Recent Record: 32-5-0   **Fall Games:** 36   **Spring Games:** 3
Camp of Clinic Dates: July 10-15, 2000
Positions Needed: Setter, Outside Hitter
Schedule: Washington University, Central College, Ohio Northern University, Muskingum College, Hope College, Wittenberg Univ.
Style of Play: We play up-tempo and use various defense formations. We have strong defense and we have fun.

College of Wooster
Academic Profile

Beall Avenue   **Phone:** (330) 263-2349
Wooster, OH 44691

Type: Public, 4 Yr., Liberal Arts,Coed   **Founded:** 1866
Website: http://www.wooster.edu   **Religion:** Presbyterian
SAT/ACT/GPA: 1000/22/3.2   **Housing:** Yes
Student/Faculty Ratio: 12:1   **Male/Female:** 48:52
Undergraduate Enrollment: 1,800   **Graduate Enrollment:** N/A
Scholarships/Academic: Yes   **Athletic:** No   **Financial Aid:** Yes
Expenses By: Year   **In State:** $ 25,000   **Out of State:** $ 25,000
Specializes In: Liberal Arts & Sciences
Degrees Conferred: BA, BMusic, BSEd., BS
Programs of Study: Art, BioChemistry, Biology, Black Studies, Business Economics, Chemistry, Chinese, Communications Studies, Communications Sciences & Disorders, Computer Science, English, Geology, International Relations, Math, Music, Physics, Political Science, Psychology, Religious Studies, Sociology & Anthropology, Theatre, Women's Studies, etc..

Women's Athletic Profile

1267 Beall Avenue   **NCAA I**
Wooster, OH 44691   Lady Scots, Black, Old Gold
Coach: Brenda Skeffington   **Phone:** (330) 263-2182
Email: **Fax:** (330) 263-2537

Estimated # of Women's Volleyball Scholarships: N/A
Conference: North Coast Athletic Conference
Program Profile: We have a brand new cyber weight room. There are two courts for practice in our main-wood floor gymnasium. The gym has 4,000 seats.
History: Our program began in 1967.
Achievements: 23 women have earned All-North Coast Athletic Conference; 2 have been Academic All-American.
Coaching: Brenda Skeffington, Head Coach, is entering her 3rd season. Her overall record is 331-255. She has coached for 15 years. She coached at St.John's Fisher College for 10 years (283-145). She coached at Robert Morris for 3 years (Division I).
Roster In State: 6   **Out of State:** 5   **Out of Country:** 0
Sophomores on Team: 1   **Seniors on Team:** 3   **Graduation %:** 100
Most Recent Record: 11-14-0   **Fall Games:** 25   **Spring Games:** 5
Camp of Clinic Dates: July 5-9 Camp; July 10- Specialty Clinic
Positions Needed: Middle Hitters, Outside Hitters, Defense
Schedule: Wittenberg, Ohio Wesleyan, Baldwin Wallace, John Carrol, Tiffin, Anderson
Style of Play: Aggressive serving, intense defense, exceptional passing, quick attacks. We need a couple of hammers to step up to the top of our conference.

Defiance College
Academic Profile

701 N. Clinton St.   **Phone:** 800-520-4632
Defiance, OH 43512

Type: Private, 4 Yr., Liberal Arts,Coed   **Founded:** 1850
Website: http://www.defiance.edu   **Religion:** United Church of Christ
SAT/ACT/GPA: 700/18/2.0   **Housing:** Yes
Student/Faculty Ratio: 13:1   **Male/Female:** 1:1
Undergraduate Enrollment: 1,000   **Graduate Enrollment:** 50

Scholarships/Academic: Yes   **Athletic:** No   **Financial Aid:** Yes
Expenses By: Year   **In State:** $ 17,870   **Out of State:** $ 17,870
Degrees Conferred: AA, BS, BA, MA, MBA
Programs of Study: Accounting, Arts, Arts & Humanities, Biology, Business Administration, Christian Education, Communication Arts, Criminal Justice, Design Graphics, Early Childhood Education, Finance, History, Human Resources Management, Information Technology, Marketing, Mathematics, Natural Science, Middle Childhood Education, Multi-Age in Health, Physical Education & Visual Arts, Psychology, Sports Medicine, Sports Management,

Women's Athletic Profile

701 N. Clinton Street   **NCAA I**
Defiance, OH 43512   Yellow Jackets, Gold, Purple
Coach: Robin Pietryk   **Phone:** (419) 783-2379
Email: rpietryk@ctdc.edu   **Fax:** (419) 783-2369

Estimated # of Women's Volleyball Scholarships: N/A
Conference: Heartland
Program Profile: We are rebuilding a program that goes from September 1 through the first weekend in November. Our gymnasium was recently renovated and has a new floor.
History: The program began in 1980. Our winning percentage over the years is about .500. We are not aware of any post-season play.
Achievements: 1995 SLIAC Coach of the Year
Coaching: Robin Pietryk, Head Coach, joined Defiance College in 1997 with a record of 10-15 overall. As a player, he was All-Conference at Bethany College three times. When he was at St. Louis he was named Intercollegiate Conference Coach of the Year.
Roster In State: 14   **Out of State:** 1   **Out of Country:** 0
Sophomores on Team: 2   **Seniors on Team:** 1   **Graduation %:** Unknown
Most Recent Record: 5-25-0   **Fall Games:** 22   **Spring Games:** 0
Camp of Clinic Dates: July 6 - 8, 1999
Positions Needed: Middle, Outside Hitters, Defense
Schedule: Hope, Calvin, Kalamazoo, Anderson, Baldwin-Wallace
Style of Play: 6-2 offense, man back defense. Need to be more aggressive at net. Strong defensive team.

Denison University
Academic Profile

C/O Athletic Department   **Phone:** (740) 578-5735
Granville, OH 43023

Type: Private, 4 Yr., Liberal Arts,Coed   **Founded:** 1831
Website: http://www.denison.edu   **Religion:** Non-Affiliated
SAT/ACT/GPA: 1060/22/3.0   **Housing:** Yes
Student/Faculty Ratio: 11:1   **Male/Female:** 1:1
Undergraduate Enrollment: 1,900   **Graduate Enrollment:** N/A
Scholarships/Academic: Yes   **Athletic:** No   **Financial Aid:** Yes
Expenses By: Year   **In State:** $ 27,450   **Out of State:** $ 27,450
Specializes In: Biology, Pre-Med
Degrees Conferred: BS, BA, B. Fine Arts
Programs of Study: Art, Biology, Black Studies, Chemistry, Cinema, Classical Studies, Communications, Computer Science, Dance, International Studies, Latin American, Mathematics, Music, Philosophy, Physical Education, Physics, Political Science, Psychology, Religion, Sociology, Anthropology, Spanish, Speech, Theatre

Women's Athletic Profile

Physical Education Center   **NCAA I**
Granville, OH 43023   Lady Big Red, Red, White
Coach: Sara Lee   **Phone:** (740) 587-6290
Email: lees@denison.edu   **Fax:** (740) 587-6362

Estimated # of Women's Volleyball Scholarships: N/A
Conference: North Coast Athletic Conference
Program Profile: We play in Livingston Gymnasium which is one of the finest facilities in Division III. We play both a traditional fall season and a non-traditional spring season. We host two tournaments a year.

Coaching: Sara Lee, became Head Coach in 1989. She was a four year letter winner in three sports at Moorhead State, Minnesota. She took the team to the NCAA tournament once. She has numerous Coach of the Year Honors.
Freshman Receiving Financial Aid/Academic: **Athletic:** 0
Roster In State: 9   **Out of State:** 5   **Out of Country:** 0
Sophomores on Team: 0   **Seniors on Team:** 2   **Graduation %:** Unknown
Most Recent Record: 17-18-0   **Fall Games:** 35   **Spring Games:** 8
Camp of Clinic Dates: Intermediate volleyball camp June 9-11, 1999
Positions Needed: Middle Hitter, Setter
Schedule: Wittenberg University, Muskegon College, Bluffton College, Hanover College, Ohio Wesleyan Univ., Mt. Vernon Nazarene
Style of Play: Strong defensive team (rotation defense) with quick offense (prefer 5-1).

Heidelberg College
Academic Profile

310 E. Market St.   **Phone:** 800-434-3352
Tiffin, OH 44883

Type: Private, 4 Yr., Liberal Arts,Coed   **Founded:** 1849
Website: http://www.heidelburg.edu   **Religion:** Church of Christ
SAT/ACT/GPA: 900/17/2.4   **Housing:** Yes
Student/Faculty Ratio: 14:1   **Male/Female:** 50:50
Undergraduate Enrollment: 1,200   **Graduate Enrollment:** 400
Scholarships/Academic: Yes   **Athletic:** No   **Financial Aid:** No
Expenses By: Year   **In State:** $ 21,000 **Out of State:** $ 21,000
Specializes In: Teacher Education, Preprofessional Law & Medicine, Music
Degrees Conferred: BA, BSC
Programs of Study: 35 majors in all fields including: Accounting, Allied Health, Anthropology, Business & Management, Biology, Chemistry, Communications, Computer Science, Education, English, French, Health Science, Philosophy, Physical Science, PreMed, Psychology, Social Science, Sport Medicine, Zoology

Women's Athletic Profile

310 E. Market Street   **NCAA I**
Tiffin, OH 44883   Princess, Red, Orange, Black
Coach: Jason Miller   **Phone:** (419) 448-2378
Email: jmiller7@heidelberg.edu   **Fax:** (419) 448-2025

Estimated # of Women's Volleyball Scholarships: N/A
Conference: Ohio Athletic Conference

Hiram College
Academic Profile

PO Box 1777   **Phone:** 800-362-5280
Hiram, OH 44234

Type: Private, 4 Yr., Liberal Arts, Coed   **Founded:** 1850
Website: http://www.hiram.edu   **Religion:** Disciples of Christ Church
SAT/ACT/GPA: Selective   **Housing:** Yes
Student/Faculty Ratio: 12:1   **Male/Female:** 1:1
Undergraduate Enrollment: 1,000   **Graduate Enrollment:** N/A
Scholarships/Academic: Yes   **Athletic:** No   **Financial Aid:** Yes
Expenses By: Year   **In State:** $ 23,000 **Out of State:** $ 23,000
Specializes In: Sciences, Business, Computers
Degrees Conferred: BA
Programs of Study: Art, Art History, Biology, Chemistry, Classical Studies, Communications, Comparative Studies, Computer Science, Economics, Elementary Education, English, Environmental Studies, French, German, History, International Economics & Management, Management, Mathematics, Music, Philosophy, Physics, Political Science, Psychology, Religion Studies, Sociology, Spanish, Theatre Arts, Exercise and Sport Science, Photography, Health Care

Women's Athletic Profile

P.O. Box 1777   **NCAA I**
Hiram, OH 44118   Lady Terriers, Scarlet, Blue
Coach: Sindie Shollenberger   **Phone:** (330) 569-5350
Email: shollenberge@hiram.edu   **Fax:** (330) 569-5293

Estimated # of Women's Volleyball Scholarships: N/A
Conference: North Coast Athletic
Program Profile: Building D III Program, fall season mid Aug-Late Oct. Hard wood floor, Price Gym. .There Will be a new facility built in 3-4 yrs.
Roster In State: 9   **Out of State:** 1   **Seniors on Team:** 1
Most Recent Record: 1-2
Positions Needed: Middle blockers, Outside hitters.
Style of Play: 5-1 offense with primary hitter system. Quick attack with specialty positions. Very positive environment with hard work and fun.

John Carroll University
Academic Profile

20700 North Park Boulevard
University Heights, OH 44118

Phone: 216-397-4294

Type: Private, 4 Yr., Liberal Arts, Coed
Website: http://www.jcu.edu
SAT/ACT/GPA: Based on a broad range of criteria.2.85
Student/Faculty Ratio: 16:1
Undergraduate Enrollment: 500
Scholarships/Academic: Yes   **Athletic:** No
Expenses By: Year   **In State:** $ 21,900
Specializes In: Business, Communications
Degrees Conferred: BA, BS, MBA, MS, MA

Founded: 1886
Religion: Jesuit (Catholic)
Housing: Yes
Male/Female: 49:51
Graduate Enrollment: 900
Financial Aid: Yes
Out of State: $ 21,900

Programs of Study: Biology, Chemistry, Computer Science, Engineering, Physics, Mathematics, Physics, Psychology, PreDental, PreLaw, PreMed, PreVet, Communications, Economics, History, Political Science, Sociology, Education, French, German, Greek, Latin, Spanish, Art History, English, Humanities, Philosophy, Religious Studies, World Literature, Accounting, Business Logistics, Economics, Finance, Management, Marketing

Women's Athletic Profile

20700 N. Park Blvd.
University Heights, OH 44118
Coach: Gretchen Weitbracht
Email: gweitbracht@jcu.edu

NCAA I
Lady Blue Streaks, Blue, Gold
Phone: (216) 397-4194
Fax: (216) 397-3043

Estimated # of Women's Volleyball Scholarships: 0
Conference: Ohio Athletic Conference
Program Profile: Our playing season is from September 1st to November. Our playing facility is Don Shula Sports Center which has 3,000 seats. We have two regulation playing courts with Senoh standards.
History: We were previous members of the President's Athletic Conference and we are currently in our 11th year in OAC. Our program began in 1982. Highlights include 2 OAC Championships and 3 consecutive NCAA post-season tournaments.
Achievements: 2 OAC Coach of the Year and Midwest Regional Coach of the Year, 1 (2x) All-American and 2 Regional Players; 3 OAC Player of the Year Recipients
Coaching: Gretchen Weitbracht, Head Coach, has been a college head coach for 17 years (1982-1990). She has taken teams at two different institutions to the NCAA playoffs.
Roster In State: 14   **Out of State:** 4   **Out of Country:** 0
Sophomores on Team: 0   **Seniors on Team:** 2   **Graduation %:** 100
Most Recent Record: 12-16-0   **Fall Games:** 28   **Spring Games:** 0
Positions Needed: Middle Hitters
Schedule: Muskingum College, Ohio Northern , Baldwin Wallace College, Mount Union College, Kalamazoo College, Ohio Wesleyan
Style of Play: Defense oriented with multiple play set attack offensively.

Kent State University
Academic Profile

PO Box 5190
Kent, OH 44242

Phone: 330-672-2444

Type: Public, 4 Yr., Coed
Website: http://www.kent.edu
SAT/ACT/GPA: 700/17
Student/Faculty Ratio: 18:1

Founded: 1910
Religion: Non-Affiliated
Housing: Yes
Male/Female: 1:4

Undergraduate Enrollment: 17,000
Scholarships/Academic: Yes
Expenses By: Year
Degrees Conferred: BA, BS, BBA, MA, MS, BFA, BM, MFA
Programs of Study: College of Arts and Sciences, College of Business Administration, College of Education, College of Fine and Professional Arts, School of Nursing, School of Technology, Honors College

Athletic: Yes
In State: $ 9,374

Graduate Enrollment: 4,500
Financial Aid: Yes
Out of State: $ 14,034

Women's Athletic Profile

P.O. Box 5190
Kent, OH 44242
Coach: Mora Kanim
Email: mkanim@kent.edu

NCAA I
Golden Flashes, Blue, Gold
Phone: (330) 672-2821
Fax: (330) 672-4471

Estimated # of Women's Volleyball Scholarships: 12
Conference: Mid-American Conference
Program Profile: We play in Memorial Athletic Convocation Center that seats 6,000. We have a fall season game.
Achievements: We were 1997 Mid-America Conference Semi-Finalist.
Coaching: Mora Kanim is our Head Coach, started in 1997 with an overall record of 32-33; 1984 National Champions at UCLA. Shannon Shuttle and Paul Zickart are the Asssitant Coaches.
Freshman Receiving Financial Aid/Academic:

Athletic: 3

Roster In State: 6
Sophomores on Team: 0
Most Recent Record: 11-21-0

Out of State: 8
Seniors on Team: 2
Fall Games: 28

Out of Country: 0
Graduation %: 100
Spring Games: 0

Camp of Clinic Dates: July 11-12; 16-20; 23-26
Positions Needed: Middle Blocker, Outside Hitter
Schedule: UCLA, Arizona, University of San Diego, Santa Clara
Style of Play: Swing offense and fast with a lot of movement.

Kenyon College
Academic Profile

Duff St.
Gambier, OH 43022

Phone: (740) 427-5000

Type: Private, 4 Yr., Liberal Arts, Coed
Website: http://www.kenyon.edu
SAT/ACT/GPA: 1100/25+/3.5
Student/Faculty Ratio: 10:1
Undergraduate Enrollment: 1,500
Scholarships/Academic: Yes
Expenses By: Year
Specializes In: Education, Liberal Arts
Degrees Conferred: BA, BS

Founded: 1824
Religion: Non-Denominational
Housing: Yes
Male/Female: 44:56
Graduate Enrollment: N/A
Financial Aid: Yes
Out of State: $ 27,800

Athletic: No
In State: $ 27,800

Programs of Study: Anthropology, Art, Biology, Chemistry, Classics, Dance & Drama, Economics, English, History, Mathematics, French, German, Spanish, Literature, Music, Philosophy, Physics, Political Science, Psychology, Religion, International Studies, Molecular Biology, African Studies, Neuroscience, American Studies, Law and Society

Women's Athletic Profile

Duff Street
Gambier, OH 43022
Coach: Jennie Bruening
Email: brueningj@kenyon.edu

NCAA I
Ladies, Purple, White
Phone: (614) 427-5256x5469
Fax: (614) 427-5402

Estimated # of Women's Volleyball Scholarships: N/A
Conference: North Coast Athletic Conference

Lake Erie College
Academic Profile

391 W Washington St.
Painesville, OH 44077

Phone: 800-916-0904

Type: Private, 4 Yr., Liberal Arts, Coed
Website: http://www.lakeerie.edu

Founded: 1856
Religion: Non-Affiliated

SAT/ACT/GPA: 850/18/2.0
Student/Faculty Ratio: 16:1
Undergraduate Enrollment: 600
Scholarships/Academic: Yes   **Athletic:** No
Expenses By: Year   **In State:** $ 17,270
Specializes In: Equestrian
Degrees Conferred: BA, BS, BFA, M.Ed., MBA

Housing: Yes
Male/Female: 1:2
Graduate Enrollment: 100
Financial Aid: Yes
Out of State: $ 17,270

Programs of Study: Accounting, Biology, Business Administration, Chemistry, Communications, English, Elementary Education, Environmental Management, Fine Arts, Health Care, Mathematics, Music, PreDental, PreLaw, PreMed, Psychology, Social Sciences

Women's Athletic Profile

391 W. Washington Street
Painesville, OH 44077
Coach: Eric Poje
Email: lecodmit@lakeerie.edu

NCAA I
Lady Storms, Green, White
Phone: (800) 533-4996
Fax: (216) 639-7861

Estimated # of Women's Volleyball Scholarships: None
Conference: Allegheny Mountain Collegiate Conference
Program Profile: Information is unavailable.
History: Information is unavailable.
Achievements: Information is unavailable.
Coaching: Eric Poje, Head Coach, is in his 1st year here. He was a high school and club coach for 6 years with an overall record of 86-44. He played with John Carroll University Club and with the LEVA Club team.
Sophomores on Team: 0   **Seniors on Team:** 2   **Graduation %:** 100
Most Recent Record: 0-13-0   **Fall Games:** 23   **Spring Games:** 0
Camp of Clinic Dates: June 21-25/1999, 8:00 a.m. to 12 noon (commuter camp)
Positions Needed: Setter, Outside Hitter
Style of Play: We stress fundamental defense and precision passing, with an efficient offense.

Malone College
Academic Profile

515 25th St. NW
Canton, OH 44709

Phone: 800-521-1146

Type: Private, 4 Yr., Liberal Arts, Coed
Website: http://www.malone.edu
SAT/ACT/GPA: 870/25/2.5
Student/Faculty Ratio: 14:1
Undergraduate Enrollment: 1,968
Scholarships/Academic: Yes   **Athletic:** Yes
Expenses By: Year   **In State:** $ 16,900
Degrees Conferred: BA, BS, MA

Founded: 1892
Religion: Evangelical Friends
Housing: Yes
Male/Female: 36:64
Graduate Enrollment: 262
Financial Aid: Yes
Out of State: $ 16,900

Programs of Study: Accounting, Art, Art Education, Bible, Biology, Business Administration, Chemistry, Commercial , Communication Arts, Computer Science, Education, Sports, Elementary Education, Psychology, Social Science, Internal Affairs, Law & Society, Liberal Arts, Management, Mathematics, Music, Nursing, Physical Education, Sport Medicine, Social Studies, Sport Science, Theology, PreMed, PrePharmacy, PrePhysical Therapy

Women's Athletic Profile

515 25th Street, NW
Canton, OH 44709
Coach: Cherie Parsons
Email:

NCAA I
Pioneers, Red, White, Blue
Phone: (330) 471-8300
Fax: (330) 471-8298

Estimated # of Women's Volleyball Scholarships: 4
Conference: American Mideast Conference
Program Profile: We are an exciting program that has a strong winning tradition. Our playing season is in the fall and we compete in a 1,200 seats gymnasium.
History: This program began in 1975 and has a number of truly outstanding seasons in the early 1980's, including several 40-win seasons.

Achievements: Numerous Conference Titles.
Coaching: Cherie Parsons, Head Coach, started coaching in 1994 at Malone with a 68-73 record through her first four years. Tanya Hockman is Assistant Coach.
Freshman Receiving Financial Aid/Academic: **Athletic:** 3
Roster In State: 14   **Out of State:** 0   **Out of Country:** 0
Sophomores on Team: 6   **Seniors on Team:** 2   **Graduation %:** 95
Most Recent Record: 15-18-0   **Fall Games:** 43   **Spring Games:** 0
Positions Needed: All
Schedule: Mt. Vernon Nazarene, Walsh, Cedarville, Rio Grande
Style of Play: Up-tempo; attacking style of play.

Marietta College
Academic Profile

215 5th St.reet
Marietta, OH 45750

Phone: 740-376-4600

Type: Private, 4 Yr., Liberal Arts, Coed
Website: http://www.marietta.edu
SAT/ACT/GPA: 1000/20/2.5
Student/Faculty Ratio: 12:1
Undergraduate Enrollment: 1,200
Scholarships/Academic: Yes   **Athletic:** No
Expenses By: Year   **In State:** $ 22,000
Specializes In: Education, Sports Medicine, Petroleum Engineering
Degrees Conferred: BA, BS, MA

Founded: 1835
Religion: Non-Affiliated
Housing: Yes
Male/Female: 50:50
Graduate Enrollment: 200
Financial Aid: Yes
Out of State: $ 22,000

Programs of Study: Computer Science, Engineering, Business, Sport Medicine, Accounting, Advertising, Athletic Training, Biology, Chemistry, Communications, Education, Marketing, Mathematics, Music, Philosophy, Geology, Political Science, Physics, Psychology, Religion

Women's Athletic Profile

215 Fifth Street
Marietta, OH 45750
Coach: Cathy Moneroso
Email: monteroc@marietta.edu

NCAA I
Lady Pioneers, Blue, White
Phone: (740) 376-4902
Fax: (740) 376-4674

Estimated # of Women's Volleyball Scholarships: N/A
Conference: Ohio Athletic Conference

Miami University - Ohio
Academic Profile

230 Millet Hall - ICA
Oxford, OH 45056

Phone: (513) 529-6241

Type: Public, 4 Yr., Liberal Arts, Coed
Website: http://www.muohio.edu
SAT/ACT/GPA: 1100/24/3.0
Student/Faculty Ratio: 17:1
Undergraduate Enrollment: 13,000
Scholarships/Academic: Yes   **Athletic:** Yes
Expenses By: Year   **In State:** $ 12,500
Specializes In: Miami is well known for several of its academic offerings.

Founded: 1809
Religion: Non-Affiliated
Housing: Yes
Male/Female: 46:54
Graduate Enrollment: 3,000
Financial Aid: Yes
Out of State: $ 17,500

Programs of Study: Accounting, American Studies, Anthropology, Architecture, Art, Athletic Training, Botany, Broadcasting, Business, Chemistry, Classics, Communications, Computer Science, Creative Writing, Criminal Justice, Earth Science, Economics, Education, Elementary Education, Engineering, English, Environmental Design, Finance, French, Geography, Geology, German, Greek, History, Journalism, Management, Marketing, Mathematics, Music, Nursing, Philosophy, Physical Education, Physics, Political Science, PreMed, Psychology, Public Administration, Public Relations, Sociology, Pathology, Sports Administration

Women's Athletic Profile

500 E. Sycamore St., Millet Hall
Miami, OH 45056
Coach: Carolyn Condit
Email: conditcj@muohio.edu

NCAA I
Redhawks, Red & White
Phone: (513) 529-6922
Fax: (513) 529-6729

Estimated # of Women's Volleyball Scholarships: 3

Conference: Mid-American Conference

Program Profile: Millett Hall is the home of the Miami University Volleyball Program. The 9,200-seat arena includes a main court for competition and a sport court for additional practice space. Miami has hosted the past four Mid-American Conference Tournaments in Millett Hall as the conference's top seed. In their 13 years competing in Millett Hall, the RedHawks have posted a 20-4 record on their home court, including an impressive 45-9 mark, a .833 winning percentage, over the past four seasons. Miami is currently on a 13 game winning streak at Millett, its longest single-season home string, which ties the longest Millett Hall winning streak. Miami competes in the 13-school Mid-American Conference. In 1998, Miami competed in 31 regular-season matches, including 18 conference battles.

History: In 1974, an intercollegiate volleyball program was created as one of the first women's varsity teams at Miami. Since that time, Miami has participated in six NCAA Tournaments in which MU has advanced to a record nine championship matches, claiming five MAC Tournament titles. Only four head coaches have mentored the program, compiling a 529-306-1 record for a .633 winning percentage.

Achievements: The Miami volleyball student-athletes have been successful both on and off the court. Over the past 15 years, under the direction of head coach Carolyn Condit, the volleyball program has attained a 100 percent graduation rate. Miami has posted four conference players of the year, including the last three. Two athletes have gone on to compete at the Olympic Sports Festival, while eight have earned all-region accolades. Miami boasts four GTE Academic All-Americans, while five student-athletes garnered academic all-district recognition.

Coaching: Head Coach Carolyn Condit, in her 16th season, is Miami's winningest volleyball coach and posts the most wins of any active Mid-American Conference coach (159), She owns a 310-175 Miami record and a 409-255 overall mark. Her teams have won five MAC titles and advanced to the NCAA Tournament five times. Condit has been named Conference Coach of the Year, a league best four times, was North Central Region Coach of the Year in 1986 and was a Division I National Coach of the Year finalist in 1985 and '86. She also received the Coach of the Year Award from the Greater Cincinnati and Northern Kentucky Women's Sports Association in the spring of 1998. Condit earned her bachelor's degree at the College of Mount Saint Joseph in 1976 and her master's from Indiana University. Lisa Dankovich, who enters her 11th season with the program, has contributed to five of Miami's MAC titles and NCAA Tournament appearances. Dankovich was a four-year letterwinner for Miami at the setter position. As the starting setter, she led MU to 95-35 record and was selected to the all-MAC team her last two years. She still holds the Miami and Mid-American Conference records for service aces in a season (99) and ranks 10th nationally in that category. Dankovich also owns the Miami record for career service aces (209) and ranks third in assists (3,242). She earned her bachelor's degree from Miami in 1987 and her master's from Indiana University in 1989. Paco Labrador is in his first season as the RedHawks' second assistant. He spent a four-year stint as a club coach on the junior Olympic level and worked hands on with the nationally ranked Miami and Maryland programs as a practice assistant. He earned his bachelor's degree from Hiram College in 1995 and his master's from Miami in 1997.

Freshman Receiving Financial Aid/Academic:

Roster In State: 7	**Out of State:** 9	**Athletic:** 3
Sophomores on Team: 1	**Seniors on Team:** 4	**Out of Country:**
Most Recent Record: 27-8	**Fall Games:** 30	**Graduation %:** 100
		Spring Games: 4

Camp of Clinic Dates: July 2000; Specialty Setter/Hitter Camp, Elite Camp

Positions Needed: Right side Hitter (1), Middle Hitters (2)

Schedule: University of Pacific (Cal), Notre Dame, N. Illinois, Western Michigan, Washington, Ball State

Style of Play: Very hard working and athletic. We make up for our lack of size in certain positions with quickness and intelligent play. Miami is a solid defensive team, and runs a versatile, quick offense.

Mount Union College
Academic Profile

1972 Clarke Avenue
Alliance, OH 44601

Phone: 800-334-6682

Type: Private, 4 Yr., Liberal Arts,Coed

Website: http://www.muc.edu

SAT/ACT/GPA: 850/18/2.2

Student/Faculty Ratio: 16:1

Undergraduate Enrollment: 1,850

Scholarships/Academic: Yes

Expenses By: Year

Specializes In: Business, Education

Degrees Conferred: BA, BS

Athletic: No

In State: $ 20,160

Founded: 1846

Religion: Methodist

Housing: Yes

Male/Female: 60:40

Graduate Enrollment: N/A

Financial Aid: Yes

Out of State: $ 20,160

Programs of Study: Accounting, American Studies, Art, Biology, Business Administration, Chemistry, Communications, Computer Science, CytoTechnology, Economics, Education, Geology, Mathematics, Medical Technology, Philosophy, Physical Education, Physics & Astronomy, Sport Management, Sport Medicine

1972 Clark Avenue
Alliance, OH 44601
Coach: Sandy Douglas
Email: douglass@muc.edu

NCAA I
Lady Raiders, Purple, White
Phone: (330) 823-4779
Fax: (330) 823-2399

Estimated # of Women's Volleyball Scholarships: N/A
Conference: Ohio Athletic Conference

Mount Vernon Nazarene College
Academic Profile

800 Martinsburg Rd.
Mount Vernon, OH 43050

Phone: (740) 397-9000

Type: Private, 4 Yr., Liberal Arts, Coed
Website: http://www.mvnc.edu
SAT/ACT/GPA: 18/2.5
Student/Faculty Ratio: 17:1
Undergraduate Enrollment: 1,800
Scholarships/Academic: Yes   **Athletic:** Yes
Expenses By: Year   **In State:** $ 14,630
Degrees Conferred: BA, BS, Associates, Masters

Founded: 1964
Religion: Nazarene
Housing: Yes
Male/Female: 40:60
Graduate Enrollment: 100
Financial Aid: Yes
Out of State: $ 14,630

Programs of Study: Accounting, Applied Art, Art, Biblical Studies, BioChemistry, Biology, Broadcasting, Business, Chemistry, Communications, Computer Science & Technology, Criminal Justice, Early Childhood Education, Education, Elementary Education, English, Health Science, History, Human Services, Liberal Arts, Literature, Management, Marketing, Mathematics, Medical Technology, Modern Languages, Music, Nursing, Philosophy, Physical Education, PreDentistry, PreLaw, PreMed, PreVet, Psychology, Religion, Science, Secondary Education, Social Sciences, Spanish, Special Education, Sports Administration, Sports Medicine, Theatre, Theology

Women's Athletic Profile

800 Martinsburg Rd.
Mt. Vernon, OH 43050
Coach: Paul Swanson
Email: pswanson@mvnc.edu

NCAA I
Lady Cougars, Blue, Green
Phone: (740) 397-9000x3100
Fax: (740) 392-5079

Estimated # of Women's Volleyball Scholarships: 3.5
Conference: American Mideast Conference
Program Profile: We play in the Physical Education Center (seating capacity of 2,000). We are in the AMC and National Christian Athletic Association. Our season starts late August or early September and ends early November. Post-season can be until early December. We play around 50 matches per season.
History: The program began in 1980.
Achievements: 2 NAIA All-Americans; 9 NCCAA All-Americans; 7 NCCAA All-National Tournament Team; 4 NAIA National Players of the Week; 2 NAIA Great Lakes Region First Team; 3 NAIA Great Lakes Region Second Team; NAIA All-District 22 Team; 2 Mid-Ohio Conference Player of the Year; Mid-Ohio Conference Freshman of the Year; 5 NAIA Academic All-Americans; GTE Academic All-American.
Coaching: Paul Swanson, Head Coach, started in 1984. His overall record is 495-190. He is a 1975 graduate of North Park College in Illinois. He earned his Master's degree from Northwestern University. He came to MVNC after a one year coaching stint at Waynesburg College. Melissa Gregory is Assistant Coach.
Freshman Receiving Financial Aid/Academic: **Athletic:** 4
Roster In State: 11   **Out of State:** 1   **Out of Country:** 0
Sophomores on Team: 0   **Seniors on Team:** 4   **Graduation %:** 75
Most Recent Record: 54-7-0   **Fall Games:** 18   **Spring Games:** 12
Positions Needed: Middle Hitters, Setter
Schedule: Madonna, Bethel, California , U of Michigan-Dearborn, Malone, Lee
Style of Play: Ball control, quick offense, movement oriented, rotational defense.

Muskingum College
Academic Profile

163 Stormont Street
New Concord, OH 43762

Phone: (740) 826-8320

Type: Private, 4 Yr., Liberal Arts, Coed

Founded: 1837

Website: http://www.muskingum.edu
SAT/ACT/GPA: 100/20/2.5
Student/Faculty Ratio: 15:1
Undergraduate Enrollment: 1,300
Scholarships/Academic: Yes
Expenses By: Year
Specializes In: Liberal Arts
Degrees Conferred: BA, BS

Athletic: No
In State: $ 16,690

Religion: Presbyterian Church, USA
Housing: Yes
Male/Female: 1:1
Graduate Enrollment: 1,000
Financial Aid: Yes
Out of State: $ 16,690

Programs of Study: Accounting, American Studies, Art, Biology, Business, Chemistry, Christian Education, Computer Science, Earth Science, Economics, Elementary Education, English, Environmental Science, French, Geology, German, History, Humanities, International Affairs, Journalism, Math, Music, Philosophy, Physical Education, Physics, Political Science, PreDentistry, PreMed, PreEngineering, PreLaw, PrePhysical Therapy

Women's Athletic Profile

163 Stormont Street
New Concord, OH 43762
Coach: Elizabeth Zicha
Email: ezicha@muskingum.edu

NCAA I
Fighting Muskies, Black, Red
Phone: (740) 826-8320
Fax: (740) 826-8300

Estimated # of Women's Volleyball Scholarships: 0
Conference: Ohio Athletic Conference
Program Profile: Our recreation center has a 2,300 seating capacity. We play a fall season.
History: We began in 1975. Our overall record since 1983 is 428-174.
Achievements: OAC Coach of the Year 1987-1989-1998. Regional Coach of the Year 1989-1998. OAC Conference titles 1987,1988,1993,1998. One All-American -Toni St.Clair
Coaching: Elizabeth Zicha, Head Coach, has an overall record of 380-156 from 1983-1998,
Freshman Receiving Financial Aid/Academic:
Roster In State: 16
Sophomores on Team: 4
Most Recent Record: 30-6-0
Camp of Clinic Dates: July 5-8; Jr. High Camp: July 12-15

Out of State: 2
Seniors on Team: 2
Fall Games: 36

Athletic: 0
Out of Country: 0
Graduation %: 100
Spring Games: 0

Positions Needed: Outside Hitter, Defensive Specialist, Setter
Schedule: Juniata, Central, Wittenberg, Hope, Ohio Northern, SUNY-Cortland
Style of Play: Strong defense style of play, fast-quick multiple offense.

Notre Dame College - Ohio
Academic Profile

4545 College Rd.
Cleveland, OH 44121
Type: Private, 4 Yr.,
Website: http://www.ndc.edu
SAT/ACT/GPA: 720+
Student/Faculty Ratio: 11:1
Undergraduate Enrollment: 865
Scholarships/Academic: Yes
Expenses By: Year

Athletic: No
In State: $ 12,240

Phone: 216-381-1680

Founded: 1922
Religion: Catholic
Housing: No
Male/Female: Women Only
Graduate Enrollment: 9
Financial Aid: Yes
Out of State: $ 12,240

Degrees Conferred: Bachelors, Masters, Associates
Programs of Study: Accounting, Communications, Education, English, History, Psychology, Spanish, Theology, Biology, Chemistry, Mathematics, Public Relations, Ministry

Women's Athletic Profile

4545 College Rd.
South Euclid, OH 44121
Coach: Shelly Miller
Email: smiller@ndc.edu

NCAA I
Lady Saints, Royal Blue, Silver
Phone: (216) 381-1680
Fax: (216) 381-3802

Did Not Return Profile

Oberlin College
Academic Profile

102 North Professor Street
Oberlin, OH 44074

Phone: 440-775-8411

Type: Private, 4 Yr., Liberal Arts, Coed
Website: http://www.oberlin.edu
SAT/ACT/GPA: No cut-off
Student/Faculty Ratio: 12:1
Undergraduate Enrollment: 2,950
Scholarships/Academic: Yes   **Athletic:** No
Expenses By: Year   **In State:** $ 31,017
Specializes In: Music, Science
Degrees Conferred: BA

Founded: 1833
Religion: Non-Affiliated
Housing: Yes
Male/Female: 2:3
Graduate Enrollment: N/A
Financial Aid: Yes
Out of State: $ 31,017

Programs of Study: Anthropology, Archaeology, Astronomy, Biochemistry, Biology, Chemistry, Computer Science, Creative Writing, Arts, Economics, Fine Arts, Geology, Law, Literature, Mathematics, Music, Education, Philosophy, Physics, Political Science, Psychology, Social Science

Women's Athletic Profile

200 Woodland Avenue
Oberlin, OH 44074
Coach: Elizabeth Ramsey
Email: elizabeth.ramsey@oberlin.edu

NCAA I
Yeowomen, Crimson, Gold
Phone: (440) 775-8505
Fax: (440) 775-8957

Estimated # of Women's Volleyball Scholarships: N/A
Conference: North Coast Athletic Conference
Program Profile: Play in the Phillip physical education center, Full athletic complex, main gym used for varsity sports only and it seats 2,500. Swimming pool, weight room , indoor track.
History: Began 1984.
Coaching: Head Coach Elizabeth Ramsey playing experience Big 10 University of Illinois, Coached at University of Nevada and Sonoma State University.

Roster In State: 2   **Out of State:** 7   **Out of Country:** 0
Sophomores on Team: 1   **Seniors on Team:** 2   **Graduation %:** 100
Most Recent Record: 9-18-0 **Fall Games:** 30   **Spring Games:**
Positions Needed: All
Schedule: Ohio Northern, Blowdin Wallace, Muskingum, John Carroll
Style of Play: Solid serving and ball control, evenly distribute.

Ohio Dominican College
Academic Profile

1216 Sunbury Rd.
Columbus, OH 43219
Type: Private, 4 Yr., Liberal Arts, Coed
Website: http://www.odc.edu
SAT/ACT/GPA: 800/22/2.5
Student/Faculty Ratio: 16:1
Undergraduate Enrollment: 1,977
Scholarships/Academic: Yes   **Athletic:** Yes
Expenses By: Year   **In State:** $ 14,070
Specializes In: Education
Degrees Conferred: BS, BA

Phone: 800-854-2670

Founded: 1911
Religion: Roman Catholic
Housing: Yes
Male/Female: 40:60
Graduate Enrollment: N/A
Financial Aid: Yes
Out of State:

Programs of Study: Accounting, Art, Biology, Business Administration, Business Administration with Fashion Merchandising Concentration, Chemistry, Communication Arts, Computer Science, Criminal Justice, Economics, Elementary Education, International Business, Mathematics, Philosophy, Political Science, Political Science With Environmental Issues Concentration, Psychology, Public Relations, Social Sciences, Social Work, Sociology, Spanish, Special Education, Teaching English to Speakers of Other Languages, Theology, Visual Communications

Women's Athletic Profile

1216 Sunbury Rd.
Columbus, OH 43219
Coach: Sandy Rowley
Email: rowleys@odc.edu

NCAA I
Lady Panthers, Black, Gold
Phone: (614) 251-4538
Fax: (614) 252-2556

Estimated # of Women's Volleyball Scholarships: 4 Partials
Conference: American Mideast Conference
Program Profile: The Panthers play their home games in Alumni Hall on the Ohio Dominican College Campus. The facility has two wooden courts, and seat approximately 1700. Ohio Dominican is currently in the largest conference in the NAIA. We currently compete with 20 other schools in the AMC for a Conference title.
History: The Ohio Dominincan Volleyball program has been around since 1997. The team has consistently been very competitive. The overall record for the program is 478-369.
Coaching: Sandy Rowley has been the Head Coach for the Panthers for the past 12 years. She graduated from Ohio Dominican College in 1984, and played volleyball for the college for four years. Kathy Earles has been with the coaching staff for 2 seasons. She is a 1996 graduate from ODC.
Freshman Receiving Financial Aid/Academic: **Athletic:** 3
Roster In State: 10   **Out of State:** 0   **Out of Country:** 0
Sophomores on Team: **Seniors on Team:** 2   **Graduation %:** 100
Most Recent Record: 27-14-0
Positions Needed: Middle Hitter, OH, Defensive Specialist
Schedule: Mount Vernon Nazarene College, Daemen College, Malone College, Cedarville College
Style of Play: We play a very quick offense out of the middle and the right side, and use the strong side hitters very effectively. We are a very aggressive defensive team, and believe that defense wins matches.

Ohio Northern University
Academic Profile

Sports Center
Ada, OH 45810

Phone: (419) 772-2558

Type: Private, 4 Yr., Liberal Arts, Engineering, Coed   **Founded:** 1871
Website: http://www.onu.edu   **Religion:** Methodist
SAT/ACT/GPA: 21+   **Housing:** Yes
Student/Faculty Ratio: 13:1   **Male/Female:** 54:46
Undergraduate Enrollment: 3,000   **Graduate Enrollment:** 400
Scholarships/Academic: Yes   **Athletic:** No   **Financial Aid:** Yes
Expenses By: Year   **In State:** $ 25,680   **Out of State:** $ 25,680
Specializes In: Engineering, Pharmacy, Business, Arts & Sciences
Degrees Conferred: BS, BA, BFA
Programs of Study: Arts & Science, Business, Education, Engineering, Health Science, Law, Pharmacy

Women's Athletic Profile

King Horn Center
Ada, OH 45810
Coach: Kate Witte
Email: k-witte@onu.edu

NCAA I
Lady Bears, Orange, Black
Phone: (419) 772-2446
Fax: (419) 772-2590

Estimated # of Women's Volleyball Scholarships: N/A
Conference: Ohio Athletic Conference
Program Profile: Since 1950, all time record in volleyball is 811-283 with a .741 in winning percentage. 16 out of 18 years in the NCAA III Tournament. We play in Kinghorn Center with a seating capacity of 3,400.
History: Our program began in 1950. Our OAC Conference Record is 811-288 equal to .741 in winning percentage. Play in 16 out of 18 NCAA Tournaments, won 12 out of 15 OAC Regular Season Titles. We won 11 out of 15 OAC Tournament Titles and placed 2nd in NCAA Division III in 1989.
Achievements: OAC Conference Coach of the Year in 1991, 1994, 1996 & 1997; Great Lakes Regional Coach of the Year in 1994, 1996 & 1997. We 1997 team 2nd team AVCA All-American-Cari Theisch.
Coaching: Kate Witte, Head Coach, started coaching the program in 1991 with a record of 206-76. Brian Hoffman, was started with the program in 1993. Jacove Stanley, Assistant Coach, started with the program in 1993.
Freshman Receiving Financial Aid/Academic: **Athletic :** 0
Roster In State: 15   **Out of State:** 2   **Out of Country:** 0
Sophomores on Team: 7   **Seniors on Team:** 2   **Graduation %:** 100
Most Recent Record: 19-13-0   **Fall Games:** 34   **Spring Games:** 0
Camp of Clinic Dates: June 18-22; July 20-24
Positions Needed: Setter, Middle Hitter, Outside Hitter
Schedule: Central College, Juniata College, Emory University, Washington University, Mt. St. Joseph, Muskingum College
Style of Play: We play fast tempo offensive system.

Ohio State University
Academic Profile

Lincoln Tower, 1800 Cannon Drive
Columbus, OH 43210

Phone: 614-292-3940

Type: Public, 4 Yr., Liberal Arts, Coed
Website: http://www.acs.ohio-state.edu
SAT/ACT/GPA: 1000/23
Student/Faculty Ratio: 14:1
Undergraduate Enrollment: 36,000
Scholarships/Academic: Yes
Expenses By: Year

Athletic: Yes
In State: $ 12,570

Founded: 1870
Religion: Non-Affiliated
Housing: Yes
Male/Female: 1:1
Graduate Enrollment: 10,000
Financial Aid: Yes
Out of State: $ 20,138

Programs of Study: The Ohio State University, with an enrollment of 36,000, is the second-largest university in the nation in terms of student population. OSU offers 25 different colleges in which to get a degree. Undergraduate degree majors: 176; Master's degree majors: 122; Doctorate degree majors: 98. Number of classes: 10,444.

Men's Athletic Profile

410 Woody Hayes Drive
Columbus, OH 43210
Coach: Peter Hanson
Email:

NCAA I
Buckeyes/Scarlet, Grey
Phone: (614) 292-5052
Fax: (614) 292-0506

Estimated # of Men's Volleyball Scholarships: 6
Conference: Midwest Intercollegiate Volleyball Association
History: The program began in 1968. We had 16 MIVA Championships and 11 NCAA Appearances. In 1977, we had a 2nd place finish. We were the first team to reach the championship match from outside of California. We had three gold medal Olympians including the current USA National team coach, Doug Beal, played at OSU.
Achievements: Pete Hanson, 4 x MIVA Coach of the Year; Pete Hanson 1998 Volleyball Magazine National Coach of the Year; Angel Aja and Rene Esteves All-Americans; 20+ wins the last two years including a 25-2 season in 1998.
Coaching: Pete Hanson has been our Head Coach for 15 years. His overall record is 282-192. His teams won 7 MIVA Championships. He played at Kellogg Community College and Ball State. He was Junior College All-American. He won the MIVA Championship in 1979 and was the team's MVP. Tim Embaugh is Assistant Coach

Freshman Receiving Financial Aid/Academic: 3
Roster In State: 3
Sophomores on Team: 3
Most Recent Record: 21-6

Out of State: 8
Seniors on Team: 1
Fall Games:

Athletic: 3
Out of Country: 3
Graduation %: 95%
Spring Games: 27

Schedule: Brigham Young University, Pepperdine, USC, IPFW, Lewis, Loyola, Ball State

Women's Athletic Profile

410 Woody Hayes Drive, Room 119, St. John Arena
Columbus, OH 43210
Coach: Jim Stone
Email: stone.9@osu.edu

NCAA I
Lady Buckeyes, Scarlet, Grey
Phone: (614) 292-5382
Fax: (614) 292-5668

Estimated # of Women's Volleyball Scholarships: 4
Conference: Big Ten Conference
Program Profile: We have ranked in the Top 25 teams in the country in the last 10 years. St. John Arena seats 13,500 and is the volleyball practice and competition facility. It has some of the most prestigious locker rooms in the country. The weight facility, training facility and coaches offices are all located in one building. Our fall season was the 2nd toughest schedule in the 1998 season.
History: Our program started in 1971. We have been in 10 AIAW appearances and 10 NCAA appearances in the last 10 years. We made two appearances in the Championship Semifinals. We have had 21 or more wins in 9 of the last 10 years. We have 12 All-Americans, 1 National Player of the Year, one former and one current member of the USA National Team.
Achievements: 3 Big Ten Championships; 10 consecutive appearances in NCAA Championships; 1991 National Coach of the Year; 3 x Big Ten Coach of the Year; 4 Ohio State Female Athlete of the Year; 4 big Ten Players of the Year.
Coaching: Jim Stone has completed his 17th year as Head Coach. He brought the team to its 10th consecutive Top 25 finish. His overall record is 381-169 record. His Big Ten record is 218-89. His career record is 431-211. He was 1999 National Team World University Games Women's coach. Gwen Leabo and Greg Smith are Assistant Coaches.

Freshman Receiving Financial Aid/Academic:
Roster In State: 2
Sophomores on Team: 3
Most Recent Record: 17-14-0

Out of State: 10
Seniors on Team: 5
Fall Games: 31

Athletic: 3
Out of Country: 1
Graduation %: 100
Spring Games: 0

Camp of Clinic Dates: July 10-11, July 17-20, July 19-22, July 21-23, July 24-26
Positions Needed: Setter, (2) Middle Hitters, Outside Hitter
Schedule: Penn State, Wisconsin, Illinois, Michigan State, Houston, Minnesota
Style of Play: Fast offensive system with a lot of play sets defensive-oriented; ball control emphasized ; technical-oriented coaching style; highly competitive.

Ohio University
Academic Profile

Convocation Center
Athens, OH 45701

Phone: 740-593-4100

Type: Public, 4 Yr., Liberal Arts, Coed
Website: http://www.ohiobobcats.com
SAT/ACT/GPA: Very Selective
Student/Faculty Ratio: 21:1
Undergraduate Enrollment: 16,000
Scholarships/Academic: Yes   **Athletic:** Yes
Expenses By: Year   **In State:** $ 14.600

Founded: 1804
Religion: Non-Affiliated
Housing: Yes
Male/Female: 20:1
Graduate Enrollment: 3,000
Financial Aid: Yes
Out of State: $ 14.600

Specializes In: Journalism, Communications, Physical Therapy, Education, Athletic Trng
Degrees Conferred: AA, AS, BA, BS, BSC, MA, MS, MBA, MFA
Programs of Study: Accounting, Advertising, Airway Sciences, Anthropology, Broadcasting, Chemical Engineering, Civil Engineering, Communications, Criminal Justice, Economics, Engineering Technology, Food Science, Geography, Languages, Marketing, Mathematics, Microbiology

Women's Athletic Profile

Convocation Center
Athens, OH 45701
Coach: Mike Lessinger
Email: lessinge@ohio.edu

NCAA I
Lady Bobcats, Green, White
Phone: (740) 593-1189
Fax: (740) 593-2420

Estimated # of Women's Volleyball Scholarships: 2
Conference: Mid-American Conference
Program Profile: The knocking you hear is coming from Athens, OH where the Ohio University Bobcats are making some noise. First year Head Coach Mike Lessinger lead the green and white to a 20-11 record and first-ever MAC East Division Championship. The 13,000 seating capacity is home to the Ohio team is sure to make some waves in the near future.
History: Ohio Volleyball completed it's most successful season in 2000. The 12-6 conference record tied the mark for most MAC wins in a season. The overall 20-11 mark was the second most wins by an Ohio squad.
Achievements: 2000 East Division Champion, Amber Merrill 1998 National B Team member.
Coaching: Mike Lassinger (Arizona State 95) Head Coach. Assistant Coaches Kirstine Jensen and Martyne Schroder.
Freshman Receiving Financial Aid/Academic: **Athletic:** 4-5
Roster In State: 5   **Out of State:** 7   **Out of Country:** 2
Seniors on Team: 4   **Graduation %:** 100
Most Recent Record: 20-11-0
Camp of Clinic Dates: July 15-19
Positions Needed: MB, OH
Schedule: Western Michigan, Ohio State, Texas Tech, Ball State, Loyola-Chicago
Style of Play: Ohio plays a fast paced game offensively. Success of the program is built on the foundation of ball control & defense.

Ohio Wesleyan University
Academic Profile

Sandusky Street
Delaware, OH 43015

Phone: 800-922-8953

Type: Private, 4 Yr., Liberal Arts, Coed
Website: http://www.owu.edu
SAT/ACT/GPA: 525 V, 573 M/25
Student/Faculty Ratio: 14:1
Undergraduate Enrollment: 1,850
Scholarships/Academic: Yes   **Athletic:** No
Expenses By: Year   **In State:** $ 27,210
Degrees Conferred: BA, BFA, BM

Founded: 1842
Religion: Methodist
Housing: Yes
Male/Female: 49:51
Graduate Enrollment: N/A
Financial Aid: Yes
Out of State: $ 27,210

Programs of Study: Botany - Microbiology, Chemistry, Economics, Education, English, Fine Arts, Geography, Geology, History, Humanities - Classics, Journalism, Mathematical Science, Modern Foreign Languages, Music, Philosophy, Physical Education, Physics, Politics & Government, Psychology, Religion, Sociology, Anthropology, Theatre & Dance, Zoology

Women's Athletic Profile

61 S. Sandusky Street
Delaware, OH 43015
Coach: Cindy Holliday
Email: cchollid@cc.owu.edu

NCAA I
Battling Bishops, Red, Black
Phone: (740) 368-3746
Fax: (740) 363-0793

Estimated # of Women's Volleyball Scholarships: N/A
Conference: North Coast Athletic Conference

Otterbein College
Academic Profile

160 Center St.
Westerville, OH 43081

Phone: 800-488-8144

Type: Private, 4 Yr., Liberal Arts, Coed		**Founded:** 1847
Website: http://www.otterbein.edu		**Religion:** Methodist
SAT/ACT/GPA: 820+/20+		**Housing:** Yes
Student/Faculty Ratio: 13:1		**Male/Female:** 43:57
Undergraduate Enrollment: 2,397		**Graduate Enrollment:** 93
Scholarships/Academic: Yes	**Athletic:** No	**Financial Aid:** Yes
Expenses By: Year	**In State:** $ 19,053	**Out of State:** $ 19,053

Degrees Conferred: BA, BS, BFA, M.Ed.
Programs of Study: Accounting, Art, Business Administration, Broadcasting, Chemistry, Communications, Education, Computer Science, Dance, Economics, Engineering, English, French, Health Education, History, Individualized Degree, International Studies, Journalism, Life Science, Mathematics, Music, Nursing, Philosophy, Physical Education, Physics/Astronomy, Political Science, PreDentistry, PreLaw, PreMed, PrePhysical Therapy, PreVet, Psychology, Public Relations, Religion, Sociology, Spanish, Sports Medicine, Theatre, Visual Arts

Women's Athletic Profile

160 Center Street
Westerville, OH 43081
Coach: Sharon Sexton
Email: ssexton@otterbein.edu

NCAA I
Lady Cardinals, Tan, Cardinal
Phone: (614) 823-3534
Fax: (614) 823-1966

Estimated # of Women's Volleyball Scholarships: N/A
Conference: Ohio Athletic Conference

Shawnee State University
Academic Profile

940 Second St.
Portsmouth, OH 45662-4344

Phone: (800) 959-2778

Type: Public, 4 Yr., Coed		**Founded:** 1986
Website: http://www.shawnee.edu		**Religion:** Non-Affiliated
SAT/ACT/GPA: Open Admission		**Housing:** Yes
Student/Faculty Ratio: 15:1		**Male/Female:** 40:60
Undergraduate Enrollment: 3,500		**Graduate Enrollment:** N/A
Scholarships/Academic: Yes	**Athletic:** Yes	**Financial Aid:** Yes
Expenses By: Quarter	**In State:** $ 7,609	**Out of State:** $ 9,952

Specializes In: Athletic Training, Plastic and Computer Engineering
Degrees Conferred: BA, BS, BFA
Programs of Study: Accounting, Applied Mathematics, Arts, Biology, Business Administration, Computer Science, Computer Technology, Dentistry, Education, Elementary Education, English, Finance, Fine Arts, Humanities, Liberal Arts, Management, Mathematics, Medical Laboratory Technology, Natural Science, Nursing, Occupational Therapy, Physical Education, Physical Science, Physical Therapy, Plastic Technology, PreLaw, PreMed, PreVet, Radiological Technology, Real Estate, Respiratory Therapy, Science, Social Science

Women's Athletic Profile

940 Second Street
Portsmouth, OH 45662
Coach: Dr. Steven Rader
Email: srader@shawnee.edu

NCAA I
Lady Bears, Blue/Dove Gray
Phone: (740) 355-2285
Fax: (740) 355-2381

Estimated # of Women's Volleyball Scholarships: 7
Conference: American Mideast Conference
Program Profile: The school was founded in 1986. All of our facilities are modern. Matches are played in James D. Rhode Athletic Center which has a 2,500 seating capacity.
History: Our program began in 1986. Athletic scholarships were suspended in 1996, but have been reinstated for 1999.
Coaching: Dr.Steve Rader, Head Coach, is in his third season. His team went 2-18 his first year. In 1998, his team improved to 12-19. Coach Rader is a full-time faculty member.
Freshman Receiving Financial Aid/Academic: **Athletic:** 0
Roster In State: 13   **Out of State:** 0   **Out of Country:** 0
Sophomores on Team: 2   **Seniors on Team:** 1   **Graduation %:** Unknown
Most Recent Record: 12-9-0   **Fall Games:** 31   **Spring Games:** 5
Positions Needed: Middle Hitters, Setter
Style of Play: 6-2 offense; coach likes quick attacks.

Tiffin University
Academic Profile

155 Miami St.
Tiffin, OH 44883

Phone: (419) 448-3453

Type: Private, 4 Yr., Liberal Arts, Coed
Website: http://www.tiffin.edu
SAT/ACT/GPA: 860/18/2.0
Student/Faculty Ratio: 12:1
Undergraduate Enrollment: 1,200
Scholarships/Academic: Yes   **Athletic:** Yes
Expenses By: Year   **In State:** $ 800

Founded: 1888
Religion: Non-Affiliated
Housing: Yes
Male/Female: 3:1
Graduate Enrollment: 120
Financial Aid: Yes
Out of State: $ 800

Specializes In: Business, Criminal Justice, Liberal Arts
Degrees Conferred: BA, BBA, BCJ, ABA
Programs of Study: Liberal Studies in Humanities, Liberal Studies in Social Sciences, Accounting, Finance, Hospitality Management, Information Studies, Sports Management, Health Care Management, Hotel & Restaurant Management, International Business, Marketing, Criminal Justice, Corrections, Forensic Psychology, Law Enforcement

Women's Athletic Profile

155 Miami Street
Tiffin, OH 44883
Coach: Bonnie Tiell
Email: btiell@tiffin.edu

NCAA I
Lady Dragons, Green, Gold
Phone: (419) 448-3261
Fax: (419) 443-5007

Estimated # of Women's Volleyball Scholarships: Partials
Conference: TBA
Program Profile: We have a year-round program. We have several players coach our USVBA teams. We open gyms year-round (winter and summer). Our best crowd was an estimated 500 for the University of Findlay game.
History: The program began in the early 1980's. We qualified for post-season in the past 10 of 11 seasons.
Achievements: We had 7 Academic All-Americans in seven years.
Coaching: Bonnie Tiell, Head Coach, started with the program in 1987 and has almost 300 wins. Dennis Roggori, Assistant Coach, graduated in 1997 and played four years. Rhonda Posey, Assistant Coach, graduated from Walsh.
Freshman Receiving Financial Aid/Academic: **Athletic:** 12
Roster In State: 11   **Out of State:** 1   **Out of Country:** 0
Sophomores on Team: 4   **Seniors on Team:** 2   **Graduation %:** 72
Most Recent Record: 20-14-0   **Fall Games:** 40   **Spring Games:** 3
Camp of Clinic Dates: Temp Camp (40 teams), July 15-17
Positions Needed: Middle
Schedule: Palm Beach Atlantic, Florida Tech, Ashland, Westminster, Wheeling Jesuit, West Virginia Wesleyan, Robert Morris
Style of Play: Relentless, scrappy defense with an aggressive offense. Relies on mental stability.

University of Akron
Academic Profile

178b Jar Arena
Akron, OH 44325-5201

Phone: 800-655-4884

Type: Public, 4 Yr., Coed
Website: http://www.uakron.edu
SAT/ACT/GPA: Taken test & completion of college
Student/Faculty Ratio: 20:1
Undergraduate Enrollment: 20,037
Scholarships/Academic: Yes
Expenses By: Year
Specializes In: Engineering

Founded: 1870
Religion: Non-Affiliated
Housing: Yes
Male/Female: 1:1
Graduate Enrollment: 3,568

Athletic: Yes
In State: $ 8,317

Financial Aid: Yes
Out of State: $ 14,167

Degrees Conferred: AA, AS, BA, BS, BFA, MA, MS, MBA
Programs of Study: Accounting, Art, Advertising, Biology, Business Administration, Chemistry, Classics, Communications, Communicative Disorder, Computer Science, Construction Technology, CytoTechnology, Dance, Economics, Elementary Education, Engineering, English, Finance, Geography, Geology, History, Humanities, Management, Marketing, Mathematics, Medical Science, Psychology, Music, Nursing, Philosophy, Political Science, Physical Education, Physics, Social Science, Social Work, Sociology, Special Education.

Women's Athletic Profile

323 Carroll St.
Akron, OH 44325
Coach: Mike Sweitzer
Email: msweitz@uakron.edu

NCAA I
Lady Zips, Blue, Gold
Phone: (330) 972-7338
Fax: (330) 972-6463

Estimated # of Women's Volleyball Scholarships: 4
Conference: Mid-American Conference
Program Profile: Playing site is in James A. Rhodes Arena and it seats 5, 942 with a wood playing surface. Playing season goes from September-November
History: Program began in 1974. Overall record of 529-390.
Achievements: Mike Sweitzer Coach of the Year 1995, East Division Title Holder 1999, 1992, 93, 95 American Volleyball Coaches Association National Award for Academic Excellence team had 13 straight semesters on Dean's List 1991-1997. Julie McDivitt was 2nd in nation in digs in 1999 and 3rd in 1998.
Coaching: Head Coach, Mike Sweitzer. Assistant Coach, John Napier
Roster In State: 10   **Out of State:** 3   **Out of Country:** 0
Seniors on Team: 4   **Graduation %:** 100
Most Recent Record: 16-14
Camp of Clinic Dates: TBA
Positions Needed: Setter, MH, OH, DS
Schedule: Western Michigan, Ball State, West Virginia, Virginia Tech, Texas Christian Univ.
Style of Play: Quick offense along with relentless defense. Team has consistently been conference leader in Digs, and Blocks.

University of Cincinnati
Academic Profile

350 Shoemaker Center
Cincinnati, OH 45221-0021

Phone: 513-556-1100

Type: Public, 4 Yr., Liberal Arts, Engineering, Coed
Website: http://www.uc.edu
SAT/ACT/GPA: 1054/22
Student/Faculty Ratio: 20:1
Undergraduate Enrollment: 17,833
Scholarships/Academic: Yes
Expenses By: Year

Founded: 1819
Religion: All-Denomination
Housing: Yes
Male/Female: 47:53
Graduate Enrollment: 4,422

Athletic: Yes
In State: $12,129

Financial Aid: Yes
Out of State: $12,129

Specializes In: Architecture, Education, Engineering, Interior Design, Medicine
Degrees Conferred: 500 undergraduates, Master's, Doctoral Degree
Programs of Study: African American Studies, Anthropology, Asian Studies, Biological Sciences, Biology, Chemistry, Classical Civilization Classics, Communications, Comparative Literature, Computer Science, Earth Science, Economics, English Literature, Environmental Science, French, Geography, Geology, German, History, International Affairs, Judaic Studies, Latin American Studies, Linguistics, Mathematics, Philosophy Physics, Political Science, Psychology, Sociology, Spanish

Women's Athletic Profile

350 Shoemaker Center
Cincinnati, OH 45221-2877
Coach: Laura Phillips Alford
Email: sunaharm@email.uc.edu

NCAA I
Lady Bearcats, Red, Black
Phone: (513) 556-0569
Fax: (513) 556-2877

Estimated # of Women's Volleyball Scholarships: 4
Conference: Conference USA
Program Profile: We have a strong program and play in the Shoemaker Center which had 13,700 attendance in the Conference USA. Our facilities for athletics are extensive with an academic support staff exclusive to athletics.
History: Our program started in 1972 and has had great success throughout its history. We had strong finishes in Conference play and one trip to the NCAA Tournament.
Achievements: 1997 Conference USA Tournament Runner-Up; Sharon Furlong (Moore) All-American National Team.
Coaching: Laura Phillips Alford, became Head Coach in 1997. She was a Runner-up in the Hawaii in 1998 National Championship. Reed Sunahara graduated from UCLA. He was a 3 time All-American and went to 3 National Championships. Darrell McLean was formerly the head coach at Thomas More College.
Freshman Receiving Financial Aid/Academic: | | **Athletic:** 5
Roster In State: 4 | **Out of State:** 10 | **Out of Country:** 2
Sophomores on Team: 2 | **Seniors on Team:** 3 | **Graduation %:** 95
Most Recent Record: 21-12-0
Camp of Clinic Dates: July 21-30
Positions Needed: Middle Hitters
Schedule: Long Beach, UCLA, Louisville, Houston, Miami of Ohio, South Florida

University of Dayton
Academic Profile

300 College Park
Dayton, OH 45469-1220
Type: Private, 4 Yr., Coed
Website: http://www.udayton.edu
SAT/ACT/GPA: 1110/22
Student/Faculty Ratio: 14.5:1
Undergraduate Enrollment: 6,000
Scholarships/Academic: Yes
Expenses By: Year
Specializes In: Comprehensive Studies
Degrees Conferred: BS, MS, Doctorate

Phone: (937) 229-2492

Founded: 1850
Religion: Catholic (Marianist)
Housing: Yes
Male/Female: 49:51
Graduate Enrollment: 3,000
Athletic: Yes | **Financial Aid:** Yes
In State: $ 19,840 | **Out of State:** $ 19,840

Programs of Study: Administration Studies, Biology, BioChemistry, Chemistry, Communications, Computer Information Systems, Computer Science, Criminal Justice, Economics, English, Environmental Biology, Environmental Geology, Geology, History, International Studies, Languages, Math, Music, Philosophy, Physical Science, Physics, Physics Computer Science, Political Science, PreLaw, PreMed, PreDental, Psychology, International Business, Management, Marketing, Health & Sport Science, Teacher Education, Engineering, Electrical, Manufacturing, Mechanical

Women's Athletic Profile

300 College Park
Dayton, OH 45469
Coach: Pete Hoyer
Email: launder@yar.udayto.edu

NCAA I
Lady Flyers, Red, Blue
Phone: (937) 229-2492
Fax: (937) 229-4461

Estimated # of Women's Volleyball Scholarships: 2
Conference: Atlantic 10 Conference
Program Profile: We are a Division I, Atlantic 10 conference program. The Flyers play in the Frericks Center on campus with a new sport court. The Center holds 5,000.
History: The varsity began in 1970. We joined the Atlantic 10 in 1995.
Achievements: 1992-MCC Tournament Championship; 1998-Atlantic 10 regular season co-champions
Coaching: Pete Hoyer, Head Coach, began his UD career in 1994. His overall record is 102-56. Xiangrong Liu and Sally Schulte are Assistant Coaches.
Freshman Receiving Financial Aid/Academic: | | **Athletic:** 2
Roster In State: 4 | **Out of State:** 5 | **Out of Country:** 3

Sophomores on Team: 2
Seniors on Team: 3
Graduation %: 100

Most Recent Record: 23-8-0
Fall Games: 31
Spring Games: 0

Camp of Clinic Dates: July 11-17, July 25-30, 1999

Positions Needed: Setter, Middle Blocker or Outside Hitter

Schedule: Wisconsin, Florida, Ohio State, Temple, North Carolina, Xavier

Style of Play: A balance attack team with strong side-out ability. All-around play, stable performance.

University of Findlay
Academic Profile

Box 14485
Findlay, OH 45840

Phone: (352) 375-4683

Type: Private, 4 Yr., Liberal Arts, Coed
Founded: 1882

Website: http://www.findlay.edu
Religion: Church of God

SAT/ACT/GPA: 740/18/2.0
Housing: Yes

Student/Faculty Ratio: 17:1
Male/Female: 1:1

Undergraduate Enrollment: 3,200
Graduate Enrollment: 400

Scholarships/Academic: Yes
Athletic: Yes
Financial Aid: Yes

Expenses By: Year
In State: $ 19,238
Out of State: $ 19,238

Degrees Conferred: AA, BA, BS, MBA

Programs of Study: Agriculture, Bilingual Education, Business and Management, Environmental and Hazardous Material Management, Equestrian Studies, Education, Health Science, PreMed, PreVet, Social Sciences

Men's Athletic Profile

1000 N. Main Street
Findlay, OH 45840
Coach: Wick R. Colchagoff
Email: colchagoff@findlay.edu

NCAA II
Oilers/Black, Orange
Phone: 419-424-5346
Fax:

Estimated # of Men's Volleyball Scholarships: 2

Conference: MIVA

Program Profile: The University of Findlay volleyball program has made great stride in 2 years in starting a NCAA DII men's volleyball program. Coach Wick Colchagoff sees a bright future for the program. The Oilers play in Croy Gymnasium, a 2200 seat facility which is currently undergoing a $700,000 renovation.

History: First season 2000

Freshman Receiving Financial Aid/Academic: 4
Athletic: 4

Roster In State: 14
Out of State: 5

Seniors on Team: 3
Graduation %: 92

Most Recent Record: 3-23

Positions Needed: Setter, OH, MH

Schedule: Ohio State, IPFW, Lewis, Ball State, Loyola, Quincy.

Women's Athletic Profile

1000 N. Main Street
Findley, OH 45840
Coach: Wick Colchagoff
Email: colchagoff@findlay.edu

NCAA I
Lady Oilers, Orange, Black
Phone: (419) 424-5346
Fax: (419) 424-4618

Estimated # of Women's Volleyball Scholarships: 3

Conference: Great Lakes Intercollegiate Athletic Conference

Program Profile: The University of Findlay volleyball program has made great stride in the last 2 years to becoming a national powerhouse in NCAA II. With a combined record of 63-22 in last to seasons and 2 national tournament appearances, Coach Wick Colchagoff sees a bright future for the program. The Oilers play in Croy Gymnasium, a 2200 seat facility which is currently undergoing a $700,000 renovation.

Achievements: 2000 GLIAC South Division Co-Champions, 2000 NCAA Great Lakes Region Semi-Finalist, 2000 Verizon Academic All-American of the Year, 1999 5th place NAIA National, 1999 NAIA Region IX Champions, 1999 NAIA Region IX Coach of the Year, 1999 GTE Academic All-American, 1999 NAIA 3rd team All-American.

Freshman Receiving Financial Aid/Academic:
Athletic: 4

Roster In State: 14
Out of State: 2
Out of Country: 0

Sophomores on Team:
Seniors on Team: 3
Graduation %: 92

Most Recent Record: 25-12
Positions Needed: Setter, OH, MH
Schedule: South Dakota State, Grand Valley State, Northwood, Northern Michigan, Hillsdale, Ferris State.

University of Rio Grande
Academic Profile

218 N. College Avenue
Rio Grande, OH 45674

Phone: 800-288-2746

Type: Private, 4 Yr., Liberal Arts, Coed
Website: http://www.rio.edu
SAT/ACT/GPA: 820/18
Student/Faculty Ratio: 20:1
Undergraduate Enrollment: 2,000
Scholarships/Academic: Yes   **Athletic:** Yes
Expenses By: Year   **In State:** $ 10,100
Degrees Conferred: AA, AS, AAS, BS, M.Ed.

Founded: 1876
Religion: Non-Affiliated
Housing: Yes
Male/Female: 50:50
Graduate Enrollment: 150
Financial Aid: Yes
Out of State: $ 10,500

Programs of Study: Accounting, Art, BioChemistry, Biology, Business & Management, Chemistry, Communications, Computer Science, Economics, Education, English, Finance, Health Sciences, Communications, Computer Science, Economics, Education, International Business, Liberal Arts, Mathematics, Music, Nursing, Physical Fitness/Exercise Science, Physical Science, Physics, PreMed, Psychology, Social Science, Special Education, Theatre

Women's Athletic Profile

MSC-734, 218 N. College Avenue
Rio Grande, OH 45674-3131
Coach: Patsy Fields
Email: pfields@urgrgcc.edu

NCAA I
Lady Redwomen, Red, White
Phone: (740) 245-5353
Fax: (740) 245-7555

Estimated # of Women's Volleyball Scholarships: N/A
Conference: Mid-Ohio Conference

University of Toledo
Academic Profile

2801 W. Bancroft St.
Toledo, OH 43606

Phone: (419) 530-2072

Type: Public, 4 Yr., Liberal Arts, Coed
Website: http://www.utoledo.edu
SAT/ACT/GPA: 900/18
Student/Faculty Ratio: 23:1
Undergraduate Enrollment: 20,000
Scholarships/Academic: Yes   **Athletic:** Yes
Expenses By: Year   **In State:** $ 11,000
Specializes In: Engineering, Education, Business, Law, Nursing, Pharmacy
Degrees Conferred: BA, BS, MA, MS, MBA, MBA, JD, Nursing

Founded: 1867
Religion: Non-Affiliated
Housing: Yes
Male/Female: 51:49
Graduate Enrollment: 2,000
Financial Aid: Yes
Out of State: $ 16,000

Programs of Study: Arts & Sciences, Business Administration, Education and Allied Professions, Engineering, Law, Pharmacy, University College, Community and Technical College. 150 undergraduate majors, more than 50 graduate and doctoral degrees.

Women's Athletic Profile

2801 W. Bancroft Street
Toledo, OH 43606
Coach: Kent Miller
Email: rocketvb@pop3.utoledo.edu

NCAA I
Rockets, Midnight Blue, Gold
Phone: (419) 530-2534
Fax: (419) 530-4428

Estimated # of Women's Volleyball Scholarships: 3
Conference: Mid-American Conference
Program Profile: We have a developing Division I program. We are focused on qualifying for the NCAA Tournament. We complete in a primary athletic facility called Savage Hall which has 8,500 seats. We schedule a high level of Conference opponents.
History: We started in 1975 in MAC. Kent Miller has coached here for 2 seasons.

Achievements: Miller coached with the National Team for 10 years; In 1997 we broke 13 school records and had the most wins since 1983; Second in Division I NCAA Series

Coaching: Kent Miller, Head Coach, started in 1997 with a record of 20-43 for ten years. He was USA Olympic Team assistant coach from 1987 to 1996. Assistant coaches are Jennifer Wrighton and Dave Chapman.

Freshman Receiving Financial Aid/Academic:

Roster In State: 6	Out of State: 7	Athletic: 4
Sophomores on Team: 0	Seniors on Team: 4	Out of Country: 1
Most Recent Record: 17-16-0	Fall Games: 33	Graduation %: 85
Camp of Clinic Dates: July 6-15		Spring Games: 10

Positions Needed: Outside Hitter, Middle Blocker, Right Side Hitter

Schedule: Penn State, Brigham Young University, Miami-OH, Michigan, Georgia, Kansas State

Style of Play: Aggressive, attack oriented team that puts pressure on our opponent. We are competitive, enthusiastic and exciting to watch.

Urbana University
Academic Profile

579 College Way
Urbana, OH 43078

Phone: 937-484-1356

Type: Private, 4 Yr., Liberal Arts, Coed
Website: http://www.urbana.edu
SAT/ACT/GPA: 18
Student/Faculty Ratio: 15:1
Undergraduate Enrollment: 956
Scholarships/Academic: Yes
Expenses By: Year

Athletic: Yes
In State: $ 13,838

Founded: 1850
Religion: Non-Affiliated
Housing: Yes
Male/Female: 5:4
Graduate Enrollment: 55
Financial Aid: Yes
Out of State: $ 13,838

Specializes In: Education, Business, Sports Medicine

Degrees Conferred: AA, BA, BS, MED

Programs of Study: Accounting, Finance, Management, Marketing, Human Resources, Biology, Chemistry, Computer, Pre-med, Teacher Education, English, Mathematics, Philosophy, Religion, Political Science, Sports Science, Criminal Justice, Pre-law, Psychology, Sports Management, Sports Medicine, History, Liberal Arts

Women's Athletic Profile

579 College Way
Urbana, OH 43078
Coach: Teresa Gentis
Email: jermso@hotmail.com

NCAA I
Lady Blue Knights, Blue, Silver
Phone: (937) 484-1325
Fax: (937) 484-1389

Estimated # of Women's Volleyball Scholarships: 15

Conference: Mid-East Conference

Program Profile: The program is on the rise and coming into its own. We play in a 3,000 seat gym, which includes a weight room, a pool and racquetball courts. Our season usually runs from late August to early November.

Achievements: Players have achieved conference honors for their play as well as numerous academic awards, including academic All-American for NAIA. The women's volleyball program won the Ohio Valley Region Junior Olympic Championship.

Coaching: Jeremy Wise, Head Coach, compiled a record of 2-25 in 1998. He was named 1st team All-District player in high school and college camps. He also worked at University of Ohio, where his team won the Ohio Valley Region Junior Olympic Championship.

Freshman Receiving Financial Aid/Academic:

Roster In State: 9	Out of State: 1	Athletic: 4
Sophomores on Team: 0	Seniors on Team: 1	Out of Country: 0
Most Recent Record: 2-25-0	Fall Games: 27-37	Graduation %: Unknown
		Spring Games: Scrimmages

Positions Needed: Middle Blocker, Setter, all around players

Schedule: Mount Vernon Nazarene, Cedarville, Grace, Walsh, Indiana Wesleyan University, University of Indianapolis

Style of Play: Quick offense, utilizing the middle hitters as much as possible. Scrappy defense, with a "never let the ball drop attitude". We work hard while having fun!

Walsh University
Academic Profile

2020 Easton St. NW
N. Canton, OH 44720

Phone: 330-490-7172

Type: Private, 4 Yr., Liberal Arts, Coed
Website: http://www.walsh.edu
SAT/ACT/GPA: 860/18/2.0

Founded: 1959
Religion: Catholic
Housing: Yes

Student/Faculty Ratio: 20:1
Undergraduate Enrollment: 1,350
Scholarships/Academic: Yes   **Athletic:** Yes
Expenses By: Year   **In State:** $ 17,000
Degrees Conferred: Assn., BA, BS, MA
Programs of Study: General Liberal Arts, Business, Nursing, Education, PreDental, PreMed, PreOptical, PreVet, PreLaw, Physical Therapy, PreNatural Resources, International Studies, Communications, Computer Science, English, History, Mathematics, Sociology, Psychology, Philosophy, Theology

Male/Female: 1:1
Graduate Enrollment: 200
Financial Aid: Yes
Out of State: $ 17,000

Women's Athletic Profile

2020 Easton St. NW
North Canton, OH 44720
Coach: Cass Dixon
Email: cdixon@walsh.edu

NCAA I
Lady Cavaliers, Maroon, Gold
Phone: (330) 490-7028
Fax: (330) 490-7038

Estimated # of Women's Volleyball Scholarships: Varies
Conference: American Mideast Conference
Program Profile: Sound program with much support from athletic department. Play on wood courts in Walsh's Physical Education Center with a seating capacity of 1, 700. Playing season is middle of August through middle of November (depends on post season spring conditioning and practice season from Jan-April. Summer conditioning schedule.
History: Program began in 1978. 7 coaches in 2 years, overall record of 608-211-3 (.740). Have won 3 conference titles and one district. Have competed in 4 NAIA Regional tournaments. 2000 season started 6 freshman and went 19-14 overall, 11-2 in the AMC. Tied for 3rd in AMC, lost in semifinal match of AMC tournament. Of the 14 losses 9 were to NAIA ranked/received votes teams.
Achievements: Three Conference titles, four appearances in NAIA regional tournament, one district 22 title, All-Conference, All-Region Players, freshman of the Year, Player of the Year and one NAIA honorable mention All-American.
Coaching: Coach Dixon enters her third season at Walsh. In 1999 Dixon guided the Cavaliers to their 3rd NAIA Regional Tournament appearance in four years and finished the season 32-13. In 2000 Dixon lost five starters to graduation and one to an ACL tear. They advanced to the semifinal match of the AMC tournament. While at the helm Dixon has produced 3 All-Region Players, 7 All-Conference Players, 2 NAIA Academic All-Americans and one Freshman Player of the Year.
Freshman Receiving Financial Aid/Academic: **Athletic:** 8
Roster In State: 10   **Out of State:** 2   **Out of Country:** 0
Sophomores on Team: **Seniors on Team:** 1   **Graduation %:** 100
Most Recent Record: 19-14-0
Positions Needed: Middle Blocker, Outside Hitter
Schedule: Cornerstone University, St. Xavier University, University of Findlay, Ashland University, Mount Vernon Nazarene College, Malone College, Houghton College, Muskingum College, Cedarville University.
Style of Play: Fast tempo, aggressive style based on sound fundamental skills. Strong, fast offensive team with also great blocking and defensive abilities.

Wilmington College - Ohio
Academic Profile

Pyle Center Box 1246
Wilmington, OH 45177

Phone: 800-341-9318

Type: Private, 4 Yr., Liberal Arts, Coed
Website: http://www.wilmington.edu
SAT/ACT/GPA: 850/20
Student/Faculty Ratio: 17:1
Undergraduate Enrollment: 1,100
Scholarships/Academic: Yes   **Athletic:** No
Expenses By: Year   **In State:** $ 18,500
Specializes In: Education, Athletic Training, Sports Management, Business
Degrees Conferred: BA, BS
Programs of Study: Accounting, Agricultural, Art, Athletic Training, Biology, Business Administration, Chemistry, Communications Arts, Computer Information Science, History, Computer Science, Criminal Justice, Elementary & Secondary Education, English, History, Mathematics, Physical Education, Psychology, Religion & Philosophy, Social & Political Studies, Social Work, Spanish, Sports Management, Theatre, PreLaw, PreMed, PreVet Science

Founded: 1870
Religion: Non-Affiliated
Housing: Yes
Male/Female: 50:50
Graduate Enrollment: N/A
Financial Aid: Yes
Out of State: $ 18,500

Women's Athletic Profile

Pyle Center
Wilmington, OH 45177
Coach: Kellie Diehl
Email: kdiehl@wilmington.edu

NCAA I
Lady Quakers, Green, White
Phone: (937) 382-6661
Fax: (937) 383-8566

Estimated # of Women's Volleyball Scholarships: N/A
Conference: Independent

Wittenberg University
Academic Profile

PO Box 720
Springfield, OH 45501

Phone: (800) 677-7558

Type: Private, 4 Yr., Liberal Arts, Coed
Website: http://www.wittenberg.edu
SAT/ACT/GPA: 1160/25/3.5
Student/Faculty Ratio: 14:1
Undergraduate Enrollment: 2,100
Scholarships/Academic: Yes
Expenses By: Year
Degrees Conferred: BA, B.Mus., BME, BEA

Athletic: No
In State: $ 26,112

Founded: 1845
Religion: Lutheran
Housing: Yes
Male/Female: 1:1
Graduate Enrollment: N/A
Financial Aid: Yes
Out of State: $ 26,112

Programs of Study: American Studies, Art, Biology, Chemistry, Computer Science, East Asian Studies, Economics, Education, English, French, Geography, Geology, German, History, Management, Mathematics, Music, Philosophy, Physics, Political Science, Psychology, Religion, Russian Area Studies, Sociology, Spanish, Theatre-Dance

Women's Athletic Profile

P.O. Box 720
Springfield, OH 45501
Coach: Connie Surowicz
Email: wittvb@aol.com

NCAA I
Lady Tigers, Red, White
Phone: (937) 327-6492
Fax: (937) 327-6428

Estimated # of Women's Volleyball Scholarships: N/A
Conference: North Coast Athletic Conference

Wright State University
Academic Profile

3640 Colonel Glenn Avenue
Dayton, OH 45435

Phone: (937) 775-2368

Type: Public, 4 Yr., Liberal Arts, Engineering, Coed
Website: http://www.wright.edu
SAT/ACT/GPA: General/2.0
Student/Faculty Ratio: 20:1
Undergraduate Enrollment: 12,000
Scholarships/Academic: Yes
Expenses By: Year
Specializes In: 107 Degrees
Degrees Conferred: BA, BS, BBA, MA, MD, MS

Athletic: Yes
In State: $ 9,365

Founded: 1964
Religion: Non-Affiliated
Housing: Yes
Male/Female: 1:1.3
Graduate Enrollment: 3,000
Financial Aid: Yes
Out of State: $ 13,295

Programs of Study: Accounting, Biology, Business Administration, Communications, Computer Science, Education, Engineering, Health Science, History, Mathematics, Philosophy, Physical Education, Physical Sciences, Social Sciences

Women's Athletic Profile

3640 Col. Glenn Hwy
Dayton, OH 45435-0001
Coach: Joylynn Tracy
Email: joylynn.tracy@wright.edu

NCAA I
Lady Raiders, Green, Gold
Phone: (937) 775-2771
Fax: (937) 775-2368

Estimated # of Women's Volleyball Scholarships: 1
Conference: Midwestern Collegiate Conference
Program Profile: We are a mid-level Division I program that competes in the Midwestern Collegiate Conference. We play in the McLin Gym in the Nutter Center, arguably the best facility in Ohio. Our gym seats 500 while the arena seats 10,000. We compete from September to December. Pre-season starts in mid-August.
History: Our program began in 1973. We went Division I in 1986. We have appeared in NIVC three years.
Achievements: Conference runner-up in 1993; 2 All-Conference Players in 1998. Made it to Division II Regional in 1983.

Coaching: Joylynn Tracy, became Head Coach in 1998. She was previously Assistant Coach here. Phil Nickel is in his first year as Assistant Coach. The 1998-99 overall record was 11-18.

Freshman Receiving Financial Aid/Academic: **Athletic:** 1

Roster In State: 11	**Out of State:** 1	**Out of Country:** 0
Sophomores on Team: 0	**Seniors on Team:** 4	**Graduation %:** 100
Most Recent Record: 11-18-0	**Fall Games:** 29	**Spring Games:** 4

Camp of Clinic Dates: July 5-8, July 18-22, 1999
Positions Needed: 2 Outside Hitter, 1 Middle Hitter, 1 Right Side Hitter
Schedule: UCLA, Texas Tech, University of Dayton, University of Wisconsin-Milwaukee, Southern Methodist
Style of Play: We run a quick, dynamic offense and play aggressive defense. We believe in hard work and discipline and pride ourselves on the continued pursuit of excellence.

Xavier University
Academic Profile

3800 Victory Parkway
Cincinnati, OH 45207

Phone: 800-344-4698

Type: Private, 4 Yr., Liberal Arts, Coed
Website: http://www.xu.edu
SAT/ACT/GPA: 900+/20+
Student/Faculty Ratio: 16:1
Undergraduate Enrollment: 3,500
Scholarships/Academic: Yes **Athletic:** Yes
Expenses By: Year **In State:** $ 18,500

Founded: 1831
Religion: Jesuit
Housing: yes
Male/Female: 46:54
Graduate Enrollment: 2,000
Financial Aid: Yes
Out of State: $ 18,500

Degrees Conferred: BA, BS, AA, BFA, BSBA, BSN
Programs of Study: Over 50 majors including: Allied Health, Business & Management, Communications, Education, Health Sciences, Letters/Literature, Psychology, Social Sciences

Women's Athletic Profile

3800 Victory Parkway
Cincinnati, Ohio 45207
Coach: Floyd Deaton
Email:

NCAA I
Musketeers, Blue/White
Phone: (513)745-3198
Fax: (513)745-4390

Estimated # of Women's Volleyball Scholarships: 0
Conference: Atlantic 10
Program Profile: Cinta Center 10,200 seats, practice gym (both wood).
History: Began 1973, record 451-399
Achievements: Atlantic 10 Tourney last 2 years. 1998 Coach of the Year, 1998-99 regular season champs.
Coaching: Floyd Deaton Head Coach, Assistant, Jackie Barnes
Freshman Receiving Financial Aid/Academic: **Athletic:** 1
Roster In State: 3 **Out of State:** 14 **Out of Country:** 0
Sophomores on Team: **Seniors on Team:** 2 **Graduation %:** 100
Most Recent Record: 23-8
Schedule: Texas Tech, South Carolina, Temple, Western Mich. George Washington
Style of Play: Fast offense, more horizontal than vertical. Defensive minded "ball doesn't hit floor, you wont lose"

Youngstown State University
Academic Profile

One University Plaza
Youngstown, OH 44555

Phone: (330) 742-1920

Type: Public, 4 Yr., Coed
Website: http://www.ysu.edu
SAT/ACT/GPA: 860/18/2.5
Student/Faculty Ratio: 20:1
Undergraduate Enrollment: 12,324
Scholarships/Academic: Yes **Athletic:** Yes
Expenses By: Year **In State:** $ Varies

Founded: 1906
Religion: Non-Affiliated
Housing: Yes
Male/Female: 45:55
Graduate Enrollment: 1,050
Financial Aid: Yes
Out of State: $ Varies

Specializes In: Health & Human Service, Education, Business, Nursing, Criminal Justice

Degrees Conferred: AA, BA, MS, Ph.D.
Programs of Study: 34 majors in College of Health & Human Services, 40 majors in College of Arts & Sciences, 20 majors in College of Business, 6 majors in College of Education, 15 majors in College of Engineering, 10 majors in College of Fine Arts & Performing Arts

Women's Athletic Profile

One University Plaza
Youngstown, OH 44555-0001
Coach: Joe Conroy
Email:

NCAA I
Penguins, Red, White, Black
Phone: (330) 742-1920
Fax: (330) 742-2968

Estimated # of Women's Volleyball Scholarships: 10
Conference: Mid-Continent Conference
Program Profile: We play in the Main Gym, Beeghly Center. Our playing season is traditional and non-traditional. Beeghly Center seats 6,000. We have a team locker room and 2 practice facilities. Our ten courts are air-conditioned.
History: We started in 1975 and have compiled an overall record of 303-382. We have won 20 or more matches in three of the last five seasons.
Achievements: Mid-Continent Conference Coach of the Year Award in 1994, 1995 and 1998.
Coaching: Joe Conroy, Head Coach, has been here from 1992 to the present. Andrea Jackson is Assistant Coach. She has been here from 1992 to the present. Our overall record is 108-106.

Freshman Receiving Financial Aid/Academic:		**Athletic:** 2
Roster In State: 9	**Out of State:** 8	**Out of Country:** 0
Sophomores on Team: 0	**Seniors on Team:** 3	**Graduation %:** 100
Most Recent Record: 20-12-0	**Fall Games:**	**Spring Games:** 20

Camp of Clinic Dates: July 7,8,9,14,15,16
Positions Needed: Setter, Middle Hitter
Schedule: Oral Roberts, Bucknell, Saint Peter, Toledo, Princeton, Navy, Iona
Style of Play: Moderate to fast pace. Quick offense.

OKLAHOMA

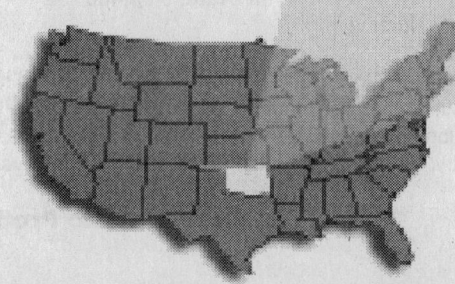

Oklahoma City

SCHOOL	CITY	AFFILIATION	PAGE
Bartlesville Wesleyan College	Bartlesville	NCCAA I/NAIA	601
Cameron University	Lawton	NCAA II	601
Oral Roberts University	Tulsa	NCAA I	602
Southern Nazarene University	Bethany	NAIA	602
Southeastern Oklahoma State Univ	Durant	NCAA II	603
University of Central Oklahoma	Edmond	NCAA II	603
University of Oklahoma	Norman	NCAA I	604
University of Tulsa	Tulsa	NCAA I	605

Bartlesville Wesleyan College
Academic Profile

2201 Silverlake Road
Bartlesville, OK 74006

Phone: (800) 468-6292

Type: Private, 4 Yr., Liberal Arts, Coed
Website: http://www.bwc.edu
SAT/ACT/GPA: 860/18/2.0
Student/Faculty Ratio: 14:1
Undergraduate Enrollment: 600
Scholarships/Academic: Yes
Expenses By: Year
Specializes In: Business, Education, Nursing
Degrees Conferred: AA, AS, BS, BA

Founded: 1909
Religion: Wesleyan
Housing: Yes
Male/Female: 38:62
Graduate Enrollment: N/A
Athletic: Yes
In State: $ 13,400

Financial Aid: Yes
Out of State: $ 13,400

Programs of Study: Accounting, Applied Computer Information System, Behavioral Sciences, Biology, Business Administration, Business Education, Chemistry, Church Music, Communications Arts, Computer Science, Cross-Cultural, Ministry, Elementary Education, English, English Education, Exercise Science, General Science, History, Political Science, LBA, MHR, Mathematics, Music Education, Nursing, Pastoral Ministry, Physical Education, PreMedicine, PrePhysical Education Therapy

Women's Athletic Profile

2201 Silver Lake Rd.
Bartlesville, OK 74003
Coach: Herb Whitehouse
Email:

NCAA I
Lady Eagles, Red, White, Blue
Phone: (918) 335-6259
Fax: (918) 335-6244

Estimated # of Women's Volleyball Scholarships: N/A
Conference: Midlands Collegiate Conference

Cameron University
Academic Profile

2800 Gore Blvd.
Lawton, OK 73505

Phone: (580) 581-2462

Type: Public, 4 Yr., Liberal Arts, Coed
Website: http://www.cameron.edu
SAT/ACT/GPA: 700/17
Student/Faculty Ratio: 28:1
Undergraduate Enrollment: 5,225
Scholarships/Academic: Yes
Expenses By: Year
Specializes In: Please refer to webpage
Degrees Conferred: AAS, AS, BA, BFA, MS
Programs of Study: Please refer to WebPages.

Founded: 1908
Religion: Non-Affiliated
Housing: Yes
Male/Female: 45:55
Graduate Enrollment: 420
Athletic: Yes
In State: $ 5,215

Financial Aid: Yes
Out of State: $ 7,867

Women's Athletic Profile

2800 Gore Boulevard
Lawton, OK 73505
Coach: Kim Vinson
Email: kimv@cameron.edu

NCAA I
Lady Aggies, Gold, Black
Phone: (580) 581-2462
Fax: (580) 581-5537

Estimated # of Women's Volleyball Scholarships: 8
Conference: Lone Star Conference
History: We were Lone Star Conference Champions in 1998 and we are looking to repeat. The last 4 seasons have all been winning ones. We made the Top 25 ranking Regional Tournament in 1998
Achievements: 1998 North Division Lone Star Coach of the Year; 1998 Lone Star Champions.
Coaching: Kim Vinson - Head Coach, was North Division Coach of the Year in 1998. She coached CU since 1989. She recently joined the 300 Win Club. Todd Caughun is Assistant Coach. He has been coaching for 12 years and is a former head coach from Alberta, Canada.

Roster In State: 0
Sophomores on Team: 3

Out of State: 8
Seniors on Team: 2

Out of Country: 2
Graduation %: 100

Most Recent Record: 29-3-0   **Fall Games:** 30   **Spring Games:** 4
Camp of Clinic Dates: Team Camp: July 27-30
Positions Needed: Outside Hitter, Setter
Schedule: West Texas A & M, Western Colorado, Metro State-Denver, Texas A & M-Kingsville, University of Central Oklahoma
Style of Play: In order to succeed, the team will have to exercise patience, focus on the goals at hand and execute on every opportunity that they face. Ball control!!!

Oral Roberts University
Academic Profile

7777 S. Lewis Avenue
Tulsa, OK 74171

Phone: 800-678-8876

Type: Private, 4 Yr., Coed
Website: http://www.oru.com
SAT/ACT/GPA: Open
Student/Faculty Ratio: 25:1
Undergraduate Enrollment: 4,500
Scholarships/Academic: Yes
Expenses By: Year
Degrees Conferred: BA, BS, BSE, MA
Programs of Study: All

Athletic: Yes
In State: $ 16,125

Founded: 1963
Religion: Non-Affiliated
Housing: Yes
Male/Female: 1:4
Graduate Enrollment: 800
Financial Aid: Yes
Out of State: $ 16,125

Women's Athletic Profile

777 S. Lewis Avenue
Tulsa, OK 74171
Coach: Amy Farber-Knowles
Email:

NCAA I
God's Squad, Navy Blue, White
Phone: (918) 495-7101
Fax: (918) 495-7123

Estimated # of Women's Volleyball Scholarships: 1
Conference: Mid-Continent Conference
Program Profile: Success Division I program with 4 straight appearances in the NCAA's. Play in the fabulous Kenneth State. Cooper Aerobics Center.
Freshman Receiving Financial Aid/Academic: **Athletic:** 7
Roster In State: 1   **Out of State:** 5   **Out of Country:** 6
Sophomores on Team: 0   **Seniors on Team:** 1   **Graduation %:** 100
Most Recent Record: 29-6-0   **Fall Games:** 33   **Spring Games:** 0
Camp of Clinic Dates: None set for 2000
Positions Needed: Middle Blocker Only
Schedule: Long Beach State, UC-Santa Barbara, University of Southern California, Arkansas, Cal-Poly, Fresno State

Southern Nazarene University
Academic Profile

6729 NW 39TH Expressway
Bethany, OK 73008

Phone: 405-491-6324

Type: Private, 4 Yr., Liberal Arts, Coed
Website: http://www.snu.edu
SAT/ACT/GPA: 19
Student/Faculty Ratio: 17:1
Undergraduate Enrollment: 1,950+
Scholarships/Academic: Yes
Expenses By: Year
Degrees Conferred: BS, Masters

Athletic: Yes
In State: $ 12,888

Founded: 1899
Religion: Nazarene
Housing: Yes
Male/Female: 2:1
Graduate Enrollment: N/A
Financial Aid: Yes
Out of State: $ 12,888

Programs of Study: Over 70 different fields of undergraduate degree options. It also offers eight convenient graduate degree programs and has two renowned adult studies programs.

Women's Athletic Profile

6729 NW 39th Expressway
Bethany, OK 73008
Coach: Kevin Ingram
Email: kingram@snu.edu

NCAA I
Lady Redskins, Cardinal, White
Phone: (405) 789-6221
Fax: (405) 491-6387

Estimated # of Women's Volleyball Scholarships: 5
Conference: Sooner
Program Profile: SNU is a small Christian College volleyball program. Our season starts in August and runs through the first of December. Our home facility is only 2 years old and holds around 5000 people. We look to be a regional contender again next season and will push towards a spot at the national tournament.
History: Our program has been around for many years and has had some years of great success as well as some years that we would consider rebuilding years. We are on our way back up and look to enjoy the fruits of our labor in the years to come.
Achievements: Many awards over the years, but in the last 2 we have turned out several Academic All-Americans as well as Conference and Regional Player.
Coaching: Head Coach Kevin Ingram

Roster In State: 2	**Out of State:** 13	**Out of Country:** 0
Sophomores on Team:	**Seniors on Team:** 5	**Graduation %:** 90-100

Most Recent Record: 14-19
Positions Needed: 5
Schedule: Lubbock Christian Univ., John Brown Univ., Univ. of Central Oklahoma, Dallas Baptist Univ.
Style of Play: Aggressive, smart, and a never say die attitude.

Southeastern Oklahoma State University
Academic Profile

University Boulevard
Durant, OK 74701-0609

Phone:

Type: Public, 4 Yr., Coed
Website:
SAT/ACT/GPA: 940/20/2.7
Student/Faculty Ratio: 19/1
Undergraduate Enrollment: 4600
Scholarships/Academic: Yes
Expenses By: Varies
Degrees Conferred: BA, BBA, MM, M.Mus
Programs of Study: Contact school for more information.

Athletic: Yes
In State:

Founded: 1901
Religion: Non-Affiliated
Housing: Yes
Male/Female: 45/55
Graduate Enrollment: 258
Financial Aid: Yes
Out of State:

Women's Athletic Profile

University Boulevard
Durant, OK 74701-0609
Coach: Cherrie Wilmoth
Email: cwilmoth@sosu.edu

NCAA I
Lady Savages, Blue, Gold
Phone: (580) 924-0121
Fax: (580) 920-7493

Estimated # of Women's Volleyball Scholarships: N/A
Conference: Independent

University of Central Oklahoma
Academic Profile

100 N. University Dr.
Edmond, OK 73034

Phone: (405) 974-2148

Type: Public, 4 Yr., Liberal Arts, Coed
Website: http://www.ucok.edu
SAT/ACT/GPA: 910/19/2.7
Student/Faculty Ratio: 23/1
Undergraduate Enrollment: 14,500
Scholarships/Academic: Yes
Expenses By: Year
Specializes In: Business, Sciences, Psychology, Education
Degrees Conferred: BA, BS, MA, MS, MBA, MED

Athletic: Yes
In State: $ 4,800

Founded: 1890
Religion: Non-Affiliated
Housing: Yes
Male/Female: 1:2
Graduate Enrollment: N/A
Financial Aid: Yes
Out of State: $ 4,200

Programs of Study: Accounting, Actuarial Science, Advertising, Applied Mathematics, Art, Art Education, Economics, Business Economics, Criminal Justice, Construction Technology, Design, Journalism, Reading Education, Nutrition, Philosophy, Photography, Graphic Arts, Food Service

Women's Athletic Profile

100 N. University Drive
Edmond, OK 73034
Coach: Mark Herrin
Email: mherrin@aix1.ucok.edu

NCAA I
Lady Bronchos, Bronze, Blue
Phone: (405) 974-2148
Fax: (405) 974-3820

Estimated # of Women's Volleyball Scholarships: 8
Conference: Lone Star Conference
Program Profile: We have a competitive Division III program. Our home court is Hamilton Fieldhouse which has 3,500 seats. Our season goes from August 15 to November 15.
History: Our first year was in 1988. Our program overall record is 365-259.
Achievements: Mark Herrin, Coach of the Year in 1994; Lone Star Champions in 1994; NCAA Regional Finalist; 14 First Team All-Conference Players; 4 All-Regional Players.
Coaching: Mark Herrin, became Head Coach in 1990. His overall record is 207-118.

Freshman Receiving Financial Aid/Academic:		**Athletic:** 3
Roster In State: 6	**Out of State:** 5	**Out of Country:** 2
Sophomores on Team: 4	**Seniors on Team:** 3	**Graduation %:** 100
Most Recent Record: 23-12-0	**Fall Games:** 35	**Spring Games:** 4

Camp of Clinic Dates: July 19-21; July 22-24
Schedule: West Texas A & M, Cameron, Texas A & M Kingsville, Ft.Hays State, Univ of Nebraska-Kearney, Eastern New Mexico
Style of Play: Disciplined.

University of Oklahoma
Academic Profile

151 W Brooks E-16
Norman, OK 73019-0201

Phone: 800-234-6868

Type: Public, 4 Yr., Liberal Arts, Engineering, Coed
Website: http://www.ou.edu
SAT/ACT/GPA: 1030/22/3.0
Student/Faculty Ratio: 21:1
Undergraduate Enrollment: 16,000
Scholarships/Academic: Yes
Expenses By: Year
Founded: 1890
Religion: Non-Affiliated
Housing: Yes
Male/Female: 1.1:1
Graduate Enrollment: 8,000

Athletic: Yes **Financial Aid:** Yes
In State: $ 7,568 **Out of State:** $ 11,349

Specializes In: Health Sports Science, Engineering, Liberal Arts
Degrees Conferred: 200 Master's and Doctoral
Programs of Study: Business, Meteorology, Education, Engineering, Fine Arts, GeoSciences, Architecture, Psychology, Marketing, Music, Political Science, Science Education, Journalism, Linguistics, Drama, Dance, Botany, Zoology, Economics, Physics, Sociology, Social Work, Special Education

Women's Athletic Profile

151 W Brooks Ave Room E-16
Norman, OK 73019
Coach: Kalani Mahi
Email: dkmahi@ou.edu

NCAA I
Sooners, Crimson, Cream
Phone: (405) 325-8364
Fax: (405) 325-7505

Estimated # of Women's Volleyball Scholarships: 3
Conference: Big 12 Conference
Program Profile: New coaching staff (1st year), building nationally competitive team. Facilities 3, 500 seat historic OU Fieldhouse will receive app. $2 million upgrade by 2003, shared only with wrestling. Volleyball has priority on court for practices and matches during season.1-4 court set-up on wood floor, 6 month old locker room with separate shower/bathroom, locker/changing, meeting, equipment, and satellite training rooms. Academic Support: we have a student athlete academic center which provides our athletes support through our academic counseling offices, computer center and career preparation center. Strength & Conditioning is done in a 16 month old weight and cardio training room, with state of the art equipment, 2 full time certified strength coaches that work with the volleyball team.
History: Program began in 1975. Three Head Coaches: Amy Dahl (1974-77), Myles Pabst (1977-99), Kalani Mahi (2000-Present). 1987 Big 8 Tournament Champions. NCAA Tournament appearances 1987, 1988 (final 8), 1997 (2nd round).
Achievements: 1987 Big 8 Conference Tournament Champion. All-American: Patrice Arrington (1997-Honorable Mention). US National Team: Marcy Crabtree (82), Patrice Arrington (87).

Coaching: Head Coach Kalani Mahi (1st season), Assistant Coaches Joel McCartney, Christy Mahi, and Andrea McCartney.

Freshman Receiving Financial Aid/Academic:

Athletic: 5

Roster In State: 2　　　　　　　　　　**Out of State:** 10　　　**Out of Country:** 1

Seniors on Team: 5

Most Recent Record: 7-19-0

Camp of Clinic Dates: July 13-15, July 16-18, July 30-Aug 2

Positions Needed: Middle Hitter, Setter

Schedule: Nebraska, Kansas State, Texas A&M, Colorado, Texas Tech, Baylor, Texas, Wake Forest, Wyoming, Kansas

Style of Play: Quick, "up-tempo" offense that involves a balanced attack (middles received highest percentage of sets in fall of 2000. Disciplined and intense defensive play. Aggressive serving team.

University of Tulsa
Academic Profile

600 S College Avenue
Tulsa, OK 74104-3189

Phone: (918) 631-2000

Type: Private, 4 Yr., Liberal Arts, Engineering, Coed

Founded: 1894

Website: http://www.utulsa.edu

Religion: Presbyterian

SAT/ACT/GPA: 1215/25/3.7

Housing: Yes

Student/Faculty Ratio: 12:1

Male/Female: 48:52

Undergraduate Enrollment: 3,300

Graduate Enrollment: 1,000

Scholarships/Academic: Yes　　　　**Athletic:** Yes　　　　**Financial Aid:** Yes

Expenses By: Year　　　　　　　　**In State:** $ 21,230　　**Out of State:** $ 21,230

Specializes In: Liberal Arts, Engineering, Business

Degrees Conferred: BA, BS, BFA, MA, MS, MBA, MFA

Programs of Study: Anthropology, Arts, Biological Science, Computer Information Systems, Chemistry, Computer Science, Economics, Education, Electrical Engineering, Engineering, Finance, History, Management, Mathematics, Philosophy, Political Science

Women's Athletic Profile

600 S. College
Tulsa, OK 74104
Coach: Matt Sonnichsen
Email: athletics@utulsa.edu

NCAA I
Golden Hurricanes, Crimson
Phone: (918) 631-3112
Fax: (918) 631-3670

Estimated # of Women's Volleyball Scholarships: N/A

Conference: Western Athletic Conference

Program Profile: We are an up and coming program. In 1998, season wins were the best since 1985. Our 1999 team will move into a $30 million dollar arena with a seating capacity of 8,300.

History: The program began in 1978.

Achievements: A new member of Western Athletic Conference.

Coaching: Matt Sonnichsen, Head Coach, is entering his first season with the program. Carey Williams is Assistant Coach.

Freshman Receiving Financial Aid/Academic:

Athletic: 3

Roster In State: 2　　　　　　　　**Out of State:** 4　　　　**Out of Country:** 4

Sophomores on Team: 3　　　　　**Seniors on Team:** 1　　**Graduation %:** 100

Most Recent Record: 11-16-0　　**Fall Games:** 30　　　　**Spring Games:** 4

Camp of Clinic Dates: June 11-12; July 7-10; July 18-20; July 25-27; July 30-31

Positions Needed: Outside Hitter, Middle Blocker

Schedule: Hawaii, Fresno State, San Jose State, Rice, SMU

Style of Play: Enthusiastic, no lack of effort, the team plays together no matter what.

OREGON

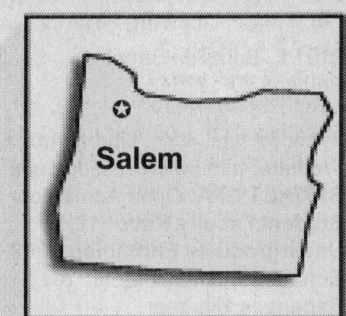

Salem

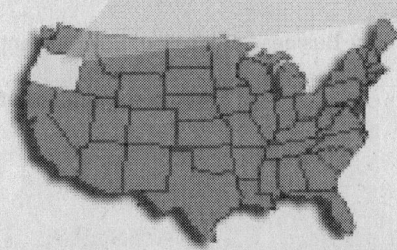

SCHOOL	CITY	AFFILIATION	PAGE
Cascade College	Portland	NCCAA	607
Chemeketa Community College	Salem	NJCAA	607
Clackamas Community College	Oregon City	NJCAA	608
Concordia University	Portland	NAIA	608
Eastern Oregon State College	La Grande	NCAA III/NAIA	609
George Fox University	Newberg	NCAA III	610
Lewis & Clark College	Portland	NCAA III	611
Linfield College	McMinnville	NCAA III	611
Oregon Institute of Technology	Klamath Falls	NAIA	612
Oregon State University	Corvallis	NCAA I	612
Pacific University	Forest Grove	NCAA III	613
Portland State University	Portland	NCAA I	613
Southern Oregon University	Ashland	NAIA	614
University of Oregon	Eugene	NCAA I	614
University of Portland	Portland	NCAA I	615
Western Baptist College	Salem	NAIA	616
Western Oregon State College	Monmouth	NCAA II/NAIA	616
Willamette University	Salem	NCAA III	617

Cascade College
Academic Profile

9101 E. Burnside Street
Portland, OR 97216

Phone: 800-550-7678

Type: Private, 4 Yr., Liberal Arts, Coed
Website: http://www.cascade.edu
SAT/ACT/GPA: Open Admission
Student/Faculty Ratio: 17:1
Undergraduate Enrollment: 309
Scholarships/Academic: Yes   **Athletic:** Yes
Expenses By: Year   **In State:** $ 12,000
Specializes In: Bible Studies
Degrees Conferred: Bachelors

Founded: 1994
Religion: Christian
Housing: Yes
Male/Female: 50:50
Graduate Enrollment: N/A
Financial Aid: Yes
Out of State: $ 12,000

Programs of Study: Bible, Ministry, Business, Education, Environmental Science, Psychology, Interdisciplinary Studies

Women's Athletic Profile

9101 E. Burnside
Portland, OR 97216
Coach: Christa Hill
Email: athletics@cascade.edu

NCAA I
Thunderbirds, Green, White
Phone: (503) 255-7060
Fax: (503) 257-1222

Estimated # of Women's Volleyball Scholarships: 6
Conference: Cascade Collegiate Conference
Program Profile: Cascade College participates in the NAIA Division II Cascade Conference. We are also members of the NCCAA. The gymnasium offers a heath and wellness center in the basement. We have newly renovated locker rooms.
History: The volleyball program is relatively young. We have just completed our fourth season as a member of the NAIA. We are a relatively young, unknown team that has nothing to lose and everything to gain.
Achievements: We have had two All-Conference players in our short 4 years of competition.
Coaching: Christa Hill, Head Coach, came from Columbia Christian College, where she won All-NCCAA honors as a freshman and All-Conference Honors as a freshman and sophomore. Christa set various assist records. Jasmine Varela is Assistant Coach.
Freshman Receiving Financial Aid/Academic: **Athletic:** 1
Roster In State: 4   **Out of State:** 7   **Out of Country:** 0
Sophomores on Team: 0   **Seniors on Team:** 5   **Graduation %:** 100
Most Recent Record: **Fall Games:** 24   **Spring Games:** 0
Camp of Clinic Dates: VB Camp 4th-6 the grades: June 21-25; 7th-9th grades: June 28-July 1st
Positions Needed: Middle Blocker, Right Hitter, Setter
Schedule: Albertson, Northwest Nazarene, Southwest Oregon University
Style of Play: We play a 5-1 offense, with a rotation defense. We try to recruit ladies who have a passion to play volleyball, enjoy being a part of a team and love to succeed.

Chemeketa Community College
Academic Profile

4000 Lancaster Drive, NE
Salem, OR 97309-7070

Phone: 503-399-5006

Type: Private, 2 Yr., Jr. College, Coed
Website: http://www.chemek.cc.or.us
SAT/ACT/GPA: Open
Student/Faculty Ratio: 16:1
Undergraduate Enrollment: 8,000
Scholarships/Academic: Yes   **Athletic:** Yes
Expenses By: Year   **In State:** $ 23,786

Founded: 1969
Religion: Non-Affiliated
Housing: Yes
Male/Female: 7:1
Graduate Enrollment: N/A
Financial Aid: Yes
Out of State: $ 23,786

Degrees Conferred: BA, BS, BFA, BLI, BM, BSSP, MA, MS, MFA
Programs of Study: Advertising, Broadcasting, Communication Disorders, Communications, Creative Writing, Dance, Film Arts, Literature, PreLaw, Public Relation, Publishing, Radio & Television, Speech, Speech Pathology, Theatre

Women's Athletic Profile

4000 Lancaster Dr. NE
Salem, OR 97309-5496
Coach: Terry McLaughlin
Email: MCLT@Chemet.CC.OR.US

NCAA I
Lady Storm, Green, Gold
Phone: (503) 399-6251
Fax: (503) 399-5496

Estimated # of Women's Volleyball Scholarships: 8
Conference: NWAACC Southern Region
Program Profile: We have an excellent gym facility. It has four courts and a capacity of 1,200.
Achievements: IWACC Coach of the Year in 1994, 1997 and 1998; 4 Conference titles; Twice NWACC Champions; 3 First Team All-Americans; 25+ Players moved to 4 year colleges in the last 11 years.
Coaching: Terry McLaughlin, Head Coach, started in 1988 and her overall record is 368-141 with a .723 winning percentage. Mark Cain is Assistant Coach.
Freshman Receiving Financial Aid/Academic: | **Athletic:** 6

Roster In State: 13	**Out of State:** 1	**Out of Country:** 0
Sophomores on Team: 0	**Seniors on Team:** 4	**Graduation %:** 90
Most Recent Record: 51-6-0	**Fall Games:** 57	**Spring Games:** 0

Camp of Clinic Dates: June 22-23, July 26-28, August 2-5
Positions Needed: None
Schedule: Mount Hood, Clackamas, Pierce, Spokane, Clark, Columbia Basin
Style of Play: Disciplined defense.

Clackamas Community College
Academic Profile

19600 South Molalla Avenue
Oregon City, OR 97045

Phone: (503) 657-6958

Type: Public, 2 Yr., Jr. College, Coed
Website: http://www.geocities.com
SAT/ACT/GPA: Open
Student/Faculty Ratio: 15:1
Undergraduate Enrollment: 13,200
Scholarships/Academic: Yes | **Athletic:** Yes
Expenses By: Year | **In State:** $ 4,500
Specializes In: General
Degrees Conferred: Associate

Founded: 1966
Religion: Non-Affiliated
Housing: No
Male/Female: 50:50
Graduate Enrollment: N/A
Financial Aid: Yes
Out of State: $ 4,500

Programs of Study: All areas - majors; Education, Business, Science, Physical Education, Health, Nursing, Criminal Justice, Computer Science, Math, Music, Arts, etc..

Women's Athletic Profile

19600 S. Molalla Ave
Oregon City, OR 97045
Coach: Kathie Woods
Email: woodsk@clackamas.cc.edu

NCAA I
Lady Cougars, Navy, Scarlet
Phone: (503) 657-6958
Fax: (503) 650-6667

Estimated # of Women's Volleyball Scholarships: 8
Conference: NWAACC
Program Profile: Our team has a winning program. We have a large gym with two courts and play a Fall season. We have excellent facilities, a great location (Portland, Oregon) arena and stress a character development program.
History: Our athletics program is approximately 25 years old. The last 4 years, we won Southern Region of NWAACC.
Achievements: Southern Region Champions in 1995,1996,1997and 1998; 4th in 1995, 3rd in 1997, 2nd in 1998; NWAACC Coach of the Year 1996,1997.
Coaching: Kathie Woods - Head Coach. Jake Harwood and Casie Ireland are Assistant Coaches.
Freshman Receiving Financial Aid/Academic: | **Athletic:** 5

Roster In State: 11	**Out of State:** 0	**Out of Country:** 0
Sophomores on Team: 0	**Seniors on Team:** 6	**Graduation %:** 100
Most Recent Record: 45-9-0	**Fall Games:** 54	**Spring Games:** 0

Camp of Clinic Dates: None
Positions Needed: Middle Blocker, Right Side
Schedule: Clackamas, Chemeketa, Spokane, Mount Hood, Columbia Basin, Lower Columbia
Style of Play: Our style is aggressive, enthusiastic, emotional, defense-oriented and team-oriented.

Concordia University
Academic Profile

2811 NE Holman St.
Portland, OR 97211

Phone: 503-280-8501

Type: Private, 4 Yr., Liberal Arts, Coed
Website: http://www.cu-portland.edu

Founded: 1905
Religion: Lutheran

SAT/ACT/GPA: 480v/18/2.5
Student/Faculty Ratio: 20/1
Undergraduate Enrollment: 935
Scholarships/Academic: Yes
Expenses By: Year
Specializes In: Education, Business
Degrees Conferred: BA, BS, MEd
Programs of Study: College of Arts & Science, College of Business, College of Education, College of Health & Social Sciences, College of Theological Studies

Athletic: Yes
In State: $ 21,000

Housing: Yes
Male/Female: 40:60
Graduate Enrollment: 105
Financial Aid: Yes
Out of State: $ 21,000

Women's Athletic Profile

2811 NE Holman
Portland, OR 97211
Coach: Joe Houck
Email: jhouck@cu-portland.edu

NCAA I
Lady Cavaliers, Navy, White
Phone: (503) 280-8689
Fax: (503) 280-8591

Estimated # of Women's Volleyball Scholarships: 4.5
Conference: Cascade Collegiate Conference
Program Profile: The NAIA competitive season runs from August-December. CU is committed to running a nationally competitive VB program and providing an alternative competitive venue for academically dedicated individuals with high Division I ability. Our gymnasium seats 750 and is an intimate setting for interaction between our fans and our teams. We recruit primarily from top area Club and HS programs, but have room for and the ability to train athletically talented individuals with little or no club experience.
History: The CUVB program has competed collegiate since 1977. Prior to 1997 the VB program was run by part time coaches. Following the legacy of 6 coaches in 8 years, CU brought stability to the program with the hiring of their first full time coach. Joseph P. Houck. In only two full seasons the Cavaliers have achieved a National ranking (26th) and are on track to become a national power.
Achievements: In 1998, Anna Gomez was named All-Conference, All-Region and All-American. Alison Gillespi was named All-Conference, Freshman of the Year and All-Region player. Coach Joseph P. Houck was named Conference Coach of the Year. Ann Houck and Heidi Day are the Assistant Coaches.
Coaching: Joseph P. Houck is our Head Coach. His first season was in 1999 with a record of 10-18 overall and conference record is 6-10. In his second season, compiled a record of 18-10 and 12-4 in the conference. He was a former assistant coach at NCAA Division I-Portland State and won 3 Oregon State 4A High School Championships in four years at San Barlow high School in Gresham. He has coached with the Cascade Juniors VBCandmost recently with the Portland Volleyball Club.
Freshman Receiving Financial Aid/Academic:

Athletic: 1
Roster In State: 7
Sophomores on Team: 0
Most Recent Record: 18-10-0

Out of State: 5
Seniors on Team: 2
Fall Games: 26

Out of Country: 0
Graduation %:
Spring Games: 6-8

Camp of Clinic Dates: Last two weeks in August
Positions Needed: Middle Blocker, Right Side, Outdie Hitter
Schedule: Lewis & Clark State, Western Oregon, Northwest Nazarene, Seattle Pacific University

Eastern Oregon State College
Academic Profile

1410 L. Avenue
La Grande, OR 97850

Phone: (541) 962-3393

Type: Public, 4 Yr., Liberal Arts, Coed
Website: http://www.eou.edu
SAT/ACT/GPA: Open/Varies
Student/Faculty Ratio: 17:1
Undergraduate Enrollment: 2,056
Scholarships/Academic: Yes
Expenses By: Year
Specializes In: Education, Business, Liberal Arts
Degrees Conferred: AA, AAS, BA, BS, MTE
Programs of Study: Anthropology, Sociology, Agriculture, Art, Biology, Business, Chemistry, Computer Science, Multimedia Studies, Education, English, Fire Science Service Administration, History, Liberal Arts, Mathematics, Multidisciplinary Studies, Music, Nursing, Philosophy, Political, Economics, Physical Education and Health, Physics, Psychology, Theatre Arts, PreProfessional Programs: PreDentistry, PreLaw, PreMed, PreOptometry, PrePharmacy, PrePhysical Therapy, PreVet

Athletic: No
In State: $ 9,822

Founded: 1929
Religion: Non-Affiliated
Housing: Yes
Male/Female: 829:965
Graduate Enrollment: 58
Financial Aid: Yes
Out of State: $ 9,822

Women's Athletic Profile

1410 L. Avenue
La Grande, OR 97850
Coach: Sharon Campbell
Email: campbes@eou.edu

NCAA I
Lady Mountaineers, Blue, Gold
Phone: (541) 962-3687
Fax: (541) 962-3577

Estimated # of Women's Volleyball Scholarships: N/A
Conference: Cascade Collegiate
Program Profile: Dual members D.III/NAIA, season begins in Aug. to Nov.
History: Began in late 60's. Conference runner-ups 87,88.
Achievements: Coach of the Year 1987.
Coaching: Head Coach Sharon Campbell was a two time MVP at Champman College.

Roster In State: 7	**Out of State:** 7	**Out of Country:** 0
Sophomores on Team: 1	**Seniors on Team:** 6	**Graduation %:**
Most Recent Record: 9-16-0	**Fall Games:** 25	**Spring Games:**

Positions Needed: OH, RS, MB
Schedule: Concordia, Portland, Southern Oregon, Simmon Fraiser
Style of Play: Up tempo and aggressive defense.

George Fox University
Academic Profile

414 N. Meridian St.
Newberg, OR 97132

Phone: 800-765-4309

Type: Private, 4 Yr., Liberal Arts, Coed
Website: http://www.georgefox.edu
SAT/ACT/GPA: Formula
Student/Faculty Ratio: 15:1
Undergraduate Enrollment: 1,350
Scholarships/Academic: Yes   **Athletic:** No
Expenses By: Year   **In State:** $ 22,315

Founded: 1891
Religion: Quaker (Friends)
Housing: Yes
Male/Female: 40:60
Graduate Enrollment: 700
Financial Aid: Yes
Out of State: $ 22,315

Degrees Conferred: BA, BS, MA, MAT, MEd, M.Div, Ed.D. Psy D
Programs of Study: Accounting, Applied Science, Art, Biblical Studies, Biology, Business & Economics, Chemistry, Christian Ministries, Cognitive Science, Communication Arts, Communication Media/Broadcast, Computer & Information Science, Elementary Education, Engineering, Family & Consumer Science, Health & Human Performance, History, Interdisciplinary Studies, International Studies, Mathematics, Music, Philosophy, Psychology, Religion , Social Work, Sociology, Spanish, Writing & Literature

Women's Athletic Profile

414 N. Meridian
Newberg, OR 97132
Coach: Steve Grant
Email: sgrant@georgefox.edu

NCAA I
Lady Bruins, Blue, Gold
Phone: (503) 538-8383
Fax: (503) 538-7234

Estimated # of Women's Volleyball Scholarships: 0
Conference: Northwest Conference of Independent Colleges
Program Profile: We have three practice courts with a seating capacity of 2,500.
History: Our program began in the early 1970's. Starting from 1982 to the present, our overall record is 405-244. Our last losing season was in 1988.
Achievements: 1998 Conference Title; 4 NAIA All-Americans in the last 5 years; 3 Conference Coach of the Year Awards in 16 seasons.
Coaching: Steve Grant - Head Coach. Coby Van Der Meer is Assistant Coach.
Freshman Receiving Financial Aid/Academic:

		Athletic: 0
Roster In State: 7	**Out of State:** 7	**Out of Country:** 0
Sophomores on Team: 4	**Seniors on Team:** 6	**Graduation %:** 100
Most Recent Record: 31-8-0	**Fall Games:** 26	**Spring Games:** 0

Positions Needed: Middle Hitter, Outside Hitter
Schedule: University of California-San Diego, Colorado College, UPS, PLU, Willamette University, Linfield College
Style of Play: Quick offense, excellent defense.

Lewis and Clark College
Academic Profile

0615 SW Palatine Hill Rd.
Portland, OR 97219

Phone: 800-444-4111

Type: Private, 4 Yr., Liberal Arts, Coed
Website: Not Available
SAT/ACT/GPA: Open
Student/Faculty Ratio: 16:1
Undergraduate Enrollment: 1,800
Scholarships/Academic: Yes
Expenses By: Year
Degrees Conferred: BA, BS, MA, MS, JD

Athletic: No
In State: $ Varies

Founded: 1867
Religion: Non-Affiliated
Housing: No
Male/Female: 4:5
Graduate Enrollment: N/A
Financial Aid: Yes
Out of State: $ Varies

Programs of Study: Anthropology, Art, Biology, Business, Chemistry, Communications, Economics, Education, English, History, Interdisciplinary, International, Management, Math, Music, Philosophy, Physics, Political Psychology, Religion, Social Science, Spanish

Women's Athletic Profile

0615 SW Palatine Hill Rd.
Portland, OR 97219
Coach: Kathy Walker
Email:

NCAA I
Lady Pioneers, Black, Orange
Phone: (503) 768-7547
Fax: (503) 768-7058

Estimated # of Women's Volleyball Scholarships: no athletic
Conference: Northwest Conference of Independent Colleges
Program Profile: The Pioneers play their traditional season segment from August to November, playing between 20 to 25 regular season matches annually, including a 16-match conference schedule. The Pamlin Sports Center, which seats 2,300 for volleyball, serves as the team's home court. They play on a wood surface. Lewis & Clark enjoyed much success in the 1980's as a member of the NAIA, appearing in two national tournaments.
History: 1969-modern day (Records are incomplete due to a facility fire that destroyed one-of-a-kind records)
11-Northwest Conference titles, 6-district championships, 3 national tourney berths (second in 1986 NAIA), over 50 all-conference players, numerous national rankings, 4 all-Americans
Coaching: Second year Head Coach Michelle Peterson is a 1995 graduate of the University of Montana, where she was a four-year letterwinner in volleyball for the Grizzlies. In addition to Lewis & Clark, she also has had head coaching stints at Adams State and Big Sky High School in Montana.
Roster In State: 1 **Out of State:** 10 **Seniors on Team:** 2
Schedule: Pacific Lutheran

Linfield College
Academic Profile

900 SE Baker
McMinnville, OR 97128-6894

Phone: 800-640-2287

Type: Private, 4 Yr., Liberal Arts, Coed
Website: http://www.linfield.edu
SAT/ACT/GPA: 900/2.8
Student/Faculty Ratio: 17:1
Undergraduate Enrollment: 1,600
Scholarships/Academic: Yes
Expenses By: Year

Athletic: No
In State: $ 26,000

Founded: 1849
Religion: Baptist
Housing: Yes
Male/Female: 45:55
Graduate Enrollment: N/A
Financial Aid: Yes
Out of State: $ 26,000

Specializes In: Business, Education, Communications, Physical Education
Programs of Study: Accounting, Anthropology, Art, Biology, Botany, Business, Chemistry, Communications, Computer Science, Creative Writing, Earth Science, Ecology, Economics, Education, English, Finance, French, German, Health Education, History, Humanities, Information Science, International Business, Japanese, Journalism, Liberal Arts, Management, Mathematics, Medical Technology, Modern Languages, Music, Natural Science, Nursing, Philosophy, Physical Education, Physics, Political Science, PreDentistry, PreLaw, PreMed, PreVet, Psychology, Public Relations, Radio & Television, Religion Science, Sociology, Spanish, Theatre

Women's Athletic Profile

900 SE Baker
McMinnville, OR 97128
Coach: Shane Kimura
Email: skimura@linfield.edu

NCAA I
Lady Wildcats, Cardinal Purple
Phone: (503) 434-2421
Fax: (503) 434-2453

Estimated # of Women's Volleyball Scholarships: N/A
Conference: Northwest Conference of Independent Colleges

Oregon Institute of Technology
Academic Profile

PO Box 2029
Klamath Falls, OR 97601-8801

Phone: (541) 885-1321

Type: Public, 4 Yr., Coed
Website: http://www.oit.edu
SAT/ACT/GPA: 1000/21/2.5
Student/Faculty Ratio: 20:1
Undergraduate Enrollment: 2,400
Scholarships/Academic: Yes
Expenses By: Year

Athletic: Yes
In State: $ 10,657

Founded: 1947
Religion: Non-Affiliated
Housing: No
Male/Female: 5:4
Graduate Enrollment: 25
Financial Aid: Yes
Out of State: $ 18,181

Specializes In: Business, Engineering, Medical
Degrees Conferred: AA, BS, AAS
Programs of Study: Applied Environmental Sciences, Applied Psychology, Civil Engineering, Computer Engineering Tech, Dental Hygiene, Diagnostic Medical Sonography, Electronics Engineering Tech, Health Sciences, Industrial Management Information Systems, Manufacturing Engineering Tech, Mechanical Engineering Tech, Nuclear Medicine, Nursing, Radiological Science, Software Engineering Tech, Surveying, Ultrasound, Vascular Technology

Women's Athletic Profile

P.O. Box 2029
Klamath Falls, OR 97601
Coach: Leon Wilcox
Email: wilcox@oit.edu

NCAA I
Hustling Owls, Navy, Gold
Phone: (541) 885-1321
Fax: (503) 885-1633

Estimated # of Women's Volleyball Scholarships: 5
Conference: Cascade Collegiate Conference
History: Our program started with the 1998 season after a six year hiatus. We finished the first season with a Conference playoff position.
Coaching: Leon Wilcox, Head Coach, started the program from scratch in the summer of 1997 and had a winning season that year. The assistant coach position is open.
Freshman Receiving Financial Aid/Academic:

Athletic: 3

Roster In State: 3
Sophomores on Team: 2
Most Recent Record:

Out of State: 7
Seniors on Team: 0
Fall Games: 31

Out of Country: 0
Graduation %: Unknown
Spring Games: 8

Camp of Clinic Dates: July 6-9, August 9-11, August 12-14
Positions Needed: 0
Schedule: Western Oregon University, Northwest Nazarene, Western Baptist, San Francisco State, Southern Oregon University, Sonoma State
Style of Play: Fast, multiple option offense. "Players" defense that allows the athlete to use experience and reaction skills. We play all-out, hard-nose defense. I expect my players to bring a very high intensity level to every practice and every match.

Oregon State University
Academic Profile

Room 110 Kerr Administration
Corvallis, OR 97331

Phone: 541-737-4411

Type: Public, 4 Yr., Coed
Website: http://www.osu.orst.edu
SAT/ACT/GPA: 970/23/3.06
Student/Faculty Ratio: 16:1
Undergraduate Enrollment: 13,400
Scholarships/Academic: Yes
Expenses By: Year

Athletic: Yes
In State: $10,115

Founded: 1868
Religion: Non-Affiliated
Housing: Yes
Male/Female: 54:46
Graduate Enrollment: 2,600
Financial Aid: Yes
Out of State: $19,565

Degrees Conferred: BA, BS, BFA, MA, MS, MAIS, MAT, Ph.D.
Programs of Study: Business, Engineering, Forestry, Health and Human Performance, Home Economics and Education, Liberal Arts, Pharmacy, Science, Anthropology, American Studies, History, Geology, Computer Science, Geography, MicroBiology, Mathematics, Music, Natural Resources, Physics, Philosophy, Political Science, Poultry Science, Psychology, Sociology, Social Sciences, Pharmacy

Gill Coliseum 105
Corvallis, OR 97331
Coach: Nancy Somera
Email: someran@ccmail.orst.edu

NCAA I
Lady Beavers, Orange, Black
Phone: (541) 737-7491
Fax: (541) 737-4002

Estimated # of Women's Volleyball Scholarships: N/A
Conference: Pacific 10 Conference

Pacific University
Academic Profile

2043 College Way
Forest Grove, OR 97116

Phone: 800-677-6712

Type: Private, 4 Yr., Liberal Arts, Coed
Website: http://www.pacifcu.edu
SAT/ACT/GPA: 1000/20
Student/Faculty Ratio: 14:1
Undergraduate Enrollment: 1,100
Scholarships/Academic: Yes
Expenses By: Year
Specializes In: Liberal Arts
Degrees Conferred: BA, BS, MA, MS

Athletic: No
In State: $ 21,000

Founded: 1842
Religion: Non-Affiliated
Housing: Yes
Male/Female: 60:40
Graduate Enrollment: 1,000
Financial Aid: Yes
Out of State: $ 21,000

Programs of Study: Accounting, Banking & Finance, Biology, Business Administration, Chemistry, Computer Science, Creative Writing, Dramatic Arts, Economics, Elementary Education, Exercise Science, French, German, History, Humanities, Japanese, Literature, Management, Marketing, Mathematics, Music, Philosophy, Physical Education, Physics, Political Science, Psychology, Science, Social Science, Sociology, Spanish

Women's Athletic Profile

2043 College Way
Forest Grove, OR 97116
Coach: Bradley Jones
Email: jonesm@pacificu.edu

NCAA I
Lady Boxers, Red, Black, White
Phone: (503) 359-3152
Fax: (503) 359-2209

Estimated # of Women's Volleyball Scholarships: N/A
Conference: Northwest Conference of Independent Colleges

Portland State University
Academic Profile

PO Box 751
Portland, OR 97207

Phone: 800-547-8887

Type: Public, 4 Yr., Liberal Arts, Coed
Website: http://www.vinkings.pdx.edu
SAT/ACT/GPA: 700/18+
Student/Faculty Ratio: 20:1
Undergraduate Enrollment: 12,000
Scholarships/Academic: Yes
Expenses By: Year
Degrees Conferred: BA, BS, MA, MS, MBA, MFA, MED, Ph.D., EdH

Athletic: Yes
In State: $ 8,000

Founded: 1924
Religion: Non-Affiliated
Housing: No
Male/Female: 50:50
Graduate Enrollment: 2,000
Financial Aid: Yes
Out of State: $ 14,000

Programs of Study: Arts, Business and Management, Business/Office and Marketing/Distribution, Communications, Education, Engineering, General Studies, Letters/Literature, PreMed, Psychology, Social Science, Social Work, Teacher Ed.

Women's Athletic Profile

P.O. Box 751
Portland, OR 97207-0751
Coach: Chris Stanley
Email: cstanpsu@upa.pdx.edu

NCAA I
Lady Vikings, Green, White
Phone: (503) 725-5115
Fax: (503) 725-5610

Estimated # of Women's Volleyball Scholarships: N/A
Conference: Big Sky Conference

Southern Oregon University
Academic Profile

1250 Siskiyous Blvd.
Ashland, OR 97520

Phone: 541-552-7672

Type: Private 4 Yr., Coed
Website: http://www.sou.edu
SAT/ACT/GPA:
Student/Faculty Ratio:
Undergraduate Enrollment: 5500
Scholarships/Academic: Yes   **Athletic:** Yes
Expenses By: Year   **In State:** $3,198
Programs of Study: Contact school for programs of study.

Founded: 1883
Religion: Non-Affiliated
Housing: Yes
Male/Female: 43/57
Graduate Enrollment: 300
Financial Aid: Yes
Out of State: $9,402

Women's Athletic Profile

1250 Siskiyou
Ashland, OR 97520
Coach: Paul Elliott
Email: peiiott@sou.edu

NCAA I
Lady Raiders, Black, Red
Phone: (541) 552-6728
Fax: (541) 552-6543

Estimated # of Women's Volleyball Scholarships: 3
Conference: Cascade Conference
Program Profile: We are one of the top NAIA programs. Our home court is called McNgal Pavilion with a seating capacity of 1,500.
History: Southern Oregon University volleyball program has an overall record of 629-444 since 1969. They had 11 consecutive play-offs appearances and finished 1998 that ranked 26th in the NAIA.
Achievements: Southern Oregon University has won 6 Conference Titles and boasts 3 All-Americans, 1 National Tournament Appearance and has 44 All-Conference players since 1978.
Coaching: Paul Elliot, Head Coach, compiled a record of 192-98 in nine years of coaching at SOU. He played volleyball and basketball at Chico State, where he graduated in 1980. He was named two-time Conference Coach of the Year. Kelly Miller is our Assistant Coach.

Freshman Receiving Financial Aid/Academic: **Athletic:** 5
Roster In State: 11   **Out of State:** 1   **Out of Country:** 0
Sophomores on Team: 0   **Seniors on Team:** 4   **Graduation %:** 100
Most Recent Record: 20-7-0 **Fall Games:** 31   **Spring Games:** Tournaments
Camp of Clinic Dates: August 11-16
Positions Needed: Hitters, Middles
Schedule: Western Oregon, Northwest Nazarene, Rockhurst College, Humboldt State, Chico State, San Francisco State
Style of Play: Wide open offense relying heavily on right side and middles. Among NAIA kills and assist leaders past three years.

University of Oregon
Academic Profile

2727 Leo Harris Pkwy
Eugene, OR 97401

Phone: (541) 346-5410

Type: Public, 4 Yr., Liberal Arts, Coed
Website: http://www.uoregon.edu
SAT/ACT/GPA: 1,000+/3.0
Student/Faculty Ratio: 19:1
Undergraduate Enrollment: 13,000
Scholarships/Academic: Yes   **Athletic:** Yes
Expenses By: Term   **In State:** $ 3,721
Specializes In: Liberal Arts, Social Sciences
Degrees Conferred: BA, BS, BFA, MA, MS, MBA, MFA, Ph.D., JD, EdD
Programs of Study: Visual & Performing Arts, Parks/Recreation, Protective Services, Public Affairs, Business & Management, Communications, Letter/Literature, Music, Psychology, Social Sciences, Teacher Education

Founded: 1876
Religion: Non-Affiliated
Housing: Yes
Male/Female: 1:1
Graduate Enrollment: 4,200
Financial Aid: Yes
Out of State: $ 6,538

Women's Athletic Profile

2727 Leo Harris Parkway
Eugene, OR 97401
Coach: Cathy Nelson
Email: cnelson@oregon.uoregon.edu

NCAA I
Lady Ducks, Green, Yellow
Phone: (541) 346-5410
Fax: (541) 346-2244

Estimated # of Women's Volleyball Scholarships: 4
Conference: Pacific 10 Conference
Program Profile: We play at McArthur Court with a seating capacity of 9,078. We play in the toughest volleyball Conference in the nation. Our team is young and our squad is moving its way into the upper echelon of the Pacific 10 Conference.
History: Our program started in 1968 and posts an all-time record of 527-463 in 31 seasons. We have advanced to the NCAA Tournament four times.
Achievements: Have had numerous All-Pacific 10 Selections; Sue Harbour, 3 time Academic All-American; Michele Krebsbach, PAC-10 Freshman of the Year; Case Crisler, 3 time Academic All-American.
Coaching: Cathy Nelson, Head Coach, has been with the program from 1995 to the present. She compiled a record of 96-102. Prentice Perkins and Didier Hemelsoct started as Assistant Coaches in 1999.
Freshman Receiving Financial Aid/Academic: **Athletic:** 4
Roster In State: 3   **Out of State:** 11   **Out of Country:** 1
Sophomores on Team: 0   **Seniors on Team:** 4   **Graduation %:** 100
Most Recent Record: 8-23-0   **Fall Games:** 30   **Spring Games:** Varies
Camp of Clinic Dates: General Skills/Setter: July 12-15; General Skills: July 17-20; High Potential:July 22-25
Positions Needed: Outside Hitter, Middle Blocker
Schedule: Stanford, University of Southern California, UCLA, Arizona, Minnesota, Washington State
Style of Play: We run a quick, diverse offense, play aggressive defense and compete in a fast-paced, energetic manner.

University of Portland
Academic Profile

5000 N. Willamette Boulevard
Portland, OR 97203

Phone: 888-627-5601

Type: Private, 4 Yr., Liberal Arts, Engineering, Coed
Website: http://www.up.edu
SAT/ACT/GPA: Individually evaluated 3.5
Student/Faculty Ratio: 15:1
Undergraduate Enrollment: 2,155
Scholarships/Academic: Yes   **Athletic:** Yes
Expenses By: Year   **In State:** $ 22,000
Founded: 1901
Religion: Roman Catholic
Housing: Yes
Male/Female: 45:55
Graduate Enrollment: 247
Financial Aid: Yes
Out of State: $ 22,000
Specializes In: Arts & Sciences, Business, Nursing, Education, Engineering
Degrees Conferred: BA, BS, BBA, Masters
Programs of Study: Business Management, Communications, Education, Engineering, Health Science, Life Science, Social Science

Women's Athletic Profile

5000 N. Williamette Blvd.
Portland, OR 97203
Coach: Patty Jayne
Email: sparksd@up.edu

NCAA I
Lady Pilots, Purple, White
Phone: (503) 283-7911
Fax: (503) 283-7399

Estimated # of Women's Volleyball Scholarships: 3
Conference: West Coast Conference
Program Profile: The Pilots play in one of the country's best volleyball conferences. The Chiles Center is one of the finest volleyball facilities on the west coast.
History: The university added women's volleyball in 1979 and in 1986 the program went Division I, affiliating with the West Coast Conference.
Achievements: (2) 1997 All-Conference Players; 2 First Team Academic All-Conference; 7th highest grade point average in the country.
Coaching: Patty Jayne, Head Coach, is in her fifth season as a head coach. Doug Sparks is assistant coach.
Freshman Receiving Financial Aid/Academic: **Athletic:** 5
Roster In State: 5   **Out of State:** 8   **Out of Country:** 0
Sophomores on Team: 0   **Seniors on Team:** 1   **Graduation %:** 100
Most Recent Record: **Fall Games:** 28   **Spring Games:** 4

Camp of Clinic Dates: July, August
Positions Needed: 3
Schedule: San Diego, Pepperdine, Loyola Marymount, Boise State, Memphis, Oregon State
Style of Play: Portland has always been known for its relentless defense, fast transitions and elite explosive middle blockers.

Western Baptist College
Academic Profile

500 Deer Park SE
Salem, OR 97301

Phone: 503-375-7005

Type: Private, 4 Yr., Liberal Arts, Coed
Website: http://www.wbc.edu
SAT/ACT/GPA: 800
Student/Faculty Ratio: 17:1
Undergraduate Enrollment: 5,720
Scholarships/Academic: Yes
Expenses By: Year
Degrees Conferred: AA, BA, BS

Athletic: Yes
In State: $ 17,570

Founded: 1939
Religion: Independent Baptist
Housing: Yes
Male/Female: 1:2
Graduate Enrollment: N/A
Financial Aid: Yes
Out of State: $ 17,000

Programs of Study: Accounting, Bible Studies, Community Services, Education, Elementary Education, English, Family Studies, Finance, Humanities, Human Performances, Interdisciplinary Studies, Liberal Arts, Management & Communications, Mathematics, Ministries, Music, PreLaw, PreNursing, Psychology, Recreation & Leisure, Religious Education, Religion, Social Science, Theology

Women's Athletic Profile

500 Deer Park Dr., SE
Salem, OR 97301
Coach: Tracy Smith
Email: tsmith@wbc.edu

NCAA I
Lady Warriors, Blue, Gold
Phone: (503) 589-8121
Fax: (503) 315-2947

Estimated # of Women's Volleyball Scholarships: Varies
Conference: Cascade Collegiate Conf.
Program Profile: C.E. Jeffers Sports Center with a capacity of 1,500. Approx. 25 matches per year, Conference members include NAIA institutions in Oregon, Washington, and Idaho.
History: Member of the NAIA since early 1980's though records have been kept just since 1989. Joined Cascade Conf. In 1994 also a member of the NCCAA.
Achievements: 1997 Cascade Conf. Tournament Champions, 1997 NCCAA Division I National Champions, NAIA top 25 ranking 1997-1999.
Freshman Receiving Financial Aid/Academic:
Roster In State: 7
Sophomores on Team:
Most Recent Record: 18-11

Out of State: 3
Seniors on Team: 1

Athletic: 3
Out of Country: 0
Graduation %: 80

Positions Needed: Hitters and defensive specialists
Schedule: Concordia, Western Oregon, Southern Oregon, Albertson College, Oregon Tech, Simon Fraser, Eastern Oregon Univ.
Style of Play: Christian student/athletes with the desire to play hard to win and represent Jesus Christ in the process.

Western Oregon State College
Academic Profile

345 Monmouth Avenue
Monmouth, OR 97361
Type: Public, 4 Yr., Liberal Arts, Coed
Website: http://www.wou.edu
SAT/ACT/GPA: 1000/21
Student/Faculty Ratio: 15:1
Undergraduate Enrollment: 4,252
Scholarships/Academic: Yes
Expenses By: Year
Degrees Conferred: AA, BA, BS, MA, MS, MED

Phone: 877-877-1593

Athletic: Yes
In State: $ 8,418

Founded: 1856
Religion: Non-Affiliated
Housing: Yes
Male/Female: 39:61
Graduate Enrollment: 251
Financial Aid: Yes
Out of State: $ 14,958

Programs of Study: Biology, Business, Chemistry, Computer, Corrections, Economics, Education, English, Fine Arts, Fire Services, Geography, History, Humanities, Interdisciplinary Studies, International Business, Languages, Law, Mathematics, Music, Natural Science, Physical Science, Physical Education, Political Science, Psychology, Public Affairs, Science, Social Science

Women's Athletic Profile

345 Monmouth Avenue
Monmouth, OR 97361
Coach: Judy Lovre
Email: lovrej@wou.edu

NCAA I
Lady Wolves, Red, Grey
Phone: (503) 838-8252
Fax: (503) 838-8370

Estimated # of Women's Volleyball Scholarships: N/A
Conference: Pacific West Conference
Program Profile: We have a three court gym that seats 3,400.
History: Our record since 1984 is 580-160.
Achievements: 1988 NAIA Coach of the Year; District 2 Coach of the Year in 1987, 1988, 1989, 1992 & 1993. Cascade Conference Coach of the Year in 1992.
Coaching: Judy Lovre, Head Coach, compiled a record of 422-127 in 12 years. Her teams were National Runner-Up 3 times. Prior to Western Oregon University, she achieved Four State Championships at Corvallis High School. Steve Smith is Assistant Coach.

Freshman Receiving Financial Aid/Academic:

		Athletic: 1
Roster In State: 14	**Out of State:** 0	**Out of Country:** 0
Sophomores on Team: 0	**Seniors on Team:** 1	**Graduation %:** 100
Most Recent Record: 28-11-0	**Fall Games:** 35-45	**Spring Games:** 3-4

Camp of Clinic Dates: First two weeks of August
Positions Needed: Outside Hitter
Style of Play: We play very technical with a fast pace, exciting defense.

Willamette University
Academic Profile

900 State St.
Salem, OR 97301

Phone: 877-542-2787

Type: Private, 4 Yr., Liberal Arts, Coed
Website: http://www.willamette.edu
SAT/ACT/GPA: 1250/27/3.8
Student/Faculty Ratio: 13:1
Undergraduate Enrollment: 1,700
Scholarships/Academic: Yes
Expenses By: Year

Athletic: No
In State: $ 21,700

Founded: 1842
Religion: Methodist
Housing: Yes
Male/Female: 40:60
Graduate Enrollment: 700
Financial Aid: Yes
Out of State: $ 21,700

Programs of Study: American Studies, Art, Biology, Business Administration, Economics, Chemistry, Comparative Literature, Computer Science, English, Environmental Science, French, German, History, Humanities, International Studies, Japanese Studies, Math, Music, Philosophy, Physics, Psychology, Religion Studies, Media Studies, Spanish

Women's Athletic Profile

900 State Street
Salem, OR 97301
Coach: Marlene Piper
Email: mpiper@willamette.edu

NCAA I
Lady Bearcats, Red, Old Gold
Phone: (503) 370-6230
Fax: (503) 370-6379

Estimated # of Women's Volleyball Scholarships: N/A
Conference: Northwest Conference of Independent Colleges
Program Profile: We play at the Lestle J. Sparks Center. Sparks Center includes volleyball courts, a new weight room and class-rooms. The building got a million dollar addition in 1995.
History: Three professional sports teams have held their pre season camps at Willamette: New York Giants, the Pittsburgh Steelers and the NBA's Portland Trailblazers.
Achievements: Northwest Conference Coach of the Year 3 times; NWC Conference Titles in 1992,1993,1994,1995 and 1996; several players named to the Olympics, World University Games, U.S. Olympic Festival and All-America teams.
Coaching: Marlene Piper, has been Head Coach for 5 years. Her 29 year career record is 781-291(.729).
Most Recent Record: 14-8-0
Style of Play: Our team is constantly improving.

PENNSYLVANIA

Harrisburg ★

SCHOOL	CITY	AFFILIATION	PAGE
Albright College	Reading	NCAA III	621
Allegheny College	Meadville	NCAA III	621
Allentown College- St. Francis De Sales	Center Valley	NCAA III	630
Alvernia College	Reading	NCAA III	622
Arcadia University	Glenside	NCAA III	622
Bryn Mawr College	Bryn Mawr	NCAA III	623
Bucknell University	Lewisburg	NCAA I	623
Cabrini College	Radnor	NCAA III	624
California University	California	NCAA II	625
Carlow College	Pittsburgh	NAIA	625
Carnegie Mellon University	Pittsburgh	NCAA III	626
Cedar Crest College	Allentown	NCAA III	626
Chatham College	Pittsburgh	NCAA III	627
Chestnut Hill College	Philadelphia	NCAA III	627
Cheyney University	Cheyney	NCAA II	628
Clarion University of Pennsylvania	Clarion	NCAA II	628
College Misericordia	Dallas	NCAA III	629
Delaware Valley College	Doylestown	NCAA III	629
Dickinson College	Carlisle	NCAA III	630
Drexel University	Philadelphia	NCAA I	631
Duquesne University	Pittsburgh	NCAA I	632
East Stroudsburg University	East Stroudsburg	NCAA II	632
Eastern College	St. Davids	NCAA III	633
Edinboro Univ of Pennsylvania	Edinboro	NCAA II	634
Elizabethtown College	Elizabethtown	NCAA III	634
Franklin & Marshall College	Lancaster	NCAA III	635
Gannon University	Erie	NCAA II	636
Geneva College	Beaver Falls	NCCAA I/NAIA	636

SCHOOL	CITY	AFFILIATION	PAGE
Gettysburg College	Gettysburg	NCAA III	637
Grove City College	Grove City	NCAA III	638
Gwynedd-Mercy College	Gwynedd-Mercy	NCAA III	638
Haverford College	Haverford	NCAA III	639
Immaculata College	Immaculata	NCAA III	639
Indiana University of Pennsylvania	Indiana	NCAA II	640
Juniata College	Huntingdon	NCAA III	640
King's College - Pennsylvania	Wilkes-Barre	NCAA III	641
Kutztown University	Kutztown	NCAA II	642
La Roche College	Pittsburgh	NCAA III	642
La Salle University	Philadelphia	NCAA I	642
Lafayette College	Easton	NCAA I	643
Lebanon Valley College	Annville	NCAA III	644
Lehigh University	Bethlehem	NCAA I	644
Lincoln University - Pennsylvania	Lincoln University	NCAA III	645
Lock Haven University	Lock Haven	NCAA II	645
Lycoming College	Williamsport	NCAA III	646
Marywood University	Scranton	NCAA III	647
Mercyhurst College	Erie	NCAA II	647
Messiah College	Gratham	NCAA III	648
Millersville University	Millersville	NCAA II	649
Moravian College	Bethlehem	NCAA III	649
Mount Aloysius College	Cresson	NAIA	649
Muhlenberg College	Allentown	NCAA III	650
Neumann College	Aston	NCAA III	651
Pennsylvania State University	University Park	NCAA I	651
Pennsylvania State University	Erie	NCAA III	652
Phila College of Textiles & Science	Philadelphia	NCAA II	653
Philadelphia College of the Bible	Langhorne	NCAA III	653
Point Park College	Pittsburgh	NAIA	654
Robert Morris College	Moon Township	NCAA I	654
Rosemont College	Rosemont	NCAA III	655
Saint Francis College	Loretto	NCAA I	656
Saint Vincent College	Latrobe	NAIA	656
Seton Hill College	Greensburg	NAIA	657
Shippensburg University	Shippensburg	NCAA II	658
Slippery Rock University	Slippery Rock	NCAA II	658
Susquehanna University	Selinsgrove	NCAA III	659
Swarthmore College	Swarthmore	NCAA III	659
Temple University	Philadelphia	NCAA I	660
Thiel College	Greenville	NCAA III	660
University of Pennsylvania	Philadelphia	NCAA I	661
Univ of Pittsburgh	Pittsburgh	NCAA I	661
Univ of Pittsburgh - Bradford	Bradford	NCAA III	662
Univ of Pittsburgh - Greensburg	Greensburg	NCAA III	663
Univ of Pittsburgh - Johnstown	Johnstown	NCAA II	663

SCHOOL	CITY	AFFILIATION	PAGE
University of Scranton	Scranton	NCAA III	664
Ursinus College	Collegeville	NCAA III	664
Villanova University	Villanova	NCAA I	665
Washington & Jefferson College	Washington	NCAA III	666
Waynesburg College	Waynesburg	NCAA III	666
West Chester University	West Chester	NCAA II	667
Westminster College	New Wilmington	NCAA II/III	667
Widener University	Chester	NCAA III	668
Wilkes University	Wilkes-Barre	NCAA III	668
Wilson College	Chambersburg	NCAA III	669
York College of Pennsylvania	York	NCAA III	670

Albright College
Academic Profile

PO Box 15234
Reading, PA 19612

Phone: 800-252-1856

Type: Private, 4 Yr., Liberal Arts, Coed
Website: http://www.albright.edu
SAT/ACT/GPA: Open
Student/Faculty Ratio: 12:1
Undergraduate Enrollment: 1,100
Scholarships/Academic: Yes   **Athletic:** No
Expenses By: Year   **In State:** $ 24,502
Specializes In: Education, Dentistry, Law, Medicine, Finance
Degrees Conferred: BA, BS

Founded: 1856
Religion: Methodist
Housing: Yes
Male/Female: 48:52
Graduate Enrollment: N/A
Financial Aid: Yes
Out of State: $ 20,000

Programs of Study: Accounting, Biology, Business, Chemistry, Computer, Economics, Education, English, Environmental, Family Studies, Fine Arts, French, German, History, Management, Marketing, Math, Medical, Nutrition, Philosophy, Physics, Political Science

Women's Athletic Profile

P.O. Box 15234
Reading, PA 19612
Coach: Mike Frankhouser
Email:

NCAA I
Lady Lions, White, Red
Phone: (610) 921-7535
Fax: (610) 921-7566

Estimated # of Women's Volleyball Scholarships: N/A
Conference: Middle Atlantic States Conference
Program Profile: We have a cavernous indoor recreational gym. Bollman Center is being renovated. It has 2,500 seats, a remodeled weight room and a state-of-the-art sound system. Our Lifesports Center has four volleyball courts.
History: We have one of the finest facilities in all of Division III.
Most Recent Record: 16-0-0   **Fall Games:** 22   **Spring Games:** 9
Schedule: Concordia, Olivet, Baldwin-Wallace, Adrian, Hope, Ohio Wesleyan, DePauw, St.Mary's, Alma

Allegheny College
Academic Profile

520 North Main Street
Meadville, PA 16335

Phone: 800-521-5293

Type: Private, 4 Yr., Coed
Website: http://www.alleg.edu
SAT/ACT/GPA: 500
Student/Faculty Ratio: 14.5:1
Undergraduate Enrollment: 1,900
Scholarships/Academic: Yes   **Athletic:** No
Expenses By: Year   **In State:** $ 24,860
Specializes In: Preprofessional Programs
Degrees Conferred: BS, BA

Founded: 1815
Religion: Methodist
Housing: Yes
Male/Female: 47:53
Graduate Enrollment: N/A
Financial Aid: Yes
Out of State: $ 24,860

Programs of Study: Art, Biology, Chemistry, Computer Science, Communication Arts, Economics, English, Environmental Studies, French, Geology, German, History, International Studies, Mathematics, Music, Neuroscience, Philosophy, Physics, Political Science, Psychology, Religious Studies, Russian, Spanish, Theatre, Women's Studies

Women's Athletic Profile

P.O. Box 34
Meadville, PA 16335
Coach: Bridget Sheehan
Email: bsheehan@admin.alleg.edu

NCAA I
Lady Gators, Blue, Gold
Phone: (814) 332-2822
Fax: (814) 333-8180

Estimated # of Women's Volleyball Scholarships: 0
Conference: North Coast Athletic Conference
Program Profile: Our facility was built in 1997. The Athletics Facility includes 6 volleyball courts, a fitness center, a pool and training facilities for injuries. Our playing season is from mid August to November.

History: We are a very competitive Division III program. We participated in 4 NCAA Post-Season Tournaments. Our program has the most wins in a season of any other athletic team at Allegheny College.
Achievements: Coach of the Year (Conference twice); NCAA Regional Coach of the Year once; 15 Conference Titles; 3 All-Americans; Most wins of any coach at Allegheny; Ranked 13th in winning % school coaches; Ranked 15th in wins in the AVCA.
Coaching: Bridget Sheehan, became Head Coach here in 1986. Her overall record is 387-178. Laurel Heilman is Assistant Coach.

Roster In State: 5	**Out of State:** 13	**Out of Country:** 0
Sophomores on Team: 4	**Seniors on Team:** 3	**Graduation %:** 100
Most Recent Record: 16-23-0	**Fall Games:** 32	**Spring Games:** 4

Camp of Clinic Dates: July 26-30
Style of Play: Quick offense-concentration of great defensive play.

Alvernia College
Academic Profile

400 Saint Bernadine St.
Reading, PA 19067

Phone: 610-796-8336

Type: Private, 4 Yr., Coed
Website: http://www.alvernia.edu
SAT/ACT/GPA: None
Student/Faculty Ratio: 12:1
Undergraduate Enrollment: 800
Scholarships/Academic: Yes   **Athletic:** No
Expenses By: Year   **In State:** $ 16,210

Founded: 1959
Religion: Catholic-Franciscan
Housing: Yes
Male/Female: 35:36
Graduate Enrollment: 800
Financial Aid: Yes
Out of State: $ 16,210

Specializes In: Criminal Justice, Physical Therapy, Education, Nursing
Degrees Conferred: BA, BSN, BS, MBA
Programs of Study: Accounting, Addictions Studies, Banking/Finance, Biology, Business, Chemistry, Communications, Computer, Criminal Justice, Education, English, Health, History, Math, Medical, Nursing, Optometry, Philosophy, Political Science, PreProfessional Programs, Psychology, Religion, Science, Secondary Education, Social Science, Spanish, Theology

Women's Athletic Profile

400 Saint Bernardine St.
Reading, PA 19607
Coach: Mike Marks
Email: hertzad@alvernia.edu

NCAA I
Lady Crusaders, Maroon/Gold
Phone: 610-796-8276
Fax: 610-796-8349

Estimated # of Women's Volleyball Scholarships: No
Conference: East Coast Athletic Conference, Pennsylvania Athletic Conference
Program Profile: We are trying to build a solid program that will consistently be successful. Each year I am able to recruit 1 or 2 quality players. This school's team will be solid and consistently competitive.
History: Prior to 1995, no records were kept. The team has improved from year to year. Our out-of-conference opponents have been upgraded as our personnel improved.
Achievements: Coach of the Year 1996, 1998; Assistant Coach Sara Martin was team MVP in 1997 & was voted to 1st Team All-Conference.
Coaching: When I started as an assistant coach in 1995, the team went 6-14. The next year, I was named Head Coach and we made it to the playoffs for the 1st time. We have been to the playoffs all the 3 years that I have been Head Coach.

Roster In State: 8	**Out of State:** 2	**Out of Country:** 0
Sophomores on Team: 0	**Seniors on Team:** 2	**Graduation %:** 100

Most Recent Record: 16-14-0
Positions Needed: Setter
Schedule: Muuhlenberg College, Susquehanna University, Widener University, Eastern College, Allentown College
Style of Play: Aggressive defense and transition into a basic offense which runs some quick and tandems.

Arcadia University
Academic Profile

450 South Easton Road
Glenside, PA 19038-3295

Phone: 215-572-2900

Type: Private, 4 Yr., Liberal Arts, Coed
Website: http://www.beaver.ed
SAT/ACT/GPA: Open
Student/Faculty Ratio: 13:1
Undergraduate Enrollment: 1,200
Scholarships/Academic: Yes   **Athletic:** No

Founded: 1853
Religion: Presbyterian
Housing: Yes
Male/Female: 30:70
Graduate Enrollment: 1,090
Financial Aid: Yes

Expenses By: Year   **In State:** $ 20,990   **Out of State:** $ 20,990
Degrees Conferred: BA, BS, BFA
Programs of Study: Accounting, Art, Art Education, Fine Arts, Biology, Business Administration, Management, Marketing, Chemistry, Communications, Computer Science, Education, Mathematics, Engineering, Optometry, Philosophy, Physical Therapy, Political Science

Women's Athletic Profile

450 S. Easton Rd.
Glenside, PA 19038
Coach: Leslie Hayes
Email: hayesl@arcadia.edu

NCAA I
Scarlet Knights, Scarlet, Grey
Phone: (215) 572-2998
Fax: (215) 572-2159

Estimated # of Women's Volleyball Scholarships: 0
Conference: Pennsylvania Athletic Conference
Achievements: Leslie Hayes- 1999 Pennsylvania Athletic Conference Coach of the Year.
Roster In State: 8   **Out of State:** 4   **Out of Country:** 0
Sophomores on Team: **Seniors on Team:** 2   **Graduation %:** 100
Most Recent Record: 5-10
Positions Needed: As needed
Schedule: Allentown College, Ursinus College, Bethany College, Eastern College

Bryn Mawr College
Academic Profile

101 North Merion Ave.
Bryn Mawr, PA 19010
Type: Private, 4 Yr., Liberal Arts, Women Only
Website: http://www.brynmawr.edu
SAT/ACT/GPA: 1150+
Student/Faculty Ratio: 9:1
Undergraduate Enrollment: 1,100
Scholarships/Academic: No   **Athletic:** No
Expenses By: Year   **In State:** $ 26,000
Degrees Conferred: AB, MA, Ph.D.

Phone: 800-262-1885

Founded: 1885
Religion: Non-Affiliated
Housing: Yes
Male/Female: Women Only
Graduate Enrollment: N/A
Financial Aid: Yes
Out of State: $ 26,000

Programs of Study: African Studies, Anthropology, Archeology, Art History, Asian Studies, Astronomy, BioChemistry, Biology, Chemistry, Classical Languages, Computer Science, Economics, English, Fine Arts, French, Geology, German, Greek, History, International Economics, Italian, Latin, Literature, Math, Music, NeuroScience, Peace Studies, Philosophy, Physics, Political Science, Psychology, Romance Languages, Russian, Social Science, Spanish, Urban Studies

Women's Athletic Profile

Schwartz Gymnasium
Bryn Mawr, PA 19010
Coach: Diane Hagan
Email: dhagan@brynmawr.edu

NCAA I
Lady Mawters, Gold, White
Phone: (610) 526-7307
Fax: (610) 526-7347

Estimated # of Women's Volleyball Scholarships: N/A
Conference: Centennial Conference
Coaching: Karen Lewis, Head Coach, graduated from Bryn Mawr in 1988 and returned to college to coach here. She coaches badminton and volleyball. She has built a fundamentally solid volleyball team.
Roster In State: 0   **Out of State:** 12   **Out of Country:** 1
Sophomores on Team: 2   **Seniors on Team:** 1   **Graduation %:** Unknown
Schedule: Eastern College, Franklin & Marshall, Wilmington, Rowan, Swarthmore, Lebanon Valley, Muhlenberg, Washington, John Hopkins, Ursinus, Haverford, Goucher, Dickinson

Bucknell University
Academic Profile

Moore Avenue
Lewisburg, PA 17837

Type: Private, 4 Yr., Liberal Arts, Engineering, Coed
Website: http://www.bucknell.edu

Phone: 570-577-1101

Founded: 1846
Religion: Non-Affiliated

SAT/ACT/GPA: Required
Student/Faculty Ratio: 12.5:1
Undergraduate Enrollment: 3,200
Scholarships/Academic: No   Athletic: No
Expenses By: Year   In State: $ 29,800
Specializes In: Engineering, Sciences
Degrees Conferred: BA, BS

Housing: No
Male/Female: 52:48
Graduate Enrollment: 200
Financial Aid: Yes
Out of State: $ Varies

Programs of Study: Accounting, Anthropology, Art, BioChemistry, Biology, Business and Management, Computer, Environmental, Engineering, Religion, Social Sciences, Statistics, Theatre, Women's Studies

Women's Athletic Profile

Davis Gymnasium
Lewisburg, PA 17837
Coach: Cindy Opalski
Email: copalski@bucknell.edu
Estimated # of Women's Volleyball Scholarships: N/A
Conference: The Patriot League

NCAA I
Lady Bison, Blue, Orange
Phone: (507) 577-3048
Fax: (507) 577-1660

Program Profile: Play double round robin conference play. Teams in the Patriot League are Army, Navy, Colgate, Lehigh, Lafayette, and Holy Cross. Davis Gymnasium is a hardwood surface which can seat 2300 comfortably. The Patriot League is a non-scholarship conference that focuses on athletics success with academic excellence.
History: The first year of the volleyball program was 1978, since then the programs record is 240-360. The program has seen three different coaches throughout its history. In 1998, the team made its first appearance in the NCAA Volleyball Tournament.
Achievements: 1993 GTE Academic All-American-Sara Mesaros
Patriot League Conference Titles in 1995, 1997 and 1998.
Coaching: Cindy Opalski, Head Coach, started here in 1990. Her best season was in 1995 with 26 victories and the League Championship. She has coached for 13 years. She worked with the U.S.Volleyball Junior Olympic Program from 1982-86. She served as Director for Nike Volleyball Camps held at Buckwell. Nikki Renninger is Assistant Coach.
Freshman Receiving Financial Aid/Academic: Athletic: 8
Roster In State: 0   Out of State: 15   Out of Country: 0
Sophomores on Team: 4   Seniors on Team: 2   Graduation %: 100
Most Recent Record: 11-11-0   Fall Games: 27   Spring Games: 0
Positions Needed: Middle and outside hitters
Schedule: Penn State, Manhattan, Colgate, Providence, Villanova, Marist, Canisius
Style of Play: Bucknell not only recruits quality athletes but quality people, matched with an aggressive style of play. This constitutes Bucknell Volleyball.

Cabrini College
Academic Profile

610 King of Prussia Rd.
Radnor, PA 19087

Phone: 800-848-1003

Type: Private, 4 Yr., Liberal Arts, Coed
Website: http://www.cabrini.edu
SAT/ACT/GPA: Open
Student/Faculty Ratio: 18:1
Undergraduate Enrollment: 850
Scholarships/Academic: Yes   Athletic: No
Expenses By: Year   In State: $ 16,950
Specializes In: Communications, Business
Degrees Conferred: BA, BS, M.Ed.

Founded: 1957
Religion: Non-Affiliated
Housing: Yes
Male/Female: 1:3
Graduate Enrollment: N/A
Financial Aid: Yes
Out of State: $ 16,950

Programs of Study: Contact school for program of study.

Women's Athletic Profile

610 King of Prussia Rd.
Radnor, PA 19087
Coach: Jim Harrigan
Email:

NCAA I
Lady Cavaliers, Blue, White
Phone: (610) 902-8386
Fax: (610) 902-8385

Estimated # of Women's Volleyball Scholarships: N/A
Conference: Pennsylvania Athletic Conference

California University - Pennsylvania
Academic Profile

250 University Avenue
California, PA 15419

Phone: 724-938-4404

Type: Public, 4 Yr., Liberal Arts, Coed
Website: http://www.cup.edu
SAT/ACT/GPA: 910/20/2.5
Student/Faculty Ratio: 20:1
Undergraduate Enrollment: 5,000
Scholarships/Academic: Yes
Expenses By: Year
Specializes In: Education, Science & Technology, Liberal Arts
Degrees Conferred: BA, BS, MA, MEd
Programs of Study: Liberal Arts, Education, Science and Technology, Human Services

Athletic: Yes
In State: $ 4,450

Founded: 1847
Religion: Non-Affiliated
Housing: Yes
Male/Female: 50:50
Graduate Enrollment: 1,000
Financial Aid: Yes
Out of State: $ 7,750

Women's Athletic Profile

900 University Avenue
California, PA 15419
Coach: Chang Limin Jin
Email: jin@cup.edu

NCAA I
Lady Vulcans, Red, Black
Phone: (724) 938-5876
Fax: (724) 938-5849

Estimated # of Women's Volleyball Scholarships: N/A
Conference: Pennsylvania State Athletic Conference

Carlow College
Academic Profile

3333 Fifth Ave.
Pittsburgh, PA 15213

Phone: 800-333-2275

Type: Private, 4 Yr., Liberal Arts
Website: http://www.carlow.edu
SAT/ACT/GPA: Students evaluated on individual basis
Student/Faculty Ratio: 15:1
Undergraduate Enrollment: 2,000
Scholarships/Academic: Yes
Expenses By: Year
Specializes In: Education, Science
Degrees Conferred: BA, BS, Bachelor of Social Work
Programs of Study: Bachelor of Science in Nursing, Master of Education in Art Education, Master of Education in Early Childhood, Master of Education in Early Childhood Supervision, Master of Education in Educational Leadership, Master of Science in Management Technology, Master of Science in Nursing, Master of Science in PreProfessional Leadership

Athletic: Yes
In State: $ 17,902

Founded: 1929
Religion: Catholic
Housing: No
Male/Female: 8:92 Women Only
Graduate Enrollment: 400
Financial Aid: Yes
Out of State: $ 17,902

Women's Athletic Profile

3333 5th Avenue
Pittsburgh, PA 15213
Coach: Julie Gaul
Email: jgaul@carlow.edu

NCAA I
Lady Celtics, Purple, Gold
Phone: (412) 578-6345
Fax: (412) 578-8704

Estimated # of Women's Volleyball Scholarships: N/A
Conference: Keystone Empire Conference
Achievements: 1991 NAIA District 18A Coach of the Year.
Coaching: George Sliman, has been Head Coach for 11 years. He is very active in USA Volleyball. He conducted setting clinics with former Olympian, Debbie Green. Julie Gaul is entering her sixth season as Assistant Coach. While playing for the University of Pittsburgh she was named team MVP and Big East MVP. They won the Big East Conference Championship at Pittsburgh that year. Gail Wildenmann-Smith started her first season as Assistant Coach. She won the Carlow Spirit Award and the Defensive Player Award.

Schedule: Bethany, Roberts Wesleyan, Chatham, Hilbert, Mt.Aloysius, Washington & Jefferson, Daemen, Seton Hill, Houghton, LaRoche
Style of Play: Potential to dominate a match hitting, serving and defensively; strong in all areas of the game

Carnegie Mellon University
Academic Profile

5000 Forbes Ave.
Pittsburgh, PA 15213-3890

Phone: 412-268-2082

Type: Private, 4 Yr., Liberal Arts, Engineering, Coed
Website: http://www.cmu.edu
SAT/ACT/GPA: 1300/30
Student/Faculty Ratio: 9:1
Undergraduate Enrollment: 4,800
Scholarships/Academic: Yes
Expenses By: Year
Founded: 1900
Religion: Non-Affiliated
Housing: Yes
Male/Female: 2:1
Graduate Enrollment: 2,700
Athletic: No   **Financial Aid:** Yes
In State: $ 30,095   **Out of State:** $ 30,095
Specializes In: Engineering, Math, Science
Degrees Conferred: BA, BS, MA, MS, Ph.D.
Programs of Study: Chemical Engineering, Civil Engineering, Electrical Engineering, Computer Engineering, Material Engineering, Mechanical Engineering, Fine Arts, Liberal Arts, Humanities, Science, Computer Science, Business Administration, Math

Women's Athletic Profile

5000 Forbes Ave.
Pittsburgh, PA 15213
Coach: Julie Webb
Email: jwebb@andrew.cmu.edu

NCAA I
Tartans, Cardinal, White, Grey
Phone: (412) 268-2193
Fax: (412)-268-3099

Estimated # of Women's Volleyball Scholarships: N/A
Conference: University Athletic Association
Program Profile: Our facilities include: an equipment room, a gym, fitness classes, a fitness room and a whirlpool . There are three volleyball courts and a seating capacity of 1,800. Season from September 1 October 29, Season includes Round Robins, Tournaments and Conference Play.
History: We are a young program. The University Athletic Association is one of the most competitive conferences in Division III.
Achievements: 1999 and 2000 ECAC South Region Champions
Coaching: Julie Webb, became Head Coach here in 1996. Previously, she coached at Morrisville-Eaton Central High School, and directed them to the Center State Conference Championship.
Freshman Receiving Financial Aid/Academic: **Athletic:** n/a
Roster In State: 1   **Out of State:** 10   **Out of Country:** 0
Sophomores on Team: **Seniors on Team:** 1   **Graduation %:** 100
Most Recent Record: 24-11-0

Cedar Crest College
Academic Profile

100 College Dr.
Allentown, PA 18104-6196

Phone: 800-360-1222

Type: Private, 4 Yr.,
Website: http://www.cedarcrest.edu
SAT/ACT/GPA: 910+
Student/Faculty Ratio: 9:1
Undergraduate Enrollment: 1,005
Scholarships/Academic: Yes
Expenses By: Year
Founded: 1867
Religion: Church of Christ
Housing: No
Male/Female: 2:98 Women Only
Graduate Enrollment: N/A
Athletic: No   **Financial Aid:** Yes
In State: $ 18,975   **Out of State:** $ 18,975
Degrees Conferred: BA, BS
Programs of Study: Contact school for programs of study.

Women's Athletic Profile

100 College Dr.
Allentown, PA 18104-6196
Coach: Dave Stever
Email: dmsteven@cedarcrest.edu

NCAA I
Classics, Yellow, White
Phone: (610) 606-740-3532
Fax: (610) 740-3794

Estimated # of Women's Volleyball Scholarships: N/A
Conference: Pennsylvania Athletic
Program Profile: It is an up and coming program. Will be competing for a conference Championship in 2001. Season last from first week in September to mid-November. Preseason camp is in August. Home games are played in Lees Hall on a wood surface. Seating capacity is 200.
History: Since 1993 program has had two winning seasons. In 2000 team had its best season winning 14 games and advancing to the conference semifinals.
Achievements: In 2000: Dave Stever was PAC Coach of the Year. Christine Feichtel was first team All-Conference. Adrienne Milot was first team Verizon Academic All-District II College Division Volleyball. In 1998 Coach Stewart Arevelo was PAC Tri-Coach of the Year and three players earned All-Conference recognition.
Coaching: Head Coach Dave Stever will be in his third season at Cedar Crest in 2001. He has grown the program in his first two years. He was a long-time successful Coach at Emmaus (PA) High School. Assistant Coach Jon Getz will also be back for a third season. He has college and high school experience.

Roster In State: 14   **Out of State:** 2   **Out of Country:** 0
Sophomores on Team: **Seniors on Team:** 0   **Graduation %:** 90
Most Recent Record: 14-13-0
Positions Needed: Outside Hitter, Middle Hitter
Schedule: Eastern, Alvernia, Misericordia, Cabrini, Neumann, Muhlenberg
Style of Play: Run quick attacks and attempt to use different options. On defense we hit the floor on every ball.

Chatham College
Academic Profile

Woodland Road
Pittsburgh, PA 15232

Phone: (800) 837-1290

Type: Private, 4 Yr., Liberal Arts
Website: http://www.chatham.edu
SAT/ACT/GPA: 1100avg/3.0-avg
Student/Faculty Ratio: 12:1
Undergraduate Enrollment: 522
Scholarships/Academic: Yes   **Athletic:** No
Expenses By: Year   **In State:** $ 23,508

Founded: 1869
Religion: Non-Affiliated
Housing: Yes
Male/Female: Women Only
Graduate Enrollment: 331
Financial Aid: Yes
Out of State: $ 23,508

Specializes In: Liberal Arts - Psychology, English, Communications
Degrees Conferred: BA, BS
Programs of Study: Accounting, Administration of Justice, Arts Management, Behavioral NeuroScience, BioChemistry, Biology, Chemistry, Communications, Cyber Communications, Economics, English, English and Dramatic, Literature, Entrepreneurial Management, Environmental Science, French, Global Policy Studies, Graphic Design, History, International Business, Marketing, Math, Music, Philosophy and Religion, Political Science, Psychology, Spanish, Theatre, Women's Studies

Women's Athletic Profile

Woodland Rd.
Pittsburgh, PA 15232
Coach: Gregory E. Lockley
Email:

NCAA I
Lady Cougars, Purple, White
Phone: (412) 365-1625
Fax: (412) 365-1724

Estimated # of Women's Volleyball Scholarships: N/A
Conference: Independent

Chestnut Hill College
Academic Profile

9601 Germantown Avenue
Philadelphia, PA 19118-2693
Type: Private, 4 Yr., Liberal Arts, Coed·
Website: http://www.chc/edu
SAT/ACT/GPA: Open
Student/Faculty Ratio: 10:1
Undergraduate Enrollment: 914
Scholarships/Academic: Yes   **Athletic:** No
Expenses By: Year   **In State:** $23,357

Phone: (215) 248-7000

Founded: 1924
Religion: Non-Affiliated
Housing: No
Male/Female: Not Available
Graduate Enrollment: 622
Financial Aid: Yes
Out of State: $23,357

Degrees Conferred: AA, BA, BS, MA, MS, M Ed., Psy.D.

Programs of Study: Art, Art History, Art Therapy, Accounting, Communications & Technology, Computer Science, Computer Technology, Criminal Justice, Economics, Education, English, Environmental Science, Finance, French, German, Gerontology, History, Management, Marketing, Mathematics, Music, Music Education, Political Science, Psychology, Religious Studies, Sociology

Women's Athletic Profile

Germantown Avenue
Philadelphia, PA 19118
Coach: Joe Gibbons
Email:

NCAA I
Lady Griffin, Brown, Gold
Phone: (215) 248-7060
Fax: (215) 248-7155

Estimated # of Women's Volleyball Scholarships: N/A
Conference: Independent
Program Profile: We want to support student-athletes in their efforts to reach high levels of athletic performance, which may include opportunities for participation in national championships, by providing all teams with adequate facilities, competent coaching and appropriate competitive opportunities.
History: We are members of the NCAA Division III.
Coaching: Joe Gibbons - Head Coach.

Cheyney University
Academic Profile

Cheyney and Creek Roads
Cheyney, PA 19319

Phone: 800-243-9369

Type: Public, 4 Yr., Coed
Website: http://www.chyney.edu
SAT/ACT/GPA: 950+
Student/Faculty Ratio: 13:1
Undergraduate Enrollment: 1,215
Scholarships/Academic: Yes
Expenses By: Year
Degrees Conferred: BA, BS, MS, M.Ed.
Programs of Study: Contact school for programs of study.

Athletic: Yes
In State: $ 7,663

Founded: 1837
Religion: Non-Affiliated
Housing: No
Male/Female: 48:52
Graduate Enrollment: 392
Financial Aid: Yes
Out of State: $ 9,927

Women's Athletic Profile

P.O. Box 350
Cheyney, PA 19319
Coach: Milt Colston
Email:

NCAA I
Lady Wolves, Royal Blue, White
Phone: (610) 399-2381
Fax: (610) 399-2352

Estimated # of Women's Volleyball Scholarships: N/A
Conference: Pennsylvania State Athletic Conference

Clarion University
Academic Profile

840 Wood Street
Clarion, PA 16214

Phone: 814-226-2306

Type: Public, 4 Yr., Coed
Website: http://www.clarion.edu
SAT/ACT/GPA: 850/21/3.0
Student/Faculty Ratio: 18:1
Undergraduate Enrollment: 5,335
Scholarships/Academic: Yes
Expenses By: Year
Specializes In: Business, Education, Health Fields, Pre-Professional
Degrees Conferred: BA, MA

Athletic: Yes
In State: $ 8,019

Founded: 1867
Religion: Non-Affiliated
Housing: Yes
Male/Female: 1.1.5
Graduate Enrollment: 430
Financial Aid: Yes
Out of State: $ 10,383

Programs of Study: Accounting, Anthropology, Art, Biology, Chemistry, Communications, Computer Science, Earth Science, Economics, English, Environmental Sciences, Finance, Geo-Sciences, French, General Studies, Geography, Geology, History, Humanities, Information Systems, Industrial Relations, Management, Mathematics, Medical Technology, Music, Molecular Biology, Natural Sciences, Philosophy, Physics, Political Science, Psychology, Sociology, Spanish, Speech Communication, Theatre

Women's Athletic Profile

Wood Street
Clarion, PA 16214
Coach: Jodi Pezek Burns
Email: spennewill@clarion.edu

NCAA I
Lady Golden Eagles, Blue, Gold
Phone: 800-672-7171
Fax: (814) 226-2063

Estimated # of Women's Volleyball Scholarships: N/A
Conference: Pennsylvania State Athletic Conference
Achievements: Coach Burns was All-Region player from 1987-90. 1988 PSAC Championship Title; 1997 GTE Academic All-American -Tracy Barnett
Coaching: Jodi Pezek Burns, is in her 4th season as Head Coach. She led the Lady Eagles to a 20-19 record in 1997 and a 2nd place finish in the PSAC-West at 7-3. She is a graduate of Clarion University. Tina Gustely is in her second season at Calrion University as Assistant Coach.

Roster In State: 15   **Out of State:** 3   **Out of Country:** 0
Sophomores on Team: 3   **Seniors on Team:** 4   **Graduation %:** Unknown
Schedule: Allegheny, Edinboro, Indiana, California, Junaita, Slippery Rock, Lock Haven, Shepard, Seton Hill, Kutztown

College Misericordia
Academic Profile

301 Lake Street
Dallas, PA 18612

Phone: (570) 674-6492

Type: Private, 4 Yr., Liberal Arts, Coed
Website: http://www.miseri.edu
SAT/ACT/GPA: Varies with the major
Student/Faculty Ratio: 14:1
Undergraduate Enrollment: 1,200
Scholarships/Academic: Yes   **Athletic:** No
Expenses By: Year   **In State:** $ 22,190
Degrees Conferred: BS, BA, MS

Founded: 1924
Religion: Catholic
Housing: Yes
Male/Female: 35:65
Graduate Enrollment: N/A
Financial Aid: Yes
Out of State: $ 22,190

Programs of Study: Accounting, Biology, Business Administration, Computer Science, Early Childhood, Elementary Education, English, History, Humanities, Management, Marketing, Mathematics, Medical Laboratory Technology, Natural Science, Nursing, Physical Therapy, PreDentistry, PreLaw, PreMed, Social Science

Women's Athletic Profile

Lake Street
Dallas, PA 18612
Coach: Jason Jones
Email:

NCAA I
Lady Cougars, Royal Blue, Gold
Phone: (570) 674-6374
Fax: (717) 6745785

Estimated # of Women's Volleyball Scholarships: N/A
Conference: ECAC

Delaware Valley College
Academic Profile

700 E. Butler Avenue
Doylestown, PA 18901

Phone: (215) 230-2963

Type: Private, 4 Yr., Coed
Website: http://www.devalcol.edu
SAT/ACT/GPA: 900/2.5
Student/Faculty Ratio: 15:1
Undergraduate Enrollment: 1,400
Scholarships/Academic: Yes   **Athletic:** No
Expenses By: Year   **In State:** $ 21,250
Specializes In: Agricultural, Biology, Chemistry, Environmental Science
Degrees Conferred: BA, BS

Founded: 1896
Religion: Jewish
Housing: Yes
Male/Female: 40:60
Graduate Enrollment: N/A
Financial Aid: Yes
Out of State: $ 21,250

Programs of Study: Marketing, Management, Criminal Justice, Business Administration, Accounting, Management Information Systems, Computer Information Systems, Biology, Micro BioTech, Environmental Biology, Animal Biology, Plant Biology, Chemistry, Mathematics, English, Secondary Education, PreVet Medicine, PreMed, PreDental Medicine, PreOptometry, AgriBusiness, Agronomy, Animal Science, Dairy Science, Food Science, Horticulture, Ornamental Horticulture, Environmental Design

Women's Athletic Profile

700 East Butler Avenue
Doylestown, PA 18901
Coach: Sandra Stoczko
Email:

NCAA I
Lady Aggies, Green, Gold
Phone: (215) 489-2240
Fax: (215) 230-2963

Estimated # of Women's Volleyball Scholarships: N/A
Conference: Middle Atlantic States Conference

De Sales University
Academic Profile

2755 Station Avenue
Center Valley, PA 18034

Phone: (610) 282-1100x 1204

Type: Private, 4 Yr., Liberal Arts, Coed
Website: http://www.desales.edu
SAT/ACT/GPA: N/A
Student/Faculty Ratio: 17/1
Undergraduate Enrollment: 1,200
Scholarships/Academic: Yes   **Athletic:** No
Expenses By: Year   **In State:** $ 18,200

Founded: 1964
Religion: Catholic
Housing: Yes
Male/Female: 1/1.5
Graduate Enrollment: 1,000
Financial Aid: Yes
Out of State: $ 18,200

Specializes In: Nursing School and Physician Assistant Program
Degrees Conferred: BA, BS
Programs of Study: Accounting, Biology, Communications, Chemistry, Computer Science, Creative Writing, Criminal Justice, Dance, Elementary Education, English, Environmental Studies, Finance, History, Human Resources Management, Legal Studies, Liberal Studies, Management, Management of Information Technology, Marketing, Marriage and Family Studies, Math, Nursing, Philosophy, Physician's Assistant, Political Science, Physical Education, Social Work, Spanish, Sport Management, Theatre, Theology, TV/Film, PreProfessional Programs

Women's Athletic Profile

2755 Station Avenue
Center Valley, PA 18034
Coach: Helen Deegan
Email:

NCAA I
Lady Centaurs, Red, Blue
Phone: (610) 282-2279x 1211
Fax: (610) 282-2279

Estimated # of Women's Volleyball Scholarships: N/A
Conference: Middle Atlantic States Conference

Dickinson College
Academic Profile

Kline Center, High Street
Carlisle, PA 17013

Phone: 800-644-1773

Type: Private, 4 Yr., Liberal Arts, Coed
Website: http://www.dickinson.edu
SAT/ACT/GPA: Not Required
Student/Faculty Ratio: 10:1
Undergraduate Enrollment: 1,950
Scholarships/Academic: Yes   **Athletic:** No
Expenses By: Year   **In State:** $ 26,260

Founded: 1773
Religion: United Methodist
Housing: Yes
Male/Female: Not Available
Graduate Enrollment: N/A
Financial Aid: Yes
Out of State: $ 26,260

Specializes In: Study Abroad Program
Degrees Conferred: BA, BS
Programs of Study: 31 majors including American Studies, Anthropology, Asian Studies, Biology, Chemistry, Computer Science, Dramatic Arts, Economics, English, Fine Arts, Foreign Languages, French, Geology, German, Greek, History, Humanities, International Studies, Latin, Mathematics, Music, Natural Sciences, Philosophy, Physics, Political Science, Psychology, Religion, Russian, Russian & Soviet Area Studies, Social Sciences, Spanish

Women's Athletic Profile

Kline Ctr., High Street
Carlisle, PA 17013
Coach: Brenda T. Clements
Email: clementsb@dickinson.edu

NCAA I
Lady Red Devils, Red, White
Phone: (717) 245-1331
Fax: (717) 245-1441

Estimated # of Women's Volleyball Scholarships: N/A
Conference: Centennial Conference
Program Profile: We play all home matches at Kline Life Sports Center. Begins September 1 and ends November or December (Post-season).
History: We are entering 23rd season as a volleyball program. Our most successful season were in the mid-80's, while in the 90's struggled in win-loss permanently.
Achievements: In 1988, was our best season in history with a record of 29-8 and became tournament winners. In 1989, our record was 23-15; ECAC Tournament.
Coaching: Brenda T. Clements, Head Coach, is entering her first season with the program. She has an overall record of 100-64 in four years. She led team to two UAC Conference Runner-Up, Mid-South Region Runner-Up with a record of 37-8; best record in school history.

Roster In State: 8	**Out of State:** 17	**Out of Country:** 1
Sophomores on Team: 3	**Seniors on Team:** 1	**Graduation %:**
Most Recent Record: 7-20-0	**Fall Games:** 22	**Spring Games:** 0

Positions Needed: Setter, Ace Attacker, Middle Blocker
Schedule: Gettysburg, Franklin Marshall, Muhlenberg, Messiah, Western Maryland
Style of Play: Fast tempo offense, combination offense (5-1 offense). Perimeter defense, aggressive style of play both offensive and defensive.

Drexel University
Academic Profile

32nd and Chestnut
Phile, PA 19104

Phone: 800-237-3935

Type: Private, 4 Yr., Coed
Website: http://www.drexel.edu
SAT/ACT/GPA: Varies
Student/Faculty Ratio: 13:1
Undergraduate Enrollment: 5,300
Scholarships/Academic: Yes **Athletic:** Yes
Expenses By: Year **In State:** $ 25,000

Founded: 1891
Religion: Non-Affiliated
Housing: None
Male/Female: 65:35
Graduate Enrollment: 2,900
Financial Aid: Yes
Out of State: $ 25,000

Specializes In: Technical and Co-op Education
Degrees Conferred: Bachelors, Masters, Doctoral
Programs of Study: Accounting, Architecture, Atmospheric Sciences, Biology, Business & Management, Chemistry, Communications, Computer Information Systems, Computer Science, Construction Management, Economics, Education, Engineering, Environmental Science, Graphic Art, Humanities, Interior Design, International Business, Literature, Management Information System, Marketing, Mathematics, Music, Natural Science, Nutrition, Operation Research, Philosophy, Photography, Physical Science, Physics, Political Science, PreVet, Psychology, Science, Science Education, Social Science, Sociology, Technical Writing

Women's Athletic Profile

3141 Chestnut Street
Philadelphia, PA 19104
Coach: Melanie K. Dahl
Email: Melanie.Kopka@drexel.edu

NCAA I
Lady Dragons, Navy Blue, Gold
Phone: (215) 895-1867
Fax: (215) 895-2038

Estimated # of Women's Volleyball Scholarships: N/A
Conference: American East Conference
Program Profile: The Walter Spiro Varsity weight room is where the Lady Dragons do their strength and conditioning training. The Drexel athletic program also benefits from the daily injury prevention and treatment provided by the University's athletic training.
History: The program began in 1982.
Achievements: 8 All-ECC, 11 All-NAC/AEC, and 1994 PSAC Coach of the Year.
Coaching: Head Coach Melanie K. Dahl former Drexel Volleyball setter. Assistant Coaches Eric Dahl and Agnieszka Lapinski.
Freshman Receiving Financial Aid/Academic: **Athletic:** 3

Roster In State: 2	**Out of State:** 11	**Out of Country:** 2

Sophomores on Team:
Most Recent Record: 9-24
Camp of Clinic Dates: July 9-13, 2001
Positions Needed: Outside Hitter, Middle Blocker
Schedule: Hofstra, New Hampshire, Northeastern
Style of Play: Team chemistry plays a big part in the Dragon's success.

Seniors on Team: 2   **Graduation %:**

Duquesne University
Academic Profile

600 Forbes Avenue
Pittsburgh, PA 15282

Phone: 412-396-5000

Type: Private, 4 Yr., Coed
Website: http://www.duq.edu
SAT/ACT/GPA: Open
Student/Faculty Ratio: 15:1
Undergraduate Enrollment: 8,000
Scholarships/Academic: Yes   **Athletic:** Yes
Expenses By: Year   **In State:** $ 21,000
Degrees Conferred: BA, BS, MA, MS, MPT, MSLP, Ph.D.
Programs of Study: Business, Education, Nursing, Health Sciences, Pharmacy, PreMed, Liberal Arts

Founded: 1878
Religion: Catholic
Housing: Yes
Male/Female: 40:60
Graduate Enrollment: 1,500
Financial Aid: Yes
Out of State: $ 21,000

Women's Athletic Profile

600 Forbes Avenue
Pittsburgh, PA 15282
Coach: Steven Operman
Email:

NCAA I
Lady Dukes, Red, Blue
Phone: (412) 396-5247
Fax: (412) 396-6210

Estimated # of Women's Volleyball Scholarships: 12
Conference: Atlantic 10 Conference
Program Profile: We play at A.J. Palumbo Center which has seating for 6,500.
Coaching: Steven Operman, Head Coach, has ten years of coaching experience. He has been head coach for 8 years. Kate Michalski has been Assistant Coach for three seasons.
Freshman Receiving Financial Aid/Academic: **Athletic:** 6
Roster In State: **Out of State:** 0   **Out of Country:** 0
Sophomores on Team: 1   **Seniors on Team:** 0   **Graduation %:**
Most Recent Record: 8-20-0
Camp of Clinic Dates: July 5-8; July 11-15
Positions Needed: Middle Hitters, Right Side
Schedule: Temple, Dayton, Xavier, Wisconsin-Milwaukee, Pittsburgh
Style of Play: A fast multi-tempo offense. Ball control and defense are major points that are stressed.

East Stroudsburg University
Academic Profile

Koehler Fieldhouse
East Stroudsburg, PA 18301

Phone: 570-422-3542

Type: Public, 4 Yr., Liberal Arts, Coed
Website: http://www.esu.edu
SAT/ACT/GPA: 1000
Student/Faculty Ratio: 21:1
Undergraduate Enrollment: 4,800
Scholarships/Academic: Yes   **Athletic:** No
Expenses By: Year   **In State:** $ 3,900
Specializes In: Computer Science, Business, Education, Sport Medicine
Programs of Study: Business, Education, Letters/Literature, Life Science, Social Science

Founded: 1893
Religion: Non-Affiliated
Housing: Yes
Male/Female: 3:5
Graduate Enrollment: 600
Financial Aid: Yes
Out of State: $ 5,600

Men's Athletic Profile

Smith & Normal
East Stroudburg, PA 18301
Coach: Sean Byron
Email:

NCAA II
Warriors/Red, Black
Phone: (717) 422-3672
Fax: (717) 422-3306

Estimated # of Men's Volleyball Scholarships: N/A
Conference: Eastern Intercollegiate Volleyball Association

Women's Athletic Profile

Smith & Normal
East Stroudsburg, PA 18301
Coach: Sean Byron
Email: sbyron@esu.edu

NCAA I
Lady Warriors, Red, Black
Phone: (717) 422-3673
Fax: (717) 422-3586

Estimated # of Women's Volleyball Scholarships: N/A
Conference: Pennsylvania State Athletic Conference
Program Profile: We play at Koehler Fieldhouse, which was newly renovated and has an indoor track allows. It has four courts set-up. We will host the Pocono Fall Classic in late October.
History: Our program began in 1974.
Achievements: We have 21 All-PSAC players, 7 All-Region and 1 All-American.
Coaching: Sean Byron - Head Coach. Tim O'Brien is our Assistant Coach.

Freshman Receiving Financial Aid/Academic:		Athletic: 3
Roster In State: 9	Out of State: 7	Out of Country: 0
Sophomores on Team: 3	Seniors on Team: 1	Graduation %: 90
Most Recent Record: 7-18-0	Fall Games: 25	Spring Games: 0

Positions Needed: Outside Hitter, Middle Blocker
Schedule: Northern Michigan, California State-Dominguez, West Texas, New Heaven, Edinboro, Saginaw State
Style of Play: Fast, good ball control, very explosive play.

Eastern College
Academic Profile

1300 Eagle Road
St. Davids, PA 19087

Phone: (610) 341-1736

Type: Private, 4 Yr., Liberal Arts, Coed
Website: http://www.eastern.edu
SAT/ACT/GPA: Varies
Student/Faculty Ratio: 14:1
Undergraduate Enrollment: 1,000
Scholarships/Academic: Yes
Expenses By: Year
Specializes In: Sciences, Education, Business
Degrees Conferred: BA, BS

Founded: 1932
Religion: Baptist, Christian
Housing: Yes
Male/Female: 1:2
Graduate Enrollment: 1,000
Athletic: No **Financial Aid:** Yes
In State: $ 19,600 **Out of State:** $ 19,600

Programs of Study: Art History, Astronomy, Biblical Studies, Biology, Business Administration, Chemistry, Communications, Elementary Education, Health & Physical Education, History, Mathematics, Medical Technology, Music, Nursing, Philosophy, Political Science, Psychology, Social Work, Sociology

Women's Athletic Profile

1300 Eagle Road
St. Davids, PA 19087
Coach: Mark Birtwistle
Email: mbirtwis@eastern.edu

NCAA I
Lady Eagles, Maroon, White
Phone: (610) 341-1736
Fax: (610) 341-1317

Estimated # of Women's Volleyball Scholarships: N/A
Conference: Pennsylvania Athletic Conference
Program Profile: The pre-season begins in the middle of August and goes through the first part of November. Division III post-season goes through December.
History: The current head coach will begin his 10th season at Eastern.
Achievements: 1990 NCCAA National Tournament Appearance - 1997 & 1998; PAC Conference Champions; 1997 & 1998 Conference Coach of the Year; 11 All-Conference Players; 3 players ranked in National statistics.
Coaching: Mark Birtwistle, Head Coach, became head coach in 1990. He has an overall record of 159-98. He played in college and in several USA Volleyball U.S. Opens (Dallas, Springfield, Massachusetts). Andy Douglas is Assistant Coach. He played college volleyball and coached boys and girls high school teams. His boys' team qualified for the State Championship twice.

Freshman Receiving Financial Aid/Academic: **Athletic:** 0

Roster In State: 4 **Out of State:** 2 **Out of Country:** 0
Sophomores on Team: 0 **Seniors on Team:** 1 **Graduation %:** 97
Most Recent Record: 22-10-0 **Fall Games:** 32 **Spring Games:** 0
Positions Needed: Setter, Middle Hitter, (2) Outside Hitters
Schedule: Franklin & Marshall, Gettysburg, Lycoming, Moravian, Salisbury State, Johns Hopkins
Style of Play: We have a strong foundation in fundamentals. Defense, both individual and team, is stressed as the most important. Then, offense becomes creative.

Edinboro University
Academic Profile

Bigger's House
Edinboro, PA 16444

Phone: (814) 732-2761

Type: Public, 4 Yr., Liberal Arts, Coed **Founded:** 1857
Website: http://www.edinboro.edu **Religion:** Non-Affiliated
SAT/ACT/GPA: 700/17 **Housing:** No
Student/Faculty Ratio: 18:1 **Male/Female:** 43:57
Undergraduate Enrollment: N/A **Graduate Enrollment:** 7,100
Scholarships/Academic: Yes **Athletic:** Yes **Financial Aid:** Yes
Expenses By: Year **In State:** $ 7,867 **Out of State:** $ 13,223
Degrees Conferred: AA, AS, BA, BS, BFA, Ma, MS, MFA, MED
Programs of Study: Accounting, Anthropology, Art, Biology, Business, Chemistry, Communications, Computer, Criminal, Earth Science, Economics, Education, English, Geography, Geology, History, Humanities, Mathematics, Medical, Natural Science, PreProfessional Programs, Psychology, Russian, Special Education, Speech, Social Science

Women's Athletic Profile

Scotland
Edinboro, PA 16444
Coach: Lynn Theehs
Email: ltheehs@edinboro.edu

NCAA I
Lady Scots, Red, White
Phone: (814) 732-2761
Fax: (814) 732-2420

Estimated # of Women's Volleyball Scholarships: N/A
Conference: Pennsylvania State Athletic Conference
Program Profile: We are affiliated with NCAA Division II. Our arena is McComb Fieldhouse and has a capacity of 4,000. We are members of the Pennsylvania State Athletic Western Division Conference. Our athletic director is Bruce Baumgartner.
History: All-time record is 575-267. We have 10 years of post-season play. We were 1994, 1996 and 1998 NCAA II Atlantic Region Champions. We were Elite Eight Qualifiers. Our all-time playoff record is 4-3. Our most recent playoff appearance was at the 1998 NCAA Division II Atlantic Regional Championships Elite Eight Qualifier.
Achievements: Coach Theehs was Coach of the Year at the PSAC West in 1994,1995 and 1997; 1996 Coach of the Year in the Atlantic Region; Conference Titles in 1980, 1981,1982, 1989, 1990, 1994, 1997 and 1998; Regional Titles in 1994, 1996 and 1998; Elite Eight appearances in 1994,1996 and 1998.
Coaching: Lynn Theehs, Head Coach, started here in 1994. Her record at Edinboro as of 1997 was 95-49.
Freshman Receiving Financial Aid/Academic: **Athletic:** 1
Roster In State: 14 **Out of State:** 4 **Out of Country:** 0
Sophomores on Team: 0 **Seniors on Team:** 6 **Graduation %:** 100
Most Recent Record: 28-8-0 **Fall Games:** 40 **Spring Games:** 0
Camp of Clinic Dates: Summer Camp July 26-30
Positions Needed: Recruiting is done
Schedule: North Dakota State University, University of Tampa, New Haven, Northern Kentucky University, Charleston, Juniata

Elizabethtown College
Academic Profile

One Alpha Drive
Elizabethtown, PA 17022-2298

Phone: (717) 361-1533

Type: Private, 4 Yr., Liberal Arts, Coed **Founded:** 1899
Website: http://www.etown.edu **Religion:** Church of Brethren
SAT/ACT/GPA: 1000 + **Housing:** Yes
Student/Faculty Ratio: 18:1 **Male/Female:** 1:3
Undergraduate Enrollment: 1,500 **Graduate Enrollment:** N/A

Scholarships/Academic: Yes   **Athletic:** No   **Financial Aid:** Yes
Expenses By: Year   **In State:** $ 22,000   **Out of State:** $ 22,000
Specializes In: Occupational Therapy, Education, Communications
Degrees Conferred: BA, BS
Programs of Study: Accounting, Anthropology, BioChemistry, Biology, Business Administration, Chemical Physics, Chemistry, Chemistry Management, Communications, Computer Engineering, Computer Science, Early Childhood Education, Economics, Education, Engineering, English, Environmental Science, History, Industrial Engineering, International Business, Mathematics, Medical Technology, Modern Languages, Music, Music Education, Music Therapy, Philosophy, Physics, Political Philosophy, Political Science, Social Studies, Social Work, Sociology

Women's Athletic Profile

One Alpha Drive
Elizabethtown, PA 17022
Coach: William Helm
Email:
Estimated # of Women's Volleyball Scholarships: N/A
Conference: Middle Atlantic States Conference

NCAA I
Lady Blue Jays, Blue, Grey
Phone: (717) 361-1137
Fax: (717) 361-1488

Franklin and Marshall College
Academic Profile

P.O. Box 3003
Lancaster, PA 17604-4440

Phone: (717) 291-4102

Type: Private, 4 Yr., Liberal Arts, Coed
Website: http://www.fandm.edu
SAT/ACT/GPA: Open
Student/Faculty Ratio: 11:1
Undergraduate Enrollment: 1,804
Scholarships/Academic: Yes   **Athletic:** No
Expenses By: Year   **In State:** $ 28,564
Specializes In: Preprofessional Programs, Business
Degrees Conferred: BA, BS

Founded: 1787
Religion: Non-Affiliated
Housing: Yes
Male/Female: 51:49
Graduate Enrollment: N/A
Financial Aid: Yes
Out of State: $ 28,564

Programs of Study: Anthropology, Art, Art History, Asian Studies, Astronomy, Biology, Business Administration, Chemistry, Classics, Computer Science, Dance, Economics, English, Environmental Science, Film, French, GeoScience, German, Government, Hebrew, History, Mathematics, Music, Philosophy, Psychology, Religion, Russian, Sociology, Spanish, Theatre

Women's Athletic Profile

College Avenue
Lancaster, PA 17604
Coach: Steve Coulson
Email: S_COULSON@ADMIN.FANAM.EDU

NCAA I
Lady Diplomats, Blue, White
Phone: (717) 291-4102
Fax: (717) 399-4440

Estimated # of Women's Volleyball Scholarships: 0
Conference: Centennial Conference
Program Profile: We have a varsity program with a 12-16 roster. Pre-season begins August 20. Regular season runs from September 4th through October 31st. Mayser Gym seats 3,000. We have seven volleyball courts and a fieldhouse.
History: We were the first women's sport at Franklin and Marshall College. Our first match was in 1973. Our overall record is 385-245 (.566). We were a member of MAC until 1993 when we joined the Centennial Conference.
Achievements: 1993 and 1994 Conference Champions; Runner up in 1995, 1996, 1997 and 1998; Conference Players of the Year in 1993, 1994 and 1996; three Academic All-Americans; Vos in 1993, Power in 1996 and Cardigan in 1997; NCAA Tournaments Appearances in 1994, 1996, 1997 and 1998.
Coaching: Steve Coulson Head Coach. His record is 188-139.
Freshman Receiving Financial Aid/Academic: **Athletic:** 0
Roster In State: 9   **Out of State:** 6   **Out of Country:** 1
Sophomores on Team: 0   **Seniors on Team:** 1   **Graduation %:** 100
Most Recent Record: 28-9-0   **Fall Games:** 37   **Spring Games:** 15
Positions Needed: Setter, Middle Hitter
Schedule: Juniata, Eastern Connecticut, Ithaca, Gettysburg, Rochester Institute of Technology, Cortland State
Style of Play: Typically, we play a 5-1 offense in a "horizontal" type system. My emphasis is on ball control through defense.

Gannon University
Academic Profile

109 University Square
Erie, PA 16541-0001

Phone: 800-426-6668

Type: Private, 4 Yr., Liberal Arts, Coed
Website: http://www.gannon.edu
SAT/ACT/GPA: 980/21/3.0
Student/Faculty Ratio: 13:1
Undergraduate Enrollment: 2,600
Scholarships/Academic: Yes   **Athletic:** Yes
Expenses By: Year   **In State:** $ 19,500

Founded: 1925
Religion: Roman Catholic
Housing: Yes
Male/Female: 1:5
Graduate Enrollment: 650
Financial Aid: Yes
Out of State: $ 19,500

Specializes In: Engineering, Business, Education, Health Sciences
Degrees Conferred: Associates, BS, Master's, Pre-Professional
Programs of Study: Offers 62 Bachelor's degrees, 10 PreProfessional Programs, 11 Associate's degrees, 16 Master's degrees through five academic areas: Business Administration, Education, Health Sciences, Humanities and Science, Engineering. The programs include: Accounting, Business, Economics, Finance, Industrial Distribution, International Business, Management, Marketing, Anthropology, Arts and Humanities, Communications, Criminal Justice, English, Languages, History, Human Services, Liberal Arts, Mental Health, PreMed, PreDentistry, PrePharmacy, PreOptometry, PreVet Medicine, Science, Early Childhood, Elementary/Second Education, Nursing, Medical, Dietetics, Special Education, Mortuary Science, Paralegal, Philosophy, Political Science, PreLaw, PreMortuary, Social Work/Science, Theology, etc.

Women's Athletic Profile

University Square
Erie, PA 16541-0001
Coach: Michele Mason
Email: mason006@gammua.edu

NCAA I
Lady Knights, Maroon, Gold
Phone: (814) 871-7245
Fax: (814) 871-7794

Estimated # of Women's Volleyball Scholarships: N/A
Conference: Great Lakes Intercollegiate Athletic Conference
Program Profile: Playing season from August-November. Games played in Hammermill Center, seating 2,800.
History: Established in 1974 All Time record 468-327. Advanced to postseason 10 times, advanced to NCAA Tournament 6 times, advanced to NCAA Elite Eight 3 times, advanced to GUAC Tournament in 1998-1999, record 20 or more wins in a season.
Achievements: 8 All GUAC members since joined to the conference in 1995. 2 AVCA All-American, 5 Academic All-American.
Coaching: Head coach Michele Mason, 2nd year, 17-12 in 1999. Assistant Coach Jen Edmonds, 1st season.
Roster In State: 10   **Out of State:** 4   **Out of Country:** 1
Seniors on Team: 3   **Most Recent Record:** 17-12
Positions Needed: All
Schedule: Northwood, Ferris State, Grand Valley State, Michigan Tech, Northern Michigan, Findlay and Edinboro
Style of Play: Hard-working, quick paced, and determined.

Geneva College
Academic Profile

3200 College Avenue
Beaver Falls, PA 15010

Phone: 800-847-8255

Type: Private, 4 Yr., Coed
Website: http://www.geneva.edu
SAT/ACT/GPA: 21
Student/Faculty Ratio: 18:1
Undergraduate Enrollment: 1,500
Scholarships/Academic: Yes   **Athletic:** Yes
Expenses By: Year   **In State:** $ 16,284

Founded: 1848
Religion: Christian
Housing: Yes
Male/Female: 45:55
Graduate Enrollment: 70
Financial Aid: Yes
Out of State: $ 16,284

Degrees Conferred: AS, BA, BS, MA
Programs of Study: Accounting, Applied Mathematics, Bible Studies, Biology, Broadcasting, Business Administration, Computer Science, Education, Electrical Engineering, Elementary Education, English, Guidance, History, Human Resources, Industrial Engineering, Medical Technology, Ministries, Music, Philosophy, Physics, Political Science, PreMed, Psychology, Radio & Television, Science, Secondary Education, Spanish, Speech, Speech Pathology

Women's Athletic Profile

3200 College Avenue
Beaver Falls, PA 15010
Coach: Cindy Guthrie
Email: cguthrie@geneva.edu

NCAA I
Golden Tornadoes, Gold, White
Phone: (724) 847-6104
Fax: (724) 847-5001

Estimated # of Women's Volleyball Scholarships: 10
Conference: American Mideast Conference
Program Profile: Geneva will try and build on their 1998 Play-Off Appearance in the first ever season in the American Mideast Conference. Geneva Plays their own matches in the 2500 seat Metheny Fieldhouse
History: Since 1997, the team has gotten gradually stronger, as evidenced by their play off appearance in the newly formed tough AMC Conference. As a third year coach, Coach Guthrie provides stability for the program.
Achievements: Stephanie Waller All-Conference AMC, NCCAA Regional All-Conference
Coaching: Cindy Guthrie-3rd year (22-45 overall)
Former Member Penn State Volleyball team
Calvin College Assistant Coach-Final Four NCAA III finish 1992
Freshman Receiving Financial Aid/Academic: **Athletic:** 7
Roster In State: 9   **Out of State:** 6
Sophomores on Team: 4   **Seniors on Team:** 1   **Graduation %:** N/A
Most Recent Record: 10-21   **Fall Games:** 31
Camp of Clinic Dates: Aug 16- Team Camp
Positions Needed: OH, MH, Setter
Schedule: Mt. Vernon Nazarene, Cedarville, Westminster, Walsh, Mt. Union, Malone
Style of Play: Geneva runs a high-energy quick offense and relentless defense. Blockin and diggin have been strengths. Our new guide offense will round out the team.

Gettysburg College
Academic Profile

300 North Washington
Gettysburg, PA 17325

Phone: 717-337-6400

Type: Private, 4 Yr., Liberal Arts, Coed
Website: http://www.gettysburg.edu
SAT/ACT/GPA: 1090-1260
Student/Faculty Ratio: 11.5/1
Undergraduate Enrollment: 2,300
Scholarships/Academic: Yes
Expenses By: Year
Degrees Conferred: BA, BS

Founded: 1832
Religion: Lutheran
Housing: Yes
Male/Female: 48/52
Graduate Enrollment: N/A
Athletic: No   **Financial Aid:** Yes
In State: $30,821   **Out of State:** $30,821

Programs of Study: Anthropology, Sociology, Art, Art History, BioChemistry, Biology, Chemistry, Classical Studies, Computer Science, Economics, English, French, German, Greek, Health and Exercise Sciences, Latin, History, Management, Mathematics, Music, Music Education, Philosophy, Physics, Political Science, Psychology, Sociology, Spanish, Theatre Arts, Women's Studies

Women's Athletic Profile

Campus Box 400
Gettysburg, PA 17325
Coach: Kim Kelly
Email: kelly@gettysburg.edu

NCAA I
Lady Bullets, Orange, Blue
Phone: (717) 337-6410
Fax: (717) 337-6528

Estimated # of Women's Volleyball Scholarships: N/A
Conference: Centennial Conference
Program Profile: We play on hard wood floor that holds two courts and our season is in the fall. Our gymnasium seats approximately 2,000 people. We also have a fieldhouse that houses for courts on a rubberized floor.
History: The program began in 1976.
Achievements: All-American (second team) under tenure here; Won Conference five consecutive years in the 6 year history of the Conference; Undefeated in the Conference for the past four years.
Coaching: Kim Kelly, became Head Coach in 1996. Her overall record is 101-18. Her team has made the Regional Finals for the past three years in a row. Ken Armacost is Assistant Coach.
Freshman Receiving Financial Aid/Academic: **Athletic:** 0

Roster In State: 6   **Out of State:** 8   **Out of Country:** 0
Sophomores on Team: 3   **Seniors on Team:** 2   **Graduation %:** 100
Most Recent Record: 31-9-0   **Fall Games:** 40   **Spring Games:** 0
Camp of Clinic Dates: June 20-24
Positions Needed: Outside Hitters, Setters
Schedule: Juniata College, Wittenberg , Emory University, Savannah Arts and Design, Ohio Northern, Muskingum College
Style of Play: 5-1 offense that moves very quickly. We run a lot of middle hitter and back row plays.

Grove City College
Academic Profile

100 Campus Drive
Grove City, PA 16127

Phone: (724) 458-2129

Type: Private, 4 Yr., Liberal Arts, Coed   **Founded:** 1876
Website: http://www.gcc.edu   **Religion:** Non-Affiliated
SAT/ACT/GPA: 1110/26/3.7   **Housing:** Yes
Student/Faculty Ratio: Not Available   **Male/Female:** 1:1
Undergraduate Enrollment: 2,200   **Graduate Enrollment:** 20
Scholarships/Academic: Yes   **Athletic:** No   **Financial Aid:** Yes
Expenses By: Year   **In State:** $ 10,600   **Out of State:** $ 10,600
Specializes In: Accounting, Business, Computers, Education, Engineering, Music
Degrees Conferred: BA, BS, BMus, BSME, BSEE
Programs of Study: Electrical & Mechanical Engineering, Elementary & Secondary Education: All Areas - Business, Economics, International Management, PreProfessional Programs, Natural Science, Mathematics & Computer Systems, Humanities and Social Sciences, Music

Women's Athletic Profile

100 Campus Drive
Grove City, PA 16127
Coach: Susan Roberts
Email:

NCAA I
Wolverines, Crimson, White
Phone: (724) 458-2129
Fax: (724) 458-3855

Estimated # of Women's Volleyball Scholarships: N/A
Conference: President's Athletic Conference
Program Profile: The Grove City Volleyball Program has continually been striving to maintain its successful beginnings. Since its inception in 1973, the volleyball program has produced one winning team after another. In 1985, the Lady Wolverines compiled a 41-0 regular season record and received the Number 1 ranking in NCAA III. We got 7 of 12 President's Athletic Conference Championships. We also got back to back ECAC championships in 1994 and 1995.
History: Our program started in 1973. The overall record is 629-225. We have ten years of NCAA playoff experience. We have seven PAC championships and 2 ECAC championships.
Achievements: 1985 Juniata Classic & Indian Invitational Champions, PAC & WKC Champions; No.1 in NCAA III in 1985; 1987 PAC Champions; 1989 PAC Champions;1992 Champions; 1993 PAC Champions; 1994 ECAC Champions; 1995 PAC and ECAC Champions; 1996 ECAC Champions; 1997 PAC second place; Becky Nelson 1997 All-PAC 1st team; Erin Mayne 1997 All-PAC 2nd team; Nicole Hable 1997 All-PAC 2nd team; Heather Oates 1997 Defensive Player of the PAC; Sarah Hamsher MVP of the PAC
Coaching: Susan Roberts, became Head Coach in 1985. Her record here is 355-177. Her overall record is 407-202. She was National Coach of the Year in 1985 when the team went 41-1.

Roster In State: 5   **Out of State:** 8   **Out of Country:** 0
Sophomores on Team: 0   **Seniors on Team:** 3   **Graduation %:** 100
Most Recent Record: 19-15-0   **Fall Games:** 30-35   **Spring Games:** 0
Positions Needed: All
Schedule: Juniata, Cortland, John Carroll, others determined by tournaments
Style of Play: Strong defensive team with quick transition.

Gwynedd Mercy College
Academic Profile

P.O. Box 901, Sumneytown Pike
Gwynedd-Mercy, PA 19437

Phone: (215) 641-5574

Type: Private, 4 Yr., Coed   **Founded:** 1948
Website: http://www.gmc.edu   **Religion:** Catholic
SAT/ACT/GPA: 900   **Housing:** Yes

Student/Faculty Ratio: 13:1
Undergraduate Enrollment: 2,100
Scholarships/Academic: Yes
Expenses By: Year
Specializes In: All majors
Degrees Conferred: Associate, BA, BS, Masters

Male/Female: 1:20
Graduate Enrollment: 300
Athletic: No
Financial Aid: Yes
In State: $ 20,100
Out of State: $ 20,100

Programs of Study: Biology, Biological Science, Secondary Education, English, Communications, Literature, PreLaw, History, Math, Psychology, Sociology, Accounting, Business Administration, Finance, Health Administration, Marketing, Business Education, Elementary Education, Early Childhood Education, Special Education, Special Elementary Education, Nursing, Medical Technology, Respiratory Care, Radiation Therapy

Women's Athletic Profile

P.O. Box 901
Gwynedd-Mercy, PA 19437
Coach: Dan Halstead
Email:

NCAA I
Griffins, Red, Gold
Phone: (215) 641-5574
Fax: (215) 542-4683

Estimated # of Women's Volleyball Scholarships: N/A
Conference: Pennsylvania Athletic Conference

Haverford College
Academic Profile

370 Lancaster Avenue
Haverford, PA 19041

Phone: 610-896-1350

Type: Private, 4 Yr., Liberal Arts, Coed
Website: http://www.haverford.edu
SAT/ACT/GPA: 1200+
Student/Faculty Ratio: 11:1
Undergraduate Enrollment: 1,200
Scholarships/Academic: No
Expenses By: Year
Degrees Conferred: BA, BS

Founded: 1833
Religion: Non-Affiliated
Housing: Yes
Male/Female: 50:50
Graduate Enrollment: N/A
Athletic: No
Financial Aid: Yes
In State: $ 29,520
Out of State: $ 29,520

Programs of Study: Archaeology, Astronomy, Biology, Chemistry, Classics, Comparative Literature, East Asian Studies, Economics, English, Fine Arts, French, Geology, German, History, History of Art, Mathematics, Music, Philosophy, Physics, Political Science, Psychology, Religion, Russian, Sociology, Anthropology

Women's Athletic Profile

370 Lancaster Avenue
Haverford, PA 19041
Coach: James Haney
Email: jhaney4971@aol.com

NCAA I
Lady Fords, Scarlet, Black
Phone: (610) 896-1127
Fax: (610) 896-1117

Estimated # of Women's Volleyball Scholarships: N/A
Conference: Centennial Conference

Immaculata College
Academic Profile

P. O. Box 642 Undergrad. Adm. Office
Immaculata, PA 19345-0642
Type: Private, 4 Yr., Women Only
Website: http://www.immaculata.edu
SAT/ACT/GPA: 900+
Student/Faculty Ratio: 12:1
Undergraduate Enrollment: 2,120
Scholarships/Academic: Yes
Expenses By: Year
Degrees Conferred: AA, AS, BA, BS, MA, EdD, Ph.D.

Phone: 877-428-6329

Founded: 1920
Religion: Catholic
Housing: No
Male/Female: Women Only
Graduate Enrollment: 220
Athletic: Yes
Financial Aid: Yes
In State: $ 19,990
Out of State: $ 19,990

Programs of Study: Accounting, Allied Health Sciences, Biology, Business Administration, Chemistry, Criminal Justice, Economics, Education (Early Childhood, Elementary, Secondary, Special), English Environmental Science, Family and Consumer Science, Fashion Marketing, Foods in Business, French, German, History, Information Technology, Institutional/Food Service Management, International Studies, Intercultural Communication, Mathematics, Music, Nursing, Nutrition, Paralegal, PreProfessional (Dental, Law, Medicine, Optometry, Veterinary), Public Policy, Psychology, Sociology, Spanish, Theatre Arts, Theology, Urban Studies, Written Communication

Women's Athletic Profile

1135 King Road
Immaculata, PA 19345
Coach: Marie Schnieder
Email:

NCAA I
Lady Mighty Macs, Blue, White
Phone: (610) 647-4400x3736
Fax: (610) 251-1668

Estimated # of Women's Volleyball Scholarships: N/A
Conference: Pennsylvania Athletic Conference

Indiana University - Pennsylvania
Academic Profile

660 S. Eleventh Street
Indiana, PA 15701

Phone: 800-442-6830

Type: Public, 4 Yr., Liberal Arts, Coed
Website: http://www.iup.edu
SAT/ACT/GPA: 950/2.7
Student/Faculty Ratio: 16:1
Undergraduate Enrollment: 12,000
Scholarships/Academic: Yes   **Athletic:** Yes
Expenses By: Year   **In State:** $ 8,366
Degrees Conferred: BA, BS, BFA, BSEd, BSN

Founded: 1875
Religion: Non-Affiliated
Housing: No
Male/Female: 4:5
Graduate Enrollment: 1,800
Financial Aid: Yes
Out of State: $ 12,866

Programs of Study: Business, Criminology, Consumer Services, Elementary & Secondary Education, Fine Arts, Food & Nutrition, Health & Physical Education, Home Economics, Medical Technology, Nursing, Respiratory Therapy, Safety Management, Art & Sciences, Computer Science, Accounting, Music

Women's Athletic Profile

Memorial Fieldhouse
Indiana, PA 15705
Coach: Carmine Cortazzo
Email:

NCAA I
Lady Indians, Crimson, Grey
Phone: (724) 357-3198
Fax: (724) 357-7804

Estimated # of Women's Volleyball Scholarships: N/A
Conference: Pennsylvania State Athletic Conference

Juniata College
Academic Profile

1700 Moore St.
Huntingdon, PA 16652-2119

Phone: (814) 641-3510

Type: Private, 4 Yr., Liberal Arts, Coed
Website: http://www.juniata.edu
SAT/ACT/GPA: 1130
Student/Faculty Ratio: 13:1
Undergraduate Enrollment: 1,250
Scholarships/Academic: Yes   **Athletic:** No
Expenses By: Year   **In State:** $ 22,200
Specializes In: Sciences, Prehealth
Degrees Conferred: BA, BS

Founded: 1876
Religion: Church of the Brethren
Housing: Yes
Male/Female: 45:55
Graduate Enrollment: N/A
Financial Aid: Yes
Out of State: $ 22,200

Programs of Study: Business, Education, PreHealth, Psychology, Sciences, Social Work

Men's Athletic Profile

1700 Monroe Street
Huntingdon, PA 16652
Coach: Ryan Patton
Email:

NCAA III
Eagles/Yale Blue, Old Gold
Phone: (814) 641-3514
Fax: (814) 641-3508

Estimated # of Men's Volleyball Scholarships: N/A
Conference: Middle Atlantic State Conference

Women's Athletic Profile

1700 Moore Street
Huntingdon, PA 16652
Coach: Larry Bock
Email: Bockl@juniata.edu

NCAA I
Lady Eagles, Yale Blue, Gold
Phone: (814) 641-3510
Fax: (814) 641-3508

Estimated # of Women's Volleyball Scholarships: N/A
Conference: Middle Atlantic States Conference
Program Profile: We play at the Kennedy Sports Center.
History: Our program began in 1977. We have been NCAA tournament qualifiers since 1981 (18 consecutive years). We have 18 MAC championships. We were NCAA second place four times, third place five times and fourth place five times. We have 21 All-Americans.
Achievements: Larry Bock was 3 times AVCA National Coach of the Year; 21 All-Americans; 5 Academic All-Americans.
Coaching: Larry Bock, has been Head Coach here for 22 years. His overall record is 816-132. Assistant Coach Ryan Patton has been here 5 years. Assistant Coach Heather Pavlik has been here 4 years.
Freshman Receiving Financial Aid/Academic: | | **Athletic:** 0
Roster In State: 10 | **Out of State:** 4 | **Out of Country:** 1
Sophomores on Team: 0 | **Seniors on Team:** 2 | **Graduation %:** 100
Most Recent Record: 38-3-0 | **Fall Games:** 22 | **Spring Games:** 4
Positions Needed: 2
Schedule: University of California-San Diego, Princeton, Central Iowa, Washington, Edinboro University, Lock Haven University
Style of Play: Fast tempo offensively, tenacious defense.

King's College - Pennsylvania
Academic Profile

133 N. River Street
Wilkes Barre, PA 18711

Phone: (570) 826-5900

Type: Private, 4 Yr., Liberal Arts, Coed
Website: http://www.kings.edu
SAT/ACT/GPA: Average 1050
Student/Faculty Ratio: 14:1
Undergraduate Enrollment: 1,700
Scholarships/Academic: Yes
Expenses By: Year

Athletic: No
In State: $ 21,000

Founded: 1946
Religion: Roman Catholic
Housing: Yes
Male/Female: 50:50
Graduate Enrollment: 100
Financial Aid: Yes
Out of State: $ 21,000

Specializes In: Education, Accounting, Business, Sports Medicine, Physician's Asst.
Degrees Conferred: BA, BS, MA
Programs of Study: Education, Biology, Psychology, Business, Accounting, Sports Medicine, Physician's Assistant, Computer Information Systems, Sociology, Physics, Chemistry, Math, Computer Science, Human Resources, Gerontology, Criminal Justice, Communications, BioMedical Technology, English, PreLaw, PreMed, International Business, Health Administration

Women's Athletic Profile

N. Main Street
Wilkes-Barre, PA 18711
Coach: Bernie Kachinko
Email:

NCAA I
Lady Monarch, Red, Gold
Phone: (717) 208-5855
Fax: (717) 208-5397

Estimated # of Women's Volleyball Scholarships: N/A
Conference: Middle Atlantic States Conference

Kutztown University
Academic Profile

Keystone Hall
Kutztown, PA 19530

Phone: (610) 683-4060

Type: Public, 4 Yr., Liberal Arts, Coed
Website: http://www.kutztown.edu
SAT/ACT/GPA: 1050 Avg.
Student/Faculty Ratio: 8:1
Undergraduate Enrollment: 6,000
Scholarships/Academic: Yes
Expenses By: Year
Specializes In: Visual & Performing Arts, Business, Education
Degrees Conferred: BA, BFA, BS, BSBA, Education, Engineering

Athletic: Yes
In State: $ 8,000

Founded: 1866
Religion: Non-Affiliated
Housing: Yes
Male/Female: 1/1.5
Graduate Enrollment: N/A
Financial Aid: Yes
Out of State: $ 13,000

Programs of Study: Accounting, Anthropology, Biology, Chemistry, Communications, Computer & Information Science, Criminal Justice, Economics, Education, English, Environmental Science, Geography, Geology, Management, Mathematics, Marketing, Music, Nursing, Philosophy, Physics, Political Science, Psychology, Sociology

Women's Athletic Profile

Keystone Hall
Kutztown, PA 19530
Coach: John Gump
Email: johngump@hotmail.edu

NCAA I
Golden Bears, Maroon, Gold
Phone: (610) 683-1333
Fax: (610) 683-1379

Estimated # of Women's Volleyball Scholarships: N/A
Conference: Pennsylvania State Athletic Conference

La Roche College
Academic Profile

9000 Babcock Blvd.
Pittsburgh, PA 15237

Phone: 800-838-4572

Type: Private, 4 Yr., Liberal Arts, Coed
Website: http://www.La Roche.edu
SAT/ACT/GPA: Varies
Student/Faculty Ratio: 20:1
Undergraduate Enrollment: 1,500
Scholarships/Academic: Yes
Expenses By: Year
Specializes In: Graphic & Interior Design
Degrees Conferred: BA, BS, MS

Athletic: No
In State: $ 15,000

Founded: 1863
Religion: Catholic
Housing: Yes
Male/Female: 40:60
Graduate Enrollment: 350
Financial Aid: Yes
Out of State: $ 15,000

Programs of Study: Accounting, Applied Art, Art, Applied Mathematics, Astronomy, Biology, Business Administration, Chemistry, Commercial Art, Communications, Computer Information Systems, Creative Writing, Earth Science, Education, English, Environmental Science, Finance, Graphic Art, History, Human Services, Interior Design, International Business, Journalism, Literature, Management, Mathematics, Medical Technology, Natural Science, Nursing, PreDentistry, PreLaw, PreMed, PreVet, Psychology, Public Relations, Radiological Technology, Religion, Respiratory Therapy, Secondary Education, Social Work, Sociology, Technical Writing

Women's Athletic Profile

9000 Babcock Boulevard
Pittsburgh, PA 15237
Coach: Kassie Ott
Email: ottk1@laroche.edu

NCAA I
Lady Redhawks, Red, White
Phone: (412) 536-1056
Fax: (412) 536-1012

Estimated # of Women's Volleyball Scholarships: N/A
Conference: Independent

La Salle University
Academic Profile

Box 805
Philadelphia, PA 19141-1199

Phone: (215) 951-1727

Type: Private, 4 Yr., Liberal Arts, Coed
Website: http://www.lasalle.edu
SAT/ACT/GPA: 1000 +/Required
Student/Faculty Ratio: 16:1
Undergraduate Enrollment: 3,000
Scholarships/Academic: Yes
Expenses By: Semester
Specializes In: Comprehensive University

Athletic: Yes
In State: $ 11,175

Founded: 1863
Religion: Christian Brothers (Catholic)
Housing: Yes
Male/Female: 46:54
Graduate Enrollment: 1,500
Financial Aid: Yes
Out of State: $ 11,175

Degrees Conferred: AA, AS, BA, BS, BSN, MBA
Programs of Study: Art History, Asian Studies, Biology, Chemistry, BioChemistry, Communications, Computer Science, Criminal Justice, Digital Arts, Economics, Education, English, Environmental Science, Fine Arts, Foreign Languages, Geology, History, Religion, Sociology, Accounting, Finance, Law, Management

Women's Athletic Profile

Box 805, 1900 W. Olney
Philadelphia, PA 19003
Coach: Jason Klotkowski
Email: klotkows@lasalle.edu

NCAA I
Lady Explorers, Blue, Gold
Phone: (215) 951-1727
Fax: (215) 951-1694

Estimated # of Women's Volleyball Scholarships: 5
Conference: Atlantic 10 Conference
Program Profile: An up and coming program, the Explorers play in the Tom Goal Arena with a seating capacity of 3,400, in the Hayman Center on La Salle's campus. The Hayman Center also includes a training room, a weight room and a pool. Our program has a fall playing season.
History: The program began in 1973. The Explorers entered the Atlantic 10 before the 1995 season.
Achievements: 1998 achievements: First place at Harvard Invitational; Melissa McCall was Tournament MVP, Melissa Hodge was GTE Academic All-American.
Coaching: Jason Klotkowski, Head Coach. He has led the Explorers to respectability in the competitive Atlantic 10 Conference and improved tremendously from 2-30 in 1996 to 18-16 in 1998. Jay Yedziniak is Assistant Coach.

Freshman Receiving Financial Aid/Academic: | | **Athletic:** 2
Roster In State: 8 | **Out of State:** 6 | **Out of Country:** 0
Sophomores on Team: 0 | **Seniors on Team:** 3 | **Graduation %:** 100
Most Recent Record: 17-16-0 | **Fall Games:** 33 | **Spring Games:** 16
Camp of Clinic Dates: August 9-13
Positions Needed: Middle Blocker
Schedule: Temple University, University of Massachusetts, University of Rhode Island, Xavier University, Virginia Tech University, University of Dayton, UNC-Evansville
Style of Play: Quick simple; 5-1 offense, perimeter defense. Key to success is quick fundamental defense. The coaching staff emphasizes ball control skills and the need to run the quick offense they have initialized.

Lafayette College
Academic Profile

A.P. Kirby Sports Center
Easton, PA 18042

Phone: (610) 330-5470

Type: Private, 4 Yr., Liberal Arts, Engineering, Coed
Website: http://www.lafayette.edu
SAT/ACT/GPA: 1150-1330
Student/Faculty Ratio: 11:1
Undergraduate Enrollment: 2179
Scholarships/Academic: Yes
Expenses By: Year
Specializes In: Liberal arts and Engineering

Athletic: Need Based
In State: $31,771

Founded: 1826
Religion: Non-Affiliated
Housing: Yes
Male/Female: 1:1
Graduate Enrollment: 0
Financial Aid: Yes
Out of State: $31,711

Degrees Conferred: MBA, MBS
Programs of Study: Engineering, International Studies, Economics & Business, Government & Law, Liberal Arts, History, Literature

Women's Athletic Profile

Pierce & Hamilton
Easton, PA 18042
Coach: Jeff Corpora
Email: corporal@lafayette.edu

NCAA I
Lady Leopards, Maroon, White
Phone: (610) 330-5475
Fax: (610) 330-5519

Estimated # of Women's Volleyball Scholarships: 0
Conference: The Patriot League
Program Profile: One of 7 Patriot League members, home games are played on a hardwood surface.
History: Began in 1974 under Head Coach Alana Desris, going 4-2; seen the reign of six head coaches; joined Patriot league play in 1991 going 8-14 overall, 3-4 league.
Coaching: First year Coach Jeff Corpora; first year Assistant Coach Rose Marie Bukks
Freshman Receiving Financial Aid/Academic: **Athletic:** 0
Roster In State: 2   **Out of State:** 9   **Out of Country:** 0
Sophomores on Team: **Seniors on Team:** 2   **Graduation %:** 100
Most Recent Record: 1-27
Schedule: Maryland , Delaware, Morgan State, Drexel, Columbia, LIU

Lebanon Valley College
Academic Profile

101 N. College Ave.   **Phone:** 800-445-6181
Annville, PA 17003

Type: Private, 4 Yr., Coed   **Founded:** 1866
Website: http://www.cuc.edu   **Religion:** Non-Affiliated
SAT/ACT/GPA: Required   **Housing:** Yes
Student/Faculty Ratio: 15:1   **Male/Female:** 50:50
Undergraduate Enrollment: 1,670   **Graduate Enrollment:** N/A
Scholarships/Academic: Yes   **Athletic:** No   **Financial Aid:** Yes
Expenses By: Year   **In State:** $ 16,630   **Out of State:** $ 16,630
Specializes In: Biology, Education, Sciences
Degrees Conferred: AA, AS, BA, BS, BM, MBA
Programs of Study: Contact school for program of study.

Women's Athletic Profile

101 N. College Avenue   **NCAA I**
Annville, PA 17003   Dutchwomen, Blue, White
Coach: Wayne Perry   **Phone:** (717) 867-6273
Email: perry@lvc.edu   **Fax:** (717) 867-6035

Estimated # of Women's Volleyball Scholarships: N/A
Conference: Middle Atlantic States Conference

Lehigh University
Academic Profile

641 Taylor St.   **Phone:** (610) 758-6111
Bethlehem, PA 18015-3187
Type: Private, 4 Yr., Liberal Arts, Engineering, Coed   **Founded:** 1865
Website: http://www.lehigh.edu   **Religion:** Non-Affiliated
SAT/ACT/GPA: Very competitive   **Housing:** Yes
Student/Faculty Ratio: 14:1   **Male/Female:** 65:35
Undergraduate Enrollment: 4,400   **Graduate Enrollment:** 2,000
Scholarships/Academic: Yes   **Athletic:** Yes   **Financial Aid:** Yes
Expenses By: Year   **In State:** $ 30,000   **Out of State:** $ 30,000
Degrees Conferred: BA, BS, MS, MBA, M.Ed., Ph.D., EdD
Programs of Study: Accounting, American Studies, Anthropology, Architecture, Art, Biology, Business & Economics, Chemistry, Classics, Computer Science, East Asian Studies, Economics, Electrical Engineering, Engineering, Engineering & Applied Science, English, French, Geology, GeoPhysics, International Careers, International Relations, Journalism, Mathematics, Molecular Biology, Music, Natural Science, Philosophy, Physics, PreDental, PreMed, Russian Studies, Science, Writing

Women's Athletic Profile

641 Taylor Street   **NCAA I**
Bethlehem, PA 18015   Lady Mountain
Coach: Patrick H. Nicholas   **Phone:** (610) 758-6111
Email: phn3@lehigh.edu   **Fax:** (610) 758-6629

Estimated # of Women's Volleyball Scholarships: N/A
Conference: The Patriot League
Program Profile: We practice and compete in our own facility-Grace Hall. We want young women that are not only very good athletes but also committed to the very best of academics.
History: The first year for women's volleyball here was 1974. In 1990, the Patriot League was formed. Lehigh has participated in every Patriot League Championship Tournament (only the top 4 go to the tournament). Lehigh won the Tournament in 1993 and in 1997. We participated in the 1997 NCAA Division I Championship Tournament.
Achievements: Patriot League Tournament Champions in 1993 and 1997; 19 All-Patriot League Selections; 28 All-Patriot League Academic Honor Roll Selections; 2 Defensive Player of the Year Selections; 1 Offensive Player of the Year Selection; 1997 Patriot League Tournament MVP; 1 District Academic All-American; Volleyball School Athlete of the Year; 2 Rookie of the Year Selections.
Coaching: Patrick H. Nicholas, started as Head Coach in 1997. His record here is 38-27. In his first year, the team won the Patriot League Championship Tournament and NCAA Play-In to Advance to the NCAA Division I Championship Tournament.

Freshman Receiving Financial Aid/Academic:		**Athletic:** 3
Roster In State: 3	**Out of State:** 6	**Out of Country:** 0
Sophomores on Team: 7	**Seniors on Team:** 3	**Graduation %:** 100
Most Recent Record: 20-15-0	**Fall Games:**	**Spring Games:** 4

Camp of Clinic Dates: Residential: July25-29; Hitters/Setters: July 31; Individual Defense/Ball Handling: August 1-5
Positions Needed: Setter, Outside Hitter, Middle Blocker
Schedule: Rice University, University of Tennessee, University of Kansas
Style of Play: A quick up-tempo pace-technically driven by fundamentals and movement. I am very passionate and we work and compete hard.

Lincoln University
Academic Profile

P.O. Box 179
Lincoln University, PA 19352

Phone: 800-790-0191

Type: Public, 4 Yr., Liberal Arts, Coed
Website: http://www.lincoln.edu
SAT/ACT/GPA: 800
Student/Faculty Ratio: 12:1
Undergraduate Enrollment: 1,270
Scholarships/Academic: Yes　　　　**Athletic:** No
Expenses By: Year　　　　**In State:** $ 7,000
Specializes In: Sciences
Degrees Conferred: BA, BS, M

Founded: 1854
Religion: Non-Affiliated
Housing: Yes
Male/Female: 40:60
Graduate Enrollment: 200
Financial Aid: Yes
Out of State: $ 9,000

Programs of Study: Accounting, Actuarial Science, Anthropology, Banking & Finance, Biology, Business Administration, Chemistry, Computer Science, Criminal Justice, Economics, Education, English, French, History, Human Services, International Relations, Journalism, Management, Mathematics, Medical Technology, Music, Nursing, Philosophy, Physical Education, Physics, Political Science, PreDental, PreEngineering, PreLaw, PreMed, PreVet, Psychology, Public Affairs, Recreation & Leisure, Recreation Therapy, Religion, Russian Work, Sociology, Spanish

Women's Athletic Profile

P.O. Box 179
Lincoln University, PA 19352
Coach: Ethel Watson
Email:

NCAA I
Lady Lions, Orange, Blue
Phone: (610) 932-83391
Fax: (610) 932-1220

Estimated # of Women's Volleyball Scholarships: N/A
Conference: Eastern College Athletic Conference

Lock Haven University
Academic Profile

Thomas Fieldhouse
Lock Haven, PA 17745

Phone: 800-233-8978

Type: Public, 4 Yr., Liberal Arts, Coed
Website: http://www.lhup.edu
SAT/ACT/GPA: 950/2.5
Student/Faculty Ratio: 17:1
Undergraduate Enrollment: 3,500

Founded: 1870
Religion: Non-Affiliated
Housing: Yes
Male/Female: 55:45
Graduate Enrollment: 200

Scholarships/Academic: Yes   **Athletic:** Yes   **Financial Aid:** Yes
Expenses By: Year   **In State:** $ 8,248   **Out of State:** $ 11,604
Specializes In: Education, Sports Medicine, Biology, Computer Science
Degrees Conferred: BA, BS, BFA, MA
Programs of Study: Early Childhood Education, Elementary Education, Secondary Education, Physical Education, Special Education, Recreation, English, History, Sociology, Psychology, Sports Medicine, Health Science, Mathematics, Art, Music, Communications, Management Science, Accounting, Computer Science, Biology, Environmental Biology, Geology, Chemistry, Physics, Fitness Management, Leisure, Commercial Management, Outdoor Management, Earth & Space Science

Women's Athletic Profile

North Fairview Street
Lock Haven, PA 17745
Coach: Tom Justice
Email: tjustice@eagle.lhup.edu

NCAA I
Lady Eagles, Crimson, White
Phone: (570) 893-2027
Fax: (570) 893-2414

Estimated # of Women's Volleyball Scholarships: 5
Conference: Pennsylvania State Athletic Conference
Program Profile: The program was ranked #1 team in the Atlantic Region. We were PSAC Champions in 1996, Atlantic Region Champions in 1997, NCAA Elite 8 in 1997 and Conference Champions in 1998. This is a program that is striving to be the best in the region and to rise to national prominence. We play a tough inter-Region and intra-Region schedule that includes opponents from Top 10 and Top 20 teams nationally.
History: This program began from ground zero in 1991 with a small group of coeds on campus who had been members of volleyball clubs. In a full Division II schedule, the first team went 0-17, but every year since then we have grown stronger to become the dominant team in the region, year in and year out. We are young and dynamic. The past three seasons have been championship ones and more championships are on the tap for the future.
Achievements: Tom Justice was named PSAC Coach of the Year; PSAC Finalist in 1995; 1996 PSAC Champions; 1997 Atlantic Region Champs; 1997 NCAA Elite 8; 1998 PSAC Regular Season Champions.
Coaching: Tom Justice, Head Coach, started coaching the team in 1991 to the present with no scholarship money, no equipment and no gym to play in. He took a lot of lumps early but he has since built a scholarship fund, 3 practice courts (9 total courts) and has had over 30 wins each of the past four years. He was named 1998 PSAC Coach of the Year. Melissa Myers, Assistant Coach, was named 1st team All-American. She played in 3 NCAA Final 4 Tournaments.
Freshman Receiving Financial Aid/Academic: **Athletic:** 3
Roster In State: 12   **Out of State:** 2   **Out of Country:** 0
Sophomores on Team: 0   **Seniors on Team:** 1   **Graduation %:** 100
Most Recent Record: 30-15-0   **Fall Games:** 45   **Spring Games:** 4
Camp of Clinic Dates: July 29 - August 1; August 2-6
Positions Needed: Middle Hitters, Opposites, Outside Hitters
Schedule: Northern Michigan, West Texas A & M, Regis University, Minnesota-Duluth, New Haven, Indiana-Purdue, Ft. Wayne
Style of Play: Quick, opportunistic, with great ball control. Outstanding passing and great diggings skills. Strong in transition. We run a spread offense from a variety of alignments. We like our hitters coming across at different angles and use play set combinations. We play a tough perimeter defense.

Lycoming College
Academic Profile

700 College Street
Williamsport, PA 17701

Phone: 570-321-4026

Type: Private, 4 Yr., Liberal Arts, Coed
Website: http://www.lycoming.edu
SAT/ACT/GPA: 900+
Student/Faculty Ratio: 14:1
Undergraduate Enrollment: 1,400
Scholarships/Academic: Yes   **Athletic:** No
Expenses By: Year   **In State:** $ 21,700
Specializes In: Liberal Arts
Degrees Conferred: BA, BS

Founded: 1812
Religion: Methodist
Housing: Yes
Male/Female: 50:50
Graduate Enrollment: N/A
Financial Aid: Yes
Out of State: $ 21,700

Programs of Study: Accounting, Actuarial Mathematics, American Studies, Art History, Art Studio, Astronomy, Biology, Business Administration, Chemistry, Communications, Computer Science, Criminal Justice, Economics, Education, English, French, German, History, International Studies, Mathematics, Music, Near East Culture & Archaeology, Nursing, Philosophy, Physics, Political Science, Psychology, Religion, Sociology-Anthropology, Spanish, Theatre

Women's Athletic Profile

Academy Street
Williamsport, PA 17701
Coach: Christen Ditzler
Email: ditzler@lycoming.edu

NCAA I
Lady Warriors, Blue, Gold
Phone: (717) 321-4252
Fax: (717) 321-4337

Estimated # of Women's Volleyball Scholarships: N/A
Conference: Middle Atlantic States Conference

Marywood University
Academic Profile

2300 Adams Avenue
Scranton, PA 18509

Phone: 800-346-5014

Type: Private, 4 Yr., Coed
Website: http://www.marywood.edu
SAT/ACT/GPA: 780+
Student/Faculty Ratio: 11:1
Undergraduate Enrollment: 1,948
Scholarships/Academic: Yes
Expenses By: Year
Degrees Conferred: AA, BA, BFA, MA, MS, MBA, MFA

Athletic: No
In State: $ 14,750

Founded: 1915
Religion: Catholic
Housing: No
Male/Female: 25:75
Graduate Enrollment: 979
Financial Aid: Yes
Out of State: $ 14,750

Programs of Study: Visual and Performing Arts, Health Sciences, Business and Management, Communications, Computer and Information Sciences, Law, Nursing, PreLaw, Social Sciences, Teacher Education

Women's Athletic Profile

2300 Adams Avenue
Scranton, PA 18509
Coach: Alan Waclawski
Email: rjnhome@epix.net

NCAA I
Lady Pacers, Green, White
Phone: (717) 961-4724
Fax: (717) 961-4730

Estimated # of Women's Volleyball Scholarships: N/A
Conference: Pennsylvania Athletic Conference

Mercyhurst College
Academic Profile

501 East 38th Street
Erie, PA 16546
Type: Private, 4 Yr., Liberal Arts, Coed
Website: http://www.mercyhurst.edu
SAT/ACT/GPA: 900/18/2.5
Student/Faculty Ratio: 18:1
Undergraduate Enrollment: 2700
Scholarships/Academic: Yes
Expenses By: Year
Specializes In: Arts, Business, Criminal Justice, Sports Medicine, Anthropology
Degrees Conferred: BA, BS, BM, MS

Phone: (814) 824-2227

Founded: 1926
Religion: Catholic
Housing: Yes
Male/Female: 54:46
Graduate Enrollment: N/A
Financial Aid: Yes

Athletic: Yes
In State: $ 18,555
Out of State: $ 18,555

Programs of Study: Accounting, Archeology, Art, Biology, Business, Chemistry, Computer Systems, Communications, Criminal Justice, Dance, Dietetics, Education, Fashion Merchandising, Graphic Design, History, Hotel and Restaurant Management, Mathematics, Music, Philosophy, Political Science, Psychology, Religious Studies, Sociology, Sports Management, Sports Medicine

Men's Athletic Profile

501 E. 38th Street
Erie, PA 16546
Coach: Craig Davic
Email: athletic@mercyhurst.edu

NCAA II
Lakers/Blue, Green
Phone: (814) 824-2227
Fax: (814) 824-2202

Estimated # of Men's Volleyball Scholarships: 4
Conference: Midwest Intercollegiate Volleyball Association

Program Profile: We have a new program that began in the 1996-97 school year as a member of the MIVA. We have made play-offs all 3 years in the MIVA. We had two consecutive winning seasons: 1998 (16-10) and 1999 (14-12). The Lakers play in the newly renovated Mercyhurst Athletic Center (MAC). It has a gym with a seating capacity of 2,000. It has new scoreboards, a sound system, bleachers and a finished wood floor.

History: In 1997, our overall record was 12-20. In 1998, our overall record was 16-10. In 1999, our overall record was 14-12.

Achievements: Mercyhurst International Champions in 1998-1999; Large/Invitational Champions in 1998; Adam Tokash ranked 5th in 1999 and 9th in 1997 in Service Aces in Division I; Matt Tamborono ranked 9th in 1998 and 16th in 1999 Blocking in Division I; Ahmed Overtorzic ranked 20th in Division I Blocking in 1999. MIVA Quarter Finalist 2000, 2 MIVA Player of the Week The team finished with a .321 attack % in 2000. 18 players have finished ranked in various categories in the MIVA.

Coaching: Coach Davic created the program in the winter of 1995. He received a USAV start up grant. In 1996 season he has a record of 42-42; in 1997 season has a record of 12-20, in 1998 has a record of 16-10, and in 1999 has a record of 14-12.

Freshman Receiving Financial Aid/Academic: 2   **Athletic:** 5

Roster In State: 9   **Out of State:** 6   **Out of Country:** 0

Seniors on Team: 2   **Graduation %:** 100%

Most Recent Record: 16-11-0

Positions Needed: MH

Schedule: Ohio State, Long Beach State, Ball State, IPFW, Loyola, Lewis, Juniata

Style of Play: 5-1 multiple quick attack of offense.

Women's Athletic Profile

501 East 38th St.
Erie, PA 16546
Coach: Carrie Roberts
Email:

NCAA I
Lady Lakers, Blue, Green
Phone: (814) 824-2227
Fax: (814) 824-2204

Estimated # of Women's Volleyball Scholarships: N/A
Conference: Midwest Intercollegiate Volleyball Association

Messiah College
Academic Profile

1 College Avenue
Grantham, PA 17027

Phone: (717) 766-2511

Type: Private, 4 Yr., Liberal Arts, Coed
Website: http://www.messiah.edu
Religion: Christian Liberal Arts College
SAT/ACT/GPA: 1000/3.0
Student/Faculty Ratio: 15:1
Undergraduate Enrollment: 2,700
Scholarships/Academic: Yes
Expenses By: Year

Athletic: No
In State: $22,000

Founded: 1909

Housing: Yes
Male/Female: 45/55
Graduate Enrollment: N/A
Financial Aid: Yes
Out of State: $22,000

Specializes In: Christian Liberal Arts & Applied Sciences

Degrees Conferred: BA, BS, BSN&E

Programs of Study: Accounting, Art, Art History, Bible, BioChemistry, Biology, Broadcasting, Telecommunications & Mass Media, Business Administration, Business Information Systems, Chemistry, Christian Ministries, Civil Engineering, Communications, Computer Science, Economics, Education, Health & Physical Education, Mechanical and Electrical Engineering, English, Environmental Studies, International Business, Journalism, Marketing, Mathematics, Music, Nursing, Nutrition & Dietetics, Philosophy, Physics, Political Science, Psychology, Recreation, Religion, Social Work, Sociology, Spanish, Sport & Exercise Science, Sports Medicine, Theatre, Therapeutic Recreation

Women's Athletic Profile

College Avenue
Gratham, PA 17027
Coach: Judi Tobias
Email: jtobias@messiah.edu

NCAA I
Lady Falcons, Blue, White
Phone: (717) 691-6044
Fax: (717) 691-6044

Estimated # of Women's Volleyball Scholarships: N/A
Conference: Middle Atlantic States Conference

Millersville University - Pennsylvania
Academic Profile

P. O. Box 1002
Millersville, PA 17551

Phone: 717-872-3824

Type: Public, 4 Yr., Coed
Website: http://www.millersville.edu
SAT/ACT/GPA: Open
Student/Faculty Ratio: 17/1
Undergraduate Enrollment: 5,300
Scholarships/Academic: Yes   **Athletic:** Yes
Expenses By: Year   **In State:** $10,234
Specializes In: Education, Arts and Sciences

Founded: 1855
Religion: Non-Affiliated
Housing: Yes
Male/Female: 45/55
Graduate Enrollment: 2,200
Financial Aid: Yes
Out of State: $ 15,922

Degrees Conferred: BA, BS, BSEd, BFA, BSN, MA, MS, MEd
Programs of Study: Art, Biology, Business Administration, Chemistry, Computer Science, Education Foundation, Elementary & Early Childhood Education, English, Foreign Languages, Geography, History, Psychology, Sociology, Anthropology, Special Education

Women's Athletic Profile

P.O. Box 1002
Millersville, PA 17551
Coach: Julie Hubbard
Email: julie.hubbard@millersville.edu

NCAA I
Lady Marauders, Black, Gold
Phone: (717) 872-3946
Fax: (717) 871-2200

Estimated # of Women's Volleyball Scholarships: N/A
Conference: Pennsylvania State Athletic Conference

Moravian College
Academic Profile

1200 Main Street
Bethlehem, PA 18018

Phone: (610) 861-3940

Type: Private, 4 Yr., Liberal Arts, Coed
Website: http://www.moravian.edu
SAT/ACT/GPA: 1000
Student/Faculty Ratio: 12:1
Undergraduate Enrollment: 1,300
Scholarships/Academic: No   **Athletic:** Yes
Expenses By: Sem   **In State:** $ 11,500
Degrees Conferred: BA, BS, B.Mus.

Founded: 1742
Religion: Non-Affiliated
Housing: Yes
Male/Female: 50:50
Graduate Enrollment: N/A
Financial Aid: Yes
Out of State: $ 11,500

Programs of Study: Business, Accounting, Biology, Economics, Chemistry, Physics, PreMed, PreDentlstry, PreVet, Nursing, Psychology, Sociology, Political Science, Religion, Art, Music, Elementary Education, Secondary Education, English, Journalism, Spanish, French, German, Classics, History, Computer Science, Allied Health, Engineering, Co-op, Mathematics, Philosophy, Natural Resource Management

Women's Athletic Profile

Main St & Elizabeth Avenue
Bethlehem, PA 18108
Coach: Shelley Sorensen-Bauder
Email:

NCAA I
Lady Greyhounds, Blue, Grey
Phone: (610) 861-1597
Fax: (610) 861-3940

Estimated # of Women's Volleyball Scholarships: N/A
Conference: Middle Atlantic States Conference

Mount Aloysius College
Academic Profile

7373 Admiral Peary Highway
Cresson, PA 16602

Phone: (814) 886-6488

Type: Private, 4 Yr., Coed
Website: http://www.mtaloy.edu
SAT/ACT/GPA: 700/16/2.0

Founded: 1939
Religion: Sisters of Mercy
Housing: Yes

Student/Faculty Ratio: 15:1
Undergraduate Enrollment: 900
Scholarships/Academic: Yes · **Athletic: Yes**
Expenses By: Year · **In State:** $14,800
Specializes In: Business
Degrees Conferred: BA, BS, AA. AS
Programs of Study: Business Administration, Criminology, Nursing, Occupational Therapy, Professional Studies

Male/Female: 1:3
Graduate Enrollment: N/A
Financial Aid: Yes
Out of State: $14,800

Women's Athletic Profile

7373 Admiral Peary Hwy.
Cresson, PA 16630
Coach: Conrad Sikirica
Email:

NCAA I
Lady Mounties, Blue, White
Phone: (814) 886-6488
Fax: (814) 886-5767

Estimated # of Women's Volleyball Scholarships: 4
Conference: Northeast Atlantic
Program Profile: We are building a solid new program. Our gym has 2,200 seats and play in the fall. The team is mostly freshmen and sophomores.
History: Our program has been here only two years. We are winless, but competitive.
Achievements: One player Second Team All-Conference. Most of our players have GPA's over 3.3
Coaching: Conrad Sikirica, Head Coach, played college volleyball at Pennsylvania State. Missy Perin is Assistant Coach. She played college volleyball at Slippery Rock.
Freshman Receiving Financial Aid/Academic: · **Athletic:** 2
Roster In State: 11 · **Out of State:** 1 · **Out of Country:** 0
Sophomores on Team: 4 · **Seniors on Team:** 1 · **Graduation %:** 100
Most Recent Record: 0-11-0 · **Fall Games:** 20 · **Spring Games:** 1
Positions Needed: All
Schedule: Pittsburgh-Johnstown, Indiana-Pennsylvania, Point Park, Daemen-New York, Roberts Wesleyan-NY, Houghton-NY
Style of Play: Fundamental; need power player (spiker).

Muhlenberg College
Academic Profile

2400 Chew Street
Allentown, PA 18104

Phone: 484-664-3200

Type: Private, 4 Yr., Liberal Arts, Coed
Website: http://www.muhlberg.edu
SAT/ACT/GPA: 1150+
Student/Faculty Ratio: 25:1
Undergraduate Enrollment: 1,900
Scholarships/Academic: Yes · **Athletic:** No
Expenses By: Year · **In State:** $ 26,000
Specializes In: Preprofessional Programs, Entrepreneurial Studies

Founded: 1848
Religion: Non-Affiliated
Housing: Yes
Male/Female: 50:50
Graduate Enrollment: N/A
Financial Aid: Yes
Out of State: $ 26,000

Degrees Conferred: BA, BS
Programs of Study: Accounting, American Studies, Art, BioChemistry, Biology, Business Administration, Chemistry, Classics, Communication Studies, Computer Science, Economics, English, Environmental Science, French, German, Greek, History, Human Resources Administration, Information Science, International Studies, Latin, Mathematics, Music, Natural Science, Philosophy, Philosophy/Political Thought, Physical Science, Physics, Political Science, Political Economy, PreLaw, PreMed, PreMinistry, Psychology, Religion, Russian Studies, Social Science, Social Work, Sociology, Spanish, Theatre Arts

Women's Athletic Profile

2400 Chew Street
Allentown, PA 18104
Coach: Jenny Warmack-Chipman
Email: jchipman@muhlenberg.edu

NCAA I
Lady Mules, Cardinal, Grey
Phone: (484)664-3669
Fax: (484)664-3537

Estimated # of Women's Volleyball Scholarships: 0
Conference: Centennial Conference
Program Profile: Intense competitive program in the top half of conference. Play in main gym Memorial Hall in mid August pre-season, then season from Sept-Nov. Wooden gym floor is resurfaced every 5 yrs or as needed.

History: Began 1979, all time record of 281-243. First sport in school's history to win 20+ games in 5 straight seasons (91-95)

Achievements: 14 All-Conference, 11 Academic selections, 1 Academic All-American since 1992.

Coaching: Jenny Warmack played at UT Austing as an outside hitter from 91-94. MVP 94 led team in 94 in digs, kills, attacks and aces. 93 UT was ranked number 1 for the majority of the year, consistently ranked in the top 10 all 4 years.

Freshman Receiving Financial Aid/Academic: **Athletic:** 0

Roster In State: 4   **Out of State:** 7   **Out of Country:** 0

Sophomores on Team: **Seniors on Team:** 1   **Graduation %:** 98

Most Recent Record: 15-7

Positions Needed: Setter, Middle, Outside

Schedule: Franklin & Marshall, Gettysburg, Western MP, John Hopkins, Moravian, Haverford.

Style of Play: 5-1, rotate and read defense, seven complex offense.

Neumann College
Academic Profile

One Newmann Drive
Aston, PA 19014

Phone: 800-963-8626

Type: Private, 4 Yr., Liberal Arts, Coed   **Founded:** 1965
Website: http://www.neumann.edu   **Religion:** Catholic
SAT/ACT/GPA: 900 avg.   **Housing:** No
Student/Faculty Ratio: 12:1   **Male/Female:** 3:1
Undergraduate Enrollment: 1,300+   **Graduate Enrollment:** 100+
Scholarships/Academic: Yes   **Athletic:** No   **Financial Aid:** Yes
Expenses By: Year   **In State:** $ 12,890   **Out of State:** $ 12,890
Degrees Conferred: AA, BA, BS, MS

Programs of Study: Accounting, Biological Science, Business Administration, Communications, Computer Science, Early Childhood Education, Elementary Education, English, Information, Science, Medical Laboratory Technology, Nursing, Political Science, PreLaw, Psychology, Religion

Women's Athletic Profile

One Newmann Drive
Aston, PA 19014
Coach: Frank Garrett
Email: garretf@newmann.edu

NCAA I
Lady Knights, Blue, Gold, White
Phone: (610) 361-5261
Fax: (610) 361-5238

Estimated # of Women's Volleyball Scholarships: N/A

Conference: Pennsylvania Athletic Conference

Program Profile: Goal oriented, NCAA Championships, intense, hard working, dedicated and loyal. Our playing season is from Aug. to Nov. and the playing surface is wood and our capacity is 750 patrons.

History: Started in 1972 but no records until 1993. Most wins were six in any season. In the past four years we are 34-6 in our conference and 10-0 in 1999 & 9-1 in 2000. We will play anyone, home or away as long as it helps us toward are goals.

Achievements: In 1999 we won our league record 10-0. The past 4 years we have players nationally ranked and our team nationally ranked.

Coaching: Head Coach Frank Garrett. Assistant Coaches Jeff Kuciapinski, Chris Harvey and Kelly Dukes.

Freshman Receiving Financial Aid/Academic: **Athletic:** 0

Roster In State: 3   **Out of State:** 8   **Out of Country:** 0

Sophomores on Team: 0   **Seniors on Team:** 1   **Graduation %:** 97

Most Recent Record: 23-5-0

Camp of Clinic Dates: July 16-20, July 23-27

Positions Needed: Middle, OH, DS

Schedule: Univ. of West Chester, Salisbury State, Frostburg State, Eastern, Haverford, Elizabethtown

Style of Play: Read, React, Adjust and take the opponents strengths away. I ask for 100% at all times. We are a hard nosed defensive team and we believe in each other.

Pennsylvania State University (Penn State)
Academic Profile

Old Main
University Park, PA 16802

Phone: (814) 863-7474

Type: Public, 4 Yr., Liberal Arts, Engineering, Coed   **Founded:** 1855
Website: http://www.psu.edu   **Religion:** Non-Affiliated

SAT/ACT/GPA: 1200/25-30/3.42 avg.
Student/Faculty Ratio: 16:1
Undergraduate Enrollment: 36,000
Scholarships/Academic: Yes   **Athletic:** Yes
Expenses By: Year   **In State:** $ 11,170
Specializes In: Engineering, Teaching, Science, Agriculture
Degrees Conferred: Baccalaureate, Masters, Doctoral, Post-Docs
Programs of Study: We have all colleges on the university park campus including: Agriculture, Architecture, Business and Management, Communications, Education, Engineering, Health Sciences, Liberal Arts, Social Sciences

Housing: Yes
Male/Female: 55:45
Graduate Enrollment: 4,000
Financial Aid: Yes
Out of State: $ 17,986

Men's Athletic Profile

Bryce Jordan Center
University Park, PA 16802
Coach: Mark Pavlik
Email:

NCAA I
Nittany Lions/Blue, White
Phone: (814) 863-7464
Fax: (814) 863-3165

Estimated # of Men's Volleyball Scholarships: N/A
Conference: Eastern College Athletic Conference

Women's Athletic Profile

111 Bryce Jordan Center
University Park, PA 16802
Coach: Russ Rose
Email: ent1@psu.edu

NCAA I
Lady Nittany Lions, Blue, White
Phone: (814) 863-7474
Fax: (814) 863-5373

Estimated # of Women's Volleyball Scholarships: 3
Conference: Big Ten Conference
Program Profile: The team competes in Recreational Hall which has 7,000 seats. We average over 2,000 fans for Big Ten Matches.
History: In 1998, our record was 36-1. We lost in the Finals for the National Championships. We won Big Ten for 3 years in a row. We placed 2nd in 1998 and 1997 in the nation.
Achievements: Numerous All-Americans; 5 AAU All-Americans; 2 Broderick Award Nominees, 2 USVBA All-Rookie Team; 6 Academic All-Americans, 10 AVCA All-Region; 5 AVCA All-District players; 5 Big Ten Player of the Year; 4 time Big Ten Coach of the Year; 1 Big Ten Freshman of the Year; 8 Atlantic 10 Player of the Year; 14 All-Atlantic 10 Conference; 4 Atlantic 10 Rookie of the Year; 6 Atlantic 10 Tournament Most Valuable Player.
Coaching: Russ Rose, Head Coach, entered his 19th year with the program. He compiled a record of 620-119. He was named 1990 & 1997 AVCA National Coach of the Year. He got 1990 & 1993 " Volleyball Monthly" National Coach of the Year. He was 1990, 1992, 1993 & 1994 NCAA Mideast Region Coach of the Year. He was 1992, 1993 & 1996 Big Ten Conference Coach of the Year. He was 1997 Big Ten Conference Co-Coach of the Year and 1996 District II Coach of the Year. Erin Appleman, Assistant Coach, entered her 6th season. Mike Schall, Assistant Coach, entered his 8th season with the program.
Freshman Receiving Financial Aid/Academic: **Athletic:** 4
Roster In State: 2   **Out of State:** 15   **Out of Country:** 1
Sophomores on Team: 3   **Seniors on Team:** 4   **Graduation %:** 100
Most Recent Record: 35-1-0   **Fall Games:** 36   **Spring Games:** 4
Camp of Clinic Dates: June 13-17; June 27-July 1; July 5-9; July 25-29, August 1-5
Positions Needed: Middle, Outside, Setter
Schedule: Nebraska, Texas, Pacific, Florida, Wisconsin, Michigan State
Style of Play: Our emphasis is on ball control and team defense. We have been in the top three hitting/blocking teams over the last five years. We play to our strengths and change according to the talents of the team.

Pennsylvania State University - Erie, Bherend College
Academic Profile

Station Road
Erie, PA 16563

Phone: 814-898-6100

Type: Public, 4 Yr., Liberal Arts, Engineering, Coed
Website: http://www.pserie.psu.edu
SAT/ACT/GPA: 1150/3.3
Student/Faculty Ratio: 17:1
Undergraduate Enrollment: 3,600
Scholarships/Academic: Yes   **Athletic:** No
Expenses By: Year   **In State:** $ 11,000

Founded: 1947
Religion: Non-Affiliated
Housing: Yes
Male/Female: 6:4
Graduate Enrollment: 300
Financial Aid: Yes
Out of State: $ 11,000

Specializes In: Plastic Engineering, Management Information Systems
Degrees Conferred: BA, BS, MBA
Programs of Study: 25 baccalaureate. Programs Including Business (Economics, Management, Accounting, Management Information System), Biology, Chemistry, Communications, Engineering, Mathematics, Political Science, Psychology, Sciences, Social Science

Women's Athletic Profile

Station Rd.
Erie, PA 16563-5400
Coach: Cindy Jacobelli
Email: CAJ9@PSU.EDU

NCAA I
Lady Lions, Blue, White, Red
Phone: (814) 898-6235
Fax: (814) 898-6322

Estimated # of Women's Volleyball Scholarships: 0
Conference: Eastern College Athletic Conference
Program Profile: NCAA Division III Program, Facility-ARC-Athletics and Recreational Center
History: The first year of Volleyball was 1976. 1984 NAIA District 18 Champions. Charter Members of AMCC Conference, 1997. AMCC Tournament 1997, 1998, 1999. Overall School record
395-415-2 (24 years) 48.8%
Achievements: 1997 Cindy Jacobelli, AMCC Coach of the Year.
Coaching: Head -Cindy Jacobelli, Assistant-Greg Jacobelli
Freshman Receiving Financial Aid/Academic:

		Athletic: 0
Roster In State: 12	**Out of State:** 0	**Out of Country:** 0
Sophomores on Team:	**Seniors on Team:** 1	**Graduation %:**

Most Recent Record: 3-7-0
Positions Needed: Setters, Middles
Schedule: Muskingum, Mt.Union, Nazareth, U of Laverne
Style of Play: Our Team is small but very quick. We rely on a quick offense and a strong defense.

Philadelphia College of Textiles & Science
Academic Profile

School House Lane & Henry Ave.
Philadelphia, PA 19144

Phone: (215) 951-2700

Type: Private, 4 Yr., Coed
Website: http://www.philacol.edu
SAT/ACT/GPA: 980/68/2.5
Student/Faculty Ratio: 14:1
Undergraduate Enrollment: 2,014
Scholarships/Academic: Yes
Expenses By: Year
Degrees Conferred: AS, BS, MS, MBA

Founded: 1884
Religion: Non-Affiliated
Housing: No
Male/Female: 42:58
Graduate Enrollment: 890
Athletic: Yes   **Financial Aid:** Yes
In State: $21,094   **Out of State:** $21,094

Programs of Study: Accounting, Applied Economics, Applied Mathematics, Architectural Studies, BioChemistry, Business and Science, Chemistry, Computer Science, Environmental Science, Fashion Apparel Management, Fashion Design, Fashion Merchandising, Finance, Graphic Design, Human Resources Management, Industrial Design Management, Interior Design, International Business, Marketing, Physician Assistant, Textile Design, Psychology

Women's Athletic Profile

School House Lane & Henry Avenue
Philadelphia, PA 19144-5497
Coach: Len Lomas
Email:

NCAA I
Rams, Maroon, White
Phone: (215) 951-2720
Fax: (215) 951-2775

Estimated # of Women's Volleyball Scholarships: N/A
Conference: Independent

Philadelphia College of the Bible
Academic Profile

200 Manor Avenue
Longhorne, PA 19047

Phone: (215)702-4405

Type: Private, 4 Yr., Coed

Founded: 1913

Website: http://www.pcb.edu
SAT/ACT/GPA: 920/19/2.0
Student/Faculty Ratio: 15:1
Undergraduate Enrollment: 775
Scholarships/Academic: Yes   **Athletic:** No
Expenses By: Year   **In State:** $ 18,545
Specializes In: Bible, Social Work, Business, Education, Music
Degrees Conferred: BS, BM, BSW
Programs of Study: Bible/Business Administration, Bible/Church Ministries, Bible/Social Work, Bible/Teacher Education

Religion: Non-Denominational
Housing: Yes
Male/Female: 40/60
Graduate Enrollment: 500
Financial Aid: Yes
Out of State: $ 18,545

Men's Athletic Profile

200 Manor Avenue
Langhorne, PA 19047
Coach: Kevin Skaer
Email: gschuyler@pcb.edu

NCCAA
Eagles/Crimson, White, Black
Phone: (215) 702-4268
Fax: (215) 702-4302

Estimated # of Men's Volleyball Scholarships: N/A
Conference: Independent

Women's Athletic Profile

200 Manor Avenue
Langhorne, PA 19047
Coach: Kevin Skaer
Email:

NCAA I
Crimson Eagles, White, Black
Phone: (215) 702-4267
Fax: (215) 702-4302

Estimated # of Women's Volleyball Scholarships: N/A
Conference: Independent

Point Park College
Academic Profile

201 Wood Street
Pittsburgh, PA 15222

Phone: 412-392-3997

Type: Private, 4 Yr., Coed
Website: http://www.ppc.edu
SAT/ACT/GPA: 850/18/2.5
Student/Faculty Ratio: 36/1
Undergraduate Enrollment: 2,557
Scholarships/Academic: Yes   **Athletic:** Yes
Expenses By: Year   **In State:** $19,314
Specializes In: Best known for our Theatre arts and Journalism programs.
Degrees Conferred: AA, AS, BA, BS, BFA, MA, MBA
Programs of Study: Accounting, Advertising, Allied Health, Applied Arts, Applied Corporate Communication, Behavioral Science, Broadcast, Business Management, Biological Sciences, Criminal Justice, Dance, Education, Engineering Technology, English, Environmental Health, Film & Video Production, Funeral Services, General Studies, Health Services, History, Human Resources Management, Information Technology, International Studies, Journalism, Legal Studies, Liberal Arts, Marketing Communications, Mass Communication, Political Science, Psychology, Public Administration, Theatre Arts

Founded: 1960
Religion: Non-Affiliated
Housing: Yes
Male/Female: 40/60
Graduate Enrollment: 285
Financial Aid: Yes
Out of State: $19,314

Women's Athletic Profile

201 Wood Street
Pittsburgh, PA 15222
Coach: Pam Donaldson
Email:

NCAA I
Lady Pioneers, Green, White
Phone: (412) 392-3844
Fax: (412) 391-1980

Robert Morris College
Academic Profile

881 Narrows Run Road
Moon Township, PA 15108-1189

Phone: 412-262-8206

Type: Private, 4 Yr., Liberal Arts, Coed

Founded: 1921

Website: http://www.robert-morris.edu
SAT/ACT/GPA: 950/21
Student/Faculty Ratio: 15:1
Undergraduate Enrollment: 3,500
Scholarships/Academic: Yes   **Athletic:** Yes
Expenses By: Year   **In State:** $ 12,628
Specializes In: Business Administration, Sport Management, Accounting, Communications
Degrees Conferred: BA, BS, BAS, MS, MBA
Programs of Study: Business Administration, Accounting, Administrative Management, Communication Management, Computer Information Systems, Economics, Finance, Health Services, Management, Marketing, Sport Management, Transportation, Arts, Secondary Teacher Certification

Religion: Non-Affiliated
Housing: Yes
Male/Female: 50:50
Graduate Enrollment: 1,500
Financial Aid: Yes
Out of State: $ 12,628

Women's Athletic Profile

881 Narrows Run Road
Moon Township, PA 15108-1189
Coach: Tim Horsmon
Email: horsmon@robert-morris.edu

NCAA I
Lady Colonials, Blue, White
Phone: (412) 262-8603
Fax: (412) 262-8557

Estimated # of Women's Volleyball Scholarships: 5
Conference: Northeast Conference
Program Profile: Robert Morris College Volleyball celebrated its 15th NCAA season in 1999 with its first ever appearance in the NCAA Tournament, capped by a repeat appearance in the 2000 season by virtue of winning their fourth and fifth Northeast Conference Championships. The teams home floor is in the Charles L. Sewall Center on the RMC main campus. The team competes in some of the nation's premier tournaments during September and has nine-match conference schedule in October and November.
History: The program existed in the early 1980's, when the AIAW had yet to merge into the NCAA. Robert Morris women's sports became NCAA-sanctioned beginning with the 1985 season. There have been nearly a dozen head coaches in the team's history, including current head coach Tim Horsmon. The team is a two-time defending conference champions.
Achievements: Horsmon: Coach of the Year, Northeast Conference, 1999. Five Northeast Conference titles in 15 seasons. Two straight conference tournament MVP's. Five all-conference selections in the past two seasons. NCAA Tournament appearances in 1999 and 2000.
Freshman Receiving Financial Aid/Academic: **Athletic:** 2.5
Roster In State: 1   **Out of State:** 10   **Out of Country:** 0
Sophomores on Team: **Seniors on Team:** 1   **Graduation %:** 100
Most Recent Record: 21-16-0
Camp of Clinic Dates: June 2000
Positions Needed: Outside and middle hitters
Schedule: UMBC, St. Francis (Pa.), Campbell, Radford, Marquette.
Style of Play: An aggressive style of play that features an emphasis on physicality and intensity. We strive to a play smart style of volleyball.

Rosemont College
Academic Profile

1400 Montgomery Avenue
Rosemont, PA 19010-1699

Phone: 800-331-0708

Type: Private, 4 Yr., Liberal Arts, Women Only
Website: http://www.rosemont.edu
SAT/ACT/GPA: 1070/3.1
Student/Faculty Ratio: 8:1
Undergraduate Enrollment: 500
Scholarships/Academic: Yes   **Athletic:** No
Expenses By: Year   **In State:** $ 21,905
Specializes In: Education, English, Psychology, Premed
Degrees Conferred: BA, BS, BFA, MA, M Ed, MS
Programs of Study: American Studies, Art History, Studio Art, BioChemistry, Biology, Business, Chemistry, Economics, English, French, German, History, Humanities, Italian Studies, Mathematics, Philosophy, Political Science, Psychology, Religious Studies, Social Science, Sociology, Spanish, Women's Studies, Education Certification, PreLaw, PreMed, Nursing, Chemical Engineering, Information Systems & Technology

Founded: 1921
Religion: Catholic
Housing: Yes
Male/Female: Women Only
Graduate Enrollment: N/A
Financial Aid: Yes
Out of State: $ 21,905

Women's Athletic Profile

1400 Montgomery Avenue
Rosemont, PA 19010
Coach: Alicia Davis
Email: admission@rosemont.edu

NCAA I
Lady Ramblers, Rose, Grey
Phone: (610) 527-0200
Fax: (610) 526-0341

Estimated # of Women's Volleyball Scholarships: N/A
Conference: Pennsylvania Athletic Conference
Roster In State: 5   **Out of State:** 5   **Out of Country:** 0
Sophomores on Team: 3   **Seniors on Team:** 3   **Graduation %:** Unknown
Most Recent Record: 6-15-0   **Fall Games:** 21   **Spring Games:** 0
Positions Needed: Open all positions
Schedule: Eastern College, Neumann College, Alvernia College, Beaver College, College Misericordia, Gwynedd Mercy College

Saint Francis College - Pennsylvania
Academic Profile

Maurice Stokes Athletic Center
Loretto, PA 15940

Phone: (814) 472-3100

Type: Private, 4 Yr., Liberal Arts, Coed
Website: http://www.sfcpa.edu
SAT/ACT/GPA: 900/2.9
Student/Faculty Ratio: 15:1
Undergraduate Enrollment: 1,280
Scholarships/Academic: Yes   **Athletic:** Yes
Expenses By: Year   **In State:** $ 21,517
Specializes In: Engineering

Founded: 1847
Religion: Franciscan 3rd Order
Housing: Yes
Male/Female: 1:2
Graduate Enrollment: 800
Financial Aid: Yes
Out of State: $ 21,517

Degrees Conferred: BA, BS, BSW, MA, MBA, M.Ed., MPT, MMT, MMS
Programs of Study: Business Administration, Humanities, Health Sciences, Social Sciences, Natural & Applied Science, PreProfessional Programs

Men's Athletic Profile

P.O. Box 600
Loretto, PA 15940
Coach: Mike Rumbaugh
Email:

NCAA I
Red Flash/Red, White
Phone: (814) 472-3018
Fax: (814) 472-3209

Estimated # of Men's Volleyball Scholarships: N/A
Conference: Eastern Intercollegiate Volleyball Association

Women's Athletic Profile

Aurice Stokes Athletic Center
Loretto, PA 15940
Coach: Michael Rumbaugh
Email:

NCAA I
Lady Red Flash, Red, White
Phone: (814) 472-3381
Fax: (814) 472-3209

Estimated # of Women's Volleyball Scholarships: N/A
Conference: Northeast Conference

Saint Vincent College
Academic Profile

300 Fraser Purchase Road
Latrobe, PA 15650-2690

Phone: (724) 539-9761

Type: Private, 4 Yr., Liberal Arts, Coed
Website: http://www.stvincent.edu
SAT/ACT/GPA: Vary
Student/Faculty Ratio: 12:1

Founded: 1846
Religion: Catholic
Housing: Yes
Male/Female: 52:48

Undergraduate Enrollment: 1,250

Scholarships/Academic: Yes   **Athletic:** Yes

Expenses By: Year   **In State:** $ 19,800

Graduate Enrollment: N/A

Financial Aid: No

Out of State: $ 19,800

Specializes In: Preprofessional Programs - Business, Law, Medicine, Sciences

Degrees Conferred: 250

Programs of Study: Anthropology, Art, Biology, BioChemistry, Business Administration, Chemistry, Communications, Computing & Information Sciences, Economics, Education Certification, Engineering, English, Environmental Sciences, Family & Consumer Sciences, Fine Arts, History, Liberal Arts, Mathematics, Medical Technology, Modern & Classics Languages, Music, Music Performance, Philosophy, Physics, Political Science, Psychology, Public Policy, Religious Education, Social Work, Sociology, Theatre

Women's Athletic Profile

300 Fraser Purchase Rd.

Latrobe, PA 15650

Coach: Susan Hozak

Email: Shozak@stvincent.edu

NCAA I

Lady Bearcats, Green, Gold

Phone: (724) 539-9761

Fax: (724) 532-5050

Estimated # of Women's Volleyball Scholarships: 2

Conference: Keystone Empire

Program Profile: Our season is from August to November.

History: We began in 1985. We won NE Region Championship in 1994 when we competed in the NAIA National Championship Tournament. We have qualified for conference playoffs 10 of the 14 years. Our current play streak is 8 years. We competed in the Regional Championships in 1994 and 1997.

Achievements: WCA/NAIA NE Region Coach of the Year in 1994; Conference Coach of the Year in 1990, 1991, 1992 and 1994; 4 All-Americans in 1994; 12 NAIA National Scholar Athletes.

Coaching: Susan Hozak, became Head Coach in 1985. Her overall school and coaches record is 236-217. She played as a college student at Waynesburg College. Waynesburg team competed for 3 nation titles during her career. She graduated in 1983.

Freshman Receiving Financial Aid/Academic: **Athletic:** 4

Roster In State: 11   **Out of State:** 9   **Out of Country:** 0

Sophomores on Team: 5   **Seniors on Team:** 0   **Graduation %:** 100

Most Recent Record: 17-10-0   **Fall Games:** 27   **Spring Games:** 10

Style of Play: Quick offense, defensive and passing concentration.

Seton Hill College
Academic Profile

Seton Hill Drive

Greensburg, PA 15601

Phone: 800-826-6234

Type: Private, 4 Yr., Liberal Arts, Women

Website: http://www.setonhill.edu

SAT/ACT/GPA: 860

Student/Faculty Ratio: 13:1

Undergraduate Enrollment: N/A

Scholarships/Academic: Yes   **Athletic:** Yes

Expenses By: Year   **In State:** $ 18,200

Founded: 1926

Religion: Catholic

Housing: Yes

Male/Female: Women Only

Graduate Enrollment: N/A

Financial Aid: Yes

Out of State: $ 18,200

Degrees Conferred: BA, BS, BFA, BMus, BSMEdTech

Programs of Study: Accounting, Art, Art Therapy, Banking/Finance, BioChemistry, Biology, Business Administration, Chemistry, Communications, Computer Science, Design, Dramatics Arts, Economics, Education, English, Fine Arts, Food Production, French, History, International Business, Journalism, Management, Marketing, Mathematics, Medical Laboratory Technology, Music, Nursing, Personnel Management, Philosophy, Photography, Physics, Political Science, PreLaw, PreMed, Psychology, Religion, Theatre

Women's Athletic Profile

Seton Hill Drive, Box 287

Greensburg, PA 15601

Coach:

Email: fogle@setonhill.edu

NCAA I

Lady Spirit, Scarlet, Gold

Phone: (724) 838-4259

Fax: (724) 834-1296

Estimated # of Women's Volleyball Scholarships: 3

Conference: American Mideast Conference

Program Profile: The team plays a Fall season.

Achievements: 3 Appearances in National Tournament; Northeast Regional Coach of the Year three times.

Freshman Receiving Financial Aid/Academic: **Athletic:** 4

Roster In State: 10
Sophomores on Team: 0
Most Recent Record: 15-17-0
Positions Needed: Middle Hitter
Schedule: Walsh, Clarion, Houghton
Style of Play: Quick sets and short hits.

Out of State: 2
Seniors on Team: 3
Fall Games: 30

Out of Country: 0
Graduation %: 100
Spring Games: 0

Shippensburg University
Academic Profile

1871 Old Main Drive
Shippensburg, PA 17257

Phone: 800-822-8028

Type: Public, 4 Yr., Liberal Arts, Coed
Website: http://www.ship.edu
SAT/ACT/GPA: Open
Student/Faculty Ratio: 20:1
Undergraduate Enrollment: 5,600
Scholarships/Academic: Yes
Expenses By: Year

Athletic: Yes
In State: $ 8,358

Founded: 1871
Religion: Non-Affiliated
Housing: Yes
Male/Female: 1:1
Graduate Enrollment: 1,000
Financial Aid: Yes
Out of State: $ 13,714

Degrees Conferred: BA, BS, BSBA, Minors and Pre-Professional Options
Programs of Study: Art, Biology, Medical Technology, Chemistry, Communications/Journalism, English, French, Geography, Earth & Space Science, Public Administration, History, Mathematics, Mathematics/Computer Science, Physics, Applied Physics, Psychology, Sociology, Speech Communication, Accounting, Business Education, Office Administration, Management, Marketing, Criminal Justice, Social Work, Elementary Education, PreLaw, PreMed, PreDentistry, PrePharmacy

Women's Athletic Profile

1871 Old Main Drive
Shippensburg, PA 17257
Coach: Randall Hood
Email:

NCAA I
Lady Raiders, Red, Blue
Phone: (717) 532-1711
Fax: (717) 530-4045

Estimated # of Women's Volleyball Scholarships: N/A
Conference: Pennsylvania State Athletic Conference

Slippery Rock University of Pennsylvania
Academic Profile

102 Morrow Field House
Slippery Rock, PA 16057-1326

Phone: (724) 738-2946

Type: Public, 4 Yr., Liberal Arts, Coed
Website: http://www.sru.edu
SAT/ACT/GPA: 950/2.5
Student/Faculty Ratio: 25:1
Undergraduate Enrollment: 7,500
Scholarships/Academic: Yes
Expenses By: Year

Athletic: Yes
In State: $ 8,470

Founded: 1889
Religion: Non-Affiliated
Housing: Yes
Male/Female: 60:40
Graduate Enrollment: 750
Financial Aid: Yes
Out of State: $ 13,822

Degrees Conferred: BA, BS, MA, MBA, Doctorate in Physical Therapy
Programs of Study: Accounting, Anthropology, Art, Athletic Training, Biology, Business Administration, Chemistry, Communications, Community Health, Computer Science, CytoTechnology, Dance, Economics, Elementary Education, English, Environmental Education, Environmental Science, Environmental Studies, Exercise Science, Finance, French, Geography, Geology, German, Gerontology, Health Education, History, International Business, Management, Marketing, Mathematics, Medical Technology, Music, Music Education, Music Therapy, Nursing, Park and Resource Management, Physics, Political Science, PreDental, PreEngineering, PreLaw, Secondary Education, Sociology, Spanish, Special Education, Sports Management, Theatre, Therapeutic Recreation, Undeclared

Women's Athletic Profile

102 Morrow Field House
Slippery Rock, PA 16057
Coach: Laurie Lokash
Email: laureen.lokash@sru.edu

NCAA I
Lady Rockets, Green, White
Phone: (724) 738-2817
Fax: (724) 738-2626

Estimated # of Women's Volleyball Scholarships: Partial

Conference: Pennsylvania State Athletic Conference
Program Profile: Volleyball is played in Morrow Fieldhouse, season goes from the middle of August to late November. The court in the Fieldhouse is wood it has been in place only since this past fall.
History: The program began as a varsity sport in 1974, it has traditionally been one of the stronger programs in the Div.II Atlantic region.
Achievements: The team has won Conference titles in 1984, 1993. Qualified for the NCAA Tournament in 1993, 94, 2000.
Coaching: Laurie Lokash, graduated from Penn State Univ. in 1984, has been Head Coaching position since 1984.
Freshman Receiving Financial Aid/Academic: **Athletic:** 2
Roster In State: 9   **Out of State:** 5   **Out of Country:** 2
Sophomores on Team: **Seniors on Team:** 3   **Graduation %:** 95
Camp of Clinic Dates: July 20-22, July 22-26 2001
Positions Needed: Setter, Outside Hitter
Style of Play: The team is defensive oriented. Passing and aggressive serving are stressed. We usually run a 5-1 offense. The right side has been emphasized the past few years as a primary attacker. Defense is our main objective.

Susquehanna University
Academic Profile

514 Universtiy Ave.
Selinsgrove, PA 17870-1001

Phone: (570)372-4273

Type: Private, 4 Yr., Liberal Arts, Coed
Website: http://www.susqu.edu
SAT/ACT/GPA:
Student/Faculty Ratio: 14:1
Undergraduate Enrollment: 1,650
Scholarships/Academic: Yes
Expenses By: Year

Founded: 1858
Religion: Evangelical Lutheran
Housing: Yes
Male/Female: 750:900
Graduate Enrollment: N/A
Athletic: No   **Financial Aid:** Yes
In State: $ 26,200   **Out of State:**

Programs of Study: The School of Art & Science offers Biochemistry, Biology, Chemistry, Classics, Computer Science, Economics, Elementary Education, English, Environmental Science, French, GeoScience, German, Greek, History, Information Systems, International Studies, Latin, Mathematics, Philosophy, Physics, Political Science, Psychology, Religion, Sociology, And Spanish. The School of Fine Arts offers Art, Art History, Communications & Theatre Arts, Music, Church Music, Music Education, And Music Performance. The Sigmund Wels School of Business offers Accounting, Business Administration, and Economics.

Women's Athletic Profile

514 University Avenue
Selinsgrove, PA 17870
Coach: Bill Switala
Email:

NCAA I
Crusaders, Orange, Maroon
Phone: (717) 372-4080
Fax: (717) 372-2758

Estimated # of Women's Volleyball Scholarships: N/A
Conference: Middle Atlantic States Conference

Swarthmore College
Academic Profile

500 College Avenue
Swarthmore, PA 19081

Phone: 800-667-3110

Type: Private, 4 Yr., Liberal Arts, Coed
Website: http://www.swarthmore.edu
SAT/ACT/GPA: 1250/21
Student/Faculty Ratio: 10:1
Undergraduate Enrollment: 1,350
Scholarships/Academic: Yes
Expenses By: Year
Degrees Conferred: BA, BS

Founded: 1864
Religion: Quaker
Housing: Yes
Male/Female: 1:1
Graduate Enrollment: N/A
Athletic: No   **Financial Aid:** Yes
In State: $ 25,900   **Out of State:** $ 25,900

Programs of Study: Art, Art History, Asian Studies, Astronomy, AstroPhysics, Biology, Black Studies, Chemistry, Classics, Computer Science, Economics, Education, Engineering, English, Literature, History, International Relations, Mathematics, Medieval Studies, Modern Languages & Literature, Music & Dance, Philosophy, Physics, Political Science, Psychology, Public Policy, Religion, Sociology & Anthropology, Special Major, Theatre Studies, Women's Studies

Women's Athletic Profile

500 College Avenue
Swarthmore, PA 19081
Coach: Chang Han
Email:

NCAA I
Lady Garnet, Grey, White
Phone: (610) 328-8218
Fax: (610) 328-7798

Estimated # of Women's Volleyball Scholarships: N/A
Conference: Centennial Conference

Temple University
Academic Profile

Vivacqua Hall, PO Box 2842
Philadelphia, PA 19122

Phone: (215) 204-7445

Type: Public, 4 Yr., Coed
Website: http://www.temple.edu
SAT/ACT/GPA: 950/2.75
Student/Faculty Ratio: 25:1
Undergraduate Enrollment: 18,000
Scholarships/Academic: Yes   **Athletic:** Yes
Expenses By: Year   **In State:** $ 8,357

Founded: 1884
Religion: Non-Affiliated
Housing: Yes
Male/Female: 48:52
Graduate Enrollment: 11,000
Financial Aid: Yes
Out of State: $ 13,927

Specializes In: Medical, 12 undergraduate schools with several majors
Degrees Conferred: AAS, BA, BS, BBA, BFA, BArch, BSN, BSEE, MA, MS, MBA, Ph.D., JD
Programs of Study: Allied Health Professions: Tyler School of Arts, Business & Management, Communications, & Theatre, Education, Engineering, Health, Physical Education, Recreation & Dance, Ester Boyer College of Music, Pharmacy, Social Administration, Architecture, Landscape Architecture and Horticulture

Women's Athletic Profile

1700 N. Broad St., 4th Floor
Philadelphia, PA 19122
Coach: Robert Bertucci
Email:

NCAA I
Lady Owls, Cherry, White
Phone: (215) 204-7445
Fax: (215) 204-7449

Estimated # of Women's Volleyball Scholarships: 3
Conference: Atlantic 10 Conference
Program Profile: The Volleyball program is headed by Bob Bertucci, with Gilad Doron as Assistant Coach. We play our games in McGonigle Hall with a capacity of 3,900. Playing season lasts from September through December. The Apollo Classic is played in the Apollo of Temple.
History: Our volleyball program began in 1975 and we have had a total of 7 coaches since then.
Achievements: Atlantic 10 Conference Champions in 1997 & 1998; 2 NCAA first round Appearances in 1997 & 1998; Bob Bertucci was named Atlantic 10 Coach of the Year in 1997.
Coaching: Robert Bertucci, Head Coach, compiled a record of 444-226 overall. During his 4 years at Temple, he compiled an 85-31 record. . Bertucci was 1997 Atlantic Coach of the Year. He was GTE Academic All-American player. He won Heidi Lombardo in 1994 & 1996. Gilad Doron is the Assistant Coach.

Roster In State: 2   **Out of State:** 10   **Out of Country:** 3
Sophomores on Team: 5   **Seniors on Team:** 3   **Graduation %:** 90
Most Recent Record: 32-10-0   **Fall Games:** 22   **Spring Games:** 0
Camp of Clinic Dates: None
Schedule: Texas A & M, Ohio State, Idaho State, LSU, University of Houston, Loyola of Chicago

Thiel College
Academic Profile

75 College Avenue
Greenville, PA 16125-2181

Phone: 800-248-4435

Type: Private, 4 Yr., Liberal Arts, Coed
Website: http://www.theil.edu
SAT/ACT/GPA: Required
Student/Faculty Ratio: 12:1
Undergraduate Enrollment: 1,000
Scholarships/Academic: Yes   **Athletic:** No
Expenses By: Year   **In State:** $ 17,080

Founded: 1866
Religion: Lutheran
Housing: Yes
Male/Female: 48:52
Graduate Enrollment: N/A
Financial Aid: Yes
Out of State: $ 17,080

Degrees Conferred: BA, BSN, AA
Programs of Study: Allied Health, Art, Biology, Business Administration, Accounting, Economics, Chemistry, Communication Arts & Science, Education, Engineering, English, Environmental Science, Geography, Geology, Spanish, Nursing, Philosophy, Political Science, Psychology, Religion, PreProfessional Programs

Women's Athletic Profile

College Avenue
Greenville, PA 16125
Coach: JoAnn Gordan
Email: jagordan@thiel.edu

NCAA I
Lady Cats, Navy, Gold
Phone: (724) 589-2164
Fax: (724) 589-2880

Estimated # of Women's Volleyball Scholarships: N/A
Conference: President's Athletic Conference

University of Pennsylvania
Academic Profile

1 College Hall
Philadelphia, PA 19104-6376

Phone: (215) 898-7507

Type: Private, 4 Yr., Liberal Arts, Engineering, Coed
Website: http://www.upenn.edu
SAT/ACT/GPA: 1200/Top 10%
Student/Faculty Ratio: 7:1
Undergraduate Enrollment: 10,000
Scholarships/Academic: Yes   **Athletic:** No
Expenses By: Year   **In State:** $ 31,664

Founded: 1740
Religion: Non-Affiliated
Housing: Yes
Male/Female: 50:50
Graduate Enrollment: 8,000
Financial Aid: Yes
Out of State: $ 31,664

Specializes In: Business, Engineering, Liberal Arts, Nursing
Degrees Conferred: BA, BS, Various Master's and Ph.D. Programs
Programs of Study: Accounting, Anthropology, BioChemistry, BioEngineering, Chemistry, Communications, Computer Science, Economics, English, Environmental Studies, Finance, Fine Arts, Geology, History, Latin American Studies, Management, Marketing

Women's Athletic Profile

1 College Hall
Philadelphia, PA 19104
Coach: Kerry Major
Email: info@admissions.ugao.upenn.edu

NCAA I
Lady Quakers, Red, Blue
Phone: (215) 898-7507
Fax: (215) 573-2095

Estimated # of Women's Volleyball Scholarships: 0
Conference: Ivy League
Program Profile: Our fall season is approximately from August 26th to November 15th (regular season). In spring, we have 10 practices and 2 competition dates. Matches are held in the historic Palestra, which seats approximately 8,500 people and has been the site of numerous sporting contests. It remains one of the oldest active buildings in the nation.
History: We began in 1977 as a varsity program and captured the Ivy League Title in the inaugural year. We are five time Ivy League Champions and have placed in the Top Two during 13 of the past 21 years. Our overall record is 372-241.
Coaching: Kerry Major, Head Coach, first year record at Penn is 11-16. and his overall record is 54-46-3. He was head coach at the University of Alaska-Anchorage for 2 years, the Assistant Coach at UAA for 1 year and was on the coaching staff for 2 years at the University of Hawaii. Orlin Jespersen has been Assistant Coach for 1 year. He was on the coaching staff at Western Washington University.
Roster In State: 1   **Out of State:** 15   **Out of Country:** 0
Sophomores on Team: 1   **Seniors on Team:** 5   **Graduation %:** 100
Most Recent Record: 11-16-0
Positions Needed: None
Schedule: Cal State-Fullerton, Georgetown, Princeton, Brown, University of San Francisco, Villanova

University of Pittsburgh, The
Academic Profile

2nd Floor Bruce Hall
Pittsburgh, PA 15260

Phone: 412-624-7488

Type: Public, 4 Yr., Liberal Arts, Engineering, Coed
Website: http://www.pitt.edu

Founded: 1787
Religion: Non-Affiliated

SAT/ACT/GPA: 1230/24
Student/Faculty Ratio: 14:1
Undergraduate Enrollment: 14,200
Scholarships/Academic: Yes **Athletic:** Yes
Expenses By: Year **In State:** $ 12,588
Housing: Yes
Male/Female: 48:52
Graduate Enrollment: 9,075
Financial Aid: Yes
Out of State: $ 19,622
Degrees Conferred: BA, BS, BSE, MA, MS, MBA, MEd, MENG, Ph.D., EdP, PsyD
Programs of Study: Biological Science, Business, Communications and the Arts, Computer and Physical Science, Education, Engineering and Environmental Design, Health Profession, Social Science. Over 90 majors offered.

Women's Athletic Profile

P.O. Box 7436 Suite #225
Pittsburgh, PA 15213
Coach: Chris Beerman
Email: cbeerman@pitt.edu
Estimated # of Women's Volleyball Scholarships: 1 or 2
Conference: Big East Conference

NCAA I
Pittsburgh Panthers, Blue, Gold
Phone: (412) 648-8337
Fax: (412) 648-9177

Program Profile: Currently we are playing in the Fitzgerald Field House which is shared with the Women's and Men's Basketball, Gymnastic, and Wrestling teams. As of January 2002 Basketball will be moving to the new Peterson Event Center which will house the academic center as well as a new weight center. 2001 will mark a new football stadium which is shared with the Pittsburg Steelers. The Field House will become an all Volleyball complex as of 2002.
History: The University of Pittsburg started their program in 1974. It has appeared in 18 Big East Championships, 10 Big East Titles, and 9 NCAA tournaments.
Freshman Receiving Financial Aid/Academic: **Athletic:** 4
Roster In State: 2 **Out of State:** 8 **Out of Country:** 1
Sophomores on Team: **Seniors on Team:** 4 **Graduation %:** 100
Most Recent Record: 22-10
Camp of Clinic Dates: July 28-31 General Development Camp, Aug. 5 Youth Camp, Aug. 6-8 Specialty Camp
Positions Needed: Middles
Schedule: Michigan, Georgia Tech, Georgia, Fairfield, Notre Dame, BYU, Long Beach State, Georgetown, George Mason.

University of Pittsburgh - Bradford
Academic Profile

300 Campus Drive
Bradford, PA 16701-2898

Phone: (814) 362-7500

Type: Public, 4 Yr., Liberal Arts, Coed
Website: http://www.upb.pitt.edu
SAT/ACT/GPA: 950/20/2.0
Student/Faculty Ratio: 14:1
Undergraduate Enrollment: 1,400
Scholarships/Academic: Yes **Athletic:** No
Expenses By: Year **In State:** $ 10,535
Degrees Conferred: BA, BS
Founded: 1963
Religion: Non-Affiliated
Housing: Yes
Male/Female: 40:60
Graduate Enrollment: N/A
Financial Aid: Yes
Out of State: $ 10,535
Programs of Study: Accounting, Actuarial Science, Administration of Justice, American Studies, Anthropology, Biology, Business, Chemistry, Communications, Computer Science, Electrical, Industrial, Manufacturing, Mechanical, English, Environmental Geology, Gerontology, History, Human Relations, International Business, International Studies, Marketing, Mathematics, Nursing, Physical Science, Physical Therapy Preparation, Political Science, PreDental, PreLaw, PreMed, Psychology, Public Relations, Radio & Television, Secondary Education, Social Sciences, Sociology, Sport & Recreation Management, Sports Medicine/Athletic Training, Writing

Women's Athletic Profile

300 Campus Drive
Bradford, PA 16701
Coach: Fred Wallace
Email: mrq22@hotmail.com

NCAA I
Lady Panthers, Navy, Gold
Phone: (814) 362-7500
Fax: (814) 362-7578

Estimated # of Women's Volleyball Scholarships: N/A
Conference: AMCC
Program Profile: Our Allegheny Mountain Collegiate Conference program is on the rise. We finished 18-12 in the 1998 season. New facilities will open in 2000, with three courts, a weight room, etc. We play in the fall.
History: The program is 15 years old and has a strong background. In 1998, the team went 18-8 in NCAA III.
Achievements: 1998 Coach of the Year AMCC; Four Players All-Conference.

Coaching: Fred Wallace, Head Coach, started in 1998. In his first year, his record was 18-12 overall and 18-8 NCAA III. He has an all-time record of 116-59. He was named coach of the year in 1996 and 1998. Helen Hartney, Assistant Coach, is also entering her first year as an Assistant Coach.

Freshman Receiving Financial Aid/Academic: **Athletic:** 0

Roster In State: 11   **Out of State:** 0   **Out of Country:** 1

Sophomores on Team: 0   **Seniors on Team:** 1   **Graduation %:** 100

Most Recent Record: 18-12-0   **Fall Games:** 35   **Spring Games:** 15

Camp of Clinic Dates: July 19-22

Positions Needed: Middles , Right Side Hitters

Schedule: Ithaca, Frostburg State, Grove City, Penn State-Behrend

Style of Play: Fast paced with equal distribution to all attack areas.

University of Pittsburgh - Greensburg
Academic Profile

1150 Mt. Pleasant Rd   **Phone:** 724-836-9880
Greensburg, PA 15601-5898

Type: Public, 4 Yr., Coed   **Founded:** 1963
Website: http://www.pitt.edu   **Religion:** Non-Affiliated
SAT/ACT/GPA: 900   **Housing:** Yes
Student/Faculty Ratio: 18:1   **Male/Female:** 45:55
Undergraduate Enrollment: 1,500   **Graduate Enrollment:** N/A
Scholarships/Academic: Yes   **Athletic:** No   **Financial Aid:** Yes
Expenses By: Year   **In State:** $ 10,354   **Out of State:** $ 17,118
Degrees Conferred: BA, BS

Programs of Study: American Studies, Biology, Environmental Science, Accounting, Management, Communications, Criminology, English, Literature, English Writing, Humanities, Information Science, Mathematics, Natural Science, Political Science, Mathematics, Natural Science, Political Science, Psychology, Social Science, PreDental, PreLaw, PreMed, PrePhysical Therapy

Women's Athletic Profile

1150 Mt. Pleasant Rd.   **NCAA I**
Greensburg, PA 15601   Lady Bobcats, Navy, Gold
Coach: Frank VanAlstine   **Phone:** (724) 836-9449
Email: upgadmit@pitt.edu   **Fax:** (724) 836-7134

Estimated # of Women's Volleyball Scholarships: N/A

Conference: Allegheny Mountain Collegiate Conference

History: The program is in its fourth year of existence and has had steady improvement. Our team compiled a record of 5-19 in 1998.

Achievements: Clara Snyder was named Freshman All-Conference.

Coaching: Frank VanAlstine, started as Head Coach in 1998, with a record of 5-19. Nathan Kubistek Assistant Coach.

Roster In State: 9   **Out of State:** 0   **Out of Country:** 0

Sophomores on Team: 5   **Seniors on Team:**   **Graduation %:** Unknown

Most Recent Record: 5-19-0   **Fall Games:** 24   **Spring Games:** 0

Schedule: Frostburg State, Penn State- Behrend, Pitt-Bradford, Lake Erie, LaRoche, Penn State Altoona

Style of Play: Defense oriented.

University of Pittsburgh - Johnstown
Academic Profile

450 School House Road   **Phone:** 800-765-4875
Johnstown, PA 15904

Type: Public, 4 Yr., Liberal Arts, Engineering, Coed   **Founded:** 1927
Website: http://www.pitt.edu   **Religion:** Non-Affiliated
SAT/ACT/GPA: 900   **Housing:** Yes
Student/Faculty Ratio: 20:1   **Male/Female:** 1:1
Undergraduate Enrollment: 3,000   **Graduate Enrollment:** N/A
Scholarships/Academic: Yes   **Athletic:** Yes   **Financial Aid:** Yes
Expenses By: Year   **In State:** $ 9,300   **Out of State:** $ 15,000
Degrees Conferred: BA, BS, M.Ed.

Programs of Study: Accounting, Biology, Business & Management, Chemistry, Communications, Computer Science, Creative Writing, Ecology, Economics, Education, Engineering, English, Finance, Geography, Geology, History, Humanities, Journalism, Literature, Mathematics, Medical Laboratory Technology, Natural Science, Political Science, PreDental, PreLaw, PreMed, PreVet, Psychology, Respiratory Therapy, Social Science, Theatre

Women's Athletic Profile

Schoolhouse Rd
Johnstown, PA 15904-2990
Coach: Clyde Horner
Email:

NCAA I
Lady Cats, Blue, Gold
Phone: (814) 269-7174
Fax: (814) 269-2026

Estimated # of Women's Volleyball Scholarships: N/A
Conference: Independent
Program Profile: Sports Center (2,400), Season runs from Sept-Oct.
History: Began in 1976. Program record is 344-217, current coach 12 of past 13 years record 234-119

Roster In State: 15	**Out of State:** 0	**Out of Country:** 0
Sophomores on Team:	**Seniors on Team:** 0	**Graduation %:** 90

Most Recent Record: 19-14
Camp of Clinic Dates: July 22-26, 2001
Positions Needed: DS, S
Schedule: St. Vincent, Haverford, West Liberty, Lebanon Valley
Style of Play: Quick Offense.

University of Scranton
Academic Profile

Linden Street
Scranton, PA 18510

Phone: 570-941-7540

Type: Private, 4 Yr., Coed
Website: http://www.uofs.edu
SAT/ACT/GPA: Open
Student/Faculty Ratio: 17:1
Undergraduate Enrollment: 3,200
Scholarships/Academic: Yes
Expenses By: Year

Athletic: No
In State: $ 23,000

Founded: 1888
Religion: Jesuit
Housing: Yes
Male/Female: 45:55
Graduate Enrollment: 250
Financial Aid: Yes
Out of State: $ 23,000

Degrees Conferred: AA, AS, BA, BS, MA, MS, MBA
Programs of Study: Accounting, Advertising, BioChemistry, Biology, BioPhysics, Broadcasting, Business, Chemistry, Classics, Communications, Computer Information System, Computer Science, Criminal Justice, Economics, Education, Engineering, English, Finance, French, German, Gerontology, History, Journalism, Marketing, Mathematics, Political Science, PreLaw, PreMed, PreVet, Psychology, Religion, Social Science, Theology

Women's Athletic Profile

John Long Center
Scranton, PA 18510
Coach: Kristin Maile
Email: mailek1@tiger.uofs.edu

NCAA I
Lady Royals, Purple, White
Phone: (717) 941-4050
Fax: (717) 941-4223

Estimated # of Women's Volleyball Scholarships: N/A
Conference: Middle Atlantic States Conference

Ursinus College
Academic Profile

Main Street, P.O. Box 1000
Collegeville, PA 19426

Phone: 610-409-3200

Type: Private, 4 Yr., Liberal Arts, Coed
Website: http://www.ursinus.edu
SAT/ACT/GPA: 1200
Student/Faculty Ratio: 12:1

Founded: 1869
Religion: United Church of Christ
Housing: Yes
Male/Female: 50:50

Undergraduate Enrollment: 1,200　　　　　　　　　　　　　　**Graduate Enrollment:** N/A
Scholarships/Academic: Yes　　　　**Athletic:** No　　**Financial Aid:** Yes
Expenses By: Year　　　　**In State:** $ 24,400　　**Out of State:** $ 24,400
Degrees Conferred: BA, BS
Programs of Study: Biology, Chemistry, Economics & Business, Exercise & Sports Science, English, History, Politics, International Relations, Psychology, French, German, Spanish, Japanese, Philosophy, Religion, Computer Science, Mathematics, Physics, PreMed, PreLaw, Education, PreEngineering

Women's Athletic Profile

Main Street
Collegeville, PA 19426
Coach: Lisa Ortlip-Cornish
Email: lcornish@acad.ursinus.edu

NCAA I
Lady Bears, Red, Gold, Black
Phone: (610) 409-3606
Fax: (610) 409-3620

Estimated # of Women's Volleyball Scholarships: N/A
Conference: Centennial Conference
Program Profile: We play at Helfferich Hall, which was built in 1972 and has a seating capacity of 1,600. Our playing season starts from August through November.
History: Our program began in 1974. Our 1998 season set a record for the most wins with 14.
Coaching: Lisa Ortlip, Head Coach, started with the program in 1995 and compiled a record of 36-19. She graduated from Villanova in 1982 and in 1981 named Whelan and Whelan Player of the Year. Phil Landis is the Assistant Coach, joined the program in 1995. He graduated from Ursinus in 1997.
Freshman Receiving Financial Aid/Academic:　　　　　　　**Athletic:** 0
Roster In State: 9　　　　**Out of State:** 6　　**Out of Country:** 0
Sophomores on Team: 2　　**Seniors on Team:** 3　　**Graduation %:** 100
Most Recent Record: 14-15-0　　**Fall Games:** 27　　**Spring Games:** 1-2
Camp of Clinic Dates: Unavailable at this time
Positions Needed: 4 Middle Hitters
Schedule: Gettysburg, Franklin & Marshall, Hood College, Allentown, Kean University, Delaware Valley
Style of Play: We play aggressive defensive.

Villanova University
Academic Profile

800 Lancaster Avenue
Villanova, PA 19085

Phone: (610) 519-4135

Type: Private, 4 Yr., Engineering, Coed　　　　　　　**Founded:** 1847
Website: http://www.villanova.com　　　　　　　**Religion:** Catholic-Augustinian
SAT/ACT/GPA: 1180-1340/27-29/3.46-3.91　　　**Housing:** Yes
Student/Faculty Ratio: 13:1　　　　　　　　　　**Male/Female:** 1:1
Undergraduate Enrollment: 6,039　　　　　　　**Graduate Enrollment:** 3,623
Scholarships/Academic: Yes　　**Athletic:** Yes　　**Financial Aid:** Yes
Expenses By: Year　　**In State:** $ 28,120　　**Out of State:** $ 28,120
Specializes In: Commerce & Finance, Engineering, Liberal Arts & Sciences, Nursing
Degrees Conferred: AA, AS, BA, BS, MA, MS, MBA, Ph.D., JD
Programs of Study: Art History, Astronomy, Classical Studies, Communications, Computer Science, Criminal Justice, Economics, Education, Engineering, English, Finance, French, Geography, German, History, Honors Program, Humanities, Human Services, Interdisciplinary Studies, International Business, Liberal Arts, Marketing, Meteorology, Military Science, Natural Science, Naval Science, Nursing, Philosophy, Physics, Political Science, PreDental, PreLaw, PreMed, PreVet, Psychology, Religion, Social Science, Spanish, Special Education

Women's Athletic Profile

800 Lancaster Rd.
Villanova, PA 19085
Coach: Allison Keely
Email:

NCAA I
Lady Wildcats, Blue, White
Phone: (610) 519-4137
Fax: (610) 519-7987

Estimated # of Women's Volleyball Scholarships: N/A
Conference: Big East Conference

Washington and Jefferson College
Academic Profile

60 South Lincoln Street
Washington, PA 15301

Phone: (724) 223-5251

Type: Private, 4 Yr., Liberal Arts, Coed
Website: http://www.washjeff.edu
SAT/ACT/GPA: 1000/20/Upper 1/3
Student/Faculty Ratio: 12:1
Undergraduate Enrollment: 1,200
Scholarships/Academic: Yes
Expenses By: Year
Specializes In: Pre-Med, Pre-Law, Business
Degrees Conferred: BA, Liberal Arts College

Athletic: No
In State: $23,950

Founded: 1787
Religion: Presbyterian
Housing: Yes
Male/Female: 50:50
Graduate Enrollment: N/A
Financial Aid: Yes
Out of State: $23,950

Programs of Study: Accounting, Art, Biology, Business Administration, Chemistry, Economics, Education, English, French, German, History, Human Resources Management, Physics, Philosophy, Political Science, Psychology, Sociology, PreLaw, PreMed, PreDentistry,

Women's Athletic Profile

Lincoln Street
Washington, PA 15301
Coach: Vicki Staton
Email: vstaton@washjeff.edu

NCAA I
Lady Presidents, Red, Black
Phone: (724) 223-6058
Fax: (724) 250-3329

Estimated # of Women's Volleyball Scholarships: N/A
Conference: President's Athletic Conference
Program Profile: Playing season is in the Fall. The Lady Presidents play in Henry Memorial Gymnasium which has wood floors, Olympic swimming pool, weight rooms, aerobic room, locker rooms and training room.
History: Program began in 1974. We have won 5 Conference Championships and 2 ECA South Division III Championships.
Achievements: Conference Titles- 1999, 1998, 1997, 1996, 1994. Coach of the Year- 1998, 1997, 1994, 1993
Coaching: Head Coach, Vicki Staton. Assistant Coach, Tedd Starkey.

Roster In State: 11
Seniors on Team: 0
Most Recent Record: 10-24-0

Out of State: 3
Graduation %: 100

Out of Country: 0

Schedule: Westminster, Grove City, Ohio Wesleyan, Allegheny, Carnegie Mellon
Style of Play: Usually play a 5-1 offense with a fast and quick style of play.

Waynesburg College
Academic Profile

College Avenue
Waynesburg, PA 15370

Phone: 800-225-7393

Type: Private, 4 Yr., Liberal Arts, Coed
Website: http://www.waynesburg.edu
SAT/ACT/GPA: Open
Student/Faculty Ratio: 16:1
Undergraduate Enrollment: 1,133
Scholarships/Academic: Yes
Expenses By: Year
Degrees Conferred: AA, AS, BA, BSN, BSBA

Athletic: No
In State: $ 15,400

Founded: 1849
Religion: Presbyterian
Housing: No
Male/Female: 47:53
Graduate Enrollment: N/A
Financial Aid: Yes
Out of State: $ 15,400

Programs of Study: Accounting, Advertising, Art, Biology, Business Administration, Chemistry, Commercial Art, Computer Science, Criminal Justice, Economics, Electronic Media, Elementary Education, English, Finance, Health Care, History, Literature, Management, Marketing, Mathematics, Medical Laboratory Technology, Nursing, Political Science, PreDental, PreLaw, PreMed, Professional Writing, Psychology, Public Administration, Secondary Education, Social Science, Sociology, Sport Broadcasting & Information, Sport Medicine, Visual Communications

Women's Athletic Profile

College Avenue
Waynesburg, PA 15370
Coach: Pat Roth
Email: proth@waynesburg.edu

NCAA I
Yellow Jackets, Orange, Black
Phone: (724) 852-3437
Fax: (724) 852-4122

Estimated # of Women's Volleyball Scholarships: N/A
Conference: President's Athletic Conference

West Chester University
Academic Profile

PE Center Room 205
West Chester, PA 19383

Phone: 877-315-2165

Type: Public, 4 Yr., Coed
Website: http://www.wcupa.edu
SAT/ACT/GPA: 840+
Student/Faculty Ratio: 19:1
Undergraduate Enrollment: 9,400
Scholarships/Academic: Yes
Expenses By: Year

Athletic: Yes
In State: $ 8,000

Founded: 1871
Religion: Non-Affiliated
Housing: No
Male/Female: 39:61
Graduate Enrollment: 1,900
Financial Aid: Yes
Out of State: $ 11,900

Degrees Conferred: AA, AS, BA, BS, BFA, MS, MBA, M.Ed.
Programs of Study: Accounting, Biology, Astronomy, Anthropology, Athletic Training, BioChemistry, Biological Science, Business, Cell Biology, Chemistry, Communications, Computer Science, Computer Information Systems, Creative Writing, Criminal Justice, Ecology, Earth Science, Education, English, Fine Arts, Forensic Studies, GeoChemistry, International Studies, Liberal Arts, Marketing, Mathematics, MicroBiology, Music, Natural Science, Nursing, Philosophy, Physical Education, Physics, Political Science, PreDental, PreLaw, PreMed, PreVet, Psychology, Public Health, Religion, Science, Social Science, Space Science, Spanish, Special Education, Speech, Speech Pathology, Speech Therapy, Sports Medicine, Theatre

Women's Athletic Profile

Health & PE Center, Rm 205
West Chester, PA 19383
Coach: Kim Happold
Email: khappold@hotmail.com

NCAA I
Lady Rams, Purple, Gold
Phone: (610) 436-3237
Fax: (610) 436-1020

Estimated # of Women's Volleyball Scholarships: N/A
Conference: Pennsylvania State Athletic Conference
Sophomores on Team: 3
Most Recent Record: 12-10
Schedule: Millersville, Cheyney, East Stroudsburg, Shippensburg, Kutztown, Wilmington

Seniors on Team: 1

Westminster College - Pennsylvania
Academic Profile

South Market Street
New Wilmington, PA 16172

Phone: 724-946-7100

Type: Private, 4 Yr., Liberal Arts, Engineering, Coed
Website: http://www.westminster.edu
SAT/ACT/GPA: 840/23/2.5
Student/Faculty Ratio: 14:1
Undergraduate Enrollment: 1,700
Scholarships/Academic: Yes
Expenses By: Year

Athletic: Yes
In State: $ 20,000

Founded: 1852
Religion: Presbyterian
Housing: Yes
Male/Female: 1:6
Graduate Enrollment: 100
Financial Aid: Yes
Out of State: $ 20,000

Specializes In: Preprofessional Programs, Business, Education
Degrees Conferred: BA, BS, B.Mus., MBA, M.Ed., MS
Programs of Study: Accounting, Art, Biology, Broadcasting, Communication, Business Administration, Chemistry, Computer Information System, Computer Science, Economics, Elementary Education, Environmental Science, Management, Political Science, Religion, Philosophy, Physics, PreLaw, PreMed, Psychology

Women's Athletic Profile

Athletic Dept.
New Wilmington, PA 16172
Coach: Tammy Swearingen
Email: swearintl@westminster.edu

NCAA I
Lady Titans, Navy Blue, White
Phone: (724) 946-7320
Fax: (724) 946-7041

Estimated # of Women's Volleyball Scholarships: 0
Conference: President's Athletic Conference
Program Profile: Team is transitioning from NCAA II to NCAA III. Facilities are being up graded with additional locker rooms and a

new 8 lane all-weather track. Gymnasium has a very nice wood floor.

History: Began in 1976 and was coached by Marjorie Walker until 1983. Team Competed NAIA and was taken over by Tammy Swearingen. The college moves from NAIA to NCAA II without additional financial aid. After hiring a new President the college was again moved to NCAA III with the 2002-2003 academic year being the first year that Westminster will be in full compliance with all D III.

Achievements: Tammy Swearingen, Coach of the Year 94-97. Conference Champs 94-97. Regional Champs 1997, NAIA Nationals 1997, 2 NAIA All-Americans 96, 97

Freshman Receiving Financial Aid/Academic: | | **Athletic:** 0
Roster In State: 1 | **Out of State:** 13 | **Out of Country:** 0
Sophomores on Team: | **Seniors on Team:** 3 | **Graduation %:** 100
Most Recent Record: 27-7-0
Camp of Clinic Dates: June 30- July 3, July 5-8
Positions Needed: DS, MH, OH
Style of Play: Aggressive defense with transition to fast pace offense

Widener University
Academic Profile

One University Place
Chester, PA 19013-5792

Phone: 888-943-3637

Type: Private, 4 Yr., Liberal Arts, Coed
Website: http://www.widener.edu
SAT/ACT/GPA: 800/18
Student/Faculty Ratio: 12:1
Undergraduate Enrollment: 2,400
Scholarships/Academic: Yes
Expenses By: Year
Founded: 1821
Religion: Non-Affiliated
Housing: Yes
Male/Female: 1:1.2
Graduate Enrollment: 2,100
Athletic: No | **Financial Aid:** Yes
In State: $ 21,800 | **Out of State:** $ 21,800

Degrees Conferred: AAS, BA, BS, MA, MS, MBA, MED, EdD, JD
Programs of Study: Business Administration, Engineering, Hospitality Management, Nursing, Human Services, Arts & Science, School of Law, Criminal Justice, Communications Studies, Physical Therapy, Physics, Psychology, Biology, Chemistry, Computer Science, Mathematics, Education, Economics

Women's Athletic Profile

One University Place
Chester, PA 19013
Coach: Diana Felker
Email: diana.m.felker@widener.edu

NCAA I
Lady Pioneers, Blue, Gold
Phone: (610) 499-4571
Fax: (610) 499-4481

Estimated # of Women's Volleyball Scholarships: N/A
Conference: Middle Atlantic States Conference
Program Profile: Large gym, wood floor, regular season from mid-Aug to end of Oct. Spring Training from Feb-April. Looking to take program to the National level. Off season consists of weight training, conditioning and VB training.
History: Began in 1982. Joined the MAC Conference in 1984. Best finish to date is 4th in 1999.
Coaching: 1st year coach at Widener, was Assistant Coach for UNC-Chapel Hill.
Roster In State: 7 | **Out of State:** 7 | **Out of Country:** 0
Seniors on Team: 2 | **Graduation %:** 100
Most Recent Record: 13-11-0
Positions Needed: MB,OH
Schedule: Juniata, Gettysburg, Haverford, Franklin & Marshall
Style of Play: Very skills oriented program. Emphasizing a lot of defense and quick transition on offense very energetic team, plays with emotion and hard working.

Wilkes University
Academic Profile

Box 111
Wilkes - Barre, PA 18766

Phone: 570-408-4400

Type: Private, 4 Yr., Liberal Arts, Engineering, Coed
Website: http://www.wilkes.edu
SAT/ACT/GPA: 950
Student/Faculty Ratio: 13:1
Undergraduate Enrollment: 1,780
Founded: 1933
Religion: Non-Affiliated
Housing: Yes
Male/Female: 1:1
Graduate Enrollment: N/A

Scholarships/Academic: Yes   **Athletic:** No   **Financial Aid:** Yes

Expenses By: Year   **In State:** $ 19,000   **Out of State:** $ 19,000

Degrees Conferred: BA, BS, MS, MA, Ph.D.

Programs of Study: Business & Management, Communication, Engineering, Health Sciences, Life Sciences, Psychology, Social Sciences

Women's Athletic Profile

P.O. Box 111
Wilkes-Barre, PA 18766
Coach: Mike Grandchamp
Email:

NCAA I
Lady Colonels, Navy, Gold
Phone: (570) 408-4031
Fax: (570) 823-9470

Estimated # of Women's Volleyball Scholarships: 0

Conference: Freedom Conference

Program Profile: Wilkes plays in the 3,500 seat Marts Center. Last season the Lady Colonels advanced to the Middle Atlantic Conference playoffs under first-year Head Coach Mike Grandchamp. The middle Atlantic Conference is the largest Division III conference in the country, and includes volleyball powers Juniata College, Moravian College and the University of Scranton. The schedule includes approximately 30 matches, including three tournaments.

History: This season marks the 26th year of varsity women's volleyball at Wilkes. Wilkes has had 18 players earn all-conference honors during that span, including one league MVP.

Coaching: Mike Grandchamp is in his second season as Head Coach of the Wilkes Women's volleyball program. A graduate of the University of Scranton, Mike served as an assistant coach there while also playing on the school's competitive men's club team. He is also a former All-American wrestler at Scranton, earning that honor during the 1998-99 season.

Freshman Receiving Financial Aid/Academic: **Athletic:** 0

Roster In State: 11   **Out of State:** 3   **Seniors on Team:** 2

Most Recent Record: 5-11

Positions Needed: Setter, Middle hitter, Outside hitter.

Schedule: New York University, University of Scranton, Eastern College, King's College, Allentown College, Lycoming College, Baptist Bible College, Muhlenberg College, Dickinson College.

Wilson College
Academic Profile

1015 Philadelphia Ave.
Chambersburg, PA 17201

Phone: (800) 421-8402

Type: Private, 4 Yr., Liberal Arts, Women   **Founded:** 1869

Website: http://www.wilson.edu   **Religion:** Presbyterian

SAT/ACT/GPA: 900/19/2.7   **Housing:** Yes

Student/Faculty Ratio: 10:1   **Male/Female:** Women Only

Undergraduate Enrollment: 300   **Graduate Enrollment:** N/A

Scholarships/Academic: Yes   **Athletic:** No   **Financial Aid:** Yes

Expenses By: Year   **In State:** $ 20,340   **Out of State:** $ 20,340

Specializes In: Liberal Arts

Degrees Conferred: BA, BS

Programs of Study: Accounting, Behavioral Science, Biology, Business and Economics, Chemistry, Criminal Justice, Economics & Finance, Education, English, Engineering Management, Environmental Studies, Equestrian Studies, Fine Arts, Foreign Languages, General Business, Graphics Design, Health Information Management, History, Humanities, Information Systems, International Studies, Latin American Studies, Legal Studies, Marketing, Management, Mass Communications, Mathematics, Mechanical Engineering, Music Education, Nuclear Medical Technology, Nursing, Physical Sciences, Philosophy and Religion, Political Science, Psychology, Sociology, Veterinary, Medical Technology

Women's Athletic Profile

1015 Philadelphia Avenue
Chambersburg, PA 17201
Coach: Kathy Murray
Email: admissions@wilson.edu

NCAA I
Lady Phoenix, Blue, White
Phone: (800) 421-8402
Fax: (717) 264-1578

Estimated # of Women's Volleyball Scholarships: 0

Conference: Atlantic Women's Colleges Conference

History: We are in our second year with NCAA.

Roster In State: 5   **Out of State:** 3   **Out of Country:** 0

Sophomores on Team: 3
Most Recent Record: 3-18-0
Camp of Clinic Dates: None
Positions Needed: Middle Hitter, Setter
Schedule: Frostburg, Hood College, College of Notre Dame at Maryland, Chatham College, Mary Baldwin College, Rosemont

Seniors on Team: 0
Fall Games: 21

Graduation %: Unknown
Spring Games: 0

York College - Pennsylvania
Academic Profile

Country Club Road
York, PA 17405-7199

Phone: 800-455-8018

Type: Private, 4 Yr., Liberal Arts, Engineering, Coed
Website: http://www.ycp.edu
SAT/ACT/GPA: 970/21
Student/Faculty Ratio: 18:1
Undergraduate Enrollment: 3,300
Scholarships/Academic: Yes   **Athletic:** No
Expenses By: Year   **In State:** $ 9,980
Degrees Conferred: BA, BS
Programs of Study: Contact school for program of study.

Founded: 1941
Religion: Non-Affiliated
Housing: Yes
Male/Female: 40:60
Graduate Enrollment: N/A
Financial Aid: Yes
Out of State: $ 9,980

Women's Athletic Profile

Country Club Rd
York, PA 17405
Coach: Sue Dumars
Email: sdumars@ycp.edu

NCAA I
Lady Spartans, Green, White
Phone: (717) 815-1770
Fax: (7170 849-1626

Estimated # of Women's Volleyball Scholarships: N/A
Conference: Capital Athletic Conference
Achievements: 1997 CAC Champions, NCAA Berth and Coach of the Year (CAC)
Coaching: Sue Dumars, Head Coach coached at Loyola College (MD) 1990-93, 2 time MAAC Champions. Assistant Coach, Kristin Hershey.
Freshman Receiving Financial Aid/Academic: **Athletic:** 0
Roster In State: 5   **Out of State:** 5   **Out of Country:** 0
Most Recent Record: 8-28-0
Positions Needed: OH, DS
Schedule: Juniata, Franklin & Marshall, Richard Stiockton, Elmira, Salisbury

RHODE ISLAND

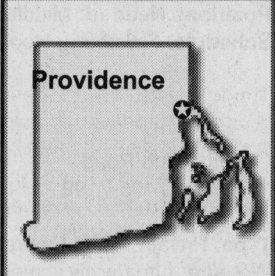

Providence

SCHOOL	CITY	AFFILIATION	PAGE
Brown University	Providence	NCAA I	672
Bryant College	Smithfield	NCAA II	672
Johnson & Wales University	Providence	NCAA III	673
Providence College	Providence	NCAA I	674
Rhode Island College	Providence	NCAA III	674
Roger Williams University	Bristol	NCAA III	675
University of Rhode Island	Kingston	NCAA I	676

Brown University
Academic Profile

P. O. Box 1932
Providence, RI 02912

Phone: (401) 863-2910

Type: Private, 4 Yr., Liberal Arts, Engineering, Coed
Website: http://www.brownbears.com
SAT/ACT/GPA: 580-680v, 640-750m
Student/Faculty Ratio: 8:1
Undergraduate Enrollment: 5,500
Scholarships/Academic: Yes   **Athletic:** No
Expenses By: Year   **In State:** $ 26,000
Specializes In: No specific course requirement outside of concentration
Degrees Conferred: BS, BA, MA, MS, MFA, Ph.D., MD

Founded: 1764
Religion: Non-Affiliated
Housing: Yes
Male/Female: 1:1
Graduate Enrollment: 1,600
Financial Aid: Yes
Out of State: $ 26,000

Programs of Study: Art, Behavioral Science, Biology, BioMedical Sciences, BioPhysics, Chemistry, Cognitive Science, Comparative Literature, Creative Writing, Electrical, Materials, Computer, Geology, GeoPhysics, NeuroScience, Religion, Theatre, Women's Studies

Women's Athletic Profile

P. O. Box 1932
Providence, RI 02912
Coach: Diane Short
Email: Diane_Short@brown.edu

NCAA I
Lady Bears, Brown, White, Red
Phone: (401) 863-7418
Fax: (401) 863-1436

Estimated # of Women's Volleyball Scholarships: N/A
Conference: Ivy Group
Program Profile: The Paul Bailey Pizzitola Memorial Sports Center was opened in 1989. It has a sports facility equal to any muti-purpose athletic facility in the Ivy League. It has a bleacher and balcony seating for 2,800 spectators. Other features include: four tennis courts, a fabric roof, a weight room, squash courts and separate rooms for wrestling and gymnastics.
History: We started in 1974. We have won two League Championships in the last three years. We won the League Championship and competed at the NCAA in 1996 and 1998.
Achievements: Last year, Brown Volleyball had the Ivy League Rookie of the Year and the Player of the Year. Brown also had a District One Academic All-American.
Coaching: Diane Short, Head Coach, has been coach for six years. She has guided the team to two Ivy League Championships and two NCAA Appearances.
Roster In State: 0   **Out of State:** 12   **Out of Country:** 1
Sophomores on Team: 2   **Seniors on Team:** 1   **Graduation %:** Unknown
Most Recent Record: 22-9-0   **Fall Games:** 31   **Spring Games:** 0
Camp of Clinic Dates: July 18-22
Positions Needed: Swing Hitter, Outside Hitter, Setter
Schedule: Loyola Marymount, George Washington, University of Rhode Island, University of Connecticut, University of Massachusetts, Rutgers
Style of Play: We have excellent defense and ball control. We are fighters and our team does not give up.

Bryant College
Academic Profile

1150 Douglas Pike
Smithfield, RI 02917-1284

Phone: 800-622-7001

Type: Private, 4 Yr., Liberal Arts, Coed
Website: http://www.bryant.edu
SAT/ACT/GPA: 820
Student/Faculty Ratio: 20:1
Undergraduate Enrollment: 2,300
Scholarships/Academic: Yes   **Athletic:** Yes
Expenses By: Year   **In State:** $ 18,500
Specializes In: Business
Degrees Conferred: AS, BA, BS, MS, MBA

Founded: 1863
Religion: Non-Affiliated
Housing: Yes
Male/Female: 1:1
Graduate Enrollment: 700
Financial Aid: Yes
Out of State: $ 18,500

Programs of Study: Accounting, Actuarial Science, Business Administration, Communications, Computer Information System, Economics, English, Finance, History, Information Science, International Studies, Management, Marketing

Women's Athletic Profile

1150 Douglas Pike
Smithfield, RI 02917
Coach: Theresa Garlacy
Email: tgarlacy@bryant.edu

NCAA I
Bulldogs, Black, Gold, White
Phone: (401) 232-6070
Fax: (401) 232-6361

Estimated # of Women's Volleyball Scholarships: 0
Conference: Northeast-10 Conference
Program Profile: We play at Bryant Gymnasium. It has three beautiful hardwood courts. There are 2,400 seats surrounding the center court. The Jarvis Fitness Center is equipped with the latest cardiovascular and strength equipment and a new aerobics room. A weight room will be open this fall. There will be 5,000 square feet of the newest in free weights and King machines. We play a fall season and a limited spring season.
History: Our program began in 1977. We had 2 NCAA bids in the past five years and three Conference Championships.
Achievements: Appearance at the 1997 NCAA Division II Tournament; 3 Conference Titles, 2 Eastern College Athletic Conference Titles.
Coaching: Theresa Garlacy, Head Coach, won the Northeast-10 Coach of the Year Award in just her second season as Bryant's head volleyball coach. Ted Garlacy is Assistant Coach.

Roster In State: 2	**Out of State:** 12	**Out of Country:** 0
Sophomores on Team: 0	**Seniors on Team:** 0	**Graduation %:** 100
Most Recent Record: 30-13-0	**Fall Games:** 37	**Spring Games:** TBA

Schedule: Pace, Bentley, Dawling, New Haven, Carson-Newman, Wingate-NC
Style of Play: Bright and exciting.

Johnson & Wales University
Academic Profile

8 Abbott Park Place
Providence, RI 02903

Phone: (800) 342-5598 x1614

Type: Private, 4 Yr., Coed
Website: http://www.jwu.edu
SAT/ACT/GPA: None/2.3 or higher
Student/Faculty Ratio: 1:25
Undergraduate Enrollment: 7,500
Scholarships/Academic: Yes   **Athletic:** No
Expenses By: Year   **In State:** $ 18,000

Founded: 1914
Religion: Non-Affiliated
Housing: Yes
Male/Female: 51:49
Graduate Enrollment: 2,000
Financial Aid: Yes
Out of State: $ 18,000

Degrees Conferred: As, BS, MS, MBA, Ph.D.
Programs of Study: Culinary Arts, Business, Criminal Justice, Hospitality, Marketing/Accounting Technology, Recreation/Leisure Management, Hotel/Restaurant Management, Travel & Tourism

Men's Athletic Profile

8 Abbott Park Place
Providence, RI 02903
Coach: Paul Amaral
Email: rbachman@jwu.edu

NCAA III
Wildcats/Scarlet, Royal, Gold
Phone: (401) 598-1000
Fax: (401) 598-4641

Estimated # of Men's Volleyball Scholarships: N/A
Conference: Independent
Program Profile: Volleyball is used to enhance and foster the process in the pursuit of excellence and success in the student-athlete both academically and athletically. We have a new $7 million facility. It has hardwood floors and 3 courts that can accommodate 1,500 fans.
History: We began in 1997. This is our 2nd year and we are building a nucleus of players that should make us a constant contender for the NECUA Championship within two years. Our ultimate goal is to be Division III national champs.
Achievements: 1996 RI Class B Coach of the Year; 1994 Class C Girls Champions
Coaching: The year 1997 was coach Amaral's first year. His record was 5-19.

Freshman Receiving Financial Aid/Academic: 7   **Athletic:** 0

Roster In State: 2	**Out of State:** 9	**Out of Country:** 1
Most Recent Record: 4-7	**Fall Games:** 6	**Spring Games:** 22

Positions Needed: all
Schedule: Roger Williams Universtiy, Sacred Heart University, D'Youville, Springfield College, Mount Saint Vincent, Kings Point/Merchant Marine
Style of Play: Ouick, multifaceted offense in which the players have freedom to be creative. An excellent work ethic is a must so as to challenge players to get out of their comfort zone.

Women's Athletic Profile

8 Abbott Park Place
Providence, RI 02903
Coach: Jamie Murray
Email: jmurray@jwu.edu

NCAA I
Wildcats, Burgundy, Blue, White
Phone: (401) 598-1194
Fax: (401) 598-1465

Estimated # of Women's Volleyball Scholarships: N/A
Conference: The Great Northeast Athletic Conference
Program Profile: Play in brand new Harborside Recreation Center. Max capacity 1500. In it's 4th year of NCAA conference runners-up last 2 years. Season begins end of Aug-mid November
History: Program began in 1994 and became official NCAA in 1996 since 96 have compiled a record of 53-24. Placed 2nd in conference championships 2 yrs in row.
Achievements: Conference runner up 97,98. Player of the Year 98, Rookie of Year 97. All-Conference player 96,97,98
Coaching: Murray, 53-24, played 4yrs RIC-Cptn 2 yrs, NEWVA-All star selection 92 Schulle, 19-11, played 3 yrs RIC-Cptn, NEWVA All star selection 91.

Roster In State: 1	**Out of State:** 1	**Out of Country:**
Sophomores on Team:	**Seniors on Team:** 5	**Graduation %:** 99
Most Recent Record: 19-11	**Fall Games:** 22	**Spring Games:** 4

Positions Needed: Middle hitters, Outside hitters
Schedule: Eastern Conn. State Univ. Spring field College, Tufts, Connecticut College, Bridewater State, US Coast Guard Academy
Style of Play: Consistent and Aggressive.

Providence College
Academic Profile

PC 222 Hawkins Hall
Providence, RI 02918

Phone: 800-721-6444

Type: Private, 4 Yr., Liberal Arts, Coed
Website: http://www.providence.edu
SAT/ACT/GPA: 1200
Student/Faculty Ratio: 13:1
Undergraduate Enrollment: 3,800
Scholarships/Academic: Yes
Expenses By: $24,600
Degrees Conferred: BA, BS, MBA, MA, MS

Founded: 1917
Religion: Catholic (Dominican)
Housing: Yes
Male/Female: 4:5
Graduate Enrollment: N/A
Financial Aid: Yes
Out of State: $ 24,600

Athletic: Yes
In State:

Programs of Study: Accountancy, African Studies, American Studies, Anthropology, Art, Asian Studies, Biology, Chemistry, Computer Science, Economics, Education, Engineering, English, Finance, Health Services, History, Humanities, Latin American Studies, Management, Marketing, Mathematics, Modern Languages, Music, Philosophy, Political Science, Psychology, Social Science, Social Work, Sociology, Theatre Arts, Theology

Women's Athletic Profile

River Avenue
Providence, RI 02918
Coach: Margot Royer
Email: mroyer@providence.edu

NCAA I
Lady Friars, Black, White
Phone: (401) 865-2028
Fax: (401) 865-2583

Estimated # of Women's Volleyball Scholarships: N/A
Conference: Big East Conference

Rhode Island College
Academic Profile

600 Mt. Pleasant Avenue
Providence, RI 02908

Phone: 800-669-5760

Type: Public, 4 Yr., Liberal Arts, Coed
Website: http://www.rhodeislandcollege.edu
SAT/ACT/GPA: Required
Student/Faculty Ratio: 15:1
Undergraduate Enrollment: 6,873

Founded: 1854
Religion: Non-Affiliated
Housing: Yes
Male/Female: 33:67
Graduate Enrollment: 1,810

Scholarships/Academic: Yes　　　　　**Athletic:** No　　　　　**Financial Aid:** Yes
Expenses By: Year　　　　　　　　　　**In State:** $ 9,500　　　　**Out of State:** $ 14,400
Specializes In: Education
Degrees Conferred: BA, BS, BFA, BM, BSN, BSW, MA, MS, MEd
Programs of Study: Accounting, Biology, Chemistry, Music, Science, Computer Science, CIS, Economics, English, History, Justice Studies, Management, Marketing, Music, Elementary Education, Music Education, Special Education, Nursing, Physical Education, Psychology, Secondary Education, Social Work, Sociology, Art History, Art Education, Film Studies

Women's Athletic Profile

600 Mount Pleasant Avenue
Providence, RI 02908
Coach: Kristen Norberg
Email: bschneck@uriacc.uri.edu

NCAA I
Anchorwomen, White, Gold
Phone: (401) 456-8156
Fax: (401) 456-8514

Estimated # of Women's Volleyball Scholarships: 0
Conference: Little East Conference
Program Profile: We practice and compete in a state-of-the-art, $ 9 million, Athletic Building with a capacity of 3,000. The facility is four years old and contains a strength/conditioning room, athletic training facilities and coaches offices.
History: Our program began in 1977 and we qualified for the ECAC Post-Season Tournament in 1986 and 1989.
Coaching: Kristen Norberg - Head Coach. She is RIC's all-time winningest coach with 210 career wins. (1984-98) Jennifer Hastings is Assistant Coach.
Freshman Receiving Financial Aid/Academic:　　　　　　　　**Athletic:** 0
Roster In State: 11　　　　　**Out of State:** 1　　　　**Out of Country:** 0
Sophomores on Team: 3　　　　**Seniors on Team:** 3　　　**Graduation %:** 100
Most Recent Record: 15-17-0　　**Fall Games:** 32　　　　**Spring Games:** 0
Positions Needed: Setter, Hitter
Schedule: Eastern Connecticut State, Western Connecticut State, Elmira, Plymouth State, Springfield College, Coast Guard
Style of Play: We are an aggressive team.

Roger Williams University
Academic Profile

One Old Ferry Road
Bristol, RI 02809

Phone: 401-254-3500

Type: Private, 4 Yr., Liberal Arts, Engineering, Coed　　　**Founded:** 1956
Website: http://www.rwu.edu　　　　　　　　　　　　　　**Religion:** Non-Affiliated
SAT/ACT/GPA: 1050　　　　　　　　　　　　　　　　　　**Housing:** Yes
Student/Faculty Ratio: 20:1　　　　　　　　　　　　　　**Male/Female:** 56:44
Undergraduate Enrollment: 2,100　　　　　　　　　　　　**Graduate Enrollment:** 465
Scholarships/Academic: Yes　　　　**Athletic:** No　　　**Financial Aid:** Yes
Expenses By: Year　　　　　　　　　**In State:** $ 22,000　**Out of State:** $ 22,000
Degrees Conferred: BA, BS, BFA, B-Arch, Juris Doctor
Programs of Study: Art & Science, Architecture, Business, Engineering, Law

Men's Athletic Profile

Old Ferry Rd.
Bristol, RI 02809
Coach: TBA
Email:

NCAA III
Hawks/Royal Blue, Gold, White
Phone: (401) 254-3050
Fax: (401) 254-3535

Estimated # of Men's Volleyball Scholarships: N/A
Conference: Eastern Intercollegiate Volleyball Association

Women's Athletic Profile

Old Ferry Rd.
Bristol, RI 02809
Coach: Ben Heroux
Email:

NCAA I
Lady Hawks, Blue, Gold, White
Phone: (401) 254-3050
Fax: (401) 254-3535

Estimated # of Women's Volleyball Scholarships: N/A
Conference: Eastern College Athletic Conference

University of Rhode Island
Academic Profile

Three Keaney Road, Ste 1
Kingston, RI 02881

Phone: (701) 874-5231

Type: Public, 4 Yr., Liberal Arts, Engineering, Coed
Website: http://www.uri.edu
SAT/ACT/GPA: 1000/24+/2.5
Student/Faculty Ratio: 16:1
Undergraduate Enrollment: 10,000
Scholarships/Academic: Yes
Expenses By: Year
Specializes In: Engineering, Ocean Sciences
Degrees Conferred: BA, BS

Founded: 1892
Religion: Non-Affiliated
Housing: Yes
Male/Female: 44:56
Graduate Enrollment: 3,000

Athletic: Yes
In State: $ 11,582

Financial Aid: Yes
Out of State: $ 19,586

Programs of Study: Arts & Science, Business Administration, Engineering, Human Science and Services, Nursing, Pharmacy, Resource Development, Finance, Accounting, Chemistry, Economics, Computer, History, Mechanical, Music, Electrical, Political Science

Women's Athletic Profile

Keaney Gymnasium Room 206
Kingston, RI 02881
Coach: Robert Schneck
Email: bschneck@uri.edu

NCAA I
Lady Rams, Blue, White
Phone: (701) 874-5231
Fax: (701) 874-2458

Estimated # of Women's Volleyball Scholarships: 12
Conference: Atlantic 10 Conference
Program Profile: We play at Keaney Gymnasium which has 7,000 seats. We play a fall season.
History: We started in 1975. We have one AIAW post-season National Championship. We made 3 NCAA First Round Appearances. We went to the NIVC Final Four.
Achievements: District I Coach of the Year in 1995 an 1996
Coaching: Bob Schneck, Head Coach, will start his 19th season here as Head Coach. His overall record is 383-225. Jill Has is Assistant Coach.
Freshman Receiving Financial Aid/Academic: **Athletic:** 12
Roster In State: 1   **Out of State:** 11   **Out of Country:** 0
Sophomores on Team: 3   **Seniors on Team:** 4   **Graduation %:** 100
Most Recent Record: 17-10-0   **Fall Games:** 30   **Spring Games:** 12
Camp of Clinic Dates: August 1-12
Positions Needed: Setter, Outside Hitter, Middle Hitter
Schedule: Washington, Wisconsin, Sacramento State, Illinois State, Ohio State
Style of Play: We are a scrappy team that is balanced offensively and defensively.

SOUTH CAROLINA

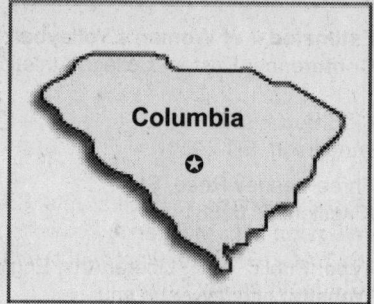

Columbia

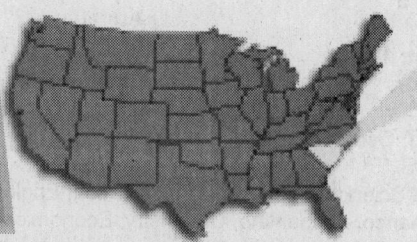

SCHOOL	CITY	AFFILIATION	PAGE
Anderson College	Anderson	NCAA II	678
Benedict College	Columbia	NAIA	678
Charleston Southern University	Charleston	NCAA I	679
Citadel	Charleston	NCAA I	679
Claflin College	Orangeburg	NAIA	680
Clemson University	Clemson	NCAA I	680
Coastal Carolina University	Conway	NCAA I	681
Coker College	Hartsville	NCAA II	682
College of Charleston	Charleston	NCAA I	682
Converse College	Spartanburgh	NCAA II	683
Francis Marion University	Florence	NCAA II	684
Furman University	Greensville	NCAA I	685
Lander University	Greenwood	NCAA II	685
Limestone College	Gaffney	NCAA II	686
Morris College	Sumter	NAIA	686
Newberry College	Newberry	NCAA II	687
North Greenville College	Tigerville	NAIA	687
Presbyterian College	Clinton	NCAA II	688
South Carolina State University	Orangeburg	NCAA I	689
Southern Wesleyan University	Central	NCCAA	689
University of South Carolina	Columbia	NCAA I	690
Univ of South Carolina - Aiken	Aiken	NCAA II	690
Univ of South Carolina-Spartanburg	Spartanburg	NCAA II	691
Voorhees College	Denmark	NAIA	692
Winthrop University	Rock Hill	NCAA I	692
Wofford College	Spartanburg	NCAA I	693

Anderson College
Academic Profile

316 Boulevard
Anderson, SC 29621

Phone: (864) 231-2030

Type: Private, 4 Yr., Liberal Arts, Coed
Website: http://www.anderson-college.edu
SAT/ACT/GPA: 1000/not available/3.0
Student/Faculty Ratio: 14:1
Undergraduate Enrollment: 1400
Scholarships/Academic: Yes
Expenses By: Year
Specializes In: Music, Art, Education
Degrees Conferred: AA, BA, BS

Athletic: Yes
In State: $ 16,400

Founded: 1911
Religion: Baptist
Housing: Yes
Male/Female: 40:60
Graduate Enrollment: n/a
Financial Aid: Yes
Out of State: $ 16,400

Programs of Study: Art, Biology, Business, Communications, Education, English, Fashion, Finances, General Studio, Graphic Art, History, Human Services & Resources, Interior Design, Journalism, Liberal Studies, Literature, Management, Marketing, Medical Technology, Music, Painting and Drawing , Physical Education, Psychology, Religion, Speech, Theatre

Women's Athletic Profile

Boulevard Street
Anderson, SC 29621
Coach: Jennifer Wilder
Email:

NCAA I
Lady Trojans, Black, Gold
Phone: (864) 231-2029
Fax: (864) 231-5601

Estimated # of Women's Volleyball Scholarships: 1.375
Conference: Carolinas - Virginia Athletic
Program Profile: Our program made a turn for the better in 1998. We more than doubled the number of victories from the previous season.
History: Anderson College won NJCAA Region X titles in 1987, 1988,1999 and 1992. Since becoming a four-year college, the program has struggled.
Achievements: Anne Poindexter NJCAA A-A, AVCA A-A 1991. Tashia Greene NJCAA A-A, AVCA A-A 1988.
Coaching: Jennifer Wilder, Head Coach, played at Dorman High School and Wofford College. She began coaching here last season.
Freshman Receiving Financial Aid/Academic:
Roster In State: 10
Sophomores on Team: 0
Most Recent Record: 17-15-0
Camp of Clinic Dates: 7/23-24,7/25-28,7/28-31
Positions Needed: Outside, Right, Middle

Out of State: 2
Seniors on Team: 2
Fall Games: 32

Athletic: 2
Out of Country: 0
Graduation %: 100
Spring Games: 0

Schedule: Lees-McRae, Charleston-West Virginia, Mt. Olive, Presbyterian, Augusta State
Style of Play: Concentration on fundamentals; keep attack from getting too concentrated; 5-1 offense; strength of defense in the back row.

Benedict College
Academic Profile

Harden Street
Columbia, SC 29204

Phone: 803-253-5143

Type: Private, 4 Yr., Liberal Arts, Coed
Website: http://www.isusc.org
SAT/ACT/GPA: 17+
Student/Faculty Ratio: 17:1
Undergraduate Enrollment: 1,265
Scholarships/Academic: Yes
Expenses By: Year
Degrees Conferred: BA, BS, BSW

Athletic: Yes
In State: $ 8,500

Founded: 1870
Religion: Baptist
Housing: No
Male/Female: 33:67
Graduate Enrollment: N/A
Financial Aid: Yes
Out of State: $ 8,500

Programs of Study: Accounting, Biological Science, Business Administration, Chemistry, Computer Science, Criminal Justice, Early Childhood Education, Elementary Education, English, Environmental Health, Journalism, Mathematics, Philosophy, Music, Physics, Religion, Social Science

Women's Athletic Profile

Harden Street
Columbia, SC 29204
Coach: Gwendolyn Rouse
Email:

NAIA
Tigeretts, Purple, Gold
Phone: (803) 253-5066
Fax: (803) 253-5434

Estimated # of Women's Volleyball Scholarships: N/A
Conference: EIAC

Charleston Southern University
Academic Profile

P.O. Box 118087
Charleston, SC 29423-8087

Phone: 843-863-7050

Type: Private, 4 Yr., Liberal Arts, Coed
Website: http://www.csuniv.edu
SAT/ACT/GPA: NCAA Standard
Student/Faculty Ratio: 14:1
Undergraduate Enrollment: 2,500
Scholarships/Academic: Yes
Expenses By: Year
Degrees Conferred: BA, BS, M Ed, MS

Athletic: Yes
In State: $ 13,516

Founded: 1964
Religion: Southern Baptist
Housing: Yes
Male/Female: 50:50
Graduate Enrollment: 500
Financial Aid: Yes
Out of State: $ 13,516

Programs of Study: Accounting, Biology, Botany, Business, Chemistry, Communications, Criminal Justice, Fine Arts, Economics, Education, English, Geology, History, Liberal Arts, Management, Mathematics, Microbiology, Music, Nursing, Political Science, Psychology, Religion

Women's Athletic Profile

P.O. Box 118087
Charleston, SC 29243-8087
Coach: Danyel Bellush
Email:

NCAA I
Lady Buccaneers, Blue, Gold
Phone: (803) 863-7078
Fax: (843) 863-7676

Estimated # of Women's Volleyball Scholarships: N/A
Conference: Big South Conference

Citadel
Academic Profile

171 Moultrie Street
Charleston, SC 29409

Phone: 800-868-1842

Type: Public, 4 Yr., Liberal Arts, Coed
Website: http://www.citadel.edu
SAT/ACT/GPA: 920/20/2.0
Student/Faculty Ratio: 17:1
Undergraduate Enrollment: 1,641
Scholarships/Academic: Yes
Expenses By: Year
Specializes In: The Military College of South Carolina
Degrees Conferred: BA, BS

Athletic: Yes
In State: $ 8,410

Founded: 1842
Religion: Non-Affiliated
Housing: Yes
Male/Female: 40:1
Graduate Enrollment: N/A
Financial Aid: Yes
Out of State: $ 18,500

Programs of Study: Biology, Business Administration, Chemistry, Civil Engineering, Computer Science, Education, Electrical Engineering, English, French, German, Health and PE, History, Mathematics, Physics, Political Science, Psychology, Spanish

Women's Athletic Profile

171 Moultrie Street
Charleston, SC 29409
Coach: Wendy Anderson
Email: Wendy.Anderson@citadel.edu

NCAA I
Lady Bulldogs, Blue, White
Phone: (843) 953-7304
Fax: (843) 953-6727

Estimated # of Women's Volleyball Scholarships: 6
Conference: Southern Conference
Program Profile: The program is in the developmental stages. We play in McAlister Fieldhouse and our playing season lasts through November.
History: Our first year was in 1998 and our record was 0-24.
Achievements: Coach of the Year while coaching at Converse College; District 6 Champions for 2 years and Runner-up for one year.
Coaching: Wendy Anderson, started as Head Coach in 1998. She played at West Virginia University as a setter. Jennifer Boeddeker is Assistant Coach.
Freshman Receiving Financial Aid/Academic: **Athletic:** 7
Roster In State: 5   **Out of State:** 9   **Out of Country:** 0
Sophomores on Team: 3   **Seniors on Team:** 0   **Graduation %:** Unknown
Most Recent Record: 0-24-0   **Fall Games:** 24   **Spring Games:** 0
Positions Needed: Setter, Outside
Schedule: Furman, Davidson, East Tennessee State, UT-Chattanooga, Appalachian, UNC-Greensboro
Style of Play: We are a new program and our focus will be defense.

Claflin College
Academic Profile

P.O Box 31, 1 Perimeter Rd.
Orangeburg, SC 29115

Phone: 803-535-5339

Type: Private, 4 Yr., Coed
Website: http://www.claflin.edu
SAT/ACT/GPA: 600+
Student/Faculty Ratio: 15:1
Undergraduate Enrollment: 885
Scholarships/Academic: No
Expenses By: Year
Degrees Conferred: BA, BS
Programs of Study: Contact school for program of study.

Founded: 1869
Religion: Methodist
Housing: No
Male/Female: 40:60
Graduate Enrollment: N/A
Financial Aid: Yes
Out of State: $ 7,413

Athletic: Yes
In State: $ 7,413

Women's Athletic Profile

700 College Avenue, NE
Orangeburg, SC 29115
Coach: Vernell Keitt
Email:

NCAA I
Pantherettes, Orange, Maroon
Phone: (803) 534-2710
Fax: (803) 531-2860

Estimated # of Women's Volleyball Scholarships: N/A
Coaching: Vernell Keitt - Head Coach. Natasha Clarkson is Statistician. Nelson Brownlee is Athletic Director.
Roster In State: 9   **Out of State:** 0   **Out of Country:** 0
Sophomores on Team: 1   **Seniors on Team:** 2   **Graduation %:** Unknown
Schedule: Paine, Morris, Benedict, Barber Scotia, Newberry, Voorhees, Columbia, Savannah, St. Augustine

Clemson University
Academic Profile

P. O. Box 31
Clemson, SC 29633

Phone: 864-656-2287

Type: Public, 4 Yr., Coed
Website: http://www.clemson.edu
SAT/ACT/GPA: Avg. 1172/3.7
Student/Faculty Ratio: 17/1
Undergraduate Enrollment: 12,710
Scholarships/Academic: Yes
Expenses By: Year
Specializes In: Agricultural
Degrees Conferred: BS, BA, Masters, Ph.D.
Programs of Study: 70 fields of study in 5 colleges: Agriculture, Forestry and Life Sciences; Architecture, Arts and Humanities; Business and Public Affairs; Engineering and Science; Health , Education and Human Development

Founded: 1889
Religion: Non-Affiliated
Housing: Yes
Male/Female: 54/46
Graduate Enrollment: 3,800
Financial Aid: Yes
Out of State: $14,836

Athletic: Yes
In State: $8,642

Women's Athletic Profile

Box 31, 1 Perimeter Rd.
Clemson, SC 29634
Coach: Jolene Jordan Hoover
Email: klarsen.@clemson.edu

NCAA I
Lady Tigers, Purple, Orange
Phone: (864) 656-1931
Fax: (864) 656-7330

Estimated # of Women's Volleyball Scholarships: 12
Conference: Atlantic Coast Conference
Program Profile: We are a top 25 program. Our volleyball facility has 1,100 seats. An expansion is planned so that we will have 2,000 seats.
History: Our program started in 1997. In the last 6 years under Jolene Hoover we have won many honors: 1997 ACC Champs, 3 ACC Rookie of the year, 5 All-ACC Freshman Team Selections, 11 All-ACC selections and 7 All-ACC Tournament MVP.
Achievements: 3 ACC Rookie of the Year selections; 5 All-ACC Freshman team selections; 11 All-ACC selections; 7 All-ACC Tournament selections; 1 ACC Tournament MVP; 4 NCAA Tournament Appearances, 11 AVCA All-District/Region selections.
Coaching: Jolene Jordan Hoover - Head Coach. She was named 1994 Coach of the Year. Her record in 1998 was 50-21 (.676) in the ACC. Her overall record was 121-49 (.712). Becky Kanitz Assistant Coach. She is in her second year here and Becky is a 1989 graduate of Purdue University. Heather Kahl, in her third year as Assistant Coach, is a 1995 Clemson graduate.

Freshman Receiving Financial Aid/Academic: | | **Athletic:** 2
Roster In State: 1 | **Out of State:** 14 | **Out of Country:** 1
Sophomores on Team: 0 | **Seniors on Team:** 5 | **Graduation %:** 100
Most Recent Record: 22-11-0 | **Fall Games:** 32 | **Spring Games:** 3 tournaments
Camp of Clinic Dates: July
Positions Needed: 4
Schedule: Michigan State, Notre Dame, Arkansas, Florida State, Texas A&M, Duke, Wake Forrest, Virginia, Maryland, Penn State

Coastal Carolina University
Academic Profile

P. O. Box 261954
Myrtle Beach, SC 29578

Phone: 800-277-7000

Type: Public, 4 Yr., Liberal Arts, Coed
Website: http://www.coastal.edu
SAT/ACT/GPA: 900/20/2.5
Student/Faculty Ratio: 17:1
Undergraduate Enrollment: 4,500
Scholarships/Academic: Yes
Expenses By: Year
Specializes In: Business, Marine Sciences
Degrees Conferred: BA, BS, MED, MBA

Founded: 1954
Religion: Non-Affiliated
Housing: Yes
Male/Female: 1:2
Graduate Enrollment: 500
Athletic: Yes | **Financial Aid:** Yes
In State: $ 8,020 | **Out of State:** $ 13,240

Programs of Study: Accounting, Finance, Management, Marketing, Elementary Education, Physical Education, Secondary Education, Biology, Chemistry, Computer Science, Marine Science, Mathematics, Sociology, Psychology, Art Studio, Dramatic Arts, English, History, Political Science

Women's Athletic Profile

755 Highway 544, PO Box 26194
Conway, SC 29528-6054
Coach: Kristen Bauer
Email: kbauer@coastal.edu

NCAA I
Chanticleers, Green, Bronze
Phone: (843) 349-2814
Fax: (843) 349-2893

Estimated # of Women's Volleyball Scholarships: 8
Conference: Big South Conference
Program Profile: Newly remodeled gymnasium, perfect crowd size for volleyball. Our court is a new wood surface. We play a fall season which begins early August to late November. Our spring season runs from February to april. Our gymnasium seats 1800.
Achievements: 2000 Big South Coach of the Year- 2000 All American Academic Team- 1999 Academic All American All District Team- Conference Player of the Year 1991, 1996- Conference Scholar Athlete of the Year 1996, 2000- Big South Tournament MVP- Big South All-Conference-Big South All Tounament
Coaching: Kristen Bauer is our head coach and she is assisted by Doneva Bays
Freshman Receiving Financial Aid/Academic: | **Athletic:** 3

Roster In State: 2   Out of State: 7   Out of Country: 2
Sophomores on Team: Seniors on Team: 1   Graduation %: N\A
Most Recent Record: 19-14
Camp of Clinic Dates: July 11-16
Positions Needed: Middle blockers and Setters
Schedule: Minnesota, Pacific, Chapel Hill, Georgia Tech, Hofstra, Pittsburgh, Radford, Liberty, Winthrop
Style of Play: We play with strong basic fundamentals and strong defensive techniques. Our practices are fast paced along with our off court sessions as well.

Coker College
Academic Profile

300 East College Avenue
Hartsville, SC 29550

Phone: 800-950-1908

Type: Private, 4 Yr., Liberal Arts, Coed
Website: http://www.coker.edu
SAT/ACT/GPA: 850/17/2.5
Student/Faculty Ratio: 10:1
Undergraduate Enrollment: 900
Scholarships/Academic: Yes   **Athletic:** Yes
Expenses By: Year   **In State:** $ 19,000
Specializes In: Preprofessional Programs, Divinity
Degrees Conferred: BA, BS, BME

Founded: 1908
Religion: Non-Affiliated
Housing: Yes
Male/Female: 47:53
Graduate Enrollment: N/A
Financial Aid: Yes
Out of State: $ 19,000

Programs of Study: Art, Biology, Chemistry, Business, Communications, Dance, Drama, Education, English, History, Political Science, Physical Education, Music, Graphic Design, Photography, French, Psychology, Mathematics, Computer Science, Sociology, Spanish, Religion, Accounting, International Studies, Criminology, Theatre, Exercise Science, Medical Technology

Women's Athletic Profile

300 East College Ave.
Hartsville, SC 29550
Coach: Ann Walters
Email: tgriggs@pascal.coker.edu

NCAA I
Lady Cobras, Navy Blue, Gold
Phone: (843) 383-8073
Fax: (843) 383-8067

Estimated # of Women's Volleyball Scholarships: N/A
Conference: Carolinas - Virginia Athletic Conference
Program Profile: We play at Timberlake Lawton Gym which has 750 seats.
Our playing season is from August until November.
Achievements: 2 All-Conference Players in 1998; Freshman of the Year in 1997.
Coaching: Ann Walters, Head Coach, has coached from 1995 to the present. Assistant Coach Kim Cantey has coached from 1996 to the present.
Freshman Receiving Financial Aid/Academic: **Athletic:** 5
Roster In State: 3   **Out of State:** 9   **Out of Country:** 1
Sophomores on Team: 2   **Seniors on Team:** 3   **Graduation %:** Unknown
Positions Needed: All positions
Schedule: Lees McRae, Queens, Mt.Oliva

College of Charleston
Academic Profile

26 George Street
Charleston, SC 29424

Phone: (843) 953-5583

Type: Public, 4 Yr., Liberal Arts, Engineering, Coed
Website: http://www.cofc.edu
SAT/ACT/GPA: 1130/25/3.1
Student/Faculty Ratio: 19:1
Undergraduate Enrollment: 11,000
Scholarships/Academic: Yes   **Athletic:** Yes
Expenses By: Year   **In State:** $ 7,290
Specializes In: Very Broad

Founded: 1770
Religion: Non-Affiliated
Housing: Yes
Male/Female: 3:1
Graduate Enrollment: 1,500
Financial Aid: Yes
Out of State: $ 10,780

Degrees Conferred: BA, BS, MA, MS, MED
Programs of Study: Accounting, Anthropology, Art, BioChemistry, Biology, Business and Management, Chemistry, Classics, Communications, Computer Information Systems, Computer Science, Economics, Education, Elementary Education, English, French, Geology, German, Greek, History, Marine Biology, Mathematics, Music, Nursing, Optometry, Philosophy, Physical Education, Physics, Podiatry, Political Science, PreDentistry ,PreMed, Psychology, Social Science, Spanish, Special Education, Theatre, Urban Studies, Veterinary Studies

Women's Athletic Profile

30 George Street
Charleston, SC 29424
Coach: Jewel Giesy
Email: giesyj@cofc.edu

NCAA I
Lady Cougars, Maroon, White
Phone: (843) 953-8246
Fax: (843) 953-8296

Estimated # of Women's Volleyball Scholarships: 1
Conference: Southern
Program Profile: Home court is in the Johnson Center in the John Kresse Arena. Facility seats 3, 500 people and was built in 1984. Play on a wood floor.
History: For many years C of C competed in the NAIA. In 1991 the program competed in the NCAA Division I. Since 1991, the volleyball program has established a winning tradition, compiling a record of 209-142.
Achievements: In the past five years , Coach Giesy has coached 2 conference Freshman of the Year, 6 AU-Conference selections and several conference Player of the Week selections.
Coaching: Head Coach Jewel Giesy played at Furman University (Div.I) and graduated in 1993. She received her Masters in Sport Management at the University of Florida. Assistant Coach Cally Geiger played at UNC Asheville in 1999.

Freshman Receiving Financial Aid/Academic: | | **Athletic:** 2
Roster In State: 4 | **Out of State:** 8 | **Out of Country:** 0
Sophomores on Team: | **Seniors on Team:** 0 | **Graduation %:** 100
Most Recent Record: 15-17
Camp of Clinic Dates: July 9-13, 2001
Positions Needed: Middle Blocker
Schedule: Univ. of Tulsa, Indiana State University, Florida International Univ., Davidson College, Univ. of Tenn-Chattanooga, Univ. of Tenn- Martin, Appalachian State, East Tennessee State University, Stetson University.
Style of Play: Very solid defensive and serve receive team (#5 in Nation in Digs/game 2000). With solid ball control the offensive options are unlimited and fun.

Converse College
Academic Profile

580 E. Main St.
Spartanburg, SC 29307

Phone: 864-596-9040

Type: Private, 4 Yr., Liberal Arts, Women Only
Website: Not Available
SAT/ACT/GPA: 1010/3.445
Student/Faculty Ratio: 9:1
Undergraduate Enrollment: 646
Scholarships/Academic: Yes
Expenses By: Year

Athletic: Yes
In State: $ 14,760

Founded: 1889
Religion: Non-Affiliated
Housing: Yes
Male/Female: Women Only
Graduate Enrollment: 98
Financial Aid: Yes
Out of State: $ 14,760

Degrees Conferred: BA, BS, BM, Mmus, MED, Masters of Liberal Arts & Educational Specialist
Programs of Study: Natural Sciences, Medical Technology, Interdisciplinary, Minor in Environmental Studies, Converse Leadership Program, Computer Information Science, Latin American and Caribbean Studies, Women's Studies, Career Professional, Arts Management, Criminal Justice and Clinical Administration, Interior Design, Publication and Media, Reserve Officer's Training Corps, Urban Planning, PreProfessional, PreMed, PreLaw, PreDentistry, PrePharmacy, PreNursing, PreMinistry

Women's Athletic Profile

580 East Main Street
Spartanburgh, SC 29307
Coach: Alex Ericson
Email:

NCAA I
Lady All Stars, Purple, Gold
Phone: (864) 577-2050
Fax: (864) 577-2054

Estimated # of Women's Volleyball Scholarships: 2
Conference: Independent

Program Profile: The program was reinstated in 1997-1998 with competition beginning in 1998-1999. Our playing season is from August through November. We play at Montgomery Gymnasium that holds 150 to 200 people.

History: Our entire athletic program was cut in 1994 and was reinstated in 1997-1998. Our first year of competition was in 1998-1999. We are NCAA Division II provisional members.

Coaching: Alex Ericson, Head Coach, was hired to restart the program in 1997. He coached a four time State Champion high school team in Tennessee along with a State and Regional Champion Club team. He was an assistant at UT.

Freshman Receiving Financial Aid/Academic:		**Athletic:** 4
Roster In State: 7	**Out of State:** 0	**Out of Country:** 1
Sophomores on Team: 2	**Seniors on Team:** 1	**Graduation %:** Unknown
Most Recent Record: 12-23-0	**Fall Games:** 35	**Spring Games:** 0

Positions Needed: Outside Hitter, Middle Blocker, Setter

Schedule: Valdosta State, West Georgia, West Alabama, Lees-McRae, Wofford, Montevallo

Style of Play: Aggressive but inconsistent. We play with a lot of heart and effort but often fail to execute on the court. We can play with anyone.

Francis Marion University
Academic Profile

P.O. Box 10057
Florence, SC 29506

Phone: (843) 661-1237

Type: Public, 4 Yr., Liberal Arts, Coed	**Founded:** 1970
Website: http://www.fmarion.edu	**Religion:** Non-Affiliated
SAT/ACT/GPA: 940/2.2	**Housing:** Yes
Student/Faculty Ratio: 18:1	**Male/Female:** 45:55
Undergraduate Enrollment: 3,400	**Graduate Enrollment:** 600
Scholarships/Academic: Yes **Athletic:** Yes	**Financial Aid:** Yes
Expenses By: Year **In State:** $ 7,420	**Out of State:** $ 10,800

Degrees Conferred: BA, BS, BBA, BGS and Graduate Degrees in Business Administration Education and Psychology

Programs of Study: Accounting, Art, Art Education, Biology, Business Administration, Economics, Chemistry, Computer Science, Education, English, Finance, Health Physics, History, International Studies, Management, Marketing, Mass Communications, Math, Medical Technology, Physics, Political Science, Psychology, Sociology, Spanish, Theatre Arts, Visual Arts, PreDental, PreEngineering, PreLaw, PreMed, PreNursing, PrePharmacy, PreVet

Women's Athletic Profile

P.O. Box 10057
Florence, SC 29506
Coach: Sonny Kirkpatrick
Email: ekirkpatrick@fmarion.edu

NCAA I
Patriots, Red, White, Blue
Phone: (843) 661-1246
Fax: (843) 661-4645

Estimated # of Women's Volleyball Scholarships: 3.5

Conference: Peach Belt Athletic Conference

Program Profile: Over the last few years the program has been at or near the top of the Peach Belt Conference. FMU won the Conference Championship in 1997 and 1998. Gym capacity is 3500. We come into camp in the beginning of August, and continue into mid-November. At this time the gym floor is a tartan floor, but we are in the process of raising money to put in a new wooden floor.

History: FMU started its program in 1977, as an NAIA school. In 1992, they made the switch to Division II in the NCAA, and have recorded a 116-26 win/loss record over the last 4+ years.

Achievements: Sonny Kirkpatrick-2x Coach of the Year (Freedom League) @ Lycoming College

Crystal Poskey 3x Regional All-American (1997-1999)

Peach Belt Conference Champions- 1997, 1998

Coaching: This is Sonny Kirkpatrick's first season at FMU. He was a two time winner of the Freedom League Coach of the Year at Lycoming College, and he comprised a record of 144wins and 103 losses in eight years there. He also led his team to the NCAA tournament in 1997+ 1998, and was ranked in the Middle Atlantic Region (1997-1999).

Freshman Receiving Financial Aid/Academic:		**Athletic:** 2
Roster In State: 2	**Out of State:** 6	**Out of Country:** 2
Sophomores on Team:	**Seniors on Team:** 2	**Graduation %:** 100
Most Recent Record: 24-11-0	**Fall Games:** 33	**Spring Games:** 4

Positions Needed: OH, MH

Schedule: Barry University, Armstrong Atlantic State University, University of North Florida, Gardener-Webb University, Wingate University, Presbyterian College

Style of Play: An aggressive style that uses tough serving to create opportunities to an advantage. We attack at any time that we feel that we have an opportunity, but we understand that there are times that you must just keep the ball in play and regroup.

Furman University
Academic Profile

3300 Poinsett Hwy.
Greenville, SC 29613

Phone: 864-294-2034

Type: Private, 4 Yr., Liberal Arts, Coed
Website: http://www.furman.edu
SAT/ACT/GPA: Open
Student/Faculty Ratio: 12:1
Undergraduate Enrollment: 2,500
Scholarships/Academic: Yes   **Athletic:** Yes
Expenses By: Year   **In State:** $ 22,000

Founded: 1820
Religion: Non-Affiliated
Housing: Yes
Male/Female: 49:51
Graduate Enrollment: 250
Financial Aid: Yes
Out of State: $ 22,000

Degrees Conferred: BA, BM, BGS, BS, MAEd, MSChem
Programs of Study: Art, Asian Studies, Biology, Chemistry, Classics, Communications, Computer Science, Drama, Earth & Environment Science, Economics, Business, Education, Engineering, English, Health & Exercise Science, History, Business, Modern Languages, Music, Philosophy, Physics, Political Sciences, PreMed, PreLaw, Psychology, Religion, Sociology, Women's Studies

Women's Athletic Profile

3300 Poinsett Hwy.
Greensville, SC 29613
Coach: Kelor Chan
Email: cole.tallman@furman.edu

NCAA I
Lady Paladins, Purple, White
Phone: (864) 294-3326
Fax: (864) 294-3061

Estimated # of Women's Volleyball Scholarships: 8
Conference: Southern Conference
Program Profile: We have a new playing facility - Timmons Arena has a seating capacity of 5,000.
Achievements: We have 2 Conference Titles, 1 Academic All-American, 3 Southern Conference, Freshman of the Year, 2 Southern Conference Players of the Year.
Coaching: Keylor Chan, Head Coach, entering his first year with the program, graduated from Florida and was an assistant coach at Kent State and Northwestern. Michelle Young is our Assistant Coach.
Freshman Receiving Financial Aid/Academic: **Athletic:** 11
Roster In State: 2   **Out of State:** 10   **Out of Country:** 0
Sophomores on Team: 3   **Seniors on Team:** 1   **Graduation %:** 89
Most Recent Record: 23-13-0   **Fall Games:** 36   **Spring Games:** 0
Camp of Clinic Dates: July 9-16
Positions Needed: Middle, Setter
Schedule: Georgia, Clemson, South Florida, Georgetown, Kansas
Style of Play: Fast and disciplined style of play.

Lander University
Academic Profile

Athletic Department
Greenwood, SC 29649

Phone: 864-388-8307

Type: Public, 4 Yr., Liberal Arts, Engineering, Coed
Website: http://www.lander.edu
SAT/ACT/GPA: 840
Student/Faculty Ratio: 16:1
Undergraduate Enrollment: 2,700
Scholarships/Academic: Yes   **Athletic:** Yes
Expenses By: Year   **In State:** $ 7,200

Founded: 1872
Religion: Non-Affiliated
Housing: Yes
Male/Female: 40:60
Graduate Enrollment: 300
Financial Aid: Yes
Out of State: $ 10,000

Degrees Conferred: BA, BS, M.Ed., MBA
Programs of Study: Biology, Business Administration, Chemistry, Computer Science, Elementary Education, Engineering, English, Health Care, Management, History, Mass Communications & Theatre, Mathematics, Allied Health, Music, Nursing, Physical Education, Political Science, Psychology, Sociology, Criminal Justice, PreLaw, PreMed, PrePharmacy, PreOptometry

Women's Athletic Profile

Stanley Avenue
Greenwood, SC 29649-2099
Coach: Doug Spears
Email: dspears@lander.edu

NCAA I
Lady Senators, Blue, Gold
Phone: (864) 388-8291
Fax: (864) 388-8889

Estimated # of Women's Volleyball Scholarships: N/A
Conference: Independent

Limestone College
Academic Profile

1115 College Drive
Gaffney, SC 29340

Phone: 800-795-7151

Type: Private, 4 Yr., Liberal Arts, Coed
Website: Not Available
SAT/ACT/GPA: 800/18
Student/Faculty Ratio: 11:1
Undergraduate Enrollment: 500
Scholarships/Academic: Yes
Expenses By: Year
Degrees Conferred: BA, BS

Athletic: Yes
In State: $ 12,500

Founded: 1845
Religion: Non-Affiliated
Housing: Yes
Male/Female: 55:45
Graduate Enrollment: N/A
Financial Aid: Yes
Out of State: $ 12,500

Programs of Study: Applied Art, Art, Biology, Business Administration, Computer Science, Early Childhood Education, Education, Elementary Education, English, Guidance, History, Humanities, Liberal Arts, Management, Math, Music, Physical Education, PreDentistry, PreLaw, PreMed, Psychology, Science, Social Work

Women's Athletic Profile

1115 College Drive
Gaffney, SC 29340-3799
Coach: Jimmy Martin
Email:

NCAA I
Lady Saints, Blue, Gold, White
Phone: (864) 488-4566
Fax: (864) 488-8360

Estimated # of Women's Volleyball Scholarships: N/A
Conference: Independent

Morris College
Academic Profile

N. Main Street
Sumter, SC 29150-3599

Phone: 888-775-1345

Type: Private, 4 Yr., Liberal Arts, Coed
Website: http://www.icusc.org/morris/mchime.htm
SAT/ACT/GPA: None
Student/Faculty Ratio: 16:1
Undergraduate Enrollment: 888
Scholarships/Academic: Yes
Expenses By: Year

Athletic: Yes
In State: $ 9,562

Founded: 1908
Religion: Baptist
Housing: No
Male/Female: 1:2
Graduate Enrollment: N/A
Financial Aid: Yes
Out of State: $ 9,562

Programs of Study: Biology, Broadcast Media, Business Administration, Christian Education, Criminal Justice History, Early Childhood Education, Elementary Education, English, Journalism, Organizational Management, Pastoral Ministry, Social Studies, Sociology

Women's Athletic Profile

100 West College Street
Sumter, SC 29150-3599
Coach: Karen K. Lockyer
Email:
Estimated # of Women's Volleyball Scholarships: 3
Conference: Great Lakes Valley

NCAA I
Lady Flyers, Red, White
Phone: (803) 934-3200
Fax: (803) 773-3687

Program Profile: We are a regionally competitive program with in a strong conference. Our home court is Neil Carey Arena which has 1,000 seats around 2 wood floors. We have a new fieldhouse with 3 courts and one sport court.

History: Our program started in 1974. Our program has been to Nationals 8 times. Our best finish was 2nd in 1981. We were Conference Champions 4 times. We are consistently Conference qualifies as the Top 4 Seed.

Achievements: Coach of the Year 3 times at the Conference Level; Regional Coach of the Year one time; All-Americans; 3 All-Region.

Coaching: Karen K. Lockyer, became Head Coach in 1975. She is the 4th Winningest coach of NCAA II. She is the 19th Winningest Coach in Division I, II and III. Barb Collens has been Assistant Coach for 3 years. She went to Nationals with KCC and then played at Tempa.

Freshman Receiving Financial Aid/Academic:

Roster In State: 11	**Out of State:** 4	**Athletic:** 6
Sophomores on Team: 3	**Seniors on Team:** 4	**Out of Country:** 0
Most Recent Record: 16-12-0	**Fall Games:**	**Graduation %:** 100
Positions Needed: 3		**Spring Games:** 4

Schedule: Tampa, Florida Southern, Edinboro, New Haven, Northern Kentucky, Indiana Purdue-Fort Wayne

Style of Play: 5-1 offense with strong middle and right side attack. We are a tall, big blocking team. We are quick.

Newberry College
Academic Profile

2100 College St.
Newberry, SC 29108

Phone: (803) 321-5164

Type: Private, 4 Yr., Liberal Arts, Coed
Website: http://www.newberry.edu
SAT/ACT/GPA: 850/20/2.5
Student/Faculty Ratio: 12:1
Undergraduate Enrollment: 744
Scholarships/Academic: Yes   **Athletic:** Yes
Expenses By: Year   **In State:** $ 17,962

Founded: 1856
Religion: Evangelical Lutheran
Housing: Yes
Male/Female: 52:48
Graduate Enrollment: N/A
Financial Aid: Yes
Out of State: $ 17,962

Specializes In: Education, Business Administration, Communications
Degrees Conferred: BA, BM, BME, BS
Programs of Study: Art, Athletic Training, Biology, Chemistry, Veterinary Technology, Accounting, Economics, Business Administration, Computer Science, Communications, Elementary Education (Special Education, Learning Disabilities), English, French, German, Spanish, History, Music Literature, Music Theory, Music Education, Performance, Physical Education, PE/Leisure Services, Sports Management, Teacher Certification

Women's Athletic Profile

2100 College Street
Newberry, SC 29108
Coach: Shena Bowman
Email:

NCAA I
Lady Indians, Scarlet, Grey
Phone: (803) 321-5155
Fax: (803) 321-5169

Estimated # of Women's Volleyball Scholarships: 2
Conference: South Atlantic Conference
Program Profile: Our program is in the process of rebuilding. Matches are played in a 1,200-seat arena. Our season begins late August and runs to mid-November.
History: The program began in 1979 as a NAIA member and then progressed to NCAA Division II in 1993.
Coaching: Shena Bowman, Head Coach,

Freshman Receiving Financial Aid/Academic:

Roster In State: 8	**Out of State:** 3	**Athletic:** 5
Sophomores on Team: 0	**Seniors on Team:** 1	**Out of Country:** 0
Most Recent Record: 1-35-0	**Fall Games:** 36	**Graduation %:** 100
Positions Needed: Middle Hitter		**Spring Games:** 0

North Greenville College
Academic Profile

Hwy. 414
Tigerville, SC 29688

Phone: 864-977-7001

Type: Private, 4 Yr., Coed
Website: http://www.scicu.org/n-greenv
SAT/ACT/GPA: 860/18/2.0
Student/Faculty Ratio: 15:1
Undergraduate Enrollment: 1,100

Founded: 1892
Religion: Southern Baptist
Housing: Yes
Male/Female: 1.2:1
Graduate Enrollment: N/A

Scholarships/Academic: Yes   **Athletic:** Yes   **Financial Aid:** Yes
Expenses By: Year   **In State:** $ 11,680   **Out of State:** $ 11,680
Specializes In: Christian Studies
Degrees Conferred: BA
Programs of Study: Art, Biological Science, Business Administration, Communication, Computer Science, General Engineering, Health Science, Liberal Arts, Music, Psychology, Religious Education, Social Science

Women's Athletic Profile

P.O. Box 1892   **NCAA I**
Tigerville, SC 29688   Lady Mounties, Scarlet, Black
Coach: Debbie Chapmen   **Phone:** (864) 977-7150
Email: **Fax:** (864) 977-7152

Estimated # of Women's Volleyball Scholarships: N/A
Conference: Mid-South Conference

Presbyterian College
Academic Profile

105 Ashland Avenue   **Phone:** (864) 833-8538
Clinton, SC 29325-2994

Type: Private, 4 Yr., Liberal Arts, Coed   **Founded:** 1880
Website: http://www.presby.edu   **Religion:** Presbyterian Church
SAT/ACT/GPA: 1000/3.0   **Housing:** Yes
Student/Faculty Ratio: 14:1   **Male/Female:** 1:1.5
Undergraduate Enrollment: 1,100   **Graduate Enrollment:** N/A
Scholarships/Academic: Yes   **Athletic:** Yes   **Financial Aid:** Yes
Expenses By: Year   **In State:** $ 22,000   **Out of State:** $ 22,000
Specializes In: Business, Education, Pre-Medical, Pre-Law, Sciences
Degrees Conferred: BS, BA
Programs of Study: Accounting, Chemistry, Computer Science, Economics, Elementary Education, Engineering, English, Fine Arts, History, Mathematics, Music, PreDental, PreLaw, PreMedical, PreVet, Physics, Political Science, Psychology, Religion, Philosophy, Social Science, Sociology, Theatre Arts, Visual Arts

Women's Athletic Profile

105 Ashland Avenue   **NCAA I**
Clinton, SC 29325   Lady Blue Horse, Blue, Cardinal
Coach: Lisa Bugay   **Phone:** (864) 833-8538
Email: Presb@aol.com   **Fax:** (864) 833-8323

Estimated # of Women's Volleyball Scholarships: 2
Conference: South Atlantic Conference
Program Profile: We play in a gymnasium that has 5,000 seats.
History: Our program started in 1986. We have been in the SAC Conference for 10 years. We have been Division II for 10 years.
Achievements: In the past 10 years: 6 (20 win) seasons; 2 Conference Titles in SAC; 3 Second place finishes; 3 Tournament Conference Championships; 1 All-American; 12 First Team All-Conference Players; 5 Academic All-Americans.
Coaching: Lisa Bugay, Head Coach. Her first year was 1998-99. At Ashland University, she played volleyball, softball and field hockey. She coached 4 seasons at the Division I level at the University of South Carolina and the University of Massachusetts.
Freshman Receiving Financial Aid/Academic: **Athletic:** 4
Roster In State: 5   **Out of State:** 7   **Out of Country:** 0
Sophomores on Team: 5   **Seniors on Team:** 2   **Graduation %:** 100
Most Recent Record: **Fall Games:** 28   **Spring Games:** 2
Camp of Clinic Dates: July 5th - 8th Individual skills; July 9-11 Setter Hitter
Positions Needed: Middle Hitter
Schedule: North Alabama, Florida Southern, West Georgia, Catawba, University of Southern California-Aiken, Francis Marion
Style of Play: Explosive offense.

South Carolina State University
Academic Profile

300 College Street, NE
Orangeburg, SC 29117-0001

Phone: 803-536-7185

Type: Public, 4 Yr., Liberal Arts, Coed
Website: http://www.scsu.edu
SAT/ACT/GPA: 950+
Student/Faculty Ratio: 19:1
Undergraduate Enrollment: 4,335
Scholarships/Academic: Yes   **Athletic:** Yes
Expenses By: Year   **In State:** $ 5,700
Specializes In: Engineering
Degrees Conferred: BA, BS, MA, M.Ed., Ph.D., EdD
Programs of Study: Contact school for programs of study.

Founded: 1896
Religion: Non-Affiliated
Housing: No
Male/Female: 41:59
Graduate Enrollment: 446
Financial Aid: Yes
Out of State: $ 8,000

Women's Athletic Profile

300 College Street, NE
Orangeburg, SC 29117-0001
Coach: Mary Hill
Email:

NCAA I
Lady Bulldogs, Garnet, Blue
Phone: (803) 533-3783
Fax: (803) 533-3634

Estimated # of Women's Volleyball Scholarships: N/A
Conference: Mid-Eastern Athletic Conference

Southern Wesleyan University
Academic Profile

PO Box 1020
Central, SC 29630

Phone: (864) 644-5302

Type: Private, 4 Yr., Liberal Arts, Coed
Website: http://www.swu.edu
SAT/ACT/GPA: 85018/
Student/Faculty Ratio: 14/1
Undergraduate Enrollment: 570
Scholarships/Academic: Yes   **Athletic:** Yes
Expenses By: Year   **In State:** $ 16,800
Specializes In: Bible, Business, Education
Degrees Conferred: BS, BA

Founded: 1906
Religion: Wesleyan
Housing: Yes
Male/Female: 46/54
Graduate Enrollment: 700
Financial Aid: Yes
Out of State: $ 16,800

Programs of Study: Accounting, Biblical Studies, Biology, Business Administration, Chemistry, Education, Elementary Education, English, History, Liberal Arts, Mathematics, Medical Technology, Ministries, Music, Music Education, Nursing, Physical Education, Psychology, Religion, Social Science, Special Education, Theology

Women's Athletic Profile

1 Wesleyan Drive
Central, SC 29630
Coach: Debbie Holcombe
Email:

NCAA I
Lady Warriors, Blue, Gold
Phone: (864) 639-2453
Fax: (864) 639-4526

Estimated # of Women's Volleyball Scholarships: 4.5
Conference: Georgia- Alabama-Carolinas Conference
Program Profile: We play at J. W. Tysinger Gymnasium which has 600 seats. We play a fall season.
History: Our Volleyball Program began in 1976.
Achievements: We were GAC Conference Champions in 1997. Bob Anderson was GAC Coach of the Year in 1997.
Coaching:
Freshman Receiving Financial Aid/Academic: **Athletic:** 2
Roster In State: 7   **Out of State:** 2   **Out of Country:** 0
Sophomores on Team: 0   **Seniors on Team:** 2   **Graduation %:** 80
Most Recent Record: **Fall Games:** 35   **Spring Games:** 0

Positions Needed: All
Schedule: La Grange, Bluefield, Georgia Southwestern, Montreat, North Greenville, Faulkner

University of South Carolina-Columbia
Academic Profile

1300 Rosewood Drive
Columbia, SC 29033

Phone: 800-868-5872

Type: Public, 4 Yr., Coed
Website: http://www.uscsports.com
SAT/ACT/GPA: 1000/3.0
Student/Faculty Ratio: 17:1
Undergraduate Enrollment: 16,000
Scholarships/Academic: Yes   **Athletic:** Yes
Expenses By: Year   **In State:** $ 8,378
Specializes In: International Business, Journalism
Degrees Conferred: 100 different bachelor degrees
Programs of Study: 70 fields of study.

Founded: 1801
Religion: Non-Affiliated
Housing: Yes
Male/Female: 46:54
Graduate Enrollment: 10,000
Financial Aid: Yes
Out of State: $ 14,232

Women's Athletic Profile

Rex Enright Athletic Center
Columbia, SC 29208
Coach: Kim Hudson-Christopher
Email: khudson@uscround.ad.sc.edu

NCAA I
Lady Gamecocks, Garnet, Black
Phone: (803) 777-7883
Fax: (803) 777-8226

Estimated # of Women's Volleyball Scholarships: 3
Conference: Southeastern Conference
Program Profile: Our facility has a seating capacity of 1,600.
Coaching: Kim Hudson-Christopher, Head Coach, was named SEC Coach of the Year in 1997, Career Achievements Award in 1991, AVCA Division II Coach of the Year in 1990, Volleyball Monthly Division II Coach of the Year in 1990, Panhandle Sports Hall of Fame Coach of the Year-All Sports in 1990, Dick Risenhoover Award for Outstanding Sport Personality in 1990.
Freshman Receiving Financial Aid/Academic: **Athletic:** 4
Roster In State: 2   **Out of State:** 10   **Out of Country:** 1
Sophomores on Team: 0   **Seniors on Team:** 2   **Graduation %:**
Most Recent Record: 22-11-0   **Fall Games:** 27   **Spring Games:** 0
Positions Needed: Middle Blocker, Outside Hitter
Schedule: Florida, UCSB, Arkansas, Florida State, Clemson, Georgia
Style of Play: We are a ball control team that runs a fast middle attack. A very defensive team that can serve teams off the court.

University of South Carolina - Aiken
Academic Profile

471 University Parkway
Aiken, SC 29801

Phone: (803) 641-3717

Type: Public, 4 Yr., Liberal Arts, Engineering, Coed
Website: http://www.usca.sc.edu
SAT/ACT/GPA: 820
Student/Faculty Ratio: 12:1
Undergraduate Enrollment: 3,300
Scholarships/Academic: Yes   **Athletic:** Yes
Expenses By: Year   **In State:** $ 6,000
Specializes In: Nursing
Degrees Conferred: 4 years Baccalaureate Degrees
Programs of Study: Accounting, Banking/Finance, Biology, Business, Chemistry, Computer Science, Criminal Justice, Education, English, History, Marketing, Mathematics, Nursing, Physical Education, Political Science, Psychology, Social Science

Founded: 1961
Religion: Non-Affiliated
Housing: Yes
Male/Female: 35:65
Graduate Enrollment: 500
Financial Aid: Yes
Out of State: $ 10,000

Women's Athletic Profile

471 University Parkway
Aiken, SC 29801
Coach: Noelle Hughes
Email: admit@sc.edu

NCAA I
Lady Pacers, Cardinal, White
Phone: (803) 648-6851
Fax: (803) 641-3441

Estimated # of Women's Volleyball Scholarships: 5
Conference: Peach Belt Athletic Conference
Program Profile: We have a fall season and our stadium has a seating capacity of 2,500.
History: Our first year was in 1990 with an overall record of 192-121.
Achievements: We have had 1 1998 Academic All-American First Team.
Coaching: Noelle Hughes, Head Coach, started coaching the program in 1998. He graduated from Florida Southern in 1996. He compiled am overall record of 14-14 for one year.
Freshman Receiving Financial Aid/Academic:

		Athletic: 3
Roster In State: 0	**Out of State:** 9	**Out of Country:** 2
Sophomores on Team: 0	**Seniors on Team:** 4	**Graduation %:** 90
Most Recent Record: 14-14-0	**Fall Games:** 32	**Spring Games:** 4

Positions Needed: 2-Middle Hitters, 3-Outside Hitters, 1-Defender
Schedule: Florida Southern, South Dakota State, University of North Florida, Bryant College, Francis Marion University
Style of Play: Rebuilding year, raw talent, very versatile players.

University of South Carolina - Spartanburg
Academic Profile

800 University Way
Spartanburg, SC 29303
Type: Public, 4 Yr., Coed
Website: http://www.uscs.sc.edu
SAT/ACT/GPA: Varies
Student/Faculty Ratio: 16:1
Undergraduate Enrollment: 3,800
Scholarships/Academic: Yes
Expenses By: Year

Phone: 800-277-8727

Founded: 1967
Religion: Non-Affiliated
Housing: Yes
Male/Female: 40:60
Graduate Enrollment: N/A
Athletic: Yes **Financial Aid:** Yes
In State: $ 7,540 **Out of State:** $ 12,000

Degrees Conferred: AA, AS, BA, BS, MA, MS
Programs of Study: More than 30 Fields of Study in Liberal Arts, Sciences, Business Administration, Nursing and Teacher Education, plus Associate Degree in Nursing. Master's degree programs are offered in Early Childhood Education and Elementary Education. Other graduate courses are offered at USCS through the Graduate Regional Studies program of the USCS system.

Women's Athletic Profile

800 University Way
Spartanburg, SC 29316
Coach: Jennifer Rakers
Email: jrichardson@uscs.edu

NCAA I
Lady Rifles, Green, White, Black
Phone: (864) 503-5000
Fax: (864) 503-5130

Estimated # of Women's Volleyball Scholarships: N/A
Conference: Peach Belt Athletic Conference
Program Profile: We are in the NCAA Division II and we have a fall season. We play at G.B. Hodge Center gymnasium, which seats 1,535 people.
History: The starting date for our program was not recorded. Our all-time record is 638-321.
Achievements: PBAC Champions - Regular Season: 1993,1994; PBAC Champions-Tournament: 1993,1994,1995; PBAC Coach of the Year: Chris Sturgill 1993; PBAC Player of the Year: Jennifer Jones 1994.
Coaching: Jennifer Rakers, became our Head Coach in 1996. Her career record is 60-42.
Freshman Receiving Financial Aid/Academic:

		Athletic: 4
Roster In State: 0	**Out of State:** 8	**Out of Country:** 2
Sophomores on Team: 0	**Seniors on Team:** 3	**Graduation %:** 100
Most Recent Record: 19-15-0	**Fall Games:** 30	**Spring Games:** 0

Positions Needed: Middle Hitter
Schedule: Campbell, Francis Marion, North Florida, Florida Southern

Voorhees College
Academic Profile

Voorhees Rd.
Denmark, SC 29042

Phone: 800-446-6250

Type: Private, 4 Yr., Liberal Arts, Coed
Website: http://www.voorhees.edu
SAT/ACT/GPA: 720 avg.
Student/Faculty Ratio: 17:1
Undergraduate Enrollment: 800
Scholarships/Academic: Yes   **Athletic:** Yes
Expenses By: Year   **In State:** $ 7,500
Degrees Conferred: BS, BA

Founded: 1897
Religion: Episcopal
Housing: No
Male/Female: 1:3
Graduate Enrollment: N/A
Financial Aid: Yes
Out of State: $ 7,400

Programs of Study: Accounting, Biology, Business Administration, Computer Science, Criminal Science, Early Childhood Education, Elementary Education, English, Health & Recreation, Mathematics, Physical Education, Political Science, Government, Sociology

Women's Athletic Profile

Voorhees Rd.
Denmark, SC 29042
Coach: Adrian West
Email:

NCAA I
Lady Tigers, Blue, White
Phone: (803) 793-3351
Fax: (803) 793-3845

Estimated # of Women's Volleyball Scholarships: N/A
Conference: EIAC

Winthrop University
Academic Profile

Winthrop Coliseum
Rock Hill, SC 29733

Phone: (803) 323-2129 ext. 6249

Type: Public, 4 Yr., Liberal Arts, Coed
Website: http://www.winthrop.edu
SAT/ACT/GPA: 850/2.75
Student/Faculty Ratio: 17:1
Undergraduate Enrollment: 4,500
Scholarships/Academic: Yes   **Athletic:** Yes
Expenses By: Year   **In State:** $ 7,850
Specializes In: Business, Education, Visual and Performing Arts
Degrees Conferred: BA, BS, BFA, MA, MS, MBA, MFA, MEd

Founded: 1886
Religion: Non-Affiliated
Housing: Yes
Male/Female: 35:65
Graduate Enrollment: 1,000
Financial Aid: Yes
Out of State: $ 11,068

Programs of Study: Art History, Biology, Business Administration, Business Education, Chemistry, Computer Science, Dance, Distributive Education, Early Childhood Education, Education, Elementary Education, English, Fine Arts, History, Home Economics, Interior Design, International Marketing, Mass Communications, Mathematics, Medical Technology, Modern Languages, Music, Music Education, Philosophy & Religion, Physical Education, Political Science, Psychology, Science Communications, Social Work, Sociology, Special Education, Speech, Theatre

Women's Athletic Profile

Winthrop Coliseum
Rock Hill, SC 29733
Coach: Cathy Ivester
Email: IvesterC@Winthrop.edu

NCAA I
Lady Eagles, Garnet, Gold
Phone: (803) 323-2129
Fax: (803) 323-2433

Estimated # of Women's Volleyball Scholarships: 6
Conference: Big South Conference
Program Profile: We play at Winthrop Coliseum which seats 6,000. Over the past 3 years, the program progressed to its first back to back winning seasons at the Division I level. The schedule consists of Big South, Southern Conference, ACC, SEC, Big Sky and Trans America Conferences.
History: In 1971, we were AIAW. In 1980 we went NAIA. Our overall record is 586-443 with a percentage of .569.
Achievements: Cathy Ivester was 1987 Coach of the Year; 1983 NAIA 10th Nationally; NAIA District 6 Champions in 1981, 1982 and 1983.
Coaching: Cathy Ivester, Head Coach, has been here from 1996 to the present. Her overall record is 142-111 (.561). She is a Limestone University graduate. She is in the Hall of Fame and was the Athlete of the Year in 1982. Kevin Campbell is Assistant Coach.

Freshman Receiving Financial Aid/Academic: **Athletic:** 2

Roster In State: 2   **Out of State:** 10   **Out of Country:** 0

Sophomores on Team: 1   **Seniors on Team:** 1   **Graduation %:** 100

Most Recent Record: 18-14-0   **Fall Games:** 29   **Spring Games:** 6

Camp of Clinic Dates: July 15-19

Positions Needed: Middles

Schedule: Clemson, Idaho, Georgia Tech, Alabama, Liberty, Georgia State

Style of Play: We play with enthusiasm, unity and confidence. We enjoy tough competition and play long rallies with stamina! We have persistence, endurance and intensity.

Wofford College
Academic Profile

429 N. Church Street   **Phone:** 864-597-4130

Spartanburg, SC 29303

Type: Private, 4 Yr., Liberal Arts, Coed   **Founded:** 1854

Website: http://www.wofford.edu   **Religion:** Methodist

SAT/ACT/GPA: 1100/3.0   **Housing:** Yes

Student/Faculty Ratio: 9:1   **Male/Female:** 52:48

Undergraduate Enrollment: 1,100   **Graduate Enrollment:** N/A

Scholarships/Academic: Yes   **Athletic:** Yes   **Financial Aid:** Yes

Expenses By: Year   **In State:** $ 21,500   **Out of State:** $ 21,500

Specializes In: Sciences

Degrees Conferred: BA, BS

Programs of Study: Accounting, Art History, Biology, Chemistry, Computer Science, Economics, Finance, English, French, German, Government, History, Humanities, Math, Philosophy, Physics, Psychology, Religion, Sociology, Spanish

Women's Athletic Profile

429 N. Church Street   **NCAA I**

Spartanburg, SC 29303-3663   Lady Terriers, Gold, Black

Coach: Joseph Bowman   **Phone:** (864) 597-4120

Email: jcbowman@ibm.net   **Fax:** (864) 597-4112

Estimated # of Women's Volleyball Scholarships: 3.5

Conference: Southern Conference

History: We were members of NAIA and NCAA Division II. We became NCAA Division I in 1997.

Coaching: Joseph Bowman, Head Coach, started in 1998. His overall record is 360-182.

Freshman Receiving Financial Aid/Academic: **Athletic:** 5

Roster In State: 5   **Out of State:** 7   **Out of Country:** 0

Sophomores on Team: 2   **Seniors on Team:** 4   **Graduation %:** 100

Most Recent Record: 8-21-0   **Fall Games:** 29   **Spring Games:** 12

Positions Needed: Setter, Opp.

Schedule: Boston College, Northwestern University, University of Tennessee-Chattanooga, Jacksonville State, Western Carolina, Appalachian State

SOUTH DAKOTA

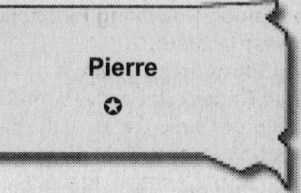

Pierre
✪

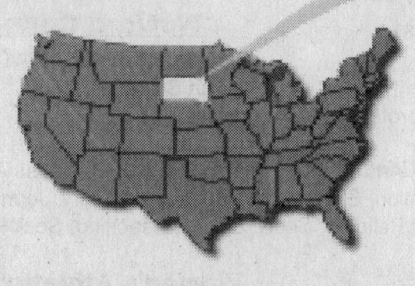

SCHOOL	CITY	AFFILIATION	PAGE
Augustana College - South Dakota	Sioux Falls	NCAA II	695
Black Hills State University	Spearfish	NAIA	695
Dakota State University	Madison	NAIA	696
Dakota Wesleyan University	Mitchell	NAIA	697
Huron University	Huron	NAIA	697
Mount Marty College	Yankton	NAIA	698
National American University	Rapid City	NAIA	698
Northern State University	Aberdeen	NCAA II	699
South Dakota State University	Brookings	NCAA II	700
University of Sioux Falls	Sioux Falls	NAIA	700
University of South Dakota	Vermillion	NCAA II	701

Augustana College
Academic Profile

2001 S. Summit Avenue
Sioux Falls, SD 57197

Phone: (605) 336-5539

Type: Private, 4 Yr., Liberal Arts, Coed
Website: http://www.augie.edu
SAT/ACT/GPA: 24
Student/Faculty Ratio: 12:1
Undergraduate Enrollment: 1,487
Scholarships/Academic: Yes
Expenses By: Year
Specializes In: Liberal Arts, Preprofessional Programs
Degrees Conferred: BA

Founded: 1860
Religion: Lutheran
Housing: Yes
Male/Female: 1:2
Graduate Enrollment: N/A

Athletic: Yes
In State: $ 17,560

Financial Aid: Yes
Out of State: $ 17,560

Programs of Study: Accounting, Art, Athletic Training, Biology, Business Administration, Chemistry, Communications, Computer Science, Economics, Deaf Education, Elementary Education, History, Journalism, MIS, Math, Medical Technology, Music, Nursing, Philosophy, Physics, Psychology, Religion, Social Studies Teaching, Social Work, Sociology, Spanish, Special Education, Theatre

Women's Athletic Profile

2001 S. Summit
Sioux Falls, SD 57197
Coach: Kim Sudbeck
Email: sudbeck@inst.augie.edu

NCAA I
Lady Vikings, Navy Blue, Gold
Phone: (605) 336-5539
Fax: (605) 336-5298

Estimated # of Women's Volleyball Scholarships: 6
Conference: North Central Collegiate Athletic Conference
Program Profile: Our facility has a seating capacity of 4,000 and was built in 1990. It has four full size volleyball courts. We reached the Top 10 in the last 3 years on a consistent basis. We won the North Central Conference in 1996 & 1997 and we were also in the NCAA playoffs in 1996 and 1997.
History: Our program began in 1972 and developed into a top NCC program in the early 1990's with back to back North Central Conference Titles in 1996 and 1997. We finished 10th in the country in 1998.
Achievements: 1997 NCC Coach of the Year; 1996 & 1997 North Central Conference Champions; 4 NCAA All-Americans; 1996 North Central Conference Player of the Year.
Coaching: Kim Sudbeck, Head Coach, started in 1995 and has an overall record of 106-31. She was 1997 North Central Conference Coach of the Year and received the 1997 Sports Writers College Coach of the Year South Dakota. She was a member of NCAA Division II National Championship Softball team.
Freshman Receiving Financial Aid/Academic:
Roster In State: 5
Sophomores on Team: 5
Most Recent Record: 25-7-0
Camp of Clinic Dates: July 12-14

Out of State: 11
Seniors on Team: 2
Fall Games: 28

Athletic: 4
Out of Country: 0
Graduation %: 100
Spring Games: 4

Schedule: North Dakota State, Tampa, Northern Michigan, South Dakota State, University of Nebraska-Omaha, North Florida
Style of Play: Augustana runs a fast, quick offense with primary focus on team defense.

Black Hills State University
Academic Profile

1200 University
Spearfish, SD 57799-9924

Phone: 800-255-2478

Type: Public, 4 Yr., Liberal Arts, Coed
Website: http://www.bhsu.edu
SAT/ACT/GPA: 860/18/2.6
Student/Faculty Ratio: 24:1
Undergraduate Enrollment: 2,800
Scholarships/Academic: Yes
Expenses By: Semester
Degrees Conferred: AA, AS, BA, BS, BSEd, Masters

Founded: 1884
Religion: Non-Affiliated
Housing: Yes
Male/Female: 45:55
Graduate Enrollment: 100

Athletic: Yes
In State: $ 2,540

Financial Aid: Yes
Out of State: $ 4,375

Programs of Study: Accounting, American Studies, Art, Biology, Business Administration & Education, Chemistry, Communications, Early Childhood Education, Elementary Education, English, Entrepreneurial Studies, Environmental, Health Services Administration, History, Human Resources Management, Instrumental Music, Marketing, Mass Communications, Middle School, Music, Mathematics, Office Administration, Outdoor Education, Physical Education, Political Science, Psychology, Physical Science, Social Science, Sociology, Spanish, Special Education, Wellness, Theatre, Technology

Women's Athletic Profile

P.O. Box 9924, 1200 University
Spearfish, SD 57799-9924
Coach: Naomi Hatfield
Email: jberry@mystic.bhsu.edu

NCAA I
Yellow Jackets, Green, Gold
Phone: (605) 642-6343
Fax: (605) 642-6539

Estimated # of Women's Volleyball Scholarships: 3
Conference: South Dakota Iowa Conference
Program Profile: The Donald Young Fitness Center has a capacity for 3 volleyball courts in the gym which seats 3,800. The facility is only 6 years old and has a beautiful hardwood floor. The Yellow Jackets usually check in for pre-season August 19, begin play the first week in September and finish the season around late November.
Achievements: BHSU has claimed the SDIC Conference Titles in 1981, 1993 and 1997. During the 1982 and 1983 seasons, the Yellow Jackets were District 12 Runner-Ups.
Coaching: Naomi Hatfield, Head Coach, started at BHSU in 1994. Her record is 58-82. Her overall college coaching record is 149-150. She was voted Rocky Mountain Athletic Conference Coach of the Year in 1993, while coaching at Chadron State College. Sarah Dittman is Assistant Coach.

Freshman Receiving Financial Aid/Academic: | | **Athletic:** 2
Roster In State: 5 | **Out of State:** 8 | **Out of Country:** 0
Sophomores on Team: 2 | **Seniors on Team:** 5 | **Graduation %:** 80
Most Recent Record: 21-10-0 | **Fall Games:** 30+ | **Spring Games:** 0
Camp of Clinic Dates: June Individual Camp; July Team Camp
Positions Needed: Setter, Middle Hitter, Outside Hitter
Schedule: Dordt College, Dickinson State, Moorhead State University, Chadron State College, National American, American Univ
Style of Play: We are a very strong defensive team.

Dakota State University
Academic Profile

820 N. Washington Ave.
Madison, SD 57042

Phone: (650) 256-5689

Type: Public, 4 Yr., Coed
Website: http://www.dsu.edu
SAT/ACT/GPA: 18
Student/Faculty Ratio: 30:1
Undergraduate Enrollment: 1,200
Scholarships/Academic: Yes
Expenses By: Year

Founded: 1881
Religion: Non-Affiliated
Housing: Yes
Male/Female: 1:1
Graduate Enrollment: New
Athletic: Yes | **Financial Aid:** Yes
In State: $ 6,026 | **Out of State:** $ 9,725

Specializes In: Business, Education, Information Systems
Degrees Conferred: BS, BA, MS, AA
Programs of Study: Elementary/Secondary Education, Business Administration, Computer Science, Computer Education, Fitness Wellness, Management Information Systems, English for Information Systems, Health Information Management, Physical Education, Respiratory Care Administration, Special Education

Women's Athletic Profile

820 N. Washington Avenue
Madison, SD 57042
Coach: Nancy Clark
Email: clark@columbia.dsu.edu

NCAA I
Lady Trojans, Blue Gold
Phone: (605) 256-5689
Fax: (605) 256-5138

Estimated # of Women's Volleyball Scholarships: 2
Conference: South Dakota-Iowa Conference
Program Profile: We play a Fall schedule with a short Spring season. We have a new gym. A community center will be added by the year 2001.
History: Our team has been in the top half of the SDIC for the last 10 years.
Achievements: 1998: one All-Conference Player; 1999: 2 All-Conference Players, 1 All-Region Player; 4th in the Conference both years.
Coaching: Nancy Clark, has been Head Coach for three years at DSU. She has been a coach for 17 years. She has one conference championship and one school winning record.

Freshman Receiving Financial Aid/Academic: **Athletic:** 3
Roster In State: 10   **Out of State:** 12   **Out of Country:** 0
Sophomores on Team: 0   **Seniors on Team:** 2   **Graduation %:** 100
Most Recent Record: 12-20-0   **Fall Games:** 32   **Spring Games:** 4 tournaments
Camp of Clinic Dates: High School/Junior High: June 21-24
Positions Needed: Middles
Schedule: Dordt College, University of Sioux Falls, North Dakota State University-Spring, South Dakota State
Style of Play: 5-1, quick.

Dakota Wesleyan University
Academic Profile

1200 University Blvd.   **Phone:** 605-996-2854
Mitchell, SD 57301

Type: Private, 4 Yr., Liberal Arts, Coed   **Founded:** 1885
Website: http://www.dwu.edu   **Religion:** Methodist
SAT/ACT/GPA: N/A   **Housing:** Yes
Student/Faculty Ratio: 17:1   **Male/Female:** 39/61
Undergraduate Enrollment: 692   **Graduate Enrollment:** 0
Scholarships/Academic: Yes   **Athletic:** Yes   **Financial Aid:** Yes
Expenses By: Year   **In State:** $ 14,863   **Out of State:** $ 14,863
Specializes In: Business, Criminal Justice, Education, Sports Medicine
Degrees Conferred: AA, BA, MA
Programs of Study: American Studies, Art, Behavioral Science, Biology, Business, Chemistry, Church and Community, Communications & Computers, Criminal Justice, Economics, Education, English, Fine Arts, History, Human Service, Mathematics, Music, Nursing, Physical Education, Political Science, Psychology, Religion and Philosophy, Sociology, Sports Medicine

Women's Athletic Profile

1200 University Boulevard   **NCAA I**
Mitchell, SD 57301   Lady Tigers, Blue, White
Coach: Geno Frugoli   **Phone:** (605) 995-2855
Email: gefrugol@dwu.edu   **Fax:** (605) 995-2699

Estimated # of Women's Volleyball Scholarships: 12
Conference: Great Plains Athletic Conference
Program Profile: DWU is a small liberal arts university of approx. 800 students with a variety of majors. It is set in the town of Mitchell, SD which has about 15,000 people. Mitchell offers great outdoor activities, and is known for hunting and fishing. It is located about 60 miles west of Sioux Falls, the largest city in South Dakota. The volleyball team has entered the GPAC conference which boasts several nationally rated teams. We play in the Wellness Center, a large two court facility that has been remodeled. The team is slowly becoming competitive playing several NAIA powerhouses and NCAA schools.
History: DWU volleyball has a great history including several teams from the late 80's and early 90's who both won the conference titles, and competed at regional and national levels.
Achievements: DWU volleyball has won several SDIC Championships, including players who are current record holders in the NAIA.
Coaching: Geno Frugoli is a first year Head Coach from Las Vegas, NV where he had a coaching record of 80-28 and never had a losing season. He was elected coach of the year in 1999 and has both conference and state runner-up titles to his credit. He also ran the All Sport Las Vegas club program which had regularly competed in the top 30 teams in the Southern California region.
Freshman Receiving Financial Aid/Academic: **Athletic:** 6
Roster In State: 6   **Out of State:** 11   **Out of Country:** 0
Sophomores on Team: **Seniors on Team:** 1   **Graduation %:** 82
Most Recent Record: 6-26
Camp of Clinic Dates: July 2001
Positions Needed: setter, outside, middles, DS
Schedule: Hastings, Dordt, Nebraska Wesleyan, St. Scholastic, National America
Style of Play: 5-1 swing offense-offense oriented-positive coaching environment

Huron University
Academic Profile

333 9th St. SW   **Phone:** 605-352-8721
Huron, SD 57350

Type: Private, 4 Yr., Liberal Arts, Coed   **Founded:** 1883
Website: http://www.huron.edu   **Religion:** Non-Affiliated

SAT/ACT/GPA: 870/18/2.0
Student/Faculty Ratio: 15:1
Undergraduate Enrollment: 600
Scholarships/Academic: Yes   **Athletic:** Yes
Expenses By: Year   **In State:** $ 13,250
Specializes In: Liberal Arts
Degrees Conferred: AA, AS, BA, BS, MBA
Programs of Study: Physical Education, Nursing, Criminal Justice, Secondary Education, Elementary Education, Business Administration, Psychology

Housing: Yes
Male/Female: 65:35
Graduate Enrollment: 70
Financial Aid: Yes
Out of State: $ 13,250

Women's Athletic Profile

333 9th Street, SW
Huron, SD 57350
Coach: Teri Holmes
Email:

NCAA I
Screaming Eagles, Silver, Grey
Phone: (605) 352-8721x26
Fax: (605) 352-7421

Estimated # of Women's Volleyball Scholarships: N/A
Conference: SDIC

Mount Marty College
Academic Profile

1105 West 8th
Yankton, SD 57078

Phone: 605-668-1268

Type: Private, 4 Yr., Liberal Arts, Coed
Website: http://www.mtmc.edu
SAT/ACT/GPA: 17 & up
Student/Faculty Ratio: 1/15
Undergraduate Enrollment: N/A
Scholarships/Academic: Yes   **Athletic:** Yes
Expenses By: Year   **In State:** $19,000
Degrees Conferred: AA, AS, BA, BS, BSEd, MED

Founded: 1936
Religion: Catholic
Housing: Yes
Male/Female: 1/2
Graduate Enrollment: N/A
Financial Aid: Yes
Out of State: $19,000

Programs of Study: Accounting, Athletic Training, Behavioral Science, Biology, Biological Science, Business Administration, Commerce, Management, Chemistry, Communications, Computer Science, Criminal Justice, PreDentistry, Elementary Education, Music, Music Education, Nursing, Radiological Technology

Women's Athletic Profile

1105 W. 8th Street
Yankton, SD 57078
Coach: Tracy Thompson
Email:

NCAA I
Lancers, Gold, White, Blue
Phone: (605) 668-1366
Fax: (605) 668-1357

Estimated # of Women's Volleyball Scholarships: N/A
Conference: South Dakota-Iowa Conference

National American University
Academic Profile

321 Kansas City Street
Rapid City, SD 57701

Phone: (800) 843-8892

Type: Private, 4 Yr., Coed
Website: http://www.national.edu
SAT/ACT/GPA: Open
Student/Faculty Ratio: 15:1
Undergraduate Enrollment: 750
Scholarships/Academic: Yes   **Athletic:** Yes
Expenses By: Year   **In State:** $13,470
Specializes In: Business, Computer Information Systems, Athletic Training, Sport Mgmt.

Founded: 1941
Religion: Great Plains
Housing: Yes
Male/Female: 60:40
Graduate Enrollment: N/A
Financial Aid: Yes
Out of State: $13,470

Degrees Conferred: BA

Programs of Study: Accounting, Athletic Training, Business Administration, Computer Information Systems, Computer Technology, Financial Management, International Business, Management Information Systems, Occupational Therapy, Paralegal Studies, Veterinary Technician, Web Developer/Web Master Microsoft Certification

Women's Athletic Profile

321 Kansas City St.
Rapid City, SD 57701
Coach: Amy Erlandson
Email:

NCAA I
Mavericks, Royal, White, Red
Phone: (605) 394-4851
Fax: (605) 394-4871

Did Not Return Profile

Northern State University
Academic Profile

1200 South Jay St.
Aberdeen, SD 57401

Phone: (605) 626-2488

Type: Public, 4 Yr., Liberal Arts, Coed
Website: http://www.northern.edu
SAT/ACT/GPA: 18/2.0
Student/Faculty Ratio: 19:1
Undergraduate Enrollment: 2,563
Scholarships/Academic: Yes
Expenses By: Year

Athletic: Yes
In State: $ 5,800

Founded: 1901
Religion: Non-Affiliated
Housing: No
Male/Female: 39:61
Graduate Enrollment: 215
Financial Aid: Yes
Out of State: $ 9,900

Specializes In: Business, Education and Fine Arts

Degrees Conferred: AA, AS, BA, BS, Pre-Professional, Bachelor of Fine Arts

Programs of Study: Accounting, Administrative Systems, Art, Biology, Business, Chemistry, Community Services, Economics, Education, English, Environmental Science, Finance, Fitness Management, Foreign Languages, Health and Physical Education, History, Industrial Technology, International Business, Management, Marketing, Mathematics, Medical Technology, Music, Political Science, Psychology, Social Science, Sociology, Special Education, Speech

Women's Athletic Profile

1200 South Jay St.
Aberdeen, SD 57401
Coach: Lisa Schriver
Email: schrivel@wolf.northern.edu

NCAA I
Lady Wolves, Maroon, Gold
Phone: (605) 626-2230
Fax: (605) 626-2238

Estimated # of Women's Volleyball Scholarships: 6

Conference: Northern Sun Intercollegiate Conference

Program Profile: We have a junior varsity and a varsity program. We play at Barnott Center which seats 8,000 and is air-conditioned. We play a fall season.

History: We played in the NAIA from 1973 to 1993. We have been a Divison II program from 1994 to the present.

Achievements: Conference Coach of the Year. 3rd place in the Conference.

Coaching: Lisa Schriver, has been Head Coach from 1996 to the present. Her overall record is 57-43. Greg Marley is Assistant Coach.

Freshman Receiving Financial Aid/Academic:
Roster In State: 9
Sophomores on Team: 0
Most Recent Record: 21-10-0

Out of State: 11
Seniors on Team: 3
Fall Games: 30

Athletic: 6
Out of Country: 0
Graduation %: 98
Spring Games: 3 tournaments

Camp of Clinic Dates: Team camp June 18-19; Individual Camp June 26-July 1

Positions Needed: Middle

Schedule: North Dakota State, Tampa, South Dakota State, Edinboro-Pennsylvania, Nebraska-Omaha, Duluth, Minnesota

Style of Play: Aggressive defensive team. Balanced attack.

South Dakota State University
Academic Profile

16th Ave. & 11th St.
Brookings, SD 57007

Phone: 800-952-3541

Type: Public, 4 Yr., Liberal Arts, Coed
Website: http://www.sdstate.edu
SAT/ACT/GPA: 22avg
Student/Faculty Ratio: 17:1
Undergraduate Enrollment: 8,100
Scholarships/Academic: Yes   **Athletic:** Yes
Expenses By: Year   **In State:** $ 6,500

Founded: 1881
Religion: Non-Affiliated
Housing: No
Male/Female: 52:48
Graduate Enrollment: 1,075
Financial Aid: Yes
Out of State: $ 10,000

Degrees Conferred: AS, BA, BS, BSN, MA, MS, Ph.D.
Programs of Study: Agricultural, Animal, Biological Science, Botany, Broadcasting, Chemistry, Engineering, Computer, Design, Dietetics, Economics, Education, Geography, Journalism, Medical, PreProfessional Programs, Parks/Recreation, Psychology

Women's Athletic Profile

16th & 11th Street
Brookings, SD 57007
Coach: Mary Byrne
Email:

NCAA I
Lady Jack Rabbits, Yellow, Blue
Phone: (605) 688-5526
Fax:

Estimated # of Women's Volleyball Scholarships: N/A
Conference: North Central Collegiate Athletic Conference

University of Sioux Falls
Academic Profile

1101 West 22nd Street
Sioux Falls, SD 57105

Phone: (605) 331-6600

Type: Private, 4 Yr., Liberal Arts, Coed
Website: http://www.thecoo.edu
SAT/ACT/GPA: 19+/2.0+
Student/Faculty Ratio: 14:1
Undergraduate Enrollment: 1,039
Scholarships/Academic: Yes   **Athletic:** Yes
Expenses By: Year   **In State:** $ 15,200

Founded: 1883
Religion: American Baptist
Housing: Yes
Male/Female: 45:55
Graduate Enrollment: N/A
Financial Aid: Yes
Out of State: $ 15,200

Specializes In: Business, Education
Degrees Conferred: AA, BA, BS, MBA, M Ed
Programs of Study: Art, Biology, Business Administration, Chemistry, Computer Science, Education, English, Exercise Science, History, Political Science, Mass Communication, Mathematics, Music, Psychology, Religious Studies, Social Science, Social Work, Sociology, Speech, Radiologic Technology, Theatre, Wellness

Women's Athletic Profile

1101 West 22nd Street
Sioux Falls, SD 57105
Coach: Lori Huisken
Email: Admissions@thecoo.edu

NCAA I
Cougars, Purple, White, Silver
Phone: (605) 331-6600
Fax: (605) 331-6615

Estimated # of Women's Volleyball Scholarships: 5 partial
Conference: South Dakota-Iowa Conference
Program Profile: We play at USF Stewart Center which has 2,000 seats. We play a fall schedule.
History: Our program began in the 1980's. We established a school record with 30 wins in 1996. We finished second in the SDIC in 1998 with a 6-1 record (19-14) under the first year that Lori Huisken was head coach.
Coaching: Lori Huisken, Head Coach, has been at USF for one year. She has a 19-14 record and led our team to second place in Conference. Kris Dunlap is Assistant Coach.
Freshman Receiving Financial Aid/Academic: **Athletic:** 6
Roster In State: 8   **Out of State:** 11   **Out of Country:** 0

Sophomores on Team: 0   **Seniors on Team:** 4   **Graduation %:** 100
Most Recent Record: 19-14-0   **Fall Games:** 40   **Spring Games:** 0
Positions Needed: Setters, Hitters
Schedule: Dordt College, Northwestern College, Black Hills State
Style of Play: Quick tempo; enthusiastic; enjoy playing the game.

University of South Dakota
Academic Profile

414 E. Clark St.
Vermillion, SD 57069

Phone: 605-677-5434

Type: Public, 4 Yr., Liberal Arts, Coed
Website: http://www.usd.edu
SAT/ACT/GPA: 20avg
Student/Faculty Ratio: 17:1
Undergraduate Enrollment: 6,025
Scholarships/Academic: Yes   **Athletic:** Yes
Expenses By: Year   **In State:** $ 6,000
Degrees Conferred: AA, BA, BFA, MA, MBA, MFA, MD
Programs of Study: Contact school for program of study.

Founded: 1862
Religion: Non-Affiliated
Housing: No
Male/Female: 45:55
Graduate Enrollment: 1,710
Financial Aid: Yes
Out of State: $ 8,450

Women's Athletic Profile

414 E. Clark Street
Vermillion, SD 57069-2390
Coach: Darin Weber
Email: dweber@usd.edu

NCAA I
Lady Coyotes, Scarlet, White
Phone: (605) 677-5936
Fax: (605) 677-5618

Estimated # of Women's Volleyball Scholarships: 8
Conference: North Central Collegiate Athletic Conference
Program Profile: The program is under new leadership and is seeing significant improvement. The Coyotes play in the Dakota Dome on a sport court. Although they set the court up in the corner of the dome the dome seats over 10,000 people. The dome also has a swimming pool, weight room, training room, and two extra courts.
History: The program began in 1973 and the overall record is 231-639-3. In Weber's 1st year the team went 10-25, the most wins since 1988 and also got the 1st conference win since 1997. The program is only in it's 3rd season of being fully funded and competes in the toughest conference in the NCAA D. II
Coaching: Coach Weber was at Western State College where his record was 82-74. Assistant Kam Heger was a former player at Western State College.
Freshman Receiving Financial Aid/Academic: **Athletic:** 3
Roster In State: 3   **Out of State:** 6   **Out of Country:** 0
Most Recent Record: 10-25
Positions Needed: Outside Hitters, Middle Hitter
Schedule: South Dakota State, Univ. Nebraska-Omaha, Univ. Northern Colorado
Style of Play: Powerful outside game with a quick tempo middle attack. We try and use athletes strengths. We play a read defense to best utilize athletic ability.

TENNESSEE

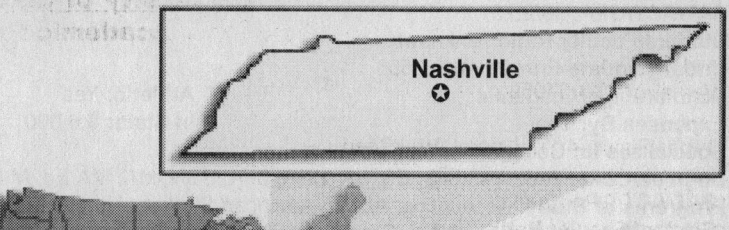

Nashville ☆

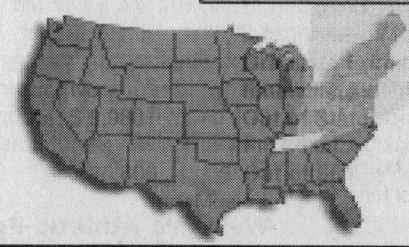

SCHOOL	CITY	AFFILIATION	PAGE
Austin Peay State University	Clarksville	NCAA I	703
Belmont University	Nashville	NCAA I	703
Bethel College	McKenzie	NAIA	704
Bryan College	Dayton	NCCAA/NAIA	704
Carson-Newman College	Jefferson City	NCAA II	705
Christian Brothers University	Memphis	NCAA II	706
East Tennessee State University	Johnson City	NCAA I	707
Fisk University	Nashville	NCAA III	707
Freed Hardeman University	Henderson	NAIA	708
King College	Bristol	NAIA	708
Lambuth University	Jackson	NAIA	709
Lane College	Jackson	NCAA II	709
Le Moyne-Owen College	Memphis	NCAA II	710
Lee University	Cleveland	NCCAA/NAIA	710
Lincoln Memorial University	Harrogate	NCAA II	711
Lipscomd University	Nashville	NAIA	711
Martin Methodist College	Pulaski	NAIA	712
Maryville College	Maryville	NCAA III	712
Middle Tennessee State University	Murfreesboro	NCAA I	713
Milligan College	Milligan College	NAIA	713
Rhodes College	Memphis	NCAA III	714
Tennessee State University	Nashville	NCAA I	714
Trevecca Nazarene University	Nashville	NAIA	715
Tusculum College	Greenville	NCAA II	716
University of Memphis	Memphis	NCAA I	716
Univ of Tennessee - Chattanooga	Chattanooga	NCAA I	717
Univers of Tennessee - Knoxville	Knoxville	NCAA I	718
University of Tennessee - Martin	Martin	NCAA I	718
University of the South	Sewanee	NCAA III	719

Austin Peay State University
Academic Profile

P.O. Box 4548
Clarksville, TN 37044

Phone: (931) 648-7661

Type: Public, 4 Yr., Liberal Arts, Coed
Website: http://www.apsu.edu
SAT/ACT/GPA: 19/2.75
Student/Faculty Ratio: Unknown
Undergraduate Enrollment: 7,508
Scholarships/Academic: Yes
Expenses By: Year
Specializes In: Comprehensive Curriculum

Founded: 1927
Religion: Non-Affiliated
Housing: Yes
Male/Female: 43:57
Graduate Enrollment: 1,000

Athletic: Yes
In State: $ 6,000

Financial Aid: Yes
Out of State: $ 11,000

Degrees Conferred: AAS, AS, BS, BA, BBA, BFA, BSN, MA, MA Ed, M Mu, MS, Ed S
Programs of Study: Accounting, African American Studies, Agriculture, Art, Allied Health, Biology, Business, Chemistry, Computer Science, Criminal Justice, CSCI, Economics, Education, English, Engineering Technology, Environmental Geography, Finance, Foreign Language, Geology, Geography, Health & Human Performance, History, International Studies, Marketing, Mass Communications, Mathematics, Medical Technology, Music, Nursing, Philosophy, Physics, Political Science, Psychology, Public Management, Public Relations, Radiology, Sociology, Special Education. Masters: Administration/Supervision, Biology, Communication, Elementary Education, English, HHP, Music, Psychology

Women's Athletic Profile

P.O. Box 4515
Clarksville, TN 37044-4576
Coach: Cheryl Holt
Email:

NCAA I
Lady Governors, Red, White
Phone: (931) 648-7661
Fax: (931) 648-7830

Estimated # of Women's Volleyball Scholarships: 10
Conference: Ohio Valley Conference
Program Profile: Dunn Athletic Center seats 9,000. We are a small Division I school.
History: We started in 1980. We are a competitive team, usually ranked 4th in the conference.
Coaching: Cheryl Holt, Head Coach, started coaching in 1982. She is in her 17th year as coach.
Freshman Receiving Financial Aid/Academic:

Athletic: 4

Roster In State: 2
Sophomores on Team: 4
Most Recent Record: 19-12-0

Out of State: 8
Seniors on Team:
Fall Games: 28

Out of Country: 0
Graduation %: 100
Spring Games: 4

Schedule: St. Louis, Dayton, Ball State, UNC Charlotte
Style of Play: Solid fundamentals. Quick. Not very tall. Good servers. Strong defensively.

Belmont University
Academic Profile

1900 Belmont Blvd.
Nashville, TN 37221

Phone: 615-460-6785

Type: Private, 4 Yr., Liberal Arts, Coed
Website: http://www.belmont.edu
SAT/ACT/GPA: 1000/21/2.5
Student/Faculty Ratio: 14:1
Undergraduate Enrollment: 3,000
Scholarships/Academic: Yes
Expenses By: Year

Founded: 1951
Religion: Christian
Housing: Yes
Male/Female: 45:55
Graduate Enrollment: 400

Athletic: Yes
In State: $ 15,500

Financial Aid: Yes
Out of State: $ 15,500

Specializes In: Business, Nursing, Music, Education, Humanities
Degrees Conferred: BA, BS, BBA, BM, BMEd, BSN, BFA, MA, MSN, MS, MBA, MEd
Programs of Study: Accounting, Art, Biology, Communications, Broadcasting, Chemistry, Child Care Administration, Church Music, Commercial Music, Computer Science, Economics, Elementary Education, English, Exercise Science, Finance, French, Graphic Design, Health, History, Hospitality Management, Marketing, Mathematics, Medical Technology, Music, Music Business, Physical Education, Physics, Political Science, Nursing, Philosophy, Psychology, Religion, Science, Social Work, Spanish, Studio Art, Theatre & Dance

Women's Athletic Profile

1900 Belmont Boulevard
Nashville, TN 37212-3757
Coach: Traci Corey
Email: coreyt@mail.belmont.edu

NCAA I
Lady Bruins, Navy, Red, White
Phone: (615) 460-6261
Fax: (615) 460-5584

Estimated # of Women's Volleyball Scholarships: 1 2001, 4 2002
Conference: TAAC
Program Profile: NCAA DI new in the TAAC Conference. Have been NAIA to independent NCAA now NCAA D.I. Young program still developing, new facility this year with locker rooms, training room, and weight room etc.
History: I started the program when the school was NAIA in 1993 and was one of the top teams. NCAA I is a big jump from NAIA. We are making quick progress and looking forward to being in the conference and expect to come in middle to upper part of the conference.
Achievements: NAIA Conference Title 1995 and Coach of the Year in 1995.
Coaching: Traci Corey has been the only Head Coach in the history of the Belmont volleyball program. Entering here eighth season with the Bruins, Corey brings a record of 94-124. Jill Simmons is entering her first season as an Assistant Coach at Belmont. Simmons brings plenty of experience as a player and coach.
Freshman Receiving Financial Aid/Academic:
Athletic: 1
Roster In State: 2 | **Out of State:** 8 | **Out of Country:** 0
Sophomores on Team: | **Seniors on Team:** 0 | **Graduation %:** 60
Most Recent Record: 12-23
Camp of Clinic Dates: TBA
Positions Needed: Middle, RS, Setter
Schedule: Georgia State, Central Florida, Mesa, Jacksonville University
Style of Play: Play a 5-1 quick offense, with an aggressive style.

Bethel College
Academic Profile

College Drive
McKenzie, TN 38201

Phone: 901-352-4030

Type: Private, 4 Yr., Coed
Website: http://www.bethel-college.edu
SAT/ACT/GPA: 14+
Student/Faculty Ratio: 15:1
Undergraduate Enrollment: 420
Scholarships/Academic: Yes | **Athletic:** Yes
Expenses By: Year | **In State:** $ 9,400
Founded: 1842
Religion: Presbyterian
Housing: No
Male/Female: 43:57
Graduate Enrollment: 40
Financial Aid: Yes
Out of State: $ 9,400
Degrees Conferred: AA, BA, BS, MA, MED
Programs of Study: Accounting, Applied Mathematics, Biological Science, Business Administration, Chemistry, Elementary Education, English, Health Education, History, Music, Physical Education, Psychology, Religion, Social Science

Women's Athletic Profile

College Drive
McKenzie, TN 38201
Coach: Tami Coleman
Email:

NCAA I
Lady Wildcats, Purple, Gold
Phone: (904) 255-1401x319
Fax: (904) 253-4231

Estimated # of Women's Volleyball Scholarships: No
Conference: Kentucky Intercollegiate
Program Profile: Baker Fieldhouse has a 2,000 seating capacity. We play a 20-25 match season.
Roster In State: 7 | **Out of State:** 3 | **Out of Country:** 0
Sophomores on Team: 0 | **Seniors on Team:** 1 | **Graduation %:** Unknown
Most Recent Record: | **Fall Games:** 25 | **Spring Games:** 0
Positions Needed: Hitter

Bryan College
Academic Profile

Box 7000
Dayton, TN 37321

Phone: 423-775-2041

Type: Private, 4 Yr., Liberal Arts, Coed

Founded: 1930

Website: http://www.bryan.edu
SAT/ACT/GPA: 860/18/2.5
Student/Faculty Ratio: 14:1
Undergraduate Enrollment: 500
Scholarships/Academic: Yes **Athletic:** Yes
Expenses By: Year **In State:** $ 15,150
Degrees Conferred: AA, AS, BA, BS

Religion: Inter-denominational
Housing: Yes
Male/Female: 45:55
Graduate Enrollment: N/A
Financial Aid: Yes
Out of State: $ 15,150

Programs of Study: Bible, Biology, Business, Christian Education, Communications, English, History, Liberal Arts, Elementary Education, Mathematics, Music, Exercise Science, Physical Education, Psychology

Women's Athletic Profile

130 Mercer Drive, P.O. Box 7000
Dayton, TN 37321
Coach: Jerri Beck
Email: admission@bryan.edu

NCAA I
Lady Lions, Red, Gold
Phone: (423) 775-2044
Fax: (423) 775-7330

Estimated # of Women's Volleyball Scholarships: N/A
Conference: Tennessee-Virginia Athletic Conference
Program Profile: We have a strong Christian commitment within our program and college. We play in Summers Gymnasium with 1,000 seat capacity. The season begins in September and continues through November.
Achievements: All-Conference player each year; Academic All-American in 1995 & 1996; All-Region Honorable Mention in 1998.
Coaching: Jerri Beck, Head Coach, started in 1993 to the present. In 1998, he compiled a record of 20-12 and his overall record is 69-78. He lettered for four years at Bryan College for volleyball and basketball. Renae Marcus, Assistant Coach, started in the 1998 season. He was a year letter-winner at Bryan and captain in 1996.
Freshman Receiving Financial Aid/Academic: **Athletic:** 1
Roster In State: 2 **Out of State:** 9 **Out of Country:** 0
Sophomores on Team: 0 **Seniors on Team:** 2 **Graduation %:** 0
Most Recent Record: 20-12-0 **Fall Games:** 32 **Spring Games:** 0
Positions Needed: Setter, Middle Hitter
Schedule: King College, Bluefield College, David Lipscomb University, Milligan College, Union University, Loyola University
Style of Play: We are quickly developing in strength and speed of offense. Our defense is well-balanced and fundamentally sound.

Carson - Newman College
Academic Profile

CNC Box 71972
Jefferson City, TN 37760

Phone: (423) 471-3424

Type: Private, 4 Yr., Liberal Arts, Coed
Website: http://www.cn.edu
SAT/ACT/GPA: 880/21
Student/Faculty Ratio: 13:1
Undergraduate Enrollment: 2,000
Scholarships/Academic: Yes **Athletic:** Yes
Expenses By: Year **In State:** $ 14,480
Specializes In: Medical Science, Business, Education, Nursing
Degrees Conferred: AA, BA, BS, MA, M.Ed.

Founded: 1851
Religion: Southern Baptist
Housing: Yes
Male/Female: 1:1
Graduate Enrollment: 200
Financial Aid: Yes
Out of State: $ 14,480

Programs of Study: All Sciences, Humanities, Mathematics, Art, Athletic Training, Nursing, Business, PreMed, PreLaw, Communication Arts, Computer Science, Education, English, Family and Consumer Services, Foreign Languages, General Studies, History, Human Studies, Math, Music, Natural and Physical Science

Women's Athletic Profile

2130 S. Branner Avenue
Jefferson City, TN 37760
Coach: Perry Robinson
Email: probinso@cncadmnt.nc.edu

NCAA I
Lady Eagles, Orange, Blue
Phone: (423) 471-9061
Fax: (423) 471-3514

Estimated # of Women's Volleyball Scholarships: 5
Conference: South Atlantic Conference
Program Profile: Our fieldhouse has 2,000 seats and was renovated in 1993.

History: Our records begin with the 1988 season. Our highest Conference finish was 3rd place in 1991. Our overall record in 1988 was 123-227.

Achievements: Holly Borham was South Atlantic Player of the Year in 1994

Coaching: Perry Robinson, became Head Coach in 1998. His overall record here is 12-21.

Freshman Receiving Financial Aid/Academic:

		Athletic: 2
Roster In State: 5	**Out of State:** 7	**Out of Country:** 0
Sophomores on Team: 0	**Seniors on Team:** 1	**Graduation %:** 76.5
Most Recent Record: 12-21-0	**Fall Games:** 33	**Spring Games:** 3

Positions Needed: All

Schedule: Gordon, Catawba, University of Montevallo, Lees-McRae, Lincoln Memorial University, Mars Hill

Style of Play: We are defense oriented and focus on ball control to facilitate an up-tempo offense.

Christian Brothers University
Academic Profile

650 E. Parkway South
Memphis, TN 38104

Phone: (901) 321-3371

Type: Private, 4 Yr., Liberal Arts, Engineering, Coed
Website: http://www.cbu.edu
SAT/ACT/GPA: 1000/22/3.0
Student/Faculty Ratio: 15:1
Undergraduate Enrollment: 1,200
Scholarships/Academic: Yes   **Athletic:** Yes
Expenses By: Year   **In State:** $ 17,400

Founded: 1871
Religion: Non-Affiliated
Housing: Yes
Male/Female: 52:48
Graduate Enrollment: 3,000
Financial Aid: Yes
Out of State: $ 17,400

Specializes In: Business, Education, Engineering, Sciences

Degrees Conferred: Bachelors, Masters

Programs of Study: Biology, Business Administration, Accounting, Chemical Engineering, Chemistry, Computer Science, Economics-Finance, Engineering, English, History, Human Development, Liberal Studies, Management, Marketing, Mathematics, Natural Science, Psychology, Physics, Religion, Telecommunications

Women's Athletic Profile

650 E. Parkway S
Memphis, TN 38104
Coach: Gary Lee
Email: glee@mail.cbu.edu

NCAA I
Buccaneers, Scarlet, Grey
Phone: (901) 321-3371
Fax: (901) 321-3370

Estimated # of Women's Volleyball Scholarships: 3

Conference: Gulf South Conference

Program Profile: We have a new Division III program. We upgraded from NAIA three years ago. We compete in the Gulf South Conference and are located in mid-town Memphis. We compete both in the Fall and the Spring.

History: Our program began with Head Coach Jennie Bradford in 1976. We were competing in the NAIA. Our NCAA II affiliation began in 1996. Our institution was allowed to compete for the first time in the post season in the NCAA II tournament in 1998.

Coaching: Gary Lee, Head Coach, started in the 1998 season. He ended the year with a 9-24 record. He coached the Delaware Blue Hens to the 1992 North Atlantic Conference Title before he came here.

Freshman Receiving Financial Aid/Academic:

		Athletic: 4
Roster In State: 3	**Out of State:** 5	**Out of Country:** 0
Sophomores on Team: 0	**Seniors on Team:** 1	**Graduation %:** 100
Most Recent Record: 9-24-0	**Fall Games:** 33	**Spring Games:** 0

Camp of Clinic Dates: July 12-23, 1999

Positions Needed: Middle Blocker, Setter

Schedule: Angelo State, Morningside, Alabama Huntsville, Drury, Henderson State, Arkansas Tech, Lane, Harding, Rhodes

Style of Play: Speed over size; defense to offense.

Women's Athletic Profile

One Cumberland Square
Lebanon, TN 37087
Coach: Dwayne Deering
Email:

NCAA I
Volleydawgs, Maroon, White
Phone: (800) 467-0562
Fax: (615) 444-2562

Estimated # of Women's Volleyball Scholarships: 3.5

Conference: Mid-South Conference
Program Profile: We were 1998 runner-up in the Mid-South. We were Conference Champs in 1991, 1993, 1994, 1995 & 1997. Dallas Floyd Recreation Center has an approximately 1,800 capacity.
History: We are not not exactly sure when the first year of the program was.
Achievements: Conference Champions in 1991, 1993, 1994, 1995 & 1997; 1 All-American; 2 Academic All-Americans (but have more in 1998); Coach of the Year in 1989, 1991, 1993, 1994 & 1997.
Coaching: Dwayne Deering, Head Coach, started coaching the team in 1988 to the present with a record of 297-127. Holly Zchel, Michelle Gunmen, Stephanie Dillard and Jill Simmons are Assistant Coaches.

Freshman Receiving Financial Aid/Academic:		**Athletic:** 8
Roster In State: 18	**Out of State:** 1	**Out of Country:** 0
Sophomores on Team: 4	**Seniors on Team:** 3	**Graduation %:** 100
Most Recent Record: 17-12-0	**Fall Games:** 29	**Spring Games:** 0

Camp of Clinic Dates: July or August
Schedule: Lipscomb, Georgetown, Lambuth, Campbellsville, Union, Cumberland
Style of Play: Fundamentals, simple, disciplined, and hustling.

East Tennessee State University
Academic Profile

University Drive & State of Franklin
Johnson City, TN 37614

Phone: (423) 439-4259

Type: Public, 4 Yr., Coed
Website: http://www.etsu.edu
SAT/ACT/GPA: NCAA Requirements
Student/Faculty Ratio: 20:1
Undergraduate Enrollment: 12,000
Scholarships/Academic: Yes
Expenses By: Year
Specializes In: Education, Medical School
Degrees Conferred: BS, MA
Programs of Study: All

Founded: 1909
Religion: Non-Affiliated
Housing: Yes
Male/Female: 1:3
Graduate Enrollment: 1,000
Athletic: Yes **Financial Aid:** Yes
In State: $ 6,482 **Out of State:** $ 11,308

Women's Athletic Profile

University Drive & State of Franklin
Johnson City, TN 37614
Coach: Kim Zenner
Email: zenner@ETSU.edu

NCAA I
Lady Buccaneers, Blue, Gold
Phone: (423) 439-4259
Fax: (423) 439-5294

Estimated # of Women's Volleyball Scholarships: 11
Conference: Southern Conference
Program Profile: ETSU is attempting to move back into the top echelon of the Southern Conference after a few years hiatus. The Buccaneers play in a perfect volleyball setting. Brooks Gym has 3, 500 seats. It will serve as the home for Blue Volleyball only in a few years.
History: The first year of competition for us was 1974. Since joining the Southern Conference in 1983, the Buccaneers have captured four regular-season and two tournament titles. ESTU has tallied 26 spots on the All-Southern Conference teams, fourteen being first-team honorees.
Achievements: ETSU captured 4 regular-season (1987,1988,.1989,1991) and 2 tournament titles (1989 & 1992); 3 ESTU players have been named Freshman of the Year; 3 players have been chosen League Player of the Year.
Coaching: The current coaching staff enters its second year at the helm of the program. Head Coach Kim Zenner, was named the Southern Conference Player of the Year in 1988. She was a two-time 1st team all-conference selection at ETSU.

Freshman Receiving Financial Aid/Academic:		**Athletic:** 2
Roster In State: 3	**Out of State:** 10	**Out of Country:** 0
Sophomores on Team: 0	**Seniors on Team:** 1	**Graduation %:** Unknown
Most Recent Record: 8-20-0	**Fall Games:** 28	**Spring Games:** 0

Schedule: University of Tennessee at Chattanooga, University of Central Florida, McNeese State, Sam Houston, Davidson, Radford
Style of Play: Fast offensive sets with a lot of miss-direction plays. The team is extremely communicative and intense on the court.

Fisk University
Academic Profile

1000 - 17th Avenue North
Nashville, TN 37208-3051

Phone: 615-329-8665

Type: 4 Yr., Coed

Founded:

Website: http://www.dubois.fisk.edu
SAT/ACT/GPA: Open
Student/Faculty Ratio:
Undergraduate Enrollment: N/A
Scholarships/Academic:　　　　　　　　**Athletic:**
Expenses By: Year　　　　　　　　　　**In State:**
Degrees Conferred:
Programs of Study: Art Education, Biological Science, Business Administration, Chemistry, Dramatic Arts, Economics, English, Fine Arts, French, History, Mathematics, Music, Music Education, Philosophy, Physics, Political Science, PreProfessional Programs, Psychology, Religion, Social Science, Spanish, Speech

Religion: Non-Affiliated
Housing: No
Male/Female:
Graduate Enrollment: N/A
Financial Aid:
Out of State:

Women's Athletic Profile

17 Avenue, N
Nashville, TN 37208
Coach: Damien Jackson
Email:

NCAA I
Lady Bulldogs, Blue, Gold
Phone: (615) 329-8668
Fax: (615) 329-8686

Estimated # of Women's Volleyball Scholarships: N/A
Conference: Independent

Freed - Hardeman University
Academic Profile

158 E. Main
Henderson, TN 38340

Phone: 800-630-3480

Type: Private, 4 Yr., Liberal Arts, Coed
Website: http://www.fhu.edu
SAT/ACT/GPA: 18
Student/Faculty Ratio: 15:1
Undergraduate Enrollment: 1,253
Scholarships/Academic: Yes　　　　　**Athletic:** Yes
Expenses By: Year　　　　　　　　　　**In State:** $ 10,500
Degrees Conferred: BA, BS, BSA, BSE, BSW, MED

Founded: 1869
Religion: Church of Christ
Housing: No
Male/Female: 47:53
Graduate Enrollment: 252
Financial Aid: Yes
Out of State: $ 10,500

Programs of Study: Accounting, Agricultural, Business Management, Banking/Finance, Biological Science, Broadcasting, Business Administration, Chemistry, Communications, Computer Science, Dramatic Arts, Education, English, Fine Arts, History, Marketing, Mathematics, Medical Laboratory Technology, Psychology, Public Relations, Religion, Social Science

Women's Athletic Profile

158 E. Main
Henderson, TN 38340
Coach: Todd Humphry
Email: thumphry@fhu.edu

NCAA I
Lions, Maroon, White, Gold
Phone: (800) 630-3480
Fax: (901) 989-6910

Estimated # of Women's Volleyball Scholarships: N/A
Conference: Tran South Conference

King College
Academic Profile

1350 King College Rd.
Bristol, TN 37620

Phone: 800-362-0014

Type: Private, 4 Yr., Liberal Arts, Coed
Website: http://www.king.edu
SAT/ACT/GPA: 950+21+
Student/Faculty Ratio: 14:1
Undergraduate Enrollment: 600
Scholarships/Academic: Yes　　　　　**Athletic:** Yes
Expenses By: Year　　　　　　　　　　**In State:** $ 14,600
Specializes In: PreMed, Humanities, Economics, Business

Founded: 1867
Religion: Presbyterian
Housing: Yes
Male/Female: 50:50
Graduate Enrollment: N/A
Financial Aid: Yes
Out of State: $ 14,600

Degrees Conferred: BA, BS
Programs of Study: PreProfessional Programs, PreMed, Health Sciences, Dentistry, Engineering, Law, Pharmaceutical Science, Physical and Occupational Therapy, Veterinary Medicine, Ministry, American Studies, Mathematics, Behavioral Science, Bible & Religion, Biology, Chemistry, Computer Information Systems, Computer Science, Economics and Business Administration, Education, English, Fine Arts, French, History, Medical Technology, Modern Languages, Physics, Political Science, Psychology, Spanish

Women's Athletic Profile

1350 King College Rd.
Bristol, TN 37620
Coach: Susan Toomey
Email: sktoomey@king.edu

NCAA I
Lady Tornado, Scarlet, Blue
Phone: (423) 652-4782
Fax: (423) 652-6041

Estimated # of Women's Volleyball Scholarships: N/A
Conference: TVAC

Lambuth University
Academic Profile

705 Lambuth Blvd.
Jackson, TN 38301

Phone: 800-526-2884

Type: Private, 4 Yr., Liberal Arts, Coed
Website: http://www.lambuth.edu
SAT/ACT/GPA: 930/20/2.5
Student/Faculty Ratio: 13:1
Undergraduate Enrollment: 1,250
Scholarships/Academic: Yes   **Athletic:** Yes
Expenses By: Year   **In State:** $ 18,808
Specializes In: Liberal Arts
Degrees Conferred: BA, BS

Founded: 1843
Religion: Methodist
Housing: Yes
Male/Female: 50:50
Graduate Enrollment: N/A
Financial Aid: Yes
Out of State: $ 18,808

Programs of Study: Accounting, Applied Arts, Art, Biblical Studies, Biology, Broadcasting, Business and Management, Business Administration, Chemistry, Communications, Computer Science, Computer Information Systems, Economics, Education, Elementary Education, English, Fashion Merchandising, History, Human Ecology, Interior Design, International Relations, Management, Marketing, Mathematics, Modern Languages, Music, Nutrition, Philosophy, Physical Education, Physical Science, Physics, Political Science, Pre-Professional Programs, Psychology, Recreation/Athletic Training, Religion, Science, Secondary Education, Social Science, Sociology, Spanish, Special Education, Speech Pathology, Speech Therapy, Theatre, Visual Art

Women's Athletic Profile

705 Lambuth Boulevard
Jackson, TN 38301
Coach: Joanie Albury
Email:

NCAA I
Lady Eagles, Blue, White
Phone: (901) 425-3379
Fax: (901) 425-3498

Estimated # of Women's Volleyball Scholarships: N/A
Conference: Mid-south Conference

Lane College
Academic Profile

545 Lane Avenue
Jackson, TN 38301

Phone: 800-960-7533

Type: 4 Yr., Coed
Website: Not Available
SAT/ACT/GPA: Open
Student/Faculty Ratio:
Undergraduate Enrollment: N/A
Scholarships/Academic: **Athletic:**
Expenses By: Year   **In State:**
Degrees Conferred: Not-Available

Founded:
Religion: Non-Affiliated
Housing: No
Male/Female:
Graduate Enrollment: N/A
Financial Aid:
Out of State:

Programs of Study: Biological Science, Business Administration, Chemistry, Civil Engineering, Communications, Computer Science, Education, Electrical Engineering, Elementary Education, English, History, Mathematics, Music, Nursing, Physical Education, PreProfessional Programs, Religion, Social Science

545 Lane Avenue
Jackson, TN 38301
Coach: James Walker, Sr.
Email:

NCAA I
Lady Dragons, Red, Blue
Phone: (901) 426-7570
Fax: (901) 423-7107

Estimated # of Women's Volleyball Scholarships: N/A
Conference: Southern Intercollegiate Conference

Le Moyne - Owen College
Academic Profile

807 Walker Avenue
Memphis, TN 36125

Phone: 901-942-7302

Type: 4 Yr.; Coed
Website: http://www.lemoyne-owen.edu
SAT/ACT/GPA: 820/17
Student/Faculty Ratio: 16:1
Undergraduate Enrollment: 1,200
Scholarships/Academic: No
Expenses By: Year
Degrees Conferred: Not-Available

Athletic: Yes
In State:

Founded: 1862
Religion: Non-Affiliated
Housing: Yes
Male/Female:
Graduate Enrollment: N/A
Financial Aid: Yes
Out of State:

Programs of Study: Accounting, Biological Science, Business Administration, Chemistry, Economics, Education, Engineering, English, Fine Arts, Health Education, History, Humanities, Mathematics, Natural Science, Physical Education, Political Science, Social Sciences

Women's Athletic Profile

807 Walker Avenue
Memphis, TN 38126
Coach: Eddie Cook
Email:

NCAA I
Lady Magicians, Purple, Gold
Phone: (901) 942-7326
Fax: (901) 942-7810

Estimated # of Women's Volleyball Scholarships: N/A
Conference: Southern Intercollegiate Conference

Lee University
Academic Profile

1120 N Ocoee Street
Cleveland, TN 37311

Phone: 1-800-LEE-9930

Type: Private, 4 Yr., Liberal Arts, Coed
Website: http://www.leeuniversity.edu
SAT/ACT/GPA: 860/18
Student/Faculty Ratio: 19:1
Undergraduate Enrollment: 2,652
Scholarships/Academic: Yes
Expenses By: Year
Specializes In: Music, Pre-Med, Religion, Education
Degrees Conferred: BA, BS

Athletic: Yes
In State: $ 9,600

Founded: 1918
Religion: Church of God
Housing: Yes
Male/Female: 49:51
Graduate Enrollment: N/A
Financial Aid: Yes
Out of State: $ 9,600

Programs of Study: Behavioral & Social Sciences, Education, Business, Bible and Christian Ministries, Language Arts, Accounting, Education, Elementary and Secondary Education, Physical Education, Secretarial & Related Programs

Women's Athletic Profile

1120 Ocoee Street
Cleveland, TN 37311
Coach: Andrea Hudson
Email: ahudon@leeuniversity.edu

NCAA I
Lady Flames, Maroon, White
Phone: (423) 614-8453
Fax: (423) 614-8443

Estimated # of Women's Volleyball Scholarships: N/A
Conference: Tran South conference

Lincoln Memorial University
Academic Profile

Cumberland Gap Parkway
Harrogate, TN 37752

Phone: (423) 869-6245

Type: Private, 4 Yr., Liberal Arts, Coed
Website: http://www.lmunet.edu
SAT/ACT/GPA: 21-26/2.3
Student/Faculty Ratio: 13:1
Undergraduate Enrollment: 1,300
Scholarships/Academic: Yes   **Athletic:** Yes
Expenses By: Year   **In State:** $ 12,620

Founded: 1897
Religion: Non-Affiliated
Housing: Yes
Male/Female: 1:3
Graduate Enrollment: 650
Financial Aid: Yes
Out of State: $ 21,620

Degrees Conferred: Associate, Bachelor's, Master's, Education Specialist
Programs of Study: Accounting, Art, Athletic Training, Business, Biology, Chemistry, Communications Arts, Economics, English, Environmental Science, General Business, Health History, Humanities, Management, Marketing, Math, Medical Technology, Nursing, Physical Education, Psychology, Social Work, Veterinary Science, Wild Life and other PreProfessional Degrees

Women's Athletic Profile

Cumberland Gap Parkway
Harrogate, TN 37752-1901
Coach: Mike Smith
Email: athletics@inetumu.Lmunet.edu

NCAA I
Lady Railsplitters, Navy, Grey
Phone: (423) 869-6239
Fax: (423) 869-6382

Estimated # of Women's Volleyball Scholarships: N/A
Conference: Gulf South Conference
Program Profile: We play in Mary Mars Gym that holds 1,000 people. We play in the fall and have a very competitive schedule. We mainly play in the south.
History: Our program will be 10 years old and our record is 106-159. In NCAA II, it is 98-94. The program has gone from NAIA to NCAA II. Our first year as NCAA II was 1989.
Achievements: All-Conference Players; 2 All-Academic All-Conference Division II Hitting % Champion for the Year.
Coaching: Mike Smith, has been Head Coach since 1994. He has taken the team to the Conference Tournament twice. No assistant coach is listed.

Roster In State: 0   **Out of State:** 9   **Out of Country:** 2
Sophomores on Team: 2   **Seniors on Team:** 3   **Graduation %:** Unknown
Most Recent Record: 24-11-0   **Fall Games:** 35   **Spring Games:** 6
Positions Needed: Outside Hitter, Setter
Schedule: North Alabama, University of Tampa, University of Alabama-Huntsville, Valdosta State, Mars Hill, Saint Joseph College
Style of Play: A quick offense that relies on defense and blocking and runs a multiple offense.

Lipscomd University
Academic Profile

3901 Granny White Pike
Nashville, TN 37204

Phone:

Type: 4 Yr.,
Website: http://www.dlu.edu
SAT/ACT/GPA: Open
Student/Faculty Ratio:
Undergraduate Enrollment: N/A
Scholarships/Academic: **Athletic:**
Expenses By: **In State:**

Founded:
Religion: Non-Affiliated
Housing: No
Male/Female:
Graduate Enrollment: N/A
Financial Aid:
Out of State:

Programs of Study: Contact school for program of study.

Women's Athletic Profile

3901 Granny White Pike
Nashville, TN 37204
Coach: Jeff Spivey
Email:

NCAA I
Lady Bisons, Purple, Gold
Phone: (615) 269-1795
Fax: (615) 269-1806

Estimated # of Women's Volleyball Scholarships: N/A
Conference: Tran South Conference

Martin Methodist College
Academic Profile

433 W. Madison St.
Pulaski, TN 38478

Phone: 800-467-1273

Type: Private, 2 Yr., Jr. College, Coed
Website: http://www.martinmethodist.edu
SAT/ACT/GPA: 860/18
Student/Faculty Ratio: 13:1
Undergraduate Enrollment: 500
Scholarships/Academic: Yes   **Athletic:** Yes
Expenses By: Year   **In State:** $ 9,585
Specializes In: Jr. College
Degrees Conferred: Associate
Programs of Study: Business, Elementary Education, Church Vocations, Human Services

Founded: 1870
Religion: United Methodist
Housing: Yes
Male/Female: 49:51
Graduate Enrollment: N/A
Financial Aid: Yes
Out of State: $ 9,585

Women's Athletic Profile

433 W. Madison St.
Pulaski, TN 38478
Coach: Rose Magers-Powell
Email: HPowell940@aol.com

NCAA I
Lady Indians, Red, White
Phone: (931) 363-9878
Fax: (931) 363-9873

Estimated # of Women's Volleyball Scholarships: N/A
Conference: Tran South Conference

Maryville College
Academic Profile

502 E. Lamar Alexander Pkwy.
Maryville, TN 37805

Phone: 800-597-2687

Type: Private, 4 Yr., Liberal Arts, Coed
Website: http://www.maryvillecollege.edu
SAT/ACT/GPA: 900/21/3.0
Student/Faculty Ratio: 14:1
Undergraduate Enrollment: 950
Scholarships/Academic: Yes   **Athletic:** No
Expenses By: Year   **In State:** $ 20,415
Specializes In: Liberal Arts
Degrees Conferred: BA, BS, BM
Programs of Study: Art Education, Biology, Business Administration, Chemistry, Computer Science, Economics, Education, English, Fine Arts, Health Science, History, International Relations, Journalism, Management, Mathematics, Music, Music Education, Nursing, Physical Therapy, Political Science, PreDental, PreEngineering, PreLaw, PreMed, Psychology, Religion, Science Education, Secondary Education, Social Science, Spanish, Speech

Founded: 1819
Religion: Presbyterian
Housing: Yes
Male/Female: 2.5:1
Graduate Enrollment: N/A
Financial Aid: Yes
Out of State: $ 20,415

Women's Athletic Profile

502 E. Lamar Alexander Parkway
Maryville, TN 37805
Coach: Kandis Schram
Email: schram@maryvilbcollege.edu

NCAA I
Lady Scots, Orange, Garnet
Phone: (423) 981-8290
Fax: (423) 981-8285

Estimated # of Women's Volleyball Scholarships: N/A
Conference: Independent
Program Profile: We are a competitive Division III South Region team. We have our own gym and training area. We play from September to November. We also have a Spring season in February.

History: We started in 1976. We hosted the first final four NCAA Division III Championships.

Achievements: 1989 Coach of Year; Conference Championship 1986, 1989, (1979,1980) NCAA playoffs in 1978, 1989, 1980, 1981, 1982, 1991.

Coaching: Kandis Schram, Head Coach, started from 1989 to the present. Her overall record is 263-191. Bill Rude, Assistant Coach, started in 1998 to the present. His overall record is 18-15.

Freshman Receiving Financial Aid/Academic: **Athletic:** 0

Roster In State: 5   **Out of State:** 8   **Out of Country:** 0

Sophomores on Team: 0   **Seniors on Team:** 1   **Graduation %:** 76

Most Recent Record: 18-15-0   **Fall Games:** 33   **Spring Games:** 6

Positions Needed: Setter, Middle, Outside

Schedule: Savannah Arts & Design, Emory, Averett, Thomas More, Westminster, Millsaps

Style of Play: The team plays with great tenacity and spirit.

Middle Tennessee State University
Academic Profile

1500 Greenland Dr.   **Phone:** 615-898-2111
Murfreesboro, TN 37132

Type: Public, 4 Yr., Liberal Arts, Coed   **Founded:** 1911
Website: http://www.mtsu.edu   **Religion:** Non-Affiliated
SAT/ACT/GPA: 950/20/2.8   **Housing:** Yes
Student/Faculty Ratio: 21:1   **Male/Female:** 1:1.2
Undergraduate Enrollment: 15,415   **Graduate Enrollment:** 2,009
Scholarships/Academic: Yes   **Athletic:** Yes   **Financial Aid:** Yes
Expenses By: Year   **In State:** $ 2,500   **Out of State:** $ 5,500
Degrees Conferred: AAS, BA, BS, BFA, BBA, BSW, MA, MS, MBA
Programs of Study: Aerospace, Art, Biology, Business, Computer, Criminal Justice, Economics, Environmental, Fashion, Finance, International, Interdisciplinary, Medical, PreProfessional Programs

Women's Athletic Profile

MTSU Box 277, 1500 Greenland Dr.   **NCAA I**
Murfreesboro, TN 37132   Lady Raiders, Blue, White
Coach: Lisa Kissee   **Phone:** (615) 898-2230
Email: lkissee@mtsu.edu   **Fax:** (615) 898-5626

Estimated # of Women's Volleyball Scholarships: N/A
Conference: Ohio Valley Conference

Milligan College
Academic Profile

P.O. Box 500   **Phone:** 800-262-8337
Milligan College, TN 37682

Type: Private, 4 Yr., Liberal Arts, Coed   **Founded:** 1881
Website: http://www.milligan.edu   **Religion:** Christian Church
SAT/ACT/GPA: 900+/20+   **Housing:** Yes
Student/Faculty Ratio: 15:1   **Male/Female:** 40:60
Undergraduate Enrollment: 900   **Graduate Enrollment:** 100
Scholarships/Academic: Yes   **Athletic:** Yes   **Financial Aid:** Yes
Expenses By: Year   **In State:** $ 15,880   **Out of State:** $ 15,880
Specializes In: Liberal Arts
Degrees Conferred: AS, BA, BS, MED, MOT
Programs of Study: Accounting, Advertising, Art, Biblical Studies, Biology, Broadcasting, Business Administration, Chemistry, Communications, Computer Science, Education, Health Music, Religious Science, English, General Engineering, History, Humanities, Human Services, Liberal Arts, Management, Mathematics, Ministries, Music, Nursing, PreDental, PreMed, PreVet, Psychology, Radio & Television, Religion, Science, Social Work, Sociology, Theatre

Women's Athletic Profile

Toll Branch Road   **NCAA I**
Milligan College, TN 37682   Lady Buffs, Orange, Black
Coach: Debra Cutshall   **Phone:** (423) 461-8724
Email: **Fax:** (423) 461-8738

Estimated # of Women's Volleyball Scholarships: N/A
Conference: TVAC

Rhodes College
Academic Profile

2000 North Parkway
Memphis, TN 38112

Phone: 800-844-5969

Type: Private, 4 Yr., Liberal Arts, Coed
Website: http://www.rhodes.edu
SAT/ACT/GPA: 1100/25/3.0
Student/Faculty Ratio: 12:1
Undergraduate Enrollment: 1,450
Scholarships/Academic: Yes   **Athletic:** No
Expenses By: Year   **In State:** $ 23,528
Specializes In: Business, Pre-professional programs
Degrees Conferred: BA, BS

Founded: 1848
Religion: Presbyterian, USA
Housing: Yes
Male/Female: 45:55
Graduate Enrollment: 10
Financial Aid: Yes
Out of State: $ 23,528

Programs of Study: Art, Biology, Chemistry, English, History, Business & Management, International Studies, Philosophy, Political Science, Psychology, Religion

Women's Athletic Profile

2000 N. Parkway
Memphis, TN 38112
Coach: Samantha Wolinski
Email: Wolinski@Rhodes.Edu

NCAA I
Lady Lynx, Red, Black
Phone: (901) 843-3168
Fax: (901) 843-3749

Estimated # of Women's Volleyball Scholarships: N/A
Conference: Southern California Athletic Conference
Program Profile: Rhodes College is a Division III School that sponsors 22 varsity sports and participates in the Southern Collegiate Athletic Conference. Volleyball season is in the fall and we play in Mallory Gymnasium which has a 2,000 capacity. It is part of the $20.5 million Bryan Campus Life Center.
History: We began in 1974 and our overall record is 310-317. Julie Bowen is the all-time winningest volleyball coach from 1990-1994 with a record of 90-46.
Achievements: Sally Mercer (1999 graduate) and Kate Maffei (1998 graduate) are all-time leaders in career kills, games played, kills per game and hitting attempts.
Coaching: Samantha Wolinski, is in her first year as Head Coach. She is 1996 graduate of Earlham College where she was a 4 year player, a 2 year captain and a middle hitter. Kate Maffei, Assistant Coach, is a 1998 graduate of Rhodes and a 3 time All-SCAC outside hitter. Jessica Bailey, Assistant Coach, was a standout setter at the University of Memphis.

Roster In State: 3   **Out of State:** 8   **Out of Country:** 0
Sophomores on Team: 3   **Seniors on Team:** 3   **Graduation %:** 100
Most Recent Record: 18-22-0   **Fall Games:** 3-5   **Spring Games:** 0
Positions Needed: 4-6
Schedule: Trinity, Milsaps, De Pauw, Southwestern, Christian Brothers, Mississippi College
Style of Play: Fast, up tempo offense; focus on accurate passing and good team defense; always being aggressive.

Tennessee State University
Academic Profile

3500 John A. Merritt Blvd.
Nashville, TN 37209-1561

Phone: (615) 963-5010

Type: Public, 4 Yr., Coed
Website: http://www.tnstate.edu
SAT/ACT/GPA: 890/19/2.25
Student/Faculty Ratio: 15:1
Undergraduate Enrollment: N/A
Scholarships/Academic: Yes   **Athletic:** Yes
Expenses By: Sem   **In State:** $ 3,571
Specializes In: Engineering, Business, Nursing

Founded: 1912
Religion: Non-Affiliated
Housing: Yes
Male/Female: 40:60
Graduate Enrollment: N/A
Financial Aid: Yes
Out of State: $ 6,105

Degrees Conferred: AA, AS, BA, BS, BBA, BSF, BSN, MA, MS, MBA, M.Ed., Ph.D., EdD
Programs of Study: Occupational Therapy, Dental Hygiene, Physical Therapy, Speech Pathology, Health Care Administration, Medical Technology, Business, Nursing, Social Work, Education, Music, Electrical Computer Engineering, Architectural and Mechanical Engineering.

Women's Athletic Profile

3500 John A. Merritt Blvd.
Nashville, TN 37208-1561
Coach: Dawn Donaldson
Email:

NCAA I
Lady Tigers, Blue, White
Phone: (615) 963-5010
Fax: (615) 963-5911

Estimated # of Women's Volleyball Scholarships: N/A
Conference: Ohio Valley Conference
Program Profile: Our program is in the rebuilding stages.
History: In 1987, our program was started and has been in the building process. Stability in the coaching staff has been a problem.
Coaching: Dawn Donaldson, Head Coach, became head coach in 1998. Her overall record is 2-26. She was All-American as a middle blocker for Northern Michigan University. Dave De Roche is Assistant Coach.

Freshman Receiving Financial Aid/Academic:		Athletic: 5
Roster In State: 1	Out of State: 9	Out of Country: 0
Sophomores on Team: 0	Seniors on Team: 1	Graduation %: 75
Most Recent Record: 2-26-0	Fall Games: 30	Spring Games: 0

Camp of Clinic Dates: July 19-22
Schedule: Cincinnati, Ohio University, Cleveland State, University of Missouri-Kansas City, North Carolina State, SF Missouri
Style of Play: The team runs a quick offense with an emphasis on mastering the basics.

Trevecca Nazarene College
Academic Profile

333 Murfreesboro Rd.
Nashville, TN 37210

Phone: 800-210-4868

Type: Private, 4 Yr., Liberal Arts, Coed
Website: http://www.trevecca.edu
SAT/ACT/GPA: 860/18/2.5
Student/Faculty Ratio: 26:1
Undergraduate Enrollment: 1,066
Scholarships/Academic: Yes   **Athletic:** Yes
Expenses By: Semester   **In State:** $ 6,010

Founded: 1901
Religion: Nazarene
Housing: Yes
Male/Female: Not Available
Graduate Enrollment: 515
Financial Aid: Yes
Out of State: $ 6,010

Specializes In: Liberal Arts
Degrees Conferred: 43 Bachelors, 6 Associates, 5 Masters
Programs of Study: Allied Health, Behavioral Science, Biological Science, Business Administration, Communications, Education, History, Information Science, Management, Mathematics, Ministries, Philosophy, Psychology, Physician's Assistant, PreLaw, Religion, Science, Social Science, Speech

Women's Athletic Profile

333 Murfressboro Rd.
Nashville, TN 37210-2877
Coach: Scott Jones
Email:

NCAA I
Lady Trojans, Purple, White
Phone: (615) 248-1271
Fax: (615) 248-7798

Estimated # of Women's Volleyball Scholarships: 3.5
Conference: Trans South Conference
Achievements: 3 All-Conference, 1 Academic All-Conference in 1998 season. Scott Jones was named Coach of the Year in the Tran South Conference in 1998.
Coaching: Scott Jones, Head Coach, compiled a record of 5-23 in the 1997 season and 32-13 in the 1998 season. There is no assistant coach listed.

Freshman Receiving Financial Aid/Academic:		Athletic: 2
Roster In State: 2	Out of State: 7	Out of Country: 1
Sophomores on Team: 2	Seniors on Team: 0	Graduation %: Unknown
Most Recent Record: 32-13-0	Fall Games: 45	Spring Games: 0

Positions Needed: Outside Hitter, Middle Blocker, RS, Setter
Schedule: Columbia, Taylor, Bethel, Georgetown, Lee, Mt. Vernon
Style of Play: Team oriented up tempo; five persons offense, aggressive defense.

Tusculum College
Academic Profile

60 Shiloh Road
Greenville, TN 37743

Phone: (423) 636-7328

Type: Private, 4 Yr., Liberal Arts, Coed
Website: http://www.tusculum.edu
SAT/ACT/GPA: 920/18/2.0
Student/Faculty Ratio: 14:1
Undergraduate Enrollment: 1200
Scholarships/Academic: Yes   **Athletic:** Yes
Expenses By: Year   **In State:** $ 17,025
Specializes In: Civic Arts, Education, Biology
Degrees Conferred: BS, BA, MA, M.Ed.

Founded: 1794
Religion: Presbyterian
Housing: Yes
Male/Female: 1:1
Graduate Enrollment: 200
Financial Aid: Yes
Out of State: $ 17,025

Programs of Study: Biology, Computer Information Systems, Computer Science, English, Mass Media, Environmental Science, History, Management, Mathematics, Medical PreProfessional, Medical Technology, Museum Studies, Physical Education, Psychology, Visual Arts, Teaching-Licensure Programs

Women's Athletic Profile

60 Shiloh Road
Greenville, TN 37743
Coach: Beth Birky
Email: bbirky@tusculum.edu

NCAA I
Lady Pioneers, Orange, Black
Phone: 423-636-7328
Fax: 423-798-1636

Estimated # of Women's Volleyball Scholarships: 12
Conference: South Atlantic Conference
Program Profile: Our arena was completed in January 1998. Our Fall season starts in mid August and goes through November. Spring season is usually about six weeks.
History: Our program started in the 1990's. We became NAIA in 1998. Now we are full members of Division II NCAA.
Achievements: Coached 2 All-Americans. The 1997-98 team was in the top 25 academically.
Coaching: Beth Birky, Head Coach, began with our program in 1997. Sara Parker is Assistant Coach.
Freshman Receiving Financial Aid/Academic: **Athletic:** 6
Roster In State: 2   **Out of State:** 9   **Out of Country:** 1
Sophomores on Team: 0   **Seniors on Team:** 2   **Graduation %:** 100
Most Recent Record: 17-19-0   **Fall Games:** 36   **Spring Games:** 3
Camp of Clinic Dates: July 26-30
Positions Needed: Middle Hitters, BR Specialist
Schedule: Gardner Webb, Mars Hill, Lincoln Memorial
Style of Play: Quickness and athleticism are focuses for our team. Variation in our attack and team communication often surprises teams that may have more height than we do.

University of Memphis
Academic Profile

570 Normal
Memphis, TN 38152

Phone: (901) 678-3570

Type: Public, 4 Yr., Coed
Website: http://www.memphis.edu
SAT/ACT/GPA: 19
Student/Faculty Ratio: 18:1
Undergraduate Enrollment: 11,656
Scholarships/Academic: Yes   **Athletic:** Yes
Expenses By: Semester   **In State:** $ 3,390
Specializes In: Business, Education
Degrees Conferred: BA, BS, MA, MS, Ph.D., EdD

Founded: 1912
Religion: Non-Affiliated
Housing: Yes
Male/Female: 1:1.38
Graduate Enrollment: 8,444
Financial Aid: Yes
Out of State: $ 5,826

Programs of Study: Accounting, Anthropology, Applied Mathematics, Art, Biology, Business & Management, Chemistry, Communications, Computer Science, Criminal Justice, Education, Economics, Geography, Geology, History, Journalism, Liberal Arts, Medical Technology, Marketing, Psychology, Physics, Physical Education, Political Science

Women's Athletic Profile

570 Normal Avenue, Suite 201
Memphis, TN 38152
Coach: Carrie Yerty
Email: memphisvb@cc.memphis.edu

NCAA I
Lady Tigers, Blue, Grey
Phone: (901) 678-3570
Fax: (901) 678-2162

Estimated # of Women's Volleyball Scholarships: 3
Conference: Conference USA
Program Profile: We practice and play in Elma Roame Fieldhouse. It has 3,000 seats.
History: The program began in 1971. We were NCAA First Round in 1994.
Coaching: Carrie Yerty, became Head Coach in 1996. She was an All Pac-10 performer at Washington State. She got Honorable Mention All-American Pac-10. She was on the USA Olympic Developmental Team. At Washington State she was leader in kills, block solos and block assists. Rob Thomas and Fiona Botten are Assistant Coaches.

Freshman Receiving Financial Aid/Academic: | | **Athletic:** 4
Roster In State: 0 | **Out of State:** 10 | **Out of Country:** 1
Sophomores on Team: 1 | **Seniors on Team:** 2 | **Graduation %:** 99
Most Recent Record: 19-14-0 | **Fall Games:** 33 | **Spring Games:** 7

Positions Needed: Setter, Outside Hitter, Middle Blocker
Schedule: Louisville, Houston, South Florida, University of Tennessee, University of Mississippi, Mississippi State
Style of Play: 5-1 offense, fast-paced with audibles. Perimeter ("man-back") defense.

University of Tennessee - Chattanooga
Academic Profile

615 McCallie Ave.
Chattanooga, TN 37403-2598

Phone: 423-755-4662

Type: Public, 4 Yr., Coed
Website: http://www.utc.edu
SAT/ACT/GPA: 750+/2.75
Student/Faculty Ratio: 19:1
Undergraduate Enrollment: 2,126
Scholarships/Academic: Yes
Expenses By: Year
Founded: 1886
Religion: Non-Affiliated
Housing: Yes
Male/Female: 45:55
Graduate Enrollment: 1,275
Athletic: Yes | **Financial Aid:** Yes
In State: $ 7,323 | **Out of State:** $ 11,505

Degrees Conferred: BA, BS, BFA, MA, MS, MBA, M.Ed.
Programs of Study: Business and Management, Business/Office & Marketing/Distribution, Computer Science, Engineering, Health Science, Psychology, Social Science, System Analysis, Teacher Education

Women's Athletic Profile

615 McCallie Avenue
Chattanooga, TN 37403-2598
Coach: Lisa Rhoades
Email: lisa-rhodes@utc.edu

NCAA I
Lady Mocs, Navy, Old Gold
Phone: (423) 755-4069
Fax: (423) 785-2160

Estimated # of Women's Volleyball Scholarships: 9
Conference: Southern Conference
Program Profile: We took a 3-35 program in 1994 to Conference Champions in 1996. There are 11 schools in the Southern Conference. We received an automatic NCAA bid.
History: Our program began as a Division I in 1983. Our first regular season championship team was in 1997 and the only one in UTC history.
Achievements: 2 time Southern Conference Coach of the Year; 3 Conference Championships in a row in 1996, 1997 and 1998.
Coaching: Lisa Rhodes, is beginning her 11th year as a Head Coach and as Division I coach. She was 5 years at University of North Carolina in Ashville. She was 5 years at University of Tennessee in Chattanooga.

Freshman Receiving Financial Aid/Academic: | | **Athletic:** 2
Roster In State: 1 | **Out of State:** 10 | **Out of Country:** 1
Sophomores on Team: 4 | **Seniors on Team:** 2 | **Graduation %:** 100
Most Recent Record: 26-10-0 | **Fall Games:** 36 | **Spring Games:** 2

Camp of Clinic Dates: Undecided
Positions Needed: Middle Blockers (2)
Schedule: South Florida, American University, Georgia State, Forman, Davidson
Style of Play: Fast defense, rotational defense, aggressive play and team chemistry.

University of Tennessee - Knoxville
Academic Profile

117 Stokely Athletic Center
Knoxville, TN 37996-3110

Phone: 423-974-2184

Type: Public, 4 Yr., Engineering, Coed
Website: http://www.utk.edu
SAT/ACT/GPA: 21/2.0
Student/Faculty Ratio: 17:1
Undergraduate Enrollment: 14,000
Scholarships/Academic: Yes   **Athletic:** Yes
Expenses By: Year   **In State:** $ 6,659

Founded: 1794
Religion: Non-Affiliated
Housing: Yes
Male/Female: 51:49
Graduate Enrollment: 4,500
Financial Aid: Yes
Out of State: $ 11,715

Specializes In: Engineering, Business Administration, Nursing
Degrees Conferred: Numerous majors nationally-ranked
Programs of Study: Accounting, Advertising, Aerospace Engineering, Animal Science, Anthropology, Architecture, Biological Science, Broadcasting, Chemical Engineering, Chemistry, Computer Science, Education, Exercise Science, Finance, Forestry, Journalism, Logistics Transportation, Management, Marketing, Nursing, Political Science, Psychology, Public Administration, Religious Studies, Speech Pathology, Statistics, Sports

Women's Athletic Profile

117 Stokely Athletic Center
Knoxville, TN 37996
Coach: Rob Patrick
Email: admission@utk.edu

NCAA I
Lady Volunteers, Orange, White
Phone: (423) 974-2184
Fax: (423) 974-6341

Estimated # of Women's Volleyball Scholarships: 12
Conference: Southeastern Conference
Program Profile: We are a building program with a newly renovated 5,000 seat "volleyball only" arena. We have the largest weight room and training room in the country. We are one of only five universities with a separate athletic department.
History: The program began in 1973. We are ranked 15th in the nation. In 1981 we were 1st round NCAA. We were 1982-2nd round NCAA. We were in the 2nd round NCAA in 1982, 1983, 1984, and 1993.
Coaching: Rob Patrick, Head Coach, started with the program in 1997 to the present with an overall record of 34-29. He was a former assistant coach at Stanford University from 1994 to 1996 with an overall record of 92-6. He got 2 National Championships. He helped coach 10 All-Americans and 14 All-Pacific 10 selections. Sherry Dunbar is Assistant Coach.

Freshman Receiving Financial Aid/Academic: **Athletic:** 5
Roster In State: 2   **Out of State:** 12   **Out of Country:** 0
Sophomores on Team: 1   **Seniors on Team:** 4   **Graduation %:** 98
Most Recent Record: 19-10-0   **Fall Games:** 29   **Spring Games:** 0
Camp of Clinic Dates: July 16-25
Positions Needed: Setter, Middle Blocker, Outside Hitter
Schedule: University of Hawaii, University of Southern California, University of Florida, University of Arkansas, University of South Carolina, University of Virginia
Style of Play: A multi-faceted offense that attacks all areas of the net and with different tempos.

University of Tennessee - Martin
Academic Profile

1037 Elm Center
Martin, TN 38238

Phone: 800-829-8861

Type: Public, 4 Yr., Coed
Website: http://www.utm.edu
SAT/ACT/GPA: 910/19/2.25
Student/Faculty Ratio: 20:1
Undergraduate Enrollment: 5,400
Scholarships/Academic: Yes   **Athletic:** Yes
Expenses By: Year   **In State:** $ 6,538

Founded: 1927
Religion: Non-Affiliated
Housing: Yes
Male/Female: 45:55
Graduate Enrollment: 400
Financial Aid: Yes
Out of State: $ 11,364

Degrees Conferred: BA, BS, MBUs, MEd, MH
Programs of Study: Agricultural, Animal, Biological, Broadcasting, Chemistry, Civil Engineering, Criminal Justice, Dental Science, Earth Space, Economics, Finance, GeoScience, History, Management, Parks/Recreation, Pharmacy, PreProfessional Programs

Women's Athletic Profile

UT Martin Elm Center
Martin, TN 38238-5021
Coach: Chris Rushing
Email: crushing@utm.edu

NCAA I
Lady Skyhawks, Blue, Orange
Phone: (901) 587-7332
Fax: (901) 587-7688

Estimated # of Women's Volleyball Scholarships: 12
Conference: Ohio Valley Conference
Program Profile: We play at volleyball only facility, which has a seating capacity of 3,000. We have volleyball only weight room and team room.
History: We became member of Division I in 1992.
Achievements: We were twice named Coach of the Year and have had Conference Titles, JC Top 20 nationally.
Coaching: Chris Rushing is our Head Coach. He is entering first season with the program and compiled a record of 15-15 in his first season. . His overall collegiate record is 62-42. National Champion as a player at Brigham Young University. Paulina Steffkova is our Assistant Coach.
Freshman Receiving Financial Aid/Academic: **Athletic:** 8

Roster In State: 4	**Out of State:** 9	**Out of Country:** 0
Sophomores on Team: 2	**Seniors on Team:** 3	**Graduation %:**
Most Recent Record: 15-15-0	**Fall Games:** 30	**Spring Games:** 0
Positions Needed: 2		

Schedule: Saint Louis, Ole Miss, Southeast Missouri, Murray State, Southwest Missouri, Valparaiso
Style of Play: We play 5-1 offense and quick-fast paced.

University of the South
Academic Profile

735 University Avenue
Sewanee, TN 37383

Phone: 800-522-2234

Type: Private, 4 Yr., Liberal Arts, Coed
Website: http://www.sewanee.edu
SAT/ACT/GPA: 1160/25/3.53
Student/Faculty Ratio: 10:1
Undergraduate Enrollment: 1,300
Scholarships/Academic: Yes   **Athletic:** No
Expenses By: Year   **In State:** $ 23,380
Degrees Conferred: BA, BS

Founded: 1858
Religion: Episcopal
Housing: Yes
Male/Female: 48:52
Graduate Enrollment: N/A
Financial Aid: Yes
Out of State: $ 23,380

Programs of Study: American Studies, Anthropology, Art History, Biology, Chemistry, Computer Literature, Computer Science, Comparative Literature, Economics, English, Fine Arts, French, Geology, German, German Studies, Greek, History, Latin, Mathematics, Mathematics and Computer Science, Medieval Studies, Music, Natural Resources, Emphasis on Forestry, Philosophy, Physics, Political Science, Psychology, Religion, Russian, Russian Area Studies, Social Science, Foreign Language, Spanish, Theatre Arts, Third World Studies

Women's Athletic Profile

735 University Avenue
Sewanee, TN 37383
Coach: Nancy Ladd
Email:

NCAA I
Lady Tigers, Purple, White
Phone: 931-598-1000
Fax:

Estimated # of Women's Volleyball Scholarships: N/A
Conference: Southern California Athletic Conference

TEXAS

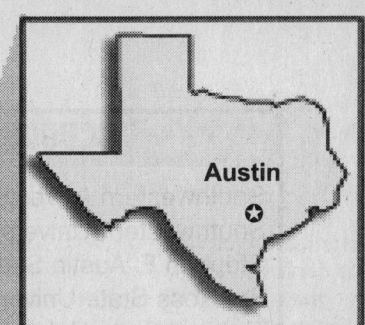

Austin

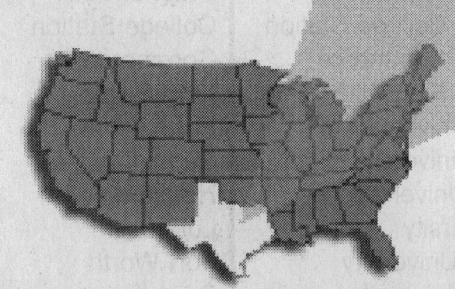

SCHOOL	CITY	AFFILIATION	PAGE
Abilene Christian University	Abilene	NCAA II	722
Angelo State University	San Angelo	NCAA II	722
Austin College	Shermant	NCAA III	723
Baylor University	Waco	NCAA I	723
Concordia University - Austin	Austin	NCAA III/NAIA	724
Dallas Baptist University	Dallas	NCAA II/NAIA	725
Dallas Christian College	Dallas	NCCAA	725
East Texas Baptist University	Marshall	NCAA III/NAIA	726
Frank Phillips College	Borger	NJCAA	726
Hardin - Simmons University	Abilene	NCAA III	727
Houston Baptist University	Houston	NAIA	727
Howard Payne University	Brownwood	NCAA III	728
Huston - Tillotson College	Austin	NAIA	728
Jarvis Christian College	Hawkins	NCAA II	729
Lamar University	Beaumont	NCAA I	729
Le Tourneau University	Longview	NCAA III	730
Lubbock Christian University	Lubbock	NAIA	731
McMurry University	Abilene	NCAA III	731
Midwestern State University	Wichita Falls	NCAA II	732
Prairie View A&M University	Prairie View	NCAA I	733
Rice University	Houston	NCAA I	733
Saint Edward's University	Austin	NCAA II	734
Saint Mary's University	San Antonio	NAIA	734
Sam Houston State University	Huntsville	NCAA I	735
San Jacinto College-Central	Pasadena	NJCAA	735
Schreiner College	Kerrville	NCAA III	736
Southern Methodist University	Dallas	NCAA I	737
Southwest Texas State University	San Marcos	NCAA I	738

SCHOOL	CITY	AFFILIATION	PAGE
Southwestern Adventist College	Keene	NAIA	738
Southwestern University	Georgetown	NCAA III	739
Stephen F. Austin State University	Nacogdoches	NCAA I	739
Sul Ross State University	Alpine	NCAA III	740
Tarleton State University	Stephenville	NCAA II	740
Texas A&M Univ- College Station	College Station	NCAA I	741
Texas A&M Univ- Commerce	Commerce	NCAA II	742
Texas A&M Univ- Kingsville	Kingsville	NCAA II	742
Texas Christian University	Forth Worth	NCAA I	743
Texas Lutheran University	Seguin	NCAA II/NAIA I	743
Texas Southern University	Houston	NCAA I	744
Texas Tech University	Lubbock	NCAA I	745
Texas Wesleyan University	Fort Worth	NCAA II/NAIA	745
Texas Woman's University	Denton	NCAA II	746
Trinity University	San Antonio	NCAA III	747
University of Dallas - Irving	Irving	NCAA III	748
University of Houston	Houston	NCAA I	748
University of Mary Hardin-Baylor	Belton	NCAA II	749
University of North Texas	Denton	NCAA I	749
Univ of Texas - Austin	Austin	NCAA I	750
Univ of Texas - Arlington	Arlington	NCAA I	751
Univ of Texas - El Paso	El Paso	NCAA I	752
Univ of Texas - Pan American	Edinburg	NCAA I	752
Univ of Texas - San Antonio	San Antonio	NCAA I	753
Univ of Texas of Permian Basin	Odessa	NAIA	753
University of the Incarnate Word	San Antonio	NCAA II/NAIA	754
Vernon Regional Junior College	Vernon	NJCAA	754
Wayland Baptist University	Plainview	NAIA	755
West Texas A&M University	Canyon	NCAA II	755
Wiley College	Marshall	NAIA	756

Abilene Christian University
Academic Profile

ACU Station, Box 27916
Abilene, TX 79699

Phone: 915-674-2650

Type: Private, 4 Yr., Liberal Arts, Coed
Website: http://www.acu.edu
SAT/ACT/GPA: 700/17
Student/Faculty Ratio: 18:1
Undergraduate Enrollment: 3,385
Scholarships/Academic: Yes   **Athletic:** No
Expenses By: Year   **In State:** $ 10,900

Founded: 1906
Religion: Church of Christ
Housing: No
Male/Female: 49:51
Graduate Enrollment: 685
Financial Aid: No
Out of State: $ 10,900

Degrees Conferred: AA, AS, BA, BS, BBA, BFA, BM, BSN, MA, MS
Programs of Study: Accounting, Advertising, Animal Science, BioChemistry, Biological Science, Communications, Computer Science, Education, French, German, Greek, Information Science, Journalism, Management, MicroBiology, Physics, Political Science, PreProfessional Programs, Psychology, Religion, Social Sciences

Women's Athletic Profile

ACU Station, Box 27916
Abilene, TX 79699
Coach: Brek Horn
Email: hornb@acu.edu

NCAA I
Lady Wildcats, Purple, White
Phone: (915) 674-2590
Fax: (915) 674-6857

Estimated # of Women's Volleyball Scholarships: N/A
Conference: Lone Star Conference
Program Profile: We play in Moody Coliseum, which is a 4, 500 seat stadium gymnasium. The floor is a hard wood floor. Our playing season is from Aug-Nov, the program is fully funded and is on the upward direction.
History: The program began in 1971. Since then the record has been 491-431 for a .534 winning percentage. In the past two years, the winning percentage has been at .746 with a 53-18 record.
Achievements: We had three 1st team All-Conference players this past year. We are returning 11 out of 13 players.
Coaching: Head Coach Brek Horn has been here for 2 years with a compiled record of 53-18. In 2000, she led the team to a 29-6 season.
Freshman Receiving Financial Aid/Academic: **Athletic:** 3
Roster In State: 12   **Out of State:** 1   **Out of Country:** 0
Sophomores on Team: **Seniors on Team:** 2   **Graduation %:** 100
Most Recent Record: 29-6
Camp of Clinic Dates: July 5-14
Positions Needed: MB, RS
Schedule: West Texas A&M, North Dakota State, Metropolitan State Univ., Cameron Univ., Michigan Tech, Eastern New Mexico Univ.
Style of Play: Up-tempo offense. We play a power game by serving tough to keep people out of their offense.

Angelo State University
Academic Profile

ASU Box 10914
San Angelo, TX 76909

Phone: (915) 942-2185

Type: Public, 4 Yr., Coed
Website: http://www.angelo.edu
SAT/ACT/GPA: 700 min
Student/Faculty Ratio: 24:1
Undergraduate Enrollment: 6,500
Scholarships/Academic: Yes   **Athletic:** Yes
Expenses By: Year   **In State:** $ 6,700

Founded: 1928
Religion: Non-Affiliated
Housing: Yes
Male/Female: 50:50
Graduate Enrollment: 2,000
Financial Aid: Yes
Out of State: $ 12,000

Degrees Conferred: AA, AS, BA, BS, BBA, BM, BSN, Masters
Programs of Study: Accounting, Animal Science, Biology, Business Administration, Chemistry, Computer Science, Economics, Education, English, Finance, French, Geology, German, History, Journalism, Kinesiology, Management, Marketing, Mathematics, Music, Nursing, Physics, Psychology, Sociology, Spanish

Women's Athletic Profile

2601 W. Avenue N
San Angelo, TX 76909
Coach: Kathleen Brasfield
Email: kathleen.brasfield@angelo.edu

NCAA I
Lady Rambelles, Blue, Gold
Phone: (915) 942-2185
Fax: (915) 942-2038

Estimated # of Women's Volleyball Scholarships: 8
Conference: Lone Star Conference
Program Profile: We have a competitive program with a solid academic reputation. A new arena is being built in 1999. Our current arena can seat 3,600 people.
History: We began in 1976. We have been to the NCAA Tournament 4 times and the LSC Championship 6 times.
Achievements: Coach of the Year 7 times; Top 10 in District II Winning Coaches.
Coaching: Kathleen Brasfield, Head Coach, started in 1978. Her overall record at ASU is 557-296-2.
Freshman Receiving Financial Aid/Academic:

Athletic: 5

Roster In State: 10	**Out of State:** 2	**Out of Country:** 0
Sophomores on Team: 0	**Seniors on Team:** 2	**Graduation %:** 100
Most Recent Record: 21-12-0	**Fall Games:** 33	**Spring Games:** 4

Camp of Clinic Dates: July 5-9
Style of Play: Up tempo transition game.

Austin College
Academic Profile

900 N Grand Avenue
Sherman, TX 75092

Phone: 800-442-5363

Type: Private, 4 Yr., Liberal Arts, Coed
Website: http://www.austinc.edu
SAT/ACT/GPA: 1000+/22/3.0
Student/Faculty Ratio: 15:1
Undergraduate Enrollment: 1,200
Scholarships/Academic: Yes
Expenses By: Year
Specializes In: Sciences, PreMed
Degrees Conferred: BA, MAT

Founded: 1849
Religion: Presbyterian
Housing: Yes
Male/Female: 50:50
Graduate Enrollment: 20

Athletic: No
In State: $ 20,000

Financial Aid: Yes
Out of State: $ 20,000

Programs of Study: American Studies, Art, BioChemistry (as an interdisciplinary major using Special Program Option), Biology, Business Administration, Chemistry, Classics, Communication Arts (Speech-Theatre-Media), Computer Science (as an interdisciplinary major using Special Program Option), Economics, English, French, German, History, International Studies, Latin, Latin American Studies, Mathematics, Music, Philosophy, Physical Education, Physics, Political Science, Psychology, Religion, Sociology, Spanish, Teacher Education (Austin Teacher Program - graduate level only)

Women's Athletic Profile

900 N. Grand Avenue, Ste. 6A
Sherman, TX 75090
Coach: Ed Garza
Email: egarza@austin.edu

NCAA I
Lady Kangaroos, Crimson, Gold
Phone: (903) 813-2515
Fax: (903) 813-3196

Estimated # of Women's Volleyball Scholarships: N/A
Conference: American Southwest Conference

Baylor University
Academic Profile

150 Bear Run
Waco, TX 76711

Phone: (254) 710-3039

Type: Private, 4 Yr., Liberal Arts, Coed
Website: http://www.baylor.edu
SAT/ACT/GPA: 1100
Student/Faculty Ratio: 18:1
Undergraduate Enrollment: 12,500
Scholarships/Academic: Yes

Founded: 1845
Religion: Baptist
Housing: Yes
Male/Female: 45:55
Graduate Enrollment: 2,500

Athletic: Yes
Financial Aid: Yes

Expenses By: Year   **In State:** $ 15,500   **Out of State:** $ 15,500
Specializes In: Education, Business, Premed, Prelaw
Degrees Conferred: BA, BS, BFA, BBA, BME, BSAC, BSN, MA, MS, MBA, Ph.D., JD
Programs of Study: College of Arts & Sciences, Engineering & Computer Science, Education, PreMed, PreLaw, Business

Women's Athletic Profile

150 Bear Run
Waco, TX 76798-7096
Coach: Brian Hosfeld
Email: angela_lightfoot@baylor.edu

NCAA I
Lady Bears, Green, Yellow
Phone: (254) 710-3039
Fax: (254) 710-3009

Estimated # of Women's Volleyball Scholarships: 12
Conference: Big 12 Conference
Program Profile: We play in Ferrell Center which has 10,500 seats and we have our own practice facility which is called Marrs McLean Gymnasium. We are building our program.
Achievements: World University Team Coach; Silver Medal in Games
Coaching: Brian Hosfeld, Head Coach, started in 1996. Our Assistant Coach, Angela Lightfoot, started in 1996. Our Assistant Coach, Jason Tanaka, started in 1998.

Freshman Receiving Financial Aid/Academic:		**Athletic:** 3
Roster In State: 5	**Out of State:** 8	**Out of Country:** 0
Sophomores on Team: 6	**Seniors on Team:** 2	**Graduation %:** 100
Most Recent Record:	**Fall Games:**	**Spring Games:** 4

Positions Needed: Middle Hitters, Outside Hitters
Schedule: Nebraska, Colorado, Texas A& M, Kansas State, Texas, Texas Tech
Style of Play: Asian style

Concordia University - Austin
Academic Profile

3400 I.H. 35 North
Austin, TX 78705

Phone: 800-865-4282

Type: Private, 4 Yr., Liberal Arts, Coed
Website: http://www.concordia.edu
SAT/ACT/GPA: 1080/19/3.0 or 4.0
Student/Faculty Ratio: 12:1
Undergraduate Enrollment: 800
Scholarships/Academic: Yes   **Athletic:** No
Expenses By: Year   **In State:** $ 14,200

Founded: 1926
Religion: Lutheran
Housing: Yes
Male/Female: 1:3
Graduate Enrollment: N/A
Financial Aid: Yes
Out of State: $ 14,200

Degrees Conferred: Bachelors, Masters in Education
Programs of Study: Behavioral Science, Biology, Business Administration, Business Management, Church Music/Conducting, Church Music/Organ, Communications, Computer Science, Early Childhood Education, Elementary Education, Secondary Education, English, Environmental Sciences, History, Liberal Arts, Mexican-American Studies, PreDental, PreLaw, PreMed, PreSeminar, Spanish

Women's Athletic Profile

IH 35 North
Austin, TX 78705
Coach: Gwen Adams
Email:

NCAA I
Lady Tornados, Purple, White
Phone: (512) 452-7662x1162
Fax: (512) 302-4365

Estimated # of Women's Volleyball Scholarships: 0
Conference: Independent
Program Profile: The volleyball program continues their success practicing and playing in the Waltman Activities Center, which is designed for a lot of cheering and support from their many fans.
History: Recognized by NAIA in 1980.
Achievements: The highest honor Concordia has received by the Conference was Conference Champ-Runner-Up. Concordia has proudly produced the All-American Athletes: Lee Kennedy, Melba Homer, and Lisa Aintz. Previous VB Coach, Linda Lowery
Coaching: First year as Head Coach. Has served one year as a Graduate Assistant Coach at Texas A&M University-Commerce. Also played four years as an out side hitter with team and conference recognition.

Freshman Receiving Financial Aid/Academic:
Roster In State: 11 | **Out of State:** 0 | **Athletic:** 0 / **Out of Country:** 0
Sophomores on Team: | **Seniors on Team:** 9 | **Graduation %:**
Most Recent Record: 10-17 | **Fall Games:** 27 | **Spring Games:** 5
Camp of Clinic Dates: June 7-11
Positions Needed: Setters, Outside Hitters, Right side hitters
Schedule: St. Edwards University, Texas Women's University, Harding University, Houston Baptist University Southwestern University, University of Mary-Hardin Baylor
Style of Play: The girls are fundamentally sound and are geared toward a quick offense with lots of positive results.

Dallas Baptist University
Academic Profile

3000 Mountain Creek Parkway
Dallas, TX 75211

Phone: 214-333-7100

Type: Private, 4 Yr., Liberal Arts, Coed | **Founded:** 1898
Website: http://www.dbu.edu | **Religion:** Southern Baptist
SAT/ACT/GPA: 910/19/2.0 | **Housing:** Yes
Student/Faculty Ratio: 19/1 | **Male/Female:** 38/62
Undergraduate Enrollment: 3,190 | **Graduate Enrollment:** 842
Scholarships/Academic: Yes | **Athletic:** Yes | **Financial Aid:** Yes
Expenses By: Semester | **In State:** $6,149.57 | **Out of State:** $ 6,149.57
Degrees Conferred: BA, BS, MBA, MED, MLA
Programs of Study: Accounting, Allied Health, Aviation Management, Banking & Finance, Biblical Studies, Biology, Broadcasting, Communications, Computer Science, Criminal Justice, Dramatic Arts, Economics, English, Fine Arts, History, Marketing, Mathematics, Music, Music Performance, Nursing, Pastoral Studies, Physical Education, Political Science, Psychology, Real Estate, Religious Education, Social Science

Women's Athletic Profile

3000 Mountain Creek Parkway
Dallas, TX 75211-9299
Coach: Kristi Arrington Moore
Email: sports@dbu.edu

NCAA I
Lady Patriots, Red, White, Blue
Phone: (214) 333-5341
Fax: (214) 333-5306

Estimated # of Women's Volleyball Scholarships: 6
Conference: Independent
Program Profile: We play in Burg Events Center which seats 3,200. We play sixty percent Division II opponents and forty percent NAIA opponents. We play 30 games a year average.
History: Our program began seventeen years ago. We blossomed in the last two years and made playoffs for the first time in 1997 and again in 1998. Our records were 24-13 in 1996 and 15-15 in 1997, we are playing more NCAA Division II programs. Our 1998 record was 14-19.
Achievements: Produced 2 All-Americans in the past six years.
Coaching: Kristi Arrington, Head Coach, in 1996 to the present. She compiled a record of 53-47. She was named NAIA Academic All-American in 1994 as a player. Angie Rogers is Assistant Coach.
Freshman Receiving Financial Aid/Academic:
Roster In State: 12 | **Out of State:** 1 | **Athletic:** 6 / **Out of Country:** 0
Sophomores on Team: 0 | **Seniors on Team:** 1 | **Graduation %:** 80
Most Recent Record: 14-19-0 | **Fall Games:** 30-32 | **Spring Games:** 0
Camp of Clinic Dates: First two weeks in June
Positions Needed: Middle Blocker, Outside Hitter
Schedule: Abilene Christian University, St. Mary's, St. Edward's, Lubbock Christian University, Angelo State, Central Arkansas

Dallas Christian College
Academic Profile

2700 Christian Pkwy
Dallas, TX 75234

Phone: 972-241-3371

Type: Private, 4 Yr., Coed | **Founded:** 1950
Website: http://www.dallas.edu | **Religion:** Non-denominational

SAT/ACT/GPA: 740/15/1.8
Student/Faculty Ratio: 10:1
Undergraduate Enrollment: 300
Scholarships/Academic: Yes   **Athletic:** No
Expenses By: Year   **In State:** $ 8,500
Specializes In: Ministry, Music, Education
Degrees Conferred: BA,BS

Housing: Yes
Male/Female: 5:4
Graduate Enrollment: N/A
Financial Aid: Yes
Out of State: $ 8,500

Programs of Study: Bible Arts, Bible Science, Bible Education, Church Music, History, English, Music Education

Women's Athletic Profile

2700 Christian Pkwy
Dallas, TX 75234
Coach: Heidi Klein
Email: dcc@dallas.edu

NCAA I
Lady Crusaders, Maroon, White
Phone: 972-241-3371
Fax: 972-241-8021

Estimated # of Women's Volleyball Scholarships: No
Conference: Interstate Conference
History: We have been playing for 10 years. We are growing in strength and wins each year.
Achievements: 2 All-Americans; 4th in Regional.
Coaching: Our coaching staff has been here 3 years. Heidi Klein is Head Coach. Velvet McWhirter is Assistant Coach.
Roster In State: 7   **Out of State:** 4   **Out of Country:** 0
Sophomores on Team: 2   **Seniors on Team:** 4   **Graduation %:** 98
Most Recent Record: 5-12-0   **Fall Games:** 25   **Spring Games:** 0
Positions Needed: Hitters, Defense
Schedule: Mid America Bible College, Nebraska Christian, University of Dallas
Style of Play: We are giving glory to God in a competitive and fun atmosphere. We are developing hard working ethics and dedication. Defensive, sound play, no showboats!

East Texas Baptist
Academic Profile

1209 North Grove Street
Marshall, TX 75670

Phone: (903) 935-7963

Type: Private, 4 Yr., Liberal Arts, Coed
Website: http://www.etbu.edu
SAT/ACT/GPA: 860/18
Student/Faculty Ratio: 16:1
Undergraduate Enrollment: 1,200+
Scholarships/Academic: Yes   **Athletic:** No
Expenses By: Year   **In State:** $ 11,500

Founded: 1917
Religion: Baptist
Housing: Yes
Male/Female: 40:60
Graduate Enrollment: 1,400
Financial Aid: Yes
Out of State: $ 11,500

Degrees Conferred: BA, BS, BAS, BSN, BBA, BSE, BM, AA, ABA, AAS
Programs of Study: Behavioral Science, Christian Ministry, English, History, Music, Psychology, Sociology, Spanish, Speech, Communications, Theatre Arts, Accounting, Biology, Business Administration, Chemistry, Computer Information System, Kinesiology, Mathematics, Medical Technology, Nursing

Women's Athletic Profile

1209 N. Grove
Marshall, TX 75670
Coach: Allison Stringfellow
Email:

NCAA I
Lady Tigers, Blue, Gold
Phone: (903) 935-7963x287
Fax: (903) 935-0162

Estimated # of Women's Volleyball Scholarships: N/A
Conference: Independent

Frank Phillips College
Academic Profile

P.O. Box 5118
Borger, TX 79008-5118

Phone: 806-274-5311

Type: Public, 2 Yr., Coed
Website: http://www.fpc.cc.tx.us

Founded: 1948
Religion: Non-Affiliated

SAT/ACT/GPA: Open
Student/Faculty Ratio: 13:1
Undergraduate Enrollment: 1,100
Scholarships/Academic: Yes   **Athletic:** Yes
Expenses By: Year   **In State:** $ 3,230
Degrees Conferred: Certificates, AA, AS
Housing: Yes
Male/Female: 1:1
Graduate Enrollment: N/A
Financial Aid: Yes
Out of State: $ 3,230
Programs of Study: Liberal & Fine Arts, Math, Science, Physical Education, Computers, Business, Accounting, Nursing, Cosmetology, Agriculture, Music, Legal Assistant, Workforce Development, Air Conditioning/Heating, Welding, Developmental Ed.

Women's Athletic Profile

1301 Roosevelt St.
Borger, TX 79008-5118
Coach: Danna Bryan
Email:

NCAA I
Lady Plainsmen, Navy/Gold
Phone: (806) 274-5311 ext. 765
Fax: (806) 273-2706

Estimated # of Women's Volleyball Scholarships: 15
Conference: Lone Star Conference
Program Profile: Our program is still in the process of becoming a better team. Our team has 15 members. Our facilities consist of a new gym floor, weights and an Olympic size pool. Our playing season goes from August to November.
History: Our volleyball program began in the fall of 1995.
Coaching: Danna Bryan, Head Coach, started in 1998. Her overall record is 22-23. Her team qualified for Regional.
Freshman Receiving Financial Aid/Academic: **Athletic:** 7
Roster In State: 7   **Out of State:** 2   **Out of Country:** 0
Sophomores on Team: 2   **Seniors on Team:** 0   **Graduation %:** 70
Most Recent Record: 22-23-0   **Fall Games:** 45   **Spring Games:** 15
Camp of Clinic Dates: July 17th
Positions Needed: Eleven openings
Schedule: Seward County College, Vernon, Navarro College
Style of Play: Our team plays with a controlled offense and defense. Our team functions as a unit.

Hardin - Simmons University
Academic Profile

HSU Box 16050
Abilene, TX 79698-6050

Phone: 800-568-2692

Type: Private, 4 Yr., Liberal Arts, Coed
Website: http://www.hsutx.edu
SAT/ACT/GPA: 990/21/"c" average
Student/Faculty Ratio: 17:1
Undergraduate Enrollment: 2200
Scholarships/Academic: Yes   **Athletic:** No
Expenses By: Year   **In State:** $11,000-13,000
Founded: 1891
Religion: Baptist
Housing: Yes
Male/Female: 5:8
Graduate Enrollment: 300
Financial Aid: Yes
Out of State: $11,000-13,000
Programs of Study: Accounting, Banking/Finance, Biology, Business Administration, Chemistry, Communications, Computer Science, Criminal Justice, Education, English, Fine Arts, History, Marketing, Math, Medical Laboratory, Nursing, Philosophy, Physical Education, Physical Therapy, Physics, Political Science, PreDentistry, PreLaw, PreMed, Religion, Social Science

Women's Athletic Profile

P.O. Box 16185
Abilene, TX 79698
Coach: Krystal Brodbeck
Email: knbrodbe@hsutx.edu

NCAA I
Cowgirls, Purple, Gold
Phone: (915) 670-1493
Fax: (915) 670-1572

Estimated # of Women's Volleyball Scholarships: N/A
Conference: American Southwest Conference

Houston Baptist University
Academic Profile

7502 Fondren Rd.
Houston, TX 77074

Phone: 800-969-3210

Type: Private, 4 Yr., Liberal Arts, Coed

Founded: 1960

Website: http://www.hbu.edu
SAT/ACT/GPA: 950 avg.
Student/Faculty Ratio: 17:1
Undergraduate Enrollment: 1,700
Scholarships/Academic: Yes   **Athletic:** Yes
Expenses By: Year   **In State:** $ 10,700
Degrees Conferred: A, BA, BS, BBA, BM, MA, MS, MBA
Programs of Study: Contact school for program of study.

Religion: Southern Baptist
Housing: No
Male/Female: 35:65
Graduate Enrollment: 500
Financial Aid: Yes
Out of State: $ 10,700

Women's Athletic Profile

7502 Fondren Rd.
Houston, TX 77074
Coach: Kaddie Platt
Email: kaddieplatt@yahoo.com

NCAA I
Lady Huskies, Royal Blue, Orange
Phone: (281) 649-3316
Fax: (281) 649-3496

Estimated # of Women's Volleyball Scholarships: N/A
Conference: Independent

Howard Payne University
Academic Profile

1000 Fisk Avenue
Brownwood, TX 76801

Phone: 915-649-8027

Type: Private, 4 Yr., Liberal Arts, Coed
Website: http://www.hputx.edu
SAT/ACT/GPA: 830/19/80%
Student/Faculty Ratio: 18:1
Undergraduate Enrollment: 1,500
Scholarships/Academic: Yes   **Athletic:** No
Expenses By: Year   **In State:** $ 10,000
Degrees Conferred: BA, BS, BBA, BAAS, BM

Founded: 1889
Religion: Non-Affiliated
Housing: Yes
Male/Female: 50:50
Graduate Enrollment: N/A
Financial Aid: Yes
Out of State: $ 10,000

Programs of Study: Accounting, Art, Biology, Business, Christian Studies, Communications, Computer, Education, History, Music, Medical Technology, Political Science, Psychology, Sociology, Social Work, PreLaw, Exercise and Sports Science

Women's Athletic Profile

508 2nd Street
Brownwood, TX 76801
Coach: Randy Lewallyn
Email: rlewally@hputx.edu

NCAA I
Lady Yellow Jackets, Gold, Blue
Phone: (915) 646-2502x5104
Fax: (915) 649-8920

Estimated # of Women's Volleyball Scholarships: N/A
Conference: American Southwest Conference

Huston-Tillotson College
Academic Profile

Phone:

Type:
Website: Not Available
SAT/ACT/GPA: Open
Student/Faculty Ratio:
Undergraduate Enrollment: N/A
Scholarships/Academic: **Athletic:**
Expenses By: **In State:**
Specializes In:
Degrees Conferred:
Programs of Study: Contact school for programs of study.

Founded:
Religion: Non-Affiliated
Housing: No
Male/Female:
Graduate Enrollment: N/A
Financial Aid:
Out of State:

Women's Athletic Profile

1820 E. 8th Street
Austin, TX 78702
Coach: Christina Carter
Email: vbcoach@flash.net

NAIA
Lady Rams, Cardinal, Gold
Phone: (512) 505-3052
Fax: (512) 474-0762

Estimated # of Women's Volleyball Scholarships: N/A
Conference: Red River Athletic Conference
Program Profile: Our season runs from August through November, small liberal arts campus in the heart of downtown Austin, Texas. historically black college. Campus make up still predominantly African-American, Hispanic and White.
History: We are not aware of program's starting date. We are starting to receive more recognition.
Achievements: 1997 & 1998 AVCA Team Academic Award in 1996-1998, NAIA All-American Scholar Athletes. In 1996, we have 4 Big State Al-Conference players, 1996 Big State Co-Conference Champions, 1997 4 Big State All-Conference players, 1997 Big State Co-Conference Champions, SW Regional Qualifiers, 1998 4 Red River All-Conference players and 1997 Coach of the Year.
Coaching: Chris Carter, Head Coach, started in 1996 with an overall record of 37-49. She played at Penn State University and was two-year captain. Stephanie Tyson, Assistant Coach, started in 1998 and played one year at Sam Houston.

Freshman Receiving Financial Aid/Academic: | | **Athletic:** 3
Roster In State: 10 | **Out of State:** 0 | **Out of Country:** 0
Sophomores on Team: 1 | **Seniors on Team:** 2 | **Graduation %:** 100
Most Recent Record: 12-18-0 | **Fall Games:** 22 | **Spring Games:** 0
Positions Needed: Middle Hitters, Defensive Specialist, Setter
Schedule: Houston Baptist, Lubbock Christian, Wayland Baptist, St. Edward's University, St. Mary's University
Style of Play: Competitive style of play. We uses all of the best attributes of the existing players. Team tends to be very athletic and plays with a lot of heart.

Jarvis Christian College
Academic Profile

P. O. Box 1470 - Highway 80 East
Hawkins, TX 75765

Phone: 800-292-9517

Type: Private, 4 Yr., Liberal Arts, Coed
Website: http://www.jarvis.edu
SAT/ACT/GPA: 800+/18+/2.0
Student/Faculty Ratio: 15:1
Undergraduate Enrollment: 500
Scholarships/Academic: Yes
Expenses By: Year

Athletic: Yes

In State: $ 9,235

Founded: 1913
Religion: Disciples of Christ
Housing: No
Male/Female: 38:62
Graduate Enrollment: N/A
Financial Aid: Yes
Out of State: $ 9,235

Specializes In: Business Administration, Computer Info Systems, Teacher Certification
Degrees Conferred: BA, BS, BBA, Bachelor of Computer Information Systems
Programs of Study: Biology, Business Administration, Chemistry, Computer Information Systems, Criminal Justice, English, Generic Special Education, History, Human Performance, Interdisciplinary Studies in Education, Mathematics, Music, Reading, Religion. Sociology, Speech, Texas Teacher Certification (Biology, Business Administration, Chemistry, English, Special Education, History, Human Performance, Mathematics, Music, Reading) Joint Degree Programs in Nursing, Mass Communications and Engineering.

Women's Athletic Profile

P.O. Drawer G
Hawkins, TX 75765
Coach: Elissia Burrell
Email:

NCAA I
Lady Bulldogs, Gold, Royal Blue
Phone: (903) 769-5764
Fax: (603) 769-4842

Estimated # of Women's Volleyball Scholarships: N/A
Conference: Big State Conference

Lamar University - Beaumont
Academic Profile

P.O. Box 10066
Beaumont, TX 77710

Phone: 409-880-8888

Type: Public, 4 Yr., Liberal Arts, Coed
Website: http://www.lamar.edu
SAT/ACT/GPA: 1000/24

Founded: 1923
Religion: Non-Affiliated
Housing: Yes

Student/Faculty Ratio: 15:1
Undergraduate Enrollment: 10,000
Scholarships/Academic: Yes   **Athletic:** Yes
Expenses By: Year   **In State:** $ 4,604
Specializes In: Engineering, Business, Education
Degrees Conferred: BA, BS, BAAS, BFA, MA, MS

Male/Female: 48:52
Graduate Enrollment: N/A
Financial Aid: Yes
Out of State: $ 7,842

Programs of Study: Accounting, Biology, Chemistry, Communications, Computer Science, Criminal Justice, Economics, Engineering: (Civil, Chemical, Electrical, Industrial and Mechanical), English, Finance, Foreign Languages, Geology, Graphic Design, Management, Marketing, Nursing, Political Science, Psychology, Sociology

Women's Athletic Profile

211 Red Bird Lane
Beaumont, TX 77710
Coach: James Barnes
Email: JEB711@aol.com

NCAA I
Lady Cardinals, Red, White
Phone: (409) 880-8888
Fax: (409) 880-2338

Estimated # of Women's Volleyball Scholarships: N/A
Conference: Southland Conference
Program Profile: Our playing facility has a seating capacity of 10,000 and includes weight facilities.
History: The program began in 1973. Our all-time record is 672-428-7 (.610). We have 3 NCAA Tournament Appearances and 3 AIAW Tournament Appearances.
Achievements: 1997 - Sun Belt Conference Champions and Sun Belt Coach of the Year; 1993 Sun Belt Conference Champions; NCAA Qualifier; 1987, 1990 America South Champions; 1983 and 1984 Southland Conference Champions; 1997 Academic All-American was Tonya Howery.
Coaching: James Barnes, Head Coach, has a career record as head coach of 61-40 in three seasons. He was a former assistant coach at McNeese State for six seasons. He was named Sun Belt Conference Coach of the Year. Jennifer Alvarez, Assistant Coach, is entering her second season with the program.
Freshman Receiving Financial Aid/Academic: **Athletic:** 4
Roster In State: 8   **Out of State:** 4   **Out of Country:** 0
Sophomores on Team: 0   **Seniors on Team:** 4   **Graduation %:** 100
Most Recent Record: 19-12-0   **Fall Games:** 31+   **Spring Games:** 4+
Camp of Clinic Dates: July 1999
Positions Needed: 2 Middle Blockers, 1 Right side Hitter
Schedule: Southwest Texas State, University of Texas-Arlington, Stephen F. Austin
Style of Play: Aggressive: Defensive and offensive system with an emphasis on consistency, mental toughness and team play.

Le Tourneau University
Academic Profile

P. O. Box 7001
Longview, TX 75607

Phone: 800-759-8811

Type: Private, 4 Yr., Liberal Arts, Engineering, Coed
Website: http://www.letu.edu
SAT/ACT/GPA: 1050/21/2.8
Student/Faculty Ratio: 10:1
Undergraduate Enrollment: 850
Scholarships/Academic: Yes   **Athletic:** No
Expenses By: Year   **In State:** $ 16,00
Specializes In: Engineering & Aviation
Degrees Conferred: BS, BA

Founded: 1948
Religion: Non-Denominational
Housing: Yes
Male/Female: 17:1
Graduate Enrollment: N/A
Financial Aid: Yes
Out of State: $ 16,000

Programs of Study: Engineering, Aviation, Liberal Arts, Natural Science, Business Administration: Nearly 40 associates and bachelors programs.

Women's Athletic Profile

2100 S. Mobberly
Longview, TX 75607
Coach: Natalie Alred
Email: nataliealred@letu.edu

NCAA I
Lady Yellow Jackets, Blue, Gold
Phone: (903) 233-7373
Fax: (903) 233-3822

Estimated # of Women's Volleyball Scholarships: N/A

Conference: American Southwest Conference

Program Profile: LeToureau has a very young program. Games are played in Solheim Arena which can seat up to 2800. Season from Sept 1-November 15th. The playing surface is wood. We have the ability to set up 4 courts when host tournaments.

History: The program began in the mid 1980's. It has struggled for some time and had numerous part time coaches. Coach Alred is the first full-time coach and has already seen stability and improvement in only her 2nd year at Le Tourneau University.

Achievements: Coach Alred has several Coach of the Year awards at the conference level, regional level and even 2 National Coach of the Year awards. Coached over 60 All-Conference players and 13 All-Americans.

Roster In State: 6	**Out of State:** 3	**Out of Country:**
Sophomores on Team:	**Seniors on Team:**	**Graduation %:** 99

Positions Needed: Setter and middle blocker

Schedule: College of the Southwest, Concordia Wisconsin, Concordia Austin, Texas Lutheran, University of Dallas.

Style of Play: Very defensive oriented. We play very aggressive on "D" and run a multiple attacking offense.

Lubbock Christian University
Academic Profile

5601-19th Street
Lubbock, TX 79407

Phone: 800-933-7601

Type: Public, 4 Yr., Coed
Website: http://www.lcu.edu
SAT/ACT/GPA: 21avg
Student/Faculty Ratio: 15:1
Undergraduate Enrollment: 1,100
Scholarships/Academic: Yes   **Athletic:** Yes
Expenses By: Year   **In State:** $ 10,000

Founded: 1957
Religion: Non-Affiliated
Housing: Yes
Male/Female: 44:56
Graduate Enrollment: N/A
Financial Aid: Yes
Out of State: $ 10,000

Degrees Conferred: AA, AS, BA, BS, BSEd, MA, MS, MBA

Programs of Study: Accounting, Agricultural Business Management, Animal Science, Banking/Finance, Biblical Studies, Biological Science, Business Administration, Chemistry, Communications, Education, Foreign Languages, History, Journalism, Kinesiology, Mathematics, Physical Education, Physics, Political Science, PreProfessional Programs, Psychology, Social Sciences, Spanish, Speech

Women's Athletic Profile

5601 W. 19th
Lubbock, TX 79407
Coach: Steven McRoberts
Email: steven.mcroberts@lcu.edu

NCAA I
Lady Chaps, Blue, Red, White
Phone: (806) 796-8800
Fax: (806) 796-8609

Estimated # of Women's Volleyball Scholarships: 8

Conference: Sooner Athletic Conference

Program Profile: Have won 4 conference championships in a row and have been to the national tournament two of the past three years. Also have finished ranked in the top 15 the past three years. Play in the brand new Rip Griffin Center (completed Fall of 2000) which seats 2,200 spectators.

History: Program was started in 1979. Program record over the past five years in 150-51.

Achievements: Conference Coach of the Year 97,98,99 Regional Coach of the Year 98,99 Conference Champions 97,98,99,00. Regional Champions 98,99 Elite Eight at National tournament 98. Several All-American players.

Freshman Receiving Financial Aid/Academic:		**Athletic:** 3
Roster In State: 13	**Out of State:** 1	**Out of Country:** 0
Sophomores on Team:	**Seniors on Team:** 1	**Graduation %:** 90

Most Recent Record: 24-13-0

Positions Needed: Middle Blocker

Schedule: Palm Beach Atlantic, Houston Baptist, John Brown, Concordia, West Texas A & M

Style of Play: Big Block and fast offense.

McMurry University
Academic Profile

14th and Sayles, Box 938
Abilene, TX 79677

Phone: 800-460-2392

Type: Private, 4 Yr., Liberal Arts, Coed
Website: http://www.mcm.edu
SAT/ACT/GPA: Open
Student/Faculty Ratio: 15:1

Founded: 1923
Religion: Methodist
Housing: Yes
Male/Female: 1:1

Undergraduate Enrollment: 1,410   **Graduate Enrollment:** N/A
Scholarships/Academic: Yes   **Athletic:** No   **Financial Aid:** Yes
Expenses By: Year   **In State:** $ 14,802   **Out of State:** $ Varies
Degrees Conferred: BA, BFA, BS, BMEd, BBA, BSN, BS
Programs of Study: Accounting, Art Education, Art/Fine Arts, Athletic Training, Biology, Biological Science, Business Administration, Commerce, Management, Ceramic Art & Design, Chemistry, Communications, Computer Information System, Computer Science, Criminal Justice, English, Elementary Education, Finance/Banking

Women's Athletic Profile

1400 Sayles Blvd.   **NCAA I**
Abilene, TX 79697   Lady Indians, Maroon, White
Coach: Cammie Petree   **Phone:** (915) 793-4635
Email: cpetree@mcmurryadm.mcm.edu   **Fax:** (915) 793-4659

Estimated # of Women's Volleyball Scholarships: N/A
Conference: American Southwest Conference
Program Profile: Positive, goal oriented program. Two hardwood floor gymnasiums, two weight rooms, wellness center with treadmills, recumbent bicycles, steppers, free weights, nautilus machines,, expanded free weight room, swimming pool, racquetball courts, sand volleyball court and training room with current therapeutic modalities. Playing season 22 weeks, traditional and non-traditional.
History: 1973. Last five years 76-63 record.
Achievements: ASC Conference Champions 1997, ASC West Division Co-Champions 1998, ASC West Division Runners-up 1999, ASC Coach of the Year 1997, 99. Individual ASC Player awards annually.
Coaching: Head Coach Cammie Petree
Freshman Receiving Financial Aid/Academic: **Athletic:** 0
Roster In State: 13   **Out of State:** 1   **Out of Country:** 0
Sophomores on Team: **Seniors on Team:** 2   **Graduation %:**
Most Recent Record: 10-16-0
Positions Needed: MB, Setter, RS
Schedule: Colorado College, Austin College, Texas Lutheran University, Southwestern Universty

Midwestern State University
Academic Profile

3410 Taft Blvd.   **Phone:** 800-842-1922
Wichita Falls, TX 76308

Type: Public, 4 Yr., Liberal Arts, Coed   **Founded:** 1922
Website: http://www.mwsu.edu   **Religion:** Non-Affiliated
SAT/ACT/GPA: 860/19   **Housing:** Yes
Student/Faculty Ratio: 20:1   **Male/Female:** 1:2
Undergraduate Enrollment: 5,500   **Graduate Enrollment:** 500
Scholarships/Academic: Yes   **Athletic:** Yes   **Financial Aid:** Yes
Expenses By: Year   **In State:** $ 5,620 **Out of State:** $ 9,905
Degrees Conferred: AAS, BA, BAAS, BBA, BS, BSW, BSIS, BSDH, BM, BSN, MA, MBA, ME, MS, MSK, MSN
Programs of Study: Accounting, Art, Art & Theatre, Applied Arts & Science, Biology, Business, Computer Information Systems, Chemical Technology, Chemistry, Computer Science, Criminal Justice, Economics, Marketing, Mass Communications, Mathematics, Medical Technology, Nursing, Political Science, Psychology, Social Work, Sociology

Women's Athletic Profile

3410 Taft   **NCAA I**
Wichita Falls, TX 76308   Lady Indians, Maroon, Gold
Coach: Pam Peetz   **Phone:** (940) 397-4471
Email: pam.peetz@nexus.mwsu.edu   **Fax:** (940) 691-8129

Estimated # of Women's Volleyball Scholarships: N/A
Conference: Lone Star Conference

Prairie View A & M University
Academic Profile

Administration Bldg. Room 003
Prairie View, TX 77446

Phone: 409-857-2626

Type: Public, 4 Yr., Liberal Arts, Coed
Website: http://www.pvamu.edu
SAT/ACT/GPA: 750/16
Student/Faculty Ratio: 25:1
Undergraduate Enrollment: 6,425
Scholarships/Academic: Yes   **Athletic:** No
Expenses By: Year   **In State:** $ 6,450
Degrees Conferred: BA, BS, MA, MS, MBA, MED

Founded: 1876
Religion: Non-Affiliated
Housing: No
Male/Female: 48:52
Graduate Enrollment: 740
Financial Aid: Yes
Out of State: $ 9,100

Programs of Study: Accounting, Agricultural Economics, Agricultural Education, Agricultural Engineering, Agronomy, Animal Science, Architecture, Biology, Broadcasting, Business Administration, Civil Engineering, Computer Engineering, Engineering Technology, Finance/Banking, Geography, Industrial Engineering Technology, Interdisciplinary Studies

Women's Athletic Profile

Administration Bldg., Rm 003
Prairie View, TX 77446
Coach: Alicia L. Pete
Email:

NCAA I
Pantherettes, Purple, Gold
Phone: (409) 857-2196
Fax: (409) 857-2408

Estimated # of Women's Volleyball Scholarships: N/A
Conference: Southwestern Athletic Conference

Rice University
Academic Profile

6100 Main-MS 548
Houston, TX 77005-1892

Phone: (713) 527-4795

Type: Private, 4 Yr., Coed
Website: http://www.riceowls.edu
SAT/ACT/GPA: 1360/
Student/Faculty Ratio: 1:6
Undergraduate Enrollment: 2,743
Scholarships/Academic: Yes   **Athletic:** Yes
Expenses By: Year   **In State:** $ 23,000
Degrees Conferred: Bachelors, Masters, Ph.D..

Founded: 1891
Religion: Non-Affiliated
Housing: Yes
Male/Female: 1:1
Graduate Enrollment: 1,525
Financial Aid: Yes
Out of State: $ 23,000

Programs of Study: Humanities, Social Sciences, Architecture, Music, Natural Sciences, Engineering, Business Administration

Women's Athletic Profile

6100 Main Street
Houston, TX 77005
Coach: Julio Morales
Email: jmorales@rice.edu

NCAA I
Lady Owls, Navy, Grey, White
Phone: (713) 527-4795
Fax: (713) 527-6191

Estimated # of Women's Volleyball Scholarships: 12
Conference: Western Athletic Conference
Program Profile: The Owls play in Autry Court which has 5,000 seats. The average attendance during the 1998 season was just shy of 400.
History: Rice University has been playing women's volleyball since 1979. The compiled overall record is 347-366.
Achievements: Tiffany Carrethers-AVCA Player of the Week, All-WAC selection and participant in the new USVL. Karolina Zelinka-training for the World University Games this summer.
Coaching: Dr. Julio Morales - Head Coach, has an overall record of 102-60 in 9 seasons. His record at Rice is 46-43. Jose Santiago and Gina Mackin are Assistant Coaches.
Freshman Receiving Financial Aid/Academic: **Athletic:** 3
Roster In State: 8   **Out of State:** 4   **Out of Country:** 1
Sophomores on Team: 0   **Seniors on Team:** 3   **Graduation %:** 100

Most Recent Record: 28-10-0   **Fall Games:** 33   **Spring Games:** 8
Camp of Clinic Dates: July 5-18
Positions Needed: Two Outside Hitters, One Middle Hitter
Schedule: Texas, Hawaii, Houston, Fresno

Saint Edward's University
Academic Profile

3001 South Congress
Austin, TX 78704

Phone: (512) 448-8480

Type: Public, 4 Yr., Liberal Arts, Coed
Website: http://www.stedwards.edu
SAT/ACT/GPA: 950/19/Top 1/2
Student/Faculty Ratio: 16:1
Undergraduate Enrollment: 1,986
Scholarships/Academic: Yes   **Athletic:** Yes
Expenses By: Year   **In State:** $ 16,198
Founded: 1885
Religion: Catholic
Housing: Yes
Male/Female: 40:60
Graduate Enrollment: 640
Financial Aid: Yes
Out of State: $ 16,198
Specializes In: Liberal Arts, Value Based Education with emphasis on learning
Degrees Conferred: BA, BS, BBA, MA, MBA
Programs of Study: Accounting, Art, BioChemistry, Biology, Business & Management, Chemistry, Communications, Computer Information Systems, Computer Science, Creative Writing, English, Finance, Criminal Justice, Economics, Education, Elementary Education, English, History, Mathematics, Management, Marketing, Philosophy, Photography, Physical Education, Political Science, PreDentistry, PreLaw , Psychology, Religion, Secondary Education, Soil Science

Women's Athletic Profile

3001 S. Congress Avenue
Austin, TX 78704
Coach: Debora Williamson
Email:

NCAA I
Lady Hilltoppers, Navy, Gold
Phone: (512) 448-8480
Fax: (512) 416-5834

Estimated # of Women's Volleyball Scholarships: N/A
Conference: Heart of Texas
Program Profile: We play at Recreation & Convocation Center which seats 2,500. We have a fall traditional season from August to December and we have a spring non-traditional season from February to April.
History: We made playoff appearances in 1983, 1985, 1986,1987, 1988, 1990, 1991, 1992, 1993, 1994, 1995, 1996, 1997 and 1998. Our championship years were 1985, 1991 and 1996. Hot tournaments and SW region tournaments were 1997.
Achievements: 1989-1999 HOT All-Conference was Suzy Bayer, Camille Smith, Tessa Kuberna, Winona Burt and Roberta Lima. SW Region Team - Suzy Bayer, Camille Smith and Tessa Kuberna. We had 1 All-American player and 3 Academic All-Americans named on our team: Suzy Bayer, Winona Burt and Kristin Wilke
Coaching: Debora Williamson, Head Coach, has been here for 9 years. Her overall record is 264-113. She played at Southwestern University and was All-American and National Runner-up.
Freshman Receiving Financial Aid/Academic: **Athletic:** 5
Roster In State: 13   **Out of State:** 0   **Out of Country:** 1
Sophomores on Team: 0   **Seniors on Team:** 6   **Graduation %:** 100
Most Recent Record: 28-15-0   **Fall Games:** 43   **Spring Games:** 4
Camp of Clinic Dates: June 7-11 (High School/8-14 years old; August 2-6 (Jr.& High School)
Schedule: Cameron University-Oklahoma, Rockhurst- Missouri, Columbia- Missouri, Angelo State-Texas, Texas A & M - Kingsville
Style of Play: Defensively strong (Top 10 in the nation in digs in 1998).

Saint Mary's University - Texas
Academic Profile

One Camino Santa Maria
San Antonio, TX 78228

Phone: (210) 436-3528

Type: Private, 4 Yr., Liberal Arts, Engineering, Coed
Website: http://www.stmarytx.edu
SAT/ACT/GPA: 950/22
Student/Faculty Ratio: 17:1
Undergraduate Enrollment: 2,600
Founded: 1852
Religion: Catholic
Housing: Yes
Male/Female: 45:55
Graduate Enrollment: 1,522

Scholarships/Academic: Yes | **Athletic:** Yes | **Financial Aid:** Yes
Expenses By: Semester | **In State:** $ 8,000 | **Out of State:** $ 8,000
Specializes In: Biology, Business, Engineering, Computer Science
Degrees Conferred: BA, BS, BAS, BBA, MA, MS, MBA, Ph.D., JD
Programs of Study: Accounting, Banking/Finance, Biology, Chemistry, Business Education, Business Administration, Communications, Computer Engineering, Computer Science, Criminal Justice, Earth Science, Economics, Education, International Relations, Management, Marketing, Mathematics, Music, Philosophy, Physics, Political Science, Psychology, Social Sciences

Women's Athletic Profile

One Camino Santa Maria
San Antonio, TX 78228-8508
Coach: Laura Groff
Email:

NCAA I
Lady Rattlers, Blue, Gold
Phone: (210) 436-3661
Fax: (210) 436-3040

Estimated # of Women's Volleyball Scholarships: N/A
Conference: Heart of Texas Conference

Sam Houston State University
Academic Profile

PO Box 2268-SHSU
Huntsville, TX 77341

Phone: 409-294-1828

Type: Public, 4 Yr., Coed
Website: http://www.shsu.edu
SAT/ACT/GPA: 1020/20
Student/Faculty Ratio: 22:1
Undergraduate Enrollment: 12,000
Scholarships/Academic: Yes | **Athletic:** Yes | **Financial Aid:** Yes
Expenses By: Semester | **In State:** $ 3,000 | **Out of State:** $ 5,500
Degrees Conferred: BBA, BS, BA, BFA, BM, BAAS, MD
Programs of Study: Agriculture, Business & Management, Communications, Education, Social Sciences, Visual & Performing Arts

Founded: 1868
Religion: Non-Affiliated
Housing: Yes
Male/Female: 1:1
Graduate Enrollment: 500

Women's Athletic Profile

P.O. Box 2268
Huntsville, TX 77340
Coach: Brenda Gray
Email:

NCAA I
Lady Bearkats, Orange, White
Phone: (409) 294-1736
Fax: (409) 294-3538

Estimated # of Women's Volleyball Scholarships: 12
Conference: Southland Conference
Program Profile: We have been members of Division I program since 1986. We are extremely competitive. We have great facilities. Our coliseum has a seating capacity of 6,100. The playing season starts mid-August and goes through mid-December. We are usually in top of the Conference.
History: The program began in 1970.
Coaching: Brenda Gray, Head Coach, is entering her 14th year with Bearkats. She was named Southland Conference Volleyball Coach of the Year in 1993 and Conference Coach of the Year honors. Jennifer Cron, Assistant Coach, is in her second season with the program. She was named Southland Conference Post-season All-Tournament Most Valuable Player.
Freshman Receiving Financial Aid/Academic: | **Athletic:** 2
Roster In State: 12 | **Out of State:** 0 | **Out of Country:** 0
Sophomores on Team: 0 | **Seniors on Team:** 3 | **Graduation %:** 90
Most Recent Record: 12-19-0 | **Fall Games:** 31 | **Spring Games:** 0
Camp of Clinic Dates: June 20-25; July 18-23
Positions Needed: Middle, Setter, Outside Hitter
Style of Play: Aggressive!!!

San Jacinto College- Central
Academic Profile

8060 Spencer Highway
Pasadena, TX 77505

Phone: (281) 476-1861

Type: Public, 2 Yr., Coed

Founded: 1961

Website: http://www.sjcd.cc.tx.us
SAT/ACT/GPA: H.S. Diploma
Student/Faculty Ratio: 24:1
Undergraduate Enrollment: 9,000
Scholarships/Academic: Yes   **Athletic:** Yes
Expenses By: Year   **In State:** $ 1,325
Specializes In: Business, Nursing, Vocational
Degrees Conferred: AA, AAS
Programs of Study: Nursing, EMS, Fire Academy, Business, Computers, Cosmetology, Kinesiology

Religion: Non-Affiliated
Housing: No
Male/Female: Not Available
Graduate Enrollment: N/A
Financial Aid: Yes
Out of State: $ 1,322

Women's Athletic Profile

8060 Spencer Highway
Pasadena, TX 77505
Coach: Becky Lidolph
Email: blidol@central.sjcd.tx.us

NCAA I
Lady Ravens, Blue, Black
Phone: (281) 476-1861
Fax: (281) 478-2729

Estimated # of Women's Volleyball Scholarships: 5,260
Conference: Region 14 Athletic Conference
Program Profile: We are a nationally ranked program. Our campus holds 9,000 students. The volleyball season is from September 1st to November 25th.
History: We began in 1974. We have 9 Conference Championships, 5 Regional Titles and 3 National 5th place finishes in 1984, 1985 and 1986. We were National Champions in 1987. We were National Runner-up in 1993.
Achievements: 16 All-Americans since 1981; District III Coach of the Year 5 times: 1984, 1985, 1986, 1987 and 1993; NJCAA National Coach of the Year in 1987; AVCA Southwest Region Coach of the Year in 1996.
Coaching: Becky Lidolph - Head Coach. Jeff Ham is Assistant Coach.
Freshman Receiving Financial Aid/Academic: **Athletic:** 7
Roster In State: 12   **Out of State:** 0   **Out of Country:** 0
Sophomores on Team: 0   **Seniors on Team:** 5   **Graduation %:** Unknown
Most Recent Record: 18-27-0   **Fall Games:** 45   **Spring Games:** 2
Positions Needed: Setters, Middle Hitters
Schedule: Galveston, University of Texas-Brownsville, Lee College
Style of Play: Quick offense, brutal defense, variety of plays depending on personnel.

Schreiner College
Academic Profile

2100 Memorial Boulevard
Kerrville, TX 78028

Phone: (830)896-5411

Type: Private, 4 Yr., Liberal Arts, Coed
Website: http://www.athletics.schreiner.edu
SAT/ACT/GPA: Rolling admission
Student/Faculty Ratio: 14:1
Undergraduate Enrollment: 675
Scholarships/Academic: Yes   **Athletic:** No
Expenses By: Year   **In State:** N/A
Specializes In: Education
Degrees Conferred: BA, BS, BBA, BGS, M.Ed.

Founded: 1923
Religion: Presbyterian
Housing: Yes
Male/Female:
Graduate Enrollment: 125
Financial Aid: Yes
Out of State: N/A

Programs of Study: Accounting, Art Education, BioChemistry, Biology, Business Administration, Chemistry, Communications, Computer Studies, Engineering (312 Program), English, Exercise Science, Finance, Fine Arts, French, German, Graphic Design, History, Humanities, Legal Studies, Management, Marketing, Mathematics, Philosophy, Religion, Studio Art, Teaching Certification

Women's Athletic Profile

2100 Memorial Boulevard
Kerrville, TX 78028
Coach: Dr. Bob Howard
Email:

NCAA I
Mountaineers, Maroon, Gold
Phone: (830) 792-7289
Fax: (830) 792-7483

Estimated # of Women's Volleyball Scholarships: 0
Conference: American Southwest Conference
Program Profile: We have a competitive Division III program. Our fall season runs from August through November and spring season runs from late February through April.

History: We started in 1984. We were originally affiliated with the NAIA, first as an independent then as a member of the Heart of Texas Conference. In 1997, we moved to NCAA Division III. In 1998, we played our inaugural season in the American Southwest Conference.

Achievements: 1998-1999 Academic All-American was Amy Ford; 6 players were named 1998-1999 Academic All-Conference; 1998-1999 NAIA 1st team All-Sectional was Amy Ford and Jimmie Jo Conn; Gretchen Goebel was Honorable Mention.

Coaching: Dr.Bob Howard, Head Coach, started with the program in 1998 to the present. In his first year, he compiled a record of 14-10. In conference play, he compiled a record of 12-3. He is the Author of "The Fundamental Contacts of Volleyball", a book published in 1995.

Roster In State: 10	**Out of State:** 1	**Out of Country:** 0
Sophomores on Team: 0	**Seniors on Team:** 1	**Graduation %:** 100
Most Recent Record: 14-10-0	**Fall Games:** 24	**Spring Games:** 15

Positions Needed: Outside Hitter (L-1), Middle Blocker (M-2), Back-up Setter

Schedule: Trinity University, Texas Lutheran University, Angelo State University, Mary Hardin Baylor University

Style of Play: Offensively, we are aggressive and look to terminate. We run a variety of quick attacks in the middle with a 2nd tempo options to the outside hitters. Defensively, we want to put up a strong block, and emphasize transition as much as digging the ball.

Southern Methodist University
Academic Profile

5990 Airline Road
Dallas, TX 75275-0216

Phone: 800-323-0672

Type: Private, 4 Yr., Liberal Arts, Engineering, Coed
Website: http://www.smumustangs.com/
SAT/ACT/GPA: 1000/25
Student/Faculty Ratio: 20:1
Undergraduate Enrollment: 5,000
Scholarships/Academic: Yes   **Athletic:** Yes
Expenses By: Year   **In State:** $ 21,000

Founded: 1911
Religion: Methodist
Housing: Yes
Male/Female: 50:50
Graduate Enrollment: 4,500
Financial Aid: Yes
Out of State: $ 21,000

Degrees Conferred: BA, BS, BFA, MA, MS, MBA, MFA, Ph.D., JD, MDiv

Programs of Study: 68 majors offered in four schools: School of Humanities & Sciences, School of Business, Arts, Engineering and Applied Science.

Women's Athletic Profile

P.O. Box 750216
Dallas, TX 75275
Coach: Lisa Seifert
Email: lseifert@mail.smu.edu

NCAA I
Lady Mustangs, Red, Blue
Phone: (214) 768-4227
Fax: (214) 768-2044

Estimated # of Women's Volleyball Scholarships: 2

Conference: Western Athletic Conference

Program Profile: We play in Moody Coliseum, which holds 9,000 seats. The season is from early August to mid December. We have 12 full scholarships. We travel and recruit nationally. Weight training and strength conditioning is our top priority. Academics are important.

History: We began in the fall of 1996. Seifert has been our only head coach. We are one of eight remaining teams of the Western Athletic Conference.

Achievements: Charity Savedra: All-WAC as defensive specialist.

Coaching: Lisa Seifert, Head Coach, was assistant coach at Texas Tech from 1989 to 1995. She has been Head Coach at SMU from 1995 to the present. Assistant Coach Gene Wood was a setter at Texas A & M from 1990 to 1993. She was a student assistant at Rice in 1995. She has been an assistant at SMU from 1997 to the present. Assistant Coach Jenny Chipman was an outside hitter at UT from 1991 to 1994. She was a graduate assistant at Wichita State in 1996. She has been assistant coach at SMU from 1997 to the present.

Freshman Receiving Financial Aid/Academic: **Athletic:** 3

Roster In State: 8	**Out of State:** 3	**Out of Country:** 0
Sophomores on Team: 3	**Seniors on Team:** 0	**Graduation %:** 100
Most Recent Record: 14-17-0	**Fall Games:** 32	**Spring Games:** 0

Camp of Clinic Dates: July 5-8, 9-11, 12-15

Positions Needed: Non—signed (2) players ; need (3) for 2000: Setter, Middle

Schedule: Texas, Hawaii, Fresno State, Baylor, Texas Tech, San Jose State

Style of Play: Our philosophy is based on ball control.

Southwest Texas State University
Academic Profile

601 University Drive
San Marcos, TX 78666

Phone: 512-245-2364

Type: Public, 4 Yr., Coed
Website: http://www.swt.edu
SAT/ACT/GPA: 920/20
Student/Faculty Ratio: 22:1
Undergraduate Enrollment: 18,500
Scholarships/Academic: Yes   **Athletic:** Yes
Expenses By: Year   **In State:** $ 7,944

Founded: 1899
Religion: Non-Affiliated
Housing: Yes
Male/Female: 47:53
Graduate Enrollment: 3,000
Financial Aid: Yes
Out of State: $ 13,364

Specializes In: Business, Education, Exercise & Sports Science, Geography, Music
Degrees Conferred: BA, BS, MA, MS, Doctorate
Programs of Study: Agriculture, Anthropology, Applied Arts, Applied Sociology, Art, Biology, Business Administration, Chemistry, Clinical Laboratory Science, Communication Disorders, Communications, Criminal Justice, Computer Science, Economics, Education, Exercise and Sport, Health Information Management, Health Professions, Health Wellness Promotion, International Studies, Mathematics, Music, Radiation Therapy, Recreational Administration, Social Work, Philosophy, Physics, Psychology, Theatre Arts

Women's Athletic Profile

Jowers Center
San Marcos, TX 78666-4615
Coach: Karen Chisum
Email:

NCAA I
Lady Bobcats, Maroon, Gold
Phone: (512) 245-2298
Fax: (512) 245-2967

Estimated # of Women's Volleyball Scholarships: N/A
Conference: Southland Conference
Program Profile: We play in Straham Coliseum with a seating capacity of 7,200.
History: Our program began in 1973 as member of Lone Star Conference. We entered the Southland Conference in 1989.
Achievements: Coach of the Year in 1991, Southland Conference Titles in 1991 & 1998.
Coaching: Karen Chisum, Head Coach, is entering her 20th year with a record of 477-309, considered winningest at Southland Conference. Jennifer LaGrange, Assistant Coach, graduated from LSU in 1994, where the team made Final Four Appearances. She is entering third year with SWT. Melissa Ferris, Assistant Coach, graduated from Arizona in 1996. She is entering her second second year at SWT. She was named to the Pac-10 All-Decade team.
Freshman Receiving Financial Aid/Academic: **Athletic:** 3
Roster In State: 13   **Out of State:** 2   **Out of Country:** 0
Sophomores on Team: 0   **Seniors on Team:** 2   **Graduation %:** 90
Most Recent Record: 25-9-0   **Fall Games:** 3   **Spring Games:** 0
Camp of Clinic Dates: July 5-9; July 10-14, 2000
Positions Needed: Outside Hitter, Setter
Schedule: Arizona State, Sacramento-CSU, Texas A&M, Rice, TCU
Style of Play: Relentless defense and mental toughness.

Southwestern Adventist College
Academic Profile

100 W. Hillcrest
Keene, TX 76059

Phone: 817-645-3921

Type: Private, 4 Yr., Coed
Website: http://www.swau.edu
SAT/ACT/GPA: 760/16/No minimal
Student/Faculty Ratio: 13:1
Undergraduate Enrollment: 1,144
Scholarships/Academic: Yes   **Athletic:** No
Expenses By: Year   **In State:** $ 13,396

Founded: 1893
Religion: Non-Affiliated
Housing: Yes
Male/Female: 45:57
Graduate Enrollment: 22
Financial Aid: Yes
Out of State: $ 13,396

Degrees Conferred: BA, BS, BFA
Programs of Study: Accounting, Biology, Biological Science, Broadcasting, Business Administration, Commerce, Management, Chemistry, Communications, Computer Programming, Computer Information Systems, Elementary Education, English, Health Services Administration, History, International Relations, Journalism, Mathematics, Medical Technology, Nursing, Physical Fitness & Exercise Science, Physics, Psychology, Religious Studies, Office Management, Social Science, Social Work, Theology

Women's Athletic Profile

P.O. Box 567
Keene, TX 76059
Coach: Mike Sarino
Email:

NCAA I
Knights, Maroon, White, Gold
Phone: (817) 645-3921
Fax: (817) 556-4744

Estimated # of Women's Volleyball Scholarships: N/A
Conference: Big State Conference

Southwestern University
Academic Profile

1001 Southwestern Blvd.
Georgetown, TX 78626-0770

Phone: (512) 863-1532

Type: Private, 4 Yr., Liberal Arts, Coed
Website: http://www.southwestern.edu
SAT/ACT/GPA: 1100/24
Student/Faculty Ratio: 11:1
Undergraduate Enrollment: 1,270
Scholarships/Academic: Yes   **Athletic:** No
Expenses By: Year   **In State:** $ 20,000

Founded: 1848
Religion: Methodist
Housing: Yes
Male/Female: 47:53
Graduate Enrollment: N/A
Financial Aid: No
Out of State: $ 20,000

Specializes In: Biology, Business, Engineering, Premed
Degrees Conferred: BS, BA, BFA, BM
Programs of Study: Accounting, American Studies, Animal Behavior, Art, Biology, Business, Chemistry, Child Study & Language Development, Communications, Computer Science, Economics, English, French, German, History, International Studies, Kinesiology, Mathematics, Music, Philosophy, Physical Science, Physics, Political Science, Psychology, Religion, Sociology, Theatre

Women's Athletic Profile

1001 Southwestern Blvd. Robertson Center
Georgetown, TX 78626-0770
Coach: Scott Mayhew
Email:

NCAA I
Lady Pirates, Black, Gold
Phone: (512) 863-1532
Fax: (512) 863-1393

Estimated # of Women's Volleyball Scholarships: N/A
Conference: Southern California Athletic Conference
Schedule: Washington University, Trinity University, Colorado College, De Pauw University, Centre College, Rhodes College

Stephen F. Austin State University
Academic Profile

1936 North Street
Nacogdoches, TX 75962

Phone: 800-731-2902

Type: Public, 4 Yr., Coed
Website: http://www.stfasu.edu
SAT/ACT/GPA: 1010/21/3.0
Student/Faculty Ratio: 20:1
Undergraduate Enrollment: 12,132
Scholarships/Academic: Yes   **Athletic:** Yes
Expenses By: Year   **In State:** $ 2,427.50

Founded: 1923
Religion: Non-Affiliated
Housing: Yes
Male/Female: 45:55
Graduate Enrollment: N/A
Financial Aid: Yes
Out of State: $ 8,817.50

Degrees Conferred: Various bachelors degrees, masters degrees, and doctorate Forestry
Programs of Study: Agriculture, Art, Biology, Chemistry, Communications, Computer Information Systems, Computer Science, Criminal Justice, Economics, English, Environmental Science, French, Geography, Gerontology, Health Science, Hearing Impaired, History, Horticulture, Humanities, Kinesiology, Management, Marketing, Mathematics, Medical Technology, Physics, Political Science, Psychology, Public Administration, Sociology, Spanish, Speech, Theatre

Women's Athletic Profile

1936 North Street
Nacogdoches, TX 75962
Coach: Debbie Humphreys
Email: dhumphreys@stanford.edu

NCAA I
Lady Jacks, Purple, White
Phone: (409) 468-2011
Fax: (409) 468-4593

Estimated # of Women's Volleyball Scholarships: 3
Conference: Southland Conference
Program Profile: The team plays at Shelton Gym that seats 1,500. We also play at William R. Johnson Coliseum which has 7,203 seats. Our playing season is from September to December.
History: We have 3 SLC Championships and 2 NCAA Tournament appearances. We had 2 NIVC appearances over the past 6 seasons.
Achievements: Coach of the Year in 1992 & 1994; 1 Player of the Year in 1994 & 1996.
Coaching: Debbie Humphreys, Head Coach, started in 1988. She compiled a record of 244-131 in 11 seasons. She played at Texas Tech University. Jennie Collings is Assistant Coach.
Freshman Receiving Financial Aid/Academic:

		Athletic: 4
Roster In State: 10	**Out of State:** 2	**Out of Country:** 0
Sophomores on Team: 2	**Seniors on Team:** 1	**Graduation %:** 78
Most Recent Record: 24-7-0	**Fall Games:** 32	**Spring Games:** 4

Camp of Clinic Dates: July 6 - 9; July 10-13; July 16-18
Positions Needed: Outside Hitter, Middle Blocker, Setter
Schedule: University of Texas-Arlington, Southwest, St. Louis, Rice
Style of Play: Quick offense centered around ball control and athletic ability. Scrappy defense.

Sul Ross State University
Academic Profile

Box C-17
Alpine, TX 79832

Phone: 915-837-8050

Type: Public, 4 Yr., Coed
Website: http://www.sulross.edu
SAT/ACT/GPA: Open
Student/Faculty Ratio: 13:1
Undergraduate Enrollment: 2,000
Scholarships/Academic: Yes
Expenses By: Year

Athletic: No
In State: $ 5,500

Founded: 1920
Religion: Non-Affiliated
Housing: Yes
Male/Female: 60:40
Graduate Enrollment: 500
Financial Aid: Yes
Out of State: $ 7,500

Specializes In: Education, Range Animal Science, Agriculture
Degrees Conferred: AAS, BA, BS, BBA, BM, MA, MS, MED, MBA
Programs of Study: Education, Animal Science, Agriculture, Biological Science, Business Administration, Communications, Criminal Justice, Fine Arts, Geology, Mathematics, Political Science, Psychology

Women's Athletic Profile

East Hwy 90
Alpine, TX 79832
Coach: Ruth McWilliams
Email:

NCAA I
Lady Lobos, Scarlet, Grey
Phone: (915) 837-8226
Fax: (915) 837-8234

Estimated # of Women's Volleyball Scholarships: N/A
Conference: American Southwest Conference

Tarleton State University
Academic Profile

Box T - 80
Stephenville, TX 76402

Phone: 254-968-9125

Type: Public, 4 Yr., Coed
Website: http://www.tarleton.edu
SAT/ACT/GPA: 930/20
Student/Faculty Ratio: 20:1
Undergraduate Enrollment: 7,354
Scholarships/Academic: Yes
Expenses By: Year

Athletic: Yes
In State: $ 5,500

Founded: 1899
Religion: Non-Affiliated
Housing: Yes
Male/Female: 50:50
Graduate Enrollment: N/A
Financial Aid: Yes
Out of State: $ 7,000

Specializes In: Education, Agriculture, Business
Degrees Conferred: BAAS, BA, BBA, BFA, BM, BS, BSW, MS, MBA, MA, MED
Programs of Study: Business/Office and Marketing/Distribution, Business Management, Communications, Computer, Education, Health, Physical Education

Women's Athletic Profile

Box T-80
Stephenville, TX 76402
Coach: TBA
Email:

NCAA I
TexAnns, Purple, White
Phone: (254) 968-9346
Fax: (254) 968-9674

Estimated # of Women's Volleyball Scholarships: 8
Conference: Lone Star Conference
Program Profile: TexAnns play home matches in their own "upper gym" at Wisdom Gym. The TexAnns have compiled a record of 287-344 since 1981.
History: Tarleton has had 21 first team All-Conference players, 9 Second team since 1978.
Most Recent Record: 5-28-0

Texas A & M University - College Station
Academic Profile

P.O. Box 30017
College Station, TX 77842-3017

Phone: (409) 845-1051

Type: Public, 4 Yr., Liberal Arts, Coed
Website: http://www.sports.tamu.edu
SAT/ACT/GPA: 920/19/2.5
Student/Faculty Ratio: 18:1
Undergraduate Enrollment: 43,000
Scholarships/Academic: Yes
Expenses By: Year
Specializes In: Business Adm., Engineering, Science, Veterinary Medicine, Med
Degrees Conferred: BA, BS, MA, MS, MBA, MD
Programs of Study: 138 fields of undergraduate study; 152 masters, 102 doctoral degrees.

Athletic: Yes
In State: $ 7,725

Founded: 1876
Religion: Non-Affiliated
Housing: Yes
Male/Female: 55:45
Graduate Enrollment: 6,774
Financial Aid: Yes
Out of State: $ 14,145

Women's Athletic Profile

Athletic Department, P.O.Box 30017
College Station, TX 77842-3017
Coach: Laurie Corbelli
Email: lcorbelli@athletics.tamu.edu

NCAA I
Lady Aggies, Maroon, White
Phone: (409) 845-1051
Fax: (409) 862-1791

Estimated # of Women's Volleyball Scholarships: N/A
Conference: Big 12 Conference
Program Profile: We play at G. Rollie White Coliseum, which has a capacity of 7,800. We have a volleyball-only facility that includes a new state-of-the-art locker room. We are in the Top 20 in the nation in attendance. We have full financial commitment form the Athletic Department.
History: The program started in 1975. Laurie Corbelli has been Head Coach since 1993. We were participants in the 13 National Championship Tournaments (AIAW & NCAA). We have been in every NCAA Tournament from 1993 to the present. We had 2 Sweet-16 Appearances.
Achievements: Laurie Corbelli: 5 times Coach of the Year (3 WCC, 2 5WC); 2 times Region/District Coach of the Year; 5 All-Americans; 2 National Team members
Coaching: Laurie Corbelli, Head Coach, has been coaching since 1986 (USF,Santa Clara, Texas A & M). Her record at Texas A & M is 141-54, .723, in 6 seasons. In 1980 and 1984, she was in the Olympic Team (1984 Silver Medalist). She received the Flo Hyman All-Time Great Player Award in 1998 and was a 2 times Major League Volleyball MVP. She is a member of the USAV Board of Directors.
Freshman Receiving Financial Aid/Academic:
Roster In State: 11
Sophomores on Team: 4
Most Recent Record: 21-9-0
Out of State: 4
Seniors on Team: 1
Fall Games: 30
Athletic: 4
Out of Country: 0
Graduation %: 100
Spring Games: 3-4
Camp of Clinic Dates: June 13-16, June 17-20, July 8-11
Positions Needed: Middle Blockers, Outside Hitters
Schedule: Nebraska, Texas, Colorado, Texas Tech, Santa Clara, Michigan State

Texas A & M University - Commerce
Academic Profile

P. O. Box 3011
Commerce, TX 75429-3011

Phone: 888-868-2682

Type: Public, 4 Yr., Coed
Website: http://www.estu.edu
SAT/ACT/GPA: 900/20/2.0
Student/Faculty Ratio: 17:1
Undergraduate Enrollment: 4,800
Scholarships/Academic: Yes   **Athletic:** Yes
Expenses By: Semester   **In State:** $ 4,000

Founded: 1889
Religion: Non-Affiliated
Housing: Yes
Male/Female: 44:56
Graduate Enrollment: 3,000
Financial Aid: Yes
Out of State: $ 7,350

Specializes In: Education, Business, Psychology, Fine Arts, Sciences
Degrees Conferred: BA, BS, BFA, MA, MS, MBA, MFA, M.Ed., Ph.D., EdD
Programs of Study: Education, Business, Psychology, Fine Arts, Technology, Agriculture, Accounting, Animal Science, Arts, Communications, Computer Information Systems, Criminal Justice, Earth Science, Economics, Computer Science, English, Finance, Geography, Geology, Management, Mathematics, Marketing, Music, Psychology, Social Work, Social Science, Theatre

Women's Athletic Profile

P.O. Box 3011
Commerce, TX 75429
Coach: Larry Blackwell
Email: Larry_Blackwell@tamu.commerce.edu

NCAA I
Lady Lions, Navy, Gold
Phone: (903) 886-5576
Fax: (903) 889-5365

Estimated # of Women's Volleyball Scholarships: 8
Conference: Lone Star Conference
Coaching: Larry Blackwell - Head Coach. Gwendolyn Adams is Assistant Coach.
Freshman Receiving Financial Aid/Academic: **Athletic:** 1
Roster In State: 6   **Out of State:** 4   **Out of Country:** 75
Sophomores on Team: 0   **Seniors on Team:** 1   **Graduation %:** Unknown
Most Recent Record: 16-19-0   **Fall Games:** 35   **Spring Games:** 0
Positions Needed: All, OH, MB, Setter
Schedule: Cameron University, Central Oklahoma, Abilene Christian, Angelo State, Harding University, Southern Arkansas
Style of Play: We play a quick, fast paced, up tempo defense.

Texas A & M University - Kingsville
Academic Profile

Campus Box 202
Kingsville, TX 78363

Phone: 800-687-6000

Type: 4 Yr., Coed
Website: Not Available
SAT/ACT/GPA: Open
Student/Faculty Ratio:
Undergraduate Enrollment: N/A
Scholarships/Academic: **Athletic:**
Expenses By: Year   **In State:**

Founded:
Religion: Non-Affiliated
Housing: No
Male/Female:
Graduate Enrollment: N/A
Financial Aid:
Out of State:

Degrees Conferred:
Programs of Study: Accounting, Agricultural Business Management, Animal Science, Biological Science, Business Administration, Chemical Engineering, Communications, Engineering, Management, Mathematics, Petroleum Engineering, Plant Science, PreProfessional Programs, Range Management

Women's Athletic Profile

Campus Box 202
Kingsville, TX 78363
Coach: Jane Atzenhoffer
Email:

NCAA I
Lady Javelinas, Blue, Gold
Phone: (361) 593-2411
Fax: (512) 593-3587

Estimated # of Women's Volleyball Scholarships: N/A
Conference: Lone Star Conference

Texas Christian University
Academic Profile

Box 297600
Fort Worth, TX 76129

Phone: (800) 828-3764

Type: Private, 4 Yr., Liberal Arts, Coed
Website: http://www.tcu.edu
SAT/ACT/GPA: 1010/22/3.0
Student/Faculty Ratio: 14:1
Undergraduate Enrollment: 5,500
Scholarships/Academic: Yes
Expenses By: Year
Specializes In: Business, Education, Sciences

Founded: 1873
Religion: Disciples of Christ
Housing: Yes
Male/Female: 43:57
Graduate Enrollment: 1,500
Athletic: Yes   **Financial Aid:** Yes
In State: $ 14,700   **Out of State:** $ 14,700

Degrees Conferred: BA, BS, BFA, BBA, B.Mus., BMEd, BSN, MA, MS, MFA, MED, Ph.D.
Programs of Study: Art, Business, Communications, Computer Science, Criminal Justice, Dance, Education, Engineering, Journalism, Kinesiology, Languages, Marketing, Music, Nursing, Nutrition & Dietetics, Physical Education, PreLaw, PreMed, Radio/Television Film, Speech Communication

Women's Athletic Profile

TCU Box 297013
Forth Worth, TX 76126
Coach: Sandra Troudt
Email: sware@tcu.edu

NCAA I
Lady Volleyfrogs, Purple, White
Phone: (817) 257-7490
Fax: (817) 257-7080

Estimated # of Women's Volleyball Scholarships: 12
Conference: Western Athletic Conference
Program Profile: This is our third year . We play from the beginning of August until Thanksgiving. A new facility is being proposed. Right now we play in our recreation facility that holds 1,000.
History: The volleyball program began in the fall of 1996. We were given 3 scholarships to begin with. TCU added three each year. In 1999, we had 12 scholarships.
Coaching: Sandra Troudt, Head Coach, started at TCU in 1996 to the present. She coached Junior National Teams for four years. A.P.Clarke and Barbara Kovacs are Assistant Coaches.
Freshman Receiving Financial Aid/Academic: **Athletic:** 5
Roster In State: 9   **Out of State:** 5   **Out of Country:** 0
Sophomores on Team: 4   **Seniors on Team:** 1   **Graduation %:** Unknown
Most Recent Record: 14-15-0   **Fall Games:** 29   **Spring Games:** 3
Camp of Clinic Dates: 6/6-9; 6/12-14; 7/17-19
Positions Needed: Setter, Outside Hitter
Schedule: Hawaii, Rice, Fresno State, San Jose State, Oregon State, Kansas
Style of Play: Fast and aggressive.

Texas Lutheran College
Academic Profile

1000 W. Court Street
Seguin, TX 78155

Phone: 800-771-8521

Type: Private, 4 Yr., Liberal Arts, Coed
Website: http://www.txlutheran.edu
SAT/ACT/GPA: 900/19/2.0
Student/Faculty Ratio: 14:1
Undergraduate Enrollment: 1,500
Scholarships/Academic: Yes
Expenses By: Year
Specializes In: Business, Kinesiology, Pre-Professional

Founded: 1891
Religion: Lutheran
Housing: Yes
Male/Female: 2:3
Graduate Enrollment: N/A
Athletic: No   **Financial Aid:** Yes
In State: $ 14,042   **Out of State:** $ 14,042

Degrees Conferred: BBA, BA, BS
Programs of Study: Accounting, Applied Science, Arts, Biology, Business Administration, Chemistry, Communication Studies, Computer Science, Early Childhood Education, Economics, English, German, History, International Studies, Kinesiology, Management Information Systems, Mathematics, MultiDisciplinary Studies, Music, Philosophy, Physical Education, Physics, Political Science, PreDental, PreMed, PreVet, Psychology, Public History, Social Science, Spanish, Theology, Social Work, Theatre

Women's Athletic Profile

1000 W. Court St.
Seguin, TX 78155
Coach: Bryan Bunn
Email: sports@txlutheran.edu

NCAA I
Lady Bulldogs, Black, Gold
Phone: (830) 372-8000
Fax: (830) 372-8008

Estimated # of Women's Volleyball Scholarships: 6
Conference: American Southwest Conference
Program Profile: We play in September or late August and continue through the National Championships in December. Matches are played in Tostengard Activity Center on campus. It seats about 250 people..
History: Our program began with the 1971 season under Coach Kathryn Yandell. Coach Susan Duke took over the reins in 1964 and remained through the 1993 season. Bunn has been head coach since 1994. While at Texas Lutheran, he qualified for 11 National Championships: six in the AIAW and five in the NAIA. We won National Titles in 1975 and 1976.
Achievements: Bunn has been Coach of the Year in the HOTC twice; Duke was Coach of the Year six times; We have won or shared 7 Conference Titles; and have had 20 All-Americans; Two players - Laurie Flachmeier and Patty Dowdell played on Olympic teams and in the volleyball major leagues.
Coaching: Bryan Bunn, Head Coach, started in 1994. His overall record in 5 years is 141-54. He is a two-time United States Volleyball Association All-American. Phil Jackson is Assistant Coach.

Freshman Receiving Financial Aid/Academic:
		Athletic: 4
Roster In State: 14	**Out of State:** 0	**Out of Country:** 0
Sophomores on Team: 2	**Seniors on Team:** 5	**Graduation %:** 100
Most Recent Record: 34-8-0	**Fall Games:** 42	**Spring Games:** 4

Positions Needed: Outside Hitter, Middle Blocker
Style of Play: We are focused and aggressive with an emphasis on offense.

Texas Southern University
Academic Profile

3100 Cleburne
Houston, TX 77004

Phone: 713-313-7472

Type: Public, 4 Yr., Coed
Website: http://www.tsu.edu
SAT/ACT/GPA: 810/68/2.5
Student/Faculty Ratio: 7:1
Undergraduate Enrollment: 8,000
Scholarships/Academic: Yes
Expenses By: Year

Athletic: Yes
In State: $ 7,024

Founded: 1947
Religion: Non-Affiliated
Housing: Yes
Male/Female: 1:4
Graduate Enrollment: N/A
Financial Aid: Yes
Out of State: $ 13,500

Specializes In: Education, Pharmacy, Law School, School of Business
Degrees Conferred: BS, BA, MBA, MS, MA, Ph.D., JhD
Programs of Study: Biology, Chemistry, Physics, Sociology, Art, Music, History, English, Spanish, French, Political Science, Public Administration, Communications, Computer Science, Psychology, Social Work, Accounting, Marketing, General Business, Elementary Education, Secondary Education, Health, Human Performance, Pharmacy, PreMed, PrePhysical Therapy, Engineering, Airway Science, Respiratory Therapy, Medical Technology, Administration

Women's Athletic Profile

3100 Cleburne
Houston, TX 77004
Coach: Dwalah Brown-Fisher
Email:

NCAA I
Lady Tigers, Maroon, Grey
Phone: (713) 313-7011
Fax: (713) 313-7273

Estimated # of Women's Volleyball Scholarships: 4
Conference: Southwestern Athletic Conference
Program Profile: Texas Southern University features top quality athletes from all over the country. Recently, the Lady Tigers had an inaugural season in the spacious health and physical education arena with a seating capacity for 8,100. The Conference stretches over four states.
History: Women's Volleyball was first introduced into the Conference in 1987. Texas Southern won the first tournament title and became a dominant force in the SWAC for years to come. We were SWAC Tournament Champions in 1987, 1989-1991 and 1994. TSU was also a part of the first-ever Play-in Game to the NCAA from the Southwestern Athletic Conference.

Achievements: Audry Ford was named Coach of the Year; 1987, 1989-1991, & 1994 Tournament Champions; 1995 Conference Champions; 1994 Play-in Game

Coaching: Dwalah Brown-Fisher, Head Coach, started in 1994 to the present. She played as a setter, started for four years and was named All-Conference and All-Tournament. Cassandra Kennedy is Assistant Coach.

Freshman Receiving Financial Aid/Academic: **Athletic:** 3

Roster In State: 13	**Out of State:** 2	**Out of Country:** 0
Sophomores on Team: 2	**Seniors on Team:** 3	**Graduation %:** 80%-90
Most Recent Record: 6-23-0	**Fall Games:** 29	**Spring Games:** 0

Positions Needed: Middle Blockers, Outside Hitters

Schedule: Southern University, Alabama A & M, Morgan State, Prairie View A&M

Style of Play: Texas Southern runs a 5-1 and 2-1-2 defense. Offense consists of numerous plays, utilizing the middle of the court as much as possible.

Texas Tech University
Academic Profile

Box 43021
Lubbock, TX 79409-3021

Phone: (806) 742-3355

Type: Public, 4 Yr., Engineering, Coed
Website: http://www.ttu.edu
SAT/ACT/GPA: 1270/29/Depends on SAT/ACT scores
Student/Faculty Ratio: 18:1
Undergraduate Enrollment: 18,136
Scholarships/Academic: Yes   **Athletic:** Yes
Expenses By: Year   **In State:** $ 7,340

Founded: 1929
Religion: Non-Affiliated
Housing: Yes
Male/Female: 1.5:1
Graduate Enrollment: 3,315
Financial Aid: Yes
Out of State: $ 13,700

Specializes In: Engineering, Law School, Medical School, Agriculture

Degrees Conferred: Bachelors, Masters, Doctorate

Programs of Study: Architecture, Business Administration, Chemistry, Communication Studies, Dietetics, Electrical Engineering, Elementary Education, Exercise and Sports Science, Family Studies, German, Human Development, Journalism, Secondary Education, Theatre Arts

Women's Athletic Profile

Box 43021
Lubbock, TX 79409
Coach: Jeff Nelson
Email: lnjne@ttu.edu

NCAA I
Red Raiders, Scarlet, Black
Phone: (806) 742-3355
Fax: (806) 742-0365

Estimated # of Women's Volleyball Scholarships: 2

Conference: Big 12 Conference

Program Profile: We are members of the Big 12 Conference. Our program was a mainstay in the NCAA Tournaments in the 1990's. We will open the United Spirit Arena in 1999 and have one of the finest facilities in the nation.

History: In 1999, we celebratd 25 years of Texas Tech volleyball. The Red Raider volleyball program began in 1975 and has enjoyed much success.

Achievements: Texas volleyball has had numerous All-Conference, All-Region and All-Academic Athletes, as well as two All-Americans and a co-side National Player of the Year in 1996.

Coaching: Jeff Nelson, Head Coach, began his tenure at Tech in 1995 and is entering his 5th season. Tech is 93-42 under his direction. We got 3 NCAA Tournaments bids. Nelson graduated form Ball State in 1986 where he played in the 1985 NCAA Final Four. Nancy Todd and Gregg Nunley are the Assistant Coaches.

Roster In State: 7	**Out of State:** 9	**Out of Country:** 0
Sophomores on Team: 0	**Seniors on Team:** 5	**Graduation %:** Unknown
Most Recent Record: 23-11-0	**Fall Games:** 34	**Spring Games:** 4

Camp of Clinic Dates: July 5-25 (5 camps)

Positions Needed: Middle, Ousitde Hitter, Setter

Schedule: University of Alaska Fairbanks, Nebraska, Texas, Colorado, Loyola Marymount, North Carolina State, Utah, Texas A & M

Style of Play: Strong ball control team that moves ball around well. Big in the middle with outstanding setting.

Texas Wesleyan University
Academic Profile

1201 Wesleyan Street
Fort Worth, TX 76105

Phone: 800-580-8980

Type: Private, 4 Yr., Coed

Founded: 1890

Website: http://www.txwesleyan.edu
SAT/ACT/GPA: 820/18/3.0
Student/Faculty Ratio: 14:1
Undergraduate Enrollment: 2,106
Scholarships/Academic: Yes
Expenses By: Year
Specializes In: Business, Education
Degrees Conferred: BA, BS, BME, BBA, MBA, MAT, ME, MHS, DJ

Religion: Methodist
Housing: Yes
Male/Female: 38:62
Graduate Enrollment: 980
Athletic: Yes   **Financial Aid:** Yes
In State: $ 13,750   **Out of State:** $ 13,750

Programs of Study: Accounting, Business Administration, Finance, Management, Marketing, Sports Management, Business Education, Business Psychology, Mass Communication, Human Learning & Development, Exercise & Sport Studies, Psychology, Reading, Bilingual Education, Art, Music, Theatre Arts, Biology, Chemistry, English, Computer Science, Spanish, History, Mathematics, Political Science, Religion

Women's Athletic Profile

1201 Wesleyan Street
Fort Worth, TX 76105
Coach: Rick Johansen
Email: ne14vb@aol.com

NCAA I
Lady Rams, Blue, Gold
Phone: (817) 531-4850
Fax: (817) 531-4208

Estimated # of Women's Volleyball Scholarships: 2
Conference: Heartland
Program Profile: Stadium Size is 1300, volleyball is played in the fall.
Roster In State: 11   **Out of State:** 1   **Out of Country:** 0
Positions Needed: Setter, Middle
Style of Play: Read Defense, floating middle attack.

Texas Woman's University
Academic Profile

P.O. Box 425349
Denton, TX 76204

Phone: (940) 898-2378

Type: Public, 4 Yr., Coed
Website: http://www.twu.edu
SAT/ACT/GPA: 910192.0
Student/Faculty Ratio: 18:1
Undergraduate Enrollment: 4,700
Scholarships/Academic: Yes
Expenses By: Year
Specializes In: Liberal Arts or Professional studies
Degrees Conferred: Bachelors, Masters, Doctoral

Founded: 1901
Religion: Non-Affiliated
Housing: Yes
Male/Female: 6/9
Graduate Enrollment: 3,900
Athletic: Yes   **Financial Aid:** Yes
In State: $7,213   **Out of State:** $13,663

Programs of Study: Bachelor of Arts, Business Administration, Fine Arts, Science and Social Work; Master of Arts, Business Administration, Fine Arts, Science, Education, Library Science, Occupational Therapy, Doctor of Philosophy and Doctor of Education

Women's Athletic Profile

P.O Box 425349
Denton, TX 76204-5349
Coach: Patty Dowdell
Email: Pdowdell@twu.edu

NCAA I
Lady Pioneers, Maroon, White
Phone: (940) 898-2378
Fax: (940) 898-2372

Estimated # of Women's Volleyball Scholarships: 8
Conference: Lone Star Conference
Program Profile: The Pioneers play in the North Division of the Lone Star Conference. They practice and compete in the brand new $ 7 million Pioneer Hall, which features Magee Arena with a seating capacity of 1,800. They play a fall season that runs from August through November.
History: We do not know the first year of our volleyball. Since 1982, the school has a record of 332-308 (.519). The program was an independent until 1989 when we joined the NCAA Division II and the Lone Star Conference.
Achievements: 1997: Patty Dowdell, LSC North Division Coach of the Year; 1997 North Division Title with a 10-0 record; 7 All-Region Selections in the past six years and 10 GTE Academic All-American District 6 Selections in the past seven years.

Coaching: Patty Dowdell, Head Coach, is entering her fourth season with the program. She was named LSC North Division Coach of the Year and has had 100 career wins. She compiled a record of 59-52 in three years. She was former assistant coach at Iowa for six years, and was a member of the 1980 US Olympic team and was a captain of the national team from 1976 to 1980. Michael Burch is Assistant Coach.

Freshman Receiving Financial Aid/Academic: | | **Athletic:** 6
Roster In State: 8 | **Out of State:** 2 | **Out of Country:** 1
Sophomores on Team: 1 | **Seniors on Team:** 0 | **Graduation %:** Unknown
Most Recent Record: 7-31-0 | **Fall Games:** 38 | **Spring Games:** 4
Camp of Clinic Dates: June 10-13; June 15-18
Positions Needed: Middle Blockers, Setter, Outside Hitters
Schedule: West Texas A & M, Cameron
Style of Play: Excellent ball control, tough serving, and 5-1 quick offense.

Trinity University
Academic Profile

715 Stadium Drive
San Antonio, TX 78212

Phone: (210) 999-8274

Type: Private, 4 Yr., Liberal Arts, Coed | **Founded:** 1869
Website: http://www.trinity.edu | **Religion:** Presbyterian
SAT/ACT/GPA: 1276/3.7 | **Housing:** Yes
Student/Faculty Ratio: 11:1 | **Male/Female:** 49:51
Undergraduate Enrollment: 2,298 | **Graduate Enrollment:** N/A
Scholarships/Academic: Yes | **Athletic:** No | **Financial Aid:** Yes
Expenses By: Year | **In State:** $ 23,000 | **Out of State:** $ 23,000
Specializes In: Liberal Arts, Education
Degrees Conferred: Bachelors, Masters
Programs of Study: Accounting, Ancient Mediterranean Studies, Anthropology, Art, Art History, BioChemistry, Biology, Business Administration, Chemistry, Chinese, Classical Studies, Communications, Computer Science, Drama, Economics, Education, Engineering, English, French, GeoScience, German, Greek, History, International Studies, Latin, Mathematics, Music, Philosophy, Physics, Political Science, Psychology, Religion, Russian, Sociology, Spanish, Speech, Urban Studies

Women's Athletic Profile

715 Stadium Drive
San Antonio, TX 78212
Coach: Julie Jenkins
Email: jjenkins@trinity.edu

NCAA I
Lady Tigers, Maroon, White
Phone: (210) 999-8274
Fax: (210) 999-8292

Estimated # of Women's Volleyball Scholarships: N/A
Conference: Southern California Athletic Conference
Program Profile: We have a new $20 million facility. Our schedule is strong and attracts nationally ranked teams. We also offer a strong spring season with a 9-10 week off-season program.
History: We have had 7 straight NCAA Tournament bids and won our 5th SCAC title in 7 years. The Lady Tigers advanced to the Sweet 16 at NCAA in 1992, 1993, 1994, 1995 and 1998. We have posted a 209-62 record over the past 7 seasons and have awarded 6 All-American honors.
Achievements: SCAC Champions in 1992, 1993, 1994, 1996 and 1998; SCAC Player of the Year in 7 of the last 8 seasons; Winners of 80 of the last 82 SCAC matches.
Coaching: Julie Jenkins, Head Coach, started in 1985. Since 1992, the team has posted a 209-62 (.771) record and an 80-2 (.976) Conference record. She was SCAC Coach of the Year in 1992,1993, 1995, 1996 and 1998.
Freshman Receiving Financial Aid/Academic: | | **Athletic:** 0
Roster In State: 7 | **Out of State:** 5 | **Out of Country:** 0
Sophomores on Team: 0 | **Seniors on Team:** 1 | **Graduation %:** 100
Most Recent Record: 36-5-0 | **Fall Games:** 36 | **Spring Games:** 7
Positions Needed: 2000/2001 Team: Middle Blocker, Outside Hitter
Schedule: University of California-San Diego, Washington University, University of Wisconsin-Whitewater, Mount St. Joseph, California State Hayward, California Lutheran, St. Olaf
Style of Play: Balanced offense: 3-4 players who can score. Fast tempo. Strong blocking team. Ball control is always the primary emphasis. Serving and passing are what determines the outcome.

University of Dallas
Academic Profile

1845 East Northgate Drive
Irving, TX 75062

Phone: 800-628-6999

Type: Private, 4 Yr., Liberal Arts, Coed
Website: http://www.udallas.edu
SAT/ACT/GPA: Individually evaluated
Student/Faculty Ratio: 11:1
Undergraduate Enrollment: 1,180
Scholarships/Academic: Yes
Expenses By: Year
Specializes In: Liberal Arts

Athletic: No
In State: $ 16,576

Founded: 1910
Religion: Catholic
Housing: Yes
Male/Female: 2:3
Graduate Enrollment: N/A
Financial Aid: Yes
Out of State: $ 16,576

Degrees Conferred: BA, BS, MA, MS, PhD, MBA, MFA, MH, etc..
Programs of Study: English, History, Art, Drama, Biology, Chemistry, Theology, Politics, Business, Engineering, Physics, Economics, Music, Spanish, German, French, Modern Languages, Mathematics, Journalism, Religious & Pastoral Studies, Management

Women's Athletic Profile

1845 E. Northgate Drive
Irving, TX 75062
Coach: Venera Flores
Email: undadmis@acad.udallas.edu

NCAA I
Lady Crusaders, Navy, White
Phone: (972) 721-5266
Fax: (972) 721-5017

Estimated # of Women's Volleyball Scholarships: N/A
Conference: American Southwest Conference
Program Profile: We have a very young team. We are in the process of building a successful program. We play in the Maher Athletic Center which seats 1,000. We had a major problem on coaching turnovers and the new staff is trying to promote stability and committment.
History: In 1992, we got original affiliation and were at the TIAA Conference (NAI). In 1997, we became a member of the NCAA Division III (ASC).
Achievements: We have had numerous selections to the All-Conference and Academic All-Conference teams.
Coaching: Venera Flores, Head Coach, started in December of 1997 with a record of 10-11. She graduated from University of Dallas with a Bachlor's Degree in Arts in 1995 and an MBA in 1998. She was a University of Dallas volleyball team captain for three years and was named TIAA All-Conference for two years. She holds three assist records at University of Dallas.

Freshman Receiving Financial Aid/Academic:
Roster In State: 3
Sophomores on Team: 0
Most Recent Record: 10-11-0

Out of State: 5
Seniors on Team: 1
Fall Games: 21

Athletic: 0
Out of Country: 0
Graduation %: 50
Spring Games: 0

Camp of Clinic Dates: June 21 - June 25
Positions Needed: Outside Hitter, Middle Blocker, Setter
Schedule: Southwestern University, Austin College, Mary-Hardin Baylor, East Texas Baptist
Style of Play: We have a young, aggressive, and enthusiastic team. We run a lot of quick plays and encourage floor play.

University of Houston
Academic Profile

3100 Cullen Blvd.
Houston, TX 77204

Phone: (713) 743-9474

Type: Public, 4 Yr., Coed
Website: http://www.uh.edu
SAT/ACT/GPA: 920-1180/19-26
Student/Faculty Ratio:
Undergraduate Enrollment: 31,000
Scholarships/Academic: Yes
Expenses By: Year

Athletic: Yes
In State: $ 2,339

Founded: 1927
Religion: Non-Affiliated
Housing: Yes
Male/Female:
Graduate Enrollment: N/A
Financial Aid: Yes
Out of State: $ 8,779

Degrees Conferred: BA, BS, Master of Arts, Science
Programs of Study: Architecture, Environmental Design, Accounting, Finance, MIS, Marketing, Education, Kinesiology, Engineering, Hotel & Restaurant Management, Art, Communications Disorder, English, History, Foreign Languages (4), Music, Radio & Television, Theatre, Speech Communications, Biology, Chemistry, Computer Science, Geology, GeoPhysics, Math, Physics, PreOptometry, PrePharmacy, Anthropology, Economics, Psychology, Human Development and Family Studies, Information System Technology

Women's Athletic Profile

3100 Cullen Boulevard Athletic Alumni Cetner
Houston, TX 77204
Coach: Bill Walton
Email: jmill@pop.uh.edu

NCAA I
Lady Cougars, Red, White
Phone: (713) 743-9472
Fax: (713) 743-9498

Estimated # of Women's Volleyball Scholarships: 4
Conference: Conference USA
Program Profile: We have one of the top programs in the country. We play and practice in a brand new (1995) 30 million dollar facility. We have three permanent practice courts (can accommodate up to 10) and we have the largest weight facility in the country with 16,500 square feet. We play at the Hofheinz Pavillion which has 8,500 seats.
History: Our program started in 1972. We are one of only 13 schools in the nation to appear in the NCAA the past 8 years. We qualified for post-season play every year for at least 10 seasons and 18 times in our 20 year history. We won 20 or more matches in 11 of the last 12 years.
Achievements: National Player of the Year - Flo Hyman; 3 Olympians, 6 first Team All-American; 17 AVCA All-Region Players, 2 Conference Titles
Coaching: Bill Walton, Head Coach, started in 1986. His overall record is 278-154. He won 210 or more matches 11 of the last 12 years here. He was 1994 AVCA South Region Coach of the Year, SWL Coach of the Year in 1994 and 1992 AVCA South Region Coach of the Year. He has coached one AVCA All-American and 16 AVCA Region Honorees.

Freshman Receiving Financial Aid/Academic: | | **Athletic:** 1
Roster In State: 6 | **Out of State:** 4 | **Out of Country:** 1
Sophomores on Team: 0 | **Seniors on Team:** 3 | **Graduation %:** 100
Most Recent Record: 21-13-0 | **Fall Games:** 34 | **Spring Games:** 4

Camp of Clinic Dates: 6/14, 6/18, 7/5-9, 7/19-23 (off campus) 7/18-20, 7/21-23, 7/25-29
Positions Needed: Middle Blockers, Outside Hitter, Right Side Hitter
Schedule: Stanford, Brigham Young University, Loyola Marymount, Arkansas, Texas, Louisville
Style of Play: We have very athletic players that will train intensely at the University of Houston. Our coach looks for athleticism and versatility. Our players are intense and aggressive - offensively and defensively.

University of Mary Hardin - Baylor
Academic Profile

Box 8010
Belton, TX 76513

Phone: 800-727-8642

Type: Public, 4 Yr., Liberal Arts, Coed
Website: http://www.umhb.edu
SAT/ACT/GPA: 900/19/Top half of senior class
Student/Faculty Ratio: 20:1
Undergraduate Enrollment: 2,479
Scholarships/Academic: Yes   **Athletic:** No
Expenses By: Year   **In State:** $ 12,000
Specializes In: Nursing

Founded: 1845
Religion: Southern Baptist
Housing: Yes
Male/Female: 40:60
Graduate Enrollment: 200
Financial Aid: Yes
Out of State: $ 12,000

Programs of Study: Accounting, Art, Business Administration, Biology, Chemistry, Computer Information Systems, Computer Science, Economics, English, History, Finance, Mathematics, Management, Marketing, Medical Technology, Music Education, Nursing, Physical Education, Political Science, Psychology, Religion, Social Work, Sociology, Spanish, Speech

Women's Athletic Profile

900 College Street
Belton, TX 76513
Coach: Alice Taylor
Email: ataylor@umhb.edu

NCAA I
Lady Crusaders, Purple, Gold, White
Phone: (254) 933-4488
Fax: (254) 933-4614

Estimated # of Women's Volleyball Scholarships: N/A
Conference: American Southwest Conference

University of North Texas
Academic Profile

PO Box 13917
Denton, TX 76203

Phone: 800-868-8211

Type: Public, 4 Yr., Coed

Founded: 1890

Website: http://www.unt.edu
SAT/ACT/GPA: 820/18
Student/Faculty Ratio: 19:1
Undergraduate Enrollment: 19,200
Scholarships/Academic: Yes   **Athletic:** Yes
Expenses By: Year   **In State:** $ 6,800
Religion: Non-Affiliated
Housing: Yes
Male/Female: 50:50
Graduate Enrollment: 6,600
Financial Aid: Yes
Out of State: $ 12,900

Specializes In: Art, Business, Music, Education, Accounting, Broadcasting
Degrees Conferred: BA, BS, BFA, BM, BSEd, MA, MS, MBA, MFA, M.Ed., Ph.D., EdD
Programs of Study: Accounting, Advertising, Anthropology, Art, Banking & Finance, BioChemistry, Biology, Broadcasting, Business, Chemistry, Communications, Computer Science, Criminal Justice, Dance, Earth Science, Economics, Education, Geography, Journalism, Mathematics, Music, Management, Marketing, Philosophy, Physics, Political Science, Social Science

Women's Athletic Profile

P.O. Box 13917
Denton, TX 76203-6737
Coach: Cassie Headrick
Email: jscott@unt.edu

NCAA I
Lady Eagles, Green, White
Phone: (940) 565-3666
Fax: (940) 565-3470

Estimated # of Women's Volleyball Scholarships: N/A
Conference: Sun Belt Conference
Program Profile: The Lady Eagles play their home games at The Snake Pit which seats 2000.
History: The program began in 1976.
Coaching: Cassie Headrick enters her 1st season with the Lady Eagles. She was an Assistant Coach at her alma maler, University of Arkansas, Little Rock, where she compiled a record of 75-43.

Roster In State: 9   **Out of State:** 2   **Out of Country:** 1
Sophomores on Team: 3   **Seniors on Team:** 3   **Graduation %:** N/A
Most Recent Record: 5-24-0   **Fall Games:** 35   **Spring Games:**
Positions Needed: Setter, MH, RSH
Schedule: Rice, Baylor, Arkansas State, Arkansas Little Rock, New Mexico State, Tulsa, Florida International
Style of Play: Very aggressive style.

University of Texas
Academic Profile

718 Belmont Hall
Austin, TX 78705

Phone: 512-475-7399

Type: Public, 4 Yr., Liberal Arts, Engineering, Coed
Website: http://www.utexas.edu
SAT/ACT/GPA: Sliding Scale
Student/Faculty Ratio: 50:50
Undergraduate Enrollment: 35,106
Scholarships/Academic: Yes   **Athletic:** Yes
Expenses By: Year   **In State:** $ 13,000+
Founded: 1883
Religion: Non-Affiliated
Housing: Yes
Male/Female: 51:49
Graduate Enrollment: 11,780
Financial Aid: Yes
Out of State: $ 18,000+

Specializes In: One of the nation's top Research, Engineering & Business Universities
Degrees Conferred: BA, BS, MA, MS
Programs of Study: See www.utexas.edu

Women's Athletic Profile

324 Belmont Hall
Austin, TX 78705
Coach: Jim Moore
Email: j_moore@mail.utexas.edu

NCAA I
Longhorns, White, Burnt Orange
Phone: (512) 471-9148
Fax: (512) 471-2177

Estimated # of Women's Volleyball Scholarships: 3
Conference: Big 12 Conference
Program Profile: Texas Volleyball has never had a losing season in its 25 years of existence. The Longhorns have advanced to each of the last 17 NCAA National Championship Tournaments and won the National Title in 1988, becoming the first school east of California to do so. The Longhorns play in the newly-renovated Gregory Gymnasium, one of the finest collegiate volleyball facilities in the country. Texas is annually ranked among the nation's leader in attendance, situated in the national top 10 in each of the last ten seasons.
History: Texas Volleyball began in 1974 and enters the 1999 season with an overall record of 749-256-14 through 999 matches. The

Longhorns have won 13 league championships and boast more than 20 All-Americans dating back to the 1981 season. In 1988 Texas became the first school east of California to win the NCAA National Title, and to this day remains the only school to go through the entire Tournament undefeated in games, beating each opponent 3-0 in the 1988 tourney.

Achievements: We have 6 Coach of the Year Awards; 34 All-Conference athletes, 21 All-Americans, 1 National Player of the Year, 1992 National Coach of the Year, 1 National Freshman of the Year, 11 Conference Players of the Year, 8 Conference Newcomer/Freshman of the Year, 5 Southwest Conference All-Decade Team members, 23 Academic All-Conference Awards.

Coaching: Jim Moore, Head Coach, has a record of 52-12 for two years at Texas. He has an overall record of 236-101 in ten years. He has led team to four conference championships, two Final Four Appearances, 1 NCAA National championships, two-time Conference Coach of the Year; 1992 National Coach of the Year.

Freshman Receiving Financial Aid/Academic:

		Athletic: 4
Roster In State: 7	**Out of State:** 6	**Out of Country:** 2
Sophomores on Team: 0	**Seniors on Team:** 2	**Graduation %:** 92
Most Recent Record: 27-5-0		

Camp of Clinic Dates: All June, July

Positions Needed: Setter, Outside Hitter

Schedule: Stanford, Nebraska, Penn State, Texas A&M, Colorado, Kansas State

Style of Play: Non-traditional swing offense where attackers have more freedom to make decisions on where to play the ball. Serve and pass oriented with emphasis on the block.

University of Texas - Arlington
Academic Profile

P.O. Box 19079
Arlington, TX 76019

Phone: 817-272-6287

Type: Public, 4 Yr., Engineering, Coed
Website: http://www.uta.edu
SAT/ACT/GPA: 900/19/2.0
Student/Faculty Ratio: 19:1
Undergraduate Enrollment: 14,844
Scholarships/Academic: Yes
Expenses By: Year
Specializes In: Business, Engineering
Degrees Conferred: 2,769 undergraduates

Athletic: Yes
In State: $ 8,000

Founded: 1895
Religion: Non-Affiliated
Housing: Yes
Male/Female: 48:52
Graduate Enrollment: 3,818
Financial Aid: Yes
Out of State: $ 14,700

Programs of Study: Architecture, Accounting, Art, Anthropology, Biology, Chemistry, Communications, Criminal Justice, Economics, Engineering (Aerospace, Civil, Computer, Electrical, Industrial Mechanical), English, Exercise Science, Exercise & Sports Studies, Foreign Language, History, Information Systems, International Business, Interior Design, Management, Marketing, Medical Technology, Music, Nursing, Philosophy, Physics, Real Estate, Social Work, Theatre Arts

Women's Athletic Profile

Box 19079
Arlington, TX 76019
Coach: Janine Smith
Email: rcooling@uta.edu

NCAA I
Mavericks, Red, White, Blue
Phone: (817) 272-2261
Fax: (817) 272-5037

Estimated # of Women's Volleyball Scholarships: N/A

Conference: Southland Conference

Program Profile: The program began in 1973. We play at the Texas Hall which "Sports Illustrated" voted best place to watch college basketball. Our best record was in 1989 when we posted 31-4. We never finished under fifth place in the Southland Conference and only placed fifth once in 1995.

History: We began in 1973 and had 14 Post-season appearances. We won 9 SLC Championships including the 1998 season. We had 6 Conference Titles in a row (1985-1990), 5 All-American players and 15 NCAA Appearances (7 since 1985). We were a NCAA Final Four team in 1989 and placed third with a 31-4 record.

Achievements: 9 SLC Championships including the 1998 season; 6 Conference Titles in a row (1985-1990); 5 All-Americans; 15 NCAA appearances (7 since 1985); NCAA Final Four team in 1989 and placed third with a 31-4 record.

Coaching: Janine Smith, Head Coach, started in 1994. She has a 84-78 overall record at UTA. She was a member of UT Austin's 1988 NCAA Championship team, She has made four trips to the NCAA Tournament. She earned second team All-SWG in 1990 and first team in 1991 and was a member of two US Olympic festival teams. Diane Saymour and Ryan Cooling are Assistant Coaches.

Freshman Receiving Financial Aid/Academic:

		Athletic: 3
Roster In State: 8	**Out of State:** 4	**Out of Country:** 0
Sophomores on Team: 3	**Seniors on Team:** 5	**Graduation %:** 100
Most Recent Record: 19-1-0	**Fall Games:** 31	**Spring Games:** 9

Camp of Clinic Dates: July
Style of Play: Hard nosed ball control and defense. Run quick tempo, middle audible offense.

University of Texas - El Paso
Academic Profile

201 Baltimore Street
El Paso, TX 79968-0579

Phone: 915-747-5576

Type: Public, 4 Yr., Coed
Website: http://www.utep.edu
SAT/ACT/GPA: 920 min
Student/Faculty Ratio: 24:1
Undergraduate Enrollment: 15,393
Scholarships/Academic: Yes   **Athletic:** Yes
Expenses By: Year   **In State:** $ 7,368
Degrees Conferred: BA, BS, BFA, MA, MS, MBA, M.Ed., Ph.D.
Programs of Study: 52 undergraduate; 60 master's degree choices.

Founded: 1914
Religion: Non-Affiliated
Housing: Yes
Male/Female: 46:54
Graduate Enrollment: 2,233
Financial Aid: Yes
Out of State: $ 13,788

Women's Athletic Profile

201 Baltimore
El Paso, TX 79968 .
Coach: Norm Brandl
Email:

NCAA I
Miners, Orange, Blue, White
Phone: (915) 747-6656
Fax: (915) 747-5162

Estimated # of Women's Volleyball Scholarships: N/A
Conference: Western Athletic Conference
Achievements: 1996 and 1997 back to back appearances in the WAC Conference Tournaments.
Coaching: Norm Brandl, Head Coach, has been here for 23 years. He is one of only 3 University of Texas at El Paso coaches with over 300 wins. Brandl developed the University of Texas at El Paso program from its infancy to its inclusion into the powerful Western Athletic Conference.
Camp of Clinic Dates: General Skills: July 15-18

University of Texas - Pan American
Academic Profile

1201 W University Drive
Edinburg, TX 78539

Phone: (956) 316-7007

Type: Public, 4 Yr., Coed
Website: http://www.panam.edu/athletics
SAT/ACT/GPA: 930/20/1.5
Student/Faculty Ratio: 20:1
Undergraduate Enrollment: 11,500
Scholarships/Academic: Yes   **Athletic:** Yes
Expenses By: Year   **In State:** $ 3,358
Specializes In: Education, International Business
Degrees Conferred: BA, BS, BFA, BSN, Masters
Programs of Study: College of Arts and Humanities, College of Business Administration, College of Education, College of Heath Sciences and Human Services, College of Science and Engineering, College of Social and Behavioral Sciences.

Founded: 1927
Religion: Non-Affiliated
Housing: Yes
Male/Female: 1:1
Graduate Enrollment: 2,500
Financial Aid: Yes
Out of State: $ 6,381

Women's Athletic Profile

1201 W. University Drive
Edinburg, TX 78539
Coach: David Thorn
Email: thorn@panam.edu

NCAA I
Lady Broncs, Green, White
Phone: (956) 381-2221
Fax: (956) 381-2011

Estimated # of Women's Volleyball Scholarships: 2
Conference: Independent
Program Profile: The Lady Broncos Volleyball team plays in the UT Pan American Fieldhouse. The fieldhouse has 5,000 seats. The

season starts the first weekend of September and ends between the middle of November and early December.

Achievements: Numerous members of the volleyball team were named to the Sun Belt Commissioner's All-Academic List; 3 girls were named to the American South Conference Commissioner's All-Academic List

Coaching: Dave Thorn - Head Coach. Christi Phillips is Assistant Coach.

Freshman Receiving Financial Aid/Academic: | | **Athletic:** 12

Roster In State: 10 | **Out of State:** 3 | **Out of Country:** 0

Sophomores on Team: 0 | **Seniors on Team:** 3 | **Graduation %:** 20

Most Recent Record: 8-15-0 | **Fall Games:** 23 | **Spring Games:** 3

Camp of Clinic Dates: UTPA Volleyball Camp: July 19-22

Positions Needed: Middle Hitters, Outside Hitters, Setter

Schedule: Texas Tech, Stephen F. Austin, University of Texas-El Paso, Southwest Texas State, Tulsa, Wichita State

Style of Play: We are fast offensive off of precision passing.

University of Texas - San Antonio
Academic Profile

6900 N. Loop 1604 W | **Phone:**
San Antonio, TX 78249

Type: Public, 4 Yr., Coed | **Founded:** 1969
Website: http://www.utsa.edu/sports | **Religion:** Non-Affiliated
SAT/ACT/GPA: Sliding Scale/2.0 | **Housing:** Yes
Student/Faculty Ratio: 21:3 | **Male/Female:** 18:82
Undergraduate Enrollment: 15,939 | **Graduate Enrollment:** 2,458
Scholarships/Academic: Yes | **Athletic:** Yes | **Financial Aid:** Yes
Expenses By: Year | **In State:** $ 1,055/12 hrs. | **Out of State:** $ 3,623/12 hr.
Specializes In: Business, Education
Degrees Conferred: BA, BBA, BS, MA, MBA, MS, Ph.D.
Programs of Study: Anthropology, Architecture, Art, Biology, Chemistry, Civil Engineering, Communications, Computer Science, Criminal Justice, Economics, Electrical Engineering, English, Finance, French, Geography, Geology, German, Health, History, Humanities, Information Systems, IDS, Interior Design, Kinesiology, Management, Management Science, Marketing, Mathematics, Mechanical Engineering, Mexican-American Studies, Music, etc..

Women's Athletic Profile

6900 N. Loop 1604 W | **NCAA I**
San Antonio, TX 78249 | Roadrunners, Orange, White
Coach: Katrinka Jo Crawford | **Phone:** (210) 458-4192
Email: Kcrawford@utsa.edu | **Fax:** (210) 458-4569

Estimated # of Women's Volleyball Scholarships: N/A
Conference: Southland Conference
Coaching: Katrinka Crawford is Head Coach. Rhonda Rust was named Assistant Coach in the summer of 1999.

University of Texas - Permian Basin
Academic Profile

4901 East University Drive | **Phone:** 915-552-2605
Odessa, TX 79762

Type: Public, 4 Yr., Liberal Arts, Coed | **Founded:** 1973
Website: http://www.utpb.edu | **Religion:** Non-Affiliated
SAT/ACT/GPA: 1100/24 | **Housing:** Yes
Student/Faculty Ratio: 16:1 | **Male/Female:** 1:2
Undergraduate Enrollment: 1,600 | **Graduate Enrollment:** 700
Scholarships/Academic: Yes | **Athletic:** No | **Financial Aid:** Yes
Expenses By: Year | **In State:** $ 4,900 | **Out of State:** $ 10,012
Specializes In: Business & Education
Degrees Conferred: BA, BS, BBA, MA, MS
Programs of Study: Art, Biology, Business Administration, Chemistry, Computer Science, Criminology, Earth Science, English, Finance, Geology, History, Humanities, Kinesiology, Management, Mass Communications, Mathematics, Political Science, Psychology, Sociology, Spanish, Speech

Women's Athletic Profile

4901 East University
Odessa, TX 79762
Coach: Steve Aicinena
Email: aicinena_s@utpe.edu
Estimated # of Women's Volleyball Scholarships: N/A
Conference: Red River Athletic Conference
Program Profile: We play a 22-24 dates per season. This requires a minimum of class time to be missed.
History: The program began in 1995 with a record 2-24. In 1996 , the record was 7-24. In 1997, the record was12-20 and in 1998 the record was 15-12 . We got second place in the Red River Athletic Conference.
Coaching: Steve Aicinena, Head Coach, has an overall record of 46-80.
Freshman Receiving Financial Aid/Academic:

NCAA I
Falcons, Orange, White, Black
Phone: (915) 552-2675
Fax: (915) 552-3675

Athletic: 0

Roster In State: 6	**Out of State:** 4	**Out of Country:** 0
Sophomores on Team: 1	**Seniors on Team:** 0	**Graduation %:** Unknown
Most Recent Record: 15-12-0	**Fall Games:** 27	**Spring Games:** 0

Camp of Clinic Dates: Summer
Positions Needed: Setter, Middle Hitter, Outside Hitter
Schedule: Houston Baptist, Lubbock Christian, Wayland Baptist

University of the Incarnate Word
Academic Profile

4301 Broadway
San Antonio, TX 78209

Phone: 800-749-9673

Type: Private, 4 Yr., Coed
Website: http://www.viwtx.edu
SAT/ACT/GPA: 960/18/2.5
Student/Faculty Ratio: 15:1
Undergraduate Enrollment: 2,500
Scholarships/Academic: Yes
Expenses By: Year
Specializes In: Nursing, Business

Founded: 1881
Religion: Catholic
Housing: Yes
Male/Female: 1:3
Graduate Enrollment: 684
Athletic: Yes
In State: $ 15,060

Financial Aid: Yes
Out of State: $ 15,060

Programs of Study: 40 undergraduate degrees in Applied Arts, Business Administration, Education, Fine Arts, Humanities, Social Sciences, Natural Science, Mathematics, Nursing, and PreProfessional Studies

Women's Athletic Profile

4301 Broadway
San Antonio, TX 78209
Coach: Mark Papich
Email: papich@universe.uiwtx.edu

NCAA I
Crusaders, Red, Black, White
Phone: (210) 805-3567
Fax: (210)829-3899

Estimated # of Women's Volleyball Scholarships: 3
Conference: Heartland Conference
Program Profile: McDermott Convocation Center seats 2, 500 people
History: Overall record 260-239, 521 (14 year history) Coach Papich is in his 5th year as Head Coach and his overall record is 94-84
Achievements: He was named NAIA Southwest Region Coach of the Year, Heart Texas Conference Coach of the Year, and the AVCA Tachikara Southwest Region Coach of the Year. His Crusader team has won a conference championship, a regional championship and led them to their first ever national tournament appearance in 1997, seeded 6th.
Freshman Receiving Financial Aid/Academic:

Athletic: 4

Roster In State: 11	**Out of State:** 2	**Out of Country:** 0
Sophomores on Team: 4	**Seniors on Team:** 1	**Graduation %:** 95
Most Recent Record: 21-15-0	**Fall Games:** 31	**Spring Games:** 4

Positions Needed: MH, Left and Setter
Schedule: Rockhurst, West Texas A & M, Regis, Abilene Christian, Eastern New Mexico State, Harding, St. Mary's.

Vernon Regional Junior College
Academic Profile

4400 College Drive
Vernon, TX 76384

Phone: (940) 552-6291

Type: Public, 2 Yr., Coed

Founded: 1975

Website: http://www.vrjc.cc.tx.us
SAT/ACT/GPA: Open
Student/Faculty Ratio:
Undergraduate Enrollment: N/A
Scholarships/Academic: Yes
Expenses By: Year

Athletic: Yes
In State: $ 1,789

Religion: Non-Affiliated
Housing: Yes
Male/Female:
Graduate Enrollment: N/A
Financial Aid: Yes
Out of State: $ 1,985

Programs of Study: Accounting, Banking/Finance, Business Administration, Communications, Dietetics, Economics, Elementary Education, English, Fine Arts, Health Education, History, Management, Marketing, Medical Therapy, Psychology, Secondary Education, Social Science, Spanish

Women's Athletic Profile

4400 College Dr.
Vernon, TX 76384
Coach: Julie A. Myers
Email: jmyers@vrjc.cc.tx.us

NCAA I
Lady Chaparrals, Blue, White
Phone: (940) 552-6291
Fax: (940) 553-3902

Estimated # of Women's Volleyball Scholarships: 14
Conference: Region II
Program Profile: We were National Tournament Qualifier in 1998. We have an entire new wood floor. (It is top of the line). We have super facilities.
History: Our program began in August of 1989. We have a scholarship program. We won Conference, District III and were National Tournament Qualifier in 1998. We have been runner-up in Conference several years.
Achievements: 1 All-American (Honorable Mention); 16 All-Conference Players; Several have gone on to play at 4 yr. colleges.
Coaching: Julie A. Myers, Head Coach, started in 1989. There is no assistant coach listed.
Freshman Receiving Financial Aid/Academic:
Roster In State: 14
Out of State: 1

Athletic: 10
Out of Country: 0

Most Recent Record: 25-19-0
Positions Needed: 7-10 players

Wayland Baptist University
Academic Profile

1900 W. 7th Street
Plainview, TX 79072

Phone: 806-296-4709

Type: Private, 4 Yr., Liberal Arts, Coed
Website: http://www.wcc.cc.il.us
SAT/ACT/GPA: 8500/
Student/Faculty Ratio: 13:1
Undergraduate Enrollment: 1,000
Scholarships/Academic: Yes
Expenses By: Year

Athletic: Yes
In State: $ 4,898

Founded: 1906
Religion: Baptist
Housing: Yes
Male/Female: 60:40
Graduate Enrollment: 100
Financial Aid: Yes
Out of State: $ 4,898

Programs of Study: Biology, Business Administration, Chemistry, Christian Studies, Composite Science, English, History, Human Services, Interdisciplinary Studies, Mass Communications, Mathematics, Music, Occupational Therapy, Physical Science

Women's Athletic Profile

1900 W. 7th Street
Plainview, TX 79072
Coach: Brad Borden
Email: bordenb@wbu1.wbu.edu

NCAA I
Flying Queens, Blue, Gold
Phone: (806) 291-5022
Fax: (806) 296-4595

Estimated # of Women's Volleyball Scholarships: N/A
Conference: Sooner Athletic Conference

West Texas A & M University
Academic Profile

WTAMU Box 60276
Canyon, TX 79016

Phone: (806) 651-2695

Type: Public, 4 Yr., Liberal Arts, Coed
Website: http://www.wtamu.edu
SAT/ACT/GPA: 950/21
Student/Faculty Ratio: 24:1

Founded: 1910
Religion: Non-Affiliated
Housing: Yes
Male/Female: Not Available

Undergraduate Enrollment: 5,200
Scholarships/Academic: Yes   **Athletic:** Yes
Expenses By: Year   **In State:** $ 3,000
Degrees Conferred: BA, BS, BFA, MA, MBA, MFA, MED

Graduate Enrollment: 1,300
Financial Aid: Yes
Out of State: $ 6,458

Programs of Study: Agribusiness, Agriculture, Biology, Chemistry, Accounting, Communications, Computer/Information Science, Education, English, Finance, History, Marketing, Music, Nursing, PreLaw, PreMed, Psychology, Physics

Women's Athletic Profile

WTAMU Box 60276
Canyon, TX 79016
Coach: Tony Graystone
Email: agraystone@mail.watamu.edu

NCAA I
Lady Buffs, Maroon, White
Phone: (806) 651-2695
Fax: (806) 651-2672

Estimated # of Women's Volleyball Scholarships: 8
Conference: Lone Star Conference
Program Profile: We are consistently one of the top Division II programs in the nation. Our fieldhouse is located on campus and seats 2,600. We average over 500 per match. Our season runs from July through December.
History: The program began in 1974 and has 3 National Championships (1990, 1991 and 1997). We had 10 NCAA Tournament appearances and 5 Conference Titles. We had five Elite and 8 appearances.
Achievements: NCAA Division II National Champions in 1990, 1991 and 1997; Lone Star Conference Champions in 1989, 1990, 1995, 1996 and 1997. We were NCAA Elite & Tournament Champions in 1989, 1990, 1991 and 1997; NCAA Post-season Tournament 10 years; 10 All-Americans; 2 National Players of the Year
Coaching: Tony Graystone, Head Coach, is entering the first season here in 1999 and was former assistant coach in 1997 & 1998. He got his B.S. from Grand Valley State University in 1992 and his M.S. from the University of Louisville in 1996. The assistant coach position is open.
Freshman Receiving Financial Aid/Academic: **Athletic:** 4
Roster In State: 7   **Out of State:** 5   **Out of Country:** 0
Sophomores on Team: 2   **Seniors on Team:** 5   **Graduation %:** Unknown
Most Recent Record: 25-7-0
Camp of Clinic Dates: July 15 - 17; July 18-22; July 26-30
Positions Needed: Middle Blocker, Outside Hitter
Schedule: Nebraska - Omaha, Northern Michigan, Metro State, Northwood, Colorado Christian, Cameron
Style of Play: Quick up-tempo offense with multiple play sets; defense and ball control highly emphasized; 5-1 offense; perimeter defense.

Wiley College
Academic Profile

711 Wiley Avenue
Marshall, TX 75670
Type: Private, 4 Yr., Liberal Arts, Coed
Website: Not Available
SAT/ACT/GPA: Open
Student/Faculty Ratio:
Undergraduate Enrollment: N/A
Scholarships/Academic: **Athletic:**
Expenses By: Year   **In State:**
Degrees Conferred: AA, BA, BS

Phone: 903-938-8341

Founded: 1873
Religion: Methodist
Housing: No
Male/Female:
Graduate Enrollment: N/A
Financial Aid:
Out of State:

Programs of Study: Biological Science, Business Administration, Chemistry, Communications, Computer Science, Education, English, Hotel/Restaurant Management, Music, Music Performance, Office Management, Philosophy, Physics, Religion, Social Science, Special Education

Women's Athletic Profile

711 Wiley Avenue
Marshall, TX 75670
Coach: W.M. Owens
Email:

NCAA I
Lady Kittens, Purple, White
Phone: (903) 927-3290
Fax: (903) 938-8100

Estimated # of Women's Volleyball Scholarships: N/A
Conference: Big State Conference

UTAH

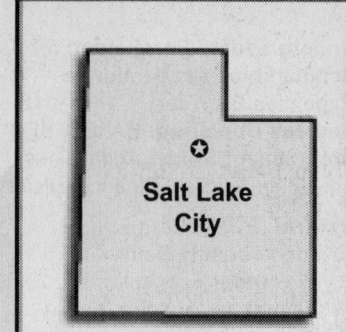

Salt Lake City

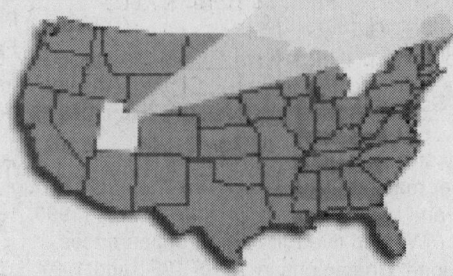

SCHOOL	CITY	AFFILIATION	PAGE
Brigham Young University	Provo	NCAA I	758
University of Utah	Salt Lake City	NCAA I	758
Utah State University	Logan	NCAA I	759
Weber State University	Ogden	NCAA I	759
Westminster College	Salt Lake City	NAIA	760

Brigham Young University
Academic Profile

248 Smith Field House
Provo, UT 84602

Phone: (801) 378-8732

Type: Private, 4 Yr., Coed
Website: http://www.byu.edu
SAT/ACT/GPA: 26/3.3
Student/Faculty Ratio: 20:1
Undergraduate Enrollment: 29,000
Scholarships/Academic: Yes
Expenses By: Year
Degrees Conferred: BA, BS, MA, MS, EDD, Ph.D., JD

Athletic: Yes
In State: $ 7,000

Founded: 1882
Religion: Non-Affiliated
Housing: Yes
Male/Female: 48:52
Graduate Enrollment: 4,000
Financial Aid: Yes
Out of State: $ 7,000

Programs of Study: Accounting, Advertising, Agriculture, Animal, Anthropology, Banking/Finance, Biology, Botany, Broadcasting, Manufacturing, Medical, Cartography, Ceramic, Engineering, Clothing/Textiles, Geography, Entomology, Fashion, Food, Humanities, International, Nursing, Nutrition, Philosophy, Psychology, Natural Resources, Special Education, Speech, Sports Medicine

Women's Athletic Profile

228 - B SFH
Provo, UT 84602
Coach: Elaine Michaelis
Email: karen_marshall@byu.edu

NCAA I
Lady Cougars, Blue, White
Phone: (801) 378-3387
Fax: (801) 378-5756

Estimated # of Women's Volleyball Scholarships: N/A
Conference: Western Athletic Conference
Achievements: 1996 WAC Mountain Division title; 42 All-Americans; six AVCA/CVCA First Team; four Volleyball Monthly First Team; three GTE Academic First Team; 1993 NCAA Final Four; 1994 Dale Rex Memorial Award; 1997 WAC Coach of the Year; IAC Coach of the Year; HCAC Coach of the Year; 1987 AVCA/TAchikara Northwest Region Coach of the Year
Coaching: Elaine Michaelis, Head Coach, has been working with the BYU program for 37 years. She has been Director of Women's Athletics for three years. Her overall record is 782-200-5. She was inducted into the Utah Summer Games Hall of Fame in 1987 and the Hall of Fame of the Utah Network for Girls and Women in Sports in 1990. Stephanie Trane is Assistant Coach. She has been here 7 years. Karen Curtis Lamb is Assistant Coach. She has been here 5 years.

Roster In State: 8
Sophomores on Team: 1
Most Recent Record: 29-6-0

Out of State: 9
Seniors on Team: 4

Out of Country: 0
Graduation %: 100

Schedule: Delaware, Rutgers, UMass, Washington State, Long Beach State, Texas Tech, Northern Illinois, Central Michigan, Wyoming, Utah, Idaho State, Utah State, San Jose State, Fresno State, Texas-El Paso, UC Santa Barbara , New Mexico, Wyoming
Style of Play: We will play each match knowing that match is key to our being able to reach our goal.

Men's Athletic Profile

P.O. Box 22241
Provo, UT 84602
Coach: Carl McGown
Email:

NCAA I
Cougars/Royal Blue, White
Phone: (801) 378-2276
Fax: (801) 378-3520

Estimated # of Men's Volleyball Scholarships: N/A
Conference: Mountain Pacific Sports Federation

University of Utah
Academic Profile

1825 E. South Campus Drive Front
Salt Lake City, UT 84112

Phone: 801-581-7281

Type: Public, 4 Yr., Coed
Website: http://www.utah.edu
SAT/ACT/GPA: 24
Student/Faculty Ratio: 21:1
Undergraduate Enrollment: 19,635
Scholarships/Academic: Yes

Athletic: Yes

Founded: 1850
Religion: Non-Affiliated
Housing: Yes
Male/Female: 55:45
Graduate Enrollment: 4,823
Financial Aid: Yes

Expenses By: Year   **In State:** $ 8,861   **Out of State:** $14,401

Specializes In: Business & Medical Related Sciences

Degrees Conferred: BA, BS, MS, MBA, MFA

Programs of Study: Architecture, Business, Education, Engineering, Fine Arts, Health, Humanities, Law, Medicine, Miners & Earth Sciences, Nursing, Pharmacy, Science, Social & Behavioral Science, Social Work

Women's Athletic Profile

1825 E. South Campus Drive Front
Salt Lake City, UT 84112-9008
Coach: Beth Launiere
Email:

NCAA I
Lady Utes, Crimson, White
Phone: (801) 581-6843
Fax: (801) 581-4358

Estimated # of Women's Volleyball Scholarships: N/A

Conference: Western Athletic Conference

Program Profile: The Utah Volleyball program has established itself as one of the top in the country. It has been a building project that was a transformation from a 1-32 record in 1989 to 21-10 in 1998.

History: Beth Launiere took over the program in 1990 and has built it into a national power. The team has had three 20 win seasons in a row and has averaged 20 wins the past six years.

Achievements: We were 1998 NCAA in second round, 1998 finished ranked 26th in country in Sagrin Ranking, four 20 win seasons in the past six years.

Coaching: Beth Launiere, Head Coach, has a record of 158-128. Cory Solomon is our Assistant Coach.

Freshman Receiving Financial Aid/Academic: **Athletic:** 2

Roster In State: 7   **Out of State:** 5   **Out of Country:** 2

Sophomores on Team: **Seniors on Team:**   **Graduation %:** 97

Most Recent Record: 21-10-0   **Fall Games:** 31   **Spring Games:** 4 Tournaments

Positions Needed: Middle Blockers

Schedule: Stanford, BYU, Notre Dame, Pepperdine, Colorado State, Texas Tech

Utah State University
Academic Profile

UMC 7400
Logan, UT 84322-1600

Phone: 435-797-1079

Type: Public, 4 Yr., Coed
Website: http://www.usu.edu
SAT/ACT/GPA: Sliding Scale
Student/Faculty Ratio: 22:1
Undergraduate Enrollment: 16,500
Scholarships/Academic: Yes   **Athletic:** Yes
Expenses By: Year   **In State:** $ 6,975

Founded: 1888
Religion: Non-Affiliated
Housing: Yes
Male/Female: 53:47
Graduate Enrollment: 4,500
Financial Aid: Yes
Out of State: $ 11,415

Degrees Conferred: BA, BS, BFA, MA, MS, MBA, MFA, M.Ed., Ph.D., EdD, AAS

Programs of Study: Agriculture, Business, Education, Engineering, Family Life, Humanities, Arts and Social Sciences, Natural Resources, and Science

Women's Athletic Profile

UMC 7400
Logan, UT 84322-7400
Coach: Tom Peterson
Email: tsp@cc.usu.edu
Estimated # of Women's Volleyball Scholarships: N/A
Conference: Big West Conference

NCAA I
Lady Aggies, Navy Blue, White
Phone: (435) 797-2068
Fax: (435) 797-1800

Weber State University
Academic Profile

1137 Univ. Circle
Ogden, UT 84408-2701

Phone: 801-626-6744

Type: Public, 4 Yr., Coed
Website: http://www.weber.edu

Founded: 1875
Religion: Non-Affiliated

SAT/ACT/GPA: Open
Student/Faculty Ratio: 17:1
Undergraduate Enrollment: 1,732
Scholarships/Academic: Yes
Expenses By: Year
Degrees Conferred: BA, BS, MA, MS

Athletic: No
In State: $ 17,826

Housing: No
Male/Female: 59:41
Graduate Enrollment: 518
Financial Aid: Yes
Out of State: $ 17,826

Programs of Study: Accounting, Art, Aviation, Biology, Business, Chemistry, Communications, Computer Science, Economics, Education, Engineering, English, Finance, History, Human Resource Management, Information Resource Management, International Business, Management, Marketing, Mathematics, Nursing, Philosophy, Physics, Political Studies, PreDental, PreLaw, PreMed, Psychology, Social Sciences, Sociology

Women's Athletic Profile

Department of Athletics
Ogden, UT 84408-2701
Coach: Al Givens
Email: apainter@weber.edu

NCAA I

Lady Wildcats, Purple, White
Phone: (801) 626-7091
Fax: (801) 626-7014

Estimated # of Women's Volleyball Scholarships: 2
Conference: Big Sky Conference
Program Profile: WSU Volleyball was started in 1974. We play all matches at the Dee Events Center Which holds 12,000. Season is Aug-Dec
History: Began in 1974 as part of the IAC. In 1988, WSU joined the Big Sky Conference and won the Championship that same year.
Achievements: BSC Champions 1988, Many 1st, 2nd Team All-Conference players
Coaching: Al Givens Head Coach- 8th season at WSU and has been coaching for 25 years. April Painter Assistant Coach 1st season.
Freshman Receiving Financial Aid/Academic:
Roster In State: 4
Sophomores on Team: 4
Most Recent Record:
Positions Needed: Setter/MB

Athletic: 4
Out of State: 9
Out of Country: 0
Seniors on Team: 2
Graduation %:
Fall Games: 26
Spring Games: 4 Tournaments

Schedule: BYU, Utah, Utah State, Sacramento State, Northern Arizona, Montana State
Style of Play: Aggressive yet Disciplined.

Westminster College - Salt Lake City
Academic Profile

1840 South 1300 East
Salt Lake City, UT 84105

Phone: (800) 748-4753

Type: Private, 4 Yr., Coed
Website: http://www.wcslc.edu
SAT/ACT/GPA: 950+
Student/Faculty Ratio: 18:1
Undergraduate Enrollment: 1,760
Scholarships/Academic: Yes
Expenses By: Year

Athletic: No
In State: $ 13,200

Founded: 1875
Religion: Presbyterian & Church of Christ
Housing: No
Male/Female: 35:65
Graduate Enrollment: 400
Financial Aid: Yes
Out of State: $ 13,200

Specializes In: Liberal Arts Core with Professional Programs
Degrees Conferred: BA, BS, BSN, MBA
Programs of Study: Accounting, Aviation Management, Biology, Business Administration, Chemistry, Communications, Computer Science, Dramatic Arts, Early Childhood, Economics, Elementary Education, English, Fine Arts, History, Human Development, Management, Marketing, Mathematics, Nursing, Philosophy, Physics, Psychology, Secondary Education, Social Science

Women's Athletic Profile

1840 S., 1300 E
Salt Lake City, UT 84105
Coach: TBA
Email:

NCAA I

Lady Parsons, NW Purple, Gold
Phone: (801) 488-4211
Fax: (801) 484-7651

Estimated # of Women's Volleyball Scholarships: N/A
Conference: RMISL

VERMONT

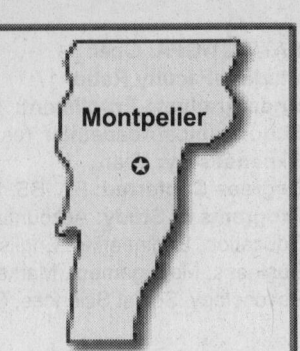

Montpelier

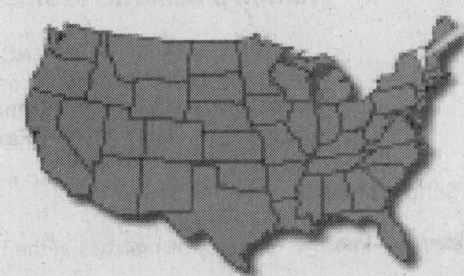

SCHOOL	CITY	AFFILIATION	PAGE
Green Mountain College	Poultney	NAIA	762
Middlebury College	Middlebury	NCAA III	762
St. Michael's College	Colchester	NCAA II	763
University of Vermont	Burlington	NCAA I	763

Green Mountain College
Academic Profile

One College Circle
Poultney, VT 05764

Phone: (802) 287-8238

Type: Private, 4 Yr., Liberal Arts, Coed
Website: http://www.greenmtn.edu
SAT/ACT/GPA: 1000/20/2.8
Student/Faculty Ratio: 20:1
Undergraduate Enrollment: 596
Scholarships/Academic: Yes
Expenses By: Year
Specializes In: Business, Education, Recreation, Environmental Studies
Degrees Conferred: BS, BA, BFA
Programs of Study: Accounting, Adventure Recreation, Arts, Behavioral Science, Business Management, Communications, History, Liberal Arts, PreLaw, PreArchitecture, Leisure Resource, Environmental Studies

Athletic: Yes
In State: $ 21,270

Founded: 1834
Religion: United Methodist
Housing: Yes
Male/Female: 49:51
Graduate Enrollment: N/A
Financial Aid: Yes
Out of State:

Women's Athletic Profile

16 College Street
Poultney, VT 05764
Coach: TBA
Email: athletic@greenmtn.edu

NCAA I
Lady Eagles, Green, Gold
Phone: (802) 287-8238
Fax: (802) 287-9428

Estimated # of Women's Volleyball Scholarships: 4
Conference: Mayflower Conference
Program Profile: We play 20 regular season games at our gym which holds 600 seats. Our season goes from August to October.
History: Our program began in 1978.
Achievements: We won two Conference Championships in the 1980's.
Coaching: TBA
Freshman Receiving Financial Aid/Academic:

Athletic: 4

Roster In State: 1
Sophomores on Team: 0
Most Recent Record: 8-10-0
Positions Needed: Setter, Outside Hitters
Schedule: Bloomfield, Plattsburg State, Teikyo, Colby Sawyer

Out of State: 7
Seniors on Team: 3
Fall Games: 20

Out of Country: 2
Graduation %: 85
Spring Games: 0

Middlebury College
Academic Profile

Memorial Fieldhouse
Middlebury, VT 05753

Phone: (802) 443-5410

Type: Private, 4 Yr., Liberal Arts, Coed
Website: http://www.middlebury.edu
SAT/ACT/GPA: 1300/29/5.1
Student/Faculty Ratio: 11:1
Undergraduate Enrollment: 2,200
Scholarships/Academic: Yes
Expenses By: Year
Specializes In: Liberal Arts
Degrees Conferred: BA, BS

Athletic: No
In State: $ 30,475

Founded: 1800
Religion: Non-Affiliated
Housing: Yes
Male/Female: 50:50
Graduate Enrollment: 200
Financial Aid: Yes
Out of State: $ 30,475

Programs of Study: American Civilization, American Literature, Art, Biology, Chemistry & BioChemistry, Chinese, Classical Studies, Computer Science, Dance, Economics, English, Environmental Science, Film, French, Geography, Geology, German, History, International Studies, International Studies, Italian, Japanese, Literary Studies, Mathematics, Molecular Biology & BioChemistry, Music, Philosophy, Physics, Political Science, PreLaw, PreMed, Psychology, Religion, Russian, Sociology-Anthropology, Spanish, Studio Art, Theatre-Dance & Film/Video, Women's Studies

Women's Athletic Profile

Memorial Fieldhouse
Middlebury, VT 05753
Coach: Sarah Raunecker
Email: raunecker_Sarah@MSMail.middlebury.edu

NCAA I
Lady Panthers, Blue, White
Phone: (802) 443-5613
Fax: (802) 443-2124

Estimated # of Women's Volleyball Scholarships: N/A
Conference: Independent
Program Profile: The volleyball season starts in early September and ends with the NESCAC Tournament in early November. We play a combination of Division II and III opponents. We play at Pepin Gymnasium. The gym contains three full volleyball courts and accommodates up to 1,200 spectators.
History: Our team has established itself as one of the solid programs in New England. We became a varsity sport in 1994. Last year we won a school-record 26 matches, including the NESCAC Championship.
Coaching: Sarah Raunecker, Head Coach, is in her fourth season. Last season, she led the team to the most wins in school history. She was named the NESCAC Coach of the Year.
Freshman Receiving Financial Aid/Academic: **Athletic:**
Roster In State: 0   **Out of State:** 12   **Out of Country:** 1
Sophomores on Team: 2   **Seniors on Team:** 3   **Graduation %:** 100
Most Recent Record: **Fall Games:** 25-30   **Spring Games:** 0

Saint Michael's College
Academic Profile

One Winooski Park
Colchester, VT 05439

Phone: (802) 654-3000

Type: Private, 4 Yr., Liberal Arts, Coed
Website: http://www.smcvt.edu
SAT/ACT/GPA: 1000+
Student/Faculty Ratio: 14:1
Undergraduate Enrollment: 1,700
Scholarships/Academic: Yes
Expenses By: Year
Specializes In: Liberal Arts
Degrees Conferred: BA, BS, MA, MS, MED

Founded: 1904
Religion: Catholic
Housing: Yes
Male/Female: 50:50
Graduate Enrollment: 200
Athletic: Yes   **Financial Aid:** Yes
In State: $ 23,400   **Out of State:** $ 23,400

Programs of Study: Accounting, American Studies, BioChemistry, Biology, Business Administration, Chemistry, Computer Science, East Asian Studies, Economics, Elementary Education, Engineering, English, Environmental Science, Fine Arts, French, History, International Business Journalism, Philosophy, Political Science, Psychology, Religious Studies, Sociology, Spanish, Theatre Arts

Women's Athletic Profile

One Winooski Park
Colchester, VT 05439
Coach: Betsy Cieplicki
Email: admission@smcvt.edu

NCAA I
Lady Knights, Purple, Gold
Phone: (802) 654-3000
Fax: (802) 654-2591

Estimated # of Women's Volleyball Scholarships: 0
Conference: Northeast-10 Conference
Program Profile: We compete at Ross Gymnasium during the fall season, which is from September to November. We practice all year long with our highly dedicated and committed team.
Roster In State: 1   **Out of State:** 8   **Out of Country:** 0
Sophomores on Team: 4   **Seniors on Team:** 0   **Graduation %:** 99
Most Recent Record: **Fall Games:** 20   **Spring Games:** 0
Camp of Clinic Dates: July 9-11, 1999
Positions Needed: Middle Hitter, Setter, Outside Hitter
Schedule: Bentley College, Bryant College, Pace, University of Massachusetts-Lowell, Middlebury College
Style of Play: Emphasis on solid defense, but we have a nice quick transition to the quick attack.

University of Vermont
Academic Profile

Athletic Department
Burlington, VT 05401

Phone: 802-656-3370

Type: Public, 4 Yr., Liberal Arts, Coed
Website: http://www.uvm.edu
SAT/ACT/GPA: Open
Student/Faculty Ratio: 15:1
Undergraduate Enrollment: 7,514

Founded: 1791
Religion: Non-Affiliated
Housing: Yes
Male/Female: 48:52
Graduate Enrollment: 1,208

Scholarships/Academic: Yes   **Athletic:** Yes   **Financial Aid:** Yes

Expenses By: Year   **In State:** $ 15,222   **Out of State:** $ 26,094

Specializes In: Eight Academic Schools

Degrees Conferred: AS, BA, BS, MA, MS, MBA, MED, Ph.D., MD

Programs of Study: Animal Science, Anthropology, International Studies, Art Education, Art History, Art Studio, Asian Studies, BioChemical Studies, Biological Studies, Biology, Botany, Business, Canadian Studies, Chemistry, Civil Engineering, Classical Civilization, Communications, Computer Science, Dental Hygiene, Dietetics, Economics, Elementary Education, English, Languages, Mathematics, Mechanical Engineering, Music, Natural Resources, Nursing, Nutrition, Physical Education, Physical Therapy, Forestry, Political Science, Theatre

Women's Athletic Profile

Patrick Gym

Burlington, VT 05405

Coach: Rick Gouse

Email: cgouse@zoo.uvm.edu

NCAA I

Lady Catamounts, Green, Gold

Phone: (802) 656-7703

Fax: (802) 656-0949

Estimated # of Women's Volleyball Scholarships: N/A

Conference: American East Conference

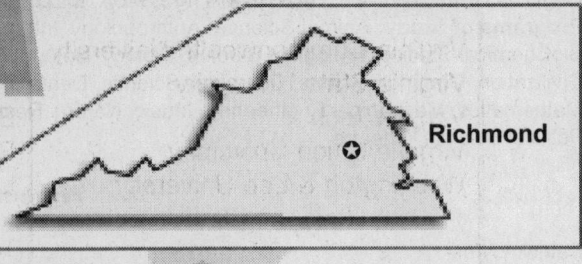

Richmond

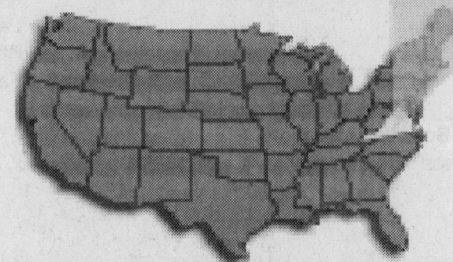

SCHOOL	CITY	AFFILIATION	PAGE
Averett College	Danville	NCAA III	767
Bluefield College	Bluefield	NAIA	767
Bridgewater College	Bridgewater	NCAA III	768
Christopher Newport University	Newport News	NCAA III	768
Clinch Valley College	Wise	NAIA	769
College of William & Mary	Williamsburg	NCAA I	770
Eastern Menonnite University	Harrisonburg	NCAA III	770
Emory and Henry College	Emory	NCAA III	771
Ferrum University	Ferrum	NCAA III	771
George Mason University	Fairfax	NCAA I	772
Hampton University	Hampton	NCAA I	773
Hollins University	Hollins University	NCAA III	773
James Madison University	Harrisonburg	NCAA I	774
Liberty University	Lynchburg	NCAA I	774
Lynchburg College	Lynchburg	NCAA III	775
Mary Baldwin College	Stauton	NCAA III	776
Mary Washington College	Fredericksburg	NCAA III	776
Marymount University	Arlington	NCAA III	777
Norfolk State University	Norfolk	NCAA I	777
Radford University	Radford	NCAA I	777
Randolph-Macon Woman's College	Lynchburg	NCAA III	778
Randolph-Macon College	Ashland	NCAA III	779
Roanoke College	Salem	NCAA III	779
Saint Paul's College	Lawrenceville	NCAA II	780
Shenandoah University	Wichester	NCAA III	780
Southern Virginia College	Springfield	NAIA	781
Sweet Briar College	Sweet Briar	NCAA III	781
University of Virginia	Charlottesville	NCAA I	782

SCHOOL	CITY	AFFILIATION	PAGE
Virginia Commonwealth University	Richmond	NCAA I	783
Virginia State University	Petersburg	NCAA II	783
Virginia Tech	Blacksburg	NCAA I	784
Virginia Union University	Richmond	NCAA II	784
Washington & Lee University	Lexington	NCAA III	785

Averett College
Academic Profile

420 West Main Street
Danville, VA 24541

Phone: 800-283-7388

Type: Private, 4 Yr., Liberal Arts, Coed
Website: http://www.averett.edu
SAT/ACT/GPA: 800
Student/Faculty Ratio: 14:1
Undergraduate Enrollment: 1,000
Scholarships/Academic: Yes
Expenses By: Year
Degrees Conferred: AS, AA, BA, BS, BAS, BBA, MAT

Founded: 1859
Religion: Virginia Baptist
Housing: Yes
Male/Female: 1:3
Graduate Enrollment: 100
Athletic: No   **Financial Aid:** Yes
In State: $ 16,800   **Out of State:**

Programs of Study: Accounting, Art, Art Education, Art History, Athletic Training, Aviation Administration, Biblical Studies, BioChemistry, Biological Science, Business, Chemistry, Commercial Art, Communications, Computer Programming, Computer Science, Creative Writing, Criminal Justice, Liberal Arts, Literature, Management, Marketing, Mathematics, Medical Laboratory, Political Science, PreLaw, PreMed, Music, Natural Science, Psychology, Public Administration, Social Science, Sports Administration, Sports Medicine

Women's Athletic Profile

420 Main Street
Danville, VA 24541
Coach: Danny Miller
Email: dmiller@averett.edu

NCAA I
Lady Cougars, Navy, Gold
Phone: (804) 791-5737
Fax: (804) 791-5740

Estimated # of Women's Volleyball Scholarships: 0
Conference: Dixie Intercollegiate Athletic Conference
Program Profile: Playing season runs from August to November traditional then a spring season from Feb to April. Play in the 3 year old Grant Center, seats 2000 people. Play about 40 matches a year with strong regional and national opponents.
History: Program began in 1983. We have won the Dixie Conference 10 consecutive years and appeared in the NCAA tournament. We are continually ranked as one of the top teams in the south region.
Achievements: Have had the Dixie conference Coach of the Year for 9 of the past 10 years. Have had the conference Player of the year for 10 consecutive years. 10 consecutive conference championships. Had Averett's first ever All-American. Multiple All-Regional Players as well as 10 Dixie Players of the Year, 40 All-Conference Players.
Coaching: Danny Miller, Head Coach, started in 1995. Coach Miller has been at Averett College as a student or coach since January 1988. He has the highest winning percentage in school history with a .717 percentage and a 167-67 record and a conference record of 80-4 a .952 percentage. Keith Richardson and Adrian Turner are Assistant Coaches.
Freshman Receiving Financial Aid/Academic: **Athletic:** 0
Roster In State: 10   **Out of State:** 3   **Out of Country:** 1
Sophomores on Team: **Seniors on Team:** 5   **Graduation %:** 98
Most Recent Record: 31-11-0
Positions Needed: Outside Hitter, Middle Hitter, Setter
Schedule: Emory University, Trinity University, SCAD, Austin College, Maryville College, Southwestern University, Centre College
Style of Play: 5-1 with a fast paced aggressive offense while playing hard defense.

Bluefield College
Academic Profile

3000 College Drive
Bluefield, VA 24605
Type: Private, 4 Yr., Liberal Arts, Coed
Website: http://www.bluefield.edu
SAT/ACT/GPA: 860/18/2.0
Student/Faculty Ratio: 27:1
Undergraduate Enrollment: 725
Scholarships/Academic: Yes
Expenses By: Year
Degrees Conferred: Baccalaureate and Associate Degrees

Phone: 800-872-0175

Founded: 1919
Religion: Baptist
Housing: Yes
Male/Female: 1;1
Graduate Enrollment: N/A
Athletic: Yes   **Financial Aid:** Yes
In State: $ 12,700   **Out of State:** $ 12,700

Programs of Study: Allied Health, Administration of Justice, Biology, Business Administration, Chemistry, Christian Ministry, Communication Arts, Criminal Justice, Drama, Education, English, Fine Arts, Health, History, Human Resources, Interdisciplinary Studies, Mathematics, Music, Organizational Management and Development, Physical Education, Psychology, Recreation, Religion and Philosophy, Humanities, Science, Social Sciences

3000 College Drive
Bluefield, VA 24065
Coach: Brenda Clements
Email:

NCAA I
Lady Rams, Blue, White, Red
Phone: (540) 326-4253
Fax: (540) 326-3682

Estimated # of Women's Volleyball Scholarships: N/A
Conference: TVAC

Bridgewater College
Academic Profile

404 E. College Street
Bridgewater, VA 22812

Phone: (540) 828-5756

Type: Private, 4 Yr., Liberal Arts, Coed
Website: http://www.bridgewater.edu
SAT/ACT/GPA: 900
Student/Faculty Ratio: 15:1
Undergraduate Enrollment: 1,050
Scholarships/Academic: Yes   **Athletic:** No
Expenses By: Year   **In State:** $ 19,980
Specializes In: Business, PreLaw, PreMed, PreVet
Degrees Conferred: BA, BS

Founded: 1880
Religion: Church of Brethren
Housing: Yes
Male/Female: 45:55
Graduate Enrollment: N/A
Financial Aid: Yes
Out of State: $ 19,980

Programs of Study: Accounting, Art, Athletic Training, Biological Science, Business Administration, Chemistry, Computer Science, Early Childhood Education, Economics, Elementary Education, English, French, German, Health Science, History, International Studies, Management, Mathematics, Medical Technology, Music, Music Education, Philosophy, Physical Education, Physical Science, Physics, Political Science, PreDental, PreLaw, PreMed, PreVet, Psychology, Religion, Science, Secondary Education, Social Science

Women's Athletic Profile

E. College Street
Bridgewater, VA 22812
Coach: Mary Heishman
Email: mheishma@bridgewater.edu

NCAA I
Lady Eagles, Crimson, Gold
Phone: (540) 828-5405
Fax: (540) 828-5611

Estimated # of Women's Volleyball Scholarships: N/A
Conference: Old Dominion Athletic Conference
Coaching: Mary Heishman is Head Coach. Mimi Knight and Dorita Puffenbarger are Assistant Coaches.
Roster In State: 10   **Out of State:** 4   **Out of Country:** 0
Sophomores on Team: 1   **Seniors on Team:** 4   **Graduation %:** 100
Most Recent Record: 23-4-0
Schedule: Ferrum, Shenandoah, Mary Washington, Emory, Washington & Lee, Greensboro, Randolph-Macon, Guilford, Averett, St.Mary's,Southern Virginia, Eastern, Messiah

Christopher Newport University
Academic Profile

50 Shoe Lane
Newport News, VA 23606

Phone: 800-333-4268

Type: Public, 4 Yr., Liberal Arts, Coed
Website: http://www.cnu.edu
SAT/ACT/GPA: Open
Student/Faculty Ratio:
Undergraduate Enrollment: N/A
Scholarships/Academic: Yes   **Athletic:** No
Expenses By: Year   **In State:** $ 8,424
Degrees Conferred: BA, BS, MS, M Ed

Founded: 1960
Religion: Non-Affiliated
Housing: Yes
Male/Female:
Graduate Enrollment: N/A
Financial Aid: Yes
Out of State: $ 13,374

Programs of Study: Teaching Education, Marketing & Business, Fine & Performing Arts, etc..

Women's Athletic Profile

50 Shoe Lane
Newport News, VA 23606
Coach: Ken Shibuya
Email: shibu@compuserve.com

NCAA I
Lady Captains, Blue, Silver
Phone: (757) 594-7352
Fax: (757) 594-7352

Estimated # of Women's Volleyball Scholarships: N/A
Conference: Dixie Intercollegiate Athletic Conference
Program Profile: Construction of Christopher Newport Athletic Center is underway. It will be a $15 million dollar facility. It will have 112,00 square feet of space. The athletic center will house a 200 meter track, three basketball-volleyball courts and an additional volleyball court in the infield of the track. It will have huge spaces for fitness and training also. It will seat approximately 2,500 for basketball and volleyball with the possibility of about 5,000 seats for convocations and concerts.
Achievements: 1985,1989,1990, and 1991 All-Dixie Conference First Team; 1989 Co-SIDA All-Academic All-District; VaDID All-Academic All-District; VaSID All-Virginia, All-Academic; 1996 VaSID-Virginia Div.II-III;
1981,1983,1984,1985,1986,1987,1988,1989,1990, 1991,1992 and 1993 Dixie Conference All-Academic
Coaching: Ken Shibuya - Head Coach. Mandy Search is Assistant Coach.
Roster In State: 8   **Out of State:** 0   **Out of Country:** 1
Sophomores on Team: 1   **Seniors on Team:** 1   **Graduation %:** Unknown
Schedule: Mary Washington, Bridgewater, Roanoke, Sweet Briar, Methodist, Averett, Ferrum, Randolph-Macon, Greensboro, North Carolina Wesleyan, Shenandoah, Emory & Henry, Marymount

Clinch Valley College
Academic Profile

7 College Avenue
Wise, VA 24293

Phone:

Type: Public, 4 Yr., Liberal Arts, Coed
Website: http://www.clinch.edu
SAT/ACT/GPA: 1000+
Student/Faculty Ratio: 17:1
Undergraduate Enrollment: Unknown
Scholarships/Academic: Yes   **Athletic:** Yes
Expenses By: Year   **In State:** $ 7,952
Degrees Conferred: BA, BS

Founded: 1954
Religion: Non-Affiliated
Housing: No
Male/Female: 2:3
Graduate Enrollment: N/A
Financial Aid: Yes
Out of State: $ 7,952

Programs of Study: Accounting, Biological, Communications, Dramatic Arts, Economics, Education, Information Science, Marketing, Mathematics, Medical, Music, Political Science, PreLaw, Secondary Education, Social Science

Women's Athletic Profile

College Avenue
Wise, VA 24293
Coach: Lisa Minton
Email:

NCAA I
Cavaliers, Cardinal, Silver Grey
Phone: (540) 328-0260
Fax: (540) 376-1023

Estimated # of Women's Volleyball Scholarships: N/A
Conference: TVAC
Program Profile: We have a well-established program. We have a pre-season camp at the end of August. We play through mid November. It is minimal but there are some spring season opportunities.
History: We began in the mid-1970's. We were part of NCCAA until mid-late 80's. Now we are NCAA - ODAC Division III. We were ODAC in 1994.
Achievements:
Coaching: Lisa Minton, Head Coach, started in 1996. Her record is 52-41. She played varsity volleyball at Messiah College in the early 1980's. She was team captain in 1984. Her team ranked 16th in national. She was Most Valued JV Player in 1981.
Freshman Receiving Financial Aid/Academic: **Athletic:** 0
Roster In State: 1   **Out of State:** 1   **Out of Country:** 2
Sophomores on Team: 2   **Seniors on Team:** 1   **Graduation %:** 98
Most Recent Record: 16-14-0   **Fall Games:** 118 **Spring Games:** 8-10
Positions Needed: OS, Middle, Setter
Schedule: Averett College, Washington and Lee, Gettysburg, Savannah College of Arts and Design, Westminster, Goshen College-Indiana
Style of Play: Consistent contenders for one of the top 3 spots in conference play. Mentally determined and consistently difficult to be defeated in less than 4 games usually 5 games a match.

College of William and Mary
Academic Profile

Box 399
Williamsburg, VA 23185

Phone: 757-221-4223

Type: Public, 4 Yr., Coed
Website: http://www.wm.edu
SAT/ACT/GPA: Open
Student/Faculty Ratio: 12:1
Undergraduate Enrollment: 5,500
Scholarships/Academic:
Expenses By: Year
Degrees Conferred: BA, BSC, BBA

Athletic:
In State: $ 9,91+

Founded: 1693
Religion: Non-Affiliated
Housing: Yes
Male/Female: Not Available
Graduate Enrollment: 2,200
Financial Aid:
Out of State: $ 20,874+

Programs of Study: American Studies, Anthropology, Art Administration, Art History, Biology, Business, Chemistry, Computer Science, Economics, English, Geology, Kinesiology, Mathematics, Music, Philosophy, Physics, Psychology, Public Policy, Religion, Sociology, Theatre

Women's Athletic Profile

P.O. Box 399
Williamsburg, VA 23187
Coach: Debbie Hill
Email:

NCAA I
Lady Tribe, Green, Gold, Silver
Phone: (757) 221-3395
Fax: (757) 221-3412

Estimated # of Women's Volleyball Scholarships: N/A
Conference: Colonial Athletic Association

Eastern Mennonite University
Academic Profile

1200 Park Road
Harrisonburg, VA 22802

Phone: (540) 432-4440

Type: Private, 4 Yr., Liberal Arts, Coed
Website: http://www.emu.edu
SAT/ACT/GPA: 880/19/2.0
Student/Faculty Ratio: 15:1
Undergraduate Enrollment: 950
Scholarships/Academic: Yes
Expenses By: Year

Athletic: No
In State: $ 19,030

Founded: 1917
Religion: Non-Affiliated
Housing: Yes
Male/Female: 40:60
Graduate Enrollment: 350
Financial Aid: Yes
Out of State: $ 19,030

Specializes In: Education, Biology, Business, Education, Nursing
Degrees Conferred: BA, BS, Masters in Business, Education ant Theology
Programs of Study: Accounting, Biology, Business and Management, Chemistry, Computer Science, Education, Health Sciences, Psychology, Letters/Literature, Life Sciences, Multi/Interdisciplinary Studies, Nursing, Philosophy, PreMed, Protective Services, Public Affairs, Religion, Theology

Men's Athletic Profile

1200 Park Rd.
Harrisonburg, VA 22802
Coach: Steve Gaston
Email: zooklr@emu.edu

NCAA III
Royals/Royal Blue, White
Phone: (540) 432-4440
Fax: (540) 432-4443

Estimated # of Men's Volleyball Scholarships: N/A
Conference: Eastern Intercollegiate Volleyball Association

Women's Athletic Profile

1200 Park Road
Harrisonburg, VA 22802
Coach: Ruth Anne Wideman
Email: widemanr@emu.edu

NCAA I
Lady Royals, Royal Blue, White
Phone: (540) 432-4440
Fax: (540) 432-4443

Estimated # of Women's Volleyball Scholarships: 0
Conference: Old Dominion Athletic Conference
Program Profile: We began 1999 construction on a new fieldhouse to include 5 volleyball courts, etc. We have a pre-season camp, extensive travel with the state and surrounding area and extended trips to mid-western states every other year. Our season goes from August to November.
History: We started in 1968. We began as part of the NCCAA and moved into the NCAA in the late 1980's to become part of the ODAC within Division III NCAA.
Achievements: ODAC Coach of the Year:1982, 1983, 1985, 1987,1990,1991,1994; 8 Regional All-Americans .
Coaching: Ruth-Anne Wideman, Head Coach, started in 1996. She played varsity volleyball at Messiah College where she ranked 16th in NCAA in her senior year. Her record here is 51-48 (.773). April King Beck is Assistant Coach.
Freshman Receiving Financial Aid/Academic: **Athletic:** 0
Roster In State: 3   **Out of State:** 5   **Out of Country:** 2
Sophomores on Team: 2   **Seniors on Team:** 1   **Graduation %:** 95
Most Recent Record: 16-14-0   **Fall Games:** 30   **Spring Games:** 10
Positions Needed: 4 players
Schedule: Salisbury State University, Moravian College, Averett, Washington and Lee, Thomas More, SCAD
Style of Play: Mentally determined to win each point. We are attempting to develop a thinking game both offensively and defensively.

Emory and Henry College
Academic Profile

PO Box 4   **Phone:** 800-848-5493
Emory, VA 24327

Type: Private, 4 Yr., Liberal Arts, Coed   **Founded:** 1836
Website: http://www.emory-henry.emory.va.us/   **Religion:** Non-Affiliated
SAT/ACT/GPA: 930/19/2.5   **Housing:** Yes
Student/Faculty Ratio: 12:1   **Male/Female:** 1:1
Undergraduate Enrollment: 1,000   **Graduate Enrollment:** N/A
Scholarships/Academic: Yes   **Athletic:** No   **Financial Aid:** Yes
Expenses By: Year   **In State:** $ 17,800 **Out of State:** $ 17,800
Degrees Conferred: BS, BA, BED, MA
Programs of Study: Accounting, Anthropology, Applied Mathematics, Art, Art Education, Biology, Business, Chemistry, Classics, Communications, Computer Information Systems, Computer Science, Creative Writing, Economics, Education, English, French, Geography, German, History, Human Services, Liberal Arts, Music, Philosophy, Physical Education, Physics, Political Science, PreLaw, PreMed, PreVet, Sociology, Sports Medicine

Women's Athletic Profile

King Athletic Center   **NCAA I**
Emory, VA 24327   Lady Wasps, Blue, Gold
Coach: Shannon Farley   **Phone:** (540) 944-6885
Email: spfarley@ehc.edu   **Fax:** (540) 944-3673

Estimated # of Women's Volleyball Scholarships: N/A
Conference: Old Dominion Athletic Conference
Program Profile: Division III program at a strong academic liberal arts college playing season goes from mid August until November, 2000 season will mark the opening of a new fitness facility.
Coaching: Head Coach-Shannon Farley-started in 1997-98
Roster In State: 17   **Out of State:** 2   **Out of Country:**
Sophomores on Team: 6   **Seniors on Team:** 1   **Graduation %:** 100
Most Recent Record: 13-16   **Fall Games:** 28   **Spring Games:** 2-3
Positions Needed: Middle Hitter
Schedule: Washington and Lee University, Maryville College, Oglethorpe University, Eastern Mennonite, Bridgewater
Style of Play: We have made up for a lack in height with a quickness, strong serving and tough defensive playing.

Ferrum University
Academic Profile

P. O. Box 1000   **Phone:** 800-868-9797
Ferrum, VA 24088

Type: Private, 4 Yr., Liberal Arts, Coed   **Founded:** 1913
Website: http://www.ferrum.edu   **Religion:** Methodist
SAT/ACT/GPA: 820/17   **Housing:** Yes

Student/Faculty Ratio: 14:1
Undergraduate Enrollment: 1,200
Scholarships/Academic: Yes **Athletic:** No
Expenses By: Year **In State:** $ 16,000
Specializes In: Business, Environmental Science, Teacher Education
Degrees Conferred: BA, BS, BSW

Male/Female: 5:4
Graduate Enrollment: N/A
Financial Aid: Yes
Out of State: $ 16,000

Programs of Study: Accounting, Agriculture, Art, Biology, Business Administration, Chemistry, Computer Science, Criminal Justice, Environmental Science, Fine Arts, French, Liberal Arts, Physical Education, Mathematical Science, Medical Technology, Philosophy, Psychology, Religion

Women's Athletic Profile

Route 40 West
Ferrum, VA 24088
Coach: Kelly Caputo
Email: kcaputo@ferrum.edu

NCAA I
Lady Panthers, Black, Gold
Phone: (540) 365-4493
Fax: (540) 365-4497

Estimated # of Women's Volleyball Scholarships: N/A
Conference: Dixie Intercollegiate Athletic Conference
Achievements: 1998 Susie Wilson All-Conference Team; Amy Robertson 1998 2X Dixie Rookie of the Week; Susie Wilson 1998 All-Tournament & MVP at Ferrum Invitational; Susie Wilson 1998 1st-team All-State; one All-American, 2 All-Region; 19 All-Conference, 11 Dixie All-Tournament Team; 32 Academic All-Conference; one Academic All-State, 3 All-State
Coaching: Kelly Caputo, Head Coach, is in her 10th year as head coach at Ferrum. She has taken three teams to Dixie Conference Tournament Championship matches. She was honored in 1990 as Dixie Conference Volleyball Coach of the year. M.J. Safewright is now in her third year as Assistant Coach. She is a Ferum 1995 graduate.

Roster In State: 11 **Out of State:** 2 **Out of Country:** 0
Sophomores on Team: 1 **Seniors on Team:** 1 **Graduation %:** Unknown
Most Recent Record: 12-14-0 **Fall Games:** 26 **Spring Games:** 0
Schedule: Hollins, Roanoke, Bridgewater, Emory & Henry , Averett, Methodist, Greensboro, N.C. Wesleyan, Lynchburg, Shenandoah

George Mason University
Academic Profile

4400 University Drive
Fairfax, VA 22030

Phone: (703) 993-3200

Type: Public, 4 Yr., Liberal Arts, Coed
Website: http://www.gmu.edu
SAT/ACT/GPA: 1070/25/3.1
Student/Faculty Ratio: 17:1
Undergraduate Enrollment: 15,262
Scholarships/Academic: Yes **Athletic:** Yes
Expenses By: Year **In State:** $9,708
Specializes In: Business, Education, Communications, Physical Therapy
Degrees Conferred: Bachelors, Professional Masters, Doctoral

Founded: 1972
Religion: Non-Affiliated
Housing: Yes
Male/Female: 45:55
Graduate Enrollment: 8,918
Financial Aid: Yes
Out of State: $18,552

Programs of Study: 104 areas of study including: Accounting, Anthropology, Banking/Finance, Biology, Business, Chemistry, Computer, International, Journalism, Management, Marketing, Parks and Recreation, PreProfessional Programs

Men's Athletic Profile

4400 University Drive
Fairfax, VA 22030-4444
Coach: Pat Kendrick
Email: toconno2@gmu.edu

NCAA I
Patriots/Dark Green, Gold
Phone: (703) 993-1000
Fax: (703) 993-2392

Estimated # of Men's Volleyball Scholarships: 4
Conference: EIVA-Tait Division
Program Profile: We play at John Linn Memorial Gymnasium which has a capacity of 2,800.
History: In 1974, the men's volleyball was established as a club team before becoming a varsity intercollegiate sports in 1975. Under the program's first head coach, Wayne Stalick, the Patriots competed under the NAIA until 1979 when the entire athletic department changed to the NCAA.
Achievements: 1984-1st ECVL Tournament; 3rd NCAA Final Four; 1985-1st ECVL Tournament; 3rd NCAA Final Four; 1988-1st EIVA Tournament; 4th NCAA Final Fours; USA National Team-Uvaldo Acosta; NCAA Championship All Tournament Team-Ric Lucas.
Freshman Receiving Financial Aid/Academic: **Athletic:** 3

Roster In State: 5 **Out of State:** 4 **Out of Country:** 3
Sophomores on Team: 1 **Seniors on Team:** 5 **Graduation %:**
Most Recent Record: 8-13-0 **Fall Games:** 0 **Spring Games:** 24
Schedule: Indiana Purdue-Fort Wayne, Lewis, Penn State, Ball State, Loyola-Chicago, New Jersey Tech
Style of Play: Based on rhythm, an understanding of tactics and a fusion of international styles.

Women's Athletic Profile

4400 University Drive
Fairfax, VA 22030-4444
Coach: Pat Kendrick
Email: pkendric@gmu.edu

NCAA I
Lady Patriots, Dark Green, Gold
Phone: (703) 993-3298
Fax: (703) 993-3239

Estimated # of Women's Volleyball Scholarships: 12
Conference: Colonial Athletic Association
Program Profile: We play at John Linn Memorial Gym which has a 2,800 capacity.
History: Our first year as a sport was 1973 and our overall record is 445-345. We have been in a number of NCAA Tournaments of which the last was in 4/1996. Our last post-season opponent was Wisconsin and we finished second. We lost 1-3.
Achievements: CAA Champions in 1992 and 1996; CAA Player of the Year 1992-97; KAEPA/AVCA All-American 1996- Virag Domkos: Pat Kendrick 1992-1994, 1996; CAA Coach of the Year-Pat Kendrick All-Virginia Coach of the Year 1993-1996.
Coaching: Pat Kendrick, Head Coach, his overall record is 269-206 and he has been here 15 years. He has had the most wins during his tenure-30. His record in 1994 was 30-5. His teams have made 4 NCAA Appearances. His team's highest national ranking was 16th in 1996. Fred Chao and Paul Koncir are Assistant Coaches.
Freshman Receiving Financial Aid/Academic: **Athletic:** 4
Roster In State: 3 **Out of State:** 4 **Out of Country:** 4
Sophomores on Team: 4 **Seniors on Team:** 3 **Graduation %:** Unknown
Most Recent Record: 7-25-0 **Fall Games:** 24 **Spring Games:** 0
Camp of Clinic Dates: July 5-9
Schedule: Auburn, Illinois, American, JMU, Georgetown
Style of Play: Up tempo, rhythmic, flexible.

Hampton University
Academic Profile

Holland Hall
Hampton, VA 23668

Phone: 757-727-5328

Type: Private, 4 Yr., Coed
Website: http://www.hamptonu.edu
SAT/ACT/GPA: 900+
Student/Faculty Ratio: 18:1
Undergraduate Enrollment: 5,343
Scholarships/Academic: Yes **Athletic:** Yes
Expenses By: Year **In State:** $ 11,226
Founded: 1868
Religion: Non-Affiliated
Housing: No
Male/Female: 37:63
Graduate Enrollment: 361
Financial Aid: Yes
Out of State: $ 11,226
Programs of Study: Biology, Chemistry, Economics, English, French, German, Greek, Greek & Latin, History, Humanities, Latin, Management Economics, Mathematics, Mathematics & Computer Science, Mathematics & Natural Science, Philosophy, Physics, Political Science, Psychology, Religion, Religion & Philosophy, Spanish

Women's Athletic Profile

Holland Hall
Hampton, VA 23668
Coach: Tiny Laster
Email:

NCAA I
Lady Pirates, Royal, Blue, White
Phone: (757) 727-5822
Fax: (757) 727-5813

Estimated # of Women's Volleyball Scholarships: N/A
Conference: Mid-Eastern Athletic Conference

Hollins College
Academic Profile

PO Box 9553
Roanoke, VA 24020

Phone: 800-456-9595

Type: Private, 4 Yr., Liberal Arts, Women Only
Website: http://www.holins.edu
Founded: 1842
Religion: Non-Affiliated

SAT/ACT/GPA: Required
Student/Faculty Ratio: 9:1
Undergraduate Enrollment: 867
Scholarships/Academic: Yes   **Athletic:** No
Expenses By: Year   **In State:** $ 21,285

Housing: Yes
Male/Female: Women Only
Graduate Enrollment: 194
Financial Aid: Yes
Out of State: $ 21,285

Degrees Conferred: BA, MA, MALS, MAT, CAS (Certificate of Advanced Studies)
Programs of Study: American Studies, Art, Biology, Chemistry, Classics, Communications, Economics, English, French, German, History, International Studies, Mathematics, Music, Philosophy, Physics, Political Science, Religion, Sociology, Spanish, Theatre

Women's Athletic Profile

Did Not Return Profile

James Madison University
Academic Profile

MSC 2301, Athletics, JMU
Harrisonburg, VA 22807

Phone: (540) 568-6518

Type: Private, 4 Yr., Liberal Arts, Coed
Website: http://www.jmu.edu
SAT/ACT/GPA: 1175/3.4-3.5
Student/Faculty Ratio: 15:1
Undergraduate Enrollment: 13,225
Scholarships/Academic: Yes   **Athletic:** Yes
Expenses By: Year   **In State:** $ 9,408
Specializes In: Liberal Arts

Founded: 1908
Religion: Non-Affiliated
Housing: Yes
Male/Female: 45:55
Graduate Enrollment: 723
Financial Aid: Yes
Out of State: $ 15,014

Degrees Conferred: BS, BA, MS, MA, MBA, MFA, EED
Programs of Study: Accounting, Anthropology, Art, Biology, Business, Communications, Chemistry, Computer Science, Dietetics, Economics, English, Finance, Foreign Languages, Grocery, Geology, Health Science, History, Integrated Science & Technology, International Affairs, International Business, Kinesiology, Management, Marketing, Mathematics, Media, Music, Nursing, Operations, Management, Physics, Philosophy & Religion, Political Science, Psychology, Public Administration, Social Science, Social Work, Sociology, Speech Communications, Theatre & Dance, Etc.

Women's Athletic Profile

S. Main Street
Harrisonburg, VA 22807
Coach: Christopher Beerman
Email: beermact@jmu.edu

NCAA I
Lady Dukes, Purple, Gold
Phone: (540) 568-6463
Fax: (540) 568-3489

Estimated # of Women's Volleyball Scholarships: 9
Conference: Colonial Athletic Association
Program Profile: We have a beautiful campus with a 2,500-seat facility. We play a very aggressive non-conference shedule. We ranked top 10 team. We play to win and we are very serious program. We have strength conditioning year-round.
History: Our program began in 1985 as a Division I. Since 1996, program is 64-29 and top 10 in the country.
Achievements: 1998 CAA Coach of the Year; 1998 CAA Regular Season Champions, 4 All-CAA players.
Coaching: Chris Beerman is our Head Coach. He had a record of 64-29 in 1996 and a record of 24-6 in CAA. He was named 2-time All-American at Ball State and CAA Coach of the Year. Anne Jackson is our Assistant Coach.
Freshman Receiving Financial Aid/Academic: **Athletic:** 1
Roster In State: 2   **Out of State:** 8   **Out of Country:** 0
Sophomores on Team: 2   **Seniors on Team:** 3   **Graduation %:** 100
Most Recent Record: 22-6-0   **Fall Games:** 33   **Spring Games:** 0
Camp of Clinic Dates: July 12-15, 2000
Positions Needed: Middle Hitter, Outside Hitter
Schedule: Long Beach State, USC, Virginia, Wyoming, Tennessee, Oral Roberts
Style of Play: We play an up-tempo, 2-passing system. Explosive, competitive, aggressive, ball control oriented.

Liberty University
Academic Profile

1971 University Boulevard
Lynchburg, VA 24502

Phone: (804) 582-2381

Type: Private, 4 Yr., Liberal Arts, Coed
Website: http://www.liberty.edu

Founded: 1971
Religion: Non Affiliated

SAT/ACT/GPA:
Student/Faculty Ratio:
Undergraduate Enrollment: 5200
Scholarships/Academic: Yes   **Athletic:** Yes
Expenses By: Year   **In State:** $14,900
Degrees Conferred: BA, MS, Ph.D., Religion

Housing: Yes
Male/Female:
Graduate Enrollment: N/A
Financial Aid: Yes
Out of State: $14,900

Programs of Study: Accounting, Advertising, Athletic Training, Biblical Studies, Biology, Business, Communication, Computer Science, Counseling, Elementary Education, English, Exercise Science & Fitness, Family & Consumer Sciences, Health Education, InterDisciplinary Studies, Journalism, Media Graphics, MultiDisciplinary Studies, Community Health Promotion, General Studies, Mathematics, Missions, Music, Nursing, Physical Education, Psychology, Philosophy, Physical Education, Psychology, Religion, Social Science, Sports Management, Theology

Women's Athletic Profile

1971 University Blvd.
Lynchburg, VA 24502-2269
Coach: Laura Miller
Email:

NCAA I
Lady Flames, Red, White, Blue
Phone: (804) 582-2609
Fax: (804) 582-2076

Estimated # of Women's Volleyball Scholarships: 11
Conference: Big South Conference
Program Profile: Hancock Athletic Center has 8,500 square feet, and a weight room with modern equipment. We have Strength and Conditioning coaches. Vines Convocation Center seats 9,000, is a hardwood arena used by men's and women's basketball and volleyball, and houses locker rooms, a video conference room and a training room. Fall is the main season and it starts in September. We travel to play non-conference matches against ACC, Colonial, SEC and WAC universities. Conference matches start in early October. The Big South Conference Tournament is the weekend before Thanksgiving. The first round of the NCAA Tournament is the first weekend in December. Spring season mostly consists of skills instruction, due to limited NCAA practice time. We usually play in 3-4 tournaments.
History: We began in 1976 by our Senior Woman Administrator Brenda Bonheim. She coached until 1980. Our program is strong and still growing. Liberty combines competitive Division I athletics with a passion for doing God's work. LU has been NCAA Division I since the Fall of 1988, and has laid the foundation for a strong program. We expect to continue to get stronger and climb higher in the NCAA Rankings.
Achievements: 1997 Big South Conference Champs; NCAA Tournament Appearances in 1997; 1998 Big South Conference Runner-Up; 1997 Liberty Invitational Champions; 1997 Commissioner's Cup.
Coaching: Laura Miller, is entering her first year as a Head Coach. She has been with the Flames for the past eight seasons. She held a career assist record until 1997 and led the team to a 2nd place finish in her first year. Kris Dorn, Assistant Coach, is entering her second year as an Assistant Coach and led the team to a 2nd place in blocking in 1997. She holds the blocking record for Taylor University.
Freshman Receiving Financial Aid/Academic: **Athletic:** 6
Roster In State: 0   **Out of State:** 11   **Out of Country:** 1
Sophomores on Team: 0   **Seniors on Team:** 3   **Graduation %:** 100
Most Recent Record: 21-14-0   **Fall Games:** 36   **Spring Games:** 3-4
Camp of Clinic Dates: Last week in July
Positions Needed: Back-up Setter, Middle Blocker, RS/DS
Schedule: Texas Tech, Wisconsin-Milwaukee, North Carolina State, University of Virginia, James Madison, Seton Hill
Style of Play: The girls are taught to play within the system that we have developed, but their athleticism and heart propel them past what they are capable of as individuals.

Lynchburg College
Academic Profile

Turner Gymnasium
Lynchburg, VA 24501

Phone: 804-544-8300

Type: Private, 4 Yr., Liberal Arts, Coed
Website: http://www.lynchburg.edu
SAT/ACT/GPA: 1010
Student/Faculty Ratio: 12:1
Undergraduate Enrollment: 2,000
Scholarships/Academic: Yes   **Athletic:** No
Expenses By: Year   **In State:** $ 21,000
Degrees Conferred: BS, BA, MBA, MED

Founded: 1903
Religion: Disciple of Christ
Housing: Yes
Male/Female: 30:70
Graduate Enrollment: 450
Financial Aid: Yes
Out of State: $ 21,000

Programs of Study: Accounting, American Studies, Biology, Chemistry, Communications, Computer Science, English, Environmental Science, German, History, International Business, Marketing, Mathematics, Medical Laboratory Technology, Music, Nursing, Philosophy, Physics, Political Science, Psychology, Religion, Secondary Education, Social Science, Spanish, Special Education, Theatre Design

Women's Athletic Profile

1501 Lakeside Drive
Lynchburg, VA 24501
Coach: Dr.Marie Lewis
Email: lewis_d@mail.lynchburg.edu

NCAA I
Lady Hornets, Crimson, Grey
Phone: (804) 544-8288
Fax: (804) 544-8365

Estimated # of Women's Volleyball Scholarships: N/A
Conference: Old Dominion Athletic Conference

Mary Baldwin College
Academic Profile

New & Frederick Street
Stauton, VA 24401

Phone: 540-887-7000

Type: Private, 4 Yr., Liberal Arts
Website: http://www.mbc.edu
SAT/ACT/GPA: Varies
Student/Faculty Ratio: 11:1
Undergraduate Enrollment: 1387
Scholarships/Academic: Yes
Expenses By: Year
Degrees Conferred: BA

Athletic: No
In State: $23,360

Founded: 1842
Religion: Presbyterian
Housing: Yes
Male/Female: Women Only
Graduate Enrollment: 64
Financial Aid: Yes
Out of State: $23,360

Programs of Study: Accounting, Advertising, Art, Art Administration, Asian Studies, BioChemistry, Biology, Business, Chemistry, Communications, Computer Science, Economics, English, French, History, Journalism, Management, Mathematics, Medical Technology, Political Science, Philosophy, Psychology, Public Relations, Sociology, Spanish, Theatre

Women's Athletic Profile

Frederick Street
Stauton, VA 24401
Coach: Sharon Spalding
Email: sspalding@mbc.edu

NCAA I
Squirrels, Yellow, White, Green
Phone: (540) 887-7217
Fax: (540) 887-7322

Estimated # of Women's Volleyball Scholarships: N/A
Conference: Independent

Mary Washington College
Academic Profile

1301 College Ave.
Fredericksburg, VA 22401
Type: Public, 4 Yr., Liberal Arts, Coed
Website: http://www.mwc.edu
SAT/ACT/GPA: Open
Student/Faculty Ratio: 17:1
Undergraduate Enrollment: 3,000
Scholarships/Academic: Yes
Expenses By: Year
Degrees Conferred: BA, BS, MFA

Phone: 800-468-5614

Athletic: No
In State: $ 9,552

Founded: 1908
Religion: Non-Affiliated
Housing: Yes
Male/Female: 1:2
Graduate Enrollment: N/A
Financial Aid: Yes
Out of State: $ 15,076

Programs of Study: American Studies, Art, Biology, Business Administration, Chemistry, Classics, Computer Science, Dance, Dramatic Arts, Economics, English, Environmental Science, French, Earth Science, Geography, Geology, Historic Preservation, International Affairs, Mathematics, Music, Performing Arts, Philosophy, Physics, Political Science, Psychology, Sociology, Religion, Spanish

Women's Athletic Profile

1301 College Avenue
Fredericksburg, VA 22401
Coach: Deborah Conway

NCAA I
Lady Eagles, Navy Blue, Grey
Phone: (540) 654-1885

Email: dconway@mwcgw.mwc.edu
Estimated # of Women's Volleyball Scholarships: N/A
Conference: Capital Athletic Conference

Fax: (540) 654-1892

Marymount University
Academic Profile

2807 North Glebe Road
Arlington, VA 22207-4299

Phone: 703-284-1500

Type: Private, 4 Yr., Liberal Arts, Coed
Website: http://www.marymount.edu
SAT/ACT/GPA: 950/21
Student/Faculty Ratio: 14 :1
Undergraduate Enrollment: 2,000
Scholarships/Academic: Yes   **Athletic:** No
Expenses By: Year   **In State:** $ 19,900
Specializes In: Nursing

Founded: 1950
Religion: Catholic
Housing: No
Male/Female: 25:75
Graduate Enrollment: 1,800
Financial Aid: Yes
Out of State: $ 19,900

Degrees Conferred: AA, AS, BA, BS, BSN, BBA, MA, MS, MBA, M.Ed.
Programs of Study: Accounting, Art, Banking and Finance, Biology, Business Administration, Communications, Computer Science, Criminal Justice, Economics, English, Environmental Science, Fashion Design, History, Human Resources, Liberal Arts, Management, Marketing, Mathematics, Nursing, Philosophy, Political Science, Psychology, Religion, Science, Theology and Religious Studies

Women's Athletic Profile

2807 N. Glebe Rd.
Arlington, VA 22207
Coach: Beth Ann Wilson
Email:

NCAA I
Lady Saints, Royal Blue, White
Phone: (703) 284-3834
Fax: (703) 527-3684

Estimated # of Women's Volleyball Scholarships: N/A
Conference: Capital Athletic Conference

Norfolk State University
Academic Profile

2401 Corprew Avenue
Norfolk, VA 23504

Phone: 757-823-8396

Type: Public, 4 Yr., Liberal Arts, Coed
Website: http://www.nsu.edu
SAT/ACT/GPA: 800/2.43
Student/Faculty Ratio: 17:1
Undergraduate Enrollment: 6,252
Scholarships/Academic: Yes   **Athletic:** Yes
Expenses By: Year   **In State:** $ 3,014/cr hr

Founded: 1935
Religion: Non-Affiliated
Housing: Yes
Male/Female: 39:61
Graduate Enrollment: 863
Financial Aid: Yes
Out of State: $ 5,474/cr hr

Degrees Conferred: AS, BS, BA, BIM, BSW, MA, MS, Psy.D, Mmus, Bmus, MSW
Programs of Study: Accounting, Allied Health, Banking/Finance, Biological Science, Business Administration, Chemistry, Arts, Geography, History, Hotel/Restaurant Management, Journalism, Languages

Women's Athletic Profile

2401 Corprew Avenue
Norfolk, VA 23504
Coach: Wilhelmina Wright-Harrison
Email:

NCAA I
Spartanettes, Green, Gold
Phone: (757) 683-2585
Fax: (757) 683-2566

Estimated # of Women's Volleyball Scholarships: N/A
Conference: MEAC

Radford University
Academic Profile

Box 6913
Radford, VA 24141

Phone: 800-890-4265

Type: Public, 4 Yr., Coed

Founded: 1910

Website: http://www.runet.edu
SAT/ACT/GPA: 850
Student/Faculty Ratio: 16:1
Undergraduate Enrollment: 8,146
Scholarships/Academic: Yes   **Athletic:** Yes
Expenses By: Year   **In State:** $ 7,458
Specializes In: Comprehensive, Committed Individualized
Degrees Conferred: BA, BS, Masters
Programs of Study: Business & Economics, Education & Human Development, Arts & Science, Nursing & Health Services, Visual & Performing Arts

Religion: Non-Affiliated
Housing: Yes
Male/Female: 45:55
Graduate Enrollment: 959
Financial Aid: Yes
Out of State: $ 12,032

Women's Athletic Profile

Box 6913
Radford, VA 24142
Coach: Jerry Pruitt
Email: jpruitt@runet.edu

NCAA I
Highlanders, Blue, Red, Green
Phone: (540) 831-5879
Fax: (703) 831-6095

Estimated # of Women's Volleyball Scholarships: 3
Conference: Big South Conference
Program Profile: We are highly competitive, progressing program with untapped potential. We play our matches in the Dedmon Central Arena (sport court surface).
History: Our program began in 1972 with an overall record of 464-345.
Achievements: 1997 NCAA first round appearances.
Coaching: Jerry Pruitt is our Head Coach. He was a former coach at Francis Marion University, which is member of NCAA II. He compiled a record of 87-12. Ranked top 25 and was 2-time Peach Belt Conference Champs, 2 Tournament Champs NCAA National Tournament bid in 1998.
Freshman Receiving Financial Aid/Academic: **Athletic:** 1
Roster In State: 7   **Out of State:** 4   **Out of Country:** 0
Sophomores on Team: 0   **Seniors on Team:** 2   **Graduation %:**
Most Recent Record: 18-12-0   **Fall Games:** 30   **Spring Games:** 4 Tournaments
Positions Needed: Setter, Middle, Outside Hitter, etc
Schedule: Tennessee, Cal-Irvine, Idaho State, Wake Forest University, Pittsburgh, Liberty University
Style of Play: Aggressive, multiple attack motion offences. Rely on athleticism over power.

Randolph - Macon Woman's College
Academic Profile

2500 Richmond Avenue
Lynchburg, VA 24053

Phone: 800-745-7692

Type: Private, 4 Yr., Liberal Arts,Coed
Website: http://www.rmc.edu
SAT/ACT/GPA: 900
Student/Faculty Ratio: 13:1
Undergraduate Enrollment: 1,100
Scholarships/Academic: Yes   **Athletic:** No
Expenses By: Year   **In State:** $ 19,100
Degrees Conferred: BA, BS
Programs of Study: Liberal Arts, Business & Management, Languages, Literature, Life Sciences, Psychology, Social Sciences

Founded: 1830
Religion: Methodist
Housing: Yes
Male/Female: 50:50
Graduate Enrollment: N/A
Financial Aid: Yes
Out of State: $ 19,100

Women's Athletic Profile

2500 Richmond Avenue
Lynchburg, VA 24503
Coach: Heather Somers
Email: hsomers@rmwc.edu

NCAA I
Lady Wildcats, Black, Gold
Phone: (804) 947-8312
Fax: (804) 947-8706

Estimated # of Women's Volleyball Scholarships: N/A
Conference: Old Dominion Athletic Conference
Program Profile: Our gym will be completely renovated in 2 years, increasing the existing space that we have, with the addition of another regulation court.
Achievements: Three players nominated for All-Conference, one first year student nominated for Conference Rookie of the Year.

Coaching: Head Coach Heather Somers enters her first year. She comes to RMWC after a highly successful playing career at Springfield College where she competed in four national championship tournaments. Was the assistant coach at Mount Holyoke and Trinity College before coming to RMWC. Assistant Coach Michelle Cunningham enters her first year.

Randolph - Macon College
Academic Profile

P. O. Box 5005
Ashland, VA 23005

Phone: 800-888-1762

Type: Private, 4 Yr., Liberal Arts, Coed
Website: http://www.rmc.edu
SAT/ACT/GPA: 1050/3.0
Student/Faculty Ratio: 12:1
Undergraduate Enrollment: 1,200
Scholarships/Academic: Yes   **Athletic:** No
Expenses By: Year   **In State:** $ 22,000
Specializes In: Liberal Arts, Education
Degrees Conferred: BA, BS

Founded: 1830
Religion: Methodist
Housing: Yes
Male/Female: 50:50
Graduate Enrollment: N/A
Financial Aid: Yes
Out of State: $ 22,000

Programs of Study: Accounting, Biology, Chemistry, Education, History, English, Business/Economics, Psychology, International Studies, Math, Political Science, Environmental Studies

Women's Athletic Profile

P.O. Box 5005
Ashland, VA 23005
Coach: Dr. Kathy Boone-Ziegler
Email: kzielger@rmc.edu

NCAA I
Yellow Jackets, Lemon, Black
Phone: (804) 752-7327
Fax: (804) 752-3748

Estimated # of Women's Volleyball Scholarships: N/A
Conference: Old Dominion Athletic Conference
Program Profile: The college is a member of D. III of the NCAA and also a charter member of the ODAC. Volleyball is in its sixth year at Randolph-Macon. We are in the process of growing and becoming a very successful program.
Roster In State: 3   **Out of State:** 4   **Out of Country:** 0
Sophomores on Team: **Seniors on Team:** 1   **Graduation %:** 100
Most Recent Record: 14-11
Camp of Clinic Dates: July/August
Positions Needed: DS, OH, MH, Setter
Schedule: Catholic, Greensboro, Averette
Style of Play: Building toward a fundamentally sound team style of play.

Roanoke College
Academic Profile

221 College Lane
Salem, VA 24153-3794

Phone: (540) 375-2382

Type: Private, 4 Yr., Liberal Arts, Coed
Website: http://www2.Roanoke.edu
SAT/ACT/GPA: 1100
Student/Faculty Ratio: 14:1
Undergraduate Enrollment: 1,700
Scholarships/Academic: Yes   **Athletic:** No
Expenses By: Year   **In State:** $ 21,935
Degrees Conferred: BS, BA, BBA

Founded: 1842
Religion: Evangelical Lutheran
Housing: Yes
Male/Female: 2:1
Graduate Enrollment: N/A
Financial Aid: Yes
Out of State: $ 21,935

Programs of Study: Art, Biology, Chemistry, Criminal Justice, Economics, English, French, History, International Relations, Music, Philosophy, Physics, Political Science, Psychology, Religion, Sociology, Spanish, Theatre, Computer Science, Computer Information Systems, Health & Physical Education, Mathematics, Medical Technology, Sports Medicine

Women's Athletic Profile

221 College Lane
Salem, VA 24153
Coach: Blair Calvert
Email:

NCAA I
Lady Maroons, Maroon, Grey
Phone: (540) 375-2338
Fax: (540) 375-2382

Estimated # of Women's Volleyball Scholarships: N/A
Conference: Old Dominion Athletic Conference
Program Profile: The team plays at C. Homer Bast Center, with a seating capacity of 2,000.
Achievements: All-Conference players were: Carolyn Bono in 1983, Stephanie Krause in 1991, Crystal Wilson in 1994 & 1995 and Blair Calvert in 1998.

Roster In State: 7	**Out of State:** 3	**Out of Country:** 0
Sophomores on Team: 0	**Seniors on Team:** 5	**Graduation %:** Unknown
Most Recent Record: 14-11-0	**Fall Games:** 25	**Spring Games:** 0

Positions Needed: Setter, Outside Hitter, Defensive Specialist

Saint Paul's College
Academic Profile

115 College Drive
Lawrenceville, VA 23868

Phone: (804) 848-3111

Type: Private, 4 Yr., Liberal Arts, Coed
Website: http://www.utoledo.edu/~wfraker/stpaul.html
SAT/ACT/GPA: 700/17/2.0
Student/Faculty Ratio: 17:1
Undergraduate Enrollment: 700
Scholarships/Academic: Yes   **Athletic:** Yes
Expenses By: Year   **In State:** $ 11,800

Founded: 1888
Religion: Episcopal
Housing: Yes
Male/Female: 1:2
Graduate Enrollment: N/A
Financial Aid: Yes
Out of State: $ 11,800

Specializes In: Education, Business, Science
Degrees Conferred: BA, BS, BSEd
Programs of Study: Aquatic Science, Biology, Business Administration, Business Education, Chemistry, Computer Science, Criminal Justice, Elementary Education, English, Environmental Science, History, Mass Communications, Mathematics, Office Administration, Political Science, PreDental, PreLaw, PreMed, PreVet, Secondary Education, Social Science

Women's Athletic Profile

115 College Drive
Lawrenceville, VA 23868
Coach: Keyonna B. Robinson
Email:

NCAA I
Lady Tigers, Black, Orange
Phone: (804) 848-3111
Fax: (804) 848-2001

Estimated # of Women's Volleyball Scholarships: 7
Conference: Central Intercollegiate Athletic Association
Program Profile: Our season goes from August through November. We play at Taylor-Whitehead Gymnasium, which has a capacity of 1,200. We have a short season in the fall only.
Achievements: Coach of the Week Honors; Coach of the Year Candidate
Coaching: Keyonna Robinson, Head Coach, started in 1996. She improved our team's ranking from 6th to 3rd. She has increased recruiting enrollment academically. As a player, she was All-CIAA Conference player 3 years. She was MVP and team captain. Her overall record is 15-47.
Freshman Receiving Financial Aid/Academic: **Athletic:** 3

Roster In State: 5	**Out of State:** 6	**Out of Country:** 0
Sophomores on Team: 4	**Seniors on Team:** 4	**Graduation %:** 100
Most Recent Record: 7-13-0	**Fall Games:** 20	**Spring Games:** 20

Positions Needed: All-Setter, Defensive Specialists, All Hitters (Middle, Outside)
Schedule: Fayetteville State, Shaw University, St. Augustine, North Carolina Central, Chowan College, Christopher Newport
Style of Play: Our team runs a 5-1 offense and a 2-1-3 defense. We play very aggressively. Our team is young and is still learning.

Shenandoah University
Academic Profile

1460 University Drive
Winchester, VA 22601

Phone: 800-432-2266

Type: Private, 4 Yr., Coed
Website: http://www.su.edu
SAT/ACT/GPA: 1000/3.1
Student/Faculty Ratio: 10:1
Undergraduate Enrollment: 1300
Scholarships/Academic: Yes   **Athletic:** No
Expenses By: Year   **In State:** $23,300

Founded: 1875
Religion: United Methodist
Housing: Yes
Male/Female: N/A
Graduate Enrollment: 1000
Financial Aid: Yes
Out of State: $23,300

Degrees Conferred: AS, BA, BS, BFA, BSM, MA, MS, MFA, MBA, Doctoral
Programs of Study: Accounting, Administration of Justice, American Studies, Arts and Sciences, Business Administration, Banking and Finance, Biology, Chemistry, Computer Information Systems, Computer Technology, Conservatory of Music, Dance, Education, English, Environmental Studies, History, Information Systems, Kinesiology, Marketing, Mass Communications, Music, Mathematics, Nursing, Occupational Therapy, Pharmacy, Philosophy, Physical Therapy, Political Science, Psychology, Religion, Respiratory Care, Sociology, Theatre

Women's Athletic Profile

1460 University Drive
Wichester, VA 22601
Coach: Ellie Tanner
Email: etanner@su.edu

NCAA I
Lady Hornets, Red, White, Blue
Phone: (540) 665-5580
Fax: (540) 665-4934

Estimated # of Women's Volleyball Scholarships: N/A
Conference: Dixie Intercollegiate Athletic Conference
Program Profile: Shingleton Gymnasium is "home of the Hornets". Shenandoah's playing season is in the fall semester with the season running from August to late October.
Achievements: 1998 All-Dixie 1st team; 1998 VASID All-State Women's Volleyball Team 1st team; 1997 All Conference 2nd team.
Coaching: Ellie Tanner is the 3rd full time Coach in the program's history.

Roster In State: 5	**Out of State:** 3	**Out of Country:**
Sophomores on Team:	**Seniors on Team:**	**Graduation %:** 100%
Most Recent Record: 12-21		
Positions Needed: All		

Southern Virginia College
Academic Profile

One College Hill Drive
Buena Vista, VA 24416

Phone: (540) 261-8400

Type: Private, 4 Yr., Liberal Arts, Coed
Website: http://www.southernvirginia.edu
SAT/ACT/GPA: 1000/20/3.0
Student/Faculty Ratio: 8:1
Undergraduate Enrollment: 286
Scholarships/Academic: Yes   **Athletic:** Yes
Expenses By: Year   **In State:** $ 14,200
Degrees Conferred: BA

Founded: 1867
Religion: Latter-Day Saints
Housing: Yes
Male/Female: 60:40
Graduate Enrollment: N/A
Financial Aid: No
Out of State: $ 14,200

Programs of Study: Liberal Studies, Business Administration, Performing Arts, English, Human Performance & Leisure Studies, American Legal Studies, General Studies, Fine Arts, Computer Assisted Design

Women's Athletic Profile

One College Hill Drive
Buena Vista, VA 24416
Coach: Diedre Dryden
Email:

NCAA I
Lady Knights, Brick Red, Green
Phone: (540) 261-8400
Fax: (540) 261-8559

Did Not Return Profile

Sweet Briar College
Academic Profile

PO Box B
Sweet Briar, VA 24595

Phone: (804) 381-6142

Type: Private, 4 Yr., Liberal Arts, W
Website: http://www.sbc.edu
SAT/ACT/GPA: 1170/24/3.5
Student/Faculty Ratio: 7:1
Undergraduate Enrollment: 740
Scholarships/Academic: Yes   **Athletic:** No

Founded: 1901
Religion: Non-Affiliated
Housing: Yes
Male/Female: 100
Graduate Enrollment: 0
Financial Aid: Yes

Expenses By: Year   **In State:** $24,940   **Out of State:** $24,940
Specializes In: Art History, Creative Writing, English, Mathematics, Sciences
Degrees Conferred: AB, BS
Programs of Study: Anthropology, Arts, Biochemistry, Computer Science, Creative Writing, Ecology, Economics, English, French, German, Greek, History, International Relations, Mathematics, Modern Language, Music, Philosophy, Political Science, Psychology, Religion, Social Science, Theater

Women's Athletic Profile

Williams Gymnasium
Sweet Briar, VA 24595
Coach: Ahmad Jumili
Email: Ajumili@sbc.edu

NCAA I
Vixens, Pink, Green
Phone: (804) 381-6441
Fax: (804) 381-6487

Estimated # of Women's Volleyball Scholarships: N/A
Conference: Old Dominion Athletic Conference

University of Virginia
Academic Profile

Miller Hall P.O. Box 9017
Charlottesville, VA 22906

Phone: 804-982-3200

Type: Public, 4 Yr., Liberal Arts, Engineering, Coed
Website: http://www.virginia.edu
SAT/ACT/GPA: 1150/3.5
Student/Faculty Ratio: 11:1
Undergraduate Enrollment: 12,500
Scholarships/Academic: Yes   **Athletic:** Yes
Expenses By: Year   **In State:** $ 9,900
Specializes In: Strong Academics
Degrees Conferred: BA, BS, Masters, Ph.D., MD

Founded: 1819
Religion: Non-Affiliated
Housing: Yes
Male/Female: 48:52
Graduate Enrollment: 6,000
Financial Aid: Yes
Out of State: $ 20,800

Programs of Study: University has ten schools: College of Arts & Sciences, Graduate School of Arts & Sciences, School of Engineering and Applied Science, School of Architecture, School of Law, McIntire School of Commerce, Darden Graduate School of Business Administration, Curry School of Education, School of Medicine, School of Nursing

Women's Athletic Profile

P. O. Box 3785, University Hall
Charlottesville, VA 22903
Coach: Melissa Aldrich-Shelton
Email: vball@virginia.edu

NCAA I
Lady Wahoos, Navy, Orange
Phone: (804) 982-5307
Fax: (804) 982-4926

Estimated # of Women's Volleyball Scholarships: 12
Conference: Atlantic Coast
Program Profile: We were an NCAA Division I Top 25 Program in 1998. Virginia is a young team on its way to becoming a regular in the polls. For the first time in 1999, the Wahoos will play in University Hall, an 8,000 seats arena.
History: Volleyball started in 1979 at UVA but it was not until recently that it has taken off. Under the guidance of Coach Shelton, the seniors of the 1998 squad were the first to graduate with a winning record since 1991.
Achievements: 1998 NCAA tournament Appearance; three All-ACC players; two All-District Players; Coach Shelton was named Virginia Coach of the Year.
Coaching: Melissa Aldrich-Shelton, Head Coach, in four seasons at UVA with a record is 77-57. She has turned the program around and has it headed to the top. Kelly P. Sheffield is Assistant Coach.
Freshman Receiving Financial Aid/Academic: **Athletic:** 2
Roster In State: 2   **Out of State:** 12   **Out of Country:** 0
Sophomores on Team: 0   **Seniors on Team:** 3   **Graduation %:** 99
Most Recent Record: 26-8-0   **Fall Games:** 32   **Spring Games:** 3
Camp of Clinic Dates: July 1999
Positions Needed: Middle Hitter, Left Side Hitter, Right Side Hitter
Schedule: Michigan, South Carolina, Clemson, Georgia Tech, Florida State, North Carolina
Style of Play: Discipline and heart are the cornerstones of UVA's team. With Virginia's ball control and powerful hitting, they are always a team to contend with.

Virginia Commonwealth University
Academic Profile

819 W. Franklin Street
Richmond, VA 23284
Type: Public, 4 Yr., Coed
Website: http://www.vcu.edu
SAT/ACT/GPA: Open
Student/Faculty Ratio: 13:1
Undergraduate Enrollment: 12,527
Scholarships/Academic: Yes   **Athletic:** Yes
Expenses By: Year   **In State:** $ 9,057
Degrees Conferred: AS, BA, BS, BFA, BSN, MA, MS, MBA, MFA, Ph.D.

Phone: 800-841-3638

Founded: 1838
Religion: Non-Affiliated
Housing: Yes
Male/Female: 40:60
Graduate Enrollment: 4,177
Financial Aid: Yes
Out of State: $ 17,219

Programs of Study: Accounting, Biology, Chemistry, Economics, Engineering, Finance, Marketing, Health, Occupational, Physical, Radiation, Real Estate, Safety and Risk, Science, Sociology, Urban, Anthropology, Art Education, Nursing, Criminal Justice, Dance, Design, Music, Psychology, Religion, Mathematics, Communications, Computer Science, Business Administration

Women's Athletic Profile

Box 8420003, 819 Franklin Street
Richmond, VA 23284-2003
Coach: Cheryl Carlson
Email: cacarlso@vcu.edu

NCAA I
Lady Rams, Black, Gold
Phone: (804) 828-3024
Fax: (804) 828-9428

Estimated # of Women's Volleyball Scholarships: N/A
Conference: Colonial Athletic Association

Virginia State University
Academic Profile

P.O. Box 9018, Office of Admissions VSU
Petersburg, VA 23806

Type: Public, 4 Yr., Coed
Website: http://www.vsu.edu
SAT/ACT/GPA: Required to take standardized test scores/"C" average
Student/Faculty Ratio: 19:1
Undergraduate Enrollment: 3,300
Scholarships/Academic: Yes   **Athletic:** Yes
Expenses By: Year   **In State:** $ 8,182
Degrees Conferred: AA, AS, BA, BS, MA, MS

Phone: 800-871-7611

Founded: 1882
Religion: Non-Affiliated
Housing: Yes
Male/Female: 40:60
Graduate Enrollment: 1,100
Financial Aid: Yes
Out of State: $ 13,726

Programs of Study: Accounting, Agricultural Business Management, Art & Design, Biological Science, Business Administration, Chemistry, Earth Science, Economics, Education, Engineering Technology, English, Geology, History, Home Economics, Information Systems & Decision Sciences, International Relations, Languages and Literature, Management and Marketing, Mathematics, Military Science, Physical Education & Recreation, Physics, Political Science, Psychology, Public Administration, Social Work, Sociology, Special Education

Women's Athletic Profile

20720 4th Ave
Petersburg, VA 23806
Coach: Steve Wallace
Email: swallace@vsu.edu

NCAA I
Trojanettes, Blue, Burnt Orange
Phone: (804) 524-5030
Fax: (804) 524-5763

Estimated # of Women's Volleyball Scholarships: 5
Conference: Central Intercollegiate Athletic Association
Program Profile: Play in the Daniel Gym with a seating capacity of 4000.
Achievements: 2000 CIAA Coach of the Week, 1999 CIAA Conference Playoffs, 1999 All-CIAA Rookie Team, 2000 All-CIAA Rookie Team.
Freshman Receiving Financial Aid/Academic: **Athletic:** 5
Roster In State: 9   **Out of State:** 3   **Out of Country:** 0
Sophomores on Team: **Seniors on Team:** 2   **Graduation %:** 85
Most Recent Record: 9-13-0
Positions Needed: Setter, Outside Hitters
Schedule: Virginia Union, Bowie State, St. Pauls College, Univ. of U.C., St. Augustines College
Style of Play: A young, aggressive, defensive minded team who plays with a lot of excitement.

Virginia Polytechnic Institute (Virginia Tech)
Academic Profile

364 Jamerson Athletic Center
Blacksburg, VA 24061-0502

Phone: (540) 231-5037

Type: Public, 4 Yr., Coed
Website: http://www.vt.edu
SAT/ACT/GPA: Not Available at this time
Student/Faculty Ratio: 17:1
Undergraduate Enrollment: 21,810
Scholarships/Academic: Yes
Expenses By: Year
Specializes In: Architecture, Business, Computer Science, Engineering
Degrees Conferred: BA, BS, MA, MS, MBA, Ph D, Ed D

Founded: 1872
Religion: Non-Affiliated
Housing: Yes
Male/Female: 60:40
Graduate Enrollment: 3,618
Athletic: Yes   **Financial Aid:** Yes
In State: $ 7,400   **Out of State:** $ 15,624

Programs of Study: Accounting, Architecture, Animal Science, BioChemistry, Biology, Chemistry, Communication Studies, Computer Science, Economics, English, Fisheries/Wildlife, Finance, Foreign Languages, Forestry, International Studies, Management, Marketing, Mathematics, Music, Physics, Political Science, Psychology, Sociology, Statistics and many more

Women's Athletic Profile

302 Cassell Coliseum
Blacksburg, VA 24061-0502
Coach: Stephanie Hawbecker
Email: mginipro@vt.edu

NCAA I
Lady Hokies, Burnt Orange
Phone: 540-231-5037
Fax: 540-231-6686

Estimated # of Women's Volleyball Scholarships: 2
Conference: Big East Atlantic -10
Program Profile: Our program has 12 scholarships. We play home matches in Cassell Coliseum which has a capacity of 10,000. Pre-season begins on August 10. The Conference Tournament is on Thanksgiving week-end. We offer strength training in a state-of-the-art facility, Merryman Center.
History: John Pierce was part-time head coach from 1977-1990. Stephanie Hawbecker has been full-time head coach from 1995 to the present. We were in the Metro Conference until 1995. We have been in the Atlantic 10 Conference from 1995 to the present.
Achievements: Lisa Pikalek was Academic All-American of the Year Division I in 1992 and on First Team in 1990, 1991; Ginny Lessman was in First Team Academic All-American in 1992.
Coaching: Stephanie Hawbecker, Head Coach, since 1991, her overall record is 157-115. She was Metro Coach of the Year in 1992. Matt Ginipro and Jennifer Arbuckle are Assistant Coaches.
Freshman Receiving Financial Aid/Academic: **Athletic:** 4
Roster In State: 7   **Out of State:** 9   **Out of Country:** 0
Sophomores on Team: 0   **Seniors on Team:** 5   **Graduation %:** 100
Most Recent Record: 21-9-0   **Fall Games:** 30   **Spring Games:** 2
Camp of Clinic Dates: Beginners Day: July 6-9; Setters: July 10; Hitters: July 11
Positions Needed: Completed 2000-2001- Setter, Opposite
Schedule: Santa Barbara, Arizona State, South Carolina, Northern Illinois, Virginia, Temple-Dayton
Style of Play: Our emphasis is on ball control, multiple quick attack (Middles & Right Side) and unselfish team play. Wanted: emotional intense, fun-loving hard workers who put academics first.

Virginia Union University
Academic Profile

1500 N. Lombardy St.
Richmond, VA 23220

Phone: 804-257-5856

Type: Private, 4 Yr., Coed
Website: Not Available
SAT/ACT/GPA: 900+
Student/Faculty Ratio: 16:1
Undergraduate Enrollment: 1,209
Scholarships/Academic: Yes
Expenses By: Year
Degrees Conferred: BA, BS, M, MDiv

Founded: 1865
Religion: American Baptist
Housing: No
Male/Female: 46:54
Graduate Enrollment: 151
Athletic: Yes   **Financial Aid:** Yes
In State: $ 11,552   **Out of State:** $ 11,552

Programs of Study: Accounting, Agriculture, Animal Science, Architecture, Art & Art History, BioChemistry, Biology, Black Studies, Botany, Chemistry, Chinese, Classics, Communications Studies, Computer Science, Engineering, Education, Geographic, Geology, Genetics, Geophysics, German, Greek, History, Italian, Marketing, Liberal Arts, Military Science, Music, Philosophy, Psychology, Plant Pathology, Physiology, Zoology

Women's Athletic Profile

1500 N. Lombardy Street
Richmond, VA 23220-1790
Coach: Stacey Jones
Email:

NCAA I
Lady Panthers, Maroon, Grey
Phone: (804) 321-2356
Fax: (804) 321-0287

Estimated # of Women's Volleyball Scholarships: N/A
Conference: Central Intercollegiate Athletic Association

Washington and Lee University
Academic Profile

PO Drawer 928
Lexington, VA 24450

Phone: 540-463-8710

Type: Private, 4 Yr., Liberal Arts, Coed
Website: http://www.wlu.edu
SAT/ACT/GPA: 1200
Student/Faculty Ratio: 10:1
Undergraduate Enrollment: 1,700
Scholarships/Academic: Yes   **Athletic:** No
Expenses By: Year   **In State:** $ 21,970
Specializes In: Law
Degrees Conferred: BA, BS, JD

Founded: 1749
Religion: Non-Affiliated
Housing: Yes
Male/Female: 55:45
Graduate Enrollment: 300
Financial Aid: Yes
Out of State: $ 21,970

Programs of Study: 40+ majors including Business & Management, Communications, Languages, Life Science, Physical Sciences, Psychology, Social Sciences

Women's Athletic Profile

Drawer 928
Lexington, VA 24450
Coach: Terri Dadio Campbell
Email: dadiot@wlu.edu

NCAA I
Lady Generals, Blue, White
Phone: (540) 463-8946
Fax: (540) 463-8173

Estimated # of Women's Volleyball Scholarships: 0
Conference: Old Dominion Athletic Conference
Achievements: 4 regular season Championships in 1998,1997,1996 and 1995; 3 Conference Championships in 1998,1997 and 1995; 2 Player of the Year, I Freshman of the Year; 2 Coach of the Year
Coaching: Terri Dadio Campbell, Head Coach, began in 1993. She has been named Coach of the Year in 1995, 1997 & 1998.
Sophomores on Team: 5   **Seniors on Team:** 2   **Graduation %:** 100
Most Recent Record: 26-2-0
Positions Needed: Setter, Outside Hitter
Schedule: Emory, Averett, Maryville, Bridgewater, Greensboro, Centre

WASHINGTON

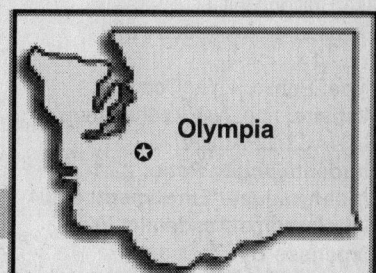

Olympia

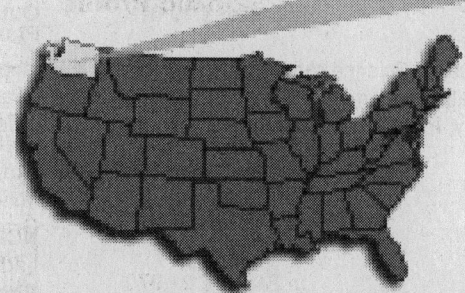

SCHOOL	CITY	AFFILIATION	PAGE
Central Washington University	Ellensburg	NCAA II	787
Eastern Washington University	Cheney	NCAA I	787
Gonzaga University	Spokane	NCAA I	788
Pacific Lutheran University	Tacoma	NCAA III	788
Saint Martin's College	Lacey	NCAA II	789
Seattle Pacific University	Seattle	NCAA II	789
Seattle University	Seattle	NCAA III	790
University of Puget Sound	Tacoma	NCAA III/NAIA	791
University of Washington	Seattle	NCAA I	791
Washington State University	Pullman	NCAA I	792
Western Washington University	Bellingham	NCAA II	793
Whitman College	Walla Walla	NCAA III	793
Whitworth College	Spokane	NCAA III	794

Central Washington University
Academic Profile

214 Buillon Hall
Ellensburg, WA 98926-7570

Phone: 509-963-3001

Type: Public, 4 Yr., Coed
Website: http://www.central.edu
SAT/ACT/GPA: 820/17
Student/Faculty Ratio: 22:1
Undergraduate Enrollment: 8,304
Scholarships/Academic: Yes
Expenses By: Year
Degrees Conferred: BA, BS, MA, MS

Athletic: Tuition
In State: $ 10,018

Founded: 1890
Religion: Non-Affiliated
Housing: Yes
Male/Female: 49:51
Graduate Enrollment: 281
Financial Aid: Yes
Out of State: $ 16,204

Programs of Study: Accounting, Actuarial Science, Anthropology, Banking & Finance, Biology, Broadcasting, Business Administration, Chemistry, Communications, Computer Science, Criminal Justice, Earth Science, Economics, Education, Engineering, Fine Arts, Geography, Geology, History, Psychology, Physics, Philosophy, Political Science

Women's Athletic Profile

400 8th Avenue
Ellensburg, WA 98926
Coach: Mario Andaya
Email:

NCAA I
Lady Wildcats, Crimson, Black
Phone: (509) 963-1983
Fax: (509) 963-2351

Estimated # of Women's Volleyball Scholarships: N/A
Conference: Pacific West Conference

Eastern Washington University
Academic Profile

526 Fifth Street
Cheney, WA 99004

Phone: 888-740-1914

Type: Public, 4 Yr., Coed
Website: http://www.ewu.edu
SAT/ACT/GPA: 720+
Student/Faculty Ratio: 20:1
Undergraduate Enrollment: 6,990
Scholarships/Academic: Yes
Expenses By: Year
Degrees Conferred: BA, BS, BFA, MA, MS, MBA, MFA, M.Ed.

Athletic: Yes
In State: $ 7,360

Founded: 1882
Religion: Non-Affiliated
Housing: No
Male/Female: 44:56
Graduate Enrollment: 1,358
Financial Aid: Yes
Out of State: $ 11,872

Programs of Study: Contact school for programs of study.

Women's Athletic Profile

MS 66, 526 5th Street
Cheney, WA 99004
Coach: Pamela Parks
Email: Pparks@ewu.edu

NCAA I
Lady Eagles, Red, White, Black
Phone: (509) 359-2511
Fax: (509) 359-2828

Estimated # of Women's Volleyball Scholarships: 12
Conference: Big Sky Conference
Program Profile: Reese Court has 5,000 seats and is a great facility for volleyball. We have a beautiful training room and a state-of-the-art weight room. We play home games and away games in the conference. We have a strong non-conference schedule.
History: Our program started in 1968. We entered the Big Sky in 1988. Our current coach has been here for 14 years with a record of 268-248. We won conference in 1989 and 1997.
Achievements: Big sky Coach of the year in 1989 and 1983; District Coach of the Year in 1989; 3 Big Sky Conference Players of the Year; 2 athletes that have been invited to the Canadian National Team; 2 Academic All-Americans
Coaching: Pamela Parks - Head Coach. Wade Benson is Assistant Coach. Both coaches are successful in college and clubs. Both coaches are involved with the Spokane Splash Club which finishes very high in competition throughout the country.

Roster In State: 10	**Out of State:** 4	**Out of Country:** 2
Sophomores on Team: 4	**Seniors on Team:** 3	**Graduation %:** 95%
Most Recent Record: 24-5-0	**Fall Games:** 30	**Spring Games:** 4

Camp of Clinic Dates: Youth: July 25-26; All Skills: July 27-30

Positions Needed: Setter, Middle (2)
Schedule: South Florida, Fresno State, California Polytechnic, California-Berkeley, Sacramento State, Oral Roberts
Style of Play: Very upbeat, scrambling defense; good ball control; smart offense; tenacious. We will not overpower you, but we will out work you.

Gonzaga University
Academic Profile

502 E Boone
Spokane, WA 99258

Phone: (509) 323-6376

Type: Private, 4 Yr., Liberal Arts, Engineering, Coed
Website: http://www.gonzaga.edu
SAT/ACT/GPA: 1000/3.2
Student/Faculty Ratio: 17:1
Undergraduate Enrollment: 4,200
Scholarships/Academic: Yes   **Athletic:** Yes
Expenses By: Year   **In State:** $ 22,160

Founded: 1887
Religion: Jesuit
Housing: Yes
Male/Female: 48:52
Graduate Enrollment: 1,300
Financial Aid: Yes
Out of State: $ 22,160

Degrees Conferred: BA, BS, BBA, B.Ed., Bachelor of Education, BSE, Bachelor of General Studies, BSN, Juris Doctor
Programs of Study: For more information please contact the University Admission at 800-323-6572.

Women's Athletic Profile

E. 502 Boone Avenue A.D. Box #66
Spokane, WA 99258
Coach: Eva Windlin-Jansen
Email: volleyball@athletics.gonzaga.edu

NCAA I
Lady Zags, Blue, White, Red
Phone: (509) 323-6376
Fax: (509) 323-5787

Estimated # of Women's Volleyball Scholarships: 3
Conference: West Coast Conference
Program Profile: We are a NCAA Division I program. Charlotte V. Martin Centre ("The Kennel") has a 4,000 seat pavilion. It is a 120,000 square foot athletic facility with a pool, an indoor track, an exercise/weight room and a racquetball court.
History: Gonzaga joined the WCC in 1986. We have made 2 post-season appearances. In the NIVC and NCAA's best season, Gonzaga was ranked 20th in "Volleyball Monthly" Final Poll. Our overall record was 12-2 in WCC where we finished in second place.
Achievements: 27 All-Conference; 2 WCC Player of the Year; 6 All-Region; 2 All-Americans; 8 Olympic Festival participants; Numerous Academic All-Conference Honorees.
Coaching: Eva Windlin-Jansen, has been Head Coach for 3 seasons. She coached at Dakota State University. In 1994 and 1995, her team won back-to-back 30-win seasons and in 1994 captured the South Dakota Iowa Conference title. She was 1994 SDIC Co-Coach of the Year. Kelley Spink and Andrea Nachtrieb are Assistant Coaches.
Freshman Receiving Financial Aid/Academic: **Athletic:** 6
Roster In State: 4   **Out of State:** 8   **Out of Country:** 3
Sophomores on Team: 0   **Seniors on Team:** 3   **Graduation %:** 100
Most Recent Record: 5-9-0
Camp of Clinic Dates: Mid July, 2000
Positions Needed: All
Schedule: Pepperdine, Loyola Marymount, Washington State, University of San Diego, Northwestern, Santa Clara
Style of Play: We play a fast, multiple offense with emphasis on ball handling and intense defense.

Pacific Lutheran University
Academic Profile

12180 Park Avenue
Tacoma, WA 98447

Phone: (253) 535-7350

Type: Private, 4 Yr., Liberal Arts, Coed
Website: http://www.plu.edu
SAT/ACT/GPA: 1200/22
Student/Faculty Ratio: 16:1
Undergraduate Enrollment: 3,000
Scholarships/Academic: Yes   **Athletic:** No
Expenses By: Year   **In State:** $ 20,570

Founded: 1890
Religion: Evangelical Lutheran
Housing: Yes
Male/Female: 1:1.5
Graduate Enrollment: 500
Financial Aid: Yes
Out of State: $ 20,570

Specializes In: Nursing, Business, Communications, Physical Education, Music
Degrees Conferred: BA, BS, BAE, BBA, BFA, BM, BME, BSN, BSPE

Programs of Study: Anthropology, Art, Biology, Chemistry, Chinese Studies, Classic, Communications, Computer Science, Earth Science, Economics, Education, English, French, German, Mathematics, Music, Philosophy, Physics, Political Science, Psychology, Religion, Social Work, Sociology, Accounting, Marketing, Management

Women's Athletic Profile

12180 Park Avenue
Tacoma, WA 98447
Coach: Kevin Aoki
Email: phed@plu.edu

NCAA I
Lady Lutes, Gold, Black
Phone: (253) 535-7350
Fax: (253) 535-7584

Estimated # of Women's Volleyball Scholarships: 0
Conference: Northwest Conference of Independent Colleges
Program Profile: Olson Auditorium has 3,400 seats and hardwood floors that were resurfaced in 1996. Pre-season practice starts in late August with the season going into early November.
Achievements: Conference tournament participant two of the past 3 seasons.
Coaching: Kevin Aoki , Head Coach, after 3 years his record is 40-46. He is a PLU graduate. He was a successful area high school coach for 12 years prior to returning to his alma mater.

Freshman Receiving Financial Aid/Academic:		**Athletic:** 0
Roster In State: 9	**Out of State:** 6	**Out of Country:** 0
Sophomores on Team: 4	**Seniors on Team:** 2	**Graduation %:** 100
Most Recent Record: 13-13-0	**Fall Games:** 25	**Spring Games:** 0
Positions Needed: All		

Schedule: Seattle Pacific, Western Washington, St. Martin's, Puget Sound, Linfield, Willamette, George Fox.

Saint Martin's College
Academic Profile

5300 Pacific Avenue S.E.
Lacey, WA 98503
Type: Private, 4 Yr., Coed
Website: http://www.stmartin.edu
SAT/ACT/GPA: 860+
Student/Faculty Ratio: 12:1
Undergraduate Enrollment: 1,000
Scholarships/Academic: Yes
Expenses By: Year

Phone: 360-438-4311

Founded: 1895
Religion: Roman Catholic
Housing: Yes
Male/Female: 42:58
Graduate Enrollment: 600

Athletic: Yes
In State: $ 19,000

Financial Aid: Yes
Out of State: $ 19,000

Specializes In: Civil & Mechanical Engineering, Education,
Degrees Conferred: AA, AS, BA, BS, MA, MBA, M.Ed.
Programs of Study: Accounting, Biology, Business Administration, Civil Engineering, Community Services, Computer, Science, Criminal Justice, Elementary Education, Secondary Education, Special Education, English, History, Japanese Studies, Mechanical Engineering, Political Science, Psychology, Religious Studies, Social Studies, Sociology and Cultural Anthropology and Theatre Arts

Women's Athletic Profile

5300 Pacific Avenue SE
Lacey, WA 98503
Coach: Clyde Reis
Email: creis@stmartin.edu

NCAA I
Lady Saints, Red, White
Phone: (360) 438-4372
Fax: (360) 438-4374

Estimated # of Women's Volleyball Scholarships: N/A
Conference: Pacific West Conference

Seattle Pacific University
Academic Profile

3307 Third Avenue, W
Seattle, WA 98119

Phone: (206) 281-2941

Type: Private, 4 Yr., Liberal Arts, Coed
Website: http://www.spu.edu
SAT/ACT/GPA: 1150/27/3.0
Student/Faculty Ratio: 17:1

Founded: 1891
Religion: Protestant
Housing: Yes
Male/Female: 40:60

Undergraduate Enrollment: 3,500

Scholarships/Academic: Yes   **Athletic:** Yes

Expenses By: Year   **In State:** $ 20,000

Specializes In: Education, Business

Degrees Conferred: BA, BS, MA, Ph.D.

Graduate Enrollment: 1,500

Financial Aid: Yes

Out of State: $ 20,000

Programs of Study: Accounting, Arts, Biology, Business, Chemistry, Communications, Computer Science, Economics, Education, Engineering, English, Fine Arts, History, Liberal Arts, Mathematics, Music, Nursing, Philosophy, Physics, Political Science, Psychology, Religion, Science, Social Science, Theology

Women's Athletic Profile

3307 3rd Avenue W
Seattle, WA 98119
Coach: JoAnn Atwell-Scrivner
Email: jaas@spu.edu

NCAA I
Lady Falcons, Maroon, White
Phone: (206) 281-2941
Fax: (206) 281-2266

Estimated # of Women's Volleyball Scholarships: 4

Conference: Pacific West Conference

Program Profile: Our volleyball program is very popular with our faculty and surrounding community.

History: Our program started in 1986. Initially, we were members of the NAIA District I. In 1991, we joined the NCAA Division II program. In 1995, we were ranked #22 and finished third place or higher in the PacWest for six of the last seven seasons.

Achievements: 1995 Pacific Coach of the Year; 4 All-Americans; 1981 NAIA District I Coach of the Year; 1989 NAIA District I Coach of the Year.

Coaching: Joann Atwell-Scrivner, is the only Head Coach that the Falcons have ever known. She has over 400 victories (412-282) in 19 years of coaching. She is a graduate of Willimette University where she was inducted into the Athletic Hall of Fame.

Roster In State: 12   **Out of State:** 0   **Out of Country:** 0

Sophomores on Team: 2   **Seniors on Team:** 1   **Graduation %:** 98

Most Recent Record: 23-7-0   **Fall Games:** 30-35   **Spring Games:** 4

Positions Needed: 2

Schedule: Mesa State, Hawaii Pacific, Brigham Young-Hawaii, University of California-Davis, Sonoma State, Western Oregon

Style of Play: Defensively focused with emphasis on blocking and diverse defensive systems. Offense is a tempo and position format with a 5-1/6-2 system.

Seattle University
Academic Profile

Broadway & Madison
Seattle, WA 98122

Phone: 800-426-7123

Type: Private, 4 Yr., Liberal Arts, Engineering, Coed

Website: http://www.seattleu.edu

SAT/ACT/GPA: 1000/3.0

Student/Faculty Ratio: 13:1

Undergraduate Enrollment: 3,300

Scholarships/Academic: Yes   **Athletic:** Yes

Expenses By: Year   **In State:** $ 21,950

Founded: 1891

Religion: Jesuit

Housing: Yes

Male/Female: 47:53

Graduate Enrollment: 1,000

Financial Aid: Yes

Out of State: $ 21,950

Degrees Conferred: BA, BS, MBA, MIT, Law School

Programs of Study: Accounting, Arts, Bible Studies, Business, Chemistry, Communications, Computer Science, Dietetics, Economics, Education, Engineering, English, Fine Arts, Food Production & Science, History, Interdisciplinary Studies, Liberal Arts, Mathematics, Music, Nursing, Nutrition, Philosophy, Physical Fitness/Exercise Science, Physics, Political Science, Psychology, Recreation & Leisure, Religion, Science, Social Science, Special Education, Theatre, Theology

Women's Athletic Profile

900 Broadway
Seattle, WA 98122
Coach: Steve Nimocks
Email:

NCAA I
Lady Chieftains, Scarlet, White
Phone: (206) 296-6426
Fax: (206) 296-2154

Estimated # of Women's Volleyball Scholarships: N/A

Conference: North Central Intercollegiate Athletic Conference

University of Puget Sound
Academic Profile

1500 N. Warner
Tacoma, WA 98416-0710

Phone: (253) 756-3412

Type: Private, 4 Yr., Liberal Arts, Coed
Website: http://www.ups.edu
SAT/ACT/GPA: 1000/3.0
Student/Faculty Ratio: 10:1
Undergraduate Enrollment: 2,800
Scholarships/Academic: Yes
Expenses By: Year
Specializes In: National Caliber Liberal Arts University
Degrees Conferred: BA, BS, MA, M.Ed
Programs of Study: Allied Health, Business & Management, Communications, Education, Letters & Literature, Life Sciences, Psychology, Social Sciences, Visual & Performing Arts

Founded: 1888
Religion: Non-Affiliated
Housing: Yes
Male/Female: .8:1
Graduate Enrollment: 100
Athletic: No
Financial Aid: Yes
In State: $ 25,000
Out of State: $ 25,000

Women's Athletic Profile

1500 N. Warner
Tacoma, WA 98416
Coach: Mark Massey
Email: mmassey@ups.edu

NCAA I
Lady Loggers, Maroon, White
Phone: (253) 756-3412
Fax: (253) 756-3634

Estimated # of Women's Volleyball Scholarships: N/A
Conference: Northwest Conference of Independent Colleges
Program Profile: Puget Sound makes the transition in 1999-2000 from one of the top NAIA volleyball teams in the nation to NCAA Division III play. Along with a change in athletic colors from green & gold to maroon & white, the team will also face new regional opponents from California, including former NCAA-III Champion UC-San Diego. UPS is one of the few schools in the U.S. where student-athletes can combine both national-caliber liberal arts education and volleyball competition, without sacrifices in either area.
History: Puget Sound has a long history of volleyball excellence, including National Player of the Year Kathy Flick and National Tournament MVP Andrea Egans. In the past decade alone, the squad has finished 1st, 2nd, 3rd and 5th nationally, making UPS one of the premier small-college volleyball programs in the country.
Achievements: Puget Sound was the first team outside of Hawaii or California to win a NAIA Volleyball National Championship; 5th place finish at Nationals in 1997; #16 national ranking in 1998;   1998 swing hitter Anna Dudek was a 2x All-American, and was nationally ranked #1 in digs and #2 in kills in her senior year.
Coaching: Mark Massey, Head Coach, has produced nine "Top 20" ranked teams in the past 14 years, including 7 All-American, 17 All-Region and 25 All-Conference performers. He was recognized in 1992 as the "Asics/Volleyball Monthly" NCAA Division II National Coach of the Year . He was a two-time recipient of the AVCA Southwest Region Coach of the Year award and was selected as the Northwest Conference Coach of the Year in 1997 after an undefeated conference season. Over the past seven years, his teams have won 75% of their matches.

Roster In State: 5
Sophomores on Team: 0
Most Recent Record: 16-6-0
Out of State: 9
Seniors on Team: 11
Fall Games: 22
Out of Country: 0
Graduation %: 100
Spring Games: 0
Camp of Clinic Dates: Skills 7/19-23; Team Swing :July 17; Setters: 7/17: 7/30-31; 8./2-4;
Positions Needed: All
Schedule: University of California - San Diego, Cal Lutheran, George Fox, California State University - Hayward, Willamette
Style of Play: Puget Sound is one of the few small-college teams in the nation to run a true"swing"style offense, patterned after the USA Men's National Team. Since adopting this fast-paced audible attack system in 1992, Coach Massey's offense has been ranked in the "Top 10" nationally each year and produced six All-American swing hitters.

University of Washington
Academic Profile

Graves Annex, Box 354080
Seattle, WA 98195-4080

Phone: (206) 543-0432

Type: Public, 4 Yr., Coed
Website: http://www.washington.edu
SAT/ACT/GPA: NCAA Qualifier/3.6
Student/Faculty Ratio: 1:11
Undergraduate Enrollment: 22,000

Founded: 1861
Religion: Non-Affiliated
Housing: Yes
Male/Female: 50:50
Graduate Enrollment: 13,000

Scholarships/Academic: Yes   **Athletic:** Yes   **Financial Aid:** Yes

Expenses By: Year   **In State:** $ 11,500   **Out of State:** $ 19,500

Specializes In: Social Sciences, Health Sciences, Engineering, Physical Science,

Degrees Conferred: BA, BS, BFA, MS, MA, MBA, MFA, Ph.D.

Programs of Study: Over 180 majors from which to chose.

Women's Athletic Profile

Box 354080

Seattle, WA 98195

Coach: Bill Neville

Email: billn@u.washington.edu

NCAA I

Lady Huskies, Purple, Gold

Phone: (206) 543-0432

Fax: (206) 685-1677

Estimated # of Women's Volleyball Scholarships: 12

Conference: Pacific 10 Conference

Program Profile: We have one of the top programs in the country with one of the most respected coaches in the world. Our facilities have been newly renovated and will open in the Spring of 2001. This puts the University of Washington at #1 in the PAC-10 and one of the best universities in the country. Our arena will have 12,000 seats.

History: Washington's volleyball program began in 1974 when we participated in the Northwest Volleyball League. In 1982, the school joined the North Pacific Volleyball League. In 1986, we joined the PAC-10 Conference. The program is perennially in the Top 25. Bill Neville, with his extensive international experience, is a top trainer for those who want to go on to the National Team.

Achievements: PAC-10 Coach of the Year; Angela Branson, First Team All-American in 1996; MaKare DeSilets was First Team All-American in 1997; Leslie Tuiasosopo was USA National Team in 1999; MaKare DeSilets was USA National Team 1997-Present; 3 others play pro in Europe; AmyTutt and Kristina Caffing are Canadian National Team candidates.

Coaching: Bill Neville, Head Coach, is in his 8th year at UW. He has a total of 30 years coaching experience. His overall career record at UW is 110-99. His total overall record is 247-214. He was Head Coach of the Canadian Men's Olympic team in 1976. He was Assistant Coach of the Gold Medal USA Men's Olympic team in 1984. He was Head Coach of the USA Men's National Team in 1998-1991. Diane Flick is Assistant Coach.

Freshman Receiving Financial Aid/Academic: **Athletic:** 5

Roster In State: 6   **Out of State:** 7   **Out of Country:** 1

Sophomores on Team: 3   **Seniors on Team:** 2   **Graduation %:** 97

Most Recent Record: 9-15-0   **Fall Games:**   **Spring Games:** 30

Camp of Clinic Dates: 16

Positions Needed: Middle Blockers, Outside Hitter

Schedule: Stanford, Wisconsin, University of Pacific, USC, Arizona, UCLA

Style of Play: Athletic, tenacious and powerful. We play Volleyball "above the rim" and on the floor.

Washington State University
Academic Profile

107 Bohler Gym P. O. Box 641610

Pullman, WA 99164-0328

Phone: 509-335-5586

Type: Public, 4 Yr., Coed

Website: http://www.wsu.edu/athletics

SAT/ACT/GPA: 700avg/17avg

Student/Faculty Ratio: 17:1

Undergraduate Enrollment: 16,000

Scholarships/Academic: Yes   **Athletic:** Yes

Expenses By: Year   **In State:** $ 7,900

Founded: 1890

Religion: Non-Affiliated

Housing: Yes

Male/Female: 53:47

Graduate Enrollment: 4,000

Financial Aid: Yes

Out of State: $ 13,000

Degrees Conferred: BA, BS, MA, MS, MBA

Programs of Study: Advertising, Animal, Anthropology, Banking/Finance, Biology, Chemistry, Communications, Computer, Criminal Justice, French, Geology, German, History, Horticulture, Hotel/Restaurant Management, Nursing, International, Parks/Recreation Management, PreProfessional Programs, Psychology, Pharmacy, Philosophy, Soil, Speech, Wildlife, Biology, Zoology

Women's Athletic Profile

107 Bohler Gym, PO Box 641610

Pullman, WA 99164-1610

Coach: Cindy Fredrick

Email: Volleyball@wsu.edu

NCAA I

Lady Cougars, Crimson, Grey

Phone: (509) 335-0277

Fax: (509) 335-0328

Estimated # of Women's Volleyball Scholarships: N/A
Conference: Pacific 10 Conference
Program Profile: The Cougar Volleyball team competes in the Bohler Gymnasium. Bohler is being renovated and is scheduled to open its doors in the spring of 2000. Meanwhile, the Cougars are playing matches in Beasley Coliseum.
History: In 1991, we had our NCAA First Round. We were the 1992 National Invitation Volleyball Champions. In 1993, we were NCAA Second Round. In 1994, we were NCAA First Round. In 1995, we were NCAA Second Round. In 1996, we were NCAA Elite 8. In 1997, we were NCAA Sweet Sixteen.
Achievements: Pac-10 Coach of the Year: Cindy Fredrick; 1995 AVCA District VIII Coach of the Year; All-Americans: Sarah Silvemail in 1995 and 1996; Stephanee Papke in 1996 and Keri Killebrew in 1997.
Coaching: Cindy Fredrick Head Coach, since 1989. Her overall record as a head coach is 270-173.
Camp of Clinic Dates: Individual: July 11-15; Team: July 18-22
Schedule: Stanford, University of California-LA, University of Southern California, University of New Mexico, Texas A & M

Western Washington University
Academic Profile

516 High Street
Bellingham, WA 98225-6597

Phone: 360-650-3440

Type: Public, 4 Yr., Liberal Arts, Coed
Website: http://www.wwu.edu
SAT/ACT/GPA: 1100
Student/Faculty Ratio: 21:1
Undergraduate Enrollment: 11,500
Scholarships/Academic: Yes   **Athletic:** Yes
Expenses By: Year   **In State:** $ 10,325
Degrees Conferred: BA, BS, BFA, BM, MA, MS, MBA, M.Ed.
Programs of Study: Arts & Sciences, Business & Economics, Fine & Performing Arts, Environmental Studies, Education, Human Services, Liberal Arts

Founded: 1899
Religion: Non-Affiliated
Housing: Yes
Male/Female: 48:52
Graduate Enrollment: 750
Financial Aid: Yes
Out of State: $ 16,508

Women's Athletic Profile

516 high Street
Bellingham, WA 98225
Coach: Michael DiMarco
Email: miked@cc.wwu.edu

NCAA I
Lady White, Blue, Silver, White
Phone: (360) 650-2849
Fax: (360) 650-3496

Estimated # of Women's Volleyball Scholarships: 4
Conference: Pacific West Conference
Program Profile: Sam Carver Gymnasium (3,100)
History: Have had 14 straight winning seasons
Achievements: 1990-placed third at NAIA National Tournament
Coaching: 1996-99 59-36
Freshman Receiving Financial Aid/Academic: **Athletic:** 2
Roster In State: 11   **Out of State:**   **Out of Country:**
Sophomores on Team: 2   **Seniors on Team:** 0   **Graduation %:**
Most Recent Record: 15-14

Whitman College
Academic Profile

345 Boyer
Walla Walla, WA 99362

Phone: (509) 521-5264

Type: Private, 4 Yr., Liberal Arts, Coed
Website: http://www.whitman.edu
SAT/ACT/GPA: 1280/3.8
Student/Faculty Ratio: 10:1
Undergraduate Enrollment: 1,300
Scholarships/Academic: Yes   **Athletic:** No
Expenses By: Year   **In State:** $ 26,000+
Specializes In: Premed, Engineering, Economics, Art
Degrees Conferred: BA
Programs of Study: Anthropology, Asian Studies, Art, Biology, Chemistry, Computer Science, Dramatic Arts, Economics, English, Environmental Studies, Fine Arts, French, Geology, German, History, Mathematics, Music, Philosophy, Physics, Political Science, PreLaw, PreMed, Psychology, Social Science, Spanish, Theatre

Founded: 1859
Religion: Non-Affiliated
Housing: Yes
Male/Female: 45:55
Graduate Enrollment: N/A
Financial Aid: Yes
Out of State: $ 26,000+

Women's Athletic Profile

345 Boyer Avenue
Walla Walla, WA 99362
Coach: Dean Snider
Email: sniderdc@whitman.edu

NCAA I
Lady Missionaries, Gold, Blue
Phone: (509) 527-5264
Fax: (509) 527-5960

Estimated # of Women's Volleyball Scholarships: N/A
Conference: Northwest Conference of Independent Colleges
History: We started in 1982.
Achievements: Coach of the Year NJCAA in 1999-91
Coaching: Dean Snider, Head Coach, since 1996. He was at WWU from 1992 to 1995. He coached at TWU from 1990 to 1991. His overall record is 156-111.
Freshman Receiving Financial Aid/Academic:

Athletic: 0

Roster In State: 8 | **Out of State:** 4 | **Out of Country:** 0
Sophomores on Team: 0 | **Seniors on Team:** 3 | **Graduation %:** 100
Most Recent Record: 13-12-0 | **Fall Games:** 25 | **Spring Games:** 0
Camp of Clinic Dates: July 21-24
Positions Needed: Middle Blockers, Outside Hitters
Style of Play: Defensive and transitional.

Whitworth College
Academic Profile

300 West Hawthorne Rd
Spokane, WA 99251

Phone: 509-527-5176

Type: Private, 4 Yr., Liberal Arts, Coed
Website: http://www.whitworth.edu
SAT/ACT/GPA: 1160 avg.
Student/Faculty Ratio: 16.5:1
Undergraduate Enrollment: 1,500
Scholarships/Academic: Yes
Expenses By: Year
Specializes In:
Degrees Conferred: BS, BA, M.Ed., MIT, MIM

Founded: 1890
Religion: Presbyterian
Housing: Yes
Male/Female: 40:60
Graduate Enrollment: 300
Athletic: Yes | **Financial Aid:** Yes
In State: $ 19,824 | **Out of State:** $ 19,824

Programs of Study: Accounting, Art, Liberal Studies, Biology, Business, Chemistry, Communications, Computer Science, Cross-Cultural Studies, Economics, Education, Engineering, English, French, History, Journalism, Math, Music, Philosophy, P.E., Physics, Political Studies, Psychology, Religion, Sociology, Spanish, Sports Medicine, Theatre

Women's Athletic Profile

300 West Hawthorne Rd.
Spokane, WA 99251
Coach: Steve Rupe
Email:

NCAA I
Pioneers, Crimson, Black
Phone: (509) 777-3235
Fax: (509) 777-3720

Estimated # of Women's Volleyball Scholarships: N/A
Conference: Northwest Conference of Independent Colleges
Program Profile: We have an improving Division III program. We play in a strong small-college conference.
History: Our program began in 1972.
Achievements: Whitworth competed in the AIAW III National Tournament 3 years in a row: 1979, 1980 and 1981; Northwest Conference Title in 1990 and 1991.
Coaching: Steve Rupe - Head Coach.
Freshman Receiving Financial Aid/Academic:

Athletic: 0

Roster In State: 6 | **Out of State:** 8 | **Out of Country:** 0
Sophomores on Team: 4 | **Seniors on Team:** 3 | **Graduation %:** 100
Most Recent Record: 3-20-0 | **Fall Games:** 25 | **Spring Games:** 0
Positions Needed: Setter
Schedule: Gonzaga University, University of Puget Sound, George Fox University, Central Washington University
Style of Play: Aggressive, energetic, team-oriented.

WEST VIRGINIA

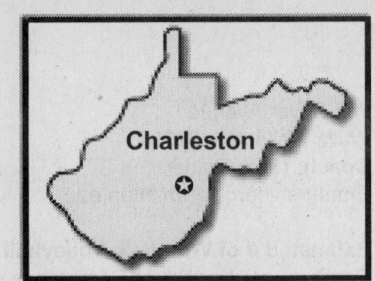

Charleston

SCHOOL	CITY	AFFILIATION	PAGE
Alderson-Broaddus College	Philippi	NCAA II	796
Bethany College	Bethany	NCAA III	796
Concord College	Athens	NCAA II	797
Fairmont State College	Fairmont	NCAA II	797
Glenville State College	Glenville	NCAA II	798
Marshall University	Huntington	NCAA I	799
Ohio Valley College	Parkersburg	NCAA II	800
Salem - Teikyo University	Salem	NCAA II	800
Shepherd College	Shepherdstown	NCAA II	801
University of Charleston	Charleston	NCAA II	801
West Liberty State College	West Liberty	NCAA II	802
West Virginia Univ Institute of Tech	Montgomery	NCAA II	802
West Virginia State College	Institute	NCAA II	803
West Virginia University	Morgantown	NCAA I	803
West Virginia Wesleyan College	Buckannon	NCAA II	804
Wheeling Jesuit University	Wheeling	NCAA II	805

Alderson - Broaddus College
Academic Profile

College Hill Road
Philippi, WV 26416

Phone: 800-263-1549

Type: Private, 4 Yr., Liberal Arts, Coed
Website: http://www.blue.ab.edu
SAT/ACT/GPA: 820/17
Student/Faculty Ratio: 13:1
Undergraduate Enrollment: 760
Scholarships/Academic: Yes
Expenses By: Year
Degrees Conferred: Associate, Bachelors

Founded: 1871
Religion: American Baptist
Housing: Yes
Male/Female: 40:60
Graduate Enrollment: 40
Athletic: Yes
Financial Aid: Yes
In State: $ 16,316
Out of State: $ 16,316

Programs of Study: Accounting, Applied Music, Biology, Business Administration, Christian Studies, Church Music, Communications, Computer Science, General Science, Education, Social Studies, Medical Technology, Environmental Science, History, Liberal Arts, Literature, Language Art, Mathematics, Music Education, Political Science, Psychology, Nursing, Radiography, Secondary Education, Elementary Education, Chemistry, Physical Education, Sociology, Speech Communications, Business, General Studies, Natural Science, Sport Medicine, Writing, Theatre

Women's Athletic Profile

Campus Box 306
Philippi, WV 26416
Coach: J.D. Long
Email: long_jd@ab.edu

NCAA I
Lady Battlers, Blue, Grey, Gold
Phone: (304) 457-6332
Fax: (304) 457-6239

Estimated # of Women's Volleyball Scholarships: N/A
Conference: West Virginia Intercollegiate Athletic Conference

Bethany College
Academic Profile

201 Cramblet Hall
Bethany, WV 26032

Phone: (304) 829-7632

Type: Private, 4 Yr., Liberal Arts, Coed
Website: http://www.bethanywvnet.edu
SAT/ACT/GPA: 1000/23/2.8
Student/Faculty Ratio: 12:1
Undergraduate Enrollment: 800
Scholarships/Academic: Yes
Expenses By: Year
Specializes In: Communications, Education, Liberal, Physical Ed., PreLaw, PreMed
Degrees Conferred: BA, BS

Founded: 1840
Religion: Disciples of Christ
Housing: Yes
Male/Female: 55:45
Graduate Enrollment: 1-12
Athletic: No
Financial Aid: Yes
In State: $ 24,696
Out of State: $ 24,696

Programs of Study: Biology, Business & Management, Chemistry, Communications, Computer Science, Economics, Education, Engineering, Environmental Science, Fine Arts, French, German, History, Journalism, Languages, Life Sciences, Mathematics, Philosophy, Physical Education, Physics, Political Science, PreDentistry, PreLaw, PreMed, Psychology, Public Administration, Religious Studies, Social Work, Sociology, Spanish, Sport Management

Women's Athletic Profile

Hummel Fieldhouse
Bethany, WV 26032
Coach: Andy Mondon
Email: Bethanywvb@aol.com

NCAA I
Lady Bison, Green, White
Phone: (831) 438-3800 x1650
Fax: (831) 438-6202

Estimated # of Women's Volleyball Scholarships: 4
Conference: President's Athletic Conference
Program Profile: We play in the Hummel Fieldhouse, which is used for volleyball only. We play a Fall season.
History: Our program is 20 years old.
Achievements: 1994 NCAA Woman of the Year Women's Volleyball; Numerous All-Conference Players
Coaching: Andy Mondon Played at Long Beach City College & California State University/Northridge
Freshman Receiving Financial Aid/Academic:
Athletic: 0
Roster In State: 7
Out of State: 1
Out of Country: 0

Sophomores on Team: 3

Seniors on Team: 5

Graduation %: N/A

Most Recent Record:

Fall Games:

Spring Games: 0

Camp of Clinic Dates: June and July

Positions Needed: All

Schedule: UC Monterey Bay, Dominican University, Pacific Union College, Point Loma College
Menlo College, College of Notre Dame, Mills College

Style of Play: Defense builds offense.

Concord College
Academic Profile

Box 1000
Athens, WV 24712

Phone: (304) 384-5342

Type: Public, 4 Yr., Liberal Arts, Coed

Website: http://www.concord.wvnet.edu

SAT/ACT/GPA: 820/17/2.0

Student/Faculty Ratio: 12:1

Undergraduate Enrollment: 2,700

Scholarships/Academic: Yes

Athletic: Yes

Expenses By: Year

In State: $ 6,238

Founded: 1871

Religion: Non-Affiliated

Housing: Yes

Male/Female: 2:1

Graduate Enrollment: N/A

Financial Aid: Yes

Out of State: $ 9,103

Specializes In: Education, Business, Social Work, Travel Management

Degrees Conferred: BS, BA, AA

Programs of Study: Business, Broadcasting, PreMed, Biology, Teacher Education, Psychology, Accounting, Communications, Travel Industry Management, Advertising & Graphic Design, Sport Management, Commercial Art, Marketing, Sciences

Women's Athletic Profile

Box 1000
Athens, WV 24712
Coach: Pat Hardin
Email: cna00045@wvnvm.wvnet.edu

NCAA I
Lady Mt.Lions, Maroon, Gray
Phone: (304) 384-5347
Fax: (304) 384-5117

Estimated # of Women's Volleyball Scholarships: 6

Conference: West Virginia Intercollegiate Athletic Conference

Program Profile: Our team participates in a 12 team Conference. We are competitive in the Conference and in team standing.

History: Our program began in the Conference in 1972. We went from NAIA to NCAA in 1993. We got WVIAC Conference Champions for three years.

Achievements: We have two previous Conference Championships and we were Conference Runner-Up twice. We were NAIA Regional Champions in 1989.

Coaching: Pat Hardin, Head Coach, is entering her sixth year at Concord. She was, at the age of 18, a high school Assistant Coach for one year. Tina Jones is Assistant Coach.

Freshman Receiving Financial Aid/Academic:

Athletic: 4

Roster In State: 3

Out of State: 7

Out of Country: 0

Sophomores on Team: 4

Seniors on Team: 2

Graduation %: 80%

Most Recent Record: 15-15-0

Fall Games: 23

Spring Games: 0

Camp of Clinic Dates: July 26-29

Positions Needed: Setter

Schedule: WV Wesleyan, U of Charleston-WV, Lincoln Memorial University, Rio Grande University (NAIA), Alderson Broaddus

Style of Play: 5-1 or 6-2 offense, aggressive defense; striving to develop intimidating offense-2 strong hitters away.

Fairmont State College
Academic Profile

1201 Locust Avenue
Fairmont, WV 26554

Phone: 800-641-5678

Type: Public, 4 Yr., Coed

Website: Not Available

SAT/ACT/GPA: 900/17/2.25

Student/Faculty Ratio: 22:1

Undergraduate Enrollment: 6,700

Scholarships/Academic: Yes

Athletic: Yes

Founded: 1867

Religion: Non-Affiliated

Housing: Yes

Male/Female: 45;55

Graduate Enrollment: N/A

Financial Aid: Yes

Expenses By: Year   **In State:** $ 5,878   **Out of State:** $ 7,946
Programs of Study: Elementary Education, Secondary Education, Business Administration, Criminal Justice, Nursing, Psychology, History, Speech, Physical Education, Health Technology, Education, Music, Chemistry, Biology, English, Marketing

Women's Athletic Profile

1201 Locust Ave   **NCAA I**
Fairmont, WV 26554   Lady Falcons, Maroon, White
Coach: Larry Hill   **Phone:** (304) 367-4279
Email: lhill@mail.fscwv.edu   **Fax:** (304) 367-0202

Estimated # of Women's Volleyball Scholarships: 3
Conference: West Virginia Intercollegiate Athletic Conference
Program Profile: The Feaster Center/Joe Retton Arena is home for the volleyball program. It is a wooden playing surface, 4000 seat facility located on the campus. Fairmont plays a very competitive regional, out of regional, and a 13 match conference schedule. Usually participating in 4 of 5 tournaments in the regular season. An off season conditioning and spring playing schedule is part of the program.
History: The program began in the mid-seventies. Over the last 13 seasons, Fairmont has won 4 conference championships, 5 conference tournaments, 5 second place finishes and qualified for post season play 4 times. In 1998 the Falcons finished 29-6 and were NCAA Atlantic regular season champions.
Achievements: In the past 13 years, Fairmont has produced 28 first team All-Conference players, 17 NCAA Atlantic All-Regional selections, 4 honorable mention All-Americans, 3 West Virginia Intercollegiate Conference Players of the Year, and 4 Coach of the Year.
Coaching: Head Coach Larry Hill is in his 17th season directing the Fairmont program. This past season was highlighted with Hill collecting his 400 win coaching volleyball at Fairmont. He has been named conference Coach of the Year 4 times and NCAA Atlantic Region Coach of the Year once.
Freshman Receiving Financial Aid/Academic: **Athletic:** 5
Roster In State: 6   **Out of State:** 6   **Out of Country:** 0
Sophomores on Team: **Seniors on Team:** 3   **Graduation %:** 75
Most Recent Record: 21-17
Positions Needed: 2 OH, 2 MH, 1 Setter
Schedule: Ferris State University, Lock Haven University, California State University of PA, Northwood, Wheeling Jesuit University, University of Charleston, Edinboro University
Style of Play: Quick. Multiple attacking offense, swing hitters is key to diversity and defense is strongly emphasized

Glenville State College
Academic Profile

200 High Street   **Phone:** (304) 462-7361
Glenville, WV 26351-1292

Type: Public, 4 Yr., Coed   **Founded:** 1872
Website: http://www.glenville.wvnet.edu   **Religion:** Non-Affiliated
SAT/ACT/GPA: 830/17/2.0   **Housing:** Yes
Student/Faculty Ratio: 15:1   **Male/Female:** 40:60
Undergraduate Enrollment: 2,278   **Graduate Enrollment:** N/A
Scholarships/Academic: Yes   **Athletic:** Yes   **Financial Aid:** Yes
Expenses By: Year   **In State:** $ 5,616 **Out of State:** $ 5,616
Specializes In: Physical Education, Multi-subjects K-12, Forestry
Degrees Conferred: AA, AS, BA, BS
Programs of Study: Bachelor of Arts in Education, Bachelor of Arts, Science, Science in Business Administration, PreProfessional, Associate in Arts, Associate in Science

Women's Athletic Profile

200 High Street   **NCAA I**
Glenville, WV 26351   Lady Pioneers, Blue, White
Coach: Tracy Fluharty   **Phone:** (304) 462-7361
Email: **Fax:** (304) 462-5593

Estimated # of Women's Volleyball Scholarships: 10
Conference: West Virginia Intercollegiate Athletic Conference
Program Profile: Our playing season is from September 1st to November 17th.

History: Our volleyball program began in 1980. In the last two years, we broke school records. In 1997, our record was 19-15. In 1998, our record was 26-13.

Achievements: All-Conference Honors in 1997:Cheryl Stout, Crystal Affolter; All-WVIAC in 1998: Cheryl Stout, Chrystal Affolter, Christy Waller.

Coaching: Tracy Lyne Fluharty is head coach.

Freshman Receiving Financial Aid/Academic: **Athletic:** 6

Roster In State: 11	**Out of State:** 2	**Out of Country:** 0
Sophomores on Team: 6	**Seniors on Team:** 1	**Graduation %:** 100%
Most Recent Record: 26-13-0	**Fall Games:** 40	**Spring Games:** 0

Camp of Clinic Dates: June 13th to 17th

Positions Needed: Hitters, Setters

Schedule: Charleston, Fairmont State, Wesleyan, Glenville State, Shepherd

Style of Play: Quick sets, alternative defensive set-ups, fast-pace play. Back row attacks.

Marshall University
Academic Profile

P. O. Box 1360
Huntington, WV 25715

Phone: (304)696-5408

Type: Public, 4 Yr., Coed
Website: http://www.herdzone.com
SAT/ACT/GPA: 910192.0
Student/Faculty Ratio: 18:1
Undergraduate Enrollment: 12,000

Founded: 1837
Religion: Non-Affiliated
Housing: Yes
Male/Female: 45:55
Graduate Enrollment: 4,000

Scholarships/Academic: Yes   **Athletic:** Yes   **Financial Aid:** Yes
Expenses By: Year   **In State:** $10,000   **Out of State:** $14,000

Specializes In: Liberal Arts

Degrees Conferred: AA, AAS, BA, BS, BFA, MA, MS, MBA

Programs of Study: Accounting, Arts, Athletic Training, Biological Science, Business, Chemistry, Communications, Dietetics, Exercise Science, Fine Arts, Finance, Forensic Science, Journalism, Labor Relations, Management, Marketing, Nursing, PreMed, Park Resources, Pathology, Public Relations, Speech.

Women's Athletic Profile

P. O. Box 1360
Huntington, WV 25715
Coach: Steffi Legall
Email: legall@marshall.edu

NCAA I
Thundering Herd, Green, White
Phone: (304) 696-4657
Fax: (304) 696-2325

Estimated # of Women's Volleyball Scholarships: 12

Conference: Mid-American Conference

Program Profile: We have a competitive Division I program in the MAC. We play a very competitive schedule in the Carn Henderson Center that was renovated in 1997 and has 9,043 seats. We play from August to November.

History: We began in 1970. Legall is the 11th coach at MU. We played at the Southern Conference until 1997. While in the Southern Conference, we won 1 regular season and 2 Tournament Titles-including an appearance in the 1995 NCAA Tournament. The program has had 20 win seasons 3 out of the last 4 years.

Achievements: 1995 SC Coach of the Year-Susan Stedman; SC Player of the Year 1995; GTE All-American-Jaki Copeland 1985; Honorable Mention All-MAC 1991-Alisha Bable; We have gone to MAC Tournament for every season since returning in 1997.

Coaching: Steffi Legall, Head Coach, started in 1997. Her record here is 32-32 in two seasons. She graduated from Florida in 1993. She was All-SEC and All-South Region in 1990 and 1991. She was a member of the German National Team in 1986-89 at Bulter prior to MU as an assistant coach for 3 years. Glenna Easterling is assistant coach. She graduated from MU in 1995. She was All-SEC in 1994. She has been Assistant Coach for 4 years.

Freshman Receiving Financial Aid/Academic: **Athletic:** 5

Roster In State: 0	**Out of State:** 11	**Out of Country:** 1
Sophomores on Team: 0	**Seniors on Team:** 3	**Graduation %:** 95%
Most Recent Record: 20-14-0	**Fall Games:** 29	**Spring Games:** 4

Camp of Clinic Dates: July 5-8 High School; July 12-15 Junior High

Positions Needed: 4: Outside Hitters, Middle Blocker, Setter

Schedule: Indiana, Miami-Ohio, Northern Illinois, Ball State, Dayton, University of Wisconsin-Milwaukee

Ohio Valley College
Academic Profile

4501 College Parkway
Parkersburg, WV 26101

Phone: 800-678-6780

Type: Private, 4 Yr.,
Website: http://www.ovc.edu
SAT/ACT/GPA: 850/18/Open
Student/Faculty Ratio: 15:1
Undergraduate Enrollment: 340
Scholarships/Academic: Yes
Expenses By: Semester
Degrees Conferred: AA, BA, BS

Athletic: Yes
In State: $ 5,724

Founded: 1960
Religion: Non-Affiliated
Housing: No
Male/Female: 176:185
Graduate Enrollment: N/A
Financial Aid: Yes
Out of State: $ 5,724

Programs of Study: Business, Accounting, Liberal Studies, Elementary Education, Psychology, Religion

Women's Athletic Profile

4501 College Parkway
Parkersburg, WV 26101
Coach: Paul Jacoby
Email:

NCAA I
Lady Scots, Royal Blue, White
Phone: (304) 485-7384
Fax: (304) 485-3106

Estimated # of Women's Volleyball Scholarships: Varies
Conference: WVIAC
Program Profile: We play in SAC
History: NCAA II second year.
Freshman Receiving Financial Aid/Athletic: 2
Roster In State: 10
Positions Needed: Middle/strong hitter, Setter, Defense
Schedule: Fairmont College, U of Charleston

Seniors on Team: 1

Most Recent Record: 4-26

Salem - Teikyo University
Academic Profile

223 W. Main Street
Salem, WV 26426

Phone: (304) 782-5252

Type: Private, 4 Yr., Liberal Arts, Coed
Website: http://www.stulib.salem-teikyo.wvnet.edu/
SAT/ACT/GPA: 17/2.0
Student/Faculty Ratio: 12:1
Undergraduate Enrollment: 650
Scholarships/Academic: Yes
Expenses By: Year
Specializes In: International Business
Degrees Conferred: AA, AS, BA, AAS, BS, MA

Athletic: Yes
In State: $ 17,049

Founded: 1888
Religion: Non-Affiliated
Housing: Yes
Male/Female: 60:40
Graduate Enrollment: 50
Financial Aid: Yes
Out of State: $ 17,049

Programs of Study: Accounting, Aeronautical Science, Airline Piloting Navigation, Biology, Equestrian Science, Broadcasting, Business Administration, Communications, Computer Science, Criminal Justice, Elementary Education, Engineering Technology, Industrial Engineering, Management, Marketing, Mathematics, Medical Laboratory Technology, Secondary Education

Women's Athletic Profile

Main Street
Salem, WV 26426
Coach: Vickie Bostic
Email: vlbcss@aol.com

NCAA I
Lady Tigers, Green, White
Phone: (304) 782-5394
Fax: (304) 782-5516

Estimated # of Women's Volleyball Scholarships: 6
Conference: West Virginia Intercollegiate Athletic Conference
Program Profile: Rebuilding program to make Volleyball more competitive and successful. Play on the Basketball court in our main gym wood floor.
Freshman Receiving Financial Aid/Academic:
Roster In State: 5
Sophomores on Team:

Out of State: 5
Seniors on Team: 1

Athletic: 4
Out of Country: 0
Graduation %: 98

Most Recent Record: 12-17-0
Positions Needed: Setter, OH, Def. Spec
Schedule: Wheeling- Jesuit, Shepherd College, Univ. of Charleston, Fairmont State

Shepherd College
Academic Profile

Butcher Athletic Center
Shepherdstown, WV 25443

Phone: 800-344-5231

Type: Public, 4 Yr., Liberal Arts, Coed
Website: http://www.shepherd.wvnet.edu
SAT/ACT/GPA: 900/17/2.0
Student/Faculty Ratio: 15:1
Undergraduate Enrollment: 4,500
Scholarships/Academic: Yes   **Athletic:** Yes
Expenses By: Year   **In State:** $ 6,800
Degrees Conferred: AA, AS, AAS, BA, BS, BFA
Programs of Study: All located on wed page over 60 degrees offered.

Founded: 1871
Religion: Non-Affiliated
Housing: Yes
Male/Female: 60:40
Graduate Enrollment: N/A
Financial Aid: Yes
Out of State: $ 9,900

Women's Athletic Profile

James Butcher Center
Shepherdstown, WV 25443
Coach: Lu Kormeluk
Email:

NCAA I
Lady Rams, Blue, Gold
Phone: (304) 876-5481
Fax: (304) 876-3267

Estimated # of Women's Volleyball Scholarships: 4
Conference: West Virginia Intercollegiate Athletic Conference
Program Profile: We play on a brand new floor at the Butcher Athletic Center.
Freshman Receiving Financial Aid/Academic: **Athletic:** 2
Roster In State: 3   **Out of State:** 10   **Out of Country:**
Sophomores on Team: **Seniors on Team:** 3   **Graduation %:** 80%
Most Recent Record: 26-9
Positions Needed: Setter, Left-side hitter, Middle hitter
Schedule: Charleston, Millersville, Wheeling Jesuit, Clarion, Fairmont State, Bridgepost, Indiana U of PA, Mount Olive
Style of Play: We play a 5-1 system, with a rotational defense and a semi quick offense.

University of Charleston
Academic Profile

2300 MacCorkle Avenue SE
Charleston, WV 25304

Phone: 800-995-4682

Type: Private, 4 Yr., Liberal Arts, Coed
Website: http://www.uchaswv.edu
SAT/ACT/GPA: 820/18
Student/Faculty Ratio: 14:1
Undergraduate Enrollment: 1,500
Scholarships/Academic: Yes   **Athletic:** Yes
Expenses By: Year   **In State:** $ 16,000
Degrees Conferred: AA, AS, BA, BS, MBA, MHRM

Founded: 1888
Religion: Non-Affiliated
Housing: Yes
Male/Female: 1:3
Graduate Enrollment: 100
Financial Aid: Yes
Out of State: $ 16,000

Programs of Study: Art, Biology, Chemistry, Education, English, Environmental Science, History, Mathematics, Music, Mass Communication, Political Science, Psychology, Social Science, Sports Science, Sports Medicine, Paralegal Studies, Accounting, Business Administration, Computer Information Systems, Nursing, Radiology, PreProfessional

Women's Athletic Profile

2300 MacCorkle Avenue SE
Charleston, WV 25304
Coach: Bren Stevens
Email: bstevens@uchaswv.edu

NCAA I
Golden Eagles, Maroon, Gold
Phone: (304) 357-4911
Fax: (304) 357-4715

Estimated # of Women's Volleyball Scholarships: N/A
Conference: West Virginia Intercollegiate Athletic Conference

Program Profile: We play in the Eddie King Gymnasium. We were formerly an NAIA member and have been a member of the NCAA II for a four year period. Our team has advanced to the NCAA Regional, three out of the last four years. In 1998 season, we advanced to the Regional Final.

History: The school has a program for seven years, and due to budget cuts, the program was suspended for five years. The program was reinstated in 1987.

Achievements: 1979 WVIAC Conference Title, 1997 WVIAC Conference Champions, 1995 & 1997 WVIAC Coach of the Year.

Coaching: Bren Stevens, Head Coach, started in 1993 to the present with an overall record of 187-55 in six years. Michael Sankoff is our Assistant coach, started in 1997 to the present.

Freshman Receiving Financial Aid/Academic:

		Athletic: 4
Roster In State: 4	**Out of State:** 11	**Out of Country:** 0
Sophomores on Team: 0	**Seniors on Team:** 11	**Graduation %:** 88%
Most Recent Record: 26-11-0	**Fall Games:** 36	**Spring Games:** 0

Camp of Clinic Dates: July 22-26, 2000

Positions Needed: 4

Schedule: Florida Southern, Elon College, Edinboro, Fairmont State, Cal Poly

Style of Play: We run a very balanced attack, which includes our outside, middle and right side attackers. We will utilize a 5-1 offense with multiple styles of defense, which are determined based on our opponents.

West Liberty State College
Academic Profile

P.O. Box 295
West Liberty, WV 26074-0296

Phone: (304) 336-8046

Type: Public, 4 Yr., Liberal Arts, Coed
Website: http://www.wlsc.wvnet.edu
SAT/ACT/GPA: 810/17/2.0
Student/Faculty Ratio: 19:1
Undergraduate Enrollment: 2,475
Scholarships/Academic: Yes

Founded: 1837
Religion: Non-Affiliated
Housing: Yes
Male/Female: 44:56
Graduate Enrollment: N/A
Athletic: Yes **Financial Aid:** Yes

Expenses By: Year **In State:** $ 6,040 **Out of State:** $ 9,480

Specializes In: Liberal Arts & Sciences, Teacher's Education

Degrees Conferred: AA, AS, BA, BS, MA, MS, MBA, Ph.D., JD

Programs of Study: Accounting, Banking/Finance, Biology, Business, Chemistry, Communications, Computer, Criminal, Dental, Nursing, Office, Economics, Education, English, Fashion, Geography, History, Interdisciplinary, Management, Marketing, Mathematics, Medical, Music, Political Science, PreProfessional Programs, Psychology, Public, Special Education

Women's Athletic Profile

Bartlell Fieldhouse
West Liberty, WV 26074
Coach: Missy Tiber
Email: tibermis@wlsc.wvnet.edu

NCAA I
Lady Hilltoppers, Gold, Black
Phone: (304) 336-8844
Fax: (304) 336-8339

Estimated # of Women's Volleyball Scholarships: N/A

Conference: West Virginia Intercollegiate Athletic Conference

Program Profile: West Liberty State has a brand new $10.5 million complex, it seats 1,200 with a state of the art maple wood floor.

History: 1980 Conference Champions, 2000 record most wins in a decade, 2 players All-WVAC, 8th place finish in WVIAC.

Coaching: Melissa Tiber Head Coach for six seasons. Most wins in a season in 2000 of 21. Continues to build a solid program improving each year.

Freshman Receiving Financial Aid/Academic:

		Athletic: 2
Roster In State: 1	**Out of State:** 11	**Seniors on Team:** 3

Most Recent Record: 21-21

Positions Needed: DS, MB, OH, Setter

Schedule: Univ. of Charleston, Wheeling Jesuit Univ.

West Virginia Institute of Technology
Academic Profile

405 Fayette Pike
Montgomery, WV 25136

Phone: 888-554-8324

Type: Public, 4 Yr., Coed
Website: Not Available
SAT/ACT/GPA: 19avg

Founded: 1895
Religion: Non-Affiliated
Housing: Yes

Student/Faculty Ratio: 18:1
Undergraduate Enrollment: 2,650
Scholarships/Academic: Yes   **Athletic:** Yes
Expenses By: Year   **In State:** $ 4,240
Degrees Conferred: AA, AS, BA, BS
Programs of Study: Accounting, Banking/Finance, Biological Science, Business, Chemistry, City/Community/Regional Planning, Computer, Education, Engineering, English, Health, History, Industrial, Music, Management, Nursing, Paper and Pulp Science, Public Administration

Male/Female: 64:36
Graduate Enrollment: 20
Financial Aid: Yes
Out of State: $ 8,410

Women's Athletic Profile

Route 61
Montgomery, WV 25136
Coach: Tim Thomas
Email:

NCAA I
Lady Golden Bears, Gold, Blue
Phone: (304) 442-3286
Fax: (304) 442-3499

Estimated # of Women's Volleyball Scholarships: N/A
Conference: West Virginia Intercollegiate Athletic Conference

West Virginia State College
Academic Profile

Campus Box 181
Institute, WV 25112

Phone: 800-987-2112

Type: Public, 4 Yr., Coed
Website: http://www.wvsc.edu
SAT/ACT/GPA: 700/17
Student/Faculty Ratio: 19:1
Undergraduate Enrollment: 4,500
Scholarships/Academic: Yes   **Athletic:** Yes
Expenses By: Year   **In State:** $ 4,240
Degrees Conferred: AA, AS, AAS, BA, BS
Programs of Study: 17 Bachelor's Degrees offered.

Founded: 1891
Religion: Non-Affiliated
Housing: No
Male/Female: 1:1
Graduate Enrollment: N/A
Financial Aid: Yes
Out of State: $ 8,410

Women's Athletic Profile

Campus Box 181
Institute, WV 25112
Coach: Denise Dietrich
Email:

NCAA I
Lady Hilltoppers, Gold, Black
Phone: (304) 766-3229
Fax: (304) 766-3364

Estimated # of Women's Volleyball Scholarships: N/A
Conference: West Virginia Intercollegiate Athletic Conference

West Virginia University
Academic Profile

P.O. Box 0877
Morgantown, WV 26507

Phone: (304) 293-4811

Type: Public, 4 Yr., Engineering, Coed
Website: http://www.wvu.edu
SAT/ACT/GPA: 950/20/2.25
Student/Faculty Ratio: 16:1
Undergraduate Enrollment: 14,000
Scholarships/Academic: Yes   **Athletic:** Yes
Expenses By: Year   **In State:** $ 7,714
Specializes In: Health & Sciences, Physical Therapy, Education, Business, Engineering
Degrees Conferred: 166 Degrees
Programs of Study: College of Agriculture, Forestry, Consumer Sciences, College of Business & Economics, College of Creative Arts, School of Dentistry, Arts & Sciences, Engineering, School of Medicine, Human Resources & Education, School of Journalism, Law, Nursing, Pharmacy, Physical Education, Social Work

Founded: 1867
Religion: Non-Affiliated
Housing: Yes
Male/Female: 2:1
Graduate Enrollment: 9,000
Financial Aid: Yes
Out of State: $ 12,898

Women's Athletic Profile

Box 0877
Morgantown, WV 26506-6201
Coach: Veronica Hammersmith
Email: uhammer@wvu.edu

NCAA I
Lady Mountaineers, Gold, Blue
Phone: (304) 293-4811
Fax: (304) 293-2525

Estimated # of Women's Volleyball Scholarships: N/A
Conference: Big East Conference
Program Profile: We have a good volleyball program in a very competitive Big East Conference. We compete in the Coliseum that seats 14,000. We have immaculate facilities for our student-athletes. We compete from August to December.
History: The volleyball program began in 1974. Coach Hammersmith has been here all but one year. We played in the Atlantic 10 making it to the NIVC in 1991. We have been in the Big East for four years, qualifying for tournaments the last two years.
Achievements: Coach Hammersmith - Atlantic 10 Coach of the Year 1991; Big East Coach of the Year in 1997
Coaching: Veronica Hammersmith, Head Coach, started here in 1975. Her overall record is 447-365. Lisa Scott Schneider, Assistant Coach, started here in 1987. Previously, she was Northeast All-Region.
Freshman Receiving Financial Aid/Academic: **Athletic:** 3
Roster In State: 1   **Out of State:** 14   **Out of Country:** 0
Sophomores on Team: 4   **Seniors on Team:** 2   **Graduation %:** 100%
Most Recent Record: 15-13-0   **Fall Games:** 28   **Spring Games:** 4
Camp of Clinic Dates: July 18-21 Individual; July 23-25 Team
Positions Needed: 2 Middles, 1 Outside
Schedule: Penn State, Kansas, Oklahoma, Notre Dame, San Jose, Northwestern
Style of Play: Good all around players that work hard, in practice and matches, thus producing an athletic team and good work ethic.

West Virginia Wesleyan College
Academic Profile

59 College Avenue
Buckhannon, WV 26201

Phone: 800-722-9933

Type: Private, 4 Yr., Liberal Arts, Coed
Website: http://www.wvwc.edu
SAT/ACT/GPA: 820/20/2.5
Student/Faculty Ratio: 15:1
Undergraduate Enrollment: 1,600
Scholarships/Academic: Yes
Expenses By: Year

Founded: 1891
Religion: Methodist
Housing: Yes
Male/Female: 45:55
Graduate Enrollment: 100
Athletic: Yes   **Financial Aid:** Yes
In State: $ 21,225   **Out of State:** $ 21,225

Specializes In: Liberal Arts, Business, Biology, Chemistry, Computer Information Sys.
Programs of Study: Art, Accounting, Biology, Business Administration, Chemistry, Computer Information Systems, Computer Science, Communications Studies, Christian Education, Dramatic Arts, Economics, Education, English, Engineering, Environmental Science, Finance, History, International Studies, Management, Marketing, Mathematics, Music, Physical Education, Sports Medicine, Philosophy, Physics, Political Science, Psychology, Public Relations, Religion, Sociology, Nursing

Women's Athletic Profile

College Avenue
Buckannon, WV 26201
Coach: Michael Burch
Email: burch_m@wvwc.edu
Estimated # of Women's Volleyball Scholarships: N/A

NCAA I
Lady Bobcats, Orange, Black
Phone: (304) 473-8219
Fax: (304) 473-8056

Conference: West Virginia Intercollegiate Athletic Conference
Program Profile: Overall Strong Program in Region for all sports. 17 sports for a small private institution. Gymnasium traditional setting, seating 4,000. Certified training program with state of the art facilities.
History: Began in 1987 won conference from 91-97. 95 5th in the country NCAA appearances in 95-97. Always fighting for conference titles.
Achievements: 4 AVCA academic awards. Last year 5th 3.43. 2000 NCAA women of the year for West Virginia.
Coaching: Michael Burch Virginia Tech, Amanda Miller Assistant, Tennessee Tech.
Roster In State: 2   **Out of State:** 7   **Out of Country:**
Sophomores on Team: **Seniors on Team:** 4   **Graduation %:** 100
Positions Needed: ALL
Schedule: Hillsdale, Edinboro, Fairmont, Wheeling Jesuit, Dowling

Style of Play: Very aggressive with non traditional offense. So capability High in the region in serving. Are over 3 aces a game able to show different tempo's in our style of play

Wheeling Jesuit University
Academic Profile

316 Washington Avenue
Wheeling, WV 26003
Type: Private, 4 Yr., Liberal Arts, Coed
Website: http://www.wju.edu
SAT/ACT/GPA: 830/17/2.0
Student/Faculty Ratio: 12:1
Undergraduate Enrollment: 1,329
Scholarships/Academic: Yes   **Athletic:** Yes
Expenses By: Year   **In State:** $ 20,200
Specializes In: Health Sciences, Business, Hi-Tech
Degrees Conferred: BS, BA, MS, MBA, MAAT

Phone: (304) 243-2365

Founded: 1954
Religion: Catholic
Housing: Yes
Male/Female: 1:1.6
Graduate Enrollment: 201
Financial Aid: Yes
Out of State: $ 20,200

Programs of Study: Accounting, Biology, Chemistry, Computer Science, Criminal Justice, Engineering, Environmental Studies, French, History, International Business, Philosophy, Literature, Management, Marketing, Mathematics, Nuclear Medical Technology, Nursing, Physics, Political & Economic Philosophy, Political Science, Professional Writing, Psychology, Respiratory Therapy, Romance, Languages, Spanish, Teacher Prep, Technical Innovation, Theology & Religious Studies, Sports Management, PreMed, PreLaw, PreVet, PreDental, PrePhysical Therapy, Master Degree Programs in Accountancy, Business Administration, Nursing, Applied Theology

Women's Athletic Profile

315 Washington Avenue
Wheeling, WV 26003
Coach: Janet Jaeger
Email: jjaeger@wju.edu

NCAA I
Lady Cardinals, Red, Gold
Phone: (304) 243-2365
Fax: (304) 243-2265

Estimated # of Women's Volleyball Scholarships: 4
Conference: West Virginia Intercollegiate Athletic Conference
Program Profile: Our facilities are top of the line, probably the best in the Conference. We will have a fall and spring season in the 1999-2000 school year. We have a very competitive program and schedule. Our program is rebuilding. We play at Alma Grace McDonough Center which has 2,200 seats.
History: The program began in 1991. We have no history or statistics by the previous coaches. The 1997-1998 record was 30-36. We have a very competitive schedule against the top teams in the Atlantic Region. Rebuilding will continue in the third season.
Achievements: None
Coaching: Janet Jaeger - Head Coach is in her third season and her overall record is 30-36. She played at the University of Cincinnati from 1987-1990. She coached a Cincinnati High School team for 1992-1995 and won the Ohio State Division I Championship in 1995.
Freshman Receiving Financial Aid/Academic: **Athletic:** 2
Roster In State: 3   **Out of State:** 5   **Out of Country:** 0
Sophomores on Team: 2   **Seniors on Team:** 2   **Graduation %:** 100%
Most Recent Record: 12-21-0   **Fall Games:** 33   **Spring Games:** 0
Positions Needed: (2) Middle Hitters, (2) Left Side Hitters, (2) All-Around Players
Schedule: Ashland, Charleston-West Virginia, University of Indianapolis, Ferris State, Northwood, University of Wisconsin-Parkside
Style of Play: We have quick paced offenses and emphasize defense. We have a variety of offensive plays that spread out the opposition's blockers and create one-on-one situations.

WISCONSIN

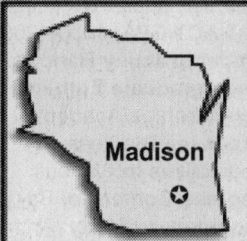

Madison

SCHOOL	CITY	AFFILIATION	PAGE
Beloit College	Beloit	NCAA III	807
Cardinal Stritch College	Milwaukee	NAIA	807
Carroll College	Waukesha	NCAA III	808
Carthage College	Kenosha	NCAA III	809
Concordia University	Mequon	NCAA III	809
Edgewood College	Madison	NCAA III	810
Lakeland College	Sheboygan	NCAA III	811
Lawrence University	Appleton	NCAA III	811
Maranatha Baptist Bible College	Watertown	NCAA III	812
Marian College of Fond du Lac	Fond du Lac	NCAA III/NAIA	812
Marquette University	Milwaukee	NCAA I	813
Milwaukee School of Engineering	Milwaukee	NCAA III	813
Northland College	Ashland	NCAA III/NAIA	814
Ripon College	Ripon	NCAA III	814
Saint Norbert College	De Pere	NCAA III	815
Univ of Wisconsin - Eau Claire	Eau Claire	NCAA III	816
Univ of Wisconsin - Green Bay	Green Bay	NCAA I	816
Univ of Wisconsin - La Crosse	LA Crosse	NCAA III	817
Univ of Wisconsin - Madison	Madison	NCAA I	817
Univ of Wisconsin - Milwaukee	Milwaukee	NCAA I	818
Univ of Wisconsin - Oshkosh	Oshkosh	NCAA III	819
Univ of Wisconsin - Parkside	Kenosha	NCAA II/NAIA	819
Univ of Wisconsin - Platteville	Platteville	NCAA III	820
Univ of Wisconsin - River Falls	River Falls	NCAA III	820
Univ of Wisconsin - Stevens Point	Stevens Point	NCAA III	821
Univ of Wisconsin - Stout	Menomonie	NCAA III	821
Univ of Wisconsin - Superior	Superior	NCAA III	822
Univ of Wisconsin - Whitewater	Whitewater	NCAA III	823
Viterbo College	La Crosse	NAIA	823
Wisconsin Lutheran College	Milwaukee	NCAA III	824

Beloit College
Academic Profile

700 College Street
Beloit, WI 53511

Phone: 800-356-0751

Type: Private, 4 Yr., Liberal Arts, Coed
Website: http://www.stu.beloit.edu.
SAT/ACT/GPA: 1050-1200/25
Student/Faculty Ratio: 12:1
Undergraduate Enrollment: 1,100
Scholarships/Academic: Yes
Expenses By: Year
Specializes In: Various
Degrees Conferred: Ba, BS

Founded: 1846
Religion: Non-Affiliated
Housing: Yes
Male/Female: 40:60
Graduate Enrollment: N/A
Athletic: No   **Financial Aid:** Yes
In State: $ 24,096   **Out of State:** $ 24,096

Programs of Study: Art, Art History, Asian Studies, Biochemistry, Biology, Business & Management, Cell Biology, Chemistry, Communications, Comparative Literature, Computer Science, Creative Writing, Economics, Education, English, Environmental Biology, German, Journalism, Mathematics, Molecular Biology, Music, Philosophy, Physics, Political Science, PreDentistry, PreLaw, PreMed, Psychology, Religion, Social Science

Women's Athletic Profile

700 College Street
Beloit, WI 53511
Coach: Vanessa MacCallum
Email: maccallu@beloit.edu

NCAA I
Lady Buccaneers, Gold, Navy
Phone: (608) 363-2236
Fax: (608) 363-2044

Estimated # of Women's Volleyball Scholarships: N/A
Conference: Midwest Conference
Program Profile: We are a very young and talented volleyball team that has taken steps toward the top of the Midwest Conference in 1998. We finished the season with a 12-17 mark in 1998.
History: The Buccaneers earned Midwest Conference wins over Carroll, 3-2 and Lawrence, 3-2 and put themselves in a position to win the North Division title over St. Norbert in 1998.
Achievements: Midwest Conference Champions in 1995 and 1998; North Division Title in 1998; Monica King - All-MWC first team in 1998.
Coaching: Head Coach Vanessa MacCallum
Roster In State: 3   **Out of State:** 13   **Out of Country:** 0
Sophomores on Team: **Seniors on Team:** 4   **Graduation %:** 100
Most Recent Record: 9-27-0
Positions Needed: Setter, MB

Cardinal Stritch College
Academic Profile

6801 N. Yates Rd.
Milwaukee, WI 53217

Phone: (414) 410-4125

Type: Private, 4 Yr., Liberal Arts, Coed
Website: http://www.stritch.edu
SAT/ACT/GPA: 20/2.5
Student/Faculty Ratio: 15:1
Undergraduate Enrollment: 1,100
Scholarships/Academic: Yes
Expenses By: Year
Specializes In: Liberal Arts
Degrees Conferred: AA, AS, BA, MA, MS, MBA, BS

Founded: 1937
Religion: Roman Catholic
Housing: Yes
Male/Female: 40:60
Graduate Enrollment: 4,400
Athletic: Yes   **Financial Aid:** Yes
In State: $ 15,400   **Out of State:** $ 15,400

Programs of Study: Accounting, Art, Biology, Business, Chemistry, Computer Science, Communications, Education, English, French, History, Mathematics, Music, Nursing, Psychology, Public Relations, Sociology, Spanish, Special Education, Theatre

Men's Athletic Profile

6801 N. Yates
Milwaukee, WI 53217
Coach: Cindi Maier
Email:

NAIA
Crusaders/Maroon, Silver
Phone: (414) 410-4121
Fax: (414) 410-4127

Estimated # of Men's Volleyball Scholarships: 5
Conference: Chicagoland Collegiate Athletic Conference
Program Profile: We will need a whole new team next year.
History: In the early 1990's our program was very good. Now, we will get a complete rebuilding.
Achievements: Many All-Conference and Academic All-Americans
Coaching: Cindi Maier Head Coach. Jennifer Wehr Assistant Coach.

Roster In State: 5	**Out of State:** 4	**Out of Country:** 0

Graduation %: 80%
Most Recent Record: 3-25
Positions Needed: All

Women's Athletic Profile

6801 N. Yates Rd.
Milwaukee, WI 53217
Coach: Cindi Maier
Email:

NCAA I
Lady Crusaders, Maroon, Silver
Phone: (414) 410-4121
Fax: (414) 410-4127

Estimated # of Women's Volleyball Scholarships: 5
Conference: Chicagoland Collegiate Athletic Conference
History: The program began in the early 1990's and we competed very well. Now we are getting a complete rebuilding.
Achievements: Many All-Conference and Academic All-Americans.
Coaching: Cindi Maier - Head Coach. Jennifer Wehr Assistant Coach.

Roster In State: 5	**Out of State:** 4	**Out of Country:** 0
Sophomores on Team: 0	**Seniors on Team:** 3	**Graduation %:** 80

Most Recent Record: 3-25-0
Positions Needed: All

Carroll College
Academic Profile

100 N. East Avenue
Waukesha, WI 53186

Phone: 800-227-7655

Type: Private, 4 Yr., Liberal Arts, Coed
Website: http://www.cc.edu
SAT/ACT/GPA: Required
Student/Faculty Ratio: 20:1
Undergraduate Enrollment: 2,445
Scholarships/Academic: Yes

Founded: 1841
Religion: Presbyterian Church
Housing: Yes
Male/Female: 1:2
Graduate Enrollment: 80

Athletic: No
In State: $ 18,140

Financial Aid: Yes
Out of State: $ 18,140

Expenses By: Year
Specializes In: Biology, Business, Chemistry, Nursing, Physical Therapy
Degrees Conferred: BA, BS, BSMT, BSN, BS(Nursing), MS(Physical Therapy), M Ed
Programs of Study: Accounting, Art, Athletic Training, Biology, Business Administration, Chemistry, Coaching, Communication, Computer Science, Criminal Justice, Education (Early Childhood, Elementary, Secondary, Masters in Education), English, Environmental Science, Fitness Management, French, Geography, German, Graphic Communication, Health Science, History, Human Services, International Relations, Journalism. Land-use Planning, Marine Biology, Mathematics, Medical Technology, Music, Nursing, Photography, Physical Education, Physical Therapy, Physics, Politics, Public Administration, Psychology, Religious Studies, Sociology, Spanish, Theatre Arts, Women's Studies. PreProfessional (PreDental, PreEngineering, PreLaw, PreMed, PreMinistry, PreVet)

Women's Athletic Profile

100 N. East Avenue
Waukesha, WI 53186
Coach: David McIntyre
Email: ccinfo@ccadmin.cc.edu

NCAA I
Pioneers, Orange, White, Navy
Phone: (414) 524-1211
Fax: (414) 524-7139

Estimated # of Women's Volleyball Scholarships: 0
Conference: Midwest Conference
Program Profile: Matches are played in Van Male Gymnasium which seats 2,500 people. Playing season is August to November (16 playing dates). Varsity and JV teams include approximately 24 total athletes.
Achievements: 8 All-Conference players in the past 3 years; 1 GTE All-Academic 3rd team member; 11 Academic All-Conference players in the past 2 years.

Coaching: David MacIntyre, Head Coach, started in the 1997 season. His overall record is 26-36. He has played for 15 years and was a 2 time All-Conference Setter in high school. He has 2 tournament MVP's with Hope College Men's Club Team. He is a member of Athletes in Action Volleyball Mission project to the Philippine Islands.

Freshman Receiving Financial Aid/Academic: **Athletic:** 0

Roster In State: 14	**Out of State:** 4	**Out of Country:** 0
Sophomores on Team: 0	**Seniors on Team:** 2	**Graduation %:** Unknown
Most Recent Record: 11-21-0	**Fall Games:** 32	**Spring Games:** 0

Positions Needed: Setter, Middle Blocker

Schedule: University of Wisconsin-Whitewater, University of Wisconsin-Plateville, North Central College, Edgewood College, University of Wisconsin-La Crosse

Style of Play: We like to play a quicker, more aggressive style. Quick tempo sets are stressed throughout the offense. Tough defense, especially our perimeter coverage, is also a strength.

Carthage College
Academic Profile

2001 Alford Park Drive
Kennosha, WI 53140

Phone: 262-551-6000

Type: Private, 4 Yr., Liberal Arts, Coed
Website: http://www.carthage.edu
SAT/ACT/GPA: Look upon individual basis
Student/Faculty Ratio: 16:1
Undergraduate Enrollment: 1,500
Scholarships/Academic: Yes   **Athletic:** No
Expenses By: Year   **In State:** $ 20,690

Founded: 1847
Religion: Lutheran
Housing: Yes
Male/Female: 52:48
Graduate Enrollment: 100
Financial Aid: Yes
Out of State: $ 20,690

Specializes In: Business, Education, Sciences

Degrees Conferred: BA

Programs of Study: Accounting, Art, Athletic Training, Biology, Biological Science, Business, Chemistry, Conservatory, Criminal Justice, Design, Economics, Education, English, Languages, Geography, Health, History, Marketing, Mathematics, Music, Natural Science, Pharmacy, Religion, Secondary Education, Speech

Women's Athletic Profile

2001 Alford Park Drive
Kenosha, WI 53140
Coach: Nancy Paulson
Email: paulson@carthage.edu

NCAA I
Lady Reds, Red, White, Black
Phone: (414) 551-6681
Fax: (414) 551-5995

Estimated # of Women's Volleyball Scholarships: N/A

Conference: College Conference of Illinois & Wisconsin

Program Profile: Our season extends from August 22 to November 15.

History: In 1975, we were two-time Conference champions. We made an appearance in 1990 in the NCAA III Championship.

Achievements: Player two-time NAIA All-American

Coaching: Nancy Paulson, Head Coach, began our program in 1997. Her overall record is 12-61. Terry Paulson, Assistant Coach.

Roster In State: 4	**Out of State:** 12	**Out of Country:** 0
Sophomores on Team: 14	**Seniors on Team:** 2	**Graduation %:** Unknown
Most Recent Record: 8-29-0	**Fall Games:** 22	**Spring Games:** 4

Camp of Clinic Dates: July/August

Positions Needed: Middle Hitter, Setter

Schedule: Elmhurst, Illinois Wesleyan, U.W. Whitewater, St. Norbert, Lake Forest, St. Mary's

Style of Play: Athletic and aggressive

Concordia University - Wisconsin
Academic Profile

12800 N. Lake Shore Drive
Mequon, WI 53097

Phone: 262-243-5700

Type: Private, 4 Yr., Liberal Arts, Coed
Website: http://www.cuw.edu
SAT/ACT/GPA: 21+
Student/Faculty Ratio: 19:1

Founded: 1881
Religion: Lutheran
Housing: Yes
Male/Female: 42:58

Undergraduate Enrollment: 3,833
Scholarships/Academic: Yes   **Athletic:** No
Expenses By: Year   **In State:** $ 17,250
Degrees Conferred: Associates, Masters, Bachelor

Graduate Enrollment: 708
Financial Aid: Yes
Out of State: $ 17,250

Programs of Study: Art, Accounting, Athletic Training, Biblical Languages, Biology, Business, Computer Science, Early Childhood, Economics, Elementary Education, English, Exercise Leadership, Exercise Physiology, Finance, Graphic Design, History, Humanities, Individualized Interior Design, Justice and Public Police, Lay Ministry, Management, Marketing Mass Communications, Mathematics, Missions, Music, Nursing, Occupational Therapy, Organizational Communications, Paralegal, Pastoral Ministry, Physical Education, Psychology, Radiological Technology, Secondary Education, Social Work, Spanish, Speech Communication, Telecasting, Theology

Women's Athletic Profile

12800 N. Lakeshore
Mequon, WI 53097
Coach: Joe Cawley
Email:

NCAA I
Lady Falcons, Blue, White
Phone: 262-243-4559
Fax:

Estimated # of Women's Volleyball Scholarships: N/A
Conference: Lake Michigan Conference

Edgewood College
Academic Profile

855 Woodrow Street
Madison, WI 53711

Phone: 608-663-2294

Type: Private, 4 Yr., Liberal Arts, Coed
Website: http://www.edgewood.edu
SAT/ACT/GPA: 850/18/2.5
Student/Faculty Ratio: 14:1
Undergraduate Enrollment: 1,000
Scholarships/Academic: Yes   **Athletic:** No
Expenses By: Year   **In State:** $ 14,000
Degrees Conferred: BS, BS, MBA, AA, MAE, MARS, MANA

Founded: 1927
Religion: Catholic
Housing: Yes
Male/Female: 1:3
Graduate Enrollment: 1,000
Financial Aid: Yes
Out of State: $ 14,000

Programs of Study: Accounting, Art, Art Therapy, Biology, Broad Fields Science, Business, Chemistry, Child Life, Computer Information Systems, Criminal Justice, CytoTechnology, Economics, Elementary Education, English, Graphic Design, History, International Relations, Mathematics, Music, Medical Technology, Nursing, Political Science, Psychology, Public Policy and Administration, Religion, Sociology, PreDentistry, PreLaw, PreMed, PrePharmacy, PreEngineering

Women's Athletic Profile

855 Woodrow Street
Madison, WI 53711
Coach: Sue Gerenstein
Email: sgerenstein@edgewood.edu

NCAA I
Lady Eagles, Red, Black
Phone: (608) 257-4861
Fax: (608) 663-6703

Estimated # of Women's Volleyball Scholarships: N/A
Conference: Lake Michigan Conference
Program Profile: Our home court is called "The Edgedome". We have a state-of-the art flooring system and a capacity for 1,100. Our season starts in late August and goes to early November. Our spring season consists of four weeks.
History: The program began in 1988. Records exist since 1991. Our overall record is 162-124. We reached NAIA District in 1991, 1992, & 1993. We went to the NAIA Regional in 1994. We got NCAA affiliation in 1995.
Achievements: Conference Champions in 1996; Conference Tournament Champions in 1994, 1995 & 1996.
Coaching: Sue Gerenstein, Head Coach, took over the program in 1997. Her record at Edgewood, after two seasons, was 32-37. Her overall career record is 88-100. Gary Paul and Scott Blackmon are Assistant Coaches.
Freshman Receiving Financial Aid/Academic: **Athletic:** 0
Roster In State: 12   **Out of State:** 1   **Out of Country:** 0
Sophomores on Team: 0   **Seniors on Team:** 6   **Graduation %:** 75-80
Most Recent Record: 18-16-0 **Fall Games:** 34   **Spring Games:** 2-4
Camp of Clinic Dates: July
Positions Needed: Middles, Lefts, Setter
Schedule: Winona, University of Wisconsin-Oshkosh, University of Wisconsin-Platteville, Marian College
Style of Play: Aggressive along net, team effort, multiple attackers and hard nosed.

Lakeland College
Academic Profile

P. O. Box 359
Sheboygan, WI 53082-0359

Phone: (920) 565-1512

Type: Private, 4 Yr., Liberal Arts, Coed
Website: http://www.lakeland.edu
SAT/ACT/GPA: 182.0
Student/Faculty Ratio: 15:1
Undergraduate Enrollment: 800
Scholarships/Academic: Yes
Expenses By: Year
Specializes In: Business and Education
Degrees Conferred: BA, MA

Athletic: No
In State: $ 16,500

Founded: 1862
Religion:
Housing: Yes
Male/Female: 1:1
Graduate Enrollment: N/A
Financial Aid: Yes
Out of State: $ 16,500

Programs of Study: Accounting, Anthropology, Art, Biology, Broad Field Social Science, Business Administration, Chemistry, Church Music, Criminal Justice, Communication, Computer Science, Early Childhood/Elementary Education, Coaching, Economics, Elementary/Middle School Education, English, English as a Second Language, Ethnic & Gender Studies, Exercise Science/Sports Studies, French, General Education, German, History, Hospitality Management, International Business, Japanese, Liberal Arts, Marketing, Mathematics, Philosophy, Physics, Political Science, Religion, Science, Secondary/Middle School Professional Sequence, Sociology, Spanish, Specialized Administration, Theatre and Speech, Writing, Athletic Training compromise 80% of students.

Women's Athletic Profile

P. O. Box 359
Sheboygan, WI 53082-0359
Coach: Chad Schreiber
Email: schreibercp@lakeland.edu

NCAA I
Muskies, Navy, Gold, White
Phone: (920) 565-1232
Fax: (920) 565-1399

Estimated # of Women's Volleyball Scholarships: 0
Conference: Lake Michigan
Program Profile: We are a competitive intercollegiate program playing nationally ranked competitors. We compete in a Fall traditional season followed by a Spring non-traditional season. Our conference receives an NCAA automatic bid. Competition takes place in the large, 3 court Todd Wehr Center.
History: We started competing in the early 1970's and saw some early success. In the mid 1990's, we saw a revitalization and we're back at the top of the program. We are now expecting regular appearances in the NCAA tournaments.
Achievements: Have finished 2nd in conference each of the past 3 seasons, and had at least 20 wins. Have had at least 3 All-Conference players each of the past 4 years.
Coaching: Chad Schreiber, Head Coach, since 1995. His overall record is 47-87. He led the men's program to a 9th place finish. He was a 3 time All-Conference Setter when he attended the University of Wisconsin-Oshkosh. Jodi Downs is Assistant Coach. She is a former All-American and a National Runner-up from the University of Wisconsin-Oshkosh.
Freshman Receiving Financial Aid/Academic:

Athletic: 0

Roster In State: 15
Sophomores on Team:
Most Recent Record: 22-12-0
Positions Needed: All

Out of State: 7
Seniors on Team: 3

Out of Country: 0
Graduation %: 98

Schedule: University of Wisconsin-River Falls, Illinois Wesleyan, University of Wisconsin-Oshkosh, University of Wisconsin-Stevens Point, Elmhurst, Marian
Style of Play: Aggressive hard swinging offense. Score on tough serving leading to easy transition points. Quick middle attack with high outside ball. Not one superstar, different leader every night.

Lawrence University
Academic Profile

P.O. Box 599
Appleton, WI 54912-0599

Phone: 800-227-0982

Type: Private, 4 Yr., Liberal Arts, Coed
Website: http://www.lawrence.edu
SAT/ACT/GPA: Open
Student/Faculty Ratio: 11:1
Undergraduate Enrollment: 1,350
Scholarships/Academic: Yes

Athletic: No

Founded: 1847
Religion: Non-Affiliated
Housing: Yes
Male/Female: 47:53
Graduate Enrollment: N/A
Financial Aid: Yes

In State: $ 21,054   **Out of State:** $ 21,054

Expenses By: Year
Specializes In: Liberal Arts, Education
Degrees Conferred: BA, BM
Programs of Study: Anthropology, Art History, Art Studio, Biology, Chemistry, Classics, Computer Science, East Asian Languages & Culture, Economics, English, French, Geology, German, Government, History, Mathematics, Music, Natural Science, Philosophy, Physics, Psychology, Religious Studies, Slavic, Spanish, Theatre & Drama, Business, PreLaw, PreMed, Engineering

Women's Athletic Profile

P.O. Box 599
Appleton, WI 54912
Coach: Kim Tatro
Email: kimberly.n.tatro@lawrence.edu

NCAA I
Lady Vikings, Navy, White
Phone: (920) 832-6975
Fax: (920) 832-7349

Estimated # of Women's Volleyball Scholarships: N/A
Conference: Midwest Conference

Maranatha Baptist Bible College
Academic Profile

745 West Main
Watertown, WI 53094

Phone: 920-261-9300

Type: Private, 4 Yr., Coed
Website: Not Available
SAT/ACT/GPA: Open
Student/Faculty Ratio: 20:1
Undergraduate Enrollment: 475
Expenses By: Year
Degrees Conferred: Bachelors, Masters

Founded: 1968
Religion: Non-Affiliated
Housing: Yes
Male/Female: 50:50
Graduate Enrollment: 20

In State: $ 8,000   **Out of State:** $ 8,000

Programs of Study: Biblical Studies, Biblical Languages, Business, Early Childhood Education, Education, Elementary Education, Humanities, Liberal Arts, Management, Ministries, Music, Nursing, Physical Education, Religion, Secondary Education, Speech, Sports Administration, Theology

Women's Athletic Profile

745 W. Main
Watertown, WI 53094
Coach: Marsha Jackson
Email: mjackson@mbbc.edu

NCAA I
Lady Crusaders, Blue, Gold
Phone: (920) 206-2351
Fax: (920) 261-9109

Estimated # of Women's Volleyball Scholarships: N/A
Conference: Independent

Marian College - Fond du Lac
Academic Profile

45 S. National Avenue
Fond Du Lac, WI 54935

Phone: 800-262-7426

Type: Private, 4 Yr., Liberal Arts, Coed
Website: http://www.marian.edu
SAT/ACT/GPA: 20
Student/Faculty Ratio: 15:1
Undergraduate Enrollment: 1,800
Scholarships/Academic: Yes   **Athletic:** No
Expenses By: Year   **In State:** $ 13,000
Specializes In: Nursing

Founded: 1936
Religion: Catholic
Housing: Yes
Male/Female: 40:60
Graduate Enrollment: 600
Financial Aid: Yes
Out of State: $ 13,000

Degrees Conferred: BA, BS, BBA, BSEd, BSN, MA
Programs of Study: Accounting, Art, Biology, Business Administration, Chemistry, Communications, Criminal Justice, CytoTechnology, Education, English, Environmental Science, History, Human Development, Human Services, Liberal Arts, Management, Marketing, Mathematics, Medical Technology, Music, Nursing, PreDentistry, PreLaw, PreMed, PreVet, Psychology, Radiological Technology, Science, Social Science, Sport Administration

Women's Athletic Profile

45 S. National Avenue
Fond du Lac, WI 54935
Coach: Doug Hammonds
Email:

NCAA I
Lady Sabres, Blue, White
Phone: (920) 923-7627
Fax: (920) 923-8134

Estimated # of Women's Volleyball Scholarships: N/A
Conference: Lake Michigan Conference

Marquette University
Academic Profile

P.O. Box 1881
Milwaukee, WI 53201-1881

Phone: (800) 222-6544

Type: Private, 4 Yr., Liberal Arts, Engineering, Coed
Website: http://www.marquette.edu
SAT/ACT/GPA: 1040/23
Student/Faculty Ratio: 15:1
Undergraduate Enrollment: 10,610
Scholarships/Academic: Yes   **Athletic:** Yes
Expenses By: Year   **In State:** $ 21,150

Founded: 1881
Religion: Catholic-Jesuit
Housing: Yes
Male/Female: 48:52
Graduate Enrollment: 3,500
Financial Aid: Yes
Out of State: $ 21,150

Specializes In: Engineering, Physical Therapy, Business Administration, Nursing
Degrees Conferred: BA, MS, Law Degree, Ph.D., AA, BBE, BCE, BIE, BSN
Programs of Study: African-American Studies, Classical Languages, English, French, German, History, Philosophy, Spanish, Theology, BioChemistry, Biology, Chemistry, Physics, Computational Math, Computer Science, Mathematics & Statistics, Anthropology, Criminology, Political Science, Psychology, Social Work, Accounting, Finance, International Business, Advertising, Journalism, Public Relations, Theatre Arts, Elementary & Secondary Education, BioMedical Engineering, Civil & Environmental Engineering, Electrical and Computer Engineering, Mechanical Engineering, Physical Therapy, Speech Pathology and Audiology, Nursing, Industrial Engineering, Medical Laboratory Technology

Women's Athletic Profile

North Rd.
Milwaukee, WI 53201-1881
Coach: Laura Farina
Email: farinal@marquette.edu

NCAA I
Lady Golden Eagles, Blue, Gold
Phone: (800) 222-6544
Fax: (414) 288-7302

Estimated # of Women's Volleyball Scholarships: 4
Conference: Conference USA
Program Profile: We are members of the 12 team Conference USA. The team plays matches in Marquette Gym which has a capacity of 3,500, including an excellent training room and weight room .
History: Marquette first fielded a women's volleyball team in 1975. The team began playing a Division I schedule in 1986. Marquette was an inagural member of Conference USA which started in 1995.
Coaching: Laura Farina, Head Coach, started in 1999. She was an All-American at Illinois. She was assistant coach at Michigan State for six years. During that time, MSU took part in 5 NCAA tournaments. Farina coached four All-Americans. Courtney Debolt and Matt Darling are Assistant Coaches.
Freshman Receiving Financial Aid/Academic: **Athletic:** 10
Roster In State: 0   **Out of State:** 100%   **Out of Country:** 10%
Sophomores on Team: 2   **Seniors on Team:** 1   **Graduation %:** 98
Most Recent Record: 10-19-0   **Fall Games:** 30-35   **Spring Games:** TBD
Camp of Clinic Dates: July
Positions Needed: Middle, Outside, Hitter
Schedule: Florida, Wisconsin, Louisville, South Florida, Purdue

Milwaukee School of Engineering
Academic Profile

1025 N. Broadway
Milwaukee, WI 53202-3109
Type: Private, 4 Yr., Engineering, Coed
Website: http://www.msoe.edu

Phone: 800-332-6763

Founded: 1903
Religion: Non-Affiliated

SAT/ACT/GPA: Open
Student/Faculty Ratio: 15:1
Undergraduate Enrollment: 2,500
Scholarships/Academic: Yes   **Athletic:** No
Expenses By: Year   **In State:** $ 18,000
Degrees Conferred: 10 Engineering Majors, Business, Nursing
Programs of Study: Business & Management, Engineering, Engineering Technology, Nursing, Technical Communications

Housing: Yes
Male/Female: 5:1
Graduate Enrollment: 500
Financial Aid: Yes
Out of State: $ 18,000

Women's Athletic Profile

1025 N. Broadway
Milwaukee, WI 53202
Coach: Marty Stufflebeam
Email:

NCAA I
Lady Raiders, Cardinal, White
Phone: (414) 277-7230
Fax: (414) 221-0610

Estimated # of Women's Volleyball Scholarships: N/A
Conference: Lake Michigan Conference

Northland College
Academic Profile

1411 Ellis Avenue
Ashland, WI 54806

Phone: (715) 682-1224

Type: Private, 4 Yr., Liberal Arts, Coed
Website: http://www.northland.edu
SAT/ACT/GPA: 920/19
Student/Faculty Ratio: 16:1
Undergraduate Enrollment: 900
Scholarships/Academic: Yes   **Athletic:** No
Expenses By: Year   **In State:** $ 17,715
Specializes In: Environmental Education
Degrees Conferred: BA, BS

Founded: 1892
Religion: Church of Christ
Housing: Yes
Male/Female: 45:55
Graduate Enrollment: N/A
Financial Aid: Yes
Out of State: $ 17,715

Programs of Study: Biology, Business Administration, Business Economics, Chemistry, Computer Science, Conflict and Peacemaking, Earth Sciences, Economics, Elementary Education, English, Environmental Studies, Fine Arts, Geology, History, Information Science, Management and Leadership, Mathematics, Meteorology , Music, Natural Resources, Occupational Therapy, Outdoor Education, Parks & Recreation, Physics, Policy Studies, PreDental, PreLaw, PreMed, Psychology, Public Administration, Religion, Secondary Education, Social Science, Sociology and Writing.

Women's Athletic Profile

1411 Ellis Avenue
Ashland, WI 54806
Coach: Rob Robinson
Email: admit@wakefield.northland.edu

NCAA I
Lumberjills, Blue, Orange
Phone: (715) 682-1224
Fax: (715) 682-1258

Estimated # of Women's Volleyball Scholarships: Yes
Conference: Independent
History: We started in 1970.
Achievements: NSCAA Champions in 1982, 1989, 1992
Coaching: Rob Robinson, Head Coach, started in 1998.
Freshman Receiving Financial Aid/Academic: **Athletic:** 1
Roster In State: 3   **Out of State:** 4   **Out of Country:** 1
Sophomores on Team: 0   **Seniors on Team:** 2   **Graduation %:** Unknown
Most Recent Record: 5-24-0   **Fall Games:** 29   **Spring Games:** 0
Positions Needed: All
Schedule: College of St. Scholastic, University of Wisconsin-Stevens Point, University of Wisconsin-Eau Claire, Hamline University

Ripon College
Academic Profile

300 Seward Street, P. O. Box 248
Ripon, WI 54971-0248

Phone: (800) 947-4766

Type: Private, 4 Yr., Liberal Arts, Coed
Website: http://www.ripon.edu

Founded: 1851
Religion: Non-Affiliated

SAT/ACT/GPA: 1140/24-25/3.20-3.30

Student/Faculty Ratio: 10:1

Undergraduate Enrollment: 700

Scholarships/Academic: Yes   **Athletic:** No

Expenses By: Year   **In State:** $ 22,640

Specializes In: Economics, Education, Fine Arts, Liberal Arts, History, Politics

Degrees Conferred: BA

Housing: Yes

Male/Female: 50:50

Graduate Enrollment: N/A

Financial Aid: Yes

Out of State: $ 22,640

Programs of Study: Anthropology, Biology, Business Management, Chemistry, Computer Science, Economics, Educational Studies, English, Environmental Studies, Foreign Languages, French, German, Global Studies, History, Latin American Studies, Letters/Literature, Life Sciences, Mathematics, Music, Philosophy, Physical Education, Physical Sciences, Physics, Politics & Government, PreProfessional (Dentistry, Law, Medicine, Physical Therapy, Veterinary,), Psychology, Science, Self-Designed Majors, Sociology/Anthropology, Spanish, Speech Communication, Theatre

Women's Athletic Profile

300 Seward Street

Ripon, WI 54971

Coach: Kelly Witte

Email: wittek@mail.ripon.edu

NCAA I

Red Hawks, Red, White, Black

Phone: (920) 748-8771

Fax: (920) 748-7386

Estimated # of Women's Volleyball Scholarships: N/A

Conference: Midwest Conference

Program Profile: There are ten schools in our conference.

Roster In State: 15   **Out of State:** 3   **Out of Country:** 0

Sophomores on Team: 0   **Seniors on Team:** 1   **Graduation %:** 95

Most Recent Record: 14-18-0   **Fall Games:** 36   **Spring Games:** 0

Positions Needed: Outside Hitter, Middle Hitter

Schedule: UW-Eau Claire, UW-Oshkosh, UW-Platteville, UW-Lacrosse, UW-River Falls, University of Dubuque

Style of Play: Solid defense set our offense up for quick kills.

Saint Norbert College
Academic Profile

100 Grant St.

DePere, WI 54115

Phone: 800-236-4878

Type: Private, 4 Yr., Liberal Arts, Coed

Website: http://www.snc.edu

SAT/ACT/GPA: No requirements

Student/Faculty Ratio: 14:1

Undergraduate Enrollment: 2,050

Scholarships/Academic: Yes   **Athletic:** No

Expenses By: Year   **In State:** $ 19,700

Specializes In: International Business, Education

Degrees Conferred: BA, BS

Founded: 1898

Religion: Roman Catholic

Housing: Yes

Male/Female: 45:55

Graduate Enrollment: 25

Financial Aid: Yes

Out of State: $ 19,700

Programs of Study: Biology, Business, Chemistry, Communications, International Studies, Business, Mathematics, PreDentistry, PreLaw, PreMed, Psychology, plus the usual Liberal Arts majors

Women's Athletic Profile

100 Grant Street

De Pere, WI 54115

Coach: Lori Sadewater

Email: admit@Mail.SNC.Edu

NCAA I

Green Knights, Green, Gold

Phone: (920) 403-3150

Fax: (920) 403-4073

Estimated # of Women's Volleyball Scholarships: N/A

Conference: Midwest Conference

Program Profile: The team plays in the Hoft Arena at the Schuldes Sports Center that seats 2,000. The team plays a 30 match regular season.

History: The volleyball program began in 1974. The team entered in the WIC - WAC Conference and won 3rd place in the Conference. In 16 years, the team has clinched a place 15 times, including 6 championships.

Achievements: Betty Roberts - 1986 1st team All-American, 1987 3rd team All-American; 1994 Academic All-District V; 1997 and 1998 team placed on Midwest Conference North Division Champion.

Coaching: Lori Sadewater, Head Coach, has an SNC career record of 81-34. As a player at Beloit College, she was named All-Conference, MVP captain of the team and Offensive Player of the Year. Ehen Erhard, Assistant Coach, is entering her third year with the program. Kurt Whitney, Volunteer Coach, is entering his first year with the program.

Freshman Receiving Financial Aid/Academic:

		Athletic: 0
Roster In State: 10	**Out of State:** 2	**Out of Country:** 0
Sophomores on Team: 0	**Seniors on Team:** 4	**Graduation %:** Unknown
Most Recent Record: 26-8-0	**Fall Games:** 34	**Spring Games:** 0

Positions Needed: Setter, Defense, Specialist
Schedule: Wisconsin-Stevens Point, Wisconsin-Eau Claire, Wisconsin-LaCrosse, Marian, Wisconsin-Oshkosh, Illinois Benedictine

University of Wisconsin - Eau Claire
Academic Profile

105 Garfield Ave.
Eau Claire, WI 54701

Phone: 715-836-5415

Type: Public, 4 Yr., Liberal Arts, Coed
Website: http://www.uwec.edu
SAT/ACT/GPA: Top half of class; 17 HS units
Student/Faculty Ratio: 20:1
Undergraduate Enrollment: 10,158
Scholarships/Academic: Yes   **Athletic:** No
Expenses By: Year   **In State:** $ 6,731

Founded: 1916
Religion: Non-Affiliated
Housing: Yes
Male/Female: 40:60
Graduate Enrollment: 516
Financial Aid: Yes
Out of State: $13,381

Specializes In: Nursing, Fine Arts, Education
Degrees Conferred: AA, AS, BA, BS, BFA, BBA, BM, BSN, MA, MS
Programs of Study: Accounting, Art, BioChemistry, Biology, Business Administration, Business Finance, Chemistry, Communications, Communicative Disorders, Comparative Studies in Religion, Computer Science, Criminal Justice, Economics, English, Elementary Education, History, Human Resources Management, Geography, Geology, German, Health Care Administration, Creative Writing, Journalism, Kinesiology, Mathematics, Management, Music, Nursing, Philosophy, Physical Education, Physical Science, Physics, Political Science, Psychology, Social Studies, Social Work, Sociology, Spanish, Special Education, Technical Writing, Theatre Arts

Women's Athletic Profile

McPhee PE Center
Eau Claire, WI 54702
Coach: Lisa Herb
Email: herblk@uwec.edu

NCAA I
Lady Blugolds, Navy, Gold
Phone: (715) 836-5475
Fax: (715) 836-4074

Estimated # of Women's Volleyball Scholarships: N/A
Conference: Wisconsin Intercollegiate Athletic Conference
Program Profile: Our season begins with a match in September with practice starting mid-August. Our conference tournament is the 1st full weekend in November with NCAA Tournament to follow.
History: In 1998 season, the Blugolds compiled a 29-7 overall record and received an NCAA Division III post-season bid.
Achievements: WIAC Coach of the Year twice, Midwest Region Coach of the Year, 7 All-Americans, consistently ranked in top 20, 7 NCAA bids, set NCAA Division III records for kills/g and assists/game in 1997
Coaching: Lisa Herb, Head Coach, begins her 13th year. She compiled a record of 593-228. She reached her 500th career victory in 1995. Herb's resume at Eau Claire also includes the direction of the successful Blugold volleyball camps and clinics. She is an assistant professor in the Department of Kinesoilogy and director of academic programs in the department. She was named Wisconsin Women's Intercollegiate Athletic (WWIAC) Coach of the Year in 1997. In 1982-1983, named Iowa Intercollegiate Athletic Conference Coach of the Year.

Roster In State: 13	**Out of State:** 9	**Out of Country:** 0
Sophomores on Team: 4	**Seniors on Team:** 3	**Graduation %:** 95%+
Most Recent Record: 14-18-0	**Fall Games:** 35	**Spring Games:** Varies

Camp of Clinic Dates: Late July, Early August
Positions Needed: Middle Hitter, Setter
Schedule: UW-Whitewater, UW-River Falls, UW-Lacrosse, St. Olaf, St. Benedict, Wartburg
Style of Play: Quick paced, team oriented and hard hitting.

University of Wisconsin - Green Bay
Academic Profile

2420 Nicolet Dr.
Green Bay, WI 54311

Phone: (920) 465-2573

Type: Public, 4 Yr., Liberal Arts, Coed

Founded: 1965

Website: http://www.uwgb.edu
SAT/ACT/GPA: Graduate top of class
Student/Faculty Ratio: 20:1
Undergraduate Enrollment: 5,282
Scholarships/Academic: Yes   **Athletic:** Yes
Expenses By: Year   **In State:** $ 7,194
Degrees Conferred: Bachelors

Religion: Non-Affiliated
Housing: Yes
Male/Female: 1:1.6
Graduate Enrollment: 137
Financial Aid: Yes
Out of State: $ 13,979

Programs of Study: Arts, Communication and the Arts, Communication Processes, English, French, German, History, Humanistic Studies, Music, Philosophy, Spanish, Theatre, Biology, Chemistry, Computer Science, Environmental Sciences, Environmental Policy & Planning, Political Science, Psychology, Human Development, Public Administration, Social Change & Development, Urban and Regional Studies, Business Administration, Education

Women's Athletic Profile

2420 Nicolet Drive
Green Bay, WI 54311
Coach: Debbie Kirch
Email: kirchd@uwgb.edu

NCAA I
Phoenix, Green, Cardinal, White
Phone: (920) 465-2573
Fax: (920) 465-2357

Estimated # of Women's Volleyball Scholarships: 3
Conference: Midwestern Collegiate Conference
Program Profile: Our volleyball team practices and plays on campus at the Phoenix Sports Center.
Coaching: Debbie Kirch, Head Coach, started in 1997. Sarah Storms, Assistant Coach.
Freshman Receiving Financial Aid/Academic: **Athletic:** 4
Roster In State: 10   **Out of State:** 4   **Out of Country:** 0
Sophomores on Team: 2   **Seniors on Team:** 1   **Graduation %:** 70
Most Recent Record: 3-30-0   **Fall Games:** 33   **Spring Games:** 3
Camp of Clinic Dates: July 18-30
Positions Needed: Middle Blockers, Setters
Schedule: Minnesota, Wisconsin, Eastern Washington, Fresno State, Oral Roberts, California Polytechnic
Style of Play: We are a small, quick, athletic team.

University of Wisconsin - La Crosse
Academic Profile

Mitchell Hall
La Crosse, WI 54601

Phone: 608-785-8939

Type: Public, 4 Yr., Coed
Website: http://www.uwlax.edu
SAT/ACT/GPA: 21
Student/Faculty Ratio: 20:1
Undergraduate Enrollment: 8,000
Scholarships/Academic: Yes   **Athletic:** No
Expenses By: Year   **In State:** $ 5,173
Degrees Conferred: AA, AS, BA, BS, MS, MBA, MED

Founded: 1909
Religion: Non-Affiliated
Housing: No
Male/Female: 45:55
Graduate Enrollment: 650
Financial Aid: Yes
Out of State: $ 10,308

Programs of Study: Accounting, Archaeology, Art, Athletic Training, Biology, Business, Chemistry, Communications, Computer, Education, Finance, Geography, History, Liberal Arts, Marketing, Math, Medical, Philosophy, Physics, Political Science

Women's Athletic Profile

Mitchelle Hall
LA Crosse, WI 54601
Coach: Sheila Perkins
Email: perkins@mail.uwlax.edu
Estimated # of Women's Volleyball Scholarships: N/A
Conference: The Great Northeast Athletic Conference

NCAA I
Lady Eagles, Maroon, Grey
Phone: (608) 785-8170
Fax: (608) 785-8674

University of Wisconsin - Madison
Academic Profile

716 Landgon Street
Madison, WI 53706-1400

Phone: 608-262-3961

Type: Public, 4 Yr., Coed

Founded:

Website: http://www.wisc.edu
SAT/ACT/GPA: Open
Student/Faculty Ratio:
Undergraduate Enrollment: N/A
Scholarships/Academic:
Expenses By: Year
Degrees Conferred:
Programs of Study: Contact school for programs of study.

Athletic:
In State:

Religion: Non-Affiliated
Housing: No
Male/Female:
Graduate Enrollment: N/A
Financial Aid:
Out of State:

Women's Athletic Profile

1440 Monroe Street
Madison, WI 53711
Coach: Pete Waite
Email:

NCAA I
Lady Badgers, Cardinal, White
Phone: (608) 263-5670
Fax: (608) 265-8051

Estimated # of Women's Volleyball Scholarships: N/A
Conference: Big Ten Conference
Program Profile: Wisconsin is one of the top programs in the country having advanced to the Finals of the NCAA Regional the last two seasons. The Badgers playing in the UW Fieldhouse, which has a seating capacity of 10,600 on a Sport Court.
History: Wisconsin began play in 1974-1975. The Badgers have competed in 7 NCAA Tournaments, won 2 NIVC Titles and 2 Big ten Championships. Wisconsin has also played host to the NCAA Champion twice setting attendance records both years.
Achievements: We have 4 All-Americans, 10 All-Districts, 2 District and All-Big Ten Coach of the Year, 14 Al-Big Ten, 1 Big Ten Player of the Year, 1 Big Ten Freshman of the Year and 2 Academic All-American.
Coaching: Pete Waite, Head coach, is entering first season with the program after spending 11 years at Northern Illinois. He has a career record of 266-102. He played at Ball State, competing in the NCAA Championship in 1979. Christy Johnson and Robert Pulliza are the Assistant Coaches.
Roster In State: 5
Sophomores on Team: 3
Most Recent Record: 30-5-0
Schedule: Penn State, Nebraska, Florida, Michigan State, Ohio State, Illinois

Out of State: 8
Seniors on Team: 3

Out of Country: 1
Graduation %:

University of Wisconsin - Milwaukee
Academic Profile

P.O. Box 413
Milwaukee, WI 53201

Phone: (414) 229-3739

Type: Public, 4 Yr., Liberal Arts, Coed
Website: http://www.uwm.edu
SAT/ACT/GPA: Adequate/Upper half of class
Student/Faculty Ratio: 18:1
Undergraduate Enrollment: 22,251
Scholarships/Academic: Yes
Expenses By: Year

Athletic: Yes
In State: $ 7,136

Founded: 1849
Religion: Non-Affiliated
Housing: Yes
Male/Female: 45:55
Graduate Enrollment: 5,500
Financial Aid: Yes
Out of State: $ 15,026

Specializes In: Business, Architecture, Education, Engineering, Fine Arts
Degrees Conferred: BA, BS, BFA, MA, MS, MBA, MFA, Ph.D.
Programs of Study: Accounting, Africology, Applied Mathematics, Architecture, Biological Aspects of Conservation, Civil Engineering, Communications, Computer Science (MIS), Dance, Education, Film, Finance, Geography, Electrical Engineering, Kinesiology, Marketing, Nursing, Psychology, Social Work, Theatre

Women's Athletic Profile

P.O. Box 413, 3415 N. Downer Avenue
Milwaukee, WI 53201
Coach: Kathy Litzau
Email: kclitzau@csd.uwm.edu

NCAA I
Lady Panthers, Gold, Black
Phone: (414) 229-3739
Fax: (414) 229-6759

Estimated # of Women's Volleyball Scholarships: 5
Conference: Midwestern Collegiate Conference
Program Profile: Our playing season is from August to December. We play at Klotche Center which has a seating capacity of 5,000.
History: Our NCAA Division I program began in 1990. We were 1997 and 1998 Conference Champions. We have gone from 3 wins to 25 wins in the last six years.
Achievements: 1996 and 1998 MCC Coach of the Year; 1997 and 1998 Conference Titles; 1998 NCAA appearance.

Coaching: Kathy Litzau - Head Coach, graduated from Notre Dame in 1990. Her overall record is 95-93. At Notre Dame, she was captain for 4 years and was voted MVP. Susie Chomko, Assistant Coach, graduated from Idaho State in 1993. In 1990, she was Big Sky Player of the Year. In 1990, she was also All-Northern Region.

Freshman Receiving Financial Aid/Academic: **Athletic:** 5

Roster In State: 5	**Out of State:** 7	**Out of Country:** 0
Sophomores on Team: 0	**Seniors on Team:** 1	**Graduation %:** 100%
Most Recent Record: 25-6-0	**Fall Games:** 31	**Spring Games:** 16

Camp of Clinic Dates: July 12-15 and July 19-22
Positions Needed: Setter, Middle Hitter, Outside Hitter, Right Side Hitter
Schedule: University of Wisconsin-Madison, Purdue, Loyola-Chicago, Butler, Eastern Illinois, Louisville
Style of Play: Quick offense with a lot of options.

University of Wisconsin - Oshkosh
Academic Profile

800 Algoma Blvd.
Oshkosh, WI 54901

Phone: 920-424-0202

Type: Public, 4 Yr., Coed   **Founded:** 1871
Website: http://www.uwosh.edu   **Religion:** Non-Affiliated
SAT/ACT/GPA: 1030/22   **Housing:** Yes
Student/Faculty Ratio: 19:1   **Male/Female:** 42/58
Undergraduate Enrollment: 9,171   **Graduate Enrollment:** 1,596
Scholarships/Academic: Yes   **Athletic:** No   **Financial Aid:** Yes
Expenses By: Year   **In State:** $6,758   **Out of State:** $14,285
Degrees Conferred: BS, BA, MA, MS, MBA
Programs of Study: 49 Majors, 15 PreProfessional programs, 24 additional Minors; Art, Business and Management, Communications, Computer Science, Education, Health Sciences, Journalism, Nursing, Parks and Recreation, PreProfessional, Protective Services, Public Affairs, Social Science

Women's Athletic Profile

800 Algoma Blvd.
Oshkosh, WI 54901
Coach: Marty Petersen
Email: petersen@uwosh.edu

NCAA I
Lady Titans, Black, Gold, White
Phone: (920) 424-1392
Fax: (920) 424-7445

Estimated # of Women's Volleyball Scholarships: N/A
Conference: Wisconsin Intercollegiate Athletic Conference
Program Profile: Outstanding facilities- Eight NCAA DIII Tournament appearances since 1990, including three trips to the Final Four.
Achievements: One national Player of the Year, 10 All-Americans, 536-333 record during last 19 years.

Roster In State: 12	**Out of State:** 3	**Seniors on Team:** 1

Most Recent Record: 29-9-0
Positions Needed: Outside Hitters
Schedule: Wis. Whitewater, Wis. Eau Claire, Washington, Trinity, Wis. River Falls, Elemhurst College, Central College, St. Olaf
Style of Play: Aggressive

University of Wisconsin - Parkside
Academic Profile

900 Wood Road
Kenosha, WI 53141

Phone: (414) 595-2412

Type: Public, 4 Yr., Liberal Arts, Coed   **Founded:** 1960
Website: http://www.uwp.edu   **Religion:** Non-Affiliated
SAT/ACT/GPA: 900/18   **Housing:** Yes
Student/Faculty Ratio: 14:1   **Male/Female:** 45/55
Undergraduate Enrollment: 4,700   **Graduate Enrollment:** 300
Scholarships/Academic: Yes   **Athletic:** Yes   **Financial Aid:** Yes
Expenses By: Year   **In State:** $ 7,700   **Out of State:** $ 13,800
Specializes In: Business, Pre-Health
Degrees Conferred: BS, BA, MBA, MA
Programs of Study: Art, Biological Sciences, Business, Communications, Computer Science, Criminal Justice, Education, Music, Nursing, PreHealth, Psychology, Social Sciences

Women's Athletic Profile

Box 2000, 900 Wood Rd.
Kenosha, WI 53141-2000
Coach: Melissa Wolter
Email:

NCAA I
Rangers, Green, White, Black
Phone: (414) 595-2127
Fax: (414) 595-2225

Did Not Return Profile

University of Wisconsin - Platteville
Academic Profile

1 University Plaza
Platteville, WI 53818-3099

Phone: 800-362-5515

Type: Public, 4 Yr., Coed
Website: http://www.uwplatt.edu
SAT/ACT/GPA: Open
Student/Faculty Ratio: 20:1
Undergraduate Enrollment: 5,000
Scholarships/Academic: Yes   **Athletic:** No
Expenses By: Year   **In State:** $ Varies
Specializes In: Engineering
Degrees Conferred: BA, MS, AS, BS

Founded: 1866
Religion: Non-Affiliated
Housing: Yes
Male/Female: 65:35
Graduate Enrollment: N/A
Financial Aid: Yes
Out of State: $ Varies

Programs of Study: Accounting, Agriculture, Art, Biology, Botany, Broadcasting, Business, Chemistry, Communications, Computer Science, Criminal Justice, Liberal Arts, Marketing, Mathematics, Economics, Education, Engineering, Geology, Geography, Philosophy, Physical Education

Women's Athletic Profile

1 University Plaza
Platteville, WI 53818
Coach: Deb Schulman
Email:

NCAA I
Lady Pioneers, Orange, Blue
Phone:
Fax: (608) 342-1576

Did Not Return Profile

University of Wisconsin - River Falls
Academic Profile

410 South 3rd St.
River Falls, WI 54022

Phone: 715-425-3500

Type: Public, 4 Yr., Coed
Website: http://www.uwrf.edu
SAT/ACT/GPA: 900/22
Student/Faculty Ratio: 18:1
Undergraduate Enrollment: 4,800
Scholarships/Academic: Yes   **Athletic:** No
Expenses By: Year   **In State:** $ 5,200
Degrees Conferred: BA, BS, BFA, BME, BSW, MA

Founded: 1874
Religion: Non-Affiliated
Housing: No
Male/Female: 45:55
Graduate Enrollment: 400
Financial Aid: Yes
Out of State: $ 9,900

Programs of Study: Accounting, Agricultural, American Studies, Animal Science, Biological Science, Chemistry, Computer Science, Conservation, Early Childhood Education, Economics, Education, English, Food Services, Languages, Geology, Geography, History, Horticulture, Journalism, Land Use, Math, Music, Physical Science, Physics, Political Science, PreProfessional Programs, etc..

Women's Athletic Profile

Karges Center
River Falls, WI 54022
Coach: Patti Ford
Email:

NCAA I
Falcons, Red, White
Phone: (715) 425-3244
Fax: (715) 425-3696

Estimated # of Women's Volleyball Scholarships: N/A
Conference: The Great Northeast Athletic Conference

History: The Falcons have had two NCAA Division III national berths. In 1998, the Falcons finished 23-11 overall and were 5-3 in the WIAC and tied for third place. The Falcons finished the 1995 season with a 38-7 record. The 38 wins is a record in a single season. They were 6-2 and placed third in the WIAC.

Coaching: Patti Ford, Head Coach, has led the Falcons to two NCAA Division III national playoffs berths. She was as assistant coach at North Dakota state before coming to UW-River Falls. She worked in all phases of the program including court coaching, scouting, recruiting, game management and organization of NDSU summer camps. From 1983-1991, she was a head coach of the Shanley North Dakota High School volleyball team. In 1991, she was named the North Dakota Coach of the Year and the East Regional Coach of the Year. She was a Coach of the Year nominee in 1988 and 1990. She was named the head coach of the 1991 Mizuno East All-Star team.

University of Wisconsin - Stevens Point
Academic Profile

4th Avenue
Stevens Point, WI 54881

Phone: (715) 346-3626

Type: Public, 4 Yr., Liberal Arts, Coed
Website: http://www.uwsp.edu
SAT/ACT/GPA: 18/2.3
Student/Faculty Ratio: 21:1
Undergraduate Enrollment: 8,500
Scholarships/Academic: Yes   **Athletic:** No
Expenses By: Year   **In State:** $ 3,000

Founded: 1894
Religion: Non-Affiliated
Housing: Yes
Male/Female: 1:1
Graduate Enrollment: N/A
Financial Aid: Yes
Out of State: $ 4,100

Degrees Conferred: AA, AS, BA, BS, MA, MS, MBA, Ph.D., JD
Programs of Study: Accounting, Anthropology, Art, Biology, Broadcasting, Business, Chemistry, Communications, Computer, Education, English, Fashion Merchandising, Fish/Game, Forestry, History, International, Liberal Arts, Math, Medical, Music, Natural Resources, PreProfessional Program, Psychology, Social Science, Speech, Theatre, Wildlife

Women's Athletic Profile

4th Avenue
Stevens Point, WI 54481
Coach: Kelly Geiger
Email: kgeiger@uwsp.edu

NCAA I
Lady Pointers, Purple, Gold
Phone: (715) 346-2151
Fax: (715) 346-3626

Estimated # of Women's Volleyball Scholarships: N/A
Conference: The Great Northeast Athletic Conference
Coaching: Kelly Geiger, begins her first season as a Head Coach of the Pointer Volleyball program and her fifth season as a member of the Pointer Volleyball coaching staff. She is a native of Deer River, Minnesota and was the team's top assistant for four seasons under Julie Johnson before accepting the head coaching duties last Spring. A graduate of the College of St. Scholastic in Duluth, Minnesota, she was an NSCAA All-American setter and a four-year letter winner for the Saints, a Benedictine Scholar at CSS and received her Master of Physical Education degree in 1992 from Idaho State University in Pocatello, graduating with a perfect 4.00 grade-point-average.

Roster In State: 21   **Out of State:** 1   **Out of Country:** 0
Sophomores on Team: 7   **Seniors on Team:** 1   **Graduation %:**
Schedule: Viterbo, Elmhurst College, Marian college, Wheaton, St. Norbert, Lakeland, UW-Superior, Eau Claire, UW-Whitewater

University of Wisconsin - Stout
Academic Profile

Johnson Fieldhouse
Menomonie, WI 54751

Phone: (715) 232-1312

Type: Public, 4 Yr., Engineering, Coed
Website: http://www.stout.edu
SAT/ACT/GPA: 1000/22/3.0
Student/Faculty Ratio: 21:1
Undergraduate Enrollment: 7,000
Scholarships/Academic: Yes   **Athletic:** No
Expenses By: Year   **In State:** $ 5,880

Founded: 1891
Religion: Non-Affiliated
Housing: Yes
Male/Female: 51:49
Graduate Enrollment: 1,000
Financial Aid: Yes
Out of State: $ 12,160

Specializes In: Early Childhood Education, Hospitality & Tourism
Degrees Conferred: BA, BS, MS, MA
Programs of Study: Apparel Design/Manufacturing, Applied Mathematics, Art, Art Education, Construction, Dietetics, Early Childhood Education, Family and Consumer Science Education, Foods Systems Technology, General Business Administration, Graphic Communications Management, Human Development & Family Studies, Industrial Technology, Manufacturing Engineering, Marketing Education, Packaging, Psychology, Retail Merchandising, Service Mangement, Technology, Telecommunications, Vocational

Women's Athletic Profile

Johnson Fieldhouse
Menomonie, WI 54751
Coach: Jill Joliff
Email: joliffj@uwstout.edu

NCAA I
Lady Blue Devils, Navy, White
Phone: 715-232-1689
Fax: 715-232-1684

Estimated # of Women's Volleyball Scholarships: 0
Conference: Wisconsin Intercollegiate Athletic Conference
Program Profile: We are a member of Division III. We play from the beginning of September throughout mid-November. We have 22 dates of competition. We play at Johnson Fiedlhouse with seats 3,500.
History: The program began in 1970 and we play in the toughest Conference in the nation.
Achievements: 1994 Conference and Regional Coach of the Year; 2 All-Americans.
Coaching: Jill Jolliff, Head Coach, started coaching the team from 1993 to the present. She compiled an overall record of 113-91. John Haggard is Assistant Coach.

Roster In State: 8 | **Out of State:** 9 | **Out of Country:** 0
Sophomores on Team: 2 | **Seniors on Team:** 2 | **Graduation %:** 88%
Most Recent Record: 22-14-0 | **Fall Games:** 36 | **Spring Games:** 10
Positions Needed: Middle Hitters
Schedule: Wisconsin-Whitewater, Wisconsin-Lacrosse, Wisconsin-River Falls, Wisconsin-Eau Claire
Style of Play: We play a semi-quick offense and we run a variety of defenses (depending on strengths of opponents), 5-1.

University of Wisconsin - Superior
Academic Profile

1800 Grand Avenue
Superior, WI 54880

Phone: (715) 394-8131

Type: Public, 4 Yr., Liberal Arts, Coed
Website: http://www.super.edu
SAT/ACT/GPA: 20/3.0
Student/Faculty Ratio: 4:1
Undergraduate Enrollment: 2,500
Scholarships/Academic: Yes
Expenses By: Year

Athletic: No
In State: $ 2,334

Founded: 1893
Religion: Non-Affiliated
Housing: Yes
Male/Female: 50:50
Graduate Enrollment: 200
Financial Aid: TAP
Out of State: $ 7,470

Specializes In: Education, Communications, Sociology, Music
Degrees Conferred: AA, BA, BFA, B.Mus., BME, BS, MA, MSEd, Specialist in Education
Programs of Study: Elementary Education, Music, Communications, Sociology, Criminal Justice, Business, Theatre, Physical Education, Human Performance Sciences, Health & Psychology

Women's Athletic Profile

Gates PE Bldg., P.O. Box 2000
Superior, WI 54880
Coach: Alena M. Krug
Email: akrug@staff.wusuperior.edu

NCAA I
Yellow Jackets, Black, Gold
Phone: (715) 394-8131
Fax: (715) 394-8110

Estimated # of Women's Volleyball Scholarships: N/A
Conference: Wisconsin Intercollegiate Athletic Association
Program Profile: We have a 3 court system, with wooden floors and a team locker room. A new field house addition will include 4 more volleyball courts.
History: The WIAC Conference is one of the strongest conferences in the nation.
Achievements: The program has produced many All-Conference players. The program also produced a few All-Americans.
Coaching: Alena M. Krug, Head Coach, her record for her first year here is 10-20. This improved the previous year's record 100%. She has previous coaching experience as an assistant coach in the University of New York at Cortland under Joan Sitterly, where her record was 97-47.
Freshman Receiving Financial Aid/Academic: | | **Athletic:** 0
Roster In State: 7 | **Out of State:** 10 | **Out of Country:** 0
Sophomores on Team: 6 | **Seniors on Team:** 0 | **Graduation %:** 100%
Most Recent Record: 10-20-0 | **Fall Games:** 20 | **Spring Games:** 3
Camp of Clinic Dates: August 2-6 the college
Positions Needed: (3) Middle Hitters, Setter, Outside Hitter
Schedule: Wisconsin-Whitewater, Wisconsin-La Crosse, Wisconsin-River Falls, Wisconsin-Stout, Wisconsin-Eau Claire
Style of Play: We play a multi-offense, back row attack, perimeter style defense and rotational. We are aggressive and adept to our opponent.

University of Wisconsin - Whitewater
Academic Profile

800 W. Main St.
Whitewater, WI 53190

Phone: 262-472-1440

Type: Public, 4 Yr., Coed
Website: http://www.uww.edu
SAT/ACT/GPA: 21
Student/Faculty Ratio: 1:21
Undergraduate Enrollment: 9,556
Scholarships/Academic: Yes   **Athletic:** No
Expenses By: Year   **In State:** $ 5,858
Specializes In: Business, Education
Degrees Conferred: BA, BBA, BFA, BM, BS

Founded: 1868
Religion: Non-Affiliated
Housing: Yes
Male/Female: 45:55
Graduate Enrollment: 1,122
Financial Aid: Yes
Out of State: $ 12,138

Programs of Study: Arts, Business, Accounting, Marketing, Elementary Education, Various Secondary Education, Mathematics, Social Work, Management Computer Systems, Office Systems, English, History, Women's Studies, Physical Education

Women's Athletic Profile

Williams Center
Whitewater, WI 53190
Coach: Kris Russell
Email: russellk@uwwvax.uww.edu

NCAA I
Lady Warhawks, Purple, White
Phone: (414) 472-5645
Fax: (414) 472-2791

Estimated # of Women's Volleyball Scholarships: N/A
Conference: Wisconsin Intercollegiate Athletic Conference
Program Profile: We are a top ten Division III program. We have eleven post-season tournament bids. We did three Elite 8 appearances and 2 Final Four appearances. We have 15 All-Americans Awards.
History: The program began in the mid-seventies. We have had 4 head coaches. Coach Russell started coaching from 1981 to the present.
Achievements: 4 Conference Coaches Awards, 3 Regional Coach of the Year Awards; twice named NCAA Division National Coach of the Year; 15 American Awards from 1988-1998.
Coaching: Kris Russell, Head Coach, is entering her 18th season with the program with a record of 605-201. Jo Lindoo and Hugh Hernesman are Assistant Coaches.
Freshman Receiving Financial Aid/Academic: **Athletic:** 0
Roster In State: 17   **Out of State:** 3   **Out of Country:** 0
Sophomores on Team: 0   **Seniors on Team:** 3   **Graduation %:** 100%
Most Recent Record: 32-6-0   **Fall Games:** 38   **Spring Games:** 4
Positions Needed: 2 Middle Blockers, 1 Outside (Left), 1 Setter
Schedule: Washington University - St. Louis, Trinity College, University of Wisconsin-River Falls, Central College, Elmhurts College, University of Wisconsin - Lacrosse
Style of Play: We are aggressive. We have quick tempo and great defense

Viterbo College
Academic Profile

815 South 9th Street
La Crosse, WI 54601

Phone: 608-796-3012

Type: Private, 4 Yr., Liberal Arts, Coed
Website: http://www.viterbo.edu/
SAT/ACT/GPA: 860/18/3.0
Student/Faculty Ratio: 16:1
Undergraduate Enrollment: 1,750
Scholarships/Academic: Yes   **Athletic:** Yes
Expenses By: Year   **In State:** $ 17,110
Degrees Conferred: BA, BS, MA, MS, MSN

Founded: 1890
Religion: Catholic
Housing: Yes
Male/Female: 26:74
Graduate Enrollment: 300
Financial Aid: Yes
Out of State: $ 17,110

Programs of Study: Biology, Business, Chemistry, Computer, Education, English, Fine Arts, Health Sciences, Humanities, Mathematics, Natural Sciences, Nursing, PreProfessional Programs (Dentistry, Medicine, Chemistry, Engineering, Pharmacy, Chiropractic, Law, Optometry) Psychology, Religious Studies, Social Science, Sociology

Women's Athletic Profile

815 S. 9th Street
La Crosse, WI 54601
Coach: Lynn Sirianni
Email: LMSIRIANNI@VITERBO.EDU

NCAA I
Lady V-Hawks, Cardinal, Silver
Phone: 608-796-3820
Fax: (608) 796-3818

Estimated # of Women's Volleyball Scholarships: N/A
Conference: MCC

Wisconsin Lutheran College
Academic Profile

8800 W. Boulevard Road
Milwaukee, WI 53226

Phone: 888-947-5884

Type: Private, 4 Yr., Liberal Arts, Coed
Website: http://www.wlc.edu
SAT/ACT/GPA: 20+/2.75
Student/Faculty Ratio: 12:1
Undergraduate Enrollment: 553
Scholarships/Academic: Yes   **Athletic:** No
Expenses By: Year   **In State:** $ 5,500

Founded: 1973
Religion: Lutheran
Housing: Yes
Male/Female: 45:55
Graduate Enrollment: N/A
Financial Aid: Yes
Out of State: $ 5,500

Degrees Conferred: BA, BS, Bachelor of Business Administration
Programs of Study: Art, Biology, Broad field Social Studies, Business Administration, Chemistry, Coaching, Communications, Communication Arts, Computer Information Systems, Education, English,
Foreign Languages, History, Liberal Arts, Mathematics, Music, Philosophy, Pre-Law, Pre-Medicine, Pre-Nursing, Pre-Pharmacy, Psychology, Secondary Education, Spanish, Theatre, Theology

Women's Athletic Profile

8800 W. Bluemound Rd.
Milwaukee, WI 53226
Coach: Julie Detjen
Email: tracy_schneider@wlc.edu

NCAA I
Lady Warriors, Green, White
Phone: (414) 443-8885
Fax: (414) 443-8505

Estimated # of Women's Volleyball Scholarships: N/A
Conference: Lake Michigan Conference
Program Profile: We play a full fall schedule and we have a Division III opponents. We begin practice in August and matches through November. Our Recreation Center is called the REX, which was completed in 1992 with a seating capacity of 2,500.
History: Our program was formed in 1987. We were a member of NAIA and won conference champions in1 989, 1990, 1991, 1992 & 1993.
Coaching: Julie Detjen, Head Coach, is entering first season with the program . She coached high school level for 8 years. As a player in 1985, she was named NCAA All-American-setter. Rachel Kuehl and April Richter are our Assistant Coaches, are entering first season with the program.

Roster In State: 10   **Out of State:** 2-5   **Out of Country:** 0
Sophomores on Team: 0   **Seniors on Team:** 8   **Graduation %:** 95%
Most Recent Record: 4-26-0   **Fall Games:** 22+   **Spring Games:** 0
Camp of Clinic Dates: Early August of 2000
Positions Needed: Setter, Defensive Specialist, Blocker
Schedule: St. Norbert, Marian College, Carroll College
Style of Play: Don't have the players yet. Would like to be aggressive at the net - "never say die" attitude.

WYOMING

Cheyenne ✪

SCHOOL	CITY	AFFILIATION	PAGE
Eastern Wyoming College	Torrington	NJCAA	826
University of Wyoming	Laramie	NCAA I	826

Eastern Wyoming College
Academic Profile

3200 West C Street
Torrington, WY 82240

Phone: (307) 532-8248

Type: Public, 2 Yr., Liberal Arts, Coed
Website: http://www.ewc.whecn.edu
SAT/ACT/GPA: GPA only must have 2.00 HS
Student/Faculty Ratio: 13:1
Undergraduate Enrollment: 600
Scholarships/Academic: Yes   **Athletic:** Yes
Expenses By: Year   **In State:** $ 4,500

Founded: 1948
Religion: Non-Affiliated
Housing: Yes
Male/Female: 1:2.5
Graduate Enrollment: N/A
Financial Aid: Yes
Out of State: $ 6,078

Specializes In: General Education and Several Technical and Certificate programs
Degrees Conferred: Associate of Applied Science and Applied Arts
Programs of Study: Accounting, AgriBusiness, Agricultural, Animal Science, Biology, Business, Computer Science, Cosmetology, Criminal Justice, Economics, Education, English, History, Mathematics, Physical Education, PreProfessional, Psychology, Veterinary Technology, Welding

Women's Athletic Profile

3200 West C. Street
Torrington, WY 82240
Coach: Verl Petsch, Jr.
Email: vpetsch@ewcl.awc.whecn.edu

NCAA I
Lady Lancers, Black, Gold
Phone: 307-532-8248
Fax: 307-532-8300

Estimated # of Women's Volleyball Scholarships: 8
Conference: Wyoming Community College Athletic
Program Profile: We play in a very strong NJCAA Division I. We have averaged 30 wins per year for the last 25 years. Our Activities Center seats 1,800. The season is from August 25th to November 15th.
History: We started in 1974. We have had 7 National Tournament Appearances and 12 Conference Championships.
Achievements: AVCA West Regional Coach of the Year 1996; NJCAA Regional Coach of the Year six times; Conference Coach of the Year 7 times; NJCAA Volleyball Hall of Fame Induction 1998
Coaching: Verl Petsch, Jr., Head Coach, started in 1974. His overall record is 805-325. Lance Petsch is Assistant Coach.
Freshman Receiving Financial Aid/Academic: **Athletic:** 4
Roster In State: 3   **Out of State:** 10   **Out of Country:** 0
Sophomores on Team: 0   **Seniors on Team:** 9   **Graduation %:** 95%
Most Recent Record: 42-22-0   **Fall Games:** 64   **Spring Games:** 0
Camp of Clinic Dates: June 14-17
Positions Needed: All
Schedule: Sheridan College, Casper College, Mid-Plains Community College
Style of Play: We are very offensive, have excellent power and very big teams.

University of Wyoming
Academic Profile

Box 3414 University Station
Laramie, WY 87071

Phone: (307) 766-5507

Type: Public, 4 Yr., Coed
Website: http://www.uwyo.edu
SAT/ACT/GPA: 810-960/20/2.75 or 3.0
Student/Faculty Ratio:
Undergraduate Enrollment: 8,806
Scholarships/Academic: Yes   **Athletic:** Yes
Expenses By: **In State:** $ 7,948

Founded: 1886
Religion: Non-Affiliated
Housing: Yes
Male/Female:
Graduate Enrollment: 2,000
Financial Aid: Yes
Out of State: $ 12,336

Specializes In: Engineering, Agriculture, Education, Science
Degrees Conferred:
Programs of Study: Agriculture, Art & Sciences, Business Education, Engineering, Health Sciences, Biology, Chemistry, Economics, English, Music, Philosophy, Psychology, History, Geology, Sociology, Broadcasting, Geography, Journalism, Math, Zoology, Finance, Chemical & Electrical Engineering, School of Nursing, School of Pharmacy, Exercise Science, Health Education

Women's Athletic Profile

Box 3414, Fieldhouse-N Addition
Laramie, WY 82071
Coach: Susan Judge
Email: suestead@uwyo.edu

NCAA I
Cowgirls, Black, Gold, White
Phone: (307) 766-4941
Fax: (307) 766-5414

Estimated # of Women's Volleyball Scholarships: 2-3
Conference: Mountain West Conference
Program Profile: Highly competitive, upper division I level program that competes in one of the top five volleyball conferences in the country. Playing venue's capacity of 1,500-15,000.
History: Our program started in 1974, 4 NCAA Tournament Appearances (2 in the 90's), best finish Elite Eight in 1989. AVCA top 25 attendance 7 of the last 10 years.
Achievements: We had have 1 All-American, 7 All-Region selections, last season had the WAC-Mountain Division Player of the Year and 3 All-Conference selections.
Coaching: Susan Judge is our Head Coach. Her 1996 overall record in three seasons is 49-43; record in conference play is 28-16. Coaches' overall record is 86-75 and led team to 1 NCAA Tournament Appearances.
Freshman Receiving Financial Aid/Academic: **Athletic:** 3
Roster In State: 4   **Out of State:** 9   **Out of Country:** 0
Sophomores on Team: 3   **Seniors on Team:** 3   **Graduation %:** 100%
Most Recent Record: 16-14-0
Positions Needed: Middle, Setter
Schedule: BYU, Colorado State, Notre Dame, Utah, Oklahoma, Pittsburgh
Style of Play: Emphasis on blocking and quick tempo offense.

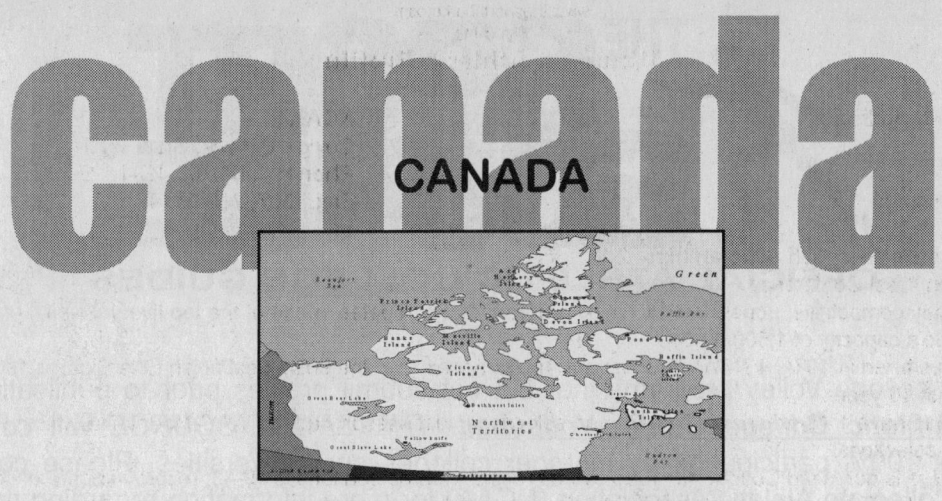

Simon Fraser University
Academic Profile

8888 University Drive
Burnaby, BC, Canada V5A 1S6

Phone: (604) 291-3224

Type: Public, 4 Yr., Coed
Website: http://www.sfu.ca
SAT/ACT/GPA: Open/3.0
Student/Faculty Ratio: 24:1
Undergraduate Enrollment: 15,000
Scholarships/Academic: Yes **Athletic:** Yes
Expenses By: Year **In State:** $ 6,300 Can
Specializes In: Engineering
Degrees Conferred: BA, BS, MA, MS, Ph.D., EdD

Founded: 1965
Religion: Non-Affiliated
Housing: Yes
Male/Female: 47:53
Graduate Enrollment: 3,000
Financial Aid: Yes
Out of State: $ 9,800 Can

Programs of Study: Anthropology, Archaeology, Bio-Chemistry, Biological Science, Business Administration, Canadian Studies, Criminology, Economics, Engineering Sciences, Geography, Liberal Arts, Mathematics, Philosophy, Physics, Political Science, Psychology, Statistics, Systems Science, Theatre

Women's Athletic Profile

8888 University Drive
Burnaby, BC V5A 1SG
Coach: Lisa Sulatycki
Email: mwk@sfu.ca

NAIA
Clan, Red, Blue, White
Phone: (604) 291-4057
Fax: (604) 291-4922

Estimated # of Women's Volleyball Scholarships: 10
Conference: WRST
Program Profile: Our team plays at Chancellor's Gym with a seating capacity of 2,500.
Coaching: Lisa Sulatycki, Head Coach, is entering her fourth season with the program.
Freshman Receiving Financial Aid/Academic: N/A **Athletic:** N/A
Roster In State: 12 **Out of State:** 0 **Out of Country:** 0
Sophomores on Team: 3 **Seniors on Team:** 1 **Graduation %:** 97
Most Recent Record: 6-22-0 **Fall Games:** 27 **Spring Games:** 0
Schedule: Portland State, Hawaii-Hilo, Hawaii Pacific, BYU-Hawaii, Chaminade, Western Oregon
Style of Play: Very solid defensively with a strong emphasis on an outside attack.

OFFICIAL ATHLETIC COLLEGE GUIDES

There are college Volley programs that did not submit profiles prior to publication of the **_Official Athletic College Guide: Volleyball_**. *THE SPORT SOURCE* will continue to encourage 100% participation by member colleges and universities. Please contact the National Collegiate Athletic Association (NCAA) for more information regarding their member institutions at (913) 339-1906, or visit the NCAA website at **http://www.ncaa.org**. You may contact the National Association of Intercollegiate Athletics (NAIA) for more information regarding their member institutions at (918) 494-8824, or visit the NAIA website at **http://www.naia.org**. For more information on the National Christian College Athletic Association (NCCAA) and their member institutions please call (765) 674-8401, or visit their website at **http://www.bright.net/~nccaa**.

Program Affilition List

College Profile Index

Additional Resources

NCAA DIVISION I PROGRAMS
(Listed in the Volleyball Athletic Guide)

SCHOOL	STATE	SCHOOL	STATE
Alabama State University	AL	East Carolina University	NC
Alcorn State University	MS	East Tennessee State University	TN
American University	DC	Eastern Illinois University	IL
Appalachian State University	NC	Eastern Kentucky University	KY
Arizona State University	AZ	Eastern Michigan University	MI
Arkansas State University	AR	Eastern Washington University	WA
Auburn University	AL	Elon College	NC
Austin Peay State University	TN	Fairfield University	CT
Ball State University	IN	Fairleigh Dickinson Univ - Teaneck	NJ
Baylor University	TX	Flagler College	FL
Belmont University	TN	Florida A&M University	FL
Bethune-Cookman College	FL	Florida Atlantic University	FL
Binghamton University	NY	Florida International University	FL
Boise State University	ID	Florida State University	FL
Boston College	MA	Fordham University	NY
Bowling Green State University	OH	Fresno State	CA
Bradley University	IL	Furman University	SC
Brigham Young University	UT	George Mason University	VA
Brown University	RI	George Washington University	DC
Bucknell University	PA	Georgetown University	DC
Butler University	IN	Georgia Southern University	GA
California State Polytechnic U - SLO	CA	Georgia State University	GA
California State Univ - Fresno	CA	Georgia Tech	GA
California State Univ - Fullerton	CA	Gonzaga University	WA
California State Univ - Northridge	CA	Grambling State University	LA
California State Univ - Sacramento	CA	Hampton University	VA
Campbell University	NC	Harvard University	MA
Canisius College	NY	Hofstra University	NY
Centenary College - Louisiana	LA	Howard University	DC
Central Connecticut State University	CT	Idaho State University	ID
Central Michigan University	MI	Illinois State University	IL
Charleston Southern University	SC	Indiana State University	IN
Chicago State University	IL	Indiana University - Bloomington	IN
Citadel	SC	Indiana University - Purdue	IN
Clemson University	SC	Iona College	NY
Cleveland State University	OH	Iowa State University	IA
Coastal Carolina University	SC	Jackson State University	MS
Colgate University	NY	Jacksonville State University	AL
College of Charleston	SC	Jacksonville University	FL
College of the Holy Cross	MA	James Madison University	VA
College of William & Mary	VA	Kansas State University	KS
Colorado State University	CO	Kent State University	OH
Columbia University-Barnard College	NY	La Salle University	PA
Coppin State College	MD	Lafayette College	PA
Cornell University	NY	Lamar University	TX
Creighton University	NE	Lehigh University	PA
Darmouth College	NH	Liberty University	VA
Davidson College	NC	Long Beach State University	CA
De Paul University	IL	Long Island University - Brooklyn	NY
Delaware State University	DE	Louisiana State University	LA
Drake University	IA	Louisiana Tech University	LA
Drexel University	PA	Loyola College	MD
Duquesne University	PA	Loyola Marymount University	CA

NCAA DIVISION I PROGRAMS
(Listed in the Volleyball Athletic Guide)

SCHOOL	STATE
Loyola University - Illinois	IL
Manhattan College	NY
Marist College	NY
Marquette University	WI
Marshall University	WV
McNeese State University	LA
Mercer University	GA
Miami University	OH
Michigan State University	MI
Middle Tennessee State University	TN
Minnesota Bible College	MN
Mississippi State University	MS
Mississippi Valley State University	MS
Montana State University - Bozeman	MT
Morehead State University	KY
Morgan State University	MD
Murray State University	KY
New Mexico State University	NM
Niagara University	NY
Nicholls State University	LA
Norfolk State University	VA
North Carolina A&T State University	NC
North Carolina State University	NC
Northeast Louisiana University	LA
Northeastern Illinois University	IL
Northeastern University	MA
Northern Arizona University	AZ
Northern Illinois University	IL
Northwestern State University	LA
Northwestern University	IL
Oakland University	MI
Ohio State University	OH
Ohio University	OH
Oral Roberts University	OK
Oregon State University	OR
Pennsylvania State University	PA
Pepperdine University	CA
Portland State University	OR
Prairie View A&M University	TX
Princeton University	NJ
Providence College	RI
Purdue University	IN
Quinnipiac College	CT
Radford University	VA
Rice University	TX
Rider University	NJ
Robert Morris College	PA
Rutgers, State Univ of New Jersey	NJ
Saint Bonaventure University	NY
Saint Francis College - New York	NY
Saint Francis College - Pennsylvania	PA
Saint John's University-New York	NY
Saint Louis University	MO

SCHOOL	STATE
Saint Mary's College - California	CA
Saint Peter's College	NJ
Sam Houston State University	TX
Samford University	AL
San Diego State University	CA
San Jose State University	CA
Santa Clara University	CA
Seton Hall University	NJ
Siena College	NY
South Carolina State University	SC
Southeast Missouri State University	MO
Southeastern Louisiana University	LA
Southern Illinois Univ - Carbondale	IL
Southern Methodist University	TX
Southern University - Baton Rouge	LA
SW Missouri State Univ-Springfield	MO
Southwest Texas State University	TX
Stanford University	CA
State University College - Oneonta	NY
State University of New York - Buffalo	NY
Stephen F. Austin State University	TX
Stetson University	FL
SUNY Martime College	NY
Syracuse University	NY
Temple University	PA
Tennessee State University	TN
Texas A&M Univ - College Station	TX
Texas Christian University	TX
Texas Southern University	TX
Texas Tech University	TX
Towson University	MD
Troy State University	AL
Tulane University	LA
United States Air Force Academy	CO
University of Akron	OH
University of Alabama - Birmingham	AL
University of Alabama - Tuscaloosa	AL
University of Albany	NY
University of Arizona	AZ
University of Arkansas - Fayetteville	AR
University of Arkansas - Little Rock	AR
University of Arkansas - Pine Bluff	AR
University of California - Berkeley	CA
University of California - Irvine	CA
University of California - Los Angeles	CA
Univ of California - Santa Barbara	CA
University of Central Florida	FL
University of Cincinnati	OH
University of Colorado	CO
University of Connecticut	CT
University of Dayton	OH
University of Delaware	DE
University of Denver	CO

NCAA DIVISION I PROGRAMS
(Listed in the Volleyball Athletic Guide)

SCHOOL	STATE
University of Evansville	IN
University of Florida	FL
University of Georgia	GA
University of Hartford	CT
University of Hawaii - Manoa	HI
University of Houston	TX
University of Idaho	ID
University of Illinois - Champaign	IL
University of Illinois - Chicago	IL
University of Iowa	IA
University of Kansas	KS
University of Kentucky	KY
University of Louisville	KY
University of Maine	ME
Univ of Maryland - Baltimore County	MD
Univ of Maryland - College Park	MD
Univ of Maryland - Eastern Shore	MD
Univ of Massachusetts - Amherst	MA
University of Memphis	TN
University of Michigan	MI
University of Minnesota-Twin Cities	MN
University of Mississippi	MS
University of Missouri - Columbia	MO
University of Missouri - Kansas City	MO
University of Montana	MT
University of Nebraska - Lincoln	NE
University of Nevada - Las Vegas	NV
University of Nevada - Reno	NV
University of New Hampshire	NH
University of New Mexico	NM
University of New Orleans	LA
Univ of North Carolina - Asheville	NC
Univ of North Carolina - Chapel Hill	NC
Univ of North Carolina - Charlotte	NC
Univ of North Carolina - Greensboro	NC
Univ of North Carolina - Wilmington	NC
University of North Texas	TX
University of Northern Iowa	IA
University of Notre Dame	IN
University of Oklahoma	OK
University of Oregon	OR
University of Pennsylvania	PA
University of Pittsburgh	PA
University of Portland	OR
University of Rhode Island	RI
University of San Diego	CA
University of San Francisco	CA
University of South Alabama	AL
University of South Carolina	SC
University of South Florida	FL
University of Southern California	CA
University of Southern Mississippi	MS
University of Southwestern Louisiana	LA

SCHOOL	STATE
Univ of Tennessee - Chattanooga	TN
Univ of Tennessee - Knoxville	TN
Univ of Tennessee - Martin	TN
University of Texas - Arlington	TX
University of Texas - Austin	TX
University of Texas - El Paso	TX
University of Texas - Pan American	TX
University of Texas - San Antonio	TX
University of the Pacific	CA
University of Toledo	OH
University of Tulsa	OK
University of Utah	UT
University of Vermont	VT
University of Virginia	VA
University of Washington	WA
University of Wisconsin - Green Bay	WI
University of Wisconsin - Madison	WI
University of Wisconsin - Milwaukee	WI
University of Wyoming	WY
US Military Academy	NY
US Naval Academy	MD
Utah State University	UT
Valparaiso University	IN
Villanova University	PA
Virginia Commonwealth University	VA
Virginia Tech	VA
Wagner College	NY
Wake Forest University	NC
Washington State University	WA
Weber State University	UT
West Virginia University	WV
Western Carolina University	NC
Western Illinois University	IL
Western Kentucky University	KY
Western Michigan University	MI
Wichita State University	KS
Winthrop University	SC
Wofford College	SC
Wright State University	OH
Xavier University	OH
Yale University	CT
Youngstown State University	OH

NCAA DIVISION II PROGRAMS

(Listed in the Volleyball Athletic Guide)

SCHOOL	STATE
Abilene Christian University	TX
Adams State College	CO
Adelphi University	NY
Alabama A&M University	AL
Albany State University - Georgia	GA
Alderson-Broaddus College	WV
American International College	MA
Anderson College	SC
Angelo State University	TX
Arkansas Tech University	AR
Armstrong Atlantic State University	GA
Ashland University	OH
Assumption College	MA
Augusta State University	GA
Augustana College - South Dakota	SD
Barry University	FL
Barton College	NC
Bellarmine College	KY
Bemidji State University	MN
Bentley College	MA
Bowie State University	MD
Brigham Young University - Hawaii	HI
Bryant College	RI
Cal State Polytechnic U-Pomona	CA
Cal State University - Bakersfield	CA
Cal State University - Chico	CA
Cal State University-Dominguez Hills	CA
Cal State University - Los Angeles	CA
Cal State University - San Bernardino	CA
Cal State University - Stanislaus	CA
California University of Pennsylvania	PA
Cameron University	OK
Carson-Newman College	TN
Catawba College	NC
Central Missouri State University	MO
Central Washington University	WA
Chadron State College	NE
Chaminade University	HI
Cheyney University of Pennsylvania	PA
Christian Brothers University	TN
Clarion University of Pennsylvania	PA
Clark Atlanta University	GA
Coker College	SC
College of Notre Dame	CA
College of Saint Rose	NY
Colorado Christian University	CO
Colorado School of Mines	CO
Columbia Union College	MD
Concord College	WV
Concordia College - New York	NY
Converse College	SC
Dominican College	NY
Dowling College	NY

SCHOOL	STATE
Drury University	MO
East Stroudsburg University	PA
Eastern New Mexico University	NM
Eckerd College	FL
Edinboro University of Pennsylvania	PA
Elizabeth City State University	NC
Emporia State University	KS
Fairmont State College	WV
Faulkner University	AL
Fayetteville State University	NC
Ferris State University	MI
Florida Institute of Technology	FL
Florida Southern College	FL
Fort Hays State University	KS
Fort Lewis College	CO
Fort Valley State University	GA
Francis Marion University	SC
Franklin Pierce College	NH
Gannon University	PA
Gardner - Webb University	NC
Glenville State College	WV
Grand Canyon University	AZ
Grand Valley State University	MI
Harding University	AR
Hawaii Pacific University	HI
Henderson State University	AR
High Point University	NC
Hillsdale College	MI
Humboldt State University	CA
Indiana University of Pennsylvania	PA
Indiana Univ-Purdue Univ-Fort Wayne	IN
Jarvis Christian College	TX
Johnson C. Smith University	NC
Kentucky State University	KY
Kentucky Wesleyan College	KY
Kutztown University of Pennsylvania	PA
Lake Superior State University	MI
Lander University	SC
Lane College	TN
Le Moyne College	NY
Le Moyne-Owen College	TN
Lees - McRae College	NC
Lenoir - Rhyne College	NC
Lewis University	IL
Limestone College	SC
Lincoln Memorial University	TN
Livingstone College	NC
Lock Haven University	PA
Long Island University - CW Post	NY
Long Island University - Southampton	NY
Lynn University	FL
Mankato State University	MN
Mars Hill College	NC

NCAA DIVISION II PROGRAMS
(Listed in the Volleyball Athletic Guide)

SCHOOL	STATE
Mercy College	NY
Mercyhurst College	PA
Merrimack College	MA
Mesa State college	CO
Metropolitan State College	CO
Michigan Technological University	MI
Midwestern State University	TX
Miles College	AL
Millersville University	PA
Mississippi University for Women	MS
Missouri Southern State College	MO
Missouri Western State College	MO
Molloy College	NY
Montana State University - Billings	MT
Moorhead State University	MN
Morningside College	IA
Morris Brown College	GA
Mount Olive College	NC
New Hampshire College	NH
New Jersey Institute of Tech	NJ
New Mexico Higlands University	NM
New York Institute of Technology	NY
Newberry College	SC
North Carolina Central University	NC
North Dakota State University	ND
Northern Kentucky University	KY
Northern Michigan University	MI
Northern State University	SD
Northwest Missouri State University	MO
Northwood University	MI
Oakland City University	IN
Ohio Valley College	WV
Ouachita Baptist University	AR
Pace University	NY
Paine College	GA
Pfeiffer University	NC
Phila College of Textiles & Science	PA
Pittsburgh State University	KS
Presbyterian College	SC
Queens College - New York	NY
Queens College - North Carolina	NC
Quincy University - Illinois	IL
Regis University	CO
Rockhurst College	MO
Rollins College	FL
Sacred Heart University	CT
Saginaw Valley State University	MI
Saint Andrews Presbyterian College	NC
Saint Anselm College	NH
Saint Augustine's College	NC
Saint Cloud State University	MN
Saint Edward's University	TX
Saint Joseph's College - Indiana	IN

SCHOOL	STATE
Saint Leo College	FL
Saint Martin's College	WA
Saint Paul's College	VA
Saint Thomas Aquinas College	NY
Salem - Teikyo University	WV
San Francisco State University	CA
Savannah State University	GA
Seattle Pacific University	WA
Shaw University	NC
Shepherd College	WV
Shippensburg University	PA
Slippery Rock University	PA
Sonoma State University	CA
South Dakota State University	SD
Southeastern Oklahoma State Univ	OK
Southern Arkansas University	AR
Southern Connecticut State Univ	CT
Southern Illinois Univ - Edwardsville	IL
Southwest Baptist University	MO
Southwest State University	MN
St. Michael's College	VT
State Univ of New York - Binghamton	NY
State Univ of New York - Stony Brook	NY
Stonehill College	MA
Tarleton State University	TX
Texas A&M University - Commerce	TX
Texas A&M University - Kingsville	TX
Texas Woman's University	TX
Truman State University	MO
Tusculum College	TN
Tuskegee University	AL
University of Alabama - Huntsville	AL
University of Alaska Anchorage	AK
University of Alaska Fairbanks	AK
University of Bridgeport	CT
University of California - Davis	CA
University of California - Riverside	CA
University of Central Arkansas	AR
University of Central Oklahoma	OK
University of Charleston	WV
Univ of Colorado at Colorado Springs	CO
University of District of Columbia	DC
University of Findlay	OH
University of Hawaii - Hilo	HI
University of Indianapolis	IN
University of Mary Hardin-Baylor	TX
University of Massachusetts - Lowell	MA
University of Minnesota - Duluth	MN
University of Minnesota - Morris	MN
University of Missouri - St. Louis	MO
University of Montevallo	AL
University of Nebraska - Kearney	NE
University of Nebraska - Omaha	NE

NCAA DIVISION II PROGRAMS
(Listed in the Volleyball Athletic Guide)

SCHOOL	STATE
University of New Haven	CT
University of North Alabama	AL
Univ of North Carolina - Pembroke	NC
University of North Dakota	ND
University of North Florida	FL
University of Northern Colorado	CO
University of Pittsburgh - Johnstown	PA
Univ of South Carolina - Aiken	SC
Univ of South Carolina - Spartanburg	SC
University of South Dakota	SD
University of Southern Colorado	CO
University of Southern Indiana	IN
University of Tampa	FL
University of West Alabama	AL
Valdosta State University	GA
Virginia State College	VA
Virginia Union University	VA
Washburn University	KS
Wayne State College - Nebraska	NE
Wayne State University - Michigan	MI
West Chester University	PA
West Liberty State College	WV
West Texas A&M University	TX
West Virginia State College	WV
West Virginia Univ Institute of Tech	WV
West Virginia Wesleyan College	WV
Western New Mexico University	NM
Western State College	CO
Western Washington University	WA
Wheeling Jesuit University	WV
Wingate University	NC
Winona State University	MN
Winston - Salem State University	NC

NCAA DIVISION III PROGRAMS
(Listed in the Volleyball Athletic Guide)

SCHOOL	STATE
Adrian College	MI
Agnes Scott College	GA
Albertus Magnus College	CT
Albion College	MI
Albright College	PA
Alfred University	NY
Allegheny College	PA
Allentown C. of St. Francis De Sales	PA
Alma College	MI
Alvernia College	PA
Amherst College	MA
Anderson University - Indiana	IN
Anna Maria College	MA
Arcadia University	PA
Augsburg College	MN
Augustana College - Illinois	IL
Aurora University	IL
Austin College	TX
Averett College	VA
Babson College	MA
Baldwin-Wallace College	OH
Baptist Bible College	PA
Bard College	NY
Baruch College	NY
Bates College	ME
Becker College	MA
Beloit College	WI
Benedictine University	IL
Bennett College	NC
Bethany College	WV
Bethel College	MN
Blackburn College	IL
Bluffton College	OH
Bowdoin College	ME
Brandies University	MA
Bridgewater College	VA
Bridgewater State College	MA
Brooklyn College	NY
Bryn Mawr College	PA
Buena Vista University	IA
Cabrini College	PA
California Institute of Technology	CA
California Lutheran University	CA
California State University - Hayward	CA
Calvin College	MI
Capital University	OH
Carleton College	MN
Carnegie Mellon University	PA
Carroll College	WI
Carthage College	WI
Case Western Reserve University	OH
Catholic University of America	DC
Cazenovia College	NY

NCAA DIVISION III PROGRAMS

(Listed in the Volleyball Athletic Guide)

SCHOOL	STATE	SCHOOL	STATE
Cedar Crest College	PA	Emory and Henry College	VA
Centenary College - New Jersey	NJ	Emory University	GA
Central College - Iowa	IA	Endicott College	MA
Centre College	KY	Eureka College	IL
Chapman University	CA	Fairleigh Dickinson Univ - Madison	NJ
Chatham College	PA	Ferrum College	VA
Chestnut Hill College	PA	Fisk University	TN
Chowan College	NC	Fitchburg State College	MA
Christopher Newport University	VA	Fontbonne College	MO
City College of New York	NY	Framingham State College	MA
Claremont-Mudd-Scripps Colleges	CA	Franklin & Marshall College	PA
Clark University	MA	Franklin College	IN
Clarke College	IA	Frostburg State University	MD
Clarkson University	NY	Gallaudet University	DC
Coe College	IA	George Fox University	OR
Colby College	ME	Gettysburg College	PA
Colby Sawyer College	NH	Gordon College	MA
College Misericordia	PA	Goucher College	MD
College of Mount St. Joseph	OH	Greensboro College	NC
College of Mount St. Vincent	NY	Greenville College	IL
College of New Rochelle	NY	Grinnell College	IA
College of Notre Dame	MD	Grove City College	PA
College of Saint Elizabeth	NJ	Guilford College	NC
College of St. Benedict	MN	Gustavus Adolphus College	MN
College of St. Catherine	MN	Gwynedd-Mercy College	PA
College of Staten Island	NY	Hamilton College	NY
College of Wooster	OH	Hamline University	MN
Colorado College	CO	Hanover College	IN
Concordia College - Moorhead	MN	Hardin - Simmons University	TX
Concordia University	IL	Hartwick College	NY
Concordia University	WI	Haverford College	PA
Connecticut College	CT	Heidelberg College	OH
Cornell College	IA	Hendrix College	AR
Daniel Webster College	NH	Hilbert College	NY
Defiance College	OH	Hiram College	OH
Delaware Valley College	PA	Hollins University	VA
Denison University	OH	Hood College	MD
DePauw University	IN	Hope College	MI
Dickinson College	PA	Howard Payne University	TX
Dominican University	IL	Hunter College	NY
Duke University	NC	Illinois College	IL
D'youville College	NY	Illinois Wesleyan University	IL
Earlham College	IN	Immaculate College	PA
Eastern College	PA	Ithaca College	NY
Eastern Connecticut State University	CT	John Carroll University	OH
Eastern Menonnite University	VA	John Hopkins University	MD
Eastern Nazarene College	MA	John Jay College of Criminal Justice	NY
Edgewood College	WI	Johnson & Wales University	RI
Elizabethtown College	PA	Juniata College	PA
Elmhurst College	IL	Kalamazoo College	MI
Elmira College	NY	Kean University	NJ
Emerson College	MA	Keene State College	NH
Emmanuel College	MA	Kenyon College	OH

NCAA DIVISION III PROGRAMS

(Listed in the Volleyball Athletic Guide)

SCHOOL	STATE	SCHOOL	STATE
Keuka College	NY	Muhlenberg College	PA
King's College - Pennsylvania	PA	Muskingum College	OH
Knox College	IL	Nazareth College	NY
La Grange College	GA	Nebraska Wesleyan University	NE
La Roche College	PA	Neumann College	PA
Lake Erie College	OH	New Jersey City University	NJ
Lake Forest College	IL	New York University	NY
Lakeland College	WI	North Carolina Wesleyan College	NC
Lasell College	MA	North Central College	IL
Lawrence University	WI	North Park University	IL
Le Tourneau University	TX	Oberlin College	OH
Lebanon Valley College	PA	Occidental College	CA
Lehman College	NY	Oglethorpe University	GA
Lewis & Clark College	OR	Ohio Northern University	OH
Lincoln University - Pennsylvania	PA	Ohio Wesleyan University	OH
Linfield College	OR	Olivet College	MI
Loras College	IA	Otterbein College	OH
Luther College	IA	Pacific Lutheran University	WA
Lycoming College	PA	Pacific University	OR
Lynchburg College	VA	Peace College	NC
Macalester College	MN	Penn State Univ - Erie, Bherend	PA
MacMurray College	IL	Philadelphia College of the Bible	PA
Manchester College	IN	Piedmont College	GA
Manhattanville College	NY	Pine Manor College	MA
Maranatha Baptist Bible College	WI	Plymouth State College	NH
Marietta College	OH	Polytechnic University	NY
Mary Baldwin College	VA	Pomona-Pitzer Colleges	CA
Mary Washington College	VA	Principia College	IL
Marymount University	VA	Ramapo College of New Jersey	NJ
Maryville College	TN	Randolph-Macon College	VA
Maryville University of Saint Louis	MO	Randolph-Macon Woman's College	VA
Marywood University	PA	Regis College - Massachusetts	MA
Mass College of Liberal Arts	MA	Rhode Island College	RI
Mass Institute of Technology	MA	Rhodes College	TN
Mass Maritime Academy	MA	Ripon College	WI
Mayville State University	ND	Rivier College	NH
McMurry University	TX	Roanoke College	VA
Medgars Evers College	NY	Rochester Institute of Technology	NY
Meredith College	NC	Rockford College	IL
Messiah College	PA	Roger Williams University	RI
Methodist College	NC	Rose-Hulman Institute of Technology	IN
Middlebury College	VT	Rosemont College	PA
Millikin University	IL	Rowan University	NJ
Mills College	CA	Russell Sage College	NY
Millsaps College	MS	Rust College	MS
Milwaukee School of Engineering	WI	Rutgers, State Univ of New Jersey	NJ
Mississippi College	MS	Rutgers, State Univ of NJ/Camden	NJ
Monmouth College	IL	Saint John Fisher College	NY
Montclair State University	NJ	Saint Joseph College - Maine	ME
Moravian College	PA	Saint Joseph's College - New York	NY
Mount Holyoke college	MA	Saint Lawrence University	NY
Mount St. Mary College	NY	Saint Mary's College - Indiana	IN
Mount Union College	OH	Saint Mary's College - Maryland	MD

NCAA DIVISION III PROGRAMS
(Listed in the Volleyball Athletic Guide)

SCHOOL	STATE
Saint Mary's University - Minnesota	MN
Saint Norbert College	WI
Saint Olaf College	MN
Salem State College	MA
Salisbury State University	MD
Savannah College of Art & Design	GA
Schreiner College	TX
Seattle University	WA
Shenandoah University	VA
Simmons College	MA
Simpson College	IA
Skidmore College	NY
Smith College	MA
Southwestern University	TX
Springfield College	MA
State Univ College - Fredonia	NY
State Univ College - New Paltz	NY
State Univ of New York - Brockport	NY
State Univ of New York - Cortland	NY
State Univ of New York - Geneseo	NY
State Univ of New York-Old Westbury	NY
State Univ of New York - Oswego	NY
State Univ of New York - Potsdam	NY
Stevens Institute of Technology	NJ
Stillman College	AL
Sul Ross State University	TX
SUNY-Plattsburgh	NY
Susquehanna University	PA
Swarthmore College	PA
Sweet Briar College	VA
Thiel College	PA
Thomas College	ME
Thomas More College	KY
Trinity College	CT
Trinity University	TX
Tufts University	MA
Union College	NY
University of California - San Diego	CA
University of California - Santa Cruz	CA
University of Chicago	IL
University of Dallas - Irving	TX
University of Dubuque	IA
University of LaVerne	CA
University of Mass - Boston	MA
University of Mass - Dartmouth	MA
University of New England	ME
University of Pittsburgh - Bradford	PA
University of Pittsburgh - Greensburg	PA
University of Redlands	CA
University of Rochester	NY
University of Saint Thomas	MN
University of Scranton	PA
University of Southern Maine	ME

SCHOOL	STATE
University of the South	TN
Univ of Wisconsin - Eau Claire	WI
Univ of Wisconsin - La Crosse	WI
Univ of Wisconsin - Oshkosh	WI
Univ of Wisconsin - Platteville	WI
Univ of Wisconsin - River Falls	WI
Univ of Wisconsin - Stevens Point	WI
Univ of Wisconsin - Stout	WI
Univ of Wisconsin - Superior	WI
Univ of Wisconsin - Whitewater	WI
Upper Iowa University	IA
Ursinus College	PA
US Coast Guard Academy	CT
US Merchant Marine Academy	NY
Utica College	NY
Vassar College	NY
Villa Julie College	MD
Washington & Jefferson College	PA
Washington & Lee University	VA
Washington College - Maryland	MD
Washington University	MO
Waynesburg College	PA
Webster University	MO
Wellesley College	MA
Wentworth Institute of Technology	MA
Wesleyan College	GA
Wesleyan University	CT
Western Connecticut State University	CT
Western Maryland College	MD
Western New England College	MA
Westfield State College	MA
Westminster College	MO
Wheaton College	MA
Wheaton College	IL
Whitman College	WA
Whittier College	CA
Whitworth College	WA
Widener University	PA
Wilkes University	PA
Willamette University	OR
William Paterson University	NJ
William Penn College	IA
Williams College	MA
Wilmington College	OH
Wilson College	PA
Wisconsin Lutheran College	WI
Wittenberg University	OH
Worcester Polytechnic Institute	MA
Worcester State College	MA
York College of Pennsylvania	PA

NAIA PROGRAMS

(Listed in the Volleyball Athletic Guide)

SCHOOL	STATE
Albertson College of Idaho	ID
Aquinas College	MI
Asbury College	KY
Atlantic Union College	MA
Avila College	MO
Azusa Pacific University	CA
Baker University	KS
Barat College	IL
Barber - Scotia College	NC
Belhaven College	MS
Bellevue University	NE
Benedict College	SC
Benedictine College	KS
Berea College	KY
Bethany College	KS
Bethany College	CA
Bethel College	KS
Bethel College	TN
Biola University	CA
Birmingham Southern College	AL
Black Hills State University	SD
Bluefield College	VA
Brenau University	GA
Brescia University	KY
Brewton Parker	GA
Briar Cliff College	IA
California Baptist College	CA
California Maritime Academy	CA
Cal State University - Monterey Bay	CA
Cardinal Stritch College	WI
Carlow College	PA
Carroll College	MT
Central Methodist College	MO
Central State University	OH
Claflin College	SC
Clinch Valley College	VA
College of the Ozarks	MO
College of the Southwest	NM
College of West Virginia	WV
Columbia College	MO
Concordia University	NE
Concordia University	CA
Concordia University	OR
Concordia University - Minnesota	MN
Cornerstone College	MI
Covenant College	GA
Culver - Stockton College	MO
Cumberland College	KY
Cumberland University	TN
Daemen College	NY
Dakota State University	SD
Dakota Wesleyan University	SD
Dana College	NE

SCHOOL	STATE
Dickinson State University	ND
Doane College	NE
Dominican College	CA
Dort College	IA
Embry-Riddle Aeronautical University	FL
Evangel College	MO
Florida Memorial College	FL
Freed Hardeman University	TN
Fresno Pacific University	CA
Friends University	KS
Georgetown College	KY
Goldey-Beacom College	DE
Goshen College	IN
Grace land College	IA
Grand View College	IA
Green Mountain College	VT
Harris-Stowe State College	MO
Hasting College	NE
Holy Names College	CA
Hope International University	CA
Houghton College	NY
Houston Baptist University	TX
Huntington College	AL
Huntington College	IN
Huron University	SD
Huston - Tillotson College	TX
Illinois Institute of Technology	IL
Indiana University Southeast	IN
Indiana Wesleyan University	IN
Iowa Wesleyan College	IA
Jamestown College	ND
John Brown University	AR
Judson College	IL
Kansas Wesleyan University	KS
Kendall College	IL
King College	TN
La Sierra University	CA
Lambuth University	TN
Lindsey Wilson College	KY
Lipscomd University	TN
Loyola University	LA
Lubbock Christian University	TX
Madonna University	MI
Malone College	OH
Marian College	IN
Martin Methodist College	TN
Marycrest International University	IA
Master's College	CA
McKendree College	IL
McPherson College	KS
Mid-America Nazarene	KS
Midland Lutheran College	NE
Midway College	KY

NAIA PROGRAMS
(Listed in the Volleyball Athletic Guide)

SCHOOL	STATE
Milligan College	TN
Minot State University	ND
Missouri Baptist College	MO
Missouri Valley College	MO
Montana State University - Northern	MT
Montana Tech of the Univ of Montana	MT
Montreat College	NC
Morris College	SC
Mount Aloysius College	PA
Mount Marty College	SD
Mount Mercy College	IA
Mount Saint Clare College	IA
Mount Vernon Nazarene College	OH
National American University	SD
Newman University	KS
North Greenville College	SC
Northwestern College	IA
Notre Dame College - Ohio	OH
Ohio Dominican College	OH
Olivet Nazarene University	IL
Oregon Institute of Technology	OR
Ottawa University	KS
Pacific Union College	CA
Palm Beach Atlantic College	FL
Park College	MO
Peru State College	NE
Pikeville College	KY
Point Loma Nazarene University	CA
Point Park College	PA
Purdue University - Calumet	IN
Robert Morris College	IL
Robert Wesleyan College	NY
Rocky Mountain College	MT
Saint Ambrose University	IA
Saint Louis College of Pharmacy	MO
Saint Mary College	KS
Saint Mary's University	TX
Saint Thomas University	FL
Saint Vincent College	PA
Saint Xavier University	IL
Sangamon State	IL
Seton Hill College	PA
Shawnee State University	OH
Siena Heights University	MI
Simon Faser University	BC
Southern California College	CA
Southern Nazarene University	OK
Southern Oregon University	OR
Southern Virginia College	VA
Southwestern Adventist College	TX
Southwestern College	KS
Spalding University	KY
Spring Arbor College	MI

SCHOOL	STATE
Sterling College	KS
Tabor College	KS
Talladega College	AL
The College of West Virginia	WV
Trevecca Nazarene University	TN
Trinity Christian College	IL
Trinity International University	IL
Tri-State University	IN
Union College	KY
University of Maine - Fort Kent	ME
University of Maine - Machias	ME
University of Maine - Presque Isle	ME
University of Mary	ND
University of Michigan - Dearborn	MI
University of Minnesota - Crookston	MN
University of Rio Grande	OH
University of Sioux Falls	SD
University of St. Francis	IN
Univ of Texas of the Permian Basin	TX
Urbana University	OH
Valley City State University	ND
Viterbo College	WI
Voorhees College	SC
Walsh University	OH
Warner Southern College	FL
Wayland Baptist University	TX
Webber College	FL
Western Baptist College	OR
Western Montana College	MT
Westminster College -Salt Lake City	UT
Westmont College	CA
Wiley College	TX
William Jewell College	MO
William Woods University	MO
Williams Baptist College	AR

NJCAA PROGRAMS
(Listed in the Volleyball Athletic Guide)

SCHOOL	STATE
Bevill State Community College	AL
Cantonsville Community College	MD
Chemeketa Community College	OR
Clackamas Community College	OR
College of Dupage	IL
Eastern Wyoming College	WY
Florida Community College	FL
Frank Phillips College	TX
Grossmont College	CA
Hagerstown Community College	MD
Illinois Central College	IL

NJCAA PROGRAMS
(Listed in the Volleyball Athletic Guide)

SCHOOL	STATE
Indian Hills Community College	IA
Jefferson College	MO
Lake County, College of	IL
Miami-Dade Community College	FL
Moorpark College	CA
Nassau Community College	NY
Northeastern Junior College	CO
Parkland College	IL
Phoenix College	AZ
San Jacinto College-Central	TX
Solano Community College	CA
SW Missouri State U-West Plains	MO
Southwestern Community College	IA
State University of NY -Cobleskill	NY
Truman College	IL
Vernon Regional Junior College	TX
Yavapai College	AZ

DUAL AFFILIATION PROGRAMS
(Listed in the Volleyball Athletic Guide)

SCHOOL	STATE
Bartlesville Wesleyan College	OK
Bethel College	IN
Bloomfield College	NJ
Bryan College	TN
Campbellsville University	KY
Cascade College	OR
Cedarville College	OH
Christian Heritage College	CA
College of Saint Scholastica	MN
Concordia University - Austin	TX
Dallas Baptist University	TX
Dallas Christian College	TX
East Texas Baptist University	TX
Eastern Oregon University	OR
Geneva College	PA
Georgia Southwestern College	GA
Grace College	IN
Hannibal-LaGrange College	MO
Husson College	ME
Judson College	AL
Kentucky Christian College	KY
Lee University	TN
Lewis - Clarke State University	ID
Lindenwood University	MO
Lyon College	AR
Marian College of Fond du Lac	WI
Martin Lutheran College	MN
Medaille College	NY
Menlo College	CA
Northland College	WI
Northwest Nazarene College	ID
Northwestern College	MN
Nova Southeastern University	FL
Nyack College	NY
Pacific Christian College	CA
Richard Stockton College of NJ	NJ
Salem College	NC
Simpson College	CA
Southern Wesleyan University	SC
Southwestern College	AZ
Spelman College	GA
Stephens College	MO
Taylor University	IN
Teikyo Post University	CT
Texas Lutheran University	TX
Texas Wesleyan University	TX
Tiffin University	OH
University of Maine - Farmington	ME
University of Puget Sound	WA
University of the Incarnate Word	TX
University of Wisconsin - Parkside	WI
Western Oregon University	OR
Westminster College - Pennsylvania	PA
Wilmington College	DE

index

SCHOOL	PAGE
College of Notre Dame	89
College of Saint Elizabeth	458
College of Saint Rose	488
College of Saint Scholastica	387
College of St. Benedict	386
College of St. Catherine	387
College of Staten Island	489
College of the Holy Cross	344
College of the Ozarks	411
College of the Southwest	472
College of William & Mary	770
College of Wooster	575
Colorado Christian University	121
Colorado College	122
Colorado School of Mines	123
Colorado State University	123
Columbia College	411
Columbia Union College	324
Columbia Univ-Barnard College	489
Concord College	797
Concordia College	370
Concordia College - Moorhead	388
Concordia College - New York	489
Concordia University	204
Concordia University	90
Concordia University	608
Concordia University	439
Concordia University	809
Concordia University - Austin	724
Concordia University - Minnesota	388
Connecticut College	134
Converse College	683
Coppin State College	325
Cornell College	259
Cornell University	490
Cornerstone College	370
Covenant College	177
Creighton University	438
Culver - Stockton College	412
Cumberland College	293

-D-

SCHOOL	PAGE
Daemen College	491
Dakota State University	696
Dakota Wesleyan University	697
Dallas Baptist University	725
Dallas Christian College	725
Dana College	439
Daniel Webster College	449
Darmouth College	450
Davidson College	539
De Paul University	204
Defiance College	576

SCHOOL	PAGE
Delaware State University	145
Delaware Valley College	629
Denison University	577
DePauw University	237
Dickinson College	630
Dickinson State University	562
Doane College	440
Dominican College	492
Dominican College	91
Dominican University	205
Dort College	260
Dowling College	492
Drake University	260
Drexel University	631
Drury University	413
Duke University	539
Duquesne University	632
D'youville College	493

-E-

SCHOOL	PAGE
Earlham College	238
East Carolina University	540
East Stroudsburg University	632
East Tennessee State University	707
East Texas Baptist University	726
Eastern College	633
Eastern Connecticut State Univ.	134
Eastern Illinois University	205
Eastern Kentucky University	293
Eastern Menonnite University	770
Eastern Michigan University	371
Eastern Nazarene College	345
Eastern New Mexico University	472
Eastern Oregon University	609
Eastern Washington University	787
Eastern Wyoming College	826
Eckerd College	155
Edgewood College	810
Edinboro Univ of Pennsylvania	634
Elizabeth City State University	541
Elizabethtown College	634
Elmhurst College	206
Elmira College	494
Elon College	541
Embry-Riddle Aeronautical Univ.	155
Emerson College	345
Emmanuel College	346
Emory and Henry College	771
Emory University	177
Emporia State University	278
Endicott College	346
Eureka College	207
Evangel College	413

SCHOOL	PAGE
-F-	
Fairfield University	135
Fairleigh Dickinson Univ- Madison	458
Fairleigh Dickinson Univ- Teaneck	459
Fairmont State College	797
Faulkner University	44
Fayetteville State University	542
Ferris State University	372
Ferrum College	771
Fisk University	707
Fitchburg State College	347
Flagler College	156
Florida A&M University	157
Florida Atlantic University	157
Florida Community College	158
Florida Institute of Technology	158
Florida International University	159
Florida Memorial College	159
Florida Southern College	160
Florida State University	160
Fontbonne College	414
Fordham University	494
Fort Hays State University	279
Fort Lewis College	124
Fort Valley State University	178
Framingham State College	348
Francis Marion University	684
Frank Phillips College	726
Franklin & Marshall College	635
Franklin College	238
Franklin Pierce College	450
Freed Hardeman University	708
Fresno Pacific University	91
Friends University	279
Frostburg State University	325
Furman University	685
-G-	
Gallaudet University	150
Gannon University	636
Gardner - Webb University	542
Geneva College	636
George Fox University	610
George Mason University	772
George Washington University	150
Georgetown College	294
Georgetown University	151
Georgia Southern University	178
Georgia Southwestern College	179
Georgia State University	179
Georgia Tech	180
Gettysburg College	637

SCHOOL	PAGE
Glenville State College	798
Goldey-Beacom College	145
Gonzaga University	788
Gordon College	349
Goshen College	239
Goucher College	326
Grace College	239
Grace land College	261
Grambling State University	305
Grand Canyon University	59
Grand Valley State University	372
Grand View College	261
Green Mountain College	762
Greensboro College	543
Greenville College	207
Grinnell College	262
Grove City College	638
Guilford College	543
Gustavus Adolphus College	389
Gwynedd-Mercy College	638
-H-	
Hagerstown Community College	326
Hamilton College	495
Hamline University	390
Hampton University	773
Hannibal-LaGrange College	415
Hanover College	240
Hardin - Simmons University	727
Harding University	66
Harris-Stowe State College	415
Hartwick College	496
Harvard University	349
Hasting College	440
Haverford College	639
Hawaii Pacific University	189
Heidelberg College	577
Henderson State University	66
Hendrix College	67
High Point University	544
Hilbert College	496
Hillsdale College	373
Hiram College	578
Hofstra University	497
Hollins University	773
Holy Names College	92
Hood College	327
Hope College	374
Hope International University	92
Houghton College	498
Houston Baptist University	727
Howard Payne University	728
Howard University	151

SCHOOL	PAGE
Humboldt State University	93
Hunter College	498
Huntington College	241
Huntington College	44
Huron University	697
Husson College	316
Huston - Tillotson College	728

-I-	
Idaho State University	194
Illinois Central College	208
Illinois College	208
Illinois Institute of Technology	209
Illinois State University	210
Illinois Wesleyan University	211
Immaculate College	639
Indian Hills Community College	262
Indiana State University	241
Indiana University - Bloomington	242
Indiana University - Purdue	243
Indiana University of Pennsylvania	640
Indiana University Southeast	244
Indiana University-PU-Fort Wayne	242
Indiana Wesleyan University	244
Iona College	499
Iowa State University	263
Iowa Wesleyan College	264
Ithaca College	499

-J-	
Jackson State University	402
Jacksonville State University	45
Jacksonville University	161
James Madison University	774
Jamestown College	562
Jarvis Christian College	729
Jefferson College	415
John Brown University	67
John Carroll University	578
John Hopkins University	328
John Jay College-Criminal Justice	484
Johnson & Wales University	673
Johnson C. Smith University	545
Judson College	45
Judson College	211
Juniata College	640

-K-	
Kalamazoo College	374
Kansas State University	280
Kansas Wesleyan University	281
Kean University	459
Keene State College	451

SCHOOL	PAGE
Kendall College	212
Kent State University	579
Kentucky Christian College	295
Kentucky State University	295
Kentucky Wesleyan College	295
Kenyon College	579
Keuka College	500
King College	708
King's College - Pennsylvania	641
Knox College	213
Kutztown University	642

-L-	
La Grange College	181
La Roche College	642
La Salle University	642
Lafayette College	643
Lake Erie College	580
Lake Forest College	213
Lake Superior State University	375
Lakeland College	811
Lamar University	729
Lambuth University	709
Lander University	685
Lane College	709
Lasell College	350
Lawrence University	811
Le Moyne College	500
Le Moyne-Owen College	710
Le Tourneau University	730
Lebanon Valley College	644
Lee University	710
Lees - McRae College	545
Lehigh University	644
Lehman College	484
Lenoir - Rhyne College	546
Lewis - Clarke State University	194
Lewis & Clark College	611
Lewis University	214
Liberty University	774
Limestone College	686
Lincoln Memorial University	711
Lincoln University - Pennsylvania	645
Lindenwood University	416
Lindsey Wilson College	296
Linfield College	611
Lipscomd University	711
Livingstone College	546
Lock Haven University	645
Long Beach State University	94
Long Island Univ- CW Post	501
Long Island Univ- Southampton	502
Long Island Univ-Brooklyn	501

SCHOOL	PAGE
Loras College	264
Louisiana State University	306
Louisiana Tech University	306
Loyola College	328
Loyola Marymount University	95
Loyola University	307
Loyola University - Illinois	215
Lubbock Christian University	731
Luther College	265
Lycoming College	646
Lynchburg College	775
Lynn University	161
Lyon College	68

-M-

SCHOOL	PAGE
Macalester College	390
MacMurray College	216
Madonna University	375
Malone College	581
Manchester College	245
Manhattan College	502
Manhattanville College	503
Maranatha Baptist Bible College	812
Marian College	246
Marian College of Fond du Lac	812
Marietta College	581
Marist College	503
Marquette University	813
Mars Hill College	547
Marshall University	799
Martin Lutheran College	392
Martin Methodist College	712
Mary Baldwin College	776
Mary Washington College	776
Marycrest International University	265
Marymount University	777
Maryville College	712
Maryville University of Saint Louis	417
Marywood University	647
Massachusetts College-Liberal Arts	353
Massachusetts Institute of Tech	351
Massachusetts Maritime Academy	351
Master's College	96
Mayville State University	563
McKendree College	216
McMurry University	731
McNeese State University	307
McPherson College	281
Medaille College	504
Medgars Evers College	505
Menlo College	96
Mercer University	181
Mercy College	505

SCHOOL	PAGE
Mercyhurst College	647
Meredith College	547
Merrimack College	352
Mesa State college	124
Messiah College	648
Methodist College	548
Metropolitan State College	125
Miami University	581
Miami-Dade Community College	162
Michigan State University	376
Mid-America Nazarene	282
Middle Tennessee State University	713
Middlebury College	762
Midland Lutheran College	441
Midway College	296
Midwestern State University	732
Miles College	46
Millersville University	649
Milligan College	713
Millikin University	217
Mills College	97
Millsaps College	403
Milwaukee School of Engineering	813
Minnesota State University	391
Minot State University	563
Mississippi College	404
Mississippi State University	404
Mississippi University for Women	405
Mississippi Valley State University	405
Missouri Baptist College	417
Missouri Southern State College	418
Missouri Valley College	418
Missouri Western State College	419
Molloy College	506
Monmouth College	218
Montana State Univ- Billings	433
Montana State Univ- Bozeman	432
Montana Tech	434
Montclair State University	460
Montreat College	549
Moorhead State University	392
Moorpark College	97
Moravian College	649
Morehead State University	297
Morgan State University	329
Morningside College	266
Morris Brown College	182
Morris College	686
Mount Aloysius College	649
Mount Holyoke college	353
Mount Marty College	698
Mount Mercy College	267
Mount Olive College	549

SCHOOL	PAGE
Mount Saint Clare College	267
Mount St. Mary College	506
Mount Union College	582
Mount Vernon Nazarene College	583
Muhlenberg College	650
Murray State University	297
Muskingum College	583

-N-

SCHOOL	PAGE
Nassau Community College	507
National American University	698
Nazareth College	507
Nebraska Wesleyan University	441
Neumann College	651
New Hampshire College	451
New Jersey City University	460
New Jersey Institute of Tech	461
New Mexico Higlands University	473
New Mexico State University	473
New York Institute of Technology	508
New York University	508
Newberry College	687
Newman University	282
Niagara University	510
Nicholls State University	308
Norfolk State University	777
North Carolina A&T State Univ	550
North Carolina Central University	550
North Carolina State University	551
North Carolina Wesleyan College	551
North Central College	218
North Dakota State University	564
North Greenville College	687
North Park University	219
Northeast Louisiana University	308
Northeastern Illinois University	219
Northeastern Junior College	126
Northeastern University	354
Northern Arizona University	60
Northern Illinois University	220
Northern Kentucky University	298
Northern Michigan University	377
Northern State University	699
Northland College	814
Northwest Missouri State Univ	420
Northwest Nazarene College	195
Northwestern College	268
Northwestern College	393
Northwestern State University	309
Northwestern University	220
Northwood University	377
Notre Dame College - Ohio	584
Nova Southeastern University	163

SCHOOL	PAGE
Nyack College	510

-O-

SCHOOL	PAGE
Oakland City University	246
Oakland University	378
Oberlin College	585
Occidental College	98
Oglethorpe University	182
Ohio Dominican College	585
Ohio Northern University	586
Ohio State University	587
Ohio University	588
Ohio Valley College	800
Ohio Wesleyan University	588
Olivet College	379
Olivet Nazarene University	221
Oral Roberts University	602
Oregon Institute of Technology	612
Oregon State University	612
Ottawa University	283
Otterbein College	589
Ouachita Baptist University	68

-P-

SCHOOL	PAGE
Pace University	510
Pacific Christian College	99
Pacific Lutheran University	788
Pacific Union College	99
Pacific University	613
Paine College	183
Palm Beach Atlantic College	163
Park College	420
Parkland College	222
Peace College	552
Pennsylvania State University	651
Pennsylvania State University	652
Pepperdine University	100
Peru State College	442
Pfeiffer University	552
Phila College of Textiles & Science	653
Philadelphia College of the Bible	653
Phoenix College	61
Piedmont College	183
Pikeville College	299
Pine Manor College	354
Pittsburgh State University	283
Plymouth State College	452
Point Loma Nazarene University	100
Point Park College	654
Polytechnic University	511
Pomona-Pitzer Colleges	101
Portland State University	613
Prairie View A&M University	733

SCHOOL	PAGE
Presbyterian College	688
Princeton University	462
Principia College	222
Providence College	674
Purdue University	247
Purdue University - Calumet	247

-Q-	
Queens College - New York	485
Queens College - North Carolina	553
Quincy University - Illinois	223
Quinnipiac College	136

-R-	
Radford University	777
Ramapo College of New Jersey	463
Randolph-Macon College	779
Randolph-Macon Woman's College	778
Regis College - Massachusetts	355
Regis University	126
Rhode Island College	674
Rhodes College	714
Rice University	733
Richard Stockton College	463
Rider University	464
Ripon College	814
Rivier College	453
Roanoke College	779
Robert Morris College	654
Robert Morris College	224
Robert Wesleyan College	511
Rochester Institute of Technology	512
Rockford College	224
Rockhurst College	421
Roger Williams University	675
Rollins College	164
Rose-Hulman Institute of Tech.	248
Rosemont College	655
Rowan University	465
Russell Sage College	513
Rust College	406
Rutgers State Univ of New Jersey	465
Rutgers State Univ of New Jersey	467
Rutgers State Univ of NJ/Camden	466

-S-	
Sacred Heart University	136
Saginaw Valley State University	379
Saint Ambrose University	269
Saint Anselm College	453
Saint Augustine's College	554
Saint Bonaventure University	513
Saint Cloud State University	393

SCHOOL	PAGE
Saint Edward's University	734
Saint Francis College	656
Saint Francis College	514
Saint John Fisher College	514
Saint John's University	515
Saint Joseph College - Maine	317
Saint Joseph's College	516
Saint Joseph's College - Indiana	249
Saint Lawrence University	516
Saint Leo College	165
Saint Louis College of Pharmacy	421
Saint Louis University	422
Saint Martin's College	789
Saint Mary College	284
Saint Mary's College - California	102
Saint Mary's College - Indiana	249
Saint Mary's College - Maryland	329
Saint Mary's University	394
Saint Mary's University	734
Saint Norbert College	815
Saint Olaf College	395
Saint Paul's College	780
Saint Peter's College	467
Saint Thomas Aquinas College	517
Saint Thomas University	165
Saint Vincent College	656
Saint Xavier University	225
Salem - Teikyo University	800
Salem State College	355
Salisbury State University	330
Sam Houston State University	735
Samford University	46
San Diego State University	102
San Francisco State University	103
San Jacinto College-Central	735
San Jose State University	104
Sangamon State	229
Santa Clara University	104
Savannah College of Art & Design	184
Savannah State University	185
Schreiner College	736
Seattle Pacific University	789
Seattle University	790
Seton Hall University	468
Seton Hill College	657
Shaw University	554
Shawnee State University	589
Shenandoah University	780
Shepherd College	801
Shippensburg University	658
Siena College	517
Siena Heights University	380
Simmons College	356

SCHOOL	PAGE
Simon Frasier	829
Simpson College	270
Simpson College	105
Skidmore College	518
Slippery Rock University	658
Smith College	356
Solano Community College	106
Sonoma State University	106
South Carolina State University	689
South Dakota State University	700
Southeast Missouri State Univ	423
Southeastern Louisiana University	310
Southeastern Oklahoma State Univ	603
Southern Arkansas University	69
Southern Connecticut State Univ.	137
Southern Illinois Univ- Carbondale	225
Southern Illinois Univ-Edwardsville	226
Southern Methodist University	737
Southern Nazarene University	602
Southern Oregon University	614
Southern University-Baton Rouge	310
Southern Virginia College	781
Southern Wesleyan University	689
Southwest Baptist University	423
Southwest Missouri State Univ	424
Southwest State University	395
Southwest Texas State University	738
Southwestern Adventist College	738
Southwestern College	284
Southwestern College	61
Southwestern Community College	271
Southwestern University	739
Spalding University	299
Spring Arbor College	380
Springfield College	357
St. Andrews Presbyterian College	553
St. Michael's College	763
Stanford University	107
State Univ College - Oneonta	524
State Univ College-Fredonia	522
State Univ College-New Paltz	522
State Univ of New York - Cortland	521
State Univ of New York - Geneseo	522
State Univ of New York - Oswego	524
State Univ of New York - Potsdam	525
State Univ of New York -Cobleskill	520
State Univ of NY - Brockport	519
State Univ of NY - Buffalo	520
State Univ of NY - Old Westbury	523
State Univ of NY - Stony Brook	526
State Univ of NY-Binghamton	519
Stephen F. Austin State University	739
Stephens College	424

SCHOOL	PAGE
Sterling College	285
Stetson University	166
Stevens Institute of Technology	468
Stillman College	47
Stonehill College	358
Sul Ross State University	740
SUNY Martime College	526
SUNY-Plattsburgh	525
Susquehanna University	659
Swarthmore College	659
Sweet Briar College	781
Syracuse University	527
-T-	
Tabor College	286
Talladega College	47
Tarleton State University	740
Taylor University	250
Teikyo Post University	137
Temple University	660
Tennessee State University	714
Texas A&M Univ- College Station	741
Texas A&M Univ- Commerce	742
Texas A&M Univ- Kingsville	742
Texas Christian University	743
Texas Lutheran University	743
Texas Southern University	744
Texas Tech University	745
Texas Wesleyan University	745
Texas Woman's University	746
Thiel College	660
Thomas College	317
Thomas More College	300
Tiffin University	590
Towson University	331
Trevecca Nazarene University	715
Trinity Christian College	227
Trinity College	138
Trinity International University	228
Trinity University	747
Tri-State University	250
Troy State University	48
Truman College	202
Truman State University	425
Tufts University	358
Tulane University	311
Tusculum College	716
Tuskegee University	49
-U-	
Union College	529
Union College	300
United States Air Force Academy	127

SCHOOL	PAGE
University of Michigan - Dearborn	381
University of Mississippi	406
University of Missouri - Columbia	425
University of Missouri - K.C.	426
University of Missouri - St. Louis	427
University of Montana	434
University of Montevallo	51
University of Nebraska - Kearney	443
University of Nebraska - Lincoln	442
University of Nebraska - Omaha	444
University of Nevada - Las Vegas	447
University of Nevada - Reno	447
University of New England	320
University of New Hampshire	454
University of New Haven	140
University of New Mexico	474
University of New Orleans	312
University of North Alabama	52
University of North Dakota	565
University of North Florida	168
University of North Texas	749
University of Northern Colorado	130
University of Northern Iowa	273
University of Notre Dame	252
University of Oklahoma	604
University of Oregon	614
University of Pennsylvania	661
University of Portland	615
University of Puget Sound	791
University of Redlands	115
University of Rhode Island	676
University of Rio Grande	594
University of Rochester	528
University of Saint Thomas	399
University of San Diego	115
University of San Francisco	116
University of Scranton	664
University of Sioux Falls	700
University of South Alabama	52
University of South Carolina	690
University of South Dakota	701
University of South Florida	169
University of Southern California	116
University of Southern Colorado	130
University of Southern Indiana	253
University of Southern Maine	320
University of Southern Mississippi	407
University of St. Francis	252
University of Tampa	169
University of Tennessee - Martin	718
University of the Incarnate Word	754
University of the Pacific	117
University of the South	719

SCHOOL	PAGE
University of Toledo	594
University of Tulsa	605
University of Utah	758
University of Vermont	763
University of Virginia	782
University of Washington	791
University of West Alabama	53
University of Wyoming	826
Upper Iowa University	273
Urbana University	595
Ursinus College	664
US Coast Guard Academy	138
US Merchant Marine Academy	530
US Military Academy	530
US Naval Academy	331
Utah State University	759
Utica College	529
-V-	
Valdosta State University	186
Valley City State University	566
Valparaiso University	254
Vanguard University	118
Vassar College	531
Vernon Regional Junior College	754
Villa Julie College	333
Villanova University	665
Virginia Commonwealth University	783
Virginia State College	783
Virginia Tech	784
Virginia Union University	784
Viterbo College	823
Voorhees College	692
-W-	
Wagner College	532
Wake Forest University	559
Walsh University	595
Warner Southern College	170
Washburn University	287
Washington & Jefferson College	666
Washington & Lee University	785
Washington College - Maryland	334
Washington State University	792
Washington University	427
Wayland Baptist University	755
Wayne State College - Nebraska	444
Wayne State University - Michigan	382
Waynesburg College	666
Webber College	171
Weber State University	759
Webster University	428
Wellesley College	361

SCHOOL	PAGE
Wentworth Institute of Technology	361
Wesleyan College	187
Wesleyan University	141
West Chester University	667
West Liberty State College	802
West Texas A&M University	755
West Virginia State College	803
West Virginia Univ Institute of Tech	802
West Virginia University	803
West Virginia Wesleyan College	804
Western Baptist College	616
Western Carolina University	559
Western Connecticut State Univ.	141
Western Illinois University	230
Western Kentucky University	302
Western Maryland College	335
Western Michigan University	382
Western New England College	362
Western New Mexico University	474
Western Oregon University	616
Western State College	131
Western Washington University	793
Westfield State College	362
Westminster College	667
Westminster College	429
Westminster College	760
Westmont College	118
Wheaton College	363
Wheaton College	231
Wheeling Jesuit University	805
Whitman College	793
Whittier College	119
Whitworth College	794
Wichita State University	287
Widener University	668
Wiley College	756
Wilkes University	668
Willamette University	617
William Jewell College	429
William Paterson University	469
William Penn College	274
William Woods University	430
Williams Baptist College	72
Williams College	363
Wilmington College	596
Wilmington College	146
Wilson College	669
Wingate University	559
Winona State University	399
Winston - Salem State University	560
Winthrop University	692
Wisconsin Lutheran College	824
Wittenberg University	597

SCHOOL	PAGE
Wofford College	693
Worcester Polytechnic Institute	364
Worcester State College	365
Wright State University	597
-X-	
Xavier University	598
-Y-	
Yale University	142
Yavapai College	63
York College of Pennsylvania	670
Youngstown State University	598

THE OFFICIAL ATHLETIC COLLEGE SCHOLARSHIP GUIDES

Yes! I am interested in receiving the current edition of:

TITLES	PRICE	# OF BOOKS
☐ *The Official Athletic College Guide: SOCCER*	$34.95 x	_____
☐ *The Official Athletic College Guide: BASEBALL*	$34.95 x	_____
☐ *The Official Athletic College Kit: SOFTBALL*	$34.95 x	_____
☐ *The Official Athletic College Guide: VOLLEYBALL*	$34.95 x	_____
☐ *Freshman College Kit:* Includes Workbook and 1 Match-Fit online access code.	$23.95 +$7 S&H x	_____
☐ *Sophomore College Kit:* Includes Workbook and three Match-Fit online access codes.	$42.95 +$7 S&H x	_____
☐ *Junior College Kit:* Includes College Guide, Workbook and 4 Match-Fit online access codes.	$64.85 +$9 S&H x	_____
☐ *Senior College Kit:* Includes College Guide, Workbook and 2 Match-Fit online access codes.	$55.85 +$9 S&H x	_____

PAYMENT: ☐ CHECK ☐ MONEY ORDER ☐ VISA ☐ MASTERCARD ☐ AMEX

Card#:_____ Exp. Date:_____

Name on card: _____

Signature: _____

(product): _____ x (price):$_____ =$_____

TAX (8.25% Texas residence only) =$_____

Shipping & handling ($7.00 per guide) =$_____

Total amount being billed =$_____

☐ Please include information regarding "Plan for Success" College Seminars

Ship to:

Name:_____

Address: _____

City: _____ State: _____

Zip:_____

Phone: _____

E-mail: _____

Fax your order to:
972-516-1754

Toll Free: 1-800-862-3092
(972)509-5707
1845 Summit Ave~Suite
402~Plano,Texas 75074

web-site:
http://www.thesportsource.com
E-mail:
sports@thesportsource.com

MATCHFIT ™

ONLINE COLLEGE IDENTIFICATION SERVICE

Jump-start your own college search with MATCHFIT™ our new online college identification service offered exclusively at **www.thesportsource.com**. Confidentially enter personal biographical data including your G.P.A., class rank, and standardized test scores, along with information specific to the type of college or university you would like to attend. Your information is matched against our extensive database to identify ten (10) college programs which match your selection criteria. Then make changes to your data and re-run the search two (2) additional times.

The net effect is three (3) sets of ten (10) colleges and universities which are compatible with your requirements for a college athletic program. Any duplications further validate that particular program as one you will want to pursue. You may select any college or university and download information specific to that program directly to your PC. This includes both a general academic profile, and a detailed athletic profile with the coach's name, mailing address, office number, fax, e-mail address, and the college web address. MATCHFIT™ is available for $34.95 and can be ordered at **www.thesportsource.com** with a MasterCard, VISA, American Express, by E-check,or order by phone.

"PLAN FOR SUCCESS" COLLEGE SEMINARS

"PLAN FOR SUCCESS" - COLLEGE SEMINARS ™ are conducted throughout the U.S. for teams, clubs, schools, and sports organizations. Our network of presenters include college coaches and experts within the field of collegiate athletics who will discuss in detail:

* * THE SPORT SOURCE™ "Action Plan for Success"
* * What college coaches look for in a player
* * NCAA / NAIA recruiting rules
* * Evaluating colleges and athletic programs
* * Writing resumes and cover letters
* * Conducting campus visits
* * Opportunities for obtaining a college athletic scholarship

"PLAN FOR SUCCESS" - COLLEGE SEMINARS™ pricing varies by group size. For more information call:

1-800-862-3092

website:http://www.thesportsource.com